Fodor's Road Guide USA

Indiana

Kentucky

Michigan

Ohio

West Virginia

First Edition

Fodor's Travel Publications
New York Toronto London Sydney Auckland
www.fodors.com

Fodor's Road Guide USA: Indiana, Kentucky, Michigan, Ohio, West Virginia

Fodor's Travel Publications
President: Bonnie Ammer
Publisher: Kris Kliemann
Executive Managing Editor: Denise DeGennaro
Editorial Director: Karen Cure
Director of Marketing Development: Jeanne Kramer
Associate Managing Editor: Linda Schmidt
Senior Editor: Constance Jones
Director of Production and Manufacturing: Chuck Bloodgood
Creative Director: Fabrizio La Rocca

Contributors
Editing: Jennifer Dowling (Kentucky), Joyce Eisenberg (Ohio), Lorraine Martindale (Indiana), Doris Maxfield (Michigan), and Alix McNamara (West Virginia), with Kim Anderson, Carissa Bluestone, Jeff Boswell, Richard Brunelli, Angela Casey, Lisa Cole, Sarah Cupp, Yvonne Daley, Daniel de Zayas, Dianne DiBlasi, Robert Fleming, Hannah Fons, Jay Hyams, Shannon Kelly, Natalie Kusz, Christa Malone, Dianna Marguleas, Liz McGeehee, JoAnn Milivojevic, Pat Hadley-Miller, Emmanuelle Morgen, Candy Moulton, Amy O'Neil, Kelly Sobel, Suzanne Venino, Susan Walton, and Kirsten Weisenberger
Writing: Alison Borgerding (Ohio dinings), Jeff Davis (Ohio), Michael Friel (West Virginia), Steven Keith (West Virginia restaurants), Susan Reigler (Kentucky), Peggy Ammerman Sailors (Indiana), Khristi Zimmeth (Michigan), and Theresa Zumwald (Ohio introductions), with Page Bierma, Michele Bloom, Alyson Borgokring, Richard Eastman, Hannah Fons, Sarah Gil, Carole Hawkins, Alia Levine, Kate Lorenz, Candy Moulton, Andrea Nelson, Sara Pepitone, Eric Reymond, Jordan Richman, Amanda Robinson, Tina Ross, Alan Ryan, Frances Schamberg, Dan Stivers, and Karla Tornabene
Research: Alex Bajoris, Joshua Greenwarld, Keisha Hutchins, Peter Jhon, Janue Johnson, Eric Joseph, Brandon Leong, LaKeisha Light, Juan Martinez, Mary Ann O'Grady, Paula Reedy, Jordana Rosenberg, Greg Temner, and Tracy Wong
Black-and-White Maps: Rebecca Baer, Robert Blake, David Lindroth, Todd Pasini
Production/Manufacturing: Bob Shields
Cover: Glen Allison/Stone (background photo), Bart Nagle (photo, illustration)
Interior Photos: Photodisc (Indiana, Michigan, and Ohio), Kentucky Department of Travel Development (Kentucky), Corbis (West Virginia)

Special Sales
Fodor's Travel Publications are available at special discounts for bulk purchases for sales promotions or premiums. Special editions, including personalized covers, excerpts of existing guides, and corporate imprints, can be created in large quantities for special needs. For more information, contact your local bookseller or write to Special Markets, Fodor's Travel Publications, 280 Park Avenue, New York, NY 10017. Inquiries from Canada should be directed to your local Canadian bookseller or sent to Random House of Canada, Ltd., Marketing Department, 2775 Matheson Boulevard East, Mississauga, Ontario L4W 4P7. Inquiries from the United Kingdom should be sent to Fodor's Travel Publications, 20 Vauxhall Bridge Road, London SW1V 2SA, England.

PRINTED IN THE UNITED STATES OF AMERICA
10 9 8 7 6 5 4 3 2 1

CONTENTS

Great Road Trips

Of all the things that went wrong with Clark Griswold's vacation, one stands out: The theme park he had driven across the country to visit was closed when he got there. Clark, the suburban bumbler played by Chevy Chase in 1983's hilarious *National Lampoon's Vacation,* is fictional, of course. But his story is poignantly true. Although most Americans get only two precious weeks of vacation a year, many set off on their journeys with surprisingly little guidance. Many travelers find out about their destination from friends and family or wait to get travel information until they arrive in their hotel, where racks of brochures dispense the "facts," along with free city magazines. But it's hard to distinguish the truth from hype in these sources. And it makes no sense to spend priceless vacation time in a hotel room reading about a place when you could be out seeing it up close and personal.

Congratulate yourself on picking up this guide. Studying it—before you leave home—is the best possible first step toward making sure your vacation fulfills your every dream.

Inside you'll find all the tools you need to plan a perfect road trip. In the hundreds of towns we describe, you'll find thousands of places to explore. So you'll always know what's around the next bend. And with the practical information we provide, you can easily call to confirm the details that matter and study up on what you'll want to see and do, before you leave home.

By all means, when you plan your trip, allow yourself time to make a few detours. Because as wonderful as it is to visit sights you've read about, it's the serendipitous experiences that often prove the most memorable: the hole-in-the-wall diner that serves a transcendent tomato soup, the historical society gallery stuffed with dusty local curiosities of days gone by. As you whiz down the highway, use the book to find out more about the towns announced by roadside signs. Consider turning off at the next exit. And always remember: In this great country of ours, there's an adventure around every corner.

HOW TO USE THIS BOOK

Alphabetical organization should make it a snap to navigate through this book. Still, in putting it together, we've made certain decisions and used certain terms you need to know about.

LOCATIONS AND CATEGORIZATIONS

Color map coordinates are given for every town in the guide.

Attractions, restaurants, and lodging places are listed under the nearest town covered in the guide.

Parks and forests are sometimes listed under the main access point.

Exact street addresses are provided whenever possible; when they were not available or applicable, directions and/or cross-streets are indicated.

CITIES

For state capitals and larger cities, attractions are alphabetized by category. Shopping sections focus on good shopping areas where you'll find a concentration of interesting shops. We include malls only if they're unusual in some way and individual stores only when they're community institutions. Restaurants and hotels are grouped by price category then arranged alphabetically.

RESTAURANTS

All are air-conditioned unless otherwise noted, and all permit smoking unless they're identified as "no-smoking."

Dress: Assume that no jackets or ties are required for men unless otherwise noted.

Family-style service: Restaurants characterized this way serve food communally, out of serving dishes as you might at home.

Meals and hours: Assume that restaurants are open for lunch and dinner unless otherwise noted. We always specify days closed and meals not available.

Prices: The price ranges listed are for dinner entrées (or lunch entrées if no dinner is served).

Reservations: They are always a good idea. We don't mention them unless they're essential or are not accepted.

Fodor's Choice: Stars denote restaurants that are Fodor's Choices—our editors' picks of the state's very best in a given price category.

LODGINGS

All are air-conditioned unless otherwise noted, and all permit smoking unless they're identified as "no-smoking."

AP: This designation means that a hostelry operates on the American Plan (AP)—-that is, rates include all meals. AP may be an option or it may be the only meal plan available; be sure to find out.

Baths: You'll find private bathrooms with bathtubs unless noted otherwise.

Business services: If we tell you they're there, you can expect a variety on the premises.

Exercising: We note if there's "exercise equipment" even when there's no designated area; if you want a dedicated facility, look for "gym."

Facilities: We list what's available but don't note charges to use them. When pricing accommodations, always ask what's included.

Hot tub: This term denotes hot tubs, Jacuzzis, and whirlpools.

MAP: Rates at these properties include two meals.

No smoking: Properties with this designation prohibit smoking.

Opening and closing: Assume that hostelries are open year-round unless otherwise noted.

Pets: We note whether or not they're welcome and whether there's a charge.

Pools: Assume they're outdoors with fresh water; indoor pools are noted.

Prices: The price ranges listed are for a high-season double room for two, excluding tax and service charge.

Telephone and TV: Assume that you'll find them unless otherwise noted.

Fodor's Choice: Stars denote hostelries that are Fodor's Choices—our editors' picks of the state's very best in a given price category.

NATIONAL PARKS

National parks protect and preserve the treasures of America's heritage, and they're always worth visiting whenever you're in the area. Many are worth a long detour. If you will travel to many national parks, consider purchasing the National Parks Pass ($50), which gets you and your companions free admission to all parks for one year. (Camping and parking are extra.) A percentage of the proceeds from sales of the pass helps to fund important projects in the parks. Both the Golden Age Passport ($10), for those 62 and older, and the Golden Access Passport (free), for travelers with disabilities, entitle holders to free entry to all national parks, plus 50% off fees for the use of many park facilities and services. You must show proof of age and of U.S. citizenship or permanent residency (such as a U.S. passport, driver's license, or birth certificate) and, if requesting Golden Access, proof of your disability. You must get your Golden Access or Golden Age passport in person; the former is available at all federal recreation areas, the latter at federal recreation areas that charge fees. You may purchase the National Parks Pass by mail or through the Internet. For information, contact the National Park Service (Department of the Interior, 1849 C St. NW, Washington, DC 20240-0001, 202/208—4747, *www.nps.gov*). To buy the National Parks Pass, write to 27540 Ave. Mentry, Valencia, CA 91355, call 888/GO—PARKS, or visit www.national-parks.org.

IMPORTANT TIP

Although all prices, opening times, and other details in this book are based on information supplied to us at press time, changes occur all the time in the travel world, and Fodor's cannot accept responsibility for facts that become outdated or for inadvertent errors or omissions. So **always confirm information when it matters,** especially if you're making a detour to visit a specific place.

Let Us Hear from You

Keeping a travel guide fresh and up-to-date is a big job, and we welcome any and all comments. We'd love to have your thoughts on places we've listed, and we're interested in hearing about your own special finds, even the ones in your own back yard. Our guides are thoroughly updated for each new edition, and we're always adding new information, so your feedback is vital. Contact us via e-mail in care of roadnotes@fodors.com (specifying the name of the book on the subject line) or via snail mail in care of Road Guides at Fodor's, 280 Park Avenue, New York, NY 10017. We look forward to hearing from you. And in the meantime, have a wonderful road trip.

THE EDITORS

Important Numbers and On-Line Info

LODGINGS

Adam's Mark	800/444—2326	www.adamsmark.com
Baymont Inns	800/428—3438	www.baymontinns.com
Best Western	800/528—1234	www.bestwestern.com
	TDD 800/528—2222	
Budget Host	800/283—4678	www.budgethost.com
Clarion	800/252—7466	www.clarioninn.com
Comfort	800/228—5150	www.comfortinn.com
Courtyard by Marriott	800/321—2211	www.courtyard.com
Days Inn	800/325—2525	www.daysinn.com
Doubletree	800/222—8733	www.doubletreehotels.com
Drury Inns	800/325—8300	www.druryinn.com
Econo Lodge	800/555—2666	www.hotelchoice.com
Embassy Suites	800/362—2779	www.embassysuites.com
Exel Inns of America	800/356—8013	www.exelinns.com
Fairfield Inn by Marriott	800/228—2800	www.fairfieldinn.com
Fairmont Hotels	800/527—4727	www.fairmont.com
Forte	800/225—5843	www.forte-hotels.com
Four Seasons	800/332—3442	www.fourseasons.com
Friendship Inns	800/453—4511	www.hotelchoice.com
Hampton Inn	800/426—7866	www.hampton-inn.com
Hilton	800/445—8667	www.hilton.com
	TDD 800/368—1133	
Holiday Inn	800/465—4329	www.holiday-inn.com
	TDD 800/238—5544	
Howard Johnson	800/446—4656	www.hojo.com
	TDD 800/654—8442	
Hyatt & Resorts	800/233—1234	www.hyatt.com
Inns of America	800/826—0778	www.innsofamerica.com
Inter-Continental	800/327—0200	www.interconti.com
La Quinta	800/531—5900	www.laquinta.com
	TDD 800/426—3101	
Loews	800/235—6397	www.loewshotels.com
Marriott	800/228—9290	www.marriott.com
Master Hosts Inns	800/251—1962	www.reservahost.com
Le Meridien	800/225—5843	www.lemeridien.com
Motel 6	800/466—8356	www.motel6.com
Omni	800/843—6664	www.omnihotels.com
Quality Inn	800/228—5151	www.qualityinn.com
Radisson	800/333—3333	www.radisson.com
Ramada	800/228—2828	www.ramada.com
	TDD 800/533—6634	
Red Carpet/Scottish Inns	800/251—1962	www.reservahost.com
Red Lion	800/547—8010	www.redlion.com
Red Roof Inn	800/843—7663	www.redroof.com
Renaissance	800/468—3571	www.renaissancehotels.com
Residence Inn by Marriott	800/331—3131	www.residenceinn.com
Ritz-Carlton	800/241—3333	www.ritzcarlton.com
Rodeway	800/228—2000	www.rodeway.com

Sheraton	800/325—3535	www.sheraton.com
Shilo Inn	800/222—2244	www.shiloinns.com
Signature Inns	800/822—5252	www.signature-inns.com
Sleep Inn	800/221—2222	www.sleepinn.com
Super 8	800/848—8888	www.super8.com
Susse Chalet	800/258—1980	www.sussechalet.com
Travelodge/Viscount	800/255—3050	www.travelodge.com
Vagabond	800/522—1555	www.vagabondinns.com
Westin Hotels & Resorts	800/937—8461	www.westin.com
Wyndham Hotels & Resorts	800/996—3426	www.wyndham.com

AIRLINES

Air Canada	888/247—2262	www.aircanada.ca
Alaska	800/426—0333	www.alaska-air.com
American	800/433—7300	www.aa.com
America West	800/235—9292	www.americawest.com
British Airways	800/247—9297	www.british-airways.com
Canadian	800/426—7000	www.cdnair.ca
Continental Airlines	800/525—0280	www.continental.com
Delta	800/221—1212	www.delta.com
Midway Airlines	800/446—4392	www.midwayair.com
Northwest	800/225—2525	www.nwa.com
SkyWest	800/453—9417	www.delta.com
Southwest	800/435—9792	www.southwest.com
TWA	800/221—2000	www.twa.com
United	800/241—6522	www.ual.com
USAir	800/428—4322	www.usair.com

BUSES AND TRAINS

Amtrak	800/872—7245	www.amtrak.com
Greyhound	800/231—2222	www.greyhound.com
Trailways	800/343—9999	www.trailways.com

CAR RENTALS

Advantage	800/777—5500	www.arac.com
Alamo	800/327—9633	www.goalamo.com
Allstate	800/634—6186	www.bnm.com/as.htm
Avis	800/331—1212	www.avis.com
Budget	800/527—0700	www.budget.com
Dollar	800/800—4000	www.dollar.com
Enterprise	800/325—8007	www.pickenterprise.com
Hertz	800/654—3131	www.hertz.com
National	800/328—4567	www.nationalcar.com
Payless	800/237—2804	www.paylesscarrental.com
Rent-A-Wreck	800/535—1391	www.rent-a-wreck.com
Thrifty	800/367—2277	www.thrifty.com

Note: Area codes are changing all over the United States as this book goes to press. For the latest updates, check www.areacode-info.com.

Fodor's Road Guide USA

Indiana
Kentucky
Michigan
Ohio
West Virginia

Indiana

With its feet firmly planted in the heartland, Indiana stands shoulder to shoulder with
Kentucky, Ohio, Michigan, and Illinois. Although modest in size, ranking 38th in the nation,
and visually unimposing, it has heart and soul. To find them, you need look no farther
than in its many small towns. The state itself is like one big small town, where a self-
sufficient and steadfast ethic is at work and locals take pride in their "Hoosier hospitality" and an optimistic outlook.

Many of the hundreds of Hoosierdom's small communities were established for
practical reasons near a roadway, a rail line, or, in the early to mid 1800s, along the Wabash
and Erie Canal, so that farmers could easily transport their produce to market. Others
grew up around an intersection of hunting and game trails or a trading post dating
back to the days of the French fur traders. Then there are charming towns that are
the picture of rural America—county seats spreading out from a small square dominated by a stately landmark courthouse dating back a century or more. Most of the
state's 92 counties have such an edifice at their center.

Less than 200 years ago the landscape that is now an orderly patchwork of fields
and towns was untamed wilderness. In the early 1800s one traveler described Indiana as "a vast forest, larger than England, just penetrated in places but the backwoods
settlers are half hunters, half farmers . . . . They are the fields of enterprise." When Indiana became the 19th state in 1816, there was a land rush to settle what was then the
western frontier. As homesteaders from the East arrived, they found prairie grass in
about a fifth of the state, mainly in the northern half, and the rest covered with dense
hardwood forests. The land proved fertile and ideal for farming, and with large-scale
settlement came wholesale cultivation. Today, only about a fifth remains wooded, mainly
the rolling highlands south of Indianapolis. The northern half lies in the Corn Belt that
extends from Ohio to Nebraska, its productive soil nurturing bumper crops of corn and

CAPITAL: INDIANAPOLIS	POPULATION: 5,803,000 (1995)	AREA: 36,291 SQUARE MI
BORDERS: OH, MI, IL, KY	TIME ZONE: EASTERN STANDARD	POSTAL ABBREVIATION: IN
WEB SITE: WWW.STATE.IN.US AND WWW.STATE.IN.US/TOURISM		

soybeans and feed for livestock, mostly hogs and cattle. Roughly three-fourths of Indiana is farmland.

Indiana relies on industry for its livelihood and is a hub of commerce. With more than 1,138 mi of interstate highways skimming across the state, several of them intersecting in Indianapolis, Indiana has long called itself the Crossroads of America. Locks and other improvements in the 1950s on the Ohio River at the state's southern border and the 1970 opening of the Burns International Harbor on Lake Michigan have made the state a major shipping center.

The opening of the port gave a crucial leg-up to the industrial northwest. The marshy Calumet region along the shores of Lake Michigan was drained in the early 1900s and became the site of one of the nation's top concentrations of heavy industry, the home of behemoth steel mills, refineries, and supporting industries. (One of Indiana's most treasured natural features, the 15-mi stretch of beaches that is now protected as the Indiana Dunes National Lakeshore, is in the thick of this industrial belt.)

Of Indiana's five largest cities, with populations over 100,000, three are in the north, Indianapolis is in the center, and Evansville sits in the extreme southwest, on the Ohio River. In contrast to Indiana's industrialized, bustling northwest, parts of the northeast seem stuck in time. In the rolling prairies and lake country of LaGrange and Elkhart counties, the pace is slow, and life is simple. Here is the nation's third-largest concentration of Amish. Having first settled in Pennsylvania, the Amish began seeking out the wide-open spaces and rich farmland of Indiana in the mid-19th century, and these "plain people" still maintain their horsedrawn buggies and a simple life centered on the farm and home.

Before Indiana was a state, it was part of the Northwest Territory, which included Ohio, Illinois, Michigan, Wisconsin, and parts of Minnesota. Indiana's oldest city, Vincennes, was the territorial capital. Scores of settlers traveled on crude plank tracks like the National Road or floated down the Wabash River and Erie Canal or the Ohio River. Today, quaint hill towns reflect the ethnic heritage of those early settlers, and those strung along the banks of the Ohio River recall the heyday of steamboats and river traffic. Under south-central Indiana's rolling hills, near Bedford, lies a thick band of limestone bedrock, and the state is the nation's leading supplier of limestone for building.

The state's writers and composers reflect its folksy, country character. Perhaps its best-loved poet is James Whitcomb Riley, who penned ditties like "Little Orphan Annie" and "When the Frost Is on the Punkin'." Songwriter Paul Dresser was inspired by the dreamy Wabash River and the gentle countryside on either side when he wrote "On the Banks of the Wabash, Far Away," now the state song. Other notable Hoosiers from the past were songwriters Cole Porter, one of America's greats, and the prolific Hoagy Carmichael, best known for "Stardust"; naturalist, photographer, and writer Gene Stratton Porter; and novelists Theodore Dreiser (*An American Tragedy*), Lew Wallace (*Ben Hur*), and Kurt Vonnegut *Slaughterhouse-Five, Cat's Cradle,* and *Breakfast of Champions*). More recent favorite sons include comedian and talk-show host David

IN Timeline

1100–1600

Roughly 12 Native American tribes of the Algonquian language group migrate to Indiana from the north and west, living there for various amounts of time. Kickapoo, Potawatomi,

Nanticoke, Wyandot, Shawnee, Munsee, Delaware, and Mohican passed through here, but the Miami, Piankashaw, and Wea were long-term residents.

1679

René-Robert Cavelier, Sieur de La Salle, a French explorer, passes through northern Indiana on his way from Canada to the Mississippi River. He is believed to have been the first

person of European descent to explore the area now called Indiana.

INTRODUCTION
HISTORY
REGIONS
WHEN TO VISIT
STATE'S GREATS
RULES OF THE ROAD
DRIVING TOURS

Letterman, TV personality Jane Pauley, the madcap Red Skelton, and cartoonist Jim Davis, creator of "Garfield". Not to mention James Dean, the 1950s Hollywood megastar who was born in Marion and buried in nearby Fairmount. The state is also known as the Mother of Vice Presidents, having produced about equal numbers of Democratic and Republican holders of the nation's second-highest office. Indiana also claims two U.S. Presidents, William Henry Harrison and his grandson Benjamin Harrison. Abraham Lincoln spent his boyhood years in southern Indiana.

If anything can excite traditionally easygoing Indiana it is basketball. Indiana University's basketball team plays in the Big Ten Conference along with Purdue University; both are perennial contenders for top honors. During high-school basketball play-offs in spring, the state is gripped from top to bottom and border to border by so-called Hoosier hysteria.

Longtime Boston Celtics star Larry Bird, long heralded as just another favorite son, earned greater kudos among locals when he returned to his home state to coach the National Basketball Association's Indiana Pacers.

History

The first known inhabitants of the Midwestern region now known as Indiana, or "land of the Indians," were members of the so-called Adena Culture, which spread across the Ohio Valley some 2,500 years ago. These Native Americans are known for the ceremonial mounds they erected near rivers. Later came the Hopewell peoples, who built still larger mounds. Remains of these groups can be seen at Mounds State Park, on the White River near Anderson. Evidence of the next group, the Mississippian Culture, is found at Angel Mounds, a state historic site and archaeological dig near Evansville. The Algonquian language group began moving into Indiana about AD 1100 to 1300. By the time the first Europeans arrived, mainly French fur trappers and traders in the mid to late 1700s, there were at least twelve Native American tribes in the region, among them the Miami, Piankashaw, and Wea. As Europeans settled the area, these Native Americans were forced to move farther west, and by 1838 very few remained in the state that would later be named after them.

The first European to reach the area was the French explorer Robert Cavelier, Sieur de La Salle, in 1679. He was soon followed by French fur trappers, traders, and missionaries who set up posts in Fort Wayne and along the Wabash River. In 1725, French Jesuit priests founded the first permanent town, Vincennes. It became the site of a French fort and later the British Fort Sackville from 1763 until 1779. The British lost the fort to George Rogers Clark and a band of frontiersmen during the Revolutionary War. That decisive battle netted the largest land conquest of the entire conflict. Vincennes later served as the capital of the Northwest Territory, a huge region bordered by Canada and the Ohio and Mississippi rivers.

After the Revolutionary War, land-hungry former colonists began pushing west against the resistance of Native Americans. One of the largest Indian revolts was led by Chief Little Turtle of the Miami. The Miami were eventually defeated, and by the mid 1790s

1710	1715		1727	
Sieur de La Salle opens the way for settlement. The French establish a thriving fur-trading enterprise in Indiana, mainly along the Wabash River and the northern part of the state.	The French build Fort Miami, a fortification and trading post at Kekionga, a Miami village near present-day Fort Wayne. A second fortification, Fort Ouiatenon, is constructed on the	Wabash River south of present-day Lafayette.	The French establish the first permanent settlement, Vincennes, on the Wabash River, 65 mi north of where the Wabash empties into the Ohio River. This is the strategic third link in the	network of French-built forts aimed at thwarting British encroachment on French trading territory.

they had turned over a large portion of northern Indiana to the U.S. government. Conflicts over territory continued into the early 1800s. The Battle of Tippecanoe, at Prophetstown, near present-day Lafayette, marked the loss of still more Native American lands. The last skirmish with Native Americans was the Battle of Mississinewa, fought near present-day Huntington, in 1812.

Four years later Indiana became the 19th state in the Union. The capital stayed in Corydon, on the southern fringes of the state, from 1816 until 1824, when it was moved to the more central Indianapolis. The last significant acquisition of land from Native Americans was the New Purchase of 1818, which opened much of central Indiana to settlement.

Communities were established and began to grow, particularly along the major transportation arteries: the Ohio River; the Great Sauk Trail (now U.S. 12); the National Road, the first federally funded "highway" (now U.S. 40); the Wabash and Erie Canal, slicing diagonally across the state; and, beginning in the 1830s, the rail lines. One of the main rail routes connected Indianapolis with Madison, on the Ohio River, from which goods could be shipped to European markets via the Mississippi River system.

By the time of the Civil War broke out, the state's population was already above 1.3 million. President Abraham Lincoln, who had spent time in Indiana as a boy, requested troops for the Union side. The only official battle on Indiana soil took place near Corydon in 1863. After the war, Indiana continued on a course of economic growth dominated by agriculture and industry, as small factories sprang up in towns across the state. By the early 1900s, heavy industry had put down roots in northwest Indiana. The turn of the century also saw the automobile industry boom in Indiana. A gasoline-powered model, the Haynes Pioneer, made its debut in Kokomo on July 4, 1894. Soon plants making more than two dozen different brands of cars dotted the state. Before Detroit took the reins as the nation's motor city in the 1920s, Indiana was the country's leading producer; over 30 manufacturers of automobiles were based here. The Indianapolis Motor Speedway opened in 1909 as a place to test cars and race them. The first 500-mi race was held there in 1911 and it is still held on the site each May.

For the first 75 years of the 20th century, Indiana's economy paralleled that of other Midwestern states, with agriculture and industries that supported motor-vehicle manufacturing playing major roles. Then the recession hit in the 1970s and Indiana suffered, as did its neighbors. By the early 1980s unemployment had hit 12 percent, and at the same time the agricultural sector was languishing; farmers were falling into debt and many went bankrupt. Recovery began in the late 1980s as manufacturers began to prosper again and the service sector—insurance, healthcare, and banking—became a major economic contender. These areas continued to flourish in the 1990s, and pharmaceutical and agricultural chemical manufacturers expanded as well. Indiana also replaced Pennsylvania as the nation's leading steel producer. Its deepwater international port on Lake Michigan and its Ohio River ports have continued to be major

1732
A fort and trading post are built at Vincennes, making the settlement a major trade center.

1754–63
The French and Indian War is the climax of a long-standing rivalry between the French and British. Although the Native American tribes are generally allied with the French, the

British win the war, and in the resulting treaty they gain French land east of the Mississippi River, including Indiana.

1763–64
Native American tribes form an alliance and, in resistance to British domination, initiate a series of conflicts known as Pontiac's War, named after the Ottawa chief. The alliance

captures seven British posts, including Fort Ouiatenon and Fort Miami, which are destroyed. The group fails to capture the key post of Fort Detroit, however, and the

INTRODUCTION
HISTORY
REGIONS
WHEN TO VISIT
STATE'S GREATS
RULES OF THE ROAD
DRIVING TOURS

shipping centers; two additional automobile manufacturers announced plans to open plants in the Hoosier state; and the Indianapolis International Airport was augmented with a major airline maintenance facility. The capital city, Indianapolis, has benefited from an ambitious growth and development plan that had invested roughly $3 billion in downtown revitalization by the mid 1990s. The crowning touch was the opening in 1995 of the $300 million Circle Centre, a 10-square-block shopping and entertainment complex built behind vintage facades of neglected downtown office buildings and department stores. During the last 10 years, Indiana has seen a strong economy based on record low unemployment rates and a state government surplus of more than $1 billion. Also, the state's economy has been boosted in the 1990s by the construction of riverboat casinos and a pari-mutuel racetrack.

Regions

1. NORTHERN ROLLING PRAIRIE AND LAKE COUNTRY

Except for the "big toe" of southwestern Indiana, the state is rectangular with the long sides running north and south. Ten thousand years ago, a series of broad ice sheets from Canadian glaciers inched southward covering almost all of the state. The most recent glacial ice sheets blanketed the northern third of the rectangle and after the glaciers retreated northern Indiana was left relatively flat yet very fertile. The glacial sheets deposited layers of glacial drift or till, which consists of sandy soil with gravel. The force of the glaciers combined with that of wind, and over time a broad band of fine sand was created along Lake Michigan's shoreline. Like Michigan, Indiana has some of the most impressive fresh-water sand dunes in the world. Lake Michigan is also a favorite destination for boating and fishing, particularly during steelhead season in spring. The dominant waterway in northwestern Indiana is the Kankakee River, which flows west from South Bend and is surrounded by a broad marshy area that has been largely drained over the years for agricultural use. More than 1,000 small kettle lakes scooped out by the ancient glaciers dot the north-central and northeastern regions. The largest naturally formed lake is Lake Wawasee, which covers 5 square mi. The dividing line between the watersheds of the Great Lakes and the Mississippi River runs near Fort Wayne in the northeast, the Maumee River flowing northeast to Lake Erie and several others flowing to the west. The rich farmland here attracted the Amish, a conservative religious community that practices old-fashioned farming methods. In many small towns in the area you can sample the country life at charming country inns, crafts and antiques shops, and friendly restaurants serving home-style food.

Towns listed: Angola, Auburn, Berne, Elkhart, Fort Wayne, Fremont, Geneva, Goshen, Hammond, Huntington, Indiana Dunes National Lakeshore, Lafayette, LaPorte, Logansport, Marion, Merrillville, Michigan City, Middlebury, Mishawaka, Muncie, Nappanee, Peru, Plymouth, Shipshewana, South Bend, Valparaiso, Wabash, Warsaw

1775–83	1778		
alliance dissolves over the next few years.	The outcome of the Revolutionary War proves to be a greater threat to Native Americans than the land claims held by the British as Americans begin streaming westward in search of land.	During the third year of the war, U.S. Lt. Col. George Rogers Clark directs a campaign to route the British from the Ohio River valley. He captures several British posts in Illinois and also takes	Vincennes. Vincennes is unprotected, as British troops were supporting efforts at Fort Detroit. Clark encounters little resistance by the predominantly French Vincennes	settlers, but by the end of the year he surrenders Vincennes to the British.

2. CENTRAL HUB AND CORRIDOR

Indianapolis, Hoosierdom's capital city, acts as the hub of an east–west corridor that divides the state into two roughly equal-size regions. The central corridor covers about a third of the state. Here you'll find Indiana's flattest terrain—and some of its richest soil, particularly in west-central Indiana, where the Illinois Grand Prairie extends across the border. As early as the 1820s, when the Indiana portion of the National Road was built, the U.S.'s first federally funded highway, the central corridor became an important transportation route. Some of the state's oldest communities and charming small towns line what remains of the National Road, now U.S. 40. Centerville, a historic town filled with brick row houses, sits on the National Road near the Ohio state line, in the center of what is known as Indiana's Antique Alley. Hundreds of antiques dealers and shops lie within a 40-mi radius of Centerville. Following the central corridor across the state and shadowing U.S. 40, I–70 was constructed in the late 1960s and now connects Indianapolis with major cities to the east and west. More interstate highways converge on Indianapolis than on any other city in the country.

Towns listed: Anderson, Brazil, Connersville, Crawfordsville, Fishers, Greencastle, Greenfield, Indianapolis, Kokomo, Marshall, New Castle, Noblesville, Richmond, Rockville, Terre Haute

3. SOUTHERN HILLS AND OHIO RIVER VALLEY

Except for a checkerboard of farm fields ringed by wooded low sandy ridges just east of Vincennes, the southern third of the state is hill country. Indiana's oldest settlement, Vincennes, sits beside the Wabash River, a 512-mi tributary of the Ohio whose course accounts for about half of the Indiana-Illinois boundary. Though glaciers once covered a large portion of southern Indiana, this region emerged from under the ice sheets sooner than the north. As a result, the forces of nature sculpted a hilly terrain, with rounded, thickly forested hills rising steeply to 200 ft and separated by narrow valleys. The wildest portion of this region is a band running north and south in the middle of the state, including the highlands a few miles north of the Ohio, where there are many forests, significant limestone cave systems, state parks, and other state-owned wildlife and recreation areas. Though few major highways pierce the area, the remote wooded countryside, lakes, and caves attract hikers, spelunkers, and anglers in droves. Sunday drivers descend on the area during the fall foliage season. Man-made Patoka Lake, Indiana's largest lake, is here. A thick band of limestone threads through the cave-riddled middle section from the Ohio River north to Bloomington. Indiana limestone from Lawrence County quarries distinguishes landmarks around the world. Among the oldest towns in the state are those perched along the Ohio; they're filled with antique steamboat-style mansions built by riverboat captains, stately brick federal town

---

1779
Clark leads a contingent of 130 U.S. and French soldiers to recapture Vincennes. This time he is victorious, and the event marks the end of British dominance over the Ohio River valley. This

strategic victory also leads to the release of land held by the British.

1787
The Northwest Ordinance organizes land claims north of the Ohio River as the Northwest Territory. Settlers, primarily from the East, begin streaming into the western frontier,

reaching Indiana by the Ohio River and Native American and trade trails. Feeling threatened, Native Americans organize resistance.

1794
Chief Little Turtle of the Miami commands a widespread revolt against the American settlement in Ohio and Indiana. Under the leadership of Gen. Anthony Wayne,

houses, and, along the main streets, 19th-century storefronts housing cozy restaurants and antiques and gift shops.

Towns listed: Aurora, Batesville, Bedford, Bloomington, Clarksville, Columbus, Corydon, Evansville, French Lick, Jasper, Jeffersonville, Madison, Metamora, Nashville, New Albany, New Harmony, Santa Claus, Vevay, Vincennes, Wyandotte

INTRODUCTION
HISTORY
REGIONS
WHEN TO VISIT
STATE'S GREATS
RULES OF THE ROAD
DRIVING TOURS

When to Visit

Temperatures are generally a few degrees higher in the southern half of the state, especially in the Ohio River Valley, which also receives more precipitation. Most of Indiana has cool winters and long, warm summers, which can be humid, particularly in the central corridor and southern hill country. In August, a string of 90°F days is not unusual.

For spring blossoms, plan to visit the state in April and May. Beginning in early April, the redbud trees bloom, followed by the lacy, flowering dogwood and crab apples. Madison is one of the few places in Indiana where shiny leafed southern magnolias grow. These trees display their huge fragrant white blossoms in June. Woodlands throughout the state are strewn with wildflowers in May.

In autumn, peak leaf color comes in early October in the northern half of the state and a couple of weeks later in southern Indiana. All across the state, fall is typically dry and comfortably warm, with few nights dipping below 32°F.

Winters, though generally mild, can also bring snow, most notably to the northern third and near Lake Michigan. All parts of Indiana can see temperatures below 0°F. Wet snow and freezing rain tend to accompany winter storms. You may encounter the "lake effect"—sudden winter storms that dump snow on isolated areas—in northern Indiana east and southeast of Lake Michigan.

CLIMATE CHART
Average High/Low Temperatures (°F) and Monthly Precipitation (in inches)

	JAN.	FEB.	MAR.	APR.	MAY	JUNE
EVANSVILLE	41/24	46/27	58/37	69/47	78/55	87/64
	3.0	3.5	5.0	4.2	4.5	3.5

	JULY	AUG.	SEPT.	OCT.	NOV.	DEC.
	88/66	71/47	57/39	45/29	55/36	43/26
	4.6	3.2	3.1	3.0	4.1	3.6

	JAN.	FEB.	MAR.	APR.	MAY	JUNE
FORT WAYNE	30/15	34/18	46/29	60/39	71/49	81/59-
	2.0	2.1	3.0	3.4	3.5	3.6

	JULY	AUG.	SEPT.	OCT.	NOV.	DEC.
	85/63	82/61	76/54	63/43	49/34	36/22
	3.5	3.4	2.6	2.5	2.8	2.9

1800 William Henry Harrison, who fought under Wayne at Fallen Timbers and later became President, is appointed the first governor of the Indiana Territory, with Vincennes designated as its capital.

1803 The eastern part of the Indiana Territory becomes Ohio. The remaining portion, which now includes Indiana, Michigan, Wisconsin, Illinois, and part of Minnesota, has a population of 5,600.

1809 Harrison persuades the Miami, Delaware, and Potawatomi to cede 3 million acres, including all of southern Indiana, to the United States. The Wea and Kickapoo tribes later

American soldiers decisively defeat Little Turtle's alliance at the Battle of Fallen Timbers, near present-day Toledo, Ohio. A year later, Wayne builds a fortress across the river from old Fort Miami and opens northeastern Indiana to settlement. In a treaty with Wayne, the Miami relinquish a large part of their land.

	JAN.	FEB.	MAR.	APR.	MAY	JUNE
GARY	32/15	36/19	48/29	61/38	73/48	83/58
	1.8	1.6	2.5	3.7	3.8	3.9
	JULY	AUG.	SEPT.	OCT.	NOV.	DEC.
	86/63	84/61	78/54	66/43	51/33	37/21
	3.6	3.5	4.3	3.0	3.4	2.7
	JAN.	FEB.	MAR.	APR.	MAY	JUNE
INDIANAPOLIS	34/17	38/21	51/32	63/42	74/52	83/61
	2.3	2.4	3.9	3.8	4.0	3.3
	JULY	AUG.	SEPT.	OCT.	NOV.	DEC.
	86/65	84/63	78/56	66/44	52/34	39/23
	4.5	3.7	2.9	2.7	3.4	3.5

FESTIVALS AND SEASONAL EVENTS

WINTER

Dec. **Conner Prairie by Candlelight.** Take a 90-minute candlelight tour of the 1836 recreated village of Prairietown, in Fishers, and chat with costumed villagers such as the doctor and blacksmith. | 317/773–0666.

Yuletide Celebration. Indianapolis celebrates all month. The Symphony Orchestra stages a dazzling holiday show downtown at the Hilbert Circle Theatre, with music, dance, and holiday classics. | 317/639–4300 or 800/366–8457.

Christmas at the Seiberling. In Kokomo, this gracious historic mansion is dressed in elegant holiday finery and presents entertainment and special events all month long. | 765/452–4314.

SPRING

Mar. **Maple Sugar Time Festival.** At the historic Chellberg Farm and Bailly Homestead in Porter, at the Indiana Dunes National Lakeshore, you can watch different methods of making maple sugar, from the 1600s up to the present day. | 219/926–7561, ext. 265.

Apr. **Heritage Week.** New Harmony hosts demonstrations of 19th-century crafts such as basket making, candle dipping, wood turning, and blacksmithing during this weeklong event. | 812/682–4488.

May–Oct. **Tri-State Antique Market.** At the fairgrounds in Lawrenceburg, near Cincinnati, Ohio, more than 250 dealers from Ohio,

---

agree to release land as well.

1810–11
Michigan and Illinois territories are separated from the Indiana territory and the state's population grows to more than 24,000. Many Native American tribes band together under

Shawnee chief Tecumseh and his brother Tenskwatawa, known as "the Prophet." Attacks are made on various American settlements throughout Indiana.

1812
Native Americans continue to resist settlement by the Americans. Near present-day Huntington, the Battle of Mississinewa with the Miami marks the end of Native American

resistance in Indiana.

INTRODUCTION
HISTORY
REGIONS
WHEN TO VISIT
STATE'S GREATS
RULES OF THE ROAD
DRIVING TOURS

Kentucky, and Indiana sell antiques and collectibles the first Sunday of each month. | 513/738–7256 | www.queencityshows.com.

May   **500 Festival.** Indianapolis presents an event practically every day of the month—among them an arts exhibit, a queen contest and coronation, a mini-marathon, and the downtown parade on the Saturday before Memorial Day weekend. | 317/636–4556.

SUMMER

June   **Annual Bill Monroe Memorial Bean Blossom Bluegrass Festival.** The longest-running bluegrass festival in the country was started by the late Bill Monroe, a legendary guitar and mandolin player who was known as the father of bluegrass (see Nashville). | 800/414–4677 or 812/988–6422 | www.beanblossom.com.

Evansville Freedom Festival. From the riverbank, you can watch the world's fastest boats race on the Ohio River, then take in a carnival downtown, a parade, fireworks, and an air show. | 812/421–2200 or 800/433–3025.

Indian Market. The Eiteljorg Museum of American Indians and Western Art, in Indianapolis, stages a juried weekend art show and sale that is among the largest of its kind in the Midwest, with Native American artwork and crafts from all over the United States plus traditional Native American food, dancers, and children's activities. | 317/636–WEST.

June, July   **Madison Regatta Presents the Indiana Governor's Cup.** On the eastern, opposite end of the Ohio River from Evansville's annual boat race and festival, the historic river town of Madison hosts its own state hydroplane racing competition over a 2½-mi course. The event also features food, music, a parade, and other entertainment. | 812/265–5000. | www.madisonregatta.com.

July   **Circus City Festival.** In Peru a three-ring circus performs under the big top next to a midway, with food and crafts booths, as the town celebrates its heritage as a world circus capital. | 765/472–3918.

Circle Fest. At the Monument Circle in downtown Indianapolis crowds of people gather to listen to bands and sample food from the city's restaurateurs. | 317/237–2222.

1813	**1816**		**1818**	**1820**
On May 11, the territorial capital is moved from Vincennes to Corydon.	In Corydon, delegates draft a petition for statehood. The U.S. Congress approves the petition, and Indiana becomes the 19th state on December 11. Indiana's present	boundaries are established.	Under the New Purchase, Native American land in central Indiana is acquired, opening almost all of the state to settlement.	A new site for the capital is chosen, near the confluence of Fall Creek and the west branch of the White River in the center of the state. Population increases to 147,178 by the time

AUTUMN

Sept.   **Penrod Art Fair.** The grande dame of all Indiana art fairs is a whopper, spreading out across the 100-acre grounds of the Indianapolis Museum of Art on the Saturday after Labor Day. A juried event, it includes more than 250 artists and musical, theater, and dance performances all day. | 317/252–9895 | www.penrod.org | jjbrown@bakerd.com.

Johnny Appleseed Festival. Fort Wayne presents fife and drum corps music, old-time food and crafts, a pioneer-era traders' village, and crafts demonstrations in the park where the famous tree planter was laid to rest in 1845. | 219/424–3700 or 800/767–7752.

Fairmount Museum Days/Remembering James Dean Festival. A huge car show of classic and vintage models, a parade, a screening of James Dean films, and a Dean look-alike contest all honor of one of the town's favorite sons. | 765/668–5435 or 800/662–9474.

Oct.   **Parke County Covered Bridge Festival.** More than six communities in the county take part in this 10-day festival, starting the second Friday of the month. Crafts, food, bridge tours, and other special events draw people from all over the state and beyond. The Rockville courthouse square is the festival headquarters. | 765/569–5226.

Mississinewa 1812. This Marion event is one of the largest War of 1812 living-history reenactments in the United States. Commemorating the Battle of Mississinewa, it features a Native American village and vendors, demonstrations of 18th-century crafts, food, and music. | 800/822–1812.

Heartland Film Festival. In Indianapolis, film screenings and an awards ceremony honor filmmakers whose works express hope and respect for positive values of life. | 317/464–9405.

Nov.–Dec.   **Old Fashioned Christmas Walk.** Carolers stroll the narrow streets of tiny Metamora, along the historic Whitewater Canal. Most of the town's many shops stay open late on Friday and Saturday evenings and all day Sunday. The Whitewater Valley Railroad carries visitors back and forth between Metamora and Connersville. | 765/647–2109; 765/825–2054 for train reservations.

1824	**1825**	**1840**	**1854**
Indianapolis, or "city of Indiana," is founded.	Four wagons carry the state government's archives from Corydon to the new capital, Indianapolis.	The state legislature convenes in Indianapolis in January. Two years later, most of the Miami relocate to Kansas.	The state's population surges to 685,866. The relatively flat and gently rolling fertile terrain of central and northern regions destine Indiana to become a productive farming state.	A total of 12 treaties are eventually signed between the Miami and the United States, ceding nearly all Miami land.

Christmas City Walkway of Lights. With more than two million twinkling lights Marion's holiday light display is one of the largest in the Midwest. | 765/668–5435 or 800/662–9474.

State's Greats

Although the interstates crisscrossing Indiana whisk travelers through the state faster than you can say "Jack Robinson," the subtle but striking natural beauty of the Indiana landscape is best savored on smaller roads. Remote farming towns and even the rugged southern hill country can be easily reached on a network of well-maintained, paved highways.

Beachgoers throng 25 mi of golden beach crowned with sand dunes that rim Lake Michigan in the northwest corner of the state. Here, for a glimpse of rural Americana from a century ago, follow the dusty country roads to tiny towns in Elkhart and LaGrange counties, the very heart of Amish country. Communities throughout this area are chock-full of crafts and antiques shops, restaurants that serve sumptuous home-style meals, and bed and breakfasts. This area is also dotted with thousands of small lakes. Straight west of Indianapolis, almost on the Illinois state line, is Rockville, the covered-bridge capital of the world. Thirty covered bridges, most of them painted dark red, dot the green landscape of surrounding Parke County.

History buffs seek out 300-year-old Vincennes, the state's oldest community and once the capital of the Northwest Territory. Quiet Corydon, the state's first capital, is also brimming with history. Before settling in Illinois, Abraham Lincoln spent his boyhood years in southern Indiana's Spencer County, not far from the Ohio River. A national memorial with an exhibit hall and the Lincoln family's reconstructed log cabin traces Lincoln's Indiana years. Madison, Evansville, Aurora, and other Ohio River towns thrived on riverboat traffic 100 years ago, and the boats' captains and the well-to-do citizenry built gracious mansions. In Madison, 100 blocks are on the National Register of Historic Places.

Outdoors enthusiasts flock to the Hoosier National Forest, the 57-mi-long Knobstone Trail, dozens of state forests, and recreation areas and lakes sprinkled across the southern hill country. Dense stands of oak, hickory, and maple crown the rounded hillsides, making a pretty show of color in fall. Nashville, seat of Brown County, is an art colony. Through the limestone belt in south-central Indiana, there are dozens of caves to tour.

Regional centers like Fort Wayne, Lafayette, Richmond, South Bend, and Evansville give you a break from the rural life. For energetic entertainment, dining, shopping, and sports, Indianapolis is a must. Riding a decade-long wave of revitalization, it's an unsung innovator.

Beaches, Forests, and Parks

Productive farmland in the north and industrial and commercial hubs have consumed most of the land, leaving only a few wild areas and federally owned parks and forests.

1860
Indiana leads the country in the production of corn, wheat, and livestock. The Wabash, the Erie Canal, the railroads, and the Ohio River transport goods east and to New Orleans, helping Indiana's

economy to grow. The state's population now stands at 1,350,428, twice that of 1840.

1861–65
The Civil War begins and Indiana responds to President Abraham Lincoln's request by entering the war on the Union side.

1863
Indiana's major military action of the Civil War comes during what becomes known as Morgan's Raid. Confederate Gen. John Hunt Morgan leads 2,500 troops to the towns of Corydon,

Salem, Dupont, and Versailles, where they loot and destroy property. Eventually, Morgan's troops are forced from the state and defeated by Union troops in Ohio.

The only beach in Indiana that mimics an ocean's is in the northwest, where the wide watery finger of Lake Michigan dips down to a 25-mi arc of sandy shoreline. Indiana's shoreline, like Michigan's to the north, offers miles of golden sand and dunes. About 15 mi of the Indiana segment is in the 13,000-acre **Indiana Dunes National Lakeshore.** Even though the property is interrupted by patches of civilization, even big steel mills at the water's edge, the beaches are pristine and inviting.

Hoosier National Forest, the only such park in the state, covers 195,000 acres and includes the state's only wilderness area, the **Charles C. Deam Wilderness.** The 13,000-acre reserve, made up of steep ridges, narrow hollows, and dense woods, is remote and accessible only on foot or horseback. The state's longest hiking trail, **Knobstone,** travels almost 60 mi through the knobby hills of **Jackson-Washington State Forest,** one of a dozen such preserves. The most rugged and primitive state-owned forests and recreation areas are in the south. The 26,000-acre **Harrison-Crawford/Wyandotte Complex,** in the high hills north of the Ohio River valley, has spectacular caves, dense forests, and upland trails. Also along the river, in Jeffersonville, is the unusual **Falls of the Ohio State Park,** where 220 acres of fossil beds are exposed when river levels are lowest from August through October. In the south near Columbus, the **Muscatatuck National Wildlife Refuge,** the only one in the state, shelters waterfowl and migratory raptors, including ospreys and eagles; river otters, reintroduced to the habitat, are thriving.

Though **Brown County State Park,** near Nashville, is the state's largest park, it is also the busiest, particularly in fall. Most of the state's 23 parks include a combination of back-to-nature amenities like nature centers, well-maintained hiking trails, and boating, as well as recreation facilities like swimming pools and tennis courts. **Chain of Lakes,** a lesser known park in the north near Fort Wayne, takes advantage of a string of eight interconnected kettle lakes, and attracts canoeists, hikers, and, in winter, cross-country skiers. **Pokagon State park,** in the state's northeast corner, has a classic lodge and is surrounded by lakes. It appeals to anglers and boaters in summer and snowbunnies in winter, with its 1/4-mi toboggan run, cross-country skiing, and ice fishing. The 250-acre **White River State Park** in Indianapolis is home to a 3-D IMAX theater, museums, a zoo, and a baseball park.

Most of the state's larger cities have municipal parks and urban and suburban pedestrian trails. A greenway system will eventually string together the 57 parks of the **Indy Parks and Recreation** system; plans are for more than 175 mi of trails on land and water following rivers, old railroad beds, and the 1836 canal towpath. One of this nation's largest developed city parks is the gargantuan but woodsy **Eagle Creek** on the outskirts of Indianapolis. Here, 3,000 acres of woodlands surround Eagle Creek Reservoir, which is dotted with canoes, sailboats and fishing boats in summer and attracts swimmers to its beach. Downtown, the **Canal Walk** skirts a 10 1/2-block vestige of historic Central Canal. Benches and fountains punctuate the wide walkways, and paddleboats troll the shallow waters.

1860–90		1886		1905–20
Agriculture continues to dominate Indiana economy fueled by invention and improvement of machinery. With increases in productivity, many farmers purchase additional land. Small factories	promote industry across Indiana. Coal mining and limestone quarrying become major industries in the south-central and southwestern regions of the state.	The discovery of natural gas in the Trenton Field, an underground reservoir extending from the Ohio Border west to Kokomo, spurs industrial growth throughout northeastern and	north-central Indiana. The supply of gas is exhausted within 20 years.	The state continues on a path of industrial growth while maintaining its status as a leading agricultural state. With the construction of a major plant on the shores of Lake Michigan by

Culture, History, and the Arts

Practically every county has its historical society and, usually, a modest museum exhibiting artifacts relating to local history. One of the most impressive is Bloomington's **Monroe County Historical Society Museum.** The Wabash and Erie Canal and railroad exhibits at the **Old City Hall Historical Museum** in downtown Fort Wayne are must-sees for fans of transportation history. The Tippecanoe County Historical Association has filled Lafayette's historic **Fowler House** with its collections. The fascinating **Northern Indiana Center for History** complex includes a museum with regional history exhibits, the 1870 **Worker's Home Museum,** which reflects the town's working-class heritage, and **Copshaholm,** a turn-of-the-century mansion. The newest historical center is the headquarters of the **Indiana Historical Society** in downtown Indianapolis, built in turn-of-the-century style.

A number of museums honor its famous sons and daughters. Two pay homage to poet James Whitcomb Riley, best known as the creator of "Little Orphan Annie." These are the **James Whitcomb Riley Birthplace and Museum** in Indianapolis and the **James Whitcomb Riley Home** in Greenfield. Two rustic homes of naturalist and author Gene Stratton Porter are also now state historic sites, one near Auburn in Rome City, the other, the **Limberlost State Historic Site,** in Geneva. Abraham Lincoln is celebrated only at his boyhood home in Lincoln City and at the **Lincoln Museum** in Fort Wayne, which displays the world's largest private collection of Lincoln artifacts and memorabilia and eye-catching films. Most larger Indiana cities have regional art, natural history, or science museums. Works by Rembrandt, Chagall, and Picasso are on view in the **Snite Museum of Art,** at the University of Notre Dame. The mix is unusual at the **Evansville Museum of Arts and Science**—art, an indoor 1900s model village, and a planetarium. Like many Hoosier towns that were important industrial and commercial centers a century ago, Evansville has a house museum, the columned **John Augustus Reitz Mansion.** In New Albany the imposing Second Empire–style **Culbertson Mansion State Historic Site** reigns over the Mansion Row historic district. In Michigan City, the **Barker Mansion** was styled after an English manor house, and the **Morris-Butler House** in Indianapolis is lavishly decorated with chandeliers and carved woodwork.

Indiana recognizes its humble beginnings and pioneer roots with **Conner Prairie,** a re-created 1836 village and living-history center in Fishers, northeast of Indianapolis. The 80-acre **Amish Acres** complex in Nappanee combines an Amish farm, a furnished farmhouse, crafts, and farming demonstrations. Several towns are practically open-air museums, most notably the river town of **Madison,** known for its 100 blocks of structures on the National Register of Historic Places. The centerpiece is the home of James F. D. Lanier, now a state historic site. **New Harmony,** in Indiana's big toe near the confluence of the Wabash and Ohio rivers, presents historic buildings from the town's two utopian communities and contemporary masterpieces by world-renowned architects. In **Columbus** Eero and Eliel Saarinen, I. M. Pei, and other internationally known architects have designed more than 50 schools, churches, and commercial buildings.

INTRODUCTION
HISTORY
REGIONS
WHEN TO VISIT
STATE'S GREATS
RULES OF THE ROAD
DRIVING TOURS

the United States Steel Corporation, the Calumet region of northwestern Indiana attracts heavy industry. The steel producer proceeds to lay out a city, naming it after chairman of the board Elbert H. Gary. The state's population is now 2,930,390, with more than half concentrated in urban and industrial areas. The automobile industry also takes off in Indiana, and soon Indianapolis rivals Detroit as the nation's automotive manufacturing center.

1928
Hoosier Cole Porter writes "Paris," which becomes the first of his many Broadway successes.

1954
I.D.E.A. manufactures the first transistor radio in Indianapolis.

The state's principal art museum, the **Indianapolis Museum of Art,** is set on 100 landscaped acres and includes major collections of American, European, Asian, and contemporary art. The **Indianapolis Motor Speedway and Hall of Fame Museum** showcases automotive history via 30 Indy 500–winning cars and classic and antique autos. At the **Auburn-Cord-Duesenberg Museum,** the automobile manufacturer's Art Deco showrooms and factory serve as the backdrop for a flashy collection of cars from the early- to mid-1900s. A contemporary adobe-style building houses the **Eiteljorg Museum of American Indians and Western Art** in downtown Indianapolis. The **Children's Museum of Indianapolis** is one of the largest in the country.

While most larger Indiana cities support a part-time symphony orchestra, Indianapolis claims the **Indianapolis Symphony Orchestra,** which presents a year-round schedule of classical, pops, and special performances. In summer, the orchestra plays on the outdoor stage at the Conner Prairie museum's grassy amphitheater in Fishers, just north of the capital; the rest of the year the venue is the **Hilbert Circle Theatre,** a renovated 1916 movie theater with superb acoustics. Indianapolis is also home to the **Indianapolis Repertory Theater,** which performs in the historic Indiana Theatre, a former downtown movie palace. Most larger towns support dance and theater groups and bring touring acts to town. Opera, Broadway shows, and top-name performers take the stage at **Clowes Hall at Butler University,** in Indianapolis. Two libraries are recognized for their collections. The **Lilly Library,** on the Indiana University campus in Bloomington, displays a copy of the Gutenberg Bible. Indiana's oldest library, with 10,000 rare volumes, is the **Cathedral Library and Museum** in Vincennes.

Sports

The very name of Indiana is inextricably associated with basketball. Fan of high-school basketball follow the sport with fervor bordering on hysteria—thus, "Hoosier hysteria"—spotlighted in the 1986 Gene Hackman film *Hoosiers,* based on a stunning last-second shot that brought the state championship to tiny Milan High. Basketball fans also flock to games at Indiana and Purdue universities, both Big Ten conference schools, and those of the professional **Indiana Pacers,** Indianapolis's NBA team, lately coached by homegrown former player Larry Bird. Other professional ball teams are the NFL's **Indianapolis Colts,** who play at the RCA Dome in Indianapolis, and the **Indianapolis Indians,** who play baseball at retro Victory Field, on the west edge of downtown.

Indianapolis calls itself the "Amateur Sports Capital of the World" because of many national and international competitions that take place in its world-class facilities. Spectators can watch the world's best swimmers, cyclists, ice skaters, and track and field stars as they compete at the IU Natatorium, Track and Field Stadium, and Tennis Center.

In the last few years, the **Indianapolis Motor Speedway** has added NASCAR races that run modified stock cars on oval courses and Formula One competition with open-wheel, light-weight, and high-speed cars to the long-standing premier auto racing event,

1969
Indianapolis-born author Kurt Vonnegut's best-known work, *Slaughterhouse-Five,* is published.

1982
Gary, Indiana–born Michael Jackson releases *Thriller,* which would become the second-best-selling album of all time.

1988
Indiana resident James Danforth Quayle becomes the 44th Vice President of the United States.

1996
Julia Carson becomes Indiana's first woman and first African-American to serve in the United States House of Representatives.

INTRODUCTION
HISTORY
REGIONS
WHEN TO VISIT
STATE'S GREATS
RULES OF THE ROAD
DRIVING TOURS

the **Indy 500.** Known as the greatest spectacle in racing, the Indy 500 races open-wheel cars that average a blinding 220 m.p.h. Indianapolis Raceway Park also stages NASCAR races and national drag strip competition.

In cities, paved trails attract walkers, cyclists, and in-line skaters. The paved 10-mi **Monon Trail** connects the north side of Indianapolis with downtown. Outside metropolitan areas, most state parks have hiking trails. The **Indiana Dunes National Lakeshore Calumet Bike Trail** covers 9 mi, southern Indiana's **Knobstone Trail** 57 mi. The trail takes its name from the Knobstone Escarpment, the flat-topped ridges that it traverses.

Anglers wet their lines in thousands of lakes; in **Lake Michigan** you can find something akin to deep-sea fishing. In the 1960s there was also an initiative to stock Lake Michigan with salmon and trout. Today, Michigan City is the self-proclaimed "coho capital of the Midwest" and catches of coho, chinook salmon, and trout set records in season, from April to November.

The Indiana Department of Natural Resources manages nine reservoirs scattered fairly evenly across the state and all but three cover at least 3,000 watery acres. **Monroe,** at 10,750 acres, and the 8,800-acre **Patoka,** both in the south, are popular for fishing, boating, water-skiing, and swimming.

Winter sports are chancy. In the north the legendary "lake effect" brings occasional sudden snowstorms. You can go cross-country skiing, ice fishing, ice skating, sledding, and tubing in Indiana Dunes National Lakeshore and most state and county parks in the area. There are also three ski resorts in southern Indiana, Perfect North Slopes, near Aurora, Nashville's Ski World, and Paoli Peaks, near French Lick. All have snowmaking, and runs can be challenging if limited in number.

There are more than 430 golf courses in the state, and roughly two-thirds of them are open to the public. Columbus's Otter Creek Golf Course, designed by Robert Trent Jones and his son Rees, is challenging. Architect Harry Weese designed the glass-walled clubhouse.

Canoeists paddle streams all over the state, including the Tippecanoe River through the eponymous state park and Sugar Creek in Turkey Run and Shades state parks. The new Indianapolis Parks Greenways includes water trails, and canoeists can rent canoes on the north side of town and put in on White River for a 3- to 4-hr leisurely float into the city center.

Rules of the Road

License Requirements: To drive in Indiana you must be at least 16 years old and have a valid driver's license. Residents of Canada and most other countries may drive with valid licenses from their home countries.

Right Turn on Red: Throughout the state, a right turn on red is permitted after a full stop, unless otherwise indicated by a no-turn-on-red sign.

Speed Limits: The speed limit on most interstate highways is 65 mph except for portions of road that travel through urban or congested areas. Watch for road signs as the speed limit can change often and quickly.

Seat Belt and Helmet Laws: Drivers and front-seat passengers must wear seat belts. Children under the age of five must use a federally approved child safety seat. Only motorcyclists under the age of 18 are required to wear helmets.

For More Information: Contact the Indiana Bureau of Motor Vehicles at 317/233–6000.

Uplands and Down Under Driving Tour

EXPLORING INDIANA'S SOUTHERN HIGHLANDS AND CAVES

Distance: 135 mi   Time: 4 days

Breaks: Stop overnight in French Lick, Bloomington, or Nashville—these towns have inns and other lodging.

Unlike northern Indiana, which was flattened by prehistoric glaciers, the landscape dips and swells south of Indianapolis. Here century-old small towns nestle in narrow

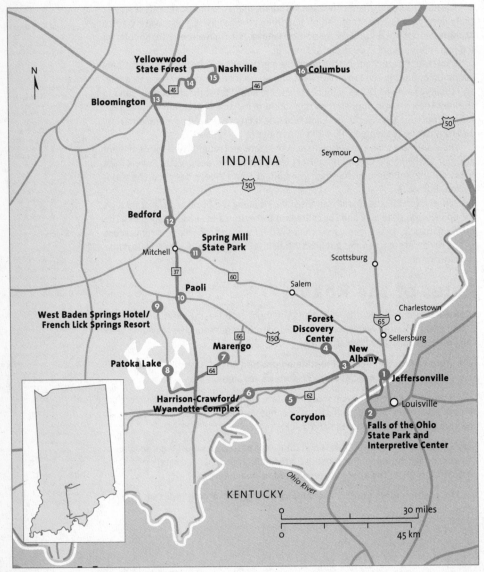

valleys amid dense forests and limestone cave systems. These hills and hollows saw a constant flow of settlers headed for the western frontier during the first half of the 19th century. Traveling on the Ohio River and following animals' trails, the settlers pressed west. Many were European immigrants whom the hilly landscape reminded of their homelands. So a number stayed on and established towns that today reflect their ethnic roots. State parks and forests protect much of the hilly terrain. The Hoosier National Forest covers a wide corridor stretching south from Lake Monroe to the Ohio River.

INTRODUCTION
HISTORY
REGIONS
WHEN TO VISIT
STATE'S GREATS
RULES OF THE ROAD
DRIVING TOURS

The history of **Jeffersonville,** one of the state's oldest cities, is inextricably linked with that of the Ohio River. Stop at the **Howard Steamboat Museum** to study the history of the Howard Shipyards, Jeffersonville's premier boat builder from 1834 to 1941. The museum is housed in the 1890 mansion of the company's owner, Edmonds J. Howard.

Leaving the museum, follow Market Street 1¾ mi west until it becomes East Riverside Avenue, and continue ¾ mi to the entrance of **Falls of the Ohio State Park and Interpretive Center,** 220 acres of shoreline fossil beds.

Four miles west of Falls of the Ohio on I–64, you'll come to **New Albany,** which grew to become the state's largest city by 1850 on the strength of Ohio River traffic. Along Mansion Row downtown are gracious homes from the town's golden era. The 20,000-square-ft Second Empire **Culbertson Mansion State Historic Site** has a rosewood staircase, marble fireplaces, and crystal chandeliers.

At the **Forest Discovery Center,** 6 mi north of New Albany, a walk-through exhibit and displays explore the topic of wood and wood processing.

Continue south along I–64 for about 3 mi to **Corydon,** the state's first capital between 1816 and 1825. Several sites here evoke the state's early days, including the modest blue limestone State Capitol building, **Governor Hendricks's Headquarters** with the **Constitution Elm** on its grounds, the **Posey House Museum** , and the **Battle of Corydon Memorial Park.**

The **Harrison-Crawford/Wyandotte Complex,** is made up of three adjacent properties: the **Wyandotte Caves State Recreation Area** , the **Wyandotte Woods State Recreation Area,** and the **Harrison-Crawford State Forest,** one of the state's largest forests at 24,000 acres. Its hills often offer fine views over the Ohio River valley. Tours of the Wyandotte caves last between 45 minutes and all day; some are easy and others require crawling, scrambling, and climbing.

From Wyandotte, go 4 mi west on I–64 to Exit 92. Follow Route 66 north about 9 mi to Marengo, site of 122-acre **Marengo Cave National Landmark,** a wide trunk-passage cave that reaches through limestone hills. Two guided tours explore the formation-filled caverns. You can rent canoes and kayaks for paddles down the scenic Blue River at nearby **Cave Country Canoes.**

Northwest of Marengo is **Patoka Lake,** the state's second-largest reservoir. Seven state recreation areas with campgrounds, hiking and bridle trails, paved bicycle trails, swimming, and picnic areas surround the sprawling lake. Exhibits at the visitors center explore the lake's formation and local wildlife, including bald eagles. More than 26,000 acres of shoreline are under state protection; elsewhere you'll find vacation homes and travelers' services.

West Baden Springs Hotel and **French Lick Springs Resort** were once rivals, spawning towns of the same names. Long before the first settlers arrived, great herds of buffalo stopped at the natural mineral springs and salt licks at what is today known as French Lick. The buffalo trace started in the bluegrass area of Kentucky then headed northwest through French Lick and Vincennes toward the Great Plains. As early as the 1840s, tourists started making the trek to the grand hotel at French Lick to partake of the mineral waters there. Soon a huge bottling plant was capping Pluto Water, a sulphurous brew thought to possess curative powers. In the early 1900s, the town was known as "the Las Vegas of the Midwest" because of its elegant casinos. Though the hotel has changed over the years, it is still in business as a golf and tennis resort and spa. The luxurious West Baden Hotel, built in 1902 less than 1 mi away, is topped by a magnificent six-story dome; you can't stay there but you can tour the structure and its formal gardens. Until 1966, when the Houston Astrodome was erected, the hotel's free-span dome was the largest in the world.

⑩ Paoli is a county seat with a majestic towered courthouse atop a hill. Quakers from North Carolina settled Paoli and named the town for the 12-year-old son of the governor of North Carolina, who had died shortly before. The courthouse was built in 1850, and the clock was added in 1856. The town calls itself the Dogwood Capital of Indiana.

⑪ From Paoli, head north for 12 mi on Rte. 37, then 3 mi east on Rte. 60 to 1,300-acre **Spring Mill State Park,** where rocky creeks wind through an 80-acre area known as Donaldson's Woods Nature Preserve. Underground, you can float down a subterranean river in one of the park's two cave systems. A reconstructed village dating back to 1815 features a gristmill and a half-dozen buildings. The park also pays homage to a local space-age hero with the Virgil I. Grissom State Memorial.

⑫ Sited roughly in the center of a wide band of limestone that stretches across the state, **Bedford** is known as the Limestone Capital of the World. Housed in the 1926 offices of Bedford's Indiana Limestone Company, the **Land of Limestone** exhibit documents quarrying and stonecutting in Lawrence County since the 1850s with photographs, tools, and artifacts. Indiana limestone was used when Chicago was rebuilt after the Great Fire of 1871, in 35 state capitol buildings, and in many buildings in Washington, D.C. Lawrence County driving and walking tours take you to residential neighborhoods, city parks, and cemeteries full of richly detailed stone carvings; the Empire Hole here was where the stone used in the Empire State Building was quarried. In **Green Hill Cemetery** don't miss the 1917 limestone monument of stone-carver Louis Baker, with a stonecutter's workbench complete with tools. At **Bluespring Caverns** a 1-mi boat tour takes you down the 20-mi-long Myst'ry River, one of the world's longest subterranean streams.

⑬ The lush, green countryside continues to **Bloomington.** The handsome Beaux Arts–style **Monroe County Courthouse,** built in 1902, towers over the low-slung downtown. The center city encompasses 11 blocks and a variety of boutiques, galleries, specialty shops, restaurants, and live music clubs. **Fountain Square,** a small shopping mall, hides behind period storefronts with a view of the courthouse square.

Indiana University was established 3 blocks from the square in 1820. The world's largest student union, the **Indiana Memorial Union** sits in the middle of campus, housing a 190-room hotel, 7 dining areas, a bookstore, bowling lanes, a billiards room, a hair salon, and the IMU Gallery. Among the landmarks on the wooded campus are the glass-and-stone I. M. Pei–designed **Indiana University Art Museum,** which houses more than 35,000 artworks from the Byzantine era to the times of Claude Monet and Pablo Picasso. **Lilly Library** is known internationally for its rare books collection. The

INTRODUCTION
HISTORY
REGIONS
WHEN TO VISIT
STATE'S GREATS
RULES OF THE ROAD
DRIVING TOURS

Monroe County Historical Museum is housed in an old Carnegie library building. The **Wylie House** was built in 1835 as the home of the university's first president, Andrew Wylie. On the far north edge of campus, the **Hilltop Garden and Nature Center** is home to one of America's oldest youth gardening programs, established in 1948, as well as display flower gardens.

🄬 **Yellowwood State Forest,** 13 mi east of Bloomington via Rte. 46, is a patch of pine, oak, and tulip poplars on the Brown County hills. A quiet lake invites boaters.

🄭 Leave Yellowwood on Rte. 46 and proceed about 5 mi east to **Nashville.** This rural village has retained its rustic airs since it caught the eyes of artists nearly a century ago. Today artists rub elbows with mobs of tourists in the tiny four-block center of town. Along nearby country roads, log cabins peek throught he woods—Brown County claims some 500 of them. Hand-painted signs point down shady lanes to artists' studios. It was a scene like this that attracted Adolph Shulz, an artist searching for the "authentic American landscape," to Brown County at the turn of the century. In 1907, the most prominent figure of the Brown County art colony, Theodore Clement Steele, built a studio and home, The House of Singing Winds, which is now part of the **T. C. Steele State Historic Site.** On the south edge of town is 15,400-acre **Brown County State Park** with horseback riding, two lakes, trails, and many miles of scenic road.

🄮 Fifteen mi east of Nashville via Rte. 46 is **Columbus,** known as the Athens of the Midwest. Notable contemporary architects have designed more than 50 buildings here, and historic buildings along the brick streets sparkle as if they were new. One- and 2-hr guided tours and self-guided tour maps are available at the **Columbus Area Visitor Center,** where displays give an overview of the community and its architectural development. The **Bartholomew Historical Society Museum,** in the Italianate brick McEwen-Samuels-Marr Home, traces the town's early history in four galleries with permanent and rotating exhibits.

East Indiana's National Road Driving Tour
150 YEARS OF HISTORY

Distance: 45 mi   Time: 2 days
Breaks: Stop overnight in Richmond or Centerville—both towns have lodging.

More than a century of history unfolds on this tour that follows the National Road and parallels I–70 from Richmond west to Greenfield in central Indiana. Launched from Cumberland, Maryland, in 1811, the Cumberland Road as it was also known, rolled across the heart of the Midwest ending in Vandalia, Illinois, nearly 30 years later. The Indiana segment, nothing more than a crude wagon road at first, was completed in 1834, after five years of cutting through thick forest and taming the wilderness. So-called pike towns sprang up overnight, serving local farmers and travelers headed west. After the road became U.S. 40 in the 1920s, about a century after the earliest towns had been established, their gas, food, and lodging establishments enjoyed a steady stream of motor traffic. Old-fashioned gas stations, remnants of former strip and cabin court motels, and roadside cafés reflect the early 20th-century chapter in the roadway's history.

● Begin your tour at Richmond's **Old National Road Welcome Center,** which stocks packets of information on the National Road and the area.

❷ **Richmond,** known as the Queen City of the Whitewater River Valley, grew up around the National Road and the East Fork of the Whitewater River. It contains numerous historic buildings dating from 1820 to 1890 in several historic districts.

Stretching along the north side of the National Road on the eastern edge of Richmond is the **Hayes Regional Arboretum,** a 355-acre natural area with a 3-mi driving tour and four hiking trails. **Glen Miller Park** is a 194-acre wooded preserve across from the arboretum with picnic shelters, spring-fed fountains, and small streams; it doesn't take its name from the band leader. It is home to several gardens, including the **E. G. Hill Memorial Rose Garden,** honoring one of the town's famed rosarians. Also in the park is the 10-ft **Madonna of the Trail Monument,** one of 12 such monuments along the National Road and U.S. 40 between Cumberland, Maryland, and California, commemorating pioneer mothers of covered-wagon days.

The 1895 stone **Wayne County Courthouse** presides over downtown. Construction of the massive structure called for 600 wagonloads of stone from Bedford quarries. To the west of town, there are impressive limestone and shale canyons along the east fork of the Whitewater River. A 7-mi hiking trail in **Whitewater Valley Gorge Park** links the falls and the remains of the Test Woolen Mills to the south. The Whitewater River Gorge Fossil Guide pinpoints prime fossil-hunting locations along the river.

Attracted by fertile land, available water, and stone for building material, the Quakers first settled Richmond in 1805. By 1847 they had established **Earlham College.** Redbrick buildings dot the shady campus. The college's **Joseph Moore Museum of Natural**

History displays an Egyptian mummy, a prehistoric mastodon, allosaurus skeletons, and other relicst.

Three miles west of Richmond on U.S. 40 lies **Historic Centerville,** one of the earliest of the National Road towns from the 1820s. It's filled with distinctive Federal-style redbrick row houses. Centerville anchors a 40-mi stretch of the National Road known as Antique Alley, where more than 900 antiques dealers do business. Immense **Webb's Antiques Mall** brings together hundreds of antiques and collectibles dealers alone on its 2 acres—all under one roof. It's a block north of the National Road in downtown Centerville.

Cambridge City, 7 mi west of Centerville on U.S. 40, was once a thriving commercial center. The National Road's heyday is reflected in the ornate cornices and fancy trim of Italianate storefronts and a former hotel, the **Vinton House,** dating from the mid-1800s. For almost 50 years, until 1955, six sisters of the Overbeck family turned out ceramic figurines and art pottery in this area. Select pieces are on display today at the **Museum of Overbeck Art Pottery.**

In **Mount Auburn,** ¼ mi west of Cambridge City on U.S. 40, the Huddleston farm was a stop for National Road travelers in the 1840s. The **Historic Huddleston Farmhouse Inn Museum** was created around the restored farm and its outbuildings, including the spring and smokehouses.

Leaving Mount Auburn, you'll pass rolling farms and stands of trees as you drive the 21 mi west toward **Knightstown,** named for Jonathan Knight, surveyor of the National Road. Three blocks north of the National Road, the dramatic Second Empire twin towers of the former Knightstown Academy, built in 1877, pierce the leafy canopy. Another dozen homes, a former hotel, and a theater were built between the mid 1860s and early 1900s. Bruce Trump has turned the 1930s Texaco gas station operated by his father into **Trump's Texaco Museum,** which displays Texaco and gas station memorabilia and collectibles.

Twelve miles farther west, **Greenfield** is a typical small Midwestern county seat with a charming courthouse square surrounded by 1880s-era storefronts and commercial buildings. A gingerbread porch graces the front of the **James Whitcomb Riley Birthplace and Museum,** the Hoosier state's most beloved children's poet of the mid- and late 1800s. The town's pride in Riley is evident in a park, school, and festival named after him.

ANDERSON

MAP 3, E4

(Nearby towns also listed: Fishers, Greenfield, Indianapolis, Muncie, New Castle, Noblesville)

Once a village of the Delaware tribe, Anderson remained a quiet community on the White River until 1887 when the first natural-gas well was sunk into an enormous underground gas reservoir that stretched from Kokomo to the Ohio border. Like other towns atop this great natural resource, Anderson boomed. Manufacturers rushed to the Queen City of the Gas Belt. The population had grown to 20,000 by the 1890s. Thought to be inexhaustible, gas wells burned around the clock; huge plumes of fire reached high above the horizon, lighting the darkness and sending farmers into their fields all night long. Then, within a decade, the supply ran out. Today, Newport-style gaslights and Victorian mansions with turrets, stained-glass, and widow's walks recall Anderson's prosperity during its gas-boom heyday. Today, the population is 60,000, and business and industry, including several large-scale manufacturers of automotive parts, support the economy.

Information: Anderson/Madison County Visitors and Convention Bureau | 6335 S. Scatterfield Rd. 46013 | 800/533–6569 | andersonvcb@iquest.net | www.madtourism.com.

Attractions

Anderson University. Established in 1917 and affiliated with the Church of God, this tree-lined campus on the edge of downtown is home to nearly 2,400 students in an undergraduate liberal-arts program and graduate programs in theology, business, and education. | 1100 E. 5th St. | 765/641–4145 or 800/428–6414 (admissions) | fax 765/641–3851 | www.anderson.edu | Free | Sept.–June, weekdays 10–5, Sat. 10–4.

Established in 1963, the **Gustav Jeeninga Museum of Bible and Near Eastern Studies** displays artifacts from Egypt, Rome, the Middle East, and Mesopotamia. Replicas of well-known Near Eastern artifacts such as the Hammurabi Law Code, the original of which is in the Louvre, and the Shalmanesar Obelisk, whose original is in the British Museum, are also displayed. | 1123 University Blvd. | 765/641–4526 | fax 765/641–3851 | www.anderson.edu | Free | Weekdays 8–5; weekends by appointment only.

The **Krannert Fine Arts Center** features a permanent art collection, including works by Warner Sallman; his Head of Christ painting is on display here. | 1100 E 5th St. | 765/641–4320 | Free | Sept.–May, weekdays 8:30–4:30; call for summer hrs.

Historic Gruenewald House. Polished dark woodwork, and Victorian furnishings dating from 1875 to 1897 fill 13 rooms of the 1860 French Second Empire–style town house in downtown Anderson. Guided tours trace the history of the house, including the lifestyle of Martin Gruenewald, an innkeeper who built the home. | 626 Main St. | 765/648–6875 | mgruenewald@netzero.net | $4 | Apr.–mid-Dec., Tues.–Fri. 10–3, or by appointment.

Historic West 8th Street. Turreted mansions and fancy Victorians with gingerbread trim dating from 1870 to 1920 reflect Anderson's late 19th-century heyday, when the town was known as the Queen City of the Gas Belt. | 765/643–5633 | www.madtourism.com | fax 765/643–9083 | Free | Daily.

Historical Military Armor Museum. More than 40 tanks, Jeeps, and other military vehicles that actually saw the battle lines from World War I through the Gulf War are displayed along with military memorabilia here. Among the highlights at the 35,000-square-ft former factory building are the 1947 Cadillac built for Harry Truman and a World War II–vintage WC56, a command vehicle believed to be part of the fleet used by General Mark Clark. | 2330 Crystal St. | 765/649–TANK | fax 765/642–0262 | $3 | Tues., Thurs., Sat. 1–4.

Hoosier Park. Indiana's first pari-mutuel horse-racing track, 8 mi south of downtown Anderson, hosts harness and thoroughbred races except in winter and shows simulcast events year-round on 275 TV monitors. You can sit in the grandstand or watch from the enclosed Homestretch Clubhouse Restaurant overlooking the track. | 4500 Dan Patch Cir. | 765/642–7223 or 800/526–7223 | fax 765/644–0467 | www.hoosierpark.com | $2 | Live racing season Apr.–Dec., Thurs.–Mon. 6 and 6:45 PM, Sun. 6:00 PM; simulcast racing daily.

Indian Trails Riverwalk, Killbuck Wetlands Nature Preserve, and Shadyside Memorial Park. Paved and boardwalk trails connect these three attractions on the banks of the Whitewater. The Riverwalk trail leads 1 mi from downtown to Killbuck Wetlands. Another short wetlands trail then connects with two trails totaling 2½ mi at the Shadyside park lake. The historic Chinese Gardens near the park entrance have been restored and are a highlight there. | 765/648–6850 | Free | Daily dawn to dusk.

Mounds State Park. Ten earthworks or mounds of the prehistoric Adena and Hopewell tribes spread along the banks of the White River in this rolling 288-acre preserve 2 mi southeast of Anderson. Four miles of easy to moderate hiking trails pass by the circular Great Mound and smaller fiddle-shape, figure-eight, and rectangular earthworks. There's also a camp-ground, a nature center, a swimming pool, and facilities for picnicking. | 4306 Mounds Rd. | 765/642–6627 | fax 765/643–0641 | www.ai.org/dnr | $2 Ind. residents, $5 non-residents | Daily.

Paramount Theatre and Ballroom. Designed by John Eberson in 1929, this ornate down-town theater is noted for its exquisite architectural details and dark blue ceiling repre-senting the midnight sky, complete with twinkling stars and wispy clouds. The original Grande Page organ, now restored, is one of only three such organs in its original installa-tion in the United States. Opera, recitals, and other theater and musical performances are presented throughout the year. | 1124 Meridian St. | 765/642–1234 or 800/523–4658 | fax 765/642–1477 | www.astralite.com/parathea | $3 | Weekdays 10–4.

One of the state's top professional community orchestras, the **Anderson Symphony Orchestra** performs holiday concerts and a total of six classical and pops concerts featuring guest artists in the exquisite theater. | 765/644–2111 | Sept.–May.

Tom St. Clair Studio Glass. The natural gas that brought the area such prosperity also fueled many glass factories in the area. Tom St. Clair, who comes from a long line of glasswork-ers in Madison County, crafts molten art glass into paperweights, perfume bottles, and other decorative accessories. | 6362 Pendleton Ave. | 765/642–7770 | Free | Fri.–Sun. 10–6.

ON THE CALENDAR

MAY: *Little 500 Festival*. This annual sprint car race runs at the Anderson Speedway. The festival, first held in 1950, has events for all ages including a fireworks display. | 765/640–2437 | www.little500.org.

OCT.: *Indian Trails Festival*. Along the downtown Riverwalk trail edging the Whitewa-ter River, you can admire the historical and cultural traditions of Native Americans with displays of artifacts, costumes, and arts and crafts. | 800/533–6569.

Dining

Cilantro's. American. Tables are draped with white cloths in this corner building in sub-urban Edgewood. There is a daily buffet of American and Indian fare plus a menu that offers up fried chicken, Swiss steak, filet mignon, rib-eye steak, sirloin steak, curried meat-balls, curried chicken, vegetables, mashed potatoes, samosas, rice, and sandwiches. | 3304 Nichol Ave. | 765/643–5335 | Closed Mon. | $7–$15 | AE, D, MC, V.

Grindstone Charley's. American. This casual, family-style restaurant is part of a multilo-cation Indiana–Ohio chain. Starter choices include chicken walnut salad and loaded potato soup, spiked with cheese, bacon, and green onions. If you have room you can move on to smothered chicken, Jack Daniel's steak, pot roast with mashed potatoes and vegetables, catfish, and barbecue pork ribs. | 5627 Scatterfield Rd. | 765/644–5021 | $8–$15 | AE, D, DC, MC, V.

Red Brick Inn. American. If you're looking for home-style cooking, this restaurant in a red-brick building is a good choice. Look for fried chicken, roast beef, ribs, shrimp, porterhouse and New York strip steaks, sandwiches, and potatoes. Chicken and noodles, served every Friday, is among the daily specials. | 6317 Pendleton Ave. | 765/649–8010 | Closed Mon. | $5–$13 | No credit cards.

Lodging

Best Inns of America. This two-story motel built in 1986 is ¼ mi from I-69, exit 26 (Ander-son), along a motel strip, 5 mi south of town. An indoor corridor leads to guest rooms. Com-plimentary Continental breakfast. Cable TV. Some pets allowed. | 5706 Scatterfield Rd. | 765/644–2000 or 800/237–8466 | fax 765/644–2000 | 93 rooms | $52 | AE, D, DC, MC, V.

Comfort Inn. This two-story motel is on the motel strip ½ mi from I-69, exit 26 (Ander-son), at the south end of town. Complimentary Continental breakfast. Microwaves (in suites), refrigerators (in suites). Cable TV. Indoor pool. Hot tub. Some pets allowed (with fee). | 2205

E. 59th St. | 765/644–4422 | fax 765/644–4422 | 56 rooms, 14 suites | $66 rooms, $71 suites | AE, D, DC, MC, V.

Holiday Inn. Built in the 1960s, this two-story Holiday Inn is one of the original chain properties on southeast Anderson's motel row. It's a full-service hotel. Restaurant, pub, room service. In-room data ports. Cable TV. 2 pools (1 indoor). Hot tub, sauna. Fitness room. Laundry facilities. Business services. | 5920 Scatterfield Rd. (Rte. 109 Bypass) | 765/644–2581 | fax 765/642–8545 | hiand@iquest.net | 158 rooms | $79 | AE, D, DC, MC, V.

Lees Inn. This relatively small two-story motel on the strip south of Anderson has a light, contemporary color scheme and contains decorative touches like chandeliers. Complimentary Continental breakfast. Cable TV. 24-hour fitness center. | 2114 E. 59th St. | 765/649–2500 or 800/733–5337 | www.leesinn.com | fax 765/643–0349 | 67 rooms | $64–$79 | AE, D, DC, MC, V.

Hawthorn Inn and Suites. It is 4 mi to the Anderson Speedway, 4 mi to Mounds State Park, and 1½ mi to Anderson Mall from this motel. Rooms have one king- or two queen-size beds. Complimentary breakfast. In-room data ports. Some microwaves. Some refrigerators. Cable TV. In-room VCRs. Indoor pool. Hot tub. Free parking. | 1836 E. 64th St. | 765/641–9980 or 800/527–1133 | fax 765/641–7984 | www.hawthorn.com | 50 | $65–$70 | AE, D, DC, MC, V.

Plum Retreat. Wicker furniture decorates the wraparound porch of this Queen Anne Victorian bed and breakfast built in 1892. Grounds are lovely grounds with their fountain, rose garden, and herb garden. Inside, stained glass doors and windows, a crystal chandelier, and antique furniture dress things up. You can eat your breakfast in the dining room, in the breakfast gazebo, or on the outdoor patio. In the Victorian suite, you'll find a sitting room, fireplace, and private balcony. The Garden Room has a walnut armoire, lace curtains, and floral wallpaper. The Irish Lace Room includes a queen canopied bed, lace curtains, and private bath. No smoking indoors. Complimentary breakfast. Library. No children under 12. | 926 W. 8th St. | 765/649–7586 | bertacchi@aol.com | 3 rooms, 1 with private bath | $70–$120 | No credit cards.

ANGOLA

MAP 3, F1

(Nearby towns also listed: Auburn, Fremont, Shipshewana)

The seat of Steuben County, "Land of 101 Lakes," Angola grew up at the intersection of the Maumee Trail and a road between Fort Wayne and Detroit. Fashioned after Boston's Faneuil Hall in 1868, its redbrick county courthouse overlooks a quaint public square where early settlers once traded with the members of the Miami and Potawatomi tribes. In the late 1800s, the great showman P. T. Barnum visited northeastern Indiana and proclaimed "all that Steuben County needs is advertising." He added that Lake James—Indiana's fourth-largest lake, 7 mi north of town—was the most beautiful body of water he had ever seen. Though tiny Angola clings to its easygoing charm most of the year, it bustles with visitors during the summer and winter vacation seasons.

Information: **Steuben County Tourism Bureau** | 207 S. Wayne St., 46703 | 800/LAKE–101 | www.lakes101.org.

Attractions

Crooked Lake. Tiny Steuben County Park touches on the southeast corner of Crooked Lake, one the larger lakes in the area after Lake James, and offers a sandy beach with swimming and boating—activities that you can also find at nearby Clear and Hamilton lakes. | Off Rte. 69 | 800/LAKE–101 | fax 219/665–5461 | www.lakes101.org | Free | Daily.

Pokagon State Park. This 1,000-acre preserve borders Lake James, the fourth-largest lake in Indiana, as well as smaller Snow Lake. The lakes sprinkled across Steuben County are kettle holes, the handiwork of an ancient glacier, as are the rockpiles scattered throughout the park's woodlands. The park's centerpiece is the classic 1920s lodge, which sits on a gentle rise overlooking the lower basin of Lake James. There's a ¼-mi toboggan run, ice fishing, and cross-country skiing in winter, fishing, boating, swimming, horseback riding, camping, picnicking, and hiking in summer, with nearly 10 mi of trails. | 450 Lane 100, Lake James | 219/833–2012 | www.ai.org/dnr | $2 state residents; $5 non-residents | Daily.

Dining

The Hatchery. American. This cozy eatery in the center of town was once a chicken hatchery. What a transformation. Meals are served by candlelight on crisp linens, or you can eat al fresco on a wooden deck with umbrellas overhead in fine weather. You'll find fresh seafood, lamb, and steaks. Entertainment Fri., Sat. | 118 S. Elizabeth St. | 219/665–9957 | No lunch. Closed Sun. | $15–$40 | AE, MC, V.

Lodging

Best Western Angola Inn. This two-story motel with room access via outside hallways is painted gray with a blue trim and is within 5 mi of outlet shopping and a flea market. The various local lakes are between 4 and 15 mi away. Take I–69, exit 148 (Angola). You'll find a restaurant and bar next door. Complimentary Continental breakfast. Cable TV. Pool. | 3155 W. U.S. 20 | 219/665–9561 | fax 219/665–9564 | www.bestwestern.com | 94 rooms | $65–$70 | AE, D, DC, MC, V.

Potawatomi Inn. This hostelry on a knoll overlooking Lake James in Pokagon State Park was originally built in the 1920s. Inside, dark wood trim accents the white walls and blue-patterned carpet and upholstery; the place still has its original lodge look and steeply pitched A-frame roof. It wraps around a garden with a rock-lined creek bed. Dining room. Cable TV. Indoor pool. Hot tubs. Volleyball court, exercise equipment. Beach, dock, boating. Cross-country skiing, tobogganing. Laundry facilities. Business services. | 6 Lane 100A, Lake James | 219/833–1077 | www.state.in.us/dnr/parklake/inns/potawatomi | fax 219/833–4087 | 126 rooms, 3 suites in 2-story inn, 16 cabins | $59–99, $109–119 suites, $47–$52 cabins | AE, D, MC, V.

AUBURN

MAP 3, F2

(Nearby towns also listed: Angola, Fort Wayne, Huntington, Shipshewana, Warsaw)

In the 1920s and 1930s during the golden age of the American automobile, the garish Auburn Boattail Speedster, the Cord front-wheel-drive sedan, and the luxurious Duesenberg put tiny Auburn on the map. This trio came to symbolize an era of motor touring in style. For more than three decades, the Auburn Automobile Company turned out cars that were regarded as benchmarks of near perfection in automotive design and engineering. With the flashy Duesenberg, the phrase "it's a doozy" was born. The factory is long gone, but this county seat in picturesque rural northeastern Indiana is still proud of its vehicular heritage, calling itself "Home of the Classics." The 12,000-square-ft Art Deco car showroom and factory building have been made into a museum, next door to another automotive and truck museum. Each September the town hosts a huge classic car festival. Manufacturers of automotive parts and other small- to medium-size companies now support the economy.

Information: **Auburn Chamber of Commerce** | 208 S. Jackson St., 46706-9998 | 219/925–2100 | auburn-in.com/index.asp.

Attractions

Auburn-Cord-Duesenberg Museum. The Auburn Automobile Company's original 1930 Art Deco showrooms and factory, near the center of town, now display over 100 classic and antique automobiles. The front-wheel-drive Cords, luxurious Duesenbergs, and stylish Auburns are highlights of the collection. The second-story design and engineering offices display drawings, drafting tools, models, and other artifacts. | 1600 S. Wayne St. | 219/925–1444 | www.acdmuseum.org | $7 | Daily 9–5.

Gene Stratton-Porter State Historic Site. The formal gardens and two-story "Cabin in Wildflower Woods" at this site 15 mi west of Auburn once belonged to author, nature photographer, and naturalist Gene Stratton-Porter. These, together with the adjoining forest, lake, and marshes, provided a rich source of material for her writing. Guided tours of the cabin let you see Porter's personal mementoes, her library, and many of the cabin's original furnishings. Tours are available on the hour. | 1205 Pleasant Point, Rome City | 219/854–3790 | www.ai.org/ism/sites/porter/ | Free | Mar.–mid-Dec., Tues.–Sat. 9–5, Sun. 1–5.

Hoosier Air Museum. In a separate building at the DeKalb County Airport, the museum has six aircraft representing different eras of aviation history such as the 1937 Stinson V–77 Gullwing. | County Rd. 62 | 219/927–0443 | www.hoosierwarbirds.org | Free, donations welcome | Tues., Thurs., and weekends 9–4.

National Automotive and Truck Museum of the United States. The former Auburn Automobile Company buildings, not far from the center of town, are filled with classic trucks from 1907 to the present as well as cars manufactured after World War II. The museum includes Corvettes, muscle cars, and one-of-a kind experimental models. Extensive exhibits trace history of model and toy vehicles as well. | 1000 Gordon M. Buerig Pl. | 219/925–9100 | www.matmus.org | fax 219/925–4563 | $4.50 | Daily.

ON THE CALENDAR

SEPT.: *Auburn-Cord-Duesenberg Festival.* Celebrating Auburn's heritage are a huge classic car auction, decorator showhouse tours, antiques and arts and crafts shows, a parade of classic and antique autos, and more. | 219/925–3600.
MAY: *Cycle Fest.* A motorcycle parade, 64-mi poker run, bike show, swap meet, music, food, and over 400 motorcycles and bikes are part of this event at the Auburn Cord Duesenberg Museum. | 219/925–3600.

Dining

The Auburn House Restaurant. American. Food is made from scratch at this family-style restaurant: barbecued brisket, Salisbury steak, lasagna, stir-fried beef and vegetables, salads, sandwiches, burgers, wraps, and more. For breakfast, they'll rustle up eggs, biscuits and gravy, hash browns, or steak and eggs; weekends, it's a breakfast buffet with omelets, French toast, and pancakes. | 131 W. 7th St. | 219/925–1102 | fax 219/925–0418 | www.theauburnhouse.com | No dinner Sun. | $6–$10 | MC, V.

Joshua's. American. Surprisingly spacious inside, this casual eatery is tucked in the corner of a strip mall on the west side of town about a mile from its center. Brass railings, potted plants, maroon plaid upholstery, and café curtains create the upbeat, comfortable feeling of a 1920s speakeasy. Try the baseball-mitt-size "Niki's Cut" T-bone steak, the shrimp scampi, or the smoked pork chops steamed in beer and herbs. | 640 N. Grandstaff Dr. | 219/925–4407 | $17–$28 | D, MC, V.

Lodging

Auburn Inn. Constructed in the 1980s, this modern two-story motel in western Auburn ¼ mi from I–69, exit 129 (Auburn/Garrette), reflects the town's classic automobile heritage: The motifs are Art Deco, and the lobby is anchored by tufted Chesterfield sofas and filled with beveled glass and brass. Side tables are antique leather automobile trunks. Guest rooms are handsomely styled in burgundy and cream with dark wood furniture. You can also munch on the inn's homemade cookies every evening. Complimentary breakfast buffet. Cable TV. Pool. Business services. | 225 Touring Dr. | 219/925–6363 or 800/44–LODGE | fax 219/925–6363 | 53 rooms | $89–$99 | AE, D, DC, MC, V.

Auburn Super 8 Motel. You can use the nearby YMCA, for free, which has a pool, spa, and health club when you stay at this two-story motel off I–69, exit 129 (Auburn/Garrette). Built in 1998, it is near golf courses, fishing sites, and several restaurants. In-room data ports. Some microwaves. Some refrigerators. Cable TV. Laundry service. | 307 Touring Dr. | 219/927–8800 or 800/800–8000 | fax 219/927–8800 | www.super8.com | 52 rooms | $57–$67 | AE, D, DC, MC, V.

Country Hearth Inn. Constructed in 1987, this small two-story motel is 1 ½ mi west of downtown. It sits close to the road 1 ½ blocks from I–69, exit 12 (Auburn/Garrette). The homey guest rooms contain light wood furniture. Complimentary Continental breakfast. Cable TV. Pool. Business services. | 1115 W. 7th St. (Rte. 8) | 219/925–1316 or 800/848–5767 | fax 219/927–8012 | www.travelbase.com/country-hearth-auburn | 76 rooms | $67 | AE, D, DC, MC, V.

Holiday Inn Express. In this hotel built in 1996, guest rooms have hair dryers, coffeemakers, irons, and ironing boards. The three-story building is in western Auburn, off I–69, exit 129 (Auburn/Garrette), and is 12 blocks from downtown. Complimentary Continental breakfast. In-room data ports, some microwaves, refrigerators. Cable TV. Indoor pool. Laundry facilities. Some pets allowed. | 404 Touring Dr. | 219/925–1900 | fax 219/927–1138 | cndmgment@aol.com | cmphotels.com | 70 rooms | $87–$108 | AE, D, DC, MC, V.

AURORA

INTRO
ATTRACTIONS
DINING
LODGING

AURORA

MAP 3, F6

(Nearby towns also listed: Batesville, Madison, Vevay; Cincinnati, OH)

In the mid 1800s, thriving on steamboat traffic on the Ohio River, Aurora rapidly spread up its steep bank. Today, street names like Importing and Exporting reflect the town's heritage as a major shipping center. Supposedly, Aurora (originally named Decatur) was the envy of Rising Sun, about 9 mi downstream. To set the town apart, one of Decatur's founders lobbied for a name change, arguing that "the Roman goddess of dawn, Aurora, comes before Rising Sun." Riverboats are again part of the local scene; there's gambling aboard two riverboat casinos in Rising Sun. In Aurora, many 19th-century homes and commercial buildings have been preserved and now house shops and restaurants. Most notable is the Steamboat Gothic Hillforest mansion overlooking downtown and the tree-bordered river.

Information: **Dearborn County Visitors Center** | 555 Eads Pkwy. E (US 50), Suite 175, Lawrenceburg, 47025 | 812/537–0814 or 800/322–8198 | dearcvb@one.net | www.dearborncvb.org.

Attractions

Hillforest. Perched on a steep hillside downtown, this Italianiate mansion with a charming rounded portico overlooks a big bend in the Ohio River and tiny Aurora. Built by industrialist and financier Thomas Gaff in the mid 1800s, the opulent home is filled with Venetian glass, parquet floors, and chandeliers. From a rooftop cupola resembling a ship's pilot house, Gaff's antique wood-and-brass telescope takes in a panoramic view of the valley. | 213 5th St. | 812/926–0087 | hillforest@seidata.com | $4 | Apr.–Dec., Tues.–Sun. 1–5; Labor Day–Memorial Day, daily 1–5.

Perfect North Slopes. One of the state's few ski areas, Perfect North draws skiers from nearby Ohio and Kentucky as well as from Indianapolis. The ski area includes over 70 acres of tree-lined trails and wide-open slopes and has five chair lifts. It's 10 mi east of Aurora. | 19074 Perfect North Rd., Lawrenceburg | 812/537–3754 or 513/381–7517 | www.perfectnorth.com/ | Dec.–mid-March, weekdays 10 AM–9:30 PM, weekends 9–3.

ON THE CALENDAR

MAY–OCT.: *Tri-State Antique Market.* Antiques hunters flock to the fairgrounds in nearby Lawrenceburg to examine the goods of more than 250 dealers from Ohio, Kentucky, and Indiana at this major event, held the first Sunday of each month. | 513/738–7256.

JUNE: *Blue Jeans Festival.* Quaint Rising Sun brings in rides, games, storytelling, an 1880s melodrama, and big-name entertainment. | 888/776–4786.

OCT.: *Farmer's Fair.* Indiana's oldest street festival opens with a parade then moves on to rides, games, food booths, and musical performances. | 812/537–0814 or 800/322–8198.

Dining

Applewood Food and Spirits. American. Art fills the walls of this restaurant set on the riverfront in an old brick building near the center of town. Go for the applewood chicken, a sautéed chicken breast topped with pecans, apples, and brandy, or the glazed ham, barbecued ribs, frog legs, two-fisted burgers, or red snapper. You can eat outdoors at umbrella-shaded tables on a porch overlooking the Ohio River or you can relax on benches and chairs in a grassy area, near the river. Sun. brunch. | 215 Judiciary St. | 812/926–1166 or 513/381–2775 | $10–$23 | AE, D, MC, V.

The Courtyard Fine Food and Spirits. American. This friendly, family-style eatery, 9 mi east of Aurora, is in the corner of a painted-brick mid-19th century row house that overlooks the Ohio River. A dark wood floor and booths distinguish the interior, and vintage photos of Rising Sun embellish the mustard-yellow walls. The kitchen is known for its steaks, fried

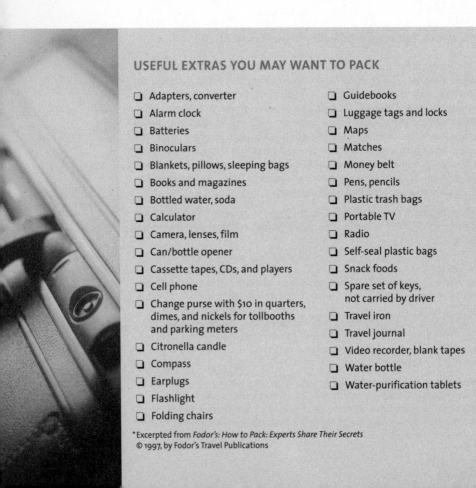

USEFUL EXTRAS YOU MAY WANT TO PACK

- ❏ Adapters, converter
- ❏ Alarm clock
- ❏ Batteries
- ❏ Binoculars
- ❏ Blankets, pillows, sleeping bags
- ❏ Books and magazines
- ❏ Bottled water, soda
- ❏ Calculator
- ❏ Camera, lenses, film
- ❏ Can/bottle opener
- ❏ Cassette tapes, CDs, and players
- ❏ Cell phone
- ❏ Change purse with $10 in quarters, dimes, and nickels for tollbooths and parking meters
- ❏ Citronella candle
- ❏ Compass
- ❏ Earplugs
- ❏ Flashlight
- ❏ Folding chairs
- ❏ Guidebooks
- ❏ Luggage tags and locks
- ❏ Maps
- ❏ Matches
- ❏ Money belt
- ❏ Pens, pencils
- ❏ Plastic trash bags
- ❏ Portable TV
- ❏ Radio
- ❏ Self-seal plastic bags
- ❏ Snack foods
- ❏ Spare set of keys, not carried by driver
- ❏ Travel iron
- ❏ Travel journal
- ❏ Video recorder, blank tapes
- ❏ Water bottle
- ❏ Water-purification tablets

*Excerpted from *Fodor's: How to Pack: Experts Share Their Secrets*
© 1997, by Fodor's Travel Publications

chicken, chef's salad, burgers, and smoked turkey sandwich on fresh baked bread. A pub is downstairs. | 135 North Front St., Rising Sun | 812/438–4035 | www.rscourtyard.com | $14–$23 | AE, D, MC, V.

Whisky's. American. The bar and paned windows are original in the redbrick building that houses this restaurant, built in 1832, and the place is filled with antique furniture. The name recalls Aurora's onetime nickname, Whiskey City—distilleries once flourished here. The menu offers barbecued ribs, chicken, steaks, and burgers. Kids' menu. In the center of town. | 334 Front St., Lawrenceburg | 513/621–2528 or 812/537–4239 | Closed Sun. No lunch Sat. | $10–$28 | AE, D, MC, V.

Lodging

Gothic Arches Bed and Breakfast. You can have afternoon tea at this restored Gothic Revival home in Aurora's National Historic District with a view of the Ohio River. Walnut and cherry Victorian beds and other period pieces furnish the rooms. Breakfast is buffet-style. Complimentary breakfast. Cable TV in some rooms. Hot tub. Library. Business services. No smoking. | 305 4th St. | 812/926–2204 or 888/747–2204 | www.seindiana.com/arches | 5, 3 with shower only | $70–$99 | AE, D, MC, V.

Mulberry Inn and Gardens Bed and Breakfast. This roomy two-story bungalow dating from the mid-1900s has been fully renovated as a bed and breakfast. It has a wide front porch with flower boxes and backyard gardens. Guest rooms have private baths and are decorated with stenciling, floral fabrics, and a combination of traditional and antique furnishings. It's in an older residential neighborhood about 9 mi from Aurora and 10 mi west of Lawrenceburg. Complimentary breakfast. Business services. | 118 S. Mulberry St., Rising Sun | 812/438–2206 or 800/235–3097 | fax 812/438–2206 | jwillis@one.net | www.bbonline.com/in/mulberry/ | 6 rooms, 1 suite | $89, $125 suite | AE, D, MC, V.

BATESVILLE

MAP 3, E6

(Nearby towns also listed: Aurora, Connersville, Metamora, Vevay)

Beginning in the 1850s, hardworking Germans from Cincinnati and the East settled this southeastern Indiana town. Like many early settlers, Christopher Hillenbrand was a cabinetmaker and was attracted by the wide stands of walnut and oak that covered the rolling countryside. In the 1880s, the Hillenbrand family started the American Furniture Company, the first of six furniture factories in Batesville by the early 1900s. Batesville is still known as a furniture-making and woodworking center, with three major manufacturers and the Weberding custom wood-carving workshop. The Hillenbrand name also continues at Hill-Rom Industries, makers of hospital beds.

Information: Brookville/Franklin County Chamber of Commerce | Box 211, Brookville, 47012 | 765/647–3177 | www.brookville47012.com | fax 765/647–4150.

Attractions

Versailles State Park. The 230-acre lake in this park is Indiana's second largest. Activities include swimming, fishing, camping, and horseback riding. You can rent paddle boats, rowboats, and canoes, and there is a nature center and picnic area. | U.S. 50, Versailles | 812/689–6424 | Daily 7 AM–11 PM.

ON THE CALENDAR

JUNE: *Batesville Music and Arts Festival.* This festival showcases the Cincinnati Pops Orchestra and country and western songs. Athletic tournaments, a juried art show, food vendors, and a run/walk also make up the festival. | 812/934–7675 | www.indianafestival.org.

Dining

Sherman House. German. Built in 1852, the facade of white stucco trimmed with dark-brown boards and decorative gables makes this downtown Batesville restaurant look as though it belongs in a Bavarian village. Inside, the ceiling is beamed, and there are rustic sconces and framed prints on the walls. Good bets on the menu: sauerbraten, sausage and sauerkraut, potato pancakes, steaks, and German chocolate cake. | 35 S. Main St. | 812/934–2407 | www.route-one.com | Breakfast also available | $8–$30 | AE, DC, MC, V.

Villa Milan Winery and Restaurant. Italian. You can eat indoors or out at this 7-½ acre vineyard in the hills 2½ mi south of Milan off Route 101. There's an indoor dining room with a chandelier, a heated patio with removable sides, and a 32-foot gazebo, which seats around 60. The menu includes pizza, calzone, spaghetti, fettuccine, veal scaloppine, pasta primavera, and Italian chicken. There's cheesecake and spumone for dessert. House wines are served. | Box 248, Milan | 812/654–3419 | www.seidata.com/villa-milan | Reservations essential on weekends | Closed Sun. | $7–$13 | AE, D, MC, V.

Lodging

Days Inn. This two-story brick motel with interior hallways is on the north side of Batesville, near I–74, exit 149 (Batesville). It opened in 1990. Several restaurants are within walking distance. Complimentary Continental breakfast. Microwaves. Refrigerators. Cable TV. Pool. | 112 Rte. 46 | 812/934–6185 or 800/544–8313 | www.daysinn.com | 60 rooms | $50–$75 | AE, D, DC, MC, V.

Sherman House. Built in 1852, the inn sits in the middle of the quiet downtown Batesville. The lobby and restaurant have heavy wood trim, rustic brass light fixtures, and murals. Guest rooms are bright with floral-print wallpaper and bedspreads, two-poster beds, and comfortable wing-back chairs. Restaurant, bar. Cable TV. Exercise equipment. Business services. No pets allowed. | 35 S. Main St. | 812/934–2407 | www.route-one.com | fax 812/934–1230 | 23 rooms | $55–$75 | AE, DC, MC, V.

BEDFORD

MAP 3, D7

(Nearby towns also listed: Bloomington, Columbus, French Lick)

A thick belt of limestone stretches across Indiana's midsection, with Bedford at the center. Blocks from Lawrence County's famed "holes," or quarries, have built dozens of state capitols and many of the landmark buildings across the nation. In 1991, stone carver Jack Kendall recalled that "I came from a stone family. Every morning I'd sit down to breakfast and all the talk was stone, stone, stone." The pride that Bedford takes in its title as Limestone Capital of the World is as durable as the legendary stone itself. You can get a feel for the life of stone, stone, stone on driving and walking tours of Bedford and Lawrence counties. Several major stonecutters still operate in Lawrence County. Underground, caves honeycomb the countryside.

Information: **Lawrence County Tourism Commission** | 1116 16th St., Box 1193, 47421 | 812/275–5998 | lctc@limestonecountry.com | www.limestonecountry.com.

Attractions

Antique Auto and Race Car Museum. Some 100 antique racing and touring cars are on display in this museum in the center of town, where a gift shop stocks automobile collectibles and limestone gifts. Along with more than a dozen Indy 500 cars are Sprint, Midget, and NASCAR race cars. And because this is Bedford, limestone carvings of cars and historic quarry photos are also part of the museum. | 3348 16th St., Stone City Mall | 812/275–0556 | www.autoracemuseum.com | $3 | Apr.–Dec., Mon.–Sat. noon–6.

Bluespring Caverns. The network of caverns 4 mi south of the center of Bedford is known for high vaulted passageways and one of the world's longest underground streams, the Myst'ry River, which flows for some 20 mi through the main cavern. The main cavern can be viewed on foot from a paved walkway and viewing platform or by boat on a 1-hour guided tour of the underground river where rare blind fish live. | Rte. 11 (Bluespring Caverns Rd.) | 812/279–9471 | www.explore-si.com/Bluespring.html | $9 | Memorial Day–Oct. 31, daily; Apr.–May, weekends.

Green Hill Cemetery. The cemetery on the southwest edge of town has some of the finest examples of limestone carving in the county, with ornate and personalized monuments such as the Lewis Baker monument, which depicts the stonecarver's workbench and tools. | 1202 18th St. | 812/275–7637 | fax 812/275–7651 | lctc@limestonecountry.com | www.limestonecountry.com | Free | Daily dawn to dusk.

Hoosier National Forest. The state's only national forest covers 196,000 acres in south-central Indiana, with two huge parcels near Bloomington and Columbus and the other stretching south from Bedford to the Ohio River. Some 230 mi of hiking, mountain biking, and equestrian trails crisscross hills that range in height from 400 ft near the Ohio River valley to above 930 ft at Browning Hill. The terrain is surprisingly diverse, from high ridges and hills along the Ohio River to underground cave and karst systems, open meadows, and old-growth forests. A number of geological features are on the forest, including an 8-acre collapsed sinkhole called Wesley Chapel Gulf; Shooting Star Cliffs, with native umbrella magnolia and rock shelters; Plaster Creek Seeps; and a horseshoe bend in the Little Blue River called Carnes Mill, where a water flume was carved out of the rocky bluff to power

LIMESTONE LEGACY

An old black-and-white picture hanging at the Land of Limestone shows a caravan of 35-ft limestone columns easing through downtown Bedford on railroad cars in the early 1900s. The mammoth pillars went on to become the building blocks of Pennsylvania's state office building. Cathedrals, Gilded Age mansions of the wealthy (including Cornelius Vanderbilt's Newport, Rhode Island, palace, The Breakers), the Empire State Building, 35 state capitols, and many other notable landmarks in the United States have been built with stone from the Hoosier state. Beginning in the 1820s, quarries centered in Bedford and Oolitic, about 7 mi north, began surrendering the stone that lay in a 10-mi-wide belt between Bloomington and Bedford. "That astonishing material," as one architect called Indiana limestone in the early 1900s, is only found in three Indiana counties.

Indiana's limestone is known for its fine grain and strength, hence its popularity as a building material and a medium for sculptors carving finely-detailed ornaments and statues. The former 1926 offices of the Indiana Limestone Company (now Bedford College Center) display tools, over 200 photographs, architectural renderings, and the geology of Indiana's limestone heritage. That heritage can also be appreciated on downtown walking or driving tours of the area (maps available at the Lawrence County Tourism Commission), one of which passes by the famous Empire Hole, where stone for the Empire State Building was quarried. Surprisingly, some of the best examples of the stonecarving can be seen at Bedford's Green Hill Cemetery.

© Corbis

a mill. The Clover Lick Barrens is a prairielike area with rock outcroppings and many rare plants, and the Tincher Area, is full of caves and other karst features. The forest also include a box-shaped sandstone canyon with waterfalls and rock shelters called Hemlock Cliffs. There are also prime fall color scenic drives, including Route 46 between Bloomington and Heltonville, Rte. 135 between Nashville and Freetown, and Rte. 58 from Bedford on to Heltonville. Near the Ohio River, the scenery is great from Derby to Tell City near the water's edge on Route 66. | 811 Constitution Ave., Bedford | 812/275–5987 | www.fs.fed.us/r9/hoosier/ | Free | Daily.

The state's only federally designated wilderness area, the 13,000-acre **Charles C. Deam Wilderness,** is filled with wooded hills and hollows near Lake Monroe in Jackson, Brown, Lawrence, and Monroe counties that can be reached only on foot or on horseback. There are almost 36 mi of trails along wooded ridges with fine views. From Bedford, take Route 50 east 10 mi to Route 446, then go 10 mi north. | Rte. 446 | 812/275–5987 | Daily.

The **Pioneer Mothers Memorial Forest** is an 88-acre preserve within the Hoosier National Forest that includes an acre of black walnut trees, one of the few such stands in the Midwest. Walnut trees reach 100 ft and measure 40 inches in diameter. Some ancient oaks here are believed to date back to the 15th century. | Free | Daily.

The Civilian Conservation Corps constructed the **Hickory Ridge Lookout Tower** in 1939. It's on the National Historic Lookout Register. In the Charles C. Deam Wilderness Area. | Rte. 446 | 812/275–5987 | Daily.

The **Rickenbaugh House** was built of sandstone in 1874 and has served as a post office and church meetinghouse. It is on the National Register of Historic Places. In the Charles C. Deam Wilderness Area. | Rte. 446 | 812/275–5987 | Daily.

Jackson-Washington State Forest. The 17,000-acre property spreads across an area known as "the Knobs." These are sugarloaf hills that poke up above the flat farm fields—considered miniature mountains in the Hoosier state—affording panoramic vistas from 300 ft above and along the 2½-mi Skyline Drive that circles the top of one of them. The 60-ft climb up the fire tower captures strikingly flat 20-mi views. In spring the cucumber magnolia, a flowering tree that seems better suited to the mountainous climes of the southeastern United States, dangles single bell-shaped flowers at the end of branches. The rugged 1-mi hike to Pinnacle Peak, the most famous of the Knobs, is well worth the effort. Another 20 mi of trails, from moderate to rugged and including a portion of the 57-mi Knobstone Trail, lace the Knobs area. There is a beach and boating at Starve Hollow State Recreation Area, next to the forest. Starve Hollow Lake covers 145 acres and is nestled in wooded hills. The forest is 35 mi east of Brookville. | 1278 E. Rte. 250, Brownstown | 812/358–2160 | www.state.in.us/dnr/forestry/htmldocs/jackwash.htm | Free | Daily.

Knobstone Trail. At some 57 mi long, this backcountry hiking trail is the state's longest. It travels through rugged, forested hills in south-central Indiana, from near Deam Lake, just north of Rte. 60 in Clark County, to Delaney Park, just east of Rte. 135 in Washington County. The trail follows narrow, flat-topped ridges or "knobs." The Knobstone Escarpment is one of Indiana's most scenic areas, and gives southern Indiana a mountainous feeling. The trail remains open during hunting season. | 317/232–4070 (maps) | fax 317–233–4648 | www.state.in.us/dnr/forestry/htmldocs/jackwash.htm | www.state.in.us/dnr/outdoor/knobston/knobston.htm | Free | Daily.

Land of Limestone Exhibit. Over 200 vintage black-and-white photographs, stone cutter's tools, architectural drawings, and other artifacts trace Lawrence County's limestone industry. In the 1850s, as quarries were opened in the countryside around Bedford and Oolitic, Lawrence County began supplying the nation with building material for its monuments; the National Cathedral, the Empire State Building, and many of the country's state capitols are built of Indiana limestone. The exhibit is on the north side of Bedford. | Bedford College Center, 405 I St. | 812/275–7637 or 800/798–0769 | Free | Weekdays 9–4:30, Sat. 9–11:30.

Lawrence County and Bedford Historical and Limestone Heritage Tours. Walking and driving tours take you to stately buildings, including the county courthouse and various churches, all made of Indiana limestone. Five tours are detailed in brochures available at the tourism commission downtown (after hours, look for the brochure rack in the front of the building); they take in limestone-turreted buildings, statues, intricately carved monuments at cemeteries, and former quarries. | Lawrence County Tourism Commission, 1116 16th St. | 812/275–7637 | www.limestonecountry.com | Free | Weekdays 10–4:30.

Lawrence County Historical Museum. The basement of the county courthouse in downtown Bedford is a treasure trove of artifacts and historical materials from the county museum's collection. Glass cases display glassware, antique dolls, a few Native American artifacts, flags, uniforms from the Civil War to World War II, and limestone architectural details and sculptures created by local carvers. | Courthouse Sq. | 812/275–4141 | Free | Weekdays 9–12 and 1–4.

Spring Mill State Park. Tucked in the 1,319-acre wooded preserve next to a trickling creek, 13 mi south of Bedford, are a re-created 1814 pioneer village and gristmill built of limestone and timbers. You can explore Twin Cave by boat and Donaldson's Cave on foot. The park also includes 80 acres of virgin forest and woodsy Spring Mill Inn. Leap ahead to the space age at the park's Grissom Memorial, which displays astronaut Virgil "Gus" Grissom's space suit and the Gemini III space capsule. The Spring Mill Inn is in the park along with a range of campsites. | Highway 60, Mitchell | 812/849–4129 | www.state.in.us/dnr/parklake | $2 per vehicle residents, $5 nonresidents | Daily.

ON THE CALENDAR

SEPT.: *Annual Persimmon Festival.* On Main Street in downtown Mitchell, persimmon pudding is served along with other persimmon novelty dishes. In addition to a bake-off, there is a parade, arts and crafts booths, a carnival, live entertainment, and displays of antique and classic autos. | 800/580–1985.

OCT: *Fort Vallonia Days.* Vallonia, about 20 mi east of Bedford, transforms itself into an early 19th-century fort and trading post for the weekend. Reenactors, storytellers, and musicians share their talent. | 812/358–3137.

Dining

Mamma's Mexican and Italian Restaurant. American. With choices of Mexican, Italian and American food on the menu, this small restaurant has one big dining room. It started as a burger joint and now serves sandwiches, shrimp, fish, grilled chicken, rib-eye steaks, grilled chicken salad, and lots of appetizers, including pepperoni bread sticks. Mexican options include chimichangas and burritos—or go Italian with spaghetti or lasagna. | 1701 M St. | 812/275–0684 | Reservations not accepted | $4–$9 | D, MC, V.

Stoll's Restaurant. American. Fried chicken is always on the menu at this Amish buffet that has three meats each day such as meatloaf, roast beef, barbecued pork, barbecued beef, barbecued ribs, beef stew, ham and beans, or minute steaks. Friday's buffet includes seafood. Everything is made from scratch including the cornbread. You can also order off a menu that has sandwiches, burgers, steaks, pork chops, catfish, shrimp, and baked fish. Most of the restaurant has good views; there's a main dining room with lots of big tables and booths, and a loft upstairs. A breakfast buffet is available. | 1801 Plaza Dr. | 812/279–8150 | Closed Sun. Breakfast also served | $5–$13 | MC, V.

Lodging

Bedford Super 8 Motel. This two-story motel opened in 2000 on the south end of town near Leatherwood Creek, 3 mi from the Blue Springs Caverns and 10 mi from Spring Mill State Park. One suite has a hot tub. Complimentary Continental breakfast. In-room data ports. Refrigerators. Cable TV. Indoor pool. Indoor hot tub. Laundry facilities. Business services. Pets allowed ($10). | 501 Bell Back Rd. | 812/275–8881 or 800/800–8000 | fax 812/275–8881 | www.super8.com | 47 rooms, 10 suites | $50–$70, suites $89–$109 | AE, D, MC, V.

Holiday Inn Express. There are at least four restaurants within a mile of this three-story hotel with interior corridors and rooms with one double bed, two queen beds, one king,

or suites. It's 1³/₁₀ mi from the Antique Auto and Race Car Museum, and 2½ mi from Blue Springs Caverns. Some microwaves, some refrigerators. Cable TV. Pool. Hot tub. Exercise equipment. Business services. Some pets allowed ($20). | 2800 Express Ln., at Rte. 37 | 812/279–1206 or 877/838–6434 | fax 812/279–1496 | www.hiexpress.com | 64 rooms | $74–$84 rooms, $84–$124 suites | AE, D, DC, MC, V.

Mark III. Built in the 1970s and constructed with stone, this small, family-owned two-story motel is four blocks from downtown. Cable TV. Some pets allowed. | 1709 M St. | 812/275–5935 | 21 rooms | $38 | AE, D, DC, MC, V.

Spring Mill Inn. This cozy inn built in 1939 of native limestone nestles amid tall oaks in Spring Mill State Park. The four-story structure has been repeatedly updated over the years but outside looks much the same as it was when it was built. Inside, you find wood floors, oak paneling, and fireplaces. Dining room. Pool. Horseback riding, boating. Video games. | Hwy. 60E, Mitchell | 877/9SP–RING or 812/849–4081 | fax 812/849–4647 | www.state.in.us/dnr/parklake | 74 rooms | $59–$89 | AE, D, MC, V.

Stonehenge. This newer three-story motel is built of native limestone and dark wood. Two or three room suites are available, and each room has its own coffee pot. It's just off the highway, approximately 1 mi west of Bedford. Restaurant, bar, room service. Cable TV. Pool. Business services. | 911 Constitution Ave. | 812/279–8111 or 800/274–2974 | fax 812/279–0172 | henge@kiva.net | www.stonehengelodge.com | 97 rooms | $66–$70 | AE, D, DC, MC, V.

BERNE

MAP 3, F3

(Nearby towns also listed: Fort Wayne, Geneva)

Fertile land and wide-open spaces first attracted a group of 70 Swiss Mennonite immigrants to northeastern Indiana near the Ohio state line in 1852. Two decades later, after the Grand Rapids and Indiana Railroad set up a depot, the town was plotted and named Berne. Today, the population is roughly 3,500, with an equal number of Amish elsewhere in Adams County. Window boxes, hanging baskets, and planters adorn the main street and half-timber buildings evoke a Swiss mountain village. The European heritage is also evident at a Swiss pioneer village, bakeries, restaurants, and two furniture factories in town.

Information: **Berne Chamber of Commerce** | 175 W. Main St., 46711 | 219/589–8080 | tourism@bernein.com | www.bernein.com/indhtm.

Attractions

Pine Lake Water Park. You will find water slides, platforms, a cable ride, paddle boats, a beach, volleyball, tennis, basketball, and food concessions at this park. | 4640 W. Rte. 218 | 219/589–8080 | Memorial Day–Labor Day, Mon.–Sat. 10–8, Sun. 12–8.

ON THE CALENDAR

JULY: *Swiss Days.* Swiss food, dancing, costumed performers, factory tours, tours of the Swiss Heritage Village, and an arts and crafts show liven up downtown Berne. | 219/589–8080.

Dining

Palmer House. Swiss. A gabled storefront downtown houses this cozy neighborhood restaurant, known for American fare, country cooking, Swiss specialties, and its Friday night smorgasbord. Try the special Swiss salad and German fries. | 118 W. Main St. | 219/589–2306 | Closed Sun. | $5–$6 | No credit cards.

Parkway Chalet Restaurant. American. Window boxes overflowing with blooms brighten this restaurant on the south edge of town offering family-style dining. Lanterns hang on the walls of the front room, which is finished with light oak. Try the roast chicken and Swiss steaks. | U.S. 27 S | 219/589–2316 | $7–$10 | No credit cards.

Lodging

Black Bear Inn and Suites. Local furniture makers designed the furniture for the various rooms of this modern two-story motel, built in 1997, 1 mi north of Berne. Extended-stay suites are available. Complimentary Continental breakfast. Indoor pool. In-room hot tubs in suites. Business services. | 1335 U.S. 27 N | 219/589–8955 | fax 219/589–8384 | 46 rooms, 9 suites | $58, $75–$100 suites | AE, D, MC, V.

Cragwood Inn Bed & Breakfast. This Queen Anne Victorian home with gingerbread trim, has four porches, a turret, and a flower garden. Inside there's oak paneling, beveled lead glass windows, and crystal chandeliers. Two rooms have their own fireplace. Complimentary breakfast. No TV. No room phones. Library. No children under 8. No smoking. | 302 N. 2nd St., Decatur | 219/728–2000 | www.bnbinns.com/cragwood.inn | 4, 2 with private bath | $60–$65 | MC, V.

Schug House Inn Lodging and Breakfast. This early 20th-century home with turrets is near downtown. The inn is enclosed by a wraparound porch with wicker furniture, and the rooms are furnished with antiques, with period lighting and inlaid wood floors. Complimentary Continental breakfast. | 706 W. Main St. | 219/589–2903 | fax 219/589–2448 | 8 rooms | $38–$40 | MC, V.

BLOOMINGTON

MAP 3, C6

(Nearby towns also listed: Bedford, Columbus, Nashville)

Nestled in the south-central Indiana hills, Bloomington is home to the oldest part of Indiana University, a Big Ten Conference college dating from 1820. In the Old Crescent Historic District of the wooded campus, nine buildings date from 1884 to 1908. One of the town's most recognizable symbols is a century-old fish weathervane atop the domed Monroe County Courthouse in the middle of the town square. About 10 years ago, the gleam was put back on the Beaux Arts–style limestone structure as part of an extensive downtown revitalization. Brick storefronts with tall windows and painted trim have all been painstakingly renovated. Bloomington's downtown now offers more than 120 specialty shops, galleries, and unusual restaurants.

Information: **Monroe County Convention and Visitors Bureau** | 2855 N. Walnut St., 47401 | 812/334–8900 or 800/800–0037 | cvb@visitbloomington.com | www. visitbloomington.com/.

Attractions

Butler Winery. This winery with a tasting room is 9 mi northeast of downtown Bloomington but there is an additional tasting room in an antique home on the north edge of downtown. Butler is known for wine from Indiana-grown grapes and also carries wine- and beer-making supplies. | In town: 15th St. and College Ave.; outside town: 6200 E. Robinson Rd. | 812/339–7233 | www.butlerwinery.com | Free | In town, daily 10–6; winery, weekends 12–6.

Fountain Square Mall. Set behind nearly a block of historic storefronts facing the courthouse downtown, Fountain Square is a multilevel mall of small, individually owned specialty shops, galleries, delis, and cafés. | Fountain Square | 812/336–7100 | fax 812/333–4680 | www.cfcincorporated.com | Free | Mon.–Sat. 10–8, Sun. 1–5.

Indiana University. This university has a wooded, 1,860-acre campus in the center of town; many Tudor-style brick buildings here date back to 1820, and the Indiana Memorial Union, which spans almost an entire city block, is the largest student union building in the United States. The Union and many of the newer buildings are built of Indiana limestone; the art museum, designed by architect I. M. Pei, is glass and stone and a striking red metal sculpture by Alexander Calder stands in front of the Musical Arts Center. The university has both graduate and undergraduate programs; the music school is one of the best in the country, especially for singing, and there are respected jouralism, medical, and law schools, among others. | 107 S. Indiana Ave. | 812/855–4848 | www.indiana.edu | Free | Daily.

The **Glenn A. Black Laboratory of Archaeology,** a major research facility near the center of Bloomington, includes a museum displaying archaeological artifacts and tracing the ethno-history of the Great Lakes and Ohio Valley regions. | 423 N. Fess St. | 812/855–9544 | Free | Sept.–May, Tues.–Fri. 9–4:30, weekends 1–4:30.

The **Hilltop Garden and Nature Center** is a peaceful, 5-acre area near the Indiana University campus, featuring demonstrations from of one of the oldest youth gardening programs in the country, as well as community gardens, a greenhouse, ponds, and flower beds. | 2301 E. 10th St. | 812/855–2799 | Free | Weekdays 1–5.

The **Indiana Memorial Union,** the university's student and faculty center, includes a hotel, restaurants, recreational facilities, a bookstore, and plenty of lounge areas. The massive limestone building overlooks an area known as Dunn Meadow in the center of campus. | 900 E. 7th St. | 812/856–6381 or 800/209–8145 | www.indiana.edu | Free | Daily 6:30–10.

The world-renowned firm of I. M. Pei and Partners designed the soaring, angular **Indiana University Art Museum.** In addition to temporary exhibits, the museum displays fine arts and artifacts from its 33,000-piece permanent collection representing nearly every major historical culture. | Fine Arts Plaza, 1133 E. 7th St. | 812/855–5445 | www.indiana.edu/~iuam | Free | Tues.–Sat. 10–5, Sun. 12–5.

The seven-story **Lilly Library** contains 400,000 books, many of them rare, and more than 7 million rare or historical manuscripts and and 100,000 pieces of sheet music. Among the library's holdings on continuing display is a copy of the Gutenberg Bible printed before 1456. The collection also includes the Coverdale Bible of 1535 (the first English printed bible), and original prints from John James Audubon's *Birds of America*. | Fine Arts Plaza, 1200 E. 7th St. | 812/855–2452 | www.indiana.edu/~liblilly | Free | Weekdays 9–6, Sat. 9–1.

Anthropological and folklore exhibits in the **Mathers Museum,** in downtown Bloomington, look at cultures around the world. | 416 N. Indiana Ave. | 812/855–6873 | www.indiana.edu/~mathers/home.html | Free | Tues.–Fri. 9–4:30, Sat.–Sun., 1–4:30, closed Mon. and during semester breaks.

Lake Monroe. Indiana's largest inland lake, at 10,750 acres, attracts scores of boaters, anglers, and swimmers. The lake has two beaches and five state recreation areas totaling 23,952 acres, and is 6 mi south of Bloomington. The Hoosier National Forest borders the southern edge of the lake. | 4850 S. Rte. 446 | 812/837–9546 or 812/837–9318 | www.ai.org/dnr | $2 per vehicle residents, $5 non-residents | Daily.

McCormick's Creek State Park. Steep ravines, limestone outcroppings, and waterfalls fill Indiana's oldest state park, part of a health retreat and sanitarium in the late 1800s. The 1,800-acre preserve is in hilly woodlands 15 mi west of Bloomington and has a swimming pool, housekeeping cabins, a lodge, and a nature center. | Rte. 5, Spencer | 812/829–4881 | www.state.in.us/dnr/statepar/parks/mccormic/mccormic.htm | $2 per vehicle residents, $5 nonresidents | Daily.

Monroe County Courthouse. A distinctive fish weathervane tops this Beaux Arts–style limestone courthouse atop a knoll in the center of downtown. Inside, a stained-glass window pierces the domed rotunda ceiling. | Courthouse Sq. | 800/800–0037 | www.cfcincorporated.com | Free | Weekdays 8–4.

Monroe County Historical Society. A Carnegie Library dating from 1918 houses this museum near downtown. Permanent exhibits trace the area's natural development and the growth of limestone quarrying, as well as its history from early settlement through the industrial era and up to the present time. Temporary exhibits focus on cultural subjects, including fashion and farming. | 202 E. 6th St. | 812/332–2517 | www.kiva.net/~mchm/museum.htm | Free | Tues.–Sat. 10–4, Sun. 1–4.

Oliver Winery. The state's oldest and largest winery, 7 mi north of downtown, produces more than 15 varieties of wine, including cabernet and a sweet honey mead. Free tours are conducted on weekends, and the grounds include a pond and picnic tables. | 8024 N. Rte. 37 | 812/876–5800 or 800/25–TASTE | Free | Mon.–Sat. 10–6, Sun. 12–6.

Wylie House Museum. The stately 1835 brick Georgian home of the university's first president, Andrew Wylie, is filled with period furnishings, described on guided tours. The garden dates from the period the house was built. Special Christmas programs are presented. It's near downtown. | 317 E. 2nd St. | 812/855–6224 | www.indiana.edu/~libwylie | Free | Mar.–Nov., Tues.–Sat. 10–2.

ON THE CALENDAR

APR.: *Little 500 Bicycle Race.* Now more than 50 years old, the Little 500 is a bicycle race held on the Indiana University campus on the third Saturday of the month. The women's Little 500 is held on Friday afternoon. Huge crowds watch teams vie for top honors on the oval track; a lot of partying goes on as well. | 812/855–9152.

SEPT: *4th Street Arts Festival.* Over 100 artists from Indiana and other states display and sell paintings, woodwork, toys, quilts, and more at this two-day juried event, usually held the first weekend of the month at the intersection of 4th and Grant streets. | 812/335–3814.

DEC.: *Madrigal Dinners.* Two weekends of Olde English music and merriment fill Alumni Hall of Indiana Memorial Union on the campus of Indiana University. | 812/855–3606.

Dining

The Irish Lion. Irish. Set behind an old storefront a block from Courthouse Square near the center of town, this lively eatery serves American and Irish fare. Dark hardwood floors, old mirrors, and Irish accoutrements make up the interior. Entrées include fresh oysters, mussels, clams, salmon, lamb, beef, poultry, and Irish pub-inspired stews. Beer and ale is served by the pint—or you might try a "yard" of beer. There's Irish music at night. | 212 W. Kirkwood Ave. | 812/336–9076 | $15–$35 | AE, D, MC, V.

Le Petit Café. Continental. Bistro cuisine fills the menu of this casual, intimate place downtown, with small tables and French posters on the walls. Try the steak Diane or the homemade pasta. Beer and wine only. | 308 W. 6th St. | 812/334–9747 | Closed Mon. | $10–$16 | MC, V.

Limestone Grille. Continental. In the evening, a neon sign shines above the doorway of this corner storefront restaurant. A hand-carved limestone bas relief covers an entire wall of the restaurant, and the white-linen covered tables are well spaced and candlelit. Several menu items make use of contemporary ingredients, such as the rainbow trout with tomatillo pineapple salsa or pasta alla rustica fusilli with red and yellow peppers, pancetta, green olives, capers, and garlic. You can also order Black Angus New York strip steak, pork chops, filet mignon, prime cut rib-eye, or chicken française. For dessert, try the bittersweet chocolate almond torte with raspberry sauce. Beer and wine only. | 2920 E. Covenanter Dr. | 812/335–8110 | www.limestonegrille.com | Closed Sun. and Mon. | $9–$18 | AE, D, MC, V.

Michael's Uptown Café. Cafe. This popular breakfast spot near the center of Bloomington, reminiscent of a bustling big-city deli, draws crowds for lunch and dinner. Photos and art works hang on the walls, and you sit in booths and at wooden chairs and tables. The cooking is American but inventive, influenced by French, Cajun, and Mediterranean cuisines; the soups are noteworthy, as are the eclectic omelets. | 102 E. Kirkwood Ave. | 812/339–0900 | Daily | $12.50–$32 | AE, D, DC, MC, V.

Nick's English Hut. American. Open since 1927, this tavern, a couple of blocks from the Indiana University campus, is a favorite hangout among locals and students. Booths line the perimeter of the room and framed news clippings, photos, and awards hang on the walls. There is a counter with bar stools and several other dining rooms beyond the main room. The Back Room is quieter than up front and has a large fireplace; the Attic Room is the place for sports fans. There are 30 televisions in all, four bars, pool tables, and seating for up to 500. Come for burgers, pizza, grilled chicken sandwiches, buffalo wings, soups, salads, and sandwiches, or entrees such as New York strip steak, filet mignon, grilled yellowfin tuna, and jambalaya. The place stays open until 2 AM daily except Sunday, when the doors close at midnight. | 423 E. Kirkwood Ave. | 812/332–4040 | www.nicksenglishhut.com | Reservations not accepted except for private parties | $5–$16 | AE, D, DC, MC, V.

Lodging

Best Western Fireside Inn. On the east side of town just 2 mi from Indiana University, and 5 mi from Lake Monroe, this two-story hotel was refurbished in 1995. Complimentary Continental breakfast. Cable TV. Pool. Laundry facilities. Some pets allowed. | 4501 E. 3rd St. | 812/332–2141 or 800/528–1234 | www.bestwestern.com | 96 rooms | $51–$84 | AE, D, DC, MC, V.

Canyon Inn. The Canyon Inn, now part of McCormick's Creek State Park, was originally the Denkewalter Sanitarium. In the 1920s the building was remodeled and given an exterior veneer of brick. Since then, new wings, a swimming pool, and a recreation center have been added. Restaurant. Pool. Video games. | State Rd. 46, Spencer | 812/829–4881 | fax 812/829–1467 | www.ai.com/dnr/ | 72 rooms, 3 floors | $59–$89 | AE, D, MC, V.

Courtyard by Marriott. This five-story hotel is across from the Convention Center and two blocks south of the Courthouse Square shops and restaurants. The guest rooms include dark wood furniture and walls are paneled. Restaurant (breakfast only). In-room data ports, microwaves (in suites), refrigerators (in suites). Cable TV. Indoor pool. Hot tub. Gym. Laundry facilities. Business services. | 310 S. College Ave. | 812/335–8000 or 800/321–2211 | fax 812/336–9997 | www.courtyard.com/bmgcy | 112 rooms, 5 suites | $89–$109, $129–$165 suites | AE, D, DC, MC, V.

Eagle Pointe Golf Resort. In the hills on the southern edge of Lake Monroe, 13 mi south of downtown Bloomington, you can stay in a condominium with views of the lake, the golf course, or the woods. All have private entrances and a balcony or patio. There are loft-style rooms as well as one-, two-, or three-bedroom units and townhouses. Most have fireplaces and full kitchens. Golf packages are available. 2 restaurants, bar. Some kitchenettes, some microwaves, some refrigerators. Cable TV, In-room VCRs (and movies). Pool. Hot tub, massage. 18-hole golf course, tennis courts. Gym, hiking. Boating, fishing, bicycles. Laundry facilities. Business services. | 2250 E. Point Rd. | 812/824–4040 or 877/324–7683 | www.eaglepointe.com | 82 rentals | $139–$419 | AE, D, DC, MC, V.

Fourwinds Resort and Marina. The three-story Fourwinds is on the shore of Lake Monroe, 13 mi south of Bloomington. Furnishings are traditional but there are occasional rustic and contemporary touches, including polished clay floor tiles, woven rugs, and bold patterned fabrics. Bar with entertainment, dining room, picnic area, snack bar, room service. Cable TV. Indoor-outdoor pool. Hot tub. Miniature golf, tennis courts. Shuffleboard, basketball courts. Marina, boating. Playground. Business services. | 9301 Fairfax Rd. | 812/824–9904 | fax 812/824–9816 | www.fourwindsresort.com | 126 rooms | $109–$144 | AE, D, DC, MC, V.

The Grant Street Inn. The courthouse is five blocks from this two-story yellow clapboard home dating from the late 1800s, now a modern lodgingplace. Guest rooms are traditional and include antique furnishings. Some have fireplaces. Some in-room hot tubs. | 310 N. Grant St. | 812/334–2353 or 800/328–4350 | fax 812/331–8673 | www.grantsinn.com | 24 rooms | $99–$169 | AE, D, MC, V.

Hampton Inn. On the outskirts of town, in a row of newer motels, this big, new four-story hotel has bright, airy rooms with dark wood furniture. Some rooms have exercise equipment. There are 25" TVs and voice mail in all rooms. Complimentary Continental breakfast. In-room data ports, some in-room hot tubs. Cable TV. Indoor pool. Gym. Business services. Some pets allowed. | 2100 N. Walnut St. | 812/334–2100 | fax 812/334–8433 | www.hamptoninn.com | 131 rooms | $63–$149 | AE, D, DC, MC, V.

Holiday Inn. Bloomington's original chain motel is on the quiet bypass that leads to downtown. The Indiana University campus is nearby. Restaurant, bar, room service. Cable TV. Indoor pool. Hot tub, sauna. Video games. Business services. | 1710 Kinser Pike | 812/334–3252 | fax 812/333–1702 | 189 rooms, 4 floors | $109–$129 | AE, D, DC, MC, V.

Indiana Memorial Union. Nestled in the heart of the Indiana University campus, the university lodging accommodations on five floors are older and modest, but well maintained with traditional furnishings. Restaurant. Cable TV. Gym. | 900 E. 7th St. | 812/856–6381 or 800/209–8145 | fax 812/855–3426 | www.iupromo.com | 186 rooms | $94–$99 | AE, MC, V, D.

TownePlace Suites by Marriott. This three-story hostelry is designed for travelers looking for more than the basics. Kitchens, in all units, have all utensils and cookware plus a dishwasher, and each unit has a desk and voicemail. There are studio, one-, and two-bedroom suites. A steakhouse and several other restaurants are in the area. In-room data ports. Kitchenettes, refrigerators. Cable TV, In-room VCRs (and movies). Pool. Exercise equipment. Laundry facilities, laundry services. Business services. | 105 S. Franklin Rd. | 812–334–1234 or 800/257–3000 | fax 812/334–1995 | www.marriott.com | 84 rooms | $69–$89 | AE, D, DC, MC, V.

BRAZIL

MAP 3, C6

(Nearby towns also listed: Greencastle, Terre Haute)

This rural town was founded in 1844 and, as the story goes, named by a resident who had read about the South American country and was intrigued with it. Today Brazil is home to many an antiques shop, and is the seat of Clay County, in the heart of west-central Indiana's coal belt. Named for the statesman Henry Clay, the county is also known for its clay resources. Brick making and pottery operations have prospered here over the years.

Information: **Brazil–Clay Co. Chamber of Commerce** | 11 N. Walnut St., Box 23, 46783 | 812/448–8457 | www.claycountychamber.com.

Attractions

Bridgeton National Historic District. A 245-ft covered bridge built in 1868 is one of the most frequently photographed bridges in this historic district 4 mi north of Brazil. It is over a waterfall with a grist mill nearby. | R.R. 1, Carbon | 765/569–5226 | www.coveredbridges.com | Free | Year-round.

Clay County Historical Museum. A former post office houses this museum, which displays artifacts and historical documents important to the county's coal-mining and clay industries and its early settlement. | 100 E. National Ave. | 812/446–4036 | Free | Mar.–Dec., weekdays 1–4, Sat. 1:30–3:30.

Forest Park. The large, shady park on the outskirts of town has two restored pioneer cabins dating from the mid 1850s, a granite fountain, picnic areas, a stadium, an outdoor pool, an 18-hole golf course, and an outdoor auditorium used for summer concerts. | Forest Ave. | 812/442–5681 | Free | Daily.

JUNE: *Clay City Lion's Pottery Festival.* Lions Pottery has been a part of this area since 1885 and this Clay City festival showcases the work of the fourth generation to be involved in the business. A craft show, flea market, antique cars and farm equipment, quilt show, and food vendors round out the activities roster. | 812/939–2626.

NOV., DEC.: *Christmas in the Park.* More than a million tiny lights sparkle throughout downtown Brazil and Forest Park during this week-long festival. You'll also find arts and crafts, holiday music performances, caroling, and an appearance from Santa. | 812/448–8457.

Dining

Company's Coming. American. This restaurant, open only for lunch, is on the first floor of a Victorian house here three rooms and a parlor are open for dining. Each has its own color scheme and is scattered with antiques and country items; one has a fireplace. The menu is home-style—there's chicken and cheese pasta, deep-dish chicken pot pie, salmon loaf, cinnamon-spiked shredded pork, and potato dill and tomato herb soups. You can also choose from salads and sandwiches. Save room for one of the homemade desserts, a hot fudge sundae, or pumpkin cheesecake in fall. | 303 N. Forest Ave. | 812/443–7963 | No dinner. Closed Sun.–Mon. | $5–$7 | MC, V.

Lodging

McGregor House Bed and Breakfast. This bed and breakfast occupies a brick-and-stone Romanesque Revival home built in 1895 in the city's historic district, four blocks from downtown. Furnishings include antiques, oriental rugs, and a baby grand piano. Rooms and suites have individual themes: the McGregor Suite shows off Scottish heritage with a queen brass bed covered with a handmade quilt, fireplace, and clawfoot tub. Other options include the European Room, the Victorian Room, and the Arts Suite. You can eat breakfast in the parlor or on the front veranda. A full gymnasium and basketball court are attached to the house. Complimentary breakfast. Refrigerator in some rooms. TV in common area. Library. No children under 11. No smoking. | 503 N. Meridian St. | 812/448–8315 | www.southernin.com/mcgregorhouse | 2 rooms, 2 suites | $80 rooms, $120 suites | No credit cards.

CLARKSVILLE

MAP 3, E8

(Nearby towns also listed: Corydon, Jeffersonville, Madison, New Albany)

This Ohio River community was the first town in the Old Northwest Territory, chartered by the state of Virginia in 1783. The Virginia Assembly rewarded General George Rogers Clark and his troops for their distinguished service against the British with a 150,000-acre land grant at the Falls of the Ohio. A few years later, Clark built a cabin on a hill overlooking the river. In 1803, explorers with the Lewis and Clark expedition met there, making the Falls of the Ohio the launching point for their trek through Louisiana Purchase territory. The huge limestone slab that creates the falls contains the largest exposed Devonian fossil beds in the world, and when water levels are low you can see 375-million-year-old fossils at Falls of the Ohio State Park.

Information: **Southern Indiana, Clark and Floyd Counties Convention and Tourism Bureau** | 315 Southern Indiana Ave., Jeffersonville, 47130 | 812/280–5566 or 800/552–3842 | fax 812/282–1904 | www.sunnysideoflouisville.org.

Attractions

Derby Dinner Playhouse. A dinner buffet and cocktails are part of this theater where you will see performances of Broadway productions. Kids' theater programs are also available.

| 525 Marriott Dr. | 812/288–8281 or 812/288–2632 | www.derbydinner.com | $25–$37 | Tues.–Sun. 6 PM–10 PM.

Falls of the Ohio State Park and Interpretive Center. The world's largest exposed Devonian-age fossil beds covering 220 acres and the 350- to 400-million-year-old fossilized coral reef are best viewed in August through October when the river is lowest. The modern Interpretive Center features an exhibit hall, a library, a wildlife observation room, an observation deck, and an auditorium for video presentations. | 201 W. Riverside Dr. | 812/280–9970 | www.fallsoftheohio.com | $2 | Daily Mon.–Sat. 9–5; Sun. 1-5; guided tours of fossil beds May–Oct.

ON THE CALENDAR
APRIL: *Thunder Over Louisville.* Along the Ohio River, near Clarksville, Louisville, and Jeffersonville, 55 tons of fireworks explode and there's an air show. | 502/228–6009.

Dining
Hometown Buffet. American. This buffet restaurant near the Green Tree Mall, which provides home-style cooking on the road. The buffet items vary daily but may include meatloaf, chicken and dumplings, hot wings, baked or fried chicken or fish, country-fried steak, barbecued ribs, fried shrimp, or carved turkey, ham, or roast beef, along with the usual potatoes, breads, vegetables, salads, and desserts. | 757 Rte. 131 | 812/285–1893 | No reservations accepted | $9 | AE, D, MC, V.

Lodging
Best Western Green Tree Inn. This single-story motel is in a suburban area 2 mi from Kentucky Kingdom water park and 4 mi from downtown Louisville. There are two shopping malls within three blocks and many food options in a half-mile radius. Restaurant. Complimentary Continental breakfast. In-room data ports. Cable TV. Pool. Hot tub. Exercise equipment. Laundry facilities. Free parking. | 1425 Broadway | 812/288–9281 or 800/950–9281 | www.bestwestern.com | 103 rooms | $69–$74 | AE, D, DC, MC, V.

COLUMBUS

MAP 3, E6

(Nearby towns also listed: Bedford, Bloomington, Nashville)

Columbus is an architectural showcase. Vintage buildings that have been restored and innovative modern ones stand side by side along the brick streets downtown. The 1874 County Courthouse with its clock tower anchors the south edge of town, and 19th-century storefronts line the main street just as in many another Indiana small town; strip malls and shopping malls have sprouted like weeds on the outskirts, as in every other prosperous community in the state. There the resemblance stops, however. While at Yale, a local boy named J. Irwin Miller roomed with Eero Saarinen, who later became a noted architect and was the son of architect Eliel Saarinen. After graduation, Miller built the family business, Cummins Engine, into an international powerhouse, the world's premier manufacturer of diesel engines. With some of the profits, he started the Columbus Engine Foundation, which, to this day, has paid the architectural fees when certain internationally renowned architects are hired for local building projects. As a result, the town has become the repository of dozens of buildings by some of the world's best-known contemporary architects, including Harry Weese, Edward Larrabee Barnes, I. M. Pei, Roche Dinkeloo, Cesar Pelli, Robert Venturi, Richard Meier, Skidmore, Owings & Merrill, Gwathney Siegel, and, of course, Eliel and Eero Saarinen; a sculpture by Henry Moore presides over the local public library, and another by Jean Tinguely is a focal point in the downtown shopping mall. In a 1991 American Institute of Architects survey Columbus was ranked sixth among U.S. cities in architectural quality and innovation, following Chicago, New York, Washington, San Francisco, and Boston. Miller also established a philanthropic foundation to donate a portion of Cummins profits to charity and made such notable minority hiring efforts at Cummins that Martin Luther King Jr. once called him "the most progressive businessman in America."

Information: **Columbus Area Visitor Center** | 506 5th St., 47202 | 812/378–2622 or 800/468–6564 | www.columbus.in.us.

Attractions

Bartholomew County Historical Museum. A restored 19th-century Italianate brick house downtown mounts exhibitions in two galleries, and documents the county's history from pioneer times to the 20th century via artifacts, art, and a Victorian parlor. | 524 3rd St. | 812/372–3541 | www.bchs.hsonline.com | Free | Tues.–Fri. 9–4.

Columbus Area Visitor Center. Two works by internationally recognized glass artist Dale Chihuly, Yellow Neon Chandelier and Persian Window, ornament this two-story Italianate house built of red brick. There's also a gift shop that carries souvenirs, handmade pottery, architectural and children's books, jewelry, glass, and clothing. | 506 5th St. | 812/372–1954 | www.columbus.in.us | Free | Dec.–Feb., Mon.–Sat. 9–5; Mar.–Nov., also Sun. 10–4.

    Architectural Tours leave from the Visitor Center and take in the city's architectural landmarks. You can also pick up maps to use for self-guided tours. | 812/378–2622 or 800/468–6564 | $7 1-hr tour, $9.50 2-hr tour | Mar.–Nov., weekdays at 10, Sat. at 10 and 2, Sun. at 11.

The Commons. Architect Cesar Pelli designed this small, one-of-a-kind mall in the center of downtown Columbus in 1973. A kinetic sculpture by Jean Tinguely dominates the huge open space at the center. Off to one side is a carpeted play area where kids can climb and slide to their hearts' content. Upstairs are a movie theater and a branch of the Indianapolis Museum of Art. Innovative though it may be, is continues to lose business to large, glitzier malls on the outskirts of town. | 4th and Washington Sts. | 812/372–4541 | Free | Mon.–Sat. 9:30–7, Sun. noon–5.

Indianapolis Museum of Art–Columbus Gallery. The only branch of the Indianapolis Museum of Art was established in 1974 in the Cesar Pelli–designed, one-of-a-kind mall in the center of downtown Columbus, the one with the Jean Tinguely sculpture in the center. The museum mounts traveling exhibits and displays works from the art museum's permanent collections in Indianapolis. | 302 Washington St. | 812/376–2597 | Free | Tues.–Thurs., Sat. 10–5, Fri. 10–8, Sun. 12–4.

Irwin Gardens. J. Irwin Miller's father, banker William G. Irwin, created these gardens surrounding his former home, a redbrick building dating from 1864, downtown. The sunken formal gardens were inspired by the great gardens of Europe and are filled with sculpted trees and shrubs, flowers, and busts of ancient Greek philosophers. | 540 5th St. | 812/372–1954 | Free | Apr.–Oct., weekends 8–4.

Mill Race Park. Where three rivers come together, landscape architect Michael Van Valkenburgh designed an 85-acre park that could withstand periodic flooding and also become, according to its designer, "a small-town equivalent of Central Park." Mill Race features an outdoor amphitheater seating 300, a restored covered bridge, trails, a lake with a fishing pier, and picnic shelters. There are wonderful displays of lighted sculptures at Christmas. | Off 5th St. | 812/376–2680 | Free | Daily.

Muscatatuck National Wildlife Refuge. The state's only federally designated wildlife refuge covers 7,802 acres of wetlands, woodlands, and open fields that were once primarily farmland. Otters were introduced in the mid-1990s and trumpeter swans in the late 1990s. The refuge is known for attracting waterfowl year-round and for migrating bald eagles, ospreys, white pelicans, white-faced ibis, American bitterns, and blue herons. The refuge is also a habitat for upland birds including bobwhites and wild turkeys. There are eight other short wildlife viewing trails and a small information center with a viewing window. The refuge is 20 mi northeast of Columbus. | 12985 E. U.S. 50, Seymour | 812/522–4352 | fax 812/522–6826 | www.fws.gov/r3pao/muscatuk | Free | Daily.

Otter Creek Golf Course. In this architecture-oriented town, it is only fitting that renowned architect Harry Weese designed the golf course clubhouse, which features a glass-walled dining room. More than 3,000 trees spread across 388 acres shading the 27-hole championship course (open to the public) designed by Robert Trent Jones and his son Rees. The course is 6 mi east of the center of Columbus. | 11522 E. Rte. 50 N | 812/579–5227 | www.ocgc.com | Mar.–Nov.

ON THE CALENDAR

SEPT.: *Chautauqua of the Arts.* More than 100 artists from 25 states display and sell fine art and crafts at scenic Mill Race Park. The festival also includes entertainment and food. | 812/378–2622 or 800/468–6564.

NOV.–DEC.: *Winter Park.* Illuminated wire-frame sculptures on holiday themes line the road in Mill Race Park; the lights are on every evening from 6 to 10. | 812/378–2622 or 800/468–6564.

Dining

Jonathan Moore's American Cafe–Ramada Inn Columbus. Contemporary. Freshly prepared American fare is served in a dining area with paintings of Brown County by local artists. A balcony in back overlooks the lake. Known for chicken, steaks, seafood, and salads. 4 mi west of downtown. Family-style dining. | 2485 Jonathan Moore Pike | 812/376–3051 or 800/849–9832 | www.ramada.hsonline.com | $10–$20 | AE, D, DC, MC, V.

Zaharako's. American. A huge old-fashioned soda fountain with its original pressed-tin ceiling welcomes you to this vintage building. Along with basic cold sandwiches plus burgers, dogs, and fries, the kitchen does a great grilled cheese sandwich with chili inside. For dessert fountain treats like sundaes are the order of the day. You eat at 1950s formica-and-chrome tables and chairs; there are a few tiny antique tables for little kids. Ask a staffer to crank up the antique orchestra music box in back. | 329 Washington St. | 812/379–9329 | $1–$4 | No supper. Closed Sun. | No credit cards.

Lodging

Columbus Inn. This bed and breakfast occupies the renovated 1895 city hall downtown. Carved woodwork and ornamental tiles decorate the lobby and lounge, and there are traditional, antique furnishings in the rooms and suites. Afternoon tea is a daily affair. Complimentary breakfast. | 445 5th St. | 812/378–4289 | fax 812/378–4289 | columbusinn@voyager.net | www.thecolumbusinn.com | 29 rooms, 5 suites | $109, $119–$200 suites | AE, D, DC, MC, V.

Holiday Inn and Conference Center. Behind a contemporary facade, this hostelry with a seven-story tower and a couple of smaller wings has a Holidome recreation center, and there's an Old English pub and a small lobby with striped awnings, touches of brass, and a scattering of Indiana collectibles. It's two blocks off I–65, exit 68 (Rte. 46), and 1 mi from downtown. Restaurant, 2 bars with entertainment. In-room data ports, room service, cable TV. Indoor pool. Beauty salon, hot tub. Exercise equipment. Video games. Business services. | 2480 Jonathan Moore Pike (Rte. 46) | 812/372–1541 | fax 812/378–9049 | www.compassworks.com/holidayinn | www.holidayinn.com/hotel/cluin | 253 rooms | $150 | AE, D, DC, MC, V.

Ramada Inn and Conference Center. Set across from the Holiday Inn on a fishing lake, this is a stylish, older three-story hotel built of fieldstone that has been totally renovated and expanded. Guest rooms include desks and work areas. Restaurant, bar, complimentary breakfast. In-room data ports, some refrigerators, room service, cable TV. 2 pools (1 indoor). Hot tub. Tennis. Exercise equipment, boating. Business services. Free parking. | 2485 Jonathan Moore Pike (Rte. 46) | 812/376–3051 or 800/842–9832 | fax 812/376–0949 | www.ramada.hson-line.net | www.ramada.hsonline.com | 166 rooms | $85–$115 | AE, D, DC, MC, V.

Ruddick-Nugent House. Four white columns rising two stories across the front of this three-story Colonial Revival house built in 1884. With its expansive front lawn, it occupies an entire city block. William's room and Lizzie's room have gasoliers (a chandelier for both gas and electric). Inez's Room is bright with yellow painted walls, an antique wardrobe, and a queen bed. Martha's room holds a queen bed with a headboard made from the original front doors of the house and a marbleized, cast-iron fireplace. You can have your breakfast by candlelight in the dining room, or on the balcony or front porch. No alcohol allowed on premises. Complimentary breakfast. Cable TV. No smoking. | 1210 16th St. | 812/379–1354 or 800/814–7478 | www.ruddick-nugent-house.com | 4 rooms | $65–$95 | AE, D, MC, V.

CONNERSVILLE

MAP 3, F5

(Nearby towns also listed: Batesville, Greenfield, Metamora, New Castle, Richmond)

Around 1808, John Conner set up a trading post near an Native American trail by the west fork of the Whitewater River. Within five years Conner had platted the town of Connersville. Three decades later the Whitewater Canal brought prosperity to this settlement in the hinterlands of Indiana. You can still see remnants of the canal today, and downtown historic buildings from the middle of the 19th century recall Connersville's heyday as a shipping center and furniture and buggy-making town. Later, automobile manufacturers set up shop here, and for a time the town was referred to as "Little Detroit." Today several automotive parts manufacturers call Connersville home.

Information: Connersville Chamber of Commerce | 504 Central Ave., 47331 | 765/825–2561 | www.connersvillein.com.

Attractions

Brookville Lake State Reservoir. Two state recreation areas with beaches look out over a 5,260-acre lake here. A scenic trail off Route 101 runs close to the lake's shoreline. Nearby is the Quakertown State Recreation Area, with more water-based activities. At Quakertown, you can visit the Treaty Line Pioneer Village, which incorporates five cabins from now-obliterated Dunlapsville, flooded when the reservoir was created. The village includes a museum in the Dunlapsville school, an 1819 gristmill, and the Quakertown General Store. The complex is 14 mi east of Connersville. | Brookville | 765/647–2658 | www.state.in.us/dnr/statepar/reserv/brook/brook.htm | $2 per vehicle residents, $5 non-residents | Daily.

Canal House. Built in 1842, this stately columned building downtown was once the headquarters for the Whitewater Valley Canal Company and is considered one of the finest examples of Greek Revival architecture in the state. The original ash, oak, and cherry floors remain, along with woodwork carved out of tulip poplar. | 111 E. 4th St. | 765/825–2561 | Free | By appointment.

Mary Gray Bird Sanctuary of the Indiana Audubon Society. The 650-acre wooded preserve is home to 60 species of birds. Follow trails that crisscross the park, then picnic in the shade or study the wildlife exhibits at the small museum. | 3499 S. Bird Sanctuary Rd. (Rte. 350 S) | 765/825–9788 | www.indianaaudubon.org | Free | Daily.

Whitewater Memorial State Park. One of the smaller state parks, Whitewater is at the northern tip of Brookville Lake and covers 1,710 acres. Twenty housekeeping cab | 1418 S. Rte. 101, Liberty | 765/458–5565 | www.ai.org/dnr | $2 per vehicle (residents), $5 per vehicle (nonresidents) | Daily.

Whitewater Valley Railroad. Indiana's longest round-trip train ride follows portions of the historic Whitewater Canal towpath along the 16-mi route to the historic canal village of Metamora. Riders can then tour Metamora, with its 100 shops and gristmill, before board-

ing the train for the return trip to Connersville. | 455 Market St. | 765/825–2054 | www.white-watervalleyrr.org/ | $14 adults, $7 for children | May–Oct., weekends noon.

ON THE CALENDAR

JULY, AUG.: *Fayette County Free Fair.* The fair covers 19 acres and features livestock contests, crafts, and carnival activities for youngsters. | 2594 Park Rd. | 765/825–2561.
SEPT: *Connersville/Fayette County Fall Festival.* Now held in conjunction with the Outlaws Car Club, several classic and street rod cars participate in this one-day event. You can visit arts and crafts booths, food vendors, and watch live entertainment. Held at Roberts Park off Park Rd. and 30th St. | 765/825–2561.

Dining

El Camino Real. Mexican. They speak Spanish at this Mexican restaurant furnished with candles, lamps, flowers, and cactus plants. There are six booths and several tables. Try the tacos, enchiladas, fajitas, burritos, quesadillas, or nachos with either chicken and steak. | 308 W. 30th St. | 765/827–9722 | Open Daily | $5–$7 | MC, V.

Lodging

The Woodridge Inn. Built in 1991, this inn has one main building and another building across the street. It's seven blocks north of 30th Street, where you'll find many restaurants and shops. Complimentary Continental breakfast. Some kitchenettes. Some refrigerators. Some in-room hot tubs. Cable TV. Pool. | 3700 Western Ave. | 765/825–4800 | fax 765/825–6035 | www.woodridgeinn.com | 92 rooms | $60–$120 | AE, D, DC, MC, V.

CORYDON

MAP 3, D8

(Nearby towns also listed: Clarksville, Jasper, Jeffersonville, New Albany, Santa Claus, Wyandotte)

Forty-three delegates met in Corydon in the shade of a huge elm tree and drafted the state's first constitution. The old state capitol, a small shuttered limestone building, served as the state's center of government from 1816 to 1825, when Indianapolis was made the new capital. Corydon was also the site of an 1863 Civil War battle, one of only a few fought on northern soil. The town takes pride in its past and preserves several historic sites. Located in the extreme south-central part of the state near the Ohio River, Corydon was settled by emigrants from the eastern seaboard who followed the Ohio River valley west. Today the town is a tourist destination and popular with outdoor recreation enthusiasts. There are a few small furniture factories in the area.

Information: Harrison County Chamber of Commerce | 310 N. Elm St., 47112 | 888/738–2137 | info@tourindiana.com | www.tourindiana.com.

Attractions

Battle of Corydon Memorial Park. On July 9, 1863, General John Hunt Morgan's Confederate troops met the Harrison County Home Guard in Corydon for the only actual Civil War battle on Hoosier soil. The Home Guard troops surrendered. | 812/738–8236 or 812/738–2137 | Free | Daily 8–5.

Corydon Capitol State Historic Site. Included at this downtown site are two buildings and the trunk of the Constitution Elm. | 202 E. Walnut St. | 812/738–4890 | fax 812/738–4904 | www.ai.org/dnr | Free (donations accepted) | Mar.–Dec., Tues.–Sat. 9–5, Sun. 1–5; shorter hrs mid-Dec.–mid-Mar.

Tall trees in the downtown square shade the restored **Capitol Building** dating from 1816. The building is only 40 square ft and is built of hand-hewn timbers and blue limestone quarried locally. Plaques inside trace the drafting of the state's first constitution and Corydon's early years as state capital.

The **Constitution Elm Monument** is a plaque near the trunk of an elm tree telling how the tree provided shade for the delegates as they labored to draft statehood papers in 1816.

A block from the old State Capitol is the preserved Federal-style home of the state's second governor. The stately **Governor Hendricks' Headquarters** is filled with period furnishings. | www.ai.org/dnr.

Corydon Scenic Railroad. A 15-mi, 90-minute round-trip train ride takes you through the rolling hills and is particularly scenic in the fall. | 210 W. Walnut St. | 812/738–8000 | $9 | May–Oct.

Marengo Cave National Landmark. Known for its stunning formations, this cave 20 mi west of Corydon offers two tours. The Dripstone Tour views soda-straw formations and totem-pole stalagmites. Huge flowstone formations are highlights of the Crystal Palace Tour, which visits massive rooms filled with formations. | Marengo | 812/365–2705 | www.marengocave.com | Crystal Palace Tour $10.50, Dripstone Tour $11, combination tour $15 | Memorial Day–Labor Day, daily 9–6; Labor Day–Memorial Day, daily 9:30–5; tours every 30 mins.

Posey House Museum. Six rooms in this 1817 Federal-style house are filled with antique furnishings. Included are an 1819 parlor piano of rosewood, farming tools, Civil War–era relics, and a kitchen with period furnishings. Call ahead; the museum is undergoing renovations at press time. | 225 Oak St. | 812/738–4890.

Squire Boone Caverns and Village. Rare rimstone dams and twisted helictite formations this system of caverns, discovered in 1790 by brothers Daniel and Squire Boone. A log-cabin village includes a gristmill, crafts demonstrations, and a display of Native American artifacts. 12 mi south of Corydon. | Rte. 135 | 812/732–4381 | www.squireboonecaverns.com | $9.50 parking $3 | Daily.

Zimmerman Art Glass. Since 1944, the Zimmerman family has been crafting paperweights, candleholders, lamps, and vases in Corydon. Watch craftsmen shape hot, molten glass, then admire the finished products. | 395 Valley Rd. | 812/738–2206 | www.corydon.iswired.com | Free | Tues.–Sat., 8–4 (glass blowing 9:30–4).

ON THE CALENDAR

JULY: *Harrison County Fair.* The week-long 140-year-old fair in downtown Corydon features agricultural displays, a carnival, and nightly grandstand shows. | 333 S. Capitol Ave. | 812/738–2137 or 888/738–2137.

OCT: *Halloween on the Square.* Celebrate in the downtown area with a parade, musical entertainment, cake walk, fortune telling, contests, and games. There's also a haunted cave walk in Wyandotte Caves, 8 mi from town. | 812/738–4890.

Dining

Bennett's. Continental. Locals say this downtown restaurant is a little upscale, but it's still fairly casual. On weekends, the tables have linen tablecloths. Eat in the bar area or the dining room. Menu items include grilled pork chops, filet mignon, catch of the day, New York strip steak, Icelandic cod, pasta, burgers, and sandwiches. You can order from one or two daily specials with a fish special on Fridays. | 400 N. Capitol Ave. | 812/738–8954 | Closed Sun.–Mon. | $10–$22 | AE, D, MC, V.

Magdalena's. American. Soups made from recipes provided by the owner's Polish grandmother, sandwiches, salads, and hot apple dumplings are served in this casual downtown eatery, brightly styled in mauve and green with floral prints on the walls. There's also an ice-cream parlor. Wine only. | 103 Chestnut St. | 812/738–8075 | No breakfast | $9–$15 | AE, D, DC, MC, V.

Lodging

Best Western Old Capitol Inn. Weathered red brick and white trim give this older but well-maintained two-story property a Colonial look. Gardens surround the pool. It's right by the I–64, exit 105 (Corydon), 3 mi from downtown. Cable TV. Pool. Business services. | Rte. 135 and I–64 | 812/738–4192 | fax 812/738–4192, ext. 316 | 77 rooms | $69 | AE, D, DC, MC, V.

Kintner House. There's a big, inviting front porch on this renovated three-story brick home with polished wood floors and antique furnishings in individually decorated guest rooms. The inn is downtown, a block from the State Capitol and square. Complimentary breakfast. No smoking, cable TV. Business services. | 101 S. Capitol Ave. | 812/738–2020 | 15 rooms | $59–$99 | AE, D, MC, V.

Hampton Inn Corydon. This three-story hotel opened in 1998. It is 2 mi from downtown, 8 mi from the Marengo Caves, and near several restaurants off I–64, exit 105 (Corydon), on Route 135 S. In-room data ports. Refrigerators. Cable TV. Indoor pool. Hot tub. Exercise equipment. Laundry facilities. | 2455 Landmark Ave. | 812/738–6688 or 800/426–7866 | fax 812/738–6699 | www.hamptoninn.com | 68 rooms | $71–$95 | AE, D, DC, MC, V.

CRAWFORDSVILLE

MAP 3, C4

(Nearby towns also listed: Lafayette, Marshall, Rockville)

The three founding fathers of Crawfordsville, on a bluff overlooking pristine Sugar Creek in west-central Indiana, rode in on horseback in 1813 and saw the potential for a settlement. But it was nearly 10 years before they returned with their families and laid out the town. Wabash College, a prestigious all-male college was founded here in 1832. Today the college has fewer than 1,000 students and is still regarded as one of the foremost private colleges in the nation. Like many small Midwestern county seats, Crawfordsville clusters around its courthouse square, where a striking granite obelisk pays homage to war veterans. The town's most celebrated native son, General Lew Wallace, served in the Civil War, officiated at the Lincoln assassination trial, and later became territorial governor of New Mexico. Wallace is best known for his epic *Ben Hur*, which he wrote at his shady estate a few blocks east of the courthouse.

Information: **Montgomery County Visitors and Convention Bureau** | 218 E. Pike St., 47933 | 765/362–5200 or 800/866–3973 | www.crawfordsville.org.

Attractions

Ben Hur Museum. The museum is in the late 1890s work study built by General Lew Wallace. Wallace wrote most of the novel *Ben Hur* on the grounds outside the building here. Furnishings original to the home and memorabilia from Wallace's colorful career as a lawyer, state senator, Civil War officer, and distinguished writer are on display. | 922 E. South Blvd. | 765/362–5769 | www.ben-hur.com/ | $3 | June–Aug., Wed.–Sat. 10–4:30, Tues., Sun. 1–4:30; Apr.–May and Sept.–Oct., Tues.–Sun. 1–4:30.

Clements Canoes. Canoe and kayak trips ranging from three hours to four days take you on Sugar Creek, an amazingly beautiful stream that threads through the rolling countryside between steep sandstone bluffs and dense pockets of woodlands. Most trips pass through Shades and Turkey Run state parks, which are honeycombed with deep wooded ravines. | 613 Lafayette Ave. | 765/362–2781 | fax 765/36–CANOE | www.clementscanoes.com/ | $23–$27 (varies with trip and craft) | Apr.–Oct., daily, 8–5 and reservations.

Henry S. Lane Historic Home. This 1845 Greek Revival home with pillars and black shutters has nine rooms furnished with Victorian antiques. The fully restored mansion in the center of town was the home of Col. Henry S. Lane, a governor of Indiana and U.S. senator during the Civil War. Lane was key in organizing the support for Abraham Lincoln's presidential nomination and lived in the home until his death in 1881. | 212 S. Water St. | 765/362–3416 | $3 | June–Aug., Wed.–Sat. 1–4, Tues., Sun. 1–4; Apr.–May and Sept.–Oct., Tues.–Sun. 1–4.

Old Jail Museum. In this restored 1882 county jail in the north end of town the cell blocks are circular and rotate with a hand crank. It's the only one of its kind in the United States. The former sheriff's living quarters have displays on local art and history. | 225 N. Washington St. | 765/362–5222 | www.crawfordsville.org | Free | June–Aug., Wed.–Sat. 10–4:30, Tues., Sun. 1–4:30; Apr.–May and Sept.–Oct., Wed.–Sun. 1–4:30.

ON THE CALENDAR

JUNE: *Strawberry Festival.* Crowds gather on the shady lawn of Historic Lane Place, which hosts an arts and crafts fair with 90 booths, strawberry desserts, a classic car show, antique tractor show, children's activities, sporting events, and entertainment. | 765/362–3058.

SEPT.: *Labor Day Breakout.* On Labor Day weekend, during the Breakout, the cells of the unusual local jail are rotated every half hour. There's food, entertainment, and a tour. | 765/362–5222.

DEC.: *Candlelight Tour of Homes.* Stroll downtown Crawfordsville to view historic and contemporary homes decorated for the holidays. | 765/362–3416.

Dining

Arni's. American. An upbeat collegiate spirit characterizes this small pizza joint, downtown, near the Wabash College campus. It's known for its super-thin-crust pizza, but you can also get sandwiches, salads, and other Italian specialties. | 114 W. Wabash Ave. | 765/362–2764 | $5–$12 | No credit cards.

Arthur's. American. In an old building downtown with a painted mural of a sidewalk café scene, this busy spot serves home-grown fare like biscuits and gravy as well as good club sandwiches and taco salads. | E. Main St. | 765/364–9938 | Breakfast also available. Closed Sun. No dinner | $4–$8.

The Bungalow and the Rendez-Vous. American. Tucked in a small mid-1900s bungalow home in the historic district downtown, the Bungalow is known for spinach melt sandwiches and spiced hot apple cider. Steaks are grilled outdoors. The Cellar Bar is in the basement. | 210 E. Pike St. | 765/362–2596 | Closed Sun. No lunch Sat., no dinner Tues. | $12–$20 | DC, MC, V.

Lodging

Days Inn. Rooms now have queen-sized beds in this two-story hotel near Route 231 S, I-74, exit 34. Complimentary Continental breakfast. Some microwaves. Some refrigerators. Cable TV. Exercise equipment. Business services. | 1040 Corey Blvd. | 765/362–0300 | www.daysinn.com | 60 rooms | $45–$54 | AE, D, DC, MC, V.

Holiday Inn. Rooms overlook the outdoor pool at this completely renovated Holiday Inn built in 1996. It's 2 mi from downtown. Restaurant, bar with entertainment. In-room data ports, some microwaves, room service, cable TV. Pool. Video games. Laundry facilities. Business services. Some pets allowed. | 2500 Lafayette Rd. | 765/362–8700 | fax 765/362–8700 | 150 rooms | $66–$166 | AE, D, DC, MC, V.

ELKHART

MAP 3, D1

(Nearby towns also listed: Goshen, Middlebury, Mishawaka, Nappanee, Shipshewana, South Bend)

The Native Americans that originally lived in this area felt that an island at the confluence of the Elkhart and St. Joseph rivers was shaped like an elk's heart—hence the name of this old-fashioned town. Today, it is a modern industrial and commercial center at the western edge of Indiana's northern Amish country, just south of I-80/90. The location makes it a gateway to the rural Amish countryside, where hitching posts line the streets of small farming towns, generous home-style cooking draws hordes to restaurants styled to look like barns, and crafts and woodworking workshops do a brisk business. Known as the Recreational Vehicle Capital of the World, Elkhart is headquarters to more than 200 vehicle and parts manufacturers. The town has been producing band instruments ever since C. G. Conn started making trumpet mouthpieces here in 1873; seven companies, many of them offshoots of Conn's original enterprise, manufacture woodwind and brass instruments.

Information: Amish Country/Elkhart County Convention and Visitors Bureau | 219 Caravan Dr., 46514 | 219/262–8161 or 800/262–8161 | ecconv@amishcountry.org | www.amish-country.org/welcome/welcome.html.

Attractions

Midwest Museum of American Art. The museum, which occupies a restored bank building downtown, displays sculpture, photography, paintings, and prints dating from the mid-1800s to the present. The noteworthy collection includes works by Alexander Calder, Norman Rockwell, and Grandma Moses. | 429 S. Main St. | 219/293–6660 | $3; free on Sun. | Tues.–Fri. 11–5, weekdays 1–4.

National New York Central Railroad Museum. Two 1915 rail coaches, a scale model of a steam locomotive, films, and 10,000 old-time photographs tell the history of the railroad in Elkhart. Also scattered across the grounds are several other locomotives and train cars. | 721 S. Main St. | 219/294–3001 | nycrrmuseum.railfan.net | $2 | Tues.–Fri. 10–2, Sat. 10–4, Sun. 12–4.

Ruthmere Museum. A. R. Beardsley, of Miles Laboratories, built this Beaux Arts–style home in 1908 and fitted out his grand mansion in opulent style with intricately painted ceilings and a marble wraparound veranda. Today you will see velvet and silk window coverings and upholstery in keeping with the overall mood along with original Tiffany lamps and a collection of fine art. It's near the center of Elkhart. | 302 E. Beardsley Ave. | 219/264–0330 | www.ruthmere.com | $6 | Guided tours only: Apr.–Dec., Tues.–Sat. at 10, 11, 1, 2 and 3; July–Aug., also Sun. at 2 and 3.

S. Ray Miller Auto Museum. Forty restored cars, many of them one-of-a-kind, along with vintage clothing and memorabilia recall the first half of the 19th century at this gallery in the northeast end of town. Featured in the collection are a 1930 Duesenberg "J" Murphy Convertible once owned by Al Capone's lawyer and a 1932 Nash. | 2130 Middlebury St. | 219/522–0539 | www.millerautomuseum.org | $6 | Weekdays 10–4, last full weekend each month noon–4.

Sunshine Animal Farm. Kids enjoy hundreds of animals in this farm setting—miniature horses, chickens, a donkey, a rabbit, and sheep. You can milk a goat and kids can ride a pony or play in the straw bales and maze. | 240 US 20, Middlebury | 800/455–9471 | www.essen-haus.com | $5.25, special rates for kids | Mon.–Sat. 9–7.

Woodlawn Nature Center. This small museum has exhibits about native plants and animals. | 604 Woodlawn Ave. | 219/264–0525 | $1 | Mar.–Oct., Tues.–Sat. 11:30–4:30; Nov.–Feb., Tues.–Fri. 1:30–4:30, Sat. 11:30–4:30.

ON THE CALENDAR

MAR.: *Wakarusa Maple Syrup Festival.* Tour a maple syrup camp in Wakarusa, then feast on pancakes smothered in real maple syrup. There's also a parade and antiques and crafts fair. | 219/262–8161 or 800/262–8161.
JUNE: *Elkhart Jazz Festival.* This premier jazz event celebrates the town's heritage as the Band Instrument Capital, with 100 internationally known jazz musicians performing everything from bebop to big band and smooth jazz in venues around town. | 219/262–8161 or 800/262–8161.

JUNE: *Festival of the Wild Rose Moon.* A living-history village is re-created in Middlebury with period artisans and entertainment, Native American dancers, and foods. | 219/262–8161 or 800/262–8161.

Dining

Matterhorn. American. This elegant restaurant on the north side of town has a dark-blue carpet and brass light fixtures, a wood-beamed vaulted ceiling, and stained glass. The menu offers salmon, walleye, and steaks. Sun. brunch. | 2041 Cassopolis St. | 219/262–1509 | No lunch Sat. | $15–$25 | AE, D, DC, MC, V.

© Artville

THE HEART OF AMISH COUNTRY

In Elkhart and neighboring LaGrange County, time seems to stand still. Fresh-faced children, boys wearing straw hats, and girls in bonnets pile in horse-drawn black-box buggies clip-clopping along dusty country roads. Plain white farmhouses are surrounded by fields that are still plowed the old-fashioned way, by a pair of sturdy draft horses. Like a flashback to a century ago, simplicity is a way of life for over 4,000 Amish in northern Indiana, which is one of the largest such settlements in the United States. The Amish started settling in the Hoosier state in the mid-1800s. Their faith dates back to the late 17th century, when Jakob Amman and a small group split from the Swiss Mennonites. Named after their leader Amman, the Amish started settling in the United States in the 1720s. They were first drawn to Lancaster County, Pennsylvania, because of the state's religious tolerance. The Amish are farmers for the most part, and over the years they have continued to migrate westward in search of fertile land. Their lives are rooted in a conservative Christian faith and literal interpretations of the Bible. Indiana's Amish country has embraced the essence of the Amish lifestyle with dozens of homey bed-and-breakfast inns, home-style restaurants in big barnlike buildings, general stores and bakeries at crossroads communities, and charming small towns filled with shops selling crafts, gifts, and antiques.

The Amish speak a German dialect known as Pennsylvania Dutch but use High German during worship. Amish children are educated in one-room schools, generally stopping at the eighth-grade level. The Amish do not own or use automobiles, electricity, radios, or TVs, and marry within their faith. Married men usually wear beards in accordance with the laws of the Hebrew scriptures and dress in a plain dark suit. Women wear long-sleeved plain colored dresses, aprons, and bonnets. Worship services are held in members' homes.

When traveling in Amish country, remember to respect their beliefs and customs. Most Amish object to being photographed. Cars share the road with buggies, so slow down, pass with care, and avoid honking your horn so as not to frighten the horses. Sunday is a day of worship for the Amish, and most businesses are closed on that day.

Lodging

Econo Lodge. In town at I–80/90, exit 92 (Elkhart), this small older motel on two floors has been maintained but not renovated. Complimentary Continental breakfast. Cable TV. Laundry facilities. Business services. Some pets allowed. | 3440 Cassopolis St. (Rte. 19) | 219/262–0540 | 35 rooms | $65 | AE, D, DC, MC, V.

Elkhart Super 8 Motel. This two-story motel was built in 1986 and has been updated. It's ¼ mi from I–80/90, exit 92 (Elkhart). Some microwaves. Some refrigerators. Cable TV. Free parking. Pets allowed. | 345 Windsor Ave. | 219/264–4457 or 800/800–8000 | fax 219/264–4457 | www.super8.com | 62 rooms | $39–$99 | AE, D, DC, MC, V.

Hampton Inn Elkhart. A shopping mall is 5 mi from this Hampton Inn, which opened in 1997. Museums are 4 mi away. The motel is off I–80/90, exit 92 (Elkhart). Cable TV. Pool. Hot tub. Exercise equipment. Business services. | 215 North Point Blvd. | 219/264–2525 or 800/426–7866 | fax 219/264–9164 | www.hamptoninn.com | 118 rooms | $80 | AE, D, DC, MC, V.

Knights Inn. This 1987 addition to Elkhart's lodging roster is a well-maintained one-story place. It's at I–80/90, exit 92 (Elkhart). Guest rooms have an antique look. | 118 rooms. In-room data ports, some kitchenettes, some microwaves, some refrigerators, cable TV. Pool. Business services. Some pets allowed (deposit). | 3252 Cassopolis St. (Rte. 19) | 219/264–4262 or 800/843–5644 | fax 219/264–4262 | 118 rooms | $33–$42 | AE, D, DC, MC, V.

Ramada Inn. Also at I–80/90, exit 92 (Elkhart), but set back off the road, this two-story hotel, built in 1974, has a stylish atrium with brown-tile floor, dark wood, and plants. Restaurant, bar with entertainment. In-room data ports, some refrigerators, room service, cable TV. 2 pools (1 indoor). Hot tub, sauna. Putting green. Exercise room. Playground. Business services. | 3011 Belvedere Rd. | 219/262–1581 | fax 219/262–1590 | 145 rooms | $89 | AE, D, DC, MC, V.

Red Roof Inn. This two-story motel is off Route 19 N 4 mi north of town. Cable TV. Some pets allowed. | 2902 Cassopolis St. (Rte. 19) | 219/262–3691 | fax 219/262–3695 | 80 rooms | $72 | AE, D, DC, MC, V.

Signature Inn. This modern-looking two-story hotel built in 1987 on the north edge of town has services and amenities for business travelers, including desks and coffee makers in the rooms. Complimentary Continental breakfast. In-room data ports, microwaves, refrigerators, cable TV. Outdoor pool. Business services. | 3010 Brittany Ct. | 219/264–7222 | www.signatureinns.com | 125 rooms | $74 | AE, D, DC, MC, V.

EVANSVILLE

(Nearby towns also listed: Jasper, New Harmony, Vincennes)

Despite the 1830s failure of the Wabash and Erie Canal, a watery transportation corridor that was supposed to link Lake Erie with the Wabash River, the town of Evansville, in Indiana's "big toe," survived. Situated at the planned terminus of the canal at the confluence of the Wabash and Ohio, Evansville went on to become one of southern Indiana's major commercial and industrial cities. By 1900, thanks in part to the staunch, enterprising work ethic of immigrant German settlers, Evansville had over 300 iron, steel, and woodworking companies and was known as a center for furniture manufacturing. Then in 1913 a devastating flood swept through the southeast side of town and 40 years later recession hit the durable goods-based economy. Once again the town rebounded, attracting nearly 30 more manufacturing firms in a 10-year period. Today restored mansions line the banks of the Ohio and the city has spearheaded an effort to preserve its architectural and cultural treasures. Owing to the recent influx of plastics manufacturers on the outskirts of town, Evansville is now known as "Plastics Valley."

Information: **Evansville Convention and Visitors Bureau** | 401 S.E. Riverside Dr., 47713 | 812/421–2200 or 800/433–3025 | tourism@evansvillecvb.org | www.evansville.cvb.org.

Attractions

Angel Mounds State Historic Site. The 103-acre site on the east side of Evansville tells the story of the Middle Mississippian Indians that lived here from AD 1100 to 1450. The Angel Mounds, 11 major earthworks, are on the property. The Central Mound is one of the largest prehistoric structures in the eastern United States. The modern interpretive center has exhibits and films on archaeological excavations of the site and the the Mississippian culture. | 8215 Pollack Ave. | 812/853–3956 | curator@angelmounds.org | Free | Mar. 15–Dec., Tues.–Sat. 9–5, Sun. 1–5.

Burdette Park. The 145-acre park on the west side of Evansville includes extensive recreation facilities amid a natural setting. Included are an Olympic-sized swimming pool, four water slides, batting cages, golf, hiking trails, and motorcross racing. | 5301 Nurrenburn Rd. | 812/435–5602 | www.vanderburgh.org/burdettepark | Free | Daily; pool Memorial Day–Labor Day.

Evansville Museum of Arts and Science. This museum, downtown on the riverfront, covers art, history, and science with a large permanent art collection, period room displays, Rivertown U.S.A.—a turn-of-the-century Main Street vignette—and a steam railroad exhibit. The Koch Planetarium and Family Place and Koch Science Center feature star shows and hands-on exhibits on science and technology. | 411 S.E. Riverside Dr. | 812/425–2406 | www.emuseum.org | Free; planetarium $2 | Tues.–Sat. 10–5, Sun. 12–5.

Mesker Park Zoo. Approximately 700 animals from Africa, Asia, and North America make their home in the large open spaces of this 70-acre zoo planted with trees and exotic flowers. Also on the grounds are a petting zoo, a train, paddleboat rides, and an unusual children's playground. | 2421 Bement Ave. | 812/428–0715 | www.meskerparkzoo.org/ | $4.75 | May–Oct., daily 9–5; butterfly house daily 10–4.

John Augustus Reitz Mansion. Bold architectural details and a mansard roof grace this French Second Empire–style home built in 1871 by a wealthy lumber baron. Period furnishings original to the home, stained glass, parquet floors, and detailed plaster moldings decorate the downtown mansion's 17 rooms. | 224 S.E. 1st St. | 812/426–1871 | www.reitzhome.evansville.net | $5 | Tues.–Sat. 11–3:30, Sun. 1–3:30.

University of Southern Indiana. Established in 1965 and the newest of the state universities, the Southern Indiana campus spreads across 300 acres on the west side of town. It includes eight academic buildings. The college enrolls nearly 9,000 undergraduates and graduates in seven degree programs. | 8600 University Blvd. | 812/464–8600 or 800/467–1965 | www.usi.edu | Free | Weekdays.

Wesselman Woods Nature Preserve. This 200-acre preserve within the city limits has hiking trails, a pond, an interpretive center, and 190 acres of virgin timber. It is 2 mi east of the center of Evansville. | 551 N. Boeke Rd. | 812/479–0989 or 812/479–0771 | www.wesselman.evansville.net | Free | Apr.–Sept., Tues.–Sun. 6–7; Oct.–Mar., Tues.–Sun. 8–4.

Willard Library. A slate roof, steep gables, and thick terra-cotta detailing give Indiana's oldest public library a look straight from the pages of a fairy tale. The majestic 1885 brick-and-stone building, located downtown, is a striking example of Italianate Gothic styling. Inside, carved oak woodwork, plaster moldings, and tall arched windows have been carefully preserved. The library houses local historical records, art books, and more than 100,000 volumes. | 21 1st Ave. | 812/425–4309 | www.willard.kib.in.us | Free | Mon.–Tues. 9–8, Wed.–Fri. 9–5:30, Sat. 9–5, Sun. 1–5.

ON THE CALENDAR

JUNE, JULY: *Evansville Freedom Festival.* Along the Riverfront Esplanade this event brings five days of festivities including musical performances, exciting hydroplane racing on the Ohio River, parades, carnivals, a beer garden, spectacular fireworks, and an airshow. | 812/434–4848 or 800/433–3025.

AUG.: *Germania Männerchor Volkfest.* A festival of German food, music, and good times. | 916 N. Fulton Ave. | 812/421–2200 or 812/422–1915.

Dining

Dogtown Tavern. American. Supposedly, the name of this tavern recalls how hunters used to tie up their dogs outside while they dined on platefuls of fiddlers (catfish), a local specialty. Beer and liquor mirrors hang on the walls. Go for the fried chicken and German fries. It's 4 mi west of Evansville, near the Ohio River. | 6201 Old Henderson Rd. | 812/423–0808 | $10–$16 | MC, V.

Elliott's Steakhouse. Steak. The tri-state area's most popular steak house, on the east side of Evansville, also serves seafood and pork dishes in a comfortable setting, with some stained glass windows. Some seafood is available. Kids' menu, early bird suppers (Sun.–Thurs.). | 4701 E. Powell Ave. | 812/473–3378 | No lunch Mon.–Sat. | $15–$45 | AE, D, DC, MC, V.

Gerst Bavarian Haus. German. Nestled in an old former hardware store, this place can be noisy at times because it often serves large parties. The German menu items include the requisite schnitzels and sauerbratens, but there's also American fare—oysters, catfish, chicken with garlic, and pasta. For dessert try warm Bavarian apple pie with ice cream. | 2100 W. Franklin St. | 812/424–1420 | $6–$15 | AE, DC, MC, V.

The Landmark. Continental. In an old home in downtown Evansville, the Landmark serves an eclectic menu with Italian, French, Middle Eastern, and American influences. Try the chicken Kiev, stuffed with mozzarella, chives, and butter, which is then breaded and sautéed. Another is seafood supreme, a mixture of clams, crabs, scallops, and shrimp with tomato sauce and herbs served on a bed of pasta. The menu also includes filet mignon, veal, and stuffed flounder. | 216 S.E. Riverside | 812/422–7701 | Reservations essential on weekends | No lunch. Closed Sun. and Mon. | $15–$19 | D, DC, MC, V.

North Main Annex. American. This café serves daily lunch specials, such as Salisbury steak, baked cod, grilled chicken, meatloaf, fried chicken, hickory-smoked baby back ribs, and spaghetti along with sandwiches. For dessert, sample the apple dumplings in cinnamon-sugar sauce. Breakfast available. | 701 N. Main St. | 812/425–4535 | Reservations not accepted | Closed Sun. No dinner Mon.–Wed. or Sat. Open at 6:30 AM for breakfast Mon.–Sat. | $5–$10 | AE, D, DC, MC, V.

Regent Court. Continental. You can look out on the Ohio River while you eat at this restaurant inside the Casino Aztar. The menu focuses on steak and seafood, and there's ribeye, New York Strip, prime rib, lobster, Chilean sea bass, rainbow trout, prawns, king crab legs, lamb, chicken, and pasta. Piano bar. Sun. brunch. | 421 N.W. Riverside Dr. | 800/342–5386 | Closed Mon. No lunch Tues.–Sat. | $15–$35 | AE, D, DC, MC, V.

Wolf's Bar-B-Q. Barbecue. Since 1927, this large, family-style restaurant on the north side of town deserves the raves it gets for barbecue sauce. The pulled pork is delicious, but you can also get barbecued beef, chicken, and pork ribs. Family-style service. | 6600 1st Ave. | 812/424–8891 | $8–$12 | D, MC, V.

Lodging

Baymont Inn and Suites Evansville East. Built in 1999, this three-story hotel is off I-164, exit 7B (Lloyd Expwy.), just 3 mi from a shopping mall and 7 mi from the local casino. Complimentary Continental breakfast. Some in-room hot tubs. Cable TV. Pool. Exercise equipment. Laundry facilities and services. | 8005 E. Division St. | 812/477–2677 | fax 812/475–0667 | www.baymontinn.com | 57 rooms | $55–$65 | AE, D, DC, MC, V.

Comfort Inn. This is a newer, three-story motel 1 ½ mi from I-164, exit 9 (Morgan Ave.), with many restaurants and the Eastland Mall nearby. Complimentary Continental break-

fast. Cable TV. Indoor pool. Hot tub. Business services. | 5006 E. Morgan Ave. | 812/477–2211 | fax 812/477–2211 | 52 rooms, 11 suites | $61–$67, $66–$72 suites | AE, D, DC, MC, V.

Country Inn and Suites. Near the intersection of Cross Point and Division Road, off I–164, exit 7B (Lloyd Expwy.), this four-story hotel is also 1 mi of Washington Square Mall. Complimentary Continental breakfast. Some microwaves. Some refrigerators. Cable TV. Pool. Exercise equipment. Business services. Free parking. | 301 Circle Front Dr. | 812/471–8399 or 800/456–4000 | fax 812/471–3133 | www.countryinns.com | 69 rooms | $55–$69, suites $80–$109 | AE, D, DC, MC, V.

EvansvilleSuper 8 Motel. Wesselman Park Nature Center is across the street from this three-story, brick motel that opened in 1989. It's near I–164, exit 9 (Morgan Ave.), on Route 62. Complimentary Continental breakfast. Some microwaves, some refrigerators. Cable TV. Pets allowed. | 4600 Morgan Ave. | 812/476–4008 or 800/800–8000 | www.super8.com | 62 rooms | $46–$64 | AE, D, DC, MC, V.

Quality Hotel and Suites. There are balconies on some rooms at this six-story hotel. It is in the city's historic district, on the riverfront, and within walking distance of the casino. Furniture is contemporary. In-room data ports. Some microwaves. Some refrigerators. Cable TV. Hot tub. Exercise equipment. Laundry services. Business services. Parking (fee). | 20 Walnut St. | 812/425–6500 | fax 812/423–7216 | www.qualityinn.com | 86 rooms | $54–$64, suites $80–$300 | AE, D, DC, MC, V.

River House Quality Hotel and Suites. Overlooking the Riverfront Esplanade park downtown, this three-story hotel, built in the 1960s, has traditional furnishings. Most guests rooms have a balcony, and some have views of the river. Restaurant, bar, complimentary breakfast buffet, room service. In-room data ports, some refrigerators. Cable TV. Hot tub. Exercise equipment. Business services. Airport shuttle. Free parking. | 20 Walnut St. | 812/425–6500 or 800/824–6710 | fax 812/423–7216 | www.qualityinn.com | 91 rooms | $69–$79 | AE, D, DC, MC, V.

Drury Inn–Evansville North. Built in 1983, this family-owned four-story motel in the northern section of town is 3½ mi south of the airport. Some rooms have a desk and recliner, and the hotel has a complimentary cocktail hour from Monday through Thursday night. Complimentary Continental breakfast. In-room data ports. Cable TV. Indoor pool. Hot tub. Exercise equipment. Laundry facilities. Business services. Free parking. Some pets allowed. | 3901 U.S. 41 N | 812/423–5818 or 800/378–7946 | www.drury-inn.com | 151 rooms | $73 | AE, D, DC, MC, V.

Fairfield Inn by Marriott. One of two Fairfield properties, built in 1995, this modern, three-story hotel is on the east side of town. Complimentary Continental breakfast. In-room data ports. Cable TV. Outdoor pool. Exercise equipment. Business services, free parking. | 7879 Eagle Crest Blvd. | 812/471–7000 | fax 812/471–7000 | 118 rooms | $66 | AE, D, DC, MC, V.

Fairfield Inn by Marriott. This four-story motel built in 1995 has spacious rooms and an upscale feel. It's on the near west side of downtown. Complimentary Continental breakfast. In-room data ports. Cable TV. Indoor pool. Exercise equipment. Business services. | 5400 Weston Rd. | 812/429–0900 | fax 812/429–0900 | 110 rooms | $69 | AE, D, DC, MC, V.

Hampton Inn–Evansville. On the east side of town at I–164, exit 7B (Lloyd Expwy.), along motel row, this Hampton Inn has five stories. It has a ⅔ mi walking trail around a lake. Complimentary Continental breakfast. Cable TV. Indoor pool. Exercise equipment. Business services. Free parking. | 8000 Eagle Crest Blvd. | 812/473–5000 | fax 812/479–1664 | www.hamptoninn.com | 143 rooms | $72 | AE, D, DC, MC, V.

Holiday Inn Airport. This older, two-story hotel on U.S. 41, is 2½ mi from the junction of Rtes. 62 and 66, and 5 mi north of the center of Evansville. Rooms have a tan and blue color scheme. Restaurant, bar. In-room data ports, room service. Cable TV. Indoor pool, wading pool. Hot tub. Exercise equipment. Video games. Laundry facilities. Playground. Business services. Airport shuttle. | 4101 U.S. 41 N | 812/424–6400 | fax 812/424–6409 | lkbandy@aol.com | 198 rooms | $89 | AE, D, DC, MC, V.

Holiday Inn Express–East. This modern two-story hotel, built in the 1970s and modernized, is on the east side of town. Guest rooms are done in soft colors. Complimentary Continental breakfast. In-room data ports. Cable TV. Pool. Business services. | 100 S. Green River Rd. | 812/473–0171 | fax 812/473–5021 | www.holiday.inn.com | 108 rooms | $64 | AE, D, DC, MC, V.

Radisson Hotel. This downtown 10-story new hotel is across the street from the city's convention center and six blocks from the riverboat casino. Restaurant. Cable TV. Indoor pool. Sauna. Health club. Business services. Some pets allowed. | 600 Walnut St. | 812/424–8000 or 800/333–3333 | fax 812/424–8999 | www.radisson.com | 471 rooms | $69 | AE, D, DC, MC, V.

Signature Inn. This two-story hotel on the east side of Evansville features contemporary architecture, with spacious rooms that include writing desks. Complimentary Continental breakfast. In-room data ports, microwaves, refrigerators. Cable TV. Pool. Business services. | 1101 N. Green River Rd. | 812/476–9626 | www.signatureinns.com | fax 812/476–9626 | 125 rooms | $68 | AE, D, DC, MC, V.

Studio Plus. This modern, three-story hotel with rooms similar to small studio apartments has all of the amenities of a suite hotel. It opened in 1997 on the east side of town. In-room data ports, full kitchens, microwaves. Cable TV. Pool. Exercise equipment. Laundry facilities. Business services. Free parking. | 301 Eagle Crest Dr. | 812/479–0103 or 800/646–8000 | fax 812/469–7172 | www.studioplus.com | 72 suites | $79 | AE, D, DC, MC, V.

FISHERS

MAP 3, D5

(Nearby towns also listed: Anderson, Indianapolis, Noblesville)

For years, the tiny community of Fishers was little more than a wide spot next to the railroad tracks in Hamilton County, off I–69. In the last 10 years, recognizing the benefit of an increased tax base, Fishers has extended its taxing authority and consumed a good portion of Hamilton County, the second-fastest-growing county in the nation. The county also claims its share of well-heeled residents, ranking eighth in the state in average adjusted gross income. Though Fishers is little more than a bedroom community 20 mi northeast of downtown Indianapolis, Hamilton County played a role in the state's early history. The redbrick home of William Conner, a trader, statesman, and one of the earliest settlers in central Indiana, is the centerpiece of Conner Prairie, a sprawling living-history settlement 3 mi north of town. It was here in 1820 that commissioners voted to move the state capital to Indianapolis.

Information: **Hamilton County, Indiana Convention and Visitors Bureau** | 11601 Municipal Dr., 46038 | 317/598–4444 or 800/776–TOUR | hccvb@netdirect.net | www.visitcentralindiana.org | www.fishers.in.us/main.html.

Attractions

Conner Prairie. This outdoor living-history museum complex, 24 mi north of downtown Indianapolis, explores early Indiana life in three areas: the Pioneer Adventure Center, an expansive museum center, and Prairietown, a re-created 1836 Indiana village made up of vintage buildings moved to the site from all over the state. On self-guided tours of the village, you can chat with costumed characters who portray a doctor, a school teacher, a potter, and other village residents. You can also tour the William Conner house, which is furnished in mid-19th-century antiques. Special programs highlight every season: the Headless Horseman at Halloween, Christmas candlelight tours, and Symphony on the Prairie, a series of summer concerts by the Indianapolis Symphony Orchestra. Prairie View Golf Club, Indiana's first course designed by Robert Trent Jones Jr. opened in spring 1997. | 13400 Allisonville Rd. | 317/776–6000 or 800/966–1836 | fax 317/776–6014 | www.conner-

prairie.org | Village and Pioneer Adventure Center $10 | Museum center Tues.–Sat. 9:30–
5, Sun. 11–5; Historic areas Apr.–Nov., Tues.–Sat. 9:30–5, Sun. 11–5.

ON THE CALENDAR
JUNE: *Fishers Freedom Festival.* Held since 1989, this festival includes a kids' parade
where the kids trim bikes, tricycles, big wheels, scooters, and other vehicles. There is a 5K
run/walk, an antique car and motorcycle show, arts and crafts booths, a puppet show,
street dance, live music, fireworks, and more. | 317/595–3195 | www.fishersfreedomfesti-
val.org.
DEC.: *Conner Prairie by Candlelight.* Candlelight tours of the 1836 re-created village
of Prairietown take a glimpse of how the villagers celebrated Christmas in pioneer
times. You can chat with costumed townsfolk then head to the museum center's
restaurant for dinner. | 317/773–0666.

Dining

Sahm's Restaurant. Continental. Since 1986 this family-owned restaurant at the corner
of Allisonville Road and 116th Street has been serving filet mignon, New York strip steak,
pork chops, baby back ribs, salmon, chicken, and pasta. House specialties are tomato basil
chicken, steak au poivre, and the fisherman's platter. Kids' menu. | 11590 Allisonville Rd. |
317/842–1577 | www.sahms.com | Daily | $9–$16 | AE, D, DC, MC, V.

Lodging

Frederick-Talbott Inn. Two older clapboard homes dating from 1890 have been joined and
refurbished as an inn, with modern conveniences. Antiques and English country pieces
mix with traditional furnishings in the guest rooms. It is across from Conner Prairie, 2 mi
north of Fishers. | 13805 Allisonville Rd. | 800/566–BEDS or 317/578–3600 | www.fredtal.com
| 10 rooms | $99–$179 | AE, D, DC, MC, V.

Holiday Inn Express. When you stay at this two-building motel built in 1983, you're 2 mi
from Geist Reservoir and 6 mi to the State Fairgrounds. One building has two stories and
the second building is three stories. There is a Bennigan's Restaurant in the hotel. Restaurant. Complimentary Continental breakfast, room service. In-room data ports. Refrigerators. Cable TV. Indoor pool. Hot tub. Exercise equipment. Business services. Some pets
allowed. | 9790 North by Northeast Blvd. | 317/578–2000 | fax 317/578–1111 | www.bassho-
tels.com | 140 | $84–$104 | AE, D, DC, MC, V.

FORT WAYNE

MAP 3, F2

*(Nearby towns also listed: Auburn, Berne, Geneva, Huntington, Shipshewana,
Warsaw)*

Three rivers come together in Fort Wayne, Indiana's second-largest city with a population of around 200,000. Tucked in the northeastern corner of the state, this strategic crossroads was favored by Miami Indians, who established a village at the headwaters
of the Maumee River, and later by fur traders and settlers. Fur trappers pushed into
the Great Lakes area starting in the 1670s, under French explorer La Salle. Each year
the region around Fort Wayne yielded 80,000 to 100,000 beaver pelts. Then for more
than a century the area was the object of conflict between the Miami, the Iroquois,
France, England, and the United States. Several fortifications were built here, although
none remains today except a replica. In 1812, territorial governor William Henry Harrison claimed victory and saved the first fort by thwarting a siege by the Shawnee under
Chief Tecumseh. Three years later a new fort was built, and in 1818, after the Treaty of
St. Mary's shifted ownership of land south of the town to the U.S. government, Fort
Wayne experienced a surge in settlement. Then came the building of the Wabash and

Erie Canal and the arrival of the railroad. Johnny Appleseed lived the last 10 years of his life near Fort Wayne and was laid to rest in Archer Cemetery in 1845. A huge pioneer-era festival held each September is named after him.

By the mid 1900s, appliance and light-duty truck manufacturers dominated the industrial sector. Like many towns in the Rust Belt, Fort Wayne suffered as the automotive industry withered in the mid-1970s and early 1980s. New life was breathed into the city in the mid-1980s as new civic and cultural centers were opened downtown and service companies became major employers along with new assembly plants and light industrial manufacturers. In addition to the city's business and industry sector it boasts a noteworthy collection of museums, a new hands-on science center, parks, and a world-class children's zoo. It is accordingly one of the most desirable Midwest cities for families, both to settle down in and to visit. Since the late 1980s and early 1990s the downtown has blossomed with a 12-mi Rivergreenway recreational trail system that links many of the town's parks.

Information: Fort Wayne/Allen County Convention and Visitors Bureau | 1021 S. Calhoun St., 46802 | 219/424–3700 or 800/767–7752 | www.visitfortwayne.com.

Attractions

Cathedral of the Immaculate Conception and Museum. The Gothic Cathedral of the Immaculate Conception is the "mother church" of the Roman Catholic Diocese of Fort Wayne-South Bend, established in 1857. Intricately detailed figures in the sanctuary and a series of stations of the cross are considered among the finest examples of wood-carving in the United States. The Bavarian-made stained-glass windows are also noteworthy. Next to the church is MacDougal Chapel, a museum displaying religious artifacts dating as far back as the mid-13th century. The cathedral and museum are downtown. | Calhoun and Lewis Sts. | 219/424–1485 | Free | Museum: Wed.–Fri. 10–2, 2nd and 4th Sun. noon–3; also by appointment.

Chain o' Lakes State Park. One of the state's most picturesque state parks, this 2,718-acre preserve includes eight interconnected small kettle lakes that were formed by ancient glaciers. Canoeists explore the lakes while trails carry hikers along the water's edge. There are family cabins and campgrounds in wooded settings. The nature center is in an old one-room schoolhouse. It's 25 mi northwest of Fort Wayne. | 2355 E. 75 S, Albion | 219/636–2654 | www.state.in.us/dnr | $2 per vehicle (residents); $5 per vehicle (nonresidents) | Daily.

Embassy Centre. This meticulously restored 1928 theater is a lavish setting for the Fort Wayne Philharmonic and other musical and theatrical performances. The theater has a rare Grade Page pipe organ. It's in downtown Fort Wayne. | 121 W. Jefferson Blvd. | 219/424–6287 | www.embassycentre.org | Free to enter building.

Foellinger-Freimann Botanical Conservatory. The downtown gardens under glass feature an arid house with species native to the desert, a tropical house with a waterfall and exotic plants, and the showcase house, which features six seasonal floral displays each year. | 1100 S. Calhoun St. | 219/427–6440 | $3 | Mon.–Sat. 10–5, Sun. noon–4.

Fort Wayne Children's Zoo. Forty acres of landscaped grounds in the northern part of the city re-create Indonesian rain-forest and African habitats, Australian landscapes, and more. A Jeep takes you through the African exhibit and there are four other rides. | 3411 Sherman Blvd. | 219/427–6800 | www.kidszoo.com/ | $5.50 | Late Apr.–mid Oct., daily 9–5.

Fort Wayne Museum of Art. A striking modern building downtown displays works from the museum's permanent collections dating from the 19th century to the present. Traveling exhibitions showcase contemporary art. | 311 E. Main St. | 219/422–6467 | www.fwmoa.org | $3 | Tues.–Sat. 10–5, Sun. 12–5.

Fort Wayne Parks and Recreation Department. The department maintains more than 2,000 acres of public land, including more than 80 parks and playgrounds. | 705 E. State Blvd. | 219/427–6000 | www.fortwayneparks.org | Free | Daily.

One of the most popular park areas is the award-winning **Lakeside Rose Garden,** which displays some 2,000 rose bushes representing about 154 varieties. | 1400 Lake Ave. | 219/483–0057 | Free | June–mid-Oct., daily.

The **Rivergreenway Recreation Trail** was conceived in the 1980s as a riverbank trail that would link various units in the local parks system. By 2000 close to 15 mi had been completed. The trail follows the St. Joseph River on the north side of the city, then the St. Mary's River. | Free | Daily dawn–dusk.

Fox Island. Operated as an Allen County park, Fox Island is a 605-acre nature preserve for mushroom hunting, swimming, cross-country skiing, fishing, hiking, and wildlife viewing. It also features a night observatory and a nature center with programs. | 7324 Yohne Rd. | 219/449–3180 | fax 219/449–3181 | $2 | Tues.–Sun. 9–6.

Allen County Public Library. The downtown library has the second-largest genealogy collection in the nation. Professional counselors are available to assist with searches. | 900 Webster St. | 219/421–1200 (general), 219/421–1225 (genealogy dept.) | fax 219/422–9268 | www.acpl.lib.in.us/ | Free | Mon.–Thurs. 9–9, Fri., Sat. 9–6; Labor Day–Memorial Day, also Sun. 1–6.

The Lincoln Museum. The downtown museum features an extensive collection of items belonging to Abraham Lincoln and his family. On display are memorabilia, photographs, the last portrait painted during the 16th President's lifetime, and the inkwell used to sign the Emancipation Proclamation. Four theaters with 18 interactive displays and 11 galleries are included in the museum. | 200 E. Berry St. | 219/455–3864 | www.thelincolnmuseum.org/ | $2.99 | Tues.–Sat. 10–5, Sun. 1–5.

Old City Hall Historical Museum. Housed in an 1893 downtown landmark built of massive stone blocks, the museum covers the region's history from the Ice Age to the present, with displays of artifacts, photographs, and documents. Also included are exhibits on Fort Wayne's railroad history and the Wabash and Erie Canal. | 302 E. Berry St. | 219/426–2882 | $3 | Feb.–Dec., Tues.–Fri. 9–5, weekends noon–5.

Science Central. Through hands-on displays and activities, the center makes science, math, and technology fun for all ages. Make a tornado or an earthquake, walk like an astronaut weighing almost nothing, or hold a starfish in your hand. The gift store is filled with science-oriented merchandise and games. The center is on the north edge of downtown. | 1950 N. Clinton St. | 219/424–2400 | fax 219/422–2899 | www.sciencecentral.org | $5.50 | Tues.–Sat. 9–5, Sun. 12–5.

ON THE CALENDAR

JUNE: *Germanfest.* Headwaters Park on the riverfront in Fort Wayne presents German bands from the United States and abroad, food, beer, and a family fest with children's activities. | 219/424–3700 or 800/767–7752 | www.wunderbar.org.

JULY: *Three Rivers Festival.* Arts, crafts, and the history and culture of Fort Wayne are showcased at Headwaters Park with a nine-day celebration. | 219/426–5556.

SEPT.: *Johnny Appleseed Festival.* Celebrate the life and times of Johnny Appleseed at a park named after the folk hero with reenactments of pioneer life, portrayals of the seed sower, period entertainers, demonstrations, crafts, and food. | 219/424–3700 or 800/767–7752 | www.johnnyappleseedfest.com.

NOV.–DEC: *Festival of Gingerbread.* Kids and adults make houses and other gingerbread structures to win prizes. There is a cookie sale and you can see gingerbread creations at the Historical Museum. | 219/426–2882.

Dining

Café Johnell. French. Oil paintings, brass, and white linens create an elegant mood for classic French cuisine on the near south side of town. There's also a well stocked wine cellar. The kitchen is known for its Dover sole and chateaubriand. Try the homemade pastries. | 2529 S. Calhoun St. | 219/456–1939 | Closed Sun.–Mon. No lunch | $20–$40 | AE, DC, MC, V.

Cindy's Diner. American. This '50s diner downtown serves two-fisted burgers, fries, and thick malts. Go for the Garbage, a popular dish of eggs, potatoes, onions, ham, and cheese all thrown together. | 830 South Harrison St. | 219/422–1957 | $4–$7 | No credit cards.

Club Soda. Steak. With a selection of 21 martinis, cigars, and steak, this restaurant is a celebration of the Rat Pack days of Dean, Frank, and Sammy. Angus beef steaks come with your choice of sauces–béarnaise, bordelaise, or peppercorn sauce—and topped with garlic, mushroom caps, and onions. Choose from a 14-oz or 18-oz strip steak, filet, rib-eye, porterhouse, sirloin, or prime rib. Or you can have New Zealand lamb chops, pork chops, stuffed chicken breast, salmon, tuna, swordfish, walleye, lobster, and pasta dishes. There's a late night menu on Fridays and Saturdays. There is piano music every evening, and jazz on Fri. and Sat. nights. | 235 E. Superior St. | 219/426–3442 | Closed Sun. No lunch Sat. | $13–$35 | MC, V.

Don Hall's—The Factory Steakhouse. Steak. This casual place on the north side of town, with black and white photos of old downtown on the walls, is known for its slow-roasted prime rib, steaks, seafood, chicken, and salads. Kids' menu. | 5811 Coldwater Rd. | 219/484–8693 | Reservations accepted for 6 or more people | $9–$21.50 | AE, D, DC, MC, V.

Hilgers Farm Restaurant. American. In this orchard and farm market 10 mi west of downtown Fort Wayne, this homey restaurant has a country flair, with paintings on the walls. There's a daily buffet. | 13210 U.S. 30 W, Fort Wayne | 219/625–4181 | $6.95–$10.95 | AE, D, DC, MC, V.

Loaf 'n Ladle. American. In this cozy, popular downtown lunch spot you'll find a long list of sandwiches, including tuna, egg, and chicken salad, as well as homemade soups and fresh-baked breads, muffins, and desserts. | 817 S. Calhoun St. | 219/422–5610 | $3.50–$6.50 | No credit cards.

Paula's Seafood Restaurant and Market. Seafood. Sea bass, yellowfin tuna, lobster, king crab legs, scallops, swordfish, crabcakes, salmon, and coconut shrimp are all available here; the Norwegian poached salmon comes with a raspberry champagne beurre blanc sauce. But there's also plenty of meat, including porterhouse steak, filet mignon, and beef medallions. Or you can opt for jambalaya with chicken. | 1732 W. Main St. | 219/422–4322 | www.paulasseafood.com | Closed Sun. No lunch Mon. and Sat. | $14–$38 | AE, MC, V.

Lodging

At the Herb Lady's Garden. This Civil War–era farmhouse has extensive gardens and the grounds include an herb garden. Furnishings at this bed and breakfast are Victorian antiques, original art, and early 20th-century family heirlooms. Complimentary full or Continental breakfast. No TV. No children under 18. No smoking. | 8214 Maysville Rd. | 219/493–8814 | fax 219/749–8093 | 2 rooms | $45–$75 | MC, V.

Best Western Airport Plaza. This two-story hotel is 4 mi east of downtown and close to the airport. Restaurant, bar, room service. Cable TV. Pool. Sauna. Golf privileges. Exercise equipment. Business services. Airport shuttle. Free parking. | 3939 Ferguson Rd. | 219/747–9171 | fax 219/747–1848 | 147 rooms | $73 | AE, D, DC, MC, V.

Comfort Suites. This three-story motel has interior corridors and an elevator, off I–69, exit 102A. Complimentary Continental breakfast. In-room data ports. Microwaves, refrigerators, some in-room hot tubs. Cable TV. Pool. Hot tub, sauna. Exercise equipment. Laundry facilities and services. Business services. | 5775 Coventry Ln. | 219/436–4300 or 800/866–2497 | fax 219/436–2030 | www.comfortsuites.com | 128 rooms | $81–$120 | AE, D, DC, MC, V.

Courtyard by Marriott. On the north side of town, this modern two-story hotel is set back off the street and is close to Glenbrook Mall and the Fort Wayne Zoo. In-room data ports, some refrigerators. Cable TV. Indoor-outdoor pool. Hot tub. Exercise equipment. Business services. Free parking. | 1619 W. Washington Center Rd. | 219/489–1500 or 800/321–2211 | www.courtyard.com | fax 219/489–3273 | 128 rooms, 14 suites | $59–$109, $119–$229 suites | AE, D, DC, MC, V.

Days Inn–East. A well-maintained, older, property 2 mi east of downtown. Restaurant, pub. Some refrigerators. Cable TV. Outdoor pool. Business services. Some pets allowed. | 3730 E. Washington Blvd. | 219/424–1980 | fax 219/422–6525 | 120 rooms | $40 | AE, D, DC, MC, V.

Don Hall's Guesthouse. This two-story member of a Fort Wayne-owned chain of hotels and restaurants with Old World style is on the north side of town, just off I–69, exit 111B (Lima Rd.). 2 restaurants, bar with entertainment, complimentary Continental breakfast, room service. In-room data ports. Cable TV. 2 pools (1 indoor). Hot tub. Exercise equipment. | 1313 W. Washington Center Rd. | 219/489–2524 or 800/348–1999 | fax 219/489–7067 | www.don-halls.com | 130 rooms | $79 | AE, D, DC, MC, V.

Hampton Inn and Suites–Ft. Wayne North. Built in 1996, this four-story motel is on the north side of town close to the Glenbrook Mall and Memorial Coliseum. Complimentary Continental breakfast. Refrigerators. Cable TV. Pool. Hot tub. Exercise equipment. Laundry facilities, laundry services. Business services. Pets allowed. | 5702 Challenger Pkwy. | 219/489–0908 | fax 219/489–9295 | www.hamptoninn.com | 90 rooms | $69, suites $109–$119 | AE, D, DC, MC, V.

Fort Wayne Hilton at the Convention Center. This downtown nine-story high-rise built in 1985 is connected to the convention center. Two lounges, live entertainment, and concierge services are included. 2 restaurants, bar. In-room data ports. Cable TV. Indoor pool. Hot tub. Exercise equipment. Business services, convention center. Airport shuttle. | 1020 S. Calhoun St. | 219/420–1100 | fax 219/424–7775 | 250 rooms | $99–$139 | AE, D, DC, MC, V.

Fort Wayne Marriott. Shades of brown with Western and rustic accents distinguish the guest rooms of this newer six-story hotel on the north side. The Red River Steaks and BBQ restaurant features Western cooking. Restaurant, bar, picnic area. In-room data ports, some refrigerators, room service. Cable TV. Indoor-outdoor pool. Hot tub. Putting green. Exercise equipment. Free parking. Laundry facilities. Business services. Airport shuttle. Some pets allowed. | 305 E. Washington Center Rd. | 219/484–0411 | www.marriott.com | fax 219/483–2892 | 223 rooms | $109 | AE, D, DC, MC, V.

Holiday Inn Hotel and Suites Downtown. This 14-story hotel is older but well-maintained. It's downtown near the convention center. Restaurant, bar with entertainment. In-room data ports. Cable TV. Indoor pool. Hot tub. Exercise equipment. Video games. Laundry facilities. Business services. Airport shuttle. | 300 E. Washington Blvd. | 219/422–5511 | fax 219/424–1511 | 208 rooms, 28 suites | $79, $134 suites | AE, D, DC, MC, V.

Lees Inn and Suites. This two-story motel, without an elevator, is near I–69, exit 111B (Lima Road), 2 mi from the Glenbrook Mall. You have a variety of room options from standard rooms with queen-size beds to larger suites; the Royal Suites have a hot tub and a king or queen bed. Complimentary breakfast. Cable TV. Pool. Hot tub. Exercise equipment. Laundry facilities. Business services. | 5707 Challenger Pkwy. | 219/489–8888 or 800/733–5337 | fax 219/489–4354 | www.leesinn.com | 73 rooms | $69–$149 | AE, D, DC, MC, V.

Residence Inn by Marriott. This all-suites hotel with fully equipped kitchens and fireplaces is on the north side of town set back one block off I–69, exit 111A (Lima Road). There are 10, two-story buildings on this property. Complimentary Continental breakfast. Kitchenettes, microwaves. Cable TV, Pool. Playground. Some pets allowed (fee). | 4919 Lima Rd. | 219/484–4700 | fax 219/484–9772 | 80 suites | $99–$159 | AE, D, DC, MC, V.

Signature Inn. Standard chain accommodations with various discount packages and basic services are a few of the features at this two-story motel on the north side of town. Complimentary Continental breakfast. In-room data ports. Cable TV. Pool. Business services. | 1734 W. Washington Center Rd. | 219/489–5554 | fax 219/489–5554, ext. 500 | 102 rooms | $58–$73 | AE, D, DC, MC, V.

Sumner Suites. A all-suite five-story hostelry is on the north side of town. There are separate living and sleeping areas. Complimentary Continental breakfast. Microwaves, refrigerators. Laundry facilities. | 111 W. Washington Center Rd. | 219/471–8522 or 800/74–SUITES | fax 219/471–9223 | www.sumnersuites.com | 122 suites | $79–$99 | AE, D, DC, MC, V.

FREMONT

(Nearby town also listed: Angola)

A trail that passed by the present-day town of Fremont in Steuben County's lake country once carried French Jesuit missionaries and later Mormon followers of Brigham Young on their westward pilgrimage. Now Fremont caters to tourists during the summer and winter lake and recreation seasons, with dozens of antiques and crafts shops and cozy cafés. Fremont is less than 3 mi from the Michigan border and 7 mi from Ohio, off I–80/90.

Information: Steuben County Tourism Bureau | 207 S. Wayne St., 46703 | 800/LAKE–101 | lakes101@locl.net | www.lakes101.org.

Attractions
Yogi Bear's Jellystone Park–Barton Lake. At this park you'll find swimming, fishing, picnicking, basketball, volleyball, horseshoes, a waterslide, a snack bar, cabin and cottage rentals, and 460 campsites. | 140 Ln. 201, Barton Lake | 219/833–1114 or 800/375–6063 | www.jellystonesbest.com | Fees vary per activity | Open Apr.–Oct.

ON THE CALENDAR
JULY: *Fremont Music Fest.* Held downtown on the first Saturday after July 4th, this festival serves up a smorgasbord of local bands performing rock, country, polka, gospel, and other music. There's also a hog roast, parade, crafts, and food vendors. The fire department usually holds a pancake and sausage breakfast. | 219/495–9010.

Dining
Mulligan's. American. Next to the golf course, on Route 120, across from the Hampton Inn and Super 8 Motel, this restaurant has many booths that are recessed into the wall. Table settings are casual with vinyl coverings. You can listen to live piano music on Wed., Fri. and Sat. nights. The menu offers cod, shrimp and halibut as well as steaks, specialty salads, chicken, and pasta; there are nightly specials. | 100 E. Route 120 | 219/495–4114 | Closed Sun. | $9–$18 | MC, V.

Lodging
Hampton Inn Fremont. Built in 1998, this three-story motel is a quarter mile from a 60-shop outlet mall. It's 2 mi from downtown, the Pokagon State Park, and Wing Haven Nature Preserve. Complimentary Continental breakfast. In-room data ports. Some microwaves. Some refrigerators. Some in-room hot tubs. Cable TV. Indoor pool. Hot tub. Exercise equipment. Laundry facilities. | 271 W. Route 120 | 219/495–9770 or 800/426–7866 | fax 219/495–9772 | www.hamptoninn.com | 75 rooms | $89–$124 | AE, D, DC, MC, V.

FRENCH LICK

(Nearby towns also listed: Bedford, Jasper)

Long before the earliest pioneers trudged through the densely forested hill country of southern Indiana, a buffalo trace used by great herds of bison passed through the present-day town of French Lick, where salt licks and mineral springs were plentiful.

As early as the 1840s, tourists started making the trek to French Lick as well, to stay at its luxurious hotel carved out of the wilderness and to take of the mineral waters. Over the next 75 years, the French Lick Springs Hotel was upgraded and expanded, and in the early 1900s the resort included a casino. Today the complex is a little more laid back, with a welcoming wide porch running along the front. It still attracts throngs with golf, tennis, and the mineral-springs spa. The elegant West Baden Hotel was built to rival French Lick in 1902. The hotel has been restored.

Information: **French Lick/West Baden Chamber of Commerce** | Box 347, 47432 | 812/936–2405. **Lincoln Hills/Patoka Lake Recreation Region** | Courthouse Annex, 125 S. 8th St., Cannelton, 47520 | 800/289–6646 | www.orangecountyin.com.

Attractions

French Lick Springs Resort. This resort and spa date back more than 150 years to when mineral springs were first tapped on the property and dubbed Pluto Water. A three-story wood-frame hotel was built by 1840. Over the years the resort has changed hands and several hotel buildings have stood on the property. Its heyday was in the Roaring Twenties, when Hollywood celebs frequented the resort and its black-tie casinos. The last of them closed in 1949. Today's multistory buff-colored brick hotel dates from the early 1900s and is in the process of being refurbished. Many of the original fixtures remain, and the 2,600-acre, 475-room resort now offers year-round lodging, golf, tennis, horseback riding, all sorts of other recreational activities, and a spa. | 8670 W. Rte. 56 | 800/457–4042 or 812/936–9300 | fax 812/936–2100 | www.frenchlick.com | Free; fees for lodging, recreation, and spa services | Daily.

Indiana Railway Museum. A two-hour train ride aboard the old cars of the French Lick West Baden and Southern line takes you to the Hoosier National Forest through deep cuts in the limestone bedrock and the 2,200-ft Burton Tunnel. The museum at the train station displays railroad memorabilia, railroad cars, and engines. | 1 Monon St. | 812/936–2405 or 800/748–7246 | Museum free; train ride $8 | Museum daily 10–4. Train rides Apr.–Oct., weekends at 10, 1, and 4, Tues. at 1.

Patoka Lake. The state's second-largest reservoir, 8,800-acre Patoka is surrounded by seven state recreation areas with 25,800 acres of wooded land. Among the facilities are an archery range, boat ramps, and more than 500 campsites. The lake is a popular spot for fishing and boating and has a swimming beach. There is a nature center with cultural and naturalist programs in summer. It's 13 mi south of French Lick. | 3084 N. Dillard Rd., Birdseye | 812/685–2464 | www.state.in.us/dnr | Free | Daily.

Ski Paoli Peaks. One of three downhill ski areas in the state, Paoli Peaks covers 65 acres and a 300-ft vertical drop ribboned by 15 trails. There's snowmaking, plus one quad lift, three triples, and one double. There's night skiing on weekends. It's 15 mi east of French Lick. | Paoli | 812/723–4698 (snow conditions) or 812/723–4696 | fax 812/723–2300 | www.skipeaks.com/home.html | Dec.–mid-Mar., daily.

West Baden Springs Hotel. At the turn of the century, French Lick Springs Resort and nearby West Baden Springs drew high-rolling movie stars and the well-to-do. In its time, West Baden was the epitome of elegance and it thrived as a resort hotel until the stock market crash in 1929. Then it fell into disrepair over the years and is only now undergoing restoration, under the supervision of the Historic Landmarks Foundation of Indiana. You can see the magnificent structure and formal gardens on guided 1-hr tours. It's 2 mi east of French Lick. | Rte. 56, West Baden | 317/639–4534 or 800/450–4534 | fax 317/639–6734 | www.historiclandmarks.org | $10 | Tours on the hour Apr.–Dec., Mon.–Sat. 10–3, Sun. 12–4.

ON THE CALENDAR

MAY: *Orange County Dogwood Festival.* Tour the countryside when the dogwoods are in bloom, then watch a parade and pageant in downtown Orleans. | 812/723–4769.

JUNE: *Lotus-Dickey Hometown Reunion.* In Paoli, folk and acoustic music, art, and food come to the Orange County Courthouse during this three-day event. | 812/723–4318.

SEPT.: *Indian Summer Festival.* In Paoli, arts, crafts, a beauty pageant, a parade, and entertainment to celebrate the last days of summer and the start of fall. | 812/723–4769.

Dining

Beechwood Country Inn. Continental. The main dining room at this inn built in the early 1900s resembles a train club car. There is a fireplace in the main dining room. A seven-course tea or cream tea is served at 2:30 PM in the Tea Room. There's always fresh seafood, like halibut or Alaskan salmon, along with veal, rack of lamb, French cut lamb chops, tenderloin filet, New York strip, and pasta. French onion gratinée and crab bisque are served daily plus several appetizers and salads. | 8313 W. State Rd. 56 | 812/936–9012 | Reservations essential for dinner | Closed Sun. and Mon. | $18–$30 | AE, D, MC, V.

Uncle Gary's Catfish Kitchen. Seafood. In the Heritage Square shopping center in West Baden Springs, this locally owned restaurant has a chef who was trained in New Orleans and who worked for a time with legendary Cajun chef, Paul Prudhomme. This influence comes through on the menu with items like jambalaya, gumbo, and crawfish etouffée. Catfish is indeed on the menu, plus whitefish, shrimp, oysters, clams, and clam chowder. Plus there's always beef, such as country-fried steak with gravy. Swampy items such as fish nets, kayaks, and a ship's wheel and oars hang on the walls—and in the middle of the room, there's a pond with a fountain. | Heritage Sq. Shopping Center, Hwy. 56, West Baden Springs | 812/936–3474 | Closed Mon.–Wed. | $6–$10 | No credit cards.

The Villager. American. You'll find home cooking in three dining areas here. Five or six daily vegetables go with main plate lunches such as fried chicken, baked steak, chicken and dumplings, and barbecued ribs. | Hwy. 56, West Baden Springs | 812/936–4926 | Open 7 days. Breakfast also served | $6–$15 | No credit cards.

Lodging

Beechwood Country Inn. Four striking white columns line the front veranda of this three-story brick home, built in the early 1900s. No two rooms are alike. The Ballard room has a 300-year-old carved bed from an Irish castle, an Italian marble fireplace, a two-person hot tub, a sitting room, and a private balcony. The Club room has rich, dark colors and the walnut bedroom suite dates to the 1800s with elaborately carved cherubs on the headboard. Restaurant. Bar. Complimentary breakfast. Cable TV. No children under 11. No smoking. | 8313 W. State Rd. 56 | 812/936–9012 | info@beechwood-inn.com | www.beechwood-inn.com | 6 rooms | $99–$229 | AE, D, MC, V.

Big Locust Farm Bed and Breakfast. On 60 acres with flower beds, a fish pond, bird-watching, and a large front porch this two-story, brick home was built in 1994 in Victorian style. It is in a quiet location in the Hoosier National Forest. The inn name comes from the 250-year-old Big Locust tree on the grounds which is the largest in the state. It's ⅓ mi to Paoli Peaks. Complimentary breakfast. TV in common area. Hiking. No smoking. | 3295 W. County Road 255, Paoli | 812/723–4856 | 3 rooms | $55–$80 | MC, V.

Braxtan House Inn. This huge three-story Queen Anne Victorian structure is actually two houses (1830 and 1893) joined together with bay windows and a wide front porch. It's furnished with antiques and situated near the courthouse square in Paoli. Complimentary breakfast. No room phones, TV in common room. | 210 N. Gospel St., Paoli | 812/723–4677 or 800/627–2982 | fax 812/723–2112 | braxtan@kiva.net | www.kiva.net/~braxtan | 6 rooms (5 with shower only) | $60–$65 | AE, D, MC, V.

French Lick Springs. This six-story resort hotel in downtown French Lick was built in 1902, and has a yellow brick exterior. The guest rooms have retained their early 1900s furnishings. Suites, with a parlor room, are available. Bar with entertainment, dining rooms, room service. In-room data ports. Cable TV. 2 pools (1 indoor). Beauty salon, hot tub, massage.

Driving range, 18-hole golf courses, tennis. Bowling, gym, horseback riding. Minature golf. Video games. Kids' programs. Business services. | 8670 W. Rte. 56 | 812/936–9300 or 800/457–4042 | fax 812/936–2100 | 471 rooms | $119 | AE, D, DC, MC, V.

White Oaks Cabins. Six newer and well-maintained cabins ranging from small, cozy retreats for two to larger spaces designed for families of 10 are set on 45 acres near Patoka Lake. Cabins are fully furnished with heat and central air-conditioning and feature fully equipped kitchens. Screened porches, a children's fishing pond, and a screened fish-cleaning station are also included. It's 16 mi south of French Lick. Picnic area. Kitchenettes. Pond. Hiking, boating. Fishing. | 2140 N. Morgan Rd., Taswell | 812/338–3120 | fax 812/338–3120 | www.patokalake.com | 6 cabins | $65–$115 | AE, MC, V.

GENEVA

MAP 3, F3

(Nearby towns also listed: Berne, Fort Wayne, Marion)

U.S. 27, which runs through Geneva 8 mi from the Ohio border, marks the continental divide between the Atlantic and Gulf of Mexico watersheds and is also known as the Amish Turnpike. The area has been settled mainly by Swiss and Old-Order Amish, who can be distinguished by their open buckboard wagons. (The LaGrange and Elkhart County Amish in northern Indiana generally favor enclosed black buggies.) While the Adams County Amish court the tourist trade with less vigor than their northern Indiana counterparts, re-created Amish villages, restaurants, bakeries, crafts shops, and inns are beginning to thrive in the area.

Information: Geneva Chamber of Commerce | Box 151, 46740 | 219/368–7288.

Attractions

Amishville. At this Amish farm a house, barn, restored mid-1880s gristmill, and other outbuildings provide an up-close look at the Amish way of life. The Essen Platz restaurant and bakery serve Amish and country-style food. You can tour the farm on your own or in an Amish horse and buggy and take a 40-minute guided tour of the house. Geneva is 4 mi south of Berne. | 844 E. Rte. 900 S | 219/589–3536 | www.amishville.com | Free; fee for buggy rides and tour | Apr.–Dec., Mon.–Sat. 9–5, Sun. 11–5.

Bearcreek Farms. The complex is a country retreat with recreation and entertainment, including a ballroom and theater with musical performances ranging from big-band orchestras to 1950s bebop nights. Also on the grounds are campgrounds, lodging, train rides, a country store, and restaurants. Throughout the summer and fall, special events are planned. It's 4 mi southeast of Geneva. | 8339 N. 400 E. Bryant | 800/288–7630 or 219/997–6822 | www.bearcreekfarms.com | Free; performances $8 | Apr.–Dec., daily; shows Tues.–Sun. 2 and 7:30.

Limberlost State Historic Site. The two-story, 14-room Limberlost cabin of naturalist, photographer, and author Gene Stratton Porter is furnished with some of the her furniture and memorabilia. Porter named the cabin home where she lived from 1895 to 1913 after the nearby wilderness area of marshlands and woodlands from which she drew inspiration for her work. Her books include *A Girl of Limberlost, Freckles,* and *Laddie.* | 200 E. 6th St. | 219/368–7428 | www.genestrattonporter.net | Free | Tues.–Sat. 9–5, Sun. 1–5.

ON THE CALENDAR

OCT: *Nostalgia Fest-Midwest.* There's a little of everything at this festival. It highlights Kroozinationals—one of the largest car and truck events in the Midwest—vendors, a die cast and toy collectibles show, flea market, antique tractors, swap meet, live entertainment, hayrides, pumpkin carving contests, and a moon-pie bash. | 219/622–6820.

Dining
Amishville USA. American. You will get a taste of Amish and Swiss cooking at this family oriented restaurant, which is in an old wooden building with hardwood floors that once was a chicken house. There are two rooms filled with wooden tables, lit by lanterns. You can order from the buffet or off the menu which includes sauerkraut and sausage, beef and noodles, pan steaks, chicken, roast beef, stuffing, rice dressing, mashed potatoes, and soup. There is a salad bar and you can order homemade pie for dessert. No smoking. No alcohol. Before you dine, take a tour or buggy ride at Amishville USA. | 844 E. 900 S | 219/589–3536 | www.amishville.com | Closed at 7 PM Sun.–Thurs., 8 PM Fri. and Sat. | $3–$10 | D, MC, V.

Lodging
Bearcreek Farms Country. There are many activities on this 200-acre farm that has lodging in courtyard units or log cabins, a billiard room, and soda shop. From mid-May through Sept. there is a county fair and carousel ride. See musical performances at the Goodtime Theatre. Shops sell everything from furniture to baked goods, collectible bears, and other country items. The cabins sleep up to four adults and four kids. Restaurant. Some microwaves. Some refrigerators. Cable TV. Pool. Shops. No smoking. | 8339 N. 400 E, Bryant | 219/997–6822 or 800/288–7630 | www.bearcreekfarms.com | 78 rooms | $99–$125 | Closed Christmas–early Mar. | D, MC, V.

GOSHEN

MAP 3, E1

(Nearby towns also listed: Elkhart, Middlebury, Mishawaka, South Bend)

Goshen, a major agricultural and trading center in northern Indiana, was settled by Mennonites from Ohio and Pennsylvania. It is in the heart of Amish country. "Maple City," as Goshen calls itself, covers less than 10 square mi and is filled with tree-lined streets and gracious older homes. The wooded 135-acre campus of Goshen College, founded by the Mennonites, stands in a downtown residential neighborhood.

Information: Goshen Chamber of Commerce | 232 S. Main St., 46526 | 219/533–2102 or 800/307–4204 | www.goshen.org.

Attractions
Bonneyville Mill. Since the 1830s, the dark-red Bonneyville Mill has been grinding grain, making it the state's oldest continuously operating gristmill. A shady park surrounds the mill and pond. Watch the mill in operation, then purchase a sack of fresh-ground cornmeal or rye, buckwheat, or wheat flour. 10 mi north of Goshen. | Rte. 131, Bristol | 219/533–2102 or 800/307–4204 | Free | May–Oct., daily 10–5.

Goshen College. The Mennonite Church owns and operates this 4-year liberal arts college that has received national attention for the value of the education for the tuition price. Most (70 percent) students spent 14 weeks in a developing nation, learning and volunteering. About 1,000 students are enrolled in 30 majors including education, nursing, social work, art, music, and business. | 1700 S. Main St. | 219/535–7000 | www.goshen.edu | Free | Daily.

Mennonite Historical Library. The Harold and Wilma Good Library houses the independent Mennonite library on the third floor, with an extensive collection of genealogical, theological, and historical material on the Mennonite Church (which is related to the Amish faith). The Good Library's art gallery occupies the lower level of the building. | 1700 S. Main St. | 219/535–7000 or 219/535–7418 | www.goshen.edu | Free | Weekdays 8–5.

The Old Bag Factory. Nineteen shops and workshops of artists and craftspeople fill the 1896 redbrick building, on the northwest end of town, that was once a paper bag factory.

Watch a potter and furniture maker at work, then browse the shops. | 1100 Chicago Ave. | 219/534–2502 | www.oldbagfactory.com | Free | Mon.–Sat. 9–5.

Ox Bow Park. On the Elkhart River, the 223-acre park features an observation tower, nature and running trails, an open-air chapel, and picnic shelters. It's 1 mi outside of Goshen. | U.S. 33, Dunlap | 219/535–6458 | $2.50 per vehicle, Apr.–Oct.; free, Nov. 1–Mar. 31 | Daily.

ON THE CALENDAR
JULY: *Elkhart County 4-H Fair.* One of the nation's largest county fairs offers family fun and gets Goshen hopping with its 4-H exhibits, demonstrations, top-name grandstand entertainment, a giant midway, and food. | 219/262–8161 or 800/262-8161.

Dining
Checkerberry. Continental. Surrounded by rural Amish countryside, this inn presents a careful blending of country and luxury. The dining room is intimate and candlelit, with just a few tables, and the kitchen has attracted the attention of no less than *Gourmet* for its seasonal menu of locally raised food. The setting is semiformal with American antiques and bright paintings. | 62644 Rte. 37 | 219/642–4445 | www.checkerberryinn.com | Reservations required | Closed Sun., Mon., and Jan. | $29–$39 for 3–course meal | AE, MC, V.

Crackers. American. At the Goshen Inn, and serving breakfast, lunch, and dinner, Crackers has prime rib specials on Friday and Saturday nights. The regular menu includes New York strip steak, ham, chicken-fried steak, shrimp tempura, pasta, chicken Alfredo, and burgers. Live music Wed.–Sat. nights. Kids' menu. | 1375 Lincolnway E | 219/533–9551 or 888/246–7435 | fax 219/533–2840 | www.gosheninn.com | No dinner Sun. | $9–$14 | AE, D, DC, MC, V.

Das Dutchman Essenhaus. American. Bright quilt-print tablecloths add color to this Amish country kitchen. The owners dish up all-you-can eat plate dinners of chicken, roast beef, baked steak, and ham with mashed potatoes, hot vegetables, salad, beverage, and dessert. They also serve soup, sandwiches, pork chops, chopped sirloin, orange roughy, scrod, shrimp tempura, and roast turkey. | 240 US 20, Middlebury | 219/825–9471 or 800/455–9471 | www.essenhaus.com | Closed Sun. Breakfast also served | $4–$15 | D, MC, V.

Town Haus Family Restaurant. American. You'll dine casually here, with fare from the buffet or menu. Salisbury steak, ribs, chicken, macaroni and cheese, mashed potatoes, and a salad bar make up the buffet. The menu lists burgers, sandwiches, baked fish, shrimp, and more. There's a buffet at breakfast. | 1105 W. Pike St. | 219/534–1004 | No reservations accepted | Open Sun.–Thurs. 5:30 AM to 11 PM, open 24 hrs on Fri. and Sat. Breakfast also served | $5–$8 | MC, V.

Lodging
Best Western Inn. A mile southeast of downtown, this older motel on two floors has renovated guest rooms with light oak contemporary furniture. Complimentary Continental breakfast. In-room data ports. Cable TV. Exercise equipment. Business services. Free parking. | 900 Lincolnway E (U.S. 33) | 219/533–0408 | fax 219/533–0408 | www.bestwestern.com/goshenin | 77 rooms | $59 | AE, D, DC, MC, V.

Checkerberry. American and country French antiques and bright furnishings create an aura of comfort at this three-story farmhouse-style inn set on 100 acres in the heart of Amish country. The restaurant features candlelight dinners, fine wines, and inventive cuisine. | 12 rooms, 2 suites. Restaurant, complimentary Continental breakfast. Pool. Putting green, tennis. Business services. No smoking. | 62644 Rte. 37 | 219/642–4445 | www.checkerberryinn.com | AE, MC, V.

Courtyard by Marriott. Warm oak furniture, a fieldstone fireplace in the lounge, and shades of green and mauve create a homey atmosphere at this new hotel. Restaurant, buffet breakfast (fee). In-room data ports. Cable TV. Indoor-outdoor pool. Gym, exercise equipment. | 1930 Lincolnway E | 219/534–3133 or 800/321–2211 | fax 219/534–6929 | www.courtyard.com | 91 rooms | $79–$89 | AE, D, DC, MC, V.

Essenhaus Country Inn. Open since 1986, the Essenhaus resembles a sprawling white Amish farmhouse. Each room is individually decorated with handcrafted Amish and country-style furnishings. Seven additional guest rooms are nearby at Dawdy Haus. | 40 rooms. Dining room. Some in-room hot tubs. Cable TV. Business services. No smoking. | 240 U.S. 20, Middlebury | 219/825–9471 | www.essenhaus.com | AE, D, MC, V.

Goshen Inn and Conference Center. In this two-story hotel in the south end of Goshen, all of the interior areas including guest rooms have been newly renovated. Contemporary oak furnishings are accented with shades of blue and mauve. Restaurant, bar, room service. Cable TV. Indoor pool. Sauna. Gym, exercise equipment. Video games. Laundry facilities. Business services. | 1375 Lincolnway E | 219/533–9551 or 888/2GOSHEN | fax 219/533–2840 | thegosheninn@aol.com | www.gosheninn.com | 207 rooms | $76–$81 | AE, D, DC, MC, V.

Holiday Inn Express. Between Shipshewana and Amish Acres this three-story hotel, built in 1997, is in the heart of Amish country. Rooms have full size, queen, or king beds. Complimentary Continental breakfast. Cable TV. Indoor pool. Hot tub. Exercise equipment. | 2309 Lincoln Way E | 219/533–0200 | fax 219/533–1528 | www.basshotels.com | 74 rooms | $67–$94 | AE, D, DC, MC, V.

Prairie Manor Bed and Breakfast. A two-story inn set on 12 acres of lawn and surrounded by shade trees, flower gardens, and woods, Prairie Manor was built in the 1920s by a New York Wall Street banker with arched doorways, wainscoting, and a wood-paneled library with window seats. The living room was designed after the owner's favorite painting in New York City's Metropolitan Museum of Art, an English baronial hall with a huge fireplace. 1 mi south of Goshen. Complimentary breakfast. Library. | 66398 U.S. 33 S | 219/642–4761 or 800/791–3952 | fax 219/642–4762 | jeston@npcc.net | www.prairiemanor.com | 4 rooms | $69–$95 | D, MC, V.

Spring View Bed and Breakfast. When you stay in this 1995 home on 48 acres, the Amish neighbors will take you on a buggy ride, and breakfast is in the sunroom, which looks out over the spring-fed pond. All rooms have king-sized beds. Complimentary breakfast. In-room data ports. In-room hot tubs. Cable TV. Boating. Fishing. Bicycles. No smoking. No alcohol. | 63189 County Rd. 31 | 219/642–3997 | fax 219/642–2697 | www.springview.com | 5 rooms | $59–$79 | AE, D, MC, V.

Stagecoach Inn Bed and Breakfast. It is believed that the stagecoach stopped here while travelling along the Lincoln Trail between Ft. Wayne and South Bend. This 1863 home has Victorian furnishings inside, with a king-sized canopy bed in the Wells Fargo room, and a queen canopied bed in the Prairie room along with antiques and quilts. In the back of the house, you'll find a patio, swing, gazebo, garden, and fountain. The B&B is on the southeast side of Goshen. Complimentary breakfast. Cable TV. No smoking. | 66063 US Hwy. 33 | 219/642–5005 or 877/219–5005 | fax 219/642–4376 | www.the-stagecoach-inn.com | 4 rooms (1 with private bath) | $60–$75 | D, MC, V.

Varns Guest House. This modest two-story home dating from 1898 is one block from the center of a small town 12 mi northeast of Goshen. The inn is handsomely furnished with traditional furniture, patterned wallpaper and fabrics, some antiques, and family mementos. Complimentary breakfast. No smoking, no TV in rooms, TV in common area. | 205 S. Main St., Middlebury | 219/825–9666 or 800/398–5424 | 5 rooms | $85–$95 | MC, V.

GREENCASTLE

MAP 3, C5

(Nearby towns also listed: Indianapolis, Rockville, Terre Haute)

Founded in 1821, Greencastle sits in an agricultural belt just off I–70 to the west of Indianapolis. It clings to its small-town character and is best known as the home of

DePauw University, two blocks from the courthouse square. A leading liberal arts college, DePauw was founded in 1837 when Greencastle claimed only around 2,000 residents.

Information: Putnam County Convention and Visitors Bureau | 12 W. Washington St., 46135 | 800/829–4639 | cbc@ccrtc.com | www.coveredbridgecountry.com.

Attractions

Buzz Bomb Memorial. J. Frank Durham of Greencastle was on his annual 2-week reserve training for explosive ordnance demolition when he noted casually that it seemed a shame to bury the obsolete captured enemy ordnance when so few Americans had ever seen such a thing. One year and much red tape later, a German V-1 bomb was delivered to Greencastle. The bomb, just over 25 ft long with a 16-ft wingspan, is the only one of its kind on public display. It is mounted on a "V"-shaped limestone pedestal on the Courthouse lawn. | One Courthouse Sq.

DePauw University. Founded over 150 years ago, this prestigious liberal arts college ranks 12th in the nation among private liberal arts colleges and universities as the baccalaureate source for Ph.D. degrees in all fields, according to a recent study. *Fortune* magazine has ranked DePauw 11th among all colleges and universities in the nation in terms of the likelihood that its graduates will become CEOs of top American companies. DePauw's red-brick buildings with white trim are Colonial in style and date from the mid- to late 1800s. The campus is on the edge of Greencastle's downtown. | 313 S. Locust St. | 765/658–4800 | www.depauw.edu | Free | Daily.

Lieber State Recreation Area. A 200-ft waterfall is one of the main sights at this 8,200-acre property on the edge of 1,400-acre Cataract Lake. Also known as Cagles Mill Reservoir, it is popular for boating, swimming, and waterskiing. It's 20 mi south of Greencastle. | 1317 W. Lieber Rd., Cloverdale | 765/795–4576 | www.state.in.us/dnr/ | $2 for residents, $5 for non-residents | Daily.

Dining

Almost Home Tea Room. Café. Most people in Greencastle will tell you that this small lunch spot serves the best cream of broccoli soup anywhere. The turkey asparagus melt is another hit. After you've finished looking at the knickknacks everywhere and playing with the lace tablecloths, you may want to save room for the strawberry pizza with cream-cheese-and-cookie crust. | 17 W. Franklin St. | 765/653–5788 | Closed Sun. No dinner Mon.–Wed. | $9–$15 | AE, D, MC, V.

Different Drummer. American. Set in the Walden Inn, a quaint country inn with handcrafted furnishings, Different Drummer serves a menu of expertly prepared regional fare. Known for its long list of sweet breads, such as chocolate, pumpkin, and orange, and rich desserts. Try the beef tournedos and fresh Atlantic salmon. It's near downtown and the college campus. | 2 Seminary Sq. | 765/653–2761 | Breakfast also available | $13–$30 | AE, D, DC, MC, V.

Lodging

Seminary Place Bed and Breakfast. This 1891 Victorian still has its original crystal chandeliers, period antiques, and parlor furnishings. The hardwood floors are covered with Oriental rugs, and the music room houses a grand piano. The garden room is done in white wicker. Complimentary breakfast. Some in-room hot tubs. | 210 E. Seminary St. | 765/653–3177 | jtesmer@indy.tdsnet.com | 4 rooms | $85–$125 | AE, D, MC, V.

Walden Inn. At this country-style inn on three floors, each guest room is individually furnished with handcrafted traditional-style wood furniture. A palette of rich burgundy and deep blues and greens adds warmth to spaces. The inn is one block from the courthouse square, next to the campus of DePauw University. The Different Drummer café is here. Restaurant, room service. Business services. | 2 Seminary Sq. | 765/653–2761 | fax 765/653–4833 | walden@ccrtc.com | www.waldeninn.com | 55 rooms | $80–$130 | AE, D, DC, MC, V.

GREENFIELD

(Nearby towns also listed: Anderson, Connersville, Indianapolis, New Castle)

Greenfield, founded on April 11, 1828, was the birthplace of 19th-century American poet James Whitcomb Riley, author of "When the Frost is on the Punkin" and many another folksy favorite. Born in 1849, Riley based many of his characters on Greenfield figures. Today, a festival, park, memorial, and museum in his hometown all bear Riley's name

THE SECRET LIFE OF SASSAFRAS

As you travel around southern Indiana, you'll see sassafras everywhere. Even if you don't spot the trees immediately, you'll spot references to sassafras at every turn. It shows up on menus as sassafras tea. Gift shops, of which there is no shortage in this neck of the woods, sell packages of sassafras teas, along with sassafras candies. In state park visitors information centers, tree identification boards invariably highlight the distinctive leaves. So what's the big deal?

Sassafras grows in a wide range of areas stretching from Ontario in the north, through the Midwest, and southward as far as Florida and Texas. At both the northern and southern edges of its range, it's little more than a shrub, but in prime growing areas, such as the Great Smoky Mountains, the tree can reach a lofty 100 feet. In Indiana, along the shore of Lake Michigan, it even finds a firm footing amid shifting sand dunes.

Because of its smooth, bright-green twigs, the Indians called it the "green-stick" tree. You'll know it also by its variety of leaves in three shapes, its short branches that spread at right angles, its flat crown, and, most distinctively, its unusual, spicy aroma. It produces greenish-yellow flowers in March and April and small, blueberry-like fruits in August and September. Fossil records of sassafras go back a hundred million years, so that enticing odor may well have attracted dinosaurs to their lunch. Today, it's a favorite of deer and a somewhat smaller creature, the Japanese beetle.

Sassafras tea is the tree's most common traditional use. It's made by boiling the bark of the roots, which are collected in spring or fall. This is easy to do because the roots grow laterally and are rarely more than twenty inches deep. Oil of sassafras, known as safrole, was long used in medicines and as a flavor for root beer, but the bark of both roots and trunk, as well as the twigs and leaves of the tree, have been identified by the Food and Drug Administration as carcinogenic and are now banned from use.

Even if you don't try the tea, you might still get some good from sassafras. Herbalists with an interest in magic tell us that sassafras is associated with the element Fire and the planet Jupiter. Some people have claimed healing powers for it and recommend it for sachets and charms. Better yet, it's said that burning a sassafras twig will bring you money. If you're short of cash, just putting a little sassafras in your wallet is supposed to help.

© Artville

and celebrate his work. Greenfield, with a current population of 15,000, is the county seat of Hancock County, which is the smallest in the central Indiana economic hub and almost a suburb of sprawling Indianapolis. In the last decade, the Victorian storefronts around the courthouse square have been restored, and shoppers from all over Indianapolis flock to the dozens of antiques and specialty shops that now fill its downtown.

Information: **Greenfield Chamber of Commerce** | 1 Courthouse Plaza, 46140 | 317/477–4188 | byates@greenfieldcc.org | www.greenfieldcc.org.

Attractions

Hancock County Courthouse. This grand Indiana limestone building, constructed in 1896, is part French Gothic, part Romanesque Revival in style. Stunning blue stained glass windows accent the dome in the Circuit Court Room on the third floor. Murals by the Works Progress Administration (WPA) cover the walls, along with plaster fleurs-de-lis. | U.S. 40 at Rte. 9 | 317/477–4188 | Free | Weekdays 8:30–4.

James Whitcomb Riley Birthplace and Museum. The poet's gingerbread-trimmed redbrick home has period furniture dating from Riley's boyhood years. An adjacent home displays photographs and memorabilia. | 250 W. Main St. | 317/462–8539 | $2 | Apr.–Oct., Tues.–Sat. 10–4, Sun. 1–4.

Old Log Jail and Chapel-in-the-Park Museums. A chapel and log jail, built in 1853, are in Riley Park on the east side of town. | 210 N. Apple St. | 317/462–7780 | 75¢ | Apr.–Oct., weekends 1–5.

ON THE CALENDAR

JUNE: *Strawberry Festival.* Members of the First Presbyterian Church host this strawberry shortcake soirée. The event is held in Plaza Square when the weather is pleasant, in the church if it's rainy. | 317/462–5349.

OCT.: *Antique and Classic Auto Show.* Some 200 cars converge on the town in all their chrome splendor. Entertaining competitions such as an Oreo Stacking Contest round things out. | 317/477–4188.

OCT.: *Riley Festival.* This celebration of the poet's life and work kicks off with tours of the poet's birthplace and home, a fine arts show, a photography contest, and antiques and crafts booths around the historic courthouse square. | 317/462–2141.

Dining

Carnegie's. Italian. White linen cloths grace the tables at this northern Italian trattoria tucked in the basement of the local Carnegie Public Library. The house favorites are lobster ravioli with brandy-cream sauce and Carnegie salmon in lemon-wine-butter sauce with green beans and potato croquettes. If those don't tickle your palate, you can try one of the two nightly pasta selections. | 100 W. North St. | 317/462–8480 | Closed Sun.–Mon., no lunch Sat. | $9–$20 | AE, MC, V.

Lodging

Lees Inn. This two-story redbrick motel is off I–70, exit 104. Complimentary Continental breakfast. Cable TV. Free parking. Some pets allowed. | 2270 N. State St. | 317/462–7112 | fax 317/462–9801 | greenfield@leesinn.com | www.leesinn.com/greenfield.htm | 100 rooms | $59 | AE, D, DC, MC, V.

HAMMOND

MAP 3, B1

(Nearby towns also listed: Merrillville, Michigan City, Valparaiso)

Hammond is one of a cluster of towns that make up the Calumet region, an area shaped by industrialization and by the waves of immigrants who settled there in the early

1900s. Originally settled before the Civil War and platted in 1871, Hammond boomed when the steel industry took hold of the region in the early 1900s. Hammond is the second-largest city in the lakeshore area of northwest Indiana and just a few blocks from the city limits of Chicago. Though Hammond is an industrial town, its residential character shines in the parks tucked among quiet bungalow neighborhoods and along Church Row, a stretch of Hohman Avenue.

Information: **Lake County Convention and Visitors Bureau** | 7770 Corinne Dr., 46323 | 800/ALL–LAKE or 219/989–7770 | lccvb@alllake.org | www.alllake.org.

Attractions

Gibson Woods Nature Preserve–Lake County Park. This 130-acre tract contains the last sizable remnant of sand-dune and swale topography in northwest Indiana. Self-guiding trail tours highlight dune geography and plant and animal habitats, and a nature center displays live animals and reptiles. | 6201 Parrish Ave. | 219/844–3188 | Free | Daily 9–5, Nature Center 11–4.

Little Red Schoolhouse. Inkwells, a school bell, a 36-star flag, and a potbelly stove like those on display in this red-painted schoolhouse were an integral part of the school day in 1869. A small museum is on the lower level. | 7205 Kennedy Ave. | 219/844–5666 | Free | Tours by appointment only.

ON THE CALENDAR

JUNE: *Little Red Schoolhouse Festival.* Arts and crafts booths, food, kiddie rides, entertainment and games are a big part of this summer celebration in Hessville Park. | 219/844–8349.

Dining

Miller Bakery Café. Contemporary. Chicagoans often make their way to the Miller Beach area of Gary, 12 mi from Hammond, to this cozy eatery in an old brick bakery building. Cornbread custard, savory bread pudding with cilantro pesto, wood-grilled New Zealand rack of lamb with whole-grain mustard sauce, and sautéed veal medallions with caramelized

ODD COUPLES OF THE DUNES PLANT KINGDOM

At the Indiana dunes, diverse ecosystems collide, creating surprising juxtapositions. Arctic bearberry thrives next to prickly pear cactus, and southern dogwood takes root just yards from northern jack pine. Astounding quirks of nature and odd plant pairings such as these intrigued botanist Henry C. Cowles of the University of Chicago in the late 1800s. Cowles studied the dune environment intensively and discovered that plant life varied from dune to dune. He pioneered many of the concepts which are basic to understanding the interrelationships between environments and plant life today. The main principle he discovered was that once a plant establishes itself, the surrounding environment is changed as well. In the midst of industrialized Gary is a stand of the forest primeval, Miller Woods. A postage-stamp-sized patch of prairie, the Hoosier Prairie, is the largest remnant in Indiana. Cowles Bog and Pinhook Bog (scheduled tours only) support carnivorous flora and thick floating mats of vegetation. At Pinhook, a boardwalk crosses a portion of the 400-acre quaking bog's surface.

mushrooms stand out on the inventive menu. | 555 S. Lake St., Gary | 219/938–2229 | Closed Mon. No lunch | $16–$24 | AE, DC, D, MC, V.

Phil Smidt's. Seafood. Lake perch, frog legs, and mouthwatering gooseberry pie have been specialties at this established restaurant since 1910. The rambling low-slung building is downtown on the lakefront. Kids' menu. | 1205 N. Calumet Ave. | 219/659–0025 | www.philsmidts.com | Closed Mon. | $15–$40 | AE, D, DC, MC, V.

Lodging

Fairfield Inn Hammond. This four-story chain hotel just off I–80 and Kennedy Avenue is two blocks from the visitors bureau. Restaurant, complimentary Continental breakfast. In-room data ports, some microwaves, some refrigerators. Cable TV. Indoor pool. Hot tub. Exercise equipment. Laundry facilities, laundry service. Business services. | 7720 Corrine Dr. | 219/845–6950 | fax 219/845–7655 | www.fairfieldinn.com | 94 rooms, 32 suites | $79, $89 suite | AE, D, DC, MC, V.

Holiday Inn Chicago Southeast–Hammond. This four-story motel is off I–80/94, exit 912 (Cline Avenue). It is 20 mi from downtown Chicago. Restaurant, bar, room service. In-room data ports. Cable TV. Pool. Exercise equipment. Laundry facilities. Business services, free parking. Some pets allowed. | 3830 179th St. | 219/844–2140 | fax 219/845–7760 | www.holiday-inn.com | 154 rooms | $90–$96 | AE, D, DC, MC, V.

Ramada Inn. Greek Revival and modern styles mix in the lobby of this motel. Management runs shuttles to the four casino boats near the hotel and to the Southshore Train Station, which will take you into Chicago. Complimentary Continental breakfast. In-room data ports, some microwaves, some refrigerators. Cable TV. Pool. Hot tub. Laundry facilities. Business services. | 4125–41 Calumet Ave. | 219/933–0500 or 800/562–5987 | fax 219/933–0506 | www.ramada.com | 89 rooms, 9 suites | $75, $150 suites | AE, D, DC, MC, V.

HUNTINGTON

MAP 3, E3

(Nearby towns also listed: Auburn, Fort Wayne, Marion, Wabash, Warsaw)

Settlement was slow in coming to Huntington, a Wabash River valley stronghold of the Miami Indians and a portage area known as the Forks of the Wabash. Like Fort Wayne to the north, Huntington saw the first European settlers in 1831. Three years later it became the county seat and pinned its hopes on the Wabash and Erie Canal, which was never fully completed. In the late 1800s, Huntington was referred to as the Limestone City because of the limestone quarries and kilns dotting the surrounding area. A century later, Huntington native J. Danforth Quayle, the former vice president, helped put the town and Indiana on the map. Indiana has provided five United States vice presidents. Today, the town is supported by a handful of small and medium-sized manufacturers of durable goods.

Information: **Huntington County Visitor and Convention Bureau** | 407 N. Jefferson St., 46750 | 800/848–4282 or 800/359–8687 | rmeldrum@visithuntington.org | www.visithuntington.org.

Attractions

The Dan Quayle Center and Museum. Memorabilia, childhood photographs, historical materials, and papers relating to Quayle's tenure as U.S. senator and vice president are on display. | 815 Warren St. | 219/356–6356 | fax 219/356–1455 | www.quaylemuseum.org | Donation | Tues.–Sat. 10–4, Sun. 1–4.

Forks of the Wabash Historic Park. The Forks was the southwest terminus of the Long Portage, one of the three major routes connecting the Great Lakes and the Mississippi watersheds. The portage was used by the Native Americans, as well as French, British, and American traders, soldiers, and settlers. It was also the site of the Miami Tribal Council House until increased settlement made conflict inevitable between the French trappers, the English settlers, and the Miami tribe, and these Native Americans were removed to Kansas in 1846. This 120-acre nature preserve tells the story. On the grounds are the Miami chief's 1830s wood-frame house, furnished to the period, along with log buildings, a visitors center, and a museum. Remnants of the Wabash and Erie Canal are also here. | Intersection of U.S. 24 and I–9 | 219/356–1903 or 800/848–4282 | www.visithuntington.org/group/forks.htm | Free | June–Sept., weekends 1–5.

Huntington County Historical Museum. Artifacts from the county's past and exhibits on the Wabash and Erie Canal, the Erie Railroad, and the Miami Indians are on display at this museum in the Huntington County Courthouse. | 315 Court St. | 219/359–8687 or 800/848–4282 | www.visithuntington.org | Free | Tues.–Sat. 1–4.

Huntington Lake State Reservoir. Wooded bluffs and 7,600 acres of land surround the 900-acre Huntington Lake, which is on Route 5, south of the I–69 exit. Two state recreation areas border the lake. There are separate trails for mountain biking, hiking and fitness, and dogsledding. Swimming, boating, and fishing are also popular. | 517 N. Warren Rd. | 219/468–2165 or 219/468–2166 | www.state.in.us/dnr/parklake/reservoirs/huntington.html | Free | May–Labor Day, daily; Labor Day–Apr., weekdays, open 10 AM–11 PM.

Wings of Freedom Museum. Military artifacts, artwork, and documents, along with restored aircraft and vehicles, are on display in this museum at the Huntington Municipal Airport, next to the Huntington Reservoir Dam on Route 5 at U.S. 224. | 1365 Warren Rd. | 219/356–1945 | wwww.hometown.aol.com/scatvii/page/index.htm | $2 | May–Oct, Sat. 10–4, Sun. 1–4.

ON THE CALENDAR
JUNE: *Huntington County Heritage Days.* A strawberry feed, arts and crafts booths, food, a parade, museum tours, and kid's activities are part of this community-wide celebration of Huntington history. | 219/356–5300.
SEPT.: *Forks of the Wabash Pioneer Festival.* Locals costumed as French voyageurs serve up buffalo stew, sing and fiddle, and demonstrate traditional crafts in the spirit of an 1800s pioneer village. Modern-day arts and crafts are also sold from more than 100 booths. | 219/356–3916 | www.visithuntington.org/pioneer.html | $2.
OCT.: *Haunted Hotel.* You will know you have arrived when you see the humongous black spider resting on the front walk of this gruesome, ghoulish haunted house. If you make it through all 22 rooms the first time, you can do it again for half the price. | $9.95 | 219/356–1701.

Dining
George's Dog House. American. In this good ol' 1950s-style diner, George used to serve only burgers and dogs, but he expanded his menu to include burger steak, ham steak, New York strip steak, grilled chicken, and shrimp baskets, all served with cole slaw or baked beans and your choice of potato. You can still get an ice-cream soda, shake, or malt to go with a burger and fries, and the Dog House breakfast is great: two eggs, a meat, toast, and potatoes at a price that's right. | 337 N. Jefferson St. | 219/358–1711 | Closed Sun. | $5–$9 | MC, V.

Lodging
Purviance House Bed & Breakfast. The founder and president of a local bank built this house on the edge of downtown in 1859, and its furnishings reflect the pre-Victorian sensibility. The parlors are suitable for relaxing after breakfast or kicking back after a busy day of sightseeing. The house is on the National Register of Historic Places. Complimentary breakfast. Cable TV, no room phones. | 326 Jefferson St. | 219/356–9215 | fax 219/356–4218 | 5 rooms | $50–$75 | D, MC, V.

INDIANA DUNES NATIONAL LAKESHORE

MAP 3, C1

(Nearby towns also listed: Hammond, Michigan City, Valparaiso)

★ Fifteen miles of Lake Michigan shoreline draw beach and nature lovers to the 15,000-acre Indiana Dunes National Lakeshore, which the National Park Service has worked to preserve since the 1960s. Today, from some viewpoints, soaring smoke stacks of steel

SINGING SANDS ALONG THE GRAND STRAND

Fortunately for Indiana and neighboring Michigan, Mother Nature has heaped the largest collection of freshwater sand dunes in the world along the sparkling southern and eastern shores of Lake Michigan. Landlocked for the most part, Indiana takes pride in its scant grand strand, the Indiana Dunes National Lakeshore, a 15-mi stretch of dune-studded beach and the centerpiece of the Lake Michigan shoreline.

The story of the Indiana dunes begins 15,000 years ago, when vast ice sheets covering much of the Great Lakes area begin to melt. 10,000 years of wind and water pummel the glacier's rock debris into sand. The dunes begin to take shape as Lake Chicago, the precursor to Lake Michigan, contracts and lake currents carry quartz particles to the south and east. Waves push the sand ashore, forming sandbars and eventually dunes follow through force of wind. The dunes that rim Lake Michigan are from 3,000 to 4,000 years old, with the youngest at the water's edge. The oldest dunes, about 3 mi inland, are now camouflaged by a thick mantle of trees, grasses, and other plants.

More than 250 years ago, Native Americans established the Great Sauk Trail, which ran between what are now Detroit and Chicago, passing through the dunes. In Gary's Miller Beach area, Octave Chanute conducted experimental glider flights in 1896, launching his craft from atop the dunes. In 1908 the South Shore Railroad laid tracks through the dunes area, advertising the dunes as the Midwest "Vacationland" with colorful travel posters. By the 1920s, a 200-ft dune called the Hoosier Slide had been flattened as 13½ million tons of sand were hauled off for glassmaking and railroad-bed fill. Today Mount Baldy, near Michigan City, is the tallest dune in the national lakeshore at 135 ft. In the early 1900s, industry set up shop along the shoreline and the Gary Works of the U.S. Steel Corporation put the hard-working town on the map as "Steel City." The national lakeshore is now in fact a patchwork, with industry and nature preserves standing side by side. Towering smokestacks rise next to long, swelling stretches of sandy beach and dunes. After the 1933 Chicago World's Fair closed, five modern houses from the Home and Industrial Arts exhibit were barged across the lake to Beverly Shores, Indiana. If you drive along Lake Front Drive you can see the House of Tomorrow, with its floor-to-ceiling windows, the flamingo-pink Florida Tropical House, the synthetic cast-stone Rostone House, the Armco Ferro House of prefabricated steel, and the Cypress House. The Cesyerton's All-Steel Home, one of 3,000 homes in the United States made from enameled steel in the 1930s and 1940s, still stands here today.

Towns listed: Hammond, La Porte, Merrillville, Michigan City, Valparaiso.

plants mar scenes of the lake. However, despite the industrialization, the area appears much the same as it did 200 years ago, when a traveler en route from Fort Wayne, Indiana, to Fort Dearborn, now Chicago, observed "a mountain of sand, about 100 feet high" along the lakeshore and marveled at the stunted pine and juniper trees and the constant movement of the dunes. The waters of Lake Michigan are still deep blue; the difference is that on clear days, from the Lakeshore's West Beach, Chicago's building-block skyline notches the horizon.

The tallest dune, 123-ft Mt. Baldy, is at the eastern end of the preserve, near Michigan City. Plant life remains diverse, as in the 1930s, when University of Chicago botanist Henry Cowles called the area a virtual laboratory of plant kingdom diversity: Arctic bearberry, usually found in cold, harsh conditions, grows next to clumps of prickly pear cactus, which normally grows only in hot desert climates. Among national parks, Indiana Dunes ranks seventh for its variety of plants. Pinhook Bog, 12 mi south of Michigan City off Route 421, is another striking area; its floor, a 3- to 6-ft-thick mat of quaking sphagnum moss, supports a lush population of orchids, tamarack trees, pitcher plants, and other unusual species.

Information: Indiana Dunes National Lakeshore | Dorothy Buell Memorial Visitor Center, U.S. 12 Kemil Rd., Beverly Shores, 46301 | www.nps.gov/indu. | 219/926–7561, ext. 225. **Porter County Visitor Center** | 800 Indian Boundary Rd., Chesterton, 46304 | 219/926–2255 or 800/283–8687 | info@casualcoast.com | www.casualcoast.com.

INDIANA DUNES
NATIONAL
LAKESHORE

INTRO
ATTRACTIONS
DINING
LODGING

Attractions

Calumet Bike Trail. This 9-mi strip of gravel path carries hikers, bikers, and in-line skaters from the Dune Acres South Shore Line station east to the Porter-La Porte County line. The trail begins at the Visitor Center. | Dorothy Buell Memorial Visitor Center, Kemil Rd. (U.S. 12), Beverly Shores | 219/926–7561, ext. 225 | Free | Daily.

Chellberg Farm. Swedish immigrants Anders and Joanna Kjellberg created this 80-acre working farm in 1874. The site is maintained the way the Kjellbergs kept it, and there are several ongoing educational and entertainment programs, like helping those on the farm feed animals and old-time craft demonstrations. | Mineral Springs Rd. | 219/926–7561, x218 | www.nps.gov/indu | Free | Grounds open daily, farm Sun 1–4.

Indiana Dunes State Park. In the center of the National Lakeshore, though not officially a part of it, is this 2,182-acre state park, which includes 3-plus mi of Lake Michigan shoreline and some 1,800 acres of woods and varied flora and fauna. The Pinery, in the eastern end, contains the last virgin pine trees in the area along with three huge dune formations: 192-ft Mt. Tom, 184-ft Mt. Holden, and 178-ft Mt. Jackson. The 9-mi Calumet Trail cycle and pedestrian path passes through the park between Dune Acres and the National Lakeshore's Mt. Baldy. The nature center explores dunes ecology and is a departure point for bird-watching walks and nature hikes all year long. In summer, there are bathhouses and concession, and there's always picnicking and camping. | 1600 N. Rte. 25 E, Chesterton | 219/926–1952 | www.state.in.us/dnr/parklake/parks/indianadunes.html, www.ai.org/dnr | $2 per vehicle residents, $5 nonresidents | Daily.

Joseph Bailly Homestead. Voyageur and fur trader Joseph Bailly settled here in the early 1820s and built this two-and-a-half story home, fastening it all together with wooden pegs. In the 1960s, it was a boarding house and restaurant. It sits south of U.S. 12, 1.5 mi west of Route 49. | Mineral Springs Rd. | 219/926–7561, ext. 218 | www.nps.gov/indu | Free | Grounds open daily, farm Sun. 1–4.

Paul H. Douglas Center for Environmental Education. Animal exhibits, pond studies, and audio-visual presentations familiarize you with the dunes ecosystem at this center named after the late Senator from Illinois (1892–1976). Lake St. | 219/926–7561, ext. 225 | www.nps.gov/indu | Free | Mon.–Fri. 10–4.

World's Fair Homes. Five unique display and model homes from the 1933 Chicago World's Fair Century of Progress exhibition (the Armco-Ferro-Mayflower House, House of Tomorrow, the Rostone House, the Florida Tropical House, and the Cypress Log House) were dismantled and shipped by barge to Beverly Shores along the lakeshore. The homes, several made of experimental materials, can be viewed on a driving tour; you can get maps from the Dorothy Buell Memorial Visitor Center, where there are also slide shows and other information. | Kemil Road and U.S. 12 | 219/926–7561, ext. 225 | www.nps.gov/indu or www.casualcoast.com/attractions.htm | Free | Daily dawn–dusk.

ON THE CALENDAR

MAR.: *Maple Sugar Time Festival.* Chellberg Farm and Bailly Homestead demonstrate present-day methods of making maple sugar. Tours are also available of both properties. | 219/926–7561, ext. 265.

INDIANAPOLIS

MAP 3, D5

(Nearby towns also listed: Anderson, Fishers, Greencastle, Greenfield, Kokomo, Noblesville)

Humorist Will Rogers quipped that Indianapolis was "the only farm I've ever seen with a monument in the center." The capital city and its most recognizable landmark, the 284-ft Soldiers' and Sailors' Monument, sit in the very center of the state surrounded by a pancake-flat checkerboard of fields. Only 4 years after attaining statehood, Indiana's General Assembly decided that the first capital, Corydon, was inconvenient. They chose instead a spot roughly at the geographical center of the state, where Fall Creek empties into the wide and lazy west fork of the White River. The move was quickly approved, and the capital city traces its beginnings to the arrival of four horse-drawn wagons piled high with the state archives and a time-worn set of leather-bound law books. While the legislators were quick to approve the placement of the capital, they wrangled for days over a proper name. Despite complaints that the name was too hard to pronounce, they finally agreed on affixing "polis," the Greek word for city, to the state's name. Natives refer to the city casually as "Indy."

Alexander Ralston, a surveyor for Washington, D.C., designer Pierre Charles L'Enfant, was hired to design and plan the city. He envisioned an orderly layout that contained the city within a square mile. Ralston overlaid a grid of roadways and parcels of land with a circle at the center and diagonal streets radiating in four directions. Since then, the Circle City has seen a steady influx of settlers, business, and industry. Ever since the early days, transportation arteries have figured prominently in the city's lifeblood. In the 1820s the National Road (now U.S. 40), and a decade later the Central Canal, carried a steady stream of people and goods. Later, the railroads laid track through the city and with the advent of the interstate highway system, Indianapolis was crisscrossed with super slabs, more than in any other city in the nation. Over the years, Ralston's orderly plan served the city well, and it has been busy filling in the triangles and squares with sleek yet unimposing high-rises and shady neighborhoods of gracious older homes. The metropolitan area now extends well beyond the original square mile, incorporating the six adjacent counties.

Since its beginning, the city's small-town character has brought mixed blessings. For years, the modest city wore the unbecoming labels "India-no-place" and "Naptown." Although Indianapolis has pursued a steady course of growth over the years, becoming the nation's 13th-largest city, until roughly 30 years ago it was truly little more than an oversized small town.

The catalyst for the city's makeover was the decision in 1970 to combine the governments of Indianapolis and Marion County. The move doubled the population to 710,000 and increased the municipality's eligibility for federal money. They then forged a public–private partnership with local business and industry leaders that called for investing $3 billion dollars in downtown Indianapolis by the mid-1990s.

The city was soon able to claim the title "Amateur Sports Capital of the World," having built world-class sports venues such as the track and field stadium and the natatorium on the combined campuses of Indiana and Purdue Universities. The headquarters of national amateur sports federations governing rowing, track and field, and gymnastics were relocated to the city.

The 1970s and the 1980s brought investments in bricks and mortar downtown with construction of a domed stadium for the newly acquired National Football League team the Colts, along with entertainment and recreation facilities. Also in the 1980s, Indianapolis was crowned "Cinderella City" by *Newsweek* and *Travel Holiday*, and began the next phase, filling in the downtown grid with museums, performance halls, and stretches of spruced-up green. Today, a zoo, several major museums and other cultural organizations, a symphony hall, and a repertory theater are all downtown, along with ample greenery. The White River State Park corridor along the White River strings together several sports and cultural attractions, including the Canal Walk, a linear park along a 10½-block remnant of the old Central Canal. By the early 1990s, the pace of development slowed and many people wondered whether the massive craters that dotted downtown would ever be filled in. Then, in fall 1995, Indianapolis unveiled Circle Centre, a mall full of shops and restaurants hidden cleverly behind the facades of staid, old, onetime office buildings and abandoned department stores. Today, the emphasis is on maintaining the city's sturdy grid framework while strategically adding new cultural and recreational facilities.

Information: Indianapolis Convention and Visitors Association | 1 RCA Dome, Ste. 100, 46225 | 317/639–4282 or 800/958–INDY | icva@indianapolis.org | www.indy.org.

WALKING TOUR

This walk through downtown Indianapolis can last between 2 and 6 hours, depending on your interests. Start at the Indiana Convention Center and RCA Dome. Heading east along Georgia Street from its intersection with Capitol Ave., you'll notice the facade of the Rost Jewelry Company, one of the historic facades rebuilt in 1995. As you turn left (north) onto Illinois Street, more of the facades will come into view on the right side of the street; in all, eight facades of landmark buildings make up the exterior of the Circle Center mall, the city's modern shopping, dining, and entertainment complex. A detour left (west) on Maryland Street for ³/₅ mi brings you to Victory Field, the 13,500-seat home of the Indianapolis Indians baseball team. Continuing north on Illinois Street brings you to Washington Street, where a glass dome houses the Center for Arts. A left (west) turn and a mile-long walk leads to the Eiteljorg Museum of American Indians and Western Art, White River State Park, and later, the Indianapolis Zoo. Heading north on South West Street brings you to the Military Park, site of the Congressional Medal of Honor Memorial, the only one of its kind in the nation. Returning to the corner of Illinois Street and Washington, continue (east) on Washington Street and then make a left (north) onto Meridian Street, which leads into Monument Circle. Among the attractions here are the Soldiers' and Sailors' Monument, a 284-ft limestone Civil War memorial crowned with a statue of Miss Victory; also on the Circle is the home of the Indianapolis Symphony Orchestra, a former movie house that dates back to the 1930s. Follow the circle going left (northwest) to Market Street, then make a right (west). Straight ahead is the limestone, marble, and granite State Capitol, where all 3 branches of the state government convene.

Continue along Market Street to the entrance of the building, then make a right (north) at Capitol Avenue. A left turn (west) onto Ohio Street and a 1,000-ft walk brings you to several attractions. The Central Canal intersects Ohio Street here, offering an expanse of park-like tranquility, including cascading waterfalls, pedestrian bridges, and a geyser. Slightly farther west on the right (north) side of the street is the Indiana Historical Society, a 165,000-square-ft archive and conservation center that also features changing exhibitions on state history. Make a right (north) at the end of Ohio Street, and continue with the Military Park on your left. Make a left (west) onto New York St., and continue about 1,000 ft until you enter the campuses of Indiana University and Purdue University Indianapolis, home of the IU Natatorium, where U.S. Olympic trials have been held since 1982. The well-manicured campus near the University Stadium is a great place to relax at the end of your tour—especially considering that the university track team may be covering greater distances in less time during their workout on the 400-meter oval. For the winded, the #3 bus heads back down New York Street toward Monument Circle every 40–60 minutes.

NEIGHBORHOODS

Meridian–Kessler and Broad Ripple. Known as America's most loved Main Street, Indianapolis's main artery Meridian Street runs precisely north and south along the line of longitude. For roughly 2 mi, the street passes stately 1930s and 1940s homes that rise up toward the rear of sweeping tree-shaded lawns. To the east, north of Kessler Boulevard, this residential section bumps up against Broad Ripple, a village that's now filled with restaurants, night clubs, shops, and galleries. As early as the late 1800s, good eats and good times brought travelers to Broad Ripple, on a horseshoe bend of the White River, 6 mi north of downtown. At the turn of the century, a 5-cent ride on the trolley carried excursionists to Broad Ripple's amusement center at what is now Broad Ripple Park. White City, Indy's Coney Island, labeled itself "the amusement park that satisfied." Broad Ripple is still the destination of choice for nighttime pleasure seekers. One terminus of the popular 10½-mi Monon Rail Trail is here as well.

Massachusetts Avenue Arts District. Massachusetts Avenue was one of the original diagonal spokes radiating out from the city's hub. It was soon lined with storefronts, factories, and warehouses, and the strip prospered. In the late 1940s, when the streetcar tracks were paved over, the avenue fell into decay. The renovation in the early 1980s of the Hammond Block, a triangular red-brick gem dating from 1874, marked its rebirth. Today, the tall, compact landmark marks the gateway to the district, which has galleries, theaters, storefront eateries, and ethnic restaurants.

Old Northside Historic District. Residential and commercial structures alike have been fixed up over the last two decades in this diverse National Register of Historic Places area, which runs between 12th street on the south and 16th street on the north, and between Pennsylvania street on the west and just beyond College Street on the east. At the turn of the 20th century, many a local bigwig lived here, including drug company founder Eli Lilly, local department store scion L.S. Ayres, novelist Booth Tarkington, former president Benjamin Harrison, and former vice-president Thomas Riley ("What this country needs is a good five-cent cigar") Marshall; the area declined during post–World War I years, when movers and shakers established other residential neighborhoods farther north and west. Construction of I–465 in the 1960s meant the end of many a fine home, and others were turned into multifamily dwellings.

Indiana Avenue District. Much of the city's rich jazz and blues heritage is linked to this street, one of the diagonal arteries in the town's original design. Pianist Erroll Grandy, known as the "godfather of Indianapolis jazz," and legendary guitarist Wes Montgomery, among others, are credited with putting the city in the national jazz spotlight. By the 1940s more than 25 jazz clubs stood shoulder to shoulder along the "Grand Ol Street." The impressive Walker Building presided over the avenue's jazz scene. Named for Madame C. J. Walker, a self-made millionaire, the 950-seat structure is still the place to go for jazz; now called the Madame Walker Urban Life Center and Theatre, it has Jazz on the Avenue every Friday night.

The blues also figured in the Indy music scene early on. By the 1920s, blues greats in the city were playing and recording hits like "Indiana Avenue Stomp." Mandolinist Yank Rachell arrived in town in the 1950s, and over the next 20 years he and other traditional blues players helped attract new interest to the genre. Today the Slippery Noodle Inn, just south of Union Station on S. Meridian Street, is synonymous with the blues. The 1850 redbrick building, the oldest commercial structure in the metropolitan area, draws local and national acts, offering basic eats and great music in a no-frills space. Blues lovers know they have arrived when they see the Noodle's red neon sign proclaiming "Dis Is It."

Attractions
ART AND ARCHITECTURE

Eiteljorg Museum of American Indians and Western Art. This large, impressive adobe-style institution opened in White River State Park in 1989 as a repository for the collections of Harrison Eiteljorg. It houses historical artifacts, an American Western collection, and works by Native American artists. Paintings and bronze sculptures by Charles Russell, Frederic Remington, Georgia O'Keeffe, and other members of the original Taos, New Mexico, artists' colony are on display. Pottery, basketry, clothing, and other works from 10 regions of North America are also exhibited. | 500 W. Washington St. | 317/636–9378 | fax 317/264–1724 | www.eiteljorg.org | $5 | Mon.–Sat. 10–5, Sun. noon–5; Labor Day–Memorial Day, Tues.–Sat. 10–5, Sun. noon–5.

Indianapolis Museum of Art. This institution is one of the nation's oldest art museums and its seventh largest. The collection of watercolors by J. M. W. Turner is the largest outside of the United Kingdom, and the Eli Lilly Collection of Chinese Art is one of the most comprehensive arrays of Asian art in the nation. Other highlights of the permanent collection include the W. J. Holliday Collection of neo-Impressionist art, the Clowes Fund Collection of Old Master paintings, and the *Love* sculpture by Robert Indiana. The former home of J. K. Lilly, built in the style of an 18th-century French chateau, is now the Lilly Pavilion of Decorative Arts, which showcases fine American, English, and German pieces. The Mary Fendrich Hulman Pavilion displays works from the Eiteljorg Collection of African Art. The museum is on 152 acres of manicured and wooded grounds. Also on the grounds are several art pavilions, the Eli Lilly Botanical Garden, a lecture hall, a greenhouse, restaurants, nature trails, and the Indianapolis Civic Theatre. | 1200 W. 38th St. | 317/923–1331 | fax 317/920–2660 | www.ima-art.org | Free; fees for special exhibitions | Tues.–Sat. 10–5, Thurs. 10–8:30, Sun. noon–5.

Morris-Butler House. Dark woodwork, Victorian antiques, and chandeliers create a luxurious look in this 16-room house built in 1865 for a well-to-do family. An Indiana-made Wooten desk and paintings by Hoosier painter Jacob Cox are among the striking pieces on view. The house is in the historic Old Northside neighborhood and was the first restoration project of the Historic Landmarks Foundation of Indiana, the largest statewide preservation organization in the United States. | 1204 N. Park Ave. | 317/636–5409 | fax 317/636–2630 | www.historiclandmarks.org/offices.htm | $5 | Tours every 30 mins Tues.–Sat. 10–4, Sun. 1–4; closed first 2 weeks in Jan.

State Capitol. The Capitol is 1½ blocks west of the Soldiers' and Sailors' Monument downtown on nine grassy acres. A dome tops the stately limestone structure. Inside are imported marble, polished granite, brass fixtures, and a massive stained-glass window. The building houses all three branches of state government. Stop in the rotunda, inside the dome, to pick up self-guided tour brochures. | 200 W. Washington St. | 317/233–5293 | Free | Weekdays 9–4.

PARKS, NATURAL SIGHTS, AND RECREATION

Eagle Creek Park and Nature Preserve. Spread across 33,000 acres with a 13,000-acre lake in the middle, this expanse is one of the largest municipal parks in the United States. Picnicking is popular, and there is an extensive network of hiking trails as well as a swimming beach, a paddleboat pond, and sailboat and rowboat rentals. When snow cover is sufficient, the park is open to cross-country skiers and rental equipment is available. The park's lake is the site of one of two rowing courses in the United States sanctioned for international competition by the International Federation of Rowing Associations. In 1994 the park hosted the World Rowing Championships. | 7840 W. 56th St. | 317/327–7110 | $2 per vehicle; holidays and weekends $3 per vehicle | Daily dawn–dusk.

Garfield Park and Conservatory. This leafy preserve is one of the city's oldest parks. The formal gardens have been restored to their original 1916 design. Replica urns and planters punctuate the sunken gardens amid the formal gardens. The conservatory contains more than 500 tropical plants and a 15-ft waterfall. Also in the park are a swimming pool, tennis courts, and baseball diamonds. | 2450 S. Shelby St. | 317/327–7184 | Free; conservatory $2.50 | Daily 10–6.

Greenways/Monon Rail Trail. The city claimed the abandoned Monon railroad track and has paved the railbed for roughly 10½ mi to create this ribbon of asphalt, which connects downtown with the north side and Broad Ripple. It's often thronged with in-line skaters, cyclists, and parents pushing strollers. | 1502 W. 16th St. | 317/327–PARK | www.indygov.org/indyparks | Free | Daily dawn–dusk.

Indianapolis Parks and Recreation. The city maintains more than 156 city and suburban parks and 175 mi of greenway corridors following rivers, old railroad beds, and an 1836 canal towpath. Eagle Creek Park and Nature Preserve, Garfield Park and Conservatory, and Greenways/Monon Rail Trail (open daily, from dawn to dusk) are three of the most popular. | 1502 W. 16th St. | 317/327–PARK | www.indygov.org/indyparks | Free | Weekdays 9–5.

Indianapolis Tennis Center. The RCA Championships are held each summer at this facility on the campus of Indiana University–Purdue University at Indianapolis. The center has six indoor courts and 18 outdoor courts and has been named an outstanding public tennis facility by the United States Tennis Association. | 755 University Blvd. | 317/278–2100 | fax 317/636–2237 | www.iupui.edu/~tennis/ | $10 per hour | Weekdays 6:30 AM–10 PM, Sat. 7 AM–10:30 PM, Sun. 8 AM–9 PM.

Indiana University Track and Soccer Stadium. The 1997 USA Track & Field National Championship and World Team selection meet were held at this stadium on the Indiana University–Purdue University at Indianapolis campus. It also hosts soccer matches. You can use the track, which has an oval, 400-m eight-lane track with a rubber all-weather surface and a jogging lane. The stadium is connected by tunnel to the Natatorium. | 901 W. New York St. | 317/274–3518 | fax 317/274–7769 | www.adaf.iupui.edu/sportscomplex/sports.htm | Free to University Place guests | Weekdays 5:30 AM–8 PM, Sun. 1–5.

I.U. Natatorium. This swim center on the campus of Indiana University–Purdue University at Indianapolis has been the site of U.S. swimming trials for every Olympics since its opening in 1982. Sixty-five American and seven world records have been set at the Natatorium. Highlights of the facility are a 50-m competition pool, an 18-ft diving well for platform and springboard diving, a 50-m instructional pool, two workout rooms with Hammer Strength weight machines, and seating for 4,700 spectators. | 901 W. New York St. | 317/274–3518 | fax 317/274–7769 | www.iunat.iupui.edu | Free to University Place guests | Competition pool weekdays 5:30–8, Sun. 1–5; conditioning room Mon.–Thurs. 5:30–8, Fri.–Sat. noon–3, Sun. 1–5.

White River State Park. This 250-acre park in the heart of downtown is the site of numerous landmarks: an IMAX 3D Theater, Victory Field baseball park, the Indianapolis Zoo, the Eiteljorg Museum of American Indians and Western Art, the National Institute for Fitness and Sport, Military Park, River Promenade, Pumphouse Visitors Center, and Celebration Plaza.

The historic Central Canal and the Washington Street Bridge, which has been renovated as a pedestrian mall and now connects to the ½-mi River Promenade on the northern edge of the Indianapolis Zoo, are also here. The Promenade, which follows the upper banks of the White River, is built from 1,272 blocks of Indiana limestone and is accented with 14 stone tablets carved with renderings of famous buildings made of Indiana limestone, including New York's Empire State Building. A focal point of the Promenade is the hand-carved Rose Window, a limestone frame measuring more than 7 ft in diameter. | 801 W. Washington St. | 317/637–4567 | www.indianapolis.org/attract.htm#white | Free | Daily.

The **Central Canal Walk** runs along the Central Canal between St. Claire and Washington streets and into White River State Park; it terminates at a 17-ft waterfall at McCormick's Rock on the White River. This water sculpture commemorates the founding of the city in 1822. Benches and fountains line the wide walkway. | www.indianapolis.org/attract.htm#central canal | Free | Daily.

Opened in 1996, the 416-seat **IMAX 3D Theater** is one of only 12 such theaters in the nation. You watch 3D films here with special polarized glasses (provided by the theater) on a six-story-high screen. | 650 W. Washington St. | 317/233–4629.

Indianapolis Zoo. This 64-acre cageless zoo, opened in 1988 in White River State Park, is one of the few recently built zoos in the United States. It includes botanical gardens. The dolphin pavilion houses the state's largest aquarium and is the world's second-largest, fully enclosed, environmentally controlled marine mammal facility. More than 3,000 animals in simulated natural habitats make their home on landscaped grounds with 1,700 species of plants. The Encounters Exploration Center uses hands-on exhibits and interactive videos to demonstrate the interconnectedness of life. In the Living Deserts of the World, a conservatory covered by a transparent dome, birds and animals roam at will. | 1200 W. Washington St. | 317/630–2001 | fax 317/630–5153 | www.indyzoo.com/default1.asp | $10, parking $3 | Weekdays 9–4, weekends 9–5.

The grassy square **Military Park** on the campus of Indiana University–Purdue University at Indianapolis was once a Civil War encampment and training field. Walkways dotted with benches crisscross the 14-acre greenspace, and there's a small shelter. | 801 W. Washington St. | Free | Daily.

National Institute for Fitness and Sport. Fitness and sports physiology research are the raison d'être of this 65,000-square-ft fitness center on the edge of the campus of Indiana University–Purdue University at Indianapolis. However, the sports facilities, including a 200-m indoor track, strength training area, and locker rooms, are open to professional and amateur athletes as well as the general public. | 250 University Blvd. | 317/274–3432 | www.nifs.org | $12 | Weekdays 5:30AM–10PM, weekends 7 AM–6 PM.

CULTURE, EDUCATION, AND HISTORY

Butler University. This co-educational university was founded in 1858 on what was then the outskirts of the city. Today, the undergraduate enrollment is 4,126, and the school is known for its music and dance programs. Older residential neighborhoods surround the 280-acre campus, which is the site of Clowes Memorial Hall, Hinkle Fieldhouse, and the Holcomb Observatory and Planetarium. | 4600 Sunset Ave. | 317/940–8000 or 888/940–8100 | www.butler.edu | Free | Daily.

Contemporary **Clowes Memorial Hall** was built in 1963 in memory of Eli Lilly Company research scientist Dr. George Henry Alexander Clowes, who envisioned the site as a center for theater arts. The building is known for its acoustics and is used by Indianapolis arts organizations as well as Butler University. A program of Broadway and touring shows is presented each year. | 4602 Sunset Ave. | 317/940–9697 or 317/940–6444 | Sept.–May, weekdays 10–5, Sat. 10–2.

The **J. I. Holcomb Observatory and Planetarium,** built in 1954, has a 38-inch Cassegrain reflector telescope, the largest public telescope in Indiana. Tours and planetarium shows are presented. | 4600 Sunset Ave. | 317/940–9333 | www.butler.edu/holcomb/ | $2.25 | Planetarium shows Aug.–Apr., Fri.–Sat. 7 and 8:15; May–July, Fri.–Sat. 8 and 9:15.

Crown Hill Cemetery. The nation's fourth largest cemetery is the resting place for such notables as President Benjamin Harrison, bank robber John Dillinger, and poet James Whitcomb Riley. | 700 W. 38th St. | 317/925–8231 | Free | Daily 9–5.

Historic Lockerbie Square. Cobbled streets crisscross this quiet, shady enclave on the east edge of downtown, which dates back to 1846. Its tall Victorian town houses and gracious brick homes have been painstakingly restored. | 317/631–5885 | Free | Daily.

Widely considered one of the most perfectly preserved Victorian houses in the United States, the **James Whitcomb Riley Home,** built in 1872, is where the Hoosier poet spent the last 23 years of his life. Many of Riley's personal mementos are displayed. The entire estate looks much the same as Riley must have left it. | 528 Lockerbie St. | 317/631–5885 | $3 | Tues.–Sat. 10–3:30, Sun. noon–3:30.

Indiana University—Purdue University Indianapolis. The 285-acre campus on the edge of downtown combines schools from Purdue and Indiana universities. The Indiana University Medical Center is one of the country's top medical research centers. Other notable schools are the Law, Nursing, Engineering, and Business schools. The campus is also home to internationally recognized amateur sports facilities, including the Natatorium, the University Track and Soccer Stadium, and the Indianapolis Tennis Center. Several national and international competitions take place here each year. | 425 University Blvd. | 317/274–5555 | Free | Daily.

Indiana World War Memorial and American Legion Mall. This impressive memorial building is the centerpiece of a five-block parklike area just north of Monument Circle downtown. The limestone and marble memorial pays homage to fallen Hoosiers from World Wars I and II, the Korean War, and the Vietnam War. The Shrine Room, with 24 stained-glass windows, is an awe-inspiring sight with a 17- by 30-ft American flag suspended in the center of the room. In the lower level, a military museum follows Indiana soldiers from the Battle of Tippecanoe through recent military conflicts. The grassy and tree-lined American Legion Mall is flanked by the American Legion state and national headquarters. Along the mall, fly flags of all 50 states. In between the memorial and the mall is University Park, with the stone DePew Fountain in the center, and statues of Abraham Lincoln, Benjamin Harrison, and Schuyler Colfax. | 431 N. Meridian St. | 317/232–7615 | Free | Wed.–Sat. 9–6.

Indianapolis Art Center. The Art Center is next to the White River in Broad Ripple Village on the Monon Trail. Primarily a teaching organization, the center hosts dozens of art classes and outreach programs. It also presents exhibitions of regional and national art. In summer, concerts play on at its riverfront open-air theater. | 820 E. 67th St. | 317/255–2464 | www.indplsartcenter.org/ | Free | Weekdays 9 AM–10 PM, Sat. 9–6, Sun. noon–3.

Madame Walker Theatre Center. African motifs accent this buff-colored corner building dating from 1927, and terra-cotta pictures of African symbols embellish the 950-seat hall inside. Music, dance, and theatre performances fill the program. In the spirit of Indiana Avenue's early 1900s heritage as a Midwestern jazz center, the theater presents Jazz on the Avenue in the Casino-Ballroom on Friday nights. | 617 Indiana Ave. | 317/236–2099 | www.mmewalkertheatre.org/ | Admission price varies | Tours by appointment.

Hilbert Circle Theatre. The stately Circle Theatre, formerly a movie palace built in 1916, overlooks the Soldiers' and Sailors' Monument. A classical structure with painted details and ornate plaster moldings, the building was carefully restored and acoustically fine-tuned, and unveiled in 1984 as the home of the Indianapolis Symphony Orchestra. It seats 1,835 and is listed on the National Register of Historic Places.

Each year the **Indianapolis Symphony Orchestra** presents more than 200 concerts and has several classical and pops series at the Hilbert Circle Theatre. One of the oldest orchestras in the country, the Indianapolis Symphony dates from 1930. It has a very popular summer program of outdoor concerts at Conner Prairie Farm, near the town of Fishers, as well as free concerts at parks throughout the city during the summer. | 45 Monument Cir. | 317/639–4300 | fax 317/262–1159 | www.indyorch.org | Admission price varies | Tours by appointment.

Soldiers' and Sailors' Monument. In the center of Monument Circle in downtown Indianapolis, the 284-ft limestone monument commemorates Indiana's soldiers and sailors who served in the Civil War. *Miss Victory,* a 30-ft statue, crowns the top. You can climb up or take an elevator to a glass-enclosed observation deck. The Colonel Eli Lilly Civil War Museum in the basement has vintage uniforms, flags, letters from soldiers, and other Civil War relics. | Monument Cir. | 317/232–7615 | Free | Wed.–Sat. 9–6.

MUSEUMS

The Children's Museum of Indianapolis. The world's largest children's museum, attracting more than 1 million visitors a year, occupies a modern five-story building 30 blocks north of the Circle. Collections and interactive exhibits explore the physical and natural sciences, history, foreign cultures, and the arts. The Science Works gallery has a 22-ft limestone climbing wall, a fossil dig, and a tunnel. Also on view are a tall water clock, a life-size dinosaur model, a log cabin, and countless cultural artifacts. In addition to a planetarium and children's theater, the museum operates the IWERKS CineDome, a large-format movie theater. | 3000 N. Meridian St. | 317/334–3322 | fax 317/921–4019 | www.childrensmuseum.org/ | $8 | Tues.–Sun. 10–5.

Hook's American Drug Store Museum. At the Indiana State Fairgrounds, this small historic brick building re-creates a mid-19th-century American drug store, with polished wood floors, shelves lined with apothecary jars, and a soda fountain. The museum is chock-full of antiques and Americana and sells old-time candy and soda-fountain treats. | 1202 E. 38th St. | 317/924–1503 | fax 317/924–5825 | Free after entering fairgrounds | Tues.–Sun. 11–5.

Indiana Historical Society. State-of-the-art climate-controlled archives, a library, and conservation areas house an extensive collection of rare documents and photographs. In the Cole Porter Room, you can listen to a wide range of Hoosier legends, including Cole Porter, John Mellencamp, Wes Montgomery, Hoagy Carmichael, Michael Jackson, Noble Sissle, and the Hampton Sisters, on a programmable CD jukebox. The Exhibitions Gallery showcases the Hoosier History Makers exhibit and other rotating displays. Finally, a 30,000-square-ft research facility houses rare books and the William Henry Smith Memorial Library, a 300-seat theater, letters, diaries, business records, maps, architectural drawings, paintings, and other material on the history of Indiana and the Old Northwest. The building itself, an impressive 165,000-square-ft, four-story structure that opened in 1999, was inspired by historic structures around the state. | 450 W. Ohio St. | 317/234–1830 | www.indianahistory.org/ | Free | Tues.–Sat. 10–5, Sun. noon–5 (except library).

Indiana Medical History Museum. The museum is housed in the Pathological Department of the former Central State Hospital. When the structure was built in 1896, it was a research and teaching center. It is now the oldest pathology laboratory in the United States. Scientific laboratory equipment and photography, and an assortment of medical equipment and devices, are on display. | 3045 W. Vermont St. | 317/635–7329 | fax 317/635–7349 | $5 | Thurs.–Sat. 10–4.

Indiana State Museum. The museum occupies the former city hall, a stately limestone building dating from the early 20th century. A 212-pound bronze Foucault pendulum is suspended 85 ft from the rotunda ceiling to the floor. Exhibits explore the cultural and natural history of the state from the Ice Age to just after the turn of the century. One of the most popular exhibits highlights the phenomenon of Indiana high school basketball, known as Hoosier hysteria. The museum's Freetown Village dramatically portrays the lives of African Americans in Indiana just after the Civil War. Special exhibits focus on sports, small-town Victorian lifestyles, and fine art. | 202 N. Alabama St. | 317/232–1637 | fax 317/232–7090 | www.ai.org/ism/museum/index.html | Free | Mon.–Sat. 9–4:45, Sun. noon–4:45.

National Art Museum of Sport (NAMOS). This unusual museum displays more than 1,000 paintings, prints, sculptures, and photographs in galleries at the University Place Conference Center and Hotel on the Indiana University–Purdue University campus. Works by Winslow Homer, Fletcher Martin, George Bellows, and Alfred Boucher depict more than

44 sports from archery to yachting. The museum was founded by Connecticut artist-sportsman Germain G. Glidden in 1959 and moved to Indianapolis in 1990. | 850 W. Michigan St. | 317/274–3627 | fax 317/274–3878 | www.namos.iupui.edu | Free | Weekdays 8–5.

President Benjamin Harrison Memorial Home. This 16-room Italianate mansion built in 1875, a northside landmark, was the home of America's 23rd president, who campaigned from here in 1888. Original Victorian furnishings, Mrs. Harrison's ball gowns, and an extensive collection of political mementos are on display in the carefully restored building. During the first Wednesday of every month (except Jan., July, and Aug.), the home hosts "Live from Delaware Street," during which costumed actors portray President and Mrs. Harrison, the household staff, and other period characters. | 1230 N. Delaware St. | 317/631–1898 | fax 317/632–5488 | www.surf-ici.com/harrison/ | $5 | Mon.–Sat. 10–3:30, Sun. 12:30–3:30.

RELIGION AND SPIRITUALITY

Scottish Rite Cathedral. Built of stone, the tower of this Gothic structure rises 212 ft above the downtown skyline. The cathedral has Russian white-oak beams and paneling and contains a 54-bell carillon, one of the nation's largest, along with a 7,000-pipe organ. Shortly after its completion in 1929, the International Association of Architects called it "one of the seven most beautiful buildings in the world." Tours are available. | 650 N. Meridian St. | 317/262–3100 | Free | Weekdays 10–3.

SHOPPING

Circle Centre. This sophisticated mall is cleverly designed with dozens of shops and department stores hidden behind the facades of Indy's old downtown buildings. The multilevel maze also includes movie theaters and restaurants. | 49 W. Maryland St. | 317/681–8000 | fax 317/681–5650 | Free | Mon.–Sat. 10–9, Sun. noon–6; entertainment venues open later.

City Market. The city's original market, on the National Register of Historic Places, dates back to 1886. Built of brick with tall windows and high ceilings, it is a favorite lunch spot for downtown workers. Some 25 vendors sell fresh produce, meats, fish, baked goods, flowers, and imported foods and coffee. During Fri. lunch hour, jazz and other musical performances are presented. | 222 E. Market St. | 317/634–9266 | Free | Mon.–Sat. 9–5.

SPECTATOR SPORTS

Hinkle Fieldhouse. You may have seen this Butler University arena in the 1980s high-school basketball movie *Hoosiers*. For more than half a century, finals of the Indiana state basketball tournament were played here, and you can still watch basketball and other collegiate sports events here. Nearby Butler Bowl is an outdoor, open-air playing field flanked by stadium seating and the home field for Butler's football team, the Bulldogs. | 510 W. 49th St. | 317/940–9390 | fax 317/940–9808 | www.butlersports.com/general/index.html | Daily.

Indiana Pacers. This National Basketball Association team plays at the Indiana Fieldhouse downtown. | 125 S. Pennsylvania St. | 317/917–2500 | fax 317/917–2799 | www.nba.com/pacers.

Indianapolis Colts. This National Football League team plays at the RCA Dome. | 100 S. Capitol Ave. | 317/297–7000 | www.colts.com.

Indianapolis Motor Speedway and Hall of Fame Museum. Built in 1909, the famed 2½ mi oval track at the Indianapolis Motor Speedway hosts the Indianapolis 500 every Memorial Day and stock-car races the rest of the year. When it is not being used for competitions or for tire testing or practice, you can take a narrated bus ride around the track. The museum showcases more than 30 winning cars from the Indianapolis 500 along with rotating displays of 75 classic and antique passenger cars. The Tony Hulman Theatre screens a film highlighting the history of the racetrack. | 4790 W. 16th St. | 317/484–6747 | fax 317/484–6449 | www.indy500.com | $3 | Daily 9–5.

Indianapolis Indians. This AAA farm team for the Milwaukee Brewers plays in a 13,500-seat open-air ballpark, opened in 1996 in White River State Park. | 501 W. Maryland St. | 317/269–3545 | Apr.–early Sept.

SIGHTSEEING TOURS

Gray Line Bus Tours. Tours of the city and metropolitan area are available along with special Indy 500 and Brickyard 400 auto race packages. Regular tours depart from the Hyatt Regency downtown, at Capitol and Washington Streets. | 9075 N. Meridian St. | 317/573–0403 or 800/447–4526 | fax 317/573–0410 | www.grayline.com.

OTHER POINTS OF INTEREST

Easley's Winery. The winery is in an old brick building on the edge of downtown. Free wine tastings are available. | 205 N. College Ave. | 317/636–4516 | Free | Weekdays 9–6, Sat. 9–5, Sun. noon–4; tours for groups of 12 or more by appointment.

Indiana Convention Center and RCA Dome. Completed in 1984, the 19-story, 60,000-seat covered stadium is the home turf of the Indianapolis Colts National Football League team and also hosts other events. RCA Dome tours cover the Indianapolis Colts locker rooms, the owner's suite, the press box, and the stadium floor. | 100 S. Capitol Ave. | 317/262–3410 | www.iccrd.com | Daily 8–5.

ON THE CALENDAR

MAY: *500 Festival.* A month of special events leads up to a giant star-studded parade and the running of the Indy 500 auto race. | 317/636–4556.

MAY: *Indianapolis 500-Mile Race.* Tradition and high-spirited celebrations surround the granddaddy of all car-racing events; the annual race covers 500 mi on the oval Speedway racetrack. The all-day event, over the Memorial Day weekend, draws roughly 250,000 spectators. | 317/481–8500.

JUNE: *Indian Market.* Native American artists and craftspeople from across North America show and sell their wares at this juried market, one of the largest such events east of the Mississippi River. The market also has Native American dancing, food, and kids' activities. | Military Park | 317/636–WEST.

AUG.: *Indiana State Fair.* The sixth-oldest fair in the country showcases the talents of youngsters with one of the largest 4-H programs in the country. The big midway has rides, food, a balloon race, and grandstand country and Western entertainment. | 1202 E. 38th St. | 317/927–7500.

OCT.: *Heartland Film Festival.* This unique film festival recognizes and honors filmmakers whose work explores the human journey by expressing hope and respect for positive values of life. | 613 N. East St. | 317/464–9405 | www.heartlandfilmfest.org.

SEPT.: *Penrod Art Fair.* This popular art fair takes place on the grounds of the Indianapolis Museum of Art. More than 250 artists display their work and music; theater and dance performances are presented. | 317/252–9895.

OCT.: *Blue River Valley Pioneer Fair.* Pioneer craft demonstrations, cooking, and musical presentations are performed by costumed settlers at the Shelby County Fairgrounds in Shelbyville. | 317/392–4634.

OCT.: *Village Tour of Homes.* Six unique homes in historic Zionsville, a small community just north of Indianapolis, are open for tours. Brick-lined Main Street and the shady avenues of Zionsville are perfect for strolling. | 135 S. Elm St., Zionsville | 317/873–3836.

DEC.: *Yuletide Celebration.* All month, the Indianapolis Symphony Orchestra stages a dazzling holiday show in the elegantly restored Hilbert Circle Theatre. The festive holiday celebration has music, dance, and classics such as *A Christmas Carol.* | 317/639–4300 or 800/366–8457.

TRANSPORTATION

Airports: Most major domestic airlines serve Indianapolis International Airport, which is southwest of the city along I–70. | 317/487–7243.

Airport Transportation: Public transportation does not serve the airport; taxis to downtown cost about $17.

Bus: Indianapolis is served by **Greyhound** lines.800/231–2222.

Intra-city Transit: The Indianapolis Public Transportation System, known as **IndyGo,** is a pretty decent way to get around the city, with 36 bus lines that link up at a main terminal. | 1501 W. Washington St. | 317/635–3344 | $1 per ride.

Driving around Town: I–65, I–70, and I–74 reach Indianapolis, crossing the city and its surrounding beltway, I–465. Navigation is easy as streets are all organized in a grid, more or less, with just about every other street running one way. All-day parking at private lots costs around $7, and there is both free and metered street parking. Traffic is heaviest during the city's frequent sporting events; unless you're going yourself, it's best to steer clear of the major venues at those times in this sports-crazed town. Weekday rush hour traffic will slow you down a little as well.

Dining
INEXPENSIVE

Bazbeaux. American. Winner of Indianapolis Monthly magazine's People's Choice Award for best pizza, this popular eatery turns out Italian fare and pizzas with no fewer than 52 toppings. It's in an old storefront in the Massachusetts Avenue arts district, and has a covered patio where you can eat outside when the weather's nice. | 334 Massachusetts Ave. | 317/636–7662 | $10–$20 | D, MC, V.

Hard Times Café. American. Chili is the staple here. You get a chili sampler when you are seated, so that you can make educated choices among the Terlingua Red (Texas style with tomato sauce and beef broth), Texas, Cincinnati, and vegetarian chilis. Also available are burgers, dogs, steaks, ribs, and salads. Country-western music plays on the juke box, and spurs, flags, and license plates fill the walls. | 121 W. Maryland St. | 317/916–9800 | $5–$16 | AE, MC, V.

Hollyhock Hill. American. In the middle of a residential neighborhood, this cheerful restaurant has a loyal following. The family-style service is like Sunday dinner at grandma's house. Plates are heaped with skillet-fried chicken, shrimp, broiled fish, and steak. Kids' menu. | 8110 N. College Ave. | 317/251–2294 | Reservations essential | Closed Mon. | $14–$17 | AE, MC, V.

Iron Skillet. American. A family-run restaurant established in 1956, this tall, century-old home overlooking Coffin Golf Course serves chicken, mashed potatoes, fried shrimp, and steak dinners family style. Kids' menu. | 2489 W. 30th St. | 317/923–6353 | Closed Mon., Tues., and 1st week of July. No lunch Wed.–Sat. | $13–$18 | AE, D, DC, MC, V.

The Rathskeller. German. This cross between a quaint German inn and a bustling beer hall is in the historic Athenaeum Building. A big Gothic fireplace, stained-glass windows, and stuffed animal heads distinguish the beer hall; live music plays in the Biergarten in summer. The hot and cold appetizers run the gamut of German staples—bratwurst, sauerkraut, red cabbage, and smoked sausage. The Ochsenschwanz suppe (soup with oxtails and port wine) is a favorite. | 401 E. Michigan St. | 317/636–0396 | fax 317/630–4652 | Closed Sun. No lunch Sat. | $14–$23 | AE, D, DC, MC, V.

Rock Bottom Brewery. American. Beer is brewed on the premises, and you can tour the brewing operation on request. In the basement, there are small- and large-screen TVs, six pool tables, and two dart alleys. You can eat at the sidewalk tables in nice weather or in the dining room, which is decorated with photographs of the Southwest. The homemade beer bread, served warm, and the Asiago cheese dip are nice starters for either the brown-ale chicken or the tenderloin with roasted garlic. | 10 W. Washington St. | 317/681–8180 | $8–$18 | AE, DC, MC, V.

Shapiro's Delicatessen and Cafeteria. Delicatessen. The strawberry cheesecake and corned beef sandwiches piled high on rye are signature items on the menu. An Indianapolis institution since 1904, this nationally known deli was voted the home of Indy's best take-out food in 1996. | 808 S. Meridian St. | 317/631–4041 | $8–$12 | No credit cards.

Slippery Noodle Inn. American. Indiana's oldest bar is a blues institution, with live music seven nights a week. The red-brick building, built in 1850, is said to have an underground link to Union Station. The back room was once a livery stable and later a house of prostitution. Now it's a rowdy spot for good eats with a Cajun flair. You can choose from Buffalo wings, garlic wings, teriyaki wings, or wings with cayenne pepper. The voodoo chicken is smothered in onions, peppers, and Cajun spices, with a splash of tequila. | 372 S. Meridian St. | 317/631–6974 | fax 317/631–6903 | $8–$20 | AE, D, DC, MV.

MODERATE

Aristocrat Pub. American. Collectibles, antique fixtures, dark paneling, and brass-and-wood booths give this Broad Ripple–area eatery the warmth and charm of an English pub. Fish and chips, burgers, and big salads can be washed down with a long list of beers and ales on tap. You can eat outside on the garden patio in good weather. Kids' menu. Sun. brunch. | 5212 N. College Ave. | 317/283–7388 | $10–$20 | AE, D, DC, MC, V.

Carvers Steaks and Chops. Steak. Perfectly prepared steaks and fresh seafood are among the specialties in this restaurant on the south side of town. You have the option of three different dining venues. One looks like the library of an English country manor, another recalls a California wine country inn, and a third is Mediterranean-style with a garden and patio. | 780 U.S. 31 N, Greenwood | 317/887–6380 | $17–$36 | AE, D, DC, MC, V.

Jazz Cooker. Cajun/Creole. This big white clapboard house with a Mardi Gras mural outside dishes up Louisiana cuisine in Broad Ripple. The spicy black bean soup and jambalaya are accompanied by live jazz on weekends, and when the weather's nice, you can eat outside on a brick patio overlooking a colorful tree- and flower-lined street. | 925 E. Westfield Blvd. | 317/253–2883 | No lunch | $12–$24 | AE, D, DC, MC, V.

Kona Jack's. Seafood. King of a family of three Jack's restaurants, all of which are in a strip shopping center roughly 9 mi north of downtown, Kona Jack's is known for creative food preparation. Light pink swordfish is marinated in Champagne and then broiled. A glaze of coconut milk and Thai spices smothers the seared red snapper. Nearby, Daddy Jack's serves up classic American fare such as steaks and baked potatoes and Deli Jack's dishes out giant specialty subs, red potato and marinated bean salads, and six kinds of fresh-baked cookies. | 9419 N. Meridian St. | 317/843–1609 | Closed Sun. No lunch Sat. | $15–$25 | AE, D, DC, MC, V.

The Majestic. Continental. This elegant downtown restaurant in the 1895 Majestic Building is one block east of the Circle Centre Mall and half a block from Conseco Field House. Great steaks vie for attention with oysters and a wide selection of fish. Specialties include the baked pompano, which comes stuffed with scallops, shrimp, and crabmeat, topped with a lobster sherry sauce. Kids' menu. | 47 S. Pennsylvania St. | 317/636–5418 | Closed Sun. | $13–$39 | AE, D, DC, MC, V.

Magic Moments Restaurant. Contemporary. The view of the Indianapolis skyline is particularly magical at this 14th-floor penthouse restaurant. Strolling magicians entertain while you feast on ostrich with black bean risotto and wild mushroom duxelles, strawberry chicken, and a bacon-wrapped filet stuffed with wild mushrooms. The interior is simple, with mirrors and tea lights. | 1 N. Pennsylvania Bldg. | 317/822–3400 | Dinner only. Closed Sun. | $12–$25 | AE, D, DC, MC, V.

Palomino Euro-Bistro. Contemporary. This upscale, upbeat eatery has vibrantly colored walls, huge oil paintings, hand-blown glass chandeliers, and a lively clientele. Wood-oven-fired pizzas are good, as are the selections of meat, roasted over either applewood or white oak. The specialties are the oven-roasted mussels in rosemary-lemon butter, authentic paella casserole, and grilled salmon with artichoke tartar sauce. | 49 W. Maryland St. | 317/974–0400 | Reservations recommended | No lunch Sun. | $13–$28 | AE, D, DC, MC, V.

EXPENSIVE

Chanteclair. Continental. A strolling violinist and beluga caviar set an elegant tone at this restaurant on the rooftop of the Holiday Inn at the airport. You can choose beef Wellington, a filet wrapped in puff pastry, or the broiled lamb chops, among other delights. | 2501 High School Rd. | 317/243–1040 | Jacket and tie | $20–$38 | AE, D, DC, MC, V.

New Orleans House. Seafood. On the northwest side of Indianapolis, this restaurant is noted for its buffet and Bluepoint oysters on the half shell, sautéed scallops, frogs' legs, and escargot. The buffet includes peel-and-eat shrimp, oysters, seafood chowder, king crab legs, shrimp Creole, and jambalaya, as well as chicken and barbecued ribs. A piano bar provides entertainment. | 8845 Township Line Rd. | 317/872–9670 | Closed Sun. Dinner only | $37 for unlimited buffet | AE, DC, MC, V.

Peter's Restaurant and Bar. Contemporary. Contemporary art and fine crafts fill the walls at this trendy, upbeat restaurant in a storefront in the small Keystone at the Crossing shopping center. American cuisine is creatively prepared here; you'll find dishes such as sweet-potato polenta in maple syrup and grilled pork loin with cranberry-apple glaze. Weather permitting, you can have cocktails outside near a waterfall with a garden view, and there's a quiet canopied veranda for open-air dining. | 8505 Keystone Crossing Blvd. | 317/465–1155 | Closed Sun. No lunch | $16–$36 | AE, DC, MC, V.

VERY EXPENSIVE

The Restaurant at the Canterbury. Continental. Much more than a typical hotel restaurant, this downtown gem next to Circle Centre is one of the city's best-kept secrets. Crisp white linens contrast with the dark paneling in the intimate dining room, and the menu includes classic fare such as Dover sole and pepper-crusted rack of lamb. Try the chocolate or raspberry soufflé for dessert. Sun. brunch. | 123 S. Illinois St. | 317/634–3000 | Jacket requested except in summer | $40–$80 | AE, D, DC, MC, V.

Ruth's Chris Steak House. Steak. This upscale chain is furnished in Old English style, complete with fireplaces and luxurious tapestries. The prime filet mignon is a star on the menu, but you can also order pork chops and seafood, and the side dishes such as potatoes au gratin and steamed asparagus, ample enough to share, are classic. Cigars and martinis are also served. | 9445 Threel Rd. | 317/844–1155 | Reservations essential | No lunch | $18–$54 | AE, D, DC, MC, V.

St. Elmo Steak House. Steak. A city landmark since 1902, this downtown establishment is still going strong. The shrimp cocktail is giant and served with sauce made from fresh-ground horseradish, and the steaks are famous. | 127 S. Illinois St. | 317/637–1811 | No lunch | $23–$38 | AE, D, DC, MC, V.

Snax/Something Different. Contemporary. Tapas and a cocktail at Snax are just enough to whet your appetite for dinner next door at the restaurant Something Different, which serves innovative American dishes like vegetarian rice-bean cassoulet laced with garlic, shallots, and wild mushrooms, and pheasant, squab, and partridge strudel. | 4939 E. 82nd St. | 317/570–7700 | $21–$33 | AE, D, DC, MC, V.

Lodging

INEXPENSIVE

Comfort Inn. This four-story motel is 2 mi north of the Indianapolis International Airport and 5½ mi from downtown. Complimentary Continental breakfast. In-room data ports, some microwaves, some refrigerators, some in-room hot tubs. Cable TV. Indoor pool. Hot tub. Exercise equipment. Playground. Laundry facilities. Business services, airport shuttle, free parking. | 5855 Rockville Rd. | 317/487–9800 | fax 317/487–1125 | 94 rooms, 24 suites | $90, $125–$200 suites | AE, D, DC, MC, V.

Comfort Inn South. This three-story motel is off I–465, exit 2B (East Street), 2 mi from downtown. Complimentary Continental breakfast. Some refrigerators. Cable TV. Pool. Business services, free parking. Some pets allowed. | 5040 S. East St. | 317/783–6711 | fax 317/787–3065 | 94 rooms | $79 | AE, D, DC, MC, V.

Country Hearth Inn. The second-floor terrace on this three-story country-style motel on the west side of town off I–465, exit 17 (West 38th Street), is one example of why this establishment prides itself on having the charm of a bed-and-breakfast with all the conveniences of a hotel. There are early evening wine and cheese receptions, and the grounds are full of trees. Complimentary breakfast. Cable TV. Pool. Business services. | 173851 Shore Dr. | 317/297–1848 or 800/217–9182 | fax 317/297–2096 | www.countryhearth.com | 84 rooms | $53–$98 | AE, D, DC, MC, V.

Courtyard Indianapolis Castleton. Trees surround this three-story chain on the northeast side of town. It's across the street from the Castleton Square shopping mall, ½ mi from I–465, exit 35 (Allisonville Rd.), and 1 mi outside Castleton. Bar. In-room data ports, some refrigerators. Cable TV. Indoor pool. Hot tub. Exercise equipment. Laundry facilities. Business services. Free parking. | 8670 Allisonville Rd. | 317/576–9559 | fax 317/576–0695 | 146 rooms | $99–$115 | AE, D, DC, MC, V.

Courtyard Indianapolis North Carmel. This four-story hotel wraps around a courtyard and joins several other hostelries across from an office park and strip shopping centers, along a busy four-lane corridor ¼ mi from I–465, exit 31. Bar. In-room data ports, some refrigerators. Cable TV. Indoor pool. Hot tub. Exercise equipment. Laundry facilities. Business services. | 10290 N. Meridian St. | 317/571–1110 | fax 317/571–0416 | www.courtyard.com | 141 rooms, 8 suites | $79–$119, $109–$119 suites | AE, D, DC, MC, V.

Courtyard by Marriott–Airport. The courtyard at this four-story Marriott contains a gazebo, a garden, and many trees. It's 1½ mi east of the airport off Airport Expressway I–465, exit 11A (Executive Dr.). Bar. Cable TV. Indoor pool. Hot tub. Exercise equipment. Business services, airport shuttle. | 5525 Fortune Cir. E | 317/248–0300 | fax 317/248–1834 | www.courtyard.com | 151 rooms | $95 | AE, D, DC, MC, V.

Crowne Plaza–Union Station. Built in 1888, Indianapolis's Union Station was the first of many in the nation. This hostelry is connected to the station, and 26 authentic Pullman train cars have been converted into guest rooms. The hotel is also linked to the Convention Center and RCA Dome and is one block from Circle Centre mall and six blocks from the center of downtown. Restaurant, bar. In-room data ports. Cable TV. Indoor pool. Hot tub. Exercise equipment. Business services. | 123 W. Louisiana St. | 317/631–2221 | fax 317/236–7474 | www.basshotels.com/crowneplaza | 276 rooms, 28 suites | $99–$169, $179–$249 suites | AE, D, DC, MC, V.

Dewolf-Allerdice House. Restored inside and out, this Italianate home is in the Old Northside district. The second floor serves as the guest wing and the entire third floor is a single suite. The parlor is equipped with a computer with Internet access, a printer, and a fax machine. Rates include a full breakfast on weekends. Complimentary Continental breakfast. TV in common area. Library. Business services. | 1224 Park Ave. | 317/822–4299 | innkeeper@dewolf-allerdicehouse.com | www.dewolf-allerdicehouse.com | 3 rooms, 1 suite | $85–$125 | AE, D MC, V.

Doubletree Guest Suites–Indianapolis and Carmel. This all-suites chain hostelry is in a quiet area on the suburban north side of town 1 mi north of I–465, exit 31 (Meridian), at the intersection of 116th and Meridian Streets. It's 17 mi from downtown and 18 mi from the airport. All units have sleeper sofas. Restaurant, bar, room service. Microwaves, refrigerators. Cable TV. Indoor-outdoor pool. Hot tub. Exercise equipment. Business services. | 11355 N. Meridian St., Carmel | 317/844–7994 | fax 317/844–2118 | www.doubletree.com | 137 suites | $99–$139 | AE, D, DC, MC, V.

Fairfield by Marriott. This three-story motel wrapped around a courtyard is in Castleton, off I–69, exit 1 (82nd St./Castleton). Complimentary Continental breakfast. In-room data ports. Cable TV. Pool. Business services. | 8325 Bash Rd., Castleton | 317/577–0455 | fax 317/577–0455 | www.fairfieldinn.com | 132 rooms | $69 | AE, D, DC, MC, V.

Hampton Inn Indianapolis–Northwest. This four-story chain is off the highway in Park 100, one of the state's largest corporate/industrial areas, ½ mi from I-465, exit 21 (71st St.), and 3 mi from I-65, exit 124 (71st St.). Complimentary Continental breakfast. In-room data ports. Cable TV. Indoor pool. Hot tub. Exercise equipment. Business services, free parking. Some pets allowed. | 7220 Woodland Dr. | 317/290–1212 | fax 317/291–1579 | www.hampton-inn.com | 124 rooms | $119 | AE, D, DC, MC, V.

Hampton Inn–East. This four-story motel is on the east side of town in an older, busy commercial strip off I-70, exit 89 (Shadeland Ave.), ½ mi west of I-465, exit 42 (Washington St.). Complimentary Continental breakfast. In-room data ports. Cable TV. Indoor pool. Hot tub. Business services. Some pets allowed. | 2311 N. Shadeland Ave. | 317/359–9900 | fax 317/359–1376 | www.hampton-inn.com | 125 rooms | $80 | AE, D, DC, MC, V.

Hampton Inn Indianapolis–Downtown Circle Centre. This nine-story hostelry is in a turn-of-the-century landmark downtown, across the street from the Circle Centre at the corner of Meridian and Maryland Streets. Take I-70, exit 79B (West St.). Restaurant, bar, complimentary Continental breakfast, room service. In-room data ports, some refrigerators, some in-room hot tubs. Cable TV. Exercise equipment. Business services, free parking. | 105 S. Meridian St. | 317/261–1200 | fax 317/261–1030 | www.hampton-inn.com | 180 rooms, 22 suites | $119, $159 suites | AE, D, DC, MC, V.

Holiday Inn–East. Car racing collectibles adorn the lobby of this motel. It's 8 mi from downtown, off I-70, exit 89 (Shadeland Ave.). Restaurant, bar, complimentary breakfast, room service. In-room data ports, cable TV. Indoor pool. Hot tub. Exercise equipment. Laundry facilities. Business services, free parking. Some pets allowed. | 6990 E. 21st St. | 317/359–5341 | fax 317/351–1666 | www.holiday-inn.com | 184 rooms | $99 | AE, D, DC, MC, V.

Holiday Inn Select–North. This older, five-story motel has a Holidome indoor recreation center. It is on the northwest side of town across from an office park, restaurants, and strip shopping centers, ½ mi from I-465, exit 27 (Michigan Rd.). Restaurant, bar, room service. In-room data ports. Cable TV. Pool. Hot tub. Putting green. Exercise equipment. Laundry facilities. Business services, free parking. | 3850 DePauw Blvd. | 317/872–9790 | fax 317/871–5608 | www.holiday-inn.com | 349 rooms | $129 | AE, D, DC, MC, V.

Homewood Suites. This three-story all-suites hostelry has apartment-style accommodations with outside entrances, bay windows, and fireplaces. Although it's tucked in the trees in a suburban residential area on the northeast side of town, there's easy access from the highway. Homewood is about 1½ mi from I-465, exit 33 (Keystone). Complimentary Continental breakfast. In-room data ports, microwaves, refrigerators. Cable TV, in-room VCRs. Pool. Hot tub. Exercise equipment. Laundry facilities. Business services, free parking. Some pets allowed (fee). | 2501 E. 86th St. | 317/253–1919 | fax 317/255–8223 | homewoodnd@gen-hotels.com | www.homewoodsuites.com | 116 suites | $124 | AE, D, DC, MC, V.

Indianapolis/KEYSTONE–Amerisuites. This six-story all-suites chain is in the same complex as Keystone at the Crossing shopping center, 1 mi from I-465, exit 33 (Keystone Ave.). Complimentary Continental breakfast. In-room data ports, microwaves, refrigerators. Cable TV, in-room VCRs (and movies). Pool. Exercise equipment. Laundry facilities. Business services, free parking. | 9104 Keystone Crossing | 317/843–0064 | fax 317/843–1851 | 126 suites | $99–$119 | AE, D, DC, MC, V.

Indianapolis Marriott. Minutes from the downtown area, this five-story chain is known for its restaurant, Durbin's, which has a railroad theme. Restaurant, bar, room service. In-room data ports. Cable TV. Indoor-outdoor pool, wading pool. Hot tub. Putting green. Exercise equipment. Laundry facilities. Business services, free parking. Some pets allowed. | 7202 E. 21st St. | 317/352–1231 | fax 317/352–9775 | www.marriott.com | 253 rooms | $111–$180 | AE, D, DC, MC, V.

La Quinta–East. This two-story motel is on the east side of town 10 mi from the Speedway and 7 mi from the RCA Dome. Complimentary Continental breakfast. In-room data ports. Cable TV. Pool. Laundry facilities. Free parking. | 7304 E. 21st St. | 317/359–1021 | fax 317/359–0578 | 122 rooms | $72 | AE, D, DC, MC, V.

Looking Glass Inn. A Classic-style mansion built in 1905, this establishment is in the Old Northside district of Indianapolis. The home is filled with Victorian and Victorian-style antiques, including queen-size sleigh beds and old Willowware plates on the walls. The Hideaway room spans the entire third floor and is 900 square ft. Complimentary breakfast. Some kitchenettes, some in-room hot tubs. Cable TV, in-room VCRs. | 1319 N. New Jersey | 317/639–9550 | fax 317/684–9536 | www.stonesoupinn.com/LGIhouse | 5 rooms, 1 suite | $105–$125, $135 suite | AE, D, MC, V.

Nestle Inn Bed & Breakfast. This three-story Victorian home was built 1896. In the Chatham Arch district, this inn has a parlor, sitting room, and lobby. The rooms are simple, with painted walls, some quilts, and lots of peace and quiet. Complimentary breakfast. In-room data ports. Cable TV, in-room VCRs. No pets. | 637 N. East St. | 310/610–5200 or 877/339–5200 | fax 317/610–5210 | btegarden@earthlink.net | www.nestleindy.com | 4 rooms, 1 suite | $95–$115, $135 suite | AE, MC, V.

Omni North. This six-story chain hotel is off I-465, exit 1 (82nd St.). The restaurant, Abruzzi's, is known for its elegant Sunday brunch, which is complete with ice sculptures. Restaurant, bar, room service. In-room data ports, some refrigerators. Cable TV. Indoor pool. Exercise equipment. Video games. Laundry facilities. | 8181 N. Shadeland Ave. | 317/849–6668 | fax 317/849–4936 | www.omnihotels.com | 215 rooms | $89–$125 | AE, D, DC, MC, V.

Renaissance Tower Historic Inn. Built in 1922, this brick tower is on the National Register of Historic Places. All guest quarters are studio suites, elegantly furnished with four-poster cherry-wood beds and bay windows. It's nine blocks from the center of downtown. In-room data ports, kitchenettes, microwaves. Cable TV. Exercise equipment. Laundry facilities. Business services, free parking. | 230 E. 9th St. | 317/261–1652 or 800/676–7786 | fax 317/262–8648 | 80 suites | $95 | AE, D, DC, MC, V.

St. Vincent Marten House Hotel and Conference Center. European and American antiques fill this well-maintained, older property on the northwest side of town next to St. Vincent's Hospital, 5 mi from I-465 via Meridian Street/U.S. 31 and 86th Street. Restaurant, bar, room service. In-room data ports, some refrigerators. Cable TV. Indoor pool. Exercise equipment. Laundry facilities. Business services, free parking. | 1801 W. 86th St. | 317/872–4111 or 800/736–5634 | fax 317/875–7162 | 176 rooms | $120 | AE, D, DC, MC, V.

Signature Indianapolis South. This modern two-story redbrick building has floor-to-ceiling windows and light color scheme. It's on the south side of town in a busy commercial and motel strip at I-65, exit 103 (Southport Rd.). Complimentary Continental breakfast. In-room data ports, microwaves, refrigerators. Cable TV. Pool. Business services, free parking. | 4402 E. Creek View Dr. | 317/784–7006 | fax 317/784–7006 | indysouth@signature-inns.com | www.signature-inns.com | 101 rooms | $78 | AE, D, DC, MC, V.

Sheraton Indianapolis Hotel & Suites. Keystone at the Crossing, a shopping area, is the site of this 12-story brown brick high-rise; it's next to the Fashion Mall, an upscale complex of shops and restaurants on the north side of town, 1 mi from I-465, exit 33 (Keystone Ave.). Extensive meeting facilities attract groups; make sure that a frat reunion is not in attendance when you visit. Restaurant, bar, room service. In-room data ports, some refrigerators. Cable TV. Indoor pool. Hot tub, sauna. Video games. Laundry service. Business services. | 8787 Keystone Crossing | 317/846–2700 | fax 317/846–6775 | www.sheraton.com | 400 rooms, 160 suites | $99–$179, $109–$209 suites | AE, D, DC, MC, V.

Speedway Bed & Breakfast. This grand white-columned inn was built in 1906 on the site of Baker's Walnut Grove. Nowadays things rev up in May, during the Indy 500. Rooms have racing themes; you can go for the 500 Room, the Nascar Room, or the Track Side Room, for instance. Some rooms have views of the garden or a pagoda on a goldfish pond. Complimentary breakfast. Some in-room hot tubs. Cable TV, room phones. Business services. | 1829

Cunningham Rd. | 317/487–6531 or 800/975–3412 | fax 317/481–1825 | speedwaybb@msn.com | www.bbonline.com/in/speedway | 5 rooms | $65–$135 | AE, MC, D, V.

Stone Soup Inn. Mission-style and Victorian antiques fill the rooms and lofts in this 1901 Colonial Revival home on the northside of Indianapolis. The color scheme of the rooms is dark and light green; some have working fireplaces or bay windows that overlook the lily pond. In the lofts, ladders connect sitting and sleeping areas. On weekends you can get hot breakfast foods as well as rolls and muffins. Complimentary Continental breakfast. Some kitchenettes, some in-room hot tubs. Cable TV, in-room VCRs. | 1304 N. Central Ave. | 317/639–9550 | fax 317/684–9536 | www.stonesoupinn.com | 4 rooms, 4 lofts | $85–$135 | AE, D, MC, V.

Tranquil Cherub Bed & Breakfast. A grand oak staircase is just inside the front door of this B&B, which opened as a bed and breakfast in 1992. Each room has either a king- or queen-size bed and antique furnishings. Perennial gardens and lily ponds dot the grounds. It's 1 mi from the Circle. Complimentary breakfast. No room phones, TV in common area. Pond. | 2164 Capital Ave. | 317/923–9036 | fax 317/923–8676 | tcherubbnb@aol.com | www.tranquilcherub.com | 4 rooms | $79–$109 | AE, D, MC, V.

MODERATE

Embassy Suites Hotel Indianapolis Downtown. Lush gardens fill the atrium of this modern, glass-walled hotel. It's downtown, connected to the Circle Centre mall via a greenery-filled skywalk. Restaurant, bar, complimentary breakfast. In-room data ports, microwaves, refrigerators. Cable TV. Indoor pool. Hot tub. Exercise equipment. Business services. | 110 W. Washington St. | 317/236–1800 | fax 317/236–1816 | www.embassysuites.com | 360 suites | $195 | AE, D, DC, MC, V.

Embassy Suites. This Mediterranean-style, all-suites chain is in the Fortune Park business district 15 mi from downtown. It has a landscaped atrium with tropical plants and waterfalls. Restaurant, bar, complimentary breakfast. In-room data ports, microwaves, refrigerators. Cable TV. Indoor pool. Hot tub, sauna. Exercise equipment. Business services. | 3912 Vincennes Blvd. | 317/872–7700 | fax 317/872–2974 | www.embassysuites.com | 221 suites | $164 | AE, D, DC, MC, V.

Omni Severin. This downtown hostelry is connected via skywalk to the Circle Centre. Furnishings are sophisticated, with antiques in the lobby, and the architectural details are classic. Rooms are also luxuriously furnished, and some have balconies. Restaurant, bar. In-room data ports, some refrigerators. Cable TV. Indoor pool. Exercise equipment. Business services. | 40 W. Jackson Pl. | 317/634–6664 | fax 317/687–3612 | www.omnihotels.com | 386 rooms, 38 suites | $175–$215, $225–$460 suites | AE, D, DC, MC, V.

The Westin Suites. Linked by skywalk to the Convention Center and RCA Dome, this 15-story chain is furnished in a contemporary style with handsome wood paneling, marble floors, and fabrics in earth tones. The hotel restaurant, Shula's Steakhouse, has a panoramic city view. Restaurant, bar, room service. In-room data ports, some minibars. Cable TV. Indoor pool. Hot tub. Exercise equipment. Business services, parking (fee). | 50 S. Capitol | 317/262–8100 | fax 317/231–3928 | www.westin.com | 573 rooms | $135–$189 | AE, D, DC, MC, V.

EXPENSIVE

★ **Canterbury.** A member of Preferred Hotels and Resorts Worldwide, this hostelry occupies a landmark structure on the National Register of Historic Places was built in 1928 of terra cotta-trimmed, brick-faced concrete; the architect was Bennett Kay, and it cost nearly $650,000 to construct and furnish, with its tile baths and a "radio receiving set" in every room. Rooms are small but elegantly furnished with wingback chairs and dark wood furniture. This lodging is downtown across from the Circle Centre mall. Restaurant, complimentary Continental breakfast. In-room data ports, minibars. Cable TV. Business services. | 123 S. Illinois St. | 317/634–3000 or 800/538–8186 | fax 317/685–2519 | www.canterburyhotel.com | 74 rooms, 25 suites | $240–$270, $360–$1550 suites | AE, D, DC, MC, V.

Hyatt Regency. This 20-story structure was one of the buildings that inspired Indy's down-town renaissance. Guest rooms open onto corridors that line a soaring 20-story atrium, which is filled with potted plants, shops, several restaurants, and a health club. The hotel is linked by skywalk to the Convention Center, RCA Dome, and Circle Centre and is 8 mi from the Indianapolis Airport and 6 mi from the Speedway. 2 restaurants, bar. In-room data ports. Cable TV. Indoor pool. Beauty salon, massage. Exercise equipment. Business services, parking (fee). | One S. Capitol St. | 317/632–1234 | fax 317/616–6079 | www.hyatt.com | 500 rooms | $85–$500 | AE, D, DC, MC, V.

University Place Conference Center and Hotel. On the campus of Indiana University–Purdue University at Indianapolis, this 30,000-square-ft complex includes a hotel, conference facilities, a food court, restaurants, and bars. Rooms have views of the university campus, the hotel courtyard, or downtown Indianapolis. Skywalks connect it to the campus and it's 1/4 mi from downtown. Restaurant, bar. In-room data ports, refrigerators. Cable TV. Business services. | 850 W. Michigan St. | 317/269–9000 or 800/627–2700 | fax 317/231–5168 | www.doubletree.com | 264 rooms, 16 suites | $169, $299–$399 suites | AE, D, DC, MC, V.

JASPER

(Nearby towns also listed: Corydon, Evansville, French Lick, Santa Claus, Terre Haute, Vincennes)

Although the town was founded in 1833, it wasn't until the bishop of Vincennes enlisted a priest from Europe who could minister to Jasper that the town attracted immigrant families from western Europe, primarily Germany. Many of the 100 immigrant families were from the Black Forest and were masters of woodworking; they knew how to make use of the thick stands of white oak and tulip poplar that dotted the landscape of this part of south central Indiana. Today, the furniture-making industry thrives. Several furniture companies are based here, and and the headquarters of Kimball International, Inc., a piano manufacturer, is here. The social life and culture of Jasper are steeped in German traditions.

Information: Dubois County Tourism Commission | 610 Main St., 47547 | 812/482–9115 or 800/968–4578 | www.duboiscounty.com.

Attractions

Dubois County Courthouse. This structure was built in the Renaissance Revival style in 1911 incorporating 50,000 bricks from the county's original courthouse. A collection of local artifacts is on display in the lobby. | One Courthouse Sq. | 812/481–7000 | Free | Weekdays 8–4.

Holy Family Church. This modern landmark contains the nation's second-largest stained-glass window, along with another window depicting *The Jasper Story.* | 950 Church Ave. | 812/482–3076 | Free | Sun.–Fri. 6 AM–8:30 PM, Sat. 6 AM–5:30 PM.

Jasper Historical Walking Tour. Jasper's German heritage and 150-year history are highlighted on a 2-mi walking tour that takes in about 20 downtown structures, from the only maypole in Indiana, to St. Joseph Church and the courthouse. Maps are available at the Chamber of Commerce. | 302 W. 6th St. | 812/482–6866 | www.duboiscounty.org/Walking.htm | Free | Chamber of commerce open weekdays 10–4:30.

Monastery of the Immaculate Conception. Known as the Castle on the Hill for its distinctive buildings, this 190-acre monastery was founded in 1867 and is home to one of the nation's largest communities of Benedictine women. Guided tours take you through the majestic domed church, the outdoor Stations of the Cross, the Lourdes Grotto, the Rosary Steps, and the Marian Heights Academy. | 802 E. 10th St., Ferdinand | 812/367–1411 | www.thedome.org | Free | Tues.–Sat. 10–4:30, Sun. 12:30–4; Tours Tues.–Fri. 10, 11, 1, 2, 3, weekends 1, 2, 3.

St. Joseph Church. The 1880 Romanesque church, in downtown Jasper, has magnificent German stained-glass windows, Austrian mosaics with 25 million stones, and pewter and marble statues. | 13th St. | 812/482–1805 | Free | Daily 8 AM–9 PM.

St. Meinrad Archabbey. Founded in 1854 by monks from Switzerland, this spiritual enclave is home to 135 Benedictine monks. Guided tours are available part of the year; you can walk around on your own all year, with self-guided tour brochures available at the Guest House office. The abbey is 55 mi east of Evansville near I–64, exit 63 (Ferdinand Santa Claus). | Rte. 62, St. Meinrad | 812/357–6585 | www.saintmeinrad.edu | Free | 9–4:30; guided tours Mar.–Nov., Sat. 1:30.

ON THE CALENDAR
AUG.: *Strassenfest*. This downtown weekend celebration of the town's German heritage, which takes place every year on the first full weekend of Aug., showcases polka and band music, German foods and a beer garden, amusement rides, games, arts and crafts, and athletic contests. | 812/482–6866.

Dining
Heichelbech's Restaurant. German. One block east of the public library is this institution known for its caraway meatballs and Jaegerschnitzel. If you aren't in the mood for German food, try the juicy steaks. | 222 E. 12th St. | 812/482–4050 | Closed Sun. | $10–$15 | AE, MC, V.

The Millhouse Restaurant. American. This family-owned eatery cooks up dishes such as bourbon-glazed salmon, ribs, and prime rib. The pizzas are homemade, from dough to sauce. The walls are sponge-painted in shades of eggplant and terra cotta, and the ceiling is mahogany. | 1340 Mill St. | 812/482–4345 | $8–$14 | D, DC, MC, V.

Schnitzelbank. German. Frequented by tourists and locals alike, and known for its Wunderbar, a lunch buffet salad bar full of marinated vegetables, turnip kraut, and homemade bread, this eatery also presents such hearty fare as beef rouladen, sauerbraten, and hickory-smoked pork chops along with red cabbage and potato pancakes. Colorful paintings of German folk and foods line the walls, with German phrases scripted under each image. | 393 3rd Ave. | 812/482–2640 | Breakfast also available. Closed Sun. | $8–$22 | D, MC, V.

Lodging
Best Western Dutchman Inn. This two-story motel is in a quiet rural area on the outskirts of town off U.S. 231. The rooms open onto a shady garden area with picnic tables, and the restaurant serves country-style fare. Restaurant, bar, picnic area. Cable TV. Pool, wading pool. Business services, free parking. | 406 E. 22nd St., Huntingburg | 812/683–2334 | fax 812/683–8474 | www.bestwestern.com | 94 rooms | $60–$100 | AE, D, DC, MC, V.

Jasper–Days Inn. This two-story motel is at the intersection of two main highways, Routes 162 and 164. Golf packages are available at a golf course ½ mi away. Complimentary Continental breakfast. Some refrigerators. Cable TV. Pool. Laundry facilities. Business services, free parking. Some pets allowed (fee). | 272 Brucke Strasse Rd. | 812/482–6000 | fax 812/482–7207 | www.daysinn.com | 84 rooms | $58–$77 | AE, D, DC, MC, V.

Holiday Inn Holidome. The stone and wood facade of this older motel has a German motif. It is in a rural area, on the outskirts of town, and has an indoor recreation center. Restaurant, bar, room service. In-room data ports. Cable TV. Indoor pool, wading pool. Hot tub. Exercise equipment. Video games. Laundry facilities. Business services. | 951 Wernsing Rd. | 812/482–5555 | fax 812/482–7908 | www.holiday-inn.com | 200 rooms | $79–$99 | AE, D, DC, MC, V.

KODAK'S TIPS FOR TAKING GREAT PICTURES

Get Closer
- Fill the frame tightly for maximum impact
- Move closer physically or use a long lens
- Continually check the viewfinder for wasted space

Choosing a Format
- Add variety by mixing horizontal and vertical shots
- Choose the format that gives the subject greatest drama

The Rule of Thirds
- Mentally divide the frame into vertical and horizontal thirds
- Place important subjects at thirds' intersections
- Use thirds' divisions to place the horizon

Lines
- Take time to notice lines
- Let lines lead the eye to a main subject
- Use the shape of lines to establish mood

Taking Pictures Through Frames
- Use foreground frames to draw attention to a subject
- Look for frames that complement the subject
- Expose for the subject, and let the frame go dark

Patterns
- Find patterns in repeated shapes, colors, and lines
- Try close-ups or overviews
- Isolate patterns for maximum impact (use a telephoto lens)

Textures that Touch the Eyes
- Exploit the tangible qualities of subjects
- Use oblique lighting to heighten surface textures
- Compare a variety of textures within a shot

Dramatic Angles
- Try dramatic angles to make ordinary subjects exciting
- Use high angles to help organize chaos and uncover patterns, and low angles to exaggerate height

Silhouettes
- Silhouette bold shapes against bright backgrounds
- Meter and expose for the background illumination
- Don't let conflicting shapes converge

Abstract Composition
- Don't restrict yourself to realistic renderings
- Look for ideas in reflections, shapes, and colors
- Keep designs simple

Establishing Size
- Include objects of known size
- Use people for scale, where possible
- Experiment with false or misleading scale

Color
- Accentuate mood through color
- Highlight subjects or create designs through color contrasts
- Study the effects of weather and lighting

From *Kodak Guide to Shooting Great Travel Pictures* © 2000 by Fodor's Travel Publications

Jasper Sleep Inn. This three-story chain is 5 mi from the courthouse in the center of town off U.S. 231. The outdoor pool has a sundeck. Complimentary Continental breakfast. In-room data ports, some refrigerators. Outdoor pool. | 75 Indiana St. | 812/481–2008 | fax 812/634–2338 | www.sleepinn.com | 56 rooms | $64–$75 | AE, D, DC, MC, V.

Powers Inn Bed & Breakfast. On the side and out back, gardens border this cozy, three-story Second Empire house built in the 1880s, downtown. It is furnished with antiques and reproductions; in some bathrooms, sinks have been built into antique dressers. The special house breakfasts include German apple pancakes and French toast stuffed with orange marmalade and cream cheese. Complimentary breakfast. No room phones, TV in common area. | 325 W. 6th St. | 812/482–3018 | 3 rooms | $55–$60 | MC, V.

JEFFERSONVILLE

MAP 3, E8

(Nearby towns also listed: Clarksville, Corydon, Madison, New Albany; Louisville, KY)

President Thomas Jefferson suggested the novel grid layout of one of the state's oldest cities, Jeffersonville, in 1802. The original scheme called for a checkerboard design, with alternating undeveloped lots acting as open-air, green-space buffers. Jefferson reasoned that congested built-up areas created hot conditions conducive to yellow fever. The design was abandoned in 1817 with the onset of a land rush. Jeffersonville later blossomed as a boat-building center. Steamboats such as the *Glendy Burke,* the *Robert E. Lee II,* and the *Mark Twain,* considered some of the finest vessels ever built, dominated the Ohio River for almost a century. Downtown, by the riverfront in the historic commercial district, the city is preserving its diverse collection of late 19th-century buildings. Many of the structures are occupied by decades-old companies such as Schimpff's Confectionery, a century-old candy maker and soda fountain in a post–Civil War brick and tile storefront with a tin ceiling. Manufacturing and commerce support the local economy today.

Information: **Southern Indiana, Clark and Floyd Counties Convention and Tourism Bureau** | 315 Southern Indiana Ave., 47130 | 812/280–5566 or 800/552–3842 | www.sunnyside-oflouisville.org.

Attractions

Howard Steamboat Museum. Models of steamboats and displays of artifacts and tools used to build the craft tell the history of the Howard Shipyards, Jeffersonville's premier boat builder from 1834 to 1941. The museum is in the 1890 mansion of the company's owner, Edmonds J. Howard, and some furnishings are original to the Howard family. Guided tours are available. | 1101 E. Market St. | 812/283–3728 | $4 | Tues.–Sat. 10–4, Sun. 1–4.

Schimpff's Confectionery. Schimpff's is known for horehound drops, cinnamon redhots, and Modjeskas, a caramel-dipped marshmallow confection named for the famous Polish-born actress, Madame Helen Modjeska, who performed in the area in 1883. The candy maker has been making confections since the 1880s and occupies a storefront in the historic downtown district with a tin ceiling, soda fountain, and candy counter. | 347 Spring St. | 812/923–5255 | Free | Weekdays 10–5, Sat. 10–3.

ON THE CALENDAR

MAY: *Victorian Chautauqua–Spring Arts and Crafts Festival.* The Howard Steamboat Museum hosts fine arts and crafts, an herb and perennial flower sale, musical entertainment, a Victorian café, and tours of the Howard Mansion with door prizes. | 812/283–3728.

SEPT.: *Steamboat Days Festival*. Musical entertainment, food booths, arts and crafts, rides, a parade, and a kids' story hour are highlights of this free downtown festival on Spring Street. | 812/284–2628.

DEC.: *Jeffersonville Christmas Tour of Homes*. During the second weekend in December some eight to 10 residents decorate their homes for the holidays and open them to visitors. Some of the houses were built in the 1800s; others are modern. | 812/282–6407.

Dining

Inn on Spring. Eclectic. This simple establishment, on the Spring Street historic strip, has a pastoral mural of a farm and vineyard on the inside back wall. The menu changes a few times per season; long-standing favorites include the crispy duck with an orange-ginger sauce and the seafood tostada—sautéed cod, shrimp, scallops, and lobster in a spicy chili sauce, covered with melted Fontina cheese. | 415 Spring St. | 812/284–5545 | Closed Sun.–Mon. No lunch Sat. | $20–$23 | AE, MC, V.

Rocky's Italian Grill. Italian. Good views of downtown Louisville and the Second Street bridge can be enjoyed from this brightly colored restaurant decked with Italian flags. The chicken with pesto dressing, tomatoes, and artichoke hearts is a house special, as is the whole-wheat pizza. Or you can try the seafood pasta, lasagna, or spinach manicotti. Kids' menu. | 715 W. Riverside Dr. | 812/282–3844 | $5–$15 | AE, D, DC, MC, V.

Lodging

Best Western Greentree Inn. This suburban property, with a curved drive-through entrance and appealing gardens in front, is 4 mi from downtown Louisville at I-65, exit 4 (Clarksville). Malls and restaurants are within ½ mi, and a health club is next door. All rooms are on the ground floor. In-room data ports. Cable TV. Pool. Business services. Some pets allowed. | 1425 Broadway St., Clarksville | 812/288–9281 | fax 812/288–9281 | www.bestwestern.com | 107 rooms | $69 | AE, D, DC, MC, V.

1877 House Country Inn. This two-story white farmhouse with dark green shutters is on 2½ acres set 6 mi from Louisville, Kentucky. Each room has a fireplace, painted hardwood floors, and either two double beds or one queen. The cottage is a three-room stone building with a tin roof that can sleep up to six. Complimentary breakfast. Some microwaves, some refrigerators. Cable TV, in-room VCRs, some room phones. | 2408 Utica-Sellersburg Rd. | 812/284–1877 | fax 812/284–1877 | 4 rooms | $75–$125 | AE, D, MC.

Holiday Inn Lakeview. A water park and a 12-acre fishing lake are on the grounds of this brick high-rise motel 1 mi from the river and 2 mi from downtown Louisville, next to the Derby Dinner Playhouse, a dinner theater. Restaurant, bar with entertainment, picnic area. Some refrigerators. Cable TV. 2 pools (1 indoor). Beauty salon. Miniature golf, tennis. Exercise equipment. Playground. Laundry facilities. Business services, airport shuttle. | 505 Marriott Dr., Clarksville | 812/283–4411 | fax 812/288–8976 | www.holiday-inn.com | 356 rooms, 13 suites | $89, $120 suites | AE, D, DC, MC, V.

Old Bridge Inn. This gray and black Georgian Colonial home, built in 1840, is two blocks from the Ohio River. Rooms have themes; the Nautical Suite displays the innkeeper's ship clock collection and has 1930s Art Deco waterfall furniture—made of wood with striped veneer that recalls a waterfall. The bathrooms are private but outside the rooms, and the inn provides robes for the jaunt. Complimentary breakfast. No room phones. Business services. | 131 W. Chestnut St. | 812/284–3580 | fax 812/284–3561 | innbridge@aol.com | www.bbon-line.con/in/oldbridge | 3 rooms | $65–$115 | AE, D, MC, V.

Ramada Inn–Riverside. The 10-story hostelry on the west side of town is along the Ohio River with a view of the Louisville skyline. It is 1½ mi from the Howard Steamboat Museum. Bar. Cable TV. Pool. Video games. Business services, airport shuttle. Some pets allowed. | 700 W. Riverside Dr. | 812/284–6711 or 800/537–3612 | fax 812/283–3686 | RamadaRVR@aol.com | 186 rooms, 20 suites | $65–$105, $145 suites | AE, D, DC, MC, V.

KOKOMO

(Nearby towns also listed: Indianapolis, Lafayette, Marion, Peru)

Known as the "City of Firsts," Kokomo claims more than a dozen significant electronic, metallurgical, automotive-related, and even culinary inventions. Among the firsts in this revitalized industrial town 40 mi north of Indianapolis were canned tomato juice, the mechanical corn picker, all-transistor radios, and the first car, which was invented by Elwood Haynes in 1894 on Pumpkinvine Pike on the edge of town. Haynes also invented stainless steel at the urging of his wife, who had expressed a desire for tarnish-free tableware. Signal seeking and push-button devices on car radios started out at the town's Delco Radio, now Delphi Electronics. Many of these inventions were spurred during a business boom that started in 1886, when it was discovered that the town is in the middle of a natural-gas belt that runs through north-central and northeastern Indiana. At the height of the gas boom, nearly 100 glass factories were crafting canning jars, goblets, and fancy decorative glass. When the supply of gas ran out almost all of the factories shut down. The only one to operate continuously since 1888 is Kokomo Opalescent Glass, which turns out sheets of colored and patterned glass for windows and lamp shades. Kokomo suffered in the 1980s, when much of the Midwest experienced a slump in the automotive industry. Chrysler and Delco have been two of the county's top employers for decades, employing more than 20,000 people, almost half of the town's population. Fortunately, Kokomo rebounded quickly and today's economy is surprisingly healthy. The courthouse square downtown has been revitalized and unusual stores and one-of-a-kind restaurants and cafés have set up shop behind the old facades. A few blocks south of the square is the Main Street antiques district.

Information: Kokomo/Howard County Visitors Bureau | 1504 N. Reed Rd., 46901 | 765/457–6802 or 800/837–0971 | kokomoin@iquest.net | www.iquest.net/kokomoin.

Attractions

City of Firsts Automotive Heritage Museum. The Pioneer Auto Club, a group of automotive enthusiasts and collectors in Kokomo, originated the idea of a museum that would showcase Kokomo's automotive heritage. The museum was opened in 1998, and today it displays dozens of classic and rare automobiles, many manufactured in Kokomo or connected to the town in other ways. There is a pedal-car exhibit and rows of antique and vintage cars, including Elwood Haynes's 1918 Pike's Peak car and the Jack Rabbit model of the Apperson, made from 1907 to 1926. Mixed in are exhibits such as a 1950s diner, a replica of the facade from one of Elwood Haynes's homes, and the Riverside Machine Shop, a replica of the bicycle and buggy shop where Elmer and Edgar Apperson built "America's first car" for inventor Elwood Haynes. | 1500 N. Reed Rd. | 765/454–9999 or 800/837–0971 | fax 765/454–9956 | www.kokomo.org | $5 | Daily 10–5.

Elwood Haynes Museum. Kokomo inventor Elwood Haynes, who specialized in metallurgy and machinery, invented the first automobile as well as stainless steel and alloys such as Stellite, which NASA still uses today. Haynes's stately brick home at the edge of Highland Park is now a museum where two floors of displays trace Haynes's inventions, document central Indiana's automotive and industrial heritage, and exhibit mementos and personal belongings of the Haynes family. Several Haynes autos are behind glass in the garage. | 1915 S. Webster St. | 317/456–7500 | Free | Tues.–Sat. 1–4, Sun. 1–5, and by appointment.

Haynes Memorial. A plaque marks the corner of Goyer and Pumpkinvine Pike, east of Hwy. 31, where inventor Elwood Haynes made the initial road test of his first automobile on July 4, 1894. | 765/457–6892 or 800/837–0971 | www.iquest.net/kokomoin | Free | Daily.

Greentown Glass Museum. During the region's natural gas boom, many glass factories were established, among them one in Greentown, by Kokomo. The Indiana Tumbler and

Goblet Company produced its distinctive styles and opaque-colored glass from 1894 to 1903. A fire put an end to the company, and for years other glassmakers were unable to reproduce the swirled color combinations unique to Greentown glass. The glassware is popular with collectors, and the story of the factory and its famous glass is now traced at a museum in the center of this quiet farming community. Holly amber and chocolate glass, two of the most popular of Greentown glass styles and colors, are a part of the museum's huge collection. | 112 N. Meridian, Greentown | 765/628–6206 | web.iquest.net/kokomoin | Free.

Kokomo Fine Arts Center. A handsome brown cottage shaded by tall trees, on the edge of Highland Park, is now home to galleries where artists and other dedicated volunteers mount exhibits of paintings, decoratively painted china, drawings, sculpture, and other works by local artists. Some of this is from the permanent collection. | 525 W. Richetts St. | 765/457–9480 | web.iquest.net/kokomoin | Free | Feb.–Dec., Tues.–Fri. 1–5.

Kokomo Parks and Recreation Department. The parks department operates more than 400 acres of parks in the city and 1,025 acres in the county. It showcases points of historical interest and maintains areas for outdoor recreation. | 1402 W. Deffenbaugh St. | 765/456–7275 | fax 765/456–7277 | web.iquest.net/kokomoin | Free | Daily.

The 80-acre **Highland Park** is a favorite in the parks system. It's in the middle of town and is the home of "Old Ben," a huge stuffed steer, and an equally impressive sycamore stump (both housed behind glass in a shelter). Old Ben, on display since 1918, was one of the largest steers ever known, weighing in at 4,720 pounds. The shady park attracts picnickers, and there are tennis courts, horseshoe courts, basketball courts, and baseball diamonds. A red covered bridge crosses Kokomo Creek, which meanders through the preserve. If you come on a Wednesday evening in summer, you can catch a band concert. | 900 W. Deffenbaugh St. | 765/452–0063 or 800/837–0971 | fax 765/456–7277 | web.iquest.net/kokomoin | Free | Daily, dawn–10 PM; concerts June–Aug., Wed. at 8 PM.

Howard County Historical Museum/Seiberling Mansion. The impressive stone-and-brick Seiberling Mansion, an intricately detailed 1891 Romanesque Revival structure, is one of Indiana's finest examples of late Victorian architecture, with its carved woodwork, brass hardware with a Moorish motif, and Art Nouveau stained-glass windows. Artifacts and artwork important to county history are on display. The Carriage House Museum next door houses antique cars. In April, the thousands of daffodils around the house are resplendent. | 1200 W. Sycamore St. | 765/452–4314 | $2 | Feb.–Dec., Tues.–Sun. 1–4.

Kokomo Opalescent Glass Factory. Victorian-era glass artist Louis Comfort Tiffany is said to have used glass from this factory for his windows and lamp shades. It is the only Indiana glass factory that has operated continuously since the local gas boom and still produces sheets of glass for churches, cathedrals, and other customers from around the world, using original formulas for colors and patterns dating from its founding in 1888. Tours give a fascinating glimpse into the glassmaking process. | 1310 S. Market St. | 765/457–1829 | www.kog.com | Free | Oct.–Apr., Mon.–Sat. 9–5; May–Sept., Mon.–Sat. 9–5, Sun. 9–1; tours Wed., Fri. at 10 (no open-toed shoes).

ON THE CALENDAR

JUNE: *Greentown Glass Festival.* Nearby Greentown celebrates its glassmaking heritage on the second weekend in June, with a festival and tours of the glass museum, a carnival, musical entertainment, arts and crafts, and a parade on Saturday. | 765/628–7953.

JULY: *Haynes Apperson Festival.* At the heart of this Fourth of July weekend festival is an antique car show, in honor of the Haynes and the Apperson, early vehicles with their roots in Kokomo. Other activities include an amateur sports tournament, live entertainment, kids' rides, a parade, a fireworks display, and food galore, all in the downtown main square. | 765/457–6802 or 800/837–0971.

DEC.: *Victorian Christmas.* The Seiberling Mansion, which is on the National Register of Historic Places, is elegantly decorated for the season and hosts special events, including wine tasting, horse-drawn carriage rides, musical entertainment, and a visit from Santa. | 765/452–4314.

Dining

Country Cook Inn. American. South-facing windows warm this passive-heated building, built into the ground. Dinner is prix fixe and includes your choice of roast beef, baked cod, or other meat, plus a vegetable, potato, homemade dinner roll, and dessert. | 10531 E. 180 S, Greentown | 765/628–7676 | Dinner reservations essential | Closed Sun.–Mon. No lunch Sat. | $11 | AE, MC, V.

Grindstone Charley's Restaurant. Eclectic. This festive, peppy spot is a good place to go with a bunch of friends who can't agree on anything. Chimichangas and rib eyes vie for attention with stir-fry, chicken and dumplings, Italian sandwiches, and pulled pork. | 3830 S. LaFountain St. | 765/453–9125 | $10–$17 | AE, MC, V.

Laughner's Cafeteria. American. Savory home-style fare such as meatloaf, ham steak, and fried chicken, along with fresh-baked pies, are served cafeteria style. | 1919 S. Reed Rd. | 765/452–1247 | $5–$9 | AE, D, DC, MC, V.

Sycamore Grille. Steak. Brass instruments hang on one wall of the main dining room of this restaurant in a turn-of-the-century building, with the original tin ceilings. The main draws are steaks and seafood, or try the the marinated Portobello mushroom sandwich. | 113 W. Sycamore St. | 765/457–2220 | Closed Sun. No lunch Sat. | $10–$20 | AE, D, DC, MC, V.

Lodging

Bavarian Inn. A white-gated entrance leads into this two-story re-creation of a German house on 9 wooded acres on the southwest side of Kokomo. All rooms have fireplaces, recliners, and either a queen- or king-size bed. Breakfast may include German potato pancakes, apple strudel, or homemade German rye bread. Complimentary breakfast. Kitchenettes, in-room hot tubs. Cable TV, in-room VCRs. | 4697 S. Dixon Rd. | 765/453–4715 | www.bavarianinn.thehideaway.com | 7 rooms | $85 | AE, MC, V.

Clarion Hotel. Rooms at this hostelry off U.S. 31 at Lincoln Road come in various configurations, including regular rooms, Jacuzzi suites, king suites, and executive suites. 1 bar, complimentary breakfast, room service. Some refrigerators. Cable TV. In-room VCRs. Indoor pool. Hot tub. Health club. Laundry facilities, laundry service. | 1709 Lincoln Rd. | 765/459–8001 | fax 765/457–6636 | ramadakoni@aol.com | 100 rooms, 32 suites | $59–$89, $99–$169 suites | AE, D, DC, MC, V.

Fairfield Inn by Marriott. This three-story motel is in a commercial area on the south side of the city, off U.S. 31, 45 mi from downtown. Complimentary Continental breakfast. In-room data ports, some microwaves, some refrigerators. Cable TV. Indoor pool. Hot tub. Business services. | 1717 E. Lincoln Rd. | 765/453–8822 | fax 765/453–8822 | www.fairfieldinn.com | 61 rooms, 20 suites | $65–$72, $80 suites | AE, D, DC, MC, V.

Holiday Inn Express and Suites. This three-story hostelry is on the south side of Kokomo off U.S. 31. Complimentary Continental breakfast. In-room data ports, microwaves, refrigerators, some in-room hot tubs. Cable TV. Indoor pool. Exercise equipment. Laundry facilities. Business services. | 511 Albany Dr. | 765/453–2222 | fax 765/453–4398 | www.holiday-inn.com | 69 rooms, 20 suites | $84, $110–$165 suites | AE, D, DC, MC, V.

Motel 6. This two-story motel is off U.S. 31 on the south side of town. Restaurant. Cable TV. Laundry facilities. | 2808 S. Reed Rd. | 765/457–8211 | fax 765/454–9774 | 93 rooms | $46 | AE, D, DC, MC, V.

Signature Inn. This two-story redbrick motel is in a commercial area 1 mi south of downtown near U.S. 31 and Alto Road. Complimentary Continental breakfast. Indoor pool. Hot tub. Exercise equipment. | 4021 S. LaFountain | 765/455–1000 | fax 765/455–1000 | www.signatureinn.com | 101 rooms | $67 | AE, D, DC, MC, V.

LAFAYETTE

(Nearby towns also listed: Crawfordsville, Kokomo)

Lafayette and its sister city, West Lafayette, straddle the Wabash River. Lafayette is the county seat of Tippecanoe County and has a population of 44,000. However, West Lafayette, although half the size, is the more prominent of the two, since it is home to Purdue University. Named after the French military officer and hero of the American Revolution, Marquis de Lafayette, the town thrived as a shipping center with as many as 15 boats a day docking along the Wabash River and Wabash-Erie Canal in the mid-1800s. It was here in 1811 that William Henry Harrison defeated the Shawnee during the Battle of Tippecanoe. In the early days, Lafayette was the subject of ridicule by Crawfordsville residents who pronounced the name "laugh-at" or "lay flat." The low hills that border the Wabash soon flatten out and stretch into expanses of rich farmland just beyond the twin cities. Today, the Lafayette area is a food processing center and home to several large automotive and machinery manufacturing companies.

Information: Greater Lafayette Convention and Visitors Bureau | 301 Frontage Rd., 47905 | 800/872–6648 | lcvb@pop.nlci.com | www.lafayette-in.com.

Attractions

Columbian Park. An amusement center with rides, a small zoo, an extensive playground, and picnic areas are on the grounds of this 67-acre wooded park. One of the largest outdoor swimming pools in the state is here, with a 65-ft slide. | 1915 Scott St. | 765/771–2220 | Free | Daily.

Columbian Park Zoo. Though small, the collection of animals in this zoo is impressive, with a snow leopard, lemurs, and a walk-through aviary. Most exhibits are outdoors. | 1915 Scott St. | 765/771–2220 | Free | Memorial Day–Labor Day, daily 11–8, Labor Day–Memorial Day, daily 11:30–4:30.

Fort Ouiatenon. Fort Ouiatenon is where the French, in 1717, established the first permanent European outpost in Indiana. The post was across the Wabash River from a Wea Indian Village. A small, square log blockhouse replicating a portion of the original stockade was constructed in the 1930s and houses a museum. | 2979 S. River Rd. | 765/476–8411 | www.tcha.mus.in.us/sites.htm | Free | Mid-Apr.–Oct., Tues.–Sun. noon–5.

Greater Lafayette Museum of Art. This low modern building displays 19th- and 20th-century American paintings, drawings, and sculptures. Three galleries display works by regional artists and craftspeople. | 101 S. 9th St. | 765/742–1128 | www.dcwi.com/~glma/ | Free | Tues.–Sun. 11–4.

Imagination Station. Hands-on science, engineering, and technology exhibits fill this museum designed to appeal to all ages. | 600 N. 4th St. | 765/420–7780 | www.nlci.com/imagination/ | $3 | Mon.–Sat. 1–5.

Jerry E. Clegg Botanical Gardens. One-and-one-half miles of trails in this 20-acre park take you along a bank high above Wildcat Creek where you can see natural woodland gardens full of wildflowers. | 1782 N. 400 E | 765/483–0303 | Free | Daily 10–6.

Purdue University. Founded in 1869 as a land-grant college, this perennial NCAA basketball championship contender is known for its agriculture, engineering, veterinary, and aerospace programs, and turns out more astronauts than any other university in the world. The campus spreads across many parklike acres dotted with more than 100 redbrick Tudor- and Colonial-style buildings. Purdue enrolls 36,000 students. Campus maps outlining self-guided tours are available at the Memorial Union, which contains an art gallery, several restaurants, a hotel, and a theater. | 1080 Schleman Hall, West Lafayette | 765/494–1776 | admissions@purdue.edu | www.cs.purdue.edu/about_purdue.html | Free | Daily.

Tippecanoe Battlefield Museum and Park. A slender stone obelisk marks the site of the Battle of Tippecanoe. Here, on November 7, 1811, William Henry Harrison defeated forces led by the Prophet, the brother of the Shawnee chief, Tecumseh. The settlers' victory opened what is now Indiana to settlement. Harrison went on to become President, although he died after a month in office. The museum, 7 mi north of Lafayette off I–65, exit 178 (State Rd. 43), tells the story of the battle from both sides. | Prophet Rock Rd. | 765/567–2147 | www.tcha.mus.in.us/battlefield.htm | $3 | March–Nov., daily 10–5, Dec.–Feb., daily 10–4.

Tippecanoe County Historical Association. The Fowler House displays pioneer tools, artifacts relating to 19th-century manufacturing, and period room settings. It also houses a library. | 909 South St. | 765/476–8411 | www.tcha.mus.in.us/fowler.htm | Free | Wed.–Sun. 1–5.

Wolf Park. Wolf packs and bison inhabit this 75-acre research and wildlife preserve. Every Friday night is a Howlnight, when the park stays open into the evening for those who want to howl with the wolves. | Battle Ground | 765/567–2265 | www.wolfpark.org | $4 | May–Dec. 1, Tues.–Sun., 1–5; Fri. 7:30 PM for Howlnight.

ON THE CALENDAR

JUNE: *Fiddlers' Gathering* Fiddlers from around the world gather at this annual event showcasing traditional fiddle and bluegrass music, food, and crafts at the Tippecanoe Battlefield. | 765/742–1419.

JUNE: *Taste of Tippecanoe.* A variety of performers and food vendors come to six stages and 30 food booths on Reihle Plaza (at the end of Main Street) the third Saturday of the month. | 765/423–2787.

OCT.: *Feast of the Hunters' Moon.* An 18th-century fur trading post is re-created to celebrate the days that Native Americans, French traders, and early settlers lived along the Wabash River south of town. Traditional crafts, food, and lifestyles are demonstrated. | 765/447–9999 or 800/872–6648.

Dining

Lafayette Brewing Co. English. With more than 13 beers on tap and Scotch eggs and shepherd's pie on the menu, this pub brings a little bit of England to Hoosierland. Brews made on premises include East Side Bitter, Black Angus Oatmeal Stout, and Big Boris Barleywine. | 662 Main St. | 765/742–2591 | $5–$13 | D, MC, V.

Maize, an American Grill. Contemporary. Off the corner of State Street and Third, this classy 1940s-style restaurant with white tablecloths has an ambitious menu. Try the jumbo ravioli or veal liver cooked in an applejack brandy and served with mashed potatoes and wilted spinach. | 112 N. Third St. | 765/429–6125 | Reservations recommended | Closed Sun.–Mon. No lunch Sat. | $21–$25 | AE, D, DC, MC, V.

Sarge Oak's. Continental. One of the only restaurants in town that can trace its history to Prohibition, this eatery is reminiscent of a 1930s game parlor, with its handsome furnishings, period lighting fixtures, and early 20th-century hand-colored photographs. It's known for aged fresh-cut steaks, seafood, and tasty french fries. | 721 Main St. | 765/742–5230 | Closed Sun.–Mon. No lunch Sat. | $12–$20 | AE, D, DC, MC, V.

Sgt. Preston's of the North. American. You can feast on large slabs of steak and grilled shrimp at this college hangout on the river. A cigar menu includes some heavy hitters like the Monte Cristo and the Honduran Padron. There's live music on the deck during the summer on Monday, Friday, and Saturday. | 6 N. Second St. | 765/742–7378 | $9–$17 | AE, D, MC, V.

Lodging

Baymont Inn and Suites. On the east side of town, off I–65, exit 172, this chain hotel has a variety of accommodations and gives you complimentary passes to a local gym. Complimentary Continental breakfast. Some in-room data ports, some refrigerators, some microwaves. Indoor pool. Hot tub. Laundry facilities, laundry service. Business services. |

312 Meijer Dr. | 765/446–2400 | fax 765/446–2401 | www.budgetel.com | 71 rooms, 6 suites | $67, $77 suite | AE, D, DC, MC, V.

Commandant's Home Bed and Breakfast. On the 130-acre grounds of the former Indiana Veterans' Home, this house built in 1895 is on the National Register of Historic Places. The Federal-style structure has 10-ft ceilings, a crystal chandelier, hardwood floors, and the original marble fireplace. Period furnishings fill the home, and the back porches overlook the Wabash River. It is 6 mi to Lafayette. Complimentary breakfast. Business services. | 3848 State Rd. 43 N, West Lafayette | 765/463–5980 | fax 765/463–5982 | rooms@commhomeb-b.com | www.commhomeb-b.com | 6 rooms | $95–$125 | AE, D, MC, V.

Fairfield Inn by Marriott. This three-story motel 5 mi from downtown is in a commercial area near I–65, exit 172. You can have dinner delivered by local restaurants. Complimentary Continental breakfast. In-room data ports, some microwaves, some refrigerators. Cable TV. Indoor pool. Hot tub. Video Games. Business services. | 4000 State Rd. 26 E | 765/449–0083 or 800/228–2800 | fax 765/449–0083 | www.fairfieldinn.com | 79 rooms, 11 suites | $68–$78, $78–$88 suites | AE, D, DC, MC, V.

Hampton Inn Lafayette. This chain is 1 mi west of I–65, exit 172, on a strip with other chain hotels and restaurants. Complimentary breakfast. In-room data ports, some microwaves, some refrigerators. Indoor pool. Hot tub. Laundry service, laundry facilities. Business services. | 3941 State Rd. 26 E | 765/447–1600 | fax 765/449–9963 | 62 rooms | $82–$103 | AE, D, DC, MC, V.

Holiday Inn. This four-story brick building is one of the few motels close to the Purdue University campus. There are small gardens in front and out back. Restaurant, bar, room service. Cable TV. Indoor pool. Sauna. Video games. Laundry service. Business services. Some pets allowed. | 5600 Rte. 43 N | 765/567–2131 | fax 765/567–2511 | www.holiday-inn.com | 150 rooms | $115 | AE, D, DC, MC, V.

Homewood Suites. A three-story all-suites hostelry with traditional English country-style furnishings, this chain is on the east side of Lafayette off I–65, exit 172, across from restaurants and shopping, 7 mi from Purdue University. Complimentary Continental breakfast. In-room data ports, kitchenettes, microwaves. Cable TV, in-room VCRs (and movies). Pool. Hot tub. Exercise equipment. Laundry facilities. Business services, airport shuttle. Some pets allowed. | 3939 Rte. 26 E | 765/448–9700 | fax 765/449–1297 | www.homewoodsuites.com | 84 suites | $95–$155 | AE, D, DC, MC, V.

Loeb House Inn. You'll find this Italianate house-turned-inn a few minutes south of Wolf Park in the Centennial District. Dating from 1888, the plaster ceiling medallions, wallpaper, hand-painted tiles, and moldings are original. Two parlors are available, one for meetings and one more formal. Antique beds, parquet floors, bay windows, and claw-foot tubs add charm to the rooms. Complimentary breakfast. Some in-room hot tubs. Cable TV, room phones. Business services. | 708 Cincinnati St. | 765/420–7737 | fax 765/420–7805 | www.loebhouseinn.com | 5 rooms | $85–$175 | AE, MC, V.

Radisson Inn. A geometric, hatlike roof shades the entrance to this chain. It's off I–65, exit 172 (State Rd. 26 E), 8 mi from downtown Lafayette and 10 mi from Purdue University. Restaurant, bar with entertainment, room service. In-room data ports, refrigerators. Cable TV. Indoor pool. Hot tub, sauna. Laundry facilities. Free parking. Some pets allowed. | 4343 State Rd. 26 E | 765/447–0575 | fax 765/447–0901 | www.radisson.com/lafayettein | 124 rooms | $79–$99 | AE, D, DC, MC, V.

Signature Inn. This two-story motel is off I–65, exit 172 (State Rd. 26 E), 8 mi from downtown. Large desks and work areas add appeal for business travelers. Complimentary Continental breakfast. Cable TV. Pool. Business services. | 4320 Rte. 26 E | 765/447–4142 | fax 765/447–4142 | www.signatureinn.com | 121 rooms | $60–$83 | AE, D, DC, MC, V.

Union Club Hotel. Purdue University's Union building, on the campus, is home to this hotel. Built in the 1920s, the structure is a traditional five-story stone building that also contains restaurants, a food court, a theater, and recreation facilities (including billiards). Restau-

rant. Cable TV. Gym. Airport shuttle. | 101 N. Grant St. | 765/494–8900 | fax 765/494–8924 | www.purdue.edu | 153 rooms | $72–$98 | AE, D, MC, V.

LA PORTE

MAP 3, C1

(Nearby towns also listed: Michigan City, South Bend, Valparaiso)

In the rolling orchard country along Indiana's Lake Michigan shoreline, La Porte was settled and named by French traders and explorers in the mid-1700s. Just south of the present-day town a natural opening in the dense forest provided a gateway to the lush, rolling prairie land. La Porte was also on the Sauk Trail, which carried pioneer wagons as well as Native Americans between Michigan, Indiana, and Illinois. The gabled red sandstone county courthouse built in 1892 stands in the center of town. Victorian storefronts facing the courthouse square now house antique shops and restaurants. Throughout the county, farmers harvest bushels of berries, peaches, apples, and vegetables, and on Saturday mornings in season a downtown farmers' market sells produce. The La Porte County Fruit and Growers Association publishes a map showing roughly 30 fruit growers and pick-your-own farms.

Information: La Porte County Convention and Visitors Bureau | 1503 S. Meer Rd., 46360 | 219/872–5055 or 800/685–7174 | lpccvb@netnitco.net | www.harborcountry-in.org.

Attractions

Door Prairie Museum. An 1886 Benz Motor Wagon and a 1903 Winton, as well as modern classics like the 1968 Daimler and 1982 DeLorean, are highlights of the Kesling Vehicle Collection, which spans more than a century. The museum, 1 mi south of La Porte on U.S. 35, also presents a mock Main Street vignette with storefronts from three different eras. Lunch is available with advance reservations. The last Sunday of August is the Classics and Antique Car Show. | 2405 Indiana Ave. | 219/326–1337 | dpmuseum@csinet.net | www.dpautomuseum.com | $5 | Apr.–Dec., Tues.–Sat. 10–4:30, Sun. noon–4:30.

Hesston Steam Museum. This 155-acre property, 9 mi north of La Porte, pays homage to the steam engine: You can take 15-minute rides on three steam trains and see stationary steam engines, a steam sawmill, and a steam light plant. One of the steam engines makes cider in fall, and *Travel Agent* magazine called the annual steam festival, Hesston's Labor Day weekend Steam and Power Show, one of Indiana's top ten annual events. | 1201 E. 1000 N, Hesston | 219/872–7405 | Free. | Memorial Day–Labor Day, weekends noon–5; Labor Day–Oct. Sun. noon–5.

Kingsbury Fish and Wildlife Area. This 5,000-acre preserve is a wetland area with an abundance of waterfowl. The fishing lake is full of catfish and bass. | 5334 Hupp Rd. | 219/393–3612 | www.ai.org/dnr | Free | Daily.

La Porte County Historical Society Museum. Heirlooms from La Porte County families, antique toys and firearms, and weapons from the W. A. Jones collection, recognized as one of the finest of its kind, are all on display in this museum as part of a collection of 20,000 artifacts. The museum also exhibits paintings and historical documents. | 809 State Rd. | 219/326–6808, ext. 276 | Free | Weekdays 10–4:30, 1st Sun. of month 1–4.

ON THE CALENDAR

AUG.–SEPT.: *Steam and Power Show.* The rural steam museum stages this event every Labor Day weekend; it attracts thousands. | 219 778–2783.

Dining

Hesston Bar and Restaurant. American. Steak and potatoes are the mainstays at this restaurant, which is 10 mi east of Michigan City and 15 mi north of La Porte. One dining room is a solarium, and another has a mural of old-town Hesston. The house specialty is the prime rib, but the New Zealand grilled lamb served with homemade mint sauce is also a favorite. Homemade desserts include cheesecake, bread pudding, and French silk pie. | Fail Rd. and 1000 N | 219/778–2938 | No lunch | $9–$41 | AE, DC, MC, V.

LOGANSPORT

MAP 3, D3

(Nearby town also listed: Peru)

Originally known as Logan's Port, the town was a major shipping center due to its location at the confluence of the Wabash and Eel rivers. As one of the Midwest's busiest rail centers, Logansport continued to flourish. The former train depot now houses the Iron Horse Museum. Gracious Victorian mansions along Banker's Row in the Point Historic District were once the homes of Logansport's elite. One of the town's best-loved landmarks is the carousel in Riverside Park. Each year 42,000 people climb aboard for a spin on one of its 50 hand-carved animals.

Information: Logansport/Cass County Chamber of Commerce | 300 E. Broadway, Ste. 103, 46947 | 219/753–6388 | lcccoc@cqc.com | www.logan-casschamber.com.

Attractions

Cass County Historical Society Museum. The museum consists of the 1853 Jeroloman-Long House, a cabin, a carriage barn, and a schoolroom. Photographs, historical documents, and artifacts depict everyday life in the 1800s. | 1004 E. Market St. | 219/753–3866 | Free | Tues.–Sat. 1–5.

France Park. At the meeting of the Wabash and Eel rivers, this scenic park has a golf course, mountain biking trails, swimming, and a log cabin. The park's quarry attracts scuba divers. | 4505 West, U.S. 24W | 219/753–2928 | Free | Daily.

Indiana Beach. Fourteen hundred-acre Lake Shafer, with its sandy swimming beach and 50 mi of shoreline, is a favorite Hoosier weekend destination. There's also tennis, horseback riding, hiking, para-sailing, two lakeside championship 18-hole golf courses, and an amusement center with three roller coasters, a carousel, rides, and entertainment. Aquatic stunt shows are presented four times a day from June through August. The *Shafer Queen,* a replica double-decker paddlewheel steamer, cruises around the lake. | 5224 E. Indiana Beach Rd., Monticello | 219/583–4141 | www.indianabeach.com | $2 | May–Labor Day, daily 11–11.

Riverside Park. A carousel dating from 1892, with hand-carved animals by Gustav Dentzel, is a focal point in this downtown park. There's also a model train and a miniature golf course. | 1212 Riverside Dr. | Park 219/753–6969, complex 219/753–8725 | Free | Park open daily; complex open Memorial Day–Labor Day weekdays 6 PM–9 PM and weekends 1–9, Labor Day–early Dec. weekends 1–5.

Tippecanoe River State Park. More than 2,760 acres of parkland surround the Tippecanoe River at the northern edge of Pulaski County. The park is known for canoeing, and also has bridle and hiking trails, a boat launch, camping, and fishing. The county owns several other state recreation and wildlife areas and portions of the Grand Kankakee Marsh. | 4200 N. U.S. 35, Winamac | 219/946–3213 | www.state.in.us/dnr/statepar/parks/tippibas/tippibas | $2 per vehicle residents, $5 nonresidents.

ON THE CALENDAR

JULY: *Cass County 4H Fair.* This weeklong fair at the Cass County Fairgrounds celebrates farms and farm life. There's a dog show and 4H Queen contest as well as animal shows, karaoke contests, country and gospel entertainment, oodles of food vendors, local merchants, and a carnival in the evening. | 219/753–7750.

JULY: *Iron Horse Festival.* Train rides recall the town's railroad heritage. You can also take a ride in an open-cockpit airplane, browse an arts and crafts show, chow down at an international food fest, and cheer on a Friday night parade. | 219/722–IRON.

Dining

Happy Burger. American. Come here with a group and dare to tackle the Hap's super supreme pizza, loaded with the works. You can get chicken by the bucket—specify white-meat only or wings. | 900 W. Market St. | 219/753–4016 | $4–$15 | AE, D, DC, MC, V.

Lodging

Inntiquity. One-and-one-half miles north of Logansport, you'll find this Colonial home and former dairy barn, which was originally built in 1849. Rooms are filled with period pieces (the owners restore furniture for a hobby), and serve meals on porcelain, with sterling silver—on the terrace in nice weather. Most rooms have four-poster canopy beds, and all have access to a balcony. Complimentary breakfast. Cable TV, room phones. Business services. | 1075 State Rd. 25 N | 219/722–2398 or 877/230–7870 | fax 219/739–2217 | inntiquity@cqc.com | www.inntiquity.com | 10 rooms | $75–$110 | D, MC, V.

MADISON

MAP 3, E7

(Nearby towns also listed: Aurora, Clarksville, Jeffersonville, New Albany)

It's hard to imagine the days when the sound of paddlewheelers trumpeting their comings and goings reverberated through quiet Madison. This proud river town of 13,000 on the southeast fringes of Indiana, founded in 1809, was the envy of every river port town along the Ohio River for its ideal location on a high shelf above one of the most navigable stretches of water. By the time the New Purchase was finalized in 1818 and the Ohio River valley began to swarm with land-hungry Easterners headed west, Madison was well positioned to be the gateway to the Western frontier. Ohio River boatmen deemed the place "highly pleasant to the imagination" and "mixed with something of the romantic." Promoters advertised Madison as "beautifully situated . . . on one of the most healthy and elegant situations . . . and near the center of the most fertile country." Madison flourished as factories crowded the riverfront, with foundries, pork-packing plants, and businesses turning out starch, wagons, boats, and saddle trees (the wooden frame of a saddle). It was during these golden years that riverboat captains, industrial tycoons, and financiers made fortunes and raised monuments to their prosperity throughout the town. Soon, Madison's tree-lined boulevards presented a staggering array of 19th-century architecture from Steamboat Gothic structures to Greek Revival mansions; what is now considered one of the finest concentrations of early Federal-style buildings west of the Allegheny Mountains is here as well. There's a bit of the charm of the Old South to Madison, which makes sense since Kentucky is just across the river. Magnolias shade front lawns, and nearly every structure in town is adorned with lacy ironwork, from gates, fences, and railings to entire fronts. In Madison's heyday tons of ironwork were forged here, then floated south to New Orleans, where it trims verandas and balconies today.

All was well in Madison for about 75 years. Then, as was the case with most 19th-century boomtowns on the nation's waterways, Madison suffered a series of setbacks. For most of the next century, Madison slumbered. As a consequence, much of Madison's historic fabric remained intact. Today, more than 130 square blocks in the downtown area alone are on the National Register of Historic Places. A number of these structures have been turned into bed-and-breakfasts; antiques shops fill old commercial buildings downtown. Just west of town is an area filled with rocky gorges gouged out by Ice Age glaciers, where miles of trails and steep wooden staircases lead to 100-ft waterfalls.

Information: Madison Area Convention and Visitors Bureau | 301 E. Main St., 47250 | 812/265–2956 or 800/559–2956 | info@visitmadison.org | www.visitmadison.org.

Attractions

Broadway Fountain. Originally cast of iron and shown at the Philadelphia Centennial Exposition in 1876, the fountain was purchased by the Madison lodge of the Independent Order of Odd Fellows and presented to the city. One hundred years later, in 1976, it was recast in bronze to commemorate the community's bicentennial. | N. Broadway and Main St. | 812/265–2956 or 800/559–2956 | www.visitmadison.org | Free | Daily.

Clifty Falls State Park. Steep ravines and high waterfalls mark this 1,300-acre reserve, a geologic relict of the Ice Age. Clifty Creek falls 70 ft, before descending another 250 ft within 3 mi; eventually it spills into the Ohio River. Four of the park's waterfalls drop more than 60 ft. Moderate to difficult trails follow steps and boardwalks to waterfall overlooks and creekbeds. | 1501 Green Rd. | 812/265–1331 or 812/265–4135 | www.ai.org/dnr | $2 per vehicle residents, $5 nonresidents | Daily.

Dr. William Hutchings Hospital Museum. The doctor's office provides a glimpse into the life of a frontier physician. The building and its contents are exactly as they were left by Dr. Hutchings on his death in 1903. | 120 W. 3rd St. | 812/265–2967 | $2 | May–Oct., Mon.–Sat. 10–4:30, Sun. 1–4:30.

Francis Costigan House. The architect of the Lanier and Shrewsbury-Windle houses completed his own residence in 1851. It is considered an architectural marvel because it incorporates complex design and construction details in a very small space. | 408 W. Third St. | 812/265–2967 | $12 | May–Oct., Mon.–Sat. 10–4:30, Sun. 1:15–4:30.

Jefferson County Historical Museum and Madison Railroad Station. Rotating historical exhibits and artifacts important to the town's local history and the heritage of the Ohio Valley are on display. Special exhibits trace southern Indiana's role in the Civil War and steamboating. The octagonal railroad station next door was constructed in 1895 and used as a passenger station until 1935. Railroading artifacts are also on display. | 615 W. 1st St. | 812/265–2335 | $3 for the combo ticket, $2 for just the railroad or just the museum | Apr. 25–Oct. 31, Mon.–Sat. 10–4:30, Sun. 1–4; Nov. 1–Apr. 24, weekdays 10–4:30.

Judge Jeremiah Sullivan House. A 19th-century Justice of the Indiana Supreme Court, Judge Jeremiah Sullivan is credited with having named Indianapolis. His 1818 home is considered the town's first mansion. The estate contains the only known fully restored Federal serving kitchen in the nation. | 304 W. 2nd St. | 812/265–2967 | $2 | House May–Oct., Mon.–Sat. 10–4:30, Sun. 1–4:30; garden daily until dusk.

The modest **Talbot-Hyatt Pioneer Garden** behind the Sullivan home is planted with herbs and vegetables of the period. | Free | Daily.

Lanier Mansion State Historic Site. On a knoll overlooking the Ohio River, this gleaming white mansion was designed by Francis Costigan, a notable architect of the time, for James F. D. Lanier, a financier and industrialist in the mid-19th century. Completed in 1844, the house is in the Greek Revival style, which was the first national style of architecture. Lanier's loans to Indiana enabled the state to equip Union troops during the Civil War. A highlight is the three-story, seemingly unsupported spiral staircase. Outside, Lanier's formal gardens have been restored and planted with varieties from the 1850s. Cutting and vegetable beds, an arbor, and dwarf fruit trees are a part of the formal pattern. Cinder paths original to the gardens were excavated as part of the restoration. | 511 W. 1st St. | 812/265–3526 | www.ai.org/ism/sites/lanier | Free | Tues.–Sat. 9–5, Sun. 1–5; tours every 30 mins.

Schofield House. The tall brick home was built in the Federal style in 1816. It is believed to be the first two-story tavern house in Madison. | 217 W. 2nd St. | 812/265–4759 or 812/867–3434 | $2 | Apr.–Oct., Mon.–Sat. 10–4:30, Sun. 1–4:30.

Shrewsbury-Windle House. Lanier House architect Francis Costigan designed this house in 1849 for Captain Charles L. Shrewsbury, a prominent figure in the riverboat industry. Costigan's signature free-floating staircase is a highlight of the house. | 301 W. 1st St. | 812/265–4481 | $2 | Apr.–Dec., daily 10–4, or by appointment.

ON THE CALENDAR
APR.–MAY: *Madison in Bloom.* The whole town seems to bloom in spring and summer, and eight private gardens are open during a garden tour sponsored by the Jefferson County Historical Society. | 812/265–2335.

JULY: *Madison Regatta Presents the Indiana Governor's Cup.* The world's fastest boats compete at speeds of over 200 mph on a 2½-mi stretch of the Ohio River; the best views of the race are from the water's edge. | 812/265–5000.

Dining
Key West Shrimp House. Seafood. Window tables along the front have good views at this cozy restaurant in an old button factory overlooking the Ohio River. Shrimp are prepared at least six different ways. The homemade Key lime pie is a favorite. Kids' menu. | 117 Ferry St. | 812/265–2831 | Closed Mon. | $16–$35 | AE, D, DC, MC, V.

Ovo Café. Contemporary. In the heart of downtown, this café is in a building constructed in the 1850s. With its burgundy and dark green color scheme, there's Mediterranean flair here. The Spanish almond chicken and the chicken piccata are specialties, and there's an appetizer sampler that includes hummus, tabbouleh, and baba ghanouj. | 209 W. Main St. | 812/273–8808 | Closed Sun.–Mon. | $11–$20 | MC, V.

Lodging
Clifty Inn. Scenery makes the difference at this plain hostelry built in 1924: Clifty Falls State Park surrounds this property, which spreads across a ridge and where many rooms overlook the park's woods and the Ohio River. Restaurant. Indoor-outdoor pool. Hot tub. | Off Routes 56 and 62 | 812/265–4135 | fax 812/273–5720 | www.state.in.us/dnr/parklake/inns/clifty/index.html | 63 rooms, 4 suites | $69–$89, $119–$129 suites | AE, D, MC, V.

Schussler House Bed & Breakfast. This 1849 Greek Revival home, listed on the National Register of Historic Places, opened as an inn in 1993. It's in the historic district, close to many shops and restaurants. Rooms have either canopy or wrought-iron beds. | 514 Jefferson St. | 812/273–2068 or 800/392–1931 | schussler@voyager.net | www.schusslerhouse.com | 3 rooms | $120–$145 | D, MC, V.

MARION

MAP 3, E3

(Nearby towns also listed: Geneva, Huntington, Kokomo, Muncie, Peru, Wabash)

In 1831, less than 20 years after the Battle of Mississinewa, the town of Marion was established 7 mi from the site of the struggle on the west bank of the Mississinewa River. With the discovery of vast natural gas reserves underground in 1887, Marion was quickly propelled to the industrial forefront; foundries and paper and glass factories were established, and then automotive plants sprang up. By 1900, in just 20 years, the town's population had grown from 3,000 to more than 17,000. Later in the century, 1950s movie idol James Dean was born in Marion, although he was raised and is buried in nearby Fairmount. Today, Marion is the seat of Grant County. A 2¾-mi riverwalk extends from downtown to Matter Park along the Mississinewa. A mix of industry and agriculture supports the economy; Thomson Consumer Electronics and General Motors are two of the six companies that each employ more than 500 Marion residents.

Information: Marion–Grant County Convention and Visitors Bureau | 217 S. Adams St., 46952 | 765/668–5435 or 800/662–9474 | marionin@comteck.com | www.comteck.com/ ~marionin.

Attractions

Cumberland Covered Bridge. This 181-ft span across Mississinewa River at Matthews was built in 1877 and is Grant County's last remaining covered bridge. Swept ¼ mi downstream during a flood in 1913, the bridge was returned to its original location, where it rests today. | 3rd and Front Sts., Matthews | 765/998–2372 | Free | Daily.

Fairmount. This town of 3,100, located 8 mi from Marion, capitalizes on the fact that James Dean grew up and was buried here after he was killed in an automobile crash in 1955. Other famous sons include CBS news correspondent Phil Jones, "Garfield" comic strip creator Jim Davis, and former National Hurricane Center director Robert Sheets.

The **Fairmount Historical Museum,** in a century-old brick home, houses an extensive collection of memorabilia and personal mementos of James Dean and other local notables. Displays trace the county's history with artifacts and artworks. A wide selection of Dean mementos and other souvenirs is on sale. | 203 E. Washington St. | 765/948–4555 | www.jamesdeanartifacts.com | $1 | Mar.–Nov., Mon.–Sat. 10–5, Sun. noon–5, or by appointment.

A gracious home on Fairmount's tree-lined Main Street, the **James Dean Memorial Gallery** houses the world's largest private collection of James Dean's personal effects. Dean's costumes, high-school yearbooks, a rare Warner Brothers life mask, original movie posters by the hundred, and books and magazines from around the world are some of the thousands of items on display, along with various tribute and novelty items produced since the 1950s. Both proprietors are avid enthusiasts, and David Loehr wrote a comprehensive guide for collectors of Dean memorabilia. | 425 N. Main St. | 765/948–3326 | www.james-deangallery.com | $3.75 | Apr.–Nov., daily 10–6; Dec.–Mar., daily 10–5.

James Dean Memorial Park. Hollywood artist Kenneth Kendall created the larger-than-life-size bronze bust of Dean that is the centerpiece of this small corner park. Benches surround the monument, which was dedicated on September 30, 1995, in commemoration of the 40th anniversary of the star's death. | 2nd and Main Sts. | 800/662–9474 | Free | Daily.

Matter Park. Shady Matter Park stretches north of downtown along the Mississinewa River. Cyclists and strollers are attracted to the park's 2¾-mi riverwalk pedestrian trail. The park also has softball fields, picnic shelters and tables, playgrounds, tennis courts, a fishing pond, soccer and football fields, and a sand volleyball court. | River and Quarry Rds. | 765/668–4453 or 800/662–9474 | fax 765/668–4443 | Free | Daily.

Wilson-Vaughn Historic Hostess House. One of Marion's most treasured historic homes, this gracious, columned brick mansion was built in the early 1900s by Samuel H. Plato, an African-American businessman and builder. In the 1940s, after it had been empty for years, a group of dedicated volunteers lovingly put the gleam back on the place and named it Hostess House, thinking of it as a place where they could entertain. Today, the house welcomes diners for lunch on weekdays and is festively decked out over the Christmas holidays. It also sells handicrafts and Hostess House fresh-baked poppy seed bread. | 723 W. 4th St. | 765/664–3755 | www.comteck.com/~marionin/ | $1 | Weekdays 10–4.

Mississinewa Battlefield. The United States Army's first victory of the War of 1812 was won at this site 7 mi north of Marion on December 17–18, 1812. Lt. Col. John B. Campbell led 600 troops on a campaign that overtook four Miami villages allied with the British. | Rte. 15 | 765/668–5435 or 800/822–1812 | www.mississinewa1812.com | Free | Daily.

Mississinewa Lake State Reservoir. More than 14,000 acres surround this 3,210-acre reservoir. In the area are the Meshingomesia Miami Indian Cemetery, and, next to it, the Frances Slocum State Forest. The Frances Slocum Trail, a scenic drive, follows the southern edge of the lake from Route 15 northwest of Marion to east of Wabash. There are four launch areas on the water, but no boat rentals. | 4673 S Rte. 625 E | 765/473–6528 | www.state.in.us/dnr/parklake/reservoirs/mississinewa.html, www.ai.org/dnr | $2 per vehicle residents, $5 non-residents | Daily.

ON THE CALENDAR

FEB.: *James Dean Birthday Celebration.* Fans of the 1950s movie idol gather during the annual birthday bash at the Fairmount Historical Museum. There are also free film showings, and tours of the museum and James Dean's childhood home. | 765/948–4555.

MAR.–APR.: *Marion Easter Pageant.* On Good Friday at 8 PM and Easter morning at 6 AM, the Passion is reenacted with music. | 765/668–5435 or 800/662–9474.

SEPT.: *Fairmount Museum Days: Remembering James Dean.* A car show brings in 2,500 classic and custom autos, and there's a James Dean look-alike contest, a 1950s dance contest, a parade, Garfield the Cat photo and art contest, a bicycle tour, a screening of Dean's three films, and live entertainment. | 765/948–3326 or 765/948–4555.

OCT.: *Mississinewa 1812.* A step back in time, this is a reenactment of the Battle of Mississinewa. It's the largest such gathering re-creating the War of 1812 in the United States. | 800/822–1812 | www.mississinewa1812.com.

Dining

Hostess House. Café. Near downtown on Route 18, this 1912 Greek Revival mansion has original fixtures and Victorian furnishings. A large selection of grilled sandwiches, salads, and soups fill the menu, and you can finish your meal with butterscotch pie. | 723 W. 4th St. | 765/664–3755 | Closed weekends. No dinner | $4–$6 | No credit cards.

Lodging

Comfort Suites. This two-story all-suites motel is on the north side of town, off I–69, exit 64 (Marion). Large columns mark the entrance. Complimentary Continental breakfast. In-room data ports, microwaves, refrigerators, some in-room hot tubs. Cable TV. Indoor pool. Hot tub. Exercise equipment. Laundry facilities. Business services, free parking. | 1345 N. Baldwin Ave. | 765/651–1006 | fax 765/651–0145 | www.comfortinn.com | 62 suites | $100–$120 | AE, D, DC, MC, V.

Golden Oak Bed & Breakfast. This 1908 Craftsman home with a checkerboard brick facade is eight blocks from the courthouse. Each room is furnished distinctively—one with antiques, one with a bridal theme, and one, the black room, named for the chalk and pencil drawings by the innkeeper's son that are its focal point. Complimentary breakfast. Cable TV. No in-room phones. | 809 W. 4th St. | 765/651–9950 | www.golden-oak-indiana.com | 5 rooms | $60–$85 | AE, MC, V.

Holiday Inn. This five-story redbrick building is the only full-service hotel in town with its own restaurant. It's in a commercial area 6 mi off I–69, exit 64 (Marion-Mt. Piliar). Restaurant, bar, room service. Cable TV. Pool. Exercise equipment. | 501 E. 4th St. | 765/668–8801 | fax 765/662–6827 | holmar@ix.netcom.com | www.holiday-inn.com | 120 rooms | $99–$109 | AE, D, DC, MC, V.

MARSHALL

MAP 3, C5

(Nearby towns also listed: Crawfordsville, Rockville)

A steel-girder arch put up in 1921–22 to commemorate soldiers who died during World War I spans the main intersection in this town. Marshall is in the heart of Parke County's covered bridge country and is a gateway to Turkey Run State Park, less than 6 mi away. As a result, although its population is fewer than 500, Marshall swells in size on weekends and holidays. Early settlers used the area's rich clay resources and timber for brickmaking, pottery, and lumbering enterprises.

Information: Parke County Convention and Visitors Bureau | 401 E. Ohio St., Rockville, 47872 | 765/569–5226 | pci@ticz.com | www.coveredbridges.com.

Attractions

Shades State Park. *(See also* Rockville.*)* The 3,084-acre wooded park is less visited than Turkey Run, roughly 10 mi away. According to one legend, its name comes from its early nickname "Shades of Death," owing to its dense forest. This primordial pocket has dramatic ravines, blanketed with moss and ferns, and delicate waterfalls. Natural mineral springs trickling through the pristine area led to the creation of a health and recreation resort in the late 1880s. Ten miles of trails, some with ladders and stairs, skirt ravines and provide lookout points 200 ft above Sugar Creek. It's 17 mi southwest of Crawfordsville | Off Rte. 47; Rte. 1, Waveland | 765/435–2810 | www.ai.org/dnr | $2 per vehicle residents, $5 nonresidents | May–Aug., daily.

Turkey Run State Park. Opened in 1916, Turkey Run was named for the wild turkeys that roost among the 50-ft reddish-brown Mansfield sandstone cliffs and rocky gorges that cut through the woodland area. A 15-mi network of trails extending from both sides of Sugar Creek follow boulder-strewn ravines. More challenging treks explore the rugged terrain in the Rocky Hollow Nature Preserve, also spanning Sugar Creek. The park also has modern amenities—an Olympic-size swimming pool, tennis courts, and a nature center. At the hub of the trail system stands the refurbished red-brick Turkey Run Inn. The stone structure blends well with its natural surroundings. A leafy canopy of tulip poplars, oaks, and maples hides practically everything but the inn's columned entrance. In the homey wood-floored dining room you can get meals of fried catfish and broiled ham. | Off Rte. 47 | 765/597–2635 | www.state.in.us/dnr/statepar/parks/turkey/turkey.htm | $2 per vehicle residents, $5 nonresidents | Daily.

ON THE CALENDAR

OCT.: *Covered Bridge Festival.* Through a county-wide festival, the town of Marshall draws covered bridge lovers from far and wide. The town's businesses have special hours to accommodate out-of-towners, and the large festival includes homemade crafts, candle-making, and food. The fire department has a fish fry to benefit the Children's Hospital. | 765/569–5226.

Dining

Marshall Restaurant Coffee and Soda Shoppe. American. This fountain shop is complete with soda bar, old-fashioned soda machine, water, and carbonated water dispensers. The dining room is done in old barn wood and beams, unmatched tables, antique lanterns, and old harnesses. Friday night's specialty is all-you-can-eat fried catfish, and Saturday night's specials include a steak and shrimp plate as well as rib-eye and porterhouse steaks. The hand-pattied hamburgers are big and juicy. | Rte. 236 (Guion Rd.) | 765/597–2045 | $5–$9 | No credit cards.

Lodging

Turkey Run Inn. Built in 1919 of native Mansfield sandstone and wood, this rustic country inn is in Turkey Run State Park. Rooms are small with simple, spare furnishings and private baths. Restaurant, picnic area. Cable TV. Indoor pool. Tennis. Hiking. Video games. Kids' programs, playground. Business services. | Off Rte. 47 | 765/597–2211 | fax 765/597–2660 | www.state.in.us/dnr | 61 rooms in lodge; 21 cabins | $59–$69 | AE, D, MC, V.

MERRILLVILLE

INTRO
ATTRACTIONS
DINING
LODGING

MERRILLVILLE

MAP 3, B1

(Nearby towns also listed: Hammond, Michigan City, Valparaiso)

Tucked in the northwest corner of the state and considered part of greater Chicagoland, Merrillville was once the junction of more than a dozen pioneer and Indian trails. The business and commercial district downtown is newer, and the community is like a modern suburb.

Information: **Lake County Convention and Visitors Bureau** | 7770 Corinne Dr., Hammond, 46323 | 219/989–7770 or 800/All–Lake | lccvb@netico.net | www.alllake.org.

Attractions

Buckley Homestead County Park. The homestead depicts three time periods with a 1910 farm, an early 19th-century one-room schoolhouse, and an 1850s log house. Special programs and crafts workshops are presented. It is 15 mi from Merrillville. | 3606 Belshaw Rd., Lowell | 219/696–0769 | www.thetimesonline.com/org/lcparks/Buckley.html | Free | Daily 7–dusk; buildings open weekends 10–5. .

Deep River County Park. In this park 5 mi from Merrillville, a three-story red gristmill grinds and sells flour, and there's a visitors center. A block away, at Deep River water park, you'll find a wave pool, tube and body slides, a lazy river you can float in an inner tube, and more. | 9410 Old Lincoln Hwy., Hobart | 219/947–7850 or 800/928–7275 | www.thetimesonline.com/org/lcparks/parks.html | $4 | Park daily 7–dusk, buildings open May–Oct. 10–5; water park Memorial Day–Labor Day 10–6.

Grand Kankakee Marsh County Park. A 900-acre portion of the Grand Kankakee Marsh is preserved in this favorite destination for bird-watchers and the migrating and nesting birds they look for. Ospreys and bald eagles are occasionally sighted as well. It's 18 mi from Merrillville. | 21690 Range Line Rd., Hebron | 219/552–9614 | www.thetimesonline.com/org/lcparks/parks.html | Free | Jan.–Sept., daily 7–dusk.

Sts. Constantine and Helen Greek Orthodox Cathedral. A 100-ft-diameter rotunda, stained-glass windows, and Byzantine mosaics fill this contemporary cathedral built in 1971. More than 1,300 Greek families worship here. | 800 Madison Ave. | 219/769–2481 | Free | Daily 10–4; tours by appointment only.

Star Plaza Theatre. Top artists and shows perform on this stage. | 8001 Delaware Pl. | 219/769–6600 | www.starplazatheatre.com.

ON THE CALENDAR

AUG.: *Lakefront Festival.* A rubber-ducky race, a hog roast, food, arts and crafts, entertainment, a kids' game area, and a beer garden are Hobart's salute to its lakefront. | 219/942–2987.

OCT.: *Buckley Homestead Days.* Buckley Homestead County Park–Lake County Park, 15 mi from Merrillville, celebrates early farm history with period crafts demonstrations, traditional music and food, a medicine show, a circus, horse-drawn hayrides, and craft activities for kids. | 3606 Belshaw Rd., Lowell | 219/696–0769.

NOV.–JAN.: *Festival of Lights.* Pop a tape of Bing Crosby into the cassette player of your car, crank up the heat, and go for a 1-mi drive through Hidden Lake Park, where local corporations and organizations sponsor 60 lighted, animated displays. Donkeys and camels enliven the nativity scene. | 800/255–5253.

Dining

J. Ginger's. Continental. Stained-glass windows separate booths in this softly lighted restaurant in the Radisson Hotel. The Caesar salad is made tableside; the chefs prepare surf and turf, capon breast, and many other meat and fish dishes. Sun. champagne brunch. | 800 E. 81st Ave. | 219/769–6311 | No lunch. No dinner Sun. | $12–$27 | AE, D, DC, MC, V.

Louis' Bon Appetit. Continental. Flowers and trees fill the garden of this Victorian home, one of the top restaurants among food-lovers in this part of the state. Weather permitting, you can have your confit of duck or pork tenderloin outside on the back porch. | 302 S. Main St., Crown Point | 219/663–6363 | Closed Mon. No lunch Tues.–Sat., no dinner Sun. | $14–$24 | AE, D, DC, MC, V.

The Patio. Mediterranean. The mural of a Mediterranean seascape in the lounge sets the scene for veal piccata, chicken kabobs, and rack of lamb, a house specialty. But contrary to what the name suggests, there's no patio. | 7706 Broadway | 219/769–7990 | Closed Sun. No lunch Sat. | $11–$36 | AE, D, DC, MC, V.

Lodging

Courtyard Merrillville. This two-story chain hostelry is off I–65, exit 253B (Merrillville), and U.S. 30, in a commercial area, 50 mi from Chicago. Restaurant, room service. In-room data ports, some microwaves, some refrigerators. Indoor-outdoor pool. Hot tub. Exercise equipment. Laundry facilities, laundry service. Business services. | 7850 Rhode Island Ave. | 219/756–1600 | fax 219/756–2080 | www.courtyard.com | 112 rooms, 23 suites | $89–$99, $109–$159 suites | AE, D, DC, MC, V.

Fairfield Inn by Marriott. This modern three-story motel is off I–65, exit 253B (Merrillville), in a busy area filled with motels and restaurants. Complimentary Continental breakfast. In-room data ports. Cable TV. Pool. Business services. | 8275 Georgia St. | 219/736–0500 | fax 219/736–5116 | www.fairfieldinn.com | 132 rooms | $59–$99 | AE, D, DC, MC, V.

Hampton Inn Merrillville. At the intersection of I–65, exit 253B (Merrillille), and U.S. 30, this three-story chain motel has some spa rooms, with queen-size bed and whilpool tub. Complimentary Continental breakfast. In-room data ports, some microwaves, some refrigerators. Indoor pool. Exercise equipment. Business services. | 8353 Georgia St. | 219/736–7600 | fax 219/736–7676 | www.hamptoninn.com | 64 rooms | $89–$139 | AE, D, DC, MC, V.

Radisson Hotel at Star Plaza. This big four-story hostelry and conference center is at the Star Plaza Theatre complex, a half hour's drive from downtown Chicago off I–65, exit 253 (Merrillville), and U.S. 30. Tropical plants fill its atrium. Restaurant, bar with entertainment. In-room data ports, some refrigerators, in-room hot tubs. Cable TV. 2 pools (1 indoor). Beauty salon, sauna. Exercise equipment. Video games. Playground. Laundry facilities. Business services. Some pets allowed. | 800 E. 81st Ave. | 219/769–6311 | fax 219/793–9025 | www.radisson.com | 347 rooms | $109–$169 | AE, D, DC, MC, V.

Red Roof Inn. This older well-maintained two-story chain is along motel row, 12 mi south of downtown off I–65, exit 253B (Merrillville). In-room data ports. Cable TV. Business services. | 8290 Georgia St. | 219/738–2430 | fax 219/738–2436 | www.redroof.com | 108 rooms | $33–$43 | AE, D, DC, MC, V.

METAMORA

INTRO
ATTRACTIONS
DINING
LODGING

METAMORA

MAP 3, F6

(Nearby towns also listed: Batesville, Connersville)

In 1847, finishing touches were put on the Whitewater Canal, running from Lawrenceburg on the Ohio River to Hagerstown. The Metamora segment had already been completed several years before, and soon the tiny town was a main stop. In the 1860s, railroad tracks went in along the canal's northern towpath, but this new arrival put a damper on Metamora's canal and the town's future as a center of commerce. Metamora slumbered. Eventually, the state of Indiana bought and restored 14 mi of the canal, the town's water-powered gristmill, and a 60-ft aqueduct that carries the canal over Duck Creek, 16 ft below. With that restoration came a community-wide rejuvenation. Canal-era wood-frame structures front the waterway and now house more than 100 gift shops and eateries.

Information: Metamora Economic Development Corporation | Main St., Box 95, 47030 | 765/647–2109 | metamora@cnz.com | www.metamora.com. .

Attractions

Whitewater Canal State Historic Site. This historic site covers 14 mi of the Whitewater Canal, which was built between 1836 and 1847. A replica flatboat takes travelers on horsedrawn boat rides, and a gristmill turns out sacks of cornmeal. The canal itself is lined with tall frame houses dating from the waterway's heyday. | 19063 N. Clayborn St. | 765/647–6512 | www.ai.org/ism/sites/whitewater/ | Free | Gristmill mid-Mar.–mid-Dec., Tues.–Sat. 9–5, Sun. 1–5; boat rides May–Oct., Tues.–Sun. 11–4.

ON THE CALENDAR

NOV., DEC.: *Old-Fashioned Christmas Walk.* The Whitewater Valley train traverses the historic canal village, and luminarias light the way to more than 100 shops, food, and entertainment venues. | 765/647–2109.

Dining

Trapper's Hog Roast. Barbecue. Since 1979, Trapper Jim has been serving up hogs from a giant tepee, equipped with porch and veranda, at the foot of the pedestrian bridge along the canal. Some 3,000 hogs later, Jim has the technique down right, slicing the hog directly into the homemade barbecue sauce. You can also feast on burgers made from buffalo (raised 6 mi away) or Black Angus, or homemade Italian sausage. | 3 Canal St. | 765/647–4446 | Closed Jan.–Mar. | $3–$7 | No credit cards.

Lodging

The Gingerbread House Bed & Breakfast. This two-story Victorian home with period furnishings is on the National Register of Historic Places. There's a minimum two-night rental, from Friday afternoon to Sunday evening, on weekends; during the week you can stay for just one night. Breakfast arrives at your doorstep in a basket. Complimentary breakfast. Microwaves, refrigerators. Cable TV, in-room VCRs. | 19072 Clayborn St. | 765/647–5518 | www.emetamora.com/gingerbreadhouse | 1 house with 2 bedrooms | $75 per week night, $200 for an enitre weekend | No credit cards.

MICHIGAN CITY

MAP 3, C1

(Nearby towns also listed: Hammond, La Porte, Merrillville, Valparaiso)

Settled by French fur trappers and pioneers, Michigan City was established on the shore of Lake Michigan at the terminus of Michigan Road, a main thoroughfare stretching south to Madison, Indiana, on the Ohio River. The town prospered beginning in the mid-1800s, and "car shops" were turning out more than 1,000 freight cars a day by 1879. On the site of the present electric-generating plant, a giant sand dune called Hoosier Slide once stood, visible all the way from Chicago, 40 mi distant. Between 1890 and 1920, it was flattened as more than 13½ million tons of sand were shipped to glass factories and to the Illinois Central Railroad to provide fill for its right-of-way. Today, the tallest dunes are under 200 ft; 135-ft Mt. Baldy is on the lakeshore and 192-ft Mt. Tom is in Indiana Dunes State Park, which the lakeshore surrounds, 10 mi from Michigan City, not far from the old Hoosier Slide. The state's only lighthouse, now a museum, presides over the harbor and lakefront at 90-acre Washington Park. Mansions of railroad barons and industrialists that rose throughout town in its heyday are now museums, bed-and-breakfasts, and restaurants. The Pullman-Standard Company operated in Michigan City for nearly 100 years until 1970. Today, many local residents commute to jobs in Chicago.

Information: **La Porte County Convention and Visitors Bureau** | 1503 S. Meer Rd., La Porte, 46360. | 219/872–5055 or 800/685–7174 | lpccvb@netnitco.net | www.harborcountry-in.org.

Attractions

Barker Mansion. Called "the house that freight cars built," this turn-of-the-century mansion was built by millionaire railroad industrialist John H. Barker and is exquisitely fitted out with rare woods, fine art, and original furniture. | 631 Washington St. | 219/873–1520 | $4 | June–Oct., daily 10–5, tours weekdays at 10, 11:30, and 1, weekends at noon and 2; Nov.–May, weekdays 10–5, tours weekdays at 10, 11:30, and 1.

Great Lakes Museum of Military History. Uniforms, photos, weapons, posters, medals, firearms, a World War II declaration of war, and a 1905 cannon are on display at this military history museum, which also houses a research library. | 360 Dunes Plaza | 219/872–2702 | $2 | Tues.–Fri. 9–4, Sat. 10–4.

John G. Blank Center for the Arts. Paintings, sculpture, and other works by regional artists are exhibited in this gallery complex in a century-old building with Tiffany-style stained-glass windows. | 312 E. 8th St. | 219/874–4900 | $3 | Tues.–Fri. 10–4, Sat. 10–2; Dec., Tues. and Sat. 10–2.; Jan., Tues 10–2.

Washington Park. These 90 acres on the lakefront include picnic areas shaded by tall trees and a public-access marina and swimming beach. | 115 Lakeshore Dr. | 219/873–1506 | Free | Daily; band concerts July–Aug., Thurs.–Sat. at 8 PM.

Indiana's only lighthouse, built in 1858, is now the **Old Lighthouse Museum.** Seven rooms of exhibits trace the Great Lakes shipping history with shipbuilding tools, nautical artifacts, and photographs, and there is a rare fourth-order Fresnel lens. | 219/872–6133 or 219/872–3273 | Free | Tues.–Sun. 1–4.

The **Washington Park Zoo** has a feline house, monkey island, and a petting barn within a wooded dune area. | 219/873–1510 | $3 | Apr.–Oct., daily 10:30–4; Memorial Day–Labor Day, 10:30–6.

ON THE CALENDAR

JULY: *Summer Festival.* A traditional patriotic program, a parade, a drum and bugle corps show, a cardboard boat race, a jet-ski race, and a fireworks display are highlights of this downtown festival, now in its fourth decade. | 219/872–5055 or 800/685–7174.
JULY: *Lakefront Music Festival.* Musicians gather together over the weekend to perform during the Michigan City Summer Festival. | 219/872–5055 or 800/685–7174.

Dining

Basil's. Continental. Named after its owner, this upbeat bistro serves inventive fare such as fresh fish with a signature champagne sauce seasoned with tarragon, honey, and cream as well as chops, seafood, and steak. Entertainment on weekends. | 521 Franklin Sq. | 219/872–4500 | No lunch on weekends | $13–$25 | AE, DC, D, MC, V.

Matey's Restaurant and Beer Garden. Seafood. Just before the bridge, at the entrance to Washington Park, this bustling joint specializes in Cajun seafood chowder. You can gorge on tavern oysters, wrapped in bacon and fried; farm-raised oysters on the half shell; or the all-you-can-eat lake perch dinner. For a good view of the lake, ask to be seated on the rooftop. | 110 Franklin St. | 219/872–9471 | $10–$19 | AE, D, DC, MC, V.

Pullman Café. Steak. Everything has a railroad theme here—the hot rail appetizers, side track sandwiches, Union Pacific dinner, and club car lounge cocktail specials. The special house steak can be ordered Oskar-style, topped with béarnaise sauce and crab meat, or as a sandwich, with toast points underneath and onion rings on top. You can also get pasta, chicken, fish, and other meats. | 711 Wabash St. | 219/879–3393 | $9–$19 | D, MC, V.

Rodini Lounge. Greek. In the front window of this restaurant, an image of the nearby lighthouse in stained glass welcomes diners who come ready for the good fish, which is prepared to order—broiled, pan-fried, and deep-fried. The seafood platter is also popular. Overstuffed chairs and two fireplaces keep things cozy. | 4125 Franklin St. | 219/879–7388 | $16–$25 | AE, D, DC, MC, V.

Lodging

Al and Sally's. This well-maintained single-story strip motel is in the Indiana Dunes National Lakeshore, 3 mi from downtown on U.S. 12. Picnic area. Refrigerators. Cable TV. Pool. Tennis. Playground. | 3221 W. Dunes Hwy. | 219/872–9131 | 16 rooms | $65 | AE, D, MC, V.

Brickstone Bed & Breakfast. This 1880 Queen Anne home is a half block from the Prime Outlets shopping nall, six blocks from Lake Michigan, and ½ mi from the Blue Chip Casino. Rooms are themed around the seasons: The winter room has a white canopy bed, the spring room has a fencelike headboard laced with silk flowers, and the fall room is done in burgundy and brown. The summer suite has a pull-out couch and its own sitting room and library. All rooms have Jacuzzis. Complimentary breakfast. No room phones, TV in common area. | 215 W. Sixth St. | 219/878–1819 | 4 rooms | $80–$140 | MC, V.

Creekwood Inn. Willow creek runs through 33 acres of oaks, pines, and walnut trees surrounding this 1930s Tudor-style country estate. Some guest rooms have fireplaces, others have French doors that open onto private terraces. Two conference areas are available for gatherings. The property is 3 mi from Michigan City off I–94, exit 40B (U.S. 20/35). You'll find inventive American cuisine at The Ferns restaurant on site. Complimentary Continental breakfast. Refrigerators. Hot tub. Hiking. Exercise equipment. Fishing. Business services. | 5727 N. 600 W. | 219/872–8357 | fax 219/872–6986 | creekwd@adsnet.com | www.creekwoodinn.com | 13 rooms | $125–$180 | Closed early Jan. | AE, DC, MC, V.

Comfort Inn. Two miles from the Lighthouse Outlet Mall and ½ mi from I–94, exit 34B, this two-story chain hostelry has one suite with an outdoor Jacuzzi. In-room data ports, some kitchenettes, some in-room hot tubs. Cable TV, some in-room VCRs. Indoor pool. Laundry facilities. Business services. | 3801 N. Frontage Rd. | 219/879–9190 | fax 219/879–0373 | www.comfortinn.com | 50 rooms | $99–$131 | AE, D, DC, MC, V.

Duneland Beach Inn. Originally built in 1920 as a 23-room, one-bath hotel, the inn has been remodeled. Now, each room has a private bath. On warm mornings, you can have breakfast on the enclosed veranda, and the wooded views are pleasing. You're a block from Lake Michigan. Complimentary breakfast. Cable TV, in-room VCRs. Hot tub. No kids under 7. No pets. | 3311 Pottawattamie Terr. | 219/874–7729 or 800/423–7729 | info@dunelandbeach.com | www.dunelandbeach.com | 7 rooms, 2 suites | $89–$119, suites $119 | MC, V.

Holiday Inn Executive Conference Center. This complex is ¼ mi from I–94, exit 34B. It has a Holidome indoor recreation center, and the Windrift Mirage restaurant serves an eclectic menu in a light and airy dining room. Restaurant, bar, room service. Some refrigerators. Cable TV. Indoor pool. Exercise equipment. Business services. | 5820 S. Franklin St. | 219/879–0311 | fax 219/879–2536 | www.holiday-inn.com | 165 rooms | $115–$125 | AE, D, DC, MC, V.

Hutchinson Mansion Inn. The stately redbrick Hutchinson Mansion Inn presides over the town's historic residential and commercial district, spanning nearly one city block, less than 1 mi from the lakefront, off I–94, exit 34B. William Hutchinson—lumber baron, world traveler, and onetime Michigan City mayor—built this elegant Queen Anne–style mansion in 1876 and outfitted it with stained-glass windows, dark wood paneling, and tall beamed ceilings with decorative moldings. The bedrooms are accented with antiques such as an 8-ft Renaissance Revival bed with inlaid burl wood and a rare four-poster Jenny Lind bed. Carriage house suites have a private terrace and a porch with a swing. Complimentary breakfast. In-room data ports. Hot tub. | 220 W. 10th St. | 219/879–1700 | 5 rooms, 5 suites | $85–$110, $110–$140 suites | AE, MC, V.

Red Roof Inn–Michigan City. This two-story motel is in a commercial area 7 mi southwest of downtown Michigan City and 1/4 mi from I–94, exit 34B. In-room data ports. Cable TV. Business services. Some pets allowed. | 110 W. Kieffer Rd. | 219/874–5251 | fax 219/874–5287 | www.redroofinn.com | 79 rooms | $79–$85 | AE, D, DC, MC, V.

MIDDLEBURY

(Nearby towns also listed: Elkhart, Goshen, Shipshewana)

Situated in the middle of the Crystal Valley Amish area, Middlebury holds fast to its rural character and simple charm despite the arrival of more than six recreational vehicle manufacturers there since the late 1960s. The Patchwork Quilt Inn, with bed-and-breakfast lodging and sumptuous country-style dinners, and Das Dutchman Essenhaus, a huge barn-like restaurant and inn, are two of the area's best-known attractions, located just a few miles from the Michigan state line.

Information: Amish Country/Elkhart County Convention and Visitors Bureau | 219 Caravan Dr., Elkhart, 46514 | 219/262–8161 or 800/262–8161 | ecconv@amishcountry.org | www.amish-country.org/welcome/welcome.html.

Attractions

Sunshine Farm. Kids get a hands-on experience with animals with guinea pigs and goats, ferrets and ponies, peacocks and rabbits. Guided tours take an hour and a half, and there are pony rides for kids. | 240 U.S. 20 | 219/825–9471 ext. 500 | www.essenhaus.com | $5.25 | Closed Sun.

ON THE CALENDAR

OCT.: *Amish Country Harvest Festival.* The first full weekend in October, on the grounds of the Das Dutchman Essenhaus, crafters, musicians, quilters, and antiques and food vendors meet to sell their wares. There is a quilt raffle, kids' activities, and entertainment. | 219/825–5129.

Dining

Das Dutchman Essenhaus. American. This Amish family restaurant, on the grounds of the Das Dutchman Essenhaus complex, is a local institution for its all-you-can-eat chicken, roast beef, baked steak, or ham family-style meals, served with mashed potatoes, noodles and gravy, bread with apple butter, soup, a drink, and dessert. If you order à la carte, consider the beef and noodles or creamed chicken and biscuits. | 240 U.S. 20 | 219/825–9471 or 800/455–9471 | Closed Sun. Breakfast also served | $2–$15 | D, MC, V.

Lodging

Essenhaus Country Inn. Built in 1986 to resemble a white Amish farm house, this inn is filled with hand-made Amish furnishings and crafts, and rooms have floral wallpaper and simple, sturdy Amish furniture and quilts. Quilt squares decorate the walls. Complimentary Continental breakfast. | 240 U.S. 20 | 219/825–9471 or 800/455–9471 | brock@essenhaus.com | www.essenhaus.com | 33 rooms | $82–$150 | AE, D, MC, V.

MISHAWAKA

(Nearby towns also listed: Elkhart, Goshen, Nappanee, Plymouth, South Bend)

Mishawaka spreads along the St. Joseph River in the middle of north-central Indiana about 5 mi downstream from South Bend, its twin city; roughly half the size, it has a population of about 42,000. In the late 1700s the dense woodlands here teemed with furbearing wildlife attracting trappers from the John Jacob Astor fur trading company as well as missionaries. It was these thick woods that inspired its name, which is thought to be a Potawatomi word for "thick woods rapids." Today, more than a half-dozen city parks line the riverbanks between the two cities. While South Bend was known for its Polonia ethnic neighborhood, Mishawaka had its Belgian Town, and in 1900 15 percent of its population was foreign-born. Riding the coattails of South Bend, Mishawaka's economy was manufacturing-based in the 1930s; now it also includes retail, service industries, and education. Notably, it is now the home of the four-wheel-drive military troop and cargo vehicle known as the Hummer. Mishawaka's AM General Corporation was awarded a $1.2-billion contract to build 57,000 of these brawny vehicles in 1987, and today the car is the preferred SUV of some of Hollywood's richest and most famous.

Information: **South Bend/Mishawaka Convention and Visitors Bureau** | 401 E. Colfax Ave., Ste. 310, South Bend, 46634-1677 | 219/234–0051 or 800/462–5258 | www.cvbinfo@ livethelegends.org.

Attractions

Richard Clay Bodine State Fish Hatchery. The hatchery releases fish into the St. Joseph River. From there the fish migrate into Lake Michigan where they live and grow for four years. After they swim upriver, the steelhead trout return to Lake Michigan and the chinook salmon die. You must have appropriate licenses and stamps to fish. | 13200 E. Jefferson | 219/255–4199 | Free | Weekdays 8–3:30.

Hannah Lindahl Children's Museum. Exhibits on local history from prehistoric times to the present day are geared toward children here. | 1402 S. Main St. | 219/258–3056 | Free | Sept.–May, Tues.–Fri., 1st and 2nd Sat. of the month, 10–5; June, Tues.–Thurs. 10–5.

Merrifield Park–Shiojiri Niwa Japanese Gardens. Landscape architect Shoji Kanaoka has created a 1-acre haven along the St. Joseph River with gracefully arched bridges over dry waterfalls and streams surrounding a tea house. | 1000 E. Mishawaka Ave. | 219/258–1664 | Free | Daily.

ON THE CALENDAR

JUNE: *Summer Fest.* Locals converge on Merrifield Park for games, kids' rides, food, and a concert. | 219/234–0051 or 800/462–5258.

Dining

Beiger Mansion Inn Restaurant. Contemporary. In this neoclassical four-story mansion with a Victorian-style dining room, you'll find innovative dishes like chicken with cream sherry–soaked apricots and a sun-dried cranberry muffin; grilled lamb chops marinated in rosemary and anchovies; and mushroom and hazelnut soup. All desserts and breads are homemade. | 317 Lincolnway E | 219/256–0365 | fax 219/259–2622 | Reservations required | Closed Sun.–Mon. No lunch Sat. | $10–$16 | AE, D, DC, MC, V.

Doc Pierce's. Steak. A landmark downtown restaurant accentuated with dark wood and Tiffany lamps that is known for its four different specialty sirloins and seafood dishes. | 120 N. Main St. | 219/255–7737 | Closed Sun. | $6–$16 | AE, D, DC, MC, V.

Pat's Colonial Pub. American. Big burgers, steak, and sautéed lake perch headline at this established casual eatery. | 901 W. 4th St. | 219/259–8282 | Closed Sun. No lunch Sat. | $9–$35 | AE, MC, V.

Lodging

Beiger Mansion Inn. This four-story neoclassical limestone building modelled after a home in Newport, Rhode Island, was built as a summer home between 1903 and 1909. Rooms are furnished with Victorian antiques. Breakfast is served in the the State Dining Room. A two-night stay is required over a Notre Dame football weekend. 1 restaurant, 1 bar with entertainment, complimentary breakfast. | 317 Lincolnway E | 219/256–0365 | fax 219/259–2622 | beiger@michiana.org | business.michiana.org/beiger/ | 6 rooms, 1 suite | $70–$150 | AE, D, DC, MC, V.

Courtyard by Marriott. This newcomer is especially convenient; it's 3 mi from Notre Dame and 5 mi from the College Football Hall of Fame. In-room data ports, some in-room hot tubs. Cable TV. Indoor pool. Laundry service. Business services. | 4825 N. Main St. | 219/273–9900 | fax 219/272–0143 | 78 rooms, 3 suites | $109–$125, $129 suites | AE, D, DC, MC, V.

Hampton Inn. Notre Dame is 3.5 mi from this hostelry. Edison Lakes Corporate Park is one block away. Complimentary breakfast. Some refrigerators. Cable TV. Pool. Gym. No smoking rooms.No pets. | 445 University Dr. | 219/273–2309 | fax 219/273–0258 | 62 rooms | $69–$90 | AE, D, DC, MC, V.

MUNCIE

MAP 3, E4

(Nearby towns also listed: Anderson, Marion, New Castle)

Named after the Munsee tribe of the Delaware Indians, Muncie was another of the Trenton natural-gas-field bonanza towns. By 1890 there were 35 gas wells in Delaware County and almost 200 manufacturers in Muncie alone. In 1886 the five Ball brothers came from Buffalo, New York, and started a glass-jar company here; their turquoise canning jars were a household staple by the early 1900s. The Ball family has made an important mark on the town. Ball State University bears their name; television's *Late Show* host David Letterman is among its alumni. The site of the Frank C. Ball family home, called Minnetrista, is now a cultural center and garden. Six acres of gardens surround another Ball family home, Oakhurst, several blocks away. Ball Corporation is still in business, still making canning jars, and the lobby of the company headquarters displays a collection. Today, Muncie is the home of "Garfield" comic-strip creator Jim Davis.

Information: **Muncie Visitors Bureau** | 425 N. High St., 47305 | 765/284–2700 or 800/568–6862 | www.muncievisitorsbureau.org

Attractions

Ball State University. TV comic David Letterman's alma mater was founded as a state institution in 1918 when the Ball family, prominent Muncie industrialists, bought the campus and buildings of the Muncie National Institute and donated them to the state. A few years later the Indiana legislature changed the school's name to Ball Teachers College, before finally naming it Ball State University. Today over 60 buildings dot the 1,000-acre campus, and the enrollment in its 200-plus undergraduate and graduate degree programs numbers just under 19,000 students. It is known for its architecture, communications, and applied sciences and technology schools as well as its teachers college. | 2000 University Ave. | 765/285–1560 | www.bsu.edu/UP/cover.html | Free | Weekdays.

The **Ball State Museum of Art** in the university's Fine Arts Building holds a collection of over 9,500 paintings, including works by Rembrandt, Edgar Degas, and Winslow Homer as well as sculpture, prints, ancient glass, and decorative arts exhibits. | Riverside Ave. at Warwick Rd. | 765/285–5242 | www.bsu.edu/artmuseum/general.asp | Free | Weekdays 9–4:30, weekends 1:30–4:30.

Winding trails outline flower gardens, prairie plantings, and a demonstration wetland area at Ball State's forested **Christy Woods.** Specializing in wild orchid species, the park is also home to the Wheeler Orchid Collection. | 2000 W. University Ave. | 765/285–2641 or 765/285–8820 | www.muncieintourism.com/local.asp | Free | Dec.–Mar., weekdays 7:30–4:30, Sat. 8–4; Apr.–Nov., weekdays 7:30–4:30, Sat. 8–4, Sun. 1–5.

Cardinal Greenway. Still under construction, this trail along the abandoned railbed of what was once the CSX Railroad will ultimately extend for 60 mi, between Gaston and Richmond. The 12-ft-wide asphalt trail, flanked on one side by a foot of crushed limestone, is intended for joggers, walkers, bikers, skaters, and skiers. In more rural sections, horse trails parallel the main trail. Trailheads and rest areas punctuate the Greenway. | Main Muncie trailhead at 614 E. Wysor St. | 765/287–0399 | fax 765/287–0396 | www.cardinalgreenway.com | Free | Dusk to dawn.

Minnetrista Cultural Center. Exhibits on Indiana's history and culture such as *The State of the Game: Why Indiana Became Basketball Country* are one focus in this modern building on the site of a former Ball family home on 35 landscaped acres; science, natural history, and art are also featured, and in summer there are outdoor concerts. Minnetrista means "a gathering place by the water." | 1200 N. Minnetrista Pkwy. | 765/282–4848 or 800/428–5887 | Tues.–Sun. 11–5.

Oakhurst Gardens. Along the banks of the White River, there are 6-acres full of yellow and blue tulips, blue bells, scillas, and daffodils and an information station. | 765/282–4848 or 800/4–CULTURE | $3 | Tues.–Sat. 10–5, Sun. 1–5.

Muncie Children's Museum. Entertaining and educational exhibits are hands-on here, and topics range from the anatomy of the human eyeball to a "Garfield" cartooning exhibit. | 515 S. High St. | 765/286–1660. www.munciechildren'smuseum.org. | $4 | Tues.–Sat. 10–5, Sun. 1–5.

National Model Aviation Museum–Academy of Model Aeronautics International Aeromodeling Center. The world headquarters for builders and pilots of model airplanes displays the largest collection of model aircraft in the United States. In July and August, Academy members fly their aircraft in competition at the 1,000-acre flying site. | 5151 E. Memorial Dr. | 765/287–1256 or 800/I–FLY–AMA | www.modelaircraft.org | $2 | Weekends 8–4:30, weekends 10–4:30. Closed Sun. from Thanksgiving to Easter.

Prairie Creek Reservoir. Prairie Creek is a 2,300-acre property with 1,252 acres of spring-fed lake for pontoon and sail boating, fishing, and swimming. The lake is stocked with bass, walleye, perch, and bluegill. | 765/747–4776 (boating) or 765/747–4886 (beach) | Free | Daily.

ON THE CALENDAR
APR.–OCT.: *Muncie Dragway.* Championship drag racing is held every Wed. and Sat. evening here. | 765/789–8470.
JULY: *Delaware County Fair.* 4-H exhibits, a midway, entertainment, and food keep things hopping. | 765/284–2700 or 800/568–6862.
NOV.: *Festival of Trees and Light.* A display of decorated trees and wreaths are accompanied by family activities with Santa. | 765/284–2700 or 800/568–6862.

Dining

Foxfires. Continental. Owned in part by cartoonist Jim Davis and his wife, this restaurant encompasses a casual dining room that serves soups, salads, lamb, steaks, fish, and pasta; and a formal room that focuses more on fish and wild game. A "Garfield" art gallery is also here. | 3300 Chadam La. | 765/284–5235 | Closed Sun. No lunch | $19–$32 | AE, D, DC, MC, V.

JR Brooks. American. This casual mauve and blue family restaurant specializes in entrée-sized salads, steak kabobs, and teriyaki chicken. | 1101 McGalliard | 765/282–1321 | $6.99–$15.99 | AE, D, DC, MC, V.

Vince's. American. People fly into Muncie airport just to chow down on a slab of Vince's prime rib. The immense hangar-themed dining room has seating upstairs and downstairs as well as a lounge. The Nutty Chicken Salad, topped with almonds and served with fresh fruit or tossed greens and a slice of banana bread, is a favorite. Save room for turtle pie, topped with caramel and loaded with whipped cream. | 5201 N. Walnut St. | 765/284–6364 | $6.99–$16.99 | AE, D, MC, V.

Lodging

Comfort Inn. Six miles off I–69, exit 41, lies this chain hotel, nestled among other chain hotels and fast food joints. Complimentary Continental breakfast. Some microwaves, some refrigerators. Indoor pool. Hot tub. Business services. | 4011 W. Bethel St. | 765/282–6666 | fax 765/282–6666 | www.comfortinn.com | 66 rooms | $54–$119 | AE, D, DC, MC, V.

Muncie Days Inn Ball State University. This two-story chain motel is about 1 mi from Ball State, 7 mi east of I–69, exit 41. Complimentary Continental breakfast. Some in-room safes, some microwaves, some refrigerators. Pets allowed (fee). | 3509 N. Everbrook La. | 765/288–2311 | fax 765/288–0485 | www.daysinn.com | 62 room | $48–$58 | AE, D, DC, MC, V.

L.A. Pittenger Student Center Hotel. These on-campus accommodations are older but well maintained. There's a food court and recreational facilities, including bowling and billiards. Cable TV. Pool tables, bowling. | 2000 University Ave. | 765/285–1555 | fax 765/285–6615 | 23 rooms, 1 suite | $45–$50 | AE, MC, V.

Lee's Inn Muncie. This place is on the north side of town, with rooms in warm hues and contemporary furnishings. There's a hot breakfast buffet every day. Minibars, complimentary Continental breakfast. Cable TV. Pool. Some pets allowed. | 3302 N. Everbrook La. | 765/282–7557 or 800/733–5337 | fax 765/282–0345 | 87 rooms, 30 suites, 3 presidential suites | $74–$159 | AE, D, MC, V.

Radisson Hotel Roberts. This 1920s hotel 11 blocks from Ball State hotel offers luxury behind its period facade. Restaurant, bar with entertainment, room service. Cable TV. Indoor pool. Hot tub. Business services. Some pets allowed. | 420 S. High St. | 765/741–7777 | fax 765/747–0067 | www.radisson.com | 130 rooms, 28 suites | $69–$99 | AE, D, DC, MC, V.

Ramada Inn. Room access is via outdoor walkways at this chain hostelry on the south side of town. Charlie's Lounge is popular for dinner. Restaurant, bar with entertainment, complimentary Continental breakfast, room service. Cable TV. Pool. Laundry facilities. Business services. Some pets allowed. | 3400 S. Madison St. | 765/288–1911 | fax 765/282–9458 | 148 rooms | $45–$99 | AE, D, DC, MC, V.

NAPPANEE

MAP 3, D2

(Nearby towns also listed: Elkhart, Mishawaka, South Bend, Warsaw)

The town of Nappanee (pop. 5,500) is as charming as its melodic name. By the 1870s three sawmills here were cutting lumber at the rate of 75,000 board feet a week, and woodworking was big business. Today several workshops pursue traditional craftsmanship; on the east edge of town, Borkholder Village sells wood crafts, gifts, and furniture. Northern Indiana's largest Amish living-history settlement is here as well.

Information: **Amish Country/Elkhart County Convention and Visitors Bureau** | 219 Caravan Dr., Elkhart, 46514 | 219/262–8161 or 800/262–8161. **Nappanee Chamber of Commerce** | 451 N. Main St., 46550 | 219/773–7812 | ecconv@amishcountry.org or nappaneecc@tln.net | www.amishcountry.org or www.nappanee.com.

Attractions

Amish Acres. This 18-building 80-acre farm complex gives an overview of Amish life. You can take horse-drawn buggy rides around the grounds and walking tours through the original house, the main house, and barn outbuildings. The documentaries *The Genesis of The Amish* and *The Exodus of the Amish* are shown at the greeting barn. A huge barnlike restaurant serves a hearty home-style meal, and professional actors at the Round Barn Theatre present the lively Broadway musical comedy about Amish love and life, *Plain and Fancy*. | 1600 W. Market St. | 219/773–4188 or 800/800–4942 | www.amishacres.com | $6.95 | Mar.–Dec., daily 10–5.

Borkholder Dutch Village. Freemon Borkholder, who started Borkholder American Vintage Furniture, converted old chicken houses into a 70,000-square-ft marketplace in 1987 complete with a flea market, arts and crafts and antiques malls, a restaurant, an events center, and village shops. Auctions are held at 8 AM on Tuesdays. | 71945 County Rd. 101 | 219/773–2828 | Free | May–Oct., Mon.–Sat. 9–5; Nov.–Apr., Mon.–Sat. 10–5 | www.borkholder.com.

ON THE CALENDAR

AUG.: *Amish Acres Arts and Crafts Festival.* Some 350 artists show up for this four-day event to market their hand-crafted wares. There's also live entertainment. | 219/773–4188.

SEPT.: *Apple Festival.* The third week of the month brings many an apple-themed event to Depot Plaza, including a beauty and talent contest for kids (resulting in the crowning of the "Apple Dumpling") as well as an apple peeling contest. Each year a 6-ft-diameter apple pie is baked, to be sold by the slice, and there's a parade, antique show, and a tractor pull. | 219/773–7812.

Dining

Country Table. American. A 40-ft-long buffet is the star at this antiques-filled family restaurant on the east side of town. Country cooking reigns; there are pastas, chicken dishes, real mashed potatoes, and all manner of hot and cold desserts. Or order à la carte. | 1401 E. Market St. | 219/773–2201 | Breakfast also served. Sun. lunch only | $5–$12 | AE, D, MC, V.

Restaurant Barn at Amish Acres. American. In this bright red, century-old barn in Amish Acres farm-museum you sit at antique tables with hand-hewn beams overhead to chow down on an all-you-can eat Threshers Dinner that includes two meats from a choice of roast beef, turkey, ham, and chicken, and side items like beef and noodles, sweet and sour cabbage salad, and mashed potatoes; the cider-baked ham and stone hearth–baked bread are famous. Kids' menu. | 1600 W. Market St. | 219/773–4188 or 800/800–4942 | www.amishacres.com | Closed Jan.–Feb. and after 7 PM Mon.–Sat. and after 6 PM Sun. | $15 | D, DC, MC, V.

Lodging

Christian S. Stahly Olde Buffalo Inn Bed and Breakfast. Construction of this Amish farm house, built in 1840, pre-dates the establishment of Nappanee itself. A white picket fence surrounds the 2.5-acre lot, where you'll also find a barn, redbrick paths, and a windmill. You are welcome to stroll, tickle the ivories of the grand piano, or play a game of chess in the common area. Victorian items and an eclectic variety of antique beds furnish the rooms. It's on 2½ acres overlooking a golf course six blocks from downtown and 50 mi from Michigan City off I–80 at the Elkhart exit, between U.S. 6 and Route 19. Complimentary breakfast. Bicycles. Airport shuttle. No pets. No smoking. | 1061 Parkwood Dr. | 219/773–2223 or 888/773–2223 | fax 219/773–4275 | www.olde-buffalo-b-b.com | 6 rooms | $69–$109 | D, MC, V.

The Victorian Guest House. An impressive turreted redbrick mansion built for Frank Coppes in 1887, this inn is the focal point of the small Amish community of Nappanee. Coppes, who manufactured free-standing kitchen cabinets known as Nappanee Dutch Kitchenettes, was a stickler for craftsmanship; when it came to building his wife's dream mansion, he pulled out all stops, outfitting it with etched glass, cross-cut oak, and stained glass—all of which remains today, set off to good advantage by antique furnishings. Some of the rooms have private balconies. The guest house is off I–80 near the Elkhart exit, between U.S. 6 and Route 19, 1 mi from Amish Acres and 25 mi south of Notre Dame University. Complimentary breakfast. Cable TV. | 302 E. Market St. | 219/773–4383 or 877–773–4383 | fax 219/773–4275 | vgh@npcc.net | www.victorianb-b.com | 6 rooms | $59–$119 | MC, V.

The Inn at Amish Acres. On the grounds of the Amish Acres complex, this building is styled after the area's white Amish barns. Patterned quilts and light pine furniture fill the rooms, and rocking chairs decorate the porches overlooking the perennial garden-ringed outdoor pool. Complimentary Continental breakfast. Some microwaves, some refrigerators. Cable TV. Pool. Business services. Complimentary airport shuttle. No pets. | 1234 W. Market St. | 219/773–2011 | fax 219/773–2078 | acres@npcc.net | www.amishacres.com | 64 rooms, 16 suites | $94–$115 | AE, D, DC, MC, V.

Nappanee Inn. Part of the Amish Acres farmstead complex ½ mi away, this dark red building is styled after the area's Amish barns. Brightly colored quilts cover guest-room beds and oak furniture adds a homey touch. Restaurant, complimentary Continental breakfast. Cable TV. Pool. Business services. | 2004 W. Market St. | 219/773–5999 or 800/800–4942 | fax 219/773–5988 | acres@npcc.net | www.amishacres.com | 66 rooms | $84–$120 | Closed Nov.–Apr. | AE, D, DC, MC, V.

NASHVILLE

MAP 3, D6

(Nearby towns also listed: Bloomington, Columbus)

Roughly 60 mi south of Indianapolis the landscape starts to dip and swell into the hills of Brown County. Artists discovered this lush countryside in the 19th century and made the area something of an artists' colony under the leadership of Adolph Shulz and American Impressionist-style painter T. C. Steele, who bought more than 200 acres here in 1907 and built his studio and home here. Later, city slickers peppered country lanes in what came to be known as Peaceful Valley with summer cabins in communities like Bean Blossom, Bear Wallow, and Possum Trot. Steele's home, the House of Singing Winds, is now a state historic site. The artists are still there. But Nashville is anything but peaceful, particularly during fall foliage season, when leaf-peepers creep through town in bumper-to-bumper traffic. One of the state's top attractions, it's crammed with shops and restaurants as well as galleries, and there are goodly numbers of trinkets among the treasures they sell. Throngs notwithstanding, Nashville's charm endures.

Information: Brown County Convention and Visitors Bureau | Box 840, 47448 | 812/988–7303 or 800/753–3255 | tour@browncounty.com | www.browncounty.com.

Attractions

Bill Monroe Bluegrass Hall of Fame. Paying homage to the father of bluegrass, the late Bill Monroe, this gallery, 5 mi north of Nashville in Bean Blossom, displays Mr. Monroe's memorabilia of his life in the business. The Bluegrass Hall of Fame room features top artists Lester Flatt and Earl Scruggs whom Monroe recognized for their contribution to Bluegrass music. Bluegrass mania climaxes in May during a weeklong annual bluegrass music festival. | 5163 Rte. 135 N | 812/988–6422 | www.beanblossom.com/ | $4 adults, $3 seniors | Dec.–Apr., Mon.–Sat. 10–4; May–Nov., Mon.–Sat. 9–5, Sun. 1–5.

Brown County Art Gallery Association. Founded in 1926, this association is one of the oldest Midwest art societies, memorializing Glen Cooper Henshaw, a Brown County artist who worked during the early and mid 1900s. | Artist Dr. and E. Main St. | 812/988–4609 | Free | Mon.–Sat. 10–5, Sun. 12–5.

Brown County Art Guild. Guild artist-members show their work in the guild's gallery. | 48 S. Van Buren St. | 812/988–6185 | Mar.–Dec., Mon.–Sat. 10–5; Sun.–11–5; Jan.–Feb. by appointment.

Brown County Historical Museum. The museum includes an 1850s pioneer cabin, an 1879 log jail, an 1897 doctor's office, a blacksmith shop, and a loom room, where there are demonstrations of spinning and weaving. | Museum La. | 812/988–4153 | Free | May–Oct., weekends 1–5.

Brown County State Park. With 15,500 acres, this rolling woodland preserve is Indiana's largest state park. A covered bridge marks one entrance, and there are six scenic overlooks along the park's ridgetop roads and a fire tower you can climb for even more amazing hill-behind-hill vistas. Weed Patch Hill is among the tallest summits in Indiana at 1,058 ft. Ten miles of trails skirt two lakes, and a special campground is reserved for equestrians. The rustic log Abe Martin Lodge serves home-style chicken and biscuit dinners; it's so popular that reservations here are hard to come by. | Rte. 46 | 812/988–6406 | www.ai.org/dnr | $2 per vehicle residents, $5 nonresidents | Daily.

Little Nashville Opry. Boot-stomping fun awaits at this northern relative of the real McCoy. Though the show itself may be dubbed "little," the headliners who appear here are anything but—unless you'd call Loretta Lynn and the Statler Brothers minor. There are concession stands on the premises so you can commemorate your trip with country music paraphernalia. | 703 State Rd. 46 | 812/998–2235 | $6 | Fri.–Sat., Mar.–Nov. only.

Nashville Express Train Tours. This narrated 20-minute, 2.5-mi tour on a simulated steam train is a fine introduction to the historic sites and local businesses in Nashville. You can watch a video while you're on board. Tours depart every half hour from most major hotels in town. | On Franklin St. at Van Buren St. | 812/988–2355 or 812/988–2308 | $4 | Daily, Apr.–Nov.

Ski World Recreation Complex. The downhill ski resort takes advantage of the hilly terrain with several challenging runs. In summer, music theater and camping are the primary activities here. | 2887 W. State Rd. 46 | 812/988–6638 | Apr.–Oct., mid-Dec.–early Mar., daily.

T. C. Steele State Historic Site. T. C. Steele moved to Brown County in 1907, with his second wife, Selma Neubacher Steele, and built a home called House of the Singing Winds.

© Corbis

AUTHENTIC AMERICAN LANDSCAPE

In the dreamy haze enfolding the hills and hollows of Brown County, a group of artists blossomed into a major art colony, with several dozen artists, mainly Impressionist painters, living and working in the hills of south-central Indiana. Brown County's art colony traces its roots to 1900, when artist Adolph Shulz, searching for the "authentic American landscape," saw an account of the area in a Chicago newspaper article. Traveling the dusty backroads of Brown County he reported: "Never before had I been so thrilled by a region. It seemed like a fairyland, with its narrow winding roads leading the traveler down into creek beds, through water pools, and up and over the hills . . . Everywhere there were rail fences almost hidden in Queen Anne's lace, goldenrod, and other interesting weeds and bushes. Picturesque cabins here and there seemed to belong to the landscape, as did the people who lived in them. All this country was enveloped in a soft opalescent haze. A sense of peace and loveliness never before experienced came over me and I felt that at last I had found the ideal sketching ground." The founders of the art colony, Shulz and Theodore Clement Steele, settled there by 1908 and were soon joined by other artists who remained seasonal or year-round residents.

Today the Brown County Art Colony is considered among the most influential in the state, with works ranking among the state's art treasures. Their rich Impressionist style put a polish on the hillfolk and the surrounding landscape, where place names like Weed Patch and Bear Willow Hill hint of the area's rustic nature. Today, painters still hang out their shingles in Brown County, and they have been joined by scores of craftspeople, all of whom welcome visitors to their studios and galleries in tiny Nashville and the surrounding countryside.

As a member of the Hoosier Group of American Regional Impressionist Painters, Steele was inspired by Brown County's tranquil, woodsy landscape and spent summers here, becoming one of the leading members in the Brown County Art Colony. The hilltop home and studio, surrounded by several acres of gardens first tended by Selma, are filled with personal mementos as well as changing exhibits of paintings from his entire career. Four trails, the Dewar Log Cabin, and the 92-acre Selma Steele Nature Preserve are also part of the 211-acre property. | 4220 T. C. Steele Rd. | 812/988–2785 | fax 812/988–8457 | www.ai.org/ism/sites/steele/ | Free | Tues.–Sat. 9–5, Sun. 1–5.

Yellowwood State Forest. At 22,000 acres, Yellowwood is one of the larger state forests with boat rentals available for the quiet lake. | Yellow and Lake Drs. on State Hwy. 46 | 812/988–7945 | www.ai.org/ism | Free | Daily.

ON THE CALENDAR
JUNE: *Annual Bill Monroe Memorial Bean Blossom Bluegrass Festival.* In Bean Blossom, the spirit of legendary artist Bill Monroe lives on with four days of music, workshops, and tours of the Bill Monroe Bluegrass Hall of Fame. | 812/988–6422.
JUNE: *Log Cabin Tour.* Historic and contemporary log cabins are tucked among the hills and hollows of scenic Brown County. | 800/753–3255.
JUNE–SEPT.: *Brown County Playhouse.* Each summer and fall (weekends), budding thespians from Indiana University present summer theater in the tiny town of Nashville. Performances feature recent off-Broadway hits and comedies. | 70 S. Van Buren St. | Box office: 812/988–2123; business office: 812/855–1103.

Dining
Hobnob Restaurant. American. Housed in Nashville's oldest commercial building, a big white storefront on a downtown corner, Hobnob is a favorite breakfast spot also serving country-style lunches and dinners, including salads, chicken, and steak. Wine only. | 17 W. Main St. | 812/988–4114 | $8–$15 | AE, D, MC, V.

Nashville House. American. Paintings by Brown County artists line the walls and red-checked tablecloths grace the tables of the rustic setting. In the heart of downtown Nashville, the family restaurant is known for its fried chicken and roast turkey dinners with fried biscuits and apple butter. Kids' menu. | 87 N. Van Buren St. | 812/988–4554 | Closed late Dec.–early Jan. and Tues. in Nov.–Sept. | $16–$22 | D, MC, V.

The Ordinary. Contemporary. Nestled within the 350 quaint shops, galleries, and studios that spread sidewalk sales regularly, the restauraunt and tavern is dressed in Early American style. Known for sandwiches, ribs, and chops. Entertainment Fri., Sat. Kids' menu. | N. Van Buren St. | 812/988–6166 | Closed Mon. in Nov.–Sept. | $10–$35 | D, MC, V.

Story Inn. American. Renovated from a 1850s general store, this old world enclave is known for fine dining by candlelight. Known for filet mignon and bourbon strip steak. Seafood and vegetarian dishes available. | 6404 S. Rte. 135, Story | www.storyinn.com | 812/988–2273 | Reservations required | Closed Mon. No lunch | $15–$25.

Lodging
Abe Martin Lodge. The lodge takes its name from artist Kin Hubbard's cartoon character Abe Martin, a popular figure with Dogpatch-like quips that appeared in the *Indianapolis News* until the 1930s. Abe Martin Lodge was built of native stone and hand-hewn oak timbers in 1932, and has been completely remodeled. There are two spacious lobbies with rustic stone fireplaces and a dining room serving country-style fare such as fried chicken and biscuits with apple butter. Resting on the south side of town, the main lodge contains 30 rooms and the newer addition 54. There are 20 newer housekeeping cabins open year-round and remodeled cabins of 1932 are open from April until November. Dining room. | Rte. 46, | 812/988–4418 | fax 812/988–7334 | 84 rooms, 76 cabins | $76–$98, $52–$120 cabins | AE, D, MC, V.

Allison House. The 1883 yellow-clapboard bed-and-breakfast on the south side of town bustles with downtown shoppers during the day. No smoking, no room phones. Cross-country and downhill skiing. | 90 S. Jefferson St. | 812/988–0814 | tammy@kiva.net | www.browncounty.org/lodging/allison/house.html | 5 rooms | $95 | No credit cards.

Always Inn. A wrap-around deck and outdoor gazebo hot tub surrounded by an idyllic garden help make this bed & breakfast a true pastoral escape. Each cozy, arboreally named room has a variety of antique furnishings. Some rooms have fireplaces and access to either private patios or decks. Complimentary full breakfast. Some in-room hot tubs. In-room VCRs. Outdoor hot tub. | 8072 E. State Rd. 46 | 812/998–2233 or 888/457–2233 | fax 812/457–2233 | www.alwaysinn.com | 5 rooms | $75–$200 | AE, D, MC, V.

Artists Colony Inn. The design of the inn recalls the Pittman Inn, an early 1900s Nashville hostelry frequented by itinerant artists. Built in 1992, this three-story wood-frame building resembles the many oversize Early American clapboard farmhouses seen in the area. It sits back off Nashville's busy main street surrounded by gardens and towering trees. Reproduction cherry-wood and painted furniture, cupboards, Windsor chairs, and woven coverlets furnish the spare yet comfortable rooms in a palette of deep blue, green, burgundy, and cream. Many of the furnishings were made by local artists and each room has been named for one of the early Hoosier School artists. Restaurant. Cable TV. Hot tub. | 105 S. Van Buren St., 47448 | 812/988–0600 | fax 812/988–9023 | www.artistscolony.com | 20 rooms, 3 suites | $69–$170, suites $120–$220 | AE, MC, V.

Brown County Inn. Built in the 1970s, wood siding covers the facade of this established motel that conveniently rests on the edge of downtown. The motel is furnished with antiques, collectibles, and country decor. Restaurant, bar with entertainment. Cable TV. Indoor-outdoor pool. Miniature golf, tennis. Playground. | 51 State Rd. 46 E | 812/988–2291 or 800/772–5249 | fax 812/988–8312 | www.browncountyinn.com | 99 rooms | $50–$109 | AE, D, DC, MC, V.

Olde Magnolia House. In the heart of Nashville, just one block from most of the shops, lies this white Victorian mansion. The homey rooms have queen-sized beds, antique furnishings, and in some rooms, gas fireplaces. Lace and wall paper make up some of the fussier rooms. If you are an early riser, you can enjoy a pre-breakfast coffee and tea service on the porch. Though some baths are across the hall from the guest room, all baths are private. | 213 S. Jefferson St. | 812/988–2434 | fax 812/988–2434 | jwwlaw@kiva.net | www.kiva.net/~jwwlaw | 4 rooms | $90–$125, rates are seasonal | D, MC, V.

Seasons Lodge. Set on a hillside off the highway, 1½ mi from downtown and across from Brown County State Park, the full-service hotel with remodeled guest rooms is built of native stone with painted timbers and in a contemporary style. Restaurant, bar with entertainment, room service. Cable TV. Indoor-outdoor pool. Playground. Business services. | 560 Rte. 46 E | 812/988–2284 or 800/365–7327 | fax 812/988–7510 | roomstsl@kiva.net | www.seasonslodge.com | 80 rooms | $50–$115 | AE, D, DC, MC, V.

NEW ALBANY

MAP 3, D8

(Nearby towns also listed: Clarksville, Corydon, Jeffersonville, Madison, Wyandotte)

During New Albany's glory days the town enjoyed constant traffic along the Ohio River and by 1850 was the largest city in Indiana. Boats built there often held racing records for the Louisville–New Orleans run. Today, handsome Federal and Victorian homes in the Mansion Row Historic District east of downtown reflect the town's heyday. The most opulent of them, a 1869 Second Empire mansion of merchant and philanthropist William S. Culbertson, is now a state historic site. North of town, ridgetop roads known as "the Knobs" are peppered with markets, orchards, and restaurants and overlook the Falls City area and Louisville.

Information: **Southern Indiana, Clark and Floyd Counties Convention and Tourism Bureau** | 315 Southern Indiana Ave., Jeffersonville, 47130 | 812/280–5566 or 800/552–3842 | www.sunnysideoflouisville.org.

Attractions

Cave Country Canoes. The Blue River is a spring-fed stream that takes on an aqua hue as it parts limestone bluffs riddled with caves. It was the first river selected for Indiana's Natural and Scenic Rivers System. Canoe and kayak trips here range from half-day, 7-mi trips to two-day and longer excursions. | Milltown | 812/365–2705 | www.cavecountrycanoes.com/trips.htm | half day $15; full day $18, two days $32 | Apr.–Oct.

Culbertson Mansion State Historic Site. The 1867 three-story French Second Empire mansion houses hand-painted ceilings, a carved rosewood staircase, marble fireplaces, and crystal chandeliers in its 25 rooms. William S. Culbertson was one of Indiana's wealthiest merchants and philanthropists. | 914 E. Main St. | 812/949–6134 | www.ai.org/ism | Free | Mar.–Dec., Tues.–Sun. 9–5.

Floyd County Museum. The Beaux Arts museum building originally housed the New Albany Public Library from 1904 until 1969 before reopening in 1971 as an art and history museum. Permanent exhibits depicting the pioneer, steamboat, and Civil War era along the Ohio River complement traveling exhibits of local history and culture. | 201 E. Spring St. | 812/944–7336 | Tues.–Sat. 1–4.

Forest Discovery Center. Visitors can stroll among the trees in a glass-enclosed skyway that connects the forest to Koetter Woodworking's state-of-the-art lumber mill and see logs transformed into finished trim products. | 533 Louis Smith Rd., Starlight | 812/923–1590 | fax 812/923–1595 | www.forestcenter.com | $5.50 | Tues.–Sat. 9–5, Sun. 1–5.

Scribner House. Framed in wood, the Federal-style two-story home was the built in 1814 by Joel and Mary Scribner. Now owned by the local chapter of the Daughters of the American Revolution, the three-bedroom, two-parlor house overlooks the Ohio River from a two-level back porch. | 201 E. Spring St. | 812/944–7330 or 812/948–2921 | Free | Sept.–July, Tues.–Sat. 10–4; tours by appointment.

ON THE CALENDAR

OCT.: *Harvest Homecoming*. Downtown streets burst with a festival marketplace complete with a parade, a carnival, and concerts jostling through more than 360 booths of family fun. | 812/945–6096.

Dining

Joe Huber's Family Farm, Orchard and Restaurant. American. What started as a roadside stand in the "Knobs" above New Albany is now a spacious, yet country-style restaurant reflecting its farming roots serving chicken and dumplings with fresh vegetables and fried biscuits as well as their famous honeyed ham. Raspberry and coconut cream pies, peach cobbler, and fresh strawberry pie (in season) complete the menu. Open-air dining on the patio overlooks a flower and vegetable garden. | 2421 Scottsville Rd., Starlight | 812/923–5255 | www.joehubers.com | $12–$15 | MC, V.

Lodging

Honeymoon Mansion Bed and Breakfast Inn and Wedding Chapel. Elegantly furnished guest rooms and a Victorian-style chapel are highlights of this intimate getaway on the east side of town. Complimentary breakfast. No smoking, some in-room hot tubs. Cable TV, in-room VCRs, no room phones. No kids under 12. Business services. | 1014 E. Main St. | 812/945–0312 or 800/759–7270 | fax 812/945–6615 | www.usagetaways.com/indiana/honeymoon | 6 rooms | $79–$159 | D, MC, V.

NEW CASTLE

MAP 3, E5

(Nearby towns also listed: Anderson, Connersville, Greenfield, Muncie, Richmond)

In 1901 the long-stemmed American Beauty rose from a grower in New Castle was displayed at the Kansas City International Rose Show, creating an instant demand. By 1910 the floral business was in full bloom in New Castle, with more than 50 greenhouses and 100 florists. Rose City continued to blossom until World War I when the automotive industry and the Hoosier Kitchen Cabinet Company became prominent. Though cabinetmaking is no longer a main enterprise today, New Castle has several small and medium-size manufacturers that make metal and plastic parts and compo-

© Artville

HOOSIER HYSTERIA

Hoosier (an Indiana resident) and Hysteria (Indiana high-school basketball fever) go together like Indy and 500. The origin of the word Hoosier (pronounced *hoo*-zhur), first used in the 1820s, is still debatable. There are at least 30 different theories about it. Here are a few of the most popular ones: Early pioneers would answer knocks on their cabin doors with "Who's yere?"

Indiana settlers were well known for using their fists rather than dialogue to settle disputes and "hush" others. The settlers became known as "hushers" which with a southern Indiana drawl was pronounced "hoosiers."

A Kentucky contractor named Samuel Hoosier hired workers from Indiana to build Louisville's Portland canal. The laborers became known as "Hoosier's men" or "Hoosiers." (The existence of Mr. Hoosier has never been proven.)

Indiana poet James Whitcomb Riley said that "Hoosier" came from the early settlers' uncivilized behavior. "They were vicious fighters," he insisted, "and frequently bit off noses and ears. This happened so often that a settler coming into the barroom after a fight would see an ear on the floor and ask, 'Whose ear?' "

Modified by the word Hoosier, hysteria refers to the fervor with which fans of high-school basketball follow the sport in Indiana. Although Dr. James Naismith, a Canadian-born instructor at a YMCA in Massachusetts, is credited with inventing the game of basketball in 1891, he himself once said that "basketball really had its origin in Indiana." Naismith nailed a peach basket to the gymnasium balcony, added a ball, and the rest is history. The name Hoosier Hysteria was adopted roughly 20 years after the game was invented, when Bloomington hosted the first high-school championship in 1911. Of the 20 biggest high-school gymnasiums in the country, Indiana claims 17. Among the most exciting high-school championship games were those in 1954, when the tiny 161-student Milan High School defeated four-time state champions Muncie Central and became the inspiration for the 1980s movie *Hoosiers*. The 1990 championship game drew more than 20,000 fans, topping national records for attendance at a high-school game. The Indiana Basketball Hall of Fame in New Castle traces Hoosier Hysteria and the history of the game in Indiana.

nents for machinery and durable goods. Like many small towns in Indiana, New Castle touts its high-school basketball prowess, and in 1959 unveiled the largest high-school gymnasium in the world, with seating for 9,314. Next door is the Indiana Basketball Hall of Fame Museum, which relocated from Indianapolis to New Castle in 1989.

Information: Henry County Convention and Visitors Bureau | 2020 S. Memorial Dr., 47362 | 765/593–0764 | info@henrycountyin.org | www.henrycountyin.org.

Attractions

Henry County Historical Society Museum. Housed in the home of Civil War general William Grose, who commanded the 36th Indiana Regiment at Chickamauga and Atlanta, American history unfolds through artifacts, artwork, and mementos. | 614 S. 14th St. | 765/529–4028 | Free | Mon.–Sat. 1–4:30.

Henry County Memorial Park. A 240-acre park with a lake, boating, fishing, playground, and picnic areas. | 765/529–1004 | Free | Daily.

Henry County Saddle Club. Within the Henry County Memorial Park is this equestrian hot spot which hosts a variety of training clinics, horse shows, and the High School Rodeo Finals. Concessions are available on event days. | 2221 N. Memorial Dr. | 765/766–5441 | Mar.–Oct.

The Indiana Basketball Hall of Fame. Until 1986, the Hall of Fame was located in Indianapolis. The New Castle Hall is in a 14,000-square-ft building of brick and glass near a 9,314-seat high school gymnasium, the world's largest. Its courtyard walks and retaining walls reflect the familiar shapes of a basketball floor surrounding a map of the state, 70 ft long and 36 ft wide. A chronological history of the game, which was invented in 1891 and played in Indiana for the first time in 1894 at the Crawfordsville YMCA, is recounted through artifacts, equipment, pictures, videos, and memorabilia. | 1 Hall of Fame Ct. | 765/529–1891 | $4 | Tues.–Sat. 10–5, Sun. 1–5.

Summit Lake State Park. One of the newer state parks, 2,500-acres of wooded preserve surround a lake and beach. Summers here are filled with activities, while the winter invites cross-country skiers to its trails. | 5993 N. Messick Rd. | 765/766–5873 | www.ai.org/ | $2 per vehicle residents, $5 non-residents | Daily.

ON THE CALENDAR

DEC.: *City Securities Hall of Fame Classic.* Eight Indiana high school teams go hoop for hoop in this two-day event for both boys' and girls' basketball titles. Four games a day and a consolation game fill the weekend with the glories of the Hoosier-dominated game. | New Castle Field House, 801 Park View Dr. | 765/529–1891.

Dining

Roberto's. Italian. Half a block away from the central Courthouse stands this building, with 13-ft-high original tin ceilings built in 1880. The 7-ft-high shelves that encircle the dining room contain antique paraphernalia including collections of cameras, plungers, spittoons and seasonal scenes. Lasagna is the house specialty, but another stick-to-your-ribs option is the combo plate, where you choose three of your favorites from the Italian menu. | 1326 Broad St. | 765/521–3999 | fax 765/521–8296 | Closed Sun. | $4–$15 | AE, D, MC, V.

Lodging

Mulberry Lane Inn. Five miles north of New Castle sits this four-story brick home with white trim. The former spook house sits on 6.5 acres, which include a huge barn and more than 45 bird houses. The three-room suite has independent access, and the kitchens are fully stocked with items that can be quickly prepared or reheated. Complimentary breakfast. In-room VCRs. Outdoor pool. | 5256 N. Country Rd. 75 W | 765/836–4500 | 1 suite, 1 room | $50–$80 | No credit cards.

NEW HARMONY

MAP 3, A8

(Nearby towns also listed: Evansville, Vincennes)

The area at the confluence of the Wabash and Ohio rivers was a wilderness in the 1800s. Then a Lutheran separatist sect known as the Harmonie Society, from Germany via Pennsylvania, came here under the leadership of charismatic Father George Rapp. Within 10 years, hardworking Harmonists had transformed the forests into a thriving community with 150 buildings. They were operating six mills and shipping goods to 22 states and 16 countries. Then, in 1824, Rapp sold the town lock, stock, and barrel to Scottish-born industrialist and philanthropist Robert Owen and William Maclure. Owen envisioned the community as a giant laboratory for creating a "New Moral World," a society based on equality and education. To make his dream a reality, Owen enlisted preeminent scientists, educators, and artists, and transported them to the Rappite settlement aboard a keelboat—dubbed the "boatload of knowledge." Where hard work had brought prosperity to the Rappites, the lack thereof doomed their intellectual successors. By 1827, the utopian vision had failed. Owen bid farewell and departed. Still, the town records several firsts: It was the site of the first free public library and the first coeducational school system. Until 1856, New Harmony was also home to the U.S. Geological Survey. Today, descendents of Robert Owen have initiated restoration efforts, and the town wears its history on its sleeve. In addition to the simple, square Harmonist cabins and architectural relics of the Owen and later periods, there are several monumental works by contemporary architects such as Richard Meier. A combination ticket admits you to your choice of ten of the many historic buildings in town; it's good for up to two days.

Information: **Historic New Harmony** | Box 579, 47631 | 812/682–4488 | harmony@usi.edu | www.newharmony.org/.

Attractions

The Atheneum–Visitors Center. Designed by contemporary architect Richard Meier, this stunning white building sits atop a low, grassy knoll overlooking the Wabash River. In addition to exhibits, the building presents a 17-minute orientation film. This is the place to buy tickets to area historic sites. | North and Arthur Sts. | 800/231–2168 | www.newharmony.org/ | Tours $8 | Mid-Mar.–Dec., daily 8:30–5.

David Lenz House. Built between 1819 and 1822, this tall, weathered frame house is a typical Harmonist family home. It is furnished with pieces of the period and is surrounded by herb, vegetable, and flower gardens. | 324 North St. | 800/231–2168 | www.newharmony.org/ | Combo ticket $8 | Mid-Mar.–Dec., daily 9–4.

Early West Street Log Structures. These reconstructed cabins, across from the Lenz House, are examples of how early Harmonists lived when they came here in the early 1800s. Cooking was done outside; the 1814 Weber Cabin lacks a chimney for that reason. The Eigner Cabin, dating from 1819, is slightly more sophisticated; whitewashed walls were intended to keep insects out and brighten the space. The Potter's Shop, built in the same year, displays pottery of the period. | West and North Sts. | 800/231–2168 | www.newharmony.org/ | Combo ticket $8 | Mid-Mar.–Dec., daily 9–4.

Doctor's Office Exhibit. An apothecary shop shows what medical practice was like in a small Midwestern town during the early 1800s. | Rte. 66 and Church St. | 800/231–2168 | www.newharmony.org/ | Combo ticket $8 | Mid-Mar.–Dec., daily 9–4.

The Keppler House. The former residence pays tribute to the state's first state geologist, David Dale Owen, who conducted geological surveys of five states from his home in New

Harmony. | Tavern and Brewery Sts. | 800/231–2168 | www.newharmony.org/ | Combo ticket $8 | Mid-Mar.–Dec., daily 9–4.

Harmonie State Park. This 3,465-acre preserve 3 mi south of New Harmony stretches from the Wabash River's flat flood plain to rolling hills. There are picnic areas, a campground, a boat launch, fishing, a good-size swimming pool, and equestrian and hiking trails. | Rte. 69 | 812/682–4821 | www.newharmony.org/ | $2 per vehicle for residents, $5 nonresidents | Daily.

Harmonist Cemetery. Here, opposite early Harmonist log cabins, you can see where 230 Harmonists rest in unmarked graves, in keeping with their religious beliefs; the site was previously a Native American burial ground. | West and Granary Sts. | 800/231–2168 | www.newharmony.org/ | Free | Daily Mar.–Dec.

John Beal House. Scientific exhibits from the Owen–Maclure period are housed in this 1829 structure. | Granary St. | 800/231–2168 | www.newharmony.org/ | Admission usually charged (varies) | Mid-Mar.–Dec., daily 9–4.

The Labyrinth. Built in 1939 on the south side of town, this maze mirrors one that was a part of the Harmonist community; their labyrinth symbolized the twists and turns along life's difficult journey to perfection. | 800/231–2168 | www.newharmony.org/ | Free | Daily.

Lichtenberger Building/Maximilian-Bodmer Exhibit. This building exhibits the Maximilian-Bodmer print collection *Travels in the Interior of North America 1832–1834*. Swiss artist Johann Karl Bodmer harvested the collection of original aquatints and lithographs during an expedition to the western United States with German naturalist Alexander Philip Maximilian, Prince of Wied. Bodmer stayed in New Harmony for six months during the Owen–Maclure period. | Tavern and Main Sts. | 800/231–2168 | www.newharmony.org/ | Combo ticket $8 | Mid-Mar.–Dec., daily 9–4.

Murphy Auditorium. Built in 1913, this structure is used for theater productions, lectures, and performing arts events. | Tavern and Main Sts. | 812/465–1635 | www.newharmony.org | Admission usually charged (varies) | Mid-Mar.–Dec., daily 9–4.

New Harmony Gallery of Contemporary Art. This storefront institution downtown on Main Street, established in 1975, promotes regional contemporary art and artists with eight shows a year. | 506 Main St. | 812/682–3156 | www.newharmony.org/ | Free | Tues.–Sat. 9–5; Sun. 12–4.

New Harmony State Historic Site. Several historic structures in New Harmony are under the conservatorship of the state of Indiana, including three-story brick Dormitory No. 2, Thrall's Opera House, Scholle House, and the Fauntleroy Home. | 410 Main St. (Rte. 66) | 812/682–3271 | fax 812/682–5526 | www.state.in.us/dnr/ | Free.

The finest surviving example of Harmonist brick architecture and construction techniques is **Dormitory No. 2,** the largest Harmonist structure in town and one of four Harmonist community buildings. Straw pillow-shaped "Dutch biscuits" insulate the structure, which was used by the Pestalozzian School during the Owen–Maclure period. Between 1858 and 1861, the Slater Print Shop here published *The New Harmony Adviser*. Tucked under the attic stairs, a German prayer from 1825 reads: "Lord with thy great help and goodness, in body and soul protect us. L. Scheel." | Granary and Main Sts. | 800/231–2168 | www.newharmony.org/ | Mid-Mar.–Dec., daily 9–4.

The wood-frame **Robert Henry Fauntleroy House,** built in 1815 as a Harmonist residence, became the home of Robert Henry Fauntleroy and his wife, Jane Owen. They enlarged and remodeled it in 1840. It is furnished to the period; besides Owen furniture, you will see memorabilia from the Owen–Maclure scientific community society and ladies-only Minerva Society. | Church and West Sts. | 800/231–2168 | www.newharmony.org/ | Mid-Mar.–Dec., daily 9–4.

Built for Harmonist shoemaker Matthias Scholle in 1822, the brick **Scholle House** now displays souvenirs of the Pestalozzian School as well as original imprints published in New Harmony from 1824 to 1838. | Tavern and Brewery Sts. | 800/231–2168 | Mid-Mar.–Dec., daily 9–4.

Built as the Harmonists' Dormitory No. 4 in 1824, the brick and frame **Thrall's Opera House** was turned into a theater during the Owen–Maclure period, and was the site of lectures and social events. In 1859 the town's dramatic association remodeled it and renamed it Union Hall. In 1888 Eugene S. Thrall became the sole owner, adding a new facade with arches over the windows and doors. The flooring is original. Performing arts events are still held here. | Rte. 66 and East St. | 812/682–3115 or 812/465–1635 | www.newharmony.org/ | June–Aug.

Roofless Church. This open-air interdenominational house of worship was designed by architect Philip Johnson and dedicated in 1960. The bronze gates and sculpture, *Descent of the Holy Spirit,* are by artist Jacques Lipchitz. | Main and North Sts. | 812/682–4431 | www.newharmony.org/ | Free | Daily dawn to dusk.

Salomon Wolf House. Built by the Harmonists in 1823, this brick building is the home of an automated *Panorama of New Harmony in 1824,* a scale model of the town as it was almost 200 years ago. | Main and Tavern Sts. | 800/231–2168 | www.newharmony.org/ | Combo ticket $8 | Mid-Mar.–Dec., daily 9–4.

Tillich Park. German theologian Paul Johannes Tillich is buried here among the pines and stones engraved with his writings. | North and Main Sts. | 800/231–2168 | www.newharmony.org/ | Free | Daily, dawn to dusk.

Workingmen's Institute. This handsome brick building set back off the street is Indiana's oldest continuously operating public lending library. It was founded in 1838 by William Maclure. Today it houses a museum, an art gallery, a public circulating library, and archives devoted to New Harmony and Posey County history. | 407 W. Tavern St. | 812/682–4806 | www.newharmony.org/ | Library free, museum $1 | Tues.–Sat. 1–4.

ON THE CALENDAR

APR.: *Heritage Week.* The 19th-century craft demonstrations throughout the community include basket making, candle dipping, wood turning, and blacksmithing. | 812/682–4488.

Dining

Bayou Grill. American. One of the restaurants in the New Harmony Inn, Bayou Grill is famed for its Sunday brunch buffet. Waffles and omelets are made to order and there are two carved items (usually beef and ham), five additional entrées, and all the shrimp you can eat. Buffets are also available Fri. and Sat. nights. | 508 North St. | 812/682–4491 | $9–$15 | AE, D, DC, MC, V.

Red Geranium. Contemporary. This restaurant has been a fixture of Indiana's culinary map for years. One narrow rectangular area has floor-to-ceiling windows, and the ceiling of the garden room is painted with images of the Wabash River. The menu offers an assortment of pasta, chicken, and steak, and the spinach salad and double-crusted pies are favorites. | 504 North St. | 812/682–4431 | Closed Mon. | $15–$22 | AE, D, MC, V.

Lodging

New Harmony Inn. Reproduction Shaker furnishings fill most of this contemporary wood hostelry, built in 1979; floors are lovely tulip poplar wood. The new wing is done with French country-style pieces. A glass-enclosed pool, tennis courts, and bicycle rentals are available. Restaurant, bar. Some refrigerators. Cable TV. Indoor pool. Tennis. Heath Spa. Business services. | 508 North St. | 812/682–4491 or 800/782–8605 | fax 812/682–4491, ext. 329 | www.redg.com | 90 rooms | $75–$85 | AE, D, MC, V.

Old Rooming House. You can sit in the front porch swing, borrow bikes and ride around town, or challenge a friend to a board game in this two-story house built in 1896. Today rooms have wood floors and a scattering of antiques, including iron beds. Refrigerators. No TV. | 916 E. Church St. | 812/682–4724 or 888/255–8256 | www.oldroominghouse.com | 3 rooms | $40–$60 | No credit cards.

NOBLESVILLE

(Nearby towns also listed: Anderson, Fishers, Indianapolis)

The restoration of the Hamilton County Courthouse, distinguished by a mansard roof and tall clock tower, has triggered a new sense of community spirit in this county seat just north of Indianapolis, which has come into its own as an upscale bedroom community of Indianapolis since the early 1990s. All around the courthouse square, merchants are busy fixing up storefronts and opening new shops. Studios of artists and craftspeople, and generations-old farms thrive in surrounding suburbs.

Information: Hamilton County Convention and Visitors Bureau | 11601 Municipal Dr., Fishers, 46038 | 317/598–4444 or 800/776–TOUR | hccvb@netdirect.net | www.hccvb.org.

Attractions

Indiana Transportation Museum. Founded to preserve Indiana's railway history, the museum operates 38 mi of tracks of what was formerly the Indianapolis & Peru line, more recently known as the Nickel Plate Railroad. On display you can see vintage railroad freight cars, diesel and electric locomotives, and a Chicago "El" car. You can also have dinner aboard the Hamiltonian. | Forest Park, Rte. 19 | 317/773–6000 | www.itm.org | $3 | Weekends 10–5.

Dining

Uptown Café. There are jukeboxes on each table of this retro knotty-pine restaurant across the street from the Court House. Specials rotate nightly between American favorites like Swiss steak, roast pork and dressing, and chicken and noodles. If you come by for breakfast, try the biscuits and gravy—they put the place on the map. | 809 Connor St. | 317/773–5341 | Closed Sun. Breakfast also served | $4–$11 | No credit cards.

Lodging

Indianapolis/Noblesville Super 8 Motel. This two-story hotel built in 1996 is off I–69 and Route 37. All rooms have recliners. Complimentary Continental breakfast. In-room data ports, some microwaves, some refrigerators, some in-room hot tubs. Indoor pool. Business services. | 17070 Dragonfly La. | 317/776–7088 | www.super8.com | 58 rooms | $48–$69 | AE, D, DC, MC, V.

PERU

INTRO
ATTRACTIONS
DINING
LODGING

PERU

(Nearby towns also listed: Kokomo, Logansport, Marion, Wabash)

The Miami tribe settled the area that is now Peru, named after the South American country. It went on to become an important trading center along the Wabash and Erie Canal during its early years. But it is most famous as the former Circus City, where many a circus troupe came to winter beginning in 1884, including the Hagenbeck Wallace, Sells Floto, John Robinson, and Howes Great London circuses. The site of the present Wallace Circus Farm on Rte. 124 was visited by many famous circus personalities, including clown Emmett Kelley and animal trainer Clyde Beatty. In addition, Peru is famous as the birthplace of songwriter Cole Porter, composer of *Kiss Me Kate, Can Can,* and nearly 30 other Broadway musicals, not to mention some of the most memorable songs in the United States.

Information: Peru/Miami County Chamber of Commerce | 2½ N. Broadway, Ste. 202, 46970 | 765/472–1923 | fax 765/472–1923 | www.miamicochamber.com.

Attractions

Circus Hall of Fame and Museum. On the site of the former Wallace Circus Winter Quarters, 3 mi southeast of town, this museum, which opened in 1990, displays collections of circus wagons, posters, memorabilia, and photographs in barns on the edge of town. Most of the collections hail from the old Circus Hall of Fame in Sarasota, Florida. A highlight of the museum is a 16- by 18-ft model of the Hagenbeck Wallace Circus of 1934, built over four decades by museum director Tom Dunwoody. | Rte. 124 | 865/472–7553 | www.circushalloffame.com | Apr.–Sept., Mon.–Sat. 9–5; Sun. 1–5.

Cole Porter Gravesite. Songwriting great Cole Porter is buried alongside his parents at the monument bearing their last name. | Logan St. between Broadway and Grant | 765/472–2493 | Free | Daily.

Miami County Museum. Displays here highlight local history from the days of the Miami and the pioneers up to the present, via the early 20th century circus years and the legacy of songwriter Cole Porter. | 51 N. Broadway | 765/473–9183 | Free | Tues.–Sat. 10–5.

ON THE CALENDAR

JULY: *Circus City Festival.* Local kids perform in a three-ring circus in trapeze, highwire, and bareback riding acts, against the backdrop of a midway, crafts booths, and food stalls. | 765/472–3918.

© Artville

CIRCUS CITY, U.S.A.

Each year in late autumn, when the circus came to town, Peru schools and businesses closed, and this sleepy rural town enjoyed life under the big top as some of the world's biggest circuses called Peru their winter home. Town residents lined the streets to watch the elephants, prancing horses, brightly-painted circus wagons, and glamorous performers deboard the train and troop down Main Street.

For roughly 50 years, beginning in the late 1800s, the big names of the big tops spent the winter in farm buildings on 220 acres outside of town. It all started in 1883 with Ben Wallace, a Peru resident who bought a bankrupt road show. A few years later, Wallace set up winter quarters for the circus on farmland southeast of town and went on to buy the Hagenbach Circus. By the early 1900s, circuses from across the globe found the Indiana rural surroundings hospitable. While they wintered there, wagons were repainted, animal trainers worked on dog acts and tamed big cats, and stars spent their time perfecting stunts and acrobatic routines. Until 1929, Ringling Brothers and Barnum and Bailey Circus wintered here too. Other circus celebrities like big-cat trainer Clyde Beatty, cowboy star Tom Mix, bareback rider Poodles Hannaford, and Peru native and clown Emmett Kelly could be seen walking the streets downtown.

Today the town celebrates its circus heritage with the annual Circus City Festival and the International Circus Hall of Fame. The museum occupies two barns, one of which was a repair shop for circus wagons on the former Wallace Circus property on Rte. 124 southeast of town. (Follow the clown signs.) Inside are circus wagons, posters, artifacts, and photographs tracing the circus world from its beginnings in 1793 to the present. Much of the collection is from the old Circus Hall of Fame in Sarasota, Florida. When the Sarasota museum went defunct, Peru managed to pick up the collection and raise additional funds for the buildings. A highlight of the museum, which opened in 1990, is a 16- by 18-ft model of the Hagenbach Wallace Circus of 1934, made over a 40-year period by the museum's director Tom Dunwoody.

Dining

Grant Street Bar and Grill. French. Old barn timbers accent this country French restaurant four blocks west of downtown. Each of the several cuts of steaks comes in a unique sauce, and there's a variety of fresh fish. The ruby-red trout, in a white wine sauce with diced tomatoes, is a treat, as are the stuffed chicken breasts. | 26 N. Grant St. | 765/472–3997 | Closed Sun. and Mon. | $11–$17 | MC, V.

Lodging

Rosewood Mansion Inn. As soon as you pass through the portico of this redbrick Victorian home you see a three-story oak staircase illuminated by stained-glass windows at every turn. Erected in 1872, the house has distinctly Victorian charm but the amenities are modern. Complimentary breakfast. In-room data ports. Business services. | 54 N. Hood St. | 765/472–7151 | fax 765/472–5575 | www.rosewoodmansion.com | 11 rooms | $70–$90 | AE, D, MC, V.

PLYMOUTH

MAP 3, D2

(Nearby towns also listed: Mishawaka, South Bend, Warsaw)

Two transcontinental highways, U.S. 30 and U.S. 31, intersect in Plymouth, county seat of Marshall County. This town of 8,291 occupies the site of the last Potawatomi settlement in Indiana, which survived until the late 1830s. Lakes scatter the countryside to the south and west—among them Indiana's second-largest natural lake, Maxinkuckee. Century-old Culver Military Academy, a prestigious prep school, is on the lake. In town, the main street is lined with late-19th-century storefronts that have been restored and painted in varied pastels. A block west of the town's center is a 1872 Georgian-style brick and stone county courthouse ringed with gracious homes. Dozens of farm markets and pick-your-own fruit farms dot country lanes outside town, and blueberries are a top local crop.

Information: Marshall County Convention and Visitors Bureau | 220 N. Center St., Box 669, 46563 | 219/936–9000 or 800/626–5353 | mccvb@blueberrycountry.org | www.blueberrycountry.org.

Attractions

Centennial Park. Of the 250 acres in Plymouth's parks system, 150 acres are devoted to this park and its performing arts center, nine tennis courts, nine baseball diamonds, seven picnic pavilions, and outdoor pool. Plans are afoot to add a golf course and horseshoe pit to the mix. | 1660 N. Michigan | 219/936–2876 | www.blueberrycountry.org/attractions/plymouthpark.html | Free | Daily 6 AM–11 PM.

Chief Menominee Monument. The Treaty of the Tippecanoe in 1832 ceded to the United States land held by the Potawatomi. Most Potawatomi chiefs signed the treaty, but Chief Menominee refused. When the tribe was being removed, Menominee was put under guard for the 900-mi march to the reservation in Kansas, a trek that became known as the Trail of Death. He was never heard of again, and is thought to have perished en route. This statue, 6 mi southwest of Plymouth, commemorates Menominee's spirit. | Peach Rd. | 219/936–9000 or 800/626–5353 | www.blueberrycountry.org | Free | Daily.

Marshall County Historical Museum. A kitchen, parlor, and child's bedroom from the era between 1870 and 1910 have been set up here, along with a woodworking room with a log-cabin facade, a textile room displaying yard goods and trim, and an agricultural room housing tools such as plows, planters, and cultivators. | 123 N. Michigan St. | 219/936–2306 | Free | Tues.–Fri. 9–5; Sat. 10–4.

SEPT.: *End of Summer Bluegrass Festival.* The third weekend of the month, everyone heads for Centennial Park to camp out for this weekend-long event. The grounds are divided into three sections; you can choose to hang out in just one area or pay a flat fee to enjoy all three areas for the entire weekend. | 1660 N. Michigan | 219/936–9000 or 800/626–5353.

SEPT.: *Marshall County Blueberry Festival.* For Labor Day weekend, the heart of blueberry country dishes up blueberry treats, food booths, and more than 600 craft and novelties booths, and there's a parade, a circus, a fireworks display, a car show, and sports events. | 888/936–5020.

Dining

The Hayloft. American. Original stone walls and timbers distingish this 125-year-old barn-turned-retaurant 1½ mi west of town; some tables are secluded in the former stalls. Prime rib and barbecued baby back ribs are the specialties of the house, but there are also adventurous options such as breaded alligator and ostrich steak. | 15147 Lincoln Hwy. | 219/936–6680 | Recommended | No lunch; closed Sun. | $9–$14 | AE, D, MC, V.

Lodging

Culver Cove. This big slate-blue building, built in the late 1980s, inspired by seashore clapboard cottages overlooks Lake Maxinkuckee. Luxury accommodations with contemporary furnishings share the grounds with peaceful wooded trails. Restaurant, bar, picnic area, complimentary Continental breakfast. In-room data ports, kitchenettes, microwaves, room service, many in-room hot tubs. Cable TV. Indoor pool, lake. Beach. Beauty salon, hot tub, massage. Tennis. Exercise equipment. Laundry facilities. Business services. Free parking. | 319 E. Jefferson St., Culver | 219/842–2683 | fax 219/842–2821 | 80 rooms | $149–$189 | AE, D, DC, MC, V.

Ev & Jayne's Irish Inn. Built in 1887, this country retreat on 10 stream-crossed, partially wooded acres became a bed and breakfast in 1997. Rooms are done in country Victorian style, but most furnishings, including the cast iron beds, are reproductions. You can cozy up to an outdoor fireplace, enjoy an early tee time at the golf course next door, or watch the sun set from the brick patio and gazebo. Complimentary breakfast. In-room data ports, in-room hot tubs. In-room VCRs. Exercise equipment. Library. | 7290 N. Michigan St. | 219/936–9190 | fax 219/936–6706 | www.evandjaynesirishinn.com/ | 12 rooms | $150–$175 | AE, MC, V.

RICHMOND

MAP 3, F5

(Nearby towns also listed: Connersville, New Castle)

The Queen City of the Whitewater River, Richmond is near the Ohio border off I–70. The city straddles a wooded gorge, which spreads 600 ft across and plunges 100 ft in spots; fossils fill the gorge walls and Thistlethwaite Falls anchors the north end. Just before the turn of the 20th century, dams were constructed along the river to supply power to flour mills, paper mills, sawmills, and the Starr Piano Company, which turned out 20,000 pianos a year in its heyday. Gennett Recording Studio, which produced up to 23 million records a year up until 1934, helped put Richmond on the map as a jazz center. Much of the city is on the east side of the river; the Wayne County Courthouse, dating from 1893, towers above the riverbank. Readily available spring water, timber, and stone attracted early settlers like the Quakers to the canyon and upland area as early as 1806. The Quakers founded Earlham College, whose graceful redbrick buildings still distinguish the town. Today, industrial and manufacturing plants and distribution facilities fuel the local economy, along with the service sector. Many stately brick structures in the East Main Street–Glen Miller Park Historic District date to the National

Road era. Lavish residences from the turn of the century reflect Main Street's later fame as Millionaires' Row. Also near the National Road are Victorian neighborhoods of the Starr Historic District and more than 200 notable structures dating from 1820 to 1890 in the Old Richmond Historic District.

Information: **Old National Road State Welcome Center** | 5701 National Rd. E, 47374 | 765/935–8687 or 800/828–8414 | askus@visitrichmond.org | www.visitrichmond.org.

Attractions
East Indiana Section–National Road National Scenic Byway. George Washington first envisioned a roadway linking the eastern seaboard with the western frontier in the 1750s. Federal funds were appropriated under president Thomas Jefferson in 1806, and by 1811 the first 10 mi had been laid west from Cumberland, Maryland. After the crude road was extended through Indiana between 1829 and 1834, Indiana's population swelled; more than 90,000 new settlers arrived each year. In the 1920s, the road was paved and became a part of U.S. 40, a major transcontinental highway. When I–70 was built in the 1960s, it bypassed U.S. 40. As a result, Indiana's stretch of the National Road provides a snapshot of westward expansion from the early 1800s to the 1950s era of motor-car touring, cabin court motels, early gas stations, and roadside cafés; the 35-mi East Indiana portion of the road has been designated as both a state and a national scenic byway. The Old National Road State Welcome Center is styled to look like a wood-frame farmhouse; you can pick up brochures of attractions along the way in rooms set up to look like a soda shop and a log cabin. | 5701 National Rd. E | 765/935–8687 or 800/828–8414 | fax 765/935–0440 | www.visitrichmond.org | Free | Weekdays 8:30–8, Sun. 10–3.

One of the first towns alog the pike, **Historic Centerville** dates from the early 1800s and is lined with 100 buildings that are listed on the National Register of Historic Places. When Centerville was established, National Road frontage was valuable. More than 200 wagons a day rumbled by; as a result, Federal-style brick row houses were built with side porches and stood flush with the road. Driveways tunneled under brick archways connecting the houses and led to stables and blacksmith shops in back in an architectural style that is unique to Indiana. | Centerville | Free | Mar.–Nov., daily 8–6; Dec.–Feb., daily 9–5.

With Centerville as its hub, **Antique Alley** is one of the premier antiquing destinations of the Midwest. More than 900 separate dealers, shops, and malls line the 33 mi of the Old National Road between Richmond and Knightstown. | U.S. 40 | 765/935–8687 or 800/828–8414 | www.visitrichmond.org.

Indiana's largest antiques mall is in the heart of Centerville. **Webb's** has 2 acres of antiques with more than 400 dealers and a restaurant that serves sandwiches, soups, salads, and homemade pies for lunch. | 200 W. Union St., Centerville | 765/855–5551 | Free | Mar.–Nov., daily 8–6; Dec.–Feb., daily 9–5).

Cambridge City, home of the **Museum of Overbeck Art Pottery,** dates from 1836. It was established at the junction of the National Road and the Whitewater Canal, and Italianate storefronts dating from the mid-1800s line the streets there. The early 1900s pottery of the six Overbeck sisters is among the museum findings here. | 33 W. Main St., Cambridge City | 765/478–3335 | Free | Mon.–Sat. 10–noon and 2–5.

The buildings containing the **Mount Auburn-Cambridge City-Huddleston Farmhouse Inn Museum** were built when the National Road was young, between 1839 and 1841. The place was not an inn, but owner John Huddleston would let travelers sleep on the floor, "the first to arrive nearest the fire." Today the complex includes a restored farmhouse, springhouse, smokehouse, and barn and tells the story of the daily life of an early Hoosier farming family. | 838 National Rd., Mount Auburn | 765/478–3172 | May–Aug., Tues.–Sat. 10–4, Sun. 1–4; Sept.–Dec. and Feb.–Apr., Tues.–Sat. 10–4.

Knightstown-Trump's Texaco Museum. Knightstown, 30 mi west of Richmond, was named after the National Road's surveyor, Jonathan Knight, and dates from 1827. A dozen buildings display a range of architectural styles. Bruce Trump has refurbished his father's former Texaco gas station, which dates from the mid 1900s, and filled it with Texaco memorabilia. Vintage pumps stand sentry out front. | 39 N. Washington St., Knightstown | 765/345–7135 | www.knightstown.com | Free | By chance or appointment.

Earlham College. The century-old 800-acre campus of this Quaker college sits on the western shore of the Whitewater River gorge near downtown Richmond. | 2500 National Rd. W | 765/983–1200 | www.earlham.edu/ | Free | Sept.–Dec. 15, and Jan. 15–May 1–Mon., Wed, Fri. 1–4; Sun. 1–5 year-round.

The **Joseph Moore Museum of Natural History** holds an Egyptian mummy, replicas of giant dinosaurs and prehistoric mammals, and the most complete fossilized beaver in the world, thought to be at least 10,000 years old. | 801 National Rd. W, # 143 | 765/983–1303 | Free | Sept.–Dec. 15, Mon., Wed., Fri. 1–4.

Glen Miller Park. Established in 1885, the park encompasses 194 wooded acres; natural springs feed ponds and creeks, and there are trails for hiking. There are also several gardens, including an All-America rose garden and a friendship garden with the German city of

© Artville

NATIONAL ROAD

The Main Street of America, the National Road, cuts through the heart of Indiana, running along the state's level central corridor from Richmond through Indianapolis west to Terre Haute. Now U.S. 40, the National Road was the first federally funded highway. Beginning in Cumberland, Maryland, in 1811, the Indiana segment was opened by 1834.

A ride along U.S. 40 and parts of the old National Road traces the 75-year history of this thoroughfare with a panorama of architectural styles and "pike towns." Five miles west of Richmond is Centerville, where clapboard and brick 1820s row houses in mellow pastels cluster along the roadside. The Huddle Farmhouse Inn, a roadside stop in the 1840s, recreates the experience of pioneer travelers. Other towns reflect the National Road's history during the heyday of automobile travel, from the 1920s to the 1950s, with cottage court motels, crossroads cafés, and vintage gas stations.

The *Madonna of the Trail* in Richmond's Glen Miller Park is one of 12 across the United States on U.S. 40. The bonnet-topped pioneer woman stands 10 ft tall and weighs five tons. Dedicated in 1928 to commemorate the pioneers' trek from the Atlantic to the Pacific, the inscription reads, "the autograph of a nation written across the face of a continent."

Madonnas of the Trail:
Maryland, Bethesda
West Virginia, Wheeling
Pennsylvania, Washington
Ohio, Springfield
Indiana, Richmond
Illinois, Vandalia
Missouri, Lexington
Kansas, Council Grove
Colorado, Lamar
New Mexico, Albuquerque
Arizona, Springerville
California, Upland

Zweibrücken, a rectangular plot filled with plants and flowers. | 2200 National Rd. E | 765/983–7275 | Free | Daily, dawn–dusk.

A fountain sits in the middle of the **E. G. Hill Memorial Rose Garden** in Glen Miller Park to honor Richmond's famed rosarian, Gurney Hill, and there's a charming white Victorian gazebo. This is an All-America Garden, with over 1,600 roses, hundreds of colorful annuals and perennials, and a lacy Victorian gazebo; it has been awarded the A.A.R.S. Display Garden designation by the All-American Rose Selection Board. Peak bloom periods are June and Sept. | 2500 National Rd. E | 765/962–1511 | Free | Daily, dawn to dusk.

The **Madonna of the Trail** statue commemorates pioneer mothers. The Richmond statue is the ninth in a series established in 12 communities along U.S. 40 between Cumberland, Maryland, and Upland, California. | 2200 National Rd. E | 765/983–7285 | Free | Daily, dawn to dusk.

Hayes Regional Arboretum. More than 350 acres of nature preserve 172 native plants, and a dairy barn-turned-information center will help you learn about how you can see it all via hiking trails and a 4-mi nature drive. | 801 Elks Rd. | 765/962–3745 | $3 for driving tour | Tues.–Sat. 9–5, Sun. 1–5.

Indiana Football Hall of Fame. The Hall of Fame is devoted to pigskin heroes and memorabilia from Indiana high school, collegiate, and professional athletes. | 815 N. A St. | 765/966–2235 | $2 | May–Sept., weekdays 10–4, Sat. 12–4; Oct.–Apr., weekdays 10–2.

Levi Coffin House State Historic Site. Built in 1839, this eight-room federal brick building, 15 mi from Richmond, was an important link of the Underground Railroad during pre–Civil War days. Providing safe passage to freedom in the northern states and Canada, Levi and Catharine Coffin helped over 2,000 slaves during their 20 years of residence here. | 113 U.S. 27 N, Fountain City | 765/847–2432 | fax 765/847–2498 | www.ai.org/ism/sites/levicoffin | $2 | June 1–Aug. 31, Tues.–Sat. 1–4; Sept. 1–Oct. 31, Sat. 1–4.

Middlefork Reservoir. Some 405 aces of woodlands surround this 177-acre fishing lake. It's stocked with largemouth bass, crappie, blue gill, and channel catfish. | Sylvan Nook Dr. | 765/983–7293 or 765/983–7275 | Free | Apr.–Sept. 7–7.

Richmond Art Museum. Dating from 1898, the Richmond museum is the only public art museum in the country in an operating high school. Permanent installations fill two galleries while the others are reserved for special shows. | 350 Hub Etchison Pkwy. | 765/966–0256 | Free | Tues.–Fri. 10–4, Sun. 1–4.

Wayne County Historical Museum. The Julia Meek Gaar Collection of art and artifacts from around the world includes an Egyptian mummy, an airplane, and a Wooten desk manufactured in Indiana. Pioneer life, early automobiles made in Richmond, and reminders of Richmond's jazz heritage are also on display. | 1150 N. A St. | 765/962–5755 | $4 | Feb. 2–Dec. 20, Tues.–Fri. 9–4, weekends 1–4.

Whitewater Valley Gorge Park. A hiking guide outlines 7 mi of trail through the gorge. It crosses nine bridges and ruins of the covered National Road bridge, vertical cliffs with fossils, quarry sites, a bird sanctuary, and the former Starr Piano Company and Gennett Recording Studio are among the sights along the trail. | 2200 National Rd. W | 765/969–6970 | Free | Daily.

ON THE CALENDAR

SEPT.: *Jazz Fest*. Once the center of U.S. jazz recording, Richmond salutes its heritage with a two-day festival where musicians of every persuasion perform. | 765/962–8151 or 800/828–8414.

SEPT.: *Pioneer Day Festival*. This weekend festival features pioneer reenactments, steam engine demonstrations, pioneer crafts, and more. | 765/962–5756.

Dining

Connie's House of Marker. Greek. The National Pork Producers Association voted the Greek-style pork chops served here, boneless and rubbed with Greek spices, among the

best in the nation. Other house specialities are the Greek salads, topped with homemade dressing, and the prime rib. Stone walls set the scene in the softly lighted dining room on the northeast side of town. It was established in 1946 and still holds its long-famed Greek nights every Wednesday, when there are five specials in addition to the regular menu entrées. | 1500 N.E. St. | 765/966–2016 | Closed Sun. No lunch Mon. | $10–$16 | AE, D, MC, V.

Olde Richmond Inn. Continental. This restored 1892 mansion in the local historic district is a local favorite for dress-up family dining. A tangy shrimp bianca and the fresh seafood are top options in the six dining rooms; all have Victorian furnishings. Kids' menu. | 138 S. 5th St. | 765/962–2247 | $11–$20 | MC, V.

Taste of the Town. Italian. One of Richmond's older restaurants, this place is furnished in a soft burgundy. Along with Italian dinners, it features prime rib, filet mignon, seafood, and roast pork with Creole apricot sauce. Entertainment Fri., Sat. Kids' menu. | 1616 E. Main St. | 765/935–5464 | Closed Sun. No lunch Sat. | $14–$24 | AE, D, MC, V.

Lodging

Best Western Imperial. These well-kept accommodations are on U.S. 40 on the east side of town, 2 mi from I–70, exit 156A. Complimentary Continental breakfast. Some microwaves, some refrigerators. Cable TV. Pool. | 3020 E. Main St. | 765/966–1505 | fax 765/935–1426 | 44 rooms | $40–$55 | AE, D, DC, MC, V.

Bridgford Bed and Breakfast. With its 14-ft-high ceilings, brick walls, and fireplaces, this 1830s redbrick house in the heart of Antique Alley retains the flavor of the era in which it was built. Complimentary breakfast. | 118 W. Main St. | 765/855–5373 | 1 room | $55 | No credit cards.

Comfort Inn. This chain motel is at I–70, exit 151, on the east side of town. Microwaves (in suites), refrigerators (in suites). Indoor pool. Hot tub. Some pets allowed. | 912 Mendelson Dr. | 765/935–4766 | fax 765/935–4766 | 52 rooms, 10 suites | $59–$89 | AE, D, DC, MC, V.

Historic Lantz House Inn. Built in 1823, these three Federal buildings, once the home of a celebrated wagonmaker, are ½ block from the middle of Centerville. Art, antiques, and books fill the guest rooms. The main living room has a fireplace, and one guest room has a Jacuzzi. Complimentary breakfast. | 214 W. Main St., Centerville | 765/855–2936 or 800/495–2689 | fax 765/855–3192 | www.inns.com | 5 rooms | $72–$92 | AE, MC, V.

Lees Inn. Along motel row, this place is just off I–70, exit 156A, on the northeast side of town. Complimentary Continental breakfast. Microwaves in some rooms, some in-room hot tubs. Cable TV. Business services. Some pets allowed. | 6030 National Rd. E | 765/966–6559 or 800/733–5337 | fax 765/966–7732 | 91 rooms, 12 suites | $64–$94 | AE, D, DC, MC, V.

Philip W. Smith Bed and Breakfast. An 1890 Queen Anne brick home with ornately carved woodwork, stained glass, and guest rooms furnished in antique traditional furniture faces Glen Miller Park on the east side of town. Cable TV. Some pets allowed. | 2039 E. Main St. | 800/966–8972 | 4 rooms | $60–$75 | MC, V.

ROCKVILLE

MAP 3, C5

(Nearby towns also listed: Crawfordsville, Greencastle, Marshall, Terre Haute)

Rockville, the county seat of Parke County, is the capital of covered bridge country, where builders left their distinctive mark over a 70-year period beginning in the 1850s. More than 30 of the red-painted beauties span Wabash River tributaries in the surrounding countryside. From Rockville's old railroad depot, signs mark five self-guided driving tours, each leading to and often driving through more than a half-dozen covered bridges. Downtown Rockville, a laid-back farming community, is dominated by a massive stone courthouse from 1882. Historic storefronts around town are home to long-established businesses like Overpeck's Hardware Store, a corner soda fountain, the gallery of the Covered Bridge Art Association, and a quaint café, the Herb Garden Restaurant. The town enjoys an easy-going pace until October when the 10-day Parke County Covered Bridge Festival turns every town in the county into a marketplace of country-style food and old-time crafts. Outdoor lovers make their way to the area to visit Turkey Run and Shades state parks, headquartered 5 mi to the east, in Marshall.

Information: Parke County Convention and Visitors Bureau | 401 E. Ohio St., 47872 | 765/569–5226 | pci@ticz.com | www.coveredbridges.com.

Attractions

Billie Creek Village. This village, with 30 historic buildings and 3 covered bridges, represents an old-time Hoosier farm town; you can pet farm animals, browse in a general store, and watch demonstrations of old-fashioned crafts. It's 1 mi east of Rockville. | U.S. 36 | 765/569–3430 | $3.50 | Daily 9–4.

Tourist Center. Originally owned by Penn Central Railways, the town's 1883 railroad depot became a tourist center when the rail lines were sold. Though no trains move through the depot now, the foot traffic of tourists keeps the station busy. If you need information about the county, just stroll up the brick walkway on the east side of the building and ask any of the staffers inside. It's three blocks east of Rockville Square. | Rte. 36 (Ohio St.) | 765/569–5226.

Raccoon Lake State Recreation Area. A 2,000-acre lake here is stocked with catfish, walleye, white bass, striped bass, and bluegill, and musical performances fill the outdoor amphitheater in season. Swimming, camping, and picnicking are also part of the mix. | 160 S. Raccoon Pkwy. | 765/344–1412 | www.ai.org/dnr | Free | Mar.–Oct., daily.

ON THE CALENDAR

FEB., MAR.: *Parke County Maple Fair.* Billie Creek Village hosts a primitive maple syrup camp and horse-drawn wagon rides during this event, held while the sap is flowing. | 765/569–3430.

JUNE: *Civil War Days.* More than 2,000 Civil War buffs re-create the period with skirmishes, pioneer cooking demonstrations, crafts, entertainment, and a grand Civil War ball where ladies in hoop-skirted gowns swirl around a ballroom. | 765/569–3430.

OCT.: *Covered Bridge Festival.* Thousands converge on the county for 10 days of crafts, food, covered bridge tours, and other special events. | 765/569–5226.

NOV., DEC.: *Parke County Covered Bridge Christmas.* The Parke County Fairgrounds and communities throughout the county decorate for the holidays and showcase arts, crafts, and country-style food. | 765/569–5226.

DEC.: *Old Fashioned Arts and Crafts Christmas.* A county-wide event that follows country roads through famous covered bridges to visit quaint village shops. | 765/569–5226.

Dining

Weber's Restaurant. American. Right on the courthouse square, this mom-and-pop joint is a popular destination for tour buses and locals alike. There are nightly all-you-can-eat specials like spaghetti, fried fish, and fried chicken, and on most nights you can also order chops, seafood, or steaks. The dining room is brightly lit, with half panelled walls hung with watercolors of outdoor scenes. | 105 S. Jefferson St. | 765/569–6153 | Breakfast also served | MC, V.

Lodging

Billie Creek Inn. Designed in the style of clapboard 19th-century buildings this place is modestly decorated in contemporary and traditional wing-back chairs in dark wood. It's next

to Billie Creek Village and overlooks two covered bridges. Complimentary Continental breakfast. Outdoor pool. Pets allowed. | U.S. 36 | 765/569–3430 | fax 765/569–3582 | www.billiecreek.org | 31 rooms, 9 suites | $49–$69, $89–$119 suites | AE, D, MC, V.

Country Oaks Resort. Each of these 1,000-square-ft log cabins, set 22 mi north of Richmond off U.S. 41, can accommodate up to eight people. There are two bedrooms and bathrooms, as well as a full kitchen with dining room. Each cabin has a gas fireplace and an outdoor grill and fire ring. The pond is stocked with fish and swimming is permitted, though no lifeguard is on duty. Some in-room hot tubs, no room phones. Cable TV, in-room VCRs. Pond. Fishing. | County Rd. 275 N | 765/569–6989 | www.coveredbridges.com | 4 cabins | $100–$165 | No credit cards.

© Artville

COVERING SPANS OF HISTORY

As one of the most recognizable symbols of rural Americana, the covered bridge has long been the subject of speculation as well as veneration. While the reasoning behind a covered bridge has run the gamut from the seemingly plausible to the purely romantic, the simple truth is that bridges were covered to protect the flooring and framework, both made of wood, from the damaging effects of weather. By design, covered bridges can withstand the test of time. Today in Parke County, Indiana's century-old original spans still carry travelers across streams. Parke County sits in the center of west-central Indiana's covered-bridge country and proudly calls itself "Covered Bridge Capital of the World," with 32 bridges, the highest concentration of any region of the United States.

Practically every community in Parke County celebrates its covered-bridge heritage during the 10-day Covered Bridge Festival held annually in mid-October. Six covered-bridge driving tours follow color-coded signs through the countryside to a handful of the red-painted beauties. (Only two of the bridges in Parke County are painted white.) Each tour departs from the Parke County Visitor's Center in Rockville's old railroad depot, and generally takes between 1 to 2½ hours of self-guided, at-your-own-pace driving. Three builders constructed most of the covered bridges in Parke County between 1856 and 1920. With a historic mill nearby and a waterfall spilling below, the 245-ft Bridgeton covered bridge, constructed in 1868, is one of the most-photographed in the county. The original Roseville bridge was built in 1866 but was destroyed by fire when two men refused by a saloon vowed to "burn their bridges behind them." The current bridge was built in 1910 and is a double span at 263 ft. At just 65 ft, the Harry Evans covered bridge over Rock Run Creek is among the shortest and newest, having been built in 1908. The 1906 Conleys Ford is Parke County's only pine bridge; others were built of tulip poplar. Supposedly, bank robber John Dillinger used the 1900 covered span over Big Rocky Fork Creek as a hideout.

Indiana's other covered bridge county is Rush County, east of Indianapolis, where six of the original 19 remain. Rush County bridges are painted white and mostly date from the 1870s to the early 1900s. They are distinguished by a modest amount of gingerbread stlye ornamentation.

SANTA CLAUS

(Nearby towns also listed: Corydon, Jasper)

More than 100 years before the town of Santa Claus was officially incorporated in 1967, a group of settlers met on Christmas Eve and decided on its famous name. In 1946, the town sprouted a roadside theme park, Santa Claus Land, which was enlarged over the years and renamed Holiday World in 1980. Still, the Yule season is the main holiday in town. The local post office goes into high gear then, churning out mail with the Santa Claus postmark in response to letters from children nationwide. Santa's Lodge is appropriately decorated for Christmas year-round, and the resident elves leave tiny candy canes on your pillow at bedtime.

Information: Dubois County Tourism Commission | 610 Main St., Box 404, 47547 | 812/482–9115 or 800/ADVENTURE | www.ind-adventure.org or www.holidayworld.com.

Attractions

Dr. Ted's Musical Marvels. The collection of restored mechanical musical instruments here is amazing. You'll learn all about them on guided tours. It's ¼ mi north of I–68, exit 57 (Dale Huntingburg). | U.S. 231, Dale | 812/937–4250 | www.explore-si.com/Dr_Teds.html | $6 | May–Sept., Mon.–Sat. 10–6, Sun. 1–6.

Holiday World and Splashin' Safari Water Park. Characters like Holidog headline in this 45-acre park, a charming small amusement park improbably set among the area's sweeping hills. The industry magazine *Amusement Today* bestowed top honors on the park in 1998, naming it the "#1 Friendliest Park"; the Raven Roller Coaster is known as one of the top wooden roller coasters among coaster buffs nationwide. Holiday World also includes a water park with the obligatory lazy river and a spate of thrilling water slides. Shows ranging from country music revues to magic and high-diving teams are also presented. | At the junction of Rte.162 and Rte. 245 | 812/937–4401, 800/GO–SANTA | www.holidayworld.com/ | $20.95–$26.95 | May–mid-Oct., 10–6.

Lincoln Boyhood National Memorial. Abraham Lincoln spent 14 years of his youth in the hinterlands of southern Indiana near the Ohio River, a few miles from his birthplace in Hodgenville, Kentucky. Lincoln's mother, Nancy Hanks Lincoln, was buried here. When you visit today you will see a visitors center where commemorative panels, exhibits, and a 24-minute film give you insight into the Civil War president's life. A cabin has been reconstructed on the southwest corner of the original Thomas Lincoln property; split rail fences surround the garden, and there are farm animals such as the family would have had. A high-spirited musical drama *Young Abe Lincoln* brings Lincoln's boyhood years to life. | Lincoln City | 812/937–4541 | www.nps.gov/libo | $2 per vehicle residents, $5 nonresidents.

Lincoln State Park. This 1,700-acre state park includes housekeeping cabins, campground, 10 mi of hiking trails, a nature center, and a small lake. It's less than 1 mi from Lincoln Boyhood National Memorial and 13 mi east of Santa Claus town center. | Rte. 162, Lincoln City | 812/937–4710 | www.state.in.us/dnr/statepar/parks/lincoln/lincoln or www.explore-si.com/MainMENU.html | $2 per vehicle residents, $5 nonresidents | Daily.

Santa Claus Post Office. The Santa Claus postmark makes this a hotspot in December. | 812/937–4469 | Free | Mon.–Fri. 7–4:30, Sat. 8–11:30.

ON THE CALENDAR

OCT.: *Fall Party.* In honor of autumn, locals and visitors converge on the campgrounds in Lincoln Boyhood National Memorial for storytelling and kids' games, and everyone decorates their camp sites. | 812/937–4541.

Dining

Christmas Light Golf Course and Banquet Center. American. It may seem odd to play 18 holes and then dine in a room with a fireplace and Christmas motif, but that's the way things are in Santa Claus. In the more casual 19th Hole (with its views of the course's 18th), the decorative theme leans more toward golf. Come here for a light meal, a chef's salad, or a pork tenderloin sandwich. | 1 E. Club House Rd. | 812/544–2252 | Breakfast also served. Closed Mon. Closed Jan. | $4–$7 | D, DC, MC, V.

Windell's. American. Thriving since 1942, this family restaurant is a local institution in Dale, 5 mi from Santa Claus; pictures of customers deck the walls. The half dozen specials each night range from fried chicken to liver and onions, from pork chops to chicken and dumplings. Kids' menu. | 6 W. Metcalf St., on Hwy. 62, Dale | 812/937–4253 | $5.50–$7.75 | AE, D, MC, V.

Lodging

Motel 6. I–64, exit 57 (Dale Huntingburg), leads to this three-story motel. Some microwaves, some refrigerators. Outdoor pool. Small pets allowed. | 20840 N. U.S. 231 | 812/937–2294 | fax 812/937–2495 | 62 rooms | $53 | AE, D, DC, MC, V.

Santa's Lodge Resort. Though you won't find Dancer or Prancer or Rudolph tramping around this rustic, two-story cedar resort built in 1995, you will find a Christmas theme, a pond for fishing and paddleboat rides, and a free shuttle to local attractions. Rooms are mistletoe-free, although a candy cane is left on your pillow at bedtime. Complimentary Continental breakfast. In-room data ports, some in-room hot tubs. Exercise equipment. Pond. Fishing, boating. Playground. Laundry facilities. Business services. | 91 W. Christmas Blvd. | 812/640–7895 or 800/640–7895 | www.santaslodge.com | 87 rooms | $90–$150 | AE, D, MC, V.

SHIPSHEWANA

MAP 3, E1

(Nearby towns also listed: Angola, Auburn, Elkhart, Fort Wayne, Middlebury)

Founded in 1889, this tiny town was named after a Potawatomi chief. Today, although it claims a population of fewer than 1,000, it is the capital of northern Indiana's huge Amish community, the second largest in the nation. Amish and Mennonite bakeries, shops, a huge flea market, and an annual quilt auction have been established here and in nearby smaller towns like Honeyville, Topeka, and LaGrange. Buyers from around the world come here to attend some of the nation's largest draft-horse and carriage auctions. Shipshewana makes a logical starting point for journeys into Amish country. Start at the Menno-Hof Mennonite-Amish visitor center to learn about Amish history and beliefs.

Information: LaGrange County Convention and Visitors Bureau | 440½ S. Van Buren St., Box 637, 46565 | 219/768–4008 or 800/254–8090 | info@backroads.org | www.backroads.org.

Attractions

Menno-Hof. An Amish barn now houses a visitors center, established in 1988, where you can learn about the lives and faiths of the Amish and Mennonite people. Tours are available. | 510 S. Van Buren | 219/768–4117 | www.mennohof.org | $4 | Apr.–Dec., Mon.–Sat. 10–5; Jan.–Mar., Tues.–Fri. noon–4; Sat. 10–4.

ON THE CALENDAR

MAY–OCT.: *Shipshewana Flea Market.* This is the largest outdoor flea market in the Midwest, with over 1,000 vendors selling everything from antiques and collectibles to general merchandise. It's held every Tues. and Wed. | 219/262–8161 or 800/262–8161.

Dining

Blue Gate Restaurant. American. Amish home dishes like chicken noodles over mashed potatoes comes all-you-can-eat family-style and à la carte in this cozy restaurant. | 195 N. Van Buren | 219/768–4725 | $7–$22 | D, MC, V.

Tiffany's Restaurant. American. A huge fireplace makes this friendly restaurant a hometown favorite in Amish country. Home cooking is the draw, with daily specials, sandwiches, and a smorgasbord. It's 11 mi south of Shipshewana. | 414 Lake St., Topeka | 219/593–2988 | $5–$7 | MC, V.

Lodging

The Farmstead Inn. This new hostelry was built to look like the big white barns that dot the countryside. Inside, there's a three-story atrium with fireplaces, and guest rooms are simple and filled with country-style furnishings. It's across from the Shipshewana Flea Market and Auction. 2 pools. Hot tub. | 370 S. Van Buren | 219/768–4129 | fax 219/768–7041 | farmstead@shipshenet.com | www.farmsteadinn.com | 85 rooms | $49–$89 | AE, D, MC, V.

The Old Carriage Inn. Taking inspiration from its Amish neighbors, the rooms in this white and brick ranch house-turned-bed and breakfast are simple, with just a bed, night table, lamp, and private bathroom. But quilts are kaleidoscopic and there are gardens, a gazebo, a porch swing, and a path that leads through the garden gate straight to the Flea Market. Complimentary Continental breakfast. No room phones, no TV. | 140 Farver St. | 219/768–7217 | www.kuntrynet.com/artoci/ | 11 rooms | $75–$85 | D, MC, V.

SOUTH BEND

MAP 3, D1

(Nearby towns also listed: Elkhart, Goshen, La Porte, Mishawaka, Nappanee, Plymouth)

The University of Notre Dame calls this northern Indiana city home. Notre Dame and college football have been practically synonymous ever since coach Knute Rockne first brought national attention to the college as a football powerhouse in the 1920s. However, industry shaped the cityscape. The modest wagon repair and horseshoeing shop etablished in 1852 by the Studebaker brothers ultimately evolved into an automotive giant known for its convertible with a bullet-nose grill before it closed in 1963. In the 1870s, the South Bend Iron Works, later known as the Oliver Chilled Plow Works, was turning out 300 plows a day using a patented process for chilling iron as it was poured; before the end of the century, its president, J. D. Oliver, had built a 1,300-seat opera house, a hotel, and a huge private mansion, Copshaholm. In the 1920s Vincent Bendix introduced a new company to South Bend, developing a self-starting device for automobiles, and later buying the patents for a four-wheel braking system that is now standard on most cars. Power for some of these firms came from the East Race of the St. Joseph River. Since the 1960s, this area has been the focal point of a 52-acre development project combining older buildings with striking new structures; the waterway itself has been rehabilitated as a concrete-sided canoeing and kayaking course, complete with artificial rapids. The sleek glass Century Center, designed by architects Philip Johnson and John Burgee, soars above the whitewater of the old West Race.

Information: **South Bend/Mishawaka Convention and Visitors Bureau** | Commerce Center, 401 E. Colfax Ave., Ste. 310, 46617 | 800/828–7881 | cubinfo@livethelegends.org | www.livethelegends.org.

Attractions

Bendix Woods. This suburban park is known for the giant hedge that spells out "Studebaker" (legible only from the air). According to the *Guinness Book of Records* it is the world's largest living sign. | 32132 State Rd. 2, New Carlisle | 219/277–4828 | www.sjchamber.org | Free | May–Oct., daily.

Century Center. The glass-and-stone structure designed by Philip Johnson and John Burgee, completed in 1977, sits on 11 acres above the East Race of the St. Joseph River, towering over downtown. It is the site of special events, conventions, and meetings. The College Football Hall of Fame and the Marriott hotel are accessible via skywalk. | 120 S. St. Joseph St. | 219/235–9711 | Free | Daily.

The **South Bend Regional Museum of Art** at the Century Center displays traveling exhibitions in a 5,000-square-ft gallery as well as a permanent collection of works by 19th- and 20th-century midwestern artists. There are 11 studio classrooms on site as well. | 219/235–9102 | www.centurycenter.org | Tues.–Fri. 11–5, weekends 1–5.

College Football Hall of Fame. This interactive downtown museum is filled with Pigskin pageantry. You can march with bands, cheer with cheerleaders, salute the mascots, and enjoy tailgating, homecoming, and other football activities. A 360-degree surround-sound theater shows game clips, the Hall of Champions recognizes 800 players, and a timeline traces the history of the sport. | 111 South St. | 219/235–9999 or 800/440–3263 | www.collegefootball.org | fax 219/235–5720 | $7 county residents, $9 nonresidents | Dec.–May, daily 10–5; June.–Nov., daily 10–7.

East Race Waterway. Built during the early 1900s this section of the St. Joseph River has been turned into an artificial whitewater course. It was the first in North America and is one of only six in the world. Kayakers, canoeists, and rafters come here to challenge the rapids. | 126 Niles | 219/233–6121 | Free | June–Aug., Wed., Thurs., weekends.

Northern Indiana Center for History. The center includes Copshaholm, built in 1895 by J. D. Oliver, president of Oliver Chilled Plow. The elegantly furnished home is full of parquet floors, leaded-glass windows, and oak, cherry, and mahogany woodwork; there are 14 fireplaces, and the furnishings are original. Also on the grounds is the Worker's Home Museum, which reflects life of a working-class family in the 1930s. The History Center explores the history of the St. Joseph River valley from prehistoric times to the present; another gallery documents the history of Notre Dame. | 808 W. Washington St. | 219/235–9664 | www.centerforhistory.org | $6 | Tues.–Sat. 10–5, Sun. 12–5.

Potawatomi Park. This 50-acre park contains Potawatami Zoo, which is home to more than 250 animals from five continents. | 500 Greenlawn | 219/235–9800 | $3 | Daily 10–5.

Among Potowatomi Park's many splendors are the **Potawatomi Greenhouse and Conservatories.** Greenhouses, built in the 1920s, host three flower shows each year. There are also three conservatories that are open to the public year-round. A small tropical bird sanctuary separates two conservatories, adjacent to which lies the desert dome, where cacti and succulents are displayed. | 2105 Mishawaka Ave. | 219/235–9442 | $1 | Weekdays 9–3:30, weekends 11–3:30.

Saint Mary's College. Founded in 1844 by four Sisters of the Holy Cross from Le Mans, France, the college now enrolls around 2,000 students in undergraduate liberal-arts programs. The college is off I–80/90, exit 77 (Notre Dame/South Bend). | State Rd. 933 (Old U.S. 31/33) | 219/284–4626 | www.saintmarys.edu/ | Free | Daily.

South Bend Civic Theatre. This old redbrick firehouse in the Park Avenue District is home to South Bend's oldest continuously operating community theater. There's programming for mainstream audiences, as well as programs for children and a series of cutting-edge plays. Seating is raked and the theater is tiny, holding only 77. | 701 Portage Ave. | 219/234–1112 | www.sbct.org.

Studebaker National Museum. From a blacksmithing operation to industrial giant, this museum tells the story of the now-defunct company via horse-drawn and motorized vehicles, photographs, and other artifacts. | 525 S. Main St. | 219/235–9714 | www.stude-bakermuseum.org | $5.50 | Mon.–Sat. 9–5, Sun. 12–5.

University of Notre Dame. The Catholic order of the Congregation of Holy Cross runs this medium-sized, coed, private university of 10,000 students with a 1,250-acre campus. Founded in 1842, it is as well known for its academics as it is for athletics and the legacy of famed football coach Knute Rockne. It offers bachelor's degree programs within the Colleges of Arts and Letters, Business Administration, and Science and Engineering and the School of Architecture. Master's and doctoral programs are available through the Graduate School, and professional studies include the Law School and an MBA program. Guided tours cover a half dozen sights and can be picked up at the Main Building, Eck Visitor Center, and points on Holy Cross Road and St. Mary's Road. | U.S. 33 | 219/631–5000 or 219/631–5726 | fax 219/632–4411 | www.nd.edu/ | Free | Campus open daily; tours mid-May–mid-Aug., daily at 9, 10, 11:30, 1:30, 2:30, and 3:30.

The **Basilica of the Sacred Heart** was built in 1886 in the shape of a Latin cross; it's ornately adorned with gold and brass as well as 19th-century paintings. | 219/631–7329 | Free | Weekdays 9–11 and 1–4, Sun. 1–4.

Adjacent to Saint Mary's Lake on the Notre Dame campus, the **Grotto of Our Lady of Lourdes** is a replica of the famed shrine in Lourdes, France. | 219/631–5726 | fax 219/632–4411 | Free | Tours mid-May–mid-Aug.

The **Notre Dame Stadium** has been the home of Notre Dame's Fighting Irish football team since 1930; it now seats 80,012. Notre Dame football teams have produced seven Heisman Trophy winners, the most of any university. | Juniper Rd. and Courtney La. | 219/631–5726 | fax 219/632–4411 | www.nd.edu/~jeremy/stadium/ | Free | Tours mid-May–mid-Aug. There are two domes to the **Joyce Athletic and Convocation Center,** the home of Fighting Irish basketball, hockey, volleyball, fencing, and swimming, as well as the athletic department's administrative offices and the Sports Heritage Hall. | Juniper Rd. and Courtney La. | 219/631–5726 | fax 219/632–4411 | Free | Tours mid-May–mid-Aug.

A focal point of the university is the **Main Building** in the middle of campus. The Golden Dome administrative building, named for its distinctive architectural feature, contains murals depicting the life of Christopher Columbus. | Holy Cross Rd. and St. Mary's Rd. | Free | Tours mid-May–mid-Aug.

The 11-story granite **Notre Dame Hesburgh Library** holds 2 million volumes and can hold half the student body. The library is named for the legendary Theodore M. Hesburgh, who served as football coach between 1952 and 1987. | Bulla Rd. and Juniper Rd. | 219/631–5252 | Free | Tours mid-May–mid-Aug.

The 69,000-square-ft **Snite Museum of Art,** opened in 1980, houses an impressive collection of 19,000 art objects that includes Rembrandt etchings, 19th-century French paintings, European photographs, and works by American artists. | Juniper Rd. | 219/631–5466 | www.nd.edu/~sniteart | Free | Tues.–Wed. 10–4, Thur.–Sat. 10–5, Sun. 1–5.

SOUTH BEND

INTRO
ATTRACTIONS
DINING
LODGING

ON THE CALENDAR

JUNE: *Ethnic Festival.* This annual weekend event brings crafts, ethnic food, rides, entertainment, a car show, and a parade to Howard Park on the east side of downtown. | 219/235–7633.

JUNE–AUG.: *Firefly Festival of the Performing Arts.* A critically acclaimed series of music, dance, and theater is presented under the stars every Saturday evening in summer in St. Patricks County Park on the north side of town. | 219/288–3472.

Dining

Basil's on the Race. American. Hardwood floors, a unique tin ceiling, and river views give this restaurant its charm; works by local artists hang on the walls. Crabcakes and swordfish, either grilled or herb-encrusted, are the house specialties. For dessert, save room for the seasonal cheesecakes, including pumpkin and white chocolate raspberry. | 501 N. Niles Ave. | 219/233–1300 | Closed Sun. No lunch | $16–$27 | AE, DC, MC, V.

Bibler's Original Pancake House. American. Apple pancakes and a dozen different omelets are the specialties of this popular breakfast and lunch spot. | 1430 N. Ironwood Dr. | 219/232–3220 | No dinner. Closed weekends | $4–$8 | MC, V.

Carriage House. Continental. Crisp white linens dress the tables of this candlelit restaurant in an old brick church in a country setting 15 mi northwest of downtown. You can dine under classic white umbrellas on a patio in fine weather. | 24460 Adams Rd. | 219/272–9220 | Closed early Jan. and Sun.–Mon. No lunch | $20–$30 | AE, DC, MC, V.

Damon's. Barbecue. This is one of a national chain of casual restaurants specializing in St. Louis–style ribs and other barbecue favorites. Kids' menu. | 52885 U.S. 31 N | 219/272–5478 | $8–$20 | AE, D, DC, MC, V.

East Bank Emporium. American. Rich woodwork, touches of brass, and plants decorate this spacious, airy restaurant across the river from downtown South Bend and the Morris Performing Arts Center. The house cuts its own steaks; prime rib is the house specialty. Try the Bourbon Street Pie, a chocolate pecan pie splashed with bourbon. | 121 S. Niles Ave. | 219/234–9000 | Lunch Mon.–Sat. Dinner daily | $8–$13 | AE, D, DC, MC, V.

Heartland & Chicago Steak House. Steak. Vintage black and white photographs of the Windy City and ticket stubs from bygone sporting events cover the walls of this Chicago-theme restaurant. The house specialty steaks are served with with peppercorn or blue cheese sauce. Grilled fish and pasta are also on the menu. The Heartland nightclub is next door. | 222 S. Michigan St. | 219/234–5200 | $7–$15 | AE, DC, MC, V.

LaSalle Grill. Contemporary. Bright paintings lend sophistication to give this restaurant in a vintage building downtown. The kitchen is known for its top sirloin steaks, but the ethnic-inspired menu changes seasonally. | 115 W. Colfax | 219/288–1155 | www.lasalle-grille.com | Closed Sun. No lunch | $14–$35 | AE, D, DC, MC, V.

Morris Inn. Amerian. When celebrities are in town for football games, they often have a meal in this traditional college restaurant at Notre Dame. An institution in itself, it overlooks the campus. Try the grilled Santa Fe pork. Kids' menu. Sun. brunch. No smoking. | Notre Dame Ave. | 219/631–2000 | Reservations required (lunch) | Breakfast also available. Closed mid-Dec.–early Jan. | $12–$22 | AE, D, DC, MC, V.

Tippecanoe Place. Steak. Tippecanoe Place occupies George M. Studebaker's lavish 40-room mansion, full of intricately carved woodwork and stained glass. The kitchen is known for its oven-roasted filet mignon medallions in whisky-peppercorn sauce. There are also seafood options on the menu. Sun. brunch. | 620 W. Washington | 219/234–9077 | No lunch Sat. | $14–$22 | AE, DC, MC, V.

Lodging

Best Inns of America. Lobby and rooms here are traditonally furnished in warm colors at this hostelry 1½ mi from the University of Notre Dame. Complimentary Continental breakfast. Cable TV. Some pets allowed. | 425 Dixie Hwy. | 219/277–7700 or 800/237–8466 | fax 219/277–7700, ext. 113 | www.bestinns.com | 93 rooms | $40–$62 | AE, D, DC, MC, V.

The Book Inn. Twelve-foot ceilings, ornate woodwork, and antiques fill this 1822 Second Empire mansion with a mansard roof, arched dormers, and rooms named for literary lions like Charlotte Brontë, Louisa May Alcott, and Jane Austen. A bookstore is on the premises. The Tippecanoe restaraunt and College Football Hall of Fame are five blocks away. Complimentary breakfast. No smoking, TV. Business services. | 508 W. Washington | 219/288–1990 | fax 219/234–2338 | bookinn@aol.com | members.aol.com/bookinn/ | 6 rooms | $90–$130 | AE, MC, V.

Airport Days Inn & Suites. This three-story concrete hotel, built in 1999, is across the street from the airport. In-room data ports, some microwaves, some refrigerators. Indoor pool. Hot tub. Exercise equipment. Laundry facilities, laundry service. Business services. | 23040 US 20 W. | 219/233–3131 | fax 219/289–6187 | 60 rooms | $65–$125 | AE, D, DC, MC, V.

Days Inn. This motel is close to Notre Dame (1½ mi) and South Bend (2 mi). Complimentary Continental breakfast. In-room data ports. Cable TV. Pool. Business services. No pets allowed. | 52757 U.S. 31 N | 219/277–0510 | fax 219/277–9316 | www.daysinn.com | 180 rooms | $49–$79 | AE, D, DC, MC, V.

Econolodge. This single-story motel is 1 mi east of the Michiana Regional Airport and 2 mi south of the Studebaker Museum. Jacuzzi and kitchenette suites are available as well as standard double rooms. Some kitchenettes, some in-room hot tubs. Business services. | 3233 Lincoln Way W | 219/232–9019 | fax 219/287–6474 | 76 rooms | $45–$70 | AE, D, DC, MC, V.

English Rose Inn, Bed, Breakfast and Antique Shoppe. Built in 1892, this Victorian home across the street from Tippecanoe Place has an antiques store on the first floor and rooms upstairs. Breakfast is delivered in a basket, to your door, and rooms are filled with old lace and linen and stocked with robes, wine, and candy from a local merchant. Complimentary breakfast. In-room VCRs, no room phones. Shops. No kids under 12. | 116 S. Taylor St. | 219/289–2114 | fax 219/287–1311 | www.bbonline.com/in/englishrose/index.html | 7 rooms | $65–$155 | MC, V.

Hampton Inn & Suites. If you take I-80/90, exit 77 (South Bend Notre Dame), you will come to this chain motel down the street from St. Mary's College and Notre Dame. Rooms range in size and scope from a simple standard to an extended stay suite. All rooms have cream-colored, textured walls and stick to a teal-and-maroon color scheme. Complimentary Continental breakfast. In-room data ports, some kitchenettes, some microwaves, some refrigerators, some in-room hot tubs. Indoor pool. Laundry facilities, laundry service. Business services. | 52709 U.S. 31 N Business | 219/277–9373 | fax 219/243–0128 | www.hamptoninn-suites.com | 90 rooms, 27 suites | $91–$115 | AE, D, DC, MC, V.

Holiday Inn City Centre. This hostelry is downtown, one block from the Century Center. Restaurant, bar, room service. Cable TV. Indoor pool. Massage. Exercise equipment. Business services. Complimentary airport shuttle. | Valley American Bank Building, 213 W. Washington St., 8th–16th floors | 219/232–3941 | fax 219/284–3715 | 177 rooms | $119–$129 | AE, D, DC, MC, V.

Holiday Inn–University Area. A Holidome recreation center is the focal point of this motel ½ mi north of Notre Dame. Restaurant, bar, picnic tables, complimentary Continental breakfast and room service. Cable TV. 2 pools (1 indoor), wading pool. Hot tub. Exercise equipment. Laundry facilities. Business services. Complimentary airport shuttle. Some pets allowed. | 515 Dixie Hwy. | 219/272–6600 | fax 219/272–5553 | www.usahotelguide.com/states/indiana/southbend/hinn_southbend.html | 220 rooms | $89–$99 | AE, D, DC, MC, V.

Holiday Inn Express. Twenty minutes northeast of South Bend, in Granger, this two-story brick chain hotel, built in 1995, is 1½ mi off I-80/90, exit 83 (Mishawaka), and a block away from the University Park Mall. Complimentary Continental breakfast. In-room data ports, some microwaves. Indoor pool. Business services. | 6701 N. Main St., Granger | 219/271–1700 | 52 rooms, 10 suites | $89–$109 | AE, D, DC, MC, V.

Inn at St. Mary's. Rooms are large and papered in subdued hues in this hostelry next to St. Mary's College and Notre Dame. Bar, complimentary Continental breakfast. In-room data ports, some microwaves, some refrigerators, some in-room hot tubs. Sauna. Gym. Shops. Laundry facilities, laundry service. Business services, airport shuttle. | 1408 N. Ivy Rd. | 219/232–4000 or 800/94–STMARY | fax 219/289–0986 | www.innatsaintmarys.com | 150 rooms | $100–$180 | AE, D, DC, MC, V.

Knights Inn. Two miles from the University of Notre Dame, this inn offers well-appointed rooms at bargain prices. Complimentary Continental breakfast. Cable TV. Pool. Some kitchenettes, some in-room hot tubs. Business services. Free parking. | 236 Dixie Way N | 219/277–2960 or 800/418–8977 | fax 219/277–0203 | www.knightsinn.com | 106 rooms | $39–$149 | AE, D, DC, MC, V.

Marriott. A skywalk links this nine-story glass-and-steel downtown landmark to Century Center. Furnishings are contemporary. Restaurant, bar. In-room data ports. Cable TV. Indoor pool. Hot tub. Exercise equipment. Business services. | 123 N. St. Joseph St. | 219/234–2000 | fax 219/234–2252 | www.marriott.com/marriott/sbnin | 300 rooms | $79–$135 | AE, D, DC, MC, V.

Morris Inn of Notre Dame. Handsomely appointed guest rooms with wing-back chairs in quiet lounge areas distinguish this fixture of the university. Restaurant, bar, room service, picnic area. Some refrigerators. Cable TV. 9-hole golf course, tennis. Exercise equipment. Business services. | Notre Dame Ave. | 219/631–2000 | fax 219/631–2017 | www.nd.edu/~morrisin | 92 rooms | $89–$106 | AE, D, DC, MC, V.

Oliver Inn Bed and Breakfast. South Bend's largest bed-and-breakfast, the huge gabled 1886 Victorian home rests on a wooded acre with a carriage house next door. Fireplaces and porches add quiet charm. It's ½ mi from Notre Dame Stadium. Picnic area, complimentary Continental breakfast. Cable TV. Putting green. Business services. Some pets allowed. No smoking. | 630 W. Washington St. | 219/232–4545 or 888/697–4466 (reservations) | fax 219/288–9788 | oliver@michiana.org | www.lodging-south-bend.com | 9 rooms, 2 share bath | $95–$149 | AE, D, MC, V.

Queen Anne Inn. A wraparound porch fronts this 1893 mansion. Furnishings are traditional, and the wooden bookcases were designed by Frank Llyod Wright. It's ½ mi from Notre Dame Stadium. Complimentary breakfast. Business services. Airport shuttle. No smoking. | 420 W. Washington St. | 219/234–5959 or 800/582–2379 (reservations) | fax 219/234–4324 | queenann@michiana.org | business.michiana.org/queenann | 6 rooms, 1 suite | $75–$115 | AE, D, MC, V.

Residence Inn by Marriott. The all-suites hotel is in a quiet area 1 mi from the Notre Dame campus. Complimentary Continental breakfast. Kitchenettes, microwaves. Cable TV. Pool. Hot tub. Exercise equipment. Playground. Laundry facilities. Business services. Some pets allowed (fee). | 716 N. Niles Ave. | 219/289–5555 | fax 219/288–4531 | www.marriott.com | 80 suites | $89–$199 | AE, D, DC, MC, V.

Signature Inn. Notre Dame is 1 mi from this motel. Complimentary Continental breakfast. In-room data ports. Cable TV. Pool. Hot tub. Exercise equipment. Business services. | 215 Dixie Way S | 219/277–3211 | fax 219/277–3211 | www.signature-inns.com | 123 rooms | $74–$84 | AE, D, DC, MC, V.

Super 8. This motel is on a main thoroughfare on the northeast side of town. Complimentary Continental breakfast. Some microwaves, some refrigerators, some in-room hot tubs. Cable TV. | 52825 U.S. 33 N | 219/272–9000 | fax 219/273–0035 | 111 rooms | $44–$49 | AE, D, DC, MC, V.

TERRE HAUTE

MAP 3, B6

(Nearby towns also listed: Greencastle, Jasper, Rockville, Vincennes)

"The river runs straight, the land is high, a beautiful place for a town," declared civil engineer William Hoggatt upon arrival of what would become Terre Haute, French for "high land." Songwriter Paul Dresser, a Terre Haute native, also loved the gentle Wabash River valley landscape of west-central Indiana's corn belt; it inspired him to write "On the Banks of the Wabash, Far Away," now the state song. During the town's infancy, residents dreamed it would become the Pittsburgh of the West and established foundries and mills, fueled by nearby coal fields. After the arrival of steamboats and fleets of barges and packet boats on the Wabash came a steady stream of traffic on the Wabash and Erie Canal. For more than a decade, the canal was the region's principal north–south transportation corridor. The Terre Haute Brewing Company occupied the E. Bleemel Building alongside the canal; by 1892 it was the nation's seventh-largest brewery. Today antiques shops surround the restored brick structure, which houses a museum, a general store filled with antiques, and a restaurant. A mix of industry and education are the mainstays of the local economy.

Information: Terre Haute Convention and Visitors Bureau of Vigo County | 643 Wabash Ave., 47807 | 812/234–5555 or 800/366–3043 | fax 812/234–6750 | info@terrehaute.com | www.terrehaute.com.

Attractions

Children's Science and Technology Museum. The hands-on exhibits here include Nature's Furries, a shadow wall, lasers, model trains, and floating rings. | 523 Wabash Ave. | 812/235–5548 | $2.50 | Tues.–Sat. 9–4.

Dobbs Park and Nature Center. More than 100 acres surround a nature center that displays hides and live wildlife. | 5170 E. Poplar St. | 812/877–1095 | www.terrehaute.com/thcvb/ | Free.

Native American costumes and artifacts are displayed in Dobbs Park's **Native American Museum.** | 5170 E. Poplar St. | 812/877–6007 | Free | Mon.–Fri. 1–5; Sun. 12–5.

Eugene V. Debs Home. The eight-room Victorian home of the early labor leader is filled with his original furniture, memorabilia, and artifacts. Debs was a Socialist Party nominee for President five times between 1900 and 1920. | 451 N. 8th St. | 812/232–2163 or 812/237–3443 | Free | Wed.–Sun. 1–4:30, and by appointment.

Farrington's Grove Historic District. Some 800 vintage structures fill in a variety of architectural styles fill this 19th-century neighborhood. The oldest building dates from 1849. | 812/234–5555 or 800/366–3043 | www.terrehaute.com/thcvb/ | Free | Daily.

Fowler Park Pioneer Village. This 1840s village includes nine log homes, a smokehouse, a barn, a sorghum mill, a church, and a gristmill. All are furnished with period pieces, and there are special programs year-round. | 3000 E. Oregon Church Rd. | 812/462–3391 | www.terrehaute.com/thcvb/ | Free | Memorial Day–Labor Day, daily 8–10; Labor Day–Memorial Day, daily dawn–dusk.

Vigo County Historical Museum. The museum, in an 1868 home, spotlights a vast collection of Midwestern material on its three floors of military artifacts from the Revolutionary War to the present. | 1411 S. 6th St. | 812/235–9717 | Free | Tues.–Sun. 1–4.

Indiana State University. This residential coed university founded in 1865 has four campuses in Terre Haute. The 92-acre main campus is on the north side of downtown. The university offers Associate, Bachelor's, Master's, and doctoral degrees in liberal arts, business, and technology. It currently has about 11,000 students. | 217 N. 6th St. | 800/742–0891 or 812/237–6311 | www.indstate.edu/community/vchs | vchs@iquest.net | Free | Mon.–Thurs. 8–6, Fri. 8–4:30.

Paul Dresser Birthplace. The pre–Civil War home of the songwriter, now in Fairbanks Park, sits a stone's throw from the inspiration for his dreamy "On the Banks of the Wabash, Far Away," Hoosierdom's state song. | First St. and Paul Dresser Dr. | 812/235–9717 | Free | May–Sept., Sun. 1–4, and by appointment.

St. Mary-of-the-Woods College. Across the river from Terre Haute is the wooded 200-acre campus of the nation's oldest Catholic liberal arts college for women, founded in 1840. There are about 1,100 students, most nonresident. At St. Anne Shell Chapel, the altar is encrusted with mussel shells from the Wabash. Our Lady of Lourdes Grotto is also on the grounds. The school's shrine of Our Lady of Providence and the Heritage Museum use dioramas to tell the story of the Sisters of Providence, the sisterhood that established the school. | Off Rte. 150 | 812/535–5106 | www.smwc.edu/ | Free | Daily.

TERRE HAUTE

INTRO
ATTRACTIONS
DINING
LODGING

Shakamak State Park. This densely wooded 1,700-acre preserve, which spreads into three counties, has three man-made lakes and an aquatic center, built in 1994. Two nearby state properties, the Greene Sullivan State Forest and Minnehaha Fish and Wildlife Area—rehabilitated former strip-mining sites—provide additional terrain for outdoor recreation. | 6265 W. State Rd. 48, Jasonville | 812/665–2158 | www.state.in.us/dnr/statepar/parks/shakamak/shakamak.htm | $2 per vehicle residents, $5 nonresidents | Daily.

Sullivan Lake. This county-owned and -operated park is centered on 468-acre Sullivan Lake, southwest of Shakamak State Park. You can camp and fish for bluegill and bass. | 990 Picnic Rd., off RR3 (Silver St.) and S Main St. | 812/268–5537.

Swope Art Museum. This Art Deco structure houses a world-class collection of 19th- and 20th-century works by American artists. | 25 S. 7th St. | 812/238–1676 | www.swope.org | Free | Tues.–Fri. 10–5, weekends 1–5.

ON THE CALENDAR

FEB.: *Maple Sugarin' Days.* At the town's Prairie Creek Park, you can watch maple sap being boiled down into syrup using an old-time wood-fired evaporator—and you can buy and taste maple syrup and candy. | 812/462–3391.

APR.: *Strassenfest.* Two bands play music continuously at this German "street fest" which precedes ISU finals week, toward the end of April. Fourth street is closed between Wabash and Ohio, and organizers erect a 60-ft x 100-ft tent for dancing, dancing, and more dancing. Townspeople make sauerkraut, potato salad, and desserts to accompany a variety of German meat dishes. | 812/234–5555 or 800/366–3043.

MAY: *Wabash Valley Festival.* Fairbanks Park fills up with food booths, a market, rides, and a flea market, and there's gospel music and nightly entertainment. | 812/232–2727.

SEPT.: *Little Italy Festival.* The town of Clinton, on the Illinois border 15 mi from Terre Haute, nods to its heritage with a Labor Day weekend festival of food, grape stomping, music, and a spaghetti-eating contest. | 765/832–8205.

Dining

Gerhardt's Bierstube. German. A local landmark serves American as well as German food on the north side of town. Try the Wiener schnitzel. | 1724 Lafayette | 812/466–9249 | Closed Mon. No lunch weekends | $11–$13 | AE, D, MC, V.

M. Moggers Brewery Restaurant. American. On the site of old Terre Haute Brewery's bottling plant, this restaurant is dominated by an immense bar, which was made by fusing one ornate, antique cherry Brunswick bar with another from the old Elks building. Beer-battered and fried dishes fill the menu; the barbecued pork sandwich is a house specialty. | 910 Poplar St. | 812/234–9202 | $7–$15 | AE, D, DC, MC, V.

Lodging

Butternut Hill Bed and Breakfast. This hilltop Greek Revival home built in 1832 is the oldest residence in Terre Haute. The porch affords great views of the city, and rooms are decorated with antiques gathered from local sources. Each has a theme and decor to match; you can choose from a nautical room, rose room, blue room, and butterfly room, among others. Complimentary breakfast. No room phones, TV in common area. | 4230 Wabash Ave. | 812/234–4352 | member.aol.com/bttrnthll | 6 rooms | $70–$95 | MC, V.

Fairfield Inn by Marriott. This new motel is a block from I–70, exit 7 (U.S. 41 N), near a shopping center and 2 mi from downtown and keeps to the traditional decor of the nationwide chain. Complimentary Continental breakfast. In-room data ports, some microwaves. Cable TV. Indoor pool. Hot tub. Business services. | 475 E. Margaret Ave. | 812/235–2444 | fax 812/235–2444 | www.marriott.com | 62 rooms | $56–$65 | AE, D, DC, MC, V.

The Farmington Bed and Breakfast. This Colonial Revival inn, with jutting bays and gables, was built between 1898 and 1901. Until it became a bed and breakfast in 1997, the building housed the Phi Delta Theta fraternity. Many exquisite details have been restored, including a hand-carved fireplace mantel and the stunning stained-glass door at the east end of the parlor. The second-floor sun porch now serves as a sitting area, and most rooms have fireplaces and full baths. Complimentary breakfast. | 931 S. 7th St. | 812/238–0524 | www.members.aol.com/abednbkfst | 5 | $75–$85 | D, MC, V.

Holiday Inn. A Holidome recreation center is the focal point of this hostelry on motel row off I–70, exit 7 (U.S. 41 S). Restaurant, bar. In-room data ports, room service. Cable TV. Indoor pool. Hot tub. Exercise equipment. Laundry service. Laundry facilities. Business services. Free parking. Some pets allowed. | 3300 U.S. 41 S | 812/232–6081 | fax 812/238–9934 | www.holiday-inn.com/terrehautein | 230 rooms | $79–$89 | AE, D, DC, MC, V.

Signature Inn. A three-story chain motel on the south side of town. Complimentary Continental breakfast. In-room data ports. Cable TV. Pool. Exercise equipment. Business services. | 3053 U.S. 41 S | 812/238–1461 | fax 812/238–1461, ext. 500 | terrehaute@signature-inns.com | 157 rooms | $49–$75 | AE, D, DC, MC, V.

VALPARAISO

(Nearby towns also listed: Hammond, LaPorte, Merrillville, Michigan City)

In 1837, sailors from the South Pacific stopped in a saloon in the northwestern town of Portersville, Indiana, and told tales of the old Chilean seaport of Valparaiso, where Commodore Porter (the county's namesake) led a gallant battle while in command of the ship *Essex*. Townsfolk liked the name and it stuck. Spanish for "vale of paradise," Valparaiso accurately evokes the pristine landscape, dotted with lakes and rolling farmland, that characterize the town. The parklike campus of Valparaiso University is the focal point with its stunning Chapel of the Resurrection, one of the world's largest college chapels. Stenciling, stained glass, and sparkling chandeliers recall the opulence of the Victorian era in the Memorial Opera House.

Information: **Porter County Convention, Recreation and Visitor Commission** | 800 Indian Boundary Rd., Chesterton, 46304 | 219/926–2255 or 800/283–8687 | Info@casualcoast.com | www.casualcoast.com.

Attractions

All-Steel Home. The All-Steel Home, dating from the 1940s, is one of fewer than 3,000 such structures built in the nation. Made of porcelain enameled steel, it is furnished with 1930s pieces by theatrical and industrial designer Norman Bel Geddes. Architecture buffs may want to cruise by, although the interior is no longer open to the public. | 411 Bowse Ave., Chesterton | $2 | May–Oct., Tues.–Sun. 1–5, or by appointment.

Dune Ridge Winery. In business since 1998, this winery is in a renovated 1940s motor lodge. The 15 varieties of wines are made and bottled on the premises. You can take a tour, taste the wine, then picnic in the wooded area behind the winery. It's 15 mi north of Valparaiso. | 1240 Bean St., Porter | 219/926–5532 | www.duneridgewinery.com | Wed., Sat., 11-5, Sun. 12-5. Jan.-Apr., weekends only.

Memorial Opera House. Built in 1893 as a memorial to Civil War veterans, the opera house hosts community theater and other performances. | 104 Indiana Ave. | 219/548–9137 | Free | Occasional performances, tours by appt. only.

Old Jail Museum. The local sheriff once lived in this Italianate brick structure, built in 1871, next to the jail. It is furnished to the period. | 153 S. Franklin St. | 219/465–3595 | Free | Wed. and weekends, 1–4.

Valparaiso University. This coed college founded in 1859 sprawls acors 310 acres on the edge of town and is home to about 3,500 students. | E. Union St. | 219/464–5000 or 888/GO–Valpo | www.valpo.edu | Free | Daily.

The contemporary Lutheran **Chapel of the Resurrection** has 100-ft stained-glass windows. It's said to be the world's largest university chapel. | Chapel Dr. and Rte. 130 | 219/464–5112 | www.valpo.edu | Free | Daily.

ON THE CALENDAR

JULY: *Porter County Fair.* Country stars take to the stage and cowboys wrangle in rodeos, against a backdrop of 4-H displays, carnival rides, and food at the Porter County Expo Center. | 219/464–0133.

AUG.: *Art Fair.* For more than four decades, the charming community of Chesterton, about 14 mi north of Valparaiso near the Indiana Dunes, has hosted this event, which features as many as 135 artists. It's at the Porter County Expo Center. | 219/926–4711.

SEPT.: *Popcorn Festival.* Downtown festivities include a unique popcorn parade, an arts and crafts fair, a 5-mi run and 5K walk, hot air balloons, children's activity areas, food, and entertainment. | 219/464–8332.

OCT.: *Northwest Indiana Story Telling Festival.* In the Nature Center at Dunes State Park in Chesterton, people of all ages gather to tell tales and hear stories of glory, ghosts, and goblins, with time blocks set aside for those approrpriate for kids. You can get a complete schedule of events by calling the Nature Center. | 1600 N. 25th E, Chesterton | 219/926–1390.

Dining

Clayton's. Contemporary. a grand piano, fresh flowers, tabletop candle lamps, and crisp white linens all enhance the dining experience of this eatery. The seasonal menu is often influenced by chef-owner Bill Potts's affinity to Thai flavors, though the offerings change regularly. | 66 W. Lincoln Way | 219/531–0612 | $15–$21 | AE, D, DC, MC, V.

The Strongbow Turkey Inn. Contemporary. This family-owned restaurant is known for serving roast turkey year-round with all the fixings. Beef, chicken, and pork entrées are also on the menu. | 2405 U.S. 30 E | 800/462–5121 | $10–$25 | AE, D, DC, MC, V.

Taste of Thailand. Thai. In this culinary escape from the Midwest, you can try lime shrimp salad with red onion, lemon grass, mint leaves, and cilantro, as well as classic satays, noodles, and curries. There are several vegetarian options. The place is about 14 mi north of Valparaiso. | 425 B Sand Creek Dr. N, Chesterton | 219/921–0092 | Closed Mon., no lunch weekends | $7–$13 | AE, D, MC, V.

Lodging

Courtyard by Marriott. Rooms have a light color scheme and contemporary furnishings in this motel on U.S. 30 near several other motels. In-room data ports. Cable TV. Indoor-outdoor pool. Exercise equipment. Business services. Free parking. | 2301 Morthland Dr./U.S. 30 | 219/465–1700 | fax 219/477–2430 | www.marriott.com | 111 rooms | $79–$109 | AE, D, DC, MC, V.

Courtyard Valparaiso. This two-story hotel is very close to campus and has mauve-and-cream-toned guest rooms. It is next door to the Strongbow Inn, known for its year-round turkey dinners. One restaurant, one bar, some in-room data ports, some microwaves, some refrigerators. Indoor-outdoor pool. Exercise equipment. Laundry facilities, laundry services. Business services. | 2301 E. Northland (U.S. 30E) | 219/465–1700 | fax 219/477–2430 | www.marriott.com | 110 rooms | $69–$179 | AE, D, DC, MC, V.

Gray Goose Inn. This handsome faux English country house, set among century-old oaks about 14 mi north of Valparaiso, was once a country retreat for a wealthy Detroit businessman. Built in the mid 1930s, the inn was named for a flock of geese that make their home on the small lake nearby. A huge stone chimney anchors one end of the white wood-frame structure, and large-paned windows admit lots of light and afford broad views of the lake. Most of the spacious guest rooms have a lake view; some have fireplaces and VCRs. Complimentary breakfast. Hot tub. | 350 Indian Boundary Rd., Chesterton | 219/926–5781 or 800/521–5127 | fax 219/926–4845 | graygoose@niia.net | www.graygooseinn.com | 8 rooms, 3 suites | $90–$121, $148–$175 suites | AE, D, MC, V.

Holiday Inn Express. This hostelry is on U.S. 30 2 mi from downtown Valparaiso. Complimentary Continental breakfast. Cable TV. Exercise equipment. Business services. | 760 Morthland Dr./U.S. 30 | 219/464–8555 | fax 219/477–2492 | 54 rooms | $79–$99 | AE, D, DC, MC, V.

Inn at Aberdeen. Set amid rolling hills and woodlands 2½ mi from downtown, this Queen Anne–style farmhouse, now a hunting lodge, was once part of a dairy farm and home to thoroughbred horses. The farmhouse has been restored and enlarged with the addition of a solarium and library. Complimentary breakfast. In-room data ports, in-room VCRs. Pool. Hot tub. Library. | 3158 S. State Rd. 2 | 219/465–3753 | fax 219/465–9227 | innaberd@net-nitco.net | www.innataberdeen.com | 11 rooms | $90–$150 | AE, D, MC, V.

Spring House Inn. This inn sits on the boundary between the Chesterton and Porter, about 15 mi from Indiana Dunes National Lakeshore headquarters and 16 mi from Valparaiso. The three-story structure, with guest wings that flank the main building, was built into a hill. All rooms have wing-back chairs, a fireplace, a private porch or balcony, and country print wallpaper and exposed dark ceiling beams. In-room data ports, some microwaves, some refrigerators, some in-room hot tubs. Indoor pool. Indoor hot tub. Gym. | 303 N. Mineral Springs Rd., Porter | 219/929–4600 or 800/366–4661 | 50 rooms | $99–$109 | AE, D, DC, MC, V.

Valparaiso Fairfield Inn. Fifteen mi inland from Lake Michigan next to Valparaiso University you'll find this three-story motel with simple double rooms and executive and Jacuzzi suites. Complimentary Continental breakfast, in-room data ports, some microwaves, some refrigerators, some in-room hot tubs. Indoor pool. Hot tub. Exercise equipment. Laundry facilities, laundry service. Business services. | 2101 E. Northland Dr./U.S. 30 | 219/465–6225 | fax 219/464–9590 | www.fairfield.com | 63 rooms, 20 suites | $79–$149 | AE, D, DC, MC, V.

VEVAY

INTRO
ATTRACTIONS
DINING
LODGING

VEVAY

MAP 3, F7

(Nearby towns also listed: Aurora, Batesville, Madison)

A group of Swiss immigrants founded this quiet, charming town in 1831. Originally it was known as New Switzerland; it was renamed Vevay (pronounced vee-*vee*). They hoped to sustain an economy based on Ohio River trade. Five Swiss families brought grape rootstock with them here and formed an association to support the cultivation of grapes. At the height of its winemaking heyday, Vevay was producing about 12,000 gallons of wine a year. By the mid-1800s, however, the winemaking industry had slowed to a trickle and the agricultural mainstays of the area came to be grains, livestock, soybeans, and tobacco. When steamboat traffic waned, Vevay slumbered, saved from obscurity only by its role as a county seat and small agricultural center. In some ways the town looks much as it did in the late 19th century. More than 300 residential and commercial structures in the modest downtown area are over 100 years old and the population has yet to exceed 2,000. A three-block stroll along Market Street, overlooking the Ohio River, leads past stately, meticulously renovated mansions built by river barons. Most are in private hands; a few are open for tours or have become bed and breakfasts.

Information: Switzerland County Welcome Center | Box 149, 47043 | 812/427–2670, 812/427–3237, or 800/435–5688 | www.vevay.net.

ON THE CALENDAR

AUG.: *Swiss Wine Festival.* This event in Paul W. Ogle Riverfront Park celebrates the local Swiss heritage with grape stomping, food, entertainment, a parade, and carnival rides. | 812/427–2670, 812/427–3237, or 800/435–5688.

OCT.: *Rollin' on the River Bike Tour and Legend of Sleepy Hollow Celebration.* A 50-mi bicycle tour through the countryside offsets an old-time festival of crafts demonstrations, caramel apples, apple cider, and other food. | 812/427–2670, or 812/427–3237, 800/435–5688.

Dining

Roxano's Restaurant. Italian. Home-cooked Italian fare, but especially pizza, is the specialty of this cozy storefront café a few doors from the Switzerland County Visitors Center downtown. | 207 S. Ferry St. | 812/427–2616 | $7–$12 | No credit cards.

Windows on the River, Ogle Haus. German, American. Traditional Bavarian fare such as sauerbraten and potato pancakes top the menu along with American favorites in this restaurant with a view. | 1013 W. Main St. | 812/427–2020 or 800/545–9360 | $11–$20 | AE, MC, V.

Lodging

Rosemont Inn Bed and Breakfast. The tall redbrick mansion on the banks of the Ohio was built by a wealthy merchant for his family in 1881. All antiques-filled guest rooms have private baths. Complimentary breakfast and afternoon snacks. No smoking. | 806 W. Market | 812/427–3050 | www.rosemontinn.com | 5 rooms | $85–$95 | D,MC,V.

Belmark Inn. This place has been a bed and breakfast for the past 150 years. Each guest room is painted in shades of blue though each room is unique with antique furnishings and a handmade quilt. Some rooms have their original oak floors; the sitting area has a computer with internet access for guest use. Complimentary breakfast. No room phones, TV in common area. Laundry facilities. | 100 E. Main St. | 812/427–9877 | www.belmarkinn.com | 5 rooms | $69 | AE, MC, V.

VINCENNES

MAP 3, B7

(Nearby towns also listed: Evansville, Jasper, New Harmony, Terre Haute)

A quiet town spread along the banks of the Wabash River, Vincennes attracts more than 150,000 visitors a year as the site of the George Rogers Clark National Historical Park. Dowtown's cornerstone is a stately, columned memorial building, with a plaza, and visitors center; historic sites from the town's years as a French settlement and territorial capital punctuate a 1-mi corridor near the river. Next to the historical park is the Old Cathedral Complex, with the 1826 Basilica of St. Francis Xavier, the French and Indian cemetery, and Indiana's oldest library with 10,000 rare books. Downtown, storefront antiques and specialty shops sit beside casual corner cafés. Here, too, is the former home of former Indiana governor and 9th U.S. president William Henry Harrison.

Information: Vincennes/Knox County Convention and Visitors Bureau | Box 602, 47591 | 812/886–0400 or 800/886–6443 | chmbr@vincennes.net | www.accessknoxcounty.com.

Attractions

Fort Knox II. In 1803, the army garrison moved to a bluff 3 mi north of town that afforded a view of the river, a good boat landing, and a nearby spring. Soon Fort Knox II was built. Posts and interpretive markers outline the site of the original fort on the north side of town, near the river. | 812/882–7422 | Free | Daily, dawn to dusk.

VACATION COUNTDOWN Your checklist for a perfect journey

Way Ahead

- ❏ Devise a trip budget.
- ❏ Write down the five things you want most from this trip. Keep this list handy before and during your trip.
- ❏ Book lodging and transportation.
- ❏ Arrange for pet care.
- ❏ Photocopy any important documentation (passport, driver's license, vehicle registration, and so on) you'll carry with you on your trip. Store the copies in a safe place at home.
- ❏ Review health and home-owners insurance policies to find out what they cover when you're away from home.

A Month Before

- ❏ Make restaurant reservations and buy theater and concert tickets. Visit fodors.com for links to local events and news.
- ❏ Familiarize yourself with the local language or lingo.
- ❏ Schedule a tune-up for your car.

Two Weeks Before

- ❏ Create your itinerary.
- ❏ Enjoy a book or movie set in your destination to get you in the mood.
- ❏ Prepare a packing list.
- ❏ Shop for missing essentials.
- ❏ Repair, launder, or dry-clean the clothes you will take with you.
- ❏ Replenish your supply of prescription drugs and contact lenses if necessary.

A Week Before

- ❏ Stop newspaper and mail deliveries.
- ❏ Pay bills.
- ❏ Stock up on film and batteries.
- ❏ Label your luggage.
- ❏ Finalize your packing list—always take less than you think you need.
- ❏ Pack a toiletries kit filled with travel-size essentials.
- ❏ Check tire treads.
- ❏ Write down your insurance agent's number and any other emergency numbers and take them with you.
- ❏ Get lots of sleep. You want to be well-rested and healthy for your impending trip.

A Day Before

- ❏ Collect passport, driver's license, insurance card, vehicle registration, and other documents.
- ❏ Check travel documents.
- ❏ Give a copy of your itinerary to a family member or friend.
- ❏ Check your car's fluids, lights, tire inflation, and wiper blades.
- ❏ Get packing!

During Your Trip

- ❏ Keep a journal/scrapbook as a personal souvenir.
- ❏ Spend time with locals.
- ❏ Take time to explore. Don't plan too much. Let yourself get lost and use your Fodor's guide to get back on track.

George Rogers Clark National Historical Park. One of the Midwest's most popular historic sites, this 26-acre riverfront park in downtown Vincennes attracts crowds of history enthusiasts every year. The striking centerpiece, a stone memorial building encircled by 16 fluted columns, towers over a riverside plaza on the site of Fort Sackville. It commemorates Lt. Col. George Rogers Clark's capture of the fort from the British on February 25, 1779, one of the most brilliant strategic feats of the American Revolution. You can watch a 23-min movie and chat with park rangers in period costumes. A graceful bridge arches across the river next to the park's plaza and marks the area where droves of buffalo, Indians, British and French troops, and Clark's militia, as well as Abraham Lincoln crossed the river. | 401 S. 2nd St. | 812/882–1776 | GERO_Ranger_Activities@nps.gov | www.nps.gov/gero | $2 | Daily.

Grouseland. A two-story columned portico fronts this grand brick estate with white trim, once the home of William Henry Harrison, who was governor of the Indiana Territory from 1800 to 1812 and the ninth president of the United States. It was built in 1803–4 and is maintained as a historic house and museum, furnished with period pieces and many of Harrison's belongings. | 3 W. Scott St. | 812/882–2096 | $5 | Jan.–Feb., daily 11–4; Mar.–Dec., daily 9–5.

Historic District. Vincennes's historic district, which spans a 12-block radius near the George Rogers Clark memorial, includes buildings erected in the 1800s and 1900s. It's unique in that none of the homes have been turned into businesses or multiple-family dwellings, and local preservationists' efforts have ensured that the homes retain their original style. | 2nd St. and Patrick Henry through 1st St. and W. Scott St. | 812/886–0400 or 800/886–6443.

Indiana Military Museum. The museum holds what is considered one of the top military collections in the country. On display are military vehicles, artillery, uniforms, insignia, equipment, and related artifacts from the Civil War to the Persian Gulf War. | 4305 Bruceville Rd. | 812/882–8668 | Free | May–Oct., daily noon–4; weekends by appointmen.

Indiana Territory Site. Built in 1805 as a tailor's workshop, the red-painted two-story building is held together with wooden pegs. The House chamber is arranged as it might have been when the Legislature met here in 1811. | 1 W. Harrison St. | 812/882–7422 | www.state. in.us/dnr/ | Free | Mid-Mar.–mid-Dec., Tues.–Sat. 9–5, Sun. 1–5.

Log Cabin Visitors Center. Originally a corn crib south of Vincennes, this structure was moved to Vincennes and rebuilt as a log cabin. Portraits of William Henry Harrison and Tecumseh, among others, hang inside. | 27 N. 3rd St. | 812/882–7422 | Free | Mid-Mar.–mid-Dec., Tues.–Sat. 9–5, Sun. 1–5.

Michel Brouillet Old French House. The home of French fur trader Michel Brouillet reflects a French Creole cottage design and is typical of French settlers' dwellings in the Mississippi Valley during the 18th and early 19th centuries. The small cottage was built in 1806 using the "posts on sill" technique—14-ft upright posts, spaced about 1½ ft apart and fitted into a horizontal beam, or sill, and capped by another horizontal beam, or plate. | 509 1st St. | 812/882–7886 | $1 | May–Sept., Tues.–Sat. 9–noon, 1–5, Sun. 1–5.

Old Cathedral Complex–Basilica of St. Francis Xavier. Construction of the fourth and current St. Francis Xavier Church began in 1826. It was still underway when Abraham Lincoln passed near the site on his move to Illinois in 1830. Four bishops are buried in the crypt of the current cathedral. | 205 Church St. | 812/882–5638 | Free | Daily 8–4.

The oldest library in the state of Indiana is at the **Old Cathedral Library and Museum.** Its inventory numbers over 10,000 rare volumes. Among the oldest manuscripts are a 13th-century illuminated manuscript on vellum of the *Officium Sanctae Mariae,* a bull issued by Pope John XXII in 1319. The oldest book is Michael de Carcano's *Sermonarium triplicatum,* printed in Venice in 1476. | 205 Church St. | 812/882–7016 | Free | Memorial Day–Labor Day, Mon.–Sat. 12:30–4.

The **Old French Cemetery,** behind the Old Cathedral, is the final resting place of more than 4,000 early Vincennes citizens. | 812/882–7016 | Free | Daily.

Old State Bank, Indiana State Memorial. The Old State Bank was built in 1838 and is the oldest bank building in Indiana. | 112 N. 2nd St. | 812/882–7422 | Free | Mid-Mar.–mid-Dec., Wed.–Sat. 9–5, Sun. 1–5.

Ouabache Trails Park. This county park on the Wabash north of town encompasses 254 acres of rolling woodlands filled with hickory, oak, sycamore, maple, and poplar trees. Four miles of trails crisscross the hills and wide, low fields. | Lower Fort Knox Rd. | 812/882–4316 | Free | Daily May–Sept.

Vincennes University. Founded in 1801, the college is Indiana's oldest college. It is also the oldest continuously operating institution of higher education west of the Allegheny Mountains and north of the Ohio River. William Henry Harrison, the first governor of the Indiana Territory and later U.S. President, was the first chairman of its board of trustees. The university offers more than 150 majors and enrolls about 2,500 students. | 1002 N. 1st St. | 800/742–9198 or 812/888–8888 | www.vinu.edu | Free | Daily.

ON THE CALENDAR

MAY: *Spirit of Vincennes Rendezvous.* The two-day event begins with a candlelight tour of the home of William Henry Harrison (Grouseland) followed by a Revolutionary War–era reenactment with battles, food, traders, and musicians. | 812/882–7472 or 800/886–6443.

AUG.: *Knox County Watermelon Festival.* This two-day outdoor celebration of both summer and its messiest bounty, the watermelon, takes place downtown either the first or second weekend in August. Melon-related activities include a seed spitting contest and a watermelon eating contest. Events include kids' rides, live music, craft booths, and a three-on-three basketball competition. | 812/886–0400 or 800/886–6443.

SEPT.: *Indiana State Chili Cook-Off.* Taste chili cooks' fare as they vie for winning entries that take them to national chili championships. Family entertainment and sidewalk sales add to the festivities. | 812/882–6440.

Dining

Market Street Restaurant and Pub. American. The original ceiling beams are exposed in some rooms of this family restaurant, and bouquets of dried flowers dangle overhead; another dining room displays a collection of 100 teapots. Expect lots of beef—grilled tenderloin or rib-eye steak are two house specialties. | 106 Honore Pl. | 812/886–5201 | Closed Sun. | $10–$18 | AE, D, DC, MC, V.

Lodging

Inn of Old Vincennes. One and a half mile from the George Rogers Clark National Historical Park and 2 mi from downtown Vincennes, this two-story brick motel has large rooms. Complimentary Continental breakfast, refrigerators, some in-room hot tubs. Outdoor pool. Exercise equipment. Pets allowed. | 1800 Old Decker Rd. | 812/882–2100 | fax 812/882–2100 | www.bestwestern.com | 40 rooms | $60–$70 | AE, D, DC, MC, V.

WABASH

MAP 3, E3

(Nearby towns also listed: Huntington, Marion, Peru)

In 1880, Wabash claimed worldwide notoriety as the first city in the world to be lighted with municipally generated electricity. Named for its river, Wabash is an old town filled with stately Greek Revival, Italianate, and Victorian buildings. Much of its early settlement was a result of the commerce generated by the creation of the Erie Canal, supported by the railroad and the Wabash River. Today the town is quiet, supported by medium-size manufacturers of automotive parts, tires, containers, and alloy products.

Information: Wabash County Convention and Visitors Bureau | Box 746, 46992 | 219/563–7171 or 800/563–1169 | wabcocvb@ctlnet.com | www.communinet.org/cvb.

Attractions

Frances Slocum Monument. Born to a Quaker family in 1773, the auburn-haired Frances was abducted by members of the Miami tribe in 1778. Her adoptive parents named her Maconaquah, or "little bear woman." Frances's second husband became Chief of the Miami and Frances became revered by pioneers and tribesman alike. She was affectionately known as the White Rose of the Miami, and this many-tiered monument, in the Frances Slocum Cemetery, pays tribute to Frances's courage and peaceful ways. | On Mississinewa Rd. | 219/563–1168.

Honeywell Center. The 1940s stone-sided center named after Wabash resident Mark C. Honeywell, hosts meetings and cultural events. It contains a gallery, a theater, and a sculpture plaza. The Honeywell Golf Course is next door. | 275 W. Market St. | 800/626–6345 | Daily.

Salamonie State Lake and Salamonie River State Forest. The name Salamonie (pronounced o-sah-mo-nee) means "yellow paint." Native Americans made yellow paint from the bloodroot that grows along the winding banks of the Salamonie River. The waterway was dammed to create the reservoir. Among the few remaining forests in cultivated northern Indiana, the forest is a riverside forest demonstration project that encompasses about 850 acres and has 9 mi of fire trails as well as bridle trails. The lake property includes five state recreation areas. | 9214 West-Lost Bridge W, Andrews | 219/468–2125 | www.state.in.us/dnr/ | Free | Daily.

Wabash County Historical Museum. The building was constructed in 1899 as a tribute to Civil War veterans and displays natural-history exhibits, Native American artifacts, pioneer-era costumes, furniture, and Civil War records. | 89 W. Hill St. | 219/563–0661 | Free | Museum is moving, will be closed until late 2001. Nov.–mid-Apr. Tues.–Sat. 9–1.

ON THE CALENDAR

JUNE: *Very Berry Strawberry Festival.* If you are passing through town on either Route 13 or Route 15 during the second weekend in June, you may run right into this daylong celebration downtown where you'll find strawberry delicacies galore, in addition to a car show, 5K run, and health fair. | 219/563–1168.

Dining

Market Street Grill. American. In this 100-year-old dining room, with original tin ceilings and glazed brick walls, a G-scale train circles over the bar. Railroad and Custer antiques, old bean pots, and lanterns are scattered throughout the dining room. House specials include prime rib, barbecued ribs, and drunken chicken—soaked in egg and buttermilk and topped with mushroom gravy. Adults over 21 only. | 90 W. Market St. | 219/563–7779 | No lunch. Closed Mon.–Tues. | $10–$18 | D, MC, V.

Lodging

Lamp Post Inn Bed and Breakfast. This Romanesque home built of Indiana limestone is a block from the Honeywell Center. All rooms are individually decorated. Complimentary breakfast. | 261 W. Hill St. | 219/563–3094 | 4 rooms | $50–$60 | No credit cards.

WARSAW

MAP 3, D2

(Nearby towns also listed: Auburn, Fort Wayne, Huntington, Nappanee, Plymouth)

Warsaw, in the heart of Kosciusko County's lake country, is primarily a summer resort area. A few blocks from the County Courthouse, a handsome French Second Empire structure completed in 1884 and restored after a fire in 1980, is one of the city's oldest businesses, Warsaw Cut Glass. Operating in the same two-story brick building since 1911, the firm displays its antiques in a first-floor showroom. Upstairs, craftsmen painstakingly fashion intricate glassware by hand.

Information: Kosciusko County Convention and Visitors Bureau | 111 Capital Dr., 46580 | 219/269–6090 or 800/800–6090 | info@koscvb.org | www.koscvb.org/.

Attractions
Kosciusko County Jail Museum. Renovated jail cells here house artifacts of the county's history. | N. Indian Rd. | 219/269–1078 | culture.kconline.com/kchs | Free | Thurs.–Sat. 10–4, Sun. 10–4.

Dining
Blue Coyote. Southwestern. Six blocks south of the courthouse, this restuarant is painted in rusty desert tones and decorated with chili pepper wreaths and wildly painted cowboy boots. Baby back ribs, a specialty of the house, can be prepared with your choice of a honey-orange or spicy barbecue sauce. Chiles rellenos, stuffed with ground beef, pecans, and yellow raisins and smothered in cheese, are spicy, sweet, and delicious. | 617 S. Buffalo | 219/269–1141 | Closed Sun.–Mon. No lunch Sat. | $8–$18 | AE, MC, V.

Dig's Diner. American. Across the street from the courthouse, in an understated brownstone building, this bright dining room is scattered with old Coke signs, neon lights, and assorted diner memorabilia. The kitchen is famous for its spicy chili, its burgers and fries, and its hearty blue plate specials. | 114 N. Buffalo St. | 219/269–9696 | $5–$15 | No credit cards.

Mosaique. Contemporary. Ingredients from the area and points farther afield, including duck and striped bass, are prepared in inventive ways in a century-old building downtown. A glass mosaic bar gives the restaurant its name. | 115 S. Buffalo St. | 219/269–5080 | Closed Sun. No lunch | $30–$45 | MC, V.

Lodging
Anchor Inn. From the rooms on the second and third floors of this home you may have tree top views of Lake Wawasee. The front porch is decked with swings and high-back chairs, and the parlor serves as a music room, housing an upright piano and an 1884 pump organ. Rooms are individually appointed with period antiques and quilts and have hardwood floors. Complimentary breakfast. No room phones, no TV. | 11007 N. State Rd. 13, Syracuse | 219/457–4714 | www.bbonline.com/in/anchorinn | 5 rooms | $50–$70 | D, MC, V.

Candlelight Inn. This inn in the heart of northern Indiana's lake country, on the east side of town, has been restored to its original 1860s appearance and is now on the National Register of Historic Places. The tasteful furnishings include many antiques, framed prints, and reproduction furniture. Cable TV. | 503 E. Fort Wayne St. | 219/267–2906 or 800/352–0640 | fax 219/269–4646 | 3 rooms | $74–$89 | AE, D, MC, V.

Prairie House Bed and Breakfast. Ten minutes north of Warsaw is this one-and-a-half-story brick home, built in 1974 and renovated in 1994. Two rooms have private baths and two rooms share a bath. Complimentary breakfast. No room phones, TV in common area. | 495 E. 900 N. Leesburg | 219/658–9211 | fax 219/453–4787 | www.prairiehouse.net | 4 rooms | $45–$64 | MC, V.

Ramada Plaza Hotel, Restaurant and Entertainment Complex. The Ramada Plaza is a large, newly renovated, full-service hotel on the east side of town right off U.S. 30. Restaurant, bar, room service. In-room data ports. Cable TV. Indoor-outdoor pool. Hot tub. Gym, exercise equipment. Laundry facilities. Business services. Free parking. Some pets allowed. | 2519 E. Center St. | 219/269–2323 | fax 219/269–2432 | 156 rooms | $89–$159 | AE, D, DC, MC, V.

White Hill Manor. This former country estate on the east side of town, built of brick in Tudor style in 1932, is surrounded by lawn and trees and filled with traditional furnishings. Picnic area, complimentary breakfast. In-room data ports. TV. No kids under 12. Business services. Some pets allowed. No smoking. | 2513 E. Center St. | 219/269–6933 | fax 219/268–1936 | 8 rooms (2 with shower only) | $86–$159 | AE, D, DC, MC, V.

WYANDOTTE

MAP 3, D8

(Nearby towns also listed: Corydon, New Albany)

A few miles from the Ohio River in southern Indiana, the tiny town of Wyandotte is known primarily as the site of the Wyandotte Caves. The whole area is heavily wooded and the Wyandotte Woods State Recreation Area and Harrison-Crawford State Forest are here, encompassing 24,000 acres of rugged forest crossed by the Blue River and several long-distance trails, such as the Adventure Trail and the American Discovery Trail.

Information: **Crawford County Tourism Bureau** | Box 99, English, 47118. **Wyandotte Woods S.R.A.** | 7240 Old Forest Rd., Corydon, 47118 | 812/738–2782 | hcwc@theremc.com | www.state.in.us/dnr.

Attractions

Harrison-Crawford/Wyandotte Complex. The Wyandotte Caves and Wyandotte Woods state recreation areas and the Harrison-Crawford State Forest make up this large preserve totalling 24,000 acres. The complex includes southern Indiana's most impressive limestone cave system in rugged, densely forested hill country. Wyandotte Woods has an Olympic-size swimming pool, a nature center, and over a dozen trails suitable for day hikes, in addition to the 100 mi of designated bridle trails and two fishing lakes. | 7240 Old Forest Rd., Corydon | 812/738–8232 | www.state.in.us/dnr/forestry/htmldocs/harcraw.htm | Free | Daily.

Big Wyandotte Cave. You tour this immense cave on easy to moderate guided tours through lighted passageways lasting anywhere from a little more than an hour to all day. The shortest trip is the Historical Tour, lasting between 1 and 1½ hours. There's also the 2-hour-long Monument Mountain tour to a 185-ft underground mountain of fallen rock in a 360- by 140-ft cavern some 500 ft down. A 1½-mi 2-hr-long tour sees helictites, rare twisted formations, and prehistoric flint quarries. By advance reservation, you can also take longer spelunking tours that include long crawls and climbing; children must be at least 12 years old or in the sixth grade for these. A junior spelunker tour allows those 8 and up to get cave exploring experience for up to 2½ hours. | 7315 S. Wyandotte Cave Rd., Leavenworth | 812/738–2782 | www.state.in.us/dnr/forestry/htmldocs/wyandtcv.htm | Apr–Oct. 9–5.

Little Wyandotte Cave. The Little Wyandotte Cave is the easiest way to get a cave experience in this area. Totally separate from Big Wyandotte Cave, the smaller cave offers a comprehensive view of flowstone and dripstone formations on ½-mi trips lasting 30 to 45 min. | 7315 S. Wyandotte Cave Rd., Leavenworth | 812/738–2782 | fax 812/738–2782 | www.state.in.us/dnr/forestry/htmldocs/wyandtcv.htm | $4 | Apr.–Oct., 9–5.

ON THE CALENDAR

JUNE: *Southern Indiana Primitive Arts Festival and Flint Knapping.* The third weekend in June a small but dedicated crowd of a few hundred converge on City Park at the river's edge to celebrate the artistry of arrowheads. Fans and craftsman make and sell the stone tools, and other activities include an Altalt (predecessor of the spear) throwing contest. | Eric's Rocks | 812/739–2358.

Lodging

Hummingbird Inn Bed and Breakfast. Three blocks east of downtown is this three-story Victorian home. Each room contains Victorian antiques and individual color schemes. The Hummingbird Room has five turreted windows and pastel floral wallpaper with a hummingbird trim. You can relax and enjoy the surroudings in either of the parlors or in the dining room. No room phones, TV in common area. No kids. | 400 E. Chestnut St., Corydon | 812/738–0625 or 877/422–0625 | 4 rooms | $81–$95 | AE, MC, V.

WYANDOTTE

Kentucky

Kentucky's nickname is, of course, the "Bluegrass State." But surprisingly the rolling countryside in which thoroughbred racehorses graze is green, not blue. If you happen to be in the horse-farm region around Lexington early in spring, the sea of tiny buds in a field of Kentucky bluegrass does indeed have a bluish-purple color.

This lush carpet of bluegrass grows in limestone-based soil, rich in calcium and phosphates. The finest racehorses in the world are bred here because they are building strong bones with every nibble.

Geology and geography have been important to many other aspects of the state's history and economy. Most of the United States' coal supply (75%) comes from mines in the eastern Kentucky mountains. Bourbon distillers claim that the water from limestone springs is what makes their whiskey smooth. The fertile soil has provided a reliable livelihood for many Kentuckians. Important crops have included corn, burley tobacco, soybeans, and until 1945, hemp.

Limestone, which is easily eroded by rainwater, accounts for the formation of more than 765 mi of known caves lying beneath the surface of the state. The famous Mammoth Cave system has some 340 mi of mapped passages—it's the longest in the world.

The northern boundary of the state is defined by the Ohio River. Beginning in the early 1800s, Kentucky goods were shipped by barge upriver to Pittsburgh and on to other eastern cities, or downstream to the Mississippi River and markets such as St. Louis, Memphis, and New Orleans. Railroads and highways now transport much of the state's products, but coal-laden barges still ply the Ohio.

Kentucky's largest city, Louisville, is situated on the banks of the Ohio River and has served as a major shipping port. Today the metropolitan area has a population of nearly one million and is a manufacturing, health care, business, and arts center. Shipping

CAPITAL: FRANKFORT	POPULATION: 3,908,100	AREA: 40,411 SQUARE MI
BORDERS: MO, IL, IN, OH, WV, VA, TN, OH RIVER, MS RIVER		TIME ZONE: EASTERN/CENTRAL
POSTAL ABBREVIATION: KY	WEB SITE: WWW.KENTUCKYTOURISM.COM.	

is still important, but most goods now leave and arrive via air rather than water, since Louisville is the site of United Parcel Service's main North American air hub.

Tourism and manufacturing are as important to the state today as thorough-breds, tobacco, bourbon, and coal. Kentucky has an extensive system of state parks for boating, fishing, hiking, and other outdoor recreation. The Daniel Boone National Forest occupies hundreds of thousands of acres in the eastern part of the state. Three major auto makers—Ford, Toyota, and General Motors—have large manufacturing plants in Kentucky, as do other major corporations such as General Electric and Kimberly-Clark.

Among the many sites are the Cumberland Gap in the southeast corner (through which Daniel Boone led the first pioneer settlers); the mansions, horse farms, and bour-bon distilleries of the central Bluegrass; and the Native American burial mounds in the western lowlands where the Ohio and Mississippi rivers meet.

Being nearly as old as the Republic itself, Kentucky has produced many famous sons and daughters. Abraham Lincoln, Mary Todd Lincoln, Jefferson Davis, and Henry Clay being among the most prominent from the Civil War era. Science Nobel laureate and geneticist Thomas Hunt Morgan was born just after the Civil War. Supreme Court Justice Louis Brandeis (1856–1941) was one of eleven Kentuckians to serve on the nation's high-est court.

The most famous figure of the temperance movement ironically was born in the state that is the United States' whiskey-producing center. Carry Nation wielded her ax in Kansas saloons but was born in Garrard County.

Guthrie native (and Nobel prize–winner for literature) Robert Penn Warren was Amer-ica's first Poet Laureate. More contemporary Kentuckians of letters include novelists Barbara Kingsolver and Bobbie Ann Mason, mystery writer Sue Grafton, and poet Wendell Berry.

The state's most famous living native son is boxing champ Muhammad Ali. Other famous sports figures include baseball Hall of Famer Pee Wee Reese and football greats Paul Hornung and Phil Simms. Butch Beard, David Cowens, and Wesley Unseld are among the NBA stars native to Kentucky. Louisvillian Tori Murden became the first woman and the first American to row solo across the Atlantic Ocean in 1999.

Some of the famous names in entertainment who were born in the state are Irene Dunne, Victor Mature, Patricia Neal, Tom Cruise, Johnny Depp, Helen Humes, Rosemary Clooney, Bill Monroe, Loretta Lynn, Crystal Gayle, Billy Ray Cyrus, and the Judds.

History

Historians have never been able to come to an agreement over the origin of the state's name, though they concur that it came from Native Americans who used Kentucky as a fertile hunting ground. Some think it was derived from a Wyandot word meaning "land of tomorrow." There's equal argument for the Iroquois phrase trans-lated as "place of meadows."

Though there is archaeological evidence of prehistoric occupation, by the time the first Europeans explored Kentucky, the Cherokee, Iroquois, and Chickasaw had no

KY Timeline

385–390 million years ago
During the Devon-ian Period, much of what is now Ken-tucky was sub-merged under an inland sea. Today, at the Falls of the Ohio, near Louisville, the world's largest

exposed Devonian fossil beds are rich in the remains of armored fish and mollusks of the period.

15,000–20,000 years ago
A great ice sheet covered North America from Canada to the Ohio River during the Pleistocene Epoch. A salt lick in what is now Boone County attracted woolly

mammoths, mastodons, giant ground sloths, and giant bison living in the area. Big Bone Lick State Park is on the site today.

significant settlements in the region. Rather, they used it as a resource for hunting and fishing, and a battleground for fighting tribal wars. The first Europeans to see Kentucky were probably French and Spanish explorers who were navigating the waters of the Mississippi and lower Ohio rivers in the late 1600s.

In 1750 Dr. Thomas Walker of Virginia led a small expedition of hunters westward through the Cumberland Gap, a narrow passageway in the otherwise daunting Appalachian Mountains. Indian attacks discouraged settlement, but in 1769 Daniel Boone brought another hunting party through the Gap and over the next few years, more settlers followed. They didn't pause in the mountains; there wasn't enough flat land for farming. Instead, they headed for the rolling Bluegrass countryside, at the time teeming with deer and bison, where today thoroughbred racehorses graze. Boonesboro was established on the Kentucky River in 1775.

Meanwhile, other settlers were coming into Kentucky via the Ohio River. A band led by Pennsylvanian James Harrod came down the Ohio and traveled up the Kentucky River to build a town at present-day Harrodsburg. It's credited with being the first permanent settlement in the state. In 1778, General George Rogers Clark established a settlement at the Falls of the Ohio that he named Louisville in honor of King Louis XVI in recognition of the aid the French were giving the Americans in the war against the British.

By 1790, so many people had poured into the territory, which politically was a county of Virginia, that a move toward statehood began. In 1792, Kentucky became the 15th state, the first west of the Appalachian Mountains.

Over the next decades, farms that shaped the state's economy to the present day were established. Corn, tobacco, and livestock provided the base. Horses were important for both transportation and agriculture. But proud owners and breeders soon began to hold race meets to show off the swiftest of their animals. (The Kentucky Jockey Club is almost as old as the state—it was started in Lexington in 1797.)

Corn was an important commodity, not only for food, but for the distillation of bourbon whiskey. Likewise, in the mountainous eastern region, coal was discovered and mining became an important industry, providing fuel for the steel mills just up the Ohio River in Pittsburgh.

Much of the state's labor was provided by black slaves and this was to be a divisive factor during the Civil War. Even though Kentucky remained in the Union, it was a slave state. At the beginning of the war, the state declared neutrality, an attempt to stay on good economic terms with both the United States and the Confederacy. Other factors pulled at the political sympathies of Kentuckians.

Both President Abraham Lincoln and Confederate President Jefferson Davis were native Kentuckians. Many citizens of the state had family ties in the southern states of Virginia and North Carolina. But almost as many others traced their roots to Pennsylvania and had relatives in Ohio and Indiana. Before the end of the war, 90,000 troops fought for the Union side and 40,000 for the Confederacy.

With the increased industrialization of the late-19th and early 20th centuries, Kentucky's coal fields gained increasing importance. They were also the sites for early

12,000 years ago	2000–1000 BC	Early 1700s	1750	1769
Paleo-Indians, who lived by hunting and gathering, were the region's first human residents.	Evidence suggests the earliest agricultural efforts produced a variety of ground squash, followed by corn, a crop that now looms large in the state's economy.	Artifacts made from materials such as brass, iron, and glass result from native peoples' first contact with European explorers.	The first documented expedition through the Cumberland Gap is led by Dr. Thomas Walker.	Daniel Boone brings an exploratory party through the Cumberland Gap.

and important organized-labor activities. The United Mine Workers unionized the miners and led sometimes violent demonstrations for improved safety conditions.

Regions

1. CUMBERLAND

The easternmost section of the state stretches from north to south along the Appalachian and Cumberland mountains. More than 75% of the coal in the nation is mined here and, for decades, it has been the industry on which the local economy has been based. Areas include the Cumberland Gap region in the southeast, through which Daniel Boone led the first pioneer settlers to Kentucky in the 1770s. Heavily forested, mountainous hiking, and camping areas include the 660,000-acre Daniel Boone National Forest and several state parks. Literary heritage includes authors Harriet Arnow (*The Dollmaker*), John Fox Jr. (*The Little Shepherd of Kingdom Come*), and Jesse Stuart (*The Thread that Runs So True*) who all wrote about life in the region. Mountain fiddle music that evolved into Bluegrass originated here from music brought by Scots/English/Irish settlers.

Towns listed: Ashland, Barbourville, Berea, Corbin, Danville, Hazard, London, Maysville, Middlesboro, Morehead, Olive Hill, Paintsville, Pikeville, Pineville, Prestonsburg, Renfro Valley, Slade, Williamsburg

2. BLUEGRASS

This inner region of the state is characterized by rolling grasslands growing over a limestone base. This region boasts the largest concentration of thoroughbred racehorse farms in the world. (HRH, Elizabeth II of Great Britain, is among the rich and famous who have horses stabled here.) Also, the bourbon whiskey industry, which accounts for the largest proportion of spirits distilled in the United States, is concentrated in this region. Tours of both the horse farms and the distilleries are available.

The state's three largest metropolitan areas—Louisville, Lexington, and Covington—are at the corners of the triangle comprising the region. The state capital, Frankfort, is also in the center of the Bluegrass on the Kentucky River.

Dining and entertainment abounds in the cities, which also are the centers for museums, galleries, and spectator sports. Scattered throughout the Bluegrass are many pioneer sites, small towns where antique hunters can turn up treasures, and charming 19th-century period-furnished inns.

Towns listed: Carrollton, Covington, Frankfort, Georgetown, Lexington, Louisville, Midway, Shelbyville, Shepherdsville, Versailles

---

1775
The first Anglo settlement in the state, at Boonesborough on the Kentucky River, is established by Daniel Boone, Judge Richard Henderson, and members of the

Transylvania Company.

1778
Louisville is founded just upstream from the Falls of the Ohio by Gen. George Rogers Clark while he is leading a Virginia military campaign against the British, hoping to take the

Northwest Territory.

1787
The first Kentucky tobacco warehouse is licensed.

INTRODUCTION
HISTORY
REGIONS
WHEN TO VISIT
STATE'S GREATS
RULES OF THE ROAD
DRIVING TOURS

3. PENNYROYAL

This region takes its name from an aromatic wildflower, a member of the mint family, that grows throughout the area. (Local pronunciation often changes the name to "pennyrile.") Traditionally farmland, the Pennyroyal is also Cave Country. The limestone basin here has been eroded away by the action of water to produce the world's largest network of caverns, part of which is contained in Mammoth Cave National Park. The largest city in the region is Bowling Green, home of General Motors' Corvette factory and the Corvette Museum. The two presidents of the American Civil War, Abraham Lincoln and Jefferson Davis, were born in the Pennyroyal, and there are memorials to each.

The largest natural area in the region is the Land Between the Lakes, a forest bounded by the state's two largest bodies of water, Kentucky Lake, and Lake Barkley, both created by Tennessee Valley Authority dams.

Towns listed: Bardstown, Bowling Green, Campbellsville, Cave City, Dawson Springs, Elizabethtown, Florence, Glasgow, Greenville, Harrodsburg, Hodgenville, Hopkinsville, Horse Cave, Jamestown, Madisonville, Mammoth Cave National Park, Monticello, Mount Vernon, Murray, Paris, Richmond, Russellville, Somerset, South Union, Springfield, Williamstown, Winchester

4. WESTERN COAL FIELD

This is a compact, circular region bounded by the Ohio River to the north. Coal is strip-mined here, most notably in Muhlenberg County, of "Take Me Back to Muhlenberg County" folksong fame. Owensboro, a city on the Ohio famous throughout the state for its barbecue, is the largest city. Henderson is the site of John James Audubon State Park, where many of the wildlife painter's works are exhibited. In spite of being the center for surface mining, there are many state parks in the area with ample outdoor recreation.

Towns listed: Brandenburg, Cadiz, Falls of Rough, Henderson, Owensboro

5. JACKSON PURCHASE

In the westernmost part of the state, the Purchase is just as flat as the Cumberland in the east is mountainous. It is notable for wetland flora and fauna. It became part of Kentucky as a result of protracted negotiations in the early 1800s between the Chickasaw Indian Nation and Isaac Shelby, first governor of Kentucky. Reelfoot Lake, now part of an ecologically unique National Wildlife Refuge, was formed during massive earthquakes along the New Madrid Fault in 1811–12. The largest city in the region is Paducah, the site of the U.S. Atomic Energy Commission's gaseous diffusion plant where spent radioactive fuel is reprocessed.

Towns listed: Gilbertsville, Mayfield, Paducah, Wickliffe

1788	**1790**	**1792**	**1808**	**1809**
Jacob Beam builds the first commercial bourbon whiskey distillery, near Bardstown.	The first coal mining begins, in Lee County.	The Commonwealth of Kentucky becomes the 15th state.	Jefferson Davis, the only President of the Confederate States of America, is born in what is now Todd County.	Abraham Lincoln, the 16th President of the United States, is born in a one-room log cabin near Hodgenville.

When to Visit

Kentucky is at its most beautiful in spring and fall with bounties of wildflowers in the former and colorful foliage during the latter. These are also the most comfortable seasons for seeing the state. Blue-skied, picture-perfect days in the 60s and 70s are most frequently encountered in May and October.

Summers are hot and humid. The eastern Cumberland, where nights cool off at the higher elevations, is the place to go to escape the often oppressive heat. As long as the rainfall stays normal and the grass green, the Bluegrass countryside will be most pleasant viewed from an air-conditioned car.

Winters are chilly and damp, and though average highs are in the 40s, cold snaps, with highs in the teens, occur nearly every year. (At least twice in the 20th century, prolonged bitter cold temperatures froze the surface of the Ohio River, which is almost 1 mi wide at Louisville, and allowed people to walk from shore to shore.)

Mountain communities often become isolated in winter due to snowy, icy roads, so stick to the central and western portions of the state if you visit in the wintertime.

CLIMATE CHART

Average High/Low Temperatures (°F) and Monthly Precipitation (in inches).

	JAN	FEB.	MAR.	APR.	MAY	JUNE
JACKSON	41/24	46/28	57/37	67/46	75/54	81/62
	3.76	3.82	4.77	3.95	4.63	4.25
	JULY	AUG.	SEPT.	OCT.	NOV.	DEC.
	84/65	83/64	77/59	67/47	56/39	46/30
	5.14	3.91	3.66	3.20	4.20	4.38
	JAN	FEB.	MAR.	APR.	MAY	JUNE
LOUISVILLE	40/23	45/27	56/36	67/45	76/55	84/63
	2.86	3.30	4.66	4.23	4.62	3.46
	JULY	AUG.	SEPT.	OCT.	NOV.	DEC.
	87/67	86/66	80/59	69/46	57/37	45/29
	4.51	3.54	3.16	2.71	3.70	3.64
	JAN	FEB.	MAR.	APR.	MAY	JUNE
PADUCAH	42/24	46/27	58/38	69/47	77/56	86/65
	3.27	3.90	4.92	5.01	4.94	4.05
	JULY	AUG.	SEPT.	OCT.	NOV.	DEC.
	89/69	87/66	81/59	71/47	58/38	46/28
	4.19	3.34	3.69	3.00	4.32	4.68

1811
A massive earthquake centered along the New Madrid fault is felt throughout the state. It creates Reelfoot Lake at the western tip of Kentucky and Tennessee.

1852
Harriet Beecher Stowe publishes the strongly-abolitionist novel, *Uncle Tom's Cabin*, inspired (it is now said) by visits to a Kentucky plantation and to a slave auction on the grounds of the Mason County courthouse.

1853
While visiting Bardstown, composer Stephen Foster writes "My Old Kentucky Home," which later becomes the state song.

1862
After defeat at the Battle of Perryville, Confederate troops are forced to retreat, and Kentucky, which had remained in the Union but had mustered many regiments of Confederate troops,

FESTIVALS AND SEASONAL EVENTS

WINTER

INTRODUCTION
HISTORY
REGIONS
WHEN TO VISIT
STATE'S GREATS
RULES OF THE ROAD
DRIVING TOURS

Jan. **Musical Tribute to Dr. Martin Luther King.** Regional singing and instrumental groups converge at the Abraham Lincoln Birthplace National Historic Site near Hodgenville to present concerts of hymns and spirituals commemorating King's birthday. The annual event is held on the Sunday before King's birthday. 2995 Lincoln Farm Rd., U.S. Highway 31E, 2½ mi south of Hodgenville. | 270/358–3137 | www.nps.gov/abli.

Feb. **National Farm Machinery Show.** The largest indoor exhibition of farm and agricultural equipment in the United States takes place annually the second week of February at Louisville's Kentucky Fair and Exposition Center which is located on Phillips Lane, across from the airport, off I–65 and 264. | 502/367–5100 | www.kyfairexpo.org.

Feb.–Apr. **Humana Festival of New American Plays.** Produced at Actors Theatre of Louisville, this is a showcase for well-known playwrights and newcomers alike. Many productions seen here first have gone on to New York and London. Festival is held annually, usually late February through late March or early April. The theatre is located at 316 W. Main St. | 502/584–1205 or 800/428–5849 | www.actorstheatre.org.

SPRING

Apr. **Hillbilly Days.** Downtown Pikeville is the site for the annual festival that pokes tongue-in-cheek fun at the hillbilly stereotype. Proceeds from crafts, food, carnival games, and a parade benefit the Shriner's Children's Hospital in Lexington. The festival is usually held the third weekend in April. | 800/844–7453 | www.tourpikecounty.com.

American Quilter's Society National Quilt Show and Contest. With more than 400 quilts on exhibit competing for $100,000 in prize money, this annual contest is the grandmother of all quilt shows. There are workshops, seminars, lectures, and displays of antique quilts and other wearable art. The show is usually held the last half week of April. | 270/898–7903 | info@aqsquilt.com | www.aqsquilt.com.

The Kentucky Derby Festival. An enormous fireworks display over the Ohio River launches this event two weeks before the Kentucky Derby. Lasting two weeks, the festival in Louisville

1866	**1875**	**1884**	**1893**
is firmly in Union hands for the remainder of the Civil War.	Thomas Hunt Morgan, Nobel Laureate in Physiology/Medicine for his discovery that genes are located on chromosomes, is born in Lexington.	The first Kentucky Derby is run at Churchill Downs, in Louisville.	John A. "Bud" Hillerich, the 18-year-old son of a Louisville woodworker, makes a bat for baseball star Pete Browning, leading to the manufacture of the famous Louisville Sluggers.	A song entitled "Good Morning to You," written by Louisville sisters Patty and Mildred Hill, is published. Its melody becomes that of "Happy Birthday to You," which eventually

has over 75 events, including a steam-boat race, hot-air balloon race, mini-marathon, and parade. | 800/928–3378 | info@kdf.org | www.kdf.org.

May **International Bar-B-Q Festival.** Grilling teams from across the country gather in Owensboro. Crafts, music, and of course, lots of ribs, chicken, pork, and mutton, are on hand. | 270/926–6938.

SUMMER

June **Great American Brass Band Festival.** Brass bands and other historical ensembles come to Danville from all over the country to provide a weekend of open-air, old-fashioned entertainment. The Saturday morning parade of the bands through downtown highlights this annual festival, which usually falls on the second or third full weekend in June. | 800/755–0076 | tourism@searnet.com | www.gabbf.com.

Equitana U.S.A. This is the largest all-breed equine exposition and horse fair and exhibit in the Western Hemisphere. It's the sister event to Germany's Equitana and to Equitana Asia/Pacific in Melbourne, Australia and has over 600 educational presentations—the most sessions of any equine event in the world. The event, held annually the third full weekend in June, takes place at the Kentucky Fair and Exposition Center in Louisville, next to the Louisville Airport. | 888/467–7371 | info@equitanausa.com | www.equitanausa.com

July **Official Kentucky State Champion Old Time Fiddlers Contest.** Fiddle, harmonica, banjo, mandolin, guitar, and jig dancing events fill this contest held annually at Rough River Dam State Resort Park, the third Friday and Saturday of the month. | 270/259–3578.

Aug. **Kentucky State Fair.** The World's Championship Horse Show, which draws an international field of competitors in dressage, highlights this event showcasing the state's agriculture. Country music greats give concerts nightly, and there's a midway. The venue is the fairgrounds, which are across from the Louisville International Airport. | 502/367–5002 | www.kyfair-expo.org.

AUTUMN

Sept. **Kentucky Bourbon Festival.** Distillery tours, train rides, barrel rolling contests, and cooking classes are all part of this cele-

1911	1937	1939	1941
replaces "God Save the King" as the most frequently sung tune on the planet.	William Smith "Bill" Monroe, known as "The Father of Bluegrass Music," is born in Ohio County.	A record flood of the Ohio River displaces 200,000 residents of Louisville and causes some 200 deaths.	Colonel Harland Sanders opens a restaurant in Corbin specializing in fried chicken made with "11 secret herbs and spices."	Mammoth Cave near Bowling Green, the world's longest underground system, is designated a National Park.

bration of the state's most famous product—it's held in Bardstown for four days with events taking place all over town. If
you're over age 21 you can attend tastings. | 800/638–4877 |
www.kybourbonfestival.com.

INTRODUCTION
HISTORY
REGIONS
WHEN TO VISIT
STATE'S GREATS
RULES OF THE ROAD
DRIVING TOURS

Oct.   **International Bluegrass Music Association Bluegrass Fan Fest.**
Performers and devotees of Bluegrass flock to Louisville and
the banks of the Ohio River from around the world for this
annual festival. Concerts and workshops are the main activities during three days of "pickin' n' singin'." Fans also enjoy 40
music-related booths. | 270/684–9025 or 888/438–4262 |
ibma@ibma.org | www.ibma.org.

Perryville Commemoration and Reenactment. Civil War reen-
actors stage an hour-by-hour re-creation of the largest Civil
War battle in Kentucky at Perryville Battlefield State Historic
Site, 2 mi outside Perryville. Living history tours of downtown
Perryville are also given. | 859/332–8631 | www.perryville.net.

State's Greats

What drew Daniel Boone and the other pioneers to Kentucky—the beauty of its landscapes—will draw you as well. Whether it's fall colors in the eastern mountains or the
rolling countryside of the Bluegrass region, tourists come to enjoy the scenery and learn
about the state's—and our country's—history. Boonesborough and Fort Harrod have
both been restored. There are two Shaker Village museums in the state, where you
can stay overnight, eat traditional food, and watch artisans in period costumes make
furniture, baskets, and other crafts.

Cities, especially Louisville and Lexington, are rich in entertainment, dining, and
cultural experiences. A visitor to Kentucky can opt for back-country camping in one
of the numerous state parks as well as the Daniel Boone National Forest, or a luxurious stay in one of the cities' grand hotels, such as Louisville's historic Seelbach (alluded
to in F. Scott Fitzgerald's *The Great Gatsby*).

Louisville is also host to the most famous horse race in America, the Kentucky Derby,
run each year on the first Saturday in May at Churchill Downs. "The Most Famous Two
Minutes in Sports" attracts tens of thousands of fans to the city every spring.

The expression "as safe as Fort Knox" alludes, of course, to the U.S. Bullion Depository at the Fort Knox garrison 40 mi south of Louisville that is also the headquarters
for the U.S. Army Armored Forces and a museum housing armored equipment.

Scores of antebellum and Victorian inns are scattered throughout Kentucky, providing you with a taste of real Southern hospitality, as well as traditional regional cooking. (Cream gravy, for example, is an art form as much as it is a food.)

1942	**1966**	**1977**	**1984**	
Olympic Gold Medalist and World Heavyweight Boxing Champion Muhammad Ali is born (as Cassius Clay) in Louisville.	The Cumberland National Forest is renamed the Daniel Boone National Forest to honor the pioneer.	The Federal Surface Mining Control and Reclamation Act is passed, which requires Kentucky to return land damaged by coal mining to its original condition.	Dr. William DeVries installs a Jarvic-7 artificial heart in the chest of Bill Schroeder during an operation at Audubon Hospital in Louisville. Schroeder survives for 620 days to	become the longest-lived recipient of an artificial heart.

In western Kentucky, Mammoth Cave National Park has tours of the world's largest system of underground caverns.

Forests and Parks

The largest forest is the **Daniel Boone National Forest,** which stretches north to south throughout nearly 700,000 acres of eastern Kentucky. Natural stone arches, heavily wooded tracts with hiking trails, and panoramic views from mountain tops are highlights of this wilderness area. The only national park in the state is **Mammoth Cave National Park** near Bowling Green. Tours of the caverns are tailored in difficulty from novice to experienced spelunkers. Additionally there's a special handicapped-accessible program.

There are 49 state parks, about a dozen of which are also designated historic sites, providing outdoor recreational activities and overnight accommodations in lodges, cabins, and campgrounds. **Land Between the Lakes** in western Kentucky is a 170,000-acre wooded peninsula set aside for passive recreation and environmental education. It's maintained by the National Forest Service. Originally, it was administered by the TVA, which created Lake Barkley and Kentucky Lake by damming the Tennessee and Cumberland Rivers in the 1940s.

Many private nature preserves dot the state, though not all are open to the public. One that is open is the **Bernheim Arboretum and Research Forest** near Bardstown. The preserve has an educational center and nature classes for all ages.

Several of the state's cities have central parks and other greenways set aside for walking. Most notable is Louisville's system of Frederick Law Olmsted–designed parks, with hundreds of acres that include trails (for both people and horses), public golf courses, and public tennis courts. And there's a unique 6.9-mi **Riverwalk** along the Ohio in Louisville that takes walkers and bicyclists through some remarkably untouched wooded areas nestled between the water and the city. The state's only zoo is also in Louisville. The **Louisville Zoological Gardens** contains 1,300 animals in landscaped habitats.

Culture, History, and the Arts

The state's most famous cultural export is probably **Bluegrass music,** which has its roots in the folk music brought to the eastern mountains by English, Scottish, and Irish settlers. Small- to medium-sized Bluegrass festivals take place around the state throughout the year. The largest festival, which draws performers and listeners from around the world, is hosted in Louisville every autumn. Of course, to make fiddle and banjo music, the musicians need instruments. Scores of crafts people, still mostly from the mountains around the town of **Berea,** make fiddles, dulcimers, and other instruments. Other handmade crafts include furniture, replicas of old farm implements, wooden games, and homearts accessories.

The state boasts many concert halls serving as stages for musical performances, from classical to country. The **Kentucky Center for the Arts,** containing three theaters,

1990
After the state Supreme Court rules that Kentucky's entire educational system is unconstitutional, the General Assembly passes the Kentucky Education Reform Act (KERA), which becomes a national model for education reform.

overlooks the Ohio River in Louisville. Central Kentucky is served by the **Norton Center for the Performing Arts** in Danville and the **Lexington Opera House.** Invited artists from around the world and traveling Broadway shows are presented in these facilities, which also act as the homes for local arts organizations. **Actors Theatre of Louisville** is housed in its own complex on Main Street.

Kentucky brims with historic sites, from the **Abraham Lincoln Birthplace National Historic Site** near Hodgenville to home museums furnished with antiques. **Locust Grove** and **Farmington** in Louisville, **Federal Hill** (aka My Old Kentucky Home) in Bardstown, and **Ashland** and the **Mary Todd Lincoln House** in Lexington are examples. Shaker Villages at **Pleasant Hill** and **South Union** are entire museum communities. For an overview of state history, visit the **Kentucky History Center** in Frankfort which has interactive exhibits as well as more traditional displays.

The most significant Civil War Battle site is at **Perryville** in central Kentucky. The largest battle fought in the state is reenacted each October.

There are several museums honoring the state's industries such as the **Oscar Getz Museum of Whiskey History** in Bardstown; the **Cumberland Museum** in Williamsburg, which has coal mining and crafts exhibits; and the **Louisville Slugger Museum,** next door to the factory where the famous baseball bats are made.

For information about the history of racing and of horses, both the **Kentucky Horse Park** near Lexington and the **Kentucky Derby Museum** at Churchill Downs in Louisville are treasure troves of facts.

If you appreciate the visual arts, the state's largest art collection is housed in the **Speed Art Museum** on the edge of the University of Louisville's campus. The **Headley-Whitney Museum** in Lexington has a fine collection of decorative art.

Sports

Naturally, thoroughbred horseracing is a prominent part of the sporting scene in Kentucky. The Kentucky Derby, the first leg of American racing's Triple Crown, is held on the first Saturday in May at **Churchill Downs.** Racing takes place at the famed track from late April until mid-July and resumes in October and November. The Downs, as it's known to the locals, also regularly takes turn hosting the Breeder's Cup event. There are three other thoroughbred tracks in the state—**Keeneland** in Lexington, **Ellis Park** in Henderson, and **Turfway Park** in Florence, near Covington.

While the state has no major league professional teams, spectator sport excitement is more than provided for by college basketball. Both the **University of Kentucky** (which plays at Rupp Arena in Lexington) and the **University of Louisville** (which plays in Freedom Hall in Louisville) have storied men's basketball programs that have each won multiple NCAA National Championships.

If you'd like to play sports rather than just watch them, there's boating, fishing, swimming, hiking, backpacking, and camping facilities. White-water rafting is excellent at both **Breaks Interstate Park** and the **Big South Fork National River.** The ultimate hiking trail in the state, the **Sheltowee Trace National Recreation Trail** runs for 260 mi through the entire length of the Daniel Boone National Forest.

Rules of the Road

License Requirements: Valid driver's license is required. Minimum age for drivers in Kentucky is 16.

Right Turn on Red: It's legal to turn right on red after a full stop throughout the state, unless otherwise posted.

Seat Belt and Helmet Laws: Seat belts are required by law, as are federally approved restraint seats for all kids under 40 inches tall. Helmets for motorcyclists are also required.

Speed Limits: On interstates and parkways, the speed limit is 65 mph. In metropolitan areas this decreases to 55 mph. If you are traveling on state roads, be aware that the limit through most towns is 35 mph. And the smaller the town, the greater the reliance on traffic-ticket revenue for the municipal coffers, so watch signs carefully.

If you should be involved in an accident or need to report one, call 800/222–5555. And for current road conditions on interstates, parkways, and other major routes, you can call 800/459–7623.

For More Information: Kentucky Department of Travel | 800/225–8747.

Louisville to Lexington Through the Bluegrass Country along Scenic U.S. 60 Driving Tour

HORSES, WHISKEY, AND MANSIONS.

Distance: 75 mi   Time: 2 days
Breaks: You can lunch at Science Hill Inn in Shelbyville and overnight in Louisville.

This route will take you through prime examples of Kentucky countryside. The highway is lined with horse farms, and small towns along the route have period homes and courthouse squares. You'll even see a couple of bourbon distilleries along the way,

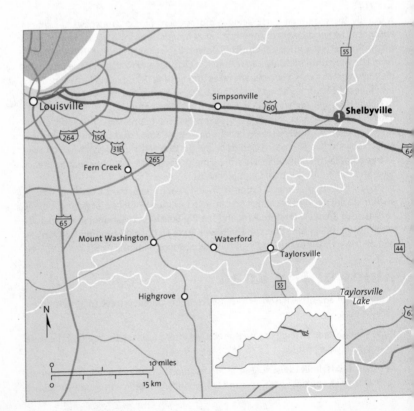

another Bluegrass state fixture. This drive is fine any time of year, though mid-April to late June can be the prettiest time, when the grass is lush green, and young thoroughbred foals can be spotted galloping by the sides of their mothers in the pastures.

To get to U.S. 60, take I–64 east out of Louisville to the Gene Snyder Freeway north. Exit onto Shelbyville Rd., which is U.S. 60, and head east.

❶ **Shelbyville** is 17 mi east of the Gene Snyder Freeway. Many of the buildings in the late-Victorian town center are listed on the National Register of Historic Places. **Science Hill** is a complex of handsome Federal-style redbrick buildings dating from 1790. It was a girls' school from 1825 to 1939. The elegant dining room (casual dress is fine at lunch) serves authentic Kentucky cuisine such as country ham, fried chicken, and hot-water cornbread. Take time to look in the shopping arcade (former classrooms and dorm rooms), but be sure to take a turn around the **Wakefield-Scearce Galleries.** The antique English and American furniture is beautiful, but the silver collection in the brick-floored basement will excite dreams of avarice.

❷ **Frankfort,** the state capital, is 20 mi west of Shelbyville on U.S. 60 and situated on the banks of the Kentucky River. The graceful Beaux Arts–style **State Capitol Building** opened in 1910. Its exterior is Indiana limestone and has 70 ionic columns and a Vermont-granite base. Marble, murals (including two depicting Daniel Boone), and paintings reflect a strongly influenced French architecture. The rotunda and dome are modeled on the Hotel Des Invalides in Paris. The grand staircase was inspired by that of the Paris Opera. And Marie Antoinette's drawing room at Versailles was copied for the State Reception Room.

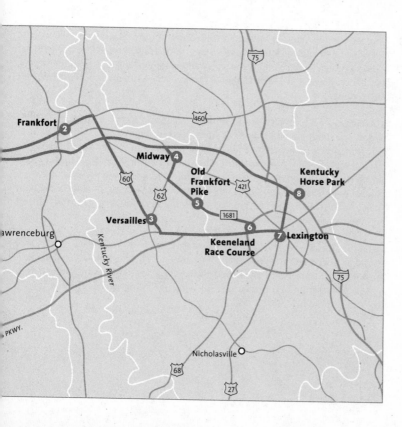

The outdoor working **Floral Clock** has a 34-ft face made up of thousands of plants that change seasonally. It is tilted above a reflecting pool so that the time can be read easily. Coins tossed into the pool are collected and donated to charities. You can overlook the city from the **Frankfort Cemetery,** where Daniel and Rebecca Boone are buried. Their grave is marked with a monument depicting scenes from the Boones' lives. If you need a little sugar fix, drop into **Rebecca-Ruth Candies,** where you can watch the original bourbon-laced chocolate candies being made—you can also sample some. And the **Kentucky History Center** is a good place to find out about state history and culture with interactive exhibits and a native trees and shrubs garden.

❸ Four miles southeast of Frankfort, near **Versailles** is **Labrot and Graham Distillery,** which has been restored to its working 19th-century condition. Limestone buildings house copper-pot stills. The visitors' center has an excellent exhibit about bourbon-making, and the tours are top-notch. There are plenty of picnic places along the creek.

❹ Tiny **Midway** is just south of I–64 at exit 65 (U.S. 62), about halfway between Frankfort and Lexington (hence, the name). It makes a good detour if you are an antiques hunter. Nineteenth-century storefronts along either side of Main Street contain dozens of shops.

❺ Go south from Midway on U.S. 62 for 5 mi to Rte. 1681, also known as **Old Frankfort Pike,** and follow the road east past some of the state's most famous horse farms. Architecture of the estate houses and horse barns is equally luxurious and ranges in style from antebellum to contemporary. **Three Chimney's** farm is home to Triple Crown winner Seattle Slew. The **Headley-Whitney Museum,** on the outskirts of Lexington, has an impressive collection of decorative art, including jewelry, Chinese porcelains, textiles, and furniture.

❻ From the Headley-Whitney Museum, take Rte. 1967 south to U.S. 60, and follow it east to Keeneland. **Keeneland Race Course** is a picture-postcard, thoroughbred course that houses a research library and is the site of thoroughbred auctions five times a year. Next door to Keeneland is fabled **Calumet Farm,** which has bred a record nine Kentucky Derby winners.

❼ In **Lexington,** there's shopping and dining along Main Street. Victorian Square is a restored block of warehouses containing retail stores and restaurants. You can spend a day in Lexington touring homes and sites. Two blocks from downtown's Broadway is the Gratz Park district with **Hunt-Morgan House.** Then go east along Main Street to **Mary Todd Lincoln House.** Also on Main Street and five minutes' drive away is Ashland. It's the home of Henry Clay, the American statesman who was Secretary of State under John Quincy Adams. Main Street becomes Richmond Road as you drive east and Ashland is at the intersection with Sycamore.

❽ Spend the afternoon at the **Kentucky Horse Park,** 6 mi north of the city center. Take I–75 north to exit 120, Iron Works Pike. The park is just off the exit and well marked. The **American Saddle Horse Museum** is also on the grounds of the park. Have dinner in the city and return to Louisville via I–64, which will take just over an hour.

From Lexington to Daniel Boone Country Driving Tour

PIONEERS AND MOUNTAIN FOLKWAYS.

Distance: 120 mi   Time: 1–2 days

Breaks: You'll lunch and shop in Berea and then overnight in Middlesboro near the Cumberland Gap.

Most of this drive is along divided highways, I–75, and and Route 25E. It is a good introduction to mountain culture and to the history of the pioneer settlement of America west of the Appalachians. Boonesborough, surviving portions of the Wilderness Road, and the Cumberland Gap are included. Spring and fall are recommended times to explore this region of Kentucky. The flowering trees and shrubs on the mountainsides are lovely in spring. Fall colors, at their peak in early to mid-October, can rival New England's if the summer hasn't been too dry. You can go in summer, but it will probably be very hot and humid. Even at night in the mountains it can be muggy. Winter is not recommended because snow and ice can make the roads hazardous, if not downright impassable.

❶ About 20 mi southeast of Lexington is **Fort Boonesborough State Park.** To get there, take I–75 to exit 95 and follow the signs. The fort, Kentucky's second permanent settlement, has been fully and faithfully reconstructed on a bank of the Kentucky River. It has log cabins, blockhouses, and is outfitted with period furnishings. Resident artisans and actors in pioneer costume reenact life as it would have been at Boonesboro when Boone and his party arrived in 1775.

❷ Since you are nearby, you may want to make a brief stop at **Boone Station State Historic Site** (Rte. 418), a few minutes from Boonesborough. When Daniel Boone left Boonesborough, he established this pioneer station. Many Boone family deaths occurred near here in the Battle of Blue Licks, and Daniel's brothers Samuel and Edward are buried here.

❸ Leaving Boonesborough, take Exit 76 off I–75 to the college town of **Berea,** which is 25 mi south of the Boone settlements. Known as the "Folk Arts and Crafts Capital of Kentucky," the town could probably contend for this title nationally. More than 50 dulcimer and fiddle makers, jewelers, weavers, quilters, and furniture and cabinet makers all have shops lining the streets of the **Old Town.** Drive along Chestnut Street past the campus of **Berea College,** established in 1855 to educate the youth of Appalachia, both white and black. This private college still provides full-tuition scholarships and only admits low-income students. All students are required to work 10–15 hours per week to help pay their expenses. Some are servers and cooks at **Boone Tavern,** where you should stop for a traditional Southern lunch. Reservations are recommended. Before leaving Berea, stop at **Churchill Weavers,** America's largest and foremost handweaving studio. The building, containing a loom room and gift shop, is surrounded by a remarkable rose garden. Self-guided tours.

❹ As you drive down I–75 you will pass **Renfro Valley,** the "Country Music Capital of Kentucky." If you enjoy country music, you might want to get tickets for a concert on your way back to Lexington. Headliners have included Loretta Lynn, Charley Pride, The Oak Ridge Boys, and Billy Ray Cyrus. If you decide to stay overnight near the Cumberland Gap and drive back the next day, there are afternoon shows on Friday and Saturday, from April through October.

❺ A half hour south of Renfro Valley, east of where the highway crosses through a portion of the Daniel Boone National Forest, is exit 38 to London. Follow the signs to **Levi Jackson Wilderness Road State Park.** Among the attractions in the park is **The Mountain Life Museum,** open April 1 through October 31. It's a reproduction of a pioneer settlement. Hiking trails include 8½ mi of the original **Wilderness Road,** constructed by Daniel Boone and his party and traveled by more than 200,000 settlers between 1774 and 1776. Also contained within the 800-acre park is **McHarges's Mill,** built on the banks of the Little Laurel River. The working mill is surrounded by the country's largest collection of millstones.

❻ Go back to I–75 and drive 9 mi to Exit 29 at Corbin. This will put you on Rte. 25E, from which it's 47 mi to **Middlesboro.** This town near Cumberland Gap is built in a bowl-shaped depression, possibly a meteor crater, and the view from the **overlook** at nearby **Cumberland Gap National Historic Park,** confirms that this is the only place for miles around where a town of any size could have been built. The view also dramatically shows the tiny break in the mountains where Boone led settlers through to Kentucky. Just outside the entrance to the park is the **Cumberland Gap Tunnel** running under the Cumberland Mountains. Among the longest of its kind in the world, the tunnel takes advantage of state-of-the-art climate control and lighting technology. If you're not claustrophobic, it's worth a drive through to Cumberland Gap, Tennessee, and dinner at **Ye Olde Tea and Coffee Shoppe,** which is housed in buildings dating from 1889.

Return to Lexington by going northwest on U.S. 25 E from Middlesboro to I–75 N. The drive will take about 2½ hours.

ABRAHAM LINCOLN BIRTHPLACE NATIONAL HISTORIC SITE

(see Hodgenville)

ASHLAND

MAP 6, H3

(Nearby towns also listed: Morehead, Olive Hill)

Eastern Kentucky's largest city is on the Ohio River, by the Ohio and West Virginia borders. It was settled in the late 1700s by the Poage family of Virginia. The area, rich in coal, timber, and limestone, became an important industrial center in the 1800s, especially for the manufacture of pig iron. The location on the river facilitated shipment of goods and made the town an important transportation center as well. The 13th-largest petroleum refining company in the United States, Ashland Oil, was founded here in 1924 and was a major force in the economy and arts in the city until it moved its corporate headquarters from Ashland to the Covington area in 1999.

A focal point of the city is Central Park in downtown, which has sports and picnic facilities, a concert bandstand, and an ancient Native American burial mound.

Information: Ashland Area Convention and Visitors Bureau | 1509 Winchester Ave., Ashland, 41101 | 606/329–1007 or 800/377–6249 | www.visitashlandky.com | aacvb@visitashlandky.com.

Attractions

Ashland Area Art Gallery. This gallery is recognized as a leader in the visual art community of the tri-state area of Kentucky, Ohio, and West Virginia. Among the gallery's collection are works by Norman Rockwell, Mitchell D. Tolle, and local artists. | 1516 Winchester Ave. | 606/329–1827 | Donations accepted | Weekdays 9–5.

Central Park. An old-fashioned bandstand where summer concerts are staged is a focal point of this 47-acre park in the middle of downtown. There's also a playground, 2 sand volleyball courts, tennis courts, picnic areas, walking and jogging trails, refrigerated ice-skating rink, pond with a fountain, 3 baseball diamonds and 1 softball diamond. You can see ancient Native American burial mounds within the park, too. | Central Ave. to Lexington Ave. and 17th to 22nd Sts. | 606/327–2046 | Free | Daily 7 AM–11 PM.

Covered Bridges. At the turn of the 19th century more than 400 covered bridges spanned the state's creeks and rivers. Today there are only a dozen left and only four of those are open to traffic, including Bennett's Mill Bridge, noted below. | Kentucky Covered Bridge Association, 62 Miami Pkwy., Ft. Thomas | 606/441–7000 | fax 606/441–2112.

The single-span **Bennett's Mill Bridge** was built in 1855 and crosses the almost 155-ft-long width of Tygart's Creek. Drive north off Rte. 7 | Rte. 1215 at Rte. 7 | Free.

The double-span **Oldtown Bridge** was built in 1880 and stretches over the Little Sandy River. Drive 9 mi south off Rte. 1. | Frazier Branch Rd. | Free | Closed to traffic.

Greenbo Lake State Resort Park. This resort park, sprawls over 3,000 acres and includes Greenbo Lake. The lodge library contains books by Kentucky author and poet Jesse Stuart, who was born and raised nearby. | Rte. 1, HC 60, Box 562, Greenup | 606/473–7324 or 800/325–0083 | www.kystateparks.com/agencies/parks/greenbo2.htm | Free | Daily.

The Highlands Museum and Discovery Center. Antique clothing and spinning and weaving equipment are among the permanent displays. You'll find a country music exhibit and kids' discovery center. | 1620 Winchester, Ashland | 606/329–8888 | $3 | Tues.–Sat. 10–4.

ASHLAND

INTRO
ATTRACTIONS
DINING
LODGING

Paramount Arts Center. Originally a movie house built in 1930 by Paramount Pictures, this cathedral-ceilinged theater was restored in 1972 to showcase live entertainment. Performances are held in the evenings and are subject to change on a regular basis. You can tour the site during the day. Many well-known artists perform here—this is where Billy Ray Cyrus recorded "Achey Breaky Heart." Call ahead or visit the website for current information on shows. | 1300 Winchester Ave. | 606/324–3175 | fax 606/324–1233 | www.paramountarts-center.com | Free to tour theatre, call for show prices | Weekdays 9–4, call for show times.

ON THE CALENDAR

MAY–SEPT.: *Central Park Concerts.* Diverse musical entertainment is held on weekends throughout the summer. | 606/329–1007 or 800/377–6249.

JUNE: *Ashland Brass Band and Hot Dog Festival.* Brass bands from Kentucky, Ohio, and West Virginia perform all afternoon in Central Park bandstand annually on the 3rd Saturday. | 606/329–1007 or 800/377–6249.

JULY: *Summer Motion.* Music, games, food, and fireworks abound for five days every 4th of July along the riverfront and in Central Park. | 606/329–1007 or 800/377–6249.

SEPT.: *Poage Landing Days Festival.* Local and national entertainers, arts and crafts, a huge woodcarving expo, a fiddle festival, and a car and motorcycle show celebrate the city's founders. There are numerous kids' activities, too. The festival is held annually every third full weekend of the month. | 606/329–1007 or 800/377–6249.

NOV.–DEC.: *Winter Wonderland of Lights.* Over 700,000 lights deck downtown, Central Park, and residential neighborhoods are decked out for the holidays. It's a spectacle not to be missed. You can see it from Thanksgiving Day through New Year's Day. | 606/329–1007 or 800/377–6249.

Dining

Around the Corner Restaurant. American. No matter what you're hungry for, chances are you'll find it Around the Corner. The menu ranges from standard homecooking to specialty dishes like chicken piccata and surf 'n turf. People keep coming back for the peach bread pudding. | 1622 Carter Ave., Ashland | 606/324–0740 | Closed Mon. | $7–$17 | AE, DC, MC, V.

C.R. Thomas Old Place. American. Old sports equipment and memorabilia and movie star photos cover the walls of this medium-sized, casual restaurant. The brick building is an 1865 landmark. Try Cajun chicken pasta, Cajun grilled sandwiches, burgers, and Snickers Crunch Pie. Breakfast not served. | 1612 Greenup Ave., Ashland | 606/325–8500 | fax 606/325–2706 | lunch: $6–$10; dinner: $8–$15 | AE, D, MC, V.

Dragon Palace. Chinese and American. You'll find an upscale, casual, yet traditional Chinese design in this redbrick contemporary building one block from the Town Center Mall. The Chinese favorites include General Tso's Chicken and Seafood Imperial; American food includes chicken, steaks, pasta, seafood, and sandwiches. Kids' menu. Reservations recommended. | 807 Carter Ave., Ashland | 606/329–8081 | $8–$17 | AE, D, MC, V.

Rosie's Restaurant. Southern. By its own admission, looks aren't everything. But with reasonable prices and huge portions of good food, Rosie's doesn't need looks. Open all night with breakfast served anytime, Rosie's claims to have the best desserts in town. | 2201 U.S. 60W | 606/928–3547 | Open 24 hrs | $3–$7 | No credit cards.

Lodging

Ashland Plaza. The upscale specialty gift shop, Angels on the Water, is locally well known and defines this 10-story contemporary high-rise with angled balconies and a lobby atrium. The top two floors have concierge service. Half the rooms overlook the Ohio River and is just south of the Ohio River Bridge. There's a contemporary, full-service restaurant on the second floor. Meals range from $9–$20. Open 6 AM–2 PM and 4–10 PM. Live music at a piano bar, Mon. to Sat. 5–9 PM. Free parking. Restaurant, bar. Cable TV. Business services.

Airport shuttle. | 1 Ashland Plaza, Ashland | 606/329–0055 or 800/346–6133 | fax 606/325–4513 | www.ashlandplaza.net | 157 rooms | $70–$85 | AE, D, DC, MC, V.

Days Inn–Ashland. This two-story no-frills outlet of the motel chain is a modern stucco building situated 8 mi from downtown Ashland. Picnic area, complimentary Continental breakfast. In-room data ports; some microwaves and refrigerators. Cable TV. Outdoor pool. Fitness room. Laundry facilities. Business facilities. Free parking and ample truck parking. Pets allowed (fee). | 12700 Rte. 180 | 606/928–3600 or 800/329–7466 | fax 606/928–6515 | ash@musselmanhotels.com | www.daysinn.com/kentucky/ashland | 63 rooms | $45–$66; high-season rack rate $55.55 plus tax | AE, D, DC, MC, V.

Fairfield Inn by Marriott. This contemporary two-story stucco is marked by a pleasant blue and rose color scheme. It's 15 minutes from the airport, off 1–64, exit 60. Complimentary Continental breakfast. Microwaves and refrigerators (in suites). Cable TV. Indoor pool. Business services. Free parking. | 10945 U.S. 60, Ashland | 606/928–1222 or 800/228–2800 | fax 606/928–1222 | 63 rooms, 8 suites | $60, $60–$70 suites | AE, D, DC, MC, V.

Greenbo Lake State Resort Park. The rustic fieldstone lodge is highlighted by large stone fireplaces in the common areas and the Jesse Stuart Library. Accommodations are on the lakefront. Restaurant. Satellite TV. Pool and seasonal use wading pool. Hiking, boating. Bicycles. Game room. Hiking trails cover 25 mi of the 3,332 wooded acres. Kids' summer programs, playground. Shuffleboard, Ping Pong, and pool table. Business services. Free parking. | HC60, Box 562, Greenup | 606/473–7324 or 800/325–0083 | fax 606/473–7741 | www.kystateparks.com | 36 rooms | $42–$69 | AE, D, DC, MC, V.

Hampton Inn–Ashland. This hotel is 2 mi from two industrial parks and 1 mi from Cedar Knoll Galleria. There is an extensive breakfast bar highlighting biscuits and gravy. Complimentary Continental breakfast. Indoor pool. Game room. Exercise equipment. | 1321 Cannonsburg Rd. | 606/928–2888 | fax 606/928–6864 | www.hampton-inns.com | 60 rooms, 7 suites, 3 hot tub suites | $60–$85 | AE, D, DC, MC, V.

Holiday Inn Express–Ashland. This inn is located 2 mi from downtown, convenient to the Paramount Arts Center, Kentucky Highland Museum, and many shops and restaurants. It is 9 mi from the Tri-State Airport in Huntington, WV. Complimentary Continental breakfast. Cable TV. Indoor pool. Some in-room hot tubs. Pets allowed (restrictions). | 4708 Winchester Ave. | 606/325–8989 or 800/465–4329 | fax 606/465–8989 | aslky@worldnet.att.net | www.exonline.com | 50 rooms, 5 hot tub suites | $58–$97 | AE, D, DC, MC, V.

Knights Inn. The Knights Inn is just 5 mi from downtown Ashland surrounded by 3 woody acres. A half dozen one-story stucco buildings comprise the motel. Parking spaces are by the room doors. Complimentary Continental breakfast. Refrigerators. Cable TV. Pool. Laundry facilities. Business services. Free parking. Some pets allowed (fee). | 7216 U.S. 60, Ashland | 606/928–9501 or 800/497–7560 | fax 606/928–4436 | 122 rooms in 6 buildings | $38–$43 | AE, D, DC, MC, V.

The Levi Hampton House Bed and Breakfast. Levi Hampton's grand, Italianate brick house dates from 1847. It's a relaxed artists' haven on Highway 23; 10 minutes south of the Ashland business district. This B&B has a sun porch, wisteria arbor where deer can be seen, and man-made fish pond. Furnished with antiques and collectibles and boasting working fireplaces. Complimentary breakfast. Some in-room hot tubs. Business services. Airport shuttle with advanced notice. | 2206 Walnut St., Catlettsburg | 606/739–8118 or 888/538–4426 | fax 606/739–8179 | dstemen!@msn.com | www.bbonline.com/ky/levihampton | 5 rooms | $75–$97 | MC, V.

BARBOURVILLE

MAP 6, G5

(Nearby towns also listed: Corbin, Daniel Boone National Forest, London, Middlesboro, Pineville, Williamsburg)

The town is named after Virginia-born pioneer James Barbour who gave Knox County 38 acres in the late 1800s with the stipulation that half the land be used for public buildings. Situated on the Cumberland River, the town celebrates its pioneer heritage with a yearly Daniel Boone Festival. Preceeding Daniel Boone through the Cumberland Gap, Dr. Thomas Walker, a physician and explorer, along with his surveying party, built a log cabin near the current site of Barbourville.

Information: **Knox County Chamber of Commerce** | 196 Daniel Boone Dr., No. 205, Barbourville, 40906 | 606/546–4300 | chamber@barbourville.com | www.barbourville.com.

Attractions

Barbourville City Recreation Park. Bring the family for a day of outdoor fun. The Brickyard Waves Water Park has a wave pool, water slide, paddleboats, kiddie pool, lazy river, and lounging areas. The park has a 9-hole miniature golf course, baseball and softball fields, picnic shelters, and playgrounds. | Allison St. | 606/546–6197 | $6, $2 landlubbers | Late May–early Sept., weekdays 11–6, Sun. 1–6.

Daniel Boone National Forest. Formerly known as the Cumberland National Forest, this roughly 690,000-acre park encompasses 21 counties, from Morehead in northeastern Kentucky down to the Tennessee state line and east again into Kentucky. The main body of the forest is divided into five ranger districts. | 1700 Bypass Rd., Winchester | 859/745–3100 | mailroom_r8_daniel_boone@fs.fed.us | www.r8web.com/boone.

Dr. Thomas Walker State Historic Site. A physician and surveyor, Walker led the first expedition through the Cumberland Gap into Kentucky in 1750. He and his small band of followers built a log cabin on the site of this 12-acre park. The original is long since gone, but officials have created a reproduction. The park is 5 mi south of Barbourville on Rte. 459. | HC 89, Box 1868, Barbourville | 606/546–4400 | fax 606/546–9366 | www.state.ky.us/agencies/parks/drwalker.htm | Free.

Kentucky Communities Crafts Village. You can take a trip back in time touring these colorful, old-fashioned crafts stores. Visit the Village Fudge Shop and the Old Town General Store in the Barbourville City Park. | U.S. 25E between Corbin and Cumberland Gap exits, Gray | 800/880–3152 | Weekdays 8–5 | Gift shop open Apr.–Oct.

ON THE CALENDAR

OCT.: *Daniel Boone Festival*. There are living history displays with costumed actors, regional food, and traditional music and crafts. This annual celebration of frontier heritage lasts six days through the first full week of the month. It's held downtown, around Court Square. | 606/546–4300.

Dining

Hillbilly Country Restaurant. Country. The only dilemma is how much to eat at Hillbilly's all-you-can-eat buffet. Help yourself to chicken and dumplings, roast beef, meatloaf, and an assortment of sides. Top it off with a dessert of homemade pie or cake. | 301 Daniel Boone Dr., Barbourville | 606/546–5910 | 6 AM–9 PM | $4–$6 | AE, MC, V.

Vintage House Historic Restaurant. Eclectic. This restaurant was a hardware store for 40 years before being renovated in 1994. The menu varies depending on the season and the chef's creativity but you can expect dishes like filet mignon, prime rib, chicken prepared with special house recipes, and Atlantic salmon. For a light lunch try a fresh pasta or quiche. | 101 N. Main St., Barbourville | 606/546–5414 | Closed Sun.–Tues. No dinner Wed. No lunch Sat. | $10–$20 | D, DC, MC, V.

BARDSTOWN

MAP 6, E4

(Nearby towns also listed: Fort Knox, Elizabethtown, Louisville, Shepardsville, Springfield)

Block after block of redbrick Federal houses and a classic courthouse square are hallmarks of this pretty town, the second-oldest in the state. Settlers who came down the Ohio River from Maryland, Pennsylvania, and Virginia were the original 1780 inhabitants. Federal Hill, the mansion in Bardstown also known as "My Old Kentucky Home," is the site that inspired Stephen Foster to write what was to become the state song. Federal Hill is also a state park. Today Bardstown is the international center of the bourbon whiskey industry, a fact commemorated with an annual festival. Nearby distilleries include Jim Beam, Heaven Hill, and Maker's Mark. Also near Bardstown is the Trappist Abbey of Gethsemani, founded in 1848 and famous as the home of monk and writer Thomas Merton.

Information: Bardstown-Nelson County Tourist and Convention Commission | Box 867, 107 Stephen Foster Ave., Bardstown, 40004 | 800/638–4877 | fax 349/502–0804 | www.bardstowntourism.com.

Attractions

Bernheim Arboretum and Research Forest. The 16,000-acre forest and arboretum is funded and maintained by a private foundation started by bourbon magnate Isaac W. Bernheim. The tree and shrub collection contains more than 1,800 labeled species. A visitors' center has a museum, start of a nature trail, and ponds on which duck and other waterfowl can be spotted. A small fee is charged for regular educational programs. The park hosts a summer concert series. | Box 130, Clermont; Drive 20 mi south of Louisville to I–65, exit 112. It's across the highway from the distillery | 502/955–8512 | nature@bernheim.org. | www.bernheim.org | Free weekdays; $5 per vehicle weekends and holidays | Daily 7–sunset.

Civil War Museum at Old Bardstown Village. You can almost smell the gunpowder and hear miniballs whizzing past as you view one of the largest collections of both North and South Civil War artifacts in existence. On display are authentic uniforms, battle flags, weapons, documents, and maps. Group tours are available with a reservation. | 310 E. Broadway, Bardstown | 502/349–0291; 502/348–5204 | $5 musuem, $2.50 village | Mar. 1–Dec. 15, Mon.–Sat. 10–5, Sun. noon–5; Jan.–Feb. Sat. 10–5, Sun. noon–5.

Jim Beam American Outpost. Beams have been making bourbon for six generations, since 1795—it's the oldest continuing business in the state. The complex includes a restored 1911 house, which was the home of T. Jeremiah Beam and is on the National Register of Historic Places. You'll find an 1800s cooperage museum and the oldest moonshine still in the country. | Drive 22 mi south of Louisville to exit 112 off I–65 | 526 Happy Hollow Rd., Clermont | 502/543–9877 | www.jimbeam.com | Free | Mon.–Sat. 9–4:30, Sun. 1–4.

Lincoln Homestead State Park. A replica log cabin is built on the site where the original family cabin stood in 1782. The park's 150 acres once consisted of the Thomas and Nancy Hanks Lincoln farm. The park's golf course is the biggest draw. There's a self-guided tour of the park which includes blacksmith and carpenter shops. | 5079 Lincoln Park Rd., Springfield | 859/336–7461 | fax 859/336–0659 | www.state.ky.us/agencies/parks/linchome | $2 | May–Sept., 10–6.

The Mansion Home Tour. This Greek Revival mansion dating from 1851 is furnished with period antiques. The Confederate flag was first raised in the State of Kentucky at this site. | 1003 N. 3rd St., Bardstown | 502/348–2586 | $5 | Daily; tours 1 and 5 daily; reservations requested.

My Old Kentucky Dinner Train. You'll ride in vintage 1940s mahogany-appointed dining cars which highlight the excursions aboard a restored train. Rides range from 2 to 2½ hours and wind through 35 mi of rolling and wooded countryside. | Trains depart from downtown, minutes from My Old Kentucky Home | 602 N. 3rd St., Bardstown | 502/348–7300 | fax 502/348–7780 | www.rjcorman.co | $36.95 plus tax lunch excursion; $59.95 plus tax dinner excursion | Tues.–Sat.; on a varied schedule by demand.

My Old Kentucky Home State Park. This redbrick mansion known as Federal Hill inspired Pittsburgh composer Stephen Foster to write "My Old Kentucky Home," in 1852. The song is now the official state song. The mansion was the home of Foster's cousin Judge John Rowan and dates from 1818. Tours of the house are given by guides in period costumes. The home is 3 blocks from Bardstown on Highway 150. | 501 E. Stephen Foster Ave., Bardstown | 502/348–3502 or 800/323–7803 | www.kystateparks.com/agencies/parks/kyhome.htm | $4.50 | Sept. 2–May 31, 9–5; June 1–Sept. 1, 8:30–6:30; closed Thanksgiving Day, the week of Christmas, New Year's Eve and Day. Candlelight tours in December.

St. Joseph Proto-Cathedral. A collection of 17th-century paintings are in the cathedral. They are said to be a gift of King Louis Philippe, who lived for a time in Bardstown during his exile from France. This is one of the first Catholic cathedrals built west of the Alleghenies in 1816. It also houses Gifts from Pope Leo XII which adorn the cathedral walls. | It's the biggest landmark in town and 3 blocks from the courthouse | 310 W. Stephen Foster Ave., Bardstown | 502/348–3126 | fax 502/349–9041 | stjoe@bardstown.com | www.stjoechurch.com | $2 (suggested) | Weekdays 9–5, Sat. 9–3, and Sun. 1–5.

Spalding Hall. Built in 1826, this building houses the Oscar Getz Museum of Whiskey History and the Bardstown Historical Museum. | The hall is next to St. Joseph Proto-Cathedral | 114 N. 5th St., Bardstown | 502/348–2999 | Free | May–Oct., daily 9–5, Sun. 1–5; Nov.–Apr., Tues.–Sat. 10–4, Sun. 1–4.

More than 200 years of Bardstown history is recounted at the **Bardstown Historical Museum** through Native American relics, pioneer kids' toys, gifts from French monarchs to the early settlers, Civil War weapons, and a replica of an 1866 covered bridge. It's a rare, old building, built in 1826 located 2 blocks off Court Square. | 114 N. 5th St., Bardstown | 502/348–2999 | fax 502/348–2999 | May 1–Oct. 31, Mon.–Sat. 9–5, Sun. 1–5; Nov. 1–Apr. 30, Tues.–Sat. 10–4, Sun. 1–4; closed Mon.

The **Oscar Getz Museum of Whiskey History** traces the history of the American whiskey industry from colonial times through the 1960s. Advertising posters, bottles, and even a copper still confiscated by government agents are among the collection's artifacts. | The museum is 2 blocks off Court Square | 114 N. 5th St., Bardstown | May 1–Oct. 31, Mon.–Sat. 9–5, Sun. 1–5; Nov. 1–Apr. 30, Tues.–Sat. 10–4, Sun. 1–4; closed Mon. | 502/348–2999 | fax 502/348–2999.

Wickland. An unusual T-shaped hallway and a gardenside carriage entrance match the main entrance in front of this 14-room mansion built in the 1820s. Wickland was home to two Kentucky governors and one governor of Louisiana. | U.S. 62E, Bardstown | 502/348–5428 | $4 | Mar.–Oct., daily, by appointment.

ON THE CALENDAR

JUNE–SEPT.: *Stephen Foster–The Musical.* This annual outdoor musical featuring the composer's famous melodies is performed on the grounds of My Old Kentucky Home State Park with period costumes. Performances every night but Mondays from the 2nd weekend of June through Labor Day. | 502/348–5971 or 800/626–1563.

SEPT.: *Kentucky Bourbon Festival.* Distillery tours, train rides, barrel rolling contests, and cooking classes are all part of this annual celebration of the state's most famous product. Usually held the 2nd week in Sept, the event has tastings and a dinner gala. You'll find the festival across the street from My Old Kentucky Home State Park. | 800/638–4877.

Dining

Dagwood's. American. Dagwood's, as the name implies, began as a sandwich shop. Over the years a more creative and sophisticated menu evolved, but the name stuck. A couple bourbon-cooking favorites are the Elijah Craig New York Strip and the Barton & Bird. All entrées come with homemade soup and salad bar. | 204 N. 3rd St., Bardstown | 502/348–4019 | Closed Sun. | $10–18 | MC, V.

Kurtz. American. This establishment is celebrated for their fried chicken—a *New York Times* food critic wrote about it. And it's said that Kurtz "outfries the Colonel." The family-run restaurant is in an English Tudor built in 1937 and has antique furniture and white tablecloths. Favorites are skillet-fried cornbread, biscuit pudding with bourbon sauce, and daily-made homemade meringue cream pies. | 418 E. Stephen Foster Ave., Bardstown | 502/348–8964 or 800/732–2384 | fax 502/349–6973 | Breakfast also available Sun. | $11–$20 | AE, D, MC, V.

Old Talbott Tavern. Southern. Once a stagecoach stop (1779), the tavern and B&B are Belgian-Flemish stone and were restored after a fire and furnished with antiques. The tavern is known for country ham, Kentucky Hot Brown, fried chicken, and homemade desserts. There's entertainment on weekends | 107 W. Stephen Foster Ave., Bardstown | 502/348–3494 or 800/482–8376 (4–TAVERN) | fax 502/348–3404 | talbott@bardstown.com | www.talbotts.com | $15–$30 | AE, MC, V.

Xavier's Restaurant. American. Formerly a seminary, this building dating back to 1829 was used as a Civil War hospital. Curved brick arches tower above as you feast on roast pork tenderloin in bourbon cinnamon sauce or pecan crusted salmon. After your dessert of bourbon pecan caramel pie, visit the lounge on weekends for live entertainment. The Oscar Getz Whiskey Museum is in the same building. | 112 Xavier Dr., Bardstown | 502/349–9464 | Tues.–Sat. 5–10, closed Sun.–Mon. | $10–$18 | AE, D, MC, V.

Lodging

Bardstown Parkview. Its name evokes the views from the rooms which have traditional American furnishings. The stone colonial inn has horse prints on the walls and is just across the street from My Old Kentucky Home State Park. Restaurant, bar, complimentary Continental breakfast. Some kitchenettes. Cable TV. Pool. Laundry facilities. Some pets allowed. Free parking. | 418 E. Stephen Foster Ave., Bardstown | 502/348–5983 or 800/732–2384 | fax 502/349–6973 | 38 rooms | $70 | AE, D, MC, V.

Best Western General Nelson. This contemporary favorite is distinguised by a 100-year-old office, a facade with archways, stained-glass, and pillars—a Southern plantation motif. There's also an outdoor gazebo in the rural, residential area; 1 mi from My Old Kentucky Home. In-room data ports, some kitchenettes. Cable TV. Pool. Therapy spa. Laundry facilities. Continental breakfast. Free parking. | 411 W. Stephen Foster Ave., Bardstown | 502/348–3977 or 800/225–3977 | fax 502/348–7596 | best@gennelson.win.net | generalnelson.win.net | 52 rooms | $49–$79 | AE, D, DC, MC, V.

Hampton Inn. This contemporary, two-story stucco building was built on the site of a former farm; the lobby has authentic and equine prints on the walls. Spacious rooms have color-coordinated modern appointments. Three rooms have working fireplaces. The motel is in the commercial area of town, close to My Old Kentucky Home. Complimentary Continental breakfast. In-room data ports. Cable TV. Indoor pool. Exercise equipment. Business services. Free parking. | 985 Chambers Blvd., Bardstown | 502/349–0100 or 800/426–7866 | fax 502/349–1191 | 106 rooms | $70–$75 | AE, D, DC, MC, V.

Holiday Inn. This is a typical roadside Holiday Inn with modern decor dominated by blues, greens, and mauves. Restaurant, bar. In-room data ports. Cable TV. Pool. Driving range, 9-hole golf course. Exercise equipment. Playground. Video games. Business services. Free parking. Some pets allowed. | 1875 New Haven Rd., Bardstown | 502/348–9253 or 800/HOLIDAY | fax 502/348–5478 | 101 rooms | $89–$95 | AE, D, DC, MC, V.

Jailer's Inn. This is your chance to experience history in a building that once served as a holding pen. It's an antique-filled B&B built in 1819 and has 30-inch-thick limestone walls and two stories. Rooms have iron bars on the windows. One room is a little-altered jail cell, complete with bunks. There's a courtyard in the rear. Complimentary Continental breakfast; afternoon snacks. Some in-room hot tubs. Cable TV, no room phones. Free parking. | 111 W. Stephen Foster Ave., Bardstown | 502/348–5551 or 800/948–5551 | fax 502/349–1837 | cpaul@jailersinn.com | www.jailersinn.com | 6 rooms | $65–$115 | Closed Jan. | AE, D, MC, V.

Old Bardstown Inn. This brick, two-story inn in the historic district looks like a little mansion. The lobby has old-fashioned lamps and the grounds have a small garden. Standard rooms each contain two queen-size beds and cherry furniture. Cable TV. Pool. Continental breakfast. Free parking. | 510 E. Stephen Foster Ave., Bardstown | 502/349–0776 or 800/894–1601 | fax 502/349–0776 | oldbardstowninn.nv.switchboard.com | 33 rooms | $58 | AE, D, MC, V.

Old Talbott Tavern/McLean House. You'll remember the place and the food. Talbott Tavern, a flemish bond stone building, is the oldest (1779) western stagecoach stop still in operation. McLean House originally was the brick post office, built in 1814. The tavern and house both have rooms. Miss Eleanor, the cook/baker for many years, is well-known in the area, especially for her home-made desserts (e.g., bourbon bread pudding) and "Miss Eleanor's Chicken Salad." The tavern is also known for its "secret recipe" Chicken Philippe (deep fried and baked chicken breast in a tarragon and white wine sauce). Complimentary Continental breakfast; on weekends, complimentary full breakfast. Cable TV. Free parking. | 107 W. Stephen Foster Ave., Bardstown | 502/348–3494 or 800/482–8376 (4–TAVERN) | talbott@bardstown.com | talbotts.com | 11 rooms | $80–$170 | AE, MC, V.

Ramada Inn. Stately white columns, large maple trees, and southern hospitality welcome you to this motel in the historic district. Continental breakfast. Cable TV. In-room data ports. Pool, hot tub, some in-room hot tubs. Pets allowed. | 523 N. 3rd St., Bardstown | 502/349–5979 | www.ramada-inn.com | 40 rooms | $48–$75 | AE, D, MC, V.

Red Carpet Inn. The area has plenty of things to see and do, so a good night's sleep here can serve you well. My Old Kentucky Home is 2 mi away, Bernheim Forest 15 mi, and the Jim Beam Distillery is 15 mi. There's golf and tennis close by. The hotel has free transportation to *Stephen Foster—The Musical*. Restaurant. Cable TV. | 1714 New Haven Rd., at 31E and Bluegrass Pkwy, Bardstown | 502/348–1112 or 800/251–1962 | fax 502/348–1114 | www.reservahost.com | 24 rooms | $46–$55 | AE, D, MC, V.

BEREA

MAP 6, G4

(Nearby towns also listed: Danville, Harrodsburg, Lexington, Richmond, Renfro Valley, Mount Vernon)

At the foot of the Cumberland Mountains, Berea was founded by the abolitionist, Reverend John Gregg Fee, and named after a city in the New Testament. Today it is the home of Berea College and a thriving community of Kentucky craftspeople.

Information: **Berea Welcome Center** | 201 N. Broadway, Berea, 40403 | 859/986–2540 or 800/598–5263 | fax 859/986–2550 | kycraftcap@berea.com | www.berea.com.

Attractions

Churchill Weavers. You'll see all aspects of the hand-weaving process, from warping and weaving to finishing at this loom house. Handwoven goods have been made here since the early 1920s. Self-guided tours are available. | Take US Highway 25 and bear off onto Highway 1016, and the loom house is ½ mi from downtown | 100 Churchill Dr., Berea | 859/986–3127 | fax 859/986–2861 | www.churchill-weavers.com | Free | Mon.–Thurs. 9–4; Fri. hrs vary; gift shop: Mon.–Sat. 9–6; Sun. noon–6.

The Studio Craftspeople of Berea. Many of the craftspeople with shops and studios in the town center formed this organization to provide information about their work. Check with the tourist and convention commission for a list of studios where you can watch crafts being made. | 201 N. Broadway, Berea | 859/986–2540 or 800/598–5263 | www.berea.com | Free.

ON THE CALENDAR

MAY, OCT.: *Kentucky Guild of Artists and Craftsmen.* Two annual exhibitions of crafts and demonstrations of their making are presented by the state's leading artisans. Weaving, woodworking, instrument making, and pottery are among the exhibits. | 859/986–3192.

OCT.: *Celebration of Traditional Music.* Mountain fiddlers and dulcimer players are among the performers at this festival hosted by Berea College. | 859/986–9341.

Dining

★ **Boone Tavern.** Southern. The white brick Victorian building on the Berea College campus was built in 1909 and is very formal. The dining room has warm wood trim and antiques. Some of the Southern traditional and regional dishes include Chicken Flakes in a Bird's Nest and Bourbon Flank Steak. Side dishes are served family-style. | 100 Main St., Berea | 859/985–3700 or 800/366–9358 | fax 859/985–3715 | $15–$24 | AE, DC, MC, V.

Dinner Bell. Southern. Dinner Bell "calls them to dinner" with regional specialties such as pork tenderloin, pinto beans, and cornbread. The restaurant has antiques and a gift-crafts shop, featuring local crafts. | I–75 Plaza Dr., Berea | 859/986–2777 | fax 859/986–7993 | Breakfast available all day | $7–$13 | AE, D, MC, V.

Papaleno's. Italian. This inviting and cozy establishment is on the edge of the Berea College campus. It has southern Italian appointments and is known for pizza and pasta, lasagna, and Italian sub sandwiches, as well as lighter fare like soups and salad. Kids' menu. | 108 Center St., Berea | 859/986–4497 | $5–$8 | AE, D, MC, V.

Lodging

Boone Tavern. Open since 1909, Berea College now runs the inn and provides much of the furniture courtesy of their artisan students. Handsome colonial style with blue, red, and green trim appointments. Restaurant. TV. | 100 Main St., Berea | 859/986–9358 or 800/366–9358 | fax 859/986–7711 | 58 rooms | $65–$90 | AE, D, DC, MC, V.

Days Inn. You'll easily spot this familiar example of the national chain when you exit the interstate. The southern-style stucco motel has arts and crafts in the lobby and hallway. | Take exit 77 off I–75. TV. Pool. Mini-golf. Business services. Pets allowed (fee). | 1202 Walnut Meadow Rd., Berea | 859/986–7373 or 800/329–7466 | fax 859/986–3144 | 60 rooms | $45–$51 | AE, D, DC, MC, V.

Holiday Inn Express, Berea. Opened in December 1998, this two-story hotel is near Berea College and the old town craft section. The adjacent Columbia Steakhouse has free delivery. Free deluxe Continental breakfast. Cable TV. Indoor pool, hot tubs. Fitness equipment. Meeting rooms. Pets allowed. | 108 Peggy Flats Rd., Berea | 859/985–1901 or 800/465–4329 | fax 859/985–8095 | spurlockgm@aol.com | www.basshotels.com | 52 rooms, 4 suites | $53–$89 | AE, D, MC, V.

Holiday Motel. This brick Colonial-style motel is subtly upscale. The comfortable and spacious rooms in this rambling, one-story motel are surprisingly quiet given the location near the interstate. | Take exit 76 off I–75. The motel is 1 mi from Berea College and ½ mi from old town Berea, also known as "The Crafts Area." Cable TV. Pool. | 100 Jane St., Berea | 859/986–9311 | fax 859/986–9311, ext. 231 | 62 rooms | $45–$65 | AE, MC, V.

Shady Lane Bed & Breakfast. This tree-shaded lot is described as a "bird-lover's paradise." The early twentieth-century (wood and vinyl siding) Southern colonial is the former home of Berea's 2nd mayor. Rooms are appointed with art from Berea craftspeople and memorabilia from the owners' worldwide travels. Enjoy breakfast on the secluded patio. After a day at nearby craft shops and studios, play horseshoes, boccie ball, or croquet on the lawn—or just head to your room and warm your toes by the fireplace. The B&B is 7 blocks from Berea College and the residential area. Complimentary breakfast and hors d'ouevres. No room phones. Hot tub. No smoking. No pets. | 123 Mt. Vernon Rd., Berea | 859/986–9851 | fax 859/986–9851 | lrwebber@aol.com | www.bbonline.com/ky/shadylane/index.html | 2 rooms | $55–$70 | No credit cards.

BOWLING GREEN

MAP 6, D5

(Nearby towns also listed: Cave City, Glasgow, Horse Cave, Mammoth Cave National Park, South Union)

The city may have been named in honor of Bowling Green, Virginia, or its designation might have referred to founder Robert Moore's "ball alley," near his home where early inhabitants played bowls on a green. Modern Bowling Green is the location of Western Kentucky University (whose faculty and students carry out research in nearby Mammoth Cave). It's also home to a major tobacco warehouse, and the General Motors assembly plant where all of the world's Corvettes are made. Gourmet and food writer, Duncan Hines (1880–1959) was born and buried here.

Information: Bowling Green Area Convention and Visitors Bureau | 352 Three Springs Rd., Bowling Green, 42104 | 270/782–0800 or 800/326–7465 | fax 270/842–2104 | tourism@bg.ky.net | www.bg.ky.net/tourism.

Attractions

Beech Bend Raceway and Amusement Park. Stock-car racing and drag racing are the spectator sports at this park. There's an amusement park and 34 more rides. You'll also find a campground, swimming pool, water slide, and go-carts for aspiring NASCAR drivers. | 798 Beech Bend Rd., Bowling Green | 270/781–7634 | fax 270/781–0524 | family@beachbend.com | www.beachbend.com | $7 | Mar.–Nov., racing; May–Aug., amusement park.

Bowling Green Civil War Driving Tour. Forts, memorials, and other landmarks are focal points. Maps are available from the Tourist and Convention Commission or at the Corvette Museum. | Bowling Green Area Convention and Visitors Bureau, 352 Three Springs Rd., Bowling Green | 270/782–0800 or 800/326–7465 | fax 270/842–2104 | tourism@bg.ky.net | www.bg.ky.net/tourism.

Capitol Arts Center. This unique theater has 1,850 seats and in addition to showing movies, it houses the Ervin G. Houchens Gallery and hosts dances, concerts, and plays. It also has two fine art galleries and a gallery on the mezzanine. Built in 1939, the theater has been beautifully restored. | 416 E. Main St., Bowling Green | 270/782–2787 or 877/694–2787 | fax 270/782–2804 | capitol@capitolarts.com | www.capitolarts.com | Mon.–Fri. 9–4, galleries and box office.

National Corvette Museum. If you're a sports-car lover, you'll revel in this museum. This is the only place in the world where the Corvette is built. The museum is across the road from the General Motors Corvette assembly plant. It houses one of the first 300 Corvettes built (in 1953), as well as the millionth. Orientation film and displays featuring aspects of design and technology are highlights. | Take exit 28 off I–65 | 350 Corvette Dr., Bowling Green | 270/781–7973 or 800/538–3883 | fax 270/745–8228 | www.corvettemuseum.com | $8 | Daily 8–5.

Riverview at Hobson Grove. You'll relish the victorian elegance that is re-created in this 1872 Italianate house with period furniture. Palladian windows and frescoed ceilings are highlights. | The house is inside Hobson Grove Park, 10 minutes from downtown Bowling Green | 1100 W. Main Ave., Bowling Green | 270/843–5565 | fax 270/843–5557 | www.bgky.org/riverview.htm | $3.50 | Feb.–mid-Dec., Tues.–Sat. 10–4; Sun. 1–4.

Timeless Treasures Antique Mall. Take a sentimental journey visiting Bowling Green's largest mall for antiques, collectibles, and gifts. Browse the 65 booths and help yourself to complimentary coffee, soda pop, and sweets. | 5521 Russellville Rd., Berea | 270/781–3898 | Mon.–Sat. 10–5; Sun. noon–5.

Western Kentucky University. The hilly 200-acre campus, built on the site of a Civil War fort boasts a current enrollment of about 14,000. The Western Kentucky Museum and the Kentucky Library are open to the public. | 1 Big Red Way, Bowling Green | 270/745–0111 | www.wku.edu | Free | Daily.

You'll experience seasonal night sky changes at the **Hardin Planetarium.** The facility has a 40-ft dome housing a Spitz A3P star projector, special-effect projectors, and seating for 150. | 1 Big Red Way, Bowling Green | 270/745–4044 | www.wku.edu | Free | Call for hrs.

Manuscripts, rare books, sheet music, photographs, and maps pertaining to Kentucky history and genealogy are housed at the **Kentucky Library** | 1 Big Red Way, Bowling Green | 270/745–5083 | www.wku.edu | Free | Mon. 8:30–7, Tues.–Fri. 8:30–4:30, Sat. 9:30–4.

Easy to spot, with its log cabin on the grounds, the **Kentucky Museum and Library** has a wide assortment of artifacts from prehistoric era through the pioneer and Civil War days. | Kentucky Bldg., Kentucky St., Bowling Green | 270/745–2592 | www.wku.edu | $2 | Tues.–Sat. 9:30–4, Sun. 1–4, closed Mon.

BOWLING GREEN

INTRO
ATTRACTIONS
DINING
LODGING

ON THE CALENDAR

JUNE: *National Corvette Homecoming.* Every year on the 1st full weekend in June, Corvette owners from around the nation gather to compare notes. | 502/245–8107 or 800/962–8387.

NOV.–DEC.: *Victorian Holiday Tours.* Period holiday trim adorns area buildings, centered on the elegant home, Riverview at Hobson Grove. | 270/843–5565.

Dining

Brickyard Cafe. Italian. Locals love the make-your-own pizza at this quaint eatery. Dine well on veal marsala, barbequed shrimp with couscous, chicken Florentine, or salmon with lemon butter. | 1026 Chestnut St., Bowling Green | 270/843–6431 | Closed Sun. | $8–$20 | AE, D, MC.

Mariah's 1818. American. It is claimed as the oldest brick structure in town—the original structure dates to 1818. The building has exposed-brick interior walls and an original facade. Hardwood tables and floors and a colorful mural depicting 19th-century Bowling Green add to the distinguished interior. Banquet facilities are available. Known at lunchtime for its chicken salad and at dinner for salmon and prime rib. Kids' menu. | 801 State St., Bowling Green | 270/842–6878 | $11.95–$18 | AE, D, DC MC, V.

Puerto Vallarta Mexican Restaurant & Cantina. Mexican. Locals claim that this is one of the most authentic Mexican restaurants north of the border. All dishes are made fresh daily. | 2800 Scottsville Rd., Bowling Green | 270/782–6264 | Mon.–Thurs. 11–10, Fri. 11–10:45, Sat. 11–10:30, Sun. 11–9 | $5–$10.

Rafferty's. American. This is the original Rafferty's, named for the rafters in its ceiling. Some know it as a chain in Kentucky, Tennessee, and North Carolina. It's crammed with collectibles, and with its wooden and stone floors, it's casual and warm. There's also an indoor sun room with shrubs, plants, and botanicals, and an outdoor deck with 10 tables under a beautiful tree. Specialties are Blackened Talapia (a white fish) with Cajun Sauce, Rustler's Roost Salmon in Orange and Bourbon Sauce, and White Chocolate Banana Cream Pie. | Take I–65 to Scottsville Rd., across from the airport | 1939 Scottsville Rd., Bowling Green | 270/842–0123 | fax 270/842–9060 | $12–$25 | AE, D, DC, MC, V.

Lodging

Best Western Motor Inn. This 3-story modern favorite has pool-side and pool-view rooms and an enclosed courtyard. The lobby is inviting with imitation wrought iron furniture and $40,000 worth of plants in their atrium and indoor pool area. | Take exit 22 off I–65. The motel is 6 mi south of the National Corvette Museum. Restaurant. Cable TV. 2 pools (1 indoor), wading pool. Hot tub. Tennis. Game room. Basketball courts, volleyball, mini golf. Playground. Laundry facilities. Business services. | 166 Cumberland Trace Rd., Bowling Green | 270/782–3800 or 800/343–2937 | fax 270/782–2384 | 179 rooms | $65–$109 | AE, D, DC, MC, V.

Days Inn. Situated along a 2-mi strip of shops, antique stores, and restuarants, you may not want to venture far. But this Days Inn is also central to points of interest like Mammoth Cave, the Kentucky Museum, Shakertown, the Hobson House Historical Landmark, and Barren River State Park. RV and truck parking is available. Restaurant, complimentary breakfast. Pool. Pets allowed. | 4617 Scottsville Rd., Bowling Green | 270/781–6470 | fax 270/781–0546 | www.daysinn.com | 65 rooms | $37–$65 | AE, D, DC, MC, V.

Fairfield Inn by Marriott. Airy, contemporary rooms evoking the chain brand. | The motel can be seen right off I–65 at exit 22. Complimentary Continental breakfast. In-room data ports. Cable TV. Pool. Business services. | 1940 Mel Browning St., Bowling Green | 270/782–6933 or 800/228–2800 | fax 270/782–6967 | 105 rooms | $60 | AE, D, DC, MC, V.

Hampton Inn. There are four floors of modern rooms with maroon and white appointments. The poolside has a gazebo and benches and lots of flowers and plants. | The motel is 1 block west of I–65, and 8 mi from the National Corvette Museum. Complimentary Continental breakfast. In-room data ports. TV. Pool. Business services. | 233 Three Springs Rd., Bowling Green | 270/842–4100 or 800/HAMPTON88 | fax 270/782–3377 | 131 rooms | $59–$79 | AE, D, DC, MC, V.

Holiday Inn I–65. This familiar favorite has modern appointments and a floral-print lobby carpet are echoed in the two floors of rooms with pleasant pink and green bedspreads. | Take exit 22 off I–65. The motel is ½ mi from Greenwood Mall and 6 mi from the National Corvette Museum. Restaurant, bar, picnic area. In-room data ports. Cable TV. Pool, wading pool. Exercise equipment. Playground. Business services. Small pets allowed. | 3240 Scottsville Rd., Bowling Green | 270/781–1500 | fax 270/842–0030 | 107 rooms | $49–$89 | AE, D, DC, MC, V.

News Inn of Bowling Green. The inn's lobby is reminiscent of a library—forest green, burgundy, and off-white, with brass lamps and oak cabinets. The one-story redbrick motel has a green roof. Rooms are in shades of red, green, and brown. The pool has a waterfall. | Take exit 22 off I–65. Picnic area. In-room data ports. Cable TV. Pool. Business services. Airport shuttle. | 3160 Scottsville Rd., Bowling Green | 270/781–3460 or 800/443–3701 | fax 270/781–3463 | 51 rooms | $44–$65 | AE, D, MC, V.

Ramada Inn–Bowling Green. The familiar chain delivers on its reputation. This large facility has spacious rooms—some are suites with king-size beds, and others have queen-size beds. Many rooms have patios on the poolside. Restaurant, complimentary breakfast. Outdoor pool. Exercise room. Playground. Business services. Pets allowed. | 4767 Scottsville Rd., Bowling Green | 502/781–3000 | fax 502/782–2591 | www.ramada.com | 118 rooms | $45–$75 | AE, D, DC, MC, V.

Travelodge Hotel. Rooms have cheerful floral bedspreads in this handsome brick-faced building. The hotel has four floors of Early American-style honey furniture in a burgundy and navy color scheme. | Take exit 22 off I–65 to Executive Way. Restaurant, bar with entertainment. Cable TV. Pool, wading pool. Business services. Airport shuttle. | 1000 Executive Way, Bowling Green | 270/781–6610 or 800/354–4394 | fax 270/781–7985 | 150 rooms | $48–$65 | AE, D, DC, MC, V.

University Plaza Hotel. This upscale hotel has a seven-floor atrium, waterfall, and a garden with a pool and fountains. It is connected to the Bowling Green/Warren County Convention Center, which has 28,000 square ft of meeting space. Restaurant. Cable TV. Indoor pool. Hot tub, sauna. Exercise equipment. Meeting space. Pets allowed. | 1021 Wilkerson Trace, Bowling Green | 270/745–0088 or 800/801–1777 or 888/294–6491 | 186 rooms, 19 Suites | $89–$129 | AE, D, DC, MC, V.

BRANDENBURG

(Nearby towns also listed: Elizabethtown, Falls of Rough, Fort Knox, Louisville)

The seat of Meade County, at a bend in the Ohio River, had many of its original buildings destroyed by a tornado in April, 1974. But just outside the town, the log and stone Doe Run Inn, originally a grist mill built in 1821, was untouched. Today, it's a bed & breakfast and restaurant. The major, non-agricultural employer in the area is Olin Chemical Corporation, which has a plant nearby. The city hosts *Christmas By the River* each year on the first Saturday after Thanksgiving.

Information: **Meade County Area Chamber of Commerce** | 737 High St., Box 483, Brandenburg, 40108 | 270/422–3626 | fax 270/422–1389 | chamber@bbtel.com | www.ltadd. org/meade.

ON THE CALENDAR
JULY: *Meade County Fair.* The event in the county! You can watch tractor pulls, a demolition derby, and a 4-H competition. You'll gorge on food, entertainment, and kids' rides. The fair is held annually, usually the third full week in July, Sun.–Sat. | 270/422–3626.
DEC.: *Christmas By The River.* The City of Brandenburg hosts this event each year on the first Saturday after Thanksgiving. The event takes place on the riverfront with arts and crafts, a karaoke contest, parade, and lighting display. The display stays lit until January 1. | Box 305, Brandenburg | 270/422–4981 | fax 270/422–4983 | bburg@bbtel.com | www.ltadd.org/brandenburg.

Attractions
Otter Creek Park Nature Center and Observatory. Follow the path from the Nature Center to the Observatory and view a moon crater close up. Explore the flora and fauna in the surrounding 2,600-acre Otter Creek Park. Visit the nature center's web site or call for year-round activities and prices. | 850 Otter Creek Park Rd., Brandenburg | 270/583–3361 | fax 270/583–9035 | ottercreek@louky.org | www.ottercreekpark.org | Free.

Dining
Doe Run Inn. Southern. You will enjoy old-fashioned breakfasts and more at this mill house and inn. It was built of limestone, from 1778–1821. Inside it has hand-hewn timbers and 2-ft-thick walls. It was first used as a wool mill, then as a grist mill. It became a country inn in 1927. The screened porch dining rooms overlook the woods and Doe Run Creek. They're known for fried chicken, country ham, and trout. They serve a Sun. buffet. | They're 3 mi outside of town off Highway 448 | 500 Doe Run Hotel Rd., Brandenburg | 270/422–2042 or 270/422–2982 | fax 270/422–4916 | doerun@bbtel.com | www.bluegrass-shopper.com/doerun | Breakfast also available | $8.50–$17 | D, DC, MC, V.

Lodging
Doe Run Inn. This is the country inn portion of the Doe Run establishment. The interior is rustic—it has murals and country antiques. Charming rooms in this stone-and-log inn are furnished with antiques. Many rooms have views of the gardens, woods, or Doe Run Creek. A separate log cabin on the grounds sleeps up to 10. Phone and TV in lobby only. Free parking. Restaurant. | 500 Doe Run Hotel Rd., Brandenburg | 270/422–2982 or 270/422–

2942 | fax 270/422–4916 | 11 rooms in lodge | Cabin prices: for up to 6 people, $85/night; $10 added for each one over 6 and up to 10 people per night. Rooms: double with private bath is $160 plus tax; 2 double beds and private bath are $70/night. 1 double bed with shared bath is $35/night | D, DC, MC, V.

Otter Creek Park. Rough it in a rustic cabin in the middle of this 2,600-acre park stretching along the Ohio River. Nature lovers and adventure-seekers can hike, bike, rock-climb (summers only), or just kick back in front of the fireplace. Pool, playground. Pets allowed (restrictions). | 850 Otter Creek Park Rd., Brandenburg | 270/583–3577 | fax 270/583–9035 | ottercreek@louky.org | www.ottercreekpark.org | 20 rooms, 10 Cabins | $50–90 rooms, $65–150 cabins | MC, V.

CADIZ

MAP 6, C5

(Nearby towns also listed: Hopkinsville, Gilbertsville, Paducah)

The seat of Trigg County has become an important tourist center because of nearby Lake Barkley. Retail shops and antiques malls abound. The unusual name of the town, founded in 1792 by North Carolinian Thomas Wadlington, is a mystery.

Information: **Cadiz/Trigg County Tourist Commission** | Box 735 TG, 22 Main St., Cadiz 42211 | 270/522–3892 or 888/446–6402.

Attractions

Barkley Dam, Lock, and Lake. A shoreline just over 1,000 mi long was created by damming the Cumberland River for flood control and recreation. A hydroelectric generating plant, canal, and navigational lock were also built. | 100 Van Morgan Dr., Golden Pond | 270/924–2000 | ww.lbl.org | Free | Daily.

Historic Walking Tour. You'll pass Victorian buildings, shops, and antiques malls along Main St. during this self-guided walking tour. | 22 Main St., Cadiz | 270/522–3892.

Hurricane Creek Public Use Area. Improved camp sites, boat launch, playground, and swimming are among the facilities. | Take exit 56 off I–24 and go 8 mi to Hurricane Camp Rd. | 25 Hurricane Camp Rd., Eddyville | 270/522–8821 | Free; $16–$19/night for RV sites | mid-Apr.–mid-Oct., daily.

Kenlake State Resort Park. (See also Gilbertsville.) The approach to the park from Cadiz will take you over two breathtaking bridges and through wooded areas belonging to the Land Between the Lakes National Recreation Area. | Take I–24 east to the Purchase Parkway south to U.S. 68E | 542 Kenlake Rd., Hardin | 270/474–2211, 270/474–2018 or 800/325–0143 | vicky.wimberly@mail.state.ky.us | www.kenlake.com.

Lake Barkley State Resort Park. (See also Land Between the Lakes in Gilbertsville.) Lake Barkley, connected by the Grand Rivers Kentucky Dam to its sister lake, Kentucky Lake, form one of the largest man-made bodies of water in the world. In 1970 the 58,000-acre park had a 120-room lodge built from huge timbers of western cedar and Douglas fir. | Take I–24 to exit 65 and then drive west on Highway 68 | Box 790, Cadiz | 270/924–1131 or 800/325–1708 | fax 270/924–0013 | www.kystateparks.com/agencies/parks/lakebark.htm.

Land Between the Lakes National Recreation Area. The scenic drive from Cadiz includes woodlands and the bridge over Lake Barkley and the Golden Pond Visitors Center. (See also Gilbertsville.) | Take I–24 to the Cadiz exit and then drive to Highway 680W | 100 Van Morgan Drive, Golden Pond | 270/924–2000 or 800/525–7077 | fax 270/924–2087 | www.lbl.org.

Original Log Cabin. This modest log cabin dating from the 19th century was a private dwelling until 1972. Furnishings include a Victorian settee and matching chair, Beckwith pump organ, and 150-year-old cradle. | 22 Main St., Cadiz | 270/522–3892 | Free | Daily.

West Cadiz Park. A picnic area, playground, boat launch, and fishing are the recreational facilities here. There's also a shelter for parties and events. | You can get to the park by way of Business Highway 68W | 270/522–3892 or 888/446–6402; to reserve the shelter, call U.S. Army Corps of Engineers at 270/362–4236 | Free | Daily dawn–dusk.

ON THE CALENDAR

OCT.: *Trigg County Ham Festival.* "It's huge and it's crowded." Devotees of that Southern delicacy, country ham, will want to pay a visit. There are vendors, live music, and wall-to-wall people. There's even a kiss-the-pig contest! The festival is held annually the 2nd full weekend of October; rain or shine. | 270/522–3892.

Dining

Cadiz Restaurant. Southern. If you're inclined to get up with the chickens you won't have to wait for breakfast here. The Cadiz Restaurant opens for breakfast at 5 AM on weekdays and 4 AM on Saturdays. Late risers can catch lunch, or the dinner buffet featuring country ham, steaks, seafood, chicken, brownies, and homemade pies. | 324 Main St., Cadiz | 270/522–6563 | Weekdays 5 AM–8 PM, Sat. 4 AM–8:30 PM, Sun. 5 AM–2 PM | $3–$9.

Patti's 1888 Restaurant and Settlement. Southern. Homestyle cooking is on the menu at family-friendly Patti's. After a meal of rib-eye steak or nationally-acclaimed 2-inch charbroiled pork chops, try the mile-high meringue pies. | 1793 J. H. O'Bryan, Grand Rivers | 888/736–2515 | $12–$19 | D, MC, V.

Lodging

Holiday Inn Express. At the gateway to the Lake Barclay area, this Holiday Inn is near Murray State University, Ft. Campbell, and the Arrowhead and Boots Randolph golf courses. Nostalgic downtown Main Street, 7 mi away, has antique malls and the 1867 Cadiz Log Cabin Museum and Visitor Center. Opened in 1998, this motel is two stories. Complimentary Continental breakfast. Cable TV. Some microwaves, some refrigerators. Some in-room hot tubs. Indoor pool. Laundry facilities. Business services. Pets allowed. | 153 Broadbent Blvd., Cadiz | 270/522–3600 | fax 270/522–0636 | holidayinncadiz@ziggycom.net | www.basshotels.com | 48 rooms, 4 hot tub suites | $60–$79 | AE, D, DC, MC, V.

Super 8 Motel. Built in 1991, this 2-story motel is located 10 mi from the Land Between the Lakes National Recreational Area. | Take I–24 to exit 65. The motel is 5 mi from Cadiz and 10 mi east of Land Between the Lakes Resort. Complimentary Continental breakfast. Cable TV. Pool. Business services. Some pets allowed (fee). | 154 Hospitality Lane, Cadiz | 270/522–7007 or 800/800–8000 | fax 270/522–3893 | 48 rooms | $45–$65 | AE, D, DC, MC, V.

Knights Inn. You'll appreciate this southern, contemporary motel with its beige and teal color scheme. The single-story layout will be welcome, too. Complimentary Continental breakfast. Some pets allowed. | 5698 Hopkinsville Rd., Cadiz | 270/522–9395 | fax 270/522–4150 | www.theknightsinn.com | 25 rooms | $44–$64 | AE, D, DC, MC, V.

Lake Barkley Lodge. The soaring, alpine-style of this facility has traditional appointments and lots of glass. The state-owned lodge has access to facilities at Lake Barkley State Resort Park. Activities include trapshooting, waterskiing, boating, hiking, tennis, and golf. There are boat-rental fees and greens fees for golf. | Take I–24 to exit 65. The lodge is 7 mi east of Land Between the Lakes. Dining room, picnic area. Kitchenettes (in cottages). TV. Pool, wading pool. Hot tub. 18-hole golf course, tennis. Gym. Beach, water sports, boating. Kids' programs, playground. Laundry facilities. Business services. Airport shuttle. | 3500 State Park Rd., Cadiz | 270/924–1131 or 800/325–1708 | fax 270/924–0013 | www.kystateparks.com | 124 rooms; 13 cottages | $55–$78, $118–$165 suites, $132–$165 cottages | AE, DC, MC, V.

CAMPBELLSVILLE

MAP 6, F5

(Nearby towns also listed: Hodgenville, Horse Cave, Jamestown)

There was a grist mill here as early as 1809; Campbellsville was established by the General Assembly eight years later. The seat of Taylor county is today an important manufacturing, medical, and education center for south-central Kentucky. Nearby Green River Lake State Park has made this a recreational area, as well.

Information: **Taylor County Tourist Commission** | Box 4021, Broadway and Court St., Campbellsville, 42719 | 270/465–3786 or 800/738–4719 | fax 270/465–3786 | ctc-chmb@kih.net | www.campbellsvilleky.com.

Attractions

Green River Lake State Park. The 1,300-acre park is on an 8,200-acre lake with one sand beach, a marina, boat launches, a bath house, and campgrounds. The park has hiking and bicycling trails, mini-golf, picnic areas, and playgrounds. Crappie, bass, and muskie are among the lake's game fish. | 179 Park Office Rd., Campbellsville | 270/465–8255 | www.kys-tateparks.com/agencies/parks/greenriv.htm | Free | Daily.

The John B. Begley Chapel at Lindsey Wilson College. Considered to be one of the most unique structures in the Southeast, the Begley Chapel sits tucked away on the Lindsey Wilson College campus 20 mi south of Campbellsville off Route 55. A breathtakingly beautiful combination of rural themes and traditional cathedral architecture, it was designed by world-renowned architect and Frank Lloyd Wright disciple E. Fay Jones. | 210 Lindsey Wilson St., Columbia | 270/384–8400 | chapel@lindsey.edu | Free | Daily 8 AM–11 PM.

ON THE CALENDAR

SEPT.: *Tebbs Bend Flea Market*. It's a 2-mi loop of yard sales, vendors, and flea markets. The annual event is appropriately held on the Tebbs Bend battle site—money raised at the market benefits the restoration of the battlefield. Look for it on the first Saturday of the month. | 800/738–4719.

NOV.: *Green River Arts and Crafts Holiday Festival and Art Show*. It's always held the Saturday and Sunday before Thanksgiving, and provides an opportunity to shop for seasonal handmade gifts. | 270/465–4431.

Dining

Creek Side. American. This local favorite is just a few blocks from Cambellsville University. The brick, contemporary architecture evokes a 1940s theme. Antiques and candlelight add to the ambience here. Inside there's a little waterfall, two artificial fireplaces, and a big-screen TV. Three dining rooms range from casual to formal. Known for its chicken finger salad and its ribeye steaks—Saturday nights it's prime rib. Salad bar. Kids' menu. Buffet. Sun. brunch. | 350 W. Broadway, Campbellsville | 270/465–7777 | $6.95–$11.95 (some steaks might be higher); daily buffet $6.95 | D, MC, V.

Druther's. Southern. This restaurant seats 200 and is decorated with antique furniture and designed for the big appetite. You can opt for the buffet or choose a hearty entrée of steak, chicken, or seafood and top it off with a slice of homemade cream pie or cobbler. | N. Columbia Ave., Campbellsville | 270/465–3870 | Sun.–Thurs. 11–9, Fri.–Sat. 11–10 | $5–$15 | AE, MC, V.

Lodging

Best Western. The two-acre grounds are very pretty—lots of trees and flowers and park benches throughout. Lobby is very contemporary and has a large-screen TV in the sitting area. Two floors of spacious rooms with modern, white wood furniture. Complimentary Continental breakfast and snacks in late afternoon. In-room data ports, some rooms have refrigerators. All rooms have cable TV plus free HBO. Pool. Hot tub. Playground. Business services. Free parking. | 1400 E. Broadway, Campbellsville | 270/465–7001 or 800/770–0430 | fax 270/465–7001 | bwestern@kyol.net | www.bestwesternlodge.com | 60 rooms | $55–$61 | AE, D, DC, MC, V.

Emerald Isle Resort and Marina. These recently-renovated condominiums overlook Green River Lake. You can hike, canoe, or rent a fishing or pontoon boat. There are facilities for private boats. Kitchenettes, microwaves, refrigerators. Cable TV. Lake. Water sports, boating, fishing. Laundry facilities. No pets. No smoking. | 1500 County Park Rd., Campbellsville | 270/465–34128 or 888/815–2000 | terry@emisresort.com | www.kih.net/emeraldisle | 10 condos | $90–$185.

Lakeview Motel, Inc. The bedford stone exterior has green trim and a green roof. There's parking by each room door. Rooms are appointed with cherry furniture. The lobby is rustic, with knotty pine paneling, wood, and a tile ceiling. The motel is less than 1 mi to Miller Park. All rooms have refrigerators. Cable TV. Olympic-sized pool. Tennis courts, 9-hole golf course. | 1291 Old Lebanon Rd., Campbellsville | 270/465–8139 or 800/242–2874 | fax 270/465–8139 | 16 rooms | $38–$45 | AE, D, MC, V.

CARROLLTON

MAP 6, F3

(Nearby towns also listed: Frankfort, Louisville, Shelbyville, Williamstown)

Originally named Port William, Carrollton was laid out by explorers Benjamin Craig and James Hawkins in 1794. It was an important stop on the river between Cincinnati and Louisville. At the confluence of the Ohio and Kentucky rivers, Carrollton has a 25-block historic district consisting of more than 350 Victorian buildings. The city is also important as a burley tobacco market.

Information: **Northern Kentucky Convention and Visitors Bureau** | 50 East River Center Blvd., Ste. 100, Covington, 41011 | 606/261–4677 | fax 606/261–5135 | info@nky-cvb.com.

Attractions

General Butler State Resort Park. A lake, mini-golf, basketball, playgrounds, and hiking are park features. Pedal boats and rowboats can be rented. A 53-room lodge and 24 cottages provide overnight accommodations. A restored, 1859 antebellum house on the property was the home of the eponymous General Butler. House tours are available. | Take exit 44 off I–71 to Highway 227 and look for signs to the park | Box 325, Carrollton | 502/732–4384 or 800/325–0078 | www.kystateparks.com/agencies/parks/genbutlr.htm | Free; house tour admission varies per group size | Jan.–Dec., except at Christmastime.

Historic District. More than 25 blocks and 350 buildings comprise the 19th-century historic district. The starting point for your walking tour begins at the Old Stone Jail, built in 1880. It housed prisoners until the late 1960s and now houses the visitor center. | Court St., Carrollton | 800/325–4290 | Free | Weekdays 9–4:30; closed weekends.

Masterson House. Built in 1790, Masterson House is the oldest two-story brick house still standing along the Ohio River between Pittsburg, PA and Cairo, IL. | 304 9th St., Carrollton | 502/732–5786 | $3 | Memorial Day–Labor Day, weekends 1:30–4:30.

ON THE CALENDAR

MAY: *Kentucky Scottish Weekend.* Highland games, bagpipes, Scottish food, and national costumes all contribute to the Gaelic festivities. | 502/239–2665.
JUNE: *Open Buddy Bass Tournament.* Point Park is the site for this summer fishing tournament. | 502/732–7036 or 800/325–4290.

SEPT.: *Two Rivers Blues Festival.* Singers and bands from throughout the region gather to celebrate blues. Held the weekend after Labor Day in Point Park. | 502/732–7036 or 800/325–4290.

Dining

Carrollton Inn. American. There's a high tin ceiling that evokes an intimate, casual place. Known for its excellent white fish and prime rib on Friday and Saturday, the lunchtime specialty is Kentucky Hot Brown—that's a piece of toast with ham, shaved turkey, bacon, and cheese sauce that's baked. Kids' menu. | 218 Main St., Carrollton | 502/732–6905 | $9–$16.95 | AE, MC, V.

Churchill Manor Restaurant. Southern. There is always a steady stream of locals who come back for the tenderloin pork and grilled cajun chicken. The menu also has classic entrées like steak and fried chicken. For dessert, save room for homemade pie. | 1408 Highland Ave., Carrollton | 502/732–6314 | 5:30 AM–9:30 PM | $5–$10 | AE, D, MC, V.

Hearthstone Inn. Southern. Leave hearth and home to sample Hearthstone's Kentucky Hot Ham, Porterhouse steaks, open-face sandwiches, and homemade pies. | 1966 Hwy. 227, Carrollton | 502/732–0510 | $5–$15 | AE, MC, V.

Lodging

Carrollton Inn. The federal-style architecture of this brick 1885 structure has a charming, wood-trimmed dining room and antiques throughout. Refurbished rooms have cherry furniture. Restaurant, bar. Cable TV. Business services. | 218 Main St., Carrollton | 502/732–6905 | 11 rooms | $49.95 | AE, MC, V.

Days Inn Carrollton. Just 13 mi from the Kentucky Speedway, this version of the familiar chain has two floors, and modern muted colors. Pool-side rooms are available. | Take exit 44 off I–71 to the motel. Complimentary breakfast buffet. In-room data ports. Cable TV. Pool. Free parking. Business services. | 61 Inn Rd., Carrollton | 502/732–9301 or 800–DAYSINN | fax 502/732–5596 | 84 rooms | $55–$59; race track events will raise price | AE, D, DC, MC, V.

General Butler Lodge. It's described as a "hilltop" lodge. It's got a stone facade and the lobby has a wood-beamed ceiling. There's an "eye-catching" two-story cathedral ceiling, and spacious rooms, many of which overlook the pool. The state-owned lodge has access to all facilities at General Butler State Resort Park. | Take exit 44 off I–71. The lodge is 2 mi outside of Carrollton. Dining room, picnic areas. Kitchenettes (in cottages). Cable TV. Pool, lake, wading pool. 9-hole golf course, mini-golf, tennis. Boating. Kids' seasonal planned recreation; several playgrounds. Business services. | 1608 Rte. 227, Carrollton | 502/732–4384 or 800/325–0078 | fax 502/732–4270 | www.kystateparks.com | 53 rooms in lodge; 24 cottages | rooms: $42–$72; cottages: $72–$162 | AE, D, MC, V.

Hampton Inn. This columned five-story hotel lies just miles from General Butler State Park and the Glenwood Hall Golf Course. Complimentary Continental breakfast. Cable TV. In-room data ports. Pool. Exercise equipment. | 7 Slumber La., Carrollton | 502/732–0700 | fax 502/732–0775 | www.hampton-inn.com | $71–$79 | AE, D, MC, V.

Holiday Inn Express. Just 3 mi from Carrollton and 13 mi from the Kentucky Speedway, this familiar favorite has a modern lobby and rooms with cherry wood furniture. | Take I–71 to exit 44 to the motel. Complimentary Continental breakfast. In-room data ports. Cable TV. Business service (fee). Free parking. Some pets (dogs, cats, birds) allowed. | 141 Inn Rd., Carrollton | 502/732–6661 or 800–HOLIDAY | fax 502/732–6661 | www.basshotels.com/hiexpress | 62 rooms | $59–$69 (except for special events) | AE, D, DC, MC, V.

Super 8–Carrollton. This two-story motel with a Southwestern exterior, is at a midpoint between Louisville and Cincinnati, and is 35 mi from Frankfort, the state capitol. It is only 2 mi from General Butler State Park. Complimentary Continental breakfast. Cable TV. Laundry facilities. | 130 Slumber La., Carrollton | 502/732–0252 or 800/800–8000 | www.Super8.com | 46 rooms | $45–$49 | AE, D, DC, M, V.

CAVE CITY

(Nearby towns also listed: Bowling Green, Glasgow, Horse Cave, Mammoth Cave National Park)

This is the center of the state's famous limestone cave region. It has the highest concentration of commercial attractions in the area.

Information: **Cave City Tourist and Convention Commission** | Box 518, Cave City, 42127 | 270/773–3131 or 800/346–8908 | cavecity@scrtc.com.

Attractions

Crystal Onyx Cave and Campgrounds. Cave City is home to Crystal Onyx Cave with its variety of beautiful formations such as delicate crystalline draperies and rimstone pools. Stalactites, stalagmites, and onyx formations, including columns, are highlights of the cave. There's a Native American burial ground, and the remains date from 680 BC. | Take Exit 53 off I–65 to Highway 90 | 8709 Happy Valley Rd., Cave City | 270/773–2359 | crystalo@caveland.net | www.mammothcave.com | $4.50–$6.50, cave tours | Feb.–Dec., daily.

Diamond Caverns. You'll experience enormous stalactites and stalagmites, projecting onyx peaks, and rock palaces, up close and personal. Guided tours are given every one and a half hours. One mi from Park City on Mammoth Cave Parkway. | Box 250, Park City | 270/749–2233 | fax 270/749–3423 | info@diamondcaverns.com | www.diamondcaverns.com | $10 | Daily, except Thanksgiving Day and Christmas Day.

Diamond Caverns Resort and Golf Club. On-site recreational facilities include an 18-hole golf course and a campground. | Take I–65 to Exit 48. The Resort is located on the entry road to Mammoth Cave National Park | 1878 Mammoth Cave Parkway, Park City | 270/749–3114 | fax 270/749–5805 | www.mammothcave.com/dcr.htm | Daily.

Kentucky Action Park. Go-carts, bumper boats, bumper cars, and a mountainside alpine sled slide are treats for thrill seekers. For the nature lover, there's horseback riding. | Take exit 53 off I–65. Go west on Highway 70 | 3057 Mammoth Cave Rd., Cave City | 270/773–2636 or 800/798–0560 | fax 270/773–3370 | kyaction@scrtc.com | www.mammothcave.com | $3–$9 | Apr.–May and Sept.–Oct., weekends 10–7; June–Aug., daily 9–9.

Mammoth Cave Chair Lift and Guntown Mountain. A re-created 1880s frontier boomtown comes to life with mock gunfights, a saloon, music, and magic shows. There's also a chairlift up the mountain. | Drive to exit 53 off I–65 and follow the signs to the fun | Box 236, Cave City | 270/773–3530 | fax 270/773–5176 | www.guntownmountain.com | $13.95 | May 1–May 31 and Aug. 15–Oct. 1, weekends; June 1–Aug. 14 and Oct. 2–Oct. 15, daily.

Mammoth Cave National Park. *(See Mammoth Cave National Park.)* The approach to the park is clogged with tacky shops and attractions, but once inside the grounds, the park is impeccably maintained by the U.S. National Park Service. | Take I–65 to exit 53 at Cave City, or exit 48 at Park City; it's 15 minutes from Cave City | Box 7, Mammoth Cave | 270/773–2111 | fax 270/758–2349.

ON THE CALENDAR

MAR.: *Mammoth Cave Amateur Ham Radio Festival.* Always on the first Saturday of the month, this is a chance for ham radio enthusiasts to meet and trade tips. | 270/773–3131 or 800/346–8908.

JUNE: *Walking Horse Show.* It's a horse of a different kind—not the state's thoroughbred, but spectacular nonetheless. Held annually one weekend of the month. | 270/773–3131 or 270/773–2188 or 800/346–8908.

AUG.: *Ohio Valley Gospel Singing Convention.* Held in the Cave City Convention Center during the last Friday and Saturday of the month, this annual festival attracts performers from a wide area and hosts concerts open to the public. | 270/773–3131 or 800/346–8908.

Dining

Joe's Diner. American. This diner/grill caters to tourists visiting nearby Mammoth Cave. There's grilled chicken and sandwiches, and a variety of burgers. Food is served with a smile and in a hurry so as to hasten your journey to the Cave. | 1004 Mammoth Cave Dr., Cave City | 270/773–3186 | Memorial Day to Labor Day, 8 AM–8 PM.

Sahara Steak House. Steak and Seafood. A great place to stop after a trip to the Wildlife Museum and Mammoth Cave—it's right next door. This place looks like a big, comfy house. There's lots of brick and wood; the vinyl tablecloths echo country casual and friendly service. They're known for New York strip filets and seafood. There's a generous salad bar and kids' menu. | 413 E. Happy Valley Rd., Cave City | 270/773–3450 | $9–$30 | AE, D, DC, MC, V.

Water Mill Restaurant. Southern. Though the old corn mill has ground to a halt, the mill wheel still stands at this country buffet. The fried chicken is popular. The restaurant is only 9 mi from Mammoth Cave. | I–65, Exit 25, Cave City | 6 AM–9 PM | $6.50–$10.

Lodging

Best Western Kentucky Inn. After a day at Mammoth Cave, drive 10 mi east to exit 53 off I–65 and you'll enjoy a bright, cheerful room with bordered wallpaper at this one-story modern motel. The lobby is formal with a Victorian-style burgundy and green theme. Cable TV. Pool, wading pool. Laundry facilities. | 1009 Doyle Ave., Cave City | 270/773–3161 | fax 270/773–5494 | 50 rooms | $30–$40 | AE, D, DC, MC, V.

Comfort Inn, Cave City. This two-story motel with connecting buildings overlooks a section of Mammoth Cave National Park's 52,830 acreas of woodlands. The park's entrance is located 5 mi from the hotel. The Wildlife Museum is only 2 ½ mi away, and the Corvette Museum is 30 mi away. Complimentary deluxe Continental breakfast. Cable TV, free local phone calls. In-room microwave and refrigerator. Outdoor heated pool. Hot tub in some rooms. Iron/ironing board. Playground. Pets allowed. | 801 Mammoth Cave St., Cave City | 270/773–2030 or 800/221–2222 | 65 rooms, 1 suite | $36–90 | AE, D, MC, V.

Days Inn. This moderately priced redbrick motel has modern, streamlined rooms. The lobby is modern with cream and brown appointments and floral prints. You'll be 10 minutes from Cave City's restaurant area and Mammoth Cave National Park. | Take exit 53 off I–65 to Highways 70 and 90. Restaurant. Cable TV. Pool, wading pool. Game room. Laundry facilities. Business services. Small pets allowed (fee). | 822 Mammoth Cave Rd., Cave City | 270/773–2151 | fax 270/773–2151 | 110 rooms | $32–$76 | AE, D, DC, MC, V.

Park Mammoth Resort. This 2,000 acre resort is 20 minutes from Mammoth Cave National Park and other cave country attractions. The lobby is rustic and has an old-fashioned organ and fireplace. The lodge is at the intersection of I–65 and 31W. Dining room. In-room data ports. Cable TV. Indoor pool, wading pool. Sauna. 36-hole golf, mini-golf, tennis. Playground. Business services. | US 31W, Park City | 270/749–4101 | fax 270/749–2524 | pmresort@caveland.net | www.caveland.net/pmr | 92 rooms | $60 | AE, D, DC, MC, V.

Parkview Motel. Rock your troubles away on the front porch at Cave City's oldest motel. All rooms have been decorated in a comfortable country style, including one "dollhouse" efficiency completely outfitted with kitchen appliances and utensils. The motel sits on 5 acres of well-manicured lawn and provides a grill and picnic tables. Mammoth Cave Park is only 2½ mi away. Restaurant, Continental breakfast. Pool. | 3906 Mammoth Cave Rd., Cave City | 270/773–3463 or 877/482–2262 | pvmotel@yahoo.com | www.parkviewmotel.com | 10 rooms, 6 cabins, 1 efficiency cabin | $28–$44 | D, MC, V.

Quality Inn. A quick 10 minutes from Mammoth Cave is this family favorite. Comfortable blue and gray rooms have king- and queen-sized beds. The lobby has cherry wood furniture. | Drive to exit 53 from I–65. Restaurant. Cable TV. Pool. Playground. Business services. Only dogs allowed. | 1006A Doyle Ave., Cave City | 270/773–2181 or 800/321–4245 | fax 270/773–3200 | 100 rooms | $28–$80 | AE, D, DC, MC, V.

Rose Manor Bed & Breakfast. This two-story brick Victorian offers spacious rooms with private baths, aromatherapy, a non-alcoholic beverage bar, late night snack, traditional country breakfast, a commons area with video and CD library. Out front there is usually a horse carriage for hire. You can also arrange for a therapeutic massage. Complimentary breakfast. Some in-room hot tubs. | 204 Duke St., Cave City | 270/773–4402 or 888/621–5900 | mammothcave.com/rose.htm | 5 rooms | $90–$110 | No credit cards.

CORBIN

MAP 6, G5

(Nearby towns also listed: Barbourville, Hazard, London, Pineville, Williamsburg)

A former important railroad crossroads, this town in the Appalachian mountains was founded around 1800 and named Lynn Camp, after Virginian William Lynn who was lost while exploring the area. The name was later changed to Corbin. It's now a visitor center for Cumberland Falls State Resort Park and the Daniel Boone National Forest and the location of Colonel Harland Sanders' first Kentucky Fried Chicken restaurant, which opened in 1930.

Information: Corbin Chamber of Commerce | 101 N. Depot St., Corbin, 40701 | 606/528–6390 or 800/528–7123.

CORBIN

INTRO
ATTRACTIONS
DINING
LODGING

Attractions

Colonel Harland Sanders' Original Restaurant. Colonel Sanders served up his first fried chicken in this little eatery *(see Dining)* that now also contains a museum with Sanders's office, a replica of his kitchen, and the equipment he used to perfect recipes with his "11 secret herbs and spices." | U.S. 25E at U.S. 25W, Corbin | 606/528–2163 | Free | Daily 9:30 AM–10 PM; Fri. and Sat. 10 AM–11 PM.

Cumberland Falls State Resort Park. You can observe a rare "moonbow" from a special observation deck overlooking the 68-ft-high Cumberland Falls. This is one of only two places in the world, the other being at Victoria Falls in Zambia, where this nocturnal equivalent of a rainbow can be observed. The falls at this state park of over 1,600 acres is inside the vast Daniel Boone National Forest. An attractive destination for birders and botanists, the park also contains several rare species of plants and animals. Various outdoor recreational facilities are available and there is an excellent, small archaeological museum with exhibits about the prehistoric geology, natural history, and anthropology of the area. | The park is at exit 25 off I–75 | 7351 Highway 90, Corbin | 606/528–4121 or 800/325–0063 | www.kystateparks.com/agencies/parks/cumbfal2.htm | Free | Daily, closed Christmas week.

Big South Fork National River/Recreation Area. The Kentucky/Tennessee border is straddled by 119,000 acres on the Cumberland Plateau. White-water canoeing, rafting, and kayaking are major draws. There are also nature trails, horseback riding trails, backpacking, and camping. Hunting and fishing areas are available. | The area is 80 mi northwest of Knoxville, between U.S. 27 on the east, and U.S. 127 on the west. Stearns Visitors Center is at Highway 92W | 4564 Leatherwood Rd., Oneida TN | 606/376–5073 or 931/879–3625 | fax 931/879–9604 | www.nps.gov/biso/index.htm | Free; fee for camping | Daily.

Sheltowee Trace Outfitters. There are guided raft trips below the falls and canoe trips above the falls of the scenic Cumberland River Gorge. Excursions usually last 5–7 hours. | The outfitters are 5 mi from Cumberland Falls on Highway 90 | Box 1060, Whitley City | 606/376–5567 or 800/541–7238 | fax 606/528–8779 | fun@ky-rafting.com | www.ky-rafting.com | Memorial Day–Labor Day, daily; Apr.–mid-May and Oct., weekends.

ON THE CALENDAR

MAR.: *Kentucky Hills Weekend.* Native American history and heritage is highlighted annually on this March weekend. | 606/528–4121 (recreation dept.) or 800/325–0063 (reservations).

APR.: *Family Outdoor Adventure Weekend.* Horseback riding, hiking, and rafting are among the activities at this weekend festival. | 606/528–4121 or 800/325–0063.

APR.: *Nature Photography Weekend.* April is the peak time for spring wildflowers, and draws shutterbugs to this annual event. Usually held the last full weekend of the month. It's suggested that attendees stay at Cumberland Falls State Parks where there are 52 lodge rooms and 24 cabins. The event goes like this: Attendees take photographs over a 24-hour period; before the weekend is over, their slides are developed and shown and a contest for five categories takes place. Each category's winner receives $25.00. | 606/528–4121 or 800/325–0063.

JUNE: *Lake Laurel Horse Show.* An all-breed horse show is held annually in the Civic Center Arena. The event is held on a Friday and Saturday mid-month. | 606/528–6390 or 800/528–7123.

AUG.: *Corbin Nibroc Funfest.* Arts, crafts, food, parades, dog show, clogging, nightly entertainment, beauty contest with scholarship prize money, and kids' activities mark this four-day event. The celebration is held the second weekend of the month. | 606/528–6390 or 800/528–7123.

Dining

Harland Sanders Café and Museum. American. This is the original Colonel Sanders—authentic 1935 wood floors and walls. Their big seller is the two-piece chicken meal. Country-style dining room is the site where the Colonel invented his famous chicken recipe. Tour Sanders's kitchen as it looked in 1940. | U.S. 25W, Corbin | 606/528–2163 | Breakfast available | $4.19–$5.67 | No credit cards.

Reno's Roadhouse. American. At Reno's you are promised Texas fun with your food. Dig into a barrel of peanuts and throw your shells on the floor and join in when the employees break into a line dance. Lunch fare is deluxe burgers and salads, or, try the catfish sandwich on Reno's special homestyle bread. Dinner includes steak, chicken, chops, BBQ ribs and seafood. Bubba's "Can't Dance" 64-oz. steak is free if you can down it in 45 minutes. | 2665 Cumberland Falls Hwy., Corbin | 606/523–5211 | $8–$18, $30 Bubba's steak.

Lodging

Baymont Inn. Modern motel decor is the rule at this chain. Some rooms have king-size beds; some rooms also have recliners. There's a modern burgundy and green lobby with a fireplace. The four floors have modern architecture and lots of plants. Complimentary Continental breakfast. Some refrigerators. Cable TV. Pool. Spa. Business services. Some pets allowed. | 174 Adams Rd., Corbin | 606/523–9040 | fax 606/523–0072 | 95 rooms | $50–$60 | AE, D, DC, MC, V.

Best Western Corbin Inn. This motel is 14 mi from the falls at exit 25 off I–75. Beige, burgundy, and green are the dominant colors in the rooms. The lobby has lots of arches, mirrors, and flowers. Complimentary Continental breakfast. Refrigerators. Cable TV. Pool. Busines services. | 2630 Cumberland Falls Hwy., Corbin | 606/528–2100 or 888/528–2100 | fax 606/523–1704 | 63 rooms | $39–$59 | AE, D, DC, MC, V.

Country Inn and Suites by Carlson. Situated on a mountaintop, this attractive stucco inn has spacious modern rooms and suites. The lobby has hardwood floors and a working fireplace, making it look like an old-fashioned living room. The inn is 16 mi from Cumberland Falls. | Take exit 25 off I–75—it's visible from the highway. Microwaves in the suites only, refrigerators. Cable TV. Pool. Business services. | 1888 Cumberland Falls Hwy., Corbin | 606/526–1400 or 800/456–4000 | fax 606/526–0974 | 44 rooms | $52–$74 | AE, D, DC, MC, V.

Dupont Lodge. This handsome stone lodge on the Laurel River blends in with the woodland surroundings. There's a large stone fireplace in the common area. The cottages are more modern than rustic, but they evoke "authentic." The state-operated lodge has access to park facilities—it's part of the Cumberland Falls Resort Park. Facilities include a museum wih Indian artifacts, 17 mi of hiking trails, fishing, whitewater rafting, and horseback riding. Dining room. Kitchenettes (in cottages). TV. Pool, wading pool. Tennis. Hiking. Business services. | 7351 Rte. 90, Corbin | 606/528–4121 or 800/325–0063 | fax 606/528–0704 | 52 rooms in lodge, 26 cottages | $32–$68, $55–$75 suites, $60–$145 cottages | Closed 5 days late Dec. | AE, D, DC, MC, V.

Hampton Inn, Corbin. There are plenty of options here if you crave a spacious room or suite. The Daniel Boone National Forest, Daniel Boone Motocross, Levi Jackson State Resort, Cumberland College and Cumberland Falls are all less than 20 mi away. This hotel opened in the spring of 2000. Complimentary breakfast. Cable TV. Pool. Hot tub. Exercise equipment. Laundry facilities. No pets. | 125 Adams Rd., Corbin | 606/523–5696 or 800/436–7800 | fax 606/523–1130 | www.hampton-inn.com | 67 rooms | $74–$84 | AE, D, DC, MC, V.

Knights Inn. This inn is 30 minutes from Cumberland Falls and 15 minutes from the Colonel Sanders Original Restaurant. The basic accommodations here are pleasant and comfortable. The lobby has floral carpeting and a brick floor evoking a country/homey look. Some kitchenettes. Cable TV. Pool. | 37 Highway 770, Corbin | 606/523–1500 | fax 606/523–5818 | 109 rooms | $36–$52 | AE, D, DC, MC, V.

Regency Inn. From this hilltop hotel you can get a scenic mountain view. The Regency is just 15 mi from Cumberland Falls and 10 mi from Laurel Lake. Complimentary Continental breakfast. Cable TV. Pool. Some in-room hot tubs. | 2560 Cumberland Falls Hwy., Corbin | 606/528–6301 | fax 606/528–6301, ext. 190 | 132 rooms | $33–$40, $90 hot tub suite | AE, D, DC, MC, V.

Super 8 Motel of Corbin/Cumberland Falls. Stone pillars mark the entrance to the glass-encased lobby of this motel. Shopping addicts can check out the adjacent Past Times Antique Mall before heading out to nearby Cumberland Falls State Park, home of the only moonbow. Parking for RVs is available. Complimentary Continental breakfast. Cable TV. Some in-room hot tubs. Laundry facilities. Pets allowed. | 171 W. Cumberland Gap Pkwy., Corbin | 606/528–8888 or 800/800–8000 | motel@gte.net | home1£gte.net | 34 rooms | $39–$79, $69–$106 suites | AE, D, DC, MC, V.

COVINGTON (CINCINNATI AIRPORT AREA)

MAP 6, F2

(Nearby towns also listed: Florence, Williamstown)

In the late 18th century, the Point (the site of present-day Covington), was a popular staging area for explorers and pioneers. Strategically located at the confluence of the Licking and Ohio rivers, the area was a military post and settlement as well. The city of Covington received its charter in 1834. About this time, an influx of Irish and German immigrants created a population boom. The new residents brought their traditional crafts with them, most notably, brewing. By the end of the century, there were dozens of independent breweries in the city. Covington's present-day economy is linked to Cincinnati, across the river, and it is also a site for office complexes.

European-style architecture arrived in the latter half of the 18th-century. Mainstrasse Village downtown has been restored to its half-timbered charm. There's a clock tower in the center and a bronze statue of the Goose Girl. The Roman Catholic Cathedral Basilica of the Assumption, completed in 1901, was modeled on Notre Dame Cathedral in Paris.

Covington is somewhat in the shadow of Cincinnati—the two cities are connected by four bridges. The Greater Cincinnati/Northern Kentucky International Airport is on

COVINGTON
(CINCINNATI
AIRPORT AREA)

INTRO
ATTRACTIONS
DINING
LODGING

the Kentucky side of the Ohio, about 10 minutes from downtown Covington. A hub for Delta Airlines, it has nonstop flights to and from several cities in Europe as well as many throughout North America.

Information: Northern Kentucky Convention and Visitors Bureau | 605 Philadelphia St., Covington, 41011 | 859/655–4159 or 800/782–9659 | fax 859/655–7668 | www. staynky.com.

Attractions

Cathedral Basilica of the Assumption. The outside is modeled on Notre Dame in Paris, and the inside is modeled on the Cathedral of St. Denis in Paris. Built at the turn of the 20th century, the basilica has 82 stained-glass windows, one of which is believed to be the largest hand-made stained glass window in the world. There are four large murals on canvas by Covington artist Frank Duveneck. | 1140 Madison Ave., Covington | 859/431–2060 | fax 859/431–8444 | www.covcathedral.com | Free | Daily 10–4; tours by appointment.

Devou Park. The 600-acre park with a view of the Ohio River has many recreational facilities, including a picnic area, swimming pool, golf course, and tennis courts. There are outdoor concerts in the summer. | 1344 Audobon Rd., Covington | 859/292–2151 | Free | Daily dawn to dusk.

The **Behringer-Crawford Museum,** in Devou Park, houses exhibits on archaeology, paleontology, local history, and local natural history. Fine arts exhibits are on display as well. | 1600 Montague Rd., Covington | 859/491–4003 | fax 859/491–4006 | $2–$3 | Tues.–Fri. 10–5; weekends 1–5.

MainStrasse Village. This is eight blocks within the 30-block area of the city that's undergoing restoration of its 19th-century German-style buildings. The district hums with shops, restaurants, and pubs. | 605 Philadelphia St., Covington | 859/491–0458 | fax 859/655–7932 | www.mainstrasse.org | Daily.

The **Carroll Chimes Bell Tower** in MainStrasse Village was named for former governor Julian Carroll; the 100-ft-tall bell tower contains a 43-bell carillon. It plays on the hour from 9 AM until dark. The tower also contains one of only two American-made animated clocks. It has 21 performing figures that act out the story of "The Pied Piper of Hamelin." | 603 Philadelphia St., Covington | 859/655–4172 or 800/354–9718 | fax 859/655–7668 | Free | Daily 9–5.

Riverboat Cruises. Cruise along the Ohio for a two-hour or day-long excursion on BB Riverboats. A paddlewheeler, steamboat, and a modern river cruiser serve lunch or dinner on longer trips. | Covington Landing, 1 Madison Ave., Covington | 859/261–8500 or 800/261–8586 | fax 859/292–2452 | www.bbriverboats.com | Fees vary | Daily.

Roebling Suspension Bridge. Engineer John Roebling was a pioneer in the design and construction of suspension bridges. Completed in 1867, the Roebling Suspension Bridge was a prototype for the Brooklyn Bridge. Find it at the foot of Court Street spanning the Ohio River. While at the waterfront, take a horse-drawn carriage ride. | State Marker 1601, Court St., Covington | 800/STAY–NKY.

ON THE CALENDAR

MAR.: *Mardi Gras.* New Orleans doesn't have a patent on Mardi Gras. This Cajun party has live entertainment, two Mardi Gras parades, food, drink, and dancing in the streets. The event is held at MainStrasse Village, an ongoing restoration of a 30-block area in west Covington located on I–75 at exit 192. Costumes are encouraged. Call for specific dates and parade times and routes. | 859/491–0458.

MAY: *Maifest.* Held in the Mainstrasse Village, there's live entertainment, arts and crafts, and plenty of German-style food and drink. It's an annual three-day Bavarian street festival that's held the full weekend after Mother's Day. | 859/491–0458.

SEPT.: *Oktoberfest.* This is the annual cool weather version of the Maifest in which the city celebrates its German heritage. It's held the full weekend after Labor day. | 513/357–6246 or 859/491–0458.

Dining

BB Riverboats. American Casual. Have lunch or dinner while cruising down the Ohio River aboard your choice of three riverboats, two of which are stern-wheelers. Casual yet elegant. Entertainment. Kids' menu. | 1 Madison Ave, Covington | 859/261–8500 or 800/261–8586 | bbriver@bbriverboats.com | www.bbriverboats.com | Reservations essential | May–Oct., daily lunch and dinner cruises; limited schedule during Nov.–Apr. | $36–$45 | AE, D, DC, MC, V.

Mike Fink. Seafood. This paddle wheel steamboat might be docked indefinitely, but diners have great views of downtown Cincinnati. Known for fresh fish dishes. They've also got a raw bar. Two recommended dishes are Halibut French Quarter and Fettuccini Alfredo. Kids' menu. | Greenup St., Covington | 859/261–4212 | fax 859/261–3941 | $14–$35 | AE, D, DC, MC, V.

Oriental Wok. Chinese, American. Bustling suburban restaurant with tropical Chinese theme. Features Cantonese as well as Szechwan fare. Fresh sea bass and General Wong's Chicken are two favorites. Open-air dining on shaded patio. Entertainment Friday and Saturday. Kids' menu. | 317 Buttermilk Pike, Fort Mitchell | 859/331–3000 | $10–$25 | AE, D, DC, MC, V.

Riverview Room. Contemporary. Revolving restaurant atop the Clarion Hotel has scenic views of the Ohio River and downtown Cincinnati. Oriental Swordfish and prime rib are favorites. Nightly harpist. Kids' menu. Sun. brunch. | 668 W. 5th St., Covington | 859/491–5300 | Jacket and tie | $18–$32 | AE, D, DC, MC, V.

South Beach Grill at the Waterfront. Contemporary. Enjoy a panorama of the Cincinnati skyline from this sophisticated floating open-air dining barge on the river. It has a two-story waterfall and live palm trees, evoking South Beach, Miami. There's an outdoor summer bar with live music, a "cigar and piano" bar, and a sushi bar. It calls itself a "four-star steak and lobster house." Two dishes are recommended: the 12-oz filet mignon, Collinsworth style (topped with crab meat and a béarnaise/mushroom sauce, with asparagus) and the coldwater, deshelled 20-oz lobster meat. | 14 Pete Rose Pier, Covington | 859/581–1414 | fax 859/392–2774 | waterfront1@fuse.net | www.waterfrontinc.com | Jacket and tie preferred | No lunch | $19–$42 | AE, DC, MC, V.

Lodging

Amos Shinkle Townhouse B&B. This bed and breakfast is an antebellum Greco-Italian mansion built in 1854. The master bedroom has a hot tub and a crystal chandelier in the bathroom. Sixteen-foot ceilings tower above antique furnishings, original cornice work, and walls with original paint and plaster. Covington is a short ride across the Roebling Suspension Bridge to Cincinnati. No pets. No smoking. | 215 Garrard St., Covington | 859/431–2118 or 800/970–7012 | fax 859/491–4551 | ashinkle@one.net | www.bbonline.com | 7 rooms | $89–$150 | AE, D, M, V.

Carneal House. This beautiful redbrick antebellum mansion in Covington's historic district was built in 1815. The inn is furnished with period antiques, a patio, and sun room overlook the Licking River. Complimentary breakfast. | 405 E. 2nd St., Covington | 859/431–6130 | fax 859/581–6041 | 6 rooms | $90–$130 | Closed Jan.–Feb. | AE, MC, V, D.

The Clarion Hotel Riverview. This landmark cylindrical hotel dominates the western edge of the skyline and overlooks the river which is 2½ blocks away. There's a great view of the river from the 18th-floor revolving restaurant. The elegant lobby is rust-colored marble and mahogany. There are florals and cherry wood in the hallways, too. 2 restaurants (*see Riverview Restaurant*); bar and grill called Kelly's Landing. In-room data ports. Some suites have hot tubs. Cable TV. Indoor-outdoor pool. Hot tub. Exercise equipment. Free laundry. Business services. Airport shuttle. | 668 W. 5th St., Covington | 859/491–1200 or 800/292–2079 | fax 859/491–0326 | www.clarioninn.com | 236 rooms | $89–$225 | AE, D, DC, MC, V.

COVINGTON
(CINCINNATI
AIRPORT AREA)

INTRO
ATTRACTIONS
DINING
LODGING

Drawbridge Inn. It's been given the nickname "the Castle" because the lobby courtyard looks out on castle-like walls. This sprawling Tudor-style complex is good for conventions and family vacations. | Take exit 186 off I–75; the inn is 7 mi north of the airport and 7 mi south of Cincinnati. 3 restaurants, 1 bar with entertainment. Cable TV. 3 pools (1 indoor). Hot tub. Tennis. Exercise equipment. Business services. Airport shuttle. Free parking. | 2477 Royal Dr., Fort Mitchell | 859/341–2800 or 800/354–9793 (outside KY), 800/352–9866 (KY) | fax 859/341–5644 | www.drawbridgeinn.com | 485 rooms | $70–$95 | AE, D, DC, MC, V.

Embassy Suites at RiverCenter. Adjacent to the Covington Landing Entertainment Complex and the Northern Kentucky Convention Center, this contemporary hotel overlooks the Ohio River. Entertainment in the restaurant and bar. The marble eight-story tropical-theme atrium lobby features a fountain, waterfalls, and lots of plants. Complimentary full, hot breakfast buffet. "Managers' reception" (unlimited cocktails and dry snacks) 5–7 PM. In-room data ports. Microwaves, refrigerators, Cable TV. Indoor pool. Hot tub. Exercise equipment. Laundry facilities. Business services. Free parking if you book overnight. | 10 E. RiverCenter Blvd., Covington | 859/261–8400 | fax 859/261–8486 | www.embassysuites.com | 226 suites | $139–$179 suites | AE, D, DC, MC, V.

Extended Stay America Efficiency Studios. These efficiency studios are designed for the value-conscious, long-term traveler. The queen studio has 300 square ft of living space including a fully-equipped kitchen with full-size refrigerator, a two-burner cooktop, microwave oven, and dining table. Cable TV. In-room data ports. Laundry facilities. | 650 West Third St., Covington | 859/581–3000 | fax 859/581–3100 | www.extstay.com | $59, $289/week | AE, D, MC, V.

Hampton Inn. Terrific location—it's ¼ mi from Covington Landing where you'll find boats and dinner cruises. The "king rooms" are equipped with sleeper sofas as well as king-sized beds—real family-friendly. The spacious lobby has a breakfast area, lots of plants, and a navy and eggplant color scheme. | Take exit 192 off I–75. Complimentary Continental breakfast. In-room data ports. Cable TV. Indoor pool. Exercise equipment. Business services. Free parking. | 200 Crescent Ave., Covington | 859/581–7800 or 800/HAMPTON | fax 859/581–8282 | www.hampton-inn.com | 151 rooms | $139–$189 | AE, D, DC, MC, V.

Holiday Inn–Cincinnati Airport. You'll relax in the atrium lobby with live plants and a fountain. This contemporary hotel has six floors and a lower terrace for lounging. Take I–275 and Mineola Pike to the service road. Restaurant, bar. In-room data ports, suites have unstocked wet bars. Some rooms have cable TV. Indoor pool. Hot tub. Dry sauna. Exercise equipment. Laundry facilities. Business services. Airport shuttle. | 1717 Airport Exchange Blvd., Erlanger | 859/371–2233 or 800–HOLIDAY | fax 859/371–5002 | cvgap@cwbusiness.com | www.holiday-inn.com | 305 rooms, 5 suites | $89–$139; suites $189 | AE, D, DC, MC, V.

Holiday Inn Riverfront. This hotel is near the Northern Kentucky Convention Center and the Central Business District of Cincinnati. Restaurant. Cable TV. Pool. Exercise equipment. Laundry facilities. Free parking. | 600 W. 3rd St., Covington | 859/291–4300 or 800/465–4329 | fax 859/491–2331 | hinn@fuse.net | www.basshotels.com | 153 rooms | $85–$125 | AE, D, DC, MC, V.

Holiday Inn–South. You'll find a modern, family-friendly place. The lobby has a cozy, elevated conversation area. Kids under 19 stay free; under 12 eat free, too. Restaurant. Cable TV. Indoor pool. Hot tub. Exercise equipment. Game room. Video games. Playground. Laundry facilities. Business services. Airport shuttle. Free parking. | 2100 Dixie Hwy., Fort Mitchell | 859/331–1500 | fax 859/331–2259 | 214 rooms | $110–$141 | AE, D, DC, MC, V.

Marriott at Rivercenter. Located on the south bank of the Ohio River, this 15-story atrium hotel has a spectacular view of the Cincinnati skyline and Ohio River from all rooms. Restaurant, room service. Baby-sitting. Laundry facilities. Business services. Free parking. | 10 West River Center Blvd., Covington | 859/261–2900 | fax 859/261–0900 | 321 rooms | $115–$145 | AE, D, MC, V.

CUMBERLAND FALLS
STATE RESORT PARK
(see Corbin)

CUMBERLAND GAP
NATIONAL HISTORICAL PARK
(see Middlesboro)

DANIEL BOONE
NATIONAL FOREST
(see Winchester)

DANVILLE

MAP 6, F4

(Nearby towns also listed: Berea, Harrodsburg, Lexington, Richmond, Springfield)

The highlight of this town, at the geographic center of the state, is the Constitution Square State Historic Site, consisting of replicas of 1780s buildings. Kentucky's constitution was drawn up here in 1792, 10 years after its founding by settler John Crow. The neoclassical campus of Centre College, a private liberal-arts college, occupies much of the town center. Also of note are the McDowell House, Apothecary, and Gardens, a restored estate of a noted pioneer surgeon, and the Pioneer Playhouse, which hosts summer theater.

Information: Danville-Boyle County Convention and Visitors Bureau | 304 S. 4th St., Danville, 40422 | 859/236–7794 or 800/755–0076 | tourism@searnet.com | www.danville-ky.com.

Attractions

Constitution Square State Historic Site. This is a reproduction of the state's first courthouse square and site of the first post office (pre-1792) west of the Appalachians. Replicas include the courthouse, jail, and meetinghouse. There's also a history museum, art gallery, museum store, and picnic area. A memorial to Kentucky's governors, the Governor's Circle—featuring a bronze plaque for each—is also here. The plans for Kentucky's independence from Virginia in 1784 were drawn up at the courthouse. | 134 S. 2nd St., Danville | 859/239–7089 | Free | Mon.–Fri. 9–5:30; Sat. 10–4; Sun. 1–4.

Herrington Lake. Bass, crappie, and walleye populations are maintained for fishing in this lake formed by the Dix Dam. Campsite hookups are available. | 606/236–7794 or 800/755–0076 | Fees for fishing and boat launch | Mar. 17–Nov. 1, daily.

McDowell House and Apothecary Shop. This is the home of renowned pioneer surgeon Ephraim McDowell, who performed the first successful ovariotomy in the world in 1809. The house was built in stages between 1792 and 1820 and is furnished with period antiques. The gardens contain wildflowers and medicinal herbs. The apothecary is stocked with old bottles and equipment. | 125 S. 2nd St., Danville | 859/236–2804 | fax 859/236–2804 | $1–$5 | Mon.–Sat. 10–noon and 1–4; Sun. 2–4; Nov. 1–Feb. 28, closed on Mon.

Norton Center for the Arts at Centre College. This important regional arts center hosts orchestras, theater companies, chamber ensembles, jazz greats, and pop music singers from around the world. The 85,000-sq-ft complex contains the 1,500-seat Newlin Hall and the intimate 360-seat theater-in-the-round, Weisiger Theatre. The Grand Foyer is used for art exhibitions. Norton Center was designed by William Wesley Peters, of the Frank Lloyd Wright Foundation, and opened in 1973. | 600 W. Walnut St., Danville | 859/236–4692 or 877/448–7469 | fax 859/238–5448 | Art exhibitions, free; performances, $35–$50 | Weekdays 10–4, and during performances.

Perryville Battlefield State Historic Site. The largest Civil War battle in the state was fought on this spot. On October 8, 1862, 16,000 Confederate troops under the command of Gen. Braxton Bragg engaged 58,000 Union soldiers led by Gen. Don Carlos Buell. The 100-acre park looks much as it did at the time of the battle. Crawford House (Confederate headquarters) and Bottom House (around which some of the heaviest fighting took place) are still standing. A museum with artifacts of the battle and maps and descriptions of the conflict is on the site. There are picnic and playground facilities, too. | The site is 9 mi west of Danville off Highway 150 | Box 296, 1825 Battlefield Rd., Perryville | 859/332–8631 or 800/755–0076 | kurt.holman@mail.state.ky.us | www.kystateparks.com | $2 | April 1–Oct. 31, daily 9–5; Nov.–Mar., by appointment.

Pioneer Playhouse Village-of-the-Arts. An 18th-century village is centered around a Wild West street which has served as a movie set. There's a music store, ice cream shop, and print shop, sometimes staffed by personnel in period costumes. The "Indian Room" has theatrical memorabilia, such as John Travolta's acting resume. This over 200-acre complex across from Centre College includes 65 wooded acres of hiking trails and campgrounds. In summer there are productions of Broadway shows, usually comedies (recent ones were by Beth Henley and Neil Simon) staged in an outdoor theater. | 840 Stanford Rd., Danville | 859/236–2747 | fax 859/236–2341 | Plays, $12; dinner and play, $20 | Plays mid-June–mid-Aug. daily; campgrounds Apr.–Dec. 1.

ON THE CALENDAR

JUNE: *Great American Brass Band Festival.* Brass bands and other ensembles gather annually from all over the country to provide open-air, old-fashioned entertainment for a full mid-month weekend. | 859/236–7794 or 800/755–0076.

SEPT.: *Historic Constitution Square Festival.* Strolling minstrels, accurate plays and reenactments, a pioneer encampment, musical entertainment, and a juried arts and crafts show are all part of this annual, three-day festival. It happens the third full weekend of the month. | 859/236–7794 or 800/755–0076.

Lodging

Holiday Inn Express. You'll find a standard stucco and brick structure. The lobby has an equestrian theme—horse prints and fabric. It's two mi from Centre College. Some larger rooms have sleeper sofas. Complimentary Continental breakfast. Cable TV. Outdoor pool. Hot tub. Laundry facilities. Free parking. Pets allowed ($50 deposit). | 96 Daniel Dr., Danville | 859/236–8600 or 800–HOLIDAY | fax 859/236–4299 | 63 rooms | $66–$89 | AE, D, DC, MC, V.

Old Crow Inn. Nestled among 27 landscaped acres of walking trails, native plants, and wildlife, Old Crow is the longest-standing stone house west of the Alleghenies. This English manor house has 23 rooms and was built in the late 1700s. After a restful night, you can take a guided tour or walk downtown to shop. In-room fireplaces. | 471 Stanford Ave., Danville | 859/236–1808 | fax 859/236–7467 | elements@searnet.com | www.oldcrowinn.com | 2 rooms, 1 suite | $75–$90 | AE, M, V.

Super 8 Motel. You'll find a familiar favorite with a modern brick style. The lobby has a purple color scheme, paintings, plants and flowers, and cherry wood furniture. There are cheerful, contemporary rooms and a landscaped lawn. Some refrigerators. Cable TV. Free Continental breakfast. Laundry room. Business services. Free parking. Some pets allowed.

| 3663 U.S. 150 Bypass, Danville | 859/236–8881 or 800/800–8000 | fax 859/236–8881, ext. 301 | 49 rooms | $50–$65 | AE, D, DC, MC, V.

Twin Hollies Retreat. This antebellum mansion built in 1833 has spacious rooms and is furnished with beautiful antiques. | You'll find it 1 block from Centre College. No kids under 12. | 406 Maple Ave., Danville | 859/236–8954 | 3 rooms | $80 | No credit cards.

DAWSON SPRINGS

(Nearby towns also listed: Greenville, Hopkinsville, Madisonville)

Because of mineral springs discovered in the 1870s, this now sleepy little town was once one of the South's booming spas, with some 17 hotels and some 50 boarding houses. But the decline of the railroads and the Great Depression effectively put the resort area out of business. Today, Dawson Springs is the gateway to the 863-acre Pennyrile Forest State Resort Park, and provides hiking, boating, and camping. An industrial park built in the 1970s provides light manufacturing jobs. Tourism is still important to the town's economy, too.

Information: Dawson Springs Chamber of Commerce, City of Dawson Springs/City Clerk's Office | Box 345, Dawson Springs, 42408 | 270/797–2781.

Attractions

Pennyrile Forest State Resort Park. This state park contains 56-acre Lake Pennyrile, which is stocked with bluegill, catfish, crappie, channel catfish, largemouth bass, yellow bullhead, warmouth, and both longear and green sunfish. The pool, beach, and lodge were renovated in 1996. Campsites with utilities are available from mid-March until the end of October. The lodge and cottages are available year-round. | 20781 Pennyrile Lodge Rd., Dawson Springs 42408 | 270/797–3421 or 800/325–1711 | www.kystateparks.com/agencies/parks/pennyril.htm | Free; fee for golf and equipment rental | Daily.

ON THE CALENDAR

MAY: *Wild Wings Weekend.* Naturalists lead hikers through trails in the Pennyrile Forest State Resort Park to observe wildflowers and birds. Hikers enjoy this annual event on the first full weekend of the month. Canoe trips are also available. | 270/797–3421.
JULY: *Dawson Springs Barbecue and Homecoming.* This annual event takes place on the Friday closest to the Fourth of July and includes cookouts and other street fair activities. | 270/797–2781.
AUG.: *"Run Through the Forest."* Runners look forward to this annual 5-km run through scenic paved roads in the Pennyrile Forest State Resort Park. | 270/797–3421.

Dining

The Place. American. This is the restaurant the locals call home. Fill up on homestyle favorites like lasagna or turkey with dressing. On Friday and Saturday the special is fresh fried catfish, and there are always homemade cream and fruit pies. | 300 E. Arcadia Ave., Dawson Springs | 270/797–5033 | Hours Mon.–Sat. 5 AM–8 PM, Sun. 6 AM–3 PM | $4–$6.

Lodging

Pennyrile Forest State Resort Park. This rustic wood and stone lodge sits on a hilltop overlooking Pennyrile Lake. There are some furnished lakeside cottages with private docks for fishing or boating. Camp sites are available. Restaurant. Some in-room fireplaces. Outdoor pool. 9-hole golf course, miniature golf, tennis. Boating, fishing. | 20781 Pennyrile Lodge Rd., Dawson Springs | 270/797–3421 or 800/325–1711 | fax 270/797–4887 | www.kystateparks.com | 24 rooms, 13 cottages | $52–$85, $75–$104 cottages | AE, D, DC, MC, V.

Springs Inn. Springs Inn is close to City Park and Tradewater Park and 8 mi from Pennyrile Forest State Resort Park. Surrounded by lush forest, the inn is busiest during deer-hunting season. | 207 Arcadia Ave., Dawson Springs | 270/797–2029 | 11 rooms, 1 suite | $28 | AE, D, MC, V.

ELIZABETHTOWN

MAP 6, E4

(Nearby towns also listed: Bardstown, Brandenburg, Fort Knox, Hodgenville)

About an hour south of Louisville's airport, E-town, as it's known locally, is a site for light manufacturing and Steinway Piano's international distribution center. It was founded as Severn's Valley Settlement circa 1790, named for area explorer John Severn. Elizabethtown was re-named in honor of the wife of Colonel Andrew Hynes from Virginia, who donated land for public buildings and town lots in 1797. Famous residents include Thomas Lincoln, Abe's father, who returned to Kentucky from Illinois and married an Elizabethtown woman after the death of his first wife. Present-day Elizabethtown is the seat of Hardin County.

Information: **Elizabethtown Tourism and Convention Bureau** | 1030 N. Mulberry St., Elizabethtown, 42701 | 270/765–2175 or 800/437–0092 | fax 270/737–6568.

Attractions

Brown-Pusey Community House. This stage coach inn dating from 1825 has been restored and is now used as a community center and genealogy library. It also has a museum of local history inside the home, called the Pusey Room. The brick Georgian house was home to Gen. George Armstrong Custer from 1871 to 1873 when his 7th Cavalry was stationed in Elizabethtown. Tours are given of the building and gardens. | 128 N. Main St., Elizabethtown | 270/765–2515 | www.kvnet.org/bph | Free; library $3 | Mon.–Sat. 10–4.

Lincoln Heritage House. There are two log cabins on the Hardin Thomas homestead, one built in 1805 with the help of Thomas's friend, Thomas Lincoln. Lincoln's craftsmanship can be seen in the woodwork, staircases, and mantelpieces. | Take I–65 to exit 94, then 3 mi to Highway 31W | Freeman Lake Park, 111 W. Dixie, Elizabethtown | 270/765–2175 or 800/437–0092 | Free | June–Aug., Tues.–Sun. 10–4.

Walking Tours. There's a guided Historic Downtown Walking Tour conducted every Thursday at 7 PM from June through September. The tour begins and ends on the town square. Brochures for three different self-guided tours of the historic district are available from the Tourism and Convention Bureau. | Elizabethtown Tourism and Convention Bureau, 1030 N. Mulberry St., Elizabethtown | 270/765–2175 or 800/437–0092.

ON THE CALENDAR

MAR.: *Central Kentucky Antique Association Showcase.* Held at Elizabethtown High School, dealers throughout the region set up booths filled with wares. It's held annually on the second Saturday of the month. | 270/765–2175.

AUG.: *Kentucky Heartland Festival.* A baby contest and a balloon glow (glow-in-the-dark) are two highlights of this event held the last full weekend of the month. There are also arts and crafts demonstrations and sales, a balloon race, an antique auto show, a parade, games, kiddie rides, fireworks, a 5-K run, a lip-synch contest, and lots of food! You'll find the whole shebang at Freeman Lake Park. | 270/765–4334.

Dining

Coffee Tree Restaurant. American. In the Holiday Inn, this is a full-service restaurant with a hearty buffet on weekdays. Dinner specialties are Porterhouse steak or ribs. There is also a salad bar and a selection of sandwiches. Kids' menu. | 1058 N. Mulberry St., Elizabethtown | 270/769–2344 | fax 270/737–2850 | $5–$15 | AE, D, DC, MC, V.

Green Bamboo. Chinese. Noted for friendly service, the Green Bamboo is filled with traditional and colorful decor. Their Mongolian Beef and Mandarin Chicken are two popular dishes. | 902 N. Dixie, Elizabethtown | 270/769–3457 | fax 270/769–2060 | $11–$25 | AE, D, MC, V.

Stone Hearth. American. Diners enjoy intimate English style dining from an older time with subdued lighting and a stone hearth. Steaks are very popular as well as the chocolate chip pecan pie. There's a salad bar, too. | 1001 N. Mulberry St., Elizabethtown | 270/765–4898 | fax 270/765–4898 | $12.95–$17.95 | AE, DC, MC, V, D.

Texas Roadhouse. Steak. Bring your appetite to this friendly Southwestern steak house that boasts, "Hearty steaks and killer ribs found nowhere else but Texas." The cedar siding sports rattlesnake skins and western memorabilia. The specialty is steak but you can also get chicken and other dishes. For dessert, try a mile-high sundae or a slab of cheesecake. | 207 Commerce Dr., Elizabethtown | 270/737–8801 | Sun.–Thurs. 4 PM–10 PM, Fri.–Sat. 4 PM–11 PM | $8–$16 | AE, MC, V.

Lodging

Best Western Cardinal Inn. This one won't remind you of a typical chain. The brick exterior and columns evoke a Southern colonial style. It has the look and ambience of a B&B rather than a motel chain. The quiet spot is ½ mi from the highway; described as off the beaten path. The inn has a one-acre back lawn with cookout grills, shuffleboard, and swings. | You'll find it at the junction of I–65N and I–65S at Exit 91. Cable TV. Pool. Playground. Laundry facilities. Some pets allowed (fee). | 642 E. Dixie, Elizabethtown | 270/765–6139 | fax 270/737–9944 or 800/528–1234 | 55 rooms | $59–$79 | AE, D, DC, MC, V.

Comfort Inn–Atrium Gardens. This contemporary motel was designed around a spacious atrium that overlooks the indoor pool and live tropical plantings. | Take exit 94 off I–65 to the motel. Complimentary full, hot breakfast. Most rooms have whirlpool tubs, microwaves, and refrigerators. Cable TV. Indoor heated pool. Putting green. Video games. Exercise room. Laundry facilities. Business services. | 1043 Executive Dr., Elizabethtown | 270/769–3030 | fax 270/769–2516 | 134 rooms | $69–$99 | AE, D, DC, MC, V.

Days Inn. Take exit 94 off I–65 to this reliable chain. There's a gift shop in the lobby and the motel shares the building with Denny's. Cable TV. Outdoor pool. Video games and pinball machine. Playground. Laundry facilities. | 2010 N. Mulberry St., Elizabethtown | 270/769–5522 or 800/DAYS–INN | fax 270/769–3211 | 120 rooms | $50–$55 | AE, D, DC, MC, V.

Hampton Inn. You'll find comfortable rooms with cherry veneer furniture. | Take I–65 to Exit 94. Complimentary Continental breakfast. Some in-room whirlpool bathtubs. Cable TV. Indoor pool. Hot tub. Business services. | 1035 Executive Dr., Elizabethtown | 270/765–6663 | fax 270/769–3151 | 60 rooms | $69–$85 | AE, D, DC, MC, V.

Holiday Inn. In the heartland of Kentucky between Louisville and Bowling Green, this motel is 2 mi from downtown Elizabethtown. The glistening white-washed building has two floors. All rooms have either two double beds or one king-size bed. Restaurant. Cable TV. In-room data ports. Pool. Laundry facilities. Pets allowed (restrictions). | 1058 N. Mulberry St., Elizabethtown | 270/769–2344 | fax 270/737–2850 | holiday@ne.infi.net | www.basshotels.com | 150 rooms | $65–$69 | AE, D, DC, MC, V.

Petticoat Junction Bed & Breakfast. Just 5 mi south of Elizabethtown, this B&B is a mix of country and Victorian—an 1875 farmhouse surrounded by gardens. You'll want to spend some time in the shops and restaurants in tiny Glendale. Complimentary breakfast. Hot tub. | 233 High St., Glendale | 270/369–8604 or 800/308–0364 | petcoatjct@aol.com | 6 rooms | $65–$80 | D, MC, V.

Ramada Limited. This Ramada, built in 1996, is just off the Blue Grass Parkway and is near Lincoln Park and the Coca-Cola Museum. There is parking for buses and RVs. Continental breakfast. Cable TV. In-room data ports. Indoor pool. Hot tub. | 108 Commerce Dr., Elizabethtown | 270/769–9683 or 888/298–2054 | www.ramada.com | 68 rooms | $48–$75 | AE, D, DC, MC, V.

Red Roof Inn. "Business king rooms" are what you'll find at this motel—Internet hookup, office furniture (including desk and lighted hutch); king-size bed, and a recliner. This place is also family-friendly. It's reported to have the biggest rooms of all the motels/hotels on the Interstate. Two of the suites have a jacuzzi, a queen-size sofa bed, and a king-size bed. There's an area for barbecuing and a gated pool. The lobby has high ceilings with fans and lots of windows where breakfast is served. | The inn is 25–30 minutes from Fort Knox and 30 minutes from Louisville; take I–65 to exit 94. Complimentary Continental breakfast. In-room data ports. Cable TV and free Showtime. Pool. Business services. Free parking. Some pets allowed (fee), with advanced notice. | 2009 N. Mulberry St., Elizabethtown | 270/765–4166 | fax 270/769–9396 | 106 rooms | $46.99–$99.99 | AE, D, DC, MC, V.

Super 8. It's a no-frills modern motel for the budget-minded. You'll like the fact that it's just 1 ½ mi to old Elizabethtown. | Take I–65 to exit 94 to the motel. Complimentary Continental breakfast. Pool. Some pets allowed. Free parking. | 2028 N. Mulberry St., Elizabethtown | 270/737–1088 | fax 270/737–1098 | 59 rooms, 1 suite | $35 | AE, D, MC, V.

FALLS OF ROUGH

MAP 6, D4

(Nearby towns also listed: Elizabethtown, Owensboro)

Falls of Rough was named for the long, steep run of rapids located at this site on the Rough River. In 1823, a dam was built. And by 1853, the local saw- and grist mill employed some 200 people, practically the entire population of the village. The mill stopped operating in 1965, but still stands.

Information: **Rough River Dam State Resort Park** | 450 Lodge Rd., Falls of Rough, 40119 | 270/257–2311 or 800/325–1713.

Attractions

Rough River Dam State Resort Park. This state park is off the Western Kentucky Parkway, 89 mi southwest of Louisville. It has over 600 acres and a lodge with a dining room and swimming pool. Hiking, boating (on Rough River Lake), and golf are the outdoor special-

PACKING IDEAS FOR HOT WEATHER

- ❏ Antifungal foot powder
- ❏ Bandanna
- ❏ Cooler
- ❏ Cotton clothing
- ❏ Day pack
- ❏ Film
- ❏ Hiking boots
- ❏ Insect repellent
- ❏ Rain jacket
- ❏ Sport sandals
- ❏ Sun hat
- ❏ Sunblock
- ❏ Synthetic ice
- ❏ Umbrella
- ❏ Water bottle

*Excerpted from *Fodor's: How to Pack: Experts Share Their Secrets*
© 1997, by Fodor's Travel Publications

ties. | 450 Lodge Rd., Falls of Rough | 270/257–2311 or 800/325–1713 | fax 270/257–8682 | Free | Daily.

ON THE CALENDAR

JULY: *The Official Kentucky State Champion Old Time Fiddler's Contest.* Fiddlers from around the nation compete for over $4,000 in prize money and the chance to become the state's Official Champion Fiddler. Competition in 15 categories and all age groups is intense. The week before is declared Old Time Fiddle Week by the Kentucky General Assembly. The annual event is held in Rough River Dam State Resort Park the third full weekend of the month. | 502/259–3578. .

Lodging

Pine Tree Inn. Here you'll find peace in the valley, hills, and hollows of the ruggedly beautiful countryside. A grocery and a restaurant are adjacent to the inn. Cable TV. Pool. | 13689 Fall of Rough Rd., Leitchfield | 270/257–2771 | fax 270/257–2761 | 20 rooms | $45–$55 | AE, D, MC, V.

Rough River Lodge. All Rough River Dam State Resort Park facilities are available to you. The modern lodge is among rolling, lakeside woodlands. | Take Highway 79N 15 minutes north from the Parkway. Dining room, picnic area. Kitchenettes (in cottages). Cable TV. Pool. Driving range, 9-hole golf, mini-golf, tennis. Playground. Laundry facilities. Business services. | 450 Lodge Rd., Falls of Rough | 502/257–2311 or 800/325–1713 | fax 502/257–8682 | 40 rooms; 17 cottages | $52–$75, $84–$115 cottages | AE, D, MC, V.

FLORENCE

MAP 6, F2

(Nearby towns also listed: Covington, Williamstown)

Florence now occupies the site that was known as Crossroads in the early 1800s for its location at the convergence of major roads between Louisville, Lexington, and Cincinnati. The Florence Mall, visible from I–71, is a regional retail and business center. Many office complexes and small manufacturing plants have sprung up here due to the town's proximity to the Greater Cincinnati/Northern Kentucky International Airport.

Information: Northern Kentucky Convention and Visitors Bureau | 605 Philadelphia, Covington, 41011 | 859/655–4155 | www.staynky.com.

Attractions

Big Bone Lick State Park. In honor of the giant sloths, bison, and mastodons that roamed the area during the last Ice Age, some 20,000 years ago, a herd of buffalo live in the park today. Outdoor recreation includes hiking, fishing, and camping. A museum houses fossils recovered from the site. | Drive south on I–75 to exit 175 | 3380 Beaver Rd., Union | 606/384–3522 | fax 606/384–4775 | www.kystateparks.com/agencies/parks/bigbone.htm | Free, $1 museum; $18 campgrounds | Apr.–Oct. campgrounds.

Turfway Park. This thoroughbred racetrack is on a 241-acre tract built in the 1950s. It was the first track in Kentucky to open for racing on Sunday. | Drive to exit 182 off I–75 and follow the signs to the park | 7500 Turfway Rd., Florence | 859/371–0200 or 800/733–0200 | $3 | Sept. 6–Oct. 6 and Nov. 26–Apr. 5, Wed.–Sun.

ON THE CALENDAR

SEPT.–OCT., NOV.–APR.: *Turfway Park.* You can enjoy thoroughbred racing in autumn and winter. The stakes race in March for 3-year-olds is a prep for the Kentucky Derby. | 800/733–0200.

Dining

Perkins Restaurant and Bakery. American. This family-friendly chain serves standard American fare for breakfast, lunch, and dinner. | 8117 U.S. Hwy. 42, Florence | 859/282–7013 | $5–12 | AE, D, DC, MC, V.

Cathay Kitchen Chinese Restaurant. Chinese. Although this restaurant is in a strip mall, it comes highly recommended by locals. If you're in the mood for a pile of golden-fried chicken chunks sided with a vat of sweet-and-sour dipping sauce, this is the place to be. The large menu here features predictably-good renditions of standard Americanized Chinese fare like chow and lo mein, General Tso's chicken, and pot-stickers. | 8049 Connector Dr., Florence | 859/282–0770 | $4–$11 | AE, D, MC, V.

Jalapeno's. Mexican. Mismatched tables and chairs in blazing primary colors characterize the main dining area at this family-friendly establishment. The extensive menu has plenty of tried-and-true Tex-Mex offerings like enchiladas and quesadillas, but further on there are more exotic items like quail-meat fajitas and red snapper broiled in banana leaves and sided with achiote sauce. Kid's menu. | 7908 Dream St., Florence | 859/746–8001 | $6–$20 | AE, MC, V.

Lodging

Best Western. This reliable outlet of the well-known chain is decorated in beige tones. The lobby is maroon, beige, and green with plants; love seats and chairs make it look like a sitting room. There's an entertainment center in the lobby (big-screen TV and Continental breakfast bar). | Take I–75 to exit 181. It's about 5 mi from the Florence Mall. Complimentary Continental breakfast. Refrigerators; some in-room hot tubs. Cable TV. Pool. Business services. | 7821 Commerce Dr., Florence | 859/525–0090 or 800/937–8376 | fax 859/525–6743 | 51 rooms | $54–$60 | AE, D, DC, MC, V.

Burlington's Willis Graves Bed & Breakfast. This elegant 1830s farmhouse in downtown Burlington is just 5 mi west of Florence on Rte. 18, 12 minutes from the Cincinnati International Airport. The Federal style B&B is Flemish bond brick and is furnished with antiques. The Burlington area is an antiques mecca. Complimentary full breakfast. Cable TV and VCR. | 5825 N. Jefferson St., Burlington | 859/689–5096 or 888/226–5096 | www.burligrave.com | 3 rooms | $75–$125 | AE, MC, V.

Cross Country Inn. Comfortable rooms are furnished with recliners, desks, and computer hook-ups. | It's 5 minutes from Florence Mall on Kentucky U.S. 18 at Exit 181. In-room data ports. Cable TV. Pool. | 7810 Commerce Dr., Florence | 606/283–2030 | fax 606/283–0171 | 112 rooms | $44–$60 | AE, D, DC, MC, V.

Fairfield Inn by Marriott. You'll find bright and cheerful rooms in light blues and pinks in this familiar chain. The lobby is homey in dark browns and maroons. The first and second floors have outside entrances and the third floor is enclosed. Complimentary Continental breakfast. In-room data ports. Cable TV. Pool. Business services. Free parking. | 50 Cavalier Blvd., Florence | 859/371–4800 | fax 859/371–4998 | 135 rooms | $49–$68 | AE, D, DC, MC, V.

Hampton Inn–Cincinnati Airport. Whether you're a horse race lover or business traveler, you'll appreciate the proximity to Turfway Park (⅛ mi) and airport (6 mi). There's a comfortable breakfast area in the country-look lobby of this typical chain hotel. Complimentary Continental breakfast. Cable TV. Pool. Business services. Airport shuttle. | 7393 Turfway Rd., Florence | 859/283–1600 | fax 859/283–0680 | 117 rooms | $79–$94 | AE, D, DC, MC, V.

Hilton Greater Cincinnati Airport. Modern, spacious rooms and fine hardwood furniture are hallmarks at this representative of the Hilton chain. Restaurant, bar. Some refrigerators. Cable TV. Pool. Exercise equipment. Business services. Airport shuttle. Free parking. | 7373 Turfway Rd., Florence | 859/371–4400 | fax 859/371–3361 | www.cincinnatiairport.hilton.com | 306 rooms | $114–$149 | AE, D, DC, MC, V.

Knights Inn. The rooms and lobby are in bright, pastel colors. There's complimentary coffee, juice, and doughnuts every day. | Take exit 180 off I–75. Some kitchenettes, some microwaves. Cable TV. Pool. Business services. Some pets allowed. | 8049 Dream St., Florence | 859/371–9711 | fax 859/371–4325 | knightsinnflorenceky.com | 115 rooms | $35–$62 | AE, D, MC, V.

Red Roof Florence. Located near Cincinnati Northern Kentucky Airport, this hotel is within walking distance of shopping districts, the Turfway Race Track, and a few restaurants. Riverfront downtown Cincinnati, is 10 mi away, the Newport Aquarium is 11 mi, and the Kentucky Speedway is 30 mi. Continental breakfast. Cable TV. In-room data ports. Some in-room hot tubs. Indoor spa. Business services. | 7454 Turfway Rd., Florence | 859/647–2700 or 800/744–7644 | fax 859/647–9131 | 51 rooms, 1 suite, 1 hot tub suite | $60–$65 | AE, D, MC, V.

Signature Inn Turfway. You'll appreciate that the Cincinnati Airport is 10 minutes away and that Turfway Park is 2 minutes away. The lobby is cozy with plants and flower-filled urns. Rooms have queen-size beds, recliners, and 12-ft-long work desks. Patterned curtains coordinate with burgundy carpeting. Complimentary Continental breakfast. In-room data ports. Cable TV. Pool. Business services. Airport shuttle. Free parking. | 30 Cavalier Ct., Florence | 859/371–0081 or 800/822–5252 | fax 859/371–0081 | 125 rooms | $75 | AE, D, DC, MC, V.

Travelodge. The modern, two-story block and concrete building is cozy and casual. Wood furniture and shades of burgundy fill the rooms of this venerable chain. Some rooms have refrigerators. Cable TV. Business services. Free parking. | 8075 Steilen Dr., Florence | 859/371–0277 | fax 859/371–0286 | 100 rooms | $40–$80 | AE, D, DC, MC, V.

Wildwood Inn. Get your choice of theme: The inn's re-creation of a tropical rainforest and a South Sea Island housed under a domed atrium. Or find other themed suites such as the Cave, Nautical, Cupid, and Oriental suites. If you opt for the Happy Days suite, you'll be sleeping in a red 1959 Cadillac convertible-turned-queen-sized bed. A re-created African Village of 12 huts decorated with artwork and pelts surrounds a small lagoon with authentic African landscaping. Ask about special packages for families and couples. Restaurant. In-room refrigerators, in-room microwaves, in-room spas. Laundry services. Indoor pool, indoor wading pool. No pets. | 7809 U.S. 42, Florence | 859/371–6300 or 800/758–2335 | fax 859/525–0829 | joyce@wildwood-inn.com | www.wildwood-inn.com | 119 rooms, 63 suites | $85–$195, $150–$285 suites | D, MC, V.

FORT KNOX

MAP 6, E4

(Nearby towns also listed: Bardstown, Brandenburg, Elizabethtown, Falls of Rough, Louisville, Shepardsville)

This U.S. Military Reservation stretches across Bullitt, Hardin, and Meade counties and was named in honor of Revolutionary War General Henry T. Knox, who became the first Secretary of War. It's the home of the 1st Armored Division, created in 1940 out of former cavalry units in order to counter German Panzer tank units; and the United States Gold Depository. The granite, steel, and concrete vault containing most of the U.S. gold reserves sits atop a bare hill. Training maneuvers for the Armored Division include artillery fire whose percussive reports can often be heard as far away as Louisville, 40 mi northeast.

Information: Radcliff/Fort Knox Tourism Commission | Box 845, Radcliff, 40159-0845 | radcliff@ne.infi.net | www.come.to/radcliff | 800/334–7540 | fax 270/352–2075.

Attractions

Bridges To The Past. Take a 1½ hour Heritage Walking Tour of old stone bridges along a stretch of the historic Louisville & Nashville Railroad ("L & N Turnpike") predating the Civil War. You get a glimpse of the area exactly as it was 150 years ago. The area, on Ft. Knox, is void of electric lines, billboards and advertising, enabling you to inspect the condition of the bridges and have a leisurely walk through a natural 19th century valley. | Fort Knox | 800/334–7540 | Free | Call for hrs.

Patton Museum of Cavalry and Armor. Named after Gen. George S. Patton, commander of the U.S. tank corps in North Africa during World War II, this museum includes tanks of American and foreign forces, other weaponry, and uniforms. Artifacts include a 10-by-12-ft section of the Berlin Wall and equipment from Operation Desert Storm. | Building 4554, Fayette Ave., Fort Knox | 502/624–3812 | Free | Weekdays 9–4:30; weekends 10–4:30; in winter weekends 10–6.

United States Bullion Depository. For obvious reasons, the public isn't allowed inside the depository, but it's clearly visible from U.S. 31W. Built in 1937 to house U.S. gold reserves, the granite-faced facility is bombproof—so secure that during World War II it served as the temporary home to the Magna Carta and the British Crown Jewels. American treasures that have resided here include the Declaration of Independence and the United States Constitution. | Gold Vault Rd., Fort Knox | 502/352–1204.

ON THE CALENDAR
JULY: *World War II Battle Reenactment.* This event is held every Fourth of July on the grounds of the Patton Museum using 1940s vehicles and equipment. | 800/334–7540.
SEPT.: *Golden Armor Festival.* It's a real spit-and-polish display of the Army's 1st Armored Division's equipment, old and new. This annual event held the first full weekend of the month also includes a race, parade, and street festival. | 270/351–4450 (chamber of commerce).

Lodging
Gold Vault Inn. This two-story motel with inside corridors is just 1 mi from Fort Knox. Children under 12 stay free with adult. Free local telephone calls and complimentary coffee in lobby. Restaurant. Cable TV. Indoor pool. Hot tub. Video games. | 1225 N. Dixie Blvd., Radcliff | 270/351–1141 | fax 270/351–1157 | www.bestwestern.com | 94 | $64–$75 | AE, D, DC, MC, V.

Quality Inn. Casual, country-style marks this branch of the budget chain. Complimentary Continental breakfast. Cable TV. Pool. Video games. Business services. | 438 S. Dixie Blvd., Radcliff | 502/351–8211 | fax 502/351–3227 | 83 rooms | $60–$80 | AE, D, DC, MC, V.

FRANKFORT

MAP 6, F3

(Nearby towns also listed: Georgetown, Harrodsburg, Lexington, Louisville, Midway, Shelbyville, Versailles)

Situated at a double bend on the Kentucky River, the capitol of Kentucky is the headquarters for the General Assembly (which meets every other year), the Kentucky Supreme Court, and the Kentucky Department for Libraries and Archives, as well as other state government agencies.

The name originated with a pioneer named Stephen Frank, who was killed in a battle at a ford on the Kentucky River. The site became known as Frank's Ford, which, in time, became Frankfort. When Kentucky became a state in 1792, Frankfort landowner Andrew Holmes wooed the new state government to Frankfort with an offer of several town lots, building materials, rents from a tobacco warehouse, cash from citizens, and promotion of the location between the large settlements of Louisville and Lexington.

During the 19th century, in addition to being the seat of state government, Frankfort was important as a manufacturing center and an agricultural market. By the end of the century, there were a dozen distilleries in the area, producing 600 barrels of bourbon daily. (Buffalo Trace Distillery still operates in the city.)

Residences downtown and along the river date from the early 1800s, lending the city a flavorful, period charm. The Greek Revival Capitol building was completed in 1830. Designed by Lexington architect Gideon Shryrock, it has a 212-ft-high dome.

Information: Frankfort/Franklin County Tourist and Convention Commission | 100 Capital Ave., Frankfort, 40601 | 502/875–8687 or 800/960–7200 | info@frankfortky.org | www.frankfortky.org.

NEIGHBORHOODS

Downtown: As Kentucky's capital, Frankfort has its share of drab government buildings. Still, on the north side of the river, there are many beautifully restored buildings. Most of the streets in the northern end of town, which is at a bend of the river, are part of downtown's historic and shopping section. Streets in this area, the city's main tourist destination, are lined with restaurants and specialty shops, from antiques stores and art galleries, bookstores and boutiques selling Kentucky-made crafts and candies and a lot in between. Brick streets, park benches and white-globed lanterns set the scene on the St. Clair mall, which offers more nifty shops including an old-fashioned general store, and restaurants that, weather permitting, serve lunch al fresco.

TRANSPORTATION

Airports: Air access to Frankfort is via Louisville International Airport (502/367-4636), about 60 mi to the west, and Lexington Bluegrass Airport (859/425-3100), 25 mi east via I–64, U.S. 60, and the scenic Old Frankfort Pike, also known as U.S. 421.

Intra-city Transit: The three bus lines around town are operated by Frankfort Area Transit. Call the main terminal at Broadway and Main St. 502/875-8565 for fares and schedules.

Driving around Town: Rush hour increases traffic, though delays are unusual. Both metered and free street parking can be found in most parts of the city; there are no meters downtown. Garage rates vary, but you can find an all-day spot in one of the city's two garages for as little as $2. You can park for free in designated sections of the Old Train Depot, at the corner of Ann Street and Broadway, just a few minutes walk to downtown attractions.

OLD FRANKFORT

(approximately 3 hours)

Walking around the center of Kentucky's 18th- and 19th-century capital town is like taking a trip back in time. The **Kentucky History Center,** at the corner of Broadway and High Street, is a fine place to start your tour since its exhibits provide the historical perspective on the city and the state. The first old structure you'll encounter upon leaving the museum is the **Lieutenant Governor's Mansion** (420 High St.) a stately but cozy pink-brick Georgian house with moss green shutters. It was the original residence of Kentucky's highest elected official before the Governor's Mansion was built behind the current Capitol Building. Backtrack to Broadway and turn right. There are several interesting shops and restaurants along the street. An active railroad track runs parallel to it, so watch for trains. Among the most interesting of the shops and good for at least an hour of a bibliophile's time, is **Poor Richard's Books** (223 Broadway), owned by Kentucky Poet Laureate Richard Taylor. It carries both current and antiquarian volumes. Half a block away, at No. 239, is the **Old Capitol Antique Mall,** housing booths from dozens of dealers. You can find everything from pressed glass to a rolltop desk. After a book or antiques browse, cross Broadway and go over the tracks at Lewis Street. One block northeast, you'll be on the tree-shaded grounds of the **Old State Capitol** where the General Assembly met from 1830 to 1910. The Greek Revival building has a unique, freestanding stone stairway that seems to defy the laws of gravity. Return to Broadway, turn right, and walk two blocks west to Wilkinson Street. Go left and at the end of the block is the L-shaped, Federal-style **Liberty Hall** (218 Wilkinson St.). It was built in 1796 as the home of Kentucky's first U.S. Senator, John Brown. The grounds include the largest formal boxwood garden in the state. On the same four-acre site is the **Orlando Brown House** (202 Wilkinson St.), another marvelous example of Greek Revival style dating from 1835, designed by Gideon Shryrock. It was built for one of Senator Brown's sons. Finish your exploration of the historic district by walking east along **Wapping Street,** just south of the Orlando Brown House. It overlooks the Kentucky River and is lined with 19th-century houses still used as residences.

Attractions
ART AND ARCHITECTURE

Liberty Hall Historic Site. Liberty Hall was the home of U.S. Senator (KY), John Brown, who started building it in 1796. The L-shape house has a Palladian window and is furnished with antiques of the period, including several Brown family items. Formal gardens behind the house stretch to the Kentucky River. | 218 Wilkinson St., Frankfort | 502/227–2560 | libhall@dcr.net | www.libertyhall.org | Free | Mar. 1–mid Dec., Tues.–Sat. 10:30, noon, 1:30, 3; Sun. 1:30, 3.

The 1835 **Orlando Brown House** is on the four-acre Liberty Hall site and was built for one of Senator Brown's sons. Its style reflects the transition from Federal to Greek Revival. Modeled on the floor plan of the older house, it contains family china, silver, brass, furniture, and paintings. | 202 Wilkinson St. | 502/227–2560 | Free | Mar. 1–mid Dec., Tues.–Sat. 10:30, noon, 1:30, 3; Sun. 1:30, 3.

Lieutenant Governor's Mansion. This Georgian mansion dates from 1798 and was the home of 33 of the state's governors, until a governor's mansion was built in 1914. It's furnished in mid-1800s style. | 420 High St., Frankfort | 502/564–3449 | Free | Tues., Thurs.

Old State Capitol Museum. State government was headquartered here from 1827 to 1910. A self-supporting central stone staircase is an architectural highlight of the Greek Revival building designed by Gideon Shryock. Upstairs are the chambers of the Kentucky House and Senate preserved with their original 19th-century wooden desks and chairs. | 300 W. Broadway, Frankfort | 502/564–1792 | Free | Tues.–Sat. 10–5; Sun. 1–5; closed Mon.

State Capitol. The graceful Beaux Arts-style Kentucky State Capitol opened in 1910. Its exterior is Indiana limestone ornamented with 70 ionic columns. It is built on a Vermont-granite base. Marble, murals (including two depicting Daniel Boone), and paintings beautify the interior, which was strongly influenced by French architecture. The rotunda and dome are modeled on Paris's Hotel Des Invalides, a model of which is also over Napoléon's tomb. The grand staircase was inspired by that of the Paris Opera. And Marie Antoinette's drawing room at Versailles was copied for the State Reception Room. The Governor's Mansion and the unique Floral Clock are on the grounds surrounding the State Capitol. | Capitol Ave., Frankfort | 502/564–3449 | capitoltoursdesk@mail.state.kentucky.us | www | Free | Weekdays 8–4:30 guided tours; Sat. 8:30–4:30; Sun. 1–4:30; no tours on Sat. or Sun.

The outdoor working **Floral Clock** has a 34-ft face made up of thousands of plants that change seasonally. It is tilted above a reflecting pool so that the time can be read easily. Coins tossed into the pool are collected and donated to kids' charities. | Capitol Ave. | 502/564–3449.

The 1914 Beaux Arts **Governor's Mansion** matches the style of the capitol building. It was modeled after Marie Antoinette's Petit Trianon, her villa at Versailles. Constructed of native limestone, it sits on a bluff overlooking the Kentucky River. | Capitol Ave. | 502/564–3449 | Free | Tues. and Thurs.

CULTURE, EDUCATION, AND HISTORY

Daniel Boone's Grave. Boone died in Missouri in 1820. In 1845 the remains of Boone and his wife, Rebecca, were moved to the Frankfort Cemetery. An obelisk-shaped monument marks the grave, which overlooks the state capital. The Kentucky Veterans War Memorial is also here—it has the names of 16,000 soldiers who died in all U.S. wars except the Civil War. Also buried here is Richard M. Johnson, Martin Van Buren's vice president. | The site is 2 blocks from the Kentucky History Center | Frankfort Cemetery, 215 E. Main St., Frankfort | 502/227–2403 | Free (donations suggested) | Daily 8 AM–dusk.

Kentucky State University. The state's only public liberal-arts university has an enrollment of 2,500 students. The 309-acre campus is joined by a 166-acre research farm and aquaculture center that is developing new crops for Kentucky farmers. Other campus highlights are the King Farouk butterfly and moth collection and Kentucky Black heritage archives. | 400 E. Main St., Frankfort | 502/597–6000 | Free | Sept.–mid-May 8–4.

Kentucky Vietnam Veterans Memorial. The granite plaza has the names of 1,062 Kentuckians killed in Vietnam etched into its stone. The shadow of a giant sundial touches the name of each person on the anniversary of his death. Names of 22 soldiers missing in action are behind the sundial so the shadow never touches them. | The memorial is on the grounds of the Kentucky Department for Library and Archives on Coffeetree Rd. It's off Highway 676 between the regional jail and the library | Coffeetree Rd., Frankfort | 502/875–8687 | Free | Daily.

Kentucky History Center. Opened April 1999, this museum is anchored by a 20,000-square-ft exhibition called "A Kentucky Journey," tracing the state's history from prehistoric time, through the pioneer days, to the present. The central atrium features a green terrazzo-marble map of Kentucky with the counties outlined in brass. Other parts of the exhibit are facades of a coal company store, a flatboat, and a western Kentucky kitchen in the 1940s, before electricity was available in the rural parts of the state. A log cabin from Owen County is a key component of the pioneer history exhibit. The center also houses the Kentucky Historical Society's Research Library (known for its genealogical information). | 100 W. Broadway, Frankfort | 502/564–1792 or 877/444–7867 | www.kyhistory.org | Free | Museum: Tues.–Sat. 10–5; Thurs. 10–8; Sun. 1–5; closed Mon. Library: Mon.–Sat. 8–4; Thurs. 8–8; closed Sun.

MUSEUMS

Kentucky Military History Museum. A collection of weapons (including the famous Kentucky long rifle), flags, uniforms, and photographs from the archives of the Kentucky Historical Society is on display at this museum. Exhibits trace two centuries of Kentucky involvement in various military campaigns. | 128 E. Main St., Frankfort | 502/564–3265 | www.kyhistory.org | Free (donations suggested) | Tues.–Sat. 10–5 and Sun. 1–5.

OTHER POINTS OF INTEREST

The Library of the Kentucky Historical Society is the state's largest genealogy library. It consists of some 80,000 volumes as well as extensive holdings of maps, photographs, manuscripts, and other documents. | 100 W. Broadway | 502/564–1792 or 877/444–7867 | Free | Mon., Tues., Wed., Fri., Sat. 8–4; Thurs. 8–8; closed Sun.

ON THE CALENDAR

JUNE: *Capital Expo Festival.* This is a festival of pride in Kentucky with arts and crafts, contests, food, fireworks, and entertainment. Capital Expo takes place annually downtown around Fountain Place on the first Thursday through Saturday of the month. | 502/875–3524.

SEPT.: *Kentucky Folklife Festival.* This is a celebration of the state's rich cultural heritage. The festival presents the living traditions of the diverse people who call Kentucky home. You'll experience it all—from the driving rhythms of the River City Drum Corps to the mouth-watering taste of western Kentucky barbecue. The annual event is held in downtown Frankfort on the last weekend of the month. | 502/564–1792, ext. 4491.

NOV.: *Kentucky Book Fair.* Held on the campus of Kentucky State University, authors native to and living in the state are on hand to sign books and greet fans. It happens annually on the Saturday before Thanksgiving. | 502/227–4556 | fax 502/227–2831 | carl-west@mis.net.

Dining

Daniel's. Contemporary. It's known for its horseradish-encrusted sea bass, pork chops, and Derby City Hot Brown (that's a regional dish—a sandwich that's baked). The interior is contemporary, but it once was a Victorian pharmacy. | 243 W. Broadway, Frankfort | 502/875–5599 | Closed Sun. | $13.95–$23.95 | AE, MC, V.

Jim's Seafood. Seafood. You'll enjoy the view of the Kentucky River in this family-owned, nautical-themed restaurant. The foundation was formerly an 18th-century hemp mill. They're known for their crab legs and their Tilapia raised in spring water. Enjoy them inside in the limestone and wood contemporary dining room, or eat lunch at picnic tables on the deck. Kids' menu. Wine and beer only. | 950 Wilkerson St., Frankfort | 502/223–7448 | fax 502/227–7419 | Closed Sun. No lunch Sat. | $11–$20 | AE, D, MC, V.

Smile of Siam. Thai. A few travel posters of Thailand are the only decoration, but the food is elegant and delicious. Coconut milk, lemon grass, lime leaves, peanuts, and cilantro flavor dishes including Thai beef stick, chicken red curry, and pad Thai (stir-fried rice noodles). | 19 Century Plaza, Frankfort | 502/227–9934 | Closed Sun. | $7–$12 | MC, V.

Lodging

INEXPENSIVE

Bluegrass Inn. Free *USA Today* and free Continental breakfast await you at this contemporary motel. The stucco and brick building has a courtyard and outdoor pool. Some rooms have king-size beds. | Take I–64 to exit 58. Some refrigerators. Cable TV and free HBO. Pool. Free parking. Pets allowed (for fee). | 635 Versailles Rd., Frankfort | 502/695–1800 or 800/322–1802 | fax 502/695–1800, ext. 333 | 61 rooms | $36–$58 | AE, D, DC, MC, V.

Days Inn. Far enough from the highway to be quiet, the complex of redbrick and black wrought-iron has a reception building and two separate lodges with contemporary rooms. Complimentary Continental breakfast. Cable TV. Pool. | 1051 U.S. 127S, Frankfort | 502/875–2200 | fax 502/875–3574 | 122 rooms in 2 lodges | $50 | AE, D, DC, MC, V.

MODERATE

Best Western Parkside Inn. The attractive white-brick facade blends with historic Frankfort. Complimentary Continental breakfast. Cable TV. Indoor-outdoor pool. Hot tub. Exercise equipment. Video games. Business services. | 80 Chenault Rd., Frankfort | 502/695–6111 | fax 502/695–6111 | 98 rooms | $65–$70 | AE, D, DC, MC, V.

Cedar Rock Farm Bed & Breakfast. This B&B, 9 mi from town, is a large cottage on 110 rolling wooded acres, some fields have been cleared to grow hay and to provide pastures for a small flock of sheep, a donkey, and two horses. Trails crisscross the farm for walks in the woods, hilltop vistas, and creekside strolls. All the rooms have antique double beds, cozy seating, hand-made rugs, and tree-top views from the windows. Outdoors there are rocking chairs, chaise lounges, and gardens. Two rooms have private baths, and a third room—tucked under the eaves—can be combined with the Green Room to create a suite with shared bath. Homemade dessert is available in the evening. Complimentary breakfast. No room phones. TV in common area. Pool. | 3569 Mink Run Rd., Frankfort | 502/747–8754 | www.bbonline.com/ky/cedar/ | 3 rooms | $65–$110 | MC, V.

Hampton Inn Frankfort. This four-story hotel, with suites available, is convenient to local points of interest, and adjacent to several full service restaurants. Near the intersection of I–64 and U.S. 127, Exit 53B. Complimentary Continental breakfast, some refrigerators, in-room data ports. Pool. Exercise equipment, health club privileges. Free parking. | 1310 U.S. 127S, Frankfort | 502/223–7600 or 800/426–7866 | fax 502/223–9881 | 123 | $79 | AE, D, DC, MC, V.

Graystone Inn Bed and Breakfast. Built from birds-eye limestone marble in 1905 for U.S. Senator Thomas Paynter, this elegant house is in Frankfort's historic district. One of the antiques-furnished rooms has a fireplace. Complimentary full breakfast. Cable TV. Business services. | 229 Shelby St., Frankfort | 502/226–6196 | fax 502/875–7919 | vaughn@dcr.net | www.bbonline.com/ky/graystone | 3 rooms | $90–$110 | AE, V, MC.

Holiday Inn–Capital Plaza. Next door to the Frankfort Civic Center, the building matches the contemporary urban architecture of this part of the capital. The attractive lobby features a dramatic fountain; rooms are spacious. Restaurants, bar. In-room data ports, some refrigerators. Cable TV. Pool. Hot tub. Exercise equipment. Video games. Business services. | 405 Wilkinson St., Frankfort | 502/227–5100 or 800/465–4329 | fax 502/875–7147 | holiday.hicp@internet.mci.com | www.holidayinnfrankfort.com | 189 rooms | $80, $125–$175 suites | AE, D, DC, MC, V.

GEORGETOWN

MAP 6, F3

(Nearby towns also listed: Frankfort, Lexington, Midway, Paris)

Named in honor of George Washington, the seat of Scott County (formerly part of Bourbon County) is an architectural jewel, with many of its Greek Revival and antebellum homes still standing. It was founded on Royal Spring, from which, legend has it, water came for the first bourbon whiskey. (The Baptist minister, Elijah Craig, is reputed to have "invented" the corn-based whiskey here, which was named after Bourbon County.) Traditionally agricultural and surrounded by horse farms, Georgetown is now the site of North America's largest Toyota plant.

Information: **Georgetown/Scott County Tourism Commission** | Box 825, 399 Outlet Center Dr., Georgetown, 40324 | 502/863–2547 or 888/863–8600 | fax 502/863–2561.

Attractions

Cardome Centre. Built in 1904, as the home of Governor J. F. Robinson, the house was later used as a convent and school for the Sisters of the Visitation. Today it functions as a community center. The museum has displays and videotapes about the history of the area. On the grounds there is a massive sculpture of buffaloes carved from a single oak tree. You can take a "pictorial self-guided tour." | 800 Cincinnati Pike (U.S. 25N), Georgetown | 502/863–1575 | Free | Weekdays 9–4, or by appointment.

Royal Spring Park. Kentucky's largest spring, which produces 25 million gallons a day, is the source of the city's water supply. The park was the site of McClelland's Fort (1776). A former slave cabin has been moved to the park and serves as a museum and information center. | Water St., Georgetown | 502/863–2547 | Free | Tues.–Sat. 10–4; closed Sun.

Scott County Courthouse. The Scott County Courthouse, built in 1877, is in the Second Empire style and was designed by Pittsburgh architect Thomas Boyd. Today it serves as an office building. | 101 E. Main St., Georgetown | 502/863–7850 | Free | Weekdays 8:30–4:30.

Toyota Motor Manufacturing, Kentucky, Inc. Take a one-hour tour with video and tram ride through the stamping, body welding, and assembly areas of the plant. There's also a visitors' center with interactive exhibitions. Production at the plant is about 400,000 cars a year. | 1001 Cherry Blossom Way, Georgetown | 502/868–3027 or 800/866–4485 | Free |

Weekdays 10, noon, and 2; also Thurs. 6. Kids must be at least in first grade; reservations required.

ON THE CALENDAR

MAY: *Bluegrass Cycling Club "Horsey Hundred."* This annual bicycling trek goes through a hundred miles of the Bluegrass on the Sat. and Sun. of Memorial Day weekend. | Box 1397, Lexington | www.bgcycling.org.

JUNE: *Morgan's Raid.* Actors in period uniforms play out the famous Confederate Raiders Civil War invasion of the town. In 1862, Captain John Hunt Morgan and his mounted soldiers entered the town, destroyed Union supplies, and camped out on the courthouse lawn for two days. This reenactment happens annually in the third full week of the month. | 502/863–2547 or 888/863–8600.

JULY, AUG.: *Cincinnati Bengals Training Camp.* You can watch the NFL team at their annual practice camp at Georgetown College from mid to late July through late August. | 502/863–2547 or 888/863–8600.

SEPT.: *Festival of the Horse.* This is the state's annual festival dedicated to Kentucky's "First Animal." Exhibitions about horses, arts and crafts, music, a Friday kids' parade, a Saturday Grand Parade, 5-km (3-mi) and 10-km (6-mi) runs, and a horse show are among the events. Look for it the last full weekend in Sept. | 502/863–2547.

Dining

Fava's Restaurant. American. In 1910, this was Louie Fava's ice cream parlor and confectionary. Reminders of that time are preserved with the display of the old soda fountain, the tin ceiling, original tile floor, and photographs of the old town. Today Fava's is an intimate eatery which seats 80, is surrounded by antique shops, and serves great home-cooked meals. The dinners include cajun dishes, "all you can eat" cat fish, prime rib, and jumbo shrimp. A hot bar and salad bar are included. | 159 East Main, Georgetown | 502/863–4383 | Breakfast also available. Closed Sun. | $5–$13 | AE, MC, V.

Lodging

Hampton Inn Georgetown. This four-story hotel with interior corridors and elevators has spacious rooms with in-room coffeemakers. Cribs are available. Complimentary Continental breakfast. In-room data ports, some refrigerators. Cable TV. Pool. Hot tub. Exercise equipment. | 128 Darby Dr., Georgetown | 502/867–4888 or 800/426–7866 | fax 502/867–7712 | www.ohwy.com/ky/h/higeorge.htm | 75 rooms | $79 | AE, D, DC, MC, V.

Shoney's Inn. The lobby is modern with brass chandeliers and lamps. It's got trees and lots of greenery. The rooms are predominantly light green. | Take I–75 to Exit 126. In-room data ports. Cable TV. Pool. Business services. Free breakfast bar across the driveway. | 200 Shoney Dr., Georgetown | 502/868–9800 or 800/552–4667 | fax 502/868–9800, ext. 141 | 119 rooms | $51–$65 | AE, D, DC, MC, V.

GILBERTSVILLE

MAP 6, B5

(Nearby towns also listed: Cadiz, Mayfield, Paducah)

Gilbertsville is the gateway to two major outdoor recreational areas: Kentucky Dam Village State Resort Park and Kentucky Lake, the largest lake in the state. The resort features a lodge (which used to be a TVA hospital), cottages, a campground, and a marina, as well as a post office and numerous shops. Boating, fishing, golf, and tennis are among the available activities.

Information: **Marshall County Tourist Commission** | Box 129, 2261 U.S. 62, Gilbertsville, 42044 | 270/362–4128 or 800/467–7145 | mctc2@ispchannel.net | www.kentuckylake.

com/mctc. **Kentucky Dam and Visitors Center** | U.S. 641N, Gilbertsville, 42044 | 270/362–4221.

Attractions

Barkley Lock and Dam. The dam provides flood control and power for a hydroelectric generating plant, while the lock and canal are navigation aids. An information and visitors center is on site for those using the lake for recreation. | U.S. 62, Gilbertsville | 270/362–4236 | Free | Weekdays.

Kenlake State Resort Park. (see also Cadiz) Situated on 160,300-acre Kentucky Lake, the park's 1,800 acres feature hiking trails, picnic areas, playgrounds, a 9-hole golf course, and indoor tennis courts. Water sports include fishing, swimming, waterskiing, and boating. Cottages and a lodge with restaurant provide accommodations; a campground is also available. | 542 Kenlake Rd., Hardin | 270/474–2211 or 800/325–0143 | Free; fees for golf course, tent and trailer sites, and equipment rental | Daily.

Kentucky Dam. About 20 mi from Paducah, this dam controls the introduction of the Tennessee River into the Ohio. At 206 ft high and 8,422 ft long, it's the largest dam in the Tennessee Valley Authority system, supporting U.S. 62/641 where the highway crosses the northern part of Kentucky Lake. There's a viewing balcony, and tours of the powerhouse are available by appointment. | U.S. 641/62 | 270/362–4221 | Free | Daily.

Kentucky Dam Village State Resort Park. The 1,351-acre park is open year-round and features a pool, a beach, a convention center, stables, a full-service marina (which supports boating, fishing, and other water sports), and a 4,000-ft airstrip. You can also play 18-hole golf, tennis, and mini-golf. | U.S. 641S, Gilbertsville | 270/362–4271 | www.kystateparks.com/agencies/parks/kydam2.htm | Fee for camping | Daily.

Land Between the Lakes National Recreation Area (LBL). Kentucky Lake (surface area 160,000 acres) and Lake Barkley (58,000 acres), the state's two largest bodies of water, border a 170,000-acre wooded finger of land containing some 200 mi of hiking and horseback trails. The lakes are noted for their excellent fishing and boating. Camping is allowed in the backwoods areas of the park year-round with a permit. Now administered by the National Forest Service, the recreational area was created in the 1940s by the Tennessee Valley Authority, when the Cumberland and Tennessee rivers were dammed for hydroelectric power. | 100 Van Morgan Dr., Golden Pond | www.lbl.org | Free | Year-round, daily.

Some of the highlights of the recreation area include animal-watching areas, historic houses, and educational facilities. A re-creation of the prairie habitat that existed here 200 years ago, the 750-acre **Elk and Bison Prairie Preserve** contains herds of bison and elk grazing on native grasses. Wild turkeys, red-tailed hawks, and several species of owl are among the large birds. A 3½-mi loop road allows car tours of the preserve. | 100 Van Morgan Dr., Golden Pond | 270/924–2000 or 800/525–7077 | www.lbl.org | $3 per vehicle | Daily, dawn to dusk.

A multimedia show about the ecology of Golden Pond and a planetarium are highlights of the **Golden Pond Visitor Center.** Exhibitions rotate with the seasons. | 100 Van Morgan Dr., Golden Pond | 270/924–2000 or 800/525–7077 | www.lbl.org | Free; $2.75 for the multimedia show | Daily 9–5.

The lifestyle and farming methods of a mid-19th-century family farm are re-created at **The Homeplace (1850).** Guides dressed in period clothes chat with visitors while going about their chores. An interpretive center has farm-life exhibitions and an audiovisual presentation. | Travel 12 mi south from the visitor center, on The Trace | 270/924–2000 or 800/525–7077 | www.lbl.org | $3.50 | Apr.–Nov., Mon.–Sat. 9–5, Sun. 10–5.

The Nature Station is an environmental education center offering live animal exhibitions and interpretive programs. You can rent a canoe or a mountain bike to explore the 5,000-acre Environmental Education Area, or take a bald eagle–viewing excursion in the winter. | From the visitor center, travel 8 mi north on The Trace. Turn on Mulberry Flat Rd., and travel another 5 mi | 270/924–2000 or 800/525–7077 | $3.50 | Mon.–Sat. 9–5; Sun. 10–5.

GILBERTSVILLE

INTRO
ATTRACTIONS
DINING
LODGING

ON THE CALENDAR

JAN.: *Gathering of Eagles.* Park guides lead tours of bald and golden eagle nesting areas. | 270/924–2000.

MAR.: *Bridge Tournament.* Enthusiasts of the game engage in a weekend of competition. | 270/924–2000.

APR.: *Log Cabin Quilting Bee and Exhibit.* Visitors can watch or practice the historic art of quilting, and view examples of traditional and contemporary work on display. | 270/924–2000 or 800/525–7077.

APR.: *Nature Photography Weekend.* Nature lovers receive tips and opportunities for capturing on film the beauty of the area. The weekend's activities are based in the Nature Station. | 270/924–2000 or 800/525–7077.

APR.: *Nature Photography Workshop.* Bring your camera and swap tips with other enthusiasts, both professional and amateur. There's a slide show and contest, too. | 270/474–2211 or 800/325–0143.

MAY: *Crafts in the Village.* Artisans of traditional arts and crafts offer their work at a weekend sale and exhibition. | 270/924–2000.

JUNE: *River Sounds Traditional Music Festival.* Bluegrass and folk-music performers gather for a weekend of entertainment. | 270/924–2000 or 800/525–7077.

OCT.: *Aurora Country Festival.* Traditional skills demonstrations and retail booths celebrate autumns of the past and present. | 270/474–2211 or 800/325–0143.

OCT.: *Fall Crafts in the Village.* This is the autumn version of the May event. | 270/362–4271.

Dining

Brass Lantern. American. Cathedral ceilings, rough cedar beams, and brick floors suggest an old-Kentucky atmosphere. The menu features prime rib, charbroiled lobster, and grasshopper pie. A salad bar and kids' menu are also available. | 16593 U.S. 68E, Aurora | 270/474–2773 | Reservations not accepted Sat. | Closed late Dec.–late Mar., and Mon.–Tues. in mid-June–mid-Aug. No lunch | $17–$29 | AE, D, DC, MC, V.

Kheeli's Cafe. American Casual. This 50's, 60's & 70's theme restaurant in the Ramada Inn has a "retro" black and white checker/formica decor with pictures of James Dean, Elvis, and other rock stars. Carry-out is available. Breakfast selections include The Jitterbug and The Diddley Bop; the lunch and dinner menu includes burgers, barbecued ribs, chicken, and catfish. Sunday brunch starts at 10 AM. One mi from the Kentucky Dam. | 2184 U.S. 62, Gilbertsville | 270/362–4278 or 800/628–6538 | www.kentuckylake.com/ramada/ | Breakfast also available. No supper Sun. | $7–$14 | AE, D, DC, MC, V.

Patti's 1880's Restaurant and Settlement. American. Set in an historical log-cabin village, this antique-furnished restaurant serves 2-inch thick pork chops, mile-high meringue pies, and flower pot bread, and features a kids' menu. The settlement has seven gift shops in old cabins along a winding stream. | 1793 J.H. O'Bryan Ave., Grand Rivers | 888/736–2515 | Closed week of Dec. 25 | $16–$26 | D, DC, M, V.

Lodging

Bel Air Motel. The Bel Air is within minutes of Kentucky Dam Village and Marina. The rooms are spacious with two queen-sized beds; studio apartments are also available. There is a shaded picnic area with tables, grills, and shuffleboard. Located just off I–24. Some kitchenettes. Cable TV. Pool. Playground. No pets. | 7428 U.S. 641N, Gilbertsville | 270/362–4254 | www.kentuckylake.com/belair | 18 rooms | $55 | D, MC, V.

Early American. This one-story motel, located 1½ mi from the town center, features modern rooms with a choice of double or king-sized beds. Picnic area. Some kitchenettes. Cable TV. Pool. Playground. Some pets allowed. | 16749 U.S. 68, Aurora | 270/474–2241 | 18 rooms | $45–$65 | AE, D, MC, V.

Kenlake Hotel. Located inside the state park, this state-owned lodge has rooms overlooking the lake, gardens, and woods. All park facilities are available to guests. Cottage lodgings include kitchenware and linens. Dining room. Picnic area. TV. Pool, wading pool. 9-hole golf course, putting green, tennis. Playground. | 542 Kenlake Rd., Aurora | 270/474–2211 or 800/325–0143 | fax 270/474–2018 | 48 rooms in lodge; 34 cottages | $42–$70; cottages $74–$100 | Closed Christmas week | AE, D, DC, MC, V.

Moors Resort & Marina. This year-round resort on Kentucky Lake has a log cabin lodge with fireplace and one-, two-, three-, and four-bedroom lakeside cottages. Their restaurant has "down home cooking." The full service marina has boat and houseboat rentals, fishing licenses, and guide service. You'll find RV sites and primative camping sites, too. Restaurant. Pool. Golf privileges, miniature golf. Beach, boating, fishing. Video games. Playground. Pets allowed. | 570 Moors Rd., Gilbertsville | 270/362–8361 or 800/626–5472 | fax 270/362–8172 | www.moorsresort.com | 24 rooms in lodge; 30 cottages | $79 | AE, D, MC, V.

Ramada Inn Resort. Located 1½ mi from Kentucky Dam Village State Resort Park, this 45-year-old hotel features three stories of rooms decorated in earth tones. Restaurant, complimentary breakfast. Pool. Hot tub. Playground. Some pets allowed. | 2184 U.S. 62, Gilbertsville | 270/362–4278 | fax 270/362–9845 | 95 rooms, 4 suites | $45–55 | AE, D, MC, V.

Village Inn Lodge. Rooms with private balconies or patios overlook woods and water at this 1950s two-story, horseshoe-shaped stucco complex. Wood-frame cabins are also available. Since it's state-owned, the lodge offers free access to all Kentucky Dam Village State Resort Park facilities. (There's a fee for use of the golf course.) Dining room, picnic area. Kitchenettes (in cottages), some microwaves. Cable TV. Pool, wading pool. 18-hole golf course, mini-golf, tennis. Marina, public beach, paddle boats. Horseback riding. Airport shuttle. | Kentucky Dam Village State Park, U.S. 641, Gilbertsville | 270/362–4271 or 800/325–0146 | fax 270/362–2981 | 72 rooms in lodge; 70 cottages | $52–$74, $86–$200 cottages | AE, D, DC, MC, V.

GLASGOW

MAP 6, E5

(Nearby towns also listed: Bowling Green, Cave City, Horse Cave, Mammoth Cave National Park)

Founded by Scottish settlers in 1799 near a large spring, Glasgow is the county seat and commercial center of Barren County. It's also the town nearest Barren River State Resort Park and Barren Lake, both recreational destinations in this part of the state, and is just 1½ mi from Mammoth Cave National Park. Named after the city in Scotland, this Glasgow celebrates that connection with an annual Highland Games weekend.

Information: **Glasgow/Barren County Chamber of Commerce** | 118 E. Public Square, Glasgow, 42141 | 270/651–3161 or 800/264–3161.

Attractions

Barren River Dam and Lake. Maintained by the Army Corps of Engineers, this dam rises 146 ft and is 3,970 ft long. The dam has created a 10,000-acre lake (noted for its bass fishing) across Barren and Allen counties. Facilities include boat ramps, as well as picnicking, swimming, and camping areas. | 11088 Finney Rd., Glasgow | 270/646–2055 | Fees for camping | Daily, 6:30–4:00.

Barren River Lake State Resort Park. This park, covering over 2,000 acres, features a lodge, a swimming pool, riding stables, nature trails, and a marina serving the lake. There are also 22 two-bedroom cottages to rent, and tent and trailer sites. Other recreational facilities include tennis courts, bicycle trails, and an 18-hole golf course. | 1149 State Park Rd., Lucas | 270/646–2151 or 800/325–0057 | www.kystateparks.com/agencies/parks/barren.htm | Fees for camping and golf | Year-round, daily.

South Central Kentucky Cultural Center. You'll find historical displays focusing on the region's relationship with coal. There are also other cultural exhibits. | 200 W. Water St., Glasgow | 270/651–9792 or 888/256–6941 | fax museum@glasgowky.com | Free | Weekdays 8–4, closed weekends.

ON THE CALENDAR

MAY: *Glasgow Highland Games.* Highland dancing and bagpipe and harp competitions provide the celebration's Gaelic flavor. Events include foot races, family activities, and a variety of amateur sports. | 1149 State Park Rd., Lucas | 270/651–3141.

SEPT.: *Bee Spring Old Timer's Day.* Held on a Saturday early in the month, the community festival features outdoor drama, BBQ, crafts, and Bluegrass music. Bee Spring is in Kentucky's caveland region on Hwy. 259, just west of Cave National Park. | 270/286–9219 or 800/624–8687 | www.cavesandlakes.com.

Dining

Bolton's Landing. American. This gray-and-blue frame family restaurant boasts a completely made-from-scratch menu which includes angel biscuits and country ham Alfredo. A kids' menu is also available. | 2433 Scottsville Rd. (U.S. 31E), Glasgow | 270/651–8008 | Closed Sun. No lunch Sat. | $7–$17 | AE, D, DC, MC, V.

The Jackson House. Southern. The restaurant features country cooking and seats 180 guests in a bright, open dining area dominated by light oak. A favorite is the lunch and dinner buffet with smoked and barbecued meats, catfish, meatloaf, and vegetables. A "table serve" menu is also available with ribeye steak, catfish, country ham, ribs, and homemade desserts. | 1463 W. Main St., Glasgow | 270/651–8890 | mammothcave.com/jackson.htm | Closed Sun. No lunch Sat. | $6–$13 | AE, MC, V.

Lodging

Comfort Inn. This two-story motel has exterior corridors and is just off Cumberland Parkway, Exit 11 at Glasgow's Business Center. Complimentary Continental breakfast, some microwaves, some refrigerators, some in-room hot tubs. Pool. | Cumberland Pky., Glasgow | 270/651–9099 or 800/228–5150 | fax 270/651–1099 | www.musselmanhotels.com | 61 rooms | $49–$55 | AE, D, DC, MC, V.

Days Inn of Glasgow. The two-story motel has inside corridors and features in–room coffee makers, and free local calls. Mini-suites are also available. Just off Cumberland Parkway, Exit 11 at Glasgow's Business Center, adjacent to U.S. 31E. Restaurant, some microwaves, some refrigerators, some in-room hot tubs. Indoor pool. Spa. | 105 Days Inn Blvd., Glasgow | 270/651–1757 or 800/329–7466 | fax 270/651–1755 | www.musselmanhotels.com | 59 rooms | $55 | AE, D, DC, MC, V.

Four Seasons Country Inn. Furnished with antique reproductions, this three-story Victorian inn is just a few minutes' drive from Barren River Lake. Complimentary Continental breakfast, refrigerators. Cable TV. Pool. Business services. | 4107 Scottsville Rd. (U.S. 31E), Glasgow | 270/678–1000 | fax 270/678–1017 | 21 rooms, 2 suites | $78–$140; suites $125 | AE, D, DC, MC, V.

Houston Inn. Chain-style basic, this two-story, family-owned establishment is 10 mi from Barren River Lake. Restaurant. Cable TV. Pool. Some pets allowed (fee). | 1003 W. Main St., Glasgow | 270/651–5191 or 800/452–7469 | fax 270/651–9233 | 78 rooms | $35–$45 | AE, D, DC, MC, V.

Louie B. Nunn Lodge. This state-owned lodge is located inside the Barren River Lake State Resort Park. Guests have access to all park facilities. Picture windows in the dining room overlook the 10,000-acre lake, and cottages dot the woods along the water. Gift shop. Dining room. Kitchenettes (in cottages). TV. Pool, wading pool. 18-hole golf course, tennis. Kids' programs in the summer. | 1149 State Park Rd., Lucas | 270/646-2151 or 800/325-0057 | fax 270/646–3645 | 51 rooms; 22 cottages | rooms $58–$78; cottages $144–$175 | Closed Christmas week | AE, D, DC, MC, V.

GREENVILLE

(Nearby towns also listed: Dawson Springs, Madisonville)

Named after Revolutionary War general Nathanael Greene, Greenville was originally settled in 1799 and incorporated as a town in 1812. Commercial center for the area's surface coal mines, Greenville is the seat of Muhlenberg County. Lake Malone State Park offers seasonal recreation including camping and boating.

Information: Greenville/Muhlenberg County Chamber of Commerce | Box 313, Greenville, 42345 | 270/338–5422.

Attractions

Duncan House Museum and Art Gallery. Learn about the area's early coal mining days. | 122 S. Cherry, Greenville | 270/338–2605 | Free | Tues.–Fri. 1–4, weekends 2–4, closed Mon.

Lake Malone State Park. The 788-acre lake is surrounded by pine-topped cliffs as high as 200 ft. Other natural features of this 338-acre park include sandstone bluffs and a natural-rock bridge. Fishing, hiking, and camping (tent and trailer) are the main recreations. | From Western Kentucky Pky., exit at Central City, then take U.S. 431 to KY 973 to the park. It's 22 mi south of Central City | KY 973, Dunmor | 270/657–2111 | www.kystateparks.com/agencies/parks/lmalone.htm | Free; fee for camping | Apr.–mid-Nov., daily.

ON THE CALENDAR

FEB., APR., JULY, OCT., DEC.: *Muhlenberg Community Theatre.* A variety of amateur productions is presented every other month throughout the year. | 502/338–7165.
MAR.: *Lone Star World Champion Rodeo.* Riding, roping, and all the usual tests of cowboy skill take place at the Agriculture and Convention Center. | 502/338–5422.
SEPT: *Everly Brothers Homecoming.* This is a Labor Day weekend tradition with Rock 'n Roll Hall of Famers and county natives the Everly Brothers. Central City hosts the annual hometown concert. Bring a lawn chair or blanket and enjoy Everly Brothers classics. The show has featured famous acts like Diamond Rio, the Kentucky Headhunters, John Prine, Chet Atkins, and John Berry. | 270/754–9603.
OCT.: *Muhlenberg County Homemakers Arts and Crafts Fair.* An exhibition and sale is held in the Greenville North Middle School. | 502/338–5422.

Dining

Brother's Bar B Que. Barbecue. Brother's, in the heart of downtown is in a circa 1893 building listed in the National Register of Historic Places. Gospel music plays in the background, autographed photographs of gospel groups hang on the walls, and antiques are displayed in the windows. The restaurant seats 65, and the menu features ribs, chicken, pork, prime rib, lasagna, potato skins, and homade pies. | 115 Main St., Greenville | 270/338–3384 | Closed Sun. No supper Sat. | $4–$11 | MC, V.

Lodging

Everly's Lake Malone Inn. Don Everly's rustic, cedar and stone, three-story resort is on 91 acres adjacent to Lake Malone State Park and a marina, about 20 mi from Greenville. Some rooms have fireplaces and balconies overlooking the lake. The inn has two 2-bedroom suites each with a sitting room, patio, and three baths. Everly Brothers' memorabilia is found throughout the inn and on Friday and Saturday evenings there are live country music performances. The country restaurant is famous for its prime rib. The inn is 17 mi south of Greenville on KY 181, east on KY 973. Restaurant. Golf privileges, tennis. Exercise equipment, hiking. Beach, boating. Playground. | 5333 KY 973, Dunmor | 270/657–2121 or 800/264–3602 | fax 270/657–2129 | everlys@pubwire.com | 59 rooms | $57 | AE, D, MC, V.

Shady Cliff Resort. This privately owned resort on 10,000 acres overlooks Lake Malone, and features a rustic-looking lodge with modern interior decor. It's about 18 mi from Greenville off Rte. 181. Dining room. Cable TV. Pool. Business services. Laundry facilities. Bring your own linens for the cabin. | 530 Lake Malone Rd., Lewisburg | 270/657–9580 | 24 rooms, 1 cabin | $42–$70, $100 cabin | AE, D, DC, MC, V.

HARRODSBURG

MAP 6, F4

(Nearby towns also listed: Danville, Lexington, Springfield)

Founded in 1774, by James Harrod, this is the oldest town in the state and the first permanent settlement. A state park, with a replica of the original fort, is near the center of town. Many buildings date from the 18th century. Morgan Row, a group of row houses on Chiles Street dating from 1807, is possibly the oldest still-standing row west of the Appalachians. Manufacturing and tourism are important components of the current economy.

Information: **Harrodsburg/Mercer County Tourist Commission** | Box 283, Dept. KTG98, 103 S. Main, Harrodsburg 40330 | 859/734–2364 or 800/355–9192 | www.harrodsburgky.com.

Attractions

Dixie Belle Riverboat Tours. Cruise on a 149-passenger paddlewheel riverboat offering daily one-hour excursions along the scenic Kentucky River Palisades—high limestone cliffs, and the High Bridge built in 1877. The riverboat is docked at Shaker Village Landing, 7 mi east of the center of Harrodsburg. | 3501 Lexington Rd., Harrodsburg | 859/734–5411 or 800/734–5611 | www.shakervillageky.org | $6 | Apr.–Oct.

Harrodsburg Pottery and Craft Shop. Watch craftspeople dip candles (regular/paraffin and beeswax) in one room of the shop. A garden and greenhouse next to the century-old building sells dried and fresh herbs. Potpourri, stoneware, soaps, dried herbs, and potted plants from the green house are among items sold in the shop. | 1026 Lexington Rd., Harrodsburg | 859/734–9991 | Free | Apr.–Dec., daily; Jan.–Mar., weekends.

Morgan Row. Located in the pre-Civil War historic district, this is possibly the oldest (circa 1807) still-standing row house west of the Appalachians. Formerly a stagecoach stop, it now contains the Harrodsburg Historical Society Museum. | 220–222 S. Chiles St., Harrodsburg | 859/734–5985 | Free | Tues.–Sat. 1–4.

Old Fort Harrod State Park. Visitors can climb around a replica of the original 1774 fort, or visit the petting zoo, blockhouses, pioneer cemetery, or period cabins—one of which was the site of Abraham Lincoln's parents' wedding. Costumed craftspeople give demonstrations of broom making, basket weaving, and blacksmithing. | 100 S. College St., Harrodsburg | 859/734–3314 | www.kystateparks.com/agencies/parks/ftharrd2.htm | $3.50 | Mar.–Nov.

Old Mud Meeting House. The mud thatch walls of this Dutch Reformed Church meetinghouse (the first west of the Appalachians) have been restored to their original condition. The building dates from the beginning of the 19th century. Contact the Mercer County Historical Society for a guided tour. | Dry Branch Pike, off U.S. 68, Harrodsburg | 859/258–3000 | Free | By appointment only.

Shaker Village of Pleasant Hill. Low stone walls crisscross 2,700 acres of rolling countryside in this restored 19th-century Shaker village. More than 30 brick and stone buildings, including the meetinghouse, trustees' house, and millhouse are furnished in the Shaker style. Men and women of the religious sect lived separately, so most buildings have two entrances and even two staircases. Costumed craftspeople give tours and make furniture, candles, brooms, and quilts, which are for sale. Allow the better part of a day to explore the village fully. Most buildings are equipped for overnight accommodations *(see Inn at Shaker Hill)*, if you want to linger. There's also a restaurant *(see Trustees House at Shaker Hill)* that serves Shaker food family-style. | 3501 Lexington Rd., Harrodsburg | 859/734–5411 or 800/734–5611 | fax 859/734–7278 | www.shakervillageky.org | $10 | Apr.–Oct.

ON THE CALENDAR

JUNE: *The Fort Harrod Heritage Festival* highlights pioneer "Living History" encampments, and re-enactments of Native American attacks on the fort. Entertainment, bluegrass and country music performances, crafts demonstrations, and an arts and crafts market are also all part of this weekend festival. | 859/734–3314.

JUNE–AUG.: *The Legend of Daniel Boone* comes to life through the dramatization of the life and adventures of Kentucky's most famous pioneer presented in the James Harrod Amphitheater. | 859/734–3346 or 800/852–6663.

AUG.: *The Pioneer Days Festival* is an arts and crafts bonanza and an annual antique car show. | 859/734–2365.

Dining

Beaumont Inn Dining Room. Southern. Once a prestigious girls' school, this 1845 mansion was converted to an inn in 1917, and has been operated by the same family ever since. Accented by period antiques, the dining room features a kids' menu, and choices such

KODAK'S TIPS FOR PHOTOGRAPHING PEOPLE

Friends' Faces
- Pose subjects informally to keep the mood relaxed
- Try to work in shady areas to avoid squints
- Let kids pick their own poses

Strangers' Faces
- In crowds, work from a distance with a telephoto lens
- Try posing cooperative subjects
- Stick with gentle lighting—it's most flattering to faces

Group Portraits
- Keep the mood informal
- Use soft, diffuse lighting
- Try using a panoramic camera

People at Work
- Capture destination-specific occupations
- Use tools for props
- Avoid flash if possible

Sports
- Fill the frame with action
- Include identifying background
- Use fast shutter speeds to stop action

Silly Pictures
- Look for or create light-hearted situations
- Don't be inhibited
- Try a funny prop

Parades and Ceremonies
- Stake out a shooting spot early
- Show distinctive costumes
- Isolate crowd reactions
- Be flexible: content first, technique second

From *Kodak Guide to Shooting Great Travel Pictures* © 2000 by Fodor's Travel Publications

as corn pudding and two-year-old Kentucky-cured country ham for adult diners. | 638 Beaumont Inn Dr., Harrodsburg | 859/734–3381 | Jacket and tie | Closed Jan.–Feb. | $20–$27 | AE, D, DC, MC, V.

Shaker Village Trustees' Office Inn. American. Part of Shaker Village at Pleasant Hill, this restaurant embraces the village's period theme, with wooden tables and chairs, and servers in period dress. Known for Shaker and traditional local dishes, the inn serves breakfast, lunch, and dinner family-style. Try the Shaker lemon pie and some of the oven-fresh bread. A kids' menu is available. There is no smoking on the premises. | Inn at Pleasant Hill, 3501 Lexington Rd., Harrodsburg | 800/734–5611 | $17–$25 | MC, V.

Lodging

Bauer Haus Bed & Breakfast. This 1880's Victorian home is listed on the National Register of Historic Places and designated a Kentucky Landmark. There are four large guest rooms on the second floor of the main house—two rooms have private baths and two rooms share a bath. The telephone, VCR, and CD player are in the commons area. The carriage house suite features a kitchenette, cable TV, VCR, CD player, telephone, whirlpool tub, and shower. Bauer Haus is within walking distance to Old Fort Harrod State Park and Historic Harrodsburg and near Lake Herrington's water sports. Complimentary breakfast. Golf packages. | 362 North College St. (U.S. 127), Harrodsburg | 859/734–6289 or 877/734–6289 | fax 859/734–9216 | www.bbonline.com/ky/bauer | 4 rooms, 1 suite | $70–$115 | AE, MC, V.

Baxter House Bed & Breakfast. This circa 1912, 2 ½-story brick home was originally built in 1840 as a two-room log cabin—today, the hand-hewn logs are visible only from the basement. The B&B, a member of the Harrodsburg Historical Society, sits on 7 acres amidst thoroughbred horse farms. A sunporch overlooks the duckpond. The commons area has a VCR and video library and all rooms have private baths, fireplace, CD player, coffee pot, and clock radio. Packages are available for local events and attractions. Complimentary breakfast. In-room data ports, microwaves, refrigerators. TV in common area. | 1677 Lexington Rd., Harrodsburg | 859/734–4877 or 888/809–4457 | baxterhouse@mindspring.com | 3 rooms | $79–$119 | AE, D, DC, MC, V.

Beaumont Inn. Complete with stately white columns, this antebellum mansion is located near Harrodsburg's historic district, among 30 acres of woods. Dining room. Cable TV. Pool, wading pool. Business services. | 638 Beaumont Inn Dr., Harrodsburg | 859/734–3381 or 800/352–3992 | fax 859/734–6897 | 33 rooms in 4 buildings | $85–$110 | Closed late Dec.–Feb. | AE, D, MC, V.

Best Western. A typical chain accommodation, this motel offers basic rooms with modern amenities. It's 3 mi south of downtown. Complimentary Continental breakfast. Some refrigerators. Cable TV. Pool. Business services. | 1680 Danville Rd., Harrodsburg | 859/734–9431 | fax 859/734–5559 | www.bestwestern.com | 69 rooms | $60–$65 | AE, D, DC, MC, V.

Inn at Pleasant Hill. Thirty restored structures are set in a bucolic Shaker Village and filled with appropriate reproduction furniture and hand-woven fabrics and rugs. You can choose from accommodations in several of the buildings, including the old mill and the spacious meetinghouse. Riverboat cruises are offered. Situated on 2,800-acres of rolling blue hills, you'll find 80 rooms in 15 buildings of this restored 18th-century Shaker village and designated national landmark. All rooms are comfortably furnished with Shaker reproductions and handwoven rugs. There are 18 museum buildings featuring Shaker artifacts. The Trustee's Office Inn restaurant is on the premises. Restaurant. No TV. Boating. Hiking, horseback riding. | 3500 Lexington Rd., Harrodsburg | 859/734–5411 or 800/734–5611 | fax 859/734–7278 | diana@shakervillageky.org | www.shakervillageky.org | 81 rooms in 18 buildings | $60–$85 rooms, $80–$200 suites and houses | closed Christmas Eve and Christmas Day | MC, V.

HAZARD

(Nearby towns also listed: Buckhorn, Daniel Boone National Forest, Pikeville, Prestonsburg)

Named in honor of Oliver Hazard Perry, hero of the Battle of Lake Erie during the War of 1812, Hazard has long been a logging and coal-mining center. Buckhorn Lake State Park is 25 mi northwest, and offers boating, camping, and fishing.

Information: Perry County Tourism Commission | 601 Main St., Suite 3, Hazard 41701 | 606/439-2659.

Attractions

Bobby Davis Memorial Park. This park was created in the late 1940s on land donated by Bobby Davis's father, to honor both his son and the other hometown boys killed in World War II. In addition to a picnic area, war memorial, and herbal garden, the grounds are planted with more than 400 varieties of trees and shrubs. | 234 Walnut St., Hazard | 606/439-4325 | Free | Daily.

The small **Bobby Davis Park Museum** on the park grounds contains collections and exhibitions relating to local history. | 234 Walnut St. | 859/439-4325 | Free | Weekdays 8-4.

Buckhorn Lake State Resort Park. Situated in the Redbird district of Daniel Boone National Forest, the park is set on 1,230 acres and includes hiking and biking trails, fishing and boating on 1,200-acre Buckhorn Lake, and overnight accommodations in an on-site lodge and cottages. | 4441 KY Hwy. 1833, Buckhorn | 606/398-7510 | www.kystateparks.com/agencies/parks/buckhorn.htm | Free | Daily.

Buckhorn Log Cathedral. This cathedral is the largest log cathedral east of the Mississippi. The Presbyterian house of worship was built circa 1928 for the students and faculty of Witherspoon College and is listed on the National Historical Register. Services are held on Sunday, and during the week the General Store across the street has a key for visitor access. | KY 28, Buckhorn | 606/398-7382 | Free | By arrangement.

Carr Creek Lake. This fishing lake of over 700 acres is 15 mi southeast of Hazard. A picnic area, a playground, and camping hook-ups are available. | Box 249, KY 15, Sassafras | 606/642-3308 | fax 606/642-3777 | Free; fee for camping | Apr.-Oct.

ON THE CALENDAR

FEB., MAR.: *East Kentucky Sport, Boat, and RV Show.* This annual event showcases the latest, state-of-the-art outdoor vehicles. | 606/439-2659.

SEPT.: *Annual Black Gold Festival.* Square dancing, clogging, folk and country music are all part of the celebration of this coal mining town's heritage. | 606/439-2659.

Dining

Cliff Hagans Ribeye. Steak. This popular meat-and-potatoes restaurant features a variety of beef steaks, chicken breast, salmon and halibut—all dinners come with potato; desserts include Kentucky Silk Pie, hot fudge cake, and pecan pie. Kids' menu and carryout. Just south of the Daniel Boone Pkwy. | 800 Morton Blvd., Hazard | 606/487-1024 | Closed Sun. | $10-$22 | AE, D, MC, V.

Frances's Diner. American. This is a local popular diner featuring homecooking and homemade pies. It's just south of the Daniel Boone Parkway on Combs Road. | 1315 Combs Rd., Hazard | 606/436-0090 | Open 24 hrs | $4-$13 | No credit cards.

Lodging

Boone Motor Inn-Hazard. This a very basic three-story motel. Bar. Cable TV. Pool. | 90 Boone Ridge Rd. (Hwy. 15N), Hazard | 606/439-5896 | 74 rooms | $36 | MC, V.

Buckhorn Lodge. Located in Buckhorn Lake State Resort Park, this state-owned stone lodge nestles on a wooded mountainside overlooking Buckhorn Lake. There are copper-hooded fireplaces in the public areas, and private balconies or patios off every guest room. Visitors have access to all facilities at Buckhorn Lake State Resort Park. Dining room, picnic area. Cable TV. Pool, wading pool. Mini-golf, tennis. Boating. Kids' programs. Business services. | 4441 Rte. 1833, Buckhorn | 606/398–7510 or 800/325–0058 | fax 606/398–7077 | www.kystateparks.com | 36 rooms | $52–$68 | AE, D, DC, MC, V.

Hazard–Days Inn. This three-story motel with outside corridors is adjacent to a 24 hour restaurant and has 24-hour free coffee in lobby. The refurbished rooms have two double beds. Kids, 17 and under, stay free with parent. Fishing is close by at Buckhorn and Carrfork Lakes. Some microwaves, some refrigerators. Cable TV. Pets allowed ($6). | 359 Morton Blvd., Hazard | 606/436–4777 | 60 rooms | $42–$59 | AE, D, DC, V.

Hazard Hotel. This two-story motel offers basic, modern rooms, each with direct outdoor access. The building is set away from the main highway, providing a certain measure of quiet. Restaurant, bar. In-room data ports. Cable TV. 2 pools (1 indoor). Hot tub. Business services. | 200 Dawahare Dr., Hazard | 606/436–4428 | fax 606/436–4428 | 72 rooms | $54–$70 | AE, D, DC, MC, V.

Super 8. No-frills, modern rooms are available in this two-story budget motel, located just off Daniel Boone Parkway. Complimentary Continental breakfast. In-room coffee. Cable TV. Business services. Hot Tub. Jacuzzi suites available. | 125 Village La., Hazard | 606/436–8888 | fax 606/439–0768 | 86 rooms | $49–$61 | AE, D, DC, MC, V.

HENDERSON

MAP 6, C4

(Nearby towns also listed: Madisonville, Owensboro)

Modern Henderson sits on part of a 200,000-acre land grant made by the 1778 Virginia Assembly to Colonel Richard Henderson of the Translyvania Company. Situated on the banks of the Ohio River, the town was also home, from 1810 to 1817, to renowned wildlife painter and ornithologist John James Audubon. Another famous resident was musician and composer W. C. Handy, "father of the blues." Henderson's riverside location has attracted several manufacturers, of products ranging from foodstuffs and furniture to aluminum and automotive accessories. Ellis Park in Henderson is the westernmost thoroughbred racetrack in the state.

Information: **Henderson County Tourist Commission** | 2961 U.S. 41N, Henderson 42420 | 270/826–3128 or 800/648–3128 | gotour@ldd.net | www.go-henderson.com.

Attractions

Ellis Park. Owned and operated by Churchill Downs, Ellis Park, on the banks of the Ohio, features an 8,500-seat grandstand and two dining rooms. There's inter-track wagering during the on-season. | 3300 U.S. 41N, Henderson | 812/425–1456 or 800/333–8110 | www.ellisparkracing.com | $2 | Live racing daily July and Aug; open year-round for off-track betting.

John James Audubon State Park. The park is a memorial to Audubon, who lived in Henderson for several years. The over-600 acres serve as both a nature preserve and a public park. You can view more than 150 species of wildflowers along its trails. For recreation, there's a 9-hole golf course and a 28-acre lake with boating. | 3100 U.S. 41N, Henderson | 270/826–2247 | www.kystateparks.com/agencies/parks/audubon2.htm | Free; fee for canoe and pedal-boat rentals | Daily.

John James Audubon Museum and Nature Center. The museum contains 435 original prints from the 1839 folio edition of *The Birds of America,* as well as relics of the artist's life. The Nature Center features an observation room overlooking a garden of native plants. The Discovery Center offers several interactive educational activities. | 3100 U.S. 41N, Henderson | 270/827–1893 | www.kystateparks.com/agencies/parks/audubon2.htm | $4 | Daily 10–5.

ON THE CALENDAR
JUNE: *W. C. Handy Blues and Barbecue Festival.* This week-long festival honors the founder of blues music, who lived here from 1892 to 1902. The festival celebrates Western Kentucky's passion for barbecue with food and live music. | 270/826–3128.
JULY–AUG.: *Ellis Park Thoroughbred Racetrack.* The track features horse races in the summer, and off-track wagering year-round. | 800/333–8110.
AUG.: *Bluegrass in the Park.* This is one of the the top Bluegrass Music festivals—drawing some of the greatest Bluegrass bands in the country. Often the venue is the Henderson Fine Arts Center and Hays Park, near the Hays Boat Landing. Bring your lawn chairs. Contact the Henderson Fine Arts Center for tickets. | 270/830–5324.
OCT.: *Big River Arts and Crafts Festival.* Over 300 exhibitors participate in this annual street festival, which offers plenty of food and entertainment. | 270/926–4433.

Dining

The Mill. Steak. This restaurant is filled with antiques, has cast iron pots hanging on the walls and even has an old player piano. The local favorites include the steaks, prime ribs and seafood specials. There is a cocktail lounge, and carry-out is available. | 528 S. Main St., Henderson | 270/881–2255 | Closed Sun. | $6–$19 | AE, D, DC, MC, V.

Planters Coffeehouse. Contemporary. The home for this two-story coffeehouse is an 1883 building and is one block from the Ohio River. The first floor is in the style of an old fashioned ice cream parlor with an atrium—it is said to be the first atrium west of the Allegheny Mountains. The second floor has a skylight and atrium, larger tables, and photographs of noted local residents, President Truman, and other famous visitors. This is a favorite place with the locals for morning coffee, muffins, rolls, and lunch. Planters is self-serve. Lunch menu selections have included: Hawaiian shrimp soup, turkey or ham croissants, grilled chicken breast, and spinach and cashew pea salads. | 130 N. Main St., Henderson | 270/830–0927 | Breakfast also available. Closed Fri.–Sun. | $5 | MC, V.

Lodging
Days Inn. Located in Henderson's busy commercial district, this motel is convenient to shops and eateries. Bar with entertainment. Some refrigerators. Cable TV. Pool. Beauty salon. Laundry facilities. Business services. | 2044 U.S. 41N, Henderson | 270/826–6600 | fax 270/826–3055 | 118 rooms | $40–$60 | AE, D, DC, MC, V.

L&N Bed and Breakfast. This century-old, two-story, brick Victorian overlooks the Ohio River downtown and is next to the tracks originally built for the old Louisville and Nashville railroad. Decorated with stained glass windows, ornate fireplaces, and polished oak floors, the house is accented with railroad-themed antiques. TV. Business services. Laundry facilities. | 327 N. Main St., Henderson | www.lnbbky.com | 270/831–1100 | fax 270/826–0075 | 4 rooms | $75 | No credit cards.

Scottish Inn. Offering basic accommodations in a quiet setting near downtown, this motel is located 1½ mi from Audubon State Park, and 1 mi from Ellis Park Race Track. A restaurant and lounge are within walking distance. Cable TV. Pool, wading pool. Business services. Some pets allowed (fee). | 2820 U.S. 41N, Henderson | 270/827–1806 or 800/251–1962 | fax 270/827–8192 | 60 rooms | $40–$45 | AE, D, DC, MC, V.

Victorian Quarters Bed & Breakfast. The scenic brick Italiannate mansion overlooks the majestic Ohio River. The suites are three rooms with kitchens, and are furnished with antiques dating back a 100 years or more. The River Suite has a commanding view of the Ohio. All rooms have private baths and there is an on-site flower shop. Complimentary breakfast, kitchenettes. Cable TV, VCRs. Pool. Hot tub. Bicycles. Business services. | 109 Clay St., Henderson | 270/831–2778 | fax 270/831–2280 | www.go-henderson.com/victorianquarters/ | 3 rooms | $85–$95 | AE, D, MC, V.

HODGENVILLE

MAP 6, E4

(Nearby towns also listed: Bardstown, Campbellsville, Elizabethtown, Horse Cave)

Famous as the hometown of Abraham Lincoln (a bronze statue of Honest Abe by A. A. Weinmann is the centerpiece of the public square), this town was established in 1789 by Englishman Robert Hodgen, who erected a mill on the Nolin River. Incorporated by the Hardin County Court in 1818, and now the county seat, Hodgenville remains, as it was when Lincoln was a farmboy, a center for agriculture.

Information: LaRue County Chamber of Commerce | Box 176, Hodgenville, 42748 | www.laruecountychambers.org. | 270/358–3411.

Attractions

Abraham Lincoln Birthplace National Historic Site. Fifty-six steps, one for each year of the president's life, lead up to the granite memorial, which houses a one-room log cabin—a replica of Lincoln's birthplace (in 1809). Above the portals is carved "With malice toward none, with charity for all," quoted from Lincoln's address to an Indiana Regiment in March, 1865. The memorial, which opened in 1911, is on the grounds of a 110-acre park that was part of the original Thomas Lincoln farm. There are also hiking trails and picnic areas. The Visitors Center houses exhibitions about, and artifacts of, the Lincoln family, including the family Bible, and has a short film about Lincoln's boyhood. | 2995 Lincoln Farm Rd., Hodgenville | 270/358–3137 | www.nps.gov/abli | Free | Memorial Day–Labor Day, daily 8–6:45; Labor Day–Memorial Day, daily 8–4:45.

Kentucky Railway Museum. The KRM, about 6 mi north of Hodgenville on US 31E, founded 1954, owns 17 mi of the old Louisville and Nashville Lebanon branch. The collection of railroad artifacts and memorabilia includes model trains and layouts, steam and first generation diesel locomotives, and over 80 pieces of rolling stock. The KRM also operates a 22-mi train ride through the scenic and historic Rolling Fork River Valley—May through December (except Mon.) and only weekends after September. Re-enactments of Civil War skirmishes and train robberies are conducted on selected weekends. For $25 you can ride in the locomotive's cab; coach fares range from $12.50–$15. | New Haven Depot U.S. 31E, New Haven | 502/549–5470 or 800/272–0152 | fax 502/549–5472 | www.kyrail.org | $3 | May–Dec.

Lincoln's Boyhood Home. This reconstructed cabin rests on the site where Lincoln lived from age two to eight, and is furnished with antiques from the period. | 7120 Bardstown Rd., Hodgenville | 502/549–3741 | $1 | Apr.–Oct. 9–5.

Lincoln Jamboree. It's billed as Kentucky's #1 country music showplace—bluegrass music lovers have been flocking to this foot-stomping hoedown since 1954. Traditional and contemporary country music is the entertainment at this family-oriented center where a regular band is featured plus guest performers. The Lincoln Jamboree restaurant is also on the premises. | 2579 Lincoln Farm Rd., Hodgenville | 270/358–3545 | $8 | Open year-round. Sat. evenings for performances; shows start at 8; reservations recommended. Closed Mon.

Lincoln Museum. Twelve dioramas with 21 life-sized wax figures in authentic scenes portray phases of Abraham Lincoln's life from cabin life to Ford's Theatre. The 94-year-old preserved building with original floors and fittings, and located on the official site of the Civil War Trail Discovery could be an attraction in its own right. It is filled with memorabilia including Civil War artifacts, artwork, and documents. | 66 Lincoln Sq., Hodgenville | 270/358-3163 | www.lincolnmuseumky.org | $3 | Mon.–Sat. 8:30–4:30, Sun. 12:30–4:30.

ON THE CALENDAR
JAN.: *Martin Luther King Jr. Birthday Observance.* Musicians offer tribute to the Civil Rights leader on the official holiday. | 270/358-3137.
FEB.: *Lincoln's Birthday Commemoration.* Speeches, concerts, programs, and a luncheon mark the birthday of our 16th president. | Feb. 12 | 270/358-3411.
FEB.: *Lincoln's Birthday Observance.* Locals and visitors can attend a wreath-laying ceremony at the Birthplace Cabin. | 270/358-3137.
MAY: *Magnolia Days.* Hodgenville's spring festival features a parade, kids' games, antique car show, beauty and baby contests, black-powder shoots, athletic and art competitions, and food booths. Larue County Chamber of Commerce, Lincoln Square, Box 176, Kentucky 42748 | 270/358-3411.
JULY: *Founders Day Weekend.* Celebrate the dedication of the park with speakers, bands, and activities that change each year. | 270/358-3411.
OCT.: *Lincoln Days Celebration.* This festival of family activities occurs on the second weekend of the month and includes games, crafts, food, and music. | 502/358-3411.

Dining
Joel Ray Sprowls' Restaurant. Southern. Joel Ray's is in the same building as the popular Saturday night Lincoln Jamboree Country Music Show which is 2½ mi south of downtown Hodgenville. The atmosphere is definitely "country" with a mix of Lincoln memorabilia, country artifacts, and country music items. Cafeteria style with steam tables. Lunch and dinner menu choices always include fried chicken, and could include salmon cakes, meat loaf, pork chops, or chicken & dumplings. On Fridays, there is a catfish or country ham special. | 2579 Lincoln Farm Road (U.S. 31E), Hodgenville | 270/358-3545 | Breakfast also available. Closed Mon. | $5 | No credit cards.

Lodging
Cruise Inn Motel. This small motel is close to the Lincoln attractions in Hodgenville. Cable TV. | 2768 Lincoln Farm Rd., Hodgenville | 270/358-9998 | 10 rooms | $38–$43 | MC, V.

Olde Gait Farm Bed & Breakfast. From this 1917 Victorian farm house walk across the road and hike the pastures and woods at Abraham Lincoln's Boyhood Home. The commons area has a TV, phone, and fireplace. There's also a separate reading parlor. Explore the barn, help groom the horses, bird-watch, or do nothing but swing on the veranda. Also available are horseback riding lessons. Stalls are available if you bring your own horse ($15 per night). Kids sharing your room are $15 extra. On the Lincoln Trail (U.S. 31E). Complimentary Continental breakfast. No room phones. Cable TV in common area. Hiking. | 7281 Bardstown Rd., Hodgenville | 502/549-7348 or 877/548-7348 | oldgate2@bardstown.com | www.bbonline.com/ky/oldgait | 3 rooms | $90 | No credit cards.

HOPKINSVILLE

MAP 6, C5

(Nearby towns also listed: Cadiz, Dawson Springs)

The town was settled in 1796 by Martha Ann and Bartholomew Wood from Jonesborough, TN (their claim was based on the husband's Revolutionary War service). It's now the county seat, as well as an important center of manufacturing and tobacco warehousing. Hopkinsville Community College is the venue for local learning. The town is a good base for visits to nearby Pennyrile Forest State Resort Park in Dawson Springs. The nation's first Poet Laureate, Robert Penn Warren, was born not far away, in Guthrie.

Information: Hopkinsville-Christian County Chamber of Commerce | 1209 S. Virginia St., Box 1382, Hopkinsville 42241 | 270/885–9096 or 800/842–9959.

Attractions

Cherokee Trail of Tears Park. This historic park is one of the few documented sites of actual trail and campsites used during the forced removal of the Cherokee people to "Indian Territory." It was used as an encampment in 1838 and 1839. The park is the burial site for two Cherokee Chiefs who died during the removal—Fly Smith and Whitepath. Every year on the first full weekend of September, the Trail of Tears Commission sponsors an intertribal Pow Wow at the park. At the intersection of U.S. 41S and Skyline Drive. | 100 Trail of Tears Dr., Hopkinsville | 270/886–8033 | fax 270/886–0034 | www.trailoftears.org | Donation | Apr.–Oct., Mon.–Sat. 10–4; Nov.–Mar., Mon.–Sat. 10–2. Closed Tue.

Fort Campbell. Located partly in Kentucky and partly in Tennessee, this 100,068-acre facility is one of the largest military bases in the nation and home to the 101st Airborne (Air Assault Division) of the U.S. Army. Opened in 1942, it was named for Col. William Bowen Campbell, an officer in the Mexican War and Whig governor of Tennessee from 1851 to 1857. Historic military items, including a rare World War II cargo glider, are displayed in the Don F. Pratt Museum in Wickham Hall. | 2334 19th and Indiana Ave., Fort Campbell | 270/798–2151 | www.campbell.army.mil/campbell.htm | Free | Mon.–Sat. 9:30–4:30. Closed Sun.

Jefferson Davis Monument State Shrine. This 20-acre state park has picnic shelters, a playground, and a gift shop. It is dedicated to the memory of Jefferson Davis, who was born nearby in 1808. In addition to being the only president of the Confederate States of America, Davis was a U.S. Senator (from Mississippi) and Secretary of War under Franklin Pierce. The centerpiece of the park is the 351-ft concrete obelisk, the fourth tallest in the world. | The monument is on U.S. 68, 9 mi east of Hopkinsville | Box 10, Fairview, KY | 270/886–1765 | www.kystateparks.com/agencies/parks/jefdav2.htm | $1 | May–Oct., daily 9–5.

Pennyroyal Area Museum. Exhibitions detailing the history of Hopkinsville and the surrounding region reside in this area museum. Special displays include those about local Civil War battles, and about Jefferson Davis, Robert Penn Warren, and Edgar Cayce, who were all born nearby. | 217 E. 9th St., Hopkinsville | 270/887–4270 | $2 | Weekdays 8:30–4:30; Sat. 10–3.

Robert Penn Warren Birthplace Museum. Author of *All the King's Men*, Warren (1905–89) won the 1947 Pulitzer Prize for fiction and Pulitzers in 1958 and 1979 for poetry. He was the United States' first Poet Laureate. Exhibitions depict Warren's life and work. | 3rd and Cherry Sts., Guthrie | 270/483–2683 | Free | Tues.–Sat. 11:30–3:30, Sun. 2–4.

ON THE CALENDAR

APR.: *Dogwood Festival.* The pink and white flowering trees planted around downtown are at their finest in late April. A street festival with food and entertainment takes place beneath the blossoms. | 270/885–9096.

MAY: *Little River Days.* Street dances, kids' activities, food, entertainment, foot and canoe races, and arts and crafts are all part of the festivities. | 270/887–4290.

MAY–OCT.: *Memorial Rides.* There's a $2 fee to ride to the top of the memorial obelisk. Hours are 9 to 5. | 270/886–1765.

JUNE: *Jefferson Davis Birthday Celebration.* Speakers, music, and other programs commemorate the June 3rd birth of the only president of the Confederacy. | 270/886–1765.

AUG.: *Western Kentucky State Fair.* Tractor contests, agricultural exhibitions, food, and rides fill the fair needs of residents who can't get to Louisville for the state fair. | 270/885–9096 or 800/842–9959.

SEPT.: *Annual Night Rider Tour.* Locals offer a unique staging of the night-rider raids during the Black Patch war over tobacco prices at the turn of the 19th century. | 270/887–4270.

Dining

J's On Main. American. J's seems to have something for everyone. They're famous for the prime rib sandwich and hamburgers, but the menu also includes a variety of sandwiches, pork chops, steaks, fish, vegetarian, enchiladas, and salads. Originally the Cayce-Yost general store, now it's a fun restaurant where works of local artists, retired football jerseys, autographs, and menus from around the world adorn the walls and bar area. | 1004 S. Main St., Hopkinsville | 270/885–2896 | www.jsonmain.com | Closed Sun. | AE, D, MC, V.

Woodshed. Southern. This small, casual restaurant offers country-style home cooking at plain wooden tables. Barbecue is the specialty of the house. | 1821 W. 7th St., Hopkinsville | 270/885–8144 | Closed Sun. | $4–$5 | No credit cards.

Lodging

Best Western Hopkinsville. This three-story motel with inside corridors and elevators is 2 mi south of town on U.S. 41. Some in-room coffeemakers and suites are available. Bar, complimentary Continental breakfast. Some in-room data ports. Cable TV. Pool. Pets allowed ($5). | 4101 Fort Campbell Blvd., Hopkinsville | 270/886–9000 | fax 270/886–9000 | ccook@commercecenter.org | 107 rooms | $59 | AE, D, DC, MC, V.

Holiday Inn. The motel lobby includes a lounge with complimentary coffee, fruit, or cookies (depending upon the time of day) and an entertainment area for kids, which offers G-rated videos. Restaurant, bar. In-room data ports. Cable TV. Indoor pool. Sauna. Exercise equipment. Business services. Free parking. Some pets allowed. | 2910 Fort Campbell Blvd., Hopkinsville | 270/886–4413 | fax 270/886–4413 | 101 rooms | $60–$80 | AE, D, DC, MC, V.

HORSE CAVE

MAP 6, E5

(Nearby towns also listed: Bowling Green, Cave City, Glasgow, Hodgenville, Mammoth Cave National Park)

Horse Cave was established in the early 1840s by Major Albert Anderson on land that had been donated for a Louisville and Nashville Railroad Station. Today, this largest town in Hart County is a center for burley tobacco marketing. The town was named for the large cave around which it grew. An underground river provided energy for an electricity generator as early as the late 1800s.

Information: Hart County Chamber of Commerce | Box 688, Munfordville 42765 | 270/524–2892.

Attractions

American Cave Museum/Hidden River Cave. Hidden River Cave's entrance can be viewed from a free Main Street overlook in downtown Horse Cave. Closed as a tourist attraction in 1943, it is now reopened after a long conservation effort which has even lured back rare blind cavefish. The cave features a subterranean river flowing 100 ft below the city and a turn-of-the-century waterworks. The museum's science and history displays include exhibits about Mammoth Cave, Horse Cave, cave exploring, groundwater, Floyd Collins and saltpeter mining. A guided tour leaves the museum every hour. Nearby is the American Cave Museum's two-story environmental education center. The "cave" with stalactites and stalagmites has exhibits on the cultural and natural resources associated with caves. | E. Main St., Horse Cave | 270/786–1466 | www.kdu.com/acm.html | $8, kids free (up to 4 years old) | 9–5; Memorial Day to Labor Day 9–7.

Horse Cave Theatre. A regional theater company presents up to six new and established plays per season by Kentuckian and nationally known playwrights in the renovated

Thomas Opera House, a 343-seat facility built in 1911. Call ahead to arrange a tour of backstage. | 101 E. Main St., Horse Cave | 270/786–1200 or 800/342–2177 | fax 270/786–5298 | June–Nov.

Kentucky Down Under/Mammoth Onyx Cave. The outback of Australia is re-created here in Kentucky Cave country. Visitors can roam through a field of kangaroos or learn an ancient aboriginal dance. Other wildlife includes brightly colored tropical birds, wallabies, wombats, and emus. The guided cave tour features unusual onyx formations. | 3700 L& N Turnpike Rd., Horse Cave | 270/786–2634 or 800/762–2869 | www.kdu.com | $16 | Daily.

ON THE CALENDAR
APR.–OCT.: *Kentucky Down Under/Kentucky Taverns.* Exhibits of Australian animals such as wallabies and wombats are the focus of this festival. There's a 45-minute guided tour of the cave. | 800/762–2869.

Dining
The Bookstore. Southern. The restaurant has 15 tables and is co-located in one large room with the used book store. One wall is decorated with old Horse Cave photographs and of course there is plenty of interesting reading material. This locals' favorite has breakfast with biscuits and gravy and a lunch standard of meat and two vegies. Specialties are fried chicken, catfish, and country ham. | 111 Water St., Horse Cave | 270/786–3084 | bookstore@horsecav.com | Closed Sun. 5 PM | $6–$14 | D, MC, V.

Lodging
Budget Host Inn. This property is located 2½ mi from downtown Horse Cave, and 14 mi from Mammoth Cave. You have a choice of rooms with double, queen, and king beds; family rooms have fold-out sleeper couches. Restaurant. Cable TV. Pool. Free parking. Some pets allowed. | Rte. 218 (Box 332), Horse Cave | 270/786–2165 | fax 270/786–2168 | 80 rooms | $30–$47 | AE, D, DC, MC, V.

Hampton Inn Horse Cave. This contemporary, two-story motel with interior corridors has comfortable spacious rooms and in-room coffeemakers. Cribs are available. The Hampton Inn is west of I–65 exit 58 and 7 mi from the Horse Cave entrance. Complimentary Continental breakfast. In-room data ports. Some refrigerators. Cable TV. Pool. Hot tub. Exercise equipment. No pets. | 750 Flint Ridge Rd., Horse Cave | 502/786–5000 or 800/426–7866 | fax 502/786–5003 | 63 rooms | $71 | AE, D, DC, MC, V.

JAMESTOWN

MAP 6, F5

(Nearby towns also listed: Campbellsville, Monticello, Somerset)

Incorporated in 1827, Jamestown was originally called Jacksonville in honor of President Andrew Jackson. But when anti-Jackson politicians were elected to the town council, the name was changed to Jamestown to honor James Woolridge, who had originally donated the land on which the town was built. Jamestown is the jumping-off point for visitors to nearby Lake Cumberland State Resort Park and Dale Hollow Lake State Resort Park. The state dock is in Jamestown—it's the place to rent houseboats, personal watercraft, fishing boats, and pontoon boats.

Information: **Russell County Tourist Commission.** | KTG, Box 64, Russell Springs, 42642 | 270/866–4333.

Attractions
Lake Cumberland Dragway. This dragway hosts IHRA drag racing—street legal vehicles only—every Friday night from early June to early November. It's south of the Cumberland

Pkwy. and U.S. 127 junction. Take U.S. 127 toward Jamestown, then turn west onto Airport Rd. | Airport Rd., Jamestown | 270/343–6101 or 270/384–3057 | $5 | June–Nov., Fri. 5 PM, closed Sat.–Thurs.

Lake Cumberland State Resort Park. The lodge and other facilities at Lake Cumberland State Resort Park were renovated in 1998. Recreation on the 50,250-acre lake includes boating, fishing, and water-skiiing. Tennis, hiking, and horseback riding are also available. The lodge has an indoor swimming pool. Other facilities include a nature center, playground, picnic area, campground, and cottages. | 5465 State Park Rd., Jamestown | 270/343–3111 | www.kystateparks.com/agencies/parks/lakecumb.htm | Free; fees for boat rental and camping | Year-round; boat rental Apr.–Nov.

ON THE CALENDAR

JUNE: *Catch a Rainbow Fishing Derby*. Fly-fishers are invited to cast for rainbow trout at nearby Wolf Creek National Fish Hatchery. | 270/866–4333.

JULY: *Lakefest*. Held at Jamestown's Monument Square, this festival occurs on the weekend (Friday and Saturday) coinciding with the Fourth of July—but not necessarily on the 4th. The Independence Day celebration features live music, crafts, games, contests, clogging, a mini-marathon, and fireworks. | 270/866–4333.

OCT.: *Pumpkin Festival*. Monument Square in downtown Jamestown turns orange with an abundance of the round squash. Carving, cooking, and all-around celebrating of the pumpkin is the rule. | 270/866–4333.

DALE HOLLOW LAKE STATE RESORT PARK

Formed in 1943 when the Army Corps of Engineers completed a dam on the Obey River in Tennessee, the lake's 27,700 acres cover parts of Kentucky and Tennessee. The waters are famous both for fine fishing (the world record small mouth bass—almost 12 pounds—was caught here), and as a stopover for migratory birds. It's not uncommon to see a great blue heron rising from a branch overhanging the shoreline early in the morning.

Hundreds of small coves and inlets make good boat tie-up sites. You can rent a houseboat equipped with a gas grill, kitchen, stateroom and bunk beds from several lake-shore marinas. You can also swim or scuba dive in these remarkably clean waters.

If you're less nautically inclined, you can stay in the 30-room state park lodge, completed in 1997. The park's 3,400-acres land area is part of both Clinton and Cumberland Counties. As a lodge resident, you can take advantage of hiking and horseback riding trails, a playground, swimming pool, and a variety of planned recreational activities. Campsites are also available.

Compared with many other of Kentucky's state resort parks, Dale Hollow is relatively undiscovered. The park and lodge are open year-round. For information, call 502/433–7431 or 800/255–TRIP. For reservations, 800/325–2282.

Related towns: Burkesville, Jamestown, Lake Cumberland State Resort Park, Monticello, Russell Springs

Dining

Loy's. Southern. Russell county locals flock to Loy's for the country cooking from breakfast to dinner. The buffet specializes in catfish on Friday and Saturday and there is always fried chicken, pork, and beef. The table-served menu includes catfish, hushpuppies, chicken, and ribeye steak. It's half way between Russell Springs and Jamestown in the Midtown Plaza and 1 mi south of the Cumberland Pkwy. | 2475 U.S. 127, Russell Springs | 270/866–8570 | Breakfast also available. No supper Sun. | $5–$8 | No credit cards.

Lodging

Cumberland Lodge. Mostly-double-bedded rooms done in shades of rose characterize this motel in the center of town. Complimentary Continental breakfast. Some refrigerators. Cable TV. Pool. Exercise equipment. | U.S. 127 and Cumberland Pkwy., Russell Springs | 270/866–4208 | fax 270/866–4206 | 53 rooms | $50 | AE, D, MC, V.

Jamestown Resort and Marina. This 300-acre complex by the lake boasts more than 800 boat slips. Lodge features suites of various sizes. Houseboats are also available for rental. Complimentary breakfast. Some kitchenettes, some minibars, refrigerators. Cable TV, in-room VCRs. Pool. Mini-golf, tennis. Hiking. Water sports, boating, fishing. Playground. Laundry facilities. | 3677 S. Hwy. 92, Jamestown | 270/343–5253 | fax 270/343–5252 | jrmarina@duo-county.com | www.jamestown-marina.com | 40 rooms; 18 cottages | $70–$130; $40–$70 cottages | AE, D, MC, V.

Lodge at Lake Cumberland State Resort Park. This state-run stone lodge overlooks the woods, and features common areas with log-burning fireplaces. Rooms have balconies with views of the lake. Guests have access to all facilities at Lake Cumberland State Resort Park. Dining room. Kitchenettes (in cottages). Cable TV. 2 pools (1 indoor), 2 wading pools. 9-hole golf course, mini-golf, putting green, tennis. Marina, water sports, boating. Kids' programs. Laundry facilities. Business services. | 5465 State Park Rd., Jamestown | 270/343–3111 or 800/325–1709 | fax 270/343–5510 | www.kystateparks.com/agencies/parks/lakecumb.htm | 48 rooms in lodge; 30 cottages | rooms $55–$145; cottages $75–$125 | AE, D, MC, V.

The Pinehurst Lodge. This one-story motel offers rooms, two-bedroom family units, and housekeeping units. The rooms in the original section have stall showers. All units are set back from the road and most overlook the large Z-shaped pool. Additional features include picnic tables, grills, shuffleboard courts, basketball court, and game room. Some kitchenettes, some refrigerators. Cable TV. Pool. No pets. | 1115 W. Cumberland Ave., Jamestown | 270/343–4143 or 877/855–4143 | www.lakecumberlandlodging.com | 26 rooms | $49 | AE, D, MC, V.

LAND BETWEEN THE LAKES

MAP 6, C5

(Nearby towns also listed: Cadiz, Gilbertsville, Murray)

Attractions

Elk & Bison Prairie. Opened in June 1996, this 750-acre is a restoration of the native prairie habitat that thrived in Western Kentucky and upper Middle Tennessee over 200 years ago. Native wildlife includes elk, bison, turkey, coyotes, redtail hawks and songbirds. Take a self-guided driving tour of the site along a 3½ mi road with three interpretive stops. | The Trace, 1 mi north of U.S. 68, Golden Pond | 270/924–2000 or 800/525–7077 | www2.lbl.org/lbl/ebbison.html | $3 per car.

Fort Donelson National Battlefield. The National Battlefield includes a visitor center and Fort Donelson National Cemetery (established 1867). It's the final resting place for Union soldiers killed at Fort Donelson and American veterans representing seven wars. The Dover Hotel (Surrender House), an adaptive restoration of the historic building where Confederate General Simon B. Buckner surrendered to Ulysses S. Grant, is also here. The Fort, open until dark, is just south of Land Between The Lakes off U.S. 79. Go to the south end of Lake Barkley in Tennessee. The visitor center is open 8–4:30. | U.S. 79, Dover, TN | 931/232–5706 | fax 931/232–6331 | www.nps.gov/fodo | Free | Daily dawn to dusk.

ON THE CALENDAR
AUG.: *Hot August Blues Festival*. The festival is held in the month from Friday evening through Sunday on the front lawn of Kenlake Hotel, Kenlake State Resort Park. | 542 Kenlake Rd., Hardin | 270/474–2211 or 800/325–0143 | $10.

Dining
Patti's 1880's Restaurant and Settlement. Southern. The restaurant is in Patti's Settlement, a re-created log cabin village with gardens, gift shops, winding streams, a miniature golf-course and arcade, and an animal park. Patti's is famous for 2-inch thick pork chops, "mile-high" meringue pies, and flower pot bread. The restaurant has received recognition from *Southern Living* magazine. Patti's is just north of the Land Between the Lakes' northern entrance. | 1793 J.H. O'Bryan Ave., Grand Rivers | 270/362–8844 or 888/736–2515 | www.pattis-settlement.com/ | $15–$22 | D, MC, V.

Lodging
Light House Landing. This full-service resort is on Kentucky Lake just 1 mi north of the Land Between the Lakes' northern entrance. The marina features guest rooms, and 12 lakeside cottages. The cottages have private sundecks overlooking the lake, or if you prefer, you can rent a 23–33 ft sailboat and stay aboard it at one of the slips. The 208-slip marina has bath-houses and a waste pump station. Rooms/cottages are equipped with a coffeemaker, air-conditioning, and some have a gas log stove. There are also barbecue grills, a game room with Ping-Pong and Foose-ball, a sailing school, and a complete ship's store with clothing and nautical gifts. The Landing is 3 mi off I–24, exit 31, on Hwy. 453. Some kitchenettes, refrigerators. Some in-room hot tubs. Cable TV, VCRs. Beach, dock, boating, fishing. No pets. | Hwy. 453, Grand Rivers | 270/362–8201 or 800/491–7245 | fax 270/362–4107 | info@lighthouse-landing.com | www.lighthouselanding.com | 26 rooms | $75–$190 | Apr.–Nov. daily; Dec.–Mar., Mon.–Sat., closed Sun. | D, MC, V.

LEXINGTON

(Nearby towns also listed: Frankfort, Georgetown, Midway, Paris, Richmond, Versailles, Winchester)

Kentucky's second-largest city is also one of its oldest. Established as a camp in 1775, it was named after the town in Massachusetts that had just been the site of an important Revolutionary War victory. The city grew rapidly after statehood as a center for commerce, the arts, and above all, horse breeding—which made the surrounding Bluegrass Region the world's thoroughbred capital. By the 1820s, Lexington was known as the "Athens of the West," and it was as easy to hear a Beethoven symphony in local concert halls as to see a beautiful race horse on one of the nearby farms.

The downtown has many notable historic districts. Just south of the city center, a neighborhood of Georgian houses reminds visitors of Georgetown in Washington, D.C. The "more antebellum" neighborhood of Gratz Park, just north of Main St., has the campus of Transylvania University, a private liberal arts college that counts Jefferson Davis among its alumni.

A central shopping and restaurant district downtown has grown up around Rupp Arena, where the University of Kentucky Wildcats play basketball. The campus of the state's land grant (and largest) university is 10 minutes south of the arena.

Lexington is the site of the world's largest burley tobacco auction as well as the famous yearling thoroughbred sales that take place in spring and fall at nearby Keeneland race course. The central tobacco warehouse district has been undergoing changes in recent years as buildings and sites are converted to new shopping and residential areas.

Information:Lexington Convention and Visitors Bureau | 301 E. Vine St., Lexington, 40507-1513 | 859/233–7299 or 800/845–3959 | vacation@visitlex.com | www.visitlex.com.

Attractions

Ashland. This 18-room mansion was the home of Henry Clay, U.S. Senator from Kentucky during the Civil War era, who also served as Speaker of the House and Secretary of State during his long political career. Clay's reputation as an orator and statesman was national and he earned the nickname, "the Great Compromiser." Furnished with Clay family artifacts and early 19th-century antiques, the house sits on 20 wooded acres. Formal gardens, an icehouse, a smokehouse, and a carriage house are among the other features. | 120 Sycamore Rd., Lexington | 859/266–8581 | www.henryclay.org | $6 | Feb.–Dec., Mon.–Sat. 10–4:30, Sun. 1–4:30.

Bluegrass Tours. Take a guided van tour of Keeneland Race Course, Red Mile Harness Race Track, and selected horse farms. Tours originate from Lexington hotels and require a minimum of three hours. | 859/252–5744 | Reservations required.

Headley-Whitney Museum. Devoted to decorative arts, this museum holds a large collection of jewelry, gold boxed, and jeweled sculptures by artist-designer George W. Headley. Other exhibitions include textiles, furniture, Chinese porcelains, and metalwork. The museum also houses a large decorative-arts library. | 4435 Old Frankfort Pike, Lexington | 859/255–6653 | www.headley-whitney.org | $4 | Tues.–Fri. 10–5; weekends noon–5.

Horse Farms. With over 400 horse farms, the Lexington area boasts the world's highest concentration of such facilities. Among the most famous are Calumet, Claiborne, and Three Chimneys. Individual farms are not open to the public, but guided tours of several are offered by Bluegrass Tours and Historic Tours of Lexington. Also, drive along Versailles Rd., Old Frankfort Pike, or Paris Pike for good views of the farms from the road. | 859/252–5744 (Bluegrass Tours) or 859/268–2906 (Historic Tours) | $20–$50 for tours | Mar.–Oct.

Hunt-Morgan House. Located in the historic Gratz Park neighborhood, this Federal-style house was built in the early 1800s by John Wesley Morgan, the first millionaire west of the Appalachians. His illustrious descendants included John Hunt Morgan, the Confederate cavalry captain who led Morgan's Raiders, and Thomas Hunt Morgan, Nobel laureate for his research in genetics. Family furnishings and a formal garden are features of the house and grounds. | 201 N. Mill St., Lexington | 859/233–3290 | $5 | Mar.–late-Dec., Tues.–Sat. 10–4; Sun. 2–5.

Keeneland. One of the most beautiful race tracks in the United States is set in the heart of thoroughbred farm country. Stately trees line the entrance and the paddock. Horse people come from all over the world for spring and fall auctions of yearling horses, and this is the only race course in America ever attended by Queen Elizabeth II, who owns some mares on a farm nearby. You can even get a true taste of Kentucky while watching the racing—burgoo, a meaty stew native to the state, is sold at concession stands. | 4201 Versailles Rd. (U.S. 60), Lexington | 859/254–3412 | www.keenland.com | $3 | Apr.–Oct.

Kentucky Horse Park. The world's only equine theme park is situated on 1,032 green, rolling acres. The International Museum of the Horse has exhibitions on evolution and all breeds, as well as films about human/horse relationships throughout history. Past exhibits included The Horses of China. During the summer, a daily Parade of Breeds occurs in the arena, where you can view horses with tack appropriate to each. Tours of the park are available in a horse-drawn trolley or by foot. The great thoroughbred Man O'War is buried here, and his grave is marked by a life-sized bronze statue. Horseback and pony rides are offered for a fee separate from admission. | 4089 Ironworks Pike, Lexington | 859/233–4303 or 800/ 568–8813 | www.imh.org/khp | $12 | Daily.

American Saddle Horse Museum. Set on the grounds of Kentucky Horse Park, the museum celebrates the Saddlebred breed, which was developed in Kentucky in the 19th century as the riding horse of choice. A multi-image presentation recounts the history and current uses of the Saddlebred and there's an interactive exhibit where you can see how you would look atop one of the horses. | 4093 Iron Works Pike | 859/259–2746 | $3 | May.– Sept., daily 9–5; Oct.–Apr., Wed.–Sun. 9–5.

Lexington Cemetery. Among the notable Lexingtonians buried here are Henry Clay, Mary Todd Lincoln's family, John Hunt Morgan, novelist James Lane Allen, and University of Kentucky basketball coach Adolph Rupp. A Civil War veterans' section and a large flower garden are features of the landscape. | 833 W. Main St. (U.S. 421), Lexington | 859/255–5522 | Free | Daily.

Lexington Children's Museum. It will take at least an hour and a half to play with the interactive exhibitions on history, civics, science, nature, and ecology here, including a walk-through cave, a simulated moon walk, and giant-soap-bubble-blowing activity. | 440 W. Short St., Lexington | 859/258–3256 | $3 | Tues.–Fri. 10–6, Sat. 10–5, Sun. 1–5.

Lexington Opera House. Now a regional performing arts center, this opulent Victorian theater opened in 1887. Touring Broadway shows and orchestra concerts are among the featured events. | 401 W. Short St., Lexington | 859/233–4567 | fax 859/253–2718 | Sept.–June.

Mary Todd Lincoln House. This 1803 Georgian house was the girlhood home of Mary Todd, who became Mrs. Abraham Lincoln. (The 16th president made three visits to the house.) Furnished with period antiques, there are also artifacts of both the Todd and Lincoln families. | 578 W. Main St., Lexington | 859/233–9999 | $7 | Mid-Mar.–Nov., Mon.–Sat. 10–4.

Transylvania University. Founded in 1780, this relatively small liberal-arts institution, with an enrollment of just under 1,000, counts Jefferson Davis among its alumni. Henry Clay taught law here. The medical school, closed in 1859, was one of the first in the nation. | 300 N. Broadway, at 3rd St., Lexington | 859/233–8120 | fax 859/233–8797 | www.transy.edu | Free | Daily.

University of Kentucky. Established as the state's land grant college in 1865, the university is the largest employer in the city. It is also Kentucky's largest university with an enrollment of more than 24,000. Tours of the campus, by both bus and foot, are available. Several museums on the campus grounds are attractions in their own right. | 500 S. Limestone St., at Euclid Ave., Lexington | 859/257–9000 | fax 859/257–1754 | www.uky.edu | Free | Daily.

Permanent collections at the U of K **Art Museum** include 20th-century photography, paintings, and works by regional 19th-century artists. A print collection, a highlight of which are WPA works, is especially strong. The museum presents traveling shows as well. | Singletary Center for the Arts, Euclid Ave. and Rose St. | 859/257–5716 | fax 859/323–1994 | www.uky.edu/artmuseum | Free | Tues.–Sun. noon–5.

Rupp Arena. This 23,000-seat arena is named in honor of legendary U of K Wildcat basketball coach Adolph Rupp. The Wildcats regularly rank in the top 10 NCAA basketball teams and have won several national championships. The arena is also home to Lexington's professional hockey team, the Thoroughblades, and is a regular venue for rock, country, and pop concerts. | 430 W. Vine St. | 859/257–4567 | Prices vary | Year-round. Exhibitions at the **William S. Webb Museum of Anthropology** recount the history of people in Kentucky from 12,000 years ago to the present. Other displays trace human evolution and the history of art and technology in global cultures. | Lafferty Hall | 859/257–8208 | www.uky.edu/as/anthropology/museum/museum.htm | Free | Weekdays 8–4:30.

Victorian Square. Shops, art galleries, and restaurants are housed in this restored block of 19th-century, ornamental brick warehouses. A 400-car parking garage with a covered walkway leads into the complex. | Vine St., Lexington | 859/252–7575 or 859/258–3253 | Daily during business hrs.

Waveland State Historic Site. The centerpiece of the 10-acre site is a restored Greek Revival manor erected in 1847. The estate depicts life on a pre-Civil War plantation. Among other buildings are an icehouse, a smokehouse, and servant's quarters. | 225 Waveland Museum La., Lexington | 859/272–3611 | www.kystateparks.com/agencies/parks/wavelan2.htm | $6 | Feb.–Dec., Mon.–Sat. 10–5, Sun. 1–5.

ON THE CALENDAR

APR.: *Blue Grass Stakes.* Part of the Keeneland Spring meet, this is one of the most important prep races for three-year-olds aspiring to compete in the Kentucky Derby. | 859/254–3412 or 800/456–3412.

APR.: *Rolex Three-Day Event and Trade Fair.* One of the world's most important cross-country, steeplechase, and dressage equestrian events is held at the Kentucky Horse Park. The simultaneously-open Trade Fair features booths selling wares from art and jewelry to horse supplies. | 859/233–4303.

APR., OCT.: *Keeneland Race Meets.* Thoroughbred horse racing occurs at this beautifully landscaped historic track, which is so quiet and civilized that, until just recently, it had no PA system. It's America's version of Ascot. | 859/254–3412.

MAY, SEPT.–OCT.: *The Red Mile Harness Track Meets.* This, America's fastest trotter track, highlights harness racing. The course was named for its red-clay surface. | 859/255–0752.

MAY: *High Hope Steeplechase.* This racing competition occurs at the Kentucky Horse Park. | 859/233–4303.

JUNE: *Egyptian Event.* This special competition features a rare horse breed that dates back to the pharaohs. Show classes, demonstrations, and art auction are also held. | 859/231–0771.

JUNE: *Festival of the Bluegrass.* Top performers of Bluegrass and gospel music gather at the Kentucky Horse Park for a weekend of outdoor concerts. | 859/846–4995.

JULY: *Junior League Horse Show.* Held at the Red Mile Harness Track, the world's largest outdoor American Saddlebred show draws visitors and competitors from across the United States and Canada. | 859/252–1893.

AUG.: *Kids First Expo.* This is a trade-fair showcase for toys, clothing, ideas, services, and activities for kids two to ten. | 859/299–0411.

SEPT.: *Roots and Heritage Festival.* A week of music, theater, poetry-reading, and art exhibitions celebrating African-American heritage culminates in a weekend street fair. | 859/233–7299 or 800/845–3959.

OCT.: *Grand Circuit Meet.* Harness-racing events occur at the track that opened in 1875. Standardbreds pull two-wheel sulkies piloted by jockey/drivers. | 859/255–0752.

NOV.–DEC.: *Southern Lights.* The Kentucky Horse Park is decorated with a 2½-mi display of more than a million white and colored holiday lights, forming fairy tale tableaux, horse-racing themes, and, of course, Santa and his reindeer. | 859/233–4303.

Dining

A La Lucie. Continental. This mall café with fabric-covered booths and fringed lampshades is reminiscent of Paris' left bank in the '20s. The cocktails here are locally praised. The menu includes fresh fish and international fare. | 159 N. Limestone St., Lexington | 859/252–5277 | www.thepacificpearl.com/lucie.html | Closed Sun. No lunch | $14–$25 | AE, D, DC, MC, V.

★ **Alfalfa Restaurant.** Eclectic. The food in this small, woody, old-fashioned restaurant is organically grown, vegetarian, and ethnic. The menu, written on a chalkboard, may include

When it Comes to Getting Cash at an ATM, Same Thing.

Whether you're in Yosemite or Yemen, using your Visa° card or ATM card with the PLUS symbol is the easiest and most convenient way to get cash. Even if your bank is in Minneapolis and you're in Miami, Visa/PLUS ATMs make getting cash so easy, you'll feel right at home. After all, Visa/PLUS ATMs are open 24 hours a day, 7 days a week, rain or shine. And if you need help finding one of Visa's 627,000 ATMs in 127 countries worldwide, visit **visa.com/pd/atm**. We'll make finding an ATM as easy as finding the Eiffel Tower, the Pyramids or even the Grand Canyon.

It's Everywhere You Want To Be.°

Find America *with a Compass*

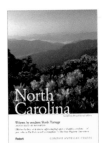

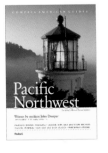

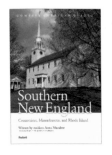

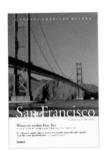

Written by local authors and illustrated throughout with images from regional photographers, Compass American Guides reveal the character and culture of America's most spectacular destinations. Covering more than 35 states and regions across the country, Compass guides are perfect for residents who want to explore their own backyards, and for visitors seeking an insider's perspective on all there is to see and do.

Fodor's Compass American Guides

At bookstores everywhere.

ham-and-apple quiche; the house salad is lavish. Each Wednesday a different cuisine—Greek, Italian, Indian—is served. | 557 S. Limestone St., Lexington | 859/253–0014 | No dinner Sun., Mon.; brunch weekends | $14–$20 | MC, V.

Atomic Cafe. Caribbean. The Bluegrass region may not seem like the place for Caribbean cuisine, but the conch fritters taste fresh off the boat. Jerk chicken and pork dishes are fiery. Shrimp lovers should check out the coconut-battered variety served here. Decor is tropical with evocative murals. | 265 N. Limestone St., Lexington | 859/254–1969 | Closed Sun.–Mon. | $10–$23 | MC, V.

Coach House. Continental. Attentive, formal service characterizes this upscale, white-tablecloth establishment. Try Dover sole, rack of lamb, and the homemade breads. Live jazz is featured Fri. and Sat. | 855 S. Broadway, Lexington | 859/252–7777 | No lunch weekends. Closed Sun. | $13–$26 | AE, D, DC, MC, V.

DeSha's Grill and Bar. Contemporary. Set on a busy corner at Victorian Square, this two-story restaurant offers an antique bar and views of downtown fountains. Known for steaks, chops, pasta, chicken and seafood, the kitchen also offers a kids' menu and Sunday brunch. | 101 N. Broadway, Lexington | 859/259–3771 | $6–$27 | AE, D, DC, MC, V.

Dudley's. American. Horse paintings accent the fine dining rooms of this renovated mid-19th-century schoolhouse. You can also choose open-air dining on the tree-shaded patio. | 380 S. Mill St., Lexington | 859/252–1010 | $12–$28 | AE, DC, MC, V.

Ed and Fred's Desert Moon Restaurant. American. The restaurant has the feel of a modern art gallery with paintings and sculptures of local artists. An eclectic menu offers choices such as sandwiches (Portobella and pepper, grilled salmon), gourmet pizzas and calzones, pastas, dungeness crab enchiladas, and Thai crab cakes. A kids' menu is available, and cocktails are served. | 148 Grand Blvd., Lexington | 859/231–1161 | deifert@earthlink.net | www.edandfredsdesertmoon.com | No lunch weekends, closed Mon. | $8–$20 | AE, D, DC, MC, V.

★ **Joe Bologna's.** Italian. Lots of carved wood and stained glass remain in this restored former church, known for its pasta and deep-dish pizza. | 120 W. Maxwell St., Lexington | 859/252–4933 | $11–$20 | AE, D, DC, MC, V.

Lynagh's Irish Pub and Grill. Irish. Dark and lively, this pub is decorated with bicycles hanging from the ceiling. Try the corned beef and cabbage or the locally-popular hamburgers. | 384 Woodland Ave., Lexington | 859/255–1292 | $11–$17 | No credit cards.

The Mansion at Griffin Gate. Continental. This 1873 Greek Revival mansion is furnished with period antiques. Dining here is like dining with Scarlett and Rhett (if they'd had a French chef). The menu includes veal, fresh seafood, and filet mignon. | 1720 Newtown Pike, Lexington | 859/288–6142 | No lunch | $27–$50 | AE, D, DC, MC, V.

Merrick Inn. Steak. The spacious, comfortable, not-too-formal restaurant is housed in a sprawling, white-columned building that was once a horse farm (circa 1890). On the extensive menu are steak, lamb, and a variety of pastas, and the specialty is fresh seasonal seafood. | 3380 Tates Creek Rd., Lexington | 859/269–5417 | Closed Sun. | $19–$35 | AE, DC, MC, V.

Pacific Pearl. Pan-Asian. This restaurant's contemporary, boldly-colored decor features a striking glass-and-metal bar, where you can sip an Oriental martini. Try the Thai bouillabaisse, crispy duck, or coconut-fried lobster. Open-air dining is available on the plant-lined patio. | 1050 Chinoe Rd., Lexington | 859/266–1611 | No lunch | $15–$32 | AE, D, DC, MC, V.

Phil Dunn's CookShop. Continental. The quilt made from jockey silks hanging on one wall identifies the bluegrass roots of this sophisticated bistro. The huge wooden counter in the middle of the room is a great place to sample an appetizer or enjoy dessert and coffee. Continental entrees include oven-roasted lamb chops, grilled Long Island duck, and spinach fettuccine with grilled vegetables. | 431 Old E. Vine St., Lexington | 859/231–0099 | No dinner Sun. | $15–$20 | AE, MC, V.

Regatta Seafood Grille. Seafood. Cheerful decor with a sailboat motif characterizes this bustling restaurant. There's open-air dining on the patio that overlooks a lake. A kids' menu is also available. | 161 Lexington Green Circle, Lexington | 859/273–7875 | $12–$32 | AE, D, DC, MC, V.

Roy and Nadine's. Contemporary. You'll find a Bohemian atmosphere and a lengthy martini list at Roy and Nadine's. There's a striking velvet sofa in the bar. Known for grilled duck, seafood, and savory appetizers, the restaurant also features a kids' menu. | 3775 Harrodsburg Rd. U.S. 27, Lexington | 859/223–0797 | No lunch Sun. | $15–$35 | AE, D, MC, V.

Lodging

Bed & Breakfast at Silver Springs Farm. Silver Springs Farm is 5 mi from downtown Lexington and is listed on the Survey of Historic Sites in Kentucky. The 21-acre farm has hand-laid stone fences and horses. It operated as a distillery from 1867 to Prohibition. The main house has three spacious rooms with queen or king beds, the two-bedroom cottage is fully furnished. If you bring your horse, there is a barn with turnout paddocks. The B&B features antiques, oak and maple floors, hand-pegged walnut doors, hand-reeded mantels, and a dog-legged stairway. One room has a private bath; the others share a bath. Complimentary breakfast. In-room data ports. Cable TV. | 3710 Leestown Pike, Lexington | 859/255–1784 or 877/255–1784 | www.bbsilverspringsfarm.com | 4 rooms | $99–$249 | MC, V.

Brand House at Rose Hill. The circa 1812 Federal style, one-story, B&B is on 1⅓ acres in the heart of Bluegrass horse country. It's listed on the National Register of Historic Places and the floor plan is registered with the Library of Congress. The house has been featured in a number of magazines. All rooms have private whirlpool baths and some rooms have fireplaces. Your breakfast may include Grand Marnier French toast, blueberry mousse, country ham souffle, fresh baked breads, and pastries. Complimentary breakfast. In-room hot tubs. Cable TV. Game room. No pets. No kids under 12. | 461 N. Limestone St., Lexington | 859/226–9464 or 800/366–4942 | fax 859/252–7940 | www.brandhouselex.com | 5 rooms | $109–$229 | AE, D, MC, V.

Campbell House Inn, Suites and Golf Club. Rooms here offer modern amenities amidst Early American-style furniture. Located 1½ mi from downtown, the facility is convenient to the airport and Keeneland Racetrack. Restaurants, bar with entertainment. In-room data ports, refrigerators. Cable TV. Pool. Beauty salon. Tennis. Exercise equipment. Video games. Laundry facilities. Business services. Airport shuttle. Free parking. | 1375 Harrodsburg Rd. (U.S. 68), Lexington | 859/255–4281 or 800/354–9235 (outside KY), 800/432–9254 (in KY) | fax 859/254–4368 | staying@campbellhouseinn.com | www.campbellhouseinn.com/ | 370 rooms | $70–$90 | AE, D, DC, MC, V.

Comfort Inn. Many of this motel's modern rooms have large corner desks, a plus for business travelers. The facility is convenient to Kentucky Horse Park. Complimentary Continental breakfast. Refrigerators. Cable TV. Indoor pool. Hot tub. Exercise equipment. Business services. | 2381 Buena Vista Dr., Lexington | 859/299–0302 | fax 859/299–2306 | 124 rooms | $70–$90 | AE, D, DC, MC, V.

Country Inns and Suites–Lexington. This four-story hotel is 3 mi east of downtown Lexington near the intersection of U.S. 60 and I–75 (Exit 110). It has 53 spacious rooms and four whirlpool suites—all units feature coffeemaker, hairdryer, iron and board, and free local phone calls. Breakfast includes bagels, an assortment of breads, muffins, cereals, fresh fruits, juices, coffee, tea, milk, and cocoa. Complimentary Continental breakfast. In-room data ports, microwaves, refrigerators, some in-room hot tubs. Indoor pool, indoor hot tub. Health club. Business services. | 2297 Executive Dr., Lexington | 859/299–8844 | fax 859/299–9688 | kpatelcountryinn@aol.com | 53 rooms, 4 suites | $65–$100 | AE, D, DC, MC, V.

Courtyard by Marriott. This handsome facility, located 3 mi outside of town, has many rooms overlooking the glass-covered, tree-lined courtyard. Bar. In-room data ports, some refrigerators. Cable TV. Indoor pool. Exercise equipment. Laundry facilities. Business services. Free parking. | 775 Newtown Ct., Lexington | 859/253–4646 | fax 859/253–9118 | 146 rooms | $70–$110 | AE, D, DC, MC, V.

Days Inn. Budget accommodations are available at this standard chain motel, located just off U.S. 75, at exit 104. Complimentary Continental breakfast. In-room data ports, some microwaves. TV. Business services. Some pets allowed. | 5575 Athens-Boonesboro Rd., Lexington | 859/263–3100 | fax 859/263–3120 | 56 rooms | $45–$65 | AE, D, DC, MC, V.

Four Points Barcelo Hotel. The three-story Barcelo Hotel is a Sheraton Starwood property featuring comfortable rooms with cherry furniture, coffeemaker, recliners, and workstation desks. Near I–75 Exit 115. Restaurant, bar. In-room data ports, some refrigerators. Cable TV. Indoor-outdoor pool. Health club. | 1938 Stanton Way, Lexington | 859/259–1311 or 800/325–3535 | fax 859/233–3658 | www.fourpoints.com | 174 rooms | $119 | AE, D, DC, MC, V.

Hampton Inn. One of the motel's room options is the "study room," which has a sofa and a desk in addition to the usual room furnishings. The facility is just off U.S. 75, at exit 110. Complimentary Continental breakfast. Cable TV. Indoor pool. Exercise equipment. | 2251 Elkhorn Rd., Lexington | 859/299–2613 | fax 859/299–9664 | www.hampton-inn.com | 125 rooms | $80–$90 | AE, D, DC, MC, V.

Hilton Suites of Lexington Green. Located 5 mi from downtown, this hotel features an atrium with a fountain, and glass-sided elevators. Suites feature wood veneer furniture and prints of horses. Restaurant, bar. In-room data ports, refrigerators, coffee. Cable TV. Pool. Exercise equipment. Business services. Airport shuttle. | 245 Lexington Green Circle, Lexington | 859/271–4000 | fax 859/273–2975 | hiltonsuites@juno.com | www.hilton.com | 174 suites | $100–$160 suites | AE, D, DC, MC, V.

Holiday Inn–North. This large chain hotel, located 2 mi north of downtown, features the Bluegrass region's largest Holidome recreation facility with indoor pool, sauna, and hot tub. The climate-controlled Holidome also has an array of exercise equipment. Restaurant, bar with entertainment. In-room data ports, microwaves, some refrigerators. Cable TV. Indoor pool. Hot tub, sauna. Exercise equipment. Video games. Laundry facilities. Business services. Free parking. Some pets allowed. | 1950 Newtown Pike, Lexington | 859/233–0512 | fax 859/231–9285 | www.holidayinn.com.ru/holiday-inn?_franchisee=lexno | 302 rooms | $110 | AE, D, DC, MC, V.

Holiday Inn–South. This stucco-and-brick hotel is just off U.S. 75, at exit 104, south of the city. Sports fans can request one of the two rooms decorated with the blue and white colors of the University of Kentucky Wildcats. Restaurant, bar with entertainment. In-room data ports. Cable TV. Pool. Exercise equipment. Laundry facilities. Business services. Free parking. Some pets allowed. | 5532 Athens-Boonesboro Rd., Lexington | 859/263–5241 | fax 859/263–4333 | 149 rooms | $60–$80 | AE, D, DC, MC, V.

Hyatt Regency. This modern hotel stands in the middle of downtown, and is connected by glass-enclosed skywalks to shopping areas, Victorian Square, and the Civic Center. Restaurants, bar. In-room data ports. Cable TV. Indoor pool. Exercise equipment. Business services. Airport shuttle. | 400 W. Vine St., Lexington | 859/253–1234 | fax 859/233–7974 | 365 rooms | $185 | AE, D, DC, MC, V.

La Quinta Inn. You'll find modern rooms and a small lobby with a bubbling fountain. The facility is located 3 mi from downtown, off U.S. 75 at exit 115. Complimentary Continental breakfast. In-room data ports. Cable TV. Pool. Business services. Free parking. Some pets allowed. | 1919 Stanton Way, Lexington | 859/231–7551 | fax 859/281–6002 | www.laquinta.com | 130 rooms | $70 | AE, D, DC, MC, V.

★ **Marriott's Griffin Gate Resort.** Located near major highways 3½ mi north of downtown, this resort boasts a two-story atrium lounge with waterfalls. Equestrian art figures prominently in the decor. Bar, dining room, picnic area. In-room data ports, refrigerators (in suites). Cable TV. 2 pools (1 indoor). Beauty salon. Hot tub. 18-hole golf course, putting green, tennis. Gym. Laundry facilities. Business services. Airport shuttle. Free parking. Some pets allowed.

| 1800 Newtown Pike Rte. 922, Lexington | 859/231–5100 | fax 859/288–6245 | www.marriott.com/lex | 409 rooms, 9 suites | $130–$170; $195–$250 suites | AE, D, DC, MC, V.

Microtel. Remodeled in 1999, this budget-priced motel offers clean and contemporary rooms 5 mi from downtown. In-room data ports. Cable TV. Business services. | 2240 Buena Vista Rd., Lexington; Take exit 110 off U.S. 75 | 859/299–9600 or 888/771–7171 | fax 859/299–8719 | 99 rooms | $43 | AE, D, DC, MC, V.

Quality Inn–Northwest. Cherry veneer furniture accents these guest rooms, some of which are equipped with desks, speaker phones, and recliner chairs. The motel is located just off the highway, 3 mi northwest of downtown. Complimentary Continental breakfast. Some microwaves. Cable TV. Pool. Playground. Business services. Free parking. Some pets allowed. | 1050 Newtown Pike Rte. 922, Lexington | 859/233–0561 | fax 859/231–6125 | 109 rooms | $45–$78 | AE, D, DC, MC, V.

Radisson Plaza Lexington. The atrium features fountains at this luxury hotel located on the main downtown square next to Rupp Arena. Restaurant, bar with entertainment. Some refrigerators. Cable TV. Indoor pool. Hot tub. Exercise equipment. Business services. Airport shuttle. | 369 W. Vine St., Lexington | 859/231–9000 | fax 859/281–3737 | www.radisson.com | 367 rooms, 21 suites | $165 | AE, D, DC, MC, V.

Ramada Inn and Conference Center. This modern hotel and conference center is located 15 mi east of downtown Versailles. The Hemburg Pavilion shopping center, which includes several restaurants, is 4 mi to the south. Rooms are decorated with floral themes and soft colors like cream and peach. Restaurant, bar (with entertainment), room service. In-room data ports. Cable TV. Pool. Hot tub, sauna. Gym. Miniature golf, tennis. Video games. Business services. | 2143 N. Broadway, Lexington | 859/299–1261 | fax 859/293–0048 | www.ramada.com | 140 rooms | $59–$99 | AE, DC, MC, V.

Red Roof Inn. Similar to other motels in the chain, this establishment offers no-frills accommodation at budget prices. The facility is located 5 mi from downtown and about ½ mi off U.S. 75. Cable TV. Business services. Some pets allowed. | 1980 Haggard Court, Lexington | 859/293–2626 | fax 859/299–8353 | 107 rooms | $53–$73 | AE, D, DC, MC, V.

Sheraton Suites Lexington. The atrium lobby here is modeled on New Orleans' French Quarter. A few conventional rooms are available in addition to suites. The facility is located 2 mi southeast of downtown. Restaurant, bar. In-room data ports, refrigerators. Cable TV, some hot tubs. Pool. Exercise equipment. Business services. Airport shuttle. | 2601 Richmond Rd., Lexington | 859/268–0060 or 800/262–3774 | fax 859/268–6209 | 155 suites | $99–$165 | AE, D, DC, MC, V.

Shoney's Inn. Rooms here are furnished with a pair of queen-size beds or a king-size bed. The facility is 2 mi southeast of downtown. Cable TV. Pool. Business services. | 2753 Richmond Rd., Lexington | 859/269–4999 or 800/552–4667 | fax 859/268–2346 | 100 rooms | $65–$75 | AE, D, DC, MC, V.

Springs Inn. Surrounded by old oak and crab apple trees, this green-and-white colonial-style hotel is across the street from a shopping mall, about 3 mi from downtown. Some suites are available. Restaurant, bar with entertainment. Some refrigerators. Cable TV. Pool, wading pool. Business services. Airport shuttle. Free parking. | 2020 Harrodsburg Rd. (U.S. 68), Lexington | 859/277–5751 or 800/354–9503 | fax 859/277–3142 | 196 rooms, 2 suites | $70 | AE, D, DC, MC, V.

Super 8. Located midway between downtown and the racing downs (5 mi to each), this chain motel offers simple, basic accommodations. A few small, single rooms are available, in addition to doubles. Cable TV. Free parking. | 2351 Buena Vista Rd., Lexington | 859/299–6241 | fax 859/299–6241 | 62 rooms | $51–$61 | AE, D, DC, MC, V.

The Swann's Nest at Cygnet Farm. This B&B is in the main home on a Lexington thoroughbred farm called Cygnet, tucked into the rolling Bluegrass countryside, 15 min. west of downtown Lexington, just off U.S. 60 to Versailles. Swann's Nest features three rooms in the main house, two spacious suites in the guest quarters, access to the commons area living room for reading and music, a den with fireplace, a screened porch, and a bricked courtyard with a bridged pond. A variety of tour and spa packages are available. Complimentary Continental breakfast, business services. | 3463 Rosalie La., Lexington | 859/226–0095 | fax 859/252–4499 | www.swannsnest.com | 5 rooms | $95–$160 | closed Dec. 15–Jan. 3 | AE, MC, V.

A True Inn Bed & Breakfast. This in-town, Richardsonian Romanesque, brick B&B built in 1843 for the Rev. John Ward, second Rector and organizer of Christ Episcopal Church, was remodeled in 1890 as an antebellum Greek Revival residence. Listed on the National Register of Historic Homes and The Bluegrass Trust, the home features a turret tower, stained and leaded glass, seven ornately carved Richardsonian and Victorian mantels, original chandeliers, spacious formal rooms and gardens. All five guest rooms have private baths, are decorated with antique furnishings, have either a full- or queen-size bed. Complimentary breakfast, some in-room refrigerators. Some in-room cable TV, cable TV in commons area, some in-room VCRs. Some in-room hot tubs. Bicycles. No pets. No kids under 12. | 467 West Second St., Lexington | 859/252–6166 or 800/374–6151 | truebandb@aol.com | www.bbonline.com/ky/trueinn | 5 rooms | $95–$150 | AE, MC, V.

LONDON

MAP 6, G5

(Nearby towns also listed: Barbourville, Corbin, Hazard, Monticello, Mount Vernon, Somerset)

Since the days of Daniel Boone, London has been a crossroads for visitors to this mountainous region. Today it is the area's commercial center, standing in the heart of the Daniel Boone National Forest. It's an important gateway to coal-mining country and supports manufacturing companies that produce baked goods, yarn, and clothing. One of Kentucky's most important pioneer historic sites is preserved at nearby Levi Jackson Wilderness Road State Park.

Information: London–Laurel County Tourist Commission. | 140 W. Daniel Boone Pkwy., London, 40741 | 606/878–6900 or 800/348–0095.

Attractions

Daniel Boone National Forest. The Daniel Boone Parkway begins near London and proceeds east into the Redbird Purchase Unit of the Forest. | Daniel Boone Pkwy. | 606/864–4163.

Laurel River Lake. Fishing in the 6,000-acre lake is principally for trout, bass, crappie, walleye, and bream. The 200-mi shoreline is characterized by steep bluffs and heavily forested hills, which are especially beautiful in fall. | The lake is located off I–75 at exit 38. Take Hwy. 92 west for 16 mi; then Hwy. 1193 | U.S. Forest Service, 761 South Laurel Rd., London | 606/864–4163 or 606/864–6412 | fax 606/878–0811 | Free | Daily.

Levi Jackson Wilderness Road State Park. Portions of the trails blazed by Daniel Boone (Wilderness Road and Boone's Trace), and used by more than 300,000 settlers between 1775 and 1800, traverse this 896-acre park. It's named after the first judge of Laurel County, who is buried in a pioneer cemetery on the grounds. | 998 Levi Jackson Mill Rd., London | 606/878–8000 | Free | Daily.

Corn-grinding demonstrations are given daily throughout the summer at **McHargue's Mill** (1812), restored in 1939. A large collection of millstones decorates the grounds. | 998 Levi Jackson Mill Rd., on state park grounds | 606/878–8000 | Free | Memorial Day–Labor Day, daily.

The **Mountain Life Museum** is a reproduction of a pioneer settlement, with log buildings and 18th-century farm tools and weapons. In addition, there's also a smokehouse and a blacksmith store. | 998 Levi Jackson Mill Rd., on state park grounds | 606/878–8000 | $1.50 | Apr.–Oct., daily 9–4:30.

London Motorplex. The regulation size drag strip, 5 mi west of I–75 on Daniel Boone Parkway, explodes into action every Saturday from April through November with a varied array of drag racing entertainment. Also, there are often races on Friday nights. | Daniel Boone Pkwy., London | 606/878–8883 | Entrance fee | Closed Dec.–Mar.

ON THE CALENDAR
MAY: *Women's National NAIA Golf Tournment.* The National Association of Intercollegiate Athletics Women's golf tournament is held in mid-month at the London Country Club. | 606/864–7849.
SEPT.: *World Chicken Festival.* Four days of "eggs-citement" in downtown London celebrate Laurel County as the home of Colonel Harland Sanders's first Kentucky Fried Chicken restaurant. You'll find entertainment, contests, a parade, a car show, a hot-air balloon race, and the world's largest skillet. There's no shortage of food. | 606/878–6900 or 800/348–0095.
OCT.: *Camp Wildcat and Civil War Reenactment.* A full-weekend living history encampment is featured on Wildcat Mountain. | 606/878–6900 or 800/348–0095.

Dining

El Dorado Mexican Restaurant. Mexican. Colorful decorations liven this festive restaurant. Besides a hefty assortment of entrees, there are many specialty dishes, including Especial El Dorado—a combination of spices, fresh vegetables, marinated beef, chorizo, shrimp, and chicken. It's grilled and served on a sizzling platter. Vegetarian dishes are available. For dessert, try a flan or *sopapilla* (fried tortilla topped with powdered sugar and honey) with ice cream. | 740 West Hwy., London | 606/877–2806 | fax 606/877–2807 | $8–$12 | AE, D, MC, V.

Ruby Tuesday. American. The standard Ruby Tuesday decor of mahogany wood, polished brass, whimsical artifacts, and Tiffany lamps creates a casual, nostalgic atmosphere. The menu includes appetizers, soups, sandwiches, chicken entrees, pasta, steaks, and fajitas. | 1916 W. Hwy. 192, London | 606/862–0015 | fax 606/862–0184 | $7–$16 | AE, D, DC, MC, V.

Lodging

Best Western Harvest Inn. You'll find moderate-priced accommodations and modern facilities with some of the amenities of more expensive motels. It's located on the highway about 1 mi north of downtown. Restaurant, complimentary Continental breakfast. Cable TV. Indoor pool. Hot tub. Free parking. | 207 W. Rte. 80, London | 606/864–2222 | fax 606/878–2825 | 100 rooms | $50–$70 | AE, D, DC, MC, V.

Budget Host–Westgate Inn. This small motel, located on the highway 1 mi north of downtown, is well-kept, and the decor is warmer than that of most chain hotels. Cable TV. Pool. Some pets allowed. | 254 W. Daniel Boone Pkwy. (Rte. 80), London | 606/878–7330 | fax 606/878–7330 | mail@budgethost.com | www.budgethost.com | 46 rooms | $47 | AE, D, DC, MC, V.

Comfort Suites. Spacious suites cater to families at this moderately-priced facility, located 2 mi west of downtown. Complimentary Continental breakfast. In-room data ports, refrigerators. Cable TV. Indoor pool. Laundry facilities. Business services. Free parking. | 1918 U.S. 192, London | 606/877–7848 | fax 606/877–7907 | 62 rooms | $65–$109 | AE, D, DC, MC, V.

Hampton Inn. Nicely appointed rooms and a spacious lobby give this motel a more luxurious atmosphere than its rates would lead you to expect. The facility is directly off the interstate, at exit 38. Complimentary Continental breakfast. In-room data ports, some refrigerators. Hot tubs in some rooms. Cable TV. Pool. Business services. Free parking. | 2075 U.S. 192, London | 606/877–1000 | fax 606/864–8560 | 82 rooms | $62–$72 | AE, D, DC, MC, V.

Holiday Inn Express–London. This comfortable two-story motel, with outside corridors, has a spacious sitting area in the lobby with a small selection of games and books. The rooms feature king- or queen-size beds, desk, movies, coffeemakers, hair dryers, irons and boards. A deluxe Continental breakfast is offered with homemade breads and Belgian waffles made to order. Near I–75 exit 41 at the junction of Hwy 80. Complimentary Continental break-fast. In-room data ports. Cable TV. Indoor–outdoor pool. Hot tub. Pets allowed (small). | 400 GOP St., London | 606/878–7678 or 800/831–3958 | fax 606/878–7654 | www.londonky.com/holidayinnexpress/ | $75 | AE, D, DC, MC, V.

LOUISVILLE

(Nearby towns also listed: Bardstown, Brandenburg, Fort Knox, Frankfort, Shelbyville, Shepardsville)

Louisville is the state's largest city, founded at the Falls of the Ohio in 1778 by Gen. George Rogers Clark. The city was named in honor of Louis XVI of France and that country's aid to the American Colonies during the Revolutionary War. Long a commercial center due to its location on the Ohio River, the city today is a center of health care and medical research (headquartered at the University of Louisville), an international air hub for United Parcel Service, and home of the largest truck-manufacturing plant in the western hemisphere, run by the Ford Motor Company. Historic residential districts include the Victorian Old Louisville, just south of downtown, and the Edwardian Cherokee Triangle to the east. Louisville's Main Street has the largest collection of cast-iron fronted buildings in the United States outside of New York City.

Attractions include historic Churchill Downs race course, home of the Kentucky Derby and the Kentucky Derby Museum; the *Belle of Louisville* paddle-wheel steamboat, which takes passengers on river excursions; the Louisville Slugger Museum attached to Hillerich and Bradsby Company, where the famous baseball bats are made; a waterfront walk stretching along 16 mi of the Ohio River; a network of parks designed by Frederick Law Olmsted; and historic homes, including Farmington (designed by Thomas Jefferson) and Locust Grove (last home of Gen. George Rogers Clark). Money is currently being raised for a museum dedicated to the life of Louisville's celebrity native, boxer Muhammad Ali. Cave Hill Cemetery, just east of downtown, is a national arboretum. A portion of its 300 acres contains the only federally-funded military cemetery in the country with both Union and Confederate graves, a reflection of Kentucky's position as a border state during the war. Reached from the Indiana shore, but in the river (so still in Kentucky), is the largest exposed Devonian fossil bed in the world, at the Falls of the Ohio.

A rich arts scene is led by the Louisville Orchestra, which gained international prominence in the 1950s for commissioning, performing, and recording works by 20th-century composers. Actors Theatre of Louisville, home of the Humana Festival of New American Plays, which has spawned several Broadway and Pulitzer Prize-winning productions is also at home in Louisville. The city also has resident professional opera, ballet, and children's theater companies. The International Bluegrass Festival is now held in the city each year.

Information: Louisville Convention and Visitors Bureau | 400 S. 1st St., Louisville, 40202 | 502/584–2121 | www.louisville-visitors.com.

NEIGHBORHOODS

Downtown: Preston and 18th Streets define downtown Louisville to the north and south, while Broadway and the Ohio River make up the eastern and western boundaries. Inside the zone, which is mostly an historic area, you'll find a variety of architectural styles and handsome museums mixed in with modern buildings. Along West Main Street you'll find 19th-century cast-iron architecture. The facade of the Hart Block at 728 W. Main Street, was built in 1884, at the height of Louisville's Victorian era, a jigsaw puzzle of cast-iron pieces bolted together. Other famous local landmarks include the

Gothic Cathedral of the Assumption, the Greek Revival Jefferson County Courthouse, and several contemporary works, including the Aegon Center, the Humana Building by architect Michael Graves, and the American Life and Accident Building. Also in the area is the Kentucky Center for the Arts and the Louisville Science Center/IMAX Theatre.

TRANSPORTATION

Airports: Most major carriers serve Louisville International Airport (502/367-4636), about 10 mi south of the city off I–65. Cab fare into the city runs about $20.
Bus Lines: The city is served by Greyhound Lines (720 W. Muhammad Ali Blvd., 800/ 231–2222).

© Corbis

THE RUN FOR THE ROSES

The fanfare of the trumpeter's electrifying "Call to the Post" sends a ripple through the stands, signalling that the horses are entering the racetrack from the paddock. Seconds later, when the first thoroughbred's hoof touches the track, a band strikes up the introduction to the state song and the crowd, 150,000 strong, breaks into "My Old Kentucky Home." Women in hats and linen frocks, men wearing jackets and horse-printed neckties, and tee-shirt-clad college kids thronging the infield are all misty-eyed, even as they're singing "Weep no more, my lady."

But minutes later, the poignancy of Stephen Foster's lyrics is forgotten, as the last powerful racehorse is loaded in the starting gate, as the gate's doors fly open, and as the Churchill Downs announcer proclaims, "They're Off!"

The Kentucky Derby is the world's most famous horse race. America's longest continually-held sporting event has been run the first Saturday in May at the historic, twin-spired Louisville racetrack since 1875. Legendary horses such as Citation, Gallant Fox, Whirlaway, and the incomparable Secretariat (whose 1973 record time of 1:59 $^2/_5$ for the 1$^1/_4$ mi race still stands) have all raced into the winner's circle to have their graceful necks adorned with the garland of roses. But this is more than just a horse race: it's a tradition. And it's a party.

The Derby is steeped in rituals, from the singing of "My Old Kentucky Home" (the lyrics are printed in the program so non-natives can participate) to the mixing of 2,000 gallons of mint juleps. (Caution: More than one will make you forget which horse you bet on.)

Louisville steps out for two full weeks leading up to the two-minute race. The Kentucky Derby Festival starts with a bang in a massive fireworks display on the downtown riverfront. Tickets for prime seats to "Thunder Over Louisville," two Saturdays before the Derby, are almost as difficult to come by as box seats for the Derby itself. During the following fortnight there are races of all sorts—a minimarathon for humans, a hot-air balloon competition, and a rivalry for river supremacy between two antique stern-wheelers—the hometown's *Belle of Louisville* and Cincinnati's *Delta Queen*. Parties, from elegant black-tie balls—with hefty ticket prices that benefit charities—to country music blowouts, grip the city in a celebratory fever. And there's a Derby Festival Parade on Broadway, with a celebrity grand marshall, not to mention lots of floats, bands, and, of course, horses.

Intra-city Transit: Public transportation within Louisville consists of buses run by the Transit Authority of River City (1000 W. Broadway, 502/585–1234). The fare is $1 during peak hours, 75¢ at all other times.

Driving around Town: Louisville is a key hub of the interstate highway system. It's intersected by I-64, which runs east-west, and by I-65, which runs north-south; I–71 comes in from the northeast, and I-264, also known as the Henry Watterson Expressway, and I-265, also known as the Gene Snyder Freeway, encircle the city with inner- and outer-beltways, respectively.

WALKING TOUR: LOUISVILLE'S HISTORIC WEST MAIN STREET
(approximately two hours)

★ Since it is only a block from the Ohio River and runs parallel to it, West Main Street was the 19th century center of Louisville commerce. Most of the Victorian-era office and warehouse buildings with cast-iron facades (the largest concentration of such architecture in America outside of New York City's SoHo district) have been preserved and refurbished. They share the street with striking new skyscrapers along a corridor of theaters, offices, and museums.

Start on the south side of Main at the corner of 3rd Street and walk west. Halfway along the block on your left will be **Actors Theatre of Louisville,** housed in the 1837 Greek Revival former bank building that was attributed to Kentucky architect Gideon Shryrock, but actually was built under his supervision from plans by New York's James Dakin. As you walk toward 4th Street, you'll see across Main the **American Life and Accident Building,** designed by Mies van der Rohe and completed in 1973. Its facade of oxidized Cor-Ten steel gives it a unique rusty color.

Walking past 30-story black box **National City Bank Tower** on the left, you'll come to the **Humana Building** on the same side of Main, and just across 5th Street. An eclectic neo-Egyptian design, with cascading fountains and pink Italian marble covering, it was designed by Michael Graves and completed in 1985. Across the street is the **Kentucky Center for the Arts,** with its collection of 20th-century sculpture. Walk through the lobby of the Arts Center to the **Belvedere,** which overlooks the Ohio. There is a bronze stature of city founder, **Gen. George Rogers Clark** with raised arm pointing to the Falls of the Ohio. Below the Belvedere, you'll see the **Belle of Louisville** paddle-wheeler docked at the foot of 4th Street.

Returning to Main Street, walk along the north (Arts Center) side to appreciate the cast-iron fronts of the buildings in the 600 and 700 block. There are several restaurants and cafés along the way; good for a coffee or lunch stop. The street's oldest building, the **St. Charles Hotel** (634) was restored as offices for the Brown–Forman Corporation in 1999. The **Hart Block** (726–730) features a marvelous jigsaw puzzle of cast-iron components on the building fronts. Housed in the former Carter Dry Goods Building at 727 is the **Louisville Science Center and IMAX Theatre.** Stop in to tour both permanent and traveling exhibits, as well as to view a 20–30 minute IMAX nature film. The other fine museum on Main St. is the **Louisville Slugger Museum.** It's a half block west and across the street from the Science Center at 800 West Main. The 6½-story replica of a bat leaning against the building is one of Louisville's newest landmarks. The good sports in charge of the plate-glass factory next door agreed to have a proportionally large baseball imbedded in one of its windows.

Attractions
ART AND ARCHITECTURE

Conrad-Caldwell House. This Victorian Romanesque Revival mansion designed by architect Arthur Loomis has elaborate stonework on the outside and detailed woodwork within. It was built in the 1890s for lumber baron Theophilus Conrad. The house is furnished with elegant Victorian antiques. Features include parquet floors, intricate tilework, and a smoking balcony. | 1402 St. James Ct., Louisville | 502/636–5023 | caldwell@iglou.com | www.old-louisville.com/museums.htm | $3.50 | Wed.–Fri. and Sun. noon–4; Sat. 10–4.

Farmington. The early 19th century redbrick Federal home of the Speed family was built from a design by Thomas Jefferson. Unusual features include octagonal rooms and a recessed staircase. The former hemp plantation has a period-style garden and stone outbuildings. Lincoln visited his friend Joshua Speed here in 1841. | 3033 Bardstown Rd. N, Louisville | 502/452–9920 | $4 | Tues.–Sat. 10–4:30, Sun. 1:30–4:30.

Jefferson County Courthouse. This Greek Revival mid-1800s courthouse was designed by Gideon Shryock. Cast iron is used inside for the floor of the 68-ft rotunda, which contains a grand cast-iron staircase and balustrade. A rose garden and statues of Thomas Jefferson and Louis XIV grace the grounds. | 527 W. Jefferson St., Louisville | 502/574–6161 | Free | Weekdays 9–5.

Locust Grove. This Georgian mansion, built in the late 18th century by the Croghan family, became the last home of George Rogers Clark when he moved here in 1809. (Lucy Croghan was Clark's sister.) The 55-acre garden has numerous stone and log outbuildings, a visitor center with orientation film and gift shop, and restored formal gardens designed by the same firm that re-created the gardens at Mt. Vernon. The mansion and outbuildings are furnished with period antiques and implements. | 561 Blankenbaker La., Louisville | 502/896–2433 | www.locustgrove.org | $4 | Daily.

Riverside, The Farnsley-Moremen Landing. This two-story, brick manor house overlooking the Ohio River dates from 1837 and has been fully restored. Period furnishings include reproductions and some original pieces. There is a dock attached to the farmstead, from which the small stern-wheeler, *The Spirit of Jefferson,* makes excursions in the summer. | 7410 Moorman Rd., Louisville | 502/935–6809 | $4 | Tues.–Sat. 10–4:30, Sun. 1–4:30.

Thomas Edison House. A room in this tiny Butchertown house was home to Thomas Edison when he worked briefly for Western Union as a teenager just after the Civil War. Displays feature several Edisonian inventions and experiments. | 731 E. Washington, Louisville | 502/585–5247 | fax 502/585–5247. | edisonhouse@edisonhouse.org | www.edisonhouse.org/ | $4 | Tues.–Sat. 10–2.

Water Tower. The headquarters and gallery for the Louisville Visual Arts Association is housed in a Grecian temple-style building dating from 1860. It was the Louisville Water Company's first pumping station. The 183-ft-tall tower is crowned by statues of Classical gods and goddesses. | 3005 River Rd., Louisville | 502/896–2146 | fax 502/896–2148 | www.louisvillevisualart.org | Free | Daily.

BEACHES, PARKS, AND NATURAL SIGHTS

E. P. "Tom" Sawyer State Park. These 370 acres in eastern Jefferson County contain a swimming pool, archery range, baseball fields, tennis courts, and picnic areas. It is the main site for the annual Corn Island Storytelling Festival. | 3000 Freys Hill Rd., Louisville | 502/426–8950 | www.kystateparks.com/agencies/parks/tomsawyr.htm | Free; fee for some activities | Daily.

Otter Creek Park. Located on the site of a riverside town destroyed in the 1937 flood, this 2,600-acre park near Fort Knox is owned by the city of Louisville. Camping and hiking are main activities; overnight accommodations are available in several cabins, as well as in a rustic lodge. Tours of the caves under the park are offered. | 850 Otter Creek Park, Brandenburg | 502/583–3577 | Free | Mar.–Nov., Tues.–Sun.

CULTURE, EDUCATION, AND HISTORY

Actors Theatre of Louisville. Honored with a Tony Award for outstanding regional theater, Actors is one of the city's most important arts organizations. Some 200 plays that have premiered here are still in production in theaters around the world. The annual Humana Festival of New American Plays is an important event for theater, and each performance season includes a mix of productions from Shakespeare and Shaw to contemporary works. The complex contains a trio of theaters. | 316 Main St., Louisville | 502/584–1205 or 800/4–ATLTIX | $15 and up | Productions year-round.

Bellarmine College. Situated on more than 100 hilly acres, this Catholic liberal-arts college is noted for its pre-med program and business school. The Thomas Merton Studies Center contains the author/monk's manuscripts, drawings, tapes, and published books. Tours of the campus are available by appointment. | 2001 Newburg Rd., Louisville | 502/452–8000 or 502/452–8187 | fax 502/452–8094 | www.bellarmine.edu | Free | Tues.–Fri., by appointment.

Cave Hill Cemetery. This historic cemetery, chartered in 1848, is the final resting place for members of many prominent Louisville families, including the Binghams and the Speeds. Among other notables buried here are Gen. George Rogers Clark, Louisville's founder, and Col. Harland Sanders, the fried-chicken mogul. Cave Hill is also a bird sanctuary and national arboretum. The central lake is populated by several species of ducks, geese, and swans. There are nearly 300 labeled species of trees. | 701 Baxter Ave., Louisville | 502/451–5630 | Free | Daily.

The Filson Club. This is the state's oldest historical society—named for John Filson, who published the first history of Kentucky in 1784. It houses some 50,000 books, periodicals, and 1½ million manuscripts. You can take a self-guided tour of the Victorian mansion headquarters. | 1310 S. 3rd St., Louisville | 502/635–5083 | www.filsonclub.org | $5 | weekdays 9–5, Sat. 9–noon.

Historic Districts. Central Louisville is a patchwork of distinctive, historic neighborhoods. The layout of the streets and courts of Old Louisville, south of downtown, was designed for the Southern Exposition of 1883 and is anchored by Central Park. Ornate Victorian homes, including the Conrad-Caldwell House (see above) line the streets. Downtown, the West Main Street Historic District has businesses, museums, and apartments housed behind the largest collection of cast-iron building facades in the nation outside of New York City. Butchertown, to the east of the business district, is characterized by shotgun houses that housed immigrant workers in the area's meat-packing plants. And the tree-filled Cherokee Triangle contains elegant homes dating from the early 20th century. | Traverse Old Louisville, between Breckinridge and 9th Sts., near Central Park. Also visit W. Main St., between 1st and 8th Sts. You'll also want to see Story Ave. west to Market St. Stop by Cherokee Triangle—Cherokee Rd. from Broadway to Eastern Pkwy. | 502/582–3732 or 800/792–5595.

Kentucky Center for the Arts. Three theaters—the 2,400-seat Whitney Hall, the 626-seat Bomhard Theater, and the intimate black box MEX (Martin Experimental Theater)—provide performance venues for local and traveling concerts, operas, plays, and dance productions. Decor includes sculpture, both inside and out, by such 20th-century artists as Alexander Calder, Jean Dubuffet, and Louise Nevelson. | 5 Riverfront Plaza, Louisville | 502/584–7777 or 800/775–7777 | Daily.

Louisville Seminary. On the seminary campus is Gardencourt, a restored 200-year-old house which is often host to chamber music concerts. There's also an Archeological Museum with Middle Eastern collections, including one of Palestinian pottery. | 1044 Alta Vista Rd., Louisville | 502/895–3411 | fax 502/895–1096 | Free | Daily.

Spalding University. Founded in 1814 by the Sisters of Charity at Nazareth, originally as a college for women, this liberal arts institution is now co-ed. The centerpiece is the Whitestone Mansion, a late-19th-century Renaissance Revival structure with stained-glass windows and a soaring, carved-wood staircase. Rooms used for seminars and by students as reading areas are furnished with period antiques. | 851 S. 4th St., Louisville | 502/585–9911 | fax 502/585–7158 | www.spalding.edu | Free | Weekdays.

University of Louisville. This sprawling urban campus contains schools of arts and sciences, engineering, music, law, social work, and business. The Federal-style administration building with a handsome rotunda is marked by a copy from the original casting of Rodin's *The*

Thinker at the entrance. Current enrollment is 23,000. Visitor information centers stand at the 3rd Street entrance and at the corner of 1st and Brandeis streets. | 2000 S. 1st St., Louisville | 502/852–6565 | www.louisville.edu | Free | Daily.

★ The **Speed Art Museum,** the oldest art museum in Kentucky (founded in 1927), is housed in a stone-front building of neoclassical design. Collections of European furniture, paintings by old and modern masters (including Picasso, Rembrandt, Monet, and Rubens), Native American art, and a modern sculpture court are highlights. A special hands-on gallery for kids allows them to create their own "masterpieces." Major traveling exhibitions come to the museum three or four times a year. | 2035 S. 3rd St. | 502/634–2700 | fax 502/636–2899 | www.speedmuseum.org | Free; fee for special exhibitions | Tues.–Fri. 10–4, Thurs. 10–8, Sat. 10–5, Sun. noon–5.

Zachary Taylor National Cemetery. President and Mrs. Zachary Taylor are buried here near the home (now a private residence) in which Taylor grew up. The national cemetery, which surrounds the Taylor family plot, was chartered in 1928. | 4701 Brownsboro Rd., Louisville | 502/893–3852 | Free | Daily.

MUSEUMS

Colonel Harland Sanders Museum. Housed in the giant white neo-antebellum "mansion" built as the corporate headquarters for Kentucky Fried Chicken, the museum contains artifacts related to the development of the Colonel's famous "secret recipe." A half-hour video about the history of the company includes an interview with the late Sanders. | 1441 Gardiner La., Louisville | 502/874–8300 | Free | Weekdays.

★ **Louisville Slugger Museum and Bat Factory.** Visitors enter this museum honoring baseball's greatest hitters through a replica of a dugout and have the opportunity to stand at a virtual home plate and swing at virtual fast balls. Bats on display include those that were swung by Ruth, Mantle, Maris, DiMaggio, and more recently, Sosa and McGwire. Guided tours of the factory, which is next door to the museum, are available. | 800 W. Main St., Louisville | 502/588–7228 | www.slugger.com/museum | $5 | Mon.–Sat. 9–5.

SPORTS AND RECREATION

Churchill Downs. The famous twin spires atop the grandstand mark Churchill Downs, the nation's oldest still-functioning thoroughbred race course. There's been racing here since 1875; the most famous meet, the Kentucky Derby, is run here on the first Saturday in May. The Downs is also one of the regular sites for the annual Breeders Cup held in the fall. | 700 Central Ave., Louisville | 502/636–4400 | fax 502/636–4430 | www.kentuckyderby.com | $2; reserved seating $4.50; Derby tickets range from $35 to $500 | Tours daily, 9–5. Racing late-Apr.–June, late-Oct.–Nov.

The **Kentucky Derby Museum** includes exhibitions celebrating the history and drama of the Kentucky Derby, including the multimedia show, "Time Machine," which features film clips of past derbies; a starting gate in which you can sit on a horse mannequin; and a beginner's guide to betting. There's even a resident live thoroughbred who lives in a paddock next to the Derby Cafe, the restaurant housed in the museum. | Gate 1 at Churchill Downs | 502/637–1111 or 502/637–7097 | www.derbymuseum.org | $6 | Weekdays 9–5, Sun. noon–5.

Kentucky Fair and Exposition Center. This is the state's largest multipurpose facility with over 1 million square ft of indoor, air-conditioned exhibition space. The on-site arena is home to University of Louisville basketball games, rock and country music concerts, an annual international horse show, and the National Farm Machinery Show. The center is also the site of the annual Kentucky State Fair. | I–65S at I–264W, Louisville | 502/367–5000 | Daily.

Riverwalk. Riverwalk's paved pathway stretches along nearly 7 mi of the city's riverfront (in some places only inches from the water), through some unexpectedly natural undeveloped areas. Some spots offer excellent views of barge traffic, McAlpine Locks and Dam at the Falls of the Ohio, and the city skyline. Parking is available at 4th Street, 8th Street, 10th Street, 31st Street and at Lannan, Shawnee, and Chickasaw Parks. | Free | Daily.

Six Flags Kentucky Kingdom. This amusement and water park, populated by staffers dressed as Warner Brothers cartoon characters, offers more than 110 rides and attractions. Among them are six roller coasters, including Chang, said to be the world's longest stand-up roller coaster. | The park is next to the Kentucky Fair and Exposition Center | 937 Phillips La., Louisville | 502/366–7508 | www.sixflags.com | $33 | Memorial Day–late Sept., daily.

SIGHTSEEING TOURS/TOUR COMPANIES

Joe and Mike's Pretty Good Tours. Daily bus tours (except major holidays) departing from downtown hotels at 9:30 and 2:30. Allow three hours. | 3744 Glenmeade Rd., Louisville | 502/459–1247.

Louisville Horse Trams, Inc. Horse-drawn carriage tours of the downtown area are offered after 6:30 PM, weather permitting. | Call for departure areas | 502/581–0100.

Riverboat Excursion. *The Belle of Louisville*, a stern-wheeler built in Pittsburgh in 1913, takes passengers on two-hour trips along the Ohio several times a day, including evening cruises. The boat races Cincinnati's *Delta Queen* each year as part of the Kentucky Derby Festival, and serenades the city daily with its steam calliope. Special dance cruises are offered in October. | 401 W. River Rd., Louisville | 502/574–BELL | $10 | May–Sept., daily.

OTHER POINTS OF INTEREST

American Printing House for the Blind. Founded in 1858, the printing house is one of the oldest facilities in the world making Braille and large-type books, maps, and other documents for the visually impaired. Tours are given of the printing plant and recording studios where "talking books" are produced. The Kentucky School for the Blind is also here. A museum in the 1883 section of the campus contains embossed and Braille books from the publisher's historic collection. | 1839 Frankfort Ave., Louisville | 502/895–2405 | Free | Mon.–Thurs.

Louisville Science Center. Housed in a restored cast-iron 19th-century warehouse, the center contains numerous hands-on exhibits geared to visitors of all ages. Permanent installations include "The World We Create" (about technology) and "The World Within Us" (human anatomy and physiology). KidZone is a special discovery area for kids under eight. IMAX films are shown in the four-story theater. | 727 W. Main St., Louisville | 502/561–6111 | lousci@bellsouth.net | www.louisvillescience.org | General admission $6; IMAX $6, together, $9 | Daily.

Louisville Zoo. Some 1,300 animals from around the world live in naturalistic settings arranged by geographic regions. The recently-opened islands exhibit features South Pacific fauna including tapirs, Galapagos tortoises, and orangutans. A small-scale train circles the zoo, and in summer there are camel and elephant rides. The indoor Herpaquarium and educational MetaZoo have reptiles, amphibians, and one of the country's largest collections of arachnids (spiders and their cousins). | 1100 Trevilian Way, Louisville | 502/459–2181 | mphan@louky.org | www.louisvillezoo.org | $7.95 | Daily.

ON THE CALENDAR

FEB.–APR.: *Humana Festival of New American Plays.* Three theaters in the historic complex on Main St. provide the stages for this Tony Award–winning festival, celebrating new plays written by established, as well as unknown, playwrights. | 502/584–1205.
APR.: *Festival of the Dogwood.* More than 40 blocks in Victorian Old Louisville are in bloom during the peak of the spring flowering tree and shrub season. | 502/582–3732.
APR.–MAY: *Kentucky Derby Festival.* Two weeks of partying celebrate America's most famous horse race. The Pegasus Parade on Broadway, the Great Steamboat Race on the Ohio, and an enormous fireworks display ("Thunder Over Louisville," on the riverfront) are among the events. | 502/584–6383 or 800/928–FEST | www.kds.org.
MAY: *Kentucky Derby.* The nation's top three-year-old thoroughbreds run 1¼ mi for a chance at racing immortality at historic Churchill Downs. | 502/636–4400.

APR.–SEPT.: *Louisville RiverBats Baseball.* Triple A minor-league professional baseball games are played at Louisville Slugger Field on Main Street. | 502/361–3100 | www.ticketmaster.com.

JUNE–JULY: *Kentucky Shakespeare Festival.* The oldest, free outdoor Shakespeare festival in the nation is held in Central Park. Two different productions are performed each season. | 502/583–8738.

AUG.: *Kentucky State Fair.* For 10 days at the Kentucky Fair and Exposition Center, you can take in displays of livestock, produce, and crafts. Cooking and other competitions and a midway full of rides are part of the fun. There are nightly country music and pops concerts by leading performers. The World's Championship Horse Show is another highlight. | 502/367–5002.

SEPT.: *Corn Island Storytelling Festival.* Storytellers from all over the country keep listeners enthralled with traditional and contemporary tales. The Ghost Stories at Long Run Park are among the most popular. Main events are held at E. P. "Tom" Sawyer Park. | 502/245–0643.

SEPT.: *Bluegrass Fan Fest.* Hosted by the International Bluegrass Music Association, a weekend of strumming, picking, and jamming attracts fiddlers and singers from around the world. | 888/438–4262.

SEPT.–MAY: *Performing Arts.* The Louisville Orchestra, Louisville Ballet, Kentucky Opera, Broadway Series, and Children's Theater each have a nine-month arts season and perform at various venues, including the Kentucky Center for the Arts and the Brown Theater. | 502/584–7777.

OCT.: *St. James Court Art Show.* One of the largest outdoor art shows in the nation is held on the sidewalks and courts under the trees in Victorian Old Louisville. | 502/635–1842.

NOV.: *Light Up Louisville.* Holiday music and food are attractions in this downtown street fair, held every year on the Friday after Thanksgiving. As soon as it's dark, Louisville's mayor throws the switch to illuminate the office towers and church steeples of the city. | 502/574–3061.

Dining
INEXPENSIVE

Baxter Station Bar and Grill. Contemporary, Latin. This historic, railroad-themed neighborhood bar includes an electric train that circles the restaurant. Try applewood smoked pork tenderloin, hot sandwiches, and beef tenderloin. | 1201 Payne St., Louisville | 502/584–1635 | Reservations not accepted | Closed Sun. | $9–$16 | AE, D, MC, V.

Come Back Inn. Italian. This very casual neighborhood hangout has a beautiful carved oak bar. It's known for Italian beef sandwich, hoagies, pizza, pasta. | 909 Swan St., Louisville | 502/627–1777 | Reservations not accepted | No dinner Mon. Closed Sun. | $9–$17 | AE, MC, V.

MODERATE

Asiatique. Pan-Asian, Contemporary. Dramatic purple and green color scheme is joined by original art in this contemporary restaurant. Try roasted mandarin quail, wok-seared sea scallops, herb-crusted chicken with mango chutney. | 106 Sears Ave., Louisville | 502/899–3578 | Jacket and tie | No lunch | $17–$30 | AE, D, DC, MC, V.

Cafe Mimosa. Vietnamese, Chinese. Asian art adds to the atmosphere here. A picture window overlooks bustling Bardstown Road. A sushi bar has been added recently. Known for chicken, pork, and shrimp. Kids' menu available. | 1216 Bardstown Rd., Louisville | 502/458–2233 | $11–$23 | AE, D, MC, V.

De La Torre's. Spanish. Enjoy a bit of Old Madrid in this white-plastered dining room with burgundy tablecloths and tile accents in the walls. Locals favor the paella, leg of lamb, and authentic tapas. | 1859 Bardstown Rd., Louisville | 502/456–4955 | Closed Sun. No lunch | $17, all entrees | AE, D, DC, MC, V.

Ferd Grisanti's. Northern Italian. Modern Italian style and art mark the dining room at Ferd Grisanti's. The sun room is especially inviting. Known for veal and pasta, the restaurant also offers a kids' menu. | 10120 Taylorsville Rd., Jeffersontown | 502/267–0050 | Closed Sun. No lunch | $11–$27 | AE, D, DC, MC, V.

Indigo Bistro and Bar. Contemporary. Giant French posters hang on the walls of this quiet, wood-trimmed dining room with art deco bar. They're known for seafood, pasta, lamb, and beef. The restaurant also features open-air dining on an awning-covered patio. | 3930 Chenoweth Sq., Louisville | 502/893–0106 | Closed Sun. | $10–$20 | AE, DC, MC, V.

★ **Lynn's Paradise Cafe.** American. Formica, concrete animals, and unattractive lamps anchor the outrageous decor. Look for a giant red coffee pot fountain out front. Known for huge breakfasts, home-cooking, and Continental entrées, pasta, the cafe also features a kids' menu. | 984 Barret Ave., Louisville | 502/583–3447 | Breakfast also available. Closed Mon. | $8–$25 | AE, MC, V.

Porcini. Northern Italian. This intimate Tuscan dining room features floral banquettes, exposed brick, and a working fountain. Try shrimp and Italian white beans, veal scallopini, or pork with marsala. | 2730 Frankfort Ave., Louisville | 502/894–8686 | Closed Sun. No lunch | $15–$27 | AE, MC, V.

Sichuan Garden. Chinese, Thai. Large frosted-glass panels create intimate spaces in this dining room set with pink tablecloths. A pianist performs Fri. and Sat. evenings. | 9850 Linn Station Rd., Louisville | 502/426–6767 | $10–$25 | AE, D, DC, MC, V.

Timothy's. Contemporary. This spot has a stylish, modern decor including a handsome, high-ceiling main dining room. There's also a cozy, antique bar. Open-air dining. | 826 E. Broadway, Louisville | 502/561–0880 | Closed Sun. No lunch Sat. | $15–$37 | AE, DC, MC, V.

211 Clover Lane Restaurant. Contemporary. Specializing in California cuisine, this intimate restaurant features French country decor, including a gravel-floored, tree-shaded dining patio. The menu features a vegetable Napoleon and Dungeness crab cakes. An espresso bar serves fancy coffee drinks. | 211 Clover La., Louisville | 502/896–9570 | Closed Mon. No dinner Sun. | $17–$32 | AE, DC, MC, V.

★ **Uptown Cafe.** Contemporary. This renovated storefront restaurant sports an arty, faux-finish decor and caters to modern, bistro-loving types. Try the vegetarian stir-fry. | 1624 Bardstown Rd., Louisville | 502/458–4212 | Closed Sun. | $9–$20 | AE, D, DC, MC, V.

Zephyr Cove. Contemporary. Featuring live jazz nightly, this restaurant offers eclectic modern decor and an enclosed sun porch. Both vegetarian dishes and wild game are on the menu. | 2330 Frankfort Ave., Louisville | 502/897–1030 | $10–$28 | AE, D, DC, MC, V.

EXPENSIVE

Café Metro. Continental. The cafe's art deco interior is accented with early 20th-century Viennese posters. Among the European-style menu items is beef tenderloin with blue cheese. | 1700 Bardstown Rd., Louisville | 502/458–4830 | Closed Sun. No lunch | $20, all entrées | AE, D, DC, MC, V.

★ **Oakroom.** Contemporary. This oak-trimmed dining room is located in a grand hotel, and offers some tables with love seats, as well as an extensive bourbon collection and cigar list. Try breast of chicken stuffed with country ham and pesto, rack of lamb, or smoked spoonfish. Sunday brunch is also available. | Seelbach Hotel, 500 S. 4th Ave., Louisville | 502/585–3200 | Collared shirt and slacks | $19–$42 | AE, D, DC, MC, V.

★ **The English Grill.** Contemporary. Stained-glass, deep armchairs, and equestrian artwork create an English gentleman's club atmosphere. Seasonal menus feature regional foods. No smoking. | 335 W. Broadway, Louisville | 502/583–1234 | Jacket and tie | No lunch | $22–$30 | AE, D, DC, MC, V.

LOUISVILLE

INTRO
ATTRACTIONS
DINING
LODGING

Le Relais. French. This elegant, art deco dining room is located in the airport administration building. The menu features fish, crab cakes, lamb chops, and you can choose open-air dining on an outdoor deck overlooking the runway. | 2817 Taylorsville Rd., Louisville | 502/451–9020 | Closed Mon. | $19–53 | AE, DC, MC, V.

★ **Lilly's.** Contemporary. Two of the four dining rooms at Lilly's feature wall-size murals. The creative menu changes weekly, and emphasizes fresh ingredients. | 1147 Bardstown Rd., Louisville | 502/451–0447 | Closed Sun. and Mon. | $20–$33 | AE, D, MC, V.

Shariat's. Contemporary. There's an open kitchen and formal service in this elegant contemporary dining room. They're known for sea bass, lamb, and vegetarian cuisine. | 2901 Brownsboro Rd., Louisville | 502/899–7878 | Closed Sun. No lunch | $18–$27 | AE, D, DC, MC, V.

Vincenzo's. Italian. This Louisville fixture keeps its regulars happy with attentive service and extremely capable chefs. Enjoy Italian fare a la carte or prix fixe. A pianist performs Fri. and Sat. | 150 S. 5th St., Louisville | 502/580–1350 | Closed Sun. No lunch Sat. | $20–$37 | AE, D, DC, MC, V.

Lodging
INEXPENSIVE

Red Roof Inn. The rooms are small but clean at this budget-priced motel, located close to two shopping malls, 8 mi east of downtown. In-room data ports. Cable TV. Business services. Free parking. Some pets allowed. | 9330 Blairwood Rd., Louisville | 502/426–7621 | fax 502/426–7933 | 108 rooms | $45–$80 | AE, D, DC, MC, V.

MODERATE

Aleksander House Bed & Breakfast. Listed on the National Register of Historic Places, the three-story, 1882 Victorian Italianate brick home, features 12-foot ceilings, original hardwood floors and moldings and five fireplaces. The five spacious guest rooms (with a suite available) are decorated in antique French furnishings. Two rooms each have a private bath. In the heart of Historic "Old Louisville," special antiquing, theater and Mystery Weekend Packages are available. A full, made-from-scratch breakfast is served to include Belgian waffles and quiche, and cater to special diets. | It's near I–65 at St. Catherine St. exit 135. Complimentary breakfast, some refrigerators. In-room TV/VCRs. Pets allowed. | 1213 S. First St., Louisville | 502/637–4985 | fax 502/635–1398 | www.bbonline/ky/aleksander | 5 rooms | $85–$149 | AE, D, MC, V.

Best Western Signature Inn. Comfortable, modern rooms, some of which are poolside, are conveniently located just off I–64 about 20 minutes from downtown. Complimentary Continental breakfast. In-room data ports, some refrigerators. Cable TV. Indoor pool. Hot tub, sauna. Laundry facilities. Business service. Free parking. | 1301 Kentucky Mills Dr., Louisville | 502/267–8100 | fax 502/269–8100 | www.bestwestern.com | 119 rooms | $73 | AE, D, DC, MC, V.

Breckinridge Inn. Spacious rooms are tucked away in this distinguished white-brick and board colonial structure, situated near the Watterson Expressway interchange. Restaurant, bar. Cable TV. 2 pools (1 indoor). Barbershop. Tennis. Exercise equipment. Business services. Airport shuttle. Free parking. Some pets allowed (fee). | 2800 Breckinridge La., Louisville | 502/456–5050 | fax 502/451–1577 | 123 rooms | $65–$95 | AE, D, DC, MC, V.

Central Park Bed & Breakfast. This three-story Victorian home is in the center of "Old Louisville." Built circa 1884, it is on the National Register of Historic Places. The craftsmanship of the era is reflected in the front porch's reverse painted glass ceiling, the home's oak woodwork and its intricately hammered brass hardware. The Central Park features a whirlpool suite, a carriage house suite with kitchen, private baths, king and queen beds, book and video library, antiques, 11 fireplaces. Complimentary breakfast. In-room data ports, some in-room hot tubs. Cable TV, some in-room VCRs. Business services. | 1353 S. Fourth St., Louisville | 502/638–1505 or 877/922–1505 | fax 502/638–1525 | www.centralparkbandb.com/ | 7 rooms | $85–$149 | AE, MC, V.

The Columbine Inn. Built in 1896, the two-story brick Victorian home, with majestic white columns, was formerly the estate of one of the "mahogany kings" of Louisville. The Columbine is graced with Honduran mahogany, a fireplace of rose marble imported from Carrara, Italy, and other examples of craftsmanship. All rooms have, queen-size beds, a love seat, private bath—some with claw-foot tubs, some rooms have a fireplace, and the common area includes a parlor, living room, and screened back porch. The gourmet breakfast includes seasonal fruit and a variety of fresh baked bread, and entrees such as crepes, lemon/orange puff pancakes, Italian frittatas, vegetable omelets, and chef/innkeeper Lorenzo Bernardini, from Cortona, Italy, will accommodate dietary restrictions. Complimentary breakfast. In-room data ports. Cable TV, in-room VCRs and movies. No kids under 12. Business services. | 1707 S. 3rd St., Louisville | 502/635–5000 or 800/635–5010 | fax 502/635–5000 | bbcolumbine@aol.com | www.bbonline.com/ky/columbine | 5 rooms (1 with shower only), 1 suite | $70–$95, $70–$115 suite | AE, DC, MC, V.

Fairfield Inn by Marriott. These economically-priced, Marriot-quality rooms are spacious and well-lit. The facility is 2½ mi southeast of Churchill Downs. Complimentary Continental breakfast. In-room data ports. Cable TV. Pool. | 9400 Blairwood Rd., Louisville | 502/339–1900 | fax 502/339–1900 | 105 rooms | $60–$85 | AE, D, DC, MC, V.

Hampton Inn. Conveniently located near the airport, fairgrounds, and downtown, this facility offers easy access to major highways. Complimentary Continental breakfast. Cable TV. Pool. Exercise equipment. Business services. Airport shuttle. | 800 Phillips La., Louisville | 502/366–8100 | fax 502/366–0700 | 130 rooms | $75–$85 | AE, D, DC, MC, V.

Inn at the Park Bed & Breakfast. Built in 1886 for the president of the Louisville & Nashville Railroad, this three-story mansion is an example of Richardsonian Romanesque architecture and showcases Queen Anne ornamentation. The B&B has a view of adjacent Central Park and features five guest rooms in the main house and two whirlpool suites in the carriage house, private baths, and eight fireplaces. Complimentary breakfast. In-room data ports. Cable TV. No pets. No kids. | 1332 S Fourth St., Louisville | 502/637–6930 or 800/700–7275 | fax 502/637–2796 | innatpark@aol.com | 7 rooms | $89–$169 | AE, D, DC MC, V.

The Inn at Woodhaven. This 1853 yellow-and-white Gothic Revival house is located near the junction of U.S. 64 and U.S. 71. The carriage house and octagonal Rose Cottage are all decorated in the style of the period. Complimentary breakfast. No smoking. Cable TV. Business services. Some pets allowed. | 401 S. Hubbards La., Louisville | 502/895–1011 or 888/895–1011 | www.bbonline.com/ky/woodhaven/index.html | fax 502/895–1011 | 7 rooms | $75–$175 | AE, D, MC, V.

Signature Inn. Rooms in contemporary decor are featured in this facility, which is convenient both to the airport and to downtown. Complimentary Continental breakfast. In-room data ports. Cable TV. Pool. Business services. Airport shuttle. Free parking. | 6515 Signature Dr., Louisville | 502/968–4100 | fax 502/968–4100 | 119 rooms | $75–$80 | AE, D, DC, MC, V.

Super 8. This budget facility is located in the suburbs south of downtown. In-room data ports. Cable TV. Business services. Airport shuttle. | 4800 Preston Hwy., Louisville | 502/968–0088 | fax 502/968–0088, ext. 347 | 100 rooms | $55 | AE, D, DC, MC, V.

EXPENSIVE

Amerisuites. Located on one of suburban Louisville's busiest thoroughfares, this hotel offers affordable and well-appointed suites. Complimentary Continental breakfast. Kitchenettes, microwaves, refrigerators. Cable TV, in-room VCRs and movies. Pool. Exercise equipment. Laundry facilities. Business services. Airport shuttle. | 701 S. Hurstbourne Pkwy., Louisville | 502/426–0119 or 800/833–1516 | fax 502/426–3013 | 123 rooms, 18 business suites | $85–$130 suites | AE, D, DC, MC, V.

Comfort Suites. These modern, spacious suites, furnished in cherry veneer, are located at the I–64 interchange, east of downtown. Complimentary Continental breakfast. Microwaves, refrigerators. Cable TV. Indoor pool. Hot tub. Business services. Airport shuttle. | 1850 Resource Way, Louisville | 502/266–6509 | fax 502/266–9014 | info@comfortsuites.com | www.comfortsuites.com | 70 suites | $80–$160 suites | AE, D, DC, MC, V.

Executive Inn. This sprawling, modern facility is near the fairgrounds, Six Flags Over Kentucky Kingdom, and the Louisville International Airport. 2 restaurants, bar. Cable TV. 2 pools (1 indoor), wading pool. Beauty salon. Gym. Business services. Airport shuttle. | 978 Phillips La., Louisville | 502/367–6161 or 800/626–2706 | fax 502/363–1880 | toeyken@exec-cinn.win.net | www.win.net/~execinn | 465 rooms, 12 suites | $95, $195–$295 suites | AE, D, DC, MC, V.

Executive West. This facility is an annex to the Executive Inn next door; together they form the state's largest motor inn complex. Six Flags Over Kentucky Kingdom Amusement Park is within walking distance. Restaurant, bar with entertainment. In-room data ports, refrigerators (in suites). Cable TV. Indoor-outdoor pool. Beauty salon. Business services. Airport shuttle. Some pets allowed. | 830 Phillips La., Louisville | 502/367–2251 or 800/626–2708 (outside KY) | fax 502/363–2087 | exwest@iglou.com | 611 rooms, 50 suites | $74–$125, $105–$240 suites | AE, D, DC, MC, V.

Hampton Inn. Offering spacious motel rooms, this facility is located on a quiet side street off busy Hurstbourne Parkway. Complimentary Continental breakfast. In-room data ports. Cable TV. Pool. Business services. | 1902 Embassy Square Blvd., Louisville | 502/491–2577 | fax 502/491–1325 | 119 rooms | $99 | AE, D, DC, MC, V.

Holiday Inn. Located east of downtown in a busy suburban commercial area, this hotel is typical of the family-welcoming chain. Restaurant, bar. In-room data ports, refrigerator (in suites). Cable TV. Indoor pool. Exercise equipment. Business services. Airport shuttle. Free parking. | 1325 S. Hurstbourne Pkwy., Louisville | 502/426–2600 | fax 502/423–1605 | 267 rooms, 7 suites | $99–$125, $125–$225 suites | AE, D, DC, MC, V.

Holiday Inn Airport. Located very near the airport, this hotel is convenient to major highways going both downtown and toward suburbs. Restaurant, bar. Complimentary breakfast. In-room data ports. Cable TV. Pool. Tennis. Exercise equipment. Video games. Laundry facilities. Business services. Airport shuttle. Free parking. Some pets allowed. | 4000 Gardiner Point Dr., Louisville | 502/452–6361 | fax 502/451–1541 | 200 rooms | $98 | AE, D, DC, MC, V.

Hyatt Regency. This hotel features an enclosed walkway leading to the convention center and nearby shopping. The modern gleaming white and wood-trimmed atrium is an attractive centerpiece. Glass-sided elevators add to the open, airy atmosphere. 2 restaurants, 1 bar. In-room data ports. Cable TV. Indoor pool. Hot tub. Tennis. Exercise equipment. Business services. | 320 W. Jefferson St., Louisville | 502/587–3434 | fax 502/581–0133 | 388 rooms, 15 suites | $90–$180, $250–$650 suites | AE, D, DC, MC, V.

Old Louisville Inn. Each room is individually styled with antiques in this stately early-20th-century house. It's close to the University of Louisville and Churchill Downs. Complimentary breakfast. Some in-room hot tubs. No room phones, TV in sitting room. Exercise equipment. Business services. | 1359 S. 3rd St., Louisville | 502/635–1574 | fax 502/637–5892 | 10 rooms, 2 suites | $75–$95, $110–$195 suites | MC, V.

Residence Inn by Marriott. Suites with cooking facilities are the big draw at this comfortable hotel, located 1½ mi east of Churchill Downs. Weekly rates are available. Complimentary Continental breakfast. In-room data ports, kitchenettes, microwaves, refrigerators. Cable TV. Pool. Hot tub. Laundry facilities. Business services. Free parking. | 120 N. Hurstbourne Pkwy., Louisville | 502/425–1821 | fax 502/425–1672 | 96 suites | $86–$106 1–bedroom suites, $109–$135 2–bedroom suites | AE, D, DC, MC, V.

Rocking Horse Manor Bed & Breakfast. This three-story 1888 Victorian mansion features rooms and suites with private baths—some with sauna, claw-foot tub or hot tub. The commons area includes a library with wet bar, a Victorian parlor, and a mini-office. Complimentary evening snacks and beverages are available. Near I–65 at St. Catherine St. exit 135. Complimentary breakfast, some in-room hot tubs. Cable TV. Business services. | 1022 S. 3rd St., Louisville | 502/583–0408 | fax 502/583–6077 | 6 | $79–$169 | AE, D, MC, V.

The Samuel Culbertson Mansion. The mansion, completed in 1897 for a 19th-century millionaire tycoon—who later was President and Chairman of Churchill Downs—is opulent, yet warm. It is built in the style of the Georgian Revival, with the Louis XVI ladies parlor, and an English manor style drawing room. There are three rooms and two suites, and a rose garden courtyard with splashing fountain enclosed by the mansion and carriage house. Near I–65 at St. Catherine St. Exit 135. Complimentary breakfast. Phones in some rooms. Cable TV, VCRs. | 1432 S. 3rd St., Louisville | 502/634–3100 | fax 502/636–3096 | bandb@culbertsonmansion.com | 5 | $99–$179 | D, MC, V.

Sheraton Suites Four Points Louisville. This former Wilson Inn, convenient to U.S. 64, was taken over in 1999 by Sheraton and remodeled to that chain's standards. In-room data ports, some kitchenettes, refrigerators. Cable TV. Business services. Airport shuttle. | 9802 Bunsen Pkwy., Louisville | 502/499–0000 | fax 502/293–2905 | 108 rooms, 30 suites | $99, $119 suites | AE, D, DC, MC, V.

VERY EXPENSIVE

The Bernheim Mansion Bed & Breakfast. This four-story Richardsonian Romanesque stone home built in 1893, is in the heart of Old Louisville's Millionaire's Row. The main exterior feature is a triple archway entry. The interior centers around a curved stairwell crowned with stained glass windows. The Bernheim provides, on request, computers and video conferencing services. Most rooms have a private bath and the carriage house has a two-bedroom suite. Near I–65 at St. Catherine St. Exit 135. Complimentary breakfast. In-room data ports, some in-room hot tubs. Cable TV, VCRs. Business services. | 1416 S. 3rd St., Louisville | 502/636–0409 or 800/303–0053 | fax 502/6360–9157 | www.bernheimmansion.com | 4 rooms, 1 suite | $119–$225 | AE, D, MC, V.

The Camberley Brown. Built in 1923, the hotel has since undergone a careful restoration that revived the intricate plaster molding, detailed woodwork, stained glass, and original crystal chandeliers. The famous Louisville Hot Brown sandwich was invented in one of the hotel's restaurant kitchens. The hotel is near the Brown and the Palace theatres. 3 restaurants, bar. In-room data ports. Cable TV. Beauty salon. Exercise equipment. Business services. Airport shuttle. Free parking. | 335 W. Broadway, Louisville | 502/583–1234 or 800/866–7666 | fax 502/587–7006 | 294 rooms, 6 suites | $190–$200, $425 suites | AE, D, DC, MC, V.

Courtyard by Marriott. Located off Hurstbourne Parkway, this brick facility with enclosed atrium can be difficult to access during rush hours. Bar. Complimentary breakfast. In-room data ports, refrigerators. Cable TV. Pool. Hot tub. Exercise equipment. Laundry facilities. Business services. Free parking. | 9608 Blairwood Rd., Louisville | 502/429–0006 | fax 502/429–5926 | 151 rooms, 12 suites | $109, $125 suites | AE, D, DC, MC, V.

Galt House. This multi-towered, downtown hotel, popular with conventioneers, is convenient to the Kentucky Center for the Arts and Main Street museums, and is directly on the riverfront. 2 restaurants, bar, dining room. Refrigerator in suites. Cable TV. Pool. Business services. Free parking. | 140 N. 4th Ave., Louisville | 502/589–5200 or 800/843–4258 | fax 502/589–3444 | info@galthouse.com | 656 rooms, 600 suites | $120–$160, $275–$475 suites | AE, D, DC, MC, V.

Holiday Inn–Downtown. This typical chain hotel is located at the southern end of the business district, near the theatres on Broadway. Restaurant, bar. In-room data ports, minibars, some refrigerators. Cable TV. Indoor pool. Business services. Airport shuttle. Some pets allowed. | 120 W. Broadway, Louisville | 502/582–2241 | fax 502/584–8591 | 287 rooms, 2 suites | $103–$125, $280–$355 suites | AE, D, DC, MC, V.

Marriott East. A striking, glass-enclosed lobby, dominates the public area of this hotel, which is located 5 mi east of downtown. Restaurant, bar. In-room data ports. Cable TV. Indoor pool. Exercise equipment. Business services. Free parking. | 1903 Embassy Square Blvd., Louisville | 502/499–6220 | fax 502/499–2480 | 254 rooms | $149–$179 | AE, D, DC, MC, V.

★ **Seelbach Hilton.** Listed on the National Register of Historic Places, this 1905 hotel boasts murals by Arthur Thomas that tell the story of settlers and Native Americans of the area. Guest rooms feature four-poster beds and and marble baths. You'll enjoy pool privileges at a nearby facility. The hotel is the site of Tom and Daisy Buchanan's wedding in F. Scott Fitzgerald's famous book, *The Great Gatsby,* and is located three blocks from the convention center. Restaurants (see Oakroom), bar with entertainment. In-room data ports. Cable TV. Business services. Airport shuttle. Parking (fee). Some pets allowed for a fee. | 500 4th Ave., Louisville | 502/585–3200 or 800/333–3399 | fax 502/585–9239 | 321 rooms, 36 suites | $180–$230, $210–$510 suites | AE, D, DC, MC, V.

MADISONVILLE

MAP 6, C5

(Nearby town also listed: Dawson Springs)

In 1807, Daniel McGary and Solomon Silkwood each donated 20 acres for a town site, naming it after then-Secretary of State James Madison. Silkwood built the first county courthouse out of logs. Today, Madisonville is the commercial hub for Kentucky's western coal-mining operations, as well as a regional medical and educational center. It is the largest city in the area of the Pennyrile State Forest.

Information: **Madison/Hopkins County Chamber of Commerce** | 15 E. Center St., Madisonville 42431 | 270/821–3435 | www.hopkinschamber.com.

Attractions

Historical Library. Historic photographs and Civil War artifacts are on display here. Also on the grounds is the two-room, 1860s log-cabin birthplace of Ruby Lafoon, governor of Kentucky from 1931 to 1935. | 107 Union St., Madisonville | 270/821–3986 | $1 | Weekdays 1–5; closed weekends.

ON THE CALENDAR

JULY–AUG.: *Hopkins County Fair.* Among the exhibits are displays of regional economic mainstays, including tobacco and coal. | 270/821–3435.

Dining

Bartholomew's. American. With two stories of dining in downtown Madisonville, this restaurant serves thin-sliced French Dip (made with prime rib) and homemade apple cobbler. Kids' menu. | 51 S. Main, Madisonville | 270/821–1061 | Closed Sun. No lunch Sat. | $17–$27 | AE, D, MC, V.

Lodging

Best Western Pennyrile Inn. Two-story accommodations are 6 mi from Madisonville and 15 mi from Pennyrile State Park. There's an adjacent campground. Take Pennyrile Parkway to Exit 37. Restaurant, complimentary breakfast buffet. Some refrigerators. Cable TV. Pool. Tennis. Exercise equipment. Laundry facilities. Business services. Airport shuttle. Pets allowed. | Pennyrile Pkwy., Mortons Gap | 270/258–5201 | fax 270/258–9072 | www.bestwestern.com | 60 rooms | $40–$50 | AE, D, DC, MC, V.

Days Inn. Large rooms and a comfortable lobby are 3 mi from downtown Madisonville. Restaurant, complimentary Continental breakfast, some room service. Cable TV. Indoor pool.

Sauna. Exercise equipment. Laundry facilities. Laundry service. Business services. Some pets allowed. | 1900 Lantaff Blvd., Madisonville | 270/821–8620 or 800/544–8313 | fax 270/825–9282 | www.daysinn.com | 143 rooms, 4 suites | $49–$75, $80–$100 suites | AE, D, DC, MC, V.

Pennyrile Lodge. Situated on a cliff overlooking Pennyrile Lake, the state-owned, wood-and-stone lodge is part of Pennyrile State Forest. Cottages have wooded or lake views, and some have private boat and fishing docks, fireplaces, or screened-in porches. Dining room, picnic table. Kitchenettes (in cottages). TV. Pool. 9-hole golf course, mini-golf, tennis. | 20781 Pennyrile Lodge Rd., Dawson Springs | 270/797–3421 or 800/325–1711 | fax 270/797–3413 | www.kystateparks.com | 24 rooms in lodge; 13 cottages | $52–$68, $74–$112 cottages | AE, D, DC, MC, V.

MAMMOTH CAVE NATIONAL PARK

MAP 6, E5

(Nearby towns also listed: Bowling Green, Cave City, Horse Cave, Glasgow)

★ Local legend says that Mammoth Cave was discovered sometime in the late 18th century, when a hunter chased a bear into the enormous opening now known as the Historic Entrance. There seems to be no real evidence of the hunter and the bear, but there is plenty of documentation about other historical aspects of the longest natural underground system in the world. Spearpoints recovered from the cave have been dated as over 12,000 years old.

The cave was an important source for saltpeter, a major ingredient in gunpowder, during the War of 1812. It supplied three quarters of the powder used by U.S. troops against the British.

Mining stopped after the war, and tourists started to arrive. To accommodate this fledgling industry, a log "hotel" and a road were built. In 1839, Dr. John Croghan of Louisville bought Mammoth Cave; terms of the deed also gave Croghan ownership of Stephen Bishop, a black slave who remains the most famous guide in the cave's history. An enthusiastic explorer, Bishop was the first person to discover the unique eyeless fish and crayfish living in the deep, underground waters. He was a popular and knowledgeable guide until his death in 1857.

Tuberculosis was a major health concern in the mid-1800s, and in 1842, Dr. Croghan began housing patients in custom-built huts inside the cave, under the premise that the cave air, with a year-round temperature of 54°F, might be beneficial to consumptives. Unfortunately, all the patients eventually died of the disease, either while still in residence or soon after leaving Mammoth Cave. The program was abandoned in 1843.

The property was handed down through the Croghan family until 1926, when the last descendant, Serena Croghan Rogers, died. Several area businessmen then lobbied Congress to have the area designated as a national park. Mammoth Cave became the nation's 26th National Park in 1941. It's still the only one in Kentucky.

Over 350 mi of caverns have been found under the 80-square-mi park, and you can take ranger-led tours underground. Above ground, rangers sponsor other activities and cultural events, and you can hike, canoe, picnic, camp, or birdwatch. Mammoth Cave is also an International Biosphere Reserve and a World Heritage Site.

Information: Mammoth Cave National Park | Box 7, Mammoth Cave 42259 | 270/758–2328 or 800/967–2283 | maca_park_information@nps.gov | www.nps.gov/maca.

TOURS AND TOUR COMPANIES

Cave Tours. A variety of tours is designed for all ages and physical abilities. Not all tours are offered every day. Call ahead for reservations.

The moderately strenuous **Cleaveland Avenue** tour ($7) leads you through two vaulted rooms—Dismal Hollow and Rocky Mountain—and curves down into elliptical Cleaveland Avenue, with its gypsum-encrusted walls. You maneuver through the Snowball Room to the narrow canyon known as Boone Avenue, and end in Thorpe's Pit, a dome-pit still being formed by water erosion. The tour is two hours long.

Frozen Niagara ($8) is one of the more spectacular tours, winding among enormous pits and domes and the great dripstone formation that resembles a rock-hewn waterfall. The two-hour tour is described as strenuous, so don't take it unless you are prepared to descend about 300 steps and climb through steep terrain.

The cave's human history is the focus of the **Historic** tour ($8). Inside, you'll see artifacts from Native Americans and European cave explorers, ruins of early mining operations, and other evidence of human presence. You must be able to climb rock stairs and a 130-step steel tower. The tour is about two hours long.

Visitors who might not be able to negotiate steps and inclines on other tours can take the **Mobility Impaired** tour ($7). An elevator descends to passageways accessible to wheelchairs. The tour is 1¼ hours long.

Even though there are some steps on the **Travertine** tour ($7), it is one of the least physically demanding, and adults with small children are usually able to take it. Sights include the Frozen Niagara, Crystal Lake, and the Drapery Room. Tour time is about 1¼ hours.

The educational **Trog** tour ($8), focusing on the cave's ecology and geology, is designed for children 8 to 12 (proof of age required). Helmets and lights are provided. Long pants and hiking shoes are required; kneepads are recommended. The tour lasts 2½ hours. Parents must accompany their children for the first 15 minutes, and pick them up punctually at tour's end.

Violet City ($9) is a lantern tour along the early explorers' route, and includes the remains of saltpeter mining, traces of pre-historic activity, huts that were used for tuberculosis patients in the 1800s, and some of the largest rooms in the park. The tour takes about three hours and is physically demanding.

The hour-long *Miss Green River* **Boat Trip** ($4) is a river tour on a twin-diesel-powered boat. Departing from inside the park and following the Green River, the route passes through valleys rich in wildlife, including white-tailed deer, beavers, and wild turkeys. | Apr.–Oct., daily; hours vary | 270/758–2328 or 800/967–2283 | fax 270/758–2349 | www.nps.gov/maca/tours.htm.

ON THE CALENDAR

APR.: *Springfest.* Wildflower walks and other nature activities punctuate a weekend of folk and bluegrass concerts and arts and crafts exhibitions. | 270/758–2328 or 800/967–2283.

OCT.: *Colorfall.* The park's cultural heritage is the focus for this weekend of crafts demonstrations, archaeological talks and tours, and oral history and genealogy seminars. | 270/758–2328 or 800/967–2283.

Dining

Joe's Happy Days Diner. American. A nostalgic, 1950's diner featuring burgers, sandwiches, shakes, and hand-dipped ice cream. | 1002 Mammoth Cave Rd., Cave City | 270/773–4255 | Breakfast also available. Labor Day–Memorial Day: no breakfast, no supper Mon.–Thurs. | $6–$8 | No credit cards.

Lodging

Mammoth Cave Hotel. You'll have your choice of rustic or modern accommodations at this hotel inside the national park. An arched bridge leads from the main building to the Mammoth Cave Park Visitor Center. 2 restaurants. Some Cable TV. Tennis. Laundry facili-

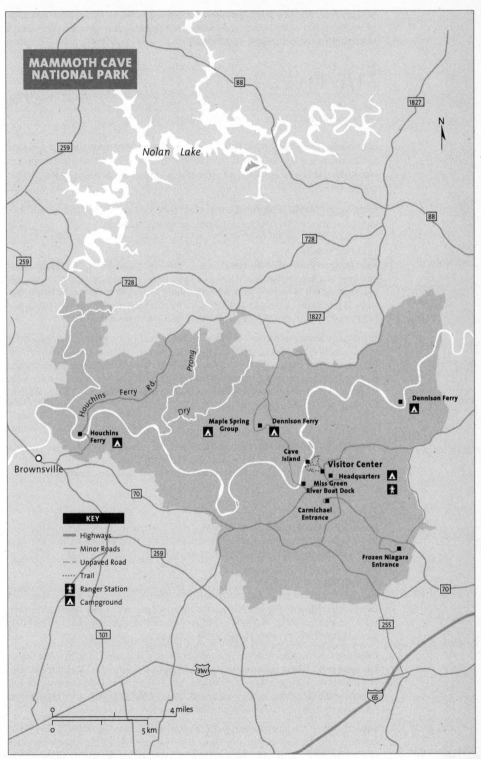

MAMMOTH CAVE NATIONAL PARK

Nolan Lake

Houchins Ferry Rd.

Dry Prong

Brownsville

Houchins Ferry

Maple Spring Group

Dennison Ferry

Dennison Ferry

Cave Island

Visitor Center

Headquarters

Miss Green River Boat Dock

Carmichael Entrance

Frozen Niagara Entrance

KEY

Highways
Minor Roads
Unpaved Road
Trail
Ranger Station
Campground

4 miles

5 km

ties (summer). Business services (winter). Some pets allowed. | Hwy. 70, Mammoth Cave | 270/758–2225 | fax 270/758–2301 | www.mammothcavehotel.com | 110 rooms | $62–$68; $72 motor lodge; $45–$52 cottages | AE, DC, MC, V.

MAYFIELD

MAP 6, B5

(Nearby towns also listed: Gilbertsville, Murray, Paducah)

Settled around 1819 by John and Nancy Anderson, Mayfield is home to the largest regional tobacco market and to the annual Fancy Farm Picnic. It is also the birthplace of contemporary novelist Bobbie Ann Mason. For many years, the town has been a center of clothing manufacturing.

Information: **Mayfield Tourism Commission** | 201 E. College St., Mayfield, 42066 | 270/247–6101 | graves@ldd.net | www.ldd.net/commerce/mayfield.

Attractions

Kaler Bottoms Public Wildlife Area. This is a primitive reserve with cypress swamps and low-lying wet terrain. Waterfowl, deer, raccoon, squirrel, turkey, great blue heron, and black vulture can be spotted. Kaler Bottoms is a site for wildlife photography, hiking, fishing, and primitive camping. Kaler Bottoms is 8 mi northeast of Mayfield. | KY 131, Mayfield | 270/759–5296 or 270/753–6913 | www.kdfwr.state.ky.us/ | Free | Daily.

Wooldridge Monuments. Over a nine-year period in the late 19th century, local horse breeder Harry C. Wooldridge erected 16 life-sized statues—including ones of his parents, brothers, favorite dogs, and himself (mounted on his favorite horse)—near what was to become his gravesite in 1899. Fifteen of the figures are carved from local sandstone. The Wooldridge and horse statue are Italian marble. | Maplewood Cemetery, U.S. 45N, Mayfield | 270/247–6101 | Free | Daily.

ON THE CALENDAR

AUG.: *Fancy Farm Picnic.* On the first Saturday of the month, officeholders (and aspiring officeholders) from around the state collect here to "press the flesh." There's also food, family activities, and a raffle. Proceeds of the picnic fund community activities. | 270/247–6101.

Dining

Majestic Pizza and Steak House. Steak. This family restaurant in the center of town is a locals' favorite for hamburgers, steaks and the buffet. Pictures of Greece adorn the walls. | 700 S. 6th St., Mayfield | 270/247–2541 | $8–$15 | MC, V.

Lodging

Days Inn. The rooms at this two-story motel, 20 mi from Kentucky Lake, are equipped with two double-beds or a king-bed. Restaurant. In-room data ports. Cable TV. Pool. Free parking. | 1101 Houseman St., Mayfield | 270/247–3700 or 800/544–8313 | fax 270/247–3135 | www.daysinn.com | 73 rooms | $49–$67 | AE, D, DC, MC, V.

Guest Inn. This two-story motel is 12 mi south of Mayfield and is only 20 mi from the Columbus Belmont Civil War museum. Refurbished in 1997, this former Holiday Inn, has comfortable rooms with in-room coffeemakers. You'll find it near Purchase Pkwy. Exit 51. Complimentary breakfast. In-room data ports. Cable TV. Pool. | KY 51N, Fulton | 270/472–2342 | fax 270/472–2347 | www.guestinnfulton.com | 80 rooms | $59 | AE, D, MC, V.

Super 8. Just off the Purchase Parkway, the motel is 2 mi from the Mayfield airport and 25 mi from the Paducah airport. The rooms were renovated in 1998. Complimentary Continental breakfast. Some refrigerators. Cable TV. Free parking. Some pets allowed. | 1100

Links La., Mayfield | 270/247–8899 or 800/800–8000 | fax 270/247–8899 | www.super8.com | 47 rooms, 4 suites | $42–$71 | AE, MC, V.

MAYSVILLE

(Nearby towns also listed: Ashland, Covington, Morehead)

Halfway between Covington and Ashland, Maysville is the birthplace of singer Rosemary Clooney, whose childhood home is on the National Register of Historic Places. Founded on the banks of the Ohio River in 1787, the town's center is still marked with 18th- and 19th-century buildings. Maysville is the seat of Mason County and the site of the nation's second-largest burley tobacco market.

Information: **Maysville Tourism Commission** | 216 Bridge St., Maysville, 41056 | 606/564–5534 or 888/875–MAYS | chrystiek@may-uky.campus.mci.net | trib.com/maysville.

Attractions

Blue Licks Battlefield State Park. The 150-acre park includes a monument to the "last battle of the Revolutionary War" fought between settlers and Native Americans a year after Cornwallis's surrender. A nature preserve within the park is home to the protected wildflower species, Short's goldenrod, which grows nowhere else in the world. Campsites, a lodge, and cottages are available. | U.S. 68, Mount Olivet | 606/289–5507 | www.kystateparks.com/agencies/parks/bluelick.htm | Free; fee for camping, pool, and other recreational facilities; museum $2 | Year-round. Museum Apr.–Oct., daily 9–5.

Historic Washington. Established in the late 18th century, this original county seat contains several restored buildings dating from 1790 to 1848 including Mefford Fort, the Old Church Museum, and the Paxton Inn. Guided tours of the town are offered. | 2116 Old Main St., Maysville, | 606/759–7411 | $1–$6 | Mon.–Fri. 11–4:30, Sat. 10:30–4:30, Sun. 1–4:30.

Marshall Key House. Now home to the "Harriet Beecher Stowe Slavery to Freedom Museum", the Marshall Key House, circa 1807, was visited by Harriet Beecher Stowe in 1833, where she witnessed a slave auction, and was inspired to write "Uncle Tom's Cabin." Included in the Old Washington Underground Railroad tour, the house is staffed on weekends enabling a separate non-tour visit. | 2124 Old Main St., Old Washington | 606/759–7411 | Tour $6 | Daily 11–3:30.

Mason County Museum. Housed in a structure dating from 1876, the Mason County Museum is today an art gallery, history museum, and genealogy center. Holdings include an area map collection. | 215 Sutton St., Maysville | 606/564–5865 | http://webpages.maysvilleky.net/masonmuseum | $3 | Apr.–Dec., Mon.–Sat. 10–4; Jan.–Mar., Tues.–Sat. 10–4.

Paxton Inn. This was a safe-house on the Underground Railroad. It was built around 1810 by James A. Paxton, a local attorney and ardent abolitionist. According to oral history, runaway slaves sat on the narrow staircase hidden next to the kitchen fireplace until they could safely be moved across the river to Ohio. The home is included in the Old Washington Underground Railroad tour. | 2030 Old Main St., Old Washington | 606/759–7411 | Tour $6 | Daily 11–3:30.

The Piedmont Art Gallery. Displaying collections of paintings and crafts by both regional and national artisans, the gallery also houses antiques, folk art, ceramics, and sculpture. | 115 W. Riverside Dr., Augusta | 606/756–2216 | Free | Thurs.–Sun., noon–5.

ON THE CALENDAR

JUNE: *Sternwheeler Annual Regatta.* Historic stern-wheeler riverboats gather at the port in neighboring Augusta. Food and entertainment are the weekend's staples. | 606/756–2183.

SEPT.: *Simon Kenton Festival.* Pioneer spirit is celebrated with crafts, demonstrations, and food in historic Washington, which is now part of greater Maysville. | 606/759–7423.

NOV.–FEB.: *Tobacco Warehouses.* Maysville is one of the world's centers for burley tobacco with re-drying sheds and looseleaf warehouses. The warehouses are open during the tobacco auction season. | 606/564–9411.

Dining

Tippedore's. Steak. Located in the French Quarter Inn, this restaurant has a wonderful view of the Ohio River, and from spring through fall you can dine on the outdoor patio watching the boat traffic. The walls are decorated with pictures of Old Maysville. Opened for breakfast and dinner, the menu includes steaks, cajun food, chicken marsala, and lots of appetizers. | 25 E McDonald Pkwy., Maysville | 606/564–8000 or 800/966–9892 | www.frenchquarter.com | Breakfast also available. No lunch; no supper Sun. | $13–$17 | AE, D, DC, MC, V.

Lodging

French Quarter Inn. The luxurious, four story, river front hotel features a whirl pool tub with every room. The French Quarter has exterior corridors, a quaint lobby bar, and gourmet dining. Rooms have cherry furniture, in-room coffeemakers, and some have a view of the Ohio River. Restaurant, bar. In-room data ports, some microwaves, some refrigerators, in-room hot tubs. Pool. Exercise equipment. | 25 E McDonald Pkwy., Maysville | 606/564–8000 or 800/966–9892 | fax 606/564–8460 | www.frenchquarter.com | 64 rooms | $82 | AE, D, DC, MC, V.

Kleier Haus Bed & Breakfast. The two-story Victorian, built in 1885, is located amongst scenic farms on the rolling hills of Maysville. The B&B has three rooms and two baths, a spacious old fashioned wrap-around porch with rocking chairs, swing, lounge and four acres of trees. A full Kentucky breakfast is served in a dining room with a fireplace and a huge window. A telephone is available in the common area. The Kleier House is adjacent to a golf course. Complimentary breakfast. Cable TV. Golf privileges. | 912 U.S. 62, Maysville | 606/759–7663 | fax 606/759–5669 | gaykleier@webtv.net | 3 rooms | $75 | Closed Nov.–Jan. | D, MC, V.

MIDDLESBORO

MAP 6, G6

(Nearby towns also listed: Barbourville, Pineville, Williamsburg)

Built between mountains in a bowl-shape depression, which may have been formed by a meteorite impact, Middlesboro is a good stopping-off point for exploring the Cumberland Gap to the west. It is also the largest town in Bell County, at the far southeastern corner of the state. The town was largely built in the 1880s by a group of British industrialists who hoped to turn Middlesboro, with its ample supply of coal, into a steel-processing center. The subsequent bankruptcies of several investors ended this idea, but many of the settlers' grand Victorian homes still form a residential neighborhood on a ridge overlooking the town center.

Information: **Bell County Tourism Commission** | 106 N. 20th St., Middlesboro, 40965 | 606/248–1075 or 800/988–1075 | www.mountaingetaway.com.

Attractions

Cumberland Gap National Historical Park. Popular with hikers, the park includes many miles of hiking trails, bordered by wildflowers in the spring and splashed by a fine display of color in the fall. It's 1/4 mi south of Middlesboro. | U.S. 25E, Middlesboro | 606/248–2817.

After winding up the 2,400-ft-high mountainside to a parking area, you can take a short walk along a wooded trail to **Pinnacle Overlook,** which provides panoramic views of the Cumberland Mountains, including glimpses of Kentucky, Virginia, and Tennessee. A map at the overlook helps in the identification of landmarks. Miles of peaks in all directions are broken only by Cumberland Gap, the depression through which Daniel Boone led settlers of the region, and by the **Cumberland Gap Tunnel.** Completed in 1992, the tunnel's 4,600-ft twin paths connect Kentucky and Tennessee via U.S. 25E. Air, temperature, and traffic in the passageways are monitored by a computer-controlled system, making this the most technologically-advanced tunnel in the world. | www.nps.gov/cuga | Free | Daily. Several Civil War forts are scattered throughout the park. The most notable, **Fort McCook,** near the Pinnacle Overlook, was built by Confederate troops to guard the passageway through the mountains. | Free | Daily.

The **Hensley Settlement** is a reconstruction of the mountain community which occupied the site from 1903 to 1951. The settlement includes log cabins and barns, has 70 acres under cultivation, and is accessible only on foot (3½-mi trail) or in a four-wheel drive vehicle. | Call park office for directions | 859/248–2817 | Free | Apr.–Oct., daily.

The **Visitors Center** features a museum with exhibitions about the history of the region and an orientation film. | U.S. 25E (Cumberland Gap Pkwy.) | 606/248–2817 | fax 606/248–7276 | www.nps.gov/cuga | Free | Daily.

Lost Squadron Museum. The centerpiece of the museum is a restored P-38 airplane, *Glacier Girl,* part of the Lost Squadron, which was forced to land in Greenland during bad weather in 1942. Other exhibits trace the story of the Lost Squadron. | Middlesboro Airport, 1400 Dorchester Ave., Middlesboro | 606/248–1149 | fax 606/248–6105 | www.thelostsquadron.com | Free | Daily 8–5.

SIGHTSEEING TOURS

Cumberland Gap Area. This three-hour guided van tour visits downtown Middlesboro, the old ironworks, and the Cumberland Gap Tunnel, among other attractions. The tour leaves daily at 9 AM and 1 PM. | Reservations necessary | Call for nearest departure point | 606/248–2626 | www.wilderness-road.com | $14.

ON THE CALENDAR

OCT.: *Cumberland Mountain Fall Festival.* Also known as "Old English Heritage Days," this three-day festival features mountain crafts, the Governor's Cup Banjo Contest, live pioneer demonstrations, and car and air shows. | 606/248–1075 or 800/988–1075.

Dining

J. Milton's Steak House. Steak. This quaint 275-seat family restaurant has been serving Middlesboro residents for more than 20 years. J. Milton's, famous for its steaks, also features a full buffet, and a full menu including chicken, seafood, catfish, and hushpuppies. Memorabilia reflecting the local history of the Cumberland Gap and the settling of Middlesboro with historical photographs create a nostalgic atmosphere. The steak house is 2 mi north of the Cumberland Gap National Park, near the Days Inn. | 910 N. 12th St. (U.S. 25E), Middlesboro | 606/248–0458 | $7–$15 | AE, D, MC, V.

Lodging

Best Western Inn. Just five blocks from the entrance to Cumberland Gap National Historical Park, the motor hotel is also 3 mi from Lincoln Museum and Cudjo Caverns. Cafeteria. Refrigerators. Cable TV. Pool. Business services. | 1623 E. Cumberland Ave., Middlesboro | 606/248–5630 | fax 606/248–0875 | www.bestwestern.com | 100 rooms | $57–$86 | AE, D, DC, MC, V.

Days Inn and Suite. This three-story hotel with inside corridors was built in 1997 and has spacious rooms—some with recliners. Some also have a view of the mountains. There's an adjacent restaurant. Complimentary Continental breakfast. Some in-room data ports, some in-room hot tubs. Cable TV. Pool. Golf privileges, tennis privileges. | 1252 N. 12th St. (U.S. 25E), Middlesboro | 606/248–6860 or 800/544–8313 | fax 606/248–6978 | 60 rooms | $64 | AE, D, DC, MC, V.

Ridgerunner Bed and Breakfast. Built in the 1890s, this Victorian mansion overlooks Middlesboro (town center is 5 mi away) and the mountains. The interior has intricate woodwork and period furnishings; outdoors there are landscaped gardens. Complimentary home-cooked breakfast. No kids under 16. | 208 Arthur Heights, Middlesboro | 606/248–4299 | www.bbonline.com./ky/ridgerunn/index.html | 4 rooms | $55–$65 | Closed Jan. | AE, D, MC, V.

MIDWAY

MAP 6, F3

(Nearby towns also listed: Frankfort, Georgetown, Lexington, Paris, Versailles)

Now a mecca for antique collectors, Midway was the first Kentucky town (circa 1833) built by a railroad company, and was named because it was the midpoint on the line between Frankfort and Lexington. It is also the home of Midway College, the state's only college for women, founded in 1847.

Information: **Woodford County Chamber of Commerce** | 110 N. Main St., Box 442, Versailles, 40383 | 859/873–5122 | www.woodfordchamber-ky.com.

ON THE CALENDAR
APR.: *Midway Village Guild Antiques Show.* A spring treasure-hunter's outing, the weekend show is brimming with local and regional antiques dealers. | 859/873–5122.
SEPT.: *Midway Fall Festival.* This event is scheduled on a weekend mid-month. There are craft demonstrations, arts and crafts exhibitors, music and dancing, and a variety of foods and snacks. | 859/873–5122.

Dining
Bistro La Belle. Continental. The decor of this intimate bistro mixes thoroughbred equine memorabilia, eclectic art, and kitsch. There's live blues music on Thursday nights. The menu features items such as: locally grown vegetables, seafood, pasta, pork chops with dried fruit—chipolte compote, creole shrimp. Nightly there are specials including seasonal lamb and game. On Sunday, there is a Chef's Whim brunch. Lunch starts at $4 and the menu includes the famous King Sandwich of peanut butter, honey and banana (an Elvis favorite!). Save room for the homemade desserts. | 117 E. Main St., Midway | 859/846–4233 | fax 859/875–2275 | bistrolabelle@aol.com | Brunch available Sun. No supper Tue., Sun. Closed Mon. | $9–$23 | AE, D, MC, V.

Lodging
Scottwood Bed and Breakfast. This circa 1795 Federal home is listed on Bluegrass Trust. All rooms have queen-size beds and two rooms share a bath. Landscaped with gardens and hemlocks, the B&B is on the scenic South Elkhorn Creek renowned for its widemouth bass fishing. You'll find a canoe there. Telephone is available in the common area. Complimentary breakfast. No in-room telephones. Cable TV, VCRs. Fishing. Pets (ask). | 2004 Leestown Rd., Midway | 859/846–5037 or 877/477–0778 | fax 859/846–4887 | www.scottwoodbb.com | 4 rooms | $95–$125 | MC, V.

MONTICELLO

(Nearby towns also listed: Jamestown, Somerset)

It was founded in 1800 and named by the county clerk after Thomas Jefferson's home. The town experienced a mini-boom in the late 1800s when oil was discovered nearby. Present industries include clothing and wood products. This, the Wayne County seat, is near Dale Hollow Lake State Resort Park.

Information: **Monticello/Wayne Co. Chamber of Commerce** | Box 566, Monticello, 42633 | 606/348–3064 | www.cedar/creek/inc.com/monticello.

Attractions

Dale Hollow Lake State Resort Park. Covering over 25,500 acres, the lake occupies space in both Kentucky and Tennessee. Many secluded inlets around the shore make this an ideal houseboat vacation destination. There's a lodge and marina in the park. | 6371 State Park Rd., Bow | 270/433–7431 | www.kystateparks.com/agencies/parks/dalehol.htm | Free | Daily.

Monticello-Wayne County Memorial Park. This 86-acre park has picnic shelters; playgrounds; horseback riding and hiking trails; and basketball, tennis, volleyball, and badminton courts. | 330 E. Michigan Ave., Monticello | 606/348–9551 | Free | Daily.

ON THE CALENDAR
MAY: *Cornbread Festival.* This event celebrates one of Kentucky's favorite foods. It takes place Memorial Day Weekend in Mill Springs Park, site of an 1840s mill that still grinds cornmeal. | 606/348–3064.

Dining

Tiffany's Restaurant. American. Chandeliers, and a position in a local hotel, make this restaurant famous for its simple, pleasant elegance. Order the pork chops or the deep-fried catfish. Barbecued ribs are the popular Fri. special. | 340 E. Rte. 90, Monticello | 606/348–9972 | $5–$6 | AE, MC, V.

Lodging

Anchor Motel. This is a modern, independently-owned motel in the downtown area. The rooms are basic with contemporary furnishings. The adjacent Anchor Restaurant serves standard American fare. Downtown shopping areas are just a few minutes away. Restaurant. Some refrigerators. Cable TV. Pool. Laundry facilities. Business services. Pets allowed. | 1077 N. Main St., Monticello | 606/348–8441 | fax 606/348–5118 | 50 rooms | $35 | AE, D, MC, V.

Grider Hill Dock and Indian Creek Lodge. You have a choice of houseboat or lodge room at this rustic facility overlooking Lake Cumberland. Houseboats come with patio tables, couches, deck chairs and microwaves. The lodge is surrounded by a variety of foliage, including hardwoods, hemlock, cedars and pines, and each room has a private deck. Restaurant. Kitchenettes (in cottages). Cable TV. Boating. | R.R. #4, Albany | 606/387–5501 | fax 606/387–7023 | www.griderhilldock.com | 22 rooms; 12 cottages, 20 houseboats | $45–$88, $74–$150 cottages; $1,100–$2,300 houseboats (for three–day weekend) | Closed Nov.–Mar. | AE, D, MC, V.

MOREHEAD

MAP 6, H3

(Nearby towns also listed: Ashland, Olive Hill, Winchester)

In 1911, a teacher named Cora Wilson Stewart turned her one-room schoolhouse into the first of her "moonlight schools," which were early models for modern adult education. Stewart's schools contributed greatly to reversing the pattern of adult illiteracy in eastern Kentucky. The schoolhouse is preserved on the campus of Morehead State University. Morehead is also one of the important staging points for visitors to the northern end of the vast Daniel Boone National Forest. Present-day economy is based on the university and the town's role as a regional medical center.

Information: **Morehead–Rowan County Tourism Commission** | 150 E. 1st St., Morehead, 40351 | 606/784–6221 | www.moreheadrowan.com.

Attractions

Cave Run Lake. Formed by a dam on the Licking River, the 8,270-acre lake is home to such sport fish as bass, bluegill, muskie, and crappie. In addition to marina facilities, there's a campground and hiking and horseback trails. | Morehead Ranger District, 2375 KY 801S, Morehead | 606/784–5624 | www.r8web.com/Boone/caverun.htm | Free | Year-round.

Minor Clark State Fish Hatchery. Fish reared here in 111 ponds on 300 acres are used for stocking Kentucky lakes. Species on display in a special pool include largemouth and smallmouth bass, rockfish, muskies, and walleye pike. | 120 Fish Hatchery Rd., Morehead | 606/784–6872 | Free | May–Sept., weekdays 7–3.

Morehead State University. Founded in 1922, the university has a current enrollment of 8,300. An early 20th-century, one-room schoolhouse stands on the grounds and is open for tour by appointment. | Howell-McDowell building, University Blvd., Morehead | 606/783–2221 | fax 606/783–5038 | www.morehead-st.edu.

Morehead State University is also home of the **Kentucky Folk Art Center.** The Center is the state's only folk-art museum, opened in 1997 and contains antique and contemporary quilts, woodcarving, primitive paintings, and other art. A seven-minute orientation video is narrated by Rosemary Clooney. | 102 W. 1st St. | 606/783–2204 | fax 606/783–5034 | www.kyfolkart.org | $3 | Mon.–Sat. 9–5, Sun. 1–5.

Books, journals, government documents, and genealogical materials are housed in the **MSU Appalachian Collection** at the Camden Carroll Library Tower. | 606/783–2829 | Free | Daily.

ON THE CALENDAR

JUNE: *Appalachian Celebration.* Held on the Morehead State University campus, this is a major festival of regional music (folk, bluegrass, country, and mountain) and draws over 100 artists and craftspeople from throughout the area. | 606/783–2077.

SEPT.: *Kentucky Hardwood Festival.* Honoring the environmental and commercial importance of the state's native hardwood trees, the weekend's activities include a parade, a car show, and arts and crafts exhibitions and sales. | 800/654–1944.

SEPT.: *Rowan County Harvest Festival.* The harvest season in Morehead is ushered in each year with a carnival, live music, craft booths, and food. | 606/784–6221.

Dining

Boomerang's. Steak. This is a gritty country roadhouse popular with local students—it's got a game room with a pool table. Steak is the main fare but the Oysters Rockefeller (oysters cooked in bacon, onion, and spinach) are equally popular. | 112 Trademore Shopping Center, Morehead | 606/784–8908 | $8–$15 | AE, D, DC, MC, V.

Fazoli's Italian Restaurant. Fast Food. Spaghetti, lasagna, calzones, and other familiar pasta and meat dishes are served up fast-food style in this brightly-lit restaurant. | 125 Flemingsburg Rd., Morehead | 606/783–9988 | $3–$5 | No credit cards.

Lodging

Best Western Plaza Inn. This inn is off I–64, at exit 137, less than 3 mi from downtown Morehead and 12 mi from Cave Run Lake. A shopping plaza, a grocery store, and several restaurants are all nearby. Complimentary Continental breakfast. In-room data ports, some in-room hot tubs. Pool. Business services. | 175 Tom Dr., Morehead | 606/784–2220 | fax 606/784–2220 | www.bestwestern.com | 45 rooms | $65 | AE, D, DC, MC, V.

Brownwood Bed & Breakfast. You'll find all wood, Amish-made furnishings in this rural B&B. The premises border the Daniel Boone State Forest and are within a half mile of Cave Run Lake, Dam, and River, 4 mi from I–64 at exit 133. Complimentary breakfast. Microwaves, refrigerators. Cable TV. No children. | 46 Carey Rd. and 1360 Rte. 801S, Morehead | 606/784–8799 | www.caverun.org | 4 cabins, 2 suites | Cabins $70, Suites $100 | AE, D, DC, MC, V.

Days Inn. Morehead State University is 3 mi from this three-story motel, and Cave Run Lake is 10 mi. Rates go up during university graduation. Complimentary Continental breakfast. Some refrigerators, some in-room hot tubs. Cable TV. Laundry facilities. Laundry service. | 170 Toms Dr., Morehead | 606/783–1484 or 800/544–8313 | fax 606/783–1484 | www.daysinn.com | 50 rooms | $40–$90 | AE, D, DC, MC, V.

Holiday Inn. Boat parking is available here, and there's a golf course nearby. The hotel is within 10 mi of Cave Run Lake and the Kentucky Folk Art Center. Restaurant. In-room data ports. Cable TV. Pool. Business services. | 1698 Flemingsburg Rd., Morehead | 606/784–7591 | fax 606/783–1859 | www.basshotels.com | 141 rooms | $60–$85 | AE, D, DC, MC, V.

Super 8. Morehead State University is 2½ mi from this facility. Restaurant. Some in-room hot tubs. Cable TV. Laundry service. | 602 Fraley Dr., Morehead | 606/784–8882 or 800/800–8000 | fax 606/784–9882 | www.super8.com | 56 rooms | $38–$61 | AE, D, DC, MC, V.

MOUNT VERNON

MAP 6, G5

(Nearby towns also listed: Berea, Danville, Hazard, London, Renfro Valley)

Part of Rockcastle County, the town originated when settlers stopped and built cabins around Spout Springs sometime before 1790. This was an important stopover along the Wilderness Road, the route (forged by Daniel Boone) that connected the Cumberland Gap to the Bluegrass region. The current economy centers around tourism and nearby Renfro Valley music center.

Information: Mount Vernon/Rockcastle County Tourist Commission | Box 1261, Mount Vernon, 40456 | 606/256–9814 or 800/252–6685.

Attractions

Isaac Shelby Cemetery State Historic Site. Isaac Shelby (1750–1826), Kentucky's first and fifth governor, had counties in nine states named after him in honor of his military, political, and educational achievements. He is buried in the family cemetery, close to the site of his former estate, which was known as Traveler's Rest. | Off U.S. 127, 5 mi south of Danville | 859/239–7089 | www.state.ky.us/agencies/parks/isshelby.htm | Free | Daily.

William Whitley House Historic Site. Originally called Sportsman's Hill, this 18th-century building was the first brick house west of the Appalachians, and served both as a shelter during skirmishes with Native Americans and as a rest stop for pioneers on the Wilderness Road. The house is furnished with period antiques. | 625 William Whitley Rd., Mount

Vernon | 606/355–2881 | www.kystateparks.com/agencies/parks/wmwhitly.htm | $3.50 | June–Aug., daily; Sept.–May, Tues.–Sun. 9–5.

ON THE CALENDAR

OCT.: *Bittersweet Festival*. Held on Main Street, the festival emphasizes regional Kentucky arts, crafts, and food. | 606/256–9814 or 800/252–6685.

Dining

Jean's. Southern. Adorning the walls are autographed photos of the Renfro Valley country entertainers who eat here. Known for catfish, pinto beans, and fried cornbread, the restaurant is 3 mi outside of town, in a freestanding brick building. | Rte. 1004, Mount Vernon | 606/256–5319 | Breakfast also available | $4–$7 | No credit cards.

Lodging

Econo Lodge. Renfro Valley is just a ½ mi from this facility, and downtown just 1½ mi. Cable TV. Pool. Some pets allowed. | 1630 Richmond St., Mount Vernon | 606/256–4621 | fax 606/256–4622 | www.econolodge.com | 35 rooms | $36–$40 | AE, D, DC, MC, V.

Kastle Inn. Weekly and monthly rates are available at this 2-story inn, situated 3 mi south of downtown, and 3 mi from Renfro Valley. Restaurant. Cable TV. Pool. Some pets allowed. | I–75 and U.S. 25, Mount Vernon | 606/256–5156 | fax 606/256–5156 | 50 rooms | $56 | AE, D, DC, MC, V.

Super 8 Motel. You'll find rooms decorated in cream, red, and green at this modern motel. Take exit 59 off I–75. You'll find Jean's Restaurant and a Pizza Hut nearby. Complimentary Continental breakfast. Cable TV. Business services. | I–75 and U.S. 25, Mount Vernon | 606/256–5313 | fax 606/256–9193 | www.super8.com | 46 rooms | $65 | AE, D, MC, V.

MURRAY

MAP 6, B6

(Nearby towns also listed: Gilbertsville, Mayfield, Paris)

Established in 1822, this is the Calloway County seat. It's also home to Murray State University, a community theater, the Western Kentucky Livestock and Exposition Center (a popular site for rodeos and horse shows), and the National Scouting Museum. Several of western Kentucky's lake and recreational areas are nearby.

Information: Murray Tourism Commission | 805 N. 12th St., Box 190, Murray 42071 | 270/759–2199 or 800/651–1603 | www.murraynet.com.

Attractions

Kenlake State Resort Park. (*See* Cadiz.)

Land Between the Lakes. (*See* Gilbertsville.)

Murray State University. This four-year public university has six colleges and enrolls 8,000 students. The first building completed on the campus was the Wrather West Kentucky Museum, the exhibits of which depict the history and development of western Kentucky. Call to schedule a campus tour. | 6606 Elizabeth, Murray | 800/272–4678 | www.mursuky.edu | Free | Daily.

National Museum, Boy Scouts of America. Chronicling the history of the Boy Scouts (founded in 1910), the museum houses interactive exhibits, including the Amazon Adventure indoor maze, and a gallery of nearly 60 original Norman Rockwell paintings. For a separate fee, you can brave the Gateway Challenge Contest, an outdoor ropes and teams course for visitors over seven years old. | Corner of 16th and Calloway Sts., Murray State University campus | 270/762–3383 or 800/303–3047 | fax 270/762–3189 | www.bsamuseum.org | $5 | Mar.–Nov., Tues.–Sat. 9–4:30, Sun. noon–4:30; Gift shop open winters.

ON THE CALENDAR
JULY: *Freedom Fest.* You'll find all the patriotic trimmings at this three-day 4th of July extravaganza, including fireworks, parades, concerts, and a street fair. | 800/715–5004.
OCT.: *Twin Lakes Star Party.* You can take part in sky viewing lessons and gazing sessions. Go to lectures, win door prizes, and see telescope and equipment displays at this annual stargazing festival held in the Golden Pond Planetarium in Land Between the Lakes. | 800/651–1603.

Dining
Log Cabin. American. Open 24 hours, except on Sundays, this actual log cabin is downtown, five blocks from the Courthouse. Locals come for the Harper's Country Ham and homemade pies. Salad bar. Kids' menu. | 505 S. 12th St., Murray | 270/753–8080 | Breakfast also available. No dinner Sun. | $5.50–$6.25 | D, MC, V.

Lodging
Amerihost Inn. An indoor pool/atrium highlights this property. It's only ¼ mi from Murray State University. Complimentary Continental breakfast. Refrigerators, data-ports, microwaves. Cable TV. Pool. Hot tub, sauna. Exercise equipment. Business services. | 1210 N. 12th St., Murray | 270/759–5910 | fax 270/759–5912 | www.amerihost.com | 60 rooms | $60–$79 | AE, D, DC, MC, V.

Days Inn. Murray State University is ½ mi from this facility. Complimentary Continental breakfast. Some kitchenettes, microwaves, refrigerators, some in-room hot tubs. Cable TV. Pool. Business services. Some pets allowed (fee). | 517 S. 12th St., Murray | 270/753–6706 or 800/544–8313 | fax 270/753–6708 | www.daysinn.com | 33 rooms, 6 suites | $43–$54, $105–$125 suites | AE, D, DC, MC, V.

Diuguid House Bed & Breakfast. This Queen Anne-style Victorian brick house dates from 1895. Inside, a smattering of antiques among the contemporary furnishings creates an eclectic mood. Twelve blocks from Murray State University, the B&B is a favorite with MSU visitors. Complimentary breakfast. TV in common area. Library. Laundry facilities. | 603 Main St., Murray | 270/753–5470 or 888/261–3028 | 3 rooms | $40 | AE, D, DC, MC, V.

Plaza Court. Weekly rates are available here, only five blocks from Murray State University. Cable TV. Free parking. Some pets allowed. | 502 S. 12th St., Murray | 270/753–2682 | 40 rooms | $36–$39 | AE, D, MC, V.

Shoney's Inn. With room colors on the bright side, the motel is ½ mi from both Murray State University and Murray State Events Center. Kentucky Lake Recreation Area is 10 mi away. In-room data ports, some microwaves, some refrigerators. Cable TV. Pool. Business services. Some pets allowed (fee). | 1503 N. 12th St., Murray | 270/753–5353 | fax 270/753–5353 | www.shoneysinn.com | 67 rooms | $49–$61, $80 suites | AE, D, DC, MC, V.

NATURAL BRIDGE STATE RESORT PARK

(see Slade)

OLIVE HILL

MAP 6, H3

(Nearby towns also listed: Ashland, Morehead)

Standing along Tygart's Creek in western Carter County, Olive Hill grew up as a trading center at the turn of the 18th century. In 1804, a road was built through it, connecting Little Sandy River's salt works to the towns of central Kentucky. Two state parks are nearby: Carter Caves and Grayson Lake.

Information: **Olive Hill Chamber of Commerce** | Box 460, Olive Hill, 41164 | 606/286–5532 | tsturgillcoh@atcc.net.

Attractions

Carter Caves State Resort Park. Covering over 1,300 acres, the park is peppered with caves, rocky cliffs, and natural bridges. The BatCave Nature preserve has a thriving population of the endangered Indiana bat. Nature trails and guided tours of some caves are available. A lodge, cottages, and campgrounds provide accommodation. | 344 Caveland Dr., Olive Hill | 606/286–4411 | www.kystateparks.com/agencies/parks/cartcave.htm | Free; fee for camping; cave tours $5 | Jan.–mid-Dec., daily.

Grayson Lake State Park. Visible from a scenic canyon on its shoreline, 1,500-acre Grayson Lake is surrounded by another 1,500 acres of park land. Fishing, boating, camping, and picnic facilities are among the attractions. | 314 Grayson Lake Park Rd., Olive Hill | 606/474–9727 | www.kystateparks.com/agencies/parks/graysonl.htm | Free; fee for camping | Year-round.

Northeastern Kentucky History Museum. For a close look at Native American and pioneer artifacts as well as items pertaining to local natural history, visit this small museum. | U.S. 182, Olive Hill | 606/474–8740 | $1 | Apr.–Oct., 9–4.

ON THE CALENDAR

JUNE–JULY: *Someday.* A musical drama set during the Civil War is performed on Fridays and Saturdays in the amphitheater at Grayson Lake State Park. | 606/286–4522.

Dining

Walker's Grill. American. This friendly country diner serves up hamburgers, soups, beans, and turkey to local customers that keep coming back. | 109 Railroad St., Olive Hill | 606/286–5931 | Closed Sun. | $3–$4 | No credit cards.

Lodging

Caveland Lodge. Rooms at this fieldstone lodge all overlook woodlands. The state-owned property offers access to all facilities at Carter Caves State Resort Park. Picnic area. Kitchenettes (in cottages), refrigerators (in cottages). 2 pools, 1 wading pool. 9-hole golf course, mini-golf, putting green, tennis. Playground. Business services. | 344 Caveland Dr., Olive Hill | 606/286–4411 or 800/325–0059 | fax 606/286–8165 | www.kystateparks.com | 28 rooms in lodge, 15 cottages | $52–$71, $96–$135 cottages | AE, D, DC, MC, V.

Travelodge. Surrounded by trees, this two-story motel supplies lovely green views. The rooms, too, are decorated in hunter-green with accents of burgundy. Right off I–64, the motel is near several restaurants and a Kmart. Complimentary Continental breakfast. In-room data ports, in-room safes, some kitchenettes, some in-room hot-tubs. Cable TV. Pool. Business services. Pets allowed (fee). | 205 U.S. 1947, Grayson | 606/474–7854 or 877/750–1222 | fax 606/474–8425 | www.travelodge.com | 60 rooms | $55 | AE, D, DC, MC, V.

OWENSBORO

(Nearby towns also listed: Henderson, Falls of Rough, Madisonville)

This city is famous for its unique style of barbecue—they cook mutton rather than pork. This largest city in western Kentucky is where William Smeathers established the first permanent settlement in 1776. Named for Colonel Abraham Owen, who died in the 1811 Battle of Tippecanoe, Owensboro is a regional agricultural and manufacturing center. Its 1,500-seat RiverPark Center hosts arts events including theater, bluegrass, and classical music.

Information: **Owensboro–Daviess County Tourist Commission** | 215 E. 2nd St., Owensboro 42303 | 270/926–1100 or 800/489–1131 | www.visitowensboro.com.

Attractions

Ben Hawes State Park. The 300-acre park has 18- and 9-hole golf courses, a softball field, a playground, picnic shelters, and hiking trails. | 400 Boothfield Rd., Owensboro | 270/684–9808 or 502/685–2011 | www.kystateparks.com/agencies/parks/benhawes.htm | Fees for golf | Year-round.

Goldy's Best Little Opryhous in Kentucky. This music hall boasts country, gospel, and bluegrass concerts all year 'round. Fridays are Talent Night. Reservations are required. | 418 Frederica St., Owensboro | 270/926–0254 | $5–$12 | Concerts at 8 PM.

Owensboro Area Museum of Science and History. Exhibition subjects include astronomy, geology, botany, anthropology, and Daviess County history. There is a notable display of live reptiles. | 220 Davies St., Owensboro | 270/687–2732 | $2 (suggested) | Tues.–Sat. 10–5, Sun. 1–4.

Owensboro Museum of Fine Art. Works by regional artists and changing exhibitions of fine and decorative art are the highlights here. Collections include five centuries of English, French, and American paintings, as well as regional folk art. | 901 Frederica St., Owensboro | 270/685–3181 | $2 (suggested) | Tues.–Fri. 10–4, weekends 1–4.

Windy Hollow Recreation Area. Windy Hollow has swimming and a 240-ft water slide on more than 200 acres. Fishing, mini-golf, and camping facilities are also available. | 5141 Windy Hollow Rd., Owensboro | 270/785–4150 | Free | Apr.–Oct., daily.

ON THE CALENDAR

MAY: *International Bar-B-Q Festival.* Crafts, music, and of course, food—lots and lots of hickory-smoked pork, beef, chicken, fish, and mutton—are on hand for this great pig-out held on the river front. The competition is hot for Barbecue Champion of the World. | 270/926–6938.

JULY–AUG.: *Daviess County Fair.* This is the region's largest agricultural and entertainment fair. | 270/926–1100 or 800/489–1131.

OCT.–APR.: *Owensboro Symphony Orchestra.* The third-largest professional orchestra in the state gives classical concerts in RiverPark Center. | 270/684–0661.

OCT.: *Taste of Owensboro.* The highlight of this annual food festival (held at Riverpark Center) is its selection of over forty wines and beers. | 800/489–1131.

Dining

Briarpatch. American. Stained-glass windows and a fireplace in the pub area characterize this 30-year-old restaurant, housed downtown in a blue barn. Filet mignon and prime rib are cooked to order, and the kitchen makes a Hoppin' John soup, with blackeyed peas, rice, and sausage. Salad bar. Kids' menu. | 2760 Veach Rd., Owensboro | 270/685–3329 | No lunch Sat. | $11–$24 | AE, D, DC, MC, V.

Colby's. Contemporary. Downtown in a late-19th-century house, the dining room is known for fresh fish and beef. Colby's Chicken Tenders are popular—batter fried in a special sauce—as is the homemade Toll House pie, with a thick cookie dough crust and hot fudge. Kids' menu. Sunday brunch. | 202 W. 3rd St., Owensboro | 270/685–4239 | Jacket and tie | $9.75–$22 | AE, MC, V.

Fazoli's Italian Restaurant. Italian. For a quick bite, stop at this location of the popular chain. Menu highlights are spaghetti, lasagna, and calzones. | 5060 Frederica St., Owensboro | 270/926–8767 | $3–$5 | AE, D, MC, V.

Moonlite Bar B-Q. Barbecue. Famous throughout the state for Western Kentucky-style barbecue and burgoo, this restaurant also serves homemade desserts like chocolate coconut pie and banana pudding. There's an original stone fireplace and pictures of local Nascar drivers in the dining area. Buffet. Kids' menu. Sunday brunch. Beer and wine only. | 2840

© Corbis

BOURBON

Mark Twain was obviously a fan of Kentucky's most famous beverage. He once wrote that "too much good bourbon is never enough," an intemperate statement, but patriotic when you consider that a joint Congressional resolution in 1964 recognized bourbon whiskey as a "distinctly American product."

What makes it so is that bourbon is distilled from (by law) at least 51%, and usually more, fermented corn, a grain indigenous to the Western Hemisphere and cultivated by Native Americans for centuries before European settlers arrived. This is the famous "sour mash" that is somewhat like an alcoholic version of sourdough. Since corn is high in sugar, bourbon is sweeter tasting than Scotch or rye whiskies.

Another condition of its production is that the whiskey must be aged in new, white oak barrels that have been charred on the inside. This gives bourbon its amber color and caramel and vanilla flavors. The barrels, after use, are often sold abroad to Scottish distillers and French cognac makers. A little taste of Kentucky thus finds its way across the Atlantic.

The aromatic flavors of bourbon are what make it a popular cooking ingredient. Virtually any recipe that calls for vanilla extract can have an equal amount of bourbon substituted.

Before Prohibition, Kentucky had over 400 distilleries. Once alcohol sales were legalized again, several which had managed to hang on by making "medicinal" bourbon merged. (By the way, it is because bourbon could be sold by prescription that modern drugstores still sell liquor.)

Today, about a dozen distilleries produce nearly 200 brands of bourbons. Most of the distilleries, which are in a geographic triangle whose points are Bardstown, Frankfort, and Louisville, have tours for visitors. But you can only look, as it's illegal to serve bourbon at a distillery. Many tours serve apple juice, which is at least a similar color.

Another irony is that, in most of Kentucky, you can't buy bourbon or any other alcoholic beverage. Out of 120 counties in the state, 75 are "dry." There are 30 "wet" counties and 15 known as "moist," where some towns have made alcohol sales legal.

W. Parish Ave., Owensboro | 270/684–8143 | Breakfast also available. No dinner Sun. | $6–$15 | AE, D, DC, MC, V.

Ruby Tuesday. American. Part of a popular chain, this eatery serves marinated steak, chicken, ribs, and fajitas. Salad bar. Kids' menu. | 5000 Frederica St., Owensboro | 270/926–8325 | $8–$15 | AE, D, DC, MC, V.

Trotter's. American. Celebrating the *other* kind of horse-racing, the dining room has a trotting horse theme. Kids' menu. Early bird suppers Mon.–Thurs. | 1100 Walnut St., Owensboro | 270/685–2771 | Closed Sun. | $16–$26 | AE, DC, MC, V.

Lodging

Days Inn. Catering to business travelers, this motel is on the outskirts of town. Restaurant. Complimentary breakfast. Room service. In-room data ports. Pool. Business services. Some pets allowed. | 3720 New Hartford Rd., Owensboro | 270/684–9621 or 800/544–8313 | fax 270/684–9626 | www.daysinn.com | 122 rooms | $32–$43 | AE, D, DC, MC, V.

The Executive Inn. The Ohio River passes by this motor hotel near the city center. 2 restaurants, bar with entertainment. Refrigerators, cable TV. 2 pools (1 indoor). Lighted indoor tennis. Exercise equipment. Air-conditioning. Free parking. Business services. Airport shuttle. | 1 Executive Blvd., Owensboro | 270/926–8000 or 800/626–1936 | fax 270/926–6442 | 145 rooms, 36 suites | $43–$70, $90–$145 suites | AE, D, DC, MC, V.

Holiday Inn. Downtown Owensboro is 1 mi from this hotel. Nearby attractions include Ben Hawes State Park (3 mi), Summitt golf course (9 mi), the Owensboro Museum of Fine Art (3 mi). Restaurant, bar with entertainment Tues.–Sat., complimentary breakfast. In-room data ports. Cable TV. Indoor pool. Hot tub, sauna. Putting green. Exercise equipment. Playground. Business services. Airport shuttle. Some pets allowed. | 3136 W. 2nd St., Owensboro | 270/685–3941 | fax 270/926–2917 | 145 rooms, 4 suites | $53–$69, $95 suites | AE, D, DC, MC, V.

Motor Lodge 231. Pink and tan wall-papered rooms in this economic motel have up-to-date furnishings and facilities. A grocery store and small shopping center are nearby. Some in-room microwaves, refrigerators. Cable TV. | 1640 Triplet St., Owensboro | 270/684–7231 | 30 rooms | $40 | MC, V.

Sleep Inn of Owensboro. This inn is nearby to the Ben Hawes State Park, the Town Square Shopping Mall, and several barbecue restaurants. Rooms are large with modern furnishings, and decorated in red tones. Complimentary Continental breakfast. Some in-room data ports, microwaves, refrigerators. Cable TV, VCRs. Pool. Hot tub. Gym. Laundry facilities. Business services. | 51 Bon Harbor Hills Dr., Owensboro | 270/691–6200 | fax 270/691–6244 | www.sleepinn.com | 66 rooms | $60 | AE, D, DC, MC, V.

WeatherBerry Bed & Breakfast. Wide porches, rooms furnished with antiques, and several 12-ft mirrors characterize this 1840 house, situated on seven acres next to a city park. Complimentary breakfast. Some pets allowed. | 2731 2nd Street W., Owensboro | 270/684–8760 | fax 270/684–8760 | weatherber@aol.com | www.bbonline.com/ky/weatherberry/index.html | 3 rooms | $65–$80 | AE, MC, V.

PADUCAH

(Nearby towns also listed: Gilbertsville, Mayfield, Wickcliffe)

Established at the confluence of the Ohio and Tennessee Rivers during the Revolutionary War, the city was named in honor of Chickasaw Chief Paduke, a statue of whom stands at the corner of 19th Street and Jefferson Blvd. The city is the headquarters for the American Quilter's Society and is the site of the U.S. Atomic Energy Commission's gaseous diffusion plant.

Information: Paducah–McCracken County Convention and Visitors Bureau | Box 90, 128 Broadway, Paducah, 42001 | 270/443–8783 or 800/723–8224 | fun@paducah-tourism.org | www.paducah-tourism.org.

Attractions

Alben W. Barkley Monument. A memorial statue honors Paducah native Alben Barkley, who was Vice President of the United States from 1949 to 1953. | Jefferson and 28th Sts., Paducah | Free | Daily.

Chief Paduke Statue. Lorado Taft sculpted this statue of the Chickasaw chief in 1909. | 19th and Jefferson Sts., Paducah | Daily.

Irvin S. Cobb Memorial. The Kentucky journalist and humorist is buried in the Oak Grove Cemetery, near his memorial. | 1613 Park Ave., Paducah | Free | Daily dawn to dusk.

Market House Complex. Built in 1905, the complex has a museum, a theater, and an art gallery. | S. 2nd St. and Broadway, Paducah

The **Market House Museum** houses the restored interior of an 1870s pharmacy, complete with apothecary equipment. Americana artifacts include Native American pottery and weapons, and memorabilia of Alben Barkley and Irvin Cobb. | 121 S. 2nd St. | 270/443–7759 | $1.50 | Mar.–Dec., Tues.–Sat. noon–4; Sun. 1–4.

The 250-seat **Market House Theatre** is the home of a community acting company. | 141 Kentucky Ave. | 270/444–6828 | www.wkynet.com/paducahnet/markethousetheatre | Box office Tues.–Fri., 10–6.

The **Yeiser Arts Center** is a regional gallery with rotating exhibitions by local and international artists. | 200 Broadway | 270/442–2453 | www.yeiser.org | $1 | Tues.–Sat. 10–4; Sun. 1–4.

Museum of the American Quilter's Society. One of the largest such museums in the country, with over 200 antique and modern quilts, the building has stained-glass panels representing several quilts in the permanent collection. Exhibitions rotate. | 215 Jefferson St., Paducah | 270/442–8856 | $5 | Apr.–Oct., Tues.–Sat. 10–5, Sun. 1–5; Nov.–Mar., Tues.–Sat. 10–5.

Paducah Railroad Museum. Learn some rail history at this freight house of the Nashville, Chattanooga, and St. Louis Railroad. Displays here showcase equipment, memorabilia and a model train layout. | 3rd and Washington St., Paducah | 270/442–4032 or 270/443–7084 | Free | Sat. 10–4, or by appointment.

Paducah Wall to Wall. Painter Robert Dafford illustrated Paducah's history with the Floodwall Murals. The 22 painted panels are on the city's floodwall, where they overlook the junction of the Ohio and Tennessee rivers. Among the murals' subjects are a view of Paducah in 1837, various Paducah industries, and representations of African-American history and Native American history. | Water St., Paducah | 270/443–8783 or 800/723–8224 | Free | Daily.

Red Line Scenic Tour. Your self-guided motor tour of Paducah will include the city hall, which is a replica of the U.S. Embassy in New Delhi, India. Maps are available at the Paducah Visitors Bureau. | Visitors Bureau, 128 Broadway, Paducah | 270/443–8783 or 800/723–8224 | www.paducah-tourism.org | Free | Daily.

Whitehaven. Dating from the mid 18th century, this classical Revival mansion now serves as a state welcome center and contains memorabilia of Alben Barkley, including the first U.S. vice presidential flag. | 1845 Lone Oak Rd., Paducah | 270/554–2077 | Free | Daily; information 8–6; tours 1–4.

ON THE CALENDAR

APR.: *Dogwood Trail Celebration.* A lighted dogwood tree trail, candlelight home tours, and other cultural events help the city welcome spring. | 800/PADUCAH.

APR.: *American Quilter's Society Quilt Show and Contest.* More than 400 quilts are entered in this annual event, held at the Executive Inn. Workshops, lectures, fashion show, and an auction are highlights. | 270/898–7903.

JULY: *Paducah Summer Festival.* A hot-air-balloon lift-off, fireworks, symphony orchestra concerts, arts and crafts, and a food fare are all part of the riverfront summer festivities. | 270/443–8783 or 800/PADUCAH.

AUG.–SEPT.: *Players Bluegrass Downs.* There's standardbreds harness racing on the track and year-round betting on racing simulcasts. | 270/444–7117.

Dining

C. C. Cohen. Contemporary. Antiques furnish the dining room in the historic Cohen Building (circa 1870). The Paducah Hot Brown—half of a hoagie roll with ham, turkey, cheddar, bacon, grilled tomato and parmesan—is popular, as is the chocolate mousse dessert. Entertainment Fri., Sat. Kids' menu. | 103 S. 2nd St., Paducah | 270/442–6391 | Closed Sun. | $15–$29 | AE, D, MC, V.

Cynthia's Ristorante. Seafood. Cynthia's is known for great fresh fish dishes and soft-shell crabs. Try the ever-popular grilled shrimp wrapped in prosciutto, the cheese tortellini tossed with roasted chicken, and the fresh mozzarella salad. With stained glass windows, a shiny tile-top bar, old-fashioned tin ceilings, and candlelit tables, this restaurant is perfect for a romantic dinner. | 125 Market House Sq., Paducah | 270/443–3319 | closed Sun.–Mon. | $11–$19 | AE, D, MC, V.

Jeremiah's. Contemporary. Originally a 19th-century bank, the building has dark wood, exposed brick walls, original tin ceilings, and a beer can collection. The kitchen serves frogs legs grilled over an open charcoal pit. There's also an on-premises microbrewery. | 225 Broadway, Paducah | 270/443–3991 | Closed Sun. No lunch | $12–$25 | AE, D, DC, MC, V.

Kirchhoff's Bakery. Cafe. Rich, hearty-baked delights reveal the heritage of this fifth generation family-owned bakery opened by German immigrants in 1873. Don't miss the cranberry-walnut bread. For lunch you can have standard deli sandwiches and salads. | 114–118 Market House Sq., Paducah | 270/442–7117 | $4–$6 | AE, D, MC, V.

Whaler's Catch. Seafood. A lively, nautical-themed interior marks this restaurant, next door to the American Quilter's Society. An outdoor dining deck overlooks downtown streets, and daily fresh fish specials are a local draw. Kids' menu. | 123 N. 2nd St., Paducah | 270/444–7701 | Closed Sun. No lunch Sat. | $17–$40 | AE, MC, V.

Lodging

Courtyard by Marriott. A tree-lined atrium dominates this three-story facility, which lies 4½ mi from the Museum of the American Quilter's Society. There are three golf courses within 3 mi of the hotel. Bar with entertainment. Complimentary breakfast. Data ports, microwaves, refrigerators, some in-room hot tubs. Cable TV. Indoor pool. Hot tub. Exercise equipment. Laundry service. Free parking. | 3835 Technology Dr., Paducah | 270/442–3600 or 800/321–2211 | fax 270/442–3619 | www.mariott.com | 100 rooms | $79, $109–$115 suites | AE, D, DC, MC, V.

Days Inn. Kentucky Oaks Mall is less than 1 mi from this two-story motel. Complimentary Continental breakfast. Data ports, some microwaves, some refrigerators. Cable TV. Pool. Business services. Free parking. | 3901 Hinkleville Rd., Paducah | 270/442–7501 | fax 270/442–7500 | www.daysinn.com | 122 rooms | $40–$90 | AE, D, DC, MC, V.

Denton Motel. Mill Springs Amusement Park is 10 minutes from this motel, and Bluegrass Downs Race track is 15 minutes. Cable TV. Business services. | 2550 Lone Oak Rd., Paducah | 270/554–1626 | fax 270/554–1626 | dentonmo@uci.net | www.denton-motel.com | 34 rooms | $52–$66 | AE, D, DC, MC, V.

Drury Inn. An atrium lobby graces this facility, which is 5 mi from Barkley airport and 2 mi from Bluegrass Downs Racetrack. Complimentary breakfast. Data ports. Cable TV.

Indoor pool. Hot tub. Some pets allowed. | 3975 Hinkleville Rd., Paducah | 270/443–3313 or 800/378–7946 | fax 270/443–3313 | www.drury-inn.com | 118 rooms, 14 suites | $80–$105, $85–$115 suites | AE, D, DC, MC, V.

1857 Bed & Breakfast. This Federalist-style B&B is in the heart of downtown Paducah. Simplicity dominates the interior; high ceilings and contemporary furnishings provide for an uncluttered look. Restaurant. Complimentary Continental breakfast, room service. Some in-room data ports. Cable TV, VCRs. Pool. Hot tub. Gym. Laundry facilities. Business services. Some pets allowed. | 127 Market House Sq., Paducah | 270/444–3690 or 800/264–5604 | fax 270/444–6309 | 3 rooms | $75–$85 | AE, MC, V.

Hickory House Inn. This 1950s vintage motel offers a good bargain. The rooms are decorated in earth tones and plaids with eclectic furnishings. Cable TV, phones. | 2504 Bridge St., Paducah | 270/442–1601 | 34 rooms | $25–$40 | AE, D, MC, V.

Holiday Inn Express. Rooms in this downtown hotel are all equipped with desks and data ports. Restaurant, picnic area, complimentary Continental breakfast. Minibars, microwaves, refrigerators. Cable TV. Indoor pool. Hot tub. Laundry facilities. Business services. Some pets allowed. | 3994 Hinkleville Rd., Paducah | 270/442–8874 | fax 270/443–3367 | pahex@apex.net | www.basshotels.com | 76 rooms | $76–$150 | AE, D, DC, MC, V.

J.R.'s. Executive Inn. Adjacent to the downtown historic district, this is the city's only full-service hotel. Many of the spacious rooms have balconies overlooking the Ohio River. Restaurant, bar with entertainment, room service. Minibars, refrigerators. Cable TV. Indoor pool. Beauty salon. Laundry facilities. Business services. Airport shuttle. | 1 Executive Blvd., Paducah | 270/443–8000 or 800/866–3636 | fax 270/444–5317 | reservations@jrsexecutiveinn.com | www.jrsexecutiveinn.com | 399 rooms, 34 suites | $59–$75, $125 suites | AE, DC, MC, V.

Quality Inn. Situated near railroad tracks, the hotel is 1½ mi from downtown, and 1 mi from the location for the Miss Kentucky Beauty Pageant. Complimentary Continental breakfast. Cable TV. Pool. Laundry facilities. Business services. Some pets allowed. | 1380 Irvin Cobb Dr., Paducah | 270/443–8751 | fax 270/442–0133 | www.qualityinn.com | 101 rooms | $49–$59 | AE, D, DC, MC, V.

Super 8. Bluegrass Downs Racetrack is 2 mi from this facility. Complimentary Continental breakfast. Microwaves, refrigerators, some in-room hot tubs. Business services. Free parking. | 5125 Old Cairo Rd., Paducah | 270/575–9605 or 800/800–8000 | fax 270/575–9605 | www.super8.com | 42 rooms | $45–$71 | AE, D, DC, MC, V.

Westowne Inn. This contemporary hotel is within ¼ mi of the Kentucky Oak Mall. Carpeted rooms have desks, dressers, and vanities. Take Exit 4 from I–24. In-room data ports. Cable TV. Pool. Pets allowed (fee). | 3901 Hinkleville Rd., Paducah | 270/442–5666 | www.westowneinn.com | 44 rooms | $41 | AE, D, DC, MC, V.

PAINTSVILLE

MAP 6, H4

(Nearby towns also listed: Pikeville, Prestonsburg)

Named for the Native American drawings that white settlers saw on its tree trunks and on the banks of the creek, Paintsville is in the heart of coal-mining Appalachia, at the junction of Paint Creek and the Levisa Fork of the Big Sandy River. Some light manufacturing has come to this mountain community in recent years, but nearly all local families are still involved in mining. Nearby Butcher Hollow was the birthplace of country music star Loretta Lynn and her sister Crystal Gayle. Paintsville Lake is an outdoor recreational area.

Information: Paintsville Tourism Commission | Box 809, 304 Main St., Paintsville, 41240 | 606/789–1469 or 800/542–5790 | http://pros.eastky.net/paintsville/chamber.

Attractions

Butcher Hollow. Sister country music stars Loretta Lynn and Crystal Gayle Webb were born at Butcher Hollow. The Webb family home and cemetery are on the grounds. Tours are available. | Miller's Creek Drive ends in Butcher Hollow | 606/789–3397 for tours | $4 | By appointment through Webb's General Store.

Mountain Homeplace. Characteristic of farms settled in the region by Scots–Irish immigrants, this farm still employs 19th-century techniques. Costumed interpreters explain their work. | 745 Rte. 2275, Staffordsville | 606/297–1850 or 800/542–5790 | http://lightning-pro-hosting.com | $5 | Apr.–Oct., daily 9–5.

ON THE CALENDAR

OCT.: *Kentucky Apple Festival.* Newly harvested fruit from regional orchards and apple pastries are the food highlights. Arts and crafts, a flea market, car show, and even an AKC dog show are included in the five-day festival. There's also square dancing, gospel singing, and a 5-km run. | 606/789–7430.

Dining

Wilma's Restaurant. Southern. Down-to-earth cooking and a friendly attitude are the hallmarks of this casual restaurant. Try the roast beef or the pork tenderloin, and any one of Wilma's homemade pies. | 212 Court St., Paintsville | 606/789–5911 | $4–$6 | No credit cards.

Lodging

Gambill Mansion Bed & Breakfast. Built in 1923 on farmland dotted with ponds, this B&B is about a half hour drive from the freeway. Choose from rooms or suites in the house or the barn. Room decorations range from Victorian to 1950s-style to safari themes. The owners offer an optional candlelight dinner. Complimentary breakfast. Some in-room kitchenettes, minibars, microwaves, refrigerators. Cable TV, VCRs. Library. Business services. | Intersection of Rtes. 32 and 201, Blaine | 606/652–3120 | fax 606/652–3120 | www.bbonline.com/ky/gambill | 3 rooms | $75–$150 | AE, D, DC, MC, V.

PARIS

INTRO
ATTRACTIONS
DINING
LODGING

PARIS

MAP 6, G3

(Nearby towns also listed: Georgetown, Lexington, Midway, Versailles, Winchester)

American whiskey may or may not have been invented in Bourbon County, but the name has persevered through legend and time. Originally called Hopewell, the county seat was renamed Paris in 1790, since the county was named for France's royal family. (Many French placenames around Kentucky are a reflection of thanks for France's assistance to Americans during the Revolutionary War.) The horse-country drive along Paris Pike (U.S. 27) from Lexington to Paris is one of the most beautiful in the state.

Information: **Paris–Bourbon County Chamber of Commerce** | 525 High St., Suite 114, Paris 40361 | 859/987–3205 or 888/987–3205 | www.parisky.com.

Attractions

Duncan Tavern Historic Shrine. Duncan Tavern was a favorite watering hole of early frontiersmen, including Daniel Boone and Simon Kenton. When the proprietor died, his widow, Ann Duncan, built the log house (1800) attached to the stone tavern and took over the inn-keeping. | U.S. Hwy., 68 Paris | 859/987–1788 | $5 | Tues.–Sat. 10–noon and 1–4.

The Hopewell Museum. Housed in the town's 1909 Beaux Arts post office building, this museum preserves the history and culture of Bourbon County. Exhibits rotate every three to six months and feature local art or historical items. | 800 Pleasant St., Paris | 859/987–7274 | $2 | Wed.–Sat. noon–5, Sun. 2–4.

Old Cane Ridge Meeting House. This 18th-century log cabin was the first church of the Disciples of Christ (a Protestant denomination founded by a former Presbyterian minister). Parishioners held tent meetings that attracted tens of thousands of worshippers at a time. The building is preserved within a native limestone superstructure. | 1655 Cane Ridge Rd., Paris | 859/987–5350 | Free | Daily.

ON THE CALENDAR

JUNE OR SEPT.: *Jazz On the Creek.* Listen to plenty of jazz at this annual festival held at Stoner Creek Dock. You can also partake in the silent auction, fill up on grill and barbecue fixings, and enjoy pontoon boat rides. | 859/987–3205.

JULY: *Bourbon County Fair and Horse Show.* Set in the heart of horse farm country, this county fair draws high-quality competition to its annual horse show. | 859/987–3205.

JULY: *Central Kentucky Steam and Gas Engine Show.* A different kind of horse power is showcased at this annual event. You can trace the history and economic impact of mechanical engines. | 859/987–3205.

Dining

Amelia's Field. Contemporary. Open for lunch and dinner by reservation only, the antiques-filled dining room is known for using regional ingredients to enliven Continental recipes. | 617 Cynthiana Rd., Paris | 859/987–5778 | Reservations essential | Jacket and tie | Closed Mon.–Wed. | $17–$29 | AE, D, MC, V.

Bourbonton Inn Restaurant. American. For traditional favorites like spaghetti, hot browns, country ham, fried fish, and cooked oysters, a stop in this casual restaurant is a must. You'll find this blue- and cream-colored eatery across the street from the courthouse. | 332 Main St., Paris | 859/987–6700 | $5–$10 | Closed Sat. | No credit cards.

Lodging

Amelia's Field. Built in the 1930s, this Colonial-style house stands in the middle of horse-farm country. Rooms are furnished with antiques but painted in bold contemporary colors. Restaurant, complimentary breakfast. TV in common room. | 617 Cynthiana Rd. | 606/987–5778 | fax 859/987–9075 | 4 rooms | $75–$100 | Closed Jan.–mid-Feb. | AE, DC, MC, V.

Bourbon House Farm Bed & Breakfast. This Georgian manor, built in 1820, is in a peaceful, rural setting. You'll find horse paddocks and a four-acre pond on the premises. Guests who come between Jan. and May might witness the birth of a baby horse. Complimentary breakfast. Cable TV. Library. Business services. No children under 12. | 584 Shropshire La., Georgetown | 859/987–8669 | 2 rooms | $95–$125 | MC, V.

Crockett's Colonial Motel. Built in the 1950s, this motel on the southern edge of downtown has an art-deco interior and mahogany furnishings. Some in-room refrigerators. Cable TV. Playground. Business services. Some pets allowed (fee). | 1493 S. Main St., Paris | 859/987–3250 | 8 rooms | $35 | No credit cards.

Howard Johnson. Standing on the edge of town, this two-story motel is within 10 mi of both Houston Oaks golf course and Hopewell Museum. Complimentary Continental breakfast. Data ports. Cable TV. Pool. Laundry service. Business services. Free parking. | 2011 Alverson Dr., Paris | 606/987–0779 or 800/406–1411 | fax 859/987–0779 | www.hojo.com | 49 rooms | $43–$80 | AE, D, DC, MC, V.

Rosedale. This 1862 Italianate brick home was once the home of a Civil War general and is now an inn furnished with antiques and Oriental rugs. Complimentary breakfast. TV in common room only. Laundry facilities. No kids under 12. | 1917 Cypress St., Paris | 859/987–1845 or 800/644–1862 | www.bbonline.com/ky/rosedale/index.html | 4 rooms (2 share baths) | $65–$100 | MC, V.

PIKEVILLE

(Nearby towns also listed: Paintsville, Prestonsburg)

Hemmed in by steep mountainsides in a river valley, Pikeville managed to create space for development in 1987. A multimillion-dollar, federally funded engineering project diverted the Lavisa Fork river channel and cut through Peach Orchard Mountain. The project helped control floods and created almost 400 acres of flat land for residential and commercial development. The town is a coal-mining center and the headquarters of several major coal companies.

Information: **Pikeville/Pike County Tourism Commission** | Box 1497 KTG, 101 Huffman Ave., Pikeville, 41502 | 606/432–5063 or 800/844–7453 | www.tourpikecounty.com.

Attractions

Breaks Interstate Park. Known as "the Grand Canyon of the South", Pine Mountain Canyon is 5 mi long and has 1,000-ft palisades. The park's 4,600 acres, maintained by both Kentucky and Virginia, contain 13 mi of hiking/biking/horseback riding trails, cottages, a lodge, and campsites. A boardwalk and viewing deck are part of the river recreation area. Laurel Lake is stocked with bluegill and bass. Whitewater rafting is among the best in the region. Moderate fees for equipment rental. | Rte. 762, 45 mi southeast of Pikeville | 606/754–5080 or 800/982–5122 | www.breakspark.com | Free | Year-round.

Fishtrap Lake. Completed in 1968 with the damming of Big Sandy River's Levisa Fork, the lake is 1,131 acres. Fishing and boating are popular, and the lake is equipped with a marina. | 2204 Fishtrap Rd., Pikeville | 606/437–7496 | Free | Daily.

Grapevine Recreation Area. Part of the Fishtrap Lake complex, this 15-acre site has a campground, playground, and picnic facilities. A very large parking lot serves the lake's launch ramp. | 2204 Fishtrap Rd., off Rte. 194, Pikeville | 606/437–7496 | Free | May–Sept., daily.

Hatfield and McCoy Historic District. The Visitor Center has maps to several sites associated with the famous mountain feud. Among the stops are the Old Pike County Jail, Augusta Dils York Mansion (home of the McCoys' lawyer), and the Dils Cemetery where many McCoys are buried. | U.S. 460 and Old U.S. 23 Bypass, Pikeville | 800/844–7453 | Free | Weekdays.

ON THE CALENDAR

APR.: *Hillbilly Days.* Parades, music, stage shows, contests, mountain arts and crafts, and traditional food (but no moonshine) are all part of this festival, which benefits the Shriner's Children's Hospital in Lexington. Everybody is an "honorary hillbilly" for the weekend. | 800/844–7453.

MAY: *Apple Blossom Festival.* This annual festival is held in nearby Elkhorn City during the first weekend of the month when the redbud-, dogwood-, and sarvice-covered mountains are splashed with colorful blossoms. Highlights of the festival are live country music, arts, crafts, and traditional local food. | 800/844–7453.

Dining

Rusty Fork Café. American. This restaurant is known for its steak, sandwiches, baby backed ribs, and homemade pies. Try the butterscotch, chocolate, or the fried-apple pie. The burgundy and green interior is complemented with antiques. | 105 S. Patty Loveless Dr., Elkhorn City | 606/754–4494 | Reservations not accepted | $6–$13 | No credit cards.

Lodging

Landmark Inn. Efficiency suites as well as regular rooms are available at this four-story hotel in downtown Pikeville, 25 mi from Breaks Park. Restaurant, bar with entertainment.

Cable TV. Pool. Laundry facilities. Some pets allowed. | 146 S. Mayo Trail, Pikeville | 606/432–2545 or 800/831–1469 | fax 606/432–2545 | 103 rooms, 2 suites | $65; $89 suites | AE, D, DC, MC, V.

Motor Lodge. Built on the canyon's rim, the state-owned lodge's rooms overlook the view. You'll have access to all facilities at the Breaks Interstate Park. Pool. Boating. Playground. Business services. | Rte. 762, within Breaks Interstate Park | 540/865–4413 or 800/982–5122 | www.state.ky.us/agencies/parks/breaks.htm | 34 rooms | $65 | AE, D, MC, V.

Super 8 Motel. This two-story motel is 2 mi from downtown. Restaurants, shopping, a golf course, and two movie theaters are nearby. Double rooms are small and practical with basic furnishings and contemporary prints on the walls. Complimentary Continental breakfast. Some in-room minibars, microwaves, refrigerators, some in-room hot tubs. Cable TV. Laundry facilities. Business services. | 198 Thompson Rd., Pikeville | 606/433–0888 | fax 606/433–0116 | www.super8.com | 74 rooms | $55 | AE, D, DC, MC, V.

PINEVILLE

MAP 6, G5

(Nearby towns also listed: Barbourville, Corbin, Middlesboro, Williamsburg)

Now the seat of Bell County, Pineville was settled in 1781, when most early travelers passed through the mountains on their way to the fertile Bluegrass region. Nearby settlement schools, many housed in log cabins, have attracted teachers from all over the U. S., serving the region's children since 1913. Nearby Pine Mountain State Resort Park contains a nature preserve made up of an old-growth forest, with many trees over 200 years old. The coal-mining industry is still how most folks here earn a living.

Information: Bell County Tourist Commission | Box 788, Middlesboro 40965 | 606/248–1075 or 800/988–1075.

Attractions
Kentucky Ridge State Forest. Kentucky's second largest state forest has 11,363 acres of forest and adjoins Pine Mountain State Resort Park. The forest is popular for its hunting, rugged hiking, and scenic overlooks. It's 5 mi southwest of Pineville. | Rte. 190, Pineville | 606/337–3011 | Free | Daily.

Pine Mountain State Resort Park. Massive Kentucky Ridge State Forest rings this 1,500-acre park, which has first-rate bird-watching and wildflower spotting. Facilities include a swimming pool, a 9-hole golf course, 10 hiking trails, and a 3000-seat amphitheater. | 1050 State Park Rd., Pineville | 606/337–3066 | www.kystateparks.com/agencies/parks/pine-myn2.htm | Free | Daily.

ON THE CALENDAR
MAY: *Mountain Laurel Festival.* The glossy, cliff-dwelling bushes explode in clouds of snowy blossoms during springtime. The seasonal celebration includes crafts, food, and folk music. | 606/337–6103.
SEPT.: *Dulcimer Festival.* This annual weekend music festival takes place at the Pine Mountain State Park Resort and celebrates the instrument called the dulcimer. You can enjoy folk music concerts, dulcimer lessons, and craft shows. | 606/337–3066.

Dining
Pine Mountain State Resort Park Dining Room. American. Kentucky hot browns are the best selling dish at this casual restaurant within the state park. | 1050 State Park Rd., Pineville | 606/337–3066 | $7–$14 | AE, D, MC, V.

Lodging

Evans Lodge. Set in the middle of the forest, this rustic, mountain-top wood lodge has access to all Pine Mountain State Park facilities. Dining room, picnic area. Kitchenettes (in cottages). Cable TV. Pool. 9-hole golf, mini-golf. Kids' programs. Business services. | 1050 Pine Mountain State Park Rd., Pineville | 606/337–3066 or 800/325–1712 | fax 606/337–7250 | 30 rooms, 19 cottages | $52–$75, $74–$120 cottages | AE, D, DC, MC, V.

Pine Mountain State Resort Park Cabins. For a secluded alternative to the park's lodge, you can elect to stay in one of the simple cabins scattered throughout the woods of the Pine Mountain State Resort Park. You will have access to the resort's pool, basketball court, miniature golf course, game room, gift shop, and playground. Kids' programs available. Kitchenettes, refrigerators. Cable TV. Business services. | 1050 State Park Rd., Pineville | 606/337–3066 or 800/325–1712 | fax 606/337–3066 | www.state.ky.us/agencies/parks/pinemtn2.htm | 30 cabins | $130 | AE, D, MC, V.

PRESTONSBURG

MAP 6, H4

(Nearby towns also listed: Paintsville, Pikeville)

Coal mining and logging were the traditional industries in this mountain community, which became less isolated when the Bert T. Combs Mountain Parkway was completed in 1962. After coal prices fell following World War II and several local mines closed, jobs shifted to the tourism industry with the opening of nearby Jenny Wiley State Resort Park and Dewey Lake.

Information: Prestonsburg Tourism Commission | 1 Hal Rogers Dr., Prestonsburg, 41653 | 606/886–1341 or 800/844–4704.

Attractions

Dewey Lake. Bass, catfish, and crappie fishing are popular on this lake, whose 52 mi of shoreline offer ample picnic space. A marina is located in the Jenny Wiley State Resort Park. You can take a tour of the 118-ft. high Dewey Lake Dam at John's Creek. | 75 Theatre Ct., Prestonsburg | Park office: 800/325–0142, Dam: 606/886–6709 | Free | May–Oct., daily. Marina: 8–6.

Jenny Wiley State Resort Park. This park was named for a pioneer woman who, in the late 1780s, escaped from captivity by Native Americans. The park has rugged mountain terrain that has hardly changed since Jenny Wiley's lifetime. A chair-lift on Sugar Camp Mountain, open in the summer, provides panoramic views. | 75 Theater Court, Prestonsburg | 606/886–2711 or 800/325–0142 | www.kystateparks.com/agencies/parks/wiley2.htm | Free | Daily.

Mountain Arts Center. Home of the Kentucky Opry, the 1,050-seat auditorium presents country, bluegrass, folk, and gospel concerts year-round. The center also contains a gift shop, art gallery, and recording studio. | 50 Hal Rogers Dr., Prestonsburg | 606/886–2623 | www.macarts.com | Daily.

ON THE CALENDAR

JUNE–AUG.: *Jenny Wiley Theatre*. Revolving shows in this summer theater include the musicals "The Legend of Jenny Wiley" by Scott Bradley, Rodgers and Hammerstein's "Cinderella and Smoke on the Mountain," and a youth theater production of "The Hatfields and the McCoys." | 606/886–9274.

Dining

Billy Ray's Restaurant. American. This small-town diner, decorated in red and white, is known best for its hamburgers. | 101 Front St., Prestonsburg | 606/886–1744 | Closed Sun. | $5–$6 | No credit cards.

Sam an Tonio's. Mexican. Enchiladas, chimichongas, steaks, and Tex-Mex cooking are served in an informal restaurant. The walls are laced with chili pepper lights. | 1566 N. Lake Dr., Prestonsburg | 606/478–3601 or 606/886–3600 | $13–$14.

Lodging

Days Inn. Downtown Pineville is 5 mi from this two-story motel. Complimentary Continental breakfast. Some in-room hot tubs. Cable TV. Pool. Exercise equipment. Business services. Some pets allowed. | 512 S. Mayo Trail, Paintsville | 606/789–3551 or 800/544–8313 | fax 606/789–9299 | www.daysinn.com | 72 rooms | $45–$65 | AE, D, DC, MC, V.

Holiday Inn. This motel is 3 mi from downtown, 2 mi from the Mountain Art Center, and 7 mi from Jenny Wiley State Park. Restaurant, bar with entertainment. In-room data ports. Cable TV. Pool. Hot tub, sauna. Exercise equipment. Laundry facilities. Business services. Some pets allowed. | 1887 N. U.S. Hwy. 23, Prestonsburg | 606/886–0001 | fax 606/886–9850 | hipburg@itiseasy.com | www.basshotels.com | 117 rooms | $58–$85 | AE, D, DC, MC, V.

May Lodge. State-owned, the secluded, pine-surrounded lodge has access to all Jenny Wiley State Resort Park facilities. Dining room, picnic area. Kitchenettes (in cottages). Cable TV. 2 pools, wading pool. 9-hole golf course. Hiking. Boating. Kids' programs, playground. Business services. | 39 Jenny Wiley Rd., Prestonsburg | 606/886–2711 or 800/325–0142 | fax 606/886–8052 | www.kystateparks.com | 49 rooms; 18 cottages | $52–$71, $65–$107 cottages | AE, D, DC, MC, V.

Microtel Inn. This motel is a ½ mi from I–23 and less than 2 mi from downtown Prestonsburg. The Mountain Arts Center is next door. Rooms are spacious with new, modern furnishings. In-room data ports. Cable TV. Gym. Laundry facilities. Business services. | 85 Hal Rogers Dr., Prestonsburg | 606/889–0331 | fax 606/889–9780 | www.microtelinn.com | 81 rooms | $55 | AE, D, DC, MC, V.

Super 8 Motel. This is a modern motel located ¼ mi from downtown. Complimentary Continental breakfast. Some in-room hot tubs. Cable TV. Business services. Pets allowed (fee). | 550 S. U.S. Hwy. 23, Prestonsburg | 606/886–3355 | www.super8.com | 80 rooms | $52 | AE, D, DC, MC, V.

RENFRO VALLEY

MAP 6, G5

(Nearby towns also listed: Berea, London, Richmond, Mount Vernon)

If you are looking for a big dose of country and bluegrass music, this entertainment center, about 45 minutes south of Lexington on I–75, is just for you. Known as "Kentucky's Country Music Capital," this country music-themed village hosts year-round concerts and is home to such annual events as the Old Joe Clark Bluegrass Festival, the All Night Gospel Sing, the Appalachian Harvest Festival, and the Fiddler Festival. Comedy and variety shows, as well as gospel music, are plentiful, and there's southern fried food to accompany them. The Renfro Valley "big barn" was completed in 1939. The town, such as it is, consists almost exclusively of the entertainment complex. Take exit 62 off I–75.

Information: Renfro Valley Entertainment Center | Rte. 25N., Renfro Valley, 40473 | 800/765–7464, ext. 700 | jthorne@renfrovalley.com | www.renfrovalley.com | Entertainment Center: free; concerts: $10–$14 | Daily.

ON THE CALENDAR

OCT.: *Fiddle Festival.* Fiddlers and fans converge for a weekend of foot-stomping, finger-flying fun, plus lots of traditional country cooking. | 800/765–7464.

Dining

Renfro Valley Lodge Restaurant. Southern. Housed in an old bus depot, this restaurant serves fried chicken, baked ham, sweet potatoes, dumplings, fried apples and other traditional fare. Stone floors, wooden furnishings and antique decorations add old-time coziness. | U.S. 25, Renfro Valley | 606/256–2638 | Reservations not accepted | Closed Mon.–Tue | $6–$8 | MC, V.

Lodging

Super 8 Motel. Rooms are decorated in cream in this standard, economic motel. The Renfro Valley Entertainment Center and several restaurants are nearby. Take exit 59 from I–75. Cable TV. Business services. | Rte. 25, Mount Vernon | 606/256–5313 | fax 606/256–9193 | www.super8.com | 46 rooms | $65 | AE, D, MC, V.

RICHMOND

(Nearby towns also listed: Berea, Danville, Lexington, Renfro Valley, Winchester)

Tree-lined streets, 19th-century homes and the handsome campus of Eastern Kentucky University make Richmond, situated at the outer edge of the Bluegrass region, seem like a small college town dreamt up by central casting. It was named after the capital of Virginia by Col. John Miller, a Revolutionary War veteran who led its settlement in 1798. Richmond was also the site of a major Civil War battle in 1862 in which Confederate Gen. Braxton Bragg led troops to a decisive victory over disorganized Union forces.

Information: Richmond Tourism Department | 345 Lancaster Ave., Richmond, 40475 | 800/866–3705 | richmondky@pcsystems.net | www.richmond-ky.com.

Attractions

Courthouse. Completed in 1850, the courthouse is a centerpiece of the downtown historic district, which consists of dozens of 19th-century houses. At one point in the Civil War, it was a hospital for both Union and Confederate armies. The lobby contains Squire Boone Rock, which was one of the markers along the Wilderness Road. | 101 W. Main St., Richmond | 859/624–4793 | Free | Daily 8–4.

Fort Boonesborough State Park. Pioneer Daniel Boone's original fort is reconstructed here on the banks of the Kentucky River. Witness such activities as candle dipping, pottery turning, soap making, and welding. There are two gift shops, a pool, miniature golf, a beach, picnic grounds, and nature trails. Kentucky River Lock and Dam #10 is also found here. From I–75, take Exit 95. | 4375 Boonesborough Rd., Richmond | 859/527–3131 | $4.50 | Daily 9–5.

Hummel Planetarium and Space Theater. The night sky and star show here covers 9.3 billion mi, and shows the sky as it would appear from each planet in our solar system. The Hummel is the 12th-largest planetarium in the country. | Kit Carson Dr., Richmond | 859/622–1547 | www.planetarium.eku.edu | $3.50 | Thurs.–Fri. 7:30, weekends 3:30, 7:30.

White Hall State Shrine. The Italianate mansion was the home of Cassius Marcellus Clay, abolitionist, Minister to Russia, newspaper publisher, and friend of Lincoln's. Many furnishings in the more than 40 rooms are original to the house. | 500 White Hall Shrine Rd., Richmond | 859/623–9178 | www.kystateparks.com/agencies/parks/whthall.htm | $4 | Apr.–Labor Day, daily 8–5:30; Labor Day–Oct., Wed.–Sun. 8–5:30.

ON THE CALENDAR

FEB.: *Richmond Area Arts Council Annual Jazz Meltdown.* You can enjoy a saxophone quartet, dinner, and dancing at this annual one-night jazz festival, sponsored by the Richmond Area Arts Center. | 859/624–4242.

JULY: *Madison County Fair and Horse Show.* Held at the Fairgrounds on Old U.S. 52, the fair highlights agricultural exhibits, food, and cooking contests in addition to the horse show. | 800/866–3705.

Dining

Woody's Fine Dining. Continental. The baked salmon filet with white wine sauce is a favorite at this elegant establishment. The filet mignon, fila-wrapped chicken breast, and crab cakes are also popular. Dine in either of two dining rooms: one is candle-lit and done in red; the other is in crisp white. You can hear live jazz bands on Thurs. nights. | 246 W. Main St., Richmond | 859/623–5130 | Closed Sun. | $14–$20 | AE, D, DC, MC, V.

Lodging

Best Western Road Star Inn. A bell tower marks this motel, which has a southwestern mission-inspired design and decor. The facility is 3 mi from East Kentucky University, and 10 mi from Fort Boonesborough State Park. Complimentary Continental breakfast. In-room data ports, some refrigerators. Cable TV. Pool. Business services. Free parking. | 1751 Lexington Rd., Richmond | 859/623–9121 | fax 859/623–3160 | www.bestwestern.com | 95 rooms | $65–$93 | AE, D, DC, MC, V.

Days Inn. Situated on the edge of town, this three-story motel is within a few miles of a mall and a golf course. Room service. Cable TV. Pool. Laundry service. Business services. Some pets allowed (fee). | 2109 Belmont Dr., Richmond | 859/624–5769 or 800/544–8313 | fax 859/624–1406 | www.daysinn.com | 70 rooms | $50–$56 | AE, D, DC, MC, V.

Econo Lodge. This modern motel is situated near a highway interchange, but far enough from the main road to be quiet. Restaurant, complimentary Continental breakfast. Cable TV. Pool. Playground. Business services. | 11165 Frontage Rd., Richmond | 606/485–4123 | fax 606/485–9322 | 60 rooms | $45–$95 | AE, D, DC, MC, V.

Econo Lodge. This lodge is less than 1 mi from Eastern Kentucky University. Richmond's main shopping area and Fort Boonesborough State Park are also nearby. Complimentary Continental breakfast. Some in-room microwaves, refrigerators. Cable TV. Pool. Laundry facilities. Business services. Pets allowed (fee). | 230 Eastern Bypass, Richmond | 859/623–8813 | fax 859/624–3482 | www.econolodge.com | 100 rooms | $48 | AE, D, DC, MC, V.

Holiday Inn. Eastern Kentucky University is ¼ mi from this facility. Restaurant, picnic area. In-room data ports, some refrigerators. Cable TV. Pool. Business services. | 100 Eastern Bypass Rte. 876, Richmond | 859/623–9220 | fax 859/624–1458 | 141 rooms | $69 | AE, D, DC, MC, V.

Super 8. Queen-size rooms are available at this two-story motel, 1 mi from Eastern Kentucky University and 4 mi from the Hummel Planetarium and a public golf course. Complimentary Continental breakfast. Cable TV. Business services. Some pets allowed (fee). | 107 N. Keeneland, Richmond | 859/624–1550 or 800/800–8000 | fax 859/624–1553 | www.super8.com | 63 rooms | $34–$68 | AE, D, DC, MC, V.

RUSSELLVILLE

MAP 6, D5

(Nearby towns also listed: Bowling Green, Hopkinsville, South Union)

Chartered in 1798, the Logan County seat is a major western Kentucky tobacco market. In 1868, the Nimrod Long Bank on South Main Street was the site of outlaw Jesse James's first bank robbery. The gang got away with $9,000.

Information: Logan County Chamber of Commerce | 116 S. Main St., Russellville, 42276 | 270/726–2206 | www.loganchamber.com.

Attractions

Logan County Glade State Nature Preserve. Populated by native prairie grasses including bluestem and sideouts, this 41-acre limestone glade demonstrates the area's pre-pioneer ecology before non-native grass species spread throughout the state. It is also the habitat for several rare plant species such as fame flower, Carolina larkspur, and glade violet. | U.S. 68 and KY 80, Russellville | 270/573–2886 | www.nr.state.ky.us/nrepc/dnr/ksnpc/index.htm | Free | Daily sunrise–sunset.

ON THE CALENDAR

OCT.: *Logan County Tobacco Festival.* A re-enactment of the local Jesse James bank robbery, arts and crafts, a car show, and tobacco judging are highlights here, as is continuous live entertainment in the town square. | 270/726–2206.

Lodging

Best Western–Briarwood Inn. Situated 1½ mi from downtown Russellville, this motel is also 10 mi from the Shaker Museum. Complimentary breakfast. Some microwaves, some refrigerators. Cable TV, in-room VCRs. Pool. Business services. | 1450 Bowling Green Rd., Russellville | 270/726–2488 | fax 270/726–3124 | www.bestwestern.com | 27 rooms | $49–$60 | AE, D, DC, MC, V.

Comfort Inn. Three miles from downtown, the rooms in this modern motel feature dark oak furnishings and marble bathroom fixtures. The carpets and bedspreads are done in hunter green and maroon. The Colonial Restaurant is across the street, and Shakerville is 10 mi away. Complimentary Continental breakfast. In-room data ports, microwaves, refrigerators, some in-room hot tubs. Cable TV, VCRs. Pool. Laundry facilities. Business services. | 1120 Bowling Green Rd., Russellville | 270/725–9771 | fax 270/725–9772 | www.comfortinn.com | 44 rooms | AE, D, DC, MC, V.

YOUR FIRST-AID TRAVEL KIT

- ❏ Allergy medication
- ❏ Antacid tablets
- ❏ Antibacterial soap
- ❏ Antiseptic cream
- ❏ Aspirin or acetaminophen
- ❏ Assorted adhesive bandages
- ❏ Athletic or elastic bandages for sprains
- ❏ Bug repellent
- ❏ Face cloth
- ❏ First-aid book
- ❏ Gauze pads and tape
- ❏ Needle and tweezers for splinters or removing ticks
- ❏ Petroleum jelly
- ❏ Prescription drugs
- ❏ Suntan lotion with an SPF rating of at least 15
- ❏ Thermometer

*Excerpted from *Fodor's: How to Pack: Experts Share Their Secrets*
© 1997, by Fodor's Travel Publications

SHELBYVILLE

(Nearby towns also listed: Frankfort, Louisville)

Founded in 1792, Shelbyville was incorporated in 1846 and named in honor of Kentucky's first governor, Isaac Shelby. Early settlers of the area included Squire Boone, Daniel's brother. Many of the Victorian homes downtown are listed on the National Register, and visitors come especially to browse the antiques shops and galleries. The farms around Shelbyville are noted for raising American saddlebred horses.

Information: Shelby County Tourism Commission | 316 Main St., Shelbyville, 40065 | 502/633–6388 or 800/680–6388 | www.shelbycountykychamber.com.

Attractions

Downtown Historic District. Most of the buildings in the late-Victorian town center are on the National Register of Historic Places. The district includes many specialty shops and antiques stores. | 3rd and 7th Sts., Shelbyville | 502/633–6388 or 800/680–6388 | www.shelbyvilleky.com | Free | Daily.

Science Hill/Wakefield-Scearce Galleries. Redbrick Federal-style buildings dating from 1790 housed a girls' school from 1825 to 1939. The complex now contains shops, a traditional Southern restaurant, and the nationally-renowned Wakefield-Scearce Antiques Galleries, with two floors of fine English and American furniture and silver displayed in room settings. A silver vault in the cellar may excite dreams of avarice. | 525 Washington St., Shelbyville | 502/633–4382 | www.wakefield-scearce.com | Free | Mon.–Sat. 9–5.

ON THE CALENDAR

JUNE: *Kentucky Dairy Festival and Antique Farm Machinery Show.* From Holsteins to Gurnsies, breeds of dairy cattle compete for prizes at the Shelby County Fairgrounds. The farm machinery show follows a technological history of state agriculture. | 502/633–6388 or 800/680–6388.
AUG.: *American Saddlebred Horse Show.* One of the nation's premier events for this smooth-gated dressage horse (first bred in Kentucky in the 19th century) occurs at Shelby County Fairgrounds. | 502/633–6388 or 800/680–6388.

Dining

Old Stone Inn. Southern. Furnished with antiques and surrounded by gardens, this inn is on the route from Louisville to Frankfort. The kitchen serves fried chicken, country ham, and hot eggplant casserole. Kids' menu. Sun. brunch. | 6905 Shelbyville Rd., Simpsonville | 502/722–8882 | Jacket and tie | Closed Mon. No dinner Sun. | $17–$25 | AE, MC, V.

Science Hill Inn. Southern. Overlooking a courtyard garden, this Georgian dining room serves fried chicken, hot-water corn bread, and bourbon biscuit pudding. Buffet. Kids' menu. Sun. brunch. | 525 Washington St., Shelbyville | 502/633–2825 | Jacket and tie | Closed Mon. No dinner Sun., Tues.–Thurs. | $16–$25 | AE, MC, V.

Lodging

Best Western Shelbyville Lodge. Reclining chairs occupy many rooms of this well-landscaped motel, which is 2 mi from downtown Shelbyville, and 3 mi from Wakefield Science Galleries. Cable TV. Pool. Exercise equipment, gym. Laundry service. Some pets allowed. | 115 Isaac Shelby Dr., Shelbyville | 502/633–4400 | fax 502/633–6818 | www.bestwestern.com | 79 rooms | $55–$60 | AE, D, DC, MC, V.

Holiday Inn Express Hotel and Suites. This modern facility was built in 1999 and overlooks a golf course. The interior is done in greens, tans, and burgundy and is accented with golf memorabilia. Take a right off I–64 at Exit 35. Complimentary Continental breakfast. In-room data ports, some in-room safes, minibars, microwaves, refrigerators. Cable TV. Pool. Gym. Business services. | 110 Club House Dr., Shelbyville | 502/647–0109 | fax 502/647–3822 | www.hiexpress.com | 81 rooms | $70 | AE, D, DC, MC, V.

Wallace House. In the heart of the antiques shopping district, this 1805 Federal house, listed on the National Register of Historic Places, has four suites with private baths and kitchen/eating areas. Weekly rates available. Complimentary Continental breakfast, fruit and snacks. Cable TV. No kids under 12. | 613 Washington St., Shelbyville | 502/633–2006 | www.bbchannel.com/bbc/p207805.asp | 4 suites | $65–$85 | AE, MC, V.

SHEPHERDSVILLE

(Nearby towns also listed: Bardstown, Elizabethtown, Fort Knox, Louisville)

This Bullitt County seat is a former rail hub between Louisville and Bowling Green. Today many residents commute to jobs in Louisville and Elizabethtown. Bernheim Arboretum and Research Forest is 7 mi away, across Rte. 245 from the Jim Beam Distillery.

Information: Bullitt County Tourism Commission | 445 Rte. 44E, Shepherdsville Sq., Suite 5, Shepherdsville, 40165 | 502/543–8687 or 800/526–2068 | ltadd.org/bullitt/bullitt_mail.html | www.ltadd.org/bullitt.

Attractions

Bernheim Arboretum and Research Forest. Funded by bourbon magnate Isaac W. Bernheim's private foundation, the 16,000-acre arboretum has more than 1,800 labeled species of trees and shrubs. A visitor center has a museum, a nature trail, and ponds on which you can spot several species of duck and other waterfowl. Educational programs are scheduled regularly (small fee). There's also a summer concert series. | Hwy. 25, Clermont | 502/955–8512 | www.bernheim.org | Daily.

Jim Beam American Outpost and Homestead. Learn about the Beam family and the Kentucky tradition of bourbon at this museum. You can take tours of the distillery and the Beam family homestead, as well as see a 19th-century cooperage display and a film about the history of bourbon. From I–65, take exit 112. | Rte. 245, Clermont | 502/543–9877 | Mon.–Sat. 9–4:30, Sun. 1–4.

ON THE CALENDAR

OCT.: *Colorfest.* You can participate in tree identification, nature hikes, bird-watching, and other outdoor activities during the third weekend of the month. | 502/955–8512.

Dining

Kitchen Family Restaurant. American. Steak, meat loaf, fried pork chops, fried chicken, catfish, and barbecued pork sandwiches are the specialties at this family-oriented restaurant. Chandeliers and abundant ivy create a cozy setting. Kids' menu. | 120 S. Lakeview Dr., Shepherdsville | 502/543–4219 | $6–$12 | MC, V.

Lodging

Best Western–South. Just outside of Shepherdsville town center (1 mi), this two-story facility is 6 mi from Bernheim Forest and Jim Beam Distillery. A golf course is 1 mi away. Restaurant, bar with entertainment, some room service. Cable TV, in-room VCRs. Pool, wading pool. Business services. Free parking. Some pets allowed. | 211 S. Lakeview Dr., Shepherdsville | 502/543–7097 | fax 502/543–2407 | www.bestwestern.com | 85 rooms | $60–$70 | AE, D, DC, MC, V.

Super 8 Motel. The large double rooms in this two-story motel are decorated in maroon and green. You'll find queen-sized beds and 26-inch TVs in each room. Several restaurants are within walking distance, and the Jefferson Mall is 10 minutes away by car. Take time to visit Shepherdsville's antique shopping area. Complimentary Continental breakfast. In-room data ports, some in-room microwaves, refrigerators, some in-room hot tubs. Cable TV. Pool. Business services. | 275 Keystone Crossroads Dr., Shepherdsville | 502/543–8870 | fax 502/921–2123 | www.super8.com | 59 rooms | $50–$70 | AE, D, DC, MC, V.

SLADE

MAP 6, G4

(Nearby towns also listed: Berea, Hazard, Richmond, Winchester)

The town serves as supply center and headquarters for surrounding recreation areas, including Red River Gorge, Natural Bridge, and Daniel Boone National Forest.

Information: Natural Bridge/Powell County Chamber of Commerce | Caboose Visitor Center, 30 E. Railroad Pl., Slade, 40376 | 606/663–9229.

Attractions

Natural Bridge State Resort Park. Stone arches (called natural bridges) and rocky cliffs dot the wooded landscape in this 1,982-acre park, attracting naturalists year-round. Several rare wildflower species are native to the park. It's also home to the Virginia big-eared bat, an endangered species. The park lodge is a regional center for folk dancing enthusiasts, and square dances are held every weekend. | 2135 Natural Bridge Rd., Slade | 606/663–2214 or 800/325–1710 | sam.devine@mail.state.ky.us | www.kystateparks.com/agencies/parks/nat-bridg.htm | Free | Year-round.

Red River Gorge. The 27,000-acre Red River Gorge National Geological Area is just a small part of vast Daniel Boone National Forest. The landscape contains sandstone cliffs and natural arch formations, rare plants and animals, and extensive hiking trails. The Red River, which carved the gorge, is the state's only National Wild and Scenic River. | Mountain Pkwy. | 606/663–9229 | www.r8web.com/Boone | Free | Daily.

Reptile Zoo. You can take in a guided tour or an educational presentation at the zoo, which exhibits more than 70 species of live reptiles from around the world. King cobras, iguanas, and crocodiles are among the residents. | 1275 Natural Bridge Rd., Slade | 606/663–9160 | www.angelfire.com/ky/reptilezoo | $3.50 | June–Aug., daily 11–6; Mar.–May and Sept.–Nov., Thurs.–Sun. 11–6.

Sky Lift. Enjoy the rugged beauty of Natural Bridge State Park from a tranquil vantage point in the sky. The ride begins a ½ mi from the park entrance. | 2135 Natural Bridge Rd., Slade | 606/663–2214 | Mid-Apr.–mid-Oct., daily.

ON THE CALENDAR
APR.: *Herpetology Weekend.* The zoo sponsors a two-day viewing of its unusual salamanders, frogs, turtles, lizards, and snakes. There's also a slide and photography competition. | 606/663–2214.
JUNE: *National Mountain Style Square Dance and Clogging Festival.* Hundreds of dancers in traditional costumes descend on the park for a weekend of floor-pounding, skirt-swirling folk dancing. | 606/663–2214.
AUG.: *Mountain Market Festival.* An open-air market held on the grounds of Natural Bridge State Park showcases local farm products and crafts. You can partake in seminars on local cooking, see lively musical performances, and enjoy an evening of square dancing. | 606/663–2214.

Dining
Hemlock Lodge. Southern. Finish off a day in the park with a down-home dinner of catfish, pork chops, or fried chicken. The Hot Browns—a platter of toast, turkey, ham, cheese

sauce and tomato, all browned in the oven—is also a favorite. Flowers and wall paintings add graceful touches to the woodsy, rustic dining room. | 2135 Natural Bridge Rd., Slade | 606/663–2214 | $8–$13 | AE, D, MC, V.

Lodging

Hemlock Lodge. Set on a cliffside overlooking the park's swimming pool, the state-owned lodge has balconied rooms and one- or two-bedroom cottages, giving you access to all facilities at Natural Bridge State Resort Park. Dining room, picnic area. Kitchenettes (in cottages). Cable TV. Pool, wading pool. Mini-golf. Boating. Playground, kids' programs. Business services. | 2135 Natural Bridge Rd., Slade | 606/663–2214 or 800/325–1710 | fax 606/663–5037 | www.state.ky.us/agencies/parks | 35 rooms; 10 cottages | $45–$82; cottages $74–$115 | AE, D, DC, MC, V.

Natural Bridge State Resort Park. The park's lodge is set deep in the woods overlooking Mill Creek Lake. Spend a day fishing, boating, or hiking on the trails in the surrounding area. You can also visit the nearby nature center, or play a few rounds of miniature golf. Stay in the lodge or in private cabins. Restaurant. Some in-room kitchenettes, minibars, microwaves, refrigerators. Cable TV. Pool. Kids' programs. Playground. Business services. | 2135 Natural Bridge Rd., Slade | 606/663–2214 | fax 606/663–5037 | 35 rooms | $72 | AE, D, DC, MC, V.

SOMERSET

(Nearby towns also listed: Jamestown, London, Monticello, Mount Vernon)

Settled in 1801 by travelers from Somerset, New Jersey, the town is today a regional medical center. Its most famous native son was John Sherman Cooper, U.S. Senator 1946–1973. Gateway to the Lake Cumberland and Big South Fork recreation areas, this is the Pulaski County seat.

Information: Somerset–Pulaski County Convention and Visitors Bureau | Box 622, Somerset 42501 | 606/679–6394 or 800/642–6287 | www.lakecumberlandtourism.com.

Attractions

Beaver Creek Wilderness. This section of the Daniel Boone National Forest is characterized by spectacular cliff formations, scenic overlooks, waterfalls, and a great variety of wild flora and fauna. Hiking trails crisscross the area's more than 4,700 acres. | U.S. 27 and KY 90 | 606/679–2010 | www.r8web.com/boone | Free | Daily.

Big South Fork Scenic Railway. An open-car passenger train takes you through 6 mi of rugged mountain scenery. Included along the way are the Cumberland River Gorge and Blue Heron, a restored mining town. | KY 92, Stearns | 606/376–5330 or 800/462–5664 | $10 | May–Oct.

General Burnside State Park. Named after the Union general whose bushy side whiskers spawned the term "sideburns," the 430-acre island park in Lake Cumberland has fishing, boating, camping, and an 18-hole golf course. It's 8 mi south of Somerset. | U.S. 27, Burnside | 606/561–4104 or 606/561–4192 | www.kystateparks.com/agencies/parks/gen-burns.htm | Free | Camping Apr.–Oct., standard fees. June–Labor Day.

Lake Cumberland. The 50,250-acre lake spreads over seven counties from Somerset to Cumberland Falls. It's one of the top lakes for fishing in the country—rich in walleye, crappie, trout, and five species of bass. The shoreline stretches for 1,200 mi. Houseboat rental is available from commercial docks. | 855 Boat Dock Rd., Somerset | 606/679–6337 | Daily.

Wolf Creek Dam. Built by the U.S. Army Corps of Engineers, the dam is over 250 ft high, more than 5,700 ft long, and creates Lake Cumberland which is over 100 mi long. | 855 Boat-dock Rd., Somerset | 606/679–6337 | Free; fee for camping | Mid-Mar.–Nov., daily.

ON THE CALENDAR

OCT.: *Battle of Mill Springs Reenactment.* The state's largest Civil War reenactment involves over 5,000 actors. Period bands, period ball, and candlelight tours of Union and Confederate camps are highlights. Proceeds benefit Civil War battlefield preservation. | 606/679–1859 | MillSprings@som-uky.campus.mci.net.

Dining

Harbor Restaurant. Seafood. Dine outdoors on one of three decks overlooking a marina. Inside, a nautical theme pervades, with models of ships, pictures of the marina's history, and a kayak suspended from the ceiling. You'll find this restaurant off Rte. 80, 4 mi west of Somerset. | 451 Lee's Ford Dock Rd., Nancy | 606/636–6426 | Closed mid-Sept.–mid-Apr. | $8–$12 | D, MC, V.

The Mill Restaurant. American. Many deep-fried specialties are served here. The chicken and cod are among the most popular. The interior is done in low-key green and peach, with rustic, unfinished woods. | 1201 S. Rte. 27, Somerset | 606/678–4021 | Reservations not accepted | $6–$13.

Rockin' Robin Cafe. American. The highlight of this 50s-themed restaurant is a 1957 Bel Air with a table built into it. The car sits in the middle of the dining room and can be reserved for parties of up to six. Classic car and old-time Coca Cola memorabilia abound. Locals come here for burgers, steaks, and southern fried chicken. Try the rattlesnake pasta—fettuccine covered in Cajun cream sauce with Cajun-style grilled chicken. | 45 S. Rte. 27, Somerset | 606/679–8575 | $4–$13 | AE, D, DC, MC, V.

Lodging

Days Inn Somerset. Functional, but not fancy, this two-story motel is 2 mi from Beaver Creek Wilderness. Complimentary Continental breakfast. In-room data ports. Cable TV. Indoor pool. Hot tub. Laundry facilities. Laundry service. Business services. Free parking. | 125 N. U.S. 27, Somerset | 606/678–2052 | fax 606/678–8477 | www.daysinn.com | 53 rooms | $52–$64, $85–$125 suites | AE, D, DC, MC, V.

Hampton Inn. You'll find cherry wood furnishings in this downtown Somerset hotel, built in 1999. Rooms on the second and third floors provide views of the surrounding mountains. The General Burnside State Park plus several restaurants are within a few miles. Complimentary Continental breakfast. In-room data ports, some in-room microwaves, refrigerators, some in-room hot tubs. Cable TV. Pool. Hot tub. Gym. Video games. Laundry facilities. Business services. | 4141 S. Rte. 27, Somerset | 606/676–8855 | www.hampton-inn.com | 72 rooms | $69–$79 | AE, D, DC, MC, V.

Holiday Inn Express. This convenient hotel is 2 mi north of downtown Somerset and 3 mi south of the Somerset Mall. You'll find several restaurants within 1 mi of the hotel. Complimentary Continental breakfast. Some in-room data ports, refrigerators, some in-room hot tubs. Cable TV. Pool. Business services. | 240 N. Rte. 27, Somerset | 606/678–2023 | fax 606/678–3055 | www.basshotels.com/holiday-inn | 59 rooms | $60 | AE, D, DC, MC, V.

Landmark Inn. Formerly a Holiday Inn, this two-story motel is 8 mi from Burnside State Park and 3 mi from Lake Cumberland. Restaurant. In-room data ports. Cable TV. Pool. Playground. Laundry facilities. Business services. | 1201 S. U.S. 27, Somerset | 606/678–8115 | 157 rooms | $36–$40 | AE, D, DC, MC, V.

The Osbornes of Cabin Hollow Bed and Breakfast. The wraparound porch of this mountainside log cabin has views of the town (4 mi away) and surrounding mountainscape. The common area has a wood stove. On the grounds, redbud and dogwood trees bloom in spring. Complimentary breakfast. No smoking. | 11 Fietz Orchard Rd., Somerset | 606/382–5495 | fax 606/382–5495 | www.usagetaways.com/osbornes/index.html | Closed Dec.–Feb. | 3 rooms | $50–$65 | MC, V.

Raintree Inn Bed & Breakfast. Built in 1872, this columned mansion was the setting for *Raintree County*, starring Elizabeth Taylor and Montgomery Clift. Grounds include a glen with a waterfall, and a sycamore tree with a nearly 20-ft circumference. Rooms have fireplaces. An adjacent two-bedroom carriage house—with private patio and courtyard—is also available. The remnants of an 1800's stagecoach way station still stand directly across the street. Complimentary breakfast. TVs in common areas. Hot tub. No smoking. | 3314 Old Rte. 90, Bronston | 606/561–5225 | www.raintree-bedandbreakfast.com | 5 rooms | $75–$85, $125 carriage house | MC, V.

Somerset Lodge. The motor lodge is 8 mi from Burnside State Park and 5 mi from Lake Cumberland. Renfro Valley is 45 mi away. Complimentary Continental breakfast. Cable TV. Pool. Business services. Free parking. Some pets allowed (fee). | 725 S. U.S. 27, Somerset | 606/678–4195 | fax 606/679–3299 | 100 rooms | $36–$50 | AE, D, DC, MC, V.

SOUTH UNION

MAP 6, D5

(Nearby towns also listed: Bowling Green, Russellville)

One of the last U.S. Shaker communities, formed in 1807 and disbanded in 1922, stood on this site. The community farmed some 6,000 acres, using crop-rotation practices. The present Shaker Tavern was built as a hotel for visiting "people of the world" (non-Shakers) in 1869.

Information: Shaker Museum at South Union | Box 30, South Union, 42283 | 502/542–4167 or 800/811–8379 | www.logantele.com/~shakmus.

Attractions

Shaker Museum. Housed in the 40-room, 1820s South Union Centre House, the museum contains Shaker furniture, tools, crafts, textiles, and other artifacts. There's also a Museum Shop. | U.S. 68, South Union | 270/542–4167 | fax 270/542–7558 | www.logantele.com/~shakmus/ | $4 | Mar.–mid-Dec., Mon.–Sat. 9–4, Sun. 1–4; mid-Dec.–Feb. by appointment.

Shaker Post Office. Don't miss stopping by the only remaining, operating Shaker post office in America for a look at a rare example of 19th-century Shaker architecture. | Rte. 73, South Union | 800/811–8379 | Free | Daily.

ON THE CALENDAR
APR.: *South Union Seminar.* This annual two-day event focuses on Shaker history. Admission price varies and can include all or some lectures, Fri. dinner, Sat. breakfast, and Sat. lunch. | 270/542–4167.
JUNE: *Shaker Festival.* Crafts and traditional farming demonstrations by artisans in Shaker costume create a living museum. There's food and traditional music, too. | 270/542–4167 or 800/811–8379.

Dining

Nan's Restaurant. Southern. The catfish steaks are an enduring favorite at this quaint, family-oriented restaurant. Try the frogs' legs, hot chicken wings, and salads, too. | 339 E. Main St., Auburn | 270/542–4611 | Reservations not accepted | $4–$7 | No credit cards.

Lodging

Federal Grove Bed & Breakfast. This Southern Colonial/Greek Revival mansion is on Rte. 103, 3 mi south of South Union, and surrounded by 15 acres of pastures and woods. There are walking trails and horses on site—you're welcome to ride. Each of the four suites evokes a theme: there's the Victorian Room, the Oak Room, the Americana Christmas Room, and the coveted Sun Porch room. This B&B is close to the many antique stores in Auburn. Restaurant, complimentary breakfast. No TV in some rooms. TV and VCR in common area. Laundry facilities. Business services. | 475 E. Main St., Auburn | 270/542–6106 | fax 270/542–6106 | www.federalgrove.com | 4 rooms | $75 | AE, D, MC, V.

Shaker Tavern. Built in the 1860s by the Shaker community for "people of the world," this Victorian inn is furnished with antiques and reproductions. The room price includes free admission to the Shaker Museum. Complimentary breakfast. No room phones. TV in common room. No smoking. | U.S. 68, South Union | 270/542–6801 | fax 270/542–7558 | www.bbonline.com/ky/shaker/index.html | 6 rooms (5 with shared bath) | $65–$75 | MC, V.

SPRINGFIELD

MAP 6, F4

(Nearby towns also listed: Bardstown, Danville, Harrodsburg, Hodgenville)

Named for the area's many limestone springs, the town was established in 1793 on 50 acres donated by Gen. Matthew Walton, a pioneer landowner. The Washington County seat, Springfield is an agricultural and light manufacturing center. Nearby, St. Catherine College is the site of the first Catholic school west of the Appalachians. It has a campus consisting of historic buildings including the Tudor Gothic St. Rose Church and Proto-Priory.

Information: **Springfield/Washington County Chamber of Commerce** | 112 Cross Main St., Springfield 40069 | 859/336–3810.

Attractions

Lincoln Homestead State Park. Abraham Lincoln's father, Thomas, grew up in a log house on the grounds of what is now this state park. The Lincoln Cabin and Blacksmith Shop contain replicas of the house and the blacksmith shop in which Thomas Lincoln was trained as a carpenter. Several furnishings in the cabin are originals. Park visitors can also tour the Berry House, where Nancy Hanks, Abraham Lincoln's mother, grew up. Other park features include an 18-hole golf course, a snack bar, a gift shop, and a picnic area. | 5079 Lincoln Park Rd., Springfield | 859/336–7461 | $1.50 | mid-May–late-Sept., daily 10–6.

ON THE CALENDAR
SEPT.: *Washington County Sorghum and Tobacco Festival.* A highlight of this weekend agricultural festival is the demonstration of sorghum molasses making. | 859/336–3810.

Dining

Linc's Restaurant. Seafood. The seafood buffet is a popular weekend tradition here, and is amply stocked with fish, crab legs, frogs' legs, and oysters. Works by local artists grace the laid-back interior of this beach house-style building. | 1007 Lincoln Park Rd., Springfield | 859/336–7493 | $7–$20 | AE, D, MC, V.

Lodging

Maple Hill Manor Bed & Breakfast. This Greek Revival mansion with Italian detail is nestled between a farm and a hill and has 14 peaceful acres to itself. Enjoy an evening on the patio or on the walking trails in the surrounding area. Call ahead of time if you are bringing children with you. Complimentary Continental breakfast, complimentary evening desserts. Some in-room hot tubs. TV in common area. Library. | 2941 Perryville Rd., Springfield | 859/339–3075 or 800/886–7546 | 7 rooms | $65–$90 | MC, V.

VERSAILLES

(Nearby towns also listed: Frankfort, Georgetown, Harrodsburg, Lexington, Midway)

This Woodford County seat, as many others in Kentucky, is named in gratitude for France's help during the Revolutionary War, although Kentuckians pronounce the name "Versales." The town is situated in the rich horse-farm country of the Bluegrass region but is also a center for "iron horse," or railroad, buffs.

KENTUCKY FLAVORS

Kentucky cuisine leans toward traditional Southern fare with staples such as pan-fried chicken, salt-cured country ham, and sautéed rainbow trout. Corn, which plays such a key role in the distillation of that Kentucky hallmark, bourbon, is often on the menu, as are grits and crunchy hot-water corn bread. (Authentic grits, by the way, are served with red-eye gravy made from ham drippings and a touch of coffee. In their uptown guise they take the form of cheese grits casserole or grits soufflé.)

Several dishes, including a mutton-and-vegetable stew called *"Burgoo,"* can claim to have originated in Kentucky. Burgoo is at its most robust in the western part of the state, which is also famous for barbecued mutton. Owensboro has many restaurants serving both.

Amateur Frankfort horticulturist John B. Bibb developed a delicate, sweet lettuce variety sometime after the Civil War. Limestone, or Bibb, lettuce has become a signature ingredient of fine dining in the region.

Because of its importance as a commercial crossroads, Louisville has been the site of a fair amount of culinary invention. The 19th-century craze for oysters, shipped up the Mississippi and Ohio Rivers on flatboats, resulted in a ready supply of the mollusks. Italian immigrant Philip Mazzoni started a bar in 1884 specializing in oysters. In addition to pan-fried and stewed varieties, he invented the rolled oyster, a hand-held snack of two or three oysters rolled in bread crumbs and deep-fried. You can still sample his invention at Mazzoni's Restaurant in present-day Louisville.

Another Louisville delicacy still served where it was created is the *Hot Brown Sandwich*. More like a casserole, the hot brown was invented by Chef Fred K. Schmidt at the Brown Hotel in the 1930s. It's a combination of sliced turkey, ham or crisp bacon, and toast, all topped with a combination of savory béchamel and mornay sauces and cooked under a broiler until the cheese is bubbly. (Some ersatz Hot Browns are made with tomato. Purists frown on this practice.)

An American classic may have been invented in another Louisville neighborhood restaurant that's still in business. One day in the 1930s, owner and kitchen manager Carl Kaelin noticed slices of American cheese stacked next to the stove and, on a whim, added a slice at the last minute to a beef patty cooking on the grill. Ever since, Kaelin's Restaurant has claimed to be the home of the first cheeseburger.

Kentuckians' sweet tooths haven't been neglected. Bread pudding with bourbon sauce is a staple dessert from the most elegant to the most humble eating establishments. And Derby Pie, a registered trademark of Kern's Kitchen, is made with pecans, chocolate chips and—surprise—bourbon. To sample the real thing, look for the trademark next to the name on restaurant menus.

Information: Woodford County Chamber of Commerce | 110 N. Main St., Box 442, Versailles, 40383 | 859/873–5122 | www.woodfordchamber-ky.com.

Attractions

Bluegrass Scenic Railway Museum. The museum displays railroad equipment and artifacts, and is a center for the reconstruction and restoration of engines and cars. A 90-minute narrated train ride takes passengers though Bluegrass horse-farm country to the scenic, rocky terrain of the Kentucky River bluffs. | Woodford County Park, U.S. 62, Versailles | 859/873–2476 or 800/755–2476 | Free; train ride, $6 | Sat. 10–4, Sun. 1–4.

Labrot and Graham Distillery. Established in 1812 and restored in the 1990s, this is the state's oldest working bourbon distillery. Hourly tours of the blue-grey limestone buildings include an orientation film and a visit to the unusual copper-pot stills. | 7855 McCracken Pike, Versailles | 800/542–1812 | www.brown-forman.com | Free | Tues.–Sat. 10–3.

Nostalgia Station Toy and Train Museum. Housed in a restored 1911 railroad station, exhibits include 1920s and 1950s Lionel toy-train store displays as well as antique toys and other model railroad accessories. | 279 Depot St., Versailles | 859/873–2497 | $3 | Wed.–Sat. 10–5, Sun. 1–5.

ON THE CALENDAR

DEC.: *Pioneer Christmas.* Jouett House, a restored late 18th-century home, is decorated for the holidays with period finery. | 859/873–7902.

Dining

Kessler's 1891 Eatery and Pub. American. You'll see the work of local artists displayed in this downtown restaurant. With high ceilings and vintage-decorated exposed brick walls, the interior generates a feel of the late 19th century. The daily lunch buffet with steak, ribs, catfish, and "barbecued everything" draws quite a crowd. | 197 S. Main St., Versailles | 859/879–3344 | www.kesslers1891.com | Closed Sun. | $9–$17.

Lodging

Sills Inn. This 1911 Victorian is painted lemon yellow with white trim, and has nearly 9,000 sq ft of floor space. Rooms are decorated with bright floral fabrics. Set on a quiet street in historic downtown Versailles, the inn is a ten-minute drive from downtown Lexington. Complimentary breakfast. In-room data ports, minibars, some refrigerators, no smoking. Cable TV, in-room VCRs. Business services. Airport shuttle. No children. | 270 Montgomery Ave., Versailles | 859/873–4478 or 800/526–9801 | fax 859/873–7099 | www.sillsinn.com | 14 rooms | $80–$160 | AE, D, DC, MC, V.

Tyrone Pike Bed & Breakfast. This contemporary gray house on a sunny lot features eclectic decor. One room has a canopy bed, another a sleigh bed, and a special honeymoon suite is available. You can visit a horse farm abutting the property, which is located in a small town outside Lexington. Picnic area, complimentary breakfast. Some kitchenettes, some refrigerators. TV. Some pets allowed. | 3820 Tyrone Pike, Versailles | 859/873–2408 or 800/736–7722 | tyronebb@uky.campus.mci.net | www.innsite.com/inns/a000708.html | 2 rooms (1 with shower only, 1 shares bath), 1 suite, 1 efficiency suite | $98–$115, $135 suite | MC, V.

WICKLIFFE

(Nearby towns also listed: Mayfield, Paducah)

Archaeology buffs often make a special trip to the Wickliffe area, since it's the site of a prehistoric Native American village. Established in 1880 at the confluence of the Ohio and Mississippi rivers (which form a large inland bay), the town was named after Confederate Gen. Charles Wickliffe. Nearby Fort Jefferson was the last western outpost of Gen. George Rogers Clark's campaign.

Information: **City of Wickliffe** | Box 175, Wickliffe, 42087 | 270/335–3557.

Attractions
Columbus-Belmont State Park. This 156-acre park was the site of the Civil War's 1861 Battle of Belmont. The bluffs and earthenworks that formed the Confederate trenches have been turned into hiking trails. The park has picnic areas, a miniature golf course, a Civil War museum, a gift shop, and a snack bar. Drive 36 mi southwest of Paducah on Rtes. 58 and 123/80. | 350 Park Rd., Columbus | 270/677–2327 | Free | Daily.

Wickliffe Mounds. A Mississippian Native American village thrived here between 700 and 1,000 years ago. Excavations include home sites, and temple and burial mounds. | 94 Green St., Wickliffe | 270/335–3681 | www.campus.murraystate.edu/org/wmar/wmrc.htm | $3.50 | Mar.–Nov. daily; Dec.–Feb. weekdays 9–4:30.

ON THE CALENDAR
SEPT.: *Wickliffe Harvest Festival.* Arts and crafts, regional food (including barbecue and burgoo), and entertainment attract visitors to the banks of the Ohio and Mississippi rivers. | 270/335–3557.

Dining
Backwoods Bar-B-Q. Barbecue. This is a small, unpretentious favorite among locals. You can't go wrong with either the chicken, the ribs, or the ham. | 94 Green St., Wickliffe | 270/335–3355 | Closed Mon.–Wed. | $6–$7 | No credit cards.

Lodging
Wickliffe Motel. This small, independently owned brick motel in downtown Wickliffe affords standard accommodation for a good price. The motel is one block from Chris's Diner. Refrigerators. Cable TV. Business services. | 520 N. 4th St., Wickliffe | 270/335–3121 | fax 270/335–3378 | 19 rooms | $32 | D, MC, V.

WILLIAMSBURG

MAP 6, G5

(Nearby towns also listed: Barbourville, Corbin, Middlesboro, Pineville)

Williamsburg is the Whitley County seat and home of Cumberland College—it's a good base of operations for a visit to the southernmost reaches of the Daniel Boone National Forest and Cumberland Falls State Resort Park.

Information: **Williamsburg Tourist Commission and Convention Center** | Box 2, Williamsburg, 40769 | 606/549–0530 or 800/552–0530 | tourky.com/williamsburg/information.htm | www.tourky.com/williamsburg.

Attractions
Cumberland Museum. The culture and history of this coal mining region are the main subjects of these exhibits. Abraham Lincoln memorabilia, Christmas dolls, mounted animal trophies, and a collection of crosses and crucifixes are also on display. | 649 S. 10th St., Williamsburg | 606/539–3100 | $4 | Mon.–Sat., 8:30–6, Sun. 9–5.

Cumberland River. The river flows through Williamsburg and onwards to Cumberland Falls State Resort Park some 18 mi north. You can take float trips along the remote regions of the river. | Williamsburg Welcome Center, I–75 N at the KY/TN border | 606/786–4474 | Free | Daily.

ON THE CALENDAR
SEPT.: *Williamsburg Annual Old-Fashioned Trading Days.* Courthouse Square bustles with arts and crafts booths and demonstrations. | 606/549–0530 or 800/552–0530.

Dining
Cumberland Inn Restaurant. American. This restaurant invites long meals and relaxation. They've got a fireplace in the center of the dining room, a self-playing piano off to the side, and shelves of books lining the walls. Try the shrimp and crab fettuccine, or the prime rib, but save room for the irresistible ice cream pie. | 649 S. 10th St., Williamsburg | 606/539–4100 | Closed daily 2 PM–5 PM | $9–$19 | AE, D, MC, V.

Lodging
Cumberland Inn. Some rooms have gas fireplaces at this neocolonial hotel, operated by Cumberland College. The inn includes an equestrian-themed Derby Suite. There's a wildlife museum on the grounds. The inn is 30 mi from Cumberland Falls. Restaurant. Cable TV. Pool. Business services. Free parking. | 649 S. 10th St., Williamsburg | 606/539–4100 | fax 606/539–4107 | www.cumberlandinn.com | 50 rooms | $69–$79, $94–$135 suites | AE, D, MC, V.

Days Inn. Cumberland Falls State Park is 8 mi from this two-story structure, which is also 15 mi from Big South Fork State Park. Complimentary Continental breakfast. Cable TV. Pool. Business services. Free parking. | 510 Rte. 92W, Williamsburg | 606/549–1500 | fax 606/549–8312 | www.daysinn.com | 86 rooms | $39–$44 | AE, D, DC, MC, V.

Super 8. Housed in three separate buildings (two 2-story and one 3-story), the motel is next door to the Briar Creek City Park and 20 mi from Cumberland Falls State Park. Complimentary Continental breakfast. In-room data ports. Cable TV. Pool. Business services. Free parking. Some pets allowed. | 30 Rte. 92W, Williamsburg | 606/549–3450 or 800/800–8000 | fax 606/549–8161 | www.super8.com | 100 rooms | $51–$65 | AE, D, DC, MC, V.

Williamsburg Motel. This 2-story motel is off I–75 at Exit 11. Rooms have double beds and are done in mauve, pink, and beige. BJ's Steak House is a block away. Complimentary breakfast. In-room data ports, some refrigerators. Cable TV. Pool. Business services. Pets allowed. | 50 Balltown Rd., Williamsburg | 606/549–2300 or 800/426–3267 | fax 606/549–8279 | 87 rooms | $43 | AE, D, MC, V.

WILLIAMSTOWN

MAP 6, F3

(Nearby towns also listed: Covington, Florence, Georgetown, Maysville)

Named for New Jersey native and Revolutionary War veteran William Arnold, who donated land for the town, Williamstown was established in 1820. At the southern edge of Northern Kentucky, the town is close to Boltz Lake, Bullock Pen Lake, Corinth Lake, and Williamstown Lake, as well as two public wildlife areas.

Information: **Grant County Visitor's Center.** | 214 S. Main St., No. 2, Williamstown, 41097 | 859/824–3451 or 800/382–7117.

Attractions
Curtis Gates Lloyd Wildlife Management Area. Hunting and fishing are the primary recreations here, in one of the state's oldest virgin forests. Shooting and archery ranges and a Leary Lake boat dock are contained within the nearly 1,200 acres. Call for hunting season dates and acceptable entry points. No camping or horseback riding. The park is ½ mi southeast of Crittenden. | U.S. 25S, Williamstown | 859/428–3193 | Free | Daily.

Kincaid Lake State Park. This 850-acre park boasts a 180-acre lake stocked with game fish such as channel catfish, bluegill, bass, and crappie. Facilities include a seasonal swimming pool, boat docks, hiking trails, and campgrounds. | Rte. 1, Box 33, Williamstown | 859/654–3531 | www.kystateparks.com/agencies/parks/kincaid2.htm | Daily.

Williamstown Lake. Williamstown's 350-acre reservoir just outside of town is a favorite local site for fishing, boating, and water skiing. Don't be surprised to see plenty of deer and even wild turkey. Horseback riding is a common pastime in this area. Call the Williamstown Marina for information on activities. | 290 Boat Dock Rd., Williamstown | 859/824–7766 | Free | Daily.

ON THE CALENDAR
JULY: *Grant County Fair and Horse Show.* Showcasing regional agriculture, the fair exhibits include annual and perennial bedding plants. | 859/824–3451 or 800/382–7117.

Dining
Country Grill. American. Serving breakfast, lunch, and dinner 4 mi from Williamstown, the café displays antiques, both hanging from its walls and for sale in an on-site gift shop. Marcos Chicken—breaded and served on a bed of spinach with mushrooms and cream sauce—is a popular menu item, as is homemade New York-style cheesecake. Kids' menu. | 21 Taft Hwy., Dry Ridge | 859/824–6000 | Breakfast also available | $10–$19 | AE, D, MC, V.

Sterling Family Restaurant. American. This relaxed eatery is locally famous for its pulled pork. Also try the Reuben or the barbecue sandwiches. | 4 Skyway Dr., Williamstown | 859/824–9764 | $7–$15 | AE, D, MC, V.

Lodging
Days Inn. Just off highways 75 and 36, this three-story motel has blue-green carpeting and blond wood furniture. Restaurant. Cable TV. Pool. Free parking. Some pets allowed. | 211 W. Rte. 36, Williamstown | 859/824–5025 or 800/544–8313 | fax 859/824–5028 | www.daysinn.com | 50 rooms | $35–$70 | AE, D, DC, MC, V.

Howard Johnson Express Inn. This motel is off I–75, 15 minutes from downtown. The Sterling Family Restaurant is next door, and the Dry Ridge Outlet Mall is about 5 mi away. Some microwaves, refrigerators. Cable TV, room phones. Pool. Business services. Pets allowed (fee). | 10 Williamstown Dr., Williamstown | 859/824–7177 | fax 859/824–7177 | www.hojo.com | 40 rooms | $38–$48 | AE, D, DC, MC, V.

WINCHESTER

MAP 6, G4

(Nearby towns also listed: Lexington, Paris, Richmond, Slade)

A marketing and manufacturing center for the Bluegrass Region, Winchester is the Clark County seat. Civil War–era U.S. Senator from Kentucky, Henry Clay ("The Great Compromiser") gave his first and last Kentucky speeches here. The state's soft drink, Ale-8-One, is bottled here.

Information: **Tourist Information Center** | 2 Maple St., Winchester 40391 | 859/744–0556 | www.winchesterky.com.

Attractions
Ale-8-One Bottling Company. The Company Store sells items (including six packs) associated with this fruit-and-gingery soft drink, made here from a secret recipe since 1926. Mail order is available. | 25 Carol Rd., Winchester | 859/744–3484 | www.aleeightone.com | Free | Mon.–Fri. 8:30–4:30.

Daniel Boone National Forest. This 694,985-acre national forest stretches across 21 counties. Popular hiking routes include the Red River Gorge National Recreation Trail, on which 36 mi of rhododendron-dotted cliffside trails overlook deep forest. The 269-mi Sheltowee Trace National Recreation Trail extends the length of the forest. The area contains more than 80 natural stone arches, a Pioneer Weapons Hunting Area (where you stalk game with a long rifle), and extensive opportunities for backcountry camping. Springtime flora include blossoming dogwoods, red buds, and mountain laurel. Fall color displays feature oak, hickory, and maple. | 1700 Bypass Rd., Winchester | 859/745–3100 | www.southernregion.fs.fed.us/boone.

Fort Boonesborough State Park. Daniel Boone's famous fort/settlement has been reconstructed on 153 acres along the Kentucky River, where costumed crafts people re-create pioneer life. The park includes campgrounds, a seasonal swimming pool, and riverside interpretive trails that highlight geological and botanical points of interest. A reenactment of the Siege of Boonesborough occurs on the last weekend in May. | 4375 Boonesborough Rd., Winchester | 859/527–3131 | www.kystateparks.com/agencies/parks/ftboones.htm | Apr.–Labor Day daily; Labor Day–Oct., Wed.–Sun.

Historic Main Street. Victorian-era storefronts house specialty shops. This area of Winchester is listed on the National Register of Historic Places. Walking tour maps are available from the tourist board. | Tourist Information Center, 2 S. Maple St., Winchester | 859/744–0556 | Free | Mon.–Sat.

Old Stone Church. Daniel Boone was one of the early members of this 1792 church, which is one of the oldest churches west of the Alleghenies. | Old Stone Church Rd., off KY 627, Winchester | 859/744–6420 | Free | By appointment.

Red River Gorge. This 25,662-acre gorge within the Daniel Boone National Forest is peppered with over 80 natural arches—geological structures sculpted by wind and water over 70 million years. Don't miss the famous Sky Bridge, a 75-ft long solid rock span. A 30-mi driving loop offers scenic overlooks of the arches, the Red River, and the bottom of the gorge. It also passes through the hand-cut Nada Tunnel, which was dug with picks and shovels in 1877. | Off the Mountain Parkway at exits 33 and 40, Winchester | 606/663–2852 | www.redrivergorge.com | Free | Daily.

Sheltowee Trace National Recreation Trail. The 269-mi hiking trail begins in Pickett State Park, Tennessee, and ends just north of Morehead, Kentucky. (All but the 10 southernmost miles of the trail are in Kentucky.) The name, which means "Big Turtle," was given to Daniel Boone by the Shawnee. The trail was followed, in part, by Boone. Sierra Club founder, John Muir, also hiked along much of its route. Portions of the trail are open to horses, mountain bikes, and motor vehicles, but you can traverse its entire length only by walking. | 100 Vaught Rd., Winchester | 859/745–3100 | Free | Year-round.

ON THE CALENDAR

APR.: *Mountain Mushroom Festival.* The 5K Fungus Run and a mushroom contest are signatures of this festival. It also includes a quilt show, car show, and food and entertainment. | 859/723–1233.

SEPT.: *Daniel Boone Pioneer Festival.* Fireworks, street dancing, arts and crafts, and a 2-mi "Walk with Friends" are highlights of this Labor Day weekend festival. | 859/744–0556.

Dining

Banana's On the River. American. A tropical theme distinguishes this large, river-view restaurant: banana trees, palm trees, and vines grace the interior dining room. Outside, two decks overlook the Kentucky River and Boonesborough State Park. Banana's is known for steak, seafood, pasta, baby back ribs, and lamb fries. Sometimes live entertainment is scheduled for the dinner hour. | 700 Ford Rd., Winchester | 859/527–3582 | Closed Sun.–Mon. | $6–$7 | AE, MC, V.

Hall's on the River. American. Part of the historic district, this country dining room serves fried, broiled, or blackened catfish and Hot Brown—an open-faced sandwich with turkey, country ham, gravy and melted cheese. Open-air dining is available on a tin-roofed deck overlooking the Kentucky River and Howard's Creek. Kids' menu. | 1225 Athens-Boonesborough Rd., Winchester | 859/527–6620 | $15–$22 | AE, MC, V.

Lodging

Best Western Country Square. You'll find king-size, queen-size, and double beds at this standard, economic motel. Fort Boonesborough is a few miles away, and several shops and restaurants are within ½ mi of the motel. Complimentary Continental breakfast. Some kitchenettes, some microwaves, refrigerators. Cable TV. Pool. Business services. Pets allowed (fee). | 1307 W. Lexington Ave., Winchester | 859/744–7210 | fax 859/744–7210 | www.best-western.com | 46 rooms | $69 | AE, D, DC, MC, V.

Hampton Inn. Downtown Winchester is 1 mi, and Fort Boonesborough State Park 6 mi, from this facility. Complimentary Continental breakfast. Cable TV. Pool. Exercise equipment. Laundry facilities. Business services. Free parking. | 1025 Early Dr., Winchester | 859/745–2000 | fax 859/745–2001 | www.hamptoninn.com | 60 rooms | $67–$74 | AE, D, DC, MC, V.

Holiday Inn. Rooms with king beds also have recliner chairs at his hotel. It's 10 mi from Fort Boonesborough State Park. Restaurant, complimentary Continental breakfast. Data ports, some refrigerators. Cable TV. Pool. Hot tub. Laundry facilities. Business services. Free parking. Some pets allowed. | 1100 Interstate Dr., Winchester | 859/744–9111 | fax 859/745–1369 | nmcwinchester@qx.net | www.basshotels.com | 64 rooms | $62–$75, $110 suites | AE, D, DC, MC, V.

Michigan

Flanked by four Great Lakes and with 2,000 mi of shoreline (even more than Califor-nia), Michigan is one of the few states identifiable from space. Divided into two penin-sulas—the Lower, which resembles a mitten and is the more densely populated, and the Upper, which is both more rugged and rural—the state spreads out over some 57,000 square mi of land and is joined at the Straits of Mackinac by the "Mighty Mac" suspen-sion bridge, a 5-mi span built in 1957. Ask a Michigander where he or she lives, and more often than not directions will be given using the palm of their hand. The south-central part of the state is even known as "the Thumb."

The state's name is attributed to the Chippewa Indians, who knew this once wild and forested terrain as *Michigama*, meaning "Big Lake." Lakes play a part both in the state's psyche and its recreational possibilities, which are both legendary and numer-ous. In summer, popular choices include canoeing, fishing, swimming, sailing, scuba diving, water and downhill skiing, and camping. In winter, trails welcome snowmo-bilers, skiers, snowshoers, dogsledders, even those daring enough to try the Midwest's only luge run, along Lake Michigan in Muskegon. The state is also blessed with some of the Midwest's most dramatic topography, including waterfalls in the Upper Penin-sula and towering dunes near Lake Michigan.

If you're less active, you can seek out rest and relaxation in one of the state's lovely resort towns, most of which date to the turn of the century and overflow with lake-side inns, boutiques, and antiques shops. You might also choose to try your luck in the burgeoning casino arena, with gaming halls that stretch across the state and are usually owned and operated by Native Americans.

The state has its share of big cities, too, including the Furniture City (Grand Rapids), the Capital City (Lansing), and the better-known Motor City (Detroit). All have vibrant arts and culture, excellent restaurants, and some of the state's top tourist attractions.

CAPITAL: LANSING	POPULATION: 9,594,300	AREA: 58,527 SQUARE MI
BORDERS: IN, OH, WI; ON, CANADA	TIME ZONE: EASTERN	POSTAL ABBREVIATION: MI
WEB SITE: WWW.MICHIGAN.ORG		

History

Michigan is a state with a rich past. Its abundant wildlife—including white-tailed deer, great schools of fish, moose, elk, and black bears—and rich natural resources nourished the Algonquin tribes for centuries before the arrival of the white man. Later arrivals included the Huron, Chippewa, Menominee, Ottawa, Miami, and Potawatomi tribes, who settled across the state. Today, many villages and rivers still have the names given them by the state's earliest inhabitants.

Etienne Brulé was the first European to arrive on the state's soil. He was sent by Samuel de Champlain, lieutenant governor of New France, who hoped to find copper and a shortcut to the Far East. Instead, Brulé sent back reports documenting the land's untamed beauty and strange new flora and fauna.

Others soon followed. Some were after Michigan's rich supply of furs, others after Native American souls. Among the most famous of these early explorers was Father Jacques Marquette, who established a settlement at Sault Ste. Marie in the mid-17th century. Marquette's accounts of his experiences brought even more opportunists, mostly fur traders such as John Jacob Astor.

One of the first settlements was Fort Pontchartrain, in 1701, marking the establishment of "La Ville d'Etroit" (the village at the straits), on the site of present-day Detroit. Within a short time, several hundred French families had settled in Michigan, many of them establishing narrow "ribbon farms" along the Detroit river. Detroit remains the oldest city in the state and is among the oldest in the Midwest. Three flags have flown over the city, those of France, England, and the United States. By 1837, when the territory known as Michigan was granted statehood, the population had grown to just over 31,000; by 1840, the number was more than 200,000.

The state's early economy revolved around farming and agriculture, with lumber becoming important in the latter half of the 19th century. Industrial giants such as Kellogg's, Upjohn, and Dow Chemical were also founded near the turn of the 20th century, giving rise to industries that flourish to this day.

Few inventions, however, had as much influence as the "horseless carriage." The 20th century brought the state's largest corporate citizens—Ford Motor Co., General Motors, and, in the 1920s, Chrysler Motors (now Daimler-Chrysler)—changing the face and the economy of the state forever. To this day, the "Big Three" maintain their world headquarters in metropolitan Detroit. Not surprisingly, automotive-related products and services are big business here.

Regions

1. DETROIT METROPOLITAN AREA

The city that put America on wheels is spread out over a wide geographic area. You'll need a car to best explore Motown and its environs. Aside from bus routes and the elevated People Mover, there aren't any big-city modes of transportation in Motor City, USA.

MI Timeline

1300–1600	1622	1634	1668
Native Americans inhabit the land known as "Michigami."	Étienne Brulé and his companions are the first Europeans to reach Michigan.	Explorer Jean Nicolet reaches the Straits of Mackinac while trying to find a new passage to China.	Father Jacques Marquette establishes Michigan's first permanent settlement at Sault Ste. Marie.

That said, there is certainly plenty to explore, from the Henry Ford Museum and Greenfield Village in nearby Dearborn (also home to Ford Motor Co.) to distinctive downtown skyscrapers built during the golden age of the American auto industry. You can also explore one of the largest island parks in the nation, Belle Isle, take tours of auto plants, and sample a full plate of ethnic eateries, everything from Polish pierogi in Hamtramck to African-American soul food in Southfield.

The metropolitan area stretches out from the city center on the Detroit riverfront. As time goes by, areas defined as suburbs have stretched farther and farther from the city into small towns like Holly, along I–75.

Towns listed: Ann Arbor, Birmingham, Bloomfield Hills, Dearborn, Detroit, Farmington/Farmington Hills, Holly, Monroe, Mt. Clemens, Pontiac, Plymouth, Rochester, Romulus, Royal Oak, Southfield, Troy, Warren, Ypsilanti

2. SOUTHWEST (INCLUDING GRAND RAPIDS)

Orchards, vineyards, dunes, beaches, and the sparkling shores of Lake Michigan are hallmarks of the state's West Coast. Many of the most popular state parks line the lakeshore, including Hoffmaster State Park, near Muskegon, which has an interpretive center with exhibits telling the story of Michigan's many sand dunes, and Warren Dunes State Park in the region's southwest corner. Biking, cross-country ski trails, fruit farms, cider mills, and wineries are among the many other attractions.

The largest city in the southwestern part of the state, and the second-largest city in Michigan, is Grand Rapids, which started out as a trading post in 1826. Today's Grand Rapids is surprisingly diverse, home to one of the largest Hispanic populations in the state and a sizable gay community, many of whom own cottages in nearby Saugatuck, a charming resort about an hour away along the Lake Michigan shore.

Towns listed: Coopersville, Douglas, Grand Haven, Grand Rapids, Greenville, Holland, Kalamazoo, Marshall, Muskegon, New Buffalo, Niles, Paw Paw, Saugatuck, South Haven, St. Joseph, Three Rivers, Whitehall/Montague

3. THE THUMB (INCLUDING FLINT/ SAGINAW METRO AREAS)

Yoked to the auto industry, Flint has experienced many cycles of boom and bust. From its early days, the site was known as a river crossing on the Pontiac Trail, part of the network of Indian routes that traversed the state. When the logging boom hit the state, Flint began making katydids—two-wheel log-hauling carts—as well as wagons and other early conveyances. Saginaw started off as a major logging town, but today it is better known for its proximity to Frankenmuth, a Bavarian-inspired tourist attraction, and to Birch Run, site of the state's largest outlet mall.

1681	**1696**	**1701**	**1754**	**1760**
Fort Michilimackinac is founded at St. Ignace in 1681.	Antoine de la Mothe Cadillac convinces King Louis of France to establish the area as a territory.	"La Ville d'Etroit," the village at the strait, is founded.	The French and Indian War erupts.	The British win the French and Indian War and take control of Canada and Michigan.

Today, Flint and Saginaw anchor the area known as Michigan's Thumb. Overlooked by some tourists because of its lack of interstates, the Thumb and its Lake Huron beaches are favored by cottagers and those seeking quieter, less-crowded retreats.

Towns listed: Bay City, Flint, Frankenmuth, Lapeer, Port Austin, Port Huron, St. Clair, Saginaw

4. NORTHEAST

Although Lake Huron ranks as the third-largest of the Great Lakes, it's the least favorite among travelers, who tend to prefer the wilder beauty of Lakes Michigan and Superior. Encompassing most of northeast Michigan, the Huron shore is a mostly undeveloped and undervisited region containing scenic state and national forests, commercial fishing businesses, and more than 100 lighthouses. It's also the area where the state reintroduced an elk herd, which now ranks as the largest free-roaming herd east of the Mississippi.

I–75 bisects northeast Michigan, heading north to the popular recreation resorts of Grayling and Gaylord before hitting the Straits of Mackinac. U.S. 23 is the more scenic coastline route, extending from Bay City to the straits. Several major golf courses lie in this area, which promotes itself as "the Sunrise Side," with the city of Alpena as its heart.

Towns listed: Alpena, Cheboygan, Houghton Lake, Gaylord, Grayling, Indian River, Mackinaw City, Oscoda, Presque Isle, Roscommon, Tawas City/East Tawas

5. CENTRAL (INCLUDING LANSING METRO AREA)

By the early 19th century, Michigan fever had caught the imagination of many pioneers. Families from throughout the East passed through Detroit and headed west along the newly completed Detroit–Chicago Road, which cut across the southern half of the state's Lower Peninsula. Their final destination was the state's rolling prairies, for sale by the federal government for just $1.25 per acre.

This rush of settlers spurred the settlement of some of the state's largest cities, including Lansing, Battle Creek, and Jackson. This pattern of migration was later extended by the Michigan Central Railroad, which by the mid-1850s had begun making regular state crossings, unloading thousands of hopeful settlers along the way. Today, the evidence of these settlers can be seen in the Greek Revival homes and East Coast-influenced architecture they left behind, as well as the high number of private colleges they founded across the state. Despite the area's simple beauty, it's often overlooked by travelers in a hurry to get to the Lake Michigan shore or to the regions farther north.

Towns listed: Alma, Battle Creek, Chesaning, Clare, Coldwater, Jackson, Lansing/East Lansing, Marshall, Midland, Mt. Pleasant, Owosso

1763	**1783**	**1787**	**1796**	**1805**
Chief Pontiac's Rebellion attempts—and fails—to end British rule in Detroit.	The Treaty of Paris awards the area known as Michigan to the newly independent United States.	The Ordinance of 1787 establishes the Northwest Territory, of which Michigan is a part.	The British evacuate Detroit and abandon its posts on the Great Lakes.	Michigan Territory is created, with Detroit as the capital.

6. NORTHWEST

Grand Traverse Bay and Little Traverse Bay are the twin anchors of the area known to many as "Michigan's Riviera"—a band of shoreline towns that have towering sand dunes, charming villages, wineries, restaurants, marinas, resorts, and more than two dozen world-class golf courses. Stretching from Ludington up to the tip of the mitten, the area is anchored by Traverse City, the cherry-growing capital of the world and site of the National Cherry Festival each July. Many popular resort towns are in the area.

Among the best-known natural attractions is Sleeping Bear Dunes National Lakeshore, near Empire. With some of the largest freshwater dunes in the world and 32 mi of Lake Michigan beach, it's one of the most popular tourist destinations in the state.

Towns listed: Bellaire, Beulah, Big Rapids, Boyne City, Cadillac, Charlevoix, Empire, Frankfort, Glen Arbor, Harbor Springs, Leland, Ludington, Manistee, Petoskey, Suttons Bay, Traverse City

7. THE UPPER PENINSULA

Larger than Massachusetts, Connecticut, and Rhode Island combined, the wild and rugged Upper Peninsula (also known as the U.P.) is dotted with small towns and laced by rivers with romantic names such as Big Two-Hearted, Tahquamenon, and Yellow Dog. The U.P. also boasts the highest hills between the Alleghenies and the Black Hills and an annual snowfall of more than 200 inches, making it one of the best skiing areas in the Midwest.

Blessed with natural wonders that include lakes, more than 150 known waterfalls, sandy beaches, and towering limestone cliffs, the U.P. is also home to a variety of wildlife, including black bears, moose, and dozens of varieties of fish. Among the many well-visited parks are the Pictured Rocks National Lakeshore and America's largest island national park—134,000-acre Isle Royale. The most popular man-made wonders include abandoned iron and copper mines, the Soo Locks, and ghost towns.

Towns listed: Brevort, Calumet, Copper Harbor, Escanaba, Fayette, Gladstone, Grand Marais, Hancock, Houghton, Iron Mountain, Ironwood, Ishpeming, Manistique, Marquette, Menominee, Munising, Newberry, Paradise, St. Ignace, Sault Ste. Marie

When to Visit

Michigan's climate is varied at its best (most of the state experiences four very noticeable seasons) and extreme at its worst (average annual snowfalls in parts of the Upper Peninsula measure more than 200 inches).

Most of the worst comments are untrue—at least most of the time. The surrounding Great Lakes give the state a mostly moderate climate for the Midwest, with generally mild winters and moderate summers, especially in the Lower Peninsula. Those along Lake Michigan and the state's other coastal areas experience a bit of a "lake effect," generally ensuring a greater snowfall than the rest of the state—a boon to skiers, snowmobilers, and winter sports enthusiasts.

1812–14	1825	1835	1837	1840
The War of 1812 leaves the British once again in control of the Great Lakes. Lewis Cass is appointed governor of Michigan Territory.	Opening the Erie Canal causes Michigan's population to more than triple to 31,639.	Stagecoaches link Detroit and Chicago. The Toledo War over the Michigan-Ohio boundary delays Michigan's admittance to the Union.	Michigan becomes the 26th state.	Douglass Houghton finds copper in the Upper Peninsula's Keweenaw Peninsula. The state's population reaches 200,000.

Many people prefer visiting in the summer, when sunny days make possible lots of warm, watery fun. When cool air rolls in from Canada, the state enjoys a dramatic fall foliage season, when Michigan blushes brilliantly from the tip of the U.P. in September to the far south by late October.

CLIMATE CHART
Average rainfall (in inches)

	JAN.	FEB.	MAR.	APR.	MAY	JUNE
DETROIT	1.93	1.71	2.73	3.2	2.85	3.53

	JULY	AUG.	SEPT.	OCT.	NOV.	DEC.
	3.07	3.3	2.28	2.17	2.39	2.49

Average High/Low Temperatures (F)

	JAN.	FEB.	MAR.	APR.	MAY	JUNE
DETROIT	30/16	33/18	44/27	58/37	70/47	79/56

	JULY	AUG.	SEPT.	OCT.	NOV.	DEC.
	83/61	81/60	74/53	62/41	48/32	35/21

Average rainfall (in inches)

	JAN.	FEB.	MAR.	APR.	MAY	JUNE
GRAND RAPIDS	2	1.53	2.61	3.57	2.86	3.68

	JULY	AUG.	SEPT.	OCT.	NOV.	DEC.
	2.95	3.14	3.24	2.69	2.87	2.59

Average High/Low Temperatures (F)

	JAN.	FEB.	MAR.	APR.	MAY	JUNE
GRAND RAPIDS	29/15	32/16	43/25	57/35	69/46	79/55
	83/60	81/58	72/50	60/39	46/30	34/21

Average rainfall (in inches)

	JAN.	FEB.	MAR.	APR.	MAY	JUNE
SAULT STE. MARIE	2.2	1.69	2.03	2.38	2.9	3.26

	JULY	AUG.	SEPT.	OCT.	NOV.	DEC.
	3	3.46	3.9	2.89	3.2	2.57

Average High/Low Temperatures (F)

	JAN.	FEB.	MAR.	APR.	MAY	JUNE
SAULT STE. MARIE	21/5	23/5	33/15	48/28	63/38	71/46

	JULY	AUG.	SEPT.	OCT.	NOV.	DEC.
	76/51	74/51	66/44	54/36	40/26	26/12

1841
The University of Michigan moves from Detroit to Ann Arbor.

1843
All land in Michigan is "acquired" by treaty after Native Americans give up the last of their holdings.

1844
The Michigan copper rush begins. Iron ore is discovered in the Upper Peninsula.

1846
Michigan is the first state to abolish the death penalty.

1847
The state capital is moved from Detroit to Lansing.

FESTIVALS AND SEASONAL EVENTS

WINTER

Jan. **North American International Auto Show.** Detroit puts on a flashy showcase for the Motor City's concept cars. | 248/643–0205 | www.nais.com.

Feb. **U.P. 200 Sled Dog Championship.** Shouts of "Mush" and "Get along lil' doggies" are heard throughout the U.P. as dogsled racers take off from Marquette. | 800/562–7134 | www.up200.org.

SPRING

Mar. **Irish Festival.** A popular parade, arts and crafts, and other events showcase Clare's Irish heritage. | 517/386–2442 | www.claremichigan.com/irish.

Apr. **Maple Syrup Festival.** Shepherd, near Mt. Pleasant, honors the nature's sweet treat, with tastings, a parade, and other activities. | 517/828–6486.

May **Tulip Time Festival.** Holland's beautiful blooms, big-name entertainment, colorful parades, and lots of Dutch treats herald the coming of spring to this western city on Lake Michigan. | 616/396–4221 or 800/822–2770 | www.tuliptime.org.

SUMMER

June **Cereal City Festival.** Battle Creek honors its livelihood with special events and attractions, including the world's longest breakfast table. | 616/962–2240 or 800/397–2240.

Detroit Grand Prix. Detroit's verdant, 1,000-acre Belle Isle Park is taken over by Formula One cars for three days of racing and events. | 313/259–7749.

Mackinac Island Lilac Festival. One of the state's most beautiful areas blooms with fragrant flowers, parades, and other special events. | 906/847–3783 or 800/4–LILACS | www.mackinacisland.org or www.mackinac.com.

July **National Cherry Festival.** Parades, cherry products, midway fun, and more make this event a family favorite in Traverse City. | 231/947–4230.

World's Championship Au Sable River Festival and Marathon. Grayling and Oscoda host this canoeing event. The race to the finish starts with a colorful run through downtown Grayling. | 517/348–2921 or 800/235–4625.

1850s	1854	1855	1857	1861–65
Lumber and agriculture dominate the state's growing economy; the population reaches nearly 400,000.	The present-day Republican Party is formed in Jackson.	The first ship travels through the newly opened Soo Locks between Lake Huron and Lake Superior.	Michigan Agricultural College opens as the first land grant college in the state (now Michigan State University).	More than 90,000 Michigan men are mustered into service in the Civil War.

Aug.   **Michigan State Fair.** Held in Detroit, the country's oldest state fair includes classic midway rides, big-name entertainment, and agricultural and livestock displays. | 313/369–8250.

AUTUMN

Sept.   **Detroit International Jazz Festival.** Riverfront Hart Plaza hosts jammers and fans from all over in the country's largest free jazz festival, held over Labor Day weekend. | 313/963–7622 | www.detroitjazzfest.com.

Mackinac Bridge Walk. The governor leads thousands of walkers across the Mighty Mac suspension bridge from St. Ignace to Mackinaw City on this annual Labor Day event. | 906/643–7600 or 888/78–GREAT | www.mackinacbridge.org.

Oktoberfest. The Bavarian-inspired mid-Michigan town of Frankenmuth honors its heritage with food, fun, music, and lots of beer. | 800/386–8696 | www.frankenmuth.org/okto-berfest.htm.

Oct.   **Fall Harvest Days.** Greenfield Village in Dearborn celebrates its agricultural roots with farming demonstrations, foods, and harvest activities. | 313/271–1620 | www.hfmgv.org.

Nov.   **America's Thanksgiving Day Parade.** An annual parade through downtown Detroit welcomes the holiday season and has more than 25 floats, 15 huge helium balloons, and 1,000 costumed marchers. | 313/923–7400 | www.theparade.org.

State's Greats

From the dramatic beauty of the Upper Peninsula waterfalls and vast natural areas to the sophisticated cultural attractions of Grand Rapids and Detroit, Michigan's attractions are as diverse as its people and its history. As far back as the Native Americans and the French fur trappers, visitors and residents have stood in awe of the state's inherent beauty and its land rich in natural resources.

"If You Seek a Pleasant Peninsula, Look About You," the state's motto insists, and the state is indeed quite pleasant, with an impressive state park system, scenic rolling hills, natural lakes (among the most numerous in the country), and recreation, camping, and sports opportunities ranked among the best in the Midwest. You can see more than 150 waterfalls in the Upper Peninsula alone. Once you've arrived, you may be impressed by the state's two faces—the urban and urbane city centers throughout the Lower Peninsula and the wild, untamed beauty that characterizes the Upper Peninsula. Both are well worth exploring.

1879	**1889**	**1897**	**1903**	**1906**
The new State Capitol, which cost $1.5 million, is dedicated in Lansing.	The Michigan Federation of Labor is organized.	Ransom Olds starts the first car factory in state.	Ford Motor Company is founded.	Kellogg starts Battle Creek Toasted Cornflake Company.

INTRODUCTION
HISTORY
REGIONS
WHEN TO VISIT
STATE'S GREATS
RULES OF THE ROAD
DRIVING TOURS

Beaches, Forests, and Parks

Four Great Lakes—Huron, Superior, Michigan, and Erie—lap at Michigan's shores, so it's not surprising that the state boasts a number of beautiful beaches. Some of the best are along the state's western shore, where temperamental Lake Michigan has sculpted both sparkling sands and wild, windswept dunes. A few of the most popular beaches in the Lower Peninsula are **Warren Dunes State Park** in Sawyer, **P. J. Hoffmaster State Park** in Muskegon, **Petoskey State Park** in Petoskey (be sure to look for the distinctive Petoskey stone, fossilized coral that is also the state stone), and the **Sleeping Bear Dunes National Lakeshore** in Empire. Quieter and less crowded beaches are spread throughout the state on its many natural lakes, including those in the north and in the **Irish Hills** in the state's southern portion. The Lake Huron shore along the state's eastern side is becoming more and more popular as real-estate prices and crowds escalate near Lake Michigan.

At one time, most of Michigan was one dense forest, a resource that gave rise to the state's unsurpassed 19th-century lumber industry. Cities such as Muskegon, Grand Haven, and Saginaw were once known for the huge quantities of lumber floated down their rivers to waiting southern sawmills. Today, remnants of those early days are in the state's forest land, including **Huron-Manistee National Forest** in Cadillac, **Hiawatha National Forest** in Escanaba, and **Ottawa National Forest** in Ironwood.

Some original stands of tall timber are still in the state parks. **Hartwick Pines State Park** near Grayling has one of the last stands of virgin white pine left in the state, as well as a lumbering museum and monument to the lumbermen and women who cleared the state.

Culture, History, and the Arts

The majority of Michigan's cultural offerings are centered in its larger cities, with Detroit, Grand Rapids, and Flint leading the way with world-class museums, symphony orchestras, and attractions ranging from homes of the auto barons to the **Motown Museum.** Although the state's tourism offices have long promoted its sand and surf, only recently have they begun promoting Michigan's considerable cultural resources.

Whatever your interest, you'll find it in Michigan. Tiny but treasure-packed maritime museums such as the **Michigan Maritime Museum** in South Haven and the **Dossin Great Lakes Museum** on Detroit's Belle Isle cover the lore and legend of the Great Lakes and attract boating enthusiasts. Art lovers flock to huge repositories of world-class masterpieces such as those at the **Detroit Institute of Arts,** one of the top ten museums in the country, and the impressive waterfront **Muskegon Museum of Art,** created with lumber-era funds.

History buff? In Lansing, a good place to get a handle on the state's diverse past is the **Michigan Library and Historical Center,** which has displays that trace Michigan's history from its days as a Native American stronghold to its current status as the world's car capital. Michigan produces 85 percent of the cars, trucks, and other automotive

1908	**1909**	**1913**	**1914**	**1920**
William Durant forms General Motors Company. The Model T Ford is manufactured.	Michigan has the first concrete road in the nation.	Upper Peninsula copper miners join in strikes advocated by the Industrial Workers of the World. Ford introduces the assembly line.	Ford's five-dollar-a-day wages draw record numbers of workers to Detroit.	Detroit's WWJ becomes the first radio station in the United States to begin regular commercial broadcasts.

vehicles made in the United States. Other exhibits tell of the state's fur trading and mining and even re-create a 1950s Detroit Auto Show. Historical and house museums across the state—including the quirky **Honolulu House** in Marshall—often bring the state's history and its economy to life through tales of its greatest resources—its people.

Theater fan? Jeff Daniels may be a well-known name around Hollywood, but he prefers tiny Chelsea, near Ann Arbor, to Tinseltown. Daniels, founder of the city's acclaimed **Purple Rose Theatre** (named after the Woody Allen film he starred in), is just one of the many well-known artists and performers who call Michigan home.

Sports

Boasting more freshwater shoreline than any other state and some 11,000 inland lakes, Michigan has varied and abundant recreational possibilities. Boating, fishing, and canoeing rank high among summer vacationers, with clear lakes and streams, such as **Houghton and Higgins Lakes,** full of bass, perch, coho salmon, pike, sturgeon, and trout. Port Austin, on the tip of the **Thumb,** has one of the highest number of charter boats in the state. In the U.P., **Lake Gogebic** has 13,380 acres of prime fishing for small-mouth bass, walleye, and other varieties of food fish.

Michigan waters also have a gold mine of underwater preserves, with almost 1,900 sq mi set aside for scuba divers who want to explore bottomland or one of the state's many shipwrecks. The **Thunder Bay Underwater Preserve** near Alpena is one of the state's most fertile hunting grounds for underwater photographers, but is open to licensed divers only.

Golf has come on strong since the 1970s, with the Grand Traverse area home to many courses, including **The Bear** at Grand Traverse Resort, designed by Jack Nicklaus, and Shanty Creek Resort's **Legend.** Gaylord boasts the most designer courses in the Midwest, including Tom Fazio's **Premier** and Rick Smith's **Masterpiece,** both at **Treetops Sylvan Resort.**

In winter, snow skiing and snowboarding attract as many fans as fishing and boating do in warmer weather. The state has more than 40 ski areas, with some of the most challenging—including **Big Powderhorn Mountain** in Bessemer and **Pine Mountain Resort** in Iron Mountain—in the Upper Peninsula. In the Lower Peninsula, **Boyne Mountain** and **Boyne Highlands Resort** reign as the top Michigan winter resorts. You can even go skiing around the Detroit area, with **Mt. Holly** and **Alpine Valley Ski Resort** serving as training grounds for hundreds of novices planning trips "up north."

More than 2,000 mi of cross-country, snowmobiling, and snowshoeing trails are available in state parks and forests. Top spots include **P. J. Hoffmaster State Park** in Muskegon and just about any park in the Upper Peninsula. Other popular pastimes include skating, sledding, and ice fishing, as well as luging. **Muskegon State Park** has the only sanctioned luge run in the Midwest.

1925	1931	1936	1941	1954
Chrysler Motors is founded.	Forty-three percent of Michigan workers are unemployed during the Depression.	A sit-down strike at the Flint GM plant is organized by the newly formed United Auto Workers.	Auto plants convert to the production of war materials and Michigan becomes known as the "Arsenal of Democracy."	Northland Center, the nation's first regional shopping mall, opens in Southfield.

INTRODUCTION
HISTORY
REGIONS
WHEN TO VISIT
STATE'S GREATS
RULES OF THE ROAD
DRIVING TOURS

Most spectator sports are grouped near the state's larger cities. Shouts of "Play Ball!" can be heard across Michigan, with the **Detroit Tigers** in Motown, the **West Michigan Whitecaps** in Grand Rapids, the **Battle Cats** in Battle Creek, and the **Lugnuts** in Lansing. Hoop fans flock to see the **Detroit Pistons** at the Palace of Auburn Hills and the **Grand Rapids Hoops** at Van Andel Arena. In fall and winter, all 80,000 seats of the Pontiac Silverdome fill with fans of the NFL's **Detroit Lions,** who'll be moving into a new stadium in downtown Detroit in 2002. Finally, Detroit isn't called HockeyTown for nothing—the NHL's **Red Wings** won their first Stanley Cup since 1955 in 1997, and repeated in 1998. They play at Joe Louis Arena.

Rules of the Road

License Requirements: Michigan's minimum driving age is 16 with a valid driver's license.

Right Turn on Red: Permitted throughout the state after a full stop unless posted signs state otherwise.

Seat Belt and Helmet Laws: Seat belts are mandatory for all front-seat passengers and back-seat passengers up to and including age 16. Children under 4 must be in an approved safety seat. Helmets are required for all motorcyclists.

Speed Limit: The speed limit on most Michigan roads and highways is 55 mph and 70 mph on freeways, unless otherwise posted. Watch signs carefully. Radar detectors are permitted in Michigan.

For More Information: Contact the state's Department of Transportation at 517/373–2090.

Best of the Upper Peninsula Driving Tour

FROM SAULT STE. MARIE TO NEWBERRY

Distance: approximately 150 mi Time: 2 days
Breaks: Try stopping overnight in Paradise, near Tahquamenon Falls State Park.

Michigan's Sault Ste. Marie, often called simply the "Soo," is the third-oldest city in the United States. Missionaries Isaac Jogues and Charles Raymbault first visited the area in 1641; later arrivals Jacques Marquette and Claude Dablon established the first mission here in 1668, and named the town in honor of the Virgin Mary.

1957	1959	1963	1974	1982
The 5-mi-long Mackinac Bridge opens.	Berry Gordy Jr. establishes Motown Records.	Martin Luther King Jr. leads 125,000 in a Detroit march.	Gerald R. Ford of Grand Rapids becomes the 38th president of the United States.	The First International Grand Prix Formula One auto race is held in Detroit.

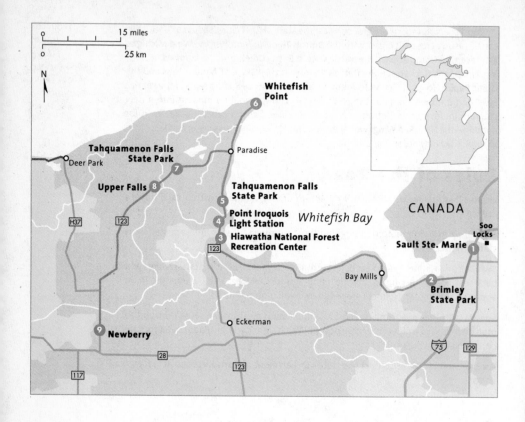

❶ Spend your first day exploring **Sault Ste. Marie** and the **Soo Locks.** Before the first white men came to the area, the Ojibway and Chippewa Indians portaged their canoes around the *bawatin* (rapids) to reach Lake Superior. The first 38-ft locks were built in 1797 to help boats pass from Lake Superior to the other Great Lakes past the powerful St. Mary's Rapids. As trade grew, the locks did too, with a set of 350-ft locks built in the 1850s. Eventually, those locks were taken over by the U.S. government, coming under the jurisdiction of the U.S. Army Corps of Engineers. Since that time the Corps has operated and maintained the locks and the surrounding parklands. An astounding 95 million tons of freight pass through the Soo each year.

Three locks remain. The MacArthur Lock, named after Gen. Douglas MacArthur, was constructed in 1943 at 800 ft in length and 80 ft in width. The 1,200-ft-long, 110-ft-wide Poe Lock, named after the Civil War officer Col. Orlando Poe, was built in 1968.

1987
Michigan celebrates its sesquicentennial.

1990
The Detroit Pistons win their second consecutive National Basketball Association Championship.

1998
The Detroit Redwings repeat as Stanley Cup champions. Chrysler Corporation merges with the German auto company Daimler-Benz, forming Daimler-Chrysler.

The Davis Lock, at 1,350 ft by 80 ft, was named for Col. Charles Davis and constructed in 1914. The Poe Lock and the Davis Lock are the longest in the world; all three locks together have been named a National Historic Site. The Visitor Viewing Area includes observation decks that come so close to the big ships you can almost touch them. The Locks Park Historic Walkway, starting at the information center, follows the waterfront for a mile and links the city's historic attractions. Day tours and dinner tours of the locks and the surrounding areas are offered by **Soo Locks Boat Tours** from June through early October. **Soo Locks Tour Trains** on the waterfront also have train rides through the Soo and over the International Bridge for a great view of the world's largest locking system. Guides describe points of interest along the way.

The Soo has other attractions besides the locks. The **Museum Ship *Valley Camp* and Great Lakes Maritime Museum** is a steam-powered freighter permanently docked in Sault Ste. Marie. First launched in 1917, the 550-ft ship weighs 11,500 tons and logged 3 million mi before being retired in 1966. Today, it's the world's largest maritime museum, with three levels of exhibits, including the pilot house, captain's quarters, an aquarium, and lifeboats from the ill-fated *Edmund Fitzgerald*, which sank with all hands during a storm on Lake Superior in 1975.

If you're feeling lucky, **Kewadin Casino,** off I–75, has Las Vegas-style gaming, including live Keno, more than 900 slots, blackjack, poker, roulette, craps, a Dreammaker Theater, and a 300-room hotel.

Once you've explored the Soo, you're ready to head out. Begin your drive in Sault Ste. Marie on I–75 Business. Follow I–75 southwest (it turns into Route H 63) to Six Mile Road and turn right.

❷ Traveling west, you'll pass open farm areas for about 17 mi until you come to **Brimley State Park.** Pick up information about the park's varied offerings at the headquarters near the parking lot.

Established in 1923, Brimley is the Upper Peninsula's oldest and most scenic state park. Within the park's 38 acres are a long swath of sandy beach, picnic areas, more than 250 campsites, and a scenic hiking trail.

As you leave the park, turn right onto Six Mile Road until it turns into Lakeshore Drive. The road follows Waiska Bay, and after about 4 mi you'll pass the Ojibway community of Bay Mills, site of one of the state's most popular casinos.

❸ Follow the shoreline as it traces Lake Superior north toward Whitefish Point. About 2 mi past Bay Mills you'll pass South Pond, followed by Spectacle and Monocle Lakes. Not far is the **Hiawatha National Forest Recreation Center,** a perfect place to stop for a picnic or beach break. In autumn, the forest is ablaze with color as stands of hardwood, including beech, birch, and maple, blush various shades of gold and crimson.

❹ Continuing on, follow Lakeshore Drive for about 1 mi until you come to **Point Iroquois Light Station,** used for more than a century to warn ships of the tight fit through Canada's Gros Cap and Point Iroquois. The station's original wooden structure, built in 1857, was replaced in 1870 by a stronger brick structure.

Follow Lakeshore approximately 5 mi through a thick forest and past Whitefish Bay. At Ranger Road and Lakeshore Drive the road becomes the Lewis Memorial Highway. Crossing Pendills Creek, the road curves to the north, with wildflowers and sandy beaches on your right. A few miles later the road meets Route 123; turn right and head north toward Whitefish Point.

⑤ About 8 mi north you'll arrive at **Tahquamenon Falls State Park,** where the lower falls of the Tahquamenon River pours into Lake Superior. The park is best known for the Upper Falls, which are more than 50 ft high and 200 ft wide. The quieter lower falls are a series of smaller waterfalls cascading around an island.

Leaving the park, continue north along Lake Superior. The shores of Whitefish Bay will be on your right. Follow the shore for about 8 mi. You'll pass through Paradise, a small resort town recognized by snowmobilers and cross-country skiers for the surrounding national forests. It's also worth a stop if you arrive during the blueberry festival.

⑥ From Paradise, head north about 10 mi to **Whitefish Point,** site of Lake Superior's first lighthouse, which is still in operation today. Overlooking the treacherous Lake Superior coastline, it once guided all ships entering and leaving Lake Superior.

A small museum at Whitefish Point honors the more than 300 shipwrecks and 320 sailors who have lost their lives in the surrounding 80-mi area, known as the "Shipwreck Coast." The most famous wreck occurred in 1975 when the *Edmund Fitzgerald* went down, an event Gordon Lightfoot memorialized in a hit song. The museum includes haunting artifacts from ships lost to Lake Superior's cold, deep waters and violent storms, including the bell from the *Edmund Fitzgerald,* as well as underwater films of exciting discoveries and vintage pictures of shipping disasters.

Nearby is the **Whitefish Point Bird Observatory,** established in 1978 to study the migration habits of Great Lakes birds. Watch for sightings of rare red-necked grebes and red-throated loons. March is the best time to visit in the spring; fall migration runs from July through mid-November.

⑦ From Whitefish, backtrack on Route 123 to Paradise. From Paradise, follow Route 123 south toward Newberry, about 43 mi away. This route allows you to take in the dramatic upper falls at **Tahquamenon Falls State Park,** one of the most popular sites on the U.P.

The shortest route to the upper Tahquamenon Falls is the leisurely drive along Route 123 from Paradise, known as "Gateway to the Tahquamenon." After about 12 mi, you'll see the entrance to Tahquamenon Falls State Park.

This state park is the second-largest in Michigan, with more than 40,000 breathtaking acres. The falls were noted in Longfellow's "Song of Hiawatha." The park can be quite crowded in July and August, when tourists pack the park and its trolley and boat rides. Spring and fall are less crowded but no less breathtaking.

⑧ Most come for the drama of the Upper Falls, which echo throughout the park. At 200 ft across, they're the country's second-largest falls next to those at Niagara, and move an amazing 50,000 gallons of water per second. You can watch the show from one of several viewing platforms or from a vantage spot along the river. Hikers often opt for the 4-mi Giant Pine Loop, which passes the falls through a thick stand of white pine. Afterward, head for the visitor's center known as Camp 33, which has handy brochures and other area information, as well as a picnic area and restaurant. The Upper Falls can also be reached by regularly scheduled boat service, including the **Toonerville Trolley,** a combination narrow gauge train and boat ride, which departs from Soo Junction.

INTRODUCTION
HISTORY
REGIONS
WHEN TO VISIT
STATE'S GREATS
RULES OF THE ROAD
DRIVING TOURS

Leave the park and head south on Route 123 toward Newberry. Close to Newberry, you'll pass areas full of dramatic white pine and cedar as well as black spruce and tamarack trees.

❾ Your drive ends about 25 mi later in Newberry, a charming 19th-century logging town where you can relax in a café or spend the night before heading on to the Straits of Mackinac. Be sure to explore the fascinating **Tahquamenon Logging Museum,** which celebrates the town's abundant forests and the industry they fueled.

"Michigan Riviera" Driving Tour
FROM LUDINGTON TO TRAVERSE CITY

Distance: approximately 125 mi Time: 2 days
Breaks: There are plenty of places to stay overnight along the way. A good midway point is Frankfort.

The northwest coast of the Lower Peninsula is sometimes referred to as "Michigan's Riviera." Filled with million-dollar resorts and unmatched natural beauty, it's a land of rolling hills, peaceful orchards, and dramatic vistas of sea and sky.

An approximately 125-mi Lake Michigan shoreline route from Ludington to Traverse City lets you take in the best of the land known as "Up North."

❶ Start in **Ludington,** a popular fishing center and port on the eastern shore of Lake Michigan. A huge illuminated cross overlooks the harbor and marks the spot where Père Jacques Marquette is thought to have died in 1675.

The town was named after James Ludington, a Wisconsin lumber baron who was instrumental in jump-starting the city's mid-19th-century industry. Be sure to check out **White Pine Village** on Lakeshore Drive, a reconstructed 19th-century community overlooking Lake Michigan with more than 30 buildings, including a blacksmith shop, a schoolhouse, and logging and maritime museums.

Ludington is also home to the **SS Badger,** a car ferry that travels between Ludington and Manitowoc, Wisconsin. More than 400 ft long, she carries up to 600 passengers and sails regularly across Lake Michigan from spring through early fall.

❷ Even if you're not stowing away, check out the **Ludington North Breakwater Lighthouse** downtown. The tower guides vessels through the channel that connects the harbor with the Père Marquette River and Lake Michigan. The stately light can be seen up to 19 mi out.

Another site worth seeing is **Ludington State Park.** To get there, turn right onto Lakeshore Drive and head north for 8 mi to the park entrance. With more than 5,000 acres of hardwoods and conifers, the area is known for its excellent hiking trails and beautiful dunes.

From Ludington, head north on Route 31. A few miles north is the **Big Sable Point Lighthouse,** one of the state's best-loved lights. Built in 1867, the 112-ft tower was originally made of brick but was later enclosed in steel plates to make it better able to withstand the strong winds off Lake Michigan.

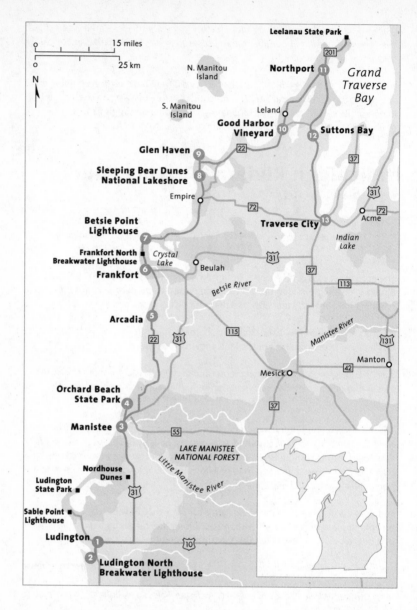

Continue on Route 31 for about 10 mi to Lake Michigan Recreation Area Road. Follow the road about 10 mi until you reach the entrance to the Nordhouse Dunes in the **Huron-Manistee National Forest,** a 4,300-acre recreation area operated by the National Forest Service. The dunes are a favorite stop for hikers, campers, and those looking for a can't-be-beat cardiovascular workout.

❸ About 10 mi north of the dunes is **Manistee,** known today as the Victorian Port City. French and English fur traders inhabited the area that the Chippewa Indians called *Manistee* (spirit of the woods) as early as the late 18th century. A 19th-century logging frenzy produced the town's mix of architectural styles, including Italianate, Shingle, and Gothic Revival. Manistee is honored in the National Forest Festival, held in early July.

Once a major logging and shipping hub, Manistee lost much of its downtown to an 1879 fire. The downtown was rebuilt closer to the water to be less susceptible to fire. Here you will want to see the **Fifth Avenue Beach,** the **Manistee North Pierhead Light, First Street Beach,** and the **Old Waterworks Building,** which was built in 1882 and today houses marine and logging exhibits.

INTRODUCTION
HISTORY
REGIONS
WHEN TO VISIT
STATE'S GREATS
RULES OF THE ROAD
DRIVING TOURS

❹ North of Manistee, Route 31 becomes Route 22. There is a fun detour about 2 mi north of Manistee on Lakeshore Road, the site of **Orchard Beach State Park.** Situated on a bluff with dramatic views of Lake Michigan, the park has a soft, sandy beach, modern campsites, and shady picnic areas.

❺ Near the small town of Arcadia, Route 22 becomes the Northwoods Highway. Continue on past Portage Lake and Onekama through the Betsie River State Game Area, a large wild wetland. Along the way, you'll be rewarded by views of Lake Michigan on your left as well as of hills, farms, and dense stands of forest.

❻ As you near Frankfort north of the Betsie River, Route 22 becomes Frankfort Avenue. Follow this into downtown **Frankfort,** which has several beaches and a lighthouse. High bluffs surround the harbor, one of Michigan's busiest ports. The resort town is known for its sandy beaches and natural harbor, a favorite of recreational boaters and fishermen. Frankfort, about halfway along on this driving tour, is also a good place to stay the night.

❼ From Frankfort, follow Route 22 north. The road skirts the shores of Crystal Lake on your left and soon passes the **Point Betsie Lighthouse,** built in 1858. If you're in the mood to explore, turn right on Betsie Road to reach the landmark light.

Leaving the lighthouse, continue north on Route 22. Follow the highway past Winetka Point on Crystal Lake and proceed another 4 mi until you reach the intersection of Route 22 and Sutter Road, then turn right onto Pine Highway. Follow Pine Highway about 2 mi to Lake Michigan Road and turn left. There's a dramatic view of the Sleeping Bear Dunes to the north (a later stop on this tour) at Platte River Point.

From the Platte River, head north on Route 22 toward Empire. A few miles outside of town, you'll be treated to rolling hills and meadows filled with apple trees.

❽ Two miles north of Empire you'll see Route 109 N and the entrance to the **Pierce Stocking Scenic Drive,** a 7½-mi loop that passes through the **Sleeping Bear Dunes National Lakeshore.** Filled with natural wonders, the drive is named after Pierce Stocking, a Michigan lumberman and naturalist who loved the area and long envisioned a route through the best of it.

You can enjoy the route from May through October on foot or by bike or car. Highlights include vintage covered bridges, the beautiful blue of Glen Lake and shallower Little Glen Lake, and Alligator Hill, a mound created by an ancient glacier. Don't miss the dune overlooks, which have incredible views of Sleeping Bear, Pyramid Point, and Glen Lake from the tops of 200-ft mountains of sand. Worth exploring is the Cottonhead Trail, a 1½-mi route that traverses a fascinating dunescape. Along the way, you may spot wildlife ranging from wood thrushes to whitetail deer. The route is especially beautiful in autumn, when the sugar maples and American beech burst into color. Watch for "ghost forests"—the bleached remains of trees that were once covered by advancing dunes, then re-exposed as the sand moved on.

Exiting the scenic loop, proceed north along the Sleeping Bear Dunes National Lakeshore on Pierce Stocking Drive.

More than 400 ft above Lake Michigan, the Sleeping Bear Dunes are one of Michigan's most beloved natural attractions. Many families love to climb to the top of them and run down (be sure to wear shoes for the best traction). A National Park Service Visitors Center near the Dune Climb and the parking lot has information, restrooms, and refreshments.

⑨ Other worthwhile stops in the expansive park include the ghost town of Glen Haven and Glen Haven Beach. Parking for the beach is in a red storage building that once housed a canning factory. The park is also home to 55 mi of marked hiking and cross-country trails, fishing and canoeing on the Platte and Crystal rivers, and a ferry from Leland that takes you to North or South Manitou islands. On South Manitou are a lighthouse, the wreck of a Liberian freighter, and a virgin white-cedar forest; on North Manitou more than 15,000 wilderness acres attract backpackers.

From the beach area, backtrack to the intersection of routes 22 and 109. Head right on Route 109. You'll skirt the shore of Sleeping Bear Bay and pass a post-glacial sandbar.

Continue north on Route 22 past Good Harbor Beach and Good Harbor Bay, both on your left. The area is a favorite of the prairie warbler, a threatened Michigan species seen here in early summer. Wild turkeys also have been spotted here.

Past Sleeping Bear Dunes you'll enter the **Leelanau Peninsula.** Extending 30 mi into Lake Michigan, the scenic peninsula was formed by a glacier and was a favored haunt of the Ojibway and Ottawa Indians. Today, the peninsula is a favorite of resort vacationers and cottagers. Full of vineyards, bed-and-breakfasts, and charming small towns, the peninsula attracts thousands of vacationers each summer, when warm temperatures are cooled by Grand Traverse Bay.

⑩ About 6 mi north of Good Harbor Beach you'll pass **Good Harbor Vineyard,** a nice place to stop and sip if you have time. About 2 mi past the winery is Leland, a popular resort town named by the fishermen who used the harbor. The small town has good restaurants, including the famous **Blue Bird; Fishtown,** a collection of shops, galleries, and art studios; and the **Leelanau Historical Museum,** with displays documenting the settlement and development of the peninsula.

⑪ Continue north along Route 22. About 13 mi north of Leland is Northport. The coastal community's small downtown has intriguing antiques shops, art galleries, and restaurants. If you love lighthouses, you may want to take a 7-mi side trip on Route 201 to **Leelanau State Park,** home to the **Grand Traverse Lighthouse** and a pebbled beach. It's also well known for its sunsets. The 1,200-acre state park has 52 campsites, most reserved well in advance.

From Northport, skirt the other end of the peninsula by following Route 22 south. From here the highway hugs the peninsula's east coast, traveling along Northport Bay on your left. Then you'll pass vineyards and the tiny town of Omena before arriving in Suttons Bay. Antiques shops and farm markets mark the way.

⑫ Once a wealthy sawmill town, **Suttons Bay** eventually turned to fruit-growing. Later, art replaced agriculture as craftspeople fled urban areas in search of a slower pace. Today's Suttons Bay has tiny art studios, galleries, and coffeehouses. It's also the site of some of the peninsula's finest restaurants, including the cosmopolitan **Hattie's,** the more casual **Boone's,** and the **Leelanau Sands Casino,** on Route 22/Bayshore Drive. The casino/resort, some 20 mi north of Traverse City, has all the usual gaming, including 900 slots, and a hotel and restaurant.

From Suttons Bay, continue south on Route 22 to **Traverse City,** about 15 mi south. Your tour ends in Traverse City, northern Michigan's largest town. Nestled on the west end of Grand Traverse Bay, this resort area has become a tourist mecca, with a pleasing blend of lacy Victorian homes on wide downtown streets, upscale restaurants, and trendy gift shops.

Among the sites worth exploring in Traverse City are **Clinch Park** and the **Clinch Park Zoo,** filled with animals native to northern Michigan; the 105-ft tall ship *Westwind,* an old clipper ship that has daily trips into the bay and functions as a floating bed-and-breakfast; and the excellent Dennos Museum Center, featuring one of the country's largest collections of Inuit art. Traverse City is also the home of the National Cherry Festival, scheduled each July and celebrating the area's status as the world's largest grower of cherries. If you have the time, don't miss the 20-mi drive via Route 37 from Traverse City to the top of the Old Mission Peninsula, site of a number of centennial farms, orchards, restaurants, and well-known wineries. To return to Ludington, head south on Route 31.

ALMA

MAP 9, D6

(Nearby towns also listed: Clare, Midland, Mt. Pleasant, Saginaw)

Near the center of the Lower Peninsula, Alma is a quiet town known primarily as the home of Alma College, one of the state's best private liberal art colleges. It's also the site of the well-loved annual Scottish Highland Festival and Games, held each Memorial Day weekend. (*Note:* Area codes in this vicinity are scheduled to change to 989 beginning April 7, 2001.)

Information: Alma Chamber of Commerce | 110 W. Superior St., Alma 48801 | 517/463–5525.

Attractions
Alma College. This private liberal arts college houses the Frank Knox Memorial Room, with career mementos of this former navy secretary, and hosts the annual Highland Festival and Games, a lively Scottish-style event with bagpipers and a Highland dance competition. | 614 W. Superior St. | 517/463–7111 | www.alma.edu | Free | Weekdays 8–5.

ON THE CALENDAR
MAY: *Highland Festival and Games.* The haunting wail of bagpipes draws visitors from all over the world for one of the largest Celtic celebrations this side of the Atlantic. This Memorial Day weekend festival also has music, dance, children's activities, crafts, and athletic competitions. | The campus of Alma College, 614 W. Superior St. | $10 | 517/463–8979 | www.almahighlandfestival.com.

Dining
Peppermill Restaurant. American. A quarter-mile from downtown, this family-style restaurant makes a mean chicken stir-fry, as well as a great wet burrito with taco meat, refried beans, a Mexican blend of cheeses and, a special sauce. Try a slice of homemade five-berry pie for dessert. Full salad bar. No alcohol. | 1480 Wright Ave. | 517/463–6222 | $6–$11 | D, MC, V.

Lodging
Comfort Inn. This chain hotel is on extensive landscaped grounds. Restaurant, bar, complimentary Continental breakfast, room service. Cable TV. Indoor pool. Hot tub. Business

services. | 3110 W. Monroe Rd. | 517/463–4400 | fax 517/463–2970 | 87 rooms | $50–$135 | AE, D, DC, MC, V.

ALPENA

MAP 9, E4

(Nearby towns also listed: Cheboygan, Gaylord, Grayling, Indian River, Oscoda, Tawas City/East Tawas)

Alpena, at the mouth of Thunder Bay in the area known as "Michigan's Sunrise Side," was one of the state's foremost 19th-century lumber towns. It's now better known for its outdoor recreation, including fishing, boating, snowmobiling, hunting, and cross-country skiing. Treasure seekers know it as the home of approximately 80 ship-wrecks sunk in the waters near Thunder Bay, making it an excellent destination for divers and lighthouse lovers. *(Note:* Area codes in this vicinity are scheduled to change to 989 beginning April 7, 2001.)

Information: Alpena Convention and Visitors Bureau | 235 W. Chisholm St., Alpena 49707 | 517/354–4181 or 800/4–ALPENA | www.oweb.com/upnorth/cvb.

Attractions

Dinosaur Gardens Prehistorical Zoo. Opened in 1934 and more than 30 years in the mak-ing, this "zoo" 10 mi south is the work of one man. Huge reproductions of more than 25 prehistoric birds and animals are along a trail through a Michigan cedar swamp. Look out for the life-size dinosaur family and 80-ft brontosaurus. | 11160 U.S. 23, Ossineke | 517/471–5477 | $5 | Mid-May–Labor Day, weekends 9–6; Labor Day–mid-Oct., weekends 10–4.

Island Park and Alpena Wildfowl Sanctuary. Nature trails, bird and wildlife viewing, and fishing make this in-town sanctuary a favorite of area outdoor lovers. It's a good place for a picnic. | Corner of U.S. 23 and Long Rapids Rd. | 517/354–4181 or 800/4–ALPENA | Free | Daily dawn to dusk.

20,000 LEAGUES UNDER THE GREAT LAKES

Go ahead, take the plunge. Michigan is home to hundreds of shipwrecks and nine underwater preserves totalling 1,900 sq mi. The preserves are open to both certi-fied divers and private charters.

One of the best preserves is in Thunder Bay in the Alpena area, which has earned the nickname "Shipwreck Alley." The Thunder Bay Underwater Preserve is an area of about 288 sq mi established in 1981 to protect the remains of some 80 ship-wrecks that lie off the Alpena coast. Wood schooners, wood and steel steamers, and other types of ships, with lengths of intact ships ranging from 148 ft to 470 ft, rest here. The earliest shipwreck is that of a passenger-carrying sidewheeler, which went down in 1849; the latest is of a German freighter stranded in 1966. The largest concentration of wrecks per square mile in the Great Lakes, it attracts divers from around the world who come to explore marked sites in waters that range from just 5 ft to more than 160 ft deep. More information and charters are available from Thunder Bay Divers at the City Marina (517/356–9336 | tbdivers@freway.net | www.alpena.net/divers).

© Corbis

Jesse Besser Museum. This regional center for art, history, and natural sciences contains galleries devoted to visual arts, early man, and lumber and agricultural exhibits. Among its most popular draws are the Sky Theatre Planetarium and the re-created 1890s street. | 491 Johnson St. | 517/356–2202 | $2 | Tues.–Sat. 10–5, Sun. 12–5, closed Mon.

Old Presque Isle Lighthouse and Museum. One of the state's oldest lighthouses, this landmark includes a museum filled with marine antiques, maps, and other artifacts. The lighthouse keeper's cottage dates from 1840. | 517/595–2787 | $2 | Mid-May–mid-Oct., daily 9–5.

Thunder Bay Underwater Preserve. The 288-square-mi area in Thunder Bay and Lake Huron allows divers to explore wildlife and some 100 shipwrecks. Dive charter services operate out of Alpena. | Thunder Bay | 800/582–1906 | www.deq.state.mi.us/shipwreck/thunderbay.html.

ON THE CALENDAR

JULY: "Art on the Bay"—Thunder Bay Art Show. Bay View Park on the Lake Huron shore hosts one of northeast Michigan's largest arts and crafts festivals, with more than 200 artists in all media. | 517/356–6678.

JULY: Michigan Brown Trout Festival. This ten-day fishing festival with competitions, name entertainment, and food runs with the "Art on the Bay" art show. | 800/425–7362.

AUG.: Alpena County Fair. A classic county fair takes place in August, with agricultural and animal displays, rides, lots of food, and more. | 517/356–1847.

Dining

Thunderbird Inn. Continental. Informal, lodge-like dining on Lake Huron has a great view and solid fare, especially seafood, steak, and prime rib. The adjacent Bird's Nest, owned by the same family, has more casual dining with burgers and sandwiches. Entertainment. Kids' menu. Sun. brunch. | 1100 State St. | 517/354–8900 | Closed Sun. | $10–$20 | MC, V.

Lodging

Best Western. This chain hotel is 2.3 mi from Lake Huron beaches. Bar. Cable TV. Indoor pool. Hot tub. Video games. | 1286 M–32 W | 517/356–9087 or 800/780–7234 | www.bestwesternmichigan.com | 36 rooms | $38–$90 | AE, D, DC, MC, V.

Fletcher Motel. This family-owned family-style motel is 1 mi north of downtown. Restaurant, bar, room service. Refrigerators, some in-room hot tubs. Cable TV. Indoor pool. Hot tub, sauna. Tennis. Some pets allowed. | 1001 U.S. 23 N | 517/354–4191 or 800/334–5920 | fax 517/354–4056 | www.fletchermotel.com | 96 rooms | $58–$64 | AE, D, DC, MC, V.

Holiday Inn. The indoor Holidome recreation center with pool and game room make this a popular choice for families. It's 2 mi from Lake Huron and the city's well-known dive preserve. Restaurant, bar (with entertainment), room service. Cable TV. Indoor pool. Hot tub. Putting green. Exercise equipment. Laundry facilities. Business services. Some pets allowed. | 1000 U.S. 23 N | 517/356–2151 or 800/465–4329 | fax 517/356–2151 | www.basshotels.com/holiday-inn | 148 rooms | $64–$84 | AE, D, DC, MC, V.

ANN ARBOR

MAP 9, E7

(Nearby towns also listed: Dearborn, Detroit, Jackson, Plymouth, Ypsilanti)

Ann Arbor is home to the powerhouse University of Michigan, which settled here in 1837 after a move from Detroit. Despite the presence of more than 100 research and high technology firms, Ann Arbor still is very much a college town. Streets are clogged with trendy eateries and shops, as well as excellent bookstores (it's the home of national chain Borders, founded here by two college students in the 1970s) and art galleries.

Information: **Ann Arbor Convention and Visitors Bureau** | 120 W. Huron St., Ann Arbor 48104 | 734/995–7281 or 800/888–9487 | www.annarbor.org.

NEIGHBORHOODS

Around State Street. One of the country's highest concentrations of book and music stores is in this bohemian area near campus. The original Borders Bookstore, established in 1971 by University of Michigan grads, is just one of them. Homes are Midwestern style with Victorian flourishes. This area is also home to two handsome movie theaters: the State Theater at State and Liberty streets and the splendid Michigan Theater at Liberty and Maynard streets.

Main Street area. The aura around Main Street is refined, amid trees and red brick and stone buildings that date from the early part of the 20th century. Many independently owned specialty stores here cater to local residents. Restaurants concentrated on Main Street between William and Huron streets, also upscale, are popular with students. Good weather gives everyone a perfect excuse to dine outdoors.

TRANSPORTATION

Airports: Ann Arbor is served by the **Detroit Metropolitan Airport,** 25 mi east of town, off I–94. | 9000 Middlebelt Rd. | 734/942–3550.

Bus Lines: The Ann Arbor bus agency, just west of campus, is served by **Greyhound.** | 116 W. Huron | 734/662–5511.

Driving Around Town: Access to the city from the east and west is provided by I–94 and from the north and south by U.S. 23. Rush hour traffic is not a problem. City streets are a good mixture of one-way and two-way, and speed limits range between 35 and 45 mph. Near the campus, there are metered spots with limits of between 30 minutes and 4 hours and a cost of 50 to 80 cents an hour. Garages around the university charge 80 to 90 cents per hour. Downtown, parking is on the street or in metered lots.

Rail: The city is served by **Amtrak.** | 325 Depot St. | 800/USA–RAIL.

Attractions

CULTURE, EDUCATION, AND HISTORY

Kempf House. Antique furnishings and local historic artifacts fill this restored house. | 312 S. Division | 734/994–4898 | $2 | Feb.–Dec., Mon., Wed., Fri., and Sat. 10–2, Sun. 12–3.

Purple Rose Theatre. The small regional theater is owned and operated by well-known Hollywood actor Jeff Daniels, who grew up here. Performances range from small, intimate plays to Midwestern premieres. | 137 Park St., Chelsea | 734/475–5817 | fax 734/475–0802 | www.purplerosetheatre.org | Prices vary with shows | Wed.–Sun.

University of Michigan. When it moved here from Detroit in 1837, the University of Michigan (U of M) had just 40 donated acres. Today it's among the largest and oldest universities in the Midwest and the main influence on the growth and economy of this city. The nationally regarded U of M campus includes more than 1,300 acres filled with libraries, museums, and the Gerald R. Ford Presidential Library. | 515 E. Jefferson St. | 734/764–1817 | www.umich.edu | Free | Daily.

A campus and area kids' favorite, the **Exhibit Museum of Natural History** houses a planetarium, dinosaur and prehistoric life exhibits, as well as displays on Michigan wildlife. | 1109 Geddes Rd. | 734/764–6085 | www.umich.edu | Free, planetarium $3 | Weekdays 9–5, Sat.–Sun. 12–5.

The **Gerald R. Ford Presidential Library** contains papers, photographs, and miscellaneous collections related to the only president from Michigan. | 1000 Beal Ave. | 734/741–2218 | www.umich.edu | Free | Weekdays 8:40–4:40.

A distinguished fieldstone building on State Street houses the **Kelsey Museum of Ancient and Medieval Archaeology,** a repository of collections gathered from years of university-sponsored Near Eastern and Mediterranean digs. | 434 S. State St. | 734/764–9304 | www.umich.edu | Free | Tues.–Fri. 9–4, weekends 1–4.

Four Gothic-style buildings rim the **Law Quadrangle** on a serene corner of the bustling campus. | 801 Monroe St. | 734/764–9322 | www.umich.edu | Free | Daily.

For more flora and fauna try the **Matthaei Botanical Gardens.** There's a conservatory featuring year-round blooming exotic plants, and outdoor nature trails spread over 250 acres emphasize local plants and shrubs. | 1800 Dixboro Rd. | 734/998–7060 | fax 734/998–6205 | www.umich.edu | $3 | Daily.

Affectionately called the "Big House," **Michigan Stadium** packs in fans like no other stadium in the country—more than 110,000 people every home game. In 1998, 5000 seats as well as two big video scoreboards were added. | 1201 S. Main | www.mgoblue.com | $35 per football ticket | Sept.–Nov.

The **Museum of Art** is ranked among the best university collections in the country. This small but distinguished art museum has Western art from the 6th century to the present, Near and Far Eastern art (including a prime collection of Japanese snuff boxes), and a well-regarded collection of prints and drawings. | 525 S. State St. | 734/764–0395 | fax 734/764–3731 | www.umich.edu | Free | Tues.–Sat. 10–5, Sun. 12–5.

The **Nichols Arboretum** contains more than 120 acres, with some 400 labeled tree species, about half of which are Michigan natives. Don't miss the peony garden in late spring or the scenic nature trails. | 827 Geddes Rd. | 734/998–7175 | www.umich.edu | Free | Daily dawn to dusk.

North Campus. The Phoenix Memorial Library, dedicated to finding peaceful uses for atomic energy, and the Gerald R. Ford Presidential Library are in this newer area of the university. Also here are a sculpture by Maya Lin, best known for Washington's Vietnam Memorial, and the School of Music and the School of Engineering, both designed by Eero Saarinen. | www.umich.edu | Free | Daily.

The classically inspired **Power Center for the Performing Arts** holds more than 1,400 seats and attracts ballet, theater, and musicians of all kinds. | 121 S. Fletcher | 734/763–3333 | www.umich.edu.

PARKS, NATURAL AREAS, AND OUTDOOR RECREATION

Huron-Clinton Metroparks. This regional parks system attracts area outdoor lovers and includes 14 parks spread throughout the Detroit/Ann Arbor area. (*See also* Detroit.) | 13000 High Ridge Dr., Brighton | 810/227–2757 | www.metroparks.com | Daily $2, weekends $3, free Wed. | Daily dawn to dusk.

Delhi. At this 53-acre park 3 mi northwest of Ann Arbor, you can go canoeing, have picnics, and enjoy other outdoor recreation, including softball, biking, and hiking. | Huron River Dr. at N. Delhi Rd. | 734/426–8211 or 800/477–3191 | www.metroparks.com | Daily $2, weekends $3, free Wed. | May–Sept.

Dexter-Huron. This park spreads across more than 120 acres along the Huron River. It is best known for shady picnic areas, fishing, and canoe launches into the Huron River. | Huron River Dr. | 734/447–3191 or 800/477–3191 | www.metroparks.com | Daily $2, weekends $3, free Wed. | Daily dawn to dusk.

Hudson Mills. This is the largest of the Ann Arbor area parks, with 1,549 acres 12 mi northwest of Ann Arbor. Hiking and biking trails, picnic areas, playgrounds, a nature trail, and canoeing (including rentals) are available. | 8801 N. Territorial Rd. | 734/227–2757, 734/426–8211, or 800/477–3191 | www.metroparks.com | Daily $2, weekends $3, free Wed. | Daily.

WALKING TOUR

A good place to begin a walking tour of Ann Arbor is on the eastern edge of campus, at the historic Kempf House, where you can learn more about Ann Arbor's history during the Victorian era. Walking east on Liberty, you will pass some of the city's funkiest shops as well as the historic Michigan Theater, a renovated vaudeville house dating from the 1920s. At State Street, turn right and walk to the Kelsey Museum, directly across the street from gothic Angell Hall. Continue down State Street another 1½ blocks. The

Museum of Art sits on the southwestern corner of the central quadrangle, housing works of masters like Rodin, Picasso, and Monet. Exit the museum and walk across South University to reach the Law Quad, where you can sit and relax in the courtyard. Continue east on South University Avenue, skirting the south side of the main quadrangle. Take a left on Church Street and follow it until you reach the intersection of Church Street, Washtenaw Court, and Geddes Road. Take a right and follow Geddes past the recreation area and past Observatory Street. On your left will be the Forest Hill Cemetery. Continue walking along Geddes until you reach Nichols Arboretum, a gorgeous park with hills, trails, and a peony garden. After exploring the arboretum, return along Geddes until you reach Observatory Street. Take a right and stroll north. On your right will be the cemetery and on your left, the university's dormitories. Stockwell, the southernmost dorm, was once the residence of a certain Ms. Ciccone, now known simply as Madonna. Continue on Observatory to Ann Street and take a left. Follow Ann to Glen Avenue and take another left. Walk one block to Huron Street to find the classically styled Power Center for the Performing Arts. You can continue west on Huron Street until you reach State and explore the area's coffee shops, eateries, and book and record stores.

ON THE CALENDAR

JUNE–JULY: *Ann Arbor Summer Festival.* This three-week-long summer festival has a variety of national dance and music performances at the Power Center, as well as movies, concerts, and an art show in the adjacent parking structure. | 734/995–7281.

JULY: *Ann Arbor Art Fairs.* One of the largest art shows in the country, the Ann Arbor Art Fairs are actually three shows in one, including the Ann Arbor Summer Art Fair, the Ann Arbor Street Art Fair, and the State Street Art Fair. More than 1,000 exhibitors line 26 blocks and attract some 500,000 browsers and buyers. | 734/994/5260 or 800/888–9487 | Free | www.artfair.org.

SEPT.: *Ann Arbor Blues and Jazz Festival.* This week-long festival has funky, soul-fired rhythm and blues open-air concerts at Gallup Park and indoor concerts at the Michigan Theater. | 734/747–9955.

NOV.–DEC.: *Domino's Farms Festival of Lights.* This popular event delights families with 800,000 outdoor lights, an indoor tree display, and nightly entertainment. | 734/930–5032.

Dining
MODERATE

Bella Ciao. Italian. This casual trattoria-style eatery has marble tabletops and intimate booths. Try pasta with caramelized sea scallops or cannelloni stuffed with spinach and veal. | 118 W. Liberty St. | 734/995–2107 | www.bellaciao.com | Closed Sun. | $15–$25 | AE, D, DC, MC, V.

Gandy Dancer. Seafood. Befitting its name, this restaurant is in a converted 1880s railroad station with many original details, including stained-glass windows, fireplaces and more. The menu reflects the Muer Corp.'s specialty, seafood, although there are other entrées as well. It's known for fresh seafood, rack of lamb, and pasta. Try the shrimp fettuccine, Charley's bucket (Maine lobster mixed with clams, red potatoes, corn on the cob, and mussels), or the signature Charley's Chowder, a hearty bouillabaisse-style stew. Homemade pasta. Entertainment. Kids' menu. Sun. brunch. | 401 Depot St. | 734/769–0592 | www.muer.com | $14–$28 | AE, D, DC, MC, V.

Paesano's. Italian. Strolling musicians add a festive air on Friday to this bright and airy casual eatery. A daily special includes a fish of the day. Among the many excellent homemade pastas are lasagna or fettuccine Alfredo. You can dine on the patio at tables with umbrellas. Kids' menu. Sun. brunch. | 3411 Washtenaw Ave. | 734/971–0484 | $8.95–$19.95 | AE, D, DC, MC, V.

Sweet Lorraine's Cafe. Eclectic. Vintage posters and bright colors complement the equally creative menu at this bistro-style favorite. Daily specials reflect a global influence, with a Burmese veggie bean soup, Spanish paella, or chili-rubbed Texas pork loin. You can dine on the patio enclosed with a wall of ivy and shaded with umbrellas during the day. Kids' menu. | 303 Detroit St. | 734/665–0700 | $10.95–$24.95 | AE, D, DC, MC, V.

Zanzibar. Eclectic. What began as a predominantly Asian-inspired restaurant has expanded its outlook for a more global approach, including palm trees, lively music, and booths upholstered in ethnic prints. The menu is equally lively, including Asian greens with fresh veggies, lemongrass vinaigrette and a warm rice patty, or the funky trans-equatorial patty cakes, made of black beans, curried potato, and plantain peanuts. Known for Asian and Mediterranean dishes. Kids' menu. No smoking. | 216 S. State St. | 734/994–7777 | $15–$23 | AE, D, MC, V.

EXPENSIVE

Earle. French. This intimate lower-level eatery is among the city's finest dining and is almost always packed. The regularly changing menu often includes entrées such as escaloped pork tenderloin sautéed with roasted peppers, cream, and goat cheese or whitefish in a walnut vinaigrette. The wine cellar has more than 800 bottles. Pianist weekdays, jazz trio weekends. | 121 W. Washington St. | 734/994–0211 | www.theearle.com | Closed Sun. June–Aug. | $16–$26 | AE, D, DC, MC, V.

Kerrytown Bistro. French. This intimate, bistro-style eatery with a vintage brick interior is accented with traditional lace curtains. Try cassoulet à la Carcassonne, coq au vin, bouillabaisse, or an excellent rack of lamb. Sun. brunch. | 415 N. 5th Ave. | 734/994–6424 | $22–$35 | AE, MC, V.

Moveable Feast. Contemporary. Dining is unhurried in this elegant late-1800s house with framed art and hand-painted walls. Try the roast duckling with apple-ginger sauce or one of the house-baked desserts. Seating is available on the front lawn for open-air dining. No smoking. | 326 W. Liberty | 734/663–3278 | Closed Sun. | $23–$34 | AE, D, DC, MC, V.

VERY EXPENSIVE

Escoffier. French. French-inspired dishes are served in this elegant dining room in the Bell Tower hotel that's across the street from concert venues and the central campus. Try continental staples, prime rib, or rack of lamb. Pianist. | 300 S. Thayer St. | 734/995–3800 | No lunch. Closed Sun. | $29–$45 | AE, DC, MC, V.

Lodging
INEXPENSIVE

Motel 6. You'll be 1 mi from the Briarwood Mall and 3 mi from the U of M campus at this motel off I-94. Complimentary coffee. In-room data ports. Satellite TV. Pool. Some pets allowed. | 3764 S. State St. | 734/665–9900 | fax 517/463–2970 | www.motel6.com | 109 rooms | $45–$62 | AE, D, DC, MC, V.

Red Roof Inn. This budget hotel is on the north side of town. Cable TV. Some pets allowed. | 3621 Plymouth Rd. | 734/996–5800 or 800/733–7663 | fax 734/996–5707 | www.redroof.com | 108 rooms | $47–$73 | AE, D, DC, MC, V.

MODERATE

Fairfield Inn by Marriott. A stay at this hotel off I-94 puts you across the street from Briarwood Mall and 3 mi from the U of M. Complimentary Continental breakfast. Refrigerators. Cable TV. Indoor pool. Hot tub. | 3285 Boardwalk | 734/995–5200 | fax 734/995–5394 | 110 rooms | $69–$109 | AE, D, DC, MC, V.

Hampton Inn-North. This chain hotel is on the north side of town. Complimentary Continental breakfast. Cable TV. Indoor pool. Hot tub. Business services. | 2300 Green Rd. | 734/996–4444 | fax 734/996–0196 | www.hampton-inn.com | 130 rooms | $79–$89 | AE, D, DC, MC, V.

Hampton Inn-South. U of M sports venues are 3 mi from this hotel. Nonsmoking rooms available. Cable TV. Indoor pool. Hot tub. Exercise equipment. Laundry facilities. Business services. | 925 Victors Way | 734/665–5000 | fax 734/665–8452 | www.hampton-inn.com | 150 rooms | $80–$90 | AE, D, DC, MC, V.

Quality Inn and Suites. Downtown and the U of M campus are 3 mi from this inn which has suite accommodations. Complimentary Continental breakfast. Cable TV. Outdoor pool. Hot tub. Business services. | 3750 Washtenaw St. | 734/971–2000 or 800/228–5151 | fax 734/971–1149 | www.qualityinn.com | 100 rooms | $69–$89 | AE, D, DC, MC, V.

EXPENSIVE

Bell Tower. This 1945 property is the winner of an award for outstanding preservation. It's at the heart of the U of M campus. Restaurant, complimentary Continental breakfast. In-room data ports. Cable TV. Business services. | 300 S. Thayer St. | 734/769–3010 or 800/562–3559 | fax 734/769–4339 | 66 rooms, 10 suites | $107–$140, $225–$240 suites | AE, DC, MC, V.

Campus Inn. Known for its great views of the city and campus, this high-rise hotel is less than 1 mi away from the U of M campus and Medical Center. Restaurant, bar. In-room data ports. Cable TV. Pool. Exercise equipment. Business services. | 615 E. Huron St. | 734/769–2200 or 800/666–8693 | fax 734/769–6222 | www.campusinn.com | 208 rooms | $139–$159 | AE, D, DC, MC, V.

Crowne Plaza. Near Briarwood Mall, this hotel has a European look, with a large lobby accented by a fireplace, marble, and lace curtains. Restaurant, bar, room service. Cable TV. Indoor pool. Hot tub. Exercise equipment. | 610 Hilton Blvd. | 734/761–7800 | fax 734/761–1040 | www.crowneplazaannarbor.com | 198 rooms | $104–$145 | AE, D, DC, MC, V.

Holiday Inn–North Campus. Downtown restaurants and shopping and the U of M campus are 2 mi from this hotel. Restaurant, bar, picnic area, room service. Cable TV. Indoor-outdoor pool. Tennis. Exercise equipment. Video games. Business services. | 3600 Plymouth Rd. | 734/769–9800 or 800/465–4329 | fax 734/761–1290 | www.basshotels.com/holiday-inn | 223 rooms | $105 | AE, D, DC, MC, V.

Residence Inn by Marriott. This extended-stay inn is a good bet if you're looking for a little extra room. Picnic area, complimentary Continental breakfast. Kitchenettes. Cable TV. Pool. Hot tub. Laundry facilities. Some pets allowed. | 800 Victors Way | 734/996–5666 | www.marriott.com | 114 suites | $99–$229 suites | AE, D, DC, MC, V.

Sheraton Inn. The central location and hot-tub suites make this hotel a business and vacationers' favorite. Restaurant, bar, room service. In-room data ports, microwaves, some refrigerators, some in-room hot tubs. Cable TV. Indoor-outdoor pool. Hot tub. Exercise equipment. Business services. | 3200 Boardwalk | 734/996–0600 or 800/325–3535 | fax 734/996–8136 | www.sheraton.com | 197 rooms | $92–$140 | AE, D, DC, MC, V.

Weber's Inn. An excellent restaurant and balcony rooms overlooking the pool/spa area make this locally owned hotel on I-94 popular. Restaurant, bar (with entertainment), room service. In-room data ports, some refrigerators. Cable TV. Indoor pool. Hot tub. Exercise equipment. Business services. | 3050 Jackson Rd. | 734/769–2500 or 800/443–3050 | fax 734/769–4743 | www.webersinn.com | 160 rooms | $90–$120 | AE, D, DC, MC, V.

BATTLE CREEK

MAP 9, D7

(Nearby towns also listed: Coldwater, Jackson, Kalamazoo, Lansing, Marshall)

Snap. Crackle. Pop. Battle Creek mainly owes its existence to its No. 1 industry—breakfast cereal. C. W. Post and W. K. Kellogg settled here at the turn of the century and their influence is still felt today in street signs, parks, and cultural institutions. In the city's scenic Oak Hill Cemetery, Post lies steps away from another famous resident, anti-slavery crusader Sojourner Truth.

Information: Greater Battle Creek Visitor and Convention Bureau | 77 E. Michigan Ave., Battle Creek 49017 | 616/962–2240 or 800/397–2240 | www.battlecreekvisitors.org.

Attractions

Binder Park Zoo. A small but highly regarded zoo, Binder Park has exotic and domestic animals in a natural environment. Wooden boardwalks and a conservation adventure station with hands-on activities are favorites for families. There are special events year-round, but Halloween and Christmas are the most popular times to visit. | 7400 Division Dr. | 616/979–1351 | fax 616/979–8834 | www.binderparkzoo.org | $7.95 | end Apr.–beg. Oct., weekdays 9–5, Sat. 9–6, Sun. 10–6.

Fort Custer State Recreation Area. Spread out over more than 3,000 acres, this popular area includes 22 mi of hiking trails, 4 mi of mountain biking trails, and 16 mi of bridle trails. You can do some cross-country skiing here. There are three mini-cabins and four rustic cabins for rent, but call well in advance to reserve them. | 5163 Fort Custer Dr. | 616/731–4200 | $4 | Daily.

Kellogg Bird Sanctuary. Operated as an experimental facility by Michigan State University, this lush sanctuary on the shores of Wintergreen Lake includes seasonal visiting wildfowl and permanent residents such as ducks, geese, swans, and birds of prey. | 12685 E. C Ave. | 616/671–2510 | www.kbs.msu.edu | $3 | Daily.

Kimball House Museum. This late-1800s house, built by a young doctor from Massachusetts, is furnished with antiques and period exhibits, including appliances, tools, and medical instruments. A special display honors civil rights activist Sojourner Truth. | 196 Capital Ave. | 616/965–2612 | Free | Fri. 1–4, closed Jan.–Apr.

Leila Arboretum. More than 70 acres and 3,000 varieties of ornamental trees and shrubs distinguish this arboretum. It's best known for its collection of mature conifers—some date back to the 1920s—and its perennial demonstration gardens. | W. Michigan Ave. at 20th St. | 616/969–0270 | Free | Daily dawn to dusk.

Michigan Battle Cats. Affiliated with the Houston Astros, this class-A Midwest League team plays at C.O. Brown Stadium. | 1392 Capital Ave. NE | 616/660–2255 | www.michiganbattlecats.com | Apr.–Sept.

Fort Custer National Cemetery. During World War II, this tranquil 770-acre site served as an important army base. In 1985, it became a National Cemetery for anyone who has served in the United States Armed Forces. Just 7 mi from Battle Creek, 14,000 people are buried there. | 15501 Dickman Rd., Augusta | 616/731–4164 | www.va.cem.gov | Daily dawn–dusk.

Sojourner Truth Grave. Sojourner Truth, the noted African-American orator and Underground Railroad leader, settled in Battle Creek when freed in the mid-19th century. Today her simple grave near the final resting place of another Battle Creek resident, cereal magnate C. W. Post, is among the Oak Hill Cemetery's most-visited. | 255 South Ave. | 616/962–2240 | Free | Daily dawn to dusk.

ON THE CALENDAR

JUNE: *Cereal City Festival.* The World's Longest Breakfast Table is the highlight of this annual downtown summer event. More than 60,000 people gather around some 250 tables to feast on cereal, doughnuts, and other breakfast treats. | 616/962–2240 or 800/397–2240.

NOV.: *International Festival of Lights.* Battle Creek ushers in the holiday season with more than a million tiny, twinkling lights and a lineup of family-style events. Other highlights are "Trees Around the World," holiday train exhibits, and lighted animal displays at Binder Park Zoo. | 800/397–2240.

Dining

Sam's Joint. Barbecue. Ribs, chicken, pasta, steak, and saltade shrimp are favorites at this family-style restaurant. Kids' menu. | 1600 Rte. 66, Athens | 616/729–5010 | Closed Sun. | $7.95–$15.45 | MC, V.

Lodging

Battle Creek Inn. A courtyard beckons lodgers to the putting green and outdoor pool. Furnished apartments and extended stay rates are available. Restaurant, bar, complimentary Continental breakfast, room service. Cable TV. 2 pools (1 indoor). Putting green. Exercise equipment. Video games. Laundry facilities. Business services. Some pets allowed. | 5050 Beckley Rd. | 616/979–1100 or 800/232–3405 | fax 616/979–1899 | www.battlecreekinn.com | 212 rooms | $58–$73 | AE, D, DC, MC, V.

Baymont Inn & Suites. Free Continental breakfast delivered to your room and in-room coffeemakers make your stay here extra nice. It is less than ½ mi from shopping and right off I–94. Complimentary Continental breakfast. Cable TV. Indoor pool. | 4725 Beckley Rd. | 616/979–5400 or 800/301–0200 | fax 616/979–3390 | www.budgetel.com | 87 rooms, 2 suites | $90, $150 suites | AE, D, DC, MC, V.

Days Inn. Downtown shopping, restaurants, and golf are within 4 mi of this single-story motel. Complimentary Continental breakfast. Some in-room hot tubs. Cable TV. Business services. Some pets allowed. | 4786 Beckley Rd. | 616/979–3561 or 800/388–7829 | fax 616/979–1400 | www.daysinn.com | 85 rooms | $49–$75 | AE, D, DC, MC, V.

Greencrest Manor. This restored, Normandy chateau–style inn built in 1934 on St. Mary's Lake is furnished with antiques and surrounded by extensive landscaping. Complimentary Continental breakfast. Some in-room hot tubs. Cable TV. Business services. No smoking. | 6174 Halbert Rd. | 616/962–8633 | fax 616/962–7254 | www.greencrestmanor.com | 8 rooms (2 with shared bath) | $95–$235 | AE, DC, MC, V.

Holiday Inn Express. A loyal business clientele frequents this motel, which is 3 mi from downtown and Binder Park Zoo. There are two restaurants next door. Complimentary Continental breakfast. Cable TV. Indoor pool. | 2590 Capitol Ave. SW | 616/965–3201 or 800/465–4329 | fax 616/965–0740 | www.basshotels.com/holdiay-inn | 102 rooms | $144 | AE, D, DC, MC, V.

McCamly Plaza. Guest rooms are larger-than-average in this elegant, restored hotel in the heart of downtown. Restaurant, bar (with entertainment). Minibars, refrigerators. Cable TV. Indoor pool. Hot tub. Exercise equipment. Shops. Business services, free parking. | 50 Capital Ave. SW | 616/963–7050 | fax 616/963–4335 | www.mccamlyplazahotel.com | 242 rooms | $119–$149 | AE, D, DC, MC, V.

Super 8. Lakeview Square Mall is next door and I–94 is 1 mi from this motel. Cable TV. | 5395 Beckley Rd. | 616/979–1828 or 800/800–8000 | fax 616/919–1828 | www.super8motels.com | 62 rooms | $39–$48 | AE, D, DC, MC, V.

BAY CITY

MAP 9, E6

(Nearby towns also listed: Flint, Frankenmuth, Midland, Port Austin, Saginaw)

Once a major lumbering center, Bay City is now a busy port known for its Victorian mansions built by lumber barons and its proliferation of antiques shops along historic Midland Street. There are a number of structures along Midland Street, including the library and bank, that date back to the late 1800s. The nearby Saginaw River and Saginaw Bay are popular sites for boating, fishing, swimming, and other watery fun. (*Note:* Area codes in this vicinity are scheduled to change to 989 beginning April 7, 2001.)

Information: **Bay Area Convention and Visitors Bureau** | 901 Saginaw St., Bay City 48708 | 517/893–4567 | fax 517/895–5594 | www.baycityarea.com.

Attractions

Bay City State Recreation Area. Just 5 mi north of Bay City, this sprawling recreation area has a visitor center with permanent and changing exhibits on life in the wetlands and a paved nature trail that leads to Tobico Marsh, a 1,700-acre refuge for more than 100 species of birds and migratory waterfowl. The park also has an observation tower, nature trails, and a 300-ft boardwalk. | 3582 State Park Dr. | 517/667–0717 | $4 per car, per day | Daily dawn to dusk.

    Jennison Nature Center. Part of the huge Bay City State Recreation Area, this excellent nature center has regularly rotating exhibits on wetland life and development and an informative 15-minute video on overdevelopment, as well as a bird observation room, a wet lab, and regular special events. | 3582 State Park Dr. | 517/667–0717 | $4 per car, per day to the park, free to the building | Tues.–Sun. 12–5.

    Tobico Marsh. With programs that emphasize some 100 Great Lakes and migratory species, this is a bird-watcher's dream. | 3582 State Park Dr. | 517/684–3020 | Free | Tues.–Sun. dawn to dusk.

Bay County Historical Museum. Bay City's heritage, from pre-Columbian days to the present, is explored in a 60,000-piece permanent collection and a number of displays, including period rooms and exhibits dedicated to the lumber industry, fur trade, and Native American culture. It also has an on-site research library and sponsors a biannual tour of historic homes. | 321 Washington Ave. | 517/893–5733 | Free | Weekdays 10–5, weekends 12–4.

City Hall and Bell Tower. A dramatic 31-ft-long tapestry in the city hall by a Polish artist depicts the history of Bay County in glowing colors and rich details. The bell tower has great views of the city and beyond. | 301 Washington Ave. | 517/894–8200 | Free | Weekdays 9-5.

ON THE CALENDAR

JUNE: *St. Stanislaus Polish Festival.* A popular parish festival has ethnic foods, a midway, bingo, beer, and entertainment. | 1503 Kosciuszko St. | 517/893–6421.

JULY: *Munger Potato Festival.* Lots of food, a carnival, games, and special events pay tribute to the area's potato farms at this event in Munger. | 517/659–3270.

Dining

Krzysiak's House. Polish. This casual, family-style restaurant serves up hearty American and Polish entrées, including *pierogi* (dumplings), *nalesniki* (blintzes), and soups. An in-restaurant shop sells homemade fudge, ice cream, and desserts. | 1605 S. Michigan Ave. | 517/894–5531 | Closed Sun. | $14–$25 | AE, D, MC, V.

Terry and Jerry's O Sole Mio. Italian. An antique piano and a stage in the dining room reflect the owners' former careers as entertainers. Today they please audiences with a wide variety of specialties, including homemade pastas and steaks cut to order. Pianist, vocalist Sat. Kids' menu. | 1005 Saginaw St. | 517/893–3496 | Closed Sun and Mon. No lunch | $12.95–$35 | AE, DC, MC, V.

Lodging

Bay Valley Hotel and Resort. You can indulge in golf, tennis, and nearby fishing at this four-season resort off I–75. The lobby is filled with antiques; rooms are less distinguished. Restaurant, bar (with entertainment), picnic area, room service. Cable TV. Indoor-outdoor pool. Hot tub. Driving range, 18-hole golf course, putting green, tennis. Gym. Playground. Business services, airport shuttle. | 2470 Old Bridge Rd. | 517/686–3500 or 800/292–5028 | fax 517/686–6931 | www.bayvalley.com | 150 rooms | $72–$125 | AE, D, DC, MC, V.

Best Western Creekside Inn. You can walk to attractions, restaurants, and the city's well-known antiques district from this modern downtown hotel. Some refrigerators. Cable TV.

Pool. Hot tub, sauna. Video games. Business services. | 6285 Westside Saginaw Rd. | 517/686–0840 or 800/780–7234 | fax 517/686–0840 | bestwesternmichigan.com | 71 rooms | $55–$70 | AE, D, DC, MC, V.

Clements Inn. A Victorian bed-and-breakfast furnished with antiques and filled with beautiful details, including intricate wood paneling and stained-glass windows, is near the city's antiques area and Saginaw River. Business services. No smoking. | 1712 Center St. | 517/894–4600 | fax 517/895–8535 | 6 rooms | $70–$175 | AE, D, DC, MC, V.

Euclid Motel. This single-level motel was built in the late 1960s. Downtown is 7 mi away. Complimentary Continental breakfast. Picnic area. Some refrigerators. Cable TV. Pool. Playground. | 809 N. Euclid Ave. | 517/684–9455 | 36 rooms | $31–$48 | AE, D, DC, MC, V.

Fairfield Inn by Marriott. Marriott's budget-minded chain is in the Bay City Mall area near city attractions and freeways. Complimentary Continental breakfast. Refrigerators. Cable TV. Indoor pool. Hot tub. | 4015 E. Wilder Rd. | 517/667–7050 | fax 734/667–7050 | www.marriott.com | 64 rooms | $75 | AE, D, DC, MC, V.

Holiday Inn. The city's shopping area is 5 mi away and the Saginaw River is 1 block from this hotel. Restaurant, bar, room service. Cable TV. Indoor pool. Hot tub, sauna. Laundry facilities. Business services. Some pets allowed. | 501 Saginaw St. | 517/892–3501 or 800/465–4329 | fax 517/892–9342 | www.basshotels.com/holiday-inn | 100 rooms | $79–$170 | AE, D, DC, MC, V.

BELLAIRE

MAP 9, D4

(Nearby towns also listed: Boyne City, Charlevoix, Gaylord, Grayling, Traverse City)

This small northwest Michigan town near Lake Michigan is best known for its golf and skiing (2,000-acre Shanty Creek is a popular year-round resort) and is the seat of Antrim County. (*Note:* Area codes in this vicinity are scheduled to change to 989 beginning April 7, 2001.)

Information: Traverse City Convention and Visitors Bureau | 101 W. Grandview Pkwy., Traverse City 49615 | 231/947–1120 or 800/TRAVERS | www.tcvisitor.com.

Attractions

Shanty Creek Resort. One of the state's best-known ski centers, this 2,000-acre four-season northern Michigan resort is known for its great downhill skiing, including two mountains with triple and double chair lifts and rope tows. More than 30 trails include a longest run of just over 1 mi and a vertical drop of 425 ft. There are also cross-country trails. In summer, you can golf on one of the four courses here, including The Legend. | 1 Shanty Creek Rd. | 231/533–8621 or 800/678–4111 | fax 231/533–7004 | www.shantycreek.com.

ON THE CALENDAR

JUNE: *Mountain Bike Race.* More than 2,500 cyclists zip up and around the hills at Shanty Creek Resort and attract more than 50,000 mountain biking fans. Events include four races divided by age and ability and a marketplace. | 231/533–8621.

Lodging

Shanty Creek Resort. This Up North-style, four-season resort is spread out over more than 2,000 acres and is known for skiing in winter and golf in summer. There's a private sand beach nearby. Mountain bikes are available for rent and you can get a box lunch if you plan to be on the trails all day. Bar, dining room, picnic area, room service. Some kitchenettes. Cable TV. 5 pools (2 indoor). Hot tub. Driving ranges, 4 18-hole golf courses, putting greens, tennis. Gym, hiking, bicycles. Ice skating, cross-country skiing, downhill skiing, sleigh rides.

Video games. Children's programs, playground. Business services, airport shuttle. | 1 Shanty Creek Rd. | 231/533–8621 or 800/678–4111 | fax 231/533–7001 | www.shantycreek.com | 590 rooms | $138–$143 | AE, D, DC, MC, V.

BEULAH

(Nearby towns also listed: Empire, Frankfort, Glen Arbor, Manistee, Traverse City)

Long a tourist attraction, scenic Beulah sits on the shores of beautiful Crystal Lake. Top draws in this tiny Up North resort town include the lake, known for its fishing, boating, and swimming, and prolific artist Gwen Frostic, who runs a studio and wildlife sanctuary in nearby Benzonia. (*Note:* Area codes in this vicinity are scheduled to change to 989 beginning April 7, 2001.)

Information: Benzie County Chamber of Commerce | Box 204, Benzonia 49616 | 231/882–5801 | www.benzie.org.

Attractions

Benzie Area Historical Museum. A century-old church houses displays honoring the town's founders, including adventurous farmers, fishermen, lumberjacks, and sailors who went West in search of a better life and the adventure of the American wilderness. There's also a nice display on native-son author Bruce Catton. | 6941 River Rd. | 231/882–5539 | $3 | May–Dec., Tues.–Sat. 10–4.

Crystal Mountain Resort. Downhill skiing and 23 trails attract skiers to this resort, which has night skiing. The longest run is approximately ½ mi, the highest vertical drop 375 ft. Snowboarding and golf are also available. | 12500 Crystal Mountain Dr. | 231/378–2000 | fax 231/378–2998 | www.crystalmtn.com | Nov.–Mar.

Gwen Frostic's Studio. All of Gwen's works can be viewed at this studio 3 mi from Beulah. From the display room you can watch 45 presses printing napkins, notepapers, and place-mats—on paper made here. | 5140 River Rd., Benzonia | 231/882–5505 | fax 231/882–4600 | heidelbergman@coslink.net | www.frostic.com/gwen | Free | Nov.–May, Mon.–Sat. 9–4:30, May–Nov. daily 9–4:30.

Platte River State Anadromous Fish Hatchery. The state raises coho and Chinook salmon here to stock in state waters. | 15210 U.S. 31 | 231/325–4611 | Free | Daily.

Dining

Brookside Inn. Continental. You can watch the brook run by when you eat on the deck sur-rounded by gardens. Steak, seafood, and desserts draw diners. Kids' menu. | 115 U.S. 31 | 231/882–9688 | www.brooksideinn.com | $6–$26 | AE, D, DC, MC, V.

Cherry Hut. American. This eatery is known as family-friendly. Some tables are under the roof of fenced patio for open-air dining. Kids' menu. | 246 U.S. 31 | 231/882–4431 | Closed late Oct.–Memorial Day | $8–$17 | D, MC, V.

Sail Inn. Seafood. True to its name, this family restaurant near downtown has a sailing theme and lots of fish on the menu. Salad bar. Kids' menu. Sun. brunch. | 1579 U.S. 31, Ben-zonia | 231/882–4971 | $11–$17 | AE, D, MC, V.

Lodging

Pine Knot Resort. This mom-and-pop-style motel east of busy U.S. 31 is approximately 8 mi from Crystal Mountain Resort and Lake Michigan beaches. Some kitchenettes, refrig-erators. Cable TV. | 171 N. Center St. | 231/882–7751 | www.wmta.org/pineknot.html | 9 rooms; 2 apartments | $80–$100, $95 apartments | AE, D, MC, V.

BIG RAPIDS

(Nearby towns also listed: Cadillac, Grand Rapids, Ludington, Mt. Pleasant)

Gateway to the Manistee National Forest, this central Michigan town was founded in the 1850s on the bank of the Muskegon River. It is the only Big Rapids in the United States and is home of Ferris State University. (*Note:* Area codes in this vicinity are scheduled to change to 989 beginning April 7, 2001.)

Information: Mecosta County Convention and Visitors Bureau | 246 N. State St., Big Rapids 49307 | 231/796–7640 or 800/833–6697 | www.mecosta.org.

Attractions

Ferris State University. Founded in 1884, this college offers such unique programs as professional golf management. The school also has excellent technology programs. | 901 S. State St. | 231/591–2000 | www.ferris.edu | Free | Daily.

Historic downtown shopping district. Browse in the specialty shops that line the red-brick sidewalk of Michigan Avenue, or order an ice-cream soda at the Old Pioneer Store and Emporium. | Michigan Ave. | 231/592–4165 | Free | Daily.

Mecosta County Parks. Picnicking, fishing, canoeing, inner tubing, bicycling, and cross-country skiing are just a few of the year-round activities at the many parks in and around Big Rapids. | 22250 Northland Dr., Paris | 231/832–3246 | www.netonecom.net/~mcpc | $5 daily pass per car to all parks | May–Sept., daily dawn to dusk.

The system includes **Brower Park,** a popular area park with swimming, boating, fishing, cross-country skiing, and a playground. | 23056 Polk Road, Stanwood | 231/823–2561 | $5 daily pass per car to all parks | Daily dawn to dusk.

Merrill Lake has two beaches that attract sun worshipers, playgrounds for the youngsters, and fishing and canoeing. You can cross-country ski on the ungroomed trails. | 3275 Evergreen Rd., Sears | 517/382–7158 | $5 daily pass per car to all parks | Daily dawn to dusk.

Wildlife watching from a designated area, picnicking, and camping lead the activities at **Paris Park.** Don't miss a walk along the fish hatchery ponds or a look at the 20-ft replica of the Eiffel Tower. | 222090 Northland Dr., Paris | 231/796–3420 | $5 daily pass per car to all parks | Daily dawn to dusk).

School Section Lake is a quiet park with a beach, picnic shelters, playgrounds, and camping. Cross-country skiing is a winter option. | 9003 90th Ave., Mecosta | 231/972–7450 | $5 daily pass per car to all parks | Daily dawn to dusk.

ON THE CALENDAR

JULY: *Mecosta County Fair.* A rodeo, rides, animal exhibits, live entertainment, and more happens at this agricultural fair at the Mecosta County Fairgrounds (210 West Ave.). | 231/796–5378.

SEPT.: *Labor Day Arts Fair.* Every Labor Day more than 200 artists and exhibitors from around the state meet at Hemlock Park for this juried riverfront event. Kids events as well as playgrounds make this a great family event. | 231/796–7649.

SEPT.: *St. Mary's Fall Festival.* The highlights of this annual festival are the antique tractor and car show and the chicken roasted in a giant barbecue pit. Kids can enjoy pony rides and a petting zoo. The festival is held the first Sunday after Labor Day on the Mecosta County Fairgrounds. | 231/796–5601.

Dining

Casey McNab's. Eclectic. Since Ferris State University is across the street, this place is filled with students as well as college memorabilia. Try their barbecued ribs or a burrito. Known for having great margaritas. | 1014 S. State St. | 231/796–1222 | $8–$9 | AE, D, MC, V.

Schuberg's Bar. American. You can sit at a knotty pine bar at this casual downtown spot, the oldest tavern in town. Burgers, chili, a great chicken caesar salad, and homemade soups are popular fare. Fine-dining on weekends. | 109 N. Michigan Ave. | 231/796–5333 | Closed Sun. | $4–$15 | AE, D, DC, MC, V.

State Street Grille. Continental. This casual, family-style restaurant is popular with both locals and Ferris State University students who crowd the outdoor patio in good weather. Try ribs, wet burritos, or the signature "smothered chicken" (chicken breast with cheese and mushrooms). Salad bar. Kids' menu. Sun. brunch. | 213 S. State St. | 231/796–8706 | $5.95–$17.95 | AE, D, MC, V.

Woody's. American. New York strip steaks and pasta primavera are popular entrées at this casual restaurant inside the Holiday Inn. Desserts include strawberry wave cheesecake and chocolate fudge cake. | 1005 Perry Ave. | 231/796–4400 | $11–$20 | AE, D, DC, MC, V.

Lodging

Holiday Inn and Conference Center. Near Ferris State University, this chain hotel is equally popular with students, families, and businesspeople. Restaurant, bar, room service. In-room data ports. Cable TV. Indoor pool. Hot tub, sauna. Driving range, 18-hole golf course, putting green. Business services. | 1005 Perry St. | 231/796–4400 or 800/465–4329 | fax 231/796–0220 | www.basshotels.com/holiday-inn | 118 rooms | $79–$89 | AE, D, DC, MC, V.

Outback Lodge & Stables. This 20-acre western retreat frequented by couples and families lies 13 mi southeast of Big Rapids in Stanwood. After your full ranch breakfast, you're free to hike, ride horseback on the trails, pitch horseshoes, or curl up in front of the fieldstone fireplace in the living room. Complimentary breakfast. Hiking, horseback riding. | 12600 Buchanan Rd., Stanwood | 231/972–7255 | outbacklodge@centurytel.net | www.bbonline.com/mi/outback | 6 rooms | $79–$119 | AE, D, DC, MC, V.

Super 8. There are two strip malls less than 1 mi from this motel, and restaurants within two blocks. Cable TV. Indoor pool. Hot tub. | 845 Water Tower Rd. | 231/796–1588 or 800/800–8000 | fax 231/796–1588 | www.super8motels.com | 49 rooms, 3 suites | $55, $130 suite | AE, D, DC, MC, V.

BIRMINGHAM

MAP 10, C2

(Nearby towns also listed: Bloomfield Hills, Dearborn, Detroit, Farmington/Farmington Hills, Holly, Royal Oak)

This tony northwest Detroit suburb is home to expensive boutiques and even more expensive art galleries. Behind the glitzy storefronts are streets lined with vintage architecture, pretty Victorian homes, and some of the state's best restaurants.

Information: Birmingham-Bloomfield Chamber of Commerce | 124 W. Maple St., Birmingham 48009 | 248/644–1700 | fax 248/644–0286 | thechamber@bbcc.com | www.bbcc.com.

Attractions

Allen House. This local history museum, housed in a Georgian-style home, is a great place to learn about the area as well as of other regional historic sites. | 556 W. Maple | 248/642–2817.

Cranbrook Educational Community. Beautiful gardens and grounds surround this boarding school for grades 6–12. Its a lovely place to take a stroll. You can explore the campus, including a library and art and science museums. Two miles from Birmingham. | 39221 Woodward Ave., Bloomfield Hills | 248/645–3492 | www.cranbrook.edu/community.

Downtown shopping district. Birmingham has a pleasantly walkable downtown and has a high ratio of art galleries to people. Check out the Hill Gallery (407 W. Brown St.), the Elizabeth Stone Gallery (536 N. Old Woodward Ave.), and the many gift shops and boutiques throughout the core downtown area (the blocks surrounding Maple St. and Old Woodward Ave.). | Woodward Ave. | 248/433–3550 | www.birmingham-mi.com | Free | Daily.

ON THE CALENDAR

MAY: *Birmingham Fine Art Festival.* More than 300 artists set up booths at this two-day outdoor festival. The annual event takes place downtown on Mother's Day weekend. | Shain Park | 248/644–1700 | www.bbcc.com.

JULY: *Jazz Fest.* Musicians such as Chuck Mangione have headlined this three-day outdoor jazz extravaganza, held downtown on the third weekend of July. | Shain Park | 248/433–3550 | www.bbcc.com.

AUG.: *Woodward Dream Cruise.* This enormous one-day event celebrates America's love affair with the auto. In the 1950s, young adults would cruise Woodward Avenue's 22 mi between Detroit and the suburbans. Today, folks interested in getting glimpse of that bygone era come to watch those wanting to relive those times as they cruise their cars through the city. Parties and live entertainment follow on the streets of Birmingham. | 248/644–1700 | www.dreamcruise.org.

SEPT.: *Fall Spectacular.* Tents go up every year behind the Townsend Hotel for this extravaganza that includes a live auction and fashion show. | 248/644–1700 | www.bbcc.com.

Dining

Big Rock Chop House. Steak. This grill in the town's late 1920s train station looks like an upscale hunting lodge. Specialties here include the 14-oz tenderloin, broiled Canadian whitefish, and sandwich "wraps." Try the grill's own beer, two varieties of which won the gold and bronze medals at the World Beer Championships in 1998. | 245 S. Eton St. | 248/647–7774 | www.bigrockchophouse.com | No lunch Sun. | $7–$32 | AE, D, DC, MC, V.

Rugby Grille. Contemporary. The "see and be seen" dining room in the posh Townsend Hotel could be in a men's club, with its rugby prints and roaring fireplace. Popular dinner entrées include chicken teriyaki, Canadian whitefish with lemon-caper buerre blanc, and baby lamb chops with fruit chutney. Much of the preparation is done tableside. The outside gallery has considerably lighter fare and looks, with daily changing spa-menu items. | 100 Townsend St. | 248/642–5999 | $20–$50 | AE, DC, MC, V.

220 and Edison's. Eclectic. This lively place serves as the town's meeting place. The decor in the former electric company office pays homage to the lightbulb. Birmingham memorabilia also is plentiful. 220 is known for its extensive wine list and luscious bone-in filet mignon. A separate entrance leads downstairs to Edison's lounge, where you can hear live jazz. | 220 Merrill St. | 248/645–2150 | Reservations recommended on weekends | Closed Sun. | $13–$30 | AE, V, MC.

Lodging

Hamilton Hotel. If you're a video-game addict, you'll enjoy the Nintendo provided in every room of this European-style hotel downtown. Afternoon tea is served each day. Complimentary breakfast, room service. In-room data ports, some in-room safes, some minibars, some refrigerators. Cable TV. Exercise equipment. Laundry service. Business services. Pets allowed. | 35270 Woodward Ave. | 248/642–6200 | fax 248/642–6567 | www.hamiltonhotel.com | 64 rooms | $119–$250 | AE, D, DC, MC, V.

Holiday Inn Express. This chain hotel is in the center of downtown and across the street from shopping and restaurants. Rooms are available in the main building or around a pleasant courtyard. Complimentary Continental breakfast. In-room data ports, refrigerators. Cable TV. Business services. | 34952 Woodward Ave. | 248/646–7300 | fax 248/646–4501 | www.hiexpress.com | 126 rooms | $149–$169 | AE, D, DC, MC, V.

Townsend Hotel. Visiting celebrities often fill the rooms of this downtown hotel across from Shain Park. Restaurant, bar, room service. In-room data ports, minibars. Cable TV. Business services, parking (fee). | 100 Townsend St. | 248/642–7900 or 800/548–4172 | fax 248/645–9061 | www.townsendhotel.com | 150 rooms, 51 one-bedroom suites | $290, $365 suites | AE, DC, MC, V.

BLOOMFIELD HILLS

(Nearby towns also listed: Birmingham, Dearborn, Detroit, Farmington/Farmington Hills, Holly, Royal Oak)

Now home to many auto industry execs, this prestigious northwest suburb traces its roots to Ellen Scripps Booth and George Booth, the owners of the *Detroit News*, who bought 300 rural acres here in 1904 as the site of the sprawling Cranbrook House estate, later an esteemed arts and educational community.

Information: Birmingham-Bloomfield Chamber of Commerce | 124 W. Maple St., Birmingham 48009 | 248/644–1700 | fax 248/644–0286 | thechamber@bbcc.com | www.bbcc.com.

Attractions

Cranbrook Educational Community. This highly regarded 315-acre campus consists of art and science museums, a graduate art school, lower, middle, and upper private schools, and a renowned house museum with elaborate gardens. The complex was founded and endowed early in the century by *Detroit News* president George G. Booth and designed by noted Finnish architect and artist Eliel Saarinen. | 39221 Woodward Ave. | 248/645–3000 | www.cranbrook.edu/community | Daily dawn to dusk.

Cranbrook Academy of Art and Museum. Founded in 1920, the museum focuses on contemporary visual arts through an excellent permanent collection and rotating special

PACKING IDEAS FOR COLD WEATHER

- Driving gloves
- Earmuffs
- Fanny pack
- Fleece neck gaiter
- Fleece parka
- Hats
- Lip balm
- Long underwear
- Scarf
- Shoes to wear indoors
- Ski gloves or mittens
- Ski hat
- Ski parka
- Snow boots
- Snow goggles
- Snow pants
- Sweaters
- Thermal socks
- Tissues, handkerchief
- Turtlenecks
- Wool or corduroy pants

*Excerpted from *Fodor's: How to Pack: Experts Share Their Secrets*
© 1997, by Fodor's Travel Publications

exhibits that sometimes include the work of Cranbrook students. Previous featured artists have included Keith Haring and Yoko Ono. Other displays include the works of some of the academy's graduates, including Finnish architect Eliel Saarinen and Swedish sculptor Carl Milles, whose work can also be seen in Cranbrook gardens. | 39221 Woodward Ave. | 248/645–3320 | www.cranbrook.edu | $5 | Tues., Wed., Fri.–Sun. 11–5, Thurs. 11–8.

Cranbrook House and Gardens. Noted Detroit architect Albert Kahn designed this English manor in 1908 for George Booth and his wife. The surrounding gardens include 40 acres of lush formal plantings, with woods, nature walks, and two on-site lakes. Self-guided tours are available. | 380 Lone Pine Rd. | 248/645–3149 | www.cranbrook.edu | $10 house and gardens, $5 gardens only | House: June–Sept., tours Thurs. 11 and 1:15, Sun. 1:30 and 3, and by appointment; gardens: May–Aug., daily 10–5; Sept., daily 11–3; Oct., weekends 11–3, tours by appointment.

Cranbrook Institute of Science. Laser-light shows, a large rock and mineral collection, and Native American artifacts are the big draws at this popular science museum. Besides the planetarium, there are also an observatory, a physics hall, and national touring exhibits, many from the Smithsonian. | 39221 N. Woodward | 248/645–3200 | www.cranbrook.edu | $7 | Sun.–Thurs., Fri. 10–10, Sat. 10–5.

Holocaust Memorial Center. On the Jewish Community Campus 10 mi west of Bloomfield Hills, this museum memorializes the Holocaust through exhibits, videos, photographs, and, dioramas. Also housed here is the Schaver Library-Archive, a research facility for the study of Jewish culture. | 6602 W. Maple Rd., West Bloomfield | 248/661–0840 | fax 248/661–4204 | info@holocaustcenter.org | www.holocaustcenter.org | Free | July–Aug., Sun.–Thurs. 10–4; Sept.–June, Sun.–Thurs. 10–4, Fri. 9–1.

Dining

Fox and Hounds. Seafood. This classy restaurant frequented by attorneys and stockbrokers is in an English Tudor-style mansion with a gold-plated turret. A stock-market ticker board runs the length of the old-fashioned mahogany bar. Favorites here include oysters, prime rib, and seafood fettuccine. | 1560 N. Woodward Ave. | 248/644–4800 | fax 248/644–0779 | www.foxhounsd.net | No lunch weekends | $8–$45 | AE, D, DC, MC, V.

The Lark. French. This local legend is well regarded nationally. The 50 seats are always filled with diners feasting on longtime chef Marcus Haight's signature rack of lamb "Genghis Khan" or the shellfish and chorizo in saffron sauce. The outdoor patio is open for drinks, cocktails, and appetizers. | 6430 Farmington Rd., West Bloomfield | 248/661–4466 | fax 248/661–8891 | larkrest@aol.com | www.thelark.com | Reservations essential | Closed Sun. and Mon. and early Jan. and early Aug., no lunch | $60–$67.50 | AE, DC, MC, V.

Lodging

Kingsley Hotel and Suites. This traditional hotel is less than 1 mi from Cranbrook Educational Community and museums. Restaurant, bar, room service. Cable TV. Indoor pool. Beauty salon, hot tub. Exercise equipment. Business services. | 39475 Woodward Ave. | 248/644–1400 or 800/544–6835 | fax 248/644–5449 | www.whg.hotels.com/kingsley | 150 rooms, 11 suites | $99–$259; $259–$399 suites | AE, D, DC, MC, V.

Wren's Nest. You'll see lots of birds and more than 9,000 tulips on the landscaped grounds of this 1840s Greek Revival inn in West Bloomfield. Two sun rooms bring extra light into the house. The quaint guest rooms, with antique four-poster beds, all have bird names such as "Red Robin's Happiness." Complimentary breakfast. TV in common area. No smoking. | 7405 West Maple Road, West Bloomfield | 248/624–6874 | fax 248/624–9869 | info@bbonline.com | www.bbonline.com/mi/wrensnest | 6 rooms | $115 | AE, D, DC, MC, V.

BOYNE CITY

(Nearby towns also listed: Bellaire, Charlevoix, Harbor Springs, Indian River, Petoskey)

An alpine-inspired northern Michigan city near Lake Charlevoix, Boyne City has a small downtown with motels and restaurants. It serves as the gateway to "Boyne Country," a popular resort area with skiing in winter, tennis and golf in summer. (*Note:* Area codes in this vicinity are scheduled to change to 989 beginning April 7, 2001.)

Information: Boyne City Chamber of Commerce | 28 S. Lake St., Boyne City 49712 | 231/582–6222 | www.boynecity.com.

Attractions

Boyne Mountain. One of the Midwest's top ski destinations has 6,000 acres and more than 40 ski runs. The longest run is more than 5,200 ft, the highest vertical drop is 500 ft. The mountain also has cross-country trails. | 1 Boyne Mountain Rd. | 800/462–6963 | fax 231/549–6093 | www.boyne.com | Nov.–Mar.

Young State Park. This 17,300-acre park includes 2 mi of white sandy beach along Lake Charlevoix and many more miles of hiking and cross-country skiing trails. | 02280 Boyne City Rd. | 231/582–7523 | www.dnr.state.mi.us | $4 per car, per day | Daily.

ON THE CALENDAR

MAY: *National Morel Mushroom Hunting Festival.* Throngs of dedicated mushroom hunters search the north woods for morels, elusive spring treats. The 1982 record was 924 morels bagged in two hours. The two-day festival includes seminars, tips, morel-inspired cuisine in area restaurants, a carnival, and a crafts show. | 231/582–6222 or 800/845–2828.

Dining

Argonne Supper Club. Seafood. Elegant in all white, this restaurant 4 mi north of downtown specializes in all-you-can eat shrimp, either batter-fried or steamed in the shell. Other popular entrées are the Alaskan king crab, local whitefish, and steaks. | 11929 Boyne City Rd. | 231/547–9331 | Closed Mon. and Tues. in winter. No lunch | $13–$30 | D, MC, V.

Pippins. Continental. This family restaurant overlooks beautiful Lake Charlevoix. Kids' menu. | 5 W. Main | 231/582–3311 | Closed Nov.–Apr., no dinner Sun. | $12–$18 | MC, V.

Stafford's One Water Street. Contemporary. Waterfront views, greenery, and an airy design make this a popular eatery. The menu reflects an all-American philosophy, with regional specialties such as fresh local fish, wild game, and more. Entertainment Fri. and Sat. Kids' menu. | 1 Water St. | 231/582–3434 | No lunch mid-Sept.–mid-June | $20–$28 | AE, MC, V.

Tannery Saloon. American. This busy Sunday brunch spot used to be the town tannery. Now it's a rustic eatery known for its baby back ribs, steaks, and roasted chicken. | 220 S. Lake St. | 231/582–2272 | $6–$16 | AE, D, DC, MC, V.

Lodging

Beardsley House. You can fish for trout or salmon in the Boyne River from the backyard of this 1898 Queen Anne Victorian three blocks east of downtown. The house contains period antiques and clawfoot bathtubs, and a functional pump organ presides over the dining room. No air-conditioning. No room phones, TV in common area. Outdoor hot tub. Fishing. No smoking. | 401 Pearl St. | 231/582–9619 | vstanden@freeway.net | www.laketo-lake.com/beardsley | 4 rooms | $90–$130 | AE, MC, V.

Boyne Mountain Resort. This popular full-service golf, tennis, and snow sports resort is one of Michigan's best-known. Its spectacular natural beauty draws visitors from around

the world. Bar, dining room. Some kitchenettes. Cable TV. 2 pools. Hot tub. One 9-hole golf course, 2 18-hole golf courses, tennis. Exercise equipment. Beach, boating, bicycles. Ice-skating, cross-country skiing, downhill skiing. Business services. | 1 Boyne Mountain Rd., Boyne Falls | 231/549–6000 or 800/GO–BOYNE | fax 231/549–6093 | www.boyne.com | 265 rooms, suites, and apartments in lodges, villas, condos | $89–$99, $124 suites, $160–$375 apartments | AE, D, DC, MC, V.

Water Street Inn. All suites in this condominium hotel one block from downtown have a bedroom, kitchen, antique furnishings, and lakeside decks. Private Lake Charlevoix beachfront is reserved for guests of the inn. Kitchenettes, in-room hot tubs. Cable TV. Beach. Business services. | 200 Front St. | 231/582–3000 or 800/456–4313 | fax 231/582–3001 | 27 rooms | $95–$195 | MC, V.

BREVORT

MAP 9, D3

(Nearby towns also listed: Manistique, Newberry, St. Ignace)

A half-hour up the Lake Michigan shore from the Mackinac Bridge, Brevort is another of the tourism-based towns that dot the shorelines of Michigan's Upper Peninsula. Former industry was mainly turn-of-the-century timber production and Depression-era fishing. The town has breathtaking vistas of Lake Michigan. (*Note:* Area codes in this vicinity are scheduled to change to 989 beginning April 7, 2001.)

Information: St. Ignace Area Chamber of Commerce | 560 N. State St., St. Ignace 49781 | 906/643–9380 or 800/338–6660 | www.stignace.com.

Attractions
Brevort Lake Campground. Most campsites at this U.S. Forest Service campground on a sandy peninsula that divides Boedne Bay and Brevort Lake are for tents, but five have RV pull-throughs. Here you can swim, launch your boat, and fish. The 4,233-acre Brevort Lake offers the largest man-made reef in an inland lake. Or you can have a picnic and hike one of the three trails. Winter sports include ice fishing and snowmobiling. | U.S. 2, Moran | 906/643–7900 | fax 906/643–8759 | 70 campsites | $12–$14 | Closed Oct.–mid-May.

Dining
G&B Restaurant. American. The only restaurant in town serves residents and visitors steaks and burgers along with perch, walleye, and whitefish. | 4340 W. U.S. 2 | 906/292–0030 | $6–$10 | No credit cards.

Lodging
Chapel Hill Motel. You can rent a single room to a five-bedroom house at this 1950s motel, which was enlarged in the 1960s and again in the 1990s. Situated off the highway, it's also nice and quiet. TV. Pool. Some pets allowed. | 4422 W. U.S. 2, St. Ignace | 906/292–5534 | 26 rooms | $39–$54 | MC, V, D.

CADILLAC

MAP 9, D5

(Nearby towns also listed: Big Rapids, Houghton Lake, Ludington, Manistee, Traverse City)

Named in honor of Antoine de la Mothe Cadillac, founder of Detroit, the city has few ties to its southern sister, preferring to emphasize its abundance of golf, tennis, and state parks and its role as headquarters for the nearby Huron-Manistee National Forest. (*Note:* Area codes in this vicinity are scheduled to change to 989 beginning April 7, 2001.)

Information: Cadillac Area Visitors Bureau | 222 Lake St., Cadillac 49601 | 231/775–0657 or 800/22–LAKES | www.cadillacmichigan.com.

Attractions

Caberfae Peaks Ski Resort. This popular ski resort has some of the Midwest's biggest vertical drops and longest runs, including a 3/4-mi novice run. You can also enjoy snowboarding, snowmobiling, and cross-country skiing. | Caberfae Rd. | 231/862–3300 | fax 231/862–3302 | www.michiweb.com/cabpeaks | Nov.–Mar.

Huron-Manistee National Forest. Covering more than 964,000 acres stretching from Manistee to Oscoda in the northern part of the Lower Peninsula, the forest is drained by the Au Sable River, once used to float logs to East Tawas and Oscoda sawmills. Here you can go swimming, cross-country and downhill skiing, hiking, and hunting for the elusive morel mushroom. Fishing and canoeing are popular on the Au Sable, Manistee, Pine, and Père Marquette Rivers. Other highlights include the Nordhouse Dunes along Lake Michigan, the Loda Lake National Wildflower Sanctuary, the River Road Scenic Byway, and the Lumberman's Monument, a bronze statue commemorating early loggers. | 1755 S. Mitchell St. | 231/775–2421 | www.fs.fed.us/r9/hmnf | $3 | Daily 8–5.

William Mitchell State Park. More than 250 scenic acres between two lakes near downtown Cadillac have camping, picnic sites, a beach, fishing, hunting, a boat launch, an interpretive hiking trail, a playground, a visitor center, and a nature study area. | 6093 E. M-115 | 231/775–7911 | fax 231/775–3322 | www.dnr.state.mi.us | $4 per car, per day | Daily dawn to dusk.

CADILLAC

INTRO
ATTRACTIONS
DINING
LODGING

ON THE CALENDAR

JULY: *Cadillac Festival of the Arts*. The third weekend of July attracts more than 200 artists to this outdoor festival in City Park. Peruse the art booths, sample international food, and listen to live jazz at the two-day event. | 231/775–0657 or 800/22–LAKES | www.cadillacmichigan.com/festivals.

Dining

Burke's Waterfront Restaurant. American. This family-friendly restaurant by Lake Cadillac has buffets for breakfast, weekday lunch, and dinner. Friday's seafood buffet includes fish, shrimp, and homemade clam chowder. You can also order pan-fried walleye, barbecue ribs, or tacos off the menu. Open-air dining on the patio in summer. | 2403 Sunnyside Dr. | 231/775–7555 | Breakfast also available | $5–$30 | AE, D, MC, V.

Hermann's European Cafe. Continental. Swedish-style wild boar, shrimp tempura, and classic Weiner schnitzel are a few of the offerings at the intimate, chef-owned European-style eatery. The chef's adjacent deli and bakery is open daily. Guest rooms are available. Kids' menu. | 214 N. Mitchell | 231/775–9563 | www.chefhermann.com | Closed Sun. | $15–$20 | D, MC, V.

Lakeside Charlie's. Continental. Family-friendly dining overlooking Lake Mitchell, a charming lakeside patio, and a nostalgic lounge with an antique bar, jukebox, and lodge-like look make this a local favorite. Entertainment Fri. and Sat. Kids' menu, early bird suppers. Sun. brunch. | 301 S. Lake Mitchell | 231/775–5332 | Closed Mon. | $11.95–$17 | AE, D, MC, V.

Marina Ristorante. Italian. This family-owned restaurant, in operation since 1959, serves up authentic veal marsala, chicken picatta, Old World sauces, and hand-rolled pasta and gnocchi. The dining area displays model boats imported from Italy, and the antique leaded-glass windows have great views of Lake Cadillac. Open-air dining on the deck in summer. | 2404 Sunnyside Dr. | 231/775–9322 | fax 231/779–1575 | Closed Tues. No lunch | $8–$26 | AE, D, DC, MC, V.

Terrace Room. Seafood. You'll have a spectacular view of the city, Lake Cadillac, and the golf course if you dine in the oak booths of this elegant restaurant at McGuire's Resort. Try the organic, locally raised Scottish Highland beef, Lake Superior whitefish, or the coconut-raspberry tempura shrimp. The Saturday dinner buffets and the Sunday brunch buffets draw large crowds. | McGuire's Resort, 7880 Mackinaw Trail | 231/775–9947 | fax 231/775–9621 | info@mcguireresort.com | www.mcguiresresort.com | $5–$23 | AE, D, DC, MC, V.

Lodging

Best Western Bill Oliver's. This single-level motel has chalet-style rooms and is 1 block from Lake Cadillac, Lake Mitchell, and hiking trails. There is also a golf course next door. Restaurant, room service. Cable TV. Indoor pool. Hot tub, sauna. Tennis. Video games. Playground. Business services. | 5676 E. M–55 | 231/775–2458 or 800/780–7234 | fax 231/775–8383 | www.bestwesternmichigan.com | 66 rooms | $58–$97 | AE, D, DC, MC, V.

Cadillac Sands Resort. This year-round resort overlooking Lake Cadillac has its own private beach and docks. Restaurant, complimentary Continental breakfast. Cable TV. Indoor pool. Putting green. Beach, dock, boating. Business services. | 6319 E. M–115 | 231/775–2407 or 800/647–2637 | fax 231/775–6422 | 54 rooms | $50–$125 | AE, D, DC, MC, V.

Days Inn. You'll be approximately 4 mi from downtown Cadillac at this chain hotel on a lake. Complimentary Continental breakfast. Some refrigerators. Cable TV. Indoor pool. Hot tub. Volleyball. Beach. Business services. | 6001 E. M–115 | 231/775–4414 or 800/388–7829 | fax 231/779–0370 | www.daysinn.com | 60 rooms | $79–$89 | AE, D, DC, MC, V.

Econo Lodge. Nestled between Lake Cadillac and Lake Mitchell, this budget chain hotel has some of the best views around. It's by two restaurants, 3 mi west of downtown on Rte. 55. In-room data ports, some kitchenettes, some microwaves, some refrigerators. Cable TV. Pets allowed. | 2501 Sunnyside Dr. | 231/775–6700 or 800/835–1934 | fax 231/775–8828 | www.econolodge.com | 29 rooms | $55–$110 | AE, D, DC, MC, V.

Hampton Inn. Less than 1 mi from downtown, this chain hotel is also within 2 mi of Lake Cadillac. Complimentary Continental breakfast. Cable TV. Indoor pool. Hot tub. Business services. | 1650 S. Mitchell St. | 231/779–2900 | fax 231/779–0846 | www.hampton-inn.com | 120 rooms | $79–$99 | AE, D, DC, MC, V.

Hermann's European Hotel. The European touches here include armoires, four-poster beds, and artwork in the spacious rooms and freshly baked pastries in the morning. The Viennese owner/chef runs the restaurant next door. Complimentary Continental breakfast. Cable TV, in-room VCRs (and movies). Laundry service. Business services. | 214 N. Mitchell St. | 231/775–9563 | fax 231/775–2090 | hermann@netonecom.net | www.chefhermann.com | 7 rooms | $65–$95 | AE, D, DC, MC, V.

McGuire's Resort. At this 327-acre modern resort, the emphasis is on recreation, from golfing to skiing to volleyball. All rooms overlook Lake Cadillac, and suites have fireplaces and hot tubs. The resort is 1 mi south of town. Restaurant, bar. In-room data ports, some microwaves, some refrigerators, some in-room hot tubs. Indoor pool. Hot tub, sauna. 18-hole golf course, 9-hole golf course, putting green, 2 tennis courts. Basketball, hiking, volleyball. Cross-country skiing, sleigh rides, snowmobiling, tobogganing. Video games. Baby-sitting, children's programs (0–16). Laundry service. Pets allowed. | 7880 Mackinaw Trail | 231/775–9947 or 888/MCGUIRES | fax 231/775–9621 | www.mcguiresresort.com | 105 rooms, 15 suites | $129–$209 | AE, D, DC, MC, V.

Sun 'n Snow Motel. On Lake Mitchell, you'll have access to a private beach and cross-country skiing and biking trails at this motel. Cable TV. Beach. Business services. Some pets allowed. | 301 S. Lake Mitchell Dr. | 231/775–9961 or 231/477–9961 (reservations) | fax 231/775–3846 | www.cadillacmichigan.com/sunnsnowmotel/ | 29 rooms | $40–$79 | D, MC, V.

Super 8. Right of I–55, there are a handful of restaurants two blocks from this single-floor motel. Complimentary Continental breakfast. Some refrigerators. Indoor pool. Hot tub. |

211 W. M–55 | 231/775–8561 or 800/800–8000 | fax 231/775–9392 | www.super8motels.com | 27 rooms | $39–$69 | AE, D, DC, MC, V.

CALUMET

MAP 9, A1

(Nearby towns also listed: Copper Harbor, Hancock, Houghton)

Calumet is a tiny Upper Peninsula mining town on the scenic Keweenaw Peninsula. The town's ornate and historic 1899 Calumet Opera House theater once attracted entertainers such as Douglas Fairbanks and Sarah Bernhardt. (*Note:* Area codes in this vicinity are scheduled to change to 989 beginning April 7, 2001.)

Information: **Keweenaw Peninsula Chamber of Commerce** | 56638 Calumet Ave., Calumet 49913 | 906/337–4579 or 800/338–7982 | www.keweenaw.org.

Attractions

Calumet Theatre. Sarah Bernhardt, Annie Oakley, Lon Chaney, Douglas Fairbanks Jr., and other stars of stage and screen once appeared in this elegant 19th-century Upper Peninsula theater. Now restored, it presents live musical and theater performances year-round and has regular tours of the 1899 structure during the summer. | 340 6th St. | 906/337–2610 | fax 906/337–4073 | $4 | Late May–mid-Sept., Tues.–Sat. 11–2.

Coppertown USA. Administered by the Keweenaw National Historical Park, Coppertown traces the evolution of the U.P. mining industry, with displays of equipment and a simulated mine. | 109 Red Jacket Rd. | 906/337–4354 | $3 | June–Oct., Mon.–Sat. 10–5.

ON THE CALENDAR

JULY: *Heritage Celebration.* Celebrate Calumet's diverse ethnic heritage at this one-day festival of food and crafts. You can choose from among French, Finnish, Croatian, and German dishes at booths in the Old Town district of Calumet. | 906/337–4570 or 800/338–7982.

Dining

Old Country Haus. German. German-American cuisine and look are staples of this family-style eatery. Salad bar. Sun. brunch. | U.S. 41, Keirsarge | 906/337–4626 | $9.95–$21.95 | AE, D, MC, V.

Shawn's. American. Lake Superior whitefish, barbecue baby back ribs, and homemade pizza are top picks at this popular sandstone restaurant and lounge 1½ mi west of Calumet. | 333 Hecla St., Laurium | 906/337–2122 | $8–$14 | MC, V.

Lodging

AmericInn Motel and Suites. You can choose from a variety of rooms at this motel close to U.P. highways, recreation, and restaurants. It's one block west of the city's visitor center. Complimentary Continental breakfast. Some refrigerators. Indoor pool. Hot tub. | 5101 S. 6th St. | 906/337–6463 | fax 906/337–4990 | www.americinn.com | 68 rooms, 15 suites | $61–$89, $95–$195 suites | AE, D, DC, MC, V.

Laurium Manor Inn & Victorian Hall. No expense was spared in building this grand 45-room 1908 Neoclassical mansion, which is 1 mi southeast of town off Route 26. The interior, done in Art Nouveau style, includes a music parlor with silver-leaf-covered ceiling, a dining room with gilded elephant-leather wall coverings, and a triple staircase of hand-carved oak. If the manor's full, you can stay next door at the Victorian Hall, a 1906 home with period antiques. Complimentary breakfast. No air-conditioning, some in-room hot tubs, some room phones, no TV in some rooms, TV in common area. No kids under 4. No

CALUMET

INTRO
ATTRACTIONS
DINING
LODGING

smoking. | 320 Tamarack St. | 906/337–2549 | fax 815/328–3692 | innkeeper@laurium-manorinn.com | www.lauriummanorinn.com | 17 rooms | $55–$150 | AE, D, DC, MC, V.

CHARLEVOIX

MAP 9, C3

(Nearby towns also listed: Bellaire, Boyne City, Harbor Springs, Indian River, Petoskey)

Charlevoix is one of Michigan's busiest resort centers in season, with a crowded Lake Michigan beach, a ferry to pristine Beaver Island, and downtown stores stocked with such necessities as fudge, sweatshirts, and preppy resort wear. Swimming, sunning, and hunting for Petoskey stones (fossilized coral) are a few of the favorite activities on Charlevoix area beaches. The beaches along Lake Michigan and Lake Charlevoix are particularly popular. (*Note:* Area codes in this vicinity are scheduled to change to 989 beginning April 7, 2001.)

Information: **Charlevoix Area Chamber of Commerce** | 408 Bridge St., Charlevoix 49720 | 231/547–2101 | info@charlevoix.org | www.charlevoix.org.

Attractions

Beaver Island Boat Co. This company has regular ferry service from downtown Charlevoix to Beaver Island, a remote island 30 mi offshore that was once a Mormon stronghold but is now better known for its fishing, hunting, and serenity. The trip takes just over two hours. | 103 Bridge Park Dr. | 231/547–2311 or 888/446–4095 | www.bibco.com | $31 round-trip | June–Sept., daily; mid-Apr.–May and Oct.–mid-Dec.

Fisherman's Island State Park. This park where you can go camping, hiking, hunting, and fishing is on 5 mi of undeveloped shoreline along Lake Michigan. It's 2 mi south of downtown Charlevoix. | Bells Bay Rd. | 231/547–6641 | $4 per car, per day | Daily.

Mt. McSauba. This steep sand dune rises amid other huge, rolling dunes on the 50-acre recreation site that slopes down to Lake Michigan. Well-maintained hiking and cross-country skiing trails run through a wooded area behind the dunes. You can also snowboard and downhill ski at this site with a vertical drop of 140 ft. | Mt. McSauba Rd. and Pleasant Rd. | 231/547–3267 | $7.

ON THE CALENDAR

JULY: *Charlevoix Craft Show.* This two-day outdoor festival held in East Park each July attracts more than 200 arts and crafts vendors from all over the Midwest. | 231/547–2101 | www.charlevoix.org.

JULY: *Venetian Festival.* Attendees deck their boats with twinkling lights for the nightly waterfront parade. Local nonprofits run music and food booths; you can also enjoy the carnival and midway. | 800/367–8557.

AUG.: *Waterfront Art Fair.* Quilts, paintings, pottery, and jewelry are highlights of this open-air show that attracts some 200 artists in all media from around the country. | 231/547–2675.

OCT.: *Apple Festival.* Downtown celebrates the apple harvest with an apple a day, apple foodstuffs and baked goods, games, rides, arts and crafts, and more. | 231/367–8557.

Dining

Grey Gables Inn. Continental. Starched linen cloths cover the tables here, and paintings, chandeliers, and antique knickknacks embellish the dining areas. The food is distinctly upscale, from escargot to pan-roasted Norwegian salmon to the homemade desserts. Full-service bar and live entertainment. | 308 Belvedere Ave. | 231/547–9261 | www.greygablesinn.com | Jacket and tie | $17–$30 | AE, D, DC, MC, V.

Judy's Restaurant. American. The locals hang out at this old-fashioned diner with a lunch counter and a dozen tables. Try "Judy's Mess" for breakfast—a skillet-fried mound of home fries, ham, cheese, green pepper, and onion. For lunch, try the meatloaf, Swedish meatballs, or lasagna. | 117 Antrim St. | 231/547–2412 | $2–$6 | No credit cards.

Rowe Inn. Contemporary. Top regional chefs and a menu that emphasizes fresh local ingredients have made this intimate eatery a northern Michigan favorite. Knotty-pine paneling and an extraordinary wine cellar add to its delights. Entrées include such favorites as wild mushroom penne, pecan stuffed morels, and local whitefish. | 6303 Rte. 48, Ellsworth | 231/588–7351 | www.roweinn.com | Reservations essential | No lunch | $19.50–$36.50 | AE, D, MC, V.

Stafford's Weathervane. American. One of a number of Stafford properties in northern Michigan, the Weathervane is a well-known local spot in a 1950s stone building that was designed by famed local architect Earl Young. The restaurant is known for seafood and steaks. Kids' menu, early bird suppers. | 106 Pine River La. | 231/547–4311 | $17.95–$34 | AE, MC, V.

Tapawingo. Contemporary. Some believe this is northern Michigan's—and the state's—finest restaurant. Harlan "Pete" Peterson's entrées range from char-grilled beef tenderloin or Colorado rack of lamb to a Polish venison stew and Thai-style tuna. No smoking. | 9502 Lake St., Ellsworth | 231/588–7971 | www.tapawingo.net | Reservations essential | Closed Nov. | $35–$57 | MC, V.

Lodging

Caine Cottage B&B. Built in 1892, this lovely Victorian is two blocks from downtown Charlevoix and three blocks from Lake Michigan. After a busy day, you can unwind in a comfy wicker chair on the front porch. Complimentary Continental breakfast. Cable TV. No smoking. | 219 Antrim St. | 231/547–6781 | www.laketolake.com/Caine | 2 rooms | $72–$125 | MC, V.

Capri Motel. This bargain motor lodge is across from the airport, about five blocks south of downtown. Ask the friendly owners about local attractions. Cable TV. Business services. | 1455 Bridge St. | 231/547–2545 | fax 231/547–7560 | caprimotel@yahoo.com | www.caprimotel-charlevoix.com | 18 rooms | $50–$100 | Closed mid-Oct.–mid-Apr. | D, MC, V.

Charlevoix Country Inn. On a bluff two blocks north of downtown, this charming 1892 inn overlooks Lake Michigan and is ¼ mi from the public pier. The cheerful floral-papered rooms have patchwork quilts on the beds. Wine and cheese are served each evening. Complimentary Continental breakfast. No air-conditioning, no room phones, no TV in some rooms, TV in common area. No smoking. | 106 W. Dixon | 231/547–5134 | fax 231/547–5336 | cci@free-way.net | www.charlevoixcountryinn.com | 8 rooms, 2 suites | $75–$145 | Closed mid Oct.–Memorial Day | MC, V.

Edgewater Inn. Overlooking Round Lake, this inn has suite-style accommodations and views of downtown, a half-block away. Restaurant, picnic area. Kitchenettes, some in-room hot tubs. Cable TV. Indoor-outdoor pool, lake. Beauty salon, hot tub. Exercise equipment. Dock. Laundry facilities. Business services. | 100 Michigan Ave. | 231/547–6044 or 800/748–0424 | fax 231/547–0038 | www.edgewater-charlevoix.com. | 60 suites | $220–$250 1–bedroom; $295–$320 2–bedroom | AE, MC, V.

Inn at Grey Gables. Built in 1887, this inn with a wraparound porch is on a quiet street four blocks from downtown. You can mingle at the afternoon wine-and-cheese social before dining at the inn's restaurant next door. Restaurant, complimentary breakfast. Some kitchenettes. No room phones. No TV. No smoking. | 306 Belvedere Ave. | 231/547–2251 or 800/280–4667 | theinnbb@hotmail.com | www.greygablesinn.com | 5 rooms, 2 suites | $110–$135 | MC, V.

Lodge of Charlevoix. Downtown restaurants and shops are three blocks from this hotel. Cable TV. Pool. Business services. | 120 Michigan Ave. | 231/547–6565 | fax 231/547–0741 | 40 rooms | $95–$155 | AE, DC, MC, V.

Pointes North Inn. This hotel next to the downtown area has suite accommodations. Complimentary Continental breakfast. Refrigerators, in-room hot tubs. Cable TV. Indoor-outdoor pool. Laundry facilities. Business services. | 101 Michigan Ave. | 231/547–0055 or 800/968–5433 | fax 231/547–2283 | www.pointesnorth.com | 23 suites | $147–$252 | AE, D, MC, V.

Sleep Inn. Overlooking a lake, this motel 2 mi from downtown is adjacent to a golf course and near other recreation. Complimentary Continental breakfast. Cable TV. Indoor pool. Business services. | 800 Petoskey Ave. | 231/547–0300 | fax 231/547–3995 | 59 rooms | $90–$140 | AE, D, MC, V.

Weathervane Terrace. At the top of a hill overlooking downtown Charlevoix, this distinctive hotel was built of Lake Michigan rocks and boulders by an eccentric local architect. Some rooms have fireplaces. The sundeck overlooks two lakes and a river. Complimentary Continental breakfast. Microwaves, refrigerators, in-room hot tubs. Cable TV. Pool. Hot tub. Business services. | 111 Pine River La. | 231/547–9955 or 800/552–0025 (MI) | fax 231/547–0070 | www.weathervane-chx.com | 68 rooms | $55–$195 | AE, D, DC, MC, V.

CHEBOYGAN

MAP 9, D3

(Nearby towns also listed: Alpena, Harbor Springs, Indian River, Mackinaw City, Petoskey)

Once a busy lumbering port, Cheboygan is today better known as a top boating area, with Great Lakes and inland waterways nearby. Cheboygan State Park covers more than 1,200 acres. (*Note:* Area codes in this vicinity are scheduled to change to 989 beginning April 7, 2001.)

Information: **Cheboygan Area Chamber of Commerce** | 124 N. Main St., Cheboygan 49721 | 231/627–7183 or 800/968–3302 | www.cheboygan.com.

Attractions

Aloha State Park. On beautiful Mullett Lake in the heart of a 40-mi inland waterway, this 95-acre park 7 mi west of Cheboygan is a favorite of summer anglers who seek northern pike, yellow perch, smallmouth bass, walleye, and lake trout. | 4347 3rd St. | 231/625–2522 | $4 per car, per day | Daily.

Cheboygan County Historical Museum. This two-story brick structure was built in 1882 and is best known for its attached county jail, which served as the sheriff's residence until the 1960s but now houses period rooms and "cells" filled with lumbering, farming, and military displays. | 404 S. Huron St. | 231/627–9597 | $2, kids free | May–Oct., weekdays 1–4.

Cheboygan Opera House. Mary Pickford, Annie Oakley, and other early artists graced the stage of this Victorian theater, now a center for local entertainment. The opera house was built in 1877 and rebuilt after a fire in 1888. | 403 N. Huron | 231/627–5432 | www.theoperahouse.org | $1 | June–Sept., Tues.–Fri. 1–4.

Cheboygan State Park. Perched on the scenic Straits of Mackinac and Lake Huron, 1,200-acre Cheboygan State Park boasts scenic Lake Huron beachfront and views of old lighthouse ruins. Three rustic cabins along the coastline are available for rent; you also can go hiking, cross-country skiing, and swimming. | 4490 Beach Rd. | 231/627–2811 | www.dnr.state.mi.us | $4 per car, per day | Daily.

The U.S. Coast Guard Cutter *Mackinaw*. Credited with extending the Great Lakes shipping season by as much as six weeks, this Coast Guard icebreaker is one of the world's largest, with an 80-man crew. It makes Cheboygan its home port and has tours when docked at the turning basin on the east side of the Cheboygan River. | 800/968–3302 | Free.

ON THE CALENDAR

JULY–AUG.: *Cheboygan County Fair*. Midway rides, agricultural and animal displays, and classic country fair fun make this an area favorite. | 231/627–8819.

SEPT.: *Buffalo Bash*. If you've never tasted buffalo before, here's your chance. You can sample buffalo sausages, ribs, and burgers while listening to live country music. The shindig is held each year in a barn 10 mi west of town. | 231/627–7183 or 800/968–3302.

Dining

Boathouse Restaurant. Seafood. This authentic old boathouse on the Cheboygan River used to store contraband whiskey from Canada during Prohibition. Now it prides itself on fresh seafood, including the honey-pecan walleye, Parmesan-crusted whitefish, and seafood gumbo. Compasses, steering wheels, and anchors point up the restaurant's nautical theme. | 106 Pine St. | 231/627–4316 | $5–$30 | AE, D, DC, MC, V.

Hack-Ma-Tack Inn. Continental. In a wooded area, this rustic inn dates from 1894 and has an Early American look. It's known for steak. Guest rooms are available. | 8131 Beebe Rd. | 231/625–2919 | Closed mid-Oct.–mid-Apr. No lunch | $15–$21 | D, DC, MC, V.

Lodging

Best Western River Terrace. The city's well-known boardwalk is 2 mi from this chain hotel that has spacious grounds and an excellent view of the river. Some in-room hot tubs. Cable TV. Indoor pool. Hot tub. Exercise equipment. Business services. | 847 S. Main St. (M–27) | 231/627–5688 or 800/780–7234 | fax 231/627–2472 | www.bestwesternmichigan.com | 53 rooms | $43–$127 | AE, D, DC, MC, V.

Birch Haus Motel. This family-owned motor lodge has bargain prices. The one-story building is nine blocks north of downtown on U.S. 23. Picnic area, complimentary Continental breakfast. Some refrigerators. Cable TV. Pets allowed. | 1301 Mackinaw Ave. | 231/627–5862 | birchhaus@webtv.net | www.cheboygan.com/lodging/birchhaus/index.phtml | 13 rooms | $40–$60 | AE, D, MC, V.

Days Inn. The Cheboygan County Historical Museum and Cheboygan Opera House are within 1 mi of this mid-downtown chain hotel. Cheboygan State Park is 5 mi away. Complimentary Continental breakfast. Refrigerators. Cable TV. Dock. Airport shuttle. Some pets allowed. | 889 S. Main St. (M–27) | 231/627–3126 or 800/388–7829 | fax 231/627–2889 | www.daysinn.com | 42 rooms | $48–$120 | AE, D, DC, MC, V.

Gables Bed & Breakfast. A few blocks from the heart of Cheboygan is this gracious Victorian mansion with a wraparound porch, period furnishings, and a Queen Anne gazebo that overlooks the garden. Dinner and dessert are available. Complimentary breakfast. Outdoor hot tub. No smoking. | 314 S. Main St. | 231/627–5079 | gables@northlink.net | www.michweb.com/gablesbb | 6 rooms | $75–$125 | AE, D, DC, MC, V.

CHESANING

(Nearby towns also listed: Flint, Frankenmuth, Owosso, Saginaw)

Founded on the banks of the Shiawassee River in 1839, this quiet town of 2,567 residents was originally called Northhampton. When the settlement was incorporated in 1853, the name was changed to Chesaning, which in the language of native Chippewa people meant "Big Rock."

Today, Chesaning is known primarily for its famous showboat, the Shiawassee Queen, which is docked on the river year-round. In summer, the boat serves as the centerpiece for Showboat Week, a local celebration featuring live performances by some surprisingly big-name recording artists. To the north of the showboat is a series of waterfalls.

Chesaning is also home to scores of lovingly preserved Victorian-era homes and buildings—particularly on the west side of town along Broad St., a picturesque boulevard—and to a number of top-notch antiques and specialty stores. (*Note:* Area codes in this vicinity are scheduled to change to 989 beginning April 7, 2001.)

Information: **Chesaning Chamber of Commerce** | Box 83, Chesaning 48616 | 517/845–3055 or 800/255–3055 | chescofc@centurytel.net | chesaningchamber.org.

Attractions

Shiawassee Queen Showboat. Docked year-round on the Shiawassee River in downtown Chesaning, this boat serves as a performance stage during Showboat Week in July. Tours and history of the boat are available. | Showboat Park | 800/255–3055 | chesaningchamber.org | Varies.

ON THE CALENDAR

JUNE: *Summer Art Fair.* Scores of artists representing every style and discipline, from primitive to postmodern, display their wares along Chesaning's historic boulevard. | 517/845–3055 or 800/255–3055 | chesaningchamber.org.

JULY: *Showboat Week.* Special events and activities are planned throughout this annual celebration, but the focus is on music—top-shelf performers from across the nation come do their thing at the Chesaning Showboat on the river. Past luminaries have included Frankie Valli and the Four Seasons, Lee Greenwood, and Kenny Rogers. Open-air seating for 7,000 is available on the river. | 517/845–3055 or 800/255–3055 | chesaningchamber.org.

NOV.: *Candlelight Walk.* Chesaning's historic district is decorated and lit for the holidays with more than 18,000 candles during this three-day event over Thanksgiving weekend. On Christmas Tree Lane (Saginaw St.), you can buy a raffle ticket for one of the festively decorated trees. A parade, arts and crafts shows, special displays at the museum, and a home tour are a few of the other events. | 517/845–3055 or 800/255–3055 | chesaningchamber.org.

Dining

Brass Bell. American. Framed art adorns the clean white walls here, contrasting nicely with the dark oak trim. Comfy (if somewhat incongruous) padded vinyl chairs pull up to large wooden tables that encourage dinner-chat. The menu here features homemade soups, hearty sandwiches, and pizza, and there are a number of Southwestern-inspired options, including the famous wet burrito—a big flour tortilla full of seasoned ground beef and beans, doused with the kitchen's special burrito sauce, cheese, tomatoes, and sour cream. | 12950 W. Brady Rd. | 517/845–9908 | $5–$8 | AE, D, MC, V.

Chesaning Heritage House. Continental. Several separate dining areas and a lounge are spread throughout this 1908 Southern-style mansion on Chesaning's historic Broad St.

The high, pillared entryway leads into the house's lofty interior, which is awash in soft golden light. Large windows on both stories look out onto the surrounding neighborhood's grand old homes and wooded lots. Menu standouts include stuffed pork tenderloin, fresh cod and whitefish from Lake Huron, and an ever-changing roster of homemade desserts. The basement-level Rathskeller lounge offers pizza and sandwiches. Entertainment on weekends. | 605 W. Broad St. | 517/845–7700 | $12–$25 | AE, D, MC, V.

Showboat Restaurant. Continental. High tin ceilings, brass chandeliers, and a broad, carpeted staircase leading to the mezzanine level characterize this downtown restaurant. A Chesaning fixture since 1965, the Showboat serves generous portions of fresh seafood and prime cuts of beef. Consider trying the mesquite-grilled salmon or the Icelandic cod filet. If you prefer your meat on the hoof, there's prime rib and filet mignon. | 244 W. Broad St. | 517/845–2830 | $12–$25 | AE, D, DC, MC, V.

Lodging

Bonnymill Inn. The building that now houses this bed and breakfast used to be a farmers' grain elevator—but don't expect to wake up with wheat-chaff in your pajamas. Marred maple hardwood is all that remains of the building's original trappings. Guest rooms are furnished with antiques, and all the beds and window-dressings are handmade. Some rooms have private balconies, others fireplaces and whirlpool tubs. Complimentary breakfast. Cable TV. Massage. | 710 Broad St. | 517/845–7780 | fax 517/845–5165 | www.bonnymillinn.com | 29 rooms | $65–$145 | AE, D, MC, V.

Victorian Gardens. In the heart of Chesaning's historic district, this Queen Anne-style home is surrounded by shade trees and dozens of examples of turn-of-the-century architecture and ornament. Both guest rooms in this bed and breakfast are decorated with period antiques. The Heritage House restaurant is right across the street. Complimentary breakfast. TV in common area. No room phones. | 504 W. Broad St. | 517/845–2511 or 888/835–2446 | victoriangardens@bigfoot.com | www.bigfoot.com/~victoriangardens | 2 | $75 | No credit cards.

CLARE

MAP 9, D5

(Nearby towns also listed: Big Rapids, Houghton Lake, Midland, Mt. Pleasant)

Settled by Irish immigrants in the mid-1800s, this central Michigan town has a well-attended Irish festival each spring and a vintage downtown hotel known as a mid-Michigan meeting spot. (*Note:* Area codes in this vicinity are scheduled to change to 989 beginning April 7, 2001.)

Information: Clare Chamber of Commerce | 429 McEwan St., Clare 48617 | 517/386–2442 | www.claremichigan.com.

Attractions

Chalet Cross-Country. Approximately 10 mi of groomed, graded cross-country ski trails attract enthusiasts from across mid-Michigan. | 5931 Clare Ave. | 517/386–9697 | Dec.–Mar.

Downtown shopping district. Some 20 specialty shops line the three central blocks of McEwan Street, selling everything from country crafts to Irish gifts. | McEwan St. | 517/386–2442 | Free | Daily.

Silver Ridge Resort. The longest of the nine runs at this popular ski area is 2500 ft; the vertical drop, 225 ft. There's also a snowboard park and more than a mile of cross-country ski trails. Night skiing is available. The resort's casual restaurant is open year-round. | 1001 Mott Mtn. Rd., Farwell | 517/588–7220 | fax 517/588–7224 | $12 weekdays, $18 weekends | Nov.–Mar.

Snow Snake Golf and Ski Area. Night skiing and more than 3 mi of cross-country ski trails are two of the attractions at this ski facility on 180 acres. The longest run is ½ mi, the vertical drop 210 ft. There's also a tubing park. In summer you can golf an 18-hole course. The area's just off U.S. 27 between Harrison and Clare. | 3407 Mannsiding Rd., Harrison | 517/539–6583 | fax 517/539–2246 | snowsnake@glccomputer.com | www.snowsnake.net | $12–$27, lift tickets; $23–$31, golf | Year-round.

Wilson State Park. This 35-acre park with 160 campsites on the shores of Budd Lake offers fishing (largemouth bass, bluegill, perch), swimming, and picnicking, volleyball, basketball, and playground facilities. The park is 20 mi south of Houghton Lake off U.S. 27, 1 mi north of Harrison. | 517/539–3021 | www.dnr.state.mi.us/www/parks/index.htm | $4 per car, per day | Daily dawn to dusk.

ON THE CALENDAR

MAR.: *Irish Festival.* Irish eyes (and everyone else's, too) are smiling during this popular annual event, a salute to the area's Emerald Isle heritage. Music, food, a 5K run, even a leprechaun contest attract revelers. | 517/386–2442 | www.claremichigan.com/irish.

MAY AND SEPT.: *Amish Arts and Crafts, Flea Market, and Quilt Auction.* Held twice yearly at a farm off U.S. 10, this festival brings together over 500 Amish and "English" (non-Amish) crafts vendors. The highlight is Saturday's Amish quilt auction at 9 AM. A cooking tent has traditional Amish noodles and pies, but also serves hamburgers and hot dogs. | Yoder Amish Farm, Leaton Rd. | 517/386–2442 | Free.

JULY: *Summerfest.* Karaoke, a beauty pageant, fishing contests, lawnmower races, and a rooster pull are all part of the the the fun at this summer event. | 517/386–2442 | www.claremichigan.com/summerfest.

JULY–AUG.: *Clare County Fair.* Classic county fair, with agricultural and livestock exhibits, carnival rides, horse races, concerts (previous bands included the Beach Boys, Faith Hill, Kenny Rogers), and fun and games for all ages. | 517/539–9011.

NOV.: *Christmas All Town/Santa Parade.* A Santa parade down Main Street kicks off the beginning of the Christmas season on the Saturday after Thanksgiving. Horse-drawn carriage rides, carolers, and shopping specials are also part of the festivities. | 888/282–5273.

Dining

Doherty Hotel. Continental. The restaurant in the Doherty Hotel is a local meeting spot that has changed little since it opened. Hand-painted walls depict nature scenes and a traditional menu includes lobster, crab legs, and baked, broiled, or pan-fried whitefish. Salad bar. Entertainment Mon., Fri., and Sat. Kids' menu. | 604 N. McEwan St. | 517/386–3441 | www.dohertyhotel.com | $9.95–$32 | AE, D, DC, MC, V.

Ruckle's Pier. American. This cozy local hangout with nautical decorations serves pizzas, burgers, and sandwiches. The daily specials include barbecued ribs on Monday night and Mexican fare on Wednesdays. | 405 N. McEwan St. | 517/386–9531 | $4–$11 | AE, D, DC, MC, V.

Whitehouse Restaurant. American. Locals line up outside this 24-hour landmark for fried-chicken dinners and killer omelettes that come in 18 varieties. You should be able to grab one of the diner's six booths if you avoid peak meal hours. | 613 McEwan St. | 517/386–9551 | $5–$7 | D, MC, V.

Lodging

Crossroads Motel. A white picket fence surrounds this quaint blue motor lodge. It's four blocks south of downtown on Business Route U.S. 27. Picnic area. Refrigerators. Cable TV. Business services. Pets allowed. | 407 S. McEwan St. | 517/386–2422 or 800/386–3950 | fax 517/386–5387 | 9 rooms | $37–$55 | AE, D, DC, MV, V.

Doherty Hotel. Antiques decorate this gracious, old-fashioned downtown hotel. It houses a popular full-service dining room with hand-painted murals. Restaurant, bar (with entertainment), complimentary breakfast. Indoor pool. Hot tub. Business services, airport shuttle. Some pets allowed. | 604 McEwan St. (U.S. 27 Bus.) | 517/386–3441 or 800/525–4115 | fax 517/386–4231 | www.dohertyhotel.com | 158 rooms, 5 suites | $60–$136; $124–$136 suites | AE, D, DC, MC, V.

Holiday Inn Express. The Soaring Eagle casino is 12 mi away and there are several golf courses within a 6 mi radius of this motel. Complimentary Continental breakfast. In-room data ports, some refrigerators. Cable TV. Indoor pool. Business services. | 10318 S. Clare Ave. | 517/386–1111 or 800/465–4329 | fax 517/386–2211 | www.hiexpress.com | 96 rooms | $69–$125 | AE, D, DC, MC, V.

COLDWATER

MAP 9, D8

(Nearby towns also listed: Battle Creek, Jackson, Marshall, Three Rivers)

Boaters flock to Coldwater Lake and the historic Tibbits Opera House, which was built in 1882 by Coldwater mayor and businessman Barton S. Tibbits, the two main attractions in this southern Michigan town. The town was once known as a major stop on the Chicago Turnpike, the primary east–west transportation route between Chicago and Detroit in the 19th century. By the 1880s it had become better known as a trading and supply center.

Information: Branch County Chamber of Commerce | 20 Division St., Coldwater 49036 | 517/278–5985 or 800/968–9333 | www.branch-county.com.

Attractions

Tibbits Opera House. Coldwater, on the main road between Chicago and Detroit, saw many 19th- and early 20th-century performers and theater companies come to town. The renovated opera house, which dates from 1882, is known for its acoustics. Today, it hosts a professional summer stock series and kids' programs from June through August, as well as community and youth programs year-round. | 14 S. Hanchett St. | 517/278–6029 | www.discover-michigan.com | Free | Weekdays 9–5, tours by appointment.

Washington Street Mercantile. This shop claims to be the largest Indian store in three states, selling a generous selection of moccasins, pottery, and silver jewelry. Don't look for crafts from the local Pottawattamie tribe, though; most of the inventory here is from the Southwest. | 226 E. Washington St. | 517/278–5100 or 888/520–6923 | fax 517/279–7021 | www.coldwaterindianstore.com | Free | Mon.–Sat. 10–6, Sun. 11:30–5.

Wing House Museum. Collections of glassware, oil paintings, and period furniture fill this Second Empire house dating from 1875. | 27 S. Jefferson St. | 517/278–2871 | $3 | Wed.–Sun. 1–5, or by appointment.

ON THE CALENDAR

FEB.: *Quincy Chain of Lakes Tip-Up Festival.* Anglers from across the county head to Quincy for this popular fishing festival, featuring contests, a Polar Bear swim, ice races, and wintry crafts. | 517/639–5493.

JUNE–AUG.: *Tibbits Professional Summer Theatre Series.* This summer stock theater group puts on a wide spectrum of performances at the Tibbits Opera House. | 517/278–6029.

JULY: *Bronson Polish Festival Days.* Food, music, dancing, and entertainment celebrate the heritage of neighboring Bronson's large Polish population. | 517/369–7334.

AUG.: *Branch County 4-H Fair.* Local 4-H students compete for ribbons and honors in a variety of agricultural events. Other highlights include horse and tractor pulling and a parade through downtown. | 517/279–8411.

SEPT.: *Applefest & Craft Show.* Apples fresh off the tree, pressed cider, and apple dumplings—as well as local crafts, wooden toys, and Halloween and Christmas decorations—are available at this festival's 120 booths. Live music, food, and games for kids make this a fun downtown event on the third Saturday of the month. | Rte. 12 and I-69 | 517/279-9375 | www.branch-county.com | Free.

Dining

Claremont House. American. In a restored train depot dating from 1888, Claremont House caters to families and those seeking a casual dining spot. Entrées range from salads to sandwiches to pastas. Favorites include prime rib, steaks, and fresh fish dishes. Salad bar. Kids' menu. | 32 Railroad St. | 517/278-5257 | Closed Sun. and Mon. | $16–$26 | AE, D, DC, MC, V.

Irma's Restaurant. American. This popular eatery is a Coldwater institution, an authentic diner with fountain drinks, burgers, fries—the whole nine yards. | 14 W. Chicago St. | 517/279-9965 | Breakfast also available | $3–$8 | No credit cards.

Lodging

Benedict Doll B&B. The former home of brewmaster Benedict Doll, this beautifully restored Queen Anne Victorian sits on nine acres of meadow, a surprising pocket of nature 1 mi from downtown. Antiques complement the theme of each guest room, and you can relax in one of the two parlors, the front porch, or the back deck. The full breakfast includes eggs Benedict Doll, the inn's signature dish. Complimentary breakfast. No room phones, TV in common area. No kids under 18. No smoking. | 665 W. Chicago St. | 517/279-2821 | benedictdoll@yahoo.com | www.benedictdoll.com | 4 rooms (3 with shared bath) | $85–$95 | D, MC, V.

Chicago Pike Inn. An elegant bed-and-breakfast is furnished with antiques. You can indulge a romantic mood with a carriage ride. Picnic area, complimentary breakfast. No air-conditioning in some rooms. Cable TV. Bicycles. No kids under 12. | 215 E Chicago St. | 517/279-8744 | fax 517/278-8597 | 8 rooms | $100–$195 | AE, MC, V.

Coldwater Super 8. There are a couple of restaurants within ½ mi of this motel. The Tibbits Opera House is four blocks away and the Wing House Museum is 3 blocks away. Some refrigerators. Hot tub. | 600 Orleans Blvd. | 517/278-8833 or 800/800-8000 | fax 517/278-2347 | www.super8motels.com | 58 rooms | $39–$69 | AE, D, DC, MC, V.

Econo Lodge. This budget red-and-white motor lodge is 3 mi west of downtown in a peaceful country location. Complimentary Continental breakfast. In-room data ports, some kitchenettes, some refrigerators. Cable TV. Business services. Pets allowed. | 884 W. Chicago Rd. | 517/278-4501 or 800/553-2666 | fax 517/278-2099 | www.econolodge.com | 46 rooms | $45–$55 | AE, D, DC, MC, V.

HideOut Bed & Breakfast. The lawn of this small inn slopes down to Craig Lake. You're welcome to swim, fish, or just admire the view. Complimentary breakfast. Lake. Outdoor hot tub. No pets. No smoking. | 260 Stevens Shores Dr. | 517/278-4210 | info@laketolake.com | www.laketolake.com/hideout | 3 rooms with shared bath | $70–$85 | MC, V.

Holiday Inn Express. This dependable chain hotel is a few miles east of downtown, off I-69, and within blocks of two restaurants. Complimentary Continental breakfast, room service. In-room data ports, some minibars, some in-room hot tubs. Cable TV. Indoor pool. Hot tub. Exercise equipment. Video games. Laundry facilities. Business services. | 630 E. Chicago St. | 517/279-0900 | fax 517/278-3775 | hiedwtr@cbpu.com | www.basshotels.com/holiday-inn | 80 rooms, 5 suites | $80–$160 | AE, D, DC, MC, V.

Quality Inn Convention Center. This New Orleans-themed hotel has an indoor courtyard and a large convention center next door. Restaurant, bar (with entertainment), complimentary breakfast, room service. Some kitchenettes. Cable TV. Indoor pool. Hot tub. Video games. Business services. Some pets allowed. | 1000 Orleans Blvd. | 517/278-2017 or 800/228-5151 | fax 517/279-7214 | www.qualityinncoldwater.com | 123 rooms | $58–$125 | AE, D, DC, MC, V.

COOPERSVILLE

(Nearby towns also listed: Grand Haven, Grand Rapids, Muskegon)

Nineteenth-century New York attorney Benjamin F. Cooper guaranteed himself Michigan immortality when he donated investment land for a new railroad station, which became Coopersville. Though the intercity railway died with the age of the interstate, town residents resurrected the line as a local tourist attraction running theme train rides. Ironically, the town also traces its rebirth to I–96, a nearby interstate highway.

Information: **Coopersville Chamber of Commerce** | 289 Danforth St., Coopersville 49404 | 616/997–9731 | www.coopersville.com.

Attractions

Coopersville Area Historical Society Museum. You can see an actual train car, a turn-of-the-century sawmill, plus other artifacts and exhibits here. The building, a former interurban train depot, is a Michigan historical site. | 363 Main St. | 616/837–6978 | www.coopersville.com/museum.html | $1 donation | Closed Mon. and Wed.–Fri.; Jan.–July, closed Sun.

The Coopersville & Marne Railway. This old-fashioned passenger train slowly rolls through the countryside on the same tracks it used 100 years ago. Theme rides and tie-ins with local festivals are regular events. Train departs from downtown Coopersville. | Main and Eastmanville Sts. | 616/837–7000 | www.coopersvilleandmarne.org.

Dining

Champp's. American. There's a sports theme at this restaurant, the only bar and grill in Coopersville. The menu ranges from sandwiches, soups, and salads to the locally famed Champp's burger. | 287 Main St. | 616/837–9227 | Closed Sun. | $2–$7 | MC, V.

Country Cafe. American. The meatloaf plate is a local favorite at this small-town diner in the heart of Coopersville. | 259 Main St. | 616/997–6572 | Brunch only on Sun. | $4–$6 | No credit cards.

Lodging

AmeriHost. This business-oriented chain hotel, built in 1995, is 2 mi west of downtown. Suites have whirlpools. Complimentary Continental breakfast. Some in-room hot tubs. Indoor pool. Hot tub, sauna. Exercise equipment. Business services. | 1040 O'Malley | 616/837–8100 or 800/434–5800 | fax 616/837–5179 | info@amerihostinn.com | www.amerihostinn.com | 59, 2 suites | $59–$199 | AE, D, V, DC, MC.

COPPER HARBOR

(Nearby towns also listed: Calumet, Hancock, Houghton)

Nestled at the top of the Keweenaw Peninsula, Copper Harbor is the U.P.'s northernmost village and the site of one of the Midwest's oldest frontier posts. Draws include fishing, mine tours, and ferry service to rugged Isle Royale. (*Note:* Area codes in this vicinity are scheduled to change to 989 beginning April 7, 2001.)

Information: **Keweenaw Peninsula Chamber of Commerce** | 1197 Calumet Ave., Calumet 49913 | 906/337–4579 or 800/338–7982 | www.keweenaw.org.

Attractions

Brockway Mountain Drive. The 9½ mi of road make up the highest above-sea-level drive between the Rockies and the Alleghenies. The route takes you through some of the Upper Peninsula's most beautiful country; it is especially popular in autumn. Lookouts provide great views of Lake Superior and nearby forests. | M–26 between Eagle Harbor and Copper Harbor | 906/774–5480 | Free | Daily.

Delaware Copper Mine Tour. Guided tours take you 110 ft down into a mid-1800s copper mine, where you can still see veins of copper. Warm clothing is recommended. There are also antique engine and indoor and outdoor train displays. | U.S. 41 | 906/289–4688 | $8 | Mid-May–mid-Oct., daily 10–5.

Ferry service to Isle Royale National Park. Isle Royale, the largest island in Lake Superior and one of the few island national parks, is a wilderness with more than 165 mi of trails. Transportation to Isle Royale is by boat or seaplane.

Ferry operators include the *Isle Royale Queen III* (Isle Royale Ferry Dock/Waterfront Landing | 906/289–4437 | $40 one-way, $80 round-trip | mid-May–Sept.), the park-owned *Ranger III* (Lakeshore Drive next to Dee Stadium, one block from downtown | 906/482–0984 | $47 one-way, $94 round-trip | mid-May–mid-Sept.), which departs from Houghton, and the *Wenonah* (National Monument Dock in Grand Portage | 715/392–2100 | www.nps.gov/isro | $33 one-way, $66 round-trip | June–Oct.), which leaves from Grand Portage, Minnesota, mid-May–Oct. Trips take 4–6 hrs one way.

Fort Wilkins State Park. This army post was built to protect copper miners from the Indians. It was abandoned in 1870 after a peaceful history. Today you can tour refurbished officers' quarters and other buildings and enjoy demonstrations of old army ways by costumed interpreters. The park also has fishing, boating, cross-country ski trails, and a museum. | U.S. 41 E | 906/289–4215 | www.dnr.state.mi.us | $4 per car, per day | Mid-May–mid-Oct., daily dawn to dusk.

ON THE CALENDAR

JAN.: *Brockway Mountain Challenge.* Lively 15K cross-country ski race takes challengers up and over Brockway Mountain. | Brockway Mountain | 906/337–4579.

Dining

Mariner North. American. Casual and more formal seating areas are in this downtown restaurant and lounge, with a maple log interior. It's known for freshwater fish, as well as fish sandwiches and hamburgers. Kids menu. | 244 Gratiot St. | 906/289–4637 | Closed Nov. | $9–$20 | AE, D, DC, MC, V.

Paradise Bar and Grill. American. An early 1900s bar, juke box, and wooden stove give this casual spot 30 mi from Copper Harbor a rustic feel. Try the barbecue ribs or a steak-and-cheese sandwich. | 122 Oneco Rd., Calumet | 906/337–0082 | $9–$16 | MC, V.

Tamarack Inn. Continental. Local favorites at this restaurant on Lake Superior are prime rib, whitefish, trout, and roasted chicken. Salad bar. Kids' menu. | 512 Gratiot St. | 906/289–4522 | Early June–mid-Oct. | $8–$16 | MC, V.

Lodging

Bella Vista Motel. This motel on Lake Superior has its own dock on the harbor and is next to the Isle Royale ferry dock. Canoes and rowboats are available. Some rooms overlook Copper Harbor. Picnic area. No air-conditioning, some kitchenettes. Cable TV. Dock, boating. | 160 6th St. | 906/289–4213 | www.bellavistamotel.com | 22 rooms, 8 cottages | $56, $40–$65 cottages | Closed mid-Oct.–mid-May | D, MC, V.

Keweenaw Mountain Lodge. Built by the Works Progress Administration (W.P.A.) in the 1930s, this rustic lodge on a gorgeous U.P. site has Up North-style rooms and cottages, some with fireplaces. It's on the Keweenaw Peninsula near Lake Superior. Restaurant, bar. No air-conditioning. Cable TV. 9-hole golf course, tennis. | U.S. 41 | 906/289–4403 | fax 906/289–4346 | www.keweenawmountainlodge.com | 8 rooms, 34 cottages | $70–$80, $75–$95 cottages | Closed mid-Oct.–mid-May | MC, V.

Minnetonka Resort. Accommodations are available in rustic cottages or in smaller, motel-style rooms. The Astor House Museum, which displays antique dolls, toys, and Native American artifacts, is on the grounds. Picnic area. No air-conditioning, some kitchenettes. Cable TV. Saunas. Some pets allowed. | 560 Gratiot St. | 904/672–1887 or 800/433–2770 | www.exploringthenorth.com | 26 rooms in 2 buildings, 12 cottages | $50–$96, $50–$95 cottages | Closed Nov.–Apr. | D, MC, V.

Norland Motel. This inn near the entrance to Fort Wilkins State Park sits on Lake Fanny Hope in a quiet, wooded area. Picnic area. No air-conditioning, some kitchenettes, refrigerators. Cable TV. | U.S. 41 | 906/289–4815 | 9 rooms | $40–$48 | Closed mid-Oct.–mid-May | No credit cards.

DEARBORN

MAP 9, F7

(Nearby towns also listed: Ann Arbor, Birmingham, Bloomfield Hills, Detroit, Monroe, Plymouth, Royal Oak, Ypsilanti)

Dearborn was once an independent village, but its rural history is overshadowed by that of one of its 19th-century sons. Automaker Henry Ford was born here in 1863, and he later chose the western Detroit suburb as the headquarters for his burgeoning Ford Motor Company. Today the city is known for its automotive-related industries and as the site of the Henry Ford Museum and Greenfield Village, one of the state's most popular tourist attractions.

Information: Dearborn Chamber of Commerce | 15544 Michigan Ave., Dearborn 48126 | 313/584–6100 | www.dearbornchamber.org.

Attractions

Henry Ford Estate–Fair Lane. Now part of the Dearborn campus of the University of Michigan, this 1913 mansion with its adjacent powerhouse was home to Henry Ford. In the combination Prairie and Scottish baronial-style house designed by William Van Tine, Ford entertained such luminaries as Charles Lindbergh, the Duke of Windsor, and president Herbert Hoover. Surprisingly modest, the 72-acre estate includes a basement bowling alley and a powerhouse where Ford and friend Thomas Edison experimented with heat, power, and light. | 4901 Evergreen Rd. | 313/593–5590 | www.umd.umich.edu/fairlane | $8 | Apr.–Dec., tours Mon.–Sat. 10–3, Sun. 1–4:30; Jan.–Mar., tours weekdays at 1, Sun. 1–4:30.

Henry Ford Museum and Greenfield Village. Once derisively called "Hank's attic," this huge museum and village is today one of the state's greatest tourist attractions and a repository of all things both great and small. Spread out over 93 acres not far from the Ford Motor Company headquarters are collections begun by Henry Ford that trace three centuries of American life. | 20900 Oakwood Blvd. | 313/271–1620 or 800/835–5237 | www.hfmgv.org | $23 for both for two days | Daily 9–5.

Greenfield Village. A favorite of area schoolchildren and adults alike, the village is a charming collection of salvaged historic buildings that trace America's evolution from a rural to an industrial society, including an 1850s stagecoach stop, the courthouse where Abraham Lincoln practiced law, a general store, a one-room schoolhouse, and the white clapboard house where Henry Ford was born. Inside the structures, workers in period dress demonstrate everything from blacksmithing to early American cooking. A steam engine makes the rounds every 20 minutes; you can also ride a vintage carousel and a Southern-style paddleboat. | 20900 Oakwood Blvd. | 313/271–1620 | www.hfmgv.org | $12.50 | Daily 9–5; interiors mid-Mar.–Dec., daily 9–5.

Henry Ford Museum. A replica of Independence Hall in Philadelphia, the museum houses a wide range of American artifacts, including George Washington's folding camp bed and the rocking chair that Lincoln was sitting in when he was shot. There are also outstanding collections of vintage planes, trains, and automobiles. "The Automobile in American Life" traces the impact of the car on 20th-century America; "Made in America" explores the history of U.S. industry. | 20900 Oakwood Blvd. | 313/271–1620 | www.hfmgv.org | $12.50 | Daily 9–5.

ON THE CALENDAR

JULY: *Colonial Life Festival.* This fun-filled summer festival at the Henry Ford Museum's Greenfield Village takes you back in time through displays of military music, musketry, and more. | 20900 Oakwood Blvd. | $12.50 | 313/271–1620 | www.hfmgv.org.

SEPT.: *Old Car Festival.* With hundreds of vintage automobiles in its permanent collection, the Henry Ford Museum is a fitting place for this celebration of the "horseless carriage." Car aficionados come from across the country for the chance to see rare models. | 20900 Oakwood Blvd. | $12.50 | 313/271–1620 | www.hfmgv.org.

OCT.: *Fall Harvest Days.* The autumn harvest is the focus of this family festival, which includes farming displays, fall foods, and more on the grounds of Greenfield Village. | 20900 Oakwood Blvd. | $12.50 | 313/271–1620 | www.hfmgv.org.

Dining

Big Fish. Seafood. Chuck Muer's stylish fish emporium is a play on words, referring to both the menu and the automobile executives who frequent it. In addition to the plentiful fresh fish, excellent pastas, lamb, and steaks are served in surroundings decorated with—what else—big fish. Try the signature Charley's Chowder and the soft, steaming rolls. French doors lead to a brick patio with open-air dining. Kids' menu. | 700 Town Center Dr. | 313/336–6350 | $12.25–$30 | AE, D, MC, V.

The Grill. Contemporary. Seasonal menus include dishes such as seared foie gras with mango and ginger tea, Muscovy duck breast with Armagnac, and Dover sole with crawfish and basil noodles. The Grill is well known for house-made desserts, including orange-chocolate mousse with kumquat compote or fresh fig tart. Buffet. Pianist, harpist. Sun. brunch. | Ritz-Carlton Hotel, 300 Town Center Dr. | 313/441–2100 | $28–$38 | AE, D, DC, MC, V.

© Corbis

10 MOST UNUSUAL THINGS IN DEARBORN'S HENRY FORD MUSEUM

1. The Rococo Revival rocking chair that President Abraham Lincoln was sitting in the night he was shot.
2. Edison's last breath, a test tube that was on the inventor's bedside table when he died and sealed after his death.
3. The 1961 Lincoln Continental limousine that President Kennedy was riding in when he was assassinated.
4. Charles A. Lindbergh's camper and motorcycle.
5. A letter from Clyde Barrow, the infamous Depression-era bank robber, to Henry Ford about his preference for Fords.
6. George Washington's folding camp bed.
7. A full-size Allegheny locomotive that's 125 ft long and weighs more than 600 tons.
8. The Oscar Mayer Wienermobile, built in 1952.
9. Edgar Allan Poe's writing desk.
10. Original McDonald's "Golden Arches" and Holiday Inn signs.

Kiernan's Steak House. Continental. The interior includes red fringed lamps, leather booths, and a clubby barroom. Steaks are the specialty, but the 16-oz lobster tails are equally famous. The restaurant is known for steak, seafood, and veal. Kids' menu. | 21931 Michigan Ave. | 313/565–4260 | No lunch weekends | $12–$21 | AE, MC, V.

La Shish. Middle Eastern. La Shish, one of Dearborn's original Middle Eastern restaurants, serves up fresh fatoush salad, *shish tawook* sandwiches (grilled chicken slathered in a tangy garlic sauce) and plenty of classic hummus and tabbouleh. The dining rooms are adorned with scenes of Lebanon, family photographs, and Middle Eastern art. The original restaurant is off I–94; other branches are in downtown Dearborn, Warren, and Farmington Hills. Entertainment. Kids' menu. | 12918 Michigan Ave. | 313/584–4477 | www.lashish.com | $8–$14 | AE, MC, V.

Lodging

Best Western Greenfield Inn. This pink, Victorian-style hotel is on I–94 and 2 mi from Greenfield Village and the Henry Ford Museum. The lobby displays the world's largest collection of old automobile prints; spacious rooms have Early American or Victorian furnishings. Restaurant, bar, room service. In-room data ports, refrigerators, some in-room hot tubs. Cable TV, in-room VCRs (and movies). Indoor pool. Hot tub. Exercise equipment. Laundry facilities. Business services, airport shuttle. | 3000 Enterprise Dr., Allen Park | 313/271–1600 or 800/780–7234 | fax 313/271–1600, ext. 7189 | www.bestwesternmichigan.com | 209 rooms | $99–$109 | AE, D, DC, MC, V.

Courtyard by Marriott. Landscaped grounds and bright, contemporary rooms await you at this hotel 3 mi from the Fairlane shopping mall and 5 mi from the Henry Ford Museum. Bar. In-room data ports, some refrigerators. Cable TV. Indoor pool. Hot tub. Exercise equipment. Laundry facilities. Business services. | 5200 Mercury Dr. | 313/271–1400 or 800/321–2211 | fax 313/271–1184 | www.courtyard.com | 147 rooms | $74–$109 | AE, D, DC, MC, V.

Dearborn Bed and Breakfast. This classic American four-square brick residence dating from the 1920s has been transformed into the city's only B & B. Rooms are furnished with Victorian renaissance period antiques, down comforters, lace, and linen. It's downtown, 3 blocks from a couple of restaurants and 1 mi from the Henry Ford Museum. Cable TV. Business services. | 22331 Morley Ave. | 313/563–2200 | fax 313/277–2962 | 4 rooms | $95–$165 | AE, D, MC, V.

Dearborn Inn, a Marriott Hotel. Henry Ford built this four-story Georgian-architecture inn in 1931 for business associates and their guests. The inn, two lodges, and five houses reproduced from homes of famous Americans sit on 23 acres of landscaped grounds and gardens in the heart of Ford Motor Co.'s business campus, less than 1 mi from Greenfield Village and the Dearborn Historical Museum. The Fairlane shopping center is 2 mi to the north. Restaurant, bar. In-room data ports, some refrigerators. Cable TV. Pool, wading pool. Tennis. Exercise equipment. Business services. | 20301 Oakwood Blvd. | 313/271–2700 or 800/228–9290 | fax 313/271–7464 | www.marriott.com | 222 rooms, 31 suites | $129–$179, $195–$210 suites | AE, D, DC, MC, V.

Hampton Inn. A family favorite is across the street from Fairlane mall, 1 mi from Henry Ford Museum and Greenfield Village, and 13 mi from Detroit sports venues. Complimentary Continental breakfast. In-room data ports, refrigerators. Cable TV. Indoor pool. Laundry facilities. Business services. | 20061 Michigan Ave. | 313/436–9600 | fax 313/436–8345 | www.hamptoninn.com/hi/dearborn | 119 rooms | $99 | AE, D, DC, MC, V.

Hyatt Regency. This 16-story hotel is the focal point of the Fairlane Town Center business, shopping, and entertainment complex near Ford Motor Co.'s world headquarters, Henry Ford Museum, and Greenfield Village. It's 9 mi from Detroit Metro Airport and 3.5 mi from the Amtrak train station. Restaurants, bars. In-room data ports, cable TV. Indoor pool. Hot tub. Exercise equipment. Business services. | 18600 Michigan Ave. | 313/593–1234 | fax 313/593–3366 | www.hyatthotels.com | 772 rooms | $119–$224 | AE, D, DC, MC, V.

Quality Inn Fairlane. Popular with families and business travelers, this hotel is 1 mi from Henry Ford Museum and Greenfield Village. Complimentary Continental breakfast. In-room data ports, refrigerators. Cable TV. Pool. Business services. | 21430 Michigan Ave. | 313/565–0800 | fax 313/565–2813 | www.choicehotels.com | 98 rooms | $75–$119 | AE, D, DC, MC, V.

Red Roof Inn. Ford Motor Co. world headquarters, Greenfield Village, Henry Ford Museum, and Fairlane Mall are within 3-½ mi of this hotel that's 15 mi from Detroit sports venues and eateries. Complimentary Continental breakfast. Cable TV. Business services. Some pets allowed. | 24130 Michigan Ave. | 313/278–9732 or 800/733–7663 | fax 313/278–9741 | www.redroof.com | 111 rooms | $80 | AE, D, DC, MC, V.

★ **Ritz-Carlton, Dearborn.** Old-world elegance describes this 11-story hotel, 3 mi from Fairlane Town Center and the Henry Ford Museum and 12 mi from Detroit sports and entertainment venues. Art and antiques from the 18th and 19th centuries adorn the hotel's public and private areas, which also have marble, crystal chandeliers, custom fabrics, and china. Restaurant, bar (with entertainment). In-room data ports, minibars, room service, cable TV. Indoor pool. Hot tub, massage. Exercise equipment. Business services. | 300 Town Center Dr. | 313/441–2000 or 800/241–3333 | fax 313/441–2051 | 308 rooms | $115–$245 | AE, D, DC, MC, V.

DETROIT

MAP 9, F7

(Suburbs also listed: Ann Arbor, Birmingham, Bloomfield Hills, Dearborn, Farmington/Farmington Hills, Mt. Clemens, Plymouth, Pontiac, Southfield, Troy, Warren, Ypsilanti)

Few realize that Detroit is one of the Midwest's oldest cities. Founded in 1701 as "la Ville d'Etroit"—the city at the straits—it was once a strategic Native American and French trading post. In the mid-19th century the city was likened to Paris because of its scenic parks and beautiful architecture, but soon evolved into the modern Motor City, the city that put the world on wheels.

BELGIAN BOWLING IN DETROIT

The diverse ethnic makeup of Detroit's east side—African-Americans, Poles, and Italians—is ever sweetening the melting pot. Among the first immigrants to arrive in the area were Belgians, who worked in many of Grosse Pointe's grand estates.

While many of the original families have integrated into other parts of the city, one vestige of the original Belgian community remains: the Cadieux Café. This small café and bar serves fine Belgian fare, including rabbit stew and Belgian-style mussels. It's also home to one of the country's few feather bowling alleys.

A cross between boccie and shuffleboard, feather bowling involves players rolling a three-pound wooden wheel about the size of a salad plate down a concave clay alley. The competitor who lands the wheel closest to the single pigeon feather at the court's end wins.

The league games, held on Thursday nights, are a good time to watch the action while sampling a Belgian brew or one of the house specialties.

The Cadieux Café is at 4300 Cadieux in Detroit, east of the Cadieux exit off I–94. | 313/882–8560.

© Corbis

With the growth of the auto industry, Detroit and its suburbs spread out across an ever-larger geographical area, eventually becoming one of the country's largest cities. While Motown and Motor City are the nicknames that stick in people's minds, Detroit is also among the world's busiest inland ports, a major steel producer, and a leader in the production of office equipment, paint, salt, garden seeds, and pharmaceuticals. The Detroit River is linked by 25 steamship companies to more than 40 countries; vessels ranging from ocean-going freighters to private yachts dock in the city's protected harbor.

A multicultural city known for high hopes and hard work, Detroit has world-class museums, theaters, and galleries, a well-run park system, extensive recreational and sports facilities, and lively ethnic neighborhoods full of friendly people and good restaurants. Those who visit the city for the first time are pleasantly surprised, and tend to echo the Convention and Visitors Bureau's slogan: "It's a Good Time in Detroit."

Information: **Detroit Metro Convention and Visitors Bureau** | 211 W. Fort St., Ste. 1000, Detroit 48226 | 800/DETROIT or 313/202–1800 | www.visitdetroit.com.

NEIGHBORHOODS

Detroit is mostly made up of working-class residential neighborhoods defined by ethnic background, among them Corktown (Irish), Mexicantown (Mexican), and the city of Hamtramck (Polish). The majority of them grew up during the heyday of the auto industry, when workers were attracted from around the world by Henry Ford's assembly line and $5 a day wages.

Greektown, bordered by Monroe and Lafayette streets downtown, is one of the city's liveliest areas, full of restaurants and shops in a restored area in the shadow of the city's Renaissance Center.

Another downtown neighborhood is **FoxTown,** bordered by I–75 and Adams Street, home to the Fox Theater, the Tigers' stadium, Comerica Park, and other entertainment venues and restaurants. The creation of millionaire Mike Ilitch, owner of the Detroit Red Wings, Detroit Tigers, and Little Caesar's pizza, it's a relatively new area built in what was once a posh residential neighborhood known as Brush Park.

Due north along Woodward Avenue is the **University Cultural Center,** bordered by Woodward Avenue and Palmer and Warren streets. Here are the city's cultural attractions, including the Detroit Institute of Arts, the Museum of African-American History, the Detroit Science Center, and the campus of Wayne State University. Also here are the Detroit Public Library, the Detroit Children's Museum, and the Detroit Historical Museum.

Closer to the river along East Jefferson Avenue at I–375 is **Bricktown,** a restored warehouse district housing shops, restaurants, and art galleries, including the innovative Detroit Artists Market.

A good bet when you get hungry is **Mexicantown,** on the city's southwest side near Clark Street and I–75. A small, busy district, it's home to much of Detroit's large Hispanic community and has some of the area's oldest churches.

TRANSPORTATION INFORMATION

Airport: Detroit and the surrounding area are served by **Detroit Metropolitan Airport,** in Romulus, a western suburb along I–94, about 15 mi from downtown. Major commercial airlines have regularly scheduled flights. | 734/AIRPORT | www.metroairport.com.
Airport Transportation: Coach service from downtown hotels to the airport is available by reservation for about $24 one way or $40 round trip. (800/351–5466 or 800/488–7433).
Amtrak: Amtrak serves the city from two stations, one in the New Center area (11 W. Baltimore Ave.), the other off Michigan Avenue in Dearborn. | 800/872–7245.
Bus Lines: Greyhound serves Detroit, with a terminal at 1001 Howard Street downtown. | 800/231–2222.

Driving Around Town: You can enter Detroit from north and south via I–75, from the west and northeast via I–94, and from the west via I–96 and I–696. All these inter-state highways lead to the downtown area. Coming from the east, Canadian Route 401 turns into Route 3 when it enters the U.S. via the Ambassador Bridge and into Route 3b when it crosses the border via the Detroit-Windsor Tunnel. Woodward Avenue, running north–south, and Jefferson Avenue, running east–west, are the main thoroughfares to the city center. Morning and evening commuting hours bring heavy congestion, which you may want to avoid. Many downtown streets are one-way, so a detailed map is a necessity if you plan to spend some time here. Parking in the area can be scarce; although there are many metered spots, they are often filled by commuters early in the day, which leaves latecomers to the many parking garages. Here, the cost can run between $3.50 and $10 for a day. Parking near Wayne State University, just north of downtown, is more affordable. If you are ticketed because your meter has expired, you are assessed $35. The boot is used only for cars with numerous outstanding tickets. Be attentive not to run lights downtown since there are many police in this area. Speed limits downtown are 35 mph and under.

Intra-city Transit: Once in the city, transportation options include city-owned buses, taxis, and the limited-stop People Mover, which links downtown attractions. The Detroit Department of Transportation has routes and schedules. | 888/DDOT–BUS | www.ci.detroit.mi.us/ddot.

Attractions
ART AND ARCHITECTURE

Detroit Institute of Arts. One of the country's top ten fine-arts museums in size, the DIA houses art from ancient to modern times, with notable collections of 17th- and 18th-century Dutch and Flemish paintings, African art, and one of the country's best German Expressionist collections. Its stunning Rivera Court has huge murals depicting a 1920s assembly line by Mexican artist Diego Rivera. | 5200 Woodward Ave. | 313/833–7900 | www.dia.org | $4 | Wed.–Fri. 11–4, weekends 11–5.

Fisher Building. The Albert Kahn-designed grande dame of Detroit architecture was built in 1928 and quickly became known as one of the world's most beautiful buildings. Inside its 11-story wings and 28-story central towers are dazzling mosaics, soaring gold-plated ceilings, and more. Today, the office building houses restaurants, boutiques, and art galleries, but is best known as the site of the Fisher Theater, which attracts Broadway and off-Broadway performances. | 3011 W. Grand Blvd. | 313/874–4444 | Free | 8 AM–9 PM.

© Corbis

WINDSOR, ONTARIO

Detroit casts a long shadow over Windsor, Ontario, its Canadian neighbor to the south (yes, south). Just across the Detroit River, Windsor is best known to Michiganders as the home of the Windsor Casino.

There's plenty more here than slot machines and poker faces. One of Canada's larger cities, Windsor has marvelous, intimate restaurants (try The Mini for Vietnamese, Spago for Italian, or La Cuisine for French), European-style shopping, and city parks with stunning views of the river and Motown beyond.

Add to this the brute strength of the American dollar, and Windsor becomes quite a bargain. The Detroit-Windsor Tunnel at the foot of the Renaissance Center and the Ambassador Bridge off I–75 near Mexicantown provide access to the city. Be sure to bring proof of citizenship—while it may look familiar, this is still a foreign country.

Fisher Mansion. This huge, Spanish mission-style estate on the bank of the Detroit River was completed in 1927 for the flamboyant owner of the Fisher Body Company. Modeled after William Randolph Hearst's San Simeon, it has ornate stone and marble accents, rare black-walnut and rosewood parquet floors, and more than 75 ounces of pure gold and silver leaf on the ceilings. Now owned by the Hare Krishnas, it's operated as a cultural center and vegetarian restaurant. | 383 Lenox Ave. | 313/331–6740 | $6 | Tours Fri.–Sun. at 12:30, 2, 3:30, and 6.

CULTURE, EDUCATION, AND HISTORY

Detroit Public Library. This white Vermont marble Italian Renaissance structure houses thousands of volumes, including the Burton Historical Collection, a Rare Book room, and the National Automotive History Collection. Its murals by Detroit artist Gari Melchers, original Pewabic tile, and intricate mosaics are worth a look. | 5201 Woodward Ave. | 313/833–1000 | www.detroit.lib.mi.us | Free | Tues., Thurs.–Sat 9:30–5:30, Wed. 1–9.

Detroit Symphony Orchestra Hall. The Detroit Symphony's Orchestra Place includes the original Orchestra Hall, known for its excellent acoustics and dating from 1919, as well as newer office space and a symphony-themed restaurant, Duet. The Detroit Symphony Orchestra performs here from September through May; in summer, it performs as part of the Meadow Brook Music Festival at Rochester's Meadow Brook Hall. | 3711 Woodward Ave. | 313/576–5111 | www.detroitsymphony.com | Sept.–May.

Fox Theater. Lavish and ornate, the restored Fox has brought life to the downtown Detroit theater district thanks to its owner, Mike Ilitch, who also owns the Red Wings and Detroit Tigers. Inside, the theater resembles a Persian temple, with gilt elephants, deities, and other figures and intricate mosaics. Year-round performances range from classic movies to top-name entertainers. | 2211 Woodward Ave. | 313/983–6611 | Box office Mon.–Sat. 10–6.

International Institute of Metropolitan Detroit. This cultural center serving new immigrants to Detroit hosts ethnic festivals and exhibits representing cultures from around the world. It also has a popular café that attracts area workers and students from nearby Wayne State University and the Center for Creative Studies. | 111 E. Kirby St. | 313/871–8600 | Free | Weekdays 8:30–5.

Wayne State University. One of the largest universities in the state, Wayne State dates from 1868 and is mainly a commuter college, with more than 35,000 students. In the University Cultural Center area, the school has some 100 buildings, many designed by well-known area architects, and is respected for its excellent medical school, its engineering program, and its two theaters, the undergraduate Bonstelle and the graduate Hillberry. | 656 Cass Ave. | 313/577–2424 or 313/577–2972 | www.wayne.edu | Free | Oct.–May, July–mid-Aug., Tues.–Sat.

MUSEUMS

Charles W. Wright Museum of African-American History. Once quartered in a small Detroit townhouse, the museum has grown into the largest museum of its kind in the world. In 1997, it moved into a breathtaking building in the city's University Cultural Center. Permanent collections and changing exhibits celebrate African-American heritage and include sections on the African village, slavery in America, and modern culture and arts. A well-stocked gift shop sells a wide range of African-American literature and art. | 315 E. Warren Ave. | 313/494–5800 | www.maah-detroit.org | $5 | Tues.–Sun. 9:30–5.

Children's Museum. This small museum across from the Detroit Institute of Arts is in the city's cultural center and is affiliated with and operated by the Detroit Public Schools. Displays include a bird room, Native American artifacts, natural history, and an art gallery. | 67 E. Kirby Ave. | 313/873–8100 | Free | Oct.–May, weekdays 1–4, Sat. 9–4.

Detroit Historical Museum. The city at the straits (Ville d'Etroit) is chronicled from its early days as a fur-trading center to its current incarnation as the world's auto capital. Highlights include exhibits about the now-closed Cadillac Assembly Plant, re-creations of the streets of Old Detroit, and an excellent 19th-century toy collection. | 5401 Woodward Ave. | 313/833–1805 | www.detroithistorical.org | $4.50, free Wed. | Tues.–Fri. 9:30–5, weekends 10–5.

Motown Museum. From this undistinguished Grand Boulevard house known as "Hitsville USA," the Motown sound went out to conquer America in the 1960s and '70s and create a lasting legacy. Here you can wander through collections of promotional materials, old sheet music, photographs, and other memorabilia—even Michael Jackson's sequined glove—or tour the restored Studio A, where hits such as "My Girl" were recorded. | 2648 W. Grand Blvd. | 313/875–2264 | $6 | Tues.–Sat. 10–5, Sun. and Mon. 12–5.

PARKS, NATURAL AREAS, AND OUTDOOR RECREATION

Belle Isle. Early French explorers once called this Hog Island because of the large number of wild swine that occupied it. Today's Belle Isle sits gracefully in the middle of the Detroit River and ranks as the country's largest island park. It sprawls over almost 1,000 acres east of downtown Detroit and has breathtaking views of the city skyline at night. The island has wooded drives and paths (including a 5-mi shoreline drive), gardens, monuments, an aquarium, a nature center, a zoo and conservatory, as well as a swimming beach, tennis courts, and a golf course. Enter the island from East Jefferson at East Grand Blvd. | 313/852–4075 | Free | Daily dawn to dusk.

Dating from the turn of the century, the **Belle Isle Aquarium** is one of the oldest public aquariums in the country, with more than 100 species of freshwater fish from Asia, South America, Africa, and, of course, the Great Lakes. | 313/852–4075 or 248/398–0900 | $2 | Daily 10–5.

A smaller outpost of the Detroit Zoological Park in Royal Oak, the 13-acre **Belle Isle Zoo** has a ¾-mi elevated wooden walkway that winds through the zoo and provides great views of uncaged animals in the natural habitats below. | 248/398–0900 | $2 | Apr.–Oct., daily.

A small maritime museum on Belle Isle's south shore, **Dossin Great Lakes Museum** focuses on the Great Lakes shipping industry. Everything from vintage sailing vessels to modern freighters are explored in displays that include a hand-carved oak lounge from a 1912 steamer, a 40-ft hydroplane, and the anchor from the ill-fated *Edmund Fitzgerald*, subject of a hit song by Gordon Lightfoot. Kids love the chance to leave a ship-to-shore message, work the periscope, and play with the radar in a working pilot house. | 313/852–4050 | $2 | Wed.–Sun. 10–5.

The **Whitcomb Conservatory** is a great place to escape winter in the city. This humid hothouse full of flowers has permanent displays of ferns, palms, and cacti, and one of the largest publicly owned orchid collections in the country. The Conservatory is surrounded by formal gardens, and sits next to the Belle Isle Aquarium. | 313/852–4065 | $2 | Daily 10–5.

Huron-Clinton Metroparks. Spread out across the metro Detroit area, this respected system includes 14 parks in Wayne, Oakland, Macomb, Washtenaw, and Livingston counties. (*See also* Ann Arbor.) | 8801 North Territorial Rd., Dexter | 734/426–8211 or 800/477–3191 | www.metroparks.com | $2 weekdays, $3 weekends, free Wed. | Daily dawn to dusk.

On the Huron River, 12 mi northwest of Ann Arbor and near the village of Dexter, **Hudson Mills Metropark** covers 1,549 acres of wooded area. At the on-site activity center you can rent bikes, cross-country skis on weekends, and snow discs. There are also soccer fields and a multipurpose room for hikers and cross-country skiers. You can enjoy the park's 3-mi hiking/biking trail, a nature trail, picnic shelters, fishing, or the 18-hole golf course. It's 2.5 mi north of North Territorial Rd. | Dexter–Pinckney Rd. | 734/426–8211 or 800/477–3191 | www.metroparks.com | $2 weekdays, $3 weekends, free Wed. | Daily dawn to dusk.

One of the newest Metroparks, **Lake Erie Metropark** has 1,607 acres and more than 3 mi of Lake Erie shore. A marina, an 18-hole golf course, and a wave-action swimming pool are among the top attractions at this park in Brownstown Township near Gibraltar. | 32481 W. Jefferson Ave., Brownstown | 800/477–2757 | www.metroparks.com | $2 weekdays, $3 weekends, free Wed. | Daily dawn to dusk.

Covering more than 4,461 acres, **Stony Creek Metropark,** between Rochester and Romeo, two northern Detroit suburbs, is open year-round so you can enjoy picnicking, swimming, fishing, boating, nature hikes, golf, and biking in summer, ice fishing, sledding, tobogganing, and cross-country skiing in winter. You can check out the exhibits at the on-site nature building, or guide yourself along the nearby trails. (*See also* Troy.) | 4300 Main Park Rd., Shelby Township | 810/781–4242 or 800/477–7756 | www.metroparks.com | $2 weekdays, $3 weekends, free Wed. | Daily dawn to dusk.

Near the cities of New Boston and Flat Rock, **Willow Metropark** covers 1,531 acres, with scenic drives and picnic areas. The park has bike and boat rentals, a swimming pool, playground, basketball, shuffleboard, and tennis courts. Fishing along the Huron River is popular year-round. | 17845 Savage Rd., Belleville | 734/753–4040 or 800/477–3182 | www.metroparks.com | $2 weekdays, $3 weekends, free Wed. | Daily dawn to dusk.

RELIGION AND SPIRITUALITY

Historic Trinity Lutheran Church. Near the site of the old Stroh's brewery in what was once a prominent German neighborhood, the neo-Gothic church was built in the early 1930s and is filled with stained glass and statues. The distinctive tower was patterned after that of a 16th-century monastery in Erfurt, Germany. | 1345 Gratiot Ave. | 313/567–3100 or 800/268–3058 (Michigan only) | fax 313/567–3209 | histtrin@aol.com | www.historictrinity.org | Free | Daily, no tours during services.

SHOPPING

Eastern Market. The city's open-air farmers' market is a sight on weekend mornings in warmer weather, when shoppers converge from across the metro area to buy fresh fruit and flowers. The rest of the year it's mostly a wholesale market. Spice shops, fruit stands, wine shops, and other indoor gourmet food emporiums are open year-round. | 2934 Russell | 313/833–1560 | Free | Wholesale market, daily 4 AM–noon; retail market, Sat. 5–5.

Renaissance Center. Five glass towers overlooking the Detroit River, housing a hotel, offices, restaurants, shops, and theaters, were designed by architect John Portman and built in the late 1970s to symbolize the "New Detroit," hence the name. Long considered a confusing maze, the structure was bought in 1997 by General Motors for conversion into its world headquarters. | 100 N. Renaissance Dr. | 313/568–5600 | Free | Daily 8–11; shops, daily 10–6.

SIGHTSEEING TOURS/TOUR COMPANIES

Washington Boulevard Trolley Car. If you're tired of driving, hop on the vintage red trolley that tools around downtown and take in some of the sights. It's the only open-top double-decker trolley car in the world. | 313/933–1300 | $1 | May–Labor Day, daily.

SPECTATOR SPORTS

Professional sports. Detroit was known as "Hockey Town" after the Red Wings' back-to-back wins of the National Hockey League's coveted Stanley Cup in 1997 and 1998. Besides the well-loved Red Wings, who play at downtown's Joe Louis Arena, Detroit is home to Detroit Tigers baseball, Detroit Lions football, Detroit Pistons basketball, and a host of smaller, lesser-known teams such as Rockers Soccer and Detroit Vipers Hockey.

Better known as "The Joe," the Joe Louis Arena (600 Civic Center Dr. | 313/396–7544 | www.detroitredwings.com) is home to the NHL's **Detroit Red Wings,** two-time winners of the Stanley Cup in the late 1990s.

The 22,000-seat Palace of Auburn Hills, north of Detroit, is home to the NBA's **Detroit Pistons** (2 Championship Dr., Auburn Hills | 248/377–0100 | www.palacenet.com), who play from October to April, as well as to the WNBA's **Detroit Shock.**

The Pontiac Silverdome (1200 Featherstone Rd., Pontiac | 248/335–4131 | www.detroitlions.com) is host to **Detroit Lions** football until 2002, when the team will move into Ford Field, a new stadium downtown near the Fox Theater.

DETROIT

INTRO
ATTRACTIONS
DINING
LODGING

The **Detroit Tigers,** long housed at the venerable stadium at Michigan and Trumbull, moved to a new stadium, Comerica Park (2100 Woodward Ave.|313/962–4000|www.detroit-tigers.com), near the Fox Theater for the 2000 season.

OTHER POINTS OF INTEREST

Civic Center. Linking the 75 acres along the downtown riverfront, Detroit's Civic Center includes Hart Plaza, Joe Louis Arena, the Renaissance Center, Cobo Arena and Conference Center, and the Veteran's Memorial Building. A "Civic Center" stop on the elevated People Mover serves the area.

City-County Building. This is the seat of Detroit's and Wayne County's government. In front is one of the most enduring symbols of the city, *The Spirit of Detroit,* by the late Michigan sculptor Marshall Fredericks. | 2 Woodward Ave. | 313/224–5585 | Free | Weekdays 8–4:30.

© Artville

MOTOWN MUSIC

"Hitsville, U.S.A.," the sign outside the house on Detroit's Grand Boulevard proclaims, "The Motown Sound, The Sound of Young America." Through all of the sixties and seventies and well into the eighties, that was certainly the truth about Motown Records.

Berry Gordy, Jr. began his music recording career in 1957, writing songs for the great Jackie Wilson, including the classics "Lonely Teardrops," "That's Why," and "I'll Be Satisfied." He quickly graduated to producing records himself. In 1959, he started his first company, Tamla Records. (He wanted to call it Tammy Records, after the Debbie Reynolds movie, but the name was already taken!) By 1961, he had founded Motown Records and the label was releasing albums in addition to single records.

Gordy's own special talent, apart from his sense of business and the marketplace, was in spotting vocal and musical talent in others. One of his earliest finds was William "Smokey" Robinson and the Miracles; Gordy had the good sense to engage Robinson not just as a performer but also as a songwriter for the label. The stars kept coming in rapid succession: Diana Ross and the Supremes, Mary Wells, the Temptations, Marvin Gaye (who had been a member of the Moonglows), Martha Reeves, Gladys Knight, the Isley Brothers, and an 11-year-old singer and harmonica player named Stevland (sic) Morris, whom Gordy quickly renamed Little Stevie Wonder.

Though all the label's records were recorded in stereo right from the start, it was the monaural single records that made the label's fortune. By the second half of the sixties, Motown reigned supreme. In the five years from 1966 to 1970, 63 of the label's singles made it to the Top 10 list. Among them, in 1969 alone, were the first six recordings by the Jackson 5.

In 1972, Gordy moved the operation to Los Angeles and he began concentrating on other parts of the entertainment business. Though Motown Records continued—today it's part of Polygram—it was never quite the same as it was in those heady days in the sixties when all the greatest stars of American pop music were regular visitors to Grand Boulevard and Hitsville, U.S.A.

Cobo Hall and Cobo Arena. Two facilities combine to make up one of the largest convention centers in the United States. The Cobo Conference and Exhibition Center covers 17 acres and ranks as one of the world's largest exhibition buildings. It hosts conventions and banquets as well as the annual Detroit Auto Show. Adjacent Cobo Arena hosts concerts and special events. | Cobo Center, 1 Washington Blvd.; Cobo Arena, 301 Civic Center Dr. | Cobo Arena, 313/983–6616; Cobo Center, 313/877–8240 | www.olympiaentertainment.com or Cobo Center, www.cobocenter.com | Daily.

Mariner's Church. Moved in the 1950s from Woodward Avenue to its present site near the tunnel to Canada and the Renaissance Center, this church is an 1849 Gothic revival church best known as the Sailor's Church. Every year it holds memorials for the crew of the *Edmund Fitzgerald* and a blessing of the fleet commemorating those who have died at sea. Tours are available on request. | 170 E. Jefferson Ave. | 313/259–2206 | Free | Weekdays 10–3, by appointment.

Dodge Fountain. Isamu Noguchi's futuristic fountain (described by some as a steel doughnut on a stick) dominates the surrounding **Hart Plaza,** a favorite of downtown lunchers and revelers who come for the city's summer ethnic festivals, held here from May through September. | Jefferson Ave. at Woodward Ave. | 313/877–8077 | Free | Daily.

WALKING TOUR

Although Detroit, the Motor City, is best experienced with a car, it makes sense to begin exploring it with a short walk around downtown. Along the Detroit River, just west of the Veteran's Memorial Building, sits Cobo Hall and Arena, the site of many rock concerts and the Detroit Auto Show. On the other side of the Veteran's Building is the Civic Center, at the heart of which is the Philip A. Hart Plaza. Crowds gather here in warm weather to relax in the open spaces, among the sculptures, and enjoy the computer-controlled Dodge Fountain. Just east of the Civic Center is the Gothic Revival Mariner's Church, built in 1849. East of this is the Renaissance Center, whose six office towers dominate the skyline. From here, you can walk north on Brush Street to Bricktown. Named for its numerous redbrick structures, it has a smattering of restaurants and shops. Take a right at Lafayette to find the many retail shops and eateries of Greektown. To return to your car, retrace your steps to the Renaissance Center or take the People Mover monorail, which has a stop on Beaubien in Greektown.

From the river, drive north on Woodward Avenue. Past the semi-circular Grand Circus Park you'll see the new Tiger Stadium, Comerica Park, on your right and the Fox Theater on your left. Approximately 2 mi north of the Fox Theater is the Detroit Symphony Orchestra Hall, an early 20th-century theater, and its newer companion building. Another 2 mi north is the neighborhood of Wayne State University. Parking is available a block east of Woodward, along Warren or Farnsworth. From these parking spaces, walk east on Warren to the Charles H. Wright Museum of African-American History. Then return to Woodward Avenue. The Detroit Institute of Arts sits directly across from the Detroit Public Library on Woodward, between Farnsworth and Kirby. A block north of these two institutions, along Kirby, are the Detroit Historical Museum, the Children's Museum, and the International Institute of Metropolitan Detroit. By car, you can continue on Woodward to Royal Oak and the Detroit Zoo.

ON THE CALENDAR

JAN.: *North American International Auto Show.* Downtown Detroit hops with car fanciers during one of Motown's glitziest and best-known events. Concept cars, new models, and more dazzle thousands of viewers from around the world. It's the only show in North America sanctioned by the prestigious Organization Internationale des Constructeurs D'Automobiles in Paris. | 248/645–6666 | www.naias.com.

MAY: *Detroit Hoedown.* The world's largest free country-music festival attracts some of the nation's top country-music talent. First held in 1983, the event at Hart Plaza attracts more than 800,000 fans who come to do-si-do and achy-breaky dance their way through the night. | 313/459–6969 or 810/399–7000.

MAY–SEPT.: *Riverfront Festivals.* A series of waterfront heritage festivals celebrates the city's rich diversity and includes the African World Festival, Detroit's largest ethnic event. | 313/224–1184.

JUNE: *Detroit Grand Prix.* Excitement builds on Belle Isle for three days each June as more than 20 Formula One cars take to the streets for high-powered competitions. More than 170,000 fans stream onto Belle Isle Park to witness the action. | 313/393–7749 | www.detroitgrandprix.com.

JULY: *International Freedom Festival.* Detroit and its nearest international neighbor, Windsor, Canada, celebrate the spirit of friendship with a double birthday bash. More than 100 free events, from bed races to a tug of war across the Detroit River to one of the country's most spectacular fireworks displays, attract more than a million spectators from both sides of the border. | 313/923–7400 | www.freedom-festival.com/.

JULY: *Michigan Taste Fest.* Southeast Michigan's premier outdoor culinary festival takes place in Detroit's New Center area, with food from more than 40 area restaurants, four stages with live entertainment, and family activities. | 313/872–0188.

AUG.: *African World Festival.* Detroit's largest ethnic festival has free music, an artists' market, international cuisine from more than 20 countries, and cultural activities for all ages. | 313/494–5835.

AUG.–SEPT.: *Michigan State Fair.* Dating from 1829, this is one of the oldest state fairs in the country, with livestock, sheep shearers, wool weavers, agricultural exhibits, and a groundbreaking live birthing area that's popular with families. The fairgrounds are at 1120 W. State Fair. | 313/369–8250 | www.mda.state.mi.us/statefair.

SEPT.: *Detroit Festival of the Arts.* Detroit's Cultural Center hosts more than 130 artists, puppeteers, and storytellers during this festival. You can also check out the special kids's fair, musical entertainment on three stages, and more. | 313/577–5088 | www.detroitfestival.com.

SEPT.: *Detroit International Jazz Festival.* Held each Labor Day weekend in riverfront Hart Plaza, the largest free jazz festival in North America has local, regional, and international jazz artists performing in more than 85 free, open-air concerts. | 313/963–7622 | www.detroitjazzfest.com.

NOV.: *America's Thanksgiving Day Parade.* A nationally televised parade through downtown Detroit ushers in the holidays and begins a three-week citywide festival. Thousands of spectators wait along Woodward Avenue for giant balloons, high-stepping local bands, and the popular Briefcase Brigade Drill Team, all decked out in suits and ties. Santa provides the big finish. | 313/923–7400 | www.theparade.org.

Dining
INEXPENSIVE

Cadieux Café. Belgian. The Euro-style Cadieux Café is all that's left of a once-sizable Belgian community on Detroit's east side. Belgian beers, mussels (a specialty), fish and chips, and other Belgian delights attract a loyal crowd. Feather bowling is available in the next alley. Entertainment. Casual. | 4300 Cadieux | 313/882–8560 | $6–$16 | AE, MC, V.

....

El Zocalo. Mexican. Colorful Mexican artifacts and paintings add spice to this popular Mexican eatery in the heart of the neighborhood known as Mexicantown. Don't miss the excellent Mexican entrées. Entertainment. Casual. Kids' menu. | 3400 Bagley | 313/841–3700 | $9–$15 | AE, D, DC, MC, V.

....

Traffic Jam and Snug. Contemporary. In a restored Detroit neighborhood near Wayne State University, this eclectic restaurant-microbrewery is a favorite of students and Cultural Center workers. Walls lined with vintage advertising signs and funky castoffs complement the menu, which ranges from the redfish sandwich on a house-baked potato roll to Cuban black bean soup or a Michigan miner's pasty. Desserts are famous, too—including the Carlotta chocolotta. Kids' menu. | 511 W. Canfield St. | 313/831–9470 | Closed Sun. No lunch Sat. | $7–$18 | AE, MC, V.

MODERATE

Blue Nile. Ethiopian. Detroit's only Ethiopian restaurant is, oddly enough, in the heart of Greektown. Richly seasoned meats and vegetables are served on communal platters with *injera*, a crepe-like flat bread used to scoop up the foods. Platters come either vegetarian or non and each includes up to 11 items. | Trappers Alley, 508 Monroe Ave. | 313/964–6699 | $13.90–$16.90 | AE, D, DC, MC, V.

Caucus Club. Continental. Open since 1949, this established downtown favorite has dark paneled walls, oil paintings, and white linen-covered tables. Barbra Streisand sang here before she became popular. It's known for lake perch and baby back embers. Entertainment weekdays. Kids' menu. | Penobscot Bldg., 150 W. Congress | 313/965–4970 | Closed Sun. No lunch Sat. | $11–$22 | AE, D, DC, MC, V.

★ **Fishbone's Rhythm Kitchen Cafe.** Cajun/Creole. Lively, colorful posters match the fiery specialties on the menu, spotlighting the cooking of New Orleans. This is one of the city's most popular Greektown eateries, so prepare for a line on weekends. Sun. brunch. | 400 Monroe St. | 313/965–4600 | Reservations for 8 or more | $14–$25 | AE, D, DC, MC, V.

Motor City Grill. Contemporary. Once a bank, this popular lunch and pre-dinner spot has an automotive theme. The menu has hand-cut steak, seafood, and prime rib. Entertainment Fri. and Sat. evenings. | 3011 W. Grand Blvd. | 313/875–7400 | Mon.–Fri. Weekends extended hours | $12–$19 | AE, D, DC, MC, V.

EXPENSIVE

Pegasus Taverna. Greek. This bustling Greektown eatery has the flavor of Greece. Spinach pies, tangy pastitsio, and an excellent *avgolemono* (chicken-lemon soup) consistently please diners. Entertainment. Kids' menu. | 558 Monroe St. | 313/964–6800 | $17–$27 | AE, D, DC, MC, V.

Tres Vite. Mediterranean. This Tuscan-inspired eatery has burnt umber walls and large picture windows overlooking Woodward Avenue. Menu items include Italian-inspired favorites like linguine with tomatoes and rock shrimp and American staples. Entertainment. Kids' menu. | 2203 Woodward Ave. | 313/471–3500 | Closed Sun. and Mon. No lunch Sat. | $16–$28 | AE, D, MC, V.

VERY EXPENSIVE

Intermezzo. Italian. This urbane spot has airy, loftlike space in a newer, whitewashed building in the burgeoning Harmonie Park district. It's known for pasta dishes. Open-air dining. Entertainment Fri. and Sat. | 1435 Randolph St. | 313/961–0707 | Closed Sun. Open Mon. for dinner | $26–$45 | AE, D, DC, MC, V.

Opus One. French. French and American furnishings reflect the menu of one of Detroit's finest and most expensive restaurants. Try escargots and spinach in phyllo, or savory strudel of duck, partridge, and pheasant. Delectable desserts include apple flan with cinnamon ice cream. Pianist Tues.–Sat. Kids' menu. | 565 E. Larned | 313/961–7766 | Jacket required | Closed Sun. No lunch Sat. | $30–$40 | AE, D, DC, MC, V.

Rattlesnake Club. Contemporary. Chef/owner Jimmy Schmidt shines on the Detroit River in two spacious, contemporary, art-filled dining areas. The creative menu includes seasonally changing dishes highlighting fresh ingredients and staples such as the dessert of homemade white chocolate ice cream with roasted macadamia nuts on purees of passion fruit and raspberry. Lake Ontario perch and veal rib chops are favorites. Open-air dining is available on a deck. Entertainment Fri. and Sat. | 300 River Pl. | 313/567–4400 | Closed Sun. No lunch Sat. $27–$42 | AE, D, DC, MC, V.

★ **The Whitney.** Continental. Arguably the city's most beautiful restaurant, this elegant dining room in a former lumber baron's Romanesque-style mansion has Tiffany stained-glass windows, crystal chandeliers, and Victorian antiques. A large menu known for classic American cuisine with a twist includes a daily selection of cold pâtés. Calamari is a favorite Whitney special. Entertainment. Sun. brunch. | 4421 Woodward Ave. | 313/832–5700 | $22–$42 | AE, DC, MC, V.

Lodging
MODERATE

Best Western Laurel Park Suites. Just 2½ mi off I–275 and 16 mi from Detroit Metro Airport, this two-story suite hotel in suburban Livonia has larger-than-average rooms. It's across the street from Laurel Park Mall and the city's many corporate parks. Complimentary Continental breakfast. In-room data ports, minibars, refrigerators, some in-room hot tubs. Cable TV. Pool. Exercise equipment. Business services. | 16999 S. Laurel Park Dr., Livonia | 734/464–0050 or 800/780–7234 | fax 734/464–5869 | www.bestwesternmichigan.com | 123 rooms | $69–$89 | AE, D, DC, MC, V.

Parkcrest Inn. One of the few lodging options in the eastern suburbs, this two-story motel is off I–94 in a residential area of Harper Woods. The formal rooms, with most of their original traditional furnishings, overlook a well-kept courtyard. Restaurant, bar, room service. Cable TV. Pool. Some pets allowed. | 20000 Harper Ave., Harper Woods | 313/884–8800 | fax 313/884–7087 | 47 rooms | $59–$68 | AE, D, DC, MC, V.

Shorecrest Motor Inn. This small, independent motel sits in the shadow of the Renaissance Center. Its proximity to downtown and the Cobo Convention Center make it popular with business travelers. It has traditional furnishings throughout the two floors. Restaurant, room service. Refrigerators. Cable TV. Business services. No pets. | 1316 E. Jefferson Ave. | 313/568–3000 or 800/992–9616 | fax 313/568–3002 | 54 rooms | $69–$89 | AE, D, DC, MC, V.

EXPENSIVE

★ **Detroit Downtown Courtyard Hotel.** Facing the Detroit River and the city's Renaissance Center, this 21-story hotel is popular with business travelers. Don't miss the great rooftop running track, with an incredible view of downtown's vintage skyscrapers. Restaurant, bar. In-room data ports, some refrigerators. Cable TV. Indoor pool. Hot tub. Beauty salon. Tennis. Gym, racquetball. Business services. | 333 E. Jefferson Ave. | 313/222–7700 or 800/321–2211 | fax 313/222–6509 | www.courtyard.com | 260 rooms, 5 suites | $154 | AE, D, DC, MC, V.

Embassy Suites. This spacious, all-suite hotel with a five-story atrium caters to business travelers. It is in suburban Livonia off I–275 near Laurel Park Mall and area corporate headquarters. Contemporary rooms have modern furnishings. Restaurant, bar, complimentary breakfast. In-room data ports, refrigerators. Cable TV. Indoor pool. Hot tub. Exercise equipment. Laundry facilities. Business services. | 19525 Victor Pkwy., Livonia | 734/462–6000 | fax 734/462–6003 | www.embassy-suites.com | 239 suites | $109–$139 suites | AE, D, DC, MC, V.

Marriott Hotel Livonia. Connected to Laurel Park Mall and off I–275, this six-story hotel caters to the business traveler. Restaurant, bar. In-room data ports. Cable TV. Indoor pool. Hot tub. Exercise equipment. Business services. | 17100 Laurel Park Dr. N, Livonia | 734/462–3100 or 800/228–9290 | fax 734/462–2815 | www.marriott.com | 221 rooms, 3 suites | $99–$149 | AE, D, DC, MC, V.

Marriott Renaissance Center. In the middle of the huge Renaissance Center, this luxury chain hotel in downtown Detroit is a premier convention center. Popular with business travelers, it is 1–6 blocks to the financial district, the Detroit River, Belle Isle, shops, and golf courses. Restaurants, bar, room service. In-room data ports, some minibars. Cable TV. Indoor pool. Beauty salon. Gym. Business services. Some pets allowed. | 48243 Jefferson Ave., Renaissance Center | 313/568–8000 or 800/228–9290 | fax 313/568–8146 | www.marriott.com | 1,306 rooms, 50 suites | $85–$175 | AE, D, DC, MC, V.

River Place. This boutique hotel in downtown Detroit is on the waterfront. Some of the Victorian-style rooms of the five floors provide views of the Detroit River and the Canadian border. Restaurant, bar. In-room data ports. Cable TV. Indoor pool. Hot tub, massage. Gym. Business services. No pets allowed. | 1000 River Pl. | 313/259–9500 or 800/890–9505 | fax 313/259–3744 | 108 rooms, 18 suites | $99–$159 | AE, D, DC, MC, V.

VERY EXPENSIVE

Atheneum Suites. This luxury hotel is in the heart of the lively Greektown entertainment district. Marble, Greek murals, and an atrium grace this elegant 10-floor structure. Suites are individually decorated, most with Mediterranean themes. Bar, room service. In-room data ports, minibars. Cable TV. Exercise equipment. Business services. | 1000 Brush Ave. | 313/962–2323 or 800/772–2323 | fax 313/962–2424 | www.hotelbook.com | 174 suites | $155–$600 suites | AE, D, DC, MC, V.

Crowne Plaza Ponchartrain. This busy downtown hotel across from Hart Plaza and Cobo Hall is popular with business travelers and convention-goers. The twenty-five floors have attractive, up-to-date rooms. Restaurant. In-room data ports, refrigerators (in suites). Cable TV. Indoor pool. Hot tub. Exercise equipment. Business services. | 2 Washington Blvd. | 313/965–0200 | fax 313/965–9464 | www.ponchartraindetroit.com | 413 rooms | $149–$169 | AE, D, DC, MC, V.

DOUGLAS

MAP 9, C7

(Nearby towns also listed: Holland, Saugatuck, South Haven)

Flower-lined streets and early American houses mark this town, the less-known neighbor of its sister city Saugatuck. Founded in 1851, it is today a tourist destination and home to gift shops and furniture stores—and is the gateway to Lake Michigan by way of the Kalamazoo River.

Information:Saugatuck-Douglas Visitors and Convention Bureau | Box 28, Saugatuck 49453 | 616/857–1701 | www.saugatuck.com.

Attractions

Party Time Cruise Lines. Cruising and dining aboard the *Par-Te-Tyme* can include port hopping on Sunday or a sunset dinner cruise. You can choose between the covered, open-air deck or the climate-controlled lower deck. | Harbour Village, Blue Star Hwy. | 616/836–2441 (boat) or 616/983–4140 (office) | $33.

Dining

Chaps. Contemporary. There's an inviting fireplace in this English-style restaurant. Locals and tourists alike come here for such menu favorites as roasted duckling with hoisin chile-garlic glaze and chicken ballotine topped with blackberry marsala sauce. | 8 Center St. | 616/257–2699 | $18–$26 | V, MC.

Everyday People Café. Contemporary. A 19th-century butcher shop originally, then a 1930s soda shop, this art deco-style restaurant has the original cooler doors and soda fountain. Pan-seared tuna with black sesame seeds, roasted Gorgonzola pork chops with carmelized onion marmalade, and fresh focaccia are specialties. Live jazz on Sunday. | 11 Center | 616/857–4240 | No reservations | Closed Wed. | $12–$22 | MC, V.

Respite Cappucino Court. Cafés. Coffee is the star here, along with good sandwiches—try the toasted tomato wraps—and homemade desserts and jam. | 48 Center St. | 616/857–5411 | $4–$8 | No credit cards.

Lodging

AmericInn. Less than a mile from downtown Douglas, this chain motel with six-inch concrete walls was built for quiet. Local artists display their works in its halls and lobby. Some suites have fireplaces. Some microwaves, some refrigerators, some in-room hot tubs. Cable TV. Indoor pool. Hot tub, sauna. Some pets allowed. | 2905 Blue Star Hwy. | 616/857–8581 | fax 616/857–3591 | americinn@americinn.com | www.americinn.com | 46 | 46 rooms | Rooms $69–$99, suites $160–$300 | V, MC, D, AE, DC.

EAST LANSING (SEE LANSING)

EMPIRE

MAP 9, C4

(Nearby towns also listed: Beulah, Frankfort, Glen Arbor, Traverse City)

First settled in 1853 by the John LaRue family, this tiny but historic northern Michigan village thrived in the 1890s because of the lumber industry. From 1950 to the early 1970s, Empire was home to Empire Air Force Station 752nd AC & W Squadron. This radar station was part of the Air Defense Command that stood watch over America's skies during the Cold War. Today, tourism dominates the economy. The town's old-fashioned downtown is within walking distance of Lake Michigan beaches. (*Note:* Area codes in this vicinity are scheduled to change to 989 beginning April 7, 2001.)

Information: **Traverse City Convention and Visitors Bureau** | 101 W. Grandview Pkwy., Traverse City 49684 | 231/947–1120 or 800/TRAVERS | www.tcvisitor.org.

Attractions

Sleeping Bear Dunes National Lakeshore. According to Chippewa legend, the dunes' name is derived from a story of a bear and her two cubs forced to swim Lake Michigan to escape a forest fire. The mother reached the shore safely and climbed to the top of a dune to await the cubs, who slipped behind and never arrived. She still waits at the top of a plateau, while the cubs have become North and South Manitou islands. Aside from this charming legend, the 75,000-acre national treasure is known for its more than 400-ft bluffs, 7-mi Pierce Stocking Scenic Drive, and 35 mi of hiking trails. At the top of the challenging Dune Climb, you have a breathtaking view of the Lake Michigan shoreline. Stop into the National Park Service Visitors Center after your climb to learn more about the area. The Sleeping Bear Coast Guard Station has a small museum illustrating area maritime history. Also within the Lakeshore are the ghost town of Glen Haven and Glen Haven Beach. | Park Headquarters, 9922 Front St. | 231/326–5134 | www.nps.gov/slbe/home.htm | $7 per car | Visitor center daily 9–6, park daily dawn to dusk.

ESCANABA

MAP 9, B3

(Nearby towns also listed: Fayette, Gladstone, Iron Mountain, Manistique, Menominee)

Headquarters for the vast 893,000-acre Hiawatha National Forest, this unspoiled Upper Peninsula port is the seat of Delta County and Lake Michigan's only ore-shipping area. Large tracts of undeveloped land and open water are magnets for bikers, hikers, skiers, and other outdoor enthusiasts. (*Note:* Area codes in this vicinity are scheduled to change to 989 beginning April 7, 2001.)

Information: **Delta County Area Chamber of Commerce** | 230 Ludington St., Escanaba 49829 | 906/786–2192 or 888/335–8264 | info@deltami.org | www.deltami.org.

Attractions

Hiawatha National Forest. This breathtaking national forest touches three Great Lakes—Huron, Superior, and Michigan—and extends between Sault Ste. Marie and Escanaba in the Upper Peninsula. You can take scenic drives, go stream fishing, hunting, swimming, boating, canoeing, camping, hiking, horseback riding, cross-country and downhill skiing, or partake in other activities on the more than 890,000 acres. You can get a great view of Lake Superior when you climb up the 65-ft tower of the forest's Point Iroquois Light Station, about 5 mi west of Bay Mills. A museum is also on the site. | Sault Ste. Marie District Ranger Station, 2727 N. Lincoln Rd. | 906/635–5311 or 906/786–4062 | www.fs.fed.us/r9/hiawatha | Free | Daily dawn to dusk.

Ludington Park. This popular park overlooking Little Bay de Noc offers a range of recreational opportunities. Here you can fish, bike along a scenic path, play tennis, and relax on the beach. The park also has playgrounds. | Ludington St./Lakeshore Dr./Jenkins Dr. | 906/786–4141 | Year-round 7 AM–11PM.

Within Ludington Park, at the east end of the lakefront, are the **Delta County Historical Museum and Sand Point Lighthouse.** The small local history complex explores the area's dependence on logging, the railroad, and shipping. The Sand Point Lighthouse has been restored to how it appeared when it was built built in 1867. You can take tours of both the lighthouse and the keeper's house. | Ludington St., off U.S. 2/41 | 906/786–3428 | Free | June–Labor Day, daily 11–7.

Pioneer Trail Park and Campground. Just 3 mi north of town, this 70-acre park on the Escanaba River has fishing along the shore, picnic areas, nature trails, miniature golf, camping, and a kid's playground. | 6822 U.S. 2/41 and M-35 | 906/786–1020 | May–Sept.

ON THE CALENDAR

AUG.: *Upper Peninsula State Fair.* Livestock showings, midway rides, and music makes this one of the Upper Peninsula's most popular summer events. | 2401 12th Ave. N | 800/533–4386 | escanaba.org/upstate.htm.

Dining

Stonehouse. Continental. This long-time local favorite has a classic fieldstone exterior. The bar has an antique car theme, while scenic oil paintings by the owner's daughter adorns the eating area. Entrées include Black Angus New York strip, Alaskan walleye, prime rib, and veal. Kids' menu. | 2223 Ludington Ave. | 906/786–5003 | Closed Sun. Sept.–Apr. No lunch weekends | $10–$29 | AE, D, DC, MC, V.

Lodging

Best Western Pioneer Inn. You're just 7 mi from Gladstone Sports Park and 12 mi from other cross-country and downhill skiing areas at this two-story chain hotel, 2 mi from Lake Michigan. For those who prefer the indoors, a casino is 13 mi away, and the mall is just 2 blocks away. Rooms are traditionally furnished; some come with hot tubs and balconies with views. Restaurant, bar. Cable TV. Indoor pool. Business services. | 2635 Ludington St. | 906/786–0602 or 800/780–7234 | fax 906/786–3938 | www.bestwesternmichigan.com | 72 rooms | $59–$149 | AE, D, DC, MC, V.

Days Inn. Snowmobile trails are in the backyard and cross-country ski trails are only 1 mi away from this four-story motel 2 mi from downtown Escanaba. It's just 5 mi from Gladstone Sports Park. Bar. Cable TV. Indoor pool. Hot tub. | 2603 N. Lincoln Rd. | 906/789–1200 or 800/388–7829 | fax 906/789–0128 | www.daysinn.com | 123 rooms | $60–$80 | AE, D, DC, MC, V.

Econo Lodge. In a commercial district less than 1 mi north of downtown, this motel is right next door to the Upper Peninsula state fairgrounds and 3 mi to Gladstone Sports Park and public beaches. The two-story motel has modern furnishings and facilities. Complimentary Continental breakfast. Cable TV. | 921 N. Lincoln Rd. | 906/789–1066 or 800/929–5997 | fax 906/789–9202 | www.econolodge.com | 50 rooms | $38–$52 | D, MC, V.

Super 8. This two-story motel is in a commercial area that's 2 mi north of downtown, yet close to city attractions and outdoor recreation. You can gamble at a casino 13 mi north, or ski at an area within 7 mi. Some in-room hot tubs. Cable TV. Some pets allowed. | 2415 N. Lincoln Ave. | 906/786–1000 or 800/800–8000 | fax 906/786–7819 | www.super8motels.com | 90 rooms | $60–$72 | AE, D, DC, MC, V.

FARMINGTON/ FARMINGTON HILLS

MAP 10, B3

(Nearby towns also listed: Birmingham, Bloomfield Hills, Dearborn, Detroit, Plymouth, Warren)

Farmington—a growing northwest Detroit suburb—has become a favorite of corporate America and a top upper-middle-class community. Beyond the sprawl is quiet Kensington Metropark, with 4,300 acres on quiet Kent Lake.

Information: **Farmington/Farmington Hills Chamber of Commerce** | 33000 Thomas St., Ste. 101, Farmington 48336 | 248/474–3440 | fax 248/474–9235 | staff@ffhchamber.com | www.ffhchamber.com.

Attractions

Kensington Metropark. One of the busiest metroparks, **Kensington Metropark** attracted 2.5 million visitors in 1998 and is the most popular year-round playground in southeast Michigan. Located 35 mi northwest of Detroit along I–96, it includes 4,357 acres and 1,200-acre Kent Lake. Here you can go boating, biking, swimming, fishing, and skating. Or hop a ride on the 66-passenger *Island Queen,* a replica of an old Mississippi riverboat. | 2240 W. Buno Rd., Milford | 248/685–1561 or 800/477–3178 | www.metroparks.com | $2 weekdays, $3 weekends, free Wed. | Daily dawn to dusk.

Marvelous Marvin's Mechanical Museum. An eccentric personal collection displays vintage mechanical marvels, including antique slot and pinball machines as well as nickelodeons, neon signs, and posters. | 31005 Orchard Lake Rd. | 248/626–5020 | Free | Mon.–Thurs. 10–9, Fri.-Sat. 10-11, Sun. 11-9.

Dining

Ah Wok. Chinese. Far beyond the usual strip-mall Chinese restaurant, Ah Wok serves both Cantonese and spicier Szechuan fare. Standouts include the honey-glazed shrimp, sea bass with black beans, and Szechuan shrimp with Chinese vegetables. | 41563 W. Ten Mile Rd., Novi | 248/349–9260 | No lunch weekends | $14–$22 | AE, DC, MC, V.

Five Lakes Grill. Contemporary. Chef Brian Polcyn trained at some of Detroit's finest restaurants, and it shows in his latest effort. This modern bistro has regional fare and fresh ingredients. Unique entrées include house-smoked brook trout with apple horseradish, firecracker shrimp, and roast Indian duckling. Kids' menu. | 424 N. Main St., Milford | 248/684–7455 | Closed Sun. No lunch | $19–$27 | AE, MC, V.

Little Italy. Italian. The dining rooms here are small and intimate and have Italian furnishings. For a romantic treat, ask for a table in one of the home's hidden nooks and crannies. Taste treats include a calamari e scungilli Napolitana, fettuccine verde al Palmino, and al dente spinach noodles covered in creamy sauce and roasted peppers. Chicken Romano and saltimbocca veal are favorite entrées. Kids' menu. | 227 Hutton St., Northville | 248/348–0575 | No lunch weekends | $13–$19 | AE, MC, V.

MacKinnon's. Contemporary. Tiffany lamps, brick walls, antique British furnishings, and original artwork fill this club-like Dickensian restaurant in a downtown storefront. Stuffed fish, deer, buffalo, and boar heads hang on the walls of the bar. The dark, quiet surroundings make for enjoyable casual or dressy dining. Chef/owner Tom MacKinnon is known for his preparation of game dishes and for his creative touches with staples, including lamb, wild turkey, and beef. Blown-up duck (air is pumped into the skin of the duck so that when baked the outside is crispy) is one entrée they say is "to die for." Try the *waterzooie*, a thick Belgian stew, or the mocha crepes with ice cream. Open-air dining during the summer. | 126 E. Main St., Northville | 248/348–1991 | Closed Sun. | $22–$34 | AE, D, DC, MC, V.

Too Chez. Contemporary. Bold colors, chalkboard wall art, and an eclectic menu featuring everything from Asian almond chicken to Cajun mahimahi mark this as one of the Detroit area's most creative and popular eateries. Try the broiled Chilean sea bass. Open-air dining during the summer. Kids' menu. | 27155 Sheraton Dr., Novi | 248/348–5555 | Closed Sun. | $16–$26 | AE, D, DC, MC, V.

Lodging

Best Western Executive Hotel and Suites. This suite hotel within 1 mi of the Novi/Farmington Hills corporate area is a favorite of business travelers. Restaurant, bar, room service. In-room data ports, some in-room hot tubs. Cable TV. Indoor pool. Exercise equipment. Business services. | 31525 W. Twelve Mile Rd., Farmington Hills | 248/553–0000 or 800/780–7234 | fax 248/553–7630 | www.bestwesternmichigan.com | 202 rooms, 44 suites | $89–$105, $109 suites | AE, D, DC, MC, V.

Comfort Inn. This four-story chain hotel is in a commercial area 1½ mi northeast of downtown. Complimentary Continental breakfast. Refrigerators (in suites). Cable TV. | 30715 Twelve Mile Rd., Farmington Hills | 248/471–9220 or 800/228–5150 | fax 248/471–2053 | www.comfortsuites.com | 135 rooms | $84–$95 | AE, D, DC, MC, V.

Courtyard by Marriott. Just 2 mi north of downtown Farmington, this three-story hotel is in a residential and commercial area. It has traditional accommodations. Restaurant, bar. In-room data ports, refrigerators (in suites). Cable TV. Indoor pool. Hot tub. Exercise equipment. Laundry facilities. Business services. | 17200 N. Laurel Park Dr., Livonia | 734/462–2000 or 800/321–2211 | fax 734/462–5907 | www.courtyard.com | 137 rooms, 12 suites | $75–$119 | AE, D, DC, MC, V.

Doubletree. A three-story atrium brings light into this hotel just off I-96. It's in a busy commercial/corporate area and near Twelve Oaks Mall. Restaurant, bar (with entertainment), room service. Cable TV. 2 pools (1 indoor). Hot tub. Exercise equipment. Business services. | 27000 Sheraton Dr., Novi | 248/348–5000 or 800/222–8733 | fax 248/348–2315 | www.hilton.com/doubletree | 217 rooms | $95–$145 | AE, D, DC, MC, V.

Hilton. Modern furnishings are throughout this seven-story hotel at I-275 and 8 Mile Road that's a choice for both business travelers and families. The hotel has a grand ballroom and amphitheater. Restaurant, bar, room service. In-room data ports, refrigerators (in suites). Cable TV. Pool. Hot tub. Exercise equipment. Business services. Some pets allowed. | 21111 Haggerty Rd., Novi | 248/349–4000 or 800/445–8667 | fax 248/349–4066 | www.hilton.com | 239 rooms | $85–$165 | AE, D, DC, MC, V.

Hotel Baronette. Among the area's nicest hotels, the Baronette has three floors of modern rooms. It borders Novi's commercial and residential areas and is next to Twelve Oaks Mall. Restaurant, bar, complimentary breakfast. Minibars. Cable TV, in-room VCRs (and movies). Indoor pool. Hot tub. Putting green. Exercise equipment. | 27790 Novi Rd., Novi | 248/349–7800 or 800/395–9009 | fax 248/349–7467 | 153 rooms | $111–$365 | AE, D, DC, MC, V.

FARMINGTON/
FARMINGTON
HILLS

INTRO
ATTRACTIONS
DINING
LODGING

Radisson Suites. This all-suites hotel borders a commercial area. The four floors have modern furnishings throughout. Restaurant, bar, complimentary Continental breakfast, room service. Refrigerators. Cable TV. Indoor pool. Hot tub. Exercise equipment. Business services. | 37529 Grand River Ave., Farmington Hills | 248/477–7800 | fax 248/477–6512 | www.radisson.com | 137 suites | $99–$189 suites | AE, D, DC, MC, V.

Red Roof Inn. A busy corporate community and area shopping and restaurants are just 1–5 mi from this two-floor chain hotel. Cable TV. Some pets allowed. | 24300 Sinacola Ct., Farmington Hills | 248/478–8640 or 800/733–7663 | fax 248/478–4842 | www.redroof.com | 108 rooms | $58–$68 | AE, D, DC, MC, V.

Ramada. This chain hotel is in a commercial area near shopping, restaurants, and highways. Complimentary Continental breakfast. Some refrigerators. Cable TV. Business services. | 21100 Haggerty Rd., Northville | 248/349–7400 or 800/298–2054 | fax 248/349–7454 | www.ramada.com | 125 rooms | $59–$79 | AE, D, DC, MC, V.

Wyndham Garden. Just off I-96, this two-story hotel is across the street from a commercial area. Modern guest rooms surround a beautifully landscaped central garden courtyard. Restaurant, bar. Cable TV. Indoor pool. Hot tub, sauna. | 42100 Crescent Blvd., Novi | 248/344–8800 or 800/996–3425 | fax 248/344–8535 | www.wyndham.com | 148 rooms, 28 suites | $115, $125 suites | AE, D, DC, MC, V.

FAYETTE

MAP 9, B3

(Nearby towns also listed: Escanaba, Gladstone, Manistique, Munising)

From 1867 to 1891, Fayette was a thriving producer of pig iron for Great Lakes steel companies because of its natural harbor and proximity to limestone, hardwood forests, and the Escanaba ore docks. The town had nearly 500 residents. Then the market died, along with Fayette. It survives today as the Fayette Historic Townsite in Fayette State Park. (*Note:* Area codes in this vicinity are scheduled to change to 989 beginning April 7, 2001.)

Information: **Delta County Area Chamber of Commerce** | 230 Ludington St., Escanaba 49829 | 906/786–2192 or 888/335–8264 | info@deltami.org | www.deltami.org.

Attractions
Fayette State Park. Between Escanaba and Manistique, this park on the Garden Peninsula is home of the Fayette Historic Townsite, a ghost town with 19 structures. You can take either self-guided or guided tours of the town's commercial buildings, residences, and the stabilized ruins of the furnace complex. You can also enjoy the park's waterfront by swimming at the beach on Sand Bay, fishing for perch, smallmouth bass, and northern pike in Big Bay de Noc, and scuba diving among the submerged artifacts of the harbor bottom. The park has 80 semi-modern campsites. | 13700 13.25 La., Garden | 906/644–2603 | www.exploringhthenorth.com/fayette/park.html or www.dnr.state.mi.us/www/parks/index.htm | Camping Apr. 15–Nov. 15.

Dining
Nahma Hotel. Contemporary. The chandelier-lit restaurant here draws locals and tourists with steaks, seafood, salads, and other basics. Ribs are a specialty, and hand-dipped ice cream from the general store next door makes for a sweet ending. | 13747 Main, Nahma | 906/644–8486 | $5–$19 | MC, V.

Lodging
Nahma Hotel. The long front porch is striking on this hotel's wooden colonial building, built in 1902. Photographs line the halls, and furnishings date from the 1920s. It's about

40 mi from Fayette Historic Townsite. Restaurant, bar, complimentary Continental breakfast. | 13747 Main, Nahma | 906/644–2486 | 17 rooms | $50–$80 | V, MC, D.

FLINT

(Nearby towns also listed: Frankenmuth, Holly, Owosso, Pontiac, Saginaw)

An important automobile producer, Flint is second only to Detroit in output. General Motors has a number of plants here and ranks as the city's largest employer. Early magnates supported the city's education and arts by founding several colleges and museums that are now part of the downtown cultural center.

Information: Flint Area Convention and Visitors Bureau | 519 S. Saginaw St., Flint 48502 | 810/232–8900 or 800/25–FLINT | www.flint.org.

Attractions

Crossroads Village/Huckleberry Railroad. This restored Genesee County village includes 30 structures dating from 1860 to 1880. You can visit an operating blacksmith, a cider mill, a gristmill, a village church, a general store, and period homes. The adjacent Huckleberry Railroad, featuring a steam engine that takes 35-minute rides through the Genesee Recreation Area, is especially popular with kids, as are the vintage carousel, wagon, and Ferris wheel rides and sight-seeing cruises on the *Genesee Belle*, a paddlewheeler. | G-6140 Bray Rd. | 810/736–7100 | www.geneseecountyparks.com | $9.25 | Weekdays 10–5:30, weekends 11–6:30 in summer, hours vary rest of year.

Flint Cultural Center. The downtown arts and cultural center includes a planetarium, an art museum, and a historical museum. It is also home to Mott Community College and University of Michigan–Flint. | 1241 E. Kearsley St. | 810/237–7330.

The **Flint Institute of Arts** in the sprawling DeWaters Art Center is the second-largest art museum in the state. The FIA houses a 5,000-piece collection that includes impressive holdings of European paintings, Renaissance tapestries, and antique French decorative objects. | 1120 E. Kearsley St. | 810/234–1695 | www.flintarts.org | Free | Tues.–Sat. 10–5, Sun. 1–5.

The popular **Longway Planetarium** has a 60-ft dome that reproduces the night sky and presents "heavenly" laser-light programs year-round. | 1310 E. Kearsley St. | 810/760–1181 | www.longwayplanetarium.com | $4 | Weekdays 8–5, weekends 1 and 2:30.

A 10,000-year-old mastodon skeleton is the highlight of the **Sloan Museum,** which also has permanent and changing exhibits on the history of Genesee County. Don't miss the section devoted to Flint's considerable automobile history, including at least 15 full-size cars. | 1221 E. Kearsley St. | 810/760–1169 | www.sloanmuseum.com | $4 | Weekdays 10–5, weekends 12–5.

Flint Generals. | Winners of the 1999–2000 Colonial Cup, this United Hockey League (UHL) team plays at the IMA Sports Arena | 3501 Lapeer Rd. | 810/742–9422 | www.flintgenerals.com | Oct.–Apr.

For-Mar Nature Preserve and Arboretum. Hikers head for this 380-acre Genesee County park and its patchwork of woodlands, restored prairies, and open fields. The park has a 113-acre arboretum full of interesting trees, shrubs, and vines, an interpretive center, and a bird collection with more than 600 stuffed and mounted specimens. | 2142 N. Genesee Rd. | 810/789–8567 | www.formar.org | Free | Daily dawn to dusk.

Genesee Recreation Area. Bicycle paths, beaches, a boat launch, camping, riding and hiking trails, and a number of picnic areas fill more than 4,540 acres along the Flint River. From Memorial Day through Labor Day, watch for colored light shows on Stepping Stone Falls, part of the dam that impounds 600-acre Mott Lake. To get there, take I–69 to I–475, then north to Exit 13. | 810/736–7100 | www.geneseecountyparks.org | Free | Daily dawn to dusk, boat launch open 24 hrs.

Dining

Coty's Westside Diner. American. You can sit on one of the 12 counter stools or in a stain-less steel booth in this 50's-style diner with neon lights and nostalgic photos. A jukebox plays 45 rpm records. Burgers and locally famous "Coney Island" hot dogs complement hand-dipped malts. Breakfast also served. | 2336 S. Ballender Hwy. | 810/238–2119 | $7–$9 | DC, MC, V.

Jerusalem Inn. Middle Eastern. Shish kabobs, shwarma, falafel, and lamb chops fill the menu in this candle-lit dining room with custom-made mohagany chairs. Belly dancers enter-tain the first Sunday evening of the month. | 1475 S. Linden Rd. | 810/720–7170. | $8–$20 | AE, D, DC, MC, V.

Makuch's Red Rooster. Continental. It's not unusual to find people dressed in everything from jeans to tuxedos in this popular French-American restaurant. The cuisine reflects a Gallic influence but isn't limited to French fare. Chefs cook entrées right at your table. Try French pepper steak and caesar salad. Kids' menu. | 3302 Davison Rd. | 810/742–9310 | Closed Sun. No lunch Sat. | $22–$40 | MC, V.

Redwood Lodge. Continental. Bear skins and mounted dear heads accent the rough wood walls of this microbrewery, the first in the county. You can see the brewery from the din-ing room. Seasonal microbrews accompany buffalo, pheasant, Black Angus steak, and occasionally duck. There's also a fireside cigar lounge. | 5304 Gateway Ctr. | 810/233–8000 | $15–$30 | AE, D, DC, MC, V.

Saltmarsh Annie's. Continental. Two 8-ft stuffed sharks hang from the ceiling of this din-ing room, where middle-aged couples and families order from a diverse menu. Atlantic salmon, pecan-crusted whitefish, and Alaskan crab legs are among the seafood special-ties. Filet mignon, top sirloin, ribs, surf and turf combos, and chicken dishes also are offered. | 2324 S. Ballenger | 810/234–1271. | $9–$19 | AE, DC, MC, V.

Lodging

Character Inn. In the heart of Flint is the city's largest hotel. With new ownership in 2000 came a wave of renovations to its 16 floors, and a new format. Some refrigerators. No smoking. Business services, airport shuttle. | 1 Riverfront Center W. | 810/239–1234 | fax 810/239–5843 | riverfront@characterinns.org | www.iblp.org | 369 rooms | $109–$129 | AE, D, DC, MC, V.

Courtyard by Marriott. This modern, upscale chain hotel 8 mi south of downtown Flint is in a suburban area near corporate offices. Three floors of guest rooms done in light col-ors surround a central courtyard, which has a gazebo. Bar, dining room, room service. Cable TV. Indoor pool, hot tub. Exercise room. Business services, airport shuttle. | 5205 Gateway Ctr. | 810/232–3500 or 800/321–2211 | fax 810/239–4022 | www.courtyard.com | 102 rooms | $79–$104 | AE, D, MC, V.

Holiday Inn Express. This five-floor chain hotel in downtown Flint has traditional accom-modations. You're across the street from the city's Cultural Center and 15 mi to Crossroads Village when you stay here. Complimentary Continental breakfast. In-room data ports. Cable TV. Business services, airport shuttle. | 1150 Robert T. Longway Blvd. | 810/238–7744 | fax 810/233–7444 | www.basshotels.com/holiday-inn | 124 rooms | $65–$85 | AE, D, DC, MC, V.

Holiday Inn Gateway Centre. Close to a business park off U.S. 23, this hotel is 7 mi south of Flint. The four floors have traditional furnishings throughout. Kids and adults can enjoy the Holidome indoor pool and sauna area, as well as the game room. Restaurant, bar, pic-nic area, room service. In-room data ports, some refrigerators. Cable TV. Indoor pool. Hot tub, sauna. Laundry facilities. Business services, airport shuttle. | 5353 Gateway Ctr. | 810/232–5300 | fax 810/232–9806 | www.basshotels.com/holiday-inn | 171 rooms | $99–$139 | AE, D, DC, MC, V.

Red Roof Inn. This two-story motel off I–75 has traditional furnishings. It's in a busy commercial area and 1 mi from Genesee Valley Mall. Cable TV. Business services. | G-3219 Miller Rd. | 810/733–1660 or 800/733–7663 | fax 810/733–6310 | www.redroof.com | 107 rooms | $37–$53 | AE, D, DC, MC, V.

Super 8. In the Flint area's busiest commercial strip, this motel is off I–75 and Miller Road and 2 mi from downtown Flint. It has three floors. Cable TV. Some pets allowed. | 3033 Claude Ave. | 810/230–7888 or 800/800–8000 | fax 810/230–7888 | www.super8motels.com | 62 rooms | $37–$48 | AE, D, DC, MC, V.

FRANKENMUTH

MAP 9, E6

(Nearby towns also listed: Bay City, Flint, Midland, Saginaw)

Settled by 15 German immigrants in 1845, this mid-Michigan village off busy I–75 now attracts thousands of tourists from around the country and the world who come to feast on Bavarian-style food and drink and enjoy the city's German attractions and architecture. (*Note:* Area codes in this vicinity are scheduled to change to 989 beginning April 7, 2001.)

Information: Frankenmuth Convention and Visitors Bureau | 635 S. Main St., Frankenmuth 48734 | 517/652–6106 or 800/386–8696 | fax 517/652–3841 | www.frankenmuth.org.

FRANKENMUTH

INTRO
ATTRACTIONS
DINING
LODGING

Attractions

Bronner's Christmas Wonderland. The self-proclaimed "World's Largest Christmas Store" celebrates the season throughout the year, with more than 50,000 decorations spread out over some 27 acres. Nativity scenes come in all colors, Bibles in all languages. There are also more than 250 decorated trees, a replica of the German chapel where "Silent Night" was penned, and a video that tells the story of how simple signmaker Wally Bronner built his considerable empire. | 25 Christmas La. | 517/652–9931 or 800/ALL–YEAR (recording) | www.bronners.com | Free | Mon.–Sat. 9–9, Sun. 12–7.

Factory Outlet Stores. Despite competition throughout the state, Prime Outlets at Birch Run ranks as the state's largest outlet-store complex, with more than 200 discount and off-price outlet stores, including Ann Taylor, Polo/Ralph Lauren, Bass, Carter's children's wear, and more. | Exit 136 off I–75, Birch Run | 517/624–7467 | Free | Daily.

Frankenmuth Historical Museum. This small museum on a bustling downtown street is a welcome respite from the crowds outside. Inside are displays that trace the evolution of the town from a simple German farming community founded on religious freedom to one of the state's top tourist attractions. A shop sells locally made crafts and Michigan products. | 613 S. Main St. | 517/652–9701 | $1 | Mon.–Sat. 10:30–5, Sun. 11–5.

Frankenmuth Riverboat Tours. Sign on for one of the sight-seeing cruises and you'll be treated to a tour of the Cass River, with the captain of the *Riverview Queen* sharing local folklore and history along the way. | 445 S. Main St. | 517/652–8844 | $6 | May–Oct.

Glockenspiel. Part of the Bavarian Inn restaurant, the 25-bell automatic carillon plays three melodies followed by a presentation of 35 carved wooden figures from the story of the Pied Piper of Hamelin. | 713 S. Main St. | 517/652–9941.

Michigan's Own Military and Space Museum. The state's military veterans of six foreign wars are honored in collections that range from uniforms, decorations, and photos to displays. One display features the World War I Michigan soldiers known as Polar Bears, because they fought in temperatures 40–50 degrees below zero. The museum also displays uniforms worn by nine Michigan-born astronauts. | 1250 S. Weiss St. | 517/652–8005 | $2.50 | Mar.–Dec., Mon.–Sat. 10–5, Sun. 11–5.

ON THE CALENDAR

JUNE: *Bavarian Festival.* Michigan's Little Bavaria rolls out the welcome mat for this annual celebration of its German heritage. You can see a huge wooden dance floor, some of the best polka bands, maypole dancers, and a large midway area with amusement rides. Afterward, quench your thirst with a stein of locally brewed ale. | 517/652–8155 or 800/386–8696.

SEPT.: *Oktoberfest.* German music, food, and dancing are found within the festival tent, while the European marketplace atmosphere of Frankenmuth's Main Street is dressed in fall colors. | 800/386–8696 | www.frankenmuth.org/oktoberfest.htm.

Dining

Bavarian Inn. German. The Bavarian Inn, in the heart of Frankenmuth, is one of the state's largest and best-loved restaurants, with seven Bavarian-theme dining rooms and more than 1,000 (usually filled) seats. Waitstaff in lederhosen and dirndls serve up house specialties, including the famous all-you-can-eat family-style chicken dinners, Weiner schnitzel, and sauerbraten. Outside is a popular Glockenspiel tower with Pied Piper figures. Kids' menu. | 713 S. Main St. | 517/652–9941 | bavarianinn@pipeline.com | www.bavarianinn.com | Closed early Jan. | $8–$23 | AE, D, MC, V.

Zehnder's. German. The Zehnder family's other restaurant (they own the Bavarian Inn across the street) has a menu similar to the Bavarian Inn's. Housed in a vintage downtown building dating from 1927, the restaurant is known for its all-you-can-eat family-style chicken dinners, steak, seafood, and homemade pastries. Kids' menu. | 730 S. Main St. | 517/652–9925 | $21–$26 | D, MC, V.

Lodging

Bavarian Inn Lodge. This large, Bavarian-style inn is ½ mi outside of town in a residential area. The lowest of its four levels is a family fun center with a game room and other recreational activities. If you prefer to be outside, there's an 18-hole golf course. The inn has antique German and Bavarian furnishings. Restaurant, bar (with entertainment), room service. Cable TV. Three indoor pools. Hot tubs. Tennis. Exercise equipment. Business services. | 1 Covered Bridge La. | 517/652–7200 or 888/775–6343 | fax 517/652–6711 | bavlodge@concentric.net | www.bavarianinn.com/lodge | 354 rooms | $135–$145 | D, MC, V.

Drury Inn. Though this four-story inn is in a commercial area 7 mi east of downtown, its Bavarian style is in keeping with the area's German theme. Cable TV. Indoor pool. Some pets allowed. | 260 S. Main St. | 517/652–2800 | fax 517/652–2800 | www.druryinn.com | 78 rooms | $60–$85 | AE, D, DC, MC, V.

Hampton Inn. This chain hotel is about 2 mi west of Frankenmuth in the busy commercial area that's home to the Prime Outlets mall, restaurants, and a golf course. King deluxe rooms have a marble shower; double rooms have traditional-style furnishings. It's ½ mi off I–75 at the Birch Run exit. Complimentary Continental breakfast. In-room data ports. Cable TV. Pool. Business services. | 13120 Tiffany Blvd., Birch Run | 517/624–2500 | fax 517/624–2501 | www.hampton-inn.com | 89 rooms | $59–$129 | AE, D, DC, MC, V.

Holiday Inn Express. You're 4 blocks from the factory outlets in Birch Run and 10 mi from Frankenmuth attractions when you stay in this motel that's ½ mi east of downtown Birch Run. Its three floors have modern furnishings. Game room. Cable TV. Indoor pool. Hot tubs. Some pets allowed. | 12150 Dixie Hwy., Birch Run | 517/624–9300 or 800/465–4329 | fax 517/732–9640 | www.basshotels.com/holiday-inn | 95 rooms | $69–$129 | AE, D, DC, MC, V.

Super 8. This two-story chain motel is off I–75 on a busy commercial strip ¼ mi to the Birch Run outlet mall and fast-food restaurants. Cable TV. Some pets allowed. | 9235 E. Birch Run

Rd. | 517/624–4440 or 800/800–8000 | fax 517/624–9439 | www.super8motels.com | 109 rooms | $38–$58 | AE, D, DC, MC, V.

Zehnder's Bavarian Haus. Meticulously landscaped grounds and European architecture set off this two-story hotel ½ mi east of town. The hotel has chalet architecture and European furnishings. Area restaurants are within 1 mi. Game room. Restaurant. Cable TV. Indoor-outdoor pool. Hot tub. Exercise equipment. Business services. | 1365 S. Main | 517/652–6144 or 800/863–7999 | fax 517/652–9777 | www.zehnders.com | 137 rooms | $55–$205 | D, MC, V.

FRANKFORT

(Nearby towns also listed: Beulah, Empire, Glen Arbor, Manistee)

This pretty Lake Michigan harbor town is noted for its excellent fishing and the nearby Sleeping Bear Dunes National Lakeshore, its two main attractions. It's also the burial site of Father Jacques Marquette, one of the state's 17th-century founders. The economy is dominated by tourism. (*Note:* Area codes in this vicinity are scheduled to change to 989 beginning April 7, 2001.)

Information: **Benzie County Chamber of Commerce** | 826 Michigan Ave., Box 204, Benzonia 49616 | 231/882–5801 or 800/882–5801 | fax 231/882–9249 | chamber@benzie.org | www.benzie.org.

Attractions

Point Betsie Lighthouse. This lighthouse once guarded one of northwest Michigan's busiest ports. North of the city of Frankfort, it marks the entrance to the Sleeping Bear Dunes National Lakeshore. You can picnic here, but the lighthouse is not open to the public. | 888/78–GREAT | Free | Daily dawn to dusk.

KODAK'S TIPS FOR NIGHT PHOTOGRAPHY

Lights at Night
· Move in close on neon signs
· Capture lights from unusual vantage points

Fireworks
· Shoot individual bursts using a handheld camera
· Capture several explosions with a time exposure
· Include an interesting foreground

Fill-In Flash
· Set the fill-in light a stop darker than the ambient light

Around the Campfire
· Keep flames out of the frame when reading the meter
· For portraits, take spot readings of faces
· Use a tripod, or rest your camera on something solid

Using Flash
· Stay within the recommended distance range
· Buy a flash with the red-eye reduction mode

From Kodak Guide to Shooting Great Travel Pictures © 2000 by Fodor's Travel Publications

Dining

Hotel Frankfort. Continental. This gingerbread Victorian hotel, built in 1902, is known for its elegant and understated dining room filled with antiques as well as for its classic cuisine. Specialties include prime rib and entrées cooked on a hot marble stone at your table. Pianist. Kids' menu. Guest rooms are available, each with a different Victorian theme. | 231 Main St. | 231/352–4303 | $11–$23 | AE, D, MC, V.

Manitou. Continental. Though the restaurant has a rustic, "Up North" look, its menu isn't standard fare. Try sautéed perch and hazelnut rack of lamb. Extra seating is available in the wine bar, and in warm weather you can enjoy open-air dining on a screened patio. Kids' menu, early bird suppers. Beer and wine only. | 4349 Scenic Hwy./Rte. 22 | 231/882–4761 | Open May–Dec. | $14–$20 | MC, V.

Wharfside. Continental. This casual Lake Michigan eatery, with a view of Betsie Bay, is a favorite of both locals and visitors. White linen tablecloths drape the tables on which globally influenced cuisine is served. Kids' menu. No smoking. | 300 Main St. | 231/352–5300 | Tues.–Sat. lunch, Wed.–Sun. dinner | $13–$22 | AE, MC, V.

Lodging

Bay Valley Inn. This motel 1 mi south of town is in a former elementary school. Accommodations include a wide range of guest rooms, including whirlpool rooms, as well as a community room with a full kitchen and a pool table. Ski areas are 15 mi away. Picnic area, complimentary Continental breakfast. Refrigerators. Cable TV. Playground. Business services. Some pets allowed. | 1561 Scenic Hwy./Rte. 22 | 231/352–7113 or 800/352–7113 | fax 231/352–7114 | 20 rooms | $60–$95, $119 penthouse | AE, D, MC, V.

Chimney Corners. Built in 1935, this old-fashioned, wood-construction resort fits in its wilderness setting. Furnishings are rustic, amenities are modern. Chimney Corners has been owned by the same family for four generations. Dining room, picnic area. No air-conditioning, some kitchenettes. Tennis. Beach, boating. Playground. Laundry facilities. Some pets allowed. | 1602 Crystal Dr./Rte. 22 | 231/352–7522 | www.benzie.com/chimneycorners | 8 rooms in lodge, 7 apartments, 13 cottages | $40–$45 lodge rooms, $760–$795/wk apartments (minimum stay), $1,100–$1,300/wk cottages (minimum stay) | Closed Nov.–Apr. | No credit cards.

Harbor Lights. Traditional rooms as well as condo-style lodgings are available at this motel, with four buildings. Rooms have decks with views of Lake Michigan and the beach. Ski areas are 17 mi away, and Traverse City is 40 mi to the northeast. No air-conditioning in some rooms, some in-room hot tubs. Cable TV. Indoor pool. Hot tub. Business services. | 15 2nd St. | 231/352–9614 or 800/346–9614 | fax 231/352–6580 | www.harborlightsmotel.com | 57 rooms, 45 condos | $60–$225, $195–$335 condos | D, MC, V.

GAYLORD

MAP 9, D4

(Nearby towns also listed: Boyne City, Bellaire, Grayling, Houghton Lake, Roscommon)

In the heart of Michigan's North Country, Gaylord was once known for its lumber industry, which shipped thousands of logs south along its many rivers to waiting furniture industries in Detroit and Grand Rapids. Today, alpine-trimmed Gaylord is better known for its four nearby rivers with excellent fishing and its approximately 150 inches of snow annually, which makes for slopeside fun. The city has developed into a golf mecca, with 26 designer courses, the most in the state, and more on the drawing boards. (*Note:* Area codes in this vicinity are scheduled to change to 989 beginning April 7, 2001.)

Information: **Gaylord Area Convention and Tourism Bureau** | 101 W. Main St., Gaylord 49735 | 517/732–4000 or 800/345–8621 | www.gaylordmichigan.com.

Attractions

Otsego Lake State Park. Not far from I–75 and U.S. 27, this park has lots of outdoor recreation, including swimming, water skiing, downhill skiing, fishing (pike, perch, bass), boating, picnicking, and a playground. You can also camp here. | 7136 Old U.S. 27 | 517/732–5485 | www.dnr.state.mi.us/www/parks/index.htm | $4 per car, per day | Daily dawn to dusk.

Treetops Sylvan Resort. This resort is well known for its skiing and golfing. The ski area has a vertical drop of 225 ft and a longest run of ½ mi, which attracts beginner and intermediate skiers. Golfers can try their skills on the Premier, Masterpiece, and other courses. | 3962 Wilkinson Rd. | 517/732–6711 or 800/444–6711 | www.treetops.com | Dec.–mid-Mar.

ON THE CALENDAR

JAN.–FEB.: *Winterfest.* "Frolic on the 45th Parallel" is the fun philosophy of this annual event featuring snowshoe walks, ice-fishing contests, an ice-sculpting competition, a cross-country ski tour, a snowmobile safari, a chili cookoff, and more. | 800/345–8621 | www.gaylordmichigan.com.

JULY: *Alpenfest.* This alpine-inspired city celebrates its heritage with a carnival, concerts, an open-air Mainstrasse featuring arts and crafts, and the world's largest coffee break. | 800/345–8621 | www.gaylordmichigan.com.

AUG.: *Otsego County Fair.* The county fair celebrates the area's harvest and its people with agricultural and livestock displays, entertainment of all kinds, and traditional fun and games. | 800/345–8621.

Dining

Schlang's Bavarian Inn. German. The roaring fireplace in winter and a German-inspired menu makes this eatery a family favorite. Popular entrées include ½-lb center cut pork chops and Weiner shnitzel. Kids' menu. | 3917 Old U.S. 27 S | 517/732–9288 | Closed Sun. No lunch | $11–$19 | MC, V.

Sugar Bowl. Continental. The same Greek family has owned this downtown restaurant, opened in 1919, for three generations. The Greek gourmet table and fireplace are inviting. American and Greek entrées include Athenian chicken, fresh Lake Superior whitefish, and roast prime rib. Some entrées are prepared on an open hearth. Kids' menu. | 216 W. Main St. | 517/732–5524 | Closed late Mar.–early Apr. | $5–$20 | AE, D, MC, V.

Lodging

Best Western Royal Crest. This two-story chain hotel is popular with skiers and golfers. It's right in town, within a commercial area off I–75 and U.S. 27. Complimentary Continental breakfast. Cable TV. Hot tub. Exercise equipment. Some pets allowed. | 803 S. Otsego Ave. | 517/732–6451 or 800/876–9252 | fax 517/732–7634 | www.bestwesternmichigan.com | 44 rooms | $69–$109 | AE, D, DC, MC, V.

Days Inn. A fireplace in the lobby and larger-than-expected guest rooms add to the comfort at this two-story motel right in town. Skiing and 18 golf courses are within 20 mi. Game room. Complimentary Continental breakfast. Refrigerators. Cable TV. Indoor pool. Hot tub. Exercise equipment. Laundry facilities. Business services. | 1201 W. Main St. | 517/732–2200 or 800/388–7829 | fax 517/732–0300 | www.daysinn.com | 95 rooms | $57–$95 | AE, D, DC, MC, V.

El Rancho Stevens. This rural, ranch-like resort (3 mi from town) is a great spot for families or couples seeking an out-of-the-way retreat. Barbecues, hayrides, entertainment, and dancing are among the many activities available. You can choose from two types of rooms—beach rooms with modern furnishings, or rooms with a rustic look. Game room. Bar, dining room, picnic area. No air-conditioning. Pool. Tennis. Beach, water sports, boating. Children's programs. Laundry facilities. | 2332 E. Dixon Lake Rd. | 517/732–5090 | fax 517/731–2819 | 32 rooms in 3 lodges | $118–$216 (2–night minimum stay) | Closed Nov.–Apr. | D, MC, V.

Garland. A beautiful resort on hundreds of hilly, wildlife-filled acres, Garland is known for golf and other recreation, including winter sleigh rides. It has the state's largest log lodge, with three floors of contemporary-style rooms. The resort also has rustic cottages with modern amenities. Garland is 3 mi outside of Gaylord. Restaurant, bar (with entertainment), picnic area, room service. Refrigerators. Cable TV. 2 pools (1 indoor). Hot tub, massage. Driving range, 72-hole golf course, putting green, tennis. Exercise equipment, hiking. Bicycles. Cross-country skiing, downhill skiing. Business services, airport shuttle. | County Road 489, HCR-1, Box 364-M, Lewiston | 517/786–2211 or 800/968–0042 | fax 517/786–2254 | www.garlandusa.com | 117 rooms, 60 cottages | $229–$239, $449–$499 cottages | Closed mid-Mar.–Apr. | AE, D, DC, MC, V.

Hampton Inn. Twenty-two golf courses, four ski areas, canoeing, and other recreation are within 15–30 mi of this three-story chain hotel just off I-75 in a commercial area. Modern furnishings are used throughout the hotel, which opened in 1997. Complimentary Continental breakfast. In-room data ports. Cable TV. Pool. Exercise equipment. Business services. | 2300 Dickerson Rd. | 517/731–4000 | fax 517/731–4710 | www.hampton-inn.com | 83 rooms | $69–$109 | AE, D, DC, MC, V.

Holiday Inn. This popular two-story Holidome hotel is three blocks from downtown restaurants and attractions and within 20 mi of canoeing and other area recreation. Rooms have traditional furnishings. Game room. Restaurant, bar, room service. Cable TV. Indoor pool. Hot tub. Exercise equipment. Laundry facilities. Business services. Some pets allowed. | 833 W. Main St. | 517/732–2431 or 800/465–4329 | fax 517/732–9640 | www.basshotels.com/holiday-inn | 140 rooms | $74–$97 | AE, D, DC, MC, V.

Marsh Ridge. Tucked away in a wilderness area 4 mi south of town, this year-round resort is popular with golfers in summer and cross-country skiers in winter. Its spa weekends also are popular. Three of the resort's seven buildings have rustic furnishings, the others have a modern look. Restaurant, picnic area. Some kitchenettes, refrigerators, some in-room hot tubs. Cable TV. Pool. Hot tub, sauna. Driving range, 18-hole golf course, putting green. Cross-country skiing. Business services. | 4815 Old U.S. 27 S | 517/732–6794 or 800/743–7529 (in Mich.) | fax 517/732–2134 | 59 rooms | $68–$205 | AE, DC, MC, V.

Quality Inn. Rooms in this two-story chain hotel have traditional furnishings. Just off I-75 and U.S. 27, it's in a commercial area that's 10–15 mi to skiing and golfing. Restaurant. Cable TV. Indoor pool. Hot tub. Exercise equipment. Business services. | 137 West St. | 517/732–7541 | fax 517/732–0930 | 117 rooms | $79–$125 | AE, D, DC, MC, V.

Treetops Sylvan Resort. Spread out over a wilderness area 2 mi from downtown, this upscale resort is popular with families and golf and ski enthusiasts. It has 81 holes of championship golf, 19 downhill runs, and lots of other sports activities. Two main buildings have a total of five floors of rooms with modern furnishings. Game room. Bar, dining room, picnic area, room service. Some kitchenettes, some refrigerators. Cable TV. 4 pools (2 indoor). Hot tubs. Driving range, 5 golf courses, putting green, tennis. Cross-country skiing, downhill skiing. Exercise equipment, hiking. Children's programs (ages 1–12), playground. Business services, airport shuttle. | 3962 Wilkinson Rd. | 517/732–6711 or 800/444–6711 | fax 517/732–6595 | www.treetops.com | 228 rooms in main buildings, 30 rooms in chalets | $114–$258 | AE, DC, MC, V.

GLADSTONE

MAP 9, B3

(Nearby towns also listed: Escanaba, Fayette, Manistique, Marquette)

Incorporated as a village in 1887 and a city in 1889, Gladstone boasts over 500 acres of parks within its city limits. Stately waterfront homes share the Lake Michigan shore with beaches and a boat launch. Because of its location on the lake's northern tip, warmer winter winds make Gladstone one of the most hospitable Upper Peninsula cities. (*Note:* Area codes in this vicinity are scheduled to change to 989 beginning April 7, 2001.)

Information: Delta County Area Chamber of Commerce | 230 Ludington St., Escanaba 49829 | 906/786–2192 or 888/335–8264 | info@deltami.org | www.deltami.org.

Attractions

Gladstone Sports Park. Snow fun abounds here, where you can snow tube, snowboard, and ski. For snowboarders, there's a terrain park and half pipe. For cross-country skiers, there's some 3 mi of trail. The downhill ski area has a vertical drop of 130 ft; the longest run is 850 ft. Night skiing. | N. Bluff Dr. | 906/428–9222 | fax 906/428–3122 | Dec.–mid-March.

Walleye's Choice. Fishing enthusiasts can reserve charter excursions for walleye fishing in Little and Big Bays de Noc—as long as the water isn't frozen! | 10132 M–35 | 906/428–1488 or 888/883–4741 | keith@walleyeschoice.com | www.walleyeschoice.com | May–Dec.

Dining

Delona Family Restaurant. American. Home-cooked meat loaf and reasonable prices are the trademarks of this rustic restaurant with a hunting lodge-style interior. | 7132 U.S. 41 | 906/786–6400 | $5–$12 | AE, D, MC, V.

Log Cabin Supper Club. Continental. At this restaurant, you'll dine in a vintage log cabin with a stone fireplace and a high ceiling with beams. Out back there's a two-level deck with patio near a trout pond. The Log Cabin has been serving up fresh fish, aged beef, and other hearty staples since 1930 (a light menu is also available). Try the raspberry chicken, signature whitefish de Noc, or Borrison stuffed filet. Salad bar. Kids' menu. | 17531 U.S. 2 | 906/786–5621 | Year-round. Closed Mon. Jan.–Mar. | $10–$25 | MC, V.

Terrace Bay Inn. American. Burgers, whitefish, and similar fare fill the menu at this casual restaurant on the the Little Bay de Noc. | 7146 P Rd. (U.S. 2/41) | 906/126–7554 | $8–$16 | AE, D, MC, V.

Lodging

Bay View Motel. A stunning view gives this inn between Escanaba and Gladstone its name. Its in a residential, 3-acre parklike area that's close to golf, cross-country ski trails, boat launches, and beaches. Two floors of traditional rooms. Picnic area. Some refrigerators. Cable TV. Indoor pool. Sauna. Playground. Business services. Some pets allowed. | 7110 U.S. 2/41 | 906/786–2843 or 800/547–1201 | fax 906/786–6218 | 23 rooms | $36–$52 | AE, D, MC, V.

Kipling House. Built as a boarding house for nearby iron ore companies in 1897, this bed and breakfast named for Rudyard Kipling is a destination for overnight guests and for sightseers. Even if you aren't spending the night, you can tour the house and learn a little about its history and that of the surrounding community. Homey touches include high-back rockers on the front porch, a gazebo, and rock garden. You can choose elegant or whimsical rooms. The Kiplinger Cottage has a free-standing fireplace and a sleeping loft. Dessert is served in the evening. Complimentary breakfast. TV in common area. Bicycles. | 1716 N. Lake Shore Dr. | 906/428–1120 or 877/905–7666 | fax 906/428–4696 | info@kiplinghouse.com | www.kiplinghouse.com | 5 rooms, 1 cottage | $75–$150 | No credit cards.

Terrace Bay Inn and Convention Center. This turn-of-century two-story hotel and resort complex overlooks Little Bay de Noc on Lake Michigan. It offers easy access to the U.P.'s famed recreation options, including cross-country and downhill skiing, snowmobiling, golfing, fishing, beaches, and state parks. The companion Terrace Bluff Golf and Country Club provides golf packages. Some rooms have private balconies overlooking the bay. Game room. Restaurant, bar. Cable TV. Indoor pool, outdoor pool. Hot tub, sauna, spa. Driving range, 18-hole golf course, tennis. Exercise equipment. Business services. | 7146 P Rd. (U.S. 2/41) | 906/786–7554 | fax 906/786–7554 | terracebay@bresnanlink.net | www.terracebay.com | 71 rooms | $48–$79 | AE, D, DC, MC, V.

GLEN ARBOR

(Nearby towns also listed: Beulah, Empire, Frankfort, Leland, Suttons Bay, Traverse City)

Just north of Sleeping Bear Dunes Lakeshore, this pretty and tiny resort town on the scenic Leelanau Peninsula caters to cottagers and vacationers with its restaurants, bed-and-breakfast inns, and a growing gallery trade. The town is also a popular starting point for canoe trips on the nearby Betsie River. (*Note:* Area codes in this vicinity are scheduled to change to 989 beginning April 7, 2001.)

Information: Traverse City Convention and Visitors Bureau | 101 W. Grandview Pkwy., Traverse City 49684 | 231/947–1120 or 800/TRAVERS | www.tcvisitor.com.

ON THE CALENDAR
JUNE: *Glen Arbor Antique Show and Festival.* Exhibitors and enthusiasts from across northern Michigan come to this annual antiques showcase. | 231/334–3238.

Dining
Boone Docks. Continental. This popular restaurant and bar has a cozy interior with lots of wood paneling and Up North accessories. In summer, the outdoor all-wood deck hops with a pared-down bar menu and lively entertainment. Menu staples include steaks and seafood. Try the lake perch or whitefish. Kids' menu. | 5858 Manitou Blvd./Rte. 22 | 231/334–6444 | $12–$20 | AE, MC, V.

Jack's Glen Lake Inn. Continental. In a small, old clapboard home, decorated with homey rose and chintz, Jack's is a local favorite. Both locals and vacationers chow on specialties such as garlic chicken or baked whitefish. No smoking. | 4566 MacFarland Rd., Maple City | 231/334–3900 | Closed Mon. and Tues. | $16–$23 | D, MC, V.

La Bécasse. French. A tiny, 40-seat restaurant known far and wide as one of the best in the state serves superb French country cooking in a whitewashed, rustic interior adorned with a few simple paintings. Try grilled escallops de veau, chicken breasts with basil mousse, or whitefish with bread crumbs, black olives, herbs, and lemon beurre blanc. Open-air dining. | 9001 S. Dunn's Farm Rd., Maple City | 231/334–3944 | Reservations essential | Closed Mon. and Tues. May–mid-June, also mid-Oct.–late Dec., mid-Mar.–early May. No lunch | $33–$45 | AE, D, MC, V.

Western Avenue Grill. American. Up North looks with lodgelike and nautical accessories adorn this laid-back eatery. The menu includes lots of casual staples, including burgers, salads, and pastas, as well as Lake Superior whitefish and steak. Open-air dining on an outdoor deck. Kids' menu. | 6410 Western Ave. | 231/334–3362 | Open daily year-round | $13–$17 | D, MC, V.

Lodging
The Homestead. This beautiful, wooded condo resort 2 mi north of town is a four-season favorite and has one- and two-bedroom accommodations with views of Lake Michigan and Sleeping Bear Dunes. Furnishings are either rustic or modern. Restaurant, bar. No air-conditioning in condos. Cable TV. 3 pools, lake. Sauna. 9-hole golf course, tennis. Beach, fishing, bicycles. Ice-skating, cross-country skiing, downhill skiing. Children's programs, playground. Business services. | 1 Woodridge Rd. | 231/334–5000 or 231/334–5100 (reservations) | fax 231/334–5120 | www.thehomesteadresort.com | 77 rooms in lodge, 210 condos | $165–$290 rooms, $238–$399 condos | Open weekends Dec. 26–mid Mar., closed Mar.–May 1 | D, MC, V.

GRAND HAVEN

(Nearby towns also listed: Coopersville, Grand Rapids, Holland, Muskegon, White-hall/Montague)

Perched at the mouth of the Grand River on the state's west side, this Ottawa County seat is a busy port and the site of popular beaches, sportfishing, and boating. It was once one of the state's busiest lumber ports, but is now better known as a vacation mecca.

According to local geologists, it's also one of the few areas where there is "singing sand"—sand made up of tiny particles that "whistle" when you walk on it. The local Coast Guard base hosts an annual festival each July.

Information: Grand Haven/Spring Lake Area Visitors Bureau | 1 S. Harbor Dr., Grand Haven 49417 | 616/842–4499 or 800/303–4096 | www.grandhavenchamber.org.

Attractions

GRAND HAVEN

INTRO
ATTRACTIONS
DINING
LODGING

Grand Haven State Park. Popular Grand Haven State Park lies along Lake Michigan. Swimming, picnicking, fishing, camping, and a playground bring a constant flow of vacationers. In winter, you can walk into the closed park. | 1001 Harbor Ave. | 616/798–3711 | www.dnr.state.mi.us/www/parks/index.htm | $4 per car, per day | Apr.–Nov., daily.

Harbor Trolleys. Routes through Grand Haven, Ferrysburg, and Spring Lake take you to city attractions, state parks, and Spring Lake. | 616/842–3200 | $1 | Daily 10–5, Memorial–Labor Day, daily 6 AM–5:30, Sat. 9–3:30.

Municipal Marina. A trolley stop and a mix of stores and restaurants are at this busy marina. | 101 N. Harbor | 616/847–3478 | Free | Daily.

Harbor Steamer. The *Harbor Steamer* excursion boat has narrated 45-minute and 1½-hour sightseeing cruises of the waterfront via Grand River and Spring Lake. Daily brown-bag lunch cruises are also available. Reservations are recommended. | 301 N. Harbor | 616/842–8950 | $5–$8 | Memorial Day–Labor Day, daily 9–5.

Musical Fountain. This large fountain on Dewey Hill near the waterfront is said to be the world's largest electronic musical fountain. Synchronized concerts combining light, music, and water begin at dusk. | 616/842–2550 | Free | Memorial Day–Labor Day, daily; Sept., weekends only.

Tri-Cities Museum. Spring Lake, Ferrysburg, and Grand Haven are the three cities whose histories are told at this museum housed in an 1870 train station. Guided tours and exhibits explain the importance of Lake Michigan and Grand Haven to the growth of such industries as fur trade, fishing, lumbering, and tourism. Besides nautical exhibits, there's a Victorian-period diorama with a parlor and dining room. | 1 N. Harbor Dr. | 616/842–0700 | tcmuseum@i2k.com | www.grandhaven.com/museum | Memorial Day–Labor Day, Tues.–Fri. 10–9:30, Sat.–Sun. 12–9:30. Labor Day–Memorial Day, Tues.–Fri. 10–9:30, Sat.–Sun. 12–4.

ON THE CALENDAR

FEB.: *Winterfest.* A citywide celebration of the season includes arts, music, and theater events, family activities, a kids' area, and lots of chilly fun, including a cardboard toboggan race and the Polar Ice Cap Golf Tournament. | 800/303–4097 | www.grandhaven-chamber.org.

MAY: *Great Lakes Stunt Kite Festival.* One of the nation's largest kite festivals has both world-class sport kite pilots as well as family high-fliers. Seminars and demonstrations are popular with families. | 616/846–7501 | www.grandhavenchamber.org.

JULY–AUG.: *National Coast Guard Festival.* The U.S. Coast Guard celebrates its birthday with ten fun-filled days and family-style entertainment. Highlights include western Michigan's largest parade, a community picnic, arts and crafts, a main street carnival, and a fireworks festival. | 888/207–2434 | www.ghcgfest.org.

Dining

Arboreal Inn. Seafood. Three separate dining rooms, each with its own look, distinguish this surprising cottagelike restaurant. The menu ranges from filet mignon to Alaskan king crab and tasty shelled shrimp boiled in beer and spices. | 18191 174th Ave., Spring Lake | 616/842–3800 | Mon.–Sat. 5 AM–10 PM, closed Sun., no lunch Sat. | $23–$28 | AE, D, MC, V.

Lodging

Best Western Beacon. This chain hotel, in a commercial area near beaches and skiing, is within ½-mi of downtown. Modern furnishings are in the two-story and three-story buildings. Picnic area. Refrigerators, some in-room hot tubs. Cable TV. Pool. Airport shuttle. | 1525 S. Beacon Blvd. | 616/842–4720 or 800/780–7234 | www.bestwesternmichigan.com | 107 rooms | $52–$110 | AE, D, DC, MC, V.

Days Inn. Modern furnishings fill the two floors of this motel in a commercial area 1 mi south of town. Cross-country and downhill skiing are a mile away. Game room. Restaurant, bar, complimentary Continental breakfast, room service. Cable TV. Indoor pool. Hot tub. Laundry facilities. Business services. | 1500 S. Beacon Blvd. | 616/842–1999 or 800/388–7829 | fax 616/842–3892 | www.daysinn.com | 100 rooms | $68–$101 | AE, D, DC, MC, V.

Fountain Inn. This traditional, older-style hotel is nice for families. Two mi outside of downtown, it has two floors and is surrounded by trees. Picnic area, complimentary Continental breakfast. Cable TV. | 1010 S. Beacon Blvd./U.S. 31 | 616/846–1800 or 800/745–8660 | fax 616/847–9287 | 47 rooms | $30–$70 | AE, D, MC, V.

Harbor House Inn. Built in 1987, this farmhouse-style bed and breakfast on the downtown waterfront has three floors and Victorian furnishings. Private baths, whirlpool bath, and views are available. Complimentary Continental breakfast. Cable TV in sitting room. No smoking. Business services. | 114 South Harbor Dr. | 616/846–0610 or 800/841–0610 | fax 616/846–0530 | www.harborhousehg.com | 17 rooms | $90–$180 | AE, MC, V.

Royal Pontaluna. This contemporary-style bed-and-breakfast inn is 3 mi north of Grand Haven on 25 acres of wilderness. Each room is furnished in a different theme and has a private bath. Complimentary Continental breakfast. Cable TV, in-room VCRs (and movies), no room phones. Indoor pool. Hot tub, sauna. Tennis. No smoking. | 1870 Pontaluna Rd., Spring Lake | 231/798–7271 or 800/865–3545 | fax 616/798–7271 | www.bbonline.com/mi/pontaluna | 5 rooms | $109–$169 | AE, DC, MC, V.

GRAND MARAIS

MAP 9, C2

(Nearby towns also listed: Manistique, Munising, Newberry, Paradise)

Blessed with a beautiful Lake Superior shoreline, this Upper Peninsula town encompasses sparkling inland lakes, beautiful beaches, and an entrance to the Pictured Rocks National Lakeshore on the city's western edge. (*Note:* Area codes in this vicinity are scheduled to change to 989 beginning April 7, 2001.)

Information: **Grand Marais Chamber of Commerce** | Box 139, Grand Marais 49839 | 906/494–2447 | www.grandmaraismichigan.com.

Attractions

Pictured Rocks National Lakeshore. Extending 40 mi along Lake Superior from Munising to Grand Marais, the Pictured Rocks are one of the state's best-loved natural areas. Cliffs that rise more than 200 ft above the lake are proof of the erosive action of waves, wind, and ice. Here you can fish in Lake Superior, walk along the 200-ft Grand Sable dunes, cross-country ski over 21 mi of scenic trails, snowmobile along the lakeshore, and camp on the Hurricane River, Little Beaver Lake, or Twelvemile Beach. The actual pictured rocks for which the lakeshore is named begin 5 mi northeast of Munising and are known for their interesting colors and formations. They're accessible only on foot or by boat—3-hour Pictured Rock Cruises leave from Munising in season. | 906/387–3700 | $15 per day | May–Oct., daily dawn to dusk.

Woodland Park. Rock hounds and mineralogists flock to the agate beaches at this park, which is three blocks from downtown on Lake Superior and adjacent to the Pictured Rocks National Lakeshore. It has playgrounds, beaches, modern and primitive campsites, picnic areas, and a recreation facility with tennis and basketball courts. | Brazel St. | 906/494–2381 | Daily, dawn to dusk.

ON THE CALENDAR
FEB.: *500–Mile Snowmobile Endurance Run.* Snowmobilers rev up for this annual race that winds its way through the state's scenic Upper Peninsula. | 800/646–2858.
JULY: *Great Lakes Kayak Symposium.* The latest in kayaking equipment and techniques are showcased at this event on the town's beaches. You can either observe or participate in the training workshops and demonstrations. | 906/494–2447 | kayak@nwpassage.com.
AUG.: *Music and Arts Festival.* Musical performances and arts and crafts by exhibitors from across the state are highlights of this annual event. | 906/494–2447.

Dining
Sportsman's Restaurant. American. This super friendly restaurant has the lake at its back, hooks over the fireplace for sodden winter wraps, and a giant stuffed moose head that's been eyeing diners since the mid-1930s. On the menu are thick steaks, whitefish, and pasties—tender beef or chicken baked in a flaky pastry crust. Try the Michigan trapper hot chocolate, a frothy cocoa fortified with brandy and creme de menthe and topped with whipped cream. | Lake St. | 906/494–2671 | $6–$11 | MC, V.

Lodging
Cabin Fever Bed and Breakfast. This inn is near a small inland lake in the woods, a few minutes from town. The single guest room in the main house is cedar-paneled and has a gorgeous water view. Two cabins that sleep 5 to 8 people are also available; they have sitting areas, wood-burning fireplaces, and fully equipped kitchens. In-room VCRs, no room phones. Fishing. | E20624 Adams Trail | 906/499–3253 | cfc@up.net | www.exploringthenorth.com/cabinfever/resort.html | 1 room, 2 cabins | $80 nightly to $450 weekly | No credit cards.

Walker's Harbor View Resort. Pretty scenery abounds at this resort on Lake Superior that has a beach and lots of trees. It's just a ¼ mi from downtown. Rooms, some with lake views, have traditional furnishings. Restaurant, bar. No air-conditioning in some rooms. Cable TV, some room phones. Indoor pool. Hot tub, sauna. Tennis. Beach. Playground. Laundry facilities. Business services. Some pets allowed. | M–77, Box 277 | 906/494–2361 | fax 906/494–2371 | 41 rooms, 9 cottages | $49–$58, $268–$353 cottages | AE, D, MC, V.

GRAND RAPIDS
MAP 9, C6

(Nearby towns also listed: Coopersville, Grand Haven, Holland, Lansing, Muskegon)

Familiarly known as the "Furniture City," in recognition of its 19th-century beginnings as a furniture manufacturing center, Grand Rapids is Michigan's second largest city. It has a surprisingly large Hispanic community. More conservative than its east-coast neighbors, it nevertheless has a lot to offer, including an extensive parks system, a number of colleges, and museums. The Gerald R. Ford Museum honors our nation's 38th president and one-time Grand Rapids resident.

Information: **Grand Rapids/Kent County Convention and Visitors Bureau** | 140 Monroe Center NW, Ste. 300, Grand Rapids 49503 | 616/459–8287 or 800/678–9859 | www.grcvb.org or www.visitgrandrapids.org.

Attractions

Blandford Nature Center. Stroll through fields and forests and past ponds and streams on this 143-acre site's noted nature trails. You can explore the natural world further at the visitor center, which has butterfly houses, a mini rain forest, and a wildlife rehabilitation program. | 1715 Hillburn Ave. NW | 616/453–6192 | Free | Weekdays 9–5, weekends 1–5.

Cannonsburg Ski Area. One of the 18 runs here will match your level of skiing skill. There's a half-pipe for snowboarders. | 6800 Cannonsburg Rd. | 616/874–6711 or 800/253–8748 | Nov.–Mar.

Fish Ladder. An interesting sculpture north of downtown on the Grand River, the Fish Ladder is a piece of environmental art designed by a local sculptor to help salmon reach their spawning grounds. Leaping fish can be seen regularly from late September to late October. On Scribner Ave. NW, south of Sixth St. | 800/678–9859 | Free | Daily.

Frederik Meijer Gardens & Sculpture Park. Funded and founded by the Meijer family, known across Michigan for their grocery/department stores, the gardens opened in the early 1990s and include both landscaped grounds accented by original sculpture and a five-story glass conservatory housing exotic plants from around the world. | 1000 Beltline NE | 616/957–1580 | www.meijergardens.org | $5 | Mon.–Sat. 9–5, Sun. 12–5.

Gerald R. Ford Museum. The star exhibit of this museum focuing on the life and career of the Grand Rapids native and the country's 38th president is the full-scale reproduction of the Oval Office, decorated as it was during Gerald R. Ford's presidency. The holographic tour of the White House is also popular. Gifts to Ford from world leaders are also on display. | 303 Pearl St. NW | 616/451–9263 | information.museum@fordmus.nara.gov | www.ford.utexas.edu | $4 | Daily 9–5.

Grand Rapids Art Museum. A renovated former courthouse and post office dating from 1903 now holds collections that include 19th- and 20th-century prints, sculpture, paintings, and photographs, with an emphasis on Grand Rapids' famous furniture-making industry. The museum also hosts touring exhibitions—a show on the life of the Italian painter Perugino made its only Midwestern stop here—and has a charming kids' gallery featuring hands-on displays. | 155 Division Ave. N | 616/459–4677 | www.gramonline.org | $5 | Tues.–Thurs. and weekends 11–6, Fri. 11–9.

Grand Rapids Children's Museum. Hands-on, interactive exhibits keep kids occupied in this institution, a true departure from the "look-but-don't-touch" variety of museum. | 22 Sheldon Ave. NE | 616/235–4726 | fax 616/235–4728 | www.grcm.org | $3 | Tues., Wed., Sat. 9:30–5, Thurs. 9:30–8.

Grand Rapids Griffins. Affiliated with the Ottawa Senators, this International Hockey League (IHL) team plays at Van Andel Arena. | 130 W. Fulton St. | 616/774–4585 | www.grgriffins.com | Oct.–Apr.

Grand Rapids Hoops. Founded in 1988, this Continental Basketball Association (CBA) team plays at Van Andel Arena. | 130 W. Fulton St. | 616/458–7788 | www.grhoops.com | Nov.–Mar.

John Ball Zoo. One of the largest and best-loved zoos in the state, the park is home to more than 1,000 animals and some 145 species from around the world. Highlights include an aquarium, a conservatory, a penguinarium, and a 60-ft waterfall near the kids' area. | 1300 W. Fulton St. | 616/336–4300 | $3.50 | Daily 10–4 | www.co.kent.mi.us/zoo.

La Grande Vitesse. A striking 42-ton work by well-known mobile artist Alexander Calder pays homage to "la grand vitesse"—the rapids after which the city takes its name. | Ottawa St. | Free | Daily.

Meyer May House. One of Frank Lloyd Wright's enduring architectural masterpieces, the landmark Meyer May house is among the best-preserved of his works, with original furnishings, carpets, light fixtures, linens, and a color scheme custom designed by Wright and his studio. The house was built in 1908 for a prominent local clothier and is part of the city's Heritage Hills Historic District. | 450 Madison Ave. SE | 616/246–4821 | Free | Tues. and Thurs. 10–1, Sun. 1–4.

Pando Ski Area. Known for its snowboarding, the complex includes a twisting half-pipe, three steep ski hills, two beginner runs, and a tubing hill. The area has a 125 ft vertical drop. | 8076 Belding Rd. NE, Rockford | 616/874–8343 | Dec.–Mar.

Robinette Appelhaus. Fresh produce, cider, and baked goods are on sale here. In the fall, you can take a horse-drawn hayride through the orchards, wander in search of the perfect pumpkin, or watch apples being pressed into cider. | 3142 Four Mile Rd. NE | 616/361–7180 | $5 | Labor Day–Christmas, Mon.–Sat. 10–5, Sun. 1–5.

Van Andel Museum Center of Grand Rapids. A partial reproduction of a working furniture factory is the centerpiece of this museum centering on the heritage and industry of Grand Rapids. Other highlights are a 76-ft whale skeleton and a working Spillman carousel dating to the turn of the 20th century, with rides for 50 cents. When you're done taking a spin, you can stroll down a restored 1890s downtown street, learn about the Native Americans who still call the land home, and peruse a well-stocked Curiosity Shop filled with goodies.

   The **Roger B. Chaffee Planetarium,** also in the center, has a domed sky theater with space and aeronautical performances. | 272 Pearl St. NW | 616/456–3977 | www.grmuseum.org | $5 | Daily 9–5.

West Michigan Whitecaps. A Minor League affiliate of the Detroit Tigers, this Class A baseball team plays at Old Kent Park in Comstock Park, 7 mi north of Grand Rapids. | 616/784–4131 | playball@whitecaps-baseball.com | www.whitecaps-baseball.com.

ON THE CALENDAR

JUNE: *Festival of the Arts.* You can enjoy music, visual arts, poetry, and live entertainment on several stages at this annual event. Food booths and kids' activities are also on tap. | 616/459–2878 | www.artsggr.org/6_festival.
JUNE: *Three Fires Indian Powwow.* The powwow is an annual gathering to celebrate the unity of three of Michigan's Native American tribes. Music, dancing, and competitions fill Riverside Park. | 616/458–8759.
JULY: *Fourth of July Celebration.* Western Michigan's biggest and brightest fireworks display begins with an afternoon family festival followed by entertainment and fireworks at dusk. | 616/459–1919.
AUG.: *Festa Italiana.* A celebrity grape stomp, a boccie ball tournament, ethnic foods, and entertainment are all part of this Italian festival. | 616/791–9422.
AUG.: *West Michigan Grand Prix.* High-powered racing machines take to the city's Scott Brayton Memorial Circuit for lots of high-energy and high-octane excitement. | 616/336–7749.

Dining

Arnie's Bakery. American. This casual restaurant is a favorite for all three meals. It serves such hearty, homemade fare as burgundy peppersteak and prime rib. There's a retail bakery on the premises as well. Pianist. Kids' menu. | 3561 28th St. SE | 616/956–7901 | No supper Sun. | $8–$11 | AE, MC, V.

Cygnus. Contemporary. In a rooftop dining room atop the 27-story Amway Grand Plaza Hotel, this restaurant is one of Grand Rapids' most romantic. It offers elegant dining and dancing under the stars. The extensive menu has fresh regional cuisine, including wild boar and other more expected (if equally creative) entrées such as free-range chicken or veal chops with lobster. It's known for steak and seafood dishes. Entertainment on weekends. | 187 Monroe Ave. NW | 616/776–6425 | Closed Mon. | $30–$40 | AE, D, MC, V.

Duba's. Continental. A Grand Rapids landmark since the late 1940s, Duba's is an upscale eatery with a stylish dining room that's both comfortable and cozy. Items on the menu range from char-broiled Alaskan halibut with citrus butter to sautéed veal liver with bacon and onions. Lobster and king crab are good bets when in season. It's known for prime rib. Kids' menu. | 420 E. Beltline NE | 616/949–1011 | Closed Sun. | $25–$31 | AE, MC, V.

Gibson's. Continental. It's hard to beat this Italianate-style 1874 mansion—a family estate and Franciscan friary—for good looks. The food is equally as good, ranging from medallions of filet mignon with shallots and wild mushrooms to sole en croute stuffed with a mousse of sea scallops and herb butter. It's known for roast lobster tails and smoked prime rib. More than 100 wines complement the extensive menu. Open-air dining in season. | 1033 Lake Dr. SE | 616/774–8535 | Closed Sun. and Mon. June–Aug. No lunch Sat. | $19–$39 | AE, D, DC, MC, V.

Great Lakes Shipping Company. Seafood. Life on the Great Lakes provides the theme that's carried out in pictures of lighthouses, ships, and other nautical artifacts and several cozy fireplaces. Not surprisingly, fresh seafood is one of the specialties, with entrées including whitefish and a fresh catch of the day. Featured dishes are prime rib and walleye. Open-air dining. Kids' menu. | 2455 Burton St. SE | 616/949–9440 | Closed Sun. | $13–$17 | AE, D, DC, MC, V.

John Brann's Steakhouse Cascade. Steak. The fare at this classic American steak house includes aged steaks, huge potatoes, and prime rib. The sizzler dinner is a favorite. Salad bar. Kids' menu, early bird dinners. Sun. brunch. | 5510 28th St. SE | 616/285–7800 | $13–$20 | AE, D, DC, MC, V.

1913 Room at the Plaza. Continental. This elegant restaurant is named for the year the ground was broken for the original hotel in which it's located. The dining room reflects the opulence of the city's lumber-baron period, with dark woods and rich furnishings of the Victorian era. The entrées on the menu are equally impressive and range from lobster-stuffed shrimp to herb-roasted pheasant. Favorites are forbidden apple dessert and grilled New York steak. Kids' menu. Sun. brunch. Parking validation is available. | 187 Monroe Ave. NW | 616/774–2000 | Closed Sun. | $19–$30 | AE, D, MC, V.

Pietro's. Italian. This cozy family-style trattoria is known for homemade pastas and Northern Italian dishes. Try the the fettuccine Michael and chicken pisano. In warm weather, the outdoor patio becomes an open-air cafe. Kids' menu. | 2780 Birchcrest St. SE | 616/452–3228 | No lunch Sat. | $7–$17 | AE, D, MC, V.

Rembrandt's. Continental. Steak, seafood, and pastas are on the menu of this comfortable yet elegant eatery at Bridgewater Place. Kids' menu. | 333 Bridge St. NW | 616/459–8900 | Closed Sun. No lunch Sat. | $22–$35 | AE, D, MC, V.

San Chez. Spanish. The colorful San Chez is one of the few Spanish restaurants in western Michigan. An eclectic crowd gravitates to its large, open dining room with tin ceilings, Spanish-style art, and dark woods. The creative menu includes grilled chicken mole with five-onion relish, saffron rice with scallions and chiles, classic paella, grilled chicken, and chorizo banderilla. | 38 W. Fulton St. | 616/774–8272 | $10–$29 | AE, D, MC, V.

Sayfee's East. Continental. This intimate spot with nightly dancing Tuesday through Saturday is a romantic favorite. It's known for chateaubriand and Dover sole. Band Tues.–Sat. Kids' menu. | 3555 Lake Eastbrook Blvd. SE | 616/949–5750 | Closed Sun. | $23–$37 | AE, D, DC, MC, V.

Schnitzelbank. German. Old-world charm prevails at this local landmark near St. Mary's Hospital. Owned by the same family since 1934, it sets the mood with wooden shutters, traditional cuckoo clocks, and scenes of Old Germany. Large portions of hearty German specialties such as sauerbraten and beef rouladen make it a family favorite, along with American staples such as whitefish and chicken. Entertainment. Kids' menu. | 342 Jefferson Ave. SE | 616/459–9527 | www.schnitzel.kvi.net | Closed Sun. No lunch Sat. | $15–$28 | AE, MC, V.

Shanghai Garden. Asian. A Japanese garden adds elegance to this Asian-style restaurant featuring diverse cuisines. Beside Chinese food, the eatery serves popular dishes such as New York strip steak, beef tenderloin, shrimp, and scallops. Sun. brunch. | 5595 28th St. SE | 616/942–5120 | No lunch in Japanese section | $13–$22 | AE, D, DC, MC, V.

Spinnaker Seafood. Seafood. The nautical theme echoes this restaurant's extensive menu of well-prepared fresh seafood. For landlubbers, it serves steak. It's near Kent County International Airport and next to the Grand Rapids Airport Hilton hotel. Kids' menu. Sun. brunch. | 4747 28th St. SE | 616/957–1111 | $23–$39 | AE, D, MC, V.

Lodging

Amerihost Inn. This two-story brick hotel is 5 mi south of town off I–96 near Van Andel Arena and Meijer Botanical Gardens. Skiing is 20 mi away. Rooms are traditionally furnished. Complimentary Continental breakfast. Some refrigerators, some in-room hot tubs. Cable TV. Indoor pool. Hot tub, sauna. Exercise equipment. Business services. | 2171 Holton Ct. NW | 616/791–8500 or 800/434–5800 | fax 616/791–8630 | info@amerihost.com | www.amerihostinn.com | 60 rooms | $66–$78 | AE, D, DC, MC, V.

Amway Grand Plaza. This elegant luxury hotel has two sides, one with 12 floors, and the other with 29 floors. The Pantlind section reflects its 1900s heritage (the hotel was formerly named the Pantlind), while the other section is contemporary. The hotel has great views and a glass tower. 7 restaurants, bars (with entertainment). Refrigerators (in suites). Cable TV. Indoor pool. Beauty salon, hot tub, massage. Tennis. Gym. Business services, airport shuttle, parking fee. | 187 Monroe Ave. NW | 616/774–2000 or 800/253–3590 | fax 616/776–6489 | www.amwaygrand.com | 682 rooms | $95–$195 | AE, D, DC, MC, V.

Bed and Breakfast of Grand Rapids. Its location in the historic Heritage Hill district and its age contributed to this 1889 Georgian Revival home being placed on the National Register of Historic Landmarks. Its surrounding gardens are a lovely place to sit and relax. Complimentary breakfast. Cable TV, no room phones. No pets. No smoking. | 510 Paris Ave. SE | 616/451–4849 or 800/551–5126 | 9 rooms | $60–$80 | AE, MC, V.

Best Western Grand Village Inn. A Victorian-inspired exterior lends character to this two-story chain hotel, with five room types, 10 mi from downtown Grand Rapids and 20 mi from Holland. It's just a mile to the massive RiverTown Crossings Regional Shopping Center. A popular atrium pool and a location near mini golf and roller skating make this a family destination. Complimentary Continental breakfast. Cable TV. Indoor pool. Laundry facilities. Business services. | 3425 Fairlane Ave., Grandville | 616/532–3222 or 800/780–7234 | fax 616/532–4959 | www.bestwesternmichigan.com | 82 rooms | $69–$130 | AE, D, DC, MC, V.

Best Western Midway. In a commercial area 4 mi from the airport, this older facility has a climate-controlled tropical atrium with pool that's a favorite of families. Modern furnishings fill the three floors of rooms. Restaurant, bar, picnic area, complimentary breakfast, room service. Some refrigerators. Cable TV. Indoor pool. Hot tub. Exercise equipment. Business services, airport shuttle. | 4101 28th St. SE | 616/942–2550 or 800/780–7234 | fax 616/942–2446 | www.bestwesternmichigan.com | 147 rooms | $85–$99 | AE, D, DC, MC, V.

Brayton House. A 20-room Georgian Revival manor in the heart of the Heritage Hill district, this 1889 inn has many original details—including a carved-oak switchback staircase and embossed-foil wallpaper. Complimentary Continental breakfast. No room phones. | 516 College SE | 616/454–6809 or 800/551–5126 | www.virtualcities.com/ons/mi/g/migb801.htm | 4 (all with shared bath) | 4 rooms with shared bath | $65–$80 | AE, MC, V.

Comfort Inn. Traditional-style furnishings fill this three-story chain hotel in a commercial area 5 mi southeast of downtown. Complimentary Continental breakfast. Cable TV. Business services. | 4155 28th St. SE | 616/957–2080 | fax 616/957–9712 | 109 rooms | $89–$110 | AE, D, DC, MC, V.

Country Inn and Suites. The lobby here has a "country manor" style—an ornate iron chandelier, antique-reproduction rugs, and a curving wooden staircase. Guest rooms are simpler. In-room data ports. Cable TV. Pool. Business services. | 5399 28th St. SE | 616/977–0909 | fax 616/977–0909 | bestlodgings.com/sites/26311/index.shtml | 61 rooms | $74–$98 | AE, D, DC, MC, V.

Courtyard by Marriott. In the heart of downtown Grand Rapids, this chain hotel has five floors. Restaurant, bar. In-room data ports, refrigerators (in suites). Cable TV. Indoor pool. Hot tub. Tennis. Exercise equipment. Laundry facilities. Business services, parking ($5). | 11 Monroe Ave. NW | 616/242–6000 or 800/321–2211 | fax 616/242–6605 | www.courtyard.com | 214 rooms, 7 suites | $79–$94 | AE, D, DC, MC, V.

Crowne Plaza. This attractive five-story hotel is 9 mi southeast of downtown and 3 mi from the airport. It's in a commercial area by I–96, next to the Centennial Country Club, and near the largest shopping mall in Michigan, Grandville's RiverTown Crossings. Rooms have traditional furnishings. The executive level is popular with business travelers. Restaurant, bar, room service. Cable TV. Indoor-outdoor pool. Hot tub. Putting green. Exercise equipment. Laundry facilities. Business services, airport shuttle. | 5700 28th St. SE | 616/957–1770 | fax 616/957–0629 | www.holiday-inn.com.ru/crowneplaza | 320 rooms | $108–$155 | AE, D, DC, MC, V.

Days Inn. A great downtown location across from the Van Andel Museum Center makes this chain hotel popular with both families and business travelers. Modern furnishings outfit the rooms on its eight floors. Restaurant, bar, room service. Refrigerators (in suites). Cable TV. Indoor pool. Hot tub. Exercise equipment. Business services. | 310 Pearl St. | 616/235–7611 or 800/388–7829 | fax 616/235–1995 | www.daysinn.com | 175 rooms | $80–$85 | AE, D, DC, MC, V.

Exel Inn. In an adjacent suburb, this two-story motel is 2 mi from Kent County International Airport, 8 mi from Fredrick Meijer Gardens, and 10 mi south of Grand Rapids. Rooms are in the traditional style. Complimentary Continental breakfast. Some pets allowed. | 4855 28th St. SE, Kentwood | 616/957–3000 | www.exelinn.com | fax 616/957–0194 | 109 rooms | $48–$110 | AE, D, DC, MC, V.

Fountain Hill Bed and Breakfast. This 1874 Italianate home has high ceilings, a polished-wood main staircase, and hardwood everywhere. Guest rooms have large desks for business travelers and thick comforters atop fluffy featherbeds. Room service is available for breakfast. In-room data ports, in-room hot tubs. Cable TV, in-room VCRs. | 222 Fountain St. NE | 616/458–6621 or 800/261–6621 | fax 616/458–6621 | www.fountainhillbandb.com | 4 rooms | 4 | $85–$125 | AE, D, MC, V.

Grand Rapids Airport Hilton. Just 2 mi to Kent County International Airport, this pleasant three-story hotel, with a backdrop of forestland, has marble floors and an attractive lobby. It's just ½ mi to a mall and 20 minutes to downtown. Restaurant, bar, room service. In-room data ports, some refrigerators. Cable TV. Indoor pool. Hot tub. Exercise equipment. Business services, airport shuttle. | 4747 28th St. SE | 616/957–0100 or 800/445–8667 | fax 616/957–2977 | www.hilton.com | 226 rooms | $89–$139 | AE, D, DC, MC, V.

Hampton Inn. The location just 3 mi to I–96 and 3 mi to Kent County International Airport makes this motel a good bet if you plan to fly into town. The two floors have modern facilities throughout. Complimentary Continental breakfast. Cable TV. Pool. Exercise equipment. Business services. | 4981 28th St. SE | 616/956–9304 | fax 616/956–6617 | www.hampton-inn.com | 120 rooms | $74–$84 | AE, D, DC, MC, V.

Hawthorn Suites Hotel. This all-suites hotel geared to business travelers is 5 mi from downtown attractions and offices. In a suburban area, it has two floors of traditional suites. Complimentary Continental breakfast. Refrigerators. Cable TV. Business services. Some pets allowed. | 2985 Kraft Ave. SE | 616/940–1777 or 800/784–8371 | fax 616/940–9809 | 40 suites | $79–$94 suites | AE, D, DC, MC, V.

Holiday Inn Airport East. This brick chain hotel houses five floors of traditional rooms as well as a popular Holidome recreation center. It's in a residential area next to the Woodland and Eastbrook shopping malls. Restaurant, bar, room service. Cable TV. Indoor pool. Hot tub, sauna. Putting green. Business services, airport shuttle. | 3333 28th St. SE | 616/949–9222 or 800/465–4329 | fax 616/949–3841 | www.basshotels.com/holiday-inn | 200 rooms | $87–$115 | AE, D, DC, MC, V.

Holiday Inn North. Just 2 mi north of downtown, this seven-story brick hotel has a scenic view of the area. Restaurant, bar (with entertainment), picnic area. Cable TV. Indoor pool. Hot tub, sauna. Video games. Laundry facilities. Business services. Some pets allowed. | 270 Ann St. NW | 616/363–9001 or 800/465–4329 | fax 616/363–0670 | www.basshotels.com/holiday-inn | 164 rooms | $79–$99 | AE, D, DC, MC, V.

Howard Johnson Plaza. An open-area recreation center and tasteful public spaces and guest rooms make this hotel a family favorite. There's a penthouse on the fifth floor. The hotel's just 5 mi from downtown, businesses, and the Van Andel Arena. Restaurant, bar, room service. In-room data ports. Cable TV. 2 pools (1 indoor). Hot tub. Exercise equipment. Business services. | 255 28th St. SW | 616/241–6444 | fax 616/241–1807 | 156 rooms | $89–$129 | AE, D, DC, MC, V.

Lexington Hotel Suites. Roomy, suite-style accommodations cater to a corporate clientele. The three-story hotel is in a residential area 7 mi southeast of downtown. Complimentary Continental breakfast. Minibars, refrigerators. Cable TV. Indoor pool. Hot tub, spa. Exercise equipment. Laundry facilities. Business services, airport shuttle. | 5401 28th St. Ct. SE | 616/940–8100 or 800/441–9628 | fax 616/940–0914 | 121 suites | $69–$104 suites | AE, D, DC, MC, V.

Peaches Bed and Breakfast. A friendly Dalmatian welcomes you to this two-story red-brick Georgian manor, with flowering shrubs. The spare, uncluttered guests rooms have work desks, big windows, and wrought-iron or four-poster beds. Complimentary breakfast. In-room data ports, cable TV. Business services. No pets. No kids. | 29 Gay Ave. SE | 616/454–8000 | fax 616/459–3692 | jl@peaches-inn.com | www.peaches-inn.com | 5 (some with shared bath) | 5 rooms, 4 with private baths | $85–$125 | AE, D, MC, V.

Quality Inn Terrace Club. This three-story chain hotel 8 mi south of downtown is near Kent County International Airport and next to a busy commercial strip. Rooms have modern furnishings. Complimentary breakfast. In-room data ports, minibars (in suites), refrigerators. Cable TV. Indoor pool. Hot tub. Exercise equipment. Laundry facilities. Business services, airport shuttle. | 4495 28th St. SE | 616/956–8080 or 800/228–5151 | fax 616/956–0619 | www.qualityinn.com | 126 rooms | $45–$80 | AE, D, DC, MC, V.

Ramada Limited. This no-frills hotel, aimed at business travelers, is 4 mi from downtown. Complimentary Continental breakfast. In-room data ports. Cable TV. Indoor pool. Laundry facilities. Business services. | 65 28th St. SW | 616/452–1461 or 800/272–6232 | fax 616/452–5115 | www.ramada.com | 56 rooms | $52–$135 | AE, D, DC, MC, V.

Red Roof Inn. Traditional rooms are in this two-story chain motel in a commercial area about 9 mi south of downtown. Cable TV. Business services. Some pets allowed. | 5131 28th St. SE | 616/942–0800 or 800/733–7663 | fax 616/942–8341 | www.redroof.com | 107 rooms | $45–$80 | AE, D, DC, MC, V.

Residence Inn by Marriott. Tudor-style suite accommodations are in this two-story hotel in a commercial area 8 mi southeast of downtown. Picnic area, complimentary Continental breakfast. Kitchenettes. Cable TV. Pool. Hot tub. Exercise equipment. Laundry facilities. Business services, airport shuttle. Some pets allowed. | 2701 E. Beltline SE | 616/957–8111 | fax 616/957–3699 | www.marriott.com | 96 suites | $104–$139 suites | AE, D, DC, MC, V.

Swan Inn. Two two-story buildings house accommodations at this inn 3 mi from downtown. Four golf courses are 2–4 mi away and skiing is 7–10 mi. Restaurant, room service. Some kitchenettes. Cable TV. Pool. Laundry facilities. Business services. | 5182 Alpine Ave. NW, Comstock Park | 616/784–1224 or 800/875–7926 | fax 616/784–6565 | 36 rooms | $42–$67 | AE, D, DC, MC, V.

Tobermory Bed and Breakfast. One of the guest rooms at this 1896 inn, which sits in the Heritage Hill district near downtown, has a sitting area in the house's turret; the views are great. Complimentary breakfast. Cable TV, no room phones. No pets. | 265 Madison Ave. SE | 616/454–1794 | fax 616/454–1794 | www.virtualcities.com/ons/mi/g/migb802.htm | 3 | 3 room with private baths | $85–$90 | AE, MC, V.

Travelodge. A quiet location makes this two-story motel popular with business travelers. Rooms have traditional-style furnishings. Restaurant, bar (with entertainment), room service. Cable TV. Indoor-outdoor pool. Sauna. Tennis. | 4041 Cascade Rd. SE | 616/949–8800 | fax 616/949–4303 | www.travelodge.com | 149 rooms | $70 | AE, D, DC, MC, V.

© Corbis

ON THE WING IN GRAYLING

Each May and June, adventurers come from around the world to this north-central lower Michigan area for just one reason: a tiny, half-ounce bird that nests in the jack pine forests of nine northern Michigan counties.

Kirtland's warbler is one of the world's rarest birds. In the 1970s, their total population hovered around 200 singing males. Their scarcity is due in part to the fact that they nest only in jack pines that are between 5 and 16 ft tall. Because our modern society doesn't like forest fires and jack pine seeds are only released by fire, the bird was slowly being pushed toward extinction.

Today, the U.S. Forest Service and the Michigan Department of Natural Resources maintain the tiny bird's habitat through controlled burns, timber harvests, and plantings. It seems to be working—by 1999 the population of singing males had increased to 905 birds.

Nesting areas are not open to the public, but the Forest Service and the state's Department of Natural Resources lead free tours from May through early July. Tours begin with a slide show and talks by a naturalist; afterward, rangers lead vehicles to a remote spot where the birds are often sighted. A mid-May festival at Kirtland Community College in Roscommon includes nature tours, photo contests, and wildlife workshops as well as crafts and entertainment. | 517/275–5121 | www.kirtland.cc.mi.us/~warbler.

GRAYLING

(Nearby towns also listed: Bellaire, Gaylord, Houghton Lake, Roscommon, Traverse City)

Once renowned for the huge fish after which the city was named, Grayling now attracts outdoorsy folk who come for canoe trips on the Au Sable River and the recreation at Hartwick Pines State Park. The seat of Crawford County, this north-central city is also the site of the World's Championship Au Sable Canoe Marathon and home to the elusive Kirtland's Warbler, a rare songbird seen in spring. *(Note:* Area codes in this vicinity are scheduled to change to 989 beginning April 7, 2001.)

Information: Grayling Area Visitors Council | 213 N. James St., Box 217, Grayling 49738 | 800/937–8837. | www.grayling-mi.com.

Attractions

Hartwick Pines State Park. Seven miles northeast of Grayling, this state park is best known for its stands of virgin pine and hemlock, some of the only such forests remaining in the once heavily forested state. A special trail lets people with disabilities see the tall trees up close. The park also has a chapel in the woods and reconstructions of buildings from an early area logging camp, as well as the Michigan Forest Visitors Center. Take Exit 259 off I–75 and head east on M–93 for approximately 3 mi. | 517/348–7068 | www.dnr.state.mi.us/www/parks/index.htm | $4 per car, per day | Daily dawn to dusk.

Wellington Farm Park. Everyday life on a Depression-era farm is the focus of this park that once was part of an actual town founded in 1881. You can take a hayride, learn whittling and carving, sample fresh apple cider, and buy produce here. | 6940 S. Military Rd. | 888/653–3276 | $2 | May–Sept., Fri.–Wed. 9–5. Sept.–May, weekends 9–5.

ON THE CALENDAR

MAY/JUNE: *Warbler Tours.* The tiny Kirtland's warbler, one of world's rarest birds, migrates to the area's woods and hollows each year to breed and raise chicks. Several local groups organize tours to the songbird's haunts. | 517/275–5121 or 800/937–8837.
JULY: *World's Championship Au Sable River Festival and Marathon.* Canoers start with a mad dash through downtown before racing to the finish in this two-city (Grayling to Oscoda) race. Hordes of race fans drive all night to follow the action in North America's longest and most difficult nonstop canoe race. | 517/348–2921 or 800/235–4625.

Dining

Patti's Towne House. American. Two reasons to visit this restaurant are its Bloody Mary, made with lots of spices and veggies, and its 1-lb pork chops, baked to tender perfection and doused with rum-raisin sauce. | 2552 S. I–75 Bus. Rte | 517/348–4331 | $10–$21 | AE, D, DC, MC, V.

Spike's Keg O' Nails. American. A town landmark, this "family tavern" dates to 1933. The click of pool balls and the buzz of local chat underscore the meals here, which can include Mexican dishes and several types of burgers. | 301 N. James St. | 517/348–7113 | manager@spikes-grayling.com | www.spikes-grayling.com | $4–$6 | AE, D, MC, V.

Steven's Family Circle. American. The gleaming, 1950s-era soda fountain here means you can order a lime phosphate—an old-time concoction of soda water and lime syrup—milk shakes, and other favorite drinks. Also on the menu are gourmet coffee, soups, sandwiches, and burgers. Barrels of penny candy are ready to satisfy your sweet tooth. | 231 Michigan Ave. | 517/348–2111 | $4–$6 | No credit cards.

Lodging

Borcher's Au Sable Canoe Livery/Bed and Breakfast. Staff at this inn lead one- to five-day canoe and kayak excursions along the leisurely Au Sable River. In winter, you can use the extensive cross-country skiing trails nearby. Balconies wrap around the two-story building. Complimentary Continental breakfast. No room phones. Cable TV. | 101 Maple St. | 517/348–4921 or 800/762–8756 | fax 517/348–2986 | chunter@borchers.com | www.borchers.com | 6 (some with shared bath) | 6 rooms | $60–$90 | AE, D, MC, V.

Days Inn. Guest rooms at this two-story motel are furnished with pleasant antique reproductions. Faux-patchwork quilts cover the beds. Complimentary Continental breakfast. In-room data ports, cable TV. Laundry facilities. Business services. | 2556 I–75 Bus. Loop S | 517/344–0204 or 800/DAYS–INN | fax 517/344–9076 | www.daysinn.com | 65 | 65 rooms | $56–$95 | AE, D, DC, MC, V.

Econo Lodge. Ten wooded acres and a central location near I–75 and Hartwick Pines State Park make this motel a popular stopping-off place throughout the year. It's on Grayling's main road. Restaurant, room service. Refrigerators, room service, cable TV. Indoor pool. Hot tub. Business services, airport shuttle. | 1232 I–75 Bus. Loop N | 517/348–8900 or 800/722–4151 | fax 517/348–6509 | www.econolodge.com | 86 rooms | $47–$135 | AE, D, DC, MC, V.

Holiday Inn. A family-focused hotel and convention center on wooded grounds, this two-floor chain hotel is 5 mi from cross country and downhill skiing and 1 mi from snowmobile trails. Restaurant, bar (with entertainment), picnic area, room service. Some refrigerators. Cable TV. Indoor pool, wading pool. Hot tub. Exercise equipment. Playground. Business services, airport shuttle. Some pets allowed. | 2650 I–75 Bus. Loop S | 517/348–7611 or 800/465–4329 | fax 517/348–7984 | www.basshotels.com/holiday-inn | 151 rooms | $69–$119 | AE, D, DC, MC, V.

North Country Lodge. This small motel in a wooded area ¼ mi north of Grayling is popular with snowmobilers, cross-country skiers, and canoeists. Fishing, swimming, and tubing are just 1 mi away. Half the rooms have a rustic, pine wood style, the other half are modern style. Some kitchenettes, some in-room hot tubs. Cable TV. Some pets allowed. | 617 I–75 Bus. Loop N | 517/348–8471 or 800/475–6300 | fax 517/348–6114 | 23 rooms | $38–$150 | AE, D, DC, MC, V.

Penrod's Au Sable River Resort. Though within the city limits, this independently owned resort is in a wooded area along the river. Cabins have furnished rustic rooms. | 14 cabins. Picnic area. Some kitchenettes. Boating. Playground. | 100 Maple St. | 517/348–2910 or 888/467–4837 | fax 517/348–2910 | penrods@grayling-mi.com | www.penrodscanoe.com | 14 cabins | $45–$90 cabins | D, MC, V.

Pointe North of Grayling. Every room in this one-floor lodge has its own country theme. You can ski on the property, which is in a wilderness area ½ mi south of downtown. Picnic area. Refrigerators. Cable TV. Cross-country skiing. | 1024 I–75 Bus. Loop S | 517/348–5950 | 21 rooms | $47–$75 | AE, D, DC, MC, V.

Super 8. You only need to travel 3 mi to reach Grayling and all kinds of outdoor recreation when you stay at this year-round motel just off I–75 in a wooded area south of town. Fishing, canoeing, cross-country and downhill skiing, and snowmobiling are among your recreational options. The motel has two floors of rooms with traditional furnishings and standard amenities. Complimentary Continental breakfast. Cable TV. Laundry facilities. Some pets allowed. | 5828 Nelson A. Miles Pkwy. | 517/348–8888 or 800/800–8000 | fax 517/348–2030 | www.super8motels.com | 60 rooms | $48–$68 | AE, D, DC, MC, V.

GREENVILLE

MAP 9, C6

(Nearby towns also listed: Alma, Grand Rapids)

Thirty-five miles northeast of Grand Rapids, Greenville is a friendly, progressive community built on gentle hills surrounded by farmland, woodlands, lakes, and streams. You'll find places to shop, parks to visit, and high-caliber golf courses. (*Note:* Area codes in this vicinity are scheduled to change to 989 beginning April 7, 2001.)

Information: **Greenville Chamber of Commerce** | 108 N. Lafayette St., Ste. C, Greenville 48838 | 616/754–5697 | info@greenvillechamber.net | www.greenvillechamber.net.

Attractions
The Barn Theatre at Montcalm Community College. The town's community theater performs here. | 407 S. Nelson St. | 517/328–2111.

ON THE CALENDAR
AUG.: *Danish Festival.* The town's heritage is commemorated at its annual Danish Festival, which is held in mid-August and has arts, crafts, music, food, and other Danish traditions celebrated throughout the town. | 616/754–6369 | www.danishfestival.org.

Dining
Huckleberry's. American. Tiffany lamps, original wood floors, and tin ceilings create surroundings where everyone from line workers to lawyers feel comfortable. Prime rib is the specialty. | 112 S. Lafayette | 616/754–0558 | Closed Sun. | $3–$20 | AE, D, MC, V.

Winter Inn. American. Victorian style and elegance surround you at this restaurant on the National Register of Historic Places. Go for old-fashioned liver and onions or walleye—a favorite of regular patrons. | 100 N. Lafayette St. | 616/754–7108 | $5–$20 | AE, D, MC, V.

Lodging
Gibson House B&B. Once owned by Charles Gibson, the founder of Frigidaire, this 1875 B&B still has some of its original fixtures and cherry woodwork. There's a game room with a pool table and fireplace. Complimentary breakfast. Cable TV, some in-room VCRs, room phones. | 311 W. Washington St. | 616/754–6691 | lformer@aol.com | 5 rooms, 2 suites | $75–$125 | No credit cards.

Winter Inn. Upstairs from the restaurant (*see* above) of the same name are 13 rooms with private baths. The building's downtown, within walking distance of all of Greenville's attractions. Cable TV, room phones. | 100 N. Lafayette St. | 616/754–7108 | 13 rooms | $46–$53 | AE, D, MC, V.

HANCOCK

MAP 9, A1

(Nearby towns also listed: Calumet, Copper Harbor, Houghton)

The influence of the Finnish farmers and Cornish miners who founded the town in 1859 can still be seen here in the nation's only Finnish-founded college and in the local popularity of the pasty, a meat pie which is a traditional lunch staple. Tours of the now-closed copper mines show the difficult lives of immigrants who settled in this U.P. town. (*Note:* Area codes in this vicinity are scheduled to change to 989 beginning April 7, 2001.)

HANCOCK

INTRO
ATTRACTIONS
DINING
LODGING

Information: **Keweenaw Peninsula Chamber of Commerce** | 326 Shelden Ave., Houghton 49931 | 906/482–5240 or 800/338–7982 | fax 906/482–5241 | keweenaw@usa.net | www.keweenaw.org.

Attractions

Hancock Beach and Recreation Area. This public park on Portage Lake, 1 mi west of Hancock, has a covered picnic pavilion, sand volleyball courts, a 300-ft sand beach, and plenty of spots to canoe and to fish for pike, walleye, and bass. | 1900 Jasberg St. | 906/482–2720.

Maasto Hiihto Ski Trail. This approximately 9-mi public cross-country ski trail is groomed daily in winter and is popular with everyone from beginners to experts. The main trail head is at the Houghton City Arena, at Birch Street. | 906/482–2388 | $2 | Dec.–Apr.

Quincy Mine Steam Hoist and Underground Tours. With the largest steam-powered hoist (790 tons) ever built, the Quincy Mine operated from 1846 to 1945. Its hoist could lift 10 tons of ore at 36 mph. Today, there are 45-minute tours of the mine, on U.S. 41. | 906/482–3101 | www.quincymine.com | $12.50 | Mid-May–mid-Oct., Sat. 9:30–5, Sun. 12:30–5.

ON THE CALENDAR

FEB.: *Annual Keweenaw Snowshoe Classic Community Snowshoe Race.* Snowshoe enthusiasts race along the Maasto Hiihto Ski Trail in this annual rite of winter. | 906/288–3000.

AUG.: *Houghton County Fair.* Agricultural and livestock displays, midway rides, classic country fair food, and games make this one of the U.P.'s most popular summer events. | 906/482–6200.

Dining

Nutini's Supper Club. Italian. Along with pizza and spaghetti, you can get a massive steak with all the trimmings here. | 321 Quincy St., Hancock | 906/482–2711 | No lunch | $6–$14 | AE, D, DC, MC, V.

Lodging

Best Western Copper Crown. This centrally located two-story motel is just off U.S. 41 and within three blocks of fishing piers, a marina, a fitness center, and restaurants. Cross-country and downhill skiing are a mile away. Complimentary Continental breakfast. Cable TV. Indoor pool. Hot tub, saunas. Business services. | 235 Hancock Ave./U.S. 41 S | 906/482–6111 | fax 906/482–0185 | www.bestwestern.com | 46 rooms | $46–$78 | AE, D, DC, MC, V.

Ramada Inn. A glass-walled atrium covers the pool area in this two-story hotel with spacious guest rooms. Restaurant, bar. In-room data ports, some in-room hot tubs. Cable TV. Pool. Hot tub, sauna. Business services. | 99 Navy St. | 906/482–8400 or 888/298–2054 | fax 906/482–8403 | www.ramada.com | 51 rooms | $45–$80 | AE, D, DC, MC, V.

HARBOR SPRINGS

MAP 9, D3

(Nearby towns also listed: Boyne City, Charlevoix, Indian River, Mackinaw City, Petoskey)

A magnet for city-weary travelers since the turn of the century, Harbor Springs sits on Little Traverse Bay's north shore. One of the state's most traveled routes—the famed "Tunnel of Trees"—starts here and ends in Cross Village. (*Note:* Area codes in this vicinity are scheduled to change to 989 beginning April 7, 2001.)

Information: **Petoskey–Harbor Springs–Boyne Country Visitors Bureau** | 401 E. Mitchell St., Petoskey 49770 | 800/845–2828 | www.boynecounty.com.

Attractions

Boyne Highlands Ski Area. One of two Boyne sister properties (the other is Boyne Mountain), Boyne Highlands has a full-service ski facility with 44 runs, a vertical drop of 500 ft, cross-country trails, a lounge, and a lodge. | 600 Highlands Dr. | 231/526–3000 or 800/GO–BOYNE | www.boynehighlands.com | Nov.–Mar., Mon.–Thurs., Sun. 9–4:30, Fri.–Sat. 9-9 | $35–$53.

Nub's Nob Ski Area. Named the "Midwest's Top Ski Only Resort" by Ski Magazine for three years running (1998–2000), Nub's Nob features 41 runs and a PSIA-certified ski school. The longest run is approximately 1 mi, the vertical drop 427 ft. There are also cross-country trails and night skiing. | 500 Nub's Nob Rd. | 231/526–2131 or 800/SKI–NUBS | info@nubsnob.com | www.nubsnob.com | Thanksgiving to Easter, 9–4:30 daily; 6 PM–10 PM Mon., Wed.–Sat. | $35–$43.

Shore Drive. One of the state's most scenic drives is Route 119, which includes the famed "Tunnel of Trees." This 20-mi stretch of road along Lake Michigan is shaded by a canopy of foliage. It passes through Harbor Springs as it winds north into Cross Village and is popular throughout the year. Autumn is spectacular, with riotous colors and crisp breezes off the water. Along the way is the Devil's Elbow and Springs area, which is reputed to be haunted. | 231/526–7999 | Free | Daily.

ON THE CALENDAR

SEPT.: *A Taste of Harbor Springs.* More than two dozen area vendors set up shop along the downtown waterfront during this event, serving up all manner of tasty treats. | 231/526–7999 | www.harborsprings-mi.com.

Dining

Legs Inn. Polish. Sitting on the bluffs of Lake Michigan, this landmark 1921 building (built by the owner's uncle) was made from local timber and named for the inverted stove legs on the roof. The waitstaff is happy to point out specialties such as goulash, pierogi (dumplings), or *lasanki* (pasta with seasoned fresh veggies, cabbage, and mushrooms). Inside, look for the hand-carved bar and wooden tables, and the stone fireplace. There is also outdoor dining, with a view of Lake Michigan. Entertainment Fri.–Sun. Kids' menu. | 6425 Lakeshore Dr., Cross Village | 231/526–2281 | Closed late-Oct.–late-May | $8–$14 | MC, V, D.

New York. Contemporary. With an urbane, downtown look, this bistro is across from the harbor in what was a turn of the century hotel, which still sports brass fixtures, etched glass, and a stamped tin ceiling. Signature dishes include char-grilled sturgeon (a delicacy fish once abundant in Michigan waters), duck breast with confit of wild rice and Traverse City dried cherries, and Great Lakes whitefish, broiled with lemon dill or sautéed with capers and white wine. Kids' menu. | 101 State St. | 231/526–1904 | www.thenewyork.com | Open daily; closed Apr. | $14–$26 | AE, MC, V.

Stafford's Pier. Continental. This popular waterfront eatery has an unpretentious look and great views of the nearby marina. Lake perch and casual fare are served in the Chart Room; the Pointer Room features more creative entrées such as baked goat cheese, wild mushroom shrimp, and grilled lavender duck. Both seating areas fill up quickly in summer and on weekends. Kids' menu. Sun. brunch. | 102 Bay St. | 231/526–6201 | www.pierat-staffords.com | $12–$22 | AE, MC, V.

Teddy Griffin Roadhouse. American. A huge stone fireplace keeps this restaurant overlooking the Boyne Highlands ski slopes warm and cozy in winter. Try the almond-grilled Canadian walleye, a fillet crusted with almond slivers and sautéed in a raspberry-Grand Marnier sauce. | 5025 Highland Rd. | 231/526–7805 | www.harborsprings-mi.com/teddys | $12–$20 | AE,D, MC, V.

Lodging

Best Western Harbor Springs. This family-run one-story chain motel is 3 mi from downtown Harbor Springs and Little Traverse Bay beaches. There's outdoor access to rooms and suites. Complimentary Continental breakfast. Cable TV. Indoor pool. Hot tub, sauna. Business services. | 8514 U.S. 119 | 231/347–9050 | fax 231/347–0837 | www.bestwestern.com | 46 rooms, 4 suites | $68–$119 | AE, D, DC, MC, V.

Birchwood Inn. Originally built as a corporate retreat, this hostelry 3 mi north of town has a main lodge and five outbuildings. It's surrounded by 40 acres of Birchwood Farms at the beginning of the scenic Tunnel of Trees route. Beaches and a nature preserve are ½ mi away. Complimentary Continental breakfast. Cable TV. Outdoor pool. Hot tub. Tennis. Playground. Business services. | 7077 Lake Shore Dr. (U.S. 119) | 231/526-2151 or 800/530–9955 | www.birchwoodinn.com | 46 rooms, 2 suites in lodge | $90–$145, $289 suites | MC, V.

Boyne Highlands Resort. Golf for summer play and skiing for winter fun make this a popular year-round resort. Accommodations include rooms in the original Bavarian-style lodge, cottages, and condominium units. Bar, dining room. Cable TV. Pools. Hot tub. 2 driving ranges, 4 18-hole golf courses, 1 9-hole golf course, 2 putting greens, tennis. Exercise equipment, hiking. Ice-skating, cross-country skiing, downhill skiing. Video games. Laundry facilities. Business services. | 600 Highlands Dr. | 231/526–3000 or 800/GO–BOYNE | fax 231/526–3100 | www.boyne.com | 418 rooms, condos, cottages | $160–$225 | AE, D, DC, MC, V.

Colonial Inn. The area's longest established resort was opened in 1894 by Civil War veteran Colonel Eaton. The landmark building is ¾ mi from downtown Harbor Springs, with a dock on Lake Michigan. Complimentary Continental breakfast. Some kitchenettes. Cable TV. Pool. Hot tub. Dock. | 210 Artesian Ave. | 231/526–2111 | www.harborsprings.com | 39 rooms | $159–249 | MC, V.

Harbor Springs Cottage Inn. Across from Little Traverse Bay and ¾ mi from downtown shops and restaurants, this one-story, traditional motel has separate entrances to rooms. Antiques, brass beds, and wicker furnish the rooms. Complimentary Continental breakfast. No air-conditioning in some rooms, some kitchenettes. Cable TV. Boating. Bicycles. | 145 Zoll St. | 231/526–5431 | fax 231/526–8094 | www.harborsprings-mi.com/cottage | 21 rooms | $90–$110 | AE, D, MC, V.

Highland Hideaway Bed and Breakfast. This hilltop inn is ½ mi from the local ski and golf areas and mere yards from an extensive network of snowmobile trails. The house has a solarium, fieldstone fireplaces, and an extensive breakfast buffet. Guest rooms are bright and modern, with satin sheets on fluffy feather beds. Complimentary breakfast. Cable TV. No room phones. Hot tub, sauna, massage. Exercise equipment. Library. No pets. No kids. No smoking. | 6767 Pleasantview Rd. | 231/526–8100 | highlandhideaway@yahoo.com | www.harborsprings-mi.com/hhbb | 5 rooms | $72–$150 | No credit cards.

Kimberly Country Estate. This plantation-style inn, with antiques and overstuffed furniture, sits on 15 acres of well-kept grounds and gardens and overlooks a pond and golf course. Guest rooms have four-poster beds and designer linens; every evening you'll find sherry and chocolate truffles on the bedside table. The inn is about 2 mi from downtown Harbor Springs shopping and restaurants, 5 mi to cross-country and downhill skiing. Complimentary Continental breakfast. No room phones. Cable TV. Pool. No pets. No kids. No smoking. | 2287 Bester Rd. | 231/526–7646 | fax 231/526–8054 | www.kimberlycountryestate.com | 8 rooms | $145–$300 | MC, V.

The Veranda. You can sit on the patio or stroll along the nearby lakeshore at this rambling Victorian mansion with arched windows, balconies, and a small turret. Complimentary breakfast. Cable TV. | 403 E. Main St. | 231/526–7782 | fax 231/526–8278 | showard@netonecom.net | www.mich-web.com/veranda | 6 rooms | $140–$225 | MC, V.

HOLLAND

MAP 9, C7

(Nearby towns also listed: Grand Haven, Grand Rapids, Muskegon, Saugatuck, South Haven)

The "Dutch Touch" reigns in this western Michigan town settled in 1847 by Dutch immigrants seeking religious freedom. The town honors its forefathers with Dutch-style architecture, shops, restaurants, and the huge Tulip Time festival held each spring.

Information: Holland Area Chamber of Commerce | 272 E. 8th St., Holland 49423 | 616/392–2389 | fax 616/392–7379 | info@holland-chamber.org | www.holland-chamber.org.

Attractions

Cappon House. The Victorian-era Cappon House was once the residence of the town's first mayor. Its interior includes detailed woodwork and hardware and a variety of original furnishings that belonged to the Cappon family. | 228 W. 9th St. | 616/392–6740 or 888/200–9123 | www.hollandmuseum.org | $2 | Late May–late Oct., Wed.–Sat. 1–4; late Oct.–late May, hours vary.

HOLLAND

INTRO
ATTRACTIONS
DINING
LODGING

Dutch Village. You'll go back to a 19th-century Netherlandish town at this 10-acre theme-park-like "village" 7 mi from Holland. Besides a working windmill, the village has canals, gardens, *klompen* dancers, a carousel, and old-fashioned swing rides. It also has a museum of Dutch culture, a gift shop, and a café serving Dutch specialties. | U.S. 31 and James St. | 616/396–1475 | www.dutchvillage.com | $7 | Mid-Apr.–mid-Oct., daily 9–5.

Holland Museum. Housed in a 1914 Classical Revival building, the museum contains exhibits on local history and the area's Dutch heritage. The extensive Dutch decorative arts collection includes pewter, furniture, and classic Delft blue-and-white pottery. The Volendam Room is an 18th-century Dutch fisherman's cottage imported from the Netherlands. | 31 W. 10th St. | 616/392–1362 or 888/200–9123 | www.hollandmuseum.org | $3 | Mon., Wed., Fri., Sat. 10–5, Thurs. 10–8, Sun. 2–5.

Holland State Park. With 143 acres that include a bathhouse, a long, broad beach, well-used sand volleyball courts, and 311 modern campsites, this is one of the Lower Peninsula's most popular and accessible (it's 10 mi from downtown Holland) parks. You can rent jet skis and boats or arrange a parasailing trip nearby. | 2215 Ottawa Beach Rd. | 616/399–9390 or 800/447–2757 | www.dnr.state.mi.us/camping | $4 per car, per day | Summer, daily 8 AM–10 PM, other seasons, daily dawn to dusk.

Hope College. Founded by the Dutch Reformed Church in America in 1866, this private liberal arts college is known for its music, dance, and theater programs. Tours are available, and there's a popular theater program in season. | 69 E. 10th St. | 616/395–7890 | fax 616/395–7991 | www.hope.edu | Free | Daily.

Veldheer Tulip Gardens. More than 250 varieties of blooms open here each spring—all available for sale. Windmills, drawbridges, and canals set off the demonstration gardens. The DeKlomp wooden shoe factory is also on the grounds; you can tour the factory for free and buy wooden shoes if you are so inclined. 12755 Quincy St. | 616/399–1900 | www.veldheertulip.com | $5 | Jan.–Apr. 12, weekdays 9–5; Apr. 15–Dec. 20, weekdays 8–6, weekends 9–5.

Windmill Island. Holland's Dutch heritage is celebrated on this 36-acre island with gardens, canals, dikes, and windmills. The huge De Zwaan windmill dates from 1780 and still produces fine graham flour. Diversions include an antique carousel and candle-making demonstrations. | 1 Lincoln Ave. | 616/355–1030 | fax 616/355–1035 | windmillisland@sirus.com | www.ci.holland.mi.us/windmill | $5.50 | April–Oct.

ON THE CALENDAR

MAY: *Tulip Time Festival.* One of Michigan's best-known festivals blooms with millions of beautiful tulips, big-name entertainment, street scrubbing, Klompen dancers, parades, fireworks, and much more. | 616/396–4221 or 800/822–2770 | www.tuliptime.org.

OCT.: *Goose Festival.* The fall migration of the stately Canada goose is marked with parades, an art fair, and food and music at this event in downtown Fennville, 6 mi south of Holland. | 616/561–6660 | www.holland.org/festivals.html.

Dining

Alpenrose. Austrian. Extensive woodwork enhances the German-Austrian look in this restaurant's two dining rooms (one for more casual dining). Entrées include both traditional German dishes such as sauerbraten, chicken shortcake, and schnitzel and classic American seafood, lamb, and duck. Open-air patio dining. Kids' menu. Sun. brunch. No smoking. | 4 E. 8th St. | 616/393–2111 | fax 616/393–0027 | www.alpenrose.com | No supper Jan.–Apr., closed Mon. | $12–$20 | AE, D, MC, V.

8th Street Grille. American. Memorabilia and photographs celebrating downtown Holland fill this eatery that seats 250. The Grille, known for its fish and chips and soup bar, has an extensive menu with fresh whitefish, steaks, quesadillas, and sandwiches. Beer and wine only. | 20 W. 8th St. | 616/392–5888 | fax 616/392–6012 | Closed Sun. | $8–$15 | AE, MC, V.

Kuipers' Sandy Point. Continental. This casual waterfront restaurant has a dock for patrons arriving by boat. The menu features the locals' favorite, Sandy Point whitefish, as well as perch and prime rib. Entertainment Fri. and Sat. Kids' menu. | 7175 Lake Shore Dr., West Olive | 616/399–6161 | Closed Sun. and Mon. | $12–$19 | AE, D, MC, V.

Pereddies. Italian. The owner's photos of Italy, wooden floors, and white tablecloths add to the old-world charm of this restaurant, bakery, deli, and gift store. It's known for its pizza, chicken cacciatore, and other standard Italian fare. Entertainment. Kids' menu. | 447 Washington Sq. | 616/394–3061 | fax 616/394–9810 | Reservations essential Fri. and Sat. | Closed Sun. | $11–$21 | AE, DC, MC, V.

Piper. American. Huge picture windows overlooking Lake Macatawa and docking facilities are part of the attraction of this restaurant long known as the Sandpiper. In its newest incarnation, it specializes in Lake Superior walleye and creative pastas. Kids menu. No smoking. | 2225 S. Shore Dr., Macatawa | 616/335–5866 | fax 616/335–6797 | www.piperrestaurant.com | Reservations essential Fri. and Sat. | Closed Sun.–Mon. in winter. No lunch | $12–$22 | AE, D, MC, V.

Queen's Inn. American. Brightly painted, beautifully carved wood is everywhere in this restaurant. Delftware china plates adorn the walls. Cabbage rolls and Wiener schnitzel are on the menu, but you can also get more familiar fare too. | 12350 James St. | 616/393–0310 | fax 616/396–1476 | $8–$12 | AE, D, MC, V.

Till Midnight. Contemporary. The eclectic menu features fresh ostrich (from a nearby farm) and panfried fresh trout, as well as homemade pastas, pizzas, and over 40 wines by the glass. Other attractions include a paté of the day, vegetarian entrées, a bakery on the premises, and sidewalk dining. Kids' menu. No smoking. | 208 College Ave. | 616/392–6883 | fax 616/392–9638 | www.tillmidnight.com | Closed Sun. | $18–$24 | AE, D, MC, V.

Lodging

Centennial Inn. Beautiful Centennial Park is across the street from this brick-and-fieldstone house. There's a big patio in back and a porch out front; some guest rooms have vaulted ceilings. Hope College is a few blocks away. Complimentary breakfast. Some in-room hot tubs. No room phones. | 8 E. 12th St. | 616/355–0998 | centbnb@iserv.net | www.yesmichigan.con/centennial | 8 | 8 rooms with private baths | $89–$115 | MC, V.

Comfort Inn. Just 3 mi from downtown Holland, this motel also is a 20-minute drive from Saugatuck beach. Complimentary Continental breakfast. Some microwaves, some refrigerators, some in-room hot tubs. Cable TV. Pool. | 422 E. 32nd St. | 616/392–1000 | fax 616/392–1421 | comfortinnholland@usa.net | www.comfortinn.com | 71 rooms | $99–$139 | AE, D, DC, MC, V.

Country Inn by Carlson. The lobby's hardwood floors, Delft tile-lined fireplace, and a large wicker-filled porch reflect the name of this motel on the north side of town. Shopping and dining are within a few blocks. Complimentary Continental breakfast. Cable TV. Business services. | 12260 James St. | 616/396–6677 or 800/456–4000 | fax 616/396–1197 | www.countryinn.com | 116 rooms | $99–$109 | AE, D, DC, MC, V.

Dutch Colonial Inn. A white clapboard built in the 1930s is home to this bed and breakfast. Antiques furnish the rooms, and there's a garden and patio. The inn is less than 2 mi from downtown, and a short drive to the area's beaches and Hope College. Picnic area, complimentary breakfast. In-room data ports, some in-room hot tubs. Cable TV. No smoking. | 560 Central Ave. | 616/396–3664 | fax 616/396–0461 | dutchcolonialinn@juneau.com | www.bbonline.com/mi/dutch | 5 rooms | $100–$160 | AE, D, MC, V.

Fairfield Inn by Marriott. Just off U.S. 31 on the north side of Holland, this three-story motor inn is within walking distance of malls and restaurants and less than 2 mi from downtown. Rooms have indoor entrances. Complimentary Continental breakfast. Cable TV. Indoor pool. Hot tub. Business services. | 2854 Westshore Dr. | 616/786–9700 | fax 616/786–9700 | www.fairfieldinn.com | 64 rooms | $89–$99 | AE, D, DC, MC, V.

Holiday Inn. A lobby filled with bright, Caribbean-style colors and paintings invites you in to this four-story chain hotel a mile from downtown Holland. Some rooms have balconies overlooking the indoor domed pool and spa area, others have outside entrances. Restaurant, two bars (with entertainment), room service. Refrigerators (in suites). Cable TV. Indoor pool. Hot tub. Exercise equipment. Laundry facilities. Business services, airport shuttle. | 650 E. 24th St. | 616/394–0111 | fax 616/394–4832 | holdyinhld@aol.com email | www.holiday-innhldmi.com | 168 rooms | $109–$139 | AE, D, DC, MC, V.

The Parsonage. This inn, which has lots of windows and a large screened porch, was built in 1908 as an actual parsonage. It's in a residential neighborhood with a number of fine homes, a few blocks away from Hope College. Complimentary breakfast. No room phones, no TV. | 6 E. 24th St. | 616/396–1316 | www.yesmichigan.com/cities/holland/parsonage | 4 rooms | $85–$112 | No credit cards.

Shaded Oaks Bed and Breakfast. The guest rooms at this Cape Cod-style house on Lake Macatawa are actually suites with separate sitting areas. You can take breakfast or afternoon coffee on the deck and enjoy the gorgeous views of water and wooded grounds. Complimentary breakfast. Cable TV, in-room VCRs (and movies), no room phones. | 444 Oak St. | 616/399–4194 | fax 616/393–0823 | jaxboat@aol.com | www.sirus.com/users/shadedoaks | 2 rooms | $125–$175 | MC, V.

Super 8. You enter your room or suite from inside this three-story motor inn that's off U.S. 31 and a short drive from Dutch Village attractions and shopping. In-room data ports. Cable TV. Laundry facilities. Business services. | 680 E. 24th St. | 616/396–8822 or 800/800–8000 | fax 616/396–2050. www.super8motels.com | 68 rooms, 6 suites | $35–$55, $105 suites | AE, D, DC, MC, V.

HOLLY

(Nearby towns also listed: Flint, Frankenmuth, Pontiac)

A major 19th-century industrial center, this village is now considered a far-flung northern suburb of Detroit. Prohibitionist Carrie Nation once paid a hatchet-wielding visit to the town's row of saloons on the street now called Battle Alley.

Information: **Holly Area Chamber of Commerce** | 120 S. Saginaw St., Holly 48502 | 248/634–1900 | fax 248/634–1049 | www.hollymi.com.

Attractions

Davisburg Candle Factory. Handcrafted candles are still produced in this factory building that was constructed circa 1840. There's a showroom and shop; candle-making demonstrations are available on weekdays by appointment. | 634 Broadway | 248/634–4214 | www.candlefactorymi.com | Free | Mon.–Sat. 10–5, Sun. 11–4.

Historic Battle Alley. Named for the bloody fights that once took place on this street full of taverns and brothels, this was where Prohibitionist Carrie Nation led her crusade against "demon rum" in 1908. It's now a restored 19th-century street full of specialty shops and antique stores. | Battle Alley.

Holly Recreation Area. At more than 8,000 acres, this park includes hardwood forests, fields of wildflowers, sparkling lakes, and several campgrounds. Rustic mini-cabins are available for rent throughout the year. You can hunt, fish, and hike, or go mountain-biking on the park's extensive trail system. Winter brings ice-fishing and cross-country skiing. | 8100 Grange Hall Rd. | 248/634–8811 | www.dnr.state.mi.us | $4 per car, per day | Daily 8–dark.

Mt. Holly Ski Area. This busy ski center, with a vertical drop of 350 ft, is the closest ski area to the Motor City and attracts metro Detroit residents with 18 runs for skiers and snowboarders. | 13536 S. Dixie Hwy. | 248/634–8269. For ski conditions: 1–800–582–7256 | www.skimtholly.com | Adult lift tickets $16–$26 | Dec.–Mar., weekdays 10–10:30, weekends 9–11.

ON THE CALENDAR

JUNE: *Pioneer and Native American Days.* Life in the early 1700s—for both the area's original inhabitants and the European settlers—is illuminated in this festival held in Holly Recreation Area. The event includes demonstrations, storytelling, and craftwork. | 248/634–8811.

AUG.–SEPT.: *Michigan Renaissance Festival.* The past comes to life during this month-long festival dedicated to the 16th century. Period fun and games, jousting, food, entertainment, and a multitude of crafts are available. | 248/634–5552 | www.michrenfest.com.

SEPT.: *Carry Nation Festival.* An annual event honoring this temperance movement leader who once brought her crusade to the city's notorious Battle Alley. | 248/634–1900 | www.hollymi.com.

NOV.–DEC.: *Dickens Christmas.* Strolling carolers, musicians, and performers spouting Dickensian phrases bring 19th-century England to life for a brief holiday period. Area stores hold open houses and sales just in time for Christmas. | 248/634–1900 | www.hollymi.com.

Dining

Historic Holly Hotel. Continental. This Victorian hotel (1891) in downtown Holly has period furnishings, including dark velvet upholstery, print wallpaper, and oak antiques. Signature dinner entrées include filet of beef Wellington and New Zealand baby rack of lamb. For lunch, try the chicken strudel. Comedy theater Thurs.–Sat., pianist Sat. evenings. Sun. brunch. Kids menu. | 110 Battle Alley | 248/634–5208 | www.hollyhotel.com | $19–$28 | AE, MC, V.

J&M Country Pub 'n' Grub. American. It's a bar, and it's a grill, but it's mostly an old-school roadhouse with Formica tables and ketchup in squirt bottles. It's also a great place to get a burger and fries—try dipping the fries in a side of ranch dressing. | 15328 Dixie Hwy. | 248/634–3115 | $4–$7 | MC, V.

Lodging

Holly Crossing Bed and Breakfast. This inn is a turn-of-the-century home with a massive fieldstone porch, soaring columns, and several balconies. Complimentary breakfast. Some in-room hot tubs. Cable TV. | 304 S. Saginaw Ave. | 248/634–7075 or 800/556–2262 | hollybb@tir.com | www.hollybandb.com | 2 | $109–$159 | AE, D, MC, V.

HOUGHTON

(Nearby towns also listed: Calumet, Copper Harbor, Hancock)

Sister city to Hancock, which it faces across Portage Lake, this Upper Peninsula town is the seat of Houghton County. It's also the site of America's first mineral strike (the mines are now closed), Michigan Tech University, and the headquarters for Isle Royale National Park. (*Note:* Area codes in this vicinity are scheduled to change to 989 beginning April 7, 2001.)

Information: Keweenaw Peninsula Chamber of Commerce | 326 Shelden Ave., Houghton 49931 | 906/482–5240 or 800/338–7982 | www.keweenaw.org.

Attractions

Ferry service to Isle Royale National Park. (*See also* Copper Harbor.) Houghton serves as the mainland headquarters for the park, and ferry service is available on the *Isle Royale Queen III.* | 906/482–0984 | www.nps.gov/isro/ | $47 one-way | Mid-May–mid-Sept.

★ **Isle Royale National Park.** The largest island in Lake Superior was named a national park in 1946 and is still 99 percent wilderness. Covering 571,000 acres, this Upper Peninsula wilderness area and International Biosphere Reserve is close to Canada, Minnesota, and Michigan. Moose, wolves, foxes, beaver, bald eagles, loons, ospreys, and more than 200 other bird species are the only inhabitants. More than 165 mi of foot trails lead to pristine inland lakes and campgrounds. The rustic Rock Harbor Lodge is open from June to Labor Day. No cars allowed. | 800 E. Lakeshore Dr., Houghton | 906/482–0984 or 906/482–0986 | www.nps.gov/isro | Mid-April–Oct.

Keweenaw Star. Departing from downtown, this excursion cruise line has sightseeing, fall foliage tours, dinner-and-dancing cruises, and floating casino nights. The 110-ft ship is also available for private bookings. | 700 Lakeshore Dr. | 906/482–0884 | fax 906/337–0863 | info@keweenawexcursions.com | www.keweenawexcursions.com | $15–$31 | Closed Nov.–Apr.

Michigan Technological University. The largest university in the Upper Peninsula, Michigan Tech dates from 1885 and has more than 6,000 students. Campus tours during the school year include stops at the Administration Building and the Seaman Mineral Museum. (1400 Townsend Dr. | 906/487–2335 or 888/MTU–1885 | mtu4u@mtu.edu | www.mtu.edu | Free | fax 906/487–2125 | Daily.

Michigan Tech's Electrical Energy Resources Center includes the **A. E. Seaman Mineral Museum,** which has displays of copper and silver specimens found in the U.P., a simulated iron manganese cave, and a collection of rare foreign and domestic mineral specimens. | 1400 Townsend Dr. | 906/487–2572 | fax 906/487–3027 | www.geo.mtu.edu/museum | Free (donations accepted) | June–Oct., weekdays 9–4:30, Sat. 12–4.

Mont Ripley Ski Area. This U.P. ski area, run by the nearby Michigan Technological University, has a vertical drop of 423 ft, 15 runs, night skiing, and cross-country trails. Follow Hwy. 26 ½ mi east of the vertical lift bridge that connects Hancock and Houghton. | Hwy. 26 | 906/487–2340 | fax 906/487–3314 | nssirden@mtu.edu | www.aux.mtu.edu/ski | Dec.1–Mar 31.

ON THE CALENDAR

JAN.–FEB.: *Winter Carnival.* Ice carving, downhill skiing, snowmobiling, food booths, and more are part of the fun at one of the Upper Peninsula's largest winter festivals. Held on the MTU campus. | 906/487–2818 | www.humtu.edu/~bluekey.

JUNE: *Bridge Fest.* A seafood extravaganza hosted by the Rotary Club is just one of the highlights of this downtown lakeside celebration. A parade, fireworks, a variety show, a bike race, a craft exhibit and sale, and a cardboard-boat race are also part of the fun. | 906/482–5240.

Dining

The Ambassador. American. Pizza, made to order with a score of toppings to choose from, is the specialty at this restaurant housed in a century-old building that was once a tavern. In the dining area, there's a nice view of the Portage Canal—and little gnomes peek out at you from the hand-painted wall murals. | 126 Shelden Ave. | 906/482–2003 | $5–$10 | AE, D, MC, V.

Library Bar and Restaurant. American. Locals and Michigan Tech students "go to the Library" for some of the best burgers in town and to sample the half-dozen home brews on tap. You can finish your meal with a massive scoop of Jack Daniels chocolate chocolate-chip ice cream. | 62 Isle Royal St. | 906/482–6211 | www.framescomplex.com/restaurant.html | $6–$11 | AE, D, MC, V.

Northern Lights. American. High atop the Best Western motel, the restaurant has huge plate-glass windows that overlook the Portage Canal. Try the beef Wellington or shrimp sautéed in garlic butter. | 820 Shelden Ave. | 906/482–4882 | www.houghtonlodging.com/restaurant.html | $10–$15 | AE, D, DC, MC, V.

Suomi Restaurant. American. In a break from the rest of its menu, this downtown family restaurant serves a fantastic Finnish breakfast, featuring novelties like custard pancakes and sweet Nisu bread. | 54 Huron St. | 906/482–3220 | $5–$7 | No credit cards.

Lodging

Best Western Franklin Square Inn. This attractive, seven-story chain hotel overlooking the canal is downtown near Michigan Tech, and a 5-minute drive to cross-country and downhill skiing in Hancock. Rooms face either the canal or the street. Restaurant, bar, room service. Cable TV. Indoor pool. Hot tub, sauna. Business services. | 820 Shelden Ave. | 906/487–1700 | fax 906/487–9432 | bwfrank@portup.com | fax 906/487–9432 | www.houghtonlodging.com | 105 rooms | $89–$99 | AE, D, DC, MC, V.

Best Western King's Inn. In the heart of downtown, this five-story chain hotel is within a few blocks of shopping, city parks, and restaurants, and ¾ mi from Michigan Tech. Complimentary Continental breakfast. Cable TV. Indoor pool. Hot tub, sauna. Some pets allowed. | 215 Shelden Ave. | 906/482–5000 | fax 906/482–9795 | www.houghtonlodging.com | 69 rooms | $69–$81 | AE, D, DC, MC, V.

Chippewa Hotel. Overlooking Chassell Bay, with its great summer and winter fishing, this small motel is one block from cross-country skiing and snowmobile trails and within walking distance of grocery stores, gift shops, taverns. Picnic area. Some kitchenettes. Cable TV. | U.S. 41, Box 470, Chassell | 906/523–4611 | www.portup.com/mainstr/chippewa/ | 15 rooms | $38–$55 | D, DC, MC, V.

L'Anse Motel and Suites. This mom-and-pop motel 30 mi south of Houghton, near Baraga State Park and Lake Superior, is decidedly off the beaten path, but good for hikers and outdoor types. It's 4 mi from cross-country skiing and a half-hour to downhill skiing. Cable TV. Some pets allowed. | U.S. 41, Box 506, L'Anse | 906/524–7820 or 800/800–6198 | fax 906/524–7247 | 21 rooms | $29–$57 | D, DC, MC, V.

Super 8–Baraga. Across the street from a casino, this modern motel is 30 mi from Houghton. Complimentary Continental breakfast. Cable TV. Business services. Pets allowed. | 790 Michigan Ave., Baraga | 906/353–6680 or 800/800–8000 | fax 906/353–7246 | www.super8motels.com | 40 rooms | $45–$57 | AE, D, DC, MC, V.

Super 8–Houghton. Lakeside rooms are available at this chain motel right on a snowmobile trail. It's two blocks from Michigan Tech. The MTU ski slope is a mile north. Complimentary Continental breakfast. Cable TV. Indoor pool. Hot tub, sauna. | 1200 E. Lakeshore Dr. | 906/482–2240 or 800/800–8000 | fax 906/482–0686 | www.qualityinn.com | 86 rooms | $65–$70 | AE, D, DC, MC, V.

Vacationland Motel. Comfortable accommodations await you at this motel 2 mi from downtown. There's an outdoor pool for summer use. Complimentary Continental breakfast. Cable TV. Pool. | U.S. 41 SE, Box 93 | 906/482–5351 or 800/822–3279 | 24 rooms | $50–$66 | AE, D, DC, MC, V.

HOUGHTON LAKE

MAP 9, D5

(Nearby towns also listed: Cadillac, Clare, Gaylord, Grayling)

More than 200,000 acres of state forest surround this year-round resort town near the state's largest inland lake. The area is popular with boaters, skiers, anglers, and snowmobilers. (*Note:* Area codes in this vicinity are scheduled to change to 989 beginning April 7, 2001.)

Information: Roscommon County/Houghton Lake Area Tourism and Convention Bureau | Box 1, Houghton Lake 48629 | 517/422–2822 or 800/676–5330 | www.roscommoncounty.com.

Attractions

Higgins Lake. More than 50 mi of sandy shoreline ring this lake that covers more than 9,000 acres. Higgins is a popular fishing and boating destination, 14 mi north of Houghton Lake. | 517/275–8760 | www.hlrcc.com.

Houghton Lake. Numerous resorts and marinas border the 70-mi shoreline of the state's largest inland lake. It's the source of the Muskegon River. | 517/366–5644 or 800/248–5253 | www.houghtonlakechamber.com.

St. Helen Lake. You can fish and boat on this smaller Roscommon County lake with 18 mi of shoreline. It's in the middle of a pine forest between I–75 and M–76. | 517/389–3725.

ON THE CALENDAR

JAN.: ***Tip-Up-Town USA Ice Festival.*** Ice fishermen and other winter sports enthusiasts head to Houghton Lake for fishing competitions, winter sports, food, and fun. | 800/248–5253 | www.houghtonlakechamber.com.

Dining

Coyles. American. This casual, family-friendly eatery is known for its traditional fare (seafood, steaks, chicken), bountiful salad bar, and lunch and dinner buffets (seafood buffet on Fri. and Sat. evenings). Stop by the gift shop and the Fred Trost trophy room before leaving. Kids' menu. | 9074 U.S. 27 | 517/422–3812 | fax 517/422–4937 | www.coylesrestaurant.com | $6–$14 | AE, D, MC, V.

Holiday on the Lake. Continental. A large dock, a stone fireplace, and an outside patio distinguish this Houghton Lake sports bar and hangout. Northern Michigan whitefish is a staple, or if you're really ready for it, try the cattleman's sizzler steak, which weighs in at a whopping 16 oz. Salad bar. Entertainment. Kids' menu. | 100 Clearview | 517/422–5195 | fax 517/422–5195 | www.holidayonthelake.com | $8–$18 | AE, D, MC, V.

Powell's Restaurant. American. Locals come here for the big hearty breakfasts of eggs, locally produced sausage, and buttermilk pancakes. If you're having lunch, you should follow it with a slice of freshly baked pie. | W. Houghton Lake Dr. | 517/366–8721 | $5–$7 | MC, V.

Lodging

American Oak Resort. You can use the resort's pristine stretch of sand beach, as well as picnic areas and grills. Rental cabins have two bedrooms, sleeper sofas, and full kitchens. There are also two-bedroom chalets with spacious sleeping lofts. Cable TV. No in-room phones. Boating. | 4440 W. Houghton Lake Dr. | 517/366–6464 | fax 517/366–1315 | mail@americanoakresort.com | www.mindspring.com~awjens/americanoakresort.htm | 7 cabins, 2 chalets | $525 weekly for cabins, $700 for chalets | AE, D, MC, V.

Lagoon Resort and Motel. This resort motel is right on the lake, with a beach for sunning and swimming, a playground for the kids, and beautiful wooded surroundings. Guest rooms are scattered throughout a collection of town houses, condos, and cottages, most with kitchens and some with private little stretches of beach. Pool. Fishing. | 6578 W. Houghton Lake Dr. | 517/422–5761 | 15 rooms | $30–$75 | MC, V.

Quality Inn. A short drive takes you to beaches, fishing, and other lake attractions from this two-story chain hotel. It's on the west end of town, just off U.S. 27. Restaurant, bar. Cable TV. Indoor pool. Hot tub, sauna. Business services. | 9285 W. Houghton Lake Dr. | 517/422–5175 or 800/228–5151 | fax 517/422–3071 | www/qualityinn.com | 100 rooms | $75–$85 | D, MC, V.

Super 8. At U.S. 27 and M–55, this modern chain hotel with basic rooms is less than 10 mi from Houghton Lake. Cable TV. Pool. Hot tub, sauna. | 9580 W. Lake City Rd. | 517/422–3119 | fax 517/422–5561 | www.super8motels.com | 70 rooms | $55–$80 | D, MC, V.

Venture Inn. This basic, small, one-story motel is next to the Houghton Lake state police post. Outdoor pool. | 8939 W. Houghton Lake Dr. | 517/422–5591 | 12 rooms | $49–$70 | MC, V.

Woodbine Villa Resort. Two-bedroom log cabins on a private Houghton Lake beach are the accommodations here. Each has a picnic table, charcoal grill, and fully outfitted kitchen. No air-conditioning. Cable TV. Sauna. Beach, dock, boating. Playground. Laundry facilities. | 12122 W. Shore Dr. | 517/422–5349 | info@woodbinevilla.com | www.woodbinevilla.com | 9 cottages | Memorial Day–Labor Day, $545/week (no single nights); after Labor Day, $345/week, $70/night | MC, V.

INDIAN RIVER

MAP 9, D3

(Nearby towns also listed: Boyne City, Cheboygan, Harbor Springs, Petoskey)

The Pigeon and Sturgeon rivers attract kayakers, canoeists, anglers, and boaters to this tiny mid-Michigan town. Others come to see the huge Cross in the Woods, listed in the Guinness Book of Records as the world's largest crucifix. (*Note:* Area codes in this vicinity are scheduled to change to 989 beginning April 7, 2001.)

Information: Indian River Chamber of Commerce and Tourist Bureau | Box 414, Indian River 49749 | 800/EXIT–310 | www.irmi.com.

Attractions

Burt Lake State Park. This 400-acre state park is known for its fishing (walleyed pike, perch), boating, and secluded picnicking spots. It also has a playground, concessions, and camping. | 6635 State Park Dr. | 231/238–9392 or 800/447–2757 | www.dnr.state.mi.us/camping | $4 per car, per day | May–Oct., daily.

Canoeing. Area liveries rent canoes, kayaks, and tubes for use on the nearby Pigeon and Sturgeon rivers. You can choose from several routes; difficulty varies with route. Reservations are advised. Try **Tomahawk Trails Canoe Livery** (Box 814 | 231/238–8703 | May–Oct.) and **Big Bear Adventures** (4271 S. Straits Hwy. | 231/238–8181 | bigbear@freeway.net | www.bigbearadventures.com | May–mid-Oct.).

Cross in the Woods. More than 55 ft tall and 22 ft across, this statue is recorded as the world's largest crucifix. The cross is carved from an Oregon redwood, and the cast bronze figure, by Michigan artist Marshall Frederick, weighs 7 tons. The surrounding 13 acres have an open-air church, flower gardens, and a religious-themed museum. | 7078 M–68 | 231/238–8973 | crossinthewoods@nmo.net | Free | Mar.–Nov., daily 9–6, church open all year.

Inland Waterways. A vast system of waterways—made up of more than 20 lakes, rivers, and streams—connects Crooked Lake near Indian River to Lake Huron. If you're the sort who hungers for a wilderness experience, you can take a canoe or kayak along the waterways and see heron, beaver, deer, and other wildlife, as well as fantastic scenery. You can hire a guide for the trip, which usually takes about two days. | 800/394–8310 | www.irmi.org.

ON THE CALENDAR
JULY: Summerfest. This downtown celebration boasts an arts-and-crafts show, a cake-walk, a dog-and-owner look-alike contest, and a big chili cook-off. | 231/238–9325 or 800/394–8310 | chamber@irmi.org | www.irmi.org.

Dining
Brown Trout Restaurant and Tavern. Contemporary. Dating from the 1930s, this town landmark's "Up North" character comes from its rustic cabin look, rough-hewn hickory furniture, and exposed beam ceilings. There's a patio out back for warm-weather dining. Try the smoked trout mousse served with bagel chips for dipping. | 4653 S. Straits Hwy. | 231/238–9441 | browntrout@browntroutmi.com | www.browntroutmi.com | Mon.–Thurs. 11–11, Fri.–Sat. 11 AM–2 PM, Sun. 10–10 | $10–$22 | AE, D, MC, V.

Lodging
Holiday Inn Express. This modern one-story motel is less than a mile from downtown Indian River, and less than 2 mi from the Cross in the Woods and Burt Lake. Complimentary Continental breakfast. Some in-room hot tubs. Cable TV. Indoor pool. Video games. Laundry facilities. | 4375 Brudy Rd. | 231/238–3000 or 800/465–4329 | fax 231/238–8992 | www.hiexpstraitsarea.com | 46 rooms, 4 suites | $99–$149 | AE, D, DC, MC, V.

Nor-Gate. Simple accommodations, including motel units, a mobile home, and one cabin, are available here. It's right off snowmobile trails and 1 mi from Burt Lake State Park. Picnic area. Some kitchenettes. Cable TV. | 4846 S. Straits Hwy. | 231/238–7788 | chamber@irmi.org | www.irmi.org | 12 rooms | $46–$70 | AE, D, MC, V.

Northwoods Lodge. This rustic, rambling log cabin hostelry has handmade log beds and furnishings. Canoe and kayak trips on Burt and Mullet Lakes are organized here. Complimentary Continental breakfast. Some in-room hot tubs. Cable TV. Sauna. Cross-country skiing. | 2390 S. Straits Hwy. | 231/238–7729 | fax 231/238–4500 | www.mich-web.com/northwoodslodge | 15 rooms | $69–$100 | D, MC, V.

IRON MOUNTAIN

MAP 9, A3

(Nearby towns also listed: Escanaba, Ishpeming, Iron River)

The rich iron deposits that gave this small (pop. 8,500) Upper Peninsula town its name, and were exploited from the 1870s to the 1940s, are no longer mined. Mine shafts are now tourist attractions and reminders of the town's heyday. (*Note:* Area codes in this vicinity are scheduled to change to 989 beginning April 7, 2001.)

Information: Tourism Association of Dickinson County | 600 S. Stephenson Ave., Box 672, Iron Mountain 49801 | 906/774–2945 or 800/236–2447 | tadca@up.net | www.ironmtntourism.org.

Attractions

Cornish Pumping Museum. The story of iron mining in the eastern Menominee Range is told through mining tools and machines, including the Cornish pumping engine designed in 1890. With a flywheel 40 ft in diameter and weighing more than 725 tons, it was once the largest engine in the country, capable of pumping 4.5 million gallons daily. The museum is 2 blocks west of U.S. 2. | 300 Kent St. | 906/774–1086 | $4 | May–Oct., Mon.–Sat. 9–5, Sun. 10–4; hours vary other seasons.

Iron Mountain Iron Mine. The source of more than 21 million tons of ore, this huge mine 10 mi east of Iron Mountain operated from the 1870s through the 1940s. Guided rail tours take you 400 ft below the surface. | W4852 U.S. 2 | 906/563–8077 | www.ironmountain-mine.com | $7 | May–mid-Oct., daily 9–5.

Menominee Range Historical Foundation Museum. Displays on the copper-rich history of Dickinson County and the Menominee Range include manuscripts, photographs, original artifacts, and other memorabilia. Highlights of the more than 100 exhibits include a turn-of-the-century general store and a replica of a typical Victorian-era parlor. | Carnegie Public Library, 300 E. Ludington St. | 906/774–4276 | $4 | May–Sept., Mon.–Sat. 10–4.

Pine Mountain Resort. When you tire of skiing, this resort has three bars, three restaurants, an indoor pool, and an on-site lodge. If you're here for the snow, Pine Mountain boasts 19 runs, including one that's ¾ mi, and a vertical drop of 400 ft. There's also an outdoor ice skating rink here. | 3332 N. Pine Mountain Rd. | 906/774–2747 or 877/553–7463 | pinemtn@uplogon.com | www.pinemountainresort.com | $23–$28 | Nov.–Apr.

U.P. Sports Hall of Fame. The achievements of Upper Peninsula athletes are showcased in this mini-museum housed in the restaurant adjacent to the Pine Mountain Lodge. Displays include photos and personal memorabilia. | 332 N. Pine Mountain Rd. | 906/774–2747 or 877/553–7463 | pinemtn@uplogon.com | www.pinemountainresort.com | Free.

ON THE CALENDAR

FEB.: *Pine Mountain Ski Jumping Tournament.* The world's best ski jumpers converge on the U.P.'s Pine Mountain for this annual high-flying event. | 3332 N. Pine Mountain Rd. | 906/774–2747.

Dining

Fontana's Supper Club. American. The beef cuts are the house specialty at this unpretentious family restaurant, which has lots of big tables, perfect for large groups. Fresh seafood and pasta also are on the menu. | 115 Stephenson | 906/774–0044 | Closed Sun., no lunch | $10–$20 | AE, D, DC, MC, V.

Romagnoli's. Italian. On an area snowmobile trail, this is a casual, "come-as-you-are" kind of place—even if you're zipped into a weatherproof coverall and moon boots, fresh out of the woods. Try the house specialty, ribs tulio: pork baby-back ribs broiled with a special sauce until tender and juicy, and served with sides of homemade bread, gnocchi, and a salad. | 1630 N. Stephenson | 906/774–7300 | pastaman@bresnanlink.net | www.exploringthenorth.com/romagnoli/rom.html | Closed Sun. | $7–$15 | MC, V.

Lodging

Best Western Executive Inn. It's easy to get to this two-story brick chain hotel from U.S. 2. Shopping and fast-food dining are in the immediate area. Downtown Iron Mountain is a mile away, and it's about 5 mi to skiing. Complimentary Continental breakfast. Cable TV. Indoor pool. Some pets allowed. | 1518 S. Stephenson Ave. | 906/774–2040 or 800/780–7234 | fax 906/774–0238 | www.bestwestern.com | 57 rooms | $58–$68 | AE, D, DC, MC, V.

Comfort Inn. Less than a mile from Iron Mountain, and within walking distance of restaurants, this standard two-story motor lodge has indoor room entrances. It's popular with business travelers. Complimentary Continental breakfast. Some refrigerators. Cable TV. Hot tub. Exercise equipment. Laundry facilities. Business services. | 1555 N. Stephenson Ave. | 906/774–5505 | fax 906/774–2631 | www.comfortinn.com | 44 rooms, 4 suites | $54–$76 | AE, D, DC, MC, V.

Days Inn. Large chain stores are across the street from this basic motel that's a mile from Iron Mountain. Complimentary Continental breakfast. Some refrigerators. Cable TV. Indoor pool. Hot tub. Laundry facilities. Business services. | 8176 N. Stephenson Ave. | 906/774–2181 or 800/388–7829 | fax 906/774–8252 | www.daysinn.com | 40 rooms, 4 suites | $59–$85 | AE, D, DC, MC, V.

Edgewater Resort Country Log Cabins. These rustic rental cabins on the Menominee River have been hosting guests since the 1940s. Cable TV, no room phones. Boating, fishing. Laundry facilities. | N4128 N. U.S. 2 | 906/774–6244 | info@edgewaterresort.com | www.edgewaterresort.com | 9 cabins | $44–$73 | MC, V.

Moon Lake Motel. This independently owned and operated motel is near fishing and snowmobiling grounds. There's prime cross-country skiing nearby, too. Some microwaves. Cable TV. | 2906 N. U.S. 2 | 906/774–3399 | fax 906/774–0054 | moonlk@exploringthenorth.com | www.exploringthenorth.com/moonlake/moon.html | 10 rooms | $34–$50 | AE, D, DC, MC, V.

Super 8 Iron Mountain. An inviting lawn surrounds this chain hotel in a quiet area 2 mi from downtown. Picnic area, complimentary Continental breakfast. Some refrigerators. Cable TV. Indoor pool. Hot tub, sauna. Laundry facilities. Business services. | 2702 N. Stephenson Ave. | 906/774–3400 or 800/800–8000 | fax 906/774–9903 | www.super8motels.com | 86 rooms, 4 suites | $59–$72 | AE, D, DC, MC, V.

Timbers Motor Lodge. Large timbers frame the entrance to this independently owned motel on U.S. 2, the main downtown drag. A cedar-paneled indoor terrace overlooks the pool area. In-room data ports. Cable TV. Indoor pool. Hot tub. Exercise equipment. Business services. | 200 S. Stephenson Ave. | 906/774–7600 or 800/433–8533 | fax 906/774–6222 | thetimebers@uplogon.com | www.thetimbers.com | 50 rooms, 2 suites | $50–$80 | AE, D, DC, MC, V.

IRON RIVER

MAP 9, A2, F3

(Nearby towns also listed: Iron Mountain, Ironwood)

Once one of the Menominee Range's largest mining towns, this Upper Peninsula village with a population of 3,000 is near the Wisconsin state line and Iron Mountain. It's known as the gateway to the Ottawa National Forest. (*Note:* Area codes in this vicinity are scheduled to change to 989 beginning April 7, 2001.)

Information: Iron County Chamber of Commerce | 50 E. Genesee St., Iron River 49935 | 906/265–3822 or 888/879–4766 | fax 906/265–5605 | www.tryiron.org.

Attractions

Harbor House Museum. This mansion was built for a state legislator in 1900 in an unusual "steamboat" style, with twin wraparound porches. The house, which is 8 mi southeast of Iron River, is now a community center and museum, with hands-on historical demonstrations, exhibits, and tours by appointment. | 17 N. 4th St., Crystal Falls | 906/875–4341 | www.iron.org/museums-harborhouse.html | Free | Closed Oct.–Mar.

Iron County Museum. This museum complex is made up of more than 22 buildings and includes a fascinating miniature logging exhibit and a historic log homestead. Very early mining tools and equipment also are on display. In summer, the museum hosts popular annual ethnic festivals. | Brady Ave. and Museum Rd., Caspian | 906/265–2617 | icmuseum@up.net | www.ironcountymuseum.com | $5 | May–Sept., Mon.–Sat. 9–5, Sun. 1–5.

Ski Brule. The longest run is 1 mi at this ski center boasting one of the highest vertical drops—500 ft—in the U.P. and 17 runs. You can also snowboard and snow tube here. A restaurant and lounge are on the property. | 119 Big Bear Rd. | 906/265–4957 or 800/362–7853 | ski-brule@up.net | www.skibrule.com | $24–$30 | Nov.–Mar., daily 9–4, Wed., Fri., Sat., 4:30–8:30.

ON THE CALENDAR

JUNE: *Pine Mountain Music Festival.* Both established and up-and-coming musicians gather in the communities of Iron County to attend workshops and seminars and to give live performances. Musical styles represented range from classical chamber music to folk and bluegrass. | 906/482–1542 or 888/309–7861 | fax 906/487–3511 | festival@pmmf.org | www.pmmf.org.

JULY: *Bass Festival.* The chance to hook the big one brings anglers from across the Upper Peninsula to celebrate this native fish. Food, fun competitions, and more abound. | 906/265–3822.

JULY: *Ferrous Frolics.* Travel back in time at the Iron County Historical Museum in Caspian, host of this popular historical festival and annual pioneer crafts show. Usually held the third or fourth weekend of the month. | 906/265–2617 | www.ironcountymuseum.com/calendar.

JULY: *Upper Peninsula Championship Rodeo.* Cowboys and cowboy wanna-bes converge on the U.P. Fairgrounds in Escanada for competitions, shows, and other horsey fun. Held the third weekend of the month. | 906/265–3822.

AUG.: *Iron County Fair.* Classic county-fair fun, with agricultural and farming displays, livestock, midway rides, and family events, is at the fairgrounds on Franklin St. the third full week of the month. | 906/265–3822.

Dining

Depot Restaurant and Bakery. Contemporary. Two authentic 1930s train cars house the restaurant; one holds the kitchen, the other the dining area. Try the filet of sole stuffed with shrimp and garlic, or the grilled swordfish sided with tomato-basil lemon-lime salsa. | 50 4th St. | 906/265–6341 | $8–$13 | MC, V.

Lodging

AmericInn Motel and Suites. A fieldstone fireplace is the focal point of the spacious lobby in this modern, three-story downtown motel with standard rooms and suites. Complimentary Continental breakfast. In-room data ports. Cable TV. Indoor pool. Hot tub. Business services. | 40 E. Adams St. | 906/265–9100 | fax 906/265–4244 | www.americinn.com | 41 rooms, 5 suites | $82–$92, $106 suites | AE, D, DC, MC, V.

Lac O' Seasons Resort. Families flock to this resort, which is on 37 acres of wooded hills a few miles from the Ski Brule slopes. Some of its 15 cabins are right on Stanley Lake, and there's a large main lodge with a game room, communal dining and kitchen areas, a lakefront porch, and a snack shop. No room phones. In-room VCRs (and movies). Boating, fishing. | 176 Stanley Lake Dr. | 906/265–4881 or 800/797–5226 | fax 906/265–4881 | www.iron.org/biz/loc/iron-index.html | 15 cabins | $580 weekly for 2–bedroom cabins, $1300 for 4–bedroom cabins | No credit cards.

IRONWOOD

MAP 9, E2

(Nearby towns also listed: Iron River, Ontonagon, Wakefield)

Once a lumbering and fur-trading center, Ironwood, with a population of 6,000, is the largest city in the Gogebic Range and a popular skiing destination, with five hills and three resorts within 30 mi. (*Note:* Area codes in this vicinity are scheduled to change to 989 beginning April 7, 2001.)

Information: **Western Upper Peninsula Convention and Visitors Bureau** | 137 E. Cloverland Dr., Ironwood 49938 | 906/932–4850 or 800/272–7000 | bigsnow@westernup.com | www.westernup.com.

Attractions

Area Waterfalls. Dozens of incredible natural rock formations dot the Upper Peninsula's waterways, creating beautiful cascades and waterfalls along rivers and streams. Most of the falls are accessible all year—in winter they turn into sparkling, multi-tiered natural ice sculptures. You can get a map of the most noteworthy sites from the visitor's bureau. | 906/932–4850 | bigsnow@westernup.com | www.westernup.com/waterfalls.

Big Powderhorn Mountain Ski Area. Winter sports dominate this popular resort 15 mi from Lake Superior. You can choose from 25 trails—the longest is 1 mi with a vertical drop of 600 ft. You can also go snowboarding, if you prefer. | N 11375 Powderhorn Rd., Bessemer | 906/932–4838 or 906/932–3100 (reservations only) | fax 906/932–2416 | info@bigpowderhorn.net | www.bigpowderhorn.net | $35 | Dec.–Mar., daily 9–4.

Blackjack Ski Area. A rustic lodge is at the heart of this U.P. resort. The longest ski run is 5,300 ft, the vertical drop 465 ft. The area also has a snowboarding park. | Blackjack Rd., Bessemer | 906/229–5115 or 906/229–5157 (reservations only) | info@skiblackjack.com | www.skiblackjack.com | $28–$33 | Nov.–Mar., daily 9–4.

Black River Harbor. Fifteen miles north of Ironwood, this is a popular departure point for Lake Superior cruises and deep-sea fishing excursions. Picnic areas, a playground, and camping are available. | 906/932–1122 or 800/280–2267 (camping reservations) | Free | Daily.

Copper Peak Ski Flying. This part of the U.P. is known as "Big Snow Country." The first stop on the Black River National Scenic Byway, 8 mi north of Ironwood, and near 5 major waterfalls on the Black River, Copper Peak has stunning scenery throughout the year. A chair lift and elevator take the adventurous to the top of a 469-ft artificial ski slide that provides great views of surrounding forests, Lake Superior, and three neighboring states. Amateurs can watch as the pros practice ski flying, a sport similar to ski jumping. Pro ski fliers reach speeds of more than 60 mph and "fly" more than 500 ft from the slide. There's also snowshoeing, dogsledding, 12 mi of mountain bike trails, hiking, and more than 50 mi of cross-country ski trails at the area. International Ski Flying competitions are sometimes held here in late January. Elevators operate in summer as well. | County Rd. 513 | 906/932–3500 | www.westernup.com/copperpeak | Skiing Oct.–Apr., elevator tours May–Oct., daily.

Hiawatha—World's Tallest Indian. A center-city landmark, this 52-ft-high statue of the legendary Iroquois warrior weighs 8 tons and looks out over the waters of Lake Superior. | Suffolk St. | Free | Daily.

Historic Ironwood Theater. Originally a movie theater, this performance space and cultural center was restored to its former glory in 1985. The theater, which is listed on the National Registry of Historic Landmarks, has a huge working pipe organ. | 113 E. Aurora St. | 906/932–0618 | www.ironwoodtheather.org | Price varies with event.

Little Girl's Point Park. Though this local park on Lake Superior is 17 mi from Ironwood, it feels far from civilization. The 32 campsites are assigned on a first-come, first-served basis; electricity is available. There's a boat launch. | 906/663–4687 | Free, charge for camping | May–Sept.

Mt. Zion Ski Area. This popular ski center is 1,150 ft above Lake Superior. The longest run of ¾ mi has a vertical drop of 300 ft. | E4946 Jackson Rd. | 906/932–3718 | Nov.–Apr.

Ottawa National Forest. Natural features and attractions fill this preserve's more than 900,000 acres. Here you can see scenic waterfalls and lakes. Popular sites include Black River Harbor, the McCormick Wilderness, the North Country National Scenic Trail, the Watersmeet Visitor Center, and Sturgeon River Gorge. Camping, fishing, hiking, and cross-country and downhill skiing are available. | Ottawa Forest Headquarters, E6248 U.S. 2 | 906/932–1330 | www.fs.fed.us/r9/ottawa | Free | Daily dawn to dusk.

AUG.: *Gogebic County Fair.* This colorful county fair celebrating the area's agricultural and livestock industries is held the second week of the month, at the fairgrounds on west U.S. 2. You can enjoy food, fun, games, and competitions. | 906/932–1420.

DEC.: *Jack Frost Parade.* This downtown event welcomes winter with a big parade, lots of sparkling lights, and an appearance by Santa himself in the town square's "Candy Cane Court." | 906/932–1122.

Dining

Branding Iron. Steak. A rough-and-ready kind of place, this restaurant 6 mi southeast of Ironwood displays spurs, chaps, and, of course, branding irons on its walls and reproduction Remington bronzes throughout the dining area. The big Formica tables here are perfect for large groups. Menu standouts include huge grilled steaks and "margaritas on tap." | 214 Silver St., Hurley WI | 715/561–4562 | Closed Sun. No lunch | $8–$15 | AE, D, MC, V.

Elk and Hound Restaurant. American. This casually elegant restaurant is adjacent to the town's country club. Seating is in wooden captain's chairs around linen-draped tables; lighting is soft and diffuse. The restaurant prides itself on its steaks, but the seafood selections are also noteworthy. | N10233 Country Club Rd. | 906/932–4545 | $10–$20 | AE, D, MC, V.

Mama Get's. Mexican. Housed in a northwoods log cabin, this restaurant features a casual, eclectic menu that includes spicy Mexican fare, steaks, and ribs. Trademark dishes include a full rack of ribs, hot chicken wings, fajitas, and quesadillas. Live music Wed. Kids' menu. | 5964 U.S. 2 | 906/932–1322 | No lunch | $12–$20 | MC, V.

Lodging

AmericInn Motel and Suites. This chain hotel is 2 mi east of M–51 on U.S. 2. Skiing is 3 mi away. Upper Peninsula mining attractions are 2 mi away and Lake Superior beaches are 12 mi to the north. In-room data ports. Cable TV. Indoor pool. Hot tub, sauna. Exercise equipment. Business services. | 1117 E. Cloverland Dr. | 906/932–7200 | fax 906/932–7222 | mbolich@zmchotels.com | www.americinn.com | 45 rooms, 4 suites | $105–$130 | AE, D, DC, MC, V.

Black River Lodge. On the Black River, this rustic stone and wood lodge 8 mi from Ironwood is a few miles from excellent skiing and hiking trails. Your accommodation options include townhouses that you can rent long-term or over night. Restaurant, bar, picnic area. No air-conditioning in some rooms, some kitchenettes, some refrigerators, some in-room hot tubs. Cable TV. Indoor pool. Hot tub. Hiking. Fishing. Video games. Playground. | 12390 Black River Rd. N. | 906/932–3857 | 25 rooms, 4 apartments, 4 townhouses | $48–$100, $100–$220 apartments/town houses | D, MC, V.

Budget Host Cloverland Motel. The basic accommodations at this motel in a commercial strip attract business travelers. Picnic area. Cable TV. Playground. | 447 W. Cloverland Dr. | 906/932–1260 or 800/283–4678 | fax 906/932–1260 | cgossen@portup.com | www.portup.com/~cgossen | 16 | $35–$75 | AE, D, DC, MC, V.

Comfort Inn. This modern two-story motor lodge, ¼ mi from downtown Ironwood, has interior corridors. Your car will start on deep-frozen winter mornings if you take advantage of the free plug-in for car batteries. Complimentary Continental breakfast. Some refrigerators. Cable TV. Indoor pool. Hot tub. Business services. | 210 E. Cloverland Dr. | 906/932–2224 or 800/228–5150 | fax 906/932–9929 | www.choicehotels.com | 63 rooms | $60–$125 | AE, D, DC, MC, V.

Davey's Motel. This two-story motel, which has a big cedar deck and many evergreens on two sides, is 12 mi from Lake Superior and 5 mi from the Wisconsin border. Some guest rooms have balconies, and all have pleasant views of the surrounding grounds. In-room data ports. Cable TV. Hot tub, sauna. Pets allowed. | 260 E. Cloverland Dr. (U.S. 2) | 906/932–2020 | fax 906/932–2020 | daveys@portup.com | www.westernup.com/daveys | 23 | $36–$150 | AE, D, MC, V.

Super 8. Two restaurants are adjacent to this two-story chain hotel on U.S. 2. Some refrigerators. Cable TV. Some pets allowed. | 160 E. Cloverland Dr. | 906/932–3395 | fax 906/932–2507 | www.super8motels.com | 42 rooms | $56–65 | AE, D, DC, MC, V.

ISHPEMING

(Nearby towns also listed: Escanaba, Iron Mountain, Marquette)

The National Ski Association was founded in this scenic U.P. town (pop. 7,200) in the 1880s, giving rise to the city's U.S. National Ski Hall of Fame and Museum and its large ski center, the area's most popular attraction. (*Note:* Area codes in this vicinity are scheduled to change to 989 beginning April 7, 2001.)

Information: **Ishpeming–Negaunee Area Chamber of Commerce** | 661 Palms Ave., Ishpeming 49849 | 906/486–4841 | fax 906/226–2099 | mqtinfo@marquette.org | www.marquette.org.

Attractions

Da Yoopers Tourist Trap. Although this is technically a gift and souvenir shop, it has so much more: You can see "the world's largest working chainsaw," named Big Gus, and "the world's largest working shotgun," named Big Ernie, which has been mounted on the back

THE UPPER PENINSULA AND YOOPERS

People in Michigan often call the Upper Peninsula the U.P., which accounts for the name people who live in that region give themselves: Yoopers.

They're a special breed, proud of their isolation and independence, proud of the beautiful summers for which the U.P. is justly famous, proud of the splendid fall foliage colors they enjoy every year, proud of the excellent fishing, and proud of . . . everything about the U.P. And that includes—in however perverse a way— the 20 to 25 ft of snow that falls on the peninsula every winter, the rusting hulks of abandoned mining equipment that dot the landscape, the long and lonely roads, and the vicious mosquitoes. There's even some local agitation, at least in the summers, to have the mosquito designated as the "state bird."

Yoopers even take pride in a local musical comedy group called Da Yoopers, whose name translates into ordinary English as The Yoopers. Da Yoopers have released a large number of CDs and tapes—you'll want to pump up the volume as you drive those long roads in the old pickup—and some of their song titles tell the whole story of typical Yooper life: "Smelting USA," "Bingo Fever," "Lonely Yooper," "Garage Sale," "Fishing Wit (sic) Fred," "Mighty Manly Hunting Men," and, perhaps not surprisingly, "Desperation Polka."

Other titles are perhaps not suitable for inclusion in a family guide book, but they also convey the self-deprecating good humor that helps local people cope with those giant mosquitoes in summer and those mountains of snow in winter. Yooper humor, in fact, is a cottage industry here and can be found in many forms, ranging from books of Yooper cartoons to bumper stickers.

Nothing in the U.P. escapes the gentle barb of Yooper humor, especially the peninsula's notorious weather. Ask a Yooper about it and he'll typically tell you, well, it's warm one day and cold all the rest of the year.

© Artville

of a truck. What really makes this one worth the trip are the stuffed deer in bawdy poses. | 490 Steel St. | 906/485–5595 | youguys1@up.net | www.dayoopers.com/thetrap.html | Free | Mon.–Sat. 9–6.

Suicide Bowl Ski Area. Despite the off-putting name, Suicide Bowl has facilities for skiers of all levels, with five basic ski-jumping hills, from a mini hill to one 70 m long. There are four cross-country trails, one of which is lighted for night skiing. The area is 1½ mi east of Ishpeming off M–28. | 906/485–1731 | www.ishpemingskiclub.com | Nov.–Mar.

U.S. National Ski Hall of Fame and Ski Museum. The big names of American skiing and the development of the sport are honored here in displays of old equipment, an antique grooming apparatus, photographs, and trophies. A 20-min film covers the history of American skiing. | 610 Palms Ave. at 2nd St. | 906/485–6323 | www.skihall.com | $3 | Mon–Sat. 10–5.

Van Riper State Park. This U.P. state park 8 mi west of Ishpeming off U.S. 41 features more than 1,000 acres on Lake Michigamme as well as swimming, water and downhill skiing, boating, fishing, hunting, picnic areas, and camping. | U.S. 41, Champion | 906/339–4461 or 800/447–2757 | www.dnr.state.mi.us/camping. | $4 per car, per day | Daily dawn to dusk.

ON THE CALENDAR

FEB.: *Annual Ski-Jumping Championships.* Ishpeming's Suicide Bowl is the site of this annual ski-jumping event, better known as the "Cardboard Classic." Usually the third weekend of the month. | 800/544–4321.

AUG.: *Renaissance Fair and Art Show.* The pageantry and spectacle of a Renaissance fair combines with the creative expression of local artists and craftspeople to make this a popular festival. You can watch a real joust, listen to post-Medieval music, and sample rustic food at the fair held at Lake Bancroft Park. | 906/942–7865.

Dining

Jasper Ridge Brewery. American. The in-house brewery here produces a range of beers, from the light and mellow to the rich and full-bodied. In the casual dining area, a big-screen TV is usually showing sporting events. Try the "awesome blossom," a whole onion creatively sliced and then beer-battered and deep-fried. The Brewery also serves juicy hamburgers and prime-grade steaks sided with stir-fried vegetables. | 1075 Country La. | 906/485–6017 | rlamere@portup.com | www.exploringthenorth.com/jasper/jasper.html | $8–$12 | AE, D, DC, MC, V.

Lodging

Best Western Country Inn. This chain hotel is 1 mi from downtown Ishpeming in the Country Village commercial development. The site has a movie theater, bowling alley, restaurants, and more than 30 shops. Cable TV. Indoor pool. Hot tub. Video games. Business services. | 850 U.S. 41 W | 906/485–6345 or 800/780–7234 | fax 906/485–6348 | www. bestwestern.com | 60 rooms | $60–$79 | AE, D, DC, MC, V.

JACKSON

MAP 9, D7

(Nearby towns also listed: Ann Arbor, Battle Creek, Coldwater, Lansing/East Lansing, Marshall)

More than 200 inland lakes ring this industrial center in south-central Michigan. Currently the seat of Jackson County (pop. 157,000), the city was the site of the naming of the Republican Party at a convention in 1854.

Information: Jackson County Convention and Visitor Bureau | 6007 Ann Arbor Rd., Jackson 49201 | 517/764–4440 or 800/245–5282 | www.jackson-mich.org.

Attractions

Brooklyn–Irish Hills. Woods, natural lakes, and sandy beaches cover this 550-acre recreational area. Golf, sailing, fishing, and shuffleboard are some of the activities you can enjoy here. Michigan International Speedway is here too. Early Irish settlers, reminded of home, named the area Irish Hills. | U.S. 12 and M–50, Brooklyn | 517/592–8907 | bihcc@frontiernet | www.brooklynmi.com.

Cascades at Sparks Foundation County Park. Huge, colorful sprays spouting from six fountains and a giant waterfall attract visitors to this 465-acre park. You can practice your sports swings here. There are two golf courses, a miniature golf course, tennis courts, and batting cages. Paddleboats and a picnic area are available too. | 1992 Warren Ave. | 517/788–4320 | www.jkncascadepks.com | Free | Memorial Day–Labor Day, daily 11–11.

The small but interesting **Cascades-Sparks Museum** depicts the history of Cascade Falls, including background on the builder, William Sparks. Original park renderings by Sparks and drawings of the falls and other park scenes by local artists are on display, as well as audiovisual exhibits and models. | 1992 Warren Ave. | 517/788–4320 | www.jkncascadepks.com | Free | Memorial Day–Labor Day.

At **Sparks Illuminated Cascades Waterfalls,** water flows more than 500 ft. The falls and six fountains are the main attractions in this large county park. | 1992 Warren Ave. | 517/788–4320 | www.jkncascadepks.com | Free | Memorial Day–Labor Day, park daily 11–11, cascades dusk–11.

Dahlem Environmental Education Center. This large preserve, owned and operated by Jackson Community College, attracts more than 20,000 visitors annually. It's best known for its 5 mi of hiking and cross-country trails as well as its year-round nature programs and events. | 7117 S. Jackson Rd. | 517/782–3453 | www.jackson.cc.mi.us | Free | Daily.

Ella Sharp Park. Biking and jogging paths and cross-country skiing and nature trails cross Jackson's largest park. An 18-hole golf course, a driving range, and picnic areas also are on the park's more than 500 partially wooded acres. For swimmers, there's an Olympic-size pool. The Ella Sharp Museum Complex also is here. | 3225 4th St. | 517/788–2320 | webmaster@jkncascadepks.com | www.jkncascadepks.com | Free | Daily.

One of mid-Michigan's best museums, the **Ella Sharp Museum Complex** includes a restored Victorian home, a pioneer log house, a barn, a wood shop, an 1885 schoolhouse, a country store, and a vintage doctor's office. Modern exhibition galleries host regular touring exhibits from across the country. | 3225 4th St. | 517/787–2320 | fax 517/787–2933 | ellasharp@dmci.net | www.ellasharp.org | $4 | Tues.–Fri. 10–4, Sat. Sun. 11–4.

Michigan Space Center. Housed in a dramatic geodesic dome, Michigan's only space museum displays a wide range of space-age exhibits, including a memorial to the ill-fated space shuttle *Challenger,* space suits, a moon rock, a model of the Hubble Space Telescope, and an Astrotheatre. You can climb into a space capsule, try out one of a number of interactive computer exhibits, or ogle the 85-ft Mercury Redstone rocket outside. Picnic facilities and a playground are on-site. | 2111 Emmons Rd. | 517/787–4425 | www.jackson.cc.mi.us/spacecenter | $4 | May–Oct., Tues.–Sat. 10–5; Nov.–Apr., Tues.–Sat. 10–5.

Republican Party Founding Site. The party itself was officially founded in neighboring Wisconsin, but Jackson claims to be the party's birthplace because the name Republican was officially adopted at a convention here in 1854. There is little to see at the site, although it's marked with a plaque. | Franklin and 2nd Sts. | Free | Daily.

Waterloo Farm Museum. This log cabin farmhouse from the 1850s hosts the Quilt and Textile Festival held each July, the October Pioneer Festival, and the Victorian Christmas. | 9998 Waterloo–Munith Rd. | 517/596–2254 | www.scs.k12.mi.us/-waterloo | $3 | June–Aug., Wed.–Sun. 1–5.

Waterloo State Recreation Area. Over a dozen small lakes dot the 20,000 acres of this state park. Swimming, beaches, water skiing, boating, and fishing are popular water activities.

On land, there's horseback riding, picnicking, and nature trails. Check out the discovery center too. | 16345 McClure Rd. | 734/475–8307 | www.dnr.state.mi.us | Daily.

ON THE CALENDAR

APR., MAY, SEPT., OCT.: *Harness Racing.* Mid-Michigan's horse-racing action attracts enthusiasts in spring and fall to Jackson County Fairgrounds. | 517/788–4500.

MAY–JUNE: *Jackson County Rose Festival.* Residents of Michigan's "Rose City" prove their point with floral displays, food, games, and special family events. | 517/787–2065.

JUNE: *Summerfest.* Outdoor concerts, car shows, and fireworks are among the attractions of the weeks-long festival. A highlight event is the Taste of Jackson day at Cascade Falls Park, where you can sample dozens of dishes from the city's top chefs. | 517/787–2065.

JUNE–AUG.: *Michigan International Speedway.* The beautiful, rolling Brooklyn–Irish Hills near Jackson are home to the high-action Michigan Speedway, which features stock-car racing during the warm-weather months. | 517/592–6666 or 800/354–1010 | www.nascar.com/tracks/michigan.

JULY: *Hot-Air Balloon Jubilee.* Balloon enthusiasts take to the sky during this colorful event featuring both competitions and public sky rides. | 517/782–1515 | www.hotairjubilee.com.

AUG.: *Civil War Muster and Battle Reenactment.* One of the state's largest Civil War reenactments presents costumed events, period games, and more. | 517/788–4320 | www.jackson-mich.org.

AUG.: *Jackson County Fair.* All the classic fun, including carnival rides, livestock displays, food, and agricultural events, are at this fair. | 517/788–4405 | www.co.jackson.mi.us/fair.

SEPT.: *Junior Achievement Mini Grand Prix.* Kids in pint-sized race cars—that's the big draw for this popular downtown event. You'll also see craft vendors, food booths, and a small carnival. | 517/782–7822 | www.jamichiganedge.com.

Dining

Brandywine Pub and Food. Continental. Barnwood walls, antique lamps and prints, and a huge fireplace add character to the four dining rooms at Brandywine. The menu, which changes seasonally, includes a thick 12-oz New York strip steak, scallops brandywine in garlic butter, broiled veal liver with bacon or onions, and golden brown, deep-fried frog legs. Kids' menu, early bird suppers. | 2125 Horton Rd. | 517/783–2777 | Closed Sun. No lunch | $8–$18 | AE, MC, V.

Gilbert's Steak House. Continental. A Jackson favorite since 1946, this roadside steak house has Tiffany lamps and comfortable booths in spacious dining rooms. Gilbert's is known for fresh fish, including Canadian walleye and whitefish and Lake Erie perch, and a generous Sunday buffet. You might try the best-selling prime rib of beef, filet mignon, or lighter options, such as chicken and pasta Modena or broiled seafood tarragon. Kids' menu. | 2323 Shirley Dr. | 517/782–7135 | www.gilbertsteakhouse.com | $10–$19 | AE, D, DC, MC, V.

Hudson's Grill. American. A John Deere tractor and two classic cars hang from the ceiling, and the walls are covered with 1950s- and 1960s-era signs. Outside, two sand volleyball courts are popular in warmer months. The menu includes juicy burgers and some Mexican dishes, but the specialties here are malts and shakes thick enough to stand a spoon in. | 2900 Springport Rd. | 517/784–4773 | $6–$12 | AE, D, MC, V.

Lodging

Baymont Inn and Suites. It's 3 mi to Jackson from this chain hotel just off I–94 and U.S. 127 at Exit 138 north. Guest rooms have large desks and lots of light, good for the working business traveler. Complimentary Continental breakfast. In-room data ports, some refrigerators. Cable TV. Video games. Laundry service. Business services. | 2035 Service Dr. | 517/789–6000 | fax 517/782–6836 | www.baymontinns.com | 66 rooms | $48–$73 | AE, D, DC, MC, V.

Country Hearth Inn. A recliner adds a homey touch to each room in this motel, housed in two buildings. It's 2 mi from downtown and several blocks from a shopping mall and restaurants. Complimentary Continental breakfast. Cable TV. Business services. | 1111 Boardman Rd. | 517/783–6404 or 800/848–5767 (reservations only) | www.countryhearth.com | 73 rooms | $63–$73 | AE, D, DC, MC, V.

Fairfield Inn by Marriott. This blue-and-white chain hotel is ¼ mi north of I–94 and two blocks from Jackson Crossing Mall, with shopping and restaurants. Complimentary Continental breakfast. Cable TV. Indoor pool. Hot tub. Business services. | 2395 Shirley Dr. | 517/784–7877 | fax 517/784–7877 | www.fairfield.com | 57 rooms | $66–$79 | AE, D, DC, MC, V.

Holiday Inn. A Holidome entertainment/pool area draws families to this chain hotel 5 mi from Jackson. It's just off I–94. Restaurant, bar, room service. Cable TV. Indoor pool. Hot tub, sauna. Miniature golf, putting green. Laundry facilities. Business services. Some pets allowed. | 2000 Holiday Inn Dr. | 517/783–2681 | fax 517/783–5744 | www.basshotels.com/holiday-inn | 184 rooms | $89–$103 | AE, D, DC, MC, V.

Rose Trellis Bed and Breakfast. The luxurious climbing rose trellis beside the front door gives this 1846 Victorian Gothic home its name. The inn, one of Jackson's older homes, is filled with period antiques. The morning spread can include fresh fruit muffins, banana-cinnamon French toast, and other specialties. Complimentary breakfast. Some in-room hot tubs. No room phones, no TV. | 603 W. Michigan Ave. | 517/787–2035 | 5 rooms | $80–$140 | AE, D, MC, V.

Super 8. Several chain restaurants are next door to this two-story chain hotel, right off I–94 at exit 138, and 5 mi from Jackson. Some refrigerators. Cable TV. Some pets allowed. | 2001 Shirley Dr. | 517/788–8780 or 800/800–8000 | fax 517/788–8780 | www.super8motels.com | 54 rooms | $59–$69 | AE, D, DC, MC, V.

KALAMAZOO

MAP 9, C7

(Nearby towns also listed: Battle Creek, Grand Rapids, Marshall, Paw Paw, South Haven, Three Rivers)

Meaning "Place Where the Water Boils," Kalamazoo's catchy name has been memorialized in song. The economy of the Kalamazoo County seat (pop. 83,000) is based on the nearby pharmaceutical industry and the presence of two major educational institutions—Western Michigan and Kalamazoo College.

Information: Kalamazoo County Convention and Visitors Bureau | 346 W. Michigan Ave., Kalamazoo 49007 | 616/381–4003 or 800/222–6363 | fax 616/343–0430 | www.kazoofun.com.

Attractions

Bittersweet Ski Area. There's a 350-ft vertical-drop hill at this ski area 2 mi west of Otsego. The 17 runs challenge all levels of skiers and snowboarders. Lighted slopes and NASTAR racing also are here. | 600 River Rd., Ostego | 616/694–2820 | www.skibittersweet.com | $20–$26 | Nov.–Mar., weekdays 10–10, Sat. 9–10:30, Sun. 9–10.

Bronson Park. Abraham Lincoln made an anti-slavery speech in this two-block downtown park in 1856. | Park & South Sts. | 616/381–4003 or 800/222–6363.

Celery Flats Interpretive Center. The region's heritage as a celery-farming center is showcased here. You can visit a 1930s-era grain elevator, a one-room schoolhouse, and a circa-1846 mansion. Tours available. | 7335 Garden La., Portage | 616/329–4522 | $4 | Daily 12–5.

Crane Park. At the crest of Westnedge Hill, this park overlooks Kalamazoo. | Westnedge Ave., north of Cork St. | 616/381–4003 or 800/222–6363 | Free | Daily dawn to dusk.

Echo Valley. Eight lighted, 60-mph toboggan runs and a 400-ft tubing hill provide thrills at this winter sports park. If ice skating is your sport, you'll find the 43,000-square-ft outdoor skating rink to your liking. Skate and tube rentals are available. A warming lodge and snack bar take away the chill. | 8495 E. H Ave. | 616/349–3291 or 616/345–5892 | www.netlink.net/echo | $8 | Dec.–Mar., Fri. 6–10, Sat. 10–10, Sun. 12–7.

Gilmore–Classic Car Club of America (CCCA) Museum. Celebrating a bygone era of the automobile, this museum's collection of more than 140 vehicles is in a group of restored red barns on 90 landscaped acres north of Gull Lake. International sports cars, classic autos, racing cars, vintage motorcycles, antique tractors, and more are in the collection. | 6865 Hickory Rd., Hickory Corners | 616/671–5089 | www.gilmorecarmuseum.org | $6 | May–Oct., daily 10–5.

Kal-Haven Trail. Just east of U.S. 131 you can get on this former Kalamazoo and South Haven Railroad track bed that's been converted to a biking, hiking, and snowmobiling trail. On it, you can travel 35 mi from the old caboose on 10th St., on the city's west side, to the shoreline city of South Haven. The trail is a Michigan linear state park. | 616/381–4003 or 800/222–6363 | www.dnr.state.mi.us | Free | Daily.

Kalamazoo Aviation History Museum. Better known as the "Kalamazoo Air Zoo," this top-flight attraction houses a collection of World War II–era warplanes, including four Grumman Cats. A menagerie of other aircraft, the Michigan Aviation Hall of Fame, and a Simulation Station that lets you pilot an amazingly realistic aircraft also are here. Rides in a 1929 Ford Tri-Motor are available May through October, weather permitting. | 3101 E. Milham Rd. | 616/382–6555 | www.airzoo.org | $10 | June–Aug., Mon.–Sat., 9–6, Wed., 9–8, Sun., 12–6; Sept.–May, Mon.–Sat. 9–5, Sun. 12–5.

Kalamazoo College. This private college founded in 1833 is one of the 100 oldest campuses in the nation. It's known nationwide for outstanding academics and the "K" plan, which involves international study and internships—85% of students study and live abroad. | 1200 Academy St. | 616/337–7000 | www.kzoo.edu | Free.

Kalamazoo Institute of Arts. More than 3,000 works of art crowd this downtown museum, with an emphasis on 20th-century American art and works of the German Expressionists. There's also a respected art school here. | 314 S. Park St. | 616/349–7775 or 616/349–3959 | www.kia.iserv.net | Sept.–July, Tues.–Sat. 10–5, Thur. 10–8, Sun. 12–5.

Kalamazoo Nature Center. A $2.5-million face-lift in 1997 spiffed up the center's exhibits, which include a butterfly house, a butterfly and hummingbird garden, a tropical rain forest, and a barn built without nails that houses farm animals. The center also has more than 1,000 surrounding acres, including a glen that was a favorite of naturalist-author James Fenimore Cooper. | 7000 N. Westnedge Ave. | 616/381–1574 | www.naturecenter.org | $4.50 | Mon.–Sat. 9–5, Sun. 1–5.

Kalamazoo Valley Museum. This downtown museum celebrates science, history, and technology. A 21st-century Digistar Theater and Planetarium, a friendly robot named O.P.U.S., simulated missions into outer space in the Challenger Center for Space Science Education, and a walk-through tornado teach with fun. There's also a children's area. | 230 N. Rose St. | 616/373–7990 or 800/772–3370 | www.kvcc.edu | Free | Mon.–Tues., Thurs.–Sat. 9–5, Wed. 9–8, Sun. 1–5.

Timber Ridge Ski Area. All-natural terrain, a 250-ft vertical drop, and 15 runs draw skiers here. You can ski at night on lighted slopes. | 07500 23½ Rd., Gobles | 616/694–9449 or 616/694–9158 (snow conditions) | www.timberridgeski.com | $15–$26 | Nov.–Mar., weekdays 10–10, weekends 9–10.

Western Michigan University. The 750-acre campus of this state college founded in 1903 is southwest of downtown. It's known for cutting-edge programs in nursing and aviation, and theatrical performances in its Shaw and York theaters. The university has an enrollment of 27,000 students. | 1903 W. Michigan Ave. | 616/387–1000 | www.wmich.edu | Free | Daily.

Wolf Lake Fisheries. You can learn about the many species of Lake Michigan game fish here as well as the history and significance of the Great Lakes fisheries. You can also feed sturgeon and grayling in a shallow breeding pond. | 34270 CR 652 | 616/668–2876 | Free | Mon.–Sat. 9–5, Sun. 12–8.

ON THE CALENDAR

MAR.: *Maple Sugaring Festival.* Tasting the harvest is one of the popular activities at this annual spring event, usually the third weekend in March. You can also see demonstrations of maple sugaring—how trees are tapped, the sap collected, and the process of boiling down 40 gal of sap to make 1 gal of syrup. | Kalamazoo Nature Center, 7000 N. Westnedge Ave. | 616/381–4003 or 800/222–6363.

JULY: *Kalamazoo County Flowerfest.* The city of Portage, the country's largest producer of bedding plants and annuals, blooms with flower displays, garden walks, and other horticultural events as well as concerts in Bronson Park. | 616/381–3597.

AUG.: *Kalamazoo County Fair.* Midway rides, agricultural and livestock displays, entertainment of all varieties, and lots of country-style cooking are some of the attractions. | 616/349–9791 | www.kalamazoocountyfair.org.

SEPT.: *National Street Rod Association Nationals.* More than 3000 pre-1949 cars are on display at the county fairgrounds during this event, which draws hundreds of admirers. | 616/383–8778 | www.nfra-usa.com.

Dining

Black Swan. Contemporary. Just a short drive from downtown, this large, open restaurant has views of the lake and surrounding countryside. Creative entrées include sautéed breast of pheasant in a poultry broth and honey-rosemary roasted New Zealand rack of lamb in a vegetable reduction. The menu changes with the season. Kids' menu. | 3501 Greenleaf Blvd. | 616/375–2105 | www.milleniumrestaurants.com | $16–$25 | AE, D, DC, MC, V.

Bravo. Italian. The mahogany wood arches and several fireplaces make this an inviting casual restaurant. It's a popular meeting place for college students. Both northern and southern Italian cooking are on the menu. Veal with morel mushrooms in a brandy and cream sauce, grilled tenderloin of beef in a chianti reduction, and cedar-planked, spice-encrusted salmon are among the choices. Kids' menu. Sun. brunch. No smoking. | 5402 Portage Rd. | 616/344–7700 | $10–$20 | AE, D, MC, V.

Francois Seafood and Steakhouse. Steak. It's the prime rib, filet mignon (nearly two inches thick), and other steaks that pull diners to this restaurant, one of Kalamazoo's few linen-and-crystal, fresh-flowers-and-piano-music establishments. The seafood side of the menu, fresh from the Great Lakes, is also good. | 116 Portage Rd. | 616/381–4958 | Reservations essential | $12–$22 | AE, D, DC, MC, V.

Jimmy John's. American. If you want a quick, economical meal made with fresh ingredients, this is the place to go. Try one of the gourmet sub sandwiches. You can take it with you or eat in a dining area that's cheerfully plastered with old road signs and 1950s-era memorabilia. | 2623 W. Michigan Ave. | 616/381–9400 | $4–$6 | No credit cards.

Oakwood Bistro. Contemporary. Polished wood and low, golden lighting combine with the soft sounds of clinking cutlery and glassware at this cozy restaurant. Try the salmon baked in parchment for dinner and creme brulee for dessert. | 3003 Oakwood Dr. | 616/344–5400 | $8–$20 | AE, D, MC, V.

Old Burdick's Bar and Grill. American. Televisions here and there make this casual place almost like a sports bar, although a brick wall separates the bar and dining areas. Try the piquant Jamaican jerk chicken if you're feeling adventurous. | 100 W. Michigan Ave. | 616/343–0032 | fax 616/381–1560 | $6–$12 | D, MC, V.

Webster's. Continental. Pages from Noah Webster's dictionary adorn the walls of this elegant restaurant in the downtown Radisson Plaza Hotel. High-backed leather chairs and dark paneling contribute to the club-like look. A changing menu can include corn crepes stuffed with seafood, herb-roasted quail, Hudson Valley duck, or salmon poached in chardonnay. Entertainment. No smoking. | 100 W. Michigan Ave. | 616/343–4444 | Jacket required | Closed Sun. | $15–$25 | AE, D, DC, MC, V.

Lodging

Baymont Inn and Suites. Business travelers and convention-goers are the primary guests of this hotel, although it's also popular with parents visiting students at nearby Western Michigan University and Kalamazoo College. Complimentary Continental breakfast. In-room data ports. Cable TV. Laundry service. Business services. Pets allowed. | 2203 S. 11th St. | 616/372–7999 or 800/301–0200 | fax 616/372–6095 | www.baymontinns.com | 70 rooms | $50–$71 | AE, D, DC, MC, V.

Best Western Kelly Inn. Just off I–94 at Exit 80, this three-story hotel 5 mi from downtown caters to business travelers. A selection of restaurants are within several blocks. Complimentary Continental breakfast. Cable TV. Indoor pool. Hot tub, sauna. Business services. | 3640 E. Cork St. | 616/381–1900 | fax 616/373–6136 | www.bestwestern.com | 124 rooms | $74–$89 | AE, D, DC, MC, V.

Clarion. This hotel bills itself as "deluxe business accommodations." Guest rooms have large dressing tables and big mirrors. Restaurant, bar, complimentary Continental breakfast. In-room data ports, some in-room hot tubs. Cable TV. Pool. Hot tub, sauna. Exercise equipment. Laundry service. Business services. | 3600 E. Cork St. | 616/385–3922 | fax 616/385–2747 | clarion@iserve.net | www.hotelchoice.com/hotel/mi003/ | 156 rooms | $86–$115 | AE, D, DC, MC, V.

Fairfield Inn by Marriott. This blue-and-white three-story chain hotel is on the outskirts of Kalamazoo, just off I–94 at Exit 80. Complimentary Continental breakfast. Cable TV. Pool. Business services. | 3800 E. Cork St. | 616/344–8300 or 800/228–9290 | fax 616/344–8300 | www.marriott.com | 133 rooms | $59–$79 | AE, D, DC, MC, V.

Hall House. The 14-room Georgian Revival mansion that is home to this bed and breakfast was built in 1923 and is in a National Historic District. An Italian marble stairway, Detroit Pewabic tile, and ceiling artwork grace the house. Complimentary Continental breakfast. Cable TV. | 106 Thompson St. | 616/343–2500 or 888/761–2525 | fax 616/343–1374 | www.hallhouse.com | 4 rooms | $89–$110 | D, MC, V.

Hampton Inn. Off I–94 in southwestern Kalamazoo, this chain hotel is ½ mi from the Air Museum and airport, making it popular with business travelers. Complimentary Continental breakfast. Cable TV. Indoor pool. Business services. | 1550 E. Kilgore Rd. | 616/344–7774 | fax 616/344–9447 | www.hampton-inn.com | 64 rooms | $62–$80 | AE, D, DC, MC, V.

Holiday Inn–Airport. In a Kalamazoo industrial district, this chain hotel is 2 mi from the airport. Restaurant, bar, room service. Cable TV. 2 pools (1 indoor). Laundry facilities. Business services, airport shuttle. Some pets allowed. | 3522 Sprinkle Rd. | 616/381–7070 or 800/465–4329 | fax 616/381–4341 | www.basshotels.com/holiday-inn | 146 rooms | $69–$79 | AE, D, DC, MC, V.

Kalamazoo House Bed and Breakfast. This three-story, moss-green brick mansion, in the heart of the historic district, has a wraparound porch and guest rooms furnished with antiques. Complimentary breakfast. Some in-room hot tubs. Cable TV, room phones. | 447 W. South St. | 616/343–5426 | 4 rooms | $80–$110 | No credit cards.

Knights Inn Kalamazoo. Rooms at this two-story motel are large enough to comfortably sleep a family. Some microwaves, some refrigerators. Cable TV. | 1211 S. Westnedge Ave. | 616/381–5000 | fax 616/344–2061 | www.the.knightsinn.com/kalamazoo008961 | 55 rooms | $35–$110 | AE, D, DC, MC, V.

Quality Inn and Suites. Southwestern adornments add a sunny touch to this chain hotel 5 mi west of downtown, off I-94 at Exit 80. It's 3 mi to Wings Stadium, site of music concerts. Complimentary Continental breakfast. Cable TV. Pool. Business services, airport shuttle. Some pets allowed. | 3750 Easy St. | 616/388-3551 | fax 616/342-9132 | www.qualityinn.com | 122 rooms | $69-$120 | AE, D, DC, MC, V.

Radisson Plaza–Kalamazoo Center. This large, full-service downtown hotel has a spacious lobby with plants, artwork, and a gallery of shops. 3 restaurants, bar. In-room data ports, refrigerators in some suites. Cable TV. Indoor pool. Hot tub, sauna. Gym. Business services, airport shuttle. | 100 W. Michigan Ave. | 616/343-3333 | fax 616/381-1560 | rhikala@radisson.com | www.radisson.com/kalamazoomi | 281 rooms | $105-$155 | AE, D, DC, MC, V.

Red Roof Inn–West. Off U.S. 131 at Exit 36-B, this two-story chain hotel is in a quiet residential area within a few miles of Kalamazoo colleges. Picnic area. Business services. Some pets allowed. | 5425 W. Michigan Ave. | 616/375-7400 or 800/733-7663 | fax 616/375-7533 | www.redroof.com | 108 rooms | $49-$59 | AE, D, DC, MC, V.

Residence Inn by Marriott. Large suites with kitchens are popular with families looking for a little more room and with long-term business travelers. Across the street from a golf course, this chain hotel in a residential area is 5 mi from downtown. Picnic area, complimentary light dinner Mon.–Thurs., complimentary breakfast. In-room data ports, kitchenettes. Cable TV. Pool. Hot tub. Exercise equipment. Laundry facilities. Business services, airport shuttle. Some pets allowed. | 1500 E. Kilgore Rd. | 616/349-0855 | fax 616/349-0855 | www.marriott.com | 83 suites | $119-$129 suites | AE, D, DC, MC, V.

Stuart Avenue Inn. This elegant bed and breakfast in the city's Stuart Avenue Historic District actually consists of two houses. The Bartlett-Upjohn House is a stunning example of Eastlake Queen Anne architecture, with the beautiful McDuffee Gardens next door. The Chappell House bears influences from the Arts and Crafts movement, with beamed ceilings and Mission and Art Nouveau details. Furnished apartments are also available in a nearby building. Complimentary Continental breakfast. Some kitchenettes. Cable TV. No smoking. | 229 Stuart Ave. | 616/342-0230 | fax 616/385-3442 | www.stuartaveinn.com | 17 rooms in 3 buildings, 6 suites | $85-$105 rooms, $130-$160 suites | AE, D, DC, MC, V.

Super 8. This three-story chain motel is 5 mi west of downtown Kalamazoo. Some refrigerators. Cable TV. Some pets allowed. | 618 Maple Hill Dr. | 616/345-0146 or 800/800-8000 | www.super8.com | 62 rooms | $55-$70 | AE, D, DC, MC, V.

LANSING AND EAST LANSING

MAP 9, D7

(Nearby towns also listed: Flint, Grand Rapids, Jackson)

Home of the first motorized buggy and of the state capital, Lansing (pop. 125,700) stretches along the banks of the Grand River in the middle of the state. Lansing was chosen as the state's capital in 1847 because lawmakers couldn't agree on a better choice. In 1855, the city was given another boost by the addition of Michigan State University in East Lansing, one of the country's first land-grant colleges. Today, Michigan State boasts some of the most beautiful grounds of any American campus, including a variety of teaching and botanical gardens, nature preserves, and arboretums.

The capital grew most dramatically after R. E. Olds created the first motorized buggy here in the late 1800s, the forerunner of the soon-to-come "merry Oldsmobile." By the turn of the century, Lansing had become a leading maker of automobiles, a title it retains today, although its economy has diversified to include other types of manufacturing as well as government and education.

LANSING AND
EAST LANSING

INTRO
ATTRACTIONS
DINING
LODGING

The city is a good place for biking, walking, and in-line skating; its 6 mi River Trail is one of the longest urban trails in the country and passes many of the city's attractions and historic sites. History buffs are attracted to the beautifully restored state capitol, one of the first designed to resemble the U.S. Capitol building.

Information: **Greater Lansing Convention and Visitors Bureau** | 1223 Turner St., Ste. 200, Lansing 48906 | 517/487–6800 or 800/968–8474 | fax 517/487–5151 | www.lansing.org.

NEIGHBORHOOD

Old Town. This area 1 mi north of the capitol is the site of Lansing's original settlement. The neighborhood contains many of the city's first residences and homes, built in the early 1800s. After the city became the capital in 1847, even more homes were built. Today, it is the site of many fine shops and galleries.As the city grew in the late 19th and early 20th centuries, construction of homes continued south of Old Town, close to the capitol building. The Victorian structures, many of which are now the property of Lansing Community College, are located along Capitol Avenue, Seymour Street, and Iona Street, all of which are west of the community college and north of the capitol. The downtown area itself has a combination of modern limestone structures, tall glass buildings, and early 20th-century stone buildings. Along Washington Avenue you'll find a high concentration of retail shops and restaurants.

TRANSPORTATION INFORMATION

Airports: Capital City Airport. Eight major airlines serve the Greater Lansing area | 517/321–6121 | www.capitalcityairport.com.

Amtrak: Amtrak serves the city from Chicago and Toronto | 800/872–7245 | www.amtrak.com.

Bus Lines: Greyhound Bus Lines operates terminals in Lansing (420 S. Grand Ave.) and East Lansing (310 W. Grand River). | 517/482–0673 (Lansing); 517/332–2569 (E. Lansing) | www.greyhound.com.

Driving Around Town. Access to Lansing is via I–127 and I–69 from the south, I–96 and I–69 from the east, U.S. 27 from the north, and I–96 from the west. I–69 and I–96 make up a beltway around the city; I–496 branches off and leads east into town, where it intersects with U.S. 127, the city's main north–south artery. Rush hour is relatively light here, and does not slow traffic significantly. Downtown, many of the east–west streets are one-way, while the north–south streets are predominantly two-way. The speed limit is 35 mph for most streets. Metered spots are plentiful downtown as are parking ramps. Meter rates are 25 cents for 20 minutes, with a maximum of either 90 minutes or two hours; long periods are available at metered spaces just south of downtown. The ramps cost $7.25 for an entire day.

Intra-City Transportation: Capital Area Transportation Authority (CATA). CATA runs a public bus system in the Greater Lansing area and parts of Ingham County. Vintage streetcar trolleys provide service on bus routes to major downtown attractions (517/394–1000. or | www.cata.org. for routes and schedules).

Attractions

ART AND ARCHITECTURE

River Sculpture and Fish Ladder. Spawning salmon and steelhead fight their way upstream in September along this contemporary sculpture in Burchard Park designed by noted artist-sculptor Joseph E. Kinnebrew and landscape architect Robert O'Boyle. | 220 Maple St., Lansing | Free | Daily.

State Capitol Building. One of the first capitols built to resemble the U.S. Capitol, the Victorian-era building was designed by architect Elijah Myers and has been restored to its 1879 condition. Tours of the public areas and House and Senate galleries are given every

45 minutes. | W. Michigan Ave., Lansing | 517/373–2353 | www.state.mi | Free | Mon.–Fri., building open 7:30–4, tours 9–4; Sat. guided tours only, 10–4.

CULTURE, EDUCATION, AND HISTORY

Boars Head Theater. Mid-Michigan's only professional theater was founded in 1966 and named for the many images of boars in Shakespeare's plays. | Center for the Arts, 425 S. Grand Ave., Lansing | 517/484–7805 | www.boarshead.org | Price varies by event.

Michigan State University. Considered one of the nation's premier land-grant universities, the school was founded in 1855 as Michigan Agricultural College. Since then it has grown from three buildings to a 5,320-acre educational complex to become one of the largest universities in the country. Due to its agricultural focus, the campus is among the United States' most scenic, with the Beal Botanical Gardens and other test gardens that are breathtaking in the spring. Other campus highlights are the MSU Museum, with three floors of permanent and changing exhibits on natural and cultural history, including a number of full-size dinosaur skeletons, the Kresge Art Museum, and the Abrams Planetarium. | East Lansing | 517/355–1855 | fax 517/353–1647 (admissions) | www.msu.edu | Free | Daily.

Turner-Dodge House and Heritage Center. Oak woodwork, leaded-glass windows, and 12-ft embossed tin ceilings helped win this 1858 Classical Revival house beside the Grand River a designation as a National Historic Landmark. | 100 E. North St., Lansing | 517/483–4220 | Free | Tours by appointment.

MUSEUMS

Impression 5 Science Center. Kid-friendly displays on the physical and natural sciences, including a computer and chemistry lab and sections on energy, biology, medicine, and physics, are the main attractions of this museum housed in a century-old building on the city's Museum Drive. | 200 Museum Dr., Lansing | 517/485–8116 | www.impression5.org | $4.50 | Mon.–Sat. 10–5, Sun. 1–5.

Michigan Library and Historical Museum. This striking, four-level building near the state capitol is built around a huge white pine—literally. (The white pine is the state tree.) The west wing houses the 4.5 million-item collection of the state library, which is well known by genealogists. In the east wing are the museum's 26 galleries with interactive exhibits. A three-story map of Michigan, a walk-through U.P. copper mine, a 1920s street scene, and a diorama from a 1950s Detroit Auto Show are a few of the displays telling Michigan's story. | 717 W. Allegan St., Lansing | 517/373–3559 | www.sos.state.mi.us/history/history.html | Free | Weekdays 9–4:30, Sat. 10–4, Sun. 1–5.

LANSING AND
EAST LANSING

INTRO
ATTRACTIONS
DINING
LODGING

I SCREAM, YOU SCREAM

Michigan State University may be known for its varied agricultural products, but few taste as good as the one you might not expect—ice cream. The scoop around East Lansing is that the university's MSU Dairy Store has some of the tastiest ice cream and cheese in the state.

The ice cream, yogurt, and cheeses are made by students in the food science and nutrition curriculums. Students, professors, and hungry office workers stop by for the goodies, which have been made here since the 1950s. Favorite scoops include cookies and cream and butter pecan. An extra-big portion is just over a buck.

Cheeses range from your basic cheddar and Swiss to a rare chocolate dessert cheese. | Farm Lane Rd., next door to Anthony Hall | 517/355–8466 | Weekdays 9–6, weekends 12–5.

© Artville

Michigan Museum of Surveying. As the nation's only museum of surveying and mapping, this institution houses a superb collection of surveying artifacts, early instruments, and historical literature. Exhibits trace the evolution of surveying from its birth more than 2000 years ago. | 220 S. Museum Dr., Lansing | 517/484–6605 | Free | Weekdays 9–4.

Michigan Women's History Center and Hall of Fame. Female artists, musicians, and writers are showcased at this small museum, which is surrounded by gorgeous gardens and public picnic areas. The center sponsors special events. | 213 W. Main St., Lansing | 517/484–1880 | Free | Weekdays 8–4.

R. E. Olds Transportation Museum. Although not well known outside Michigan, Ransom E. Olds was an important figure in the development of the early automobile. The pioneering creator of the "merry Oldsmobile" was a local resident. His career and those of other Lansing-based automotive celebrities are traced here through exhibits that include the first Olds, built in 1897, and the first Olds Toronado, which rolled off the assembly line in 1966. Lansing-built carriages, bikes, and planes are also on display. | 240 Museum Dr., Lansing | 517/372–0422 | www.reolds.com | $4 | Tue.–Sat. 10–5, Sun. 12–5; Nov.–Mar., closed Sun.

PARKS, NATURAL AREAS, AND OUTDOOR RECREATION

Carl G. Fenner Nature Center. Hikers come to hit the 4 mi of nature trails, gardeners for the fragrant herb garden, and families for the visitor center with reptiles, amphibians, native birds, and environmental displays. The interactive learning center hosts the popular Maple Syrup Festival in March and the Apple Butter Festival in October. | 2020 E. Mt. Hope Rd., Lansing | 517/483–4224 | Free | Daily, 8 AM–dusk.

The Ledges. More than 280 million years old, these 60 ft ledges of quartz sandstone are a favorite destination of local rock climbers. For a more leisurely appreciation, trails wind above and below in 76-acre Fitzgerald Park. | 133 Fitgerald Park Dr., Grand Ledge | 517/627–7351 | fax 517/627–4234 | $2 per car, per day | Daily.

Potter Park Zoo. You can see more than 400 wildlife species at this small but popular zoo spread out over a 100-acre park on the Red Cedar River. Kangaroos, Siberian tigers, penguins, reptiles, and wolves are just a few. Exhibits include an aviary and a Trappers' Cabin. There's also a farmyard petting zoo, and pony and camel rides are available in summer. | 1301 S. Pennsylvania Ave., Lansing | 517/483–4221 | www.ci.lansing.mi.us/depts/zoo/zoo.html | $5 | Memorial Day–Labor Day, daily 9–7; Labor Day–Memorial Day, daily 9–5.

Woldumar Nature Center. Fields, forest, and wetlands along the Grand River fill more than 188 acres. You can hike or cross-country ski 4 mi of trails, or stop by for indoor exhibits and programs on nature and the environment. | 5739 Old Lansing Rd., Lansing | 517/322–0030 | woldumar@tir.org | www.woldumar.org | $1 | Weekdays 8 AM–dusk.

SPECTATOR SPORTS

Lansing Lugnuts. Oldsmobile Park in downtown Lansing is home to this Class "A" Midwest League baseball team, an affiliate of the Chicago Cubs. | 505 E. Michigan Ave. | 517/485–4500 | info@lansinglugnuts.com | www.lansinglugnuts.com.

WALKING TOUR

Begin in the downtown area at the State Capitol, built in 1879, its dome towering over the imposing building. Step inside to see, among the many elegant architectural details, the rotunda's glass floor. Walk west on Allegan Street two blocks to the Michigan Library and Historical Museum, an expansive, contemporary structure that houses many exhibits telling Michigan's history. Exit the museum at Washtenaw Street and walk east five blocks to Washington Avenue, the downtown's shopping strip. Walk south on Washington one block to Kalamazoo Street and take a left. One block east on Kalamazoo you'll find the Center for the Arts and the Boars Head Theater. Continue a block and a half east, across the Grand River, to find the River Trail and Riverfront Park, the 6-mi stretch of public park that runs along the Grand.

As you walk north, you'll find a series of museums on your right. The first you come to is the R. E. Olds Transportation Museum, where you can see an assortment of antique cars, bikes, and carriages. North of this is the Michigan Museum of Surveying, and north of this, the Impression 5 Science Center, in a renovated late 19th-century structure. Continue past the Riverwalk Theater to Riverfront Plaza. You'll be at Michigan Avenue and Cedar Street. If you follow Michigan west you'll reach the capitol.

Next visit Michigan State University in East Lansing. Drive east on Michigan Avenue approximately 2½ mi to Harrison Avenue, take a right, and follow Harrison to Shaw Lane. Shaw takes you east to the center of campus, where you can park around Spartan Stadium. Walk east along Shaw to the Abrams Planetarium. Then backtrack west along Shaw toward the stadium. From the northern side of the stadium walk north toward the Red Cedar River and cross the small pedestrian bridge to the Beal Botanical Gardens, established in 1873 with over 5,000 types of plants. Walk in a northeasterly direction, with the main library on your right, until you come to Circle Drive, on which sits the red brick MSU Museum. Built in 1857, it's one of the Midwest's oldest museums. After exploring the exhibits, walk south, the main library still on your right, until you reach the Red Cedar River. Walk east along the river until you reach the Kresge Art Museum, just south of Physics Road and east of the auditorium. Return to your car by backtracking along the river until you reach a foot bridge.

ON THE CALENDAR

MAY: *East Lansing Art Festival.* More than 225 artists from across the country share the spotlight with three stages featuring live performances in downtown East Lansing. | 517/319–6804 | www.elartfest.com.

MAY: *Mexican Fiesta.* Continuous performances by dancers and musicians, traditional crafts, and Mexican fare make this a popular annual event on the campus of Michigan State University. | 517/485–3267.

JULY: *Ingham County Fair.* This county fair in Mason highlights the diversity and quality of Michigan's agricultural industry and provides a showcase for area youth. You can see the livestock, midway, and more. | 517/676–2428 | www.ingham.org.

AUG.: *National Folk Festival.* The streets of East Lansing come alive mid-month for the oldest and largest annual celebration of the nation's traditional visual and performing arts. Musicians, dancers, and craftspeople from across the country participate in this annual event featuring several stages of live performances and storytelling. | 517/351–2735 | www.nff.net.

OCT.: *Old Town Art and Octoberfest.* Dancing in the streets brings revelers to the Lansing's Old Town district for music, merriment, and a community art exhibit. | 517/482–3333 | www.messagemakers.com/Octoberfest.html.

NOV.–DEC.: *Wonderland of Lights.* Potter Park Zoo is bedecked with thousands of lights during this event that features animal exhibits and holiday displays. | 517/483–4221 | www.ci.lansing.mi.us/depts/zoo/lights.html.

Dining
INEXPENSIVE

Brick House. American. Meal-sized sandwiches and eternal favorites like prime rib and top sirloin are served at this restaurant housed in a turn-of-century building in the heart of the old town. | 311 E. Grand River Ave., Lansing | 517/372–3659 | $9–$15 | AE, D, MC, V.

Coscarelli's. Italian. You're encouraged to sip a glass of wine at this cozy, family-run restaurant while you wait for made-to-order specialties such as shrimp, mussels, and calamari sauteed and served in the family's own sauce. | 2400 S. Cedar St., Lansing | 517/482–4919 | $7–$12 | AE, D, MC, V.

LANSING AND
EAST LANSING

INTRO
ATTRACTIONS
DINING
LODGING

El Azteco. Tex-Mex. A local favorite with many devoted regulars, "El Az" is often crowded and raucous, particularly Monday through Wednesday nights, when margaritas go for 95 cents. | 225 Ann St., East Lansing | 517/351–9111 | $6–$11 | D, MC, V.

Lamai Thai Egg Roll Kitchen. Thai. The dining area in this popular restaurant may be non-descript, but the food's not. Try an appetizer of pork satay with spicy peanut dipping sauce and an entrée of Gang Ped Pla, a fish fillet in curry sauce. | 401 E. Grand River Ave., Lansing | 517/374–6390 | $6–$8 | No credit cards.

MODERATE

Beggar's Banquet. American. Original works by local potters, painters, and photographers adorn this funky and popular campus eatery. The eclectic and seasonal menu includes sandwiches, salads, and entrées such as vegetarian garden strudel and pork Normandy. | 218 Abbott Rd., East Lansing | 517/351–4540 | fax 517/351–3585 | www.beggarsbanquet.com | $7.50–$20 | AE, D, MC, V.

Clara's. Continental. A sister of the eatery of the same name in Battle Creek, Clara's is housed in a vintage train station built in 1903 and filled with antiques, including advertising paraphernalia, posters, train memorabilia, and more. The 16-page menu features everything from a classic Caesar salad with chicken to a surf and turf combination. Sun. brunch. | 637 E. Michigan Ave., Lansing | 517/372–7120 | fax 517/372–0157 | www.claras.com | $7–$17 | AE, DC, MC, V.

Michaelangelo's. Italian. Directly across from the MSU campus, this restaurant is popular with visiting parents. The dining area is spacious and well-appointed with crisp tablecloths and substantial cutlery. Try the complex but delicate vegetarian lasagna. | 213 E. Grand River Ave., East Lansing | 517/332–4825 | $12–$20 | AE, D, DC, MC, V.

Parthenon. Greek. In the heart of downtown, this restaurant is where the city's movers and shakers convene for power lunches and early breakfast meetings. At lunch the place is packed with legislators and state employees jockeying for Greek specialties such as pastitsio (a Greek-style lasagna) or spanakopita (a spinach and feta cheese in phyllo dough). All entrées are served with cheese, olives, and garlic toast. Kids' menu. | 227 S. Washington Square, Lansing | 517/484–0573 | Closed Sun. | $12–$16 | AE, D, DC, MC, V.

Lodging
INEXPENSIVE

Days Inn. This chain hotel, in a mostly commercial strip, provides no-frills accommodations. Restaurant, bar. Cable TV. Pool. Exercise equipment. Business services. | 6501 S. Pennsylvania Ave., Lansing | 517/393–1350 or 800/388–7829 | fax 517/393–9633 | www.daysinn.com | 147 rooms | $49–$159 | AE, D, DC, MC, V.

Ramada Limited. Guest rooms at this motel have large desks if you've brought your work and roll-away beds if you've brought the kids. Complimentary Continental breakfast. In-room data ports. Cable TV. Pool. | 6741 S. Cedar St., Lansing | 517/694–1454 or 888/298–2054 | fax 517/694–7087 | www.ramada.com | 100 rooms | $32–$94 | AE, D, DC, MC, V.

Red Roof Inn–East. This two-story motel is north of the junction of I–496 and I–96 and 5 mi from downtown Lansing. Business services. Some pets allowed. | 3615 Dunckel Rd., Lansing | 517/332–2575 or 800/733–7663 | fax 517/332–1459 | www.redroof.com | 80 rooms | $56–$72 | AE, D, DC, MC, V.

Rose Lake Center. Its quiet, wooded, semi-rural environment adds charm to this bed and breakfast, which is about 10 mi northeast of downtown Lansing. A pond and small waterfall are on the grounds. Complimentary breakfast. No room phones, no TV. | 7187 Drumheller Rd., Bath | 517/641–6201 | fax 517/641–6201 | 1 room | $45–$65 | No credit cards.

MODERATE

Ask Me House. This 1911 arts-and-crafts-era home stands 10 blocks from the state capitol. The interior boasts such extravagant touches as fluted oak columns and a beautiful hand-painted mural in the dining room. Here, you sleep in a four-poster bed and eat a gourmet breakfast on antique Limoges china. Complimentary breakfast. No room phones, no TV. | 1027 Seymour Ave., Lansing | 517/484–3127 | fax 517/484–4193 | www.bedandbreakfast.com | 2 rooms | $55–$77 | MC, V.

Hampton Inn. These lodgings are ½ mi from I–96 and 10 mi west of downtown. Restaurants and shopping are five to ten blocks away. Complimentary Continental breakfast. Some in-room refrigerators. Cable TV. Exercise equipment. Business services. | 525 N. Canal Rd., Lansing | 517/627–8381 | fax 517/627–5502 | www.hampton-inn.com | 107 rooms | $71–$99 | AE, D, DC, MC, V.

EXPENSIVE

Best Western Midway. Easy access to I–96 and a welcoming lobby with a fireplace are the main attractions at this basic hotel. Shopping is two blocks away and it's 15 mi to downtown Lansing. Restaurant, bar, room service. Cable TV. Indoor pool. Hot tub, sauna. Exercise equipment. Video games. Business services., airport shuttle. Some pets allowed. | 7711 W. Saginaw, Lansing | 517/627–8471 or 800/780–7234 | fax 517/627–8597 | www.bestwestern-michigan.com | 149 rooms | $78–$108 | AE, D, DC, MC, V.

Comfort Inn. Shopping and fast-food and sit-down restaurants are within two blocks of this chain hotel in a growing area off I–96. It's 2 mi east of Michigan State University. Complimentary Continental breakfast. Some in-room hot tubs. Cable TV. Pool. Hot tub, sauna, steam room. Exercise equipment. Business services. | 2209 University Park Dr., Okemos | 517/349–8700 | fax 517/349–5638 | www.choicehotels.com | 160 rooms, 160 suites | $89–$109, $109–$159 suites | AE, D, DC, MC, V.

Courtyard Marriott–Lansing. Some suites are available at this chain hotel just off U.S. 127. It's 3 mi to Michigan State University and 7 mi to downtown Lansing. Picnic area. Cable TV. Indoor pool. Hot tub. Exercise equipment. Laundry facilities. Business services. | 2710 Lake Lansing Rd., Lansing | 517/482–0500 | fax 517/482–0557 or 800/321–2211 | www.courtyard.com | 129 rooms, 17 suites | $79–$109, $115–$149 suites | AE, D, DC, MC, V.

English Inn. Housed in a 1927 mansion built for an Oldsmobile executive, this bed and breakfast and its 15-acre estate with formal gardens and wooded trails overlook the Grand River. The main house has six bedrooms and is furnished with antiques throughout. There's a charming on-site restaurant-pub. Restaurant, complimentary Continental breakfast. Cable TV. Pool. Business services. No kids under 12. No smoking. | 677 S. Michigan Rd., Eaton Rapids | 517/663–2500 or 800/858–0598 | fax 517/663–2643 | www.englishinn.com | 10 rooms | $75–$175 | AE, D, MC, V.

Fairfield Inn by Marriott. This chain hotel is 8 mi from downtown Lansing, 2 mi from Michigan State University, and 2 mi from Meridian Mall. Complimentary Continental breakfast. Some refrigerators, some in-room hot tubs. Cable TV. Indoor pool. Hot tub. Exercise equipment. | 2335 Woodlake Dr., Okemos | 517/347–1000 | fax 517/347–5092 | www.marriott.com | 79 rooms | $89–$109, $109–$159 suites | AE, D, DC, MC, V.

Harley Hotel. There are plenty of facilities for kids at this two-story hotel built in the late 1960s, 5 mi west of downtown and the capitol. Restaurant, bar, room service. Cable TV. 2 pools (1 indoor). Hot tub, sauna. Putting green, tennis. Exercise equipment. Video games. Business services, airport shuttle. | 3600 Dunckel Rd., Lansing | 517/351–7600 | fax 517/351–4640 | 150 rooms | $75–$129 | AE, D, DC, MC, V.

Hawthorn Suites. A sunny garden atrium welcomes you to this well-kept hotel near I–96 and Route 43, 7 mi west of downtown. A 24-hour convenience store is on the premises. Complimentary breakfast. Refrigerators. Cable TV. Hot tub, sauna. Exercise equipment. Busi-

LANSING AND
EAST LANSING

INTRO
ATTRACTIONS
DINING
LODGING

ness services, airport shuttle. | 901 Delta Commerce Dr., Lansing | 517/886–0600 | fax 517/886–0103 | www.hawthorn.com | 117 suites | $89–$129 suites | AE, D, DC, MC, V.

Residence Inn by Marriott. The spacious, suite-size rooms make this hotel a favorite of families and business travelers. It's one block from MSU, in the East Lansing shopping district. Picnic area, complimentary Continental breakfast. Kitchenettes. Cable TV. Pool. Hot tub. Laundry facilities. Business services. | 1600 E. Grand River Ave., East Lansing | 517/332–7711 | fax 517/332–7711, ext. 6005 | www.marriott.com | 60 suites | $79–$175 | AE, D, DC, MC, V.

VERY EXPENSIVE

East Lansing Marriott University Place. One block north of Michigan State University, this hotel is often crowded with visiting professors and parents. Lush plantings fill the lobby's open atrium. Restaurant, bar, room service. Cable TV. Indoor pool. Hot tub, sauna. Exercise equipment. Laundry facilities. Business services, airport shuttle. | 300 Mac Ave., East Lansing | 517/337–4440 | fax 517/337–5001 | www.marriott.com | 180 rooms | $139–$199 | AE, D, DC, MC, V.

Holiday Inn–South. Extensive landscaping, including fountains in the courtyard, and its location ½ mi from I–96, 5 mi south of downtown, make this chain hotel and convention center popular with business travelers. Restaurant, bar. Refrigerators. Cable TV. Indoor pool. Hot tub, sauna. Exercise equipment. Video games. Business services, airport shuttle. | 6820 S. Cedar St., Lansing | 517/694–8123 or 800/465–4329 | fax 517/699–3753 | www.basshotels.com/holiday-inn | 300 rooms | $126–$169 | AE, D, DC, MC, V.

Radisson. A great location in the heart of the city and a two-block walk to the capitol, downtown shopping, and restaurants help make this one of the area's busiest hotels. Restaurant, bar. Some in-room refrigerators. Cable TV. Indoor pool. Hot tub. Exercise equipment. Business services, airport shuttle. | 111 N. Grand Ave., Lansing | 517/482–0188 | fax 517/487–6646 | www.radisson.com | 257 rooms | $129–$199 | AE, D, DC, MC, V.

Sheraton. Rooms face an interior courtyard at this hotel near the intersection of I–496 and I–96. Downtown Lansing is 7 mi away. Restaurant, bar, room service. Some refrigerators. Cable TV. Indoor pool. Hot tub, sauna. Exercise equipment. Business services airport shuttle. | 925 S. Creyts Rd., Lansing | 517/323–7100 or 800/325–3535 | fax 517/323–2180 | sheraton_lansing@acd.net | www.sheratonlansing.com | 219 rooms | $145–$155 | AE, D, DC, MC, V.

LAPEER

MAP 9, E6

(Nearby towns also listed: Flint, Pontiac, Port Huron)

Lapeer, the county seat of Lapeer County, sits just north of the high-tech corridors of Oakland County. Still a small town (population 9,000), all signs say that it will grow quickly. Many of the downtown's original facades have been restored, making for a pleasant mix of 21st century growth and early 20th-century charm. (*Note:* Area codes in this vicinity are scheduled to change to 989 beginning April 7, 2001.)

Information: **Lapeer Area Chamber of Commerce** | 92 W. Nepessing St., Lapeer 48446 | 810/664–6647 | fax 810/664–4349 | www.lapeerareachamber.org.

Attractions

Lapeer County Courthouse. The oldest courthouse in Michigan still in use, and one of the ten oldest in the United States, this structure is not so much a tourist site as it is an icon. It was the subject of a PBS documentary in 1997. | 255 Clay St. | 810/664–8248 | Weekdays 10–5.

PIX Theatre. This downtown movie house—built in 1931 and restored in 1998—is a fine example of art deco design. It shows films, comedy acts, music, lectures, live theater, and children's performances. | 172 W. Nepessing St.

Dining

Calvelli's Eatery & Spirits. American. The 1950s look, good burgers, and a legendary burrito make this a fun spot. Streets surrounding the restaurant are blocked off Wednesday nights in the summer, while proud car owners get to show off their shiny autos, amidst D.J.'s, music and food. | 44 W. Park St. | 810/667–6877 | Closed Sun. | $7–$13 | AE, D, MC, V.

The Villa. Italian. Italian classics compete with steaks for top billing in an elegant yet casual downtown landmark. | 393 W. Nepessing | 810/664–3519 | Closed Sun.–Mon. | $10–$20 | AE, D, MC, V.

Lodging

Best Western/Lapeer Inn. You choose standard rooms or suites at this chain hotel. Three suites have heart-shape whirlpool tubs. Parlor suites have a whirlpool with one large room; the divided suite has a living room and a bedrooms and a whirlpool. Restaurant, complimentary Continental breakfast. In-room data ports, some microwaves, some refrigerators, some in-room hot tubs. In-room VCRs (and movies). Indoor pool, outdoor pool. Hot tub, sauna. | 770 West St. | 810/667–9444 | 60 rooms, 30 suites | Rooms $70–$75, $80–$135 suites | AE, MC, V.

Fairfield Inn. This is a chain hotel designed for and by business travelers. Spacious rooms have ample work space and in-room data ports. In-room data ports. Cable TV. Indoor pool. Hot tub. | 927 Demille St. | 810/245–7700 | fax 810/245–7294 | www.fairfieldinn.com | 72 rooms | $59–$84 | AE, D, MC, V.

LELAND

MAP 9, C4

(Nearby towns also listed: Empire, Glen Arbor, Suttons Bay, Traverse City)

Touristy "Fishtown" is all that's left of the 19th-century fishing industry that once dominated this scenic Lake Michigan harbor. Today, Leland is one of northern Michigan's and the Leelanau Peninsula's most popular resort areas. (*Note:* Area codes in this vicinity are scheduled to change to 989 beginning April 7, 2001.)

Information: Leelanau Peninsula Chamber of Commerce | 105 Philips, Box 336, Lake Leelanau 49653 | 231/256–9895 | fax 231/256–2559 | info@leelanauchamber.com | www.leelanauchamber.com.

Attractions

Boat trips to Manitou Islands. Manitou Island Transit has boat trips to both North and South Manitou islands. Departure is from Fishtown. | 207 W. River St. | 231/256–9061 | www.leelanau.com/manitou | $22 | South Manitou Island: June–Aug., daily; North Manitou Island: June–Labor Day, daily.

Fishtown. Small shops and art galleries occupy the restored yet rustic shantylike town on the Lake Michigan waterfront. | River St. W of Main St. | 231/947–1120 or 800/872–8377 | www.fish-town.com | Free | Memorial Day–Labor Day, daily 9–9.

Good Harbor Vineyard. Tours and tastings are available at this popular Leelanau Peninsula vineyard and winery. | 34 S. Manitou Trail, Lake Leelanau | 231/256–7165 | info@goodharbor.com | www.goodharbor.com | Free | May–Oct., Mon.–Sat. 11-5, Sun. 12–5; Nov.–May, Sat. 12–5 or by appt.

Leelanau Historical Museum. Permanent and changing displays document the settlement and development of the peninsula and celebrate area artists. | 203 E. Cedar St. | 231/256–7475 | www.leelanauhistory.org | $2 | June–Labor Day, Tues.–Sat. 10–4, Sun. 1–4; Labor Day–May, Fri.–Sat. 1–4.

Leelanau State Park/Grand Traverse Lighthouse. Coastal dunes and a picnic and recreation area surround this scenic 19th-century lighthouse, as well as 8 mi of hiking trails. Lighthouse tours are by appointment in summer. | 15310 Lighthouse Point Rd., Northport | 231/386–5422 or 800/447–2757 | www.dnr.state.mi.us/camping or www.grandtraverse-lighthouse.com | $4 per car, per day | Daily dawn to dusk.

ON THE CALENDAR

JUNE: *Leland Wine and Food Festival.* Wine and food tastings, cooking demonstrations, and music highlight this one-day event held in historic Fishtown to celebrate the region's agricultural bounty. | 231/947–1120.

Dining

Blue Bird. American. What began as a soda shop in 1927 is now a bustling family-owned restaurant that seats 250 diners. Tables overlook gardens and the Leland River. It's well known for fresh Lake Michigan whitefish and the huge cinnamon rolls served hot each morning. Kids' menu. Salad bar. | 102 River St. | 231/256–9081 | bluebird@voyager.net | www.leelanau.com/bluebird/ | Closed Apr.–mid-June, Labor Day–late Nov., and Mon. | $15–$21 | D, MC, V.

The Cove. Seafood. In summer the outdoor decks are hopping at this casual restaurant on a dam above the little Carp River. You can watch salmon leap up the falls and witness breathtaking Lake Michigan sunsets as you dine. Seafood is king. Try the have-it-your-way fresh whitefish and the cream base seafood chowder. Kids' menu. | 111 River St. | 231/256–9834 | Closed mid-Oct.–mid-May | $12–$16 | AE, MC, V.

Leelanau Country Inn. Seafood. In a (some say haunted!) house that dates from the 1880s, this relaxed inn and restaurant is as close to a British-style house-hotel as one finds in northern Michigan. Seafood is the specialty, with a fresh catch flown in daily from Boston and an ever-changing menu that often includes swordfish piccata, pan-fried perch with lemon butter sauce, and even pan-fried alligator. The delectable Swiss onion soup was once featured in *Gourmet*. Guest rooms are available. Kids' menu, early bird suppers. | 149 E. Harbor Hwy., Maple City | 231/228–5060 | JSisson@leelanaucountryinn.com | www.leelanaucountryinn.com | No lunch | $17–$26 | MC, V.

Riverside Inn. Contemporary. You get fabulous water views and both indoor and outdoor seating at this restaurant a block off Main Street. It's a casual, friendly place. Many diners come in off their boats to enjoy such dishes as Michigan ostrich—a thick ostrich fillet flash-seared, then baked medium-rare and topped with a rich hunter sauce. The Inn uses only fresh, hydroponically grown vegetables and greens, and it makes fresh soups and desserts daily. | 302 E. River St. | 231/256–9971 | Reservations essential | Closed Jan.–Apr. and Tuesdays. No lunch | $18–$25 | AE, D, MC, V.

Lodging

Falling Waters Lodge. This modern bed and breakfast has some of the best views of any accommodations in town. You can see Lakes Michigan and Leelanau, the Leland River, and a waterfall or two from any given guest room, and there are several waterfront decks. A penthouse room, accessible by a spiral staircase, is also available. Cable TV. Fishing. Pets allowed. | 200 W. Cedar St. | 231/256–9832 | fax 231/256–9832 | 11 rooms, 10 suites | $140–$225 | AE, D, MC, V.

Leland Lodge. This spacious New England-style inn is 4 blocks from the heart of town. A main lodge, built in 1927, and cabins are next to a private golf course and within blocks of both Lake Michigan and Lake Leelanau beaches. Restaurant, bar, complimentary Continental breakfast, room service. Cable TV. Business services. | 565 E. Pearl St. | 231/256–9848 | fax 231/256–8812 | kstimac@ifco-jgb.com | www.lelandlodge.com | 18 rooms, 6 cabins | $89–$159 | MC, V.

Manitou Manor. Sitting on 6 acres of land, among cherry orchards and bordering woods, this bed and breakfast, parts of which were built as early as 1873, has theme rooms with private decks. It's 2½ mi south of Leland, 3 mi to Good Harbor Bay. Complimentary breakfast. No air-conditioning, refrigerators, TV in common area. Library. No smoking. | 147 N. Manitou Trail W, Lake Leelanau | 231/256–7712 | fax 231/257–7941 | www.bbhost.com/manitoumanorbb | 6 rooms | $100–$140 | D, MC, V.

LUDINGTON

(Nearby towns also listed: Big Rapids, Cadillac, Frankfort, Manistee, Whitehall/ Montague)

This western Michigan town, with an off-season population of 9,000, borders Lake Michigan and the Père Marquette River, a popular stream for king salmon, chinook, and coho fishers. A passenger ferry which crosses Lake Michigan between Ludington and Manitowoc, Wisconsin, and a generous stretch of beach make it a popular summer destination. (*Note:* Area codes in this vicinity are scheduled to change to 989 beginning April 7, 2001.)

Information: Ludington Area Convention and Visitors Bureau | 5827 W. U.S. 10, Ludington 49431 | 231/845–5430 or 800/542–4600 | fax 231/845–6857 | assistant@carriter.net | www.ludingtoncvb.com.

Attractions

Auto ferry service. The SS *Badger* has four-hour cruises and auto ferry service from Ludington to Manitowoc, Wisconsin. Onboard amenities include a museum, video game room, movie theater, staterooms, and 2 restaurants. | 701 Maritime Dr. | 231/845–5555 or 800/841–4243 | www.ssbadger.com | $63 round-trip | May–Oct., daily.

Big Sable Point Lighthouse. This classic and often-photographed 1867 lighthouse is 6 mi north of town in Ludington State Park. | Lakeshore Dr./M–116 | 231/843–8671 or 800/447–2757 | www.dnr.state.mi.us/camping | $4 per car, per day.

Harbor View Marina. You can see dozens of watercraft, both afloat and docked for repairs, here. There's also a restaurant, a resort, and a boat shop. Kids enjoy feeding the gulls, so bring some stale crackers. | 400 S. Rath St. | 231/843–6032 | Free.

Ludington State Park. Lake Michigan and Hamlin Lake border this park, which has 6 mi of Lake Michigan beach and sand dunes. Hiking and cross-country trails meander for miles, while a canoe trail follows the Hamlin Lake shoreline. The park also has a visitor center. | Lakeshore Dr./M–116 | 231/843–8671 or 800/447–2757 | www.dnr.state.mi.us/camping | $4 per car, per day | Daily dawn to dusk.

Mason County Campground and Picnic Area. Kids love the playground near this popular site for picnicking and camping. | 5906 W. Chauvez Rd. | 231/845–7609 | $15 per night | Memorial Day–Labor Day.

Père Marquette Memorial Cross. Marking the spot where Father Jacques Marquette is thought to have died in 1675, this huge, illuminated cross overlooks the harbor. | S. Lakeshore Dr. | 231/845–5430 or 800/542–4600 | whitepine@masoncounty.net | www.lumanet.org/whitepine | Free | Daily.

Stearns and Waterworks Parks. You can sun on the beach, put your boat in the water, and go fishing at these two adjoining parks along the city's western border. They also share a picnic area and miniature golf. Don't pass up a walk to the Breakwater Lighthouse. | 201 S. William | 231/845–6237 | www.harborviewmarina.com or www.ludingtoncvb.com | Free | Daily.

White Pine Village. Twenty buildings, including a blacksmith shop, a courthouse, a hardware store, and a school overlook Lake Michigan from a reconstructed 19th-century community. The site includes logging and maritime museums. | 1687 S. Lakeshore Dr. | 231/843–4808 | www.lumanet.org/whitepine | $5 | Mid-June–Labor Day, Tues.–Sat. 11–5, Labor Day–late Oct., Tues.–Sat. 11–4.

ON THE CALENDAR

JUNE: _Harbor Festival._ Ludington past and present is celebrated at this festival sprawled throughout town. Venues include the city park and a huge parking lot near the boat ramps. Events include carnival rides, a parade, a half-marathon, a 5K race, an arts-and-crafts show, logging demonstrations, and a community fish fry. | 231/845–0324.

Dining

Gibbs Restaurant. American. Hearty homestyle cooking and huge, gooey buns that stick to your teeth and your ribs are the specialty at this restaurant on U.S. 10. Menus change regularly and often include a theme, such as Autumn Fest, Christmas in July, or the spring Mushroom Festival. Salad bar. Kids' menu. | 3951 U.S. 10 W | 231/845–0311 | www.gibbsrestaurant.com | Closed Jan. | $9–$19 | AE, D, MC, V.

Historic Nickerson Inn. Contemporary. The allure of dining on an all-season porch overlooking Lake Michigan is one of the attractions of this restaurant. The health-conscious, creative menu emphasizes fresh, locally grown vegetables, meat, and poultry. Signature dishes include a forest mushroom appetizer and raspberry port Cornish hen. No smoking. | 262 W. Lowell St., Pentwater | 231/869–6731 | info@nickersoninn.com | www.nickersoninn.com | No lunch Mon.–Sat. | $12–$25 | D, MC, V.

Jamesport Brewing Company. American. This restaurant in the heart of the James Street district was the city's first brew pub. Antique signs and maritime memorabilia hang on its exposed-brick walls. Hearty pub fare, like deluxe burgers and thick steaks, is the focus of the menu. | 410 S. James St. | 231/845–7263 | $8–$12 | AE, D, MC, V.

P. M. Steamers. American. You get fabulous water views from this restaurant across from the city marina. You can dine outdoors or in the casual, nautically themed dining room. Popular dishes include nutty walleye, a lightly breaded, panfried filet, and chicken Caesar salad, with lots of Parmesan cheese and just a hint of anchovy. | 502 W. Loomis Ave. | 231/843–9555 | $7–$12 | AE, D, MC, V.

Scotty's. American. You can enjoy the street scene on Ludington Avenue while waiting for your meal at this popular bistro. Natives and tourists alike come for seafood, lasagna and spaghetti, and thick cuts of prime rib in three sizes. Kids' menu. | 5910 E. Ludington Ave./U.S. 10 | 231/843–4033 | rdscott@t-one.net | No lunch Sat., no dinner Sun. | $10–$20 | AE, MC, V.

Lodging

Four Seasons. A pleasant sun room, extensive garden, and popular home-made breakfast make this year-round resort seem homey. This suite hotel is the closest lodgings to the SS _Badger_ car ferry to Manitowoc, Wisconsin. Complimentary breakfast. Cable TV. Bicycles. Airport shuttle. No smoking. | 717 E. Ludington Ave. | 231/843–3448 or 800/968–0180 | www.fourseasonsmotel.com | 33 rooms | $86–$150 | AE, D, MC, V.

Historic Nickerson Inn. Built in 1914, this inn has a grand lawn and porches. Theme rooms range from a nature motif to a sunrise suite. Rooms have private baths and individual heating and air conditioning units. Overlooking Lake Michigan, the inn is 2 mi from the beach and area shopping. Restaurant, complimentary breakfast. Some in-room hot tubs. No room phones. No kids under 11. | 262 W. Lowell St., Pentwater | 231/869–6731 or 800/742–1288 | fax 231/869–6151 | info@nickersoninn.com | www.nickersoninn.com | 13 rooms (4 with shower only) | $85–$185 | D, MC, V.

Lakeside Inn. This independently owned motel, 3 blocks from downtown, overlooks the city park's Lake Michigan beach. A miniature golf course and boat launching ramp are across the street. Cable TV. Pool. Business services. | 808 W. Ludington Ave. | 231/843–3458 or 800/843–2177 | fax 231/843–3450 | 52 rooms | $99–$135 | AE, D, MC, V.

Lamplighter Bed and Breakfast. There are many different ways to relax outdoors at this 1894 Victorian home that's a stone's throw from the lake: it has a gazebo, a large back patio, and a deck. All guest rooms are outfitted with period antiques and deluxe linens. Complimentary breakfast. In-room data ports. Cable TV. | 602 E. Ludington Ave. | 800/301–9792 | fax 231/845–6070 | www.ludington-michigan.com | 5 rooms | $110–$135 | AE, D, MC, V.

Lands Inn. Nice landscaping and a sun room add charm to this pleasant hotel. It's 3 mi east of Ludington next to the popular Gibbs Restaurant. Restaurant, bar (with entertainment), room service. Cable TV. Indoor pool. Hot tub, sauna. Laundry facilities. Video games. Business services. | 4079 U.S. 10 W | 231/845–7311 | fax 231/843–8551 | www.landsinn.com | 116 rooms | $59–$99 | AE, D, DC, MC, V.

Nader's Lakeshore Motor Lodge. The beach is 1 block away from this family-style motel with a main lodge and annex. It's 1 mi to downtown and the state park. The city's golf course, marina, and boat docks are nearby too. Picnic area. Some kitchenettes, refrigerators. Cable TV. Pool. Basketball. Some pets allowed. | 612 N. Lakeshore Dr. | 231/843–8757 or 800/968–0109 | www.t-one.net/~naders | 25 rooms | $75–$100 | Closed Dec.–Apr. | AE, D, DC, MC, V.

Snyder's Shoreline Inn. Most rooms have a view of the Lake Michigan at this independently owned motel a few blocks from downtown. Accommodations are in three modern two-story buildings near golf courses, the marina, and boat docks. Complimentary Continental breakfast. Some refrigerators. Cable TV. Pool. Hot tub. Beach. Business services, airport shuttle. | 903 W. Ludington Ave. | 231/845–1261 | fax 231/843–4441 | sharon@snydersshore.com | www.snydersshoreinn.com | 44 rooms, 8 suites | $79–$149, $149–$259 suites | Closed Nov.–Apr. | AE, D, DC, MC, V.

Timberlane Long Lake Resort. The rental cottages at this resort, nestled in the heart of the Manistee National Forest 17 mi east of Ludington, sleep four to six people. It has screened porches, small kitchenettes, and private picnic areas. Charcoal grills are available. Picnic area. Kitchenettes. No room phones, no TV. Hiking. Playground. | 7410 E. U.S. 10, Walhalla | 231/757–2142 or 800/227–2142 | 19 cottages | $82–$115 | D, MC, V.

Ventura Motel. This downtown motel is 3 blocks from Lake Michigan, the car ferry, and beaches. Some in-room hot tubs. Cable TV. Business services, airport shuttle. | 604 W. Ludington Ave. | 231/845–5124 or 800/968–1440 | fax 231/843–7929 | www.ventura-motel.com | 25 rooms | $89–$99 | AE, D, MC, V.

Viking Arms. Flowerbeds and a gas log fireplace in the lobby distinguish this one-story country motel that's a half mile from downtown and 1 mi from Lake Michigan and Mason County Airport. Some rooms have fireplaces. Complimentary Continental breakfast. Some in-room hot tubs. Cable TV, in-room VCRs (and movies). Pool. Hot tub. Business services, airport shuttle. | 930 E. Ludington Ave. | 231/843–3441 | fax 231/845–7703 | innkeeper@vikingarmsinn.com | www.vikingarmsinn.com/main.html | 45 rooms | $69–$150 | AE, D, DC, MC, V.

Waterside Resort Marina. This lakeside resort has 19 small guest cabins and two larger rental houses, all with kitchenettes, picnic areas, and adjacent outdoor grills. A small shop sells snacks, some household items, and fishing bait. Picnic area. Kitchenettes. Cable TV. Golf course. Boating, fishing. | 3298 N. Lakeshore Dr. | 231/843–8481 | 19 cottages, 2 3-bedroom houses | $78–$110 | MC, V.

MACKINAC ISLAND

MAP 9, D3

(Nearby towns also listed: Mackinaw City, St. Ignace)

Just 3 mi long and 2 mi wide, this limestone outcropping in the middle of the Straits of Mackinac was known by Native Americans as Michilimackinac—"Great Turtle." Over the years, the name was shortened by lazy American tongues to Mackinac (pronounced Mack-in-aw), a name given to the island, its surrounding body of water, and the nearest city on the southern bank of the straits (though the city's name was given a "w" ending).

A frontier outpost in the 18th century, the island truly came into its own a century later when it became the summer resort of choice for wealthy Midwesterners. Vestiges of the island's past can be seen and heard in the many Victorian inns and storefronts and in the horse-drawn carriages that still clip-clop down village streets. Cars are outlawed here. Bicycles are a popular means of exploring, with tandems and cycling families common sights near natural features such as Arch Rock and Devil's Point and on the round-the-island shoreline route. You can bring your own bicycle on ferries from Mackinaw City or St. Ignace or rent one from a number of Main Street liveries on the island.

Be forewarned that the island can be very crowded in summer, when day-trippers jam the place in search of fun. For a truer (and quieter) sense of the island and its personality, visit in spring or fall or plan on staying at least one night in one of the island's fine vintage inns. You'll be better able to appreciate Mackinac Island's magic after the crowds have left on the last ferry. (*Note:* Area codes in this vicinity are scheduled to change to 989 beginning April 7, 2001.)

Information: Mackinac Island Chamber of Commerce | Box 451, Mackinac Island 49757 | 800/4–LILACS | fax 906/847–3571 | www.mackinacisland.org.

Attractions

Butterfly House of Mackinac Island. More than 400 butterflies from around the world live at this conservatory. Tours are available. | 1308 McGulpin St. | 906/847–3972 | $3 | Daily 10–6.

Ferry services. Three popular lines service Mackinac Island from both St. Ignace and Mackinaw City every 15–20 minutes in season: **Arnold Transit Co.** (906/847–3351 or 800/542–8528 | fax 906/847–3892 | tonyfrazier@portup.com | www.arnoldline.com | $14.50 round-trip | May–Dec., daily); **Shepler's Mackinac Island Ferry** (231/436–5023 or 800/828–6157 | fax 231/436–7521 | sheplers@freeway.net | www.sheplers.com | $14.50 round-trip | Early May–Oct., daily); **Star Line Ferry** (567 N. State St., St. Ignace | 231/436–5045 or 800/638–9892 | fax 906/643–9856 | www.mackinacferry.com | $14.50 round-trip | May–Oct., daily).

The Haunted Theater. Wax monsters inhabit this creepy old theater downtown. Haunted-house sounds and special effects make for a scary show. | Huron St. | 906/847–6545 | $4.50 | Daily 10–6.

Mackinac Island Carriage Tours. Founded by a co-op of local families, the island's carriage tours start in the center of the shopping district on Main Street and take in more than 20 scenic and historic sites, including Fort Mackinac, Arch Rock, Skull Cave, and the Governor's Mansion. Tours take approximately two hours. | 100 Market St. | 906/847–3573 | www.mict.com | $14 | June–Oct., daily.

Mackinac Island State Park. Michigan's first state park has scenic views of Lakes Michigan and Huron and encompasses almost 80 percent of the 3-mi-long, 1,800-acre island. In summer, shoreline roads fill with bicyclists, hikers, and equestrians, many of whom come to see the island's natural geological formations such as Arch Rock, Devil's Point, and Sugar Loaf, as well as experience the sights and sounds of 19th-century military life at Fort

Mackinac. | 231/436–4100 (winter), 906/847–3328 (summer), or 800/447–2757 | fax 906–847–3571 | mackinacparks@state.mi.us | www.mackinac.com/historicparks | Free | Daily.

Benjamin Blacksmith Shop. In this working forge you can watch demonstrations of 19th- and 20th-century blacksmithing techniques. | Market St. | 231/436–4100 (winter), 906/847–3328 (summer), or 800/447–2757 | mackinacparks@state.mi.us | www.mackinac.com/historic parks | Included in admission to Fort Mackinac | Mid-June–Labor Day, daily 9–6.

The **Dr. Beaumont Museum and American Fur Company Store** commemorates Dr. William Beaumont, known for his work on the human digestive system. Displays of medical tools and equipment are explained by costumed interpreters. | 231/436–4100 (winter), 906/847–3328 (summer), or 800/447–2757 | mackinacparks@state.mi.us | www.mackinac.com/historicparks | Included in admission to Fort Mackinac | Mid-June–Labor Day, daily 9–6.

The restored 17th- and 18th-century British **Fort Mackinac** stands on a bluff overlooking the harbor and the nearby straits. You can explore 14 original buildings, some with limestone ramparts, with period settings, audio-visual presentations, and costumed guides. Popular activities include reenactments, military music, and cannon firings. | 231/436–4100 (winter), 906/847–3328 (summer), or 800/447–2757 | mackinacparks@state.mi.us | www.mackinac.com/historicparks | $7.50 | Mid-May–mid-Oct., 9–6.

The **Indian Dormitory** was built in 1838 to house Native Americans. It now holds Native American exhibits and period rooms, including murals depicting scenes from Longfellow's "Song Of Hiawatha." | 231/436–4100 (winter), 906/847–3328 (summer), or 800/447–2757 | mackinacparks@state.mi.us | www.mackinac.com/historicparks | Included in admission to Fort Mackinac | Mid-June–Labor Day, daily 9–6.

Other places worth exploring on the island and in the park are the Biddle House, with early 19th-century furnishings and crafts demonstrations, and the McGulpin House, a rare surviving example of French-Canadian architecture.

Marquette Park. This small downtown park at the foot of Fort Mackinac, and across from the marina, has a statue of the missionary Marquette and is surrounded by more than 65 varieties of lilacs. | Main St. | 906/847–3783 | Free | Daily.

ON THE CALENDAR

JUNE: *Lilac Festival.* An annual event celebrates the arrival of another summer season to this Victorian-era island. Parades, open houses, horticultural events, and lots of beautiful blooms are highlights. | 906/847–3783 or 800/4–LILACS | www.mackinacisland.org or www.mackinac.com.

JULY: *Sailing Races.* Hundreds of boats converge on Mackinac Island during the annual Chicago to Mackinac races, one of the state's largest and most colorful summer events. | 906/847–3783 or 800/4–LILACS | www.mackinacisland.org or www.mackinac.com.

AUG.: *Blacksmith Convention.* More than a dozen regional blacksmiths meet for the convention at the Benjamin Blacksmith Shop at Fort Mackinac. They use traditional smithing tools to complete group projects and give demonstrations. | 906/847–3328.

Dining

Carriage House. Continental. Outstanding views of the surrounding Straits of Mackinac can be enjoyed from both dining rooms in this Iroquois Hotel restaurant. Entrées include a grilled seafood sandwich at lunch and traditional fillet or prime rib with blue cheese bread pudding at dinner. For dessert, don't miss the sinful Mackinac Island Fudge cream puff. Open-air dining on the veranda. Kids' menu. | Main St. | 906/847–3321 | www.iroquoishotel.com | Closed mid-Oct.–mid May | $17–$26 | D, MC, V.

French Outpost. American. The Trapper Burger served here is rumored to be the island's best burger. There's outdoor seating on a large open-air patio and live music nightly. | Cadotte and Mahoney Aves. | 906/847–3772 | $8–$15 | D, MC, V.

Governor's Dining Room. Contemporary. This restaurant in the Island House combines traditional interiors with a harbor view. A creative menu includes pan-roasted lamb chops and sesame-seared tuna. Known for the chicken Mackinac with forest mushrooms and

the salmon Florentine with artichokes and tomatoes. Entertainment except Mon. | 1 Lakeshore Dr. (Main St.) | 906/847–3347 | www.theislandhouse.com | Closed late-Oct.–mid-May | $19–$35 | MC, V.

Pilot House. American. The vast gourmet breakfast buffet attracts swarms of diners to this restaurant housed in the Lake View Hotel; there's also an outrageously tasty filet mignon for dinner. The restaurant is stately, with linen-draped tables and votive candles, and it has an excellent view of busy Main Street. Outdoor seating on a big porch is available. | 1 Huron St. | 906/847–3384 | Reservations essential | $20–$40 | AE, D, DC, MC, V.

Lodging

Bay View at Mackinac. Guest rooms are on three levels of this grand Victorian-style house built in 1891. The only waterfront Mackinac Island bed and breakfast sits next to the state marina and a deck. Complimentary Continental breakfast. Some in-room VCRs. No kids. No smoking. | Huron St. | 906/847–3295 | fax 906/847–6219 | bayviewbnb@aol.com | www.mackinacbayview.com | 20 rooms (10 with shower only) | $125–$325 | Closed Nov.–Apr. | AE, D, MC, V.

Cloghaun Bed and Breakfast. This inn, whose name is pronounced "clah-haun" ("cloghaun" is Gaelic for "stony ground"), is 4 blocks from downtown. It's in one of the island's oldest Victorian homes and has been run by a single family for more than a century. Some of the antiques-furnished guest rooms have balconies. Complimentary Continental breakfast. No room phones, no TV. Library. | Market St. | 906/847–3885 | cloghaun@aol.com | www.cloghaun.com | 11 rooms, some with shared baths | $100–$165 | No credit cards.

Grand Hotel. This legendary structure is the world's largest summer hotel. Built in 1887 and extensively renovated in 1993, it is known for its porch—the world's longest at 600 ft—its excellent restaurants, and its 321 rooms, each individually decorated by noted White House designer Carleton Varney. The hotel sits on the west bluff of Mackinac Island. The hotel and island were showcased beautifully in the film "Somewhere in Time." Restaurant, bar, room service. Cable TV. Pool. Hot tub, sauna. 18-hole golf course, putting green, tennis. Hiking. Bicycles. | Grand Ave. | 906/847–3331 | fax 906/847–3259 | www.grandhotel.com | 343 rooms | $190–$540, $285–$780 suites | Closed Nov.–Apr. | AE, D, MC, V.

Iroquois Hotel. Perched on the water's edge, this inn claims some of the best views of the harbor, the straits, and the "Mighty Mac" bridge. The 1902 Victorian house, which has been operated as an inn by the current owners since 1954, has a sunny three-room lobby overlooking Main Street. Restaurant, room service. No air-conditioning. Beach. Business services. | Main St. | 906/847–3321 | fax 906/847–6274 | www.iroquoishotel.com | 46 rooms | $220–$290, $375 suites | Closed Nov.–Apr. | D, MC, V.

Island House. Built in 1910, this great Victorian house is the only hotel on Mackinac Island within Mackinac Island State Park. Restaurant, bar (with entertainment). No air-conditioning in some rooms. Indoor pool. Hot tub, steam room. Business services, airport shuttle. | 101 Main St. | 906/847–3347 or 800/626–6304 | fax 906/847–3819 | www.theislandhouse.com | 97 rooms | $140–$250 | Closed Nov.–Apr. | MC, V.

Lake View Hotel. The island's oldest continuously operating inn, since 1858, is across from the Straits of Mackinac on quiet Huron Street. The white-clapboard building houses a beautiful four-story atrium. Restaurant. No air-conditioning in some rooms. Indoor pool. Hot tub, sauna. Business services. | 1 Huron St. | 906/847–3384 | fax 906/847–6283 | lakeview@mackinac.com | www.mackinac.com/LVH | 85 rooms | $179–$274 | Closed mid-Oct.–Apr. | D, MC, V.

Lilac Tree Hotel. Public rooms and guest suites are filled with antique and reproduction furnishings, plus marble and gold appointments. Built after a tragic fire in downtown in 1987, it was the first new hotel built on the island in a span of 75 years. Restaurant. In-room data ports, refrigerators. Cable TV. Shops. | Main St. | 906/847–6575 | fax 906/847–3501 | www.mackinac.com/lilactree | 39 suites | $140–$295 suites | Closed Nov.–Apr. | AE, D, MC, V.

Mission Point Resort. Weekend sunset cruises and nightly movies are two favorite activities at this upscale family-style resort on 18 acres of lakefront outside of town. Guest rooms are decked out in a Ralph Lauren/lodge style. Lilac gardens surround the lodge. Bar, dining room, picnic area, room service. Cable TV. Pool. Hot tub. Tennis. Exercise equipment. Boating, bicycles. Video games. Children's programs (4–12). Business services. | 1 Lakeshore Dr. | 906/847–3312 or 800/833–7711 | fax 906/847–3833 | www.missionpoint.com | 242 rooms, 92 suites | $119–$359, $309–$409 suites | Closed Nov.–Apr. | AE, D, MC, V.

Murray Hotel. A mid-1880s building with an old-fashioned boardwalk porch and wraparound balconies houses this hotel in the heart of downtown. A deluxe fudge-making company is also on the premises. Restaurant, complimentary Continental breakfast. Cable TV. | Main St. | 800/462–2546 | fax 906/847–6110 | mackinac@mich.com | www.4mackinac.com/murray.html | 69 rooms | $84–$245 | MC, V.

MACKINAW CITY

MAP 9, D3

(Nearby towns also listed: Mackinac Island, St. Ignace)

Anchoring the southern end of the Mackinac Bridge, this small city is the only place where you can see the sun rise on one of the Great Lakes (Huron) and set on another (Michigan). Once a French trading post, it now sees thousands of northward-bound travelers during the summer season. (*Note:* Area codes in this vicinity are scheduled to change to 989 beginning April 7, 2001.)

Information: Greater Mackinaw Area Chamber of Commerce | Box 856, Mackinaw City 49701 | 231/436–5574 or 800/666–0160 | www.mackinawcity.com.

Attractions

Colonial Michilimackinac. At the southern end of the Mackinac Bridge (west off I-75, Exit 339), this restored colonial fur-trading village is one of northern Michigan's most-visited sites. Archaeologists and students can be seen at work in season, as the country's oldest

DIG THIS

Archaeologists dust off their trowels and brushes each June for a season of exploration at Mackinaw City's Colonial Michilimackinac, the oldest ongoing archaeological dig in the country.

The fort, a walled fortress and fur-trading village, was built by the French in 1715 but was later occupied by British soldiers during the 1760s and 1770s. During the American Revolution, American soldiers moved the fort to a 150-ft bluff on nearby Mackinac Island and renamed it Fort Mackinac. They burned what was left of Michilimackinac so other British troops couldn't occupy it.

During the past four decades of work, animal bones, lead shot, ceramic and glass shards, cuff links, and uniform buttons were among the artifacts found. Those items are in the fort's "Treasures from the Sand" exhibit, open daily in summer. You can watch the dig in progress every day from June through late August, weather permitting. An interpreter is on hand to answer questions.

For more information, contact Colonial Michilimackinac at | 906/847–3328 | www.mackinac.com/historicparks/index.html.

© Artville

ongoing dig occurs here. Other highlights are costumed interpreters, military and music demonstrations, pioneer cooking and crafts, and daily cannon firing. | 906/847–3328 (summer) or 231/436–4100 (winter) | mackinacparks@state.mi.us | www.mackinac.com/historicparks | $7.50 | May–mid-Oct., daily hrs. vary.

Historic Mill Creek. You can explore the first industrial buildings built on the Great Lakes at this 625-acre site with restored structures from the 1790s. At the complex, 3.5 mi south of Mackinaw City on U.S. 23, you can also watch sawyers and loggers use antique pit saws to cut wood, observe beavers at work on their dam, or stroll along miles of nature trails. | U.S. 23 | 906/847–3328 or 231/436–4100 | mackinaw.com/historicparks | $6.50 | Daily 9–6, closed Apr.–Nov.

Mackinac Bridge. Completed in 1957, the 5-mi "Mighty Mac" is an engineering marvel that reduced the once arduous ferry crossing between Michigan's peninsulas to a quick, 10-minute sprint. The bridge's main towers, from which the 8,614 ft suspension bridge—one of the longest in the world—hangs, rise 552 ft above the Straits of Mackinac. The Mackinac Bridge Walk, held each Labor Day, lets you get an up-close look. | 906/643–7600 | www.mackinacbridge.org | $1.50 per car.

Mackinac Island ferries. Three long-standing, family-run companies have regular 15–20-minute trips to Mackinac Island: **Arnold Transit Company** (906/847–3351 | fax 906/847–3892 | tonyfrazier@portup.com | www.arnoldline.com | $14.50 round-trip | May–Dec., daily); **Shepler's Mackinac Island Ferry** (231/436–5023 or 800/828–6157 | fax 231/436–7521 | sheplers@freeway.net | www.sheplers.com | $14.50 round-trip | Early May–Oct., daily); **Star Line Ferry** (231/436–5045 or 800/638–9892 | fax 906/643–9856 | www.mackinacferry.com | $14.50 round-trip | May–Oct., daily).

Sea Shell City. Inside this wooden building that resembles both an airport hangar and a machine shed are thousands of the most kitschy, campy souvenirs and gewgaws ever made, like rubber tomahawks, animal figurines made of seashells, and feather earrings (with sparkles!). If you don't really need a Mackinaw City bumper sticker or embossed coffee mug, at least stop in to see the 500-lb "man-killing" clam displayed in the entry hall. | 7075 Levring Rd. | 231/627–2066 | Free | Mon.–Sat. 9–6.

Wilderness State Park. This nature lovers' paradise 11 mi west of Mackinaw City spans more than 8,000 acres. Here you can stroll 26 mi of Lake Michigan shoreline and hike 16 mi of trails. Twelve miles of cross-country trails are winter favorites. Some of the nine rustic cabins for rent are on the beach. | 898 Wilderness Park Dr., Carp Lake | 231/436–5381 or 800/447–2757 | mackinacparks@state.mi.us | www.dnr.state.mi.us/camping | $4 per car, per day | Daily dawn to dusk.

ON THE CALENDAR

MAY: *Colonial Michilimackinac Pageant.* A popular re-creation of original music, military demonstrations, and actual events from the period 1715–63, when this fort was occupied by the British, takes place Memorial Day weekend at Colonial Michilimackinac. | 231/436–4100.

JULY–SEPT.: *Vesper Cruises.* Free Sunday cruises take you under the Mackinac Bridge while weaving colorful tales of the area's rich history. Trips take off from the Old State Dock in Mackinaw City. | 231/436–5622.

SEPT.: *Mackinac Bridge Walk.* The governor leads the way across the Mighty Mac followed by thousands of hoofers during this annual Labor Day event. | 800/666–0160 | www.mackinacbridge.org/walk.html.

Dining

Admiral's Table. Seafood. Fish dominate both the look and the menu at this laid-back eatery across from the Arnold Ferry Line Dock. Fresh fish is delivered daily. Steaks, chicken, sandwiches, and a wide range of salads are also available. Salad bar. Entertainment. Kids' menu. | 502 S. Huron St. | 231/436–5687 | Closed Oct.–Apr. | $15–$25 | AE, D, DC, MC, V.

Audie's. American. Two separate dining areas divide this restaurant. The "family room" is noisy and casual, with big tables, spacious booths, and high chairs. The Chippewa Room, with vintage photos of the Mackinac Bridge on the walls, is more quiet and refined. The specialty is grilled whitefish with lemon and herbs. | 314 Nicolet St. | 231/436–5744 | $7–$12 | AE, D, MC, V.

Darrow's. American. This small, family-run spot, which displays many old pictures of the town, is two blocks from Colonial Michilimackinac. It's known for homemade soups and delicious pies and other baked goods. | 303 Louvingney St. | 231/436–5514 | $$–$6 | MC, V.

Embers. Seafood. This casual country dining spot in downtown Mackinaw City by the Arnold Ferry Line Docks is known for its seafood-dominated smorgasbord (lunch and dinner) and plentiful breakfast buffet. A small gift shop sells nautical items, dolls, and Teddy bears. Buffet. | 810 S. Huron Ave. | 231/436–5773 | Closed mid-Nov.–early Apr. | $10–$15 | D, MC, V.

The Fort. Continental. Family owned for more than 30 years, this casual family-friendly restaurant across from Fort Michilimackinac serves up popular breakfast, lunch, and dinner buffets. Salad bar. Buffet. Kids' menu. | 400 N. Louvingney | 231/436–5453 | Closed Nov.–Mar. | $9–$15 | D, MC, V.

Goldie's Cafe. American. This casual, down-home restaurant, 5 mi from Mackinaw City, has cedar-beamed ceilings, floral-print valances, checkered tablecloths, and an old-fashioned ice-cream-parlor counter. Try one of the hot beef sandwiches served with gravy-doused mashed potatoes. | 6492 Paradise Trail, Carp Lake | 231/537–4089 | No supper | $5–$10 | MC, V.

Island Outpost. Seafood. With a Caribbean theme, this lakeside restaurant boasts bright colors, tropical flowers, and strategically placed bamboo accents. You can order whitefish broiled, fried, or lightly battered, followed by homemade key lime pie. | 806 S. Huron Ave. | 231/436–8757 | $6–$12 | D, MC, V.

Mackinaw Bakery and Coffeehouse. Café. Excellent sandwiches and pastries are served at this small cafe across the street from Shepler's ferry dock. | 110 Langlade St. | 231/436–5525 | No supper | $2–$5 | No credit cards.

'Neath the Birches. American. Tangy barbecued ribs and steak and seafood specialties attract both locals and "fudgies" (tourists) to this popular Mackinaw City eatery, a mile from town. Salad bar. Kids' menu, early bird suppers. | Old U.S. 31 | 231/436–5401 | Closed late Oct.–mid-May. No lunch | $11–$24 | AE, D, DC, MC, V.

Pancake Chef. American. Banana, blueberry, whole wheat—hot cakes are the star here, and you can have them your way. This family favorite has a large array of breakfast specials as well as inexpensive lunches and dinners, including a well-stocked salad bar and a daily buffet. Salad bar. Buffet. | 327 Central Ave. | 231/436–5578 | $15–$23 | D, DC, MC, V.

Scalawag's. Seafood. The nautical-themed dining area here, with its buoys, nets, shells, and ropes, evokes the menu's fresh-from-the-Great-Lakes bounty. Whitefish, prepared a half-dozen different ways, is the standout; fish chowder is another winner. | 226 E. Center Ave. | 231/436–7777 | $8–$14 | No credit cards.

Squealy Downing's Family Restaurant. American. The culinary claim to fame of this large and lofty pig-themed restaurant is the 19-ft buffet loaded with dozens of choices at each meal. Breakfast is also available. | 707 N. Huron Ave. | 231/436–7330 | $7–$16 | D, MC, V.

Lodging

Beachcomber Motel. You can soak up sun on the sandy Lake Huron beach of this motel on a busy tourist strip. Picnic area. Cable TV. Beach. Some pets allowed. | 1011 S. Huron Ave. | 231/436–8451 | 22 rooms | $39–$125 | AE, D, MC, V.

Best Western. The city's largest pool makes this a good bet for Mackinac-bound families. Complimentary Continental breakfast. In-room data ports, refrigerators, some in-room hot

tubs. Cable TV. Indoor pool. Hot tub. Laundry facilities. | 112 U.S. 31 | 231/436–5544 or 800/
780–7234 | fax 231/436–7180 | www.bestwesternmichigan.com | 73 rooms | $34–$119 | Closed
Nov.–Apr. | AE, D, DC, MC, V.

Best Western Dockside. Spacious lakefront rooms overlook this popular waterfront chain
hotel's 300 ft of private Lake Huron beach. It's the closest lodging to Shepler's and Arnold
Line ferries. Complimentary Continental breakfast. Refrigerators (in suites). Cable TV. | 505
S. Huron Ave. | 231/436–5001 or 800/774–1794 | fax 231/436–5933 | www.bestwestern-
michigan.com. | 112 rooms, 19 suites | $55–$125, $128–$169 suites | Closed Nov.–Apr. | AE, D,
DC, MC, V.

Brigadoon Bed and Breakfast. Guest rooms at this inn near Lake Huron's edge are opulent, and they all have water views. They also have heated marble floors in the bathrooms,
large working fireplaces, balconies, canopy beds, and carved wooden details everywhere.
Complimentary breakfast. Cable TV. | 207 Langlade Ave. | 231/436–8882 | fax 231/436–5987
| bayviewbnb@aol.com | www.bayviewbnb.com | 8 rooms | $95–$225 | AE, D, MC, V.

Capri Motel. This small, independently run motel has basic guest rooms but a surprisingly
charming lobby with antique-reproduction furniture and chintz swags on the windows.
Cable TV. Pool. Pets allowed. | 801 S. Nicolet St. | 231/436–5498 | fax 231/436–7328 | 27 rooms
| $69–$150 | AE, D, MC, V.

Chippewa Motor Lodge. Nicely landscaped grounds surround this modern motor inn
that has one of the area's largest beaches on Lake Huron. One block to ferries. Game room.
Restaurant, Picnic area. Cable TV. Indoor pool. Hot tub. Beach. Playground. Business ser-
vices. | 929 S. Huron Ave. | 231/436–8661 or 800/748–0124 | 39 rooms | $28–$89 | Closed mid-
Oct.–Apr. | D, MC, V.

Comfort Inn. This waterfront chain hotel is next to the ferries and a short walk to shops,
fishing, and restaurants. Refrigerators. Cable TV. Indoor pool. Hot tub. Beach. | 611 S. Huron
Ave. | 231/436–5057 or 800/228–5150 | fax 231/436–7385 | www.comfortinn.com | 60 rooms
| $38–$139 | Closed Nov.–May | AE, D, DC, MC, V.

Days Inn. The ferry docks are next door to this family-friendly chain hotel. Shuffleboard
is one of the on-site activities. Game room. Restaurant, picnic area, room service. Cable TV.
Indoor pool. Hot tub, sauna. Putting green. Playground, laundry facilities. | 825 S. Huron
Ave. | 231/436–5557 or 800/388–7829 | fax 231/436–5703 | www.daysinn.com | 84 rooms | $28–
$119 | Closed Nov.–May | AE, D, DC, MC, V.

Deer Head Lodge. This Arts-and-Crafts-era stucco house has a big, shady porch outside
and lots of leather, wood, and Mission-style furniture inside. Guest rooms have pencil-post
beds and prominently displayed hunting trophies like bearskin rugs, stuffed coyotes, and
deer heads. Complimentary Continental breakfast. Cable TV. | 109 Henry St. | 231/436–5498
| 4 rooms | $100–$200 | No credit cards.

EconoLodge at the Bridge. This simple, quiet motel, a block from Colonial Michilimackinac and within sight of the Mackinaw Bridge, has a small, sandy beach for sunning and
swimming. Restaurant, bar. In-room data ports. Cable TV. Beach. Laundry service. Business
services. | 412 N. Nicolet St. | 231/436–5026 or 800/553–2666 | fax 231/436–4172 |
www.econolodge.com | 32 rooms | $35–$120 | AE, D, MC, V.

Grand Mackinaw Inn and Suites. Some rooms here have private balconies; others have
lake views, perfect for watching the ferry boats come and go. In-room data ports. Cable
TV. Laundry service. Business services. | 907 S. Huron Ave. | 231/436–8831 | fax 231/436–8851
| 60 suites | $55–$295 | AE, D, DC, MC, V.

Hampton Inn. This business-oriented lodging is within 5 mi of both the Mackinaw City
attractions and the Mackinac Island ferries. In-room data ports. Cable TV. Pool. Sauna. Laun-
dry service. Business services. | 726 S. Huron Ave. | 231/436–7829 | fax 231/436–9881 |
www.hamptoninn.com | 62 rooms | $120–$220 | AE, D, DC, MC, V.

Holiday Inn Express. Attractions, ferries, and restaurants are within a few blocks to this chain hotel. Complimentary Continental breakfast. Some refrigerators. Cable TV, in-room VCRs (and movies). Indoor pool. Hot tub. Exercise equipment. Game room. Laundry facilities. Business services. | 364 Louvingny St. | 231/436–7100 or 800465–4329 | fax 231/436–7070 | www.basshotels/holiday-inn | 71 rooms | $35–$135 | AE, D, DC, MC, V.

La Mirage Motel. This cozy, family-style inn is near the maritime museum and overlooks Mackinaw's largest lakeshore park and historic lighthouse. Refrigerators, some in-room hot tubs. Cable TV. Indoor pool. Hot tub, sauna. Beach. Some pets allowed. | 699 N. Huron Ave. | 231/436–5304 or 800/729–0998 | fax 231/436–5304 | www.lighthouseviewmotel.com | 25 rooms | $35–$125 | Closed Nov.–Apr. | AE, D, DC, MC, V.

Motel 6. Basic lodgings are available at this chain motel one block from downtown. Some refrigerators. Cable TV. Indoor pool. Hot tub. Some pets allowed. | 206 Nicolet St. | 231/436–8961 or 800/388–9508 | fax 231/436–7317 | www.motel6.com | 53 rooms | $29–$58 | AE, D, DC, MC, V.

Parkside Inn–Bridgeside. A nice, friendly motel close to Colonial Michilimackinac State Park. Picnic area. Cable TV. Indoor pool. Hot tub. Game room. Some pets allowed. | 102 Nicolet St. | 231/436–8301 or 800/827–8301 | 44 rooms | $38–$110 | Closed Nov.–Apr. | AE, D, MC, V.

Quality Inn Beachfront. You get striking views of Mackinac Island and the Mighty Mac bridge at this chain hotel at the edge of town. The 270-ft private sandy beach is a family favorite. Picnic area. Some refrigerators. Cable TV. Indoor pool. Hot tub, sauna. Beach. Playground. Business services. Some pets allowed. | 917 S. Huron Ave. | 231/436–5051 | fax 231/436–7221 | 60 rooms | $24–$119 | AE, D, DC, MC, V.

Ramada Convention Center. The boat docks and shopping are within walking distance of this centrally located full-service hotel. Restaurant, bar, room service. Refrigerators, some in-room hot tubs. Cable TV. Indoor pool. Hot tub, sauna. Cross-country skiing. Game room. Laundry facilities. | 450 S. Nicolet St./Rte. 108 | 231/436–5535 or 800/298–2054 | fax 231/436–5489 | www.ramada.com | 162 rooms | $39–$190 | AE, D, DC, MC, V.

Ramada Limited–Waterfront. Balconies at this modern, beachfront hotel overlook the Straits and Mackinac Island. It's at the ferry docks. Complimentary Continental breakfast. Refrigerators. Cable TV. Indoor pool. Hot tub Beach. Business services. | 723 S. Huron Ave. | 231/436–5055 or 800/298–2054 | fax 231/436–5921 | www.ramada.com | 42 rooms | $42–$169 | AE, D, DC, MC, V.

Starlite Budget Inns. This no-frills motel is off the highway. Refrigerators. Cable TV. Pool. Playground. Some pets allowed. | 116 Old U.S. 31 | 231/436–5959 or 800/288–8190 | fax 231/436–5101 | 33 rooms | $28–$89 | Closed Nov.–Apr. | AE, D, DC, MC, V.

Super 8. This year-round chain motel near the bridge is just a mile to area snowmobile trails. Cable TV. Indoor pool. Hot tub, sauna. Game room. Laundry facilities. Some pets allowed. | 601 N. Huron Ave. | 231/436–5252 or 800/800–8000 | fax 231/436–7004 | www.super8motels.com | 50 rooms | $32–$135 | AE, D, DC, MC, V.

Surf. Simple, family-style accommodations overlooking Lake Huron and within walking distance of ferries can be had here. There is a view of the bridge and the island. Refrigerators. Cable TV. Indoor pool. Hot tub. Beach. Playground. Business services. Some pets allowed. | 907 S. Huron Ave. | 231/436–8831 or 800/822–8314 | 40 rooms | $30–$85 | Closed Nov.–Apr. | AE, D, MC, V.

Waterfront Inn. Kids love the 600-ft private beach on Lake Huron, Mackinaw City's largest, at this independent motor inn. Picnic area. Cable TV. Pool. Hot tub. Beach. Playground. Some pets allowed. | 1009 S. Huron Ave. | 231/436–5527 or 800/962–9832 | 69 rooms | $28–$89 | AE, D, MC, V.

MANISTEE

MAP 9, B5

(Nearby towns also listed: Cadillac, Frankfort, Ludington)

Named "Spirit of the Woods" by the native Americans, this town in the northwest corner of the state was once a busy lumber capital. Today its mainstays are salt, fruit, and tourism. (*Note:* Area codes in this vicinity are scheduled to change to 989 beginning April 7, 2001.)

Information: Manistee Area Chamber of Commerce | 11 Cypress St., Manistee 49660 | 231/723–2575 or 800/288–2286 | www.manistee.com.

Attractions

Fifth Avenue Beach. This popular downtown beach along Lake Michigan has volleyball, swimming, and a children's playground. | 231/723–2575 or 800/288–2286 | Free | Daily.

First Street Beach. Sunbathers like this in-town beach on Lake Michigan known for its picnic spots and sandy shoreline. | 231/723–2575 or 800/288–2286 | Free | Daily.

Huron-Manistee National Forest. *(See also* Cadillac.) The only National Forest in the Lower Peninsula, Huron-Manistee has almost a million acres extending across the state from Lake Michigan to Lake Huron. | S. Mitchell St., Cadillac | 231/723–2211 or 800/821–6263 | www.fs.fed.us/r9/hmnf/hmindex.htm | $3 | Daily 8–5.

Manistee County Historical Museum. A restored 19th-century drugstore is the home of the Manistee Historical Museum. Displays trace the city's heyday during the lumber boom of the 1800s. Exhibits include antiques and local memorabilia from pioneer and Civil War days, a vintage drug store, and a recreated country store. You can also pick up walking tours of the city's restored Victorian neighborhoods here. | Lyman Building, 425 River St. | 231/723–5531 | $1.50 | June–Sept., daily 10–5; Oct.–May, Tues.–Sat. 10–5.

Built in 1882, the **Old Waterworks Building** houses marine and logging exhibits. | W. 1st St. | 231/723–5531 | Free | Mid-June–Labor Day, Tues.–Sat. 10:30–4:30.

Manistee North Pierhead Light. A 19th-century light and catwalk on the city's pier are popular with vacationers and photographers. The interior is closed to the public. | 231/723–2575 or 800/288–2286 | Free | Daily.

Orchard Beach State Park. Grassy picnic areas and a sandy Lake Michigan beach beckon at this park north of Manistee. A ½-mi self-guided nature trail and 1 mi of hiking trails are next to the campground, which has modern campsites. | M–110 | 231/723–7422 or 800/447–2757 | www.dnr.state.mi.us/camping | $4 per car, per day | Daily dawn to dusk.

Ramsdell Theatre and Hall. Built at the turn of the 20th century by a prominent pioneer attorney, this lavish building now houses the city's Civic Players, with community theater productions throughout the year as well as occasional art and museum exhibits. | 101 Maple St. | 231/723–9948 or 231/723–7188 | June–Aug., Wed. and Sat.; Sept.–May, by appointment.

ON THE CALENDAR

MAR.: *St. Patrick's Day Parade.* Billed as the world's shortest parade, this march runs for barely two blocks downtown. Participants wind up at a pub and spend the afternoon making merry and competing in games to benefit local nonprofit groups. | 231/723–1031.

JULY: *National Forest Festival.* This four-day festival honors the local Manistee National Forest and the city's ties to the lumber industry with a grand parade, a vintage boat show, a Venetian boat parade, lumberjack demonstrations, beach entertainment, and more. | 231/723–2575.

SEPT.: *Victorian Port City Festival.* The age of Victoria comes alive throughout downtown Manistee, one of the state's best-preserved 19th-century cities, during this event. Arts and crafts, parades, and food booths are part of the fun. | 888/584–9862.

Dining

Armedos. American. Both Mexican and Italian fare share menu space with classic American entrees here. | 1569 S. U.S. 31 | 231/723–3561 | $6–$13 | AE, D, DC, MC, V.

Four Forty West. Steak. Huge windows give you a view of the Manistee River at this downtown restaurant. It serves steak house classics, but the house specialty is grilled perch drizzled with an herb-butter sauce. | 440 River St. | 231/723–7902 | No lunch | $20–$30 | AE, D, MC, V.

Lodging

Carriage Inn. Tranquil color schemes are used throughout this hotel that's a across from Lake Manistee. You can take the River Walk, a sidewalk which borders shops and the Manistee River, into downtown. Restaurant, bar. Cable TV. Indoor pool. Exercise equipment. Cross-country skiing. Game room. Business services, airport shuttle. | 200 Arthur St. | 231/723–9949 | fax 231/723–9949 | 72 rooms | $36–$120 | AE, D, DC, MC, V.

Days Inn. The well-known River Walk, a sidewalk alongside the Manistee River and shops, is near this chain hotel on the southern edge of town. Cable TV. Indoor pool. Hot tub. Cross-country skiing. Game room. Laundry facilities. Business services, airport shuttle. | 1462 U.S. 31 S | 231/723–8385, ext. 112 | fax 231/723–8385 | www.daysinn.com | 90 rooms | $36–$150 | AE, D, DC, MC, V.

Inn Wick-A-Te-Wah. This bed and breakfast in a 1912 bungalow is perched on the shores of Lake Portage in downtown. It has big windows, hardwood floors, and unusual furnishings. Complimentary breakfast. No room phones, no TV. | 3813 Lakeshore Dr. | 231/889–4396 | 4 rooms, some with shared bath | $80–$115 | No credit cards.

Lake Shore Bed and Breakfast. A private sandy beach and lakeside deck make this Western-style cedar house a good spot for relaxing. It's 3 mi west of downtown, and Orchard Beach State Park is a few miles away. Cable TV. Beach. | 3440 Lakeshore Dr. | 231/723–7644 | 1 suite, 4 rooms, some with shared bath | $120 | No credit cards.

Manistee Inn and Marina. This updated two-story downtown hotel with a private dock is a favorite of boaters. Complimentary Continental breakfast. Cable TV, in-room VCRs (and movies). Laundry facilities. Business services. | 378 River St. | 231/723–4000 or 800/968–6277 | fax 231/723–0007 | 25 rooms | $32–$75 | AE, D, DC, MC, V.

MANISTIQUE

MAP 9, C3

(Nearby towns also listed: Brevort, Escanaba, Fayette, Gladstone, Munising, Newberry)

Seat of the Upper Peninsula's Schoolcraft County, Manistique is the gateway to more than 300 nearby lakes and streams and the Lake Superior State Forest. It's known for its fine fishing and other recreation, and as the location of Kitch-iti-ki-pi, a clear spring 12 mi west that measures 200 ft wide and 40 ft deep. (*Note:* Area codes in this vicinity are scheduled to change to 989 beginning April 7, 2001.)

Information: **Schoolcraft County Chamber of Commerce** | Box 72, U.S. 2, Manistique 49854 | 906/341–5010 | chamber@upmail.com | www.manistique.com.

Attractions

Indian Lake State Park. Indian Lake, 5 mi west of town, is an 8,400-acre park with a mile of sandy beach. Swimming, angling (bass, bluegill, pike, perch, walleye), and camping are some of the outdoor activities you can do here. | Off County Rd. 442 | 906/341–2355 or 800/447–2757 | www.dnr.state.mi.us/camping | $4 per car, per day | Daily dawn to dusk.

Manistique Boardwalk. You can walk from the downtown marina for almost 2 mi on this wooden sidewalk running along Lake Michigan. The walk, which is particularly nice in the early morning and at sunset, takes you past the town's lighthouse and over three small bridges. | Daily.

Palms-Book State Park. This 300-acre park, 12 mi northwest of Manistique, has the state's largest spring, Kitch-iti-ki-pi, a 40-ft-deep spring that can be viewed from a self-operated observation raft throughout the year. Picnic areas and concessions are available but no camping is allowed. | M–149 | 906/341–2355 | www.dnr.state.mi.us/www/parks/index.htm | Free | Daily dawn to dusk.

ON THE CALENDAR
JULY: *Folkfest.* Held the second week of July, this ethnic celebration includes two days of entertainment, games, food, arts and crafts booths, and more in downtown on Cedar St. | 906/341–5010.
AUG.: *Schoolcraft County Fair.* Exibits, displays, horse shows, food, games, entertainment, queen, little prince and princess contests, much more are part of this annual county fair. It takes place at the fairgrounds behind the hospital. | 906/341–5010.
SEPT.: *Manistique Merchants Car & Antique Snowmobile Show.* A car parade kicks off this show that also showcases snowmobiles. A tractor pull and other events are part of the fun downtown on Cedar St. | 906/341–5010.

Dining
Big Spring Inn. American. Snowmobilers, fishermen, and hunters flock to this roadhouse-like spot, established in 1928, for the big burgers, 16-oz porterhouse steaks, and hearty pub sandwiches. The original oak bar remains, joined now by a jukebox, video games, and dart boards. It's on a snowmobile route. | M–149 | 906/644–2506 | www.bigspring.com | $6–$16 | No credit cards.

Harbor Inn. American. You can have a a pre- or post-dinner drink at the inn's century-old tavern, the town's first watering hole, which has 12-ft embossed tin ceilings and a solid oak bar. At the restaurant, which was added on later, try spaghetti marinara or a thick rib-eye steak. | 242 S. Cedar St. | 906/341–8393 | $7–$15 | D, MC, V.

Sunny Shores. Seafood. The smaller front dining area here has Formica-topped tables, condiment caddies, and old-fashioned glass sugar shakers. The rear area has murals of outdoor scenes painted on the walls, reflecting the views out the windows. Specialties include fried lake perch, fried shrimp, and lemon-pepper chicken. | 19 East Lakeshore Dr. | 906/341–5582 | Closed Dec.–Mar. | $6–$12 | MC, V.

Teddy's Pub and Bistro. American. More pub than bistro, Teddy's has a dance floor, colored lights, and a clientele that can get rowdy as the night wears on. The seafood is excellent. Try the panfried whitefish, blackened cod, or broiled swordfish with dill or lemon butter. | 100 S. 2nd St. | 906/341–8212 | $8–$20 | MC, V.

Lodging
Best Western Breakers. This chain hotel just 2 mi from downtown caters to families. Every room overlooks Lake Michigan. Snowmobiling trails start at the motel. Cable TV. Indoor-outdoor pool. Hot tub. | 1199 West Lakeshore Dr. | 906/341–2410 or 800/780–7234 | fax 906/341–2207 | www.bestwesternmichigan.com | 40 rooms | $45–$89 | AE, D, DC, MC, V.

Celibeth House Bed and Breakfast. An 1895 country manor houses this inn, which has a cozy fireplace in the living room. Everyone's welcome to make reservations for afternoon teas on Wednesdays and Sundays in Miss Mary's Tea Room. Picnic area, complimentary breakfast. No room phones. Cross-country skiing. Library. No smoking. | M–77, Blaney Park | 906/283–3409 | info@celibethhouse.com | www.celibethhouse.com | 7 rooms, with private baths | $50–$78 | Closed Dec.–Apr. | MC, V.

Comfort Inn. The lakeside boardwalk is 100 yards away and downtown is a mile away from this motel that's oriented to business travelers. In-room data ports. Cable TV. | 726 E. Lakeshore Dr. | 906/341–6981 or 800/228–5150 | fax 906/341–6339 | www.confortsuites.com | 57 | $64–$124 | AE, D, DC, MC, V.

Econo Lodge. The Lake Michigan boardwalk is across the street from this chain hotel. Complimentary Continental breakfast. Cable TV. Some pets allowed. | 209 E. Lake Shore | 906/341–6014 or 800/553–2666 | fax 906/341–2979 | www.econolodge.com | 31 rooms | $38–$66 | AE, D, DC, MC, V.

Elk Street Lodge. If you're a hunter, you may appreciate the gun racks in the guest rooms of this huge, three-story, red-brick inn that was at various times the county poor farm, a nursing home, and an adult foster-care center. Some room phones, no TV. | 906 W. Elk St. | 906/341–1122 or 877/341–1122 | fax 906/341–8573 | 9 rooms | $60–$70 | D, MC, V.

Holiday Motel. Schoolcraft County Airport is across the highway from these family-owned accommodations, 4 mi from town. Shuttles run from town to motel as well as to the casino, a mile away. The motel's 14 acres of evergreens are connected to snowmobile trails. Picnic area, complimentary Continental breakfast. No air-conditioning. Cable TV. Pool. Playground. Some pets allowed. | U.S. 2 | 906/341–2710 | 20 rooms | $32–$49 | AE, D, MC, V.

Manistique Motor Inn/Budget Host. A popular snowmobilers' hangout, this motel has basic, comfortable lodgings. Bar. No air-conditioning in some rooms. Cable TV. Pool. Cross-country skiing. Business services, airport shuttle. | U.S. 2 E, Box 1505 | 906/341–2552 | www.best-lodging.com | 26 rooms | $35–$75 | AE, D, DC, MC, V.

Northshore Motor Inn. Comfortable lodgings overlook Lake Michigan. Here you're near the boardwalk, skiing, and beaches. Picnic area. Cable TV. Beach. | 1967 E. Lakeshore Dr. | 906/341–2420 or 800/297–7107 | 12 rooms | $27–$56 | AE, D, DC, MC, V.

Royal Rose Bed and Breakfast. The boardwalk along Lake Michigan is across the street from this 1903 Dutch Colonial house, which has a big wraparound porch, crystal chandeliers in the dining room, and a fine antique collection. Some rooms have private balconies and separate sitting areas; all rooms have private baths. Complimentary breakfast. No room phones, no TV. | 230 Arbutus Ave. | 906/341–4886 | fax 906/341–4886 | gsablack@up.net | 4 rooms | $65–$85 | D, MC, V.

TUCKED IN A TEPEE

Sick of sleeping bags? Next time you're looking for a new twist on your camping experience, think about a night in a tepee.

Eight state parks across Michigan rent tepees for approximately $20 per night. The 20-ft-tall canvas tepees come equipped with cots or bunk beds, some even with coolers and propane stoves. Participating state parks include Indian Lake outside Manistique in the Upper Peninsula, Interlochen State Park near Traverse City, and Holly Recreation Area northwest of Detroit. | 888/78–GREAT | www.dnr.state.mi.us/camping.

© Artville

MARQUETTE

MAP 9, B2

(Nearby towns also listed: Gladstone, Houghton, Ishpeming, Munising)

Named for explorer and missionary Father Jacques Marquette, this town, the largest in the U.P., is surrounded by forests, beaches, and orchards. Northern Michigan University is here, as is the Great Lakes Sports Training Center, the world's largest such facility. *(Note:* Area codes in this vicinity are scheduled to change to 989 beginning April 7, 2001.)

Information: **Marquette Area Chamber of Commerce** | 501 S. Front St., Marquette 49855 | 906/226–6591 | fax 906/226–2099 | mqtinfo@marquette.org | www.marquette.org.

Attractions

Marquette County Historical Museum. Tracing the rich history of Marquette and the surrounding region, this small museum features permanent exhibits that include a fur-trading post, an Ojibway family diorama, and an 18th-century survey party. The on-site Longyear Library has extensive collections of materials on regional history. | 213 N. Front St. | 906/226–3571 | $3 | Weekdays 10–5.

Marquette Maritime Museum. Shipwrecks are the focus of many exhibits at this site in the Water Works Building on Lake Superior. Lighthouse lenses, a functioning 40-ft World War II periscope, and other nautical memorabilia also are on display. | 300 Lakeshore Dr. | 906/226–2006 | $3 | Daily, 10–5; closed Oct.–early May.

Marquette Mountain Ski Area. A more than 600-ft vertical drop and 16 runs attract both novices and mogul-bashing experts. The area holds NASTAR races. | Co. Rd. 553 | 906/225–1155 | www.marquettemountain.com | Nov.–Mar.

Mt. Marquette Scenic Outlook Area. A beautiful view of the surrounding Upper Peninsula is yours at this overlook area along Route 41. | Free | May–mid-Oct., daily.

Northern Michigan University. Dating from the turn of the century, this 300-acre campus is one of the largest in the Upper Peninsula. Among the important sites are the 5-acre technology and applied sciences center, the Olson Library, and the Superior Dome, the largest wooden dome in the world. | 906/227–2888 or 906/227–1700 | www.nmu.edu | Free | Daily.

Presque Isle Park. A scenic drive, great for viewing fall foliage, winds around this 238-acre park northeast of the city that juts out into Lake Superior. The Midwest's largest outdoor pool attracts visitors in summer. You can also hike nature trails, hunt for rocks, and take bog walks here. In winter trails are open for showshoeing and cross-country skiing. | Lake Shore Blvd. | 906/228–0460 | Free | May–Oct., daily; Nov.–Apr., daily for winter sports only. Part of Presque Isle Park, the **Upper Harbor ore dock** provides excellent views of the impressive iron-ore boat ramp and visiting freighters. Millions of tons of ore are shipped annually from this site. | Free | Daily.

Statue of Father Marquette. Marquette honors its founder with this downtown landmark built on a site overlooking the city's first settlement. | Marquette Park, 501 S. Front | 906/228–7749 | Free | Daily.

Upper Peninsula Children's Museum. Here your kids can touch snakes, turtles, and fish, or slide down a giant toilet. They also can see the fuselage of an airplane and a "fantastic forest." | 123 W. Baraga St. | 906/CANDY–11 | $4.50 | Daily, 10–6.

ON THE CALENDAR

FEB.: *UP 200 Dog Sled Race.* More than 10,000 people attend the start of this race at City Hall. Eighty mushers race to Escanaba and back to Marquette in a weekend. | 906/226–6591 | www.up200.org.

MAR.: *Noquemanon Ski Marathon.* Cross-country skiers and other winter sports enthusiasts enjoy a 150-ft luge run and the beautiful groomed trails around Marquette as part of this annual race. Events start with a spaghetti dinner the night before and culminate with five different races. | Blueberry Ridge Ski Parkway | 800/544–4321 | www.noquemanon.com.

JULY: *Art on the Rocks.* More than 100 artists in all mediums meet in the city's Presque Isle Park for art demonstrations and sales. This is one of the U.P.'s largest art events. | Presque Isle Park | 800/544–4321.

JULY: *Hiawatha Music Festival.* Performers from across the state converge on Tourist Park for this open-air music festival. | 800/544–4321 | www.portup.com/hiawatha.

JULY: *International Food Festival.* Pierogis, pasties, and all kinds of ethnic foods attract the culinarily curious to the city's Harbor Park. | 800/544–4321 | www.marquette.org.

AUG.–SEPT.: *Seafood Festival.* Fish, fish, and more fish supply the theme for this sea-worthy event in the city's Harbor Park. Food, fishing events, and kid's fun attract families. | Ellwood Mattson Lower Harbor Park | 800/544–4321 | www.marquette.org.

Dining

Heritage Room. Seafood. A large 100-year-old antique brass chandelier hangs in the dining room at this restaurant in the Landmark Inn. The menu varies, but the specialty is fresh seafood. On Friday nights there's a seafood buffet. Breakfast is also available. | 230 N. Front St. | 906/228–2580 or 888/7–LANDMARK | $14–$25 | AE, D, DC, MC, V.

Northland Pub. American. This pub at the Landmark Inn has 1920s furniture from a pub in England, along with stained glass windows and sports memorabilia. Burgers, salads, soups, sandwiches, and barbecued ribs are the favorites. | 230 N. Front St. | 906/228–2580 or 888/7–LANDMARK | $5–$10 | AE, D, DC, MC, V.

Northwoods Supper Club. American. A cutting garden lends homeyness to this onetime cabin in the woods, since expanded into a dining room, banquet room, and lounge. Fred Klumb started the family business in the mid-1930s; today the Klumb family still serves up tasty chicken as well as a wide range of other offerings. Salad bar. Entertainment Fri.–Sun. Kids' menu. | 260 Northwoods Rd. | 906/228–4343 | $20–$38 | AE, D, MC, V.

Sky Room. Contemporary. You see panoramic city views from this sixth-floor restaurant in the Landmark Inn. A local artist painted the large ceiling mural. Try seared salmon in a puff pastry served with dill, or shrimp mousse under a champagne saffron sauce. | 230 N. Front St. | 906/228–2580 or 888/7–LANDMARK | Reservations essential | No lunch. No dinner Sun.–Thurs. | Prix fixe $35 | AE, D, DC, MC, V.

Vierling Restaurant and Harbor Brewery. American. Established in 1883, this restaurant at Main and Front streets overlooks Lake Superior. The bar is a century old, and there are stained glass partitions and original artwork from Martin Vierling's collection. The menu has hot and cold sandwiches (smoked ham, Reuben, cream cheese and turkey), steaks, chicken, and pasta. Local whitefish is the specialty. | 119 S. Front St. | 906/228–3533 | No lunch Sat. Closed Sun. | $4–$19 | AE, D, MC, V.

Lodging

Blueberry Ridge Bed and Breakfast. Trees and gardens surround this B&B. The Rose Room's balcony has views of the garden, and the Fireside Room has a large fireplace. All rooms have antiques and handmade quilts. Complimentary breakfast. No room phones, no TV. No pets. No smoking. | 18 Oakridge Dr. | 906/249–9246 | fax 906/249–9246 | members.aol.com/blueberr18 | 4 rooms | $55–$95 | MC, V.

Cedar Motor Inn. Simple, comfortable lodgings are at this motel that also has a sundeck. Snowmobiling, beaches, and cross-country skiing are all nearby. In-room data ports. Cable TV. Indoor pool. Hot tub, sauna. Business services. | 2523 U.S. 41 W | 906/228–2280 | 44 rooms | $44–$58 | AE, D, DC, MC, V.

Comfort Suites. This year-round all-suite hotel is popular with snowmobilers and outdoor recreation lovers. Complimentary Continental breakfast. Refrigerators. Cable TV. Indoor pool. Hot tub. Gym. | 2463 U.S. 41 W | 906/228–0028 or 800/228–5150 | fax 906/228–0028 | www.comfortsuites.com | 60 suites | $68–$115 suites | AE, D, DC, MC, V.

Days Inn. This no-frills lodging is popular with outdoor recreation enthusiasts. Complimentary Continental breakfast. Some refrigerators. Cable TV. Indoor pool. Hot tub, sauna. | 2403 U.S. 41 W | 906/225–1393, ext. 177 or 800/388–7829 | fax 906/225–1393 | www.daysinn.com | 65 rooms | $50–$65 | AE, D, DC, MC, V.

Holiday Inn. Family-centered accommodations are available at this chain hotel. The rustic style includes a huge stone fireplace in the lobby. Restaurant, bar, picnic area, room service. Cable TV. Indoor pool. Hot tub, sauna. Cross-country and downhill skiing. Business services, airport shuttle. Some pets allowed. | 1951 U.S. 41 W | 906/225–1351 or 800/465–4329 | fax 906/228–4329 | www.basshotels.com/holiday-inn | 203 rooms | $75–$79 | AE, D, DC, MC, V.

Imperial Motel. Snowmobilers flock to this small but neat facility near snowmobile runs and cross-country and downhill skiing areas. Cable TV. Indoor pool. Sauna. Game room. Business services. | 2493 U.S. 41 W | 906/228–7430 or 800/424–9514 | fax 906/228–3883 | 43 rooms | $36–$50 | AE, D, DC, MC, V.

Landmark Inn. Built in 1929, the upscale six-story inn was restored and reopened in 1997. Rooms have antiques and rich colors. One room has gold, floral-patterned bed covers and draperies and rich purple-striped wallpaper. Some rooms have lake or downtown views. 3 restaurants, 2 bars, room service. In-room data ports, some in-room hot tubs. Cable TV. 2 spas, sauna. Gym. Shops, library. Laundry service. Airport shuttle. No pets. | 230 N. Front St. | 906/228–2580 or 888/7–LANDMARK | fax 906/228–5676 | 61 rooms | $99–$199 | AE, D, DC, MC, V.

Our Paradise Bed and Breakfast. Twelve miles east of town, this home is on 600 ft of private sandy beach. The Lake Room has a private bath and a porch facing the lake. There's a 2½ mi cross-country skiing trail across the highway. Complimentary breakfast. No room phones, TV in common area. Hiking. Beach, water sports. Cross-country skiing. No pets. No smoking. | 2441 M–28 | 906/343–6541 | ourparadise343@aol.com | 2 rooms (1 with private bath), 1 carriage house | $90–$110 | MC, V.

Ramada Inn. Downtown recreation and shopping are near this comfortable chain hotel. Restaurant, bar, room service. Cable TV. Indoor pool. Hot tub, sauna. Laundry facilities. Business services, airport shuttle. Some pets allowed. | 412 W. Washington St./U.S. 41 Bus. | 906/228–6000 or 800/298–2054 | fax 906/228–2963 | www.ramada.com | 113 rooms | $77–$87 | AE, D, DC, MC, V.

Tiroler Hof Inn. Billed "as a touch of Austria in Michigan's Upper Peninsula," this motor lodge is in a wooded area overlooking Lake Superior. Restaurant, picnic area. No air-conditioning in some rooms. Cable TV. Pond. Sauna. Cross-country and downhill skiing. Playground. Laundry facilities. | 150 Carp River Hills/U.S. 41 S | 906/226–7516 or 800/892–9376 | 44 rooms | $48–$54 | AE, D, MC, V.

Value Host. These no-frills lodgings are near downtown. Picnic area, complimentary Continental breakfast. Some refrigerators. Cable TV. Hot tub, sauna. Business services. | 1101 U.S. 41 W | 906/225–5000 | fax 906/225–5096 | 52 rooms | $35–$55 | D, MC, V.

MARSHALL

MAP 9, D7

(Nearby towns also listed: Battle Creek, Coldwater, Jackson, Kalamazoo, Lansing)

A finalist in the bid for state capital, Marshall went on to build beautiful homes during its 19th-century heyday. Many remain today, with more than 30 historical markers throughout the city, including one in Triangle Park, site of an important anti-slavery event. A September home tour is one of the state's most popular.

Information: **Marshall Chamber of Commerce** | 109 E. Michigan Ave., Marshall 49068 | 616/781–5163 or 800/877–5163 | www.marshallmi.org. .

Attractions

American Museum of Magic. Housed in a small downtown storefront, this small, independent museum was the work of a collector who wanted to share his fascination with the world of magic. Inside are vintage posters, magician's equipment, and other intriguing paraphernalia. | 107 E. Michigan Ave. | 616/781–7674 | www.marshallmich.com/history/museumofmagic.shtml | $3 | By appointment.

Honolulu House Museum. This lavish Hawaiian-inspired residence with pagodas and island motifs was built in the 19th century for Abner Pratt, a Supreme Court justice who later became U.S. Consul to Hawaii. Outside are pagoda-topped towers, a raised verandah, and other Hawaiian touches; inside are 15-ft murals hand-painted in elaborate Victorian style. | 107 N. Kalamazoo Ave. | 800/877–5163 | www.marshallmich.com/history/HonoluluHouse.shtml | $3 | May–Oct., daily 12–5; Nov.–Apr., weekends 12–5.

Marshall Historic District. Hundreds of 19th- and early 20th-century homes and other structures distinguish this town. Stop in the Chamber of Commerce for maps to the buildings and cemeteries. | 616/781–5163.

ON THE CALENDAR

JULY: *Welcome to My Garden Tour.* This popular city-wide garden tour takes you behind the scenes and into the backyards of the residences of Marshall's historic district, home to some of the state's best preserved Victorian-era architecture. | 616/781–8547.
AUG.: *Calhoun County Fair.* The state's oldest county fair is held the second full week in August at the County Fairgrounds. Enjoy parades, livestock competitions, carnival rides, arts and crafts booths, and food vendors. | 616/781–8161.
SEPT.: *Historic Home Tour.* One of the state's busiest and most popular home tours, this annual event sponsored by the local historical society takes the curious inside the city's renowned 19th-century residences. Home styles vary from Eastlake to Shingle to Queen Anne. | 616/781–5163 | www.marshallmich.com/hometourbro.html.

Dining

Copper Bar, Inc. American. Along with the burgers, televisions are plentiful at this local bar with a yellow facade. Inside, exposed beams crisscross the vaulted ceiling. | 133 W. Michigan Ave. | 616/781–5400 | $3–$5 | No credit cards.

Cornwell's Turkeyville. American. This quirky country restaurant and dinner theater talks turkey daily and serves up everything from turkey tacos to turkey hash and classic turkey sandwiches. Open-air dining. Kids' menu. | 18935 15½ Mile Rd. | 616/781–4293 | Closed late Dec.–mid-Jan. | $11–$20 | MC, V.

Schuler's of Marshall. American. Wise and witty words adorn the dining room rafters in this longtime mid-Michigan favorite, once a bowling alley and livery stable. Four generations of the Schuler family serve up the restaurant's trademark prime rib as well as lighter fare and some vegetarian dishes. There's a bakery on the premises and the menu changes seasonally. Open-air dining on patio. Kids' menu. Sun. brunch. | 115 S. Eagle St. | 616/781–0600 | $25–$36 | AE, D, DC, MC, V.

Lodging

Amerihost Inn. This motor inn is on a busy commercial strip near downtown. Complimentary Continental breakfast. Some refrigerators. Cable TV. Indoor pool. Hot tub, sauna. | 204 Winston St. | 616/789–7890 | fax 616/789–7891 | 61 rooms, 5 whirlpool suites | $70–$85, $99–$125 suites | AE, D, DC, MC, V.

Arbor Inn. Pleasant accommodations are available at this motor inn on a busy strip outside of downtown. Complimentary Continental breakfast. Some refrigerators. Cable TV. Indoor pool. | 15435 W. Michigan Ave. | 616/781–7772 | fax 616/781–2660 | 48 rooms | $40–$55 | AE, D, DC, MC, V.

McCarthy's Bear Creek. Guest rooms at this upscale country-style bed and breakfast are in the main house and a former barn (1948). The look is decidedly country, with some antiques. Picnic area, complimentary Continental breakfast. No room phones. Cross-country skiing. | 15230 C Dr. N. | 616/781–8255 | 14 rooms | $70–$110 | AE, MC, V.

National House Inn. Antiques furnish this popular bed and breakfast housed in the state's oldest operating inn. The original was a stagecoach stop between Detroit and Chicago. Complimentary Continental breakfast. Cable TV. Cross-country skiing. Business services, airport shuttle. | 102 S. Parkview | 616/781–7374 | fax 616/781–4510 | 16 rooms | $56–$130 | AE, MC, V.

Rose Hill Inn Bed and Breakfast. Once the home of William Boyce, founder of the Boy Scouts of America, this 1860 mansion with a city view is nestled among 100-year-old pines on three acres once owned by James Fenimore Cooper. Inside there are 12-ft ceilings, fireplaces, Tiffany glass, and antiques; down comforters keep you cozy after dark. Three rooms have fireplaces. Complimentary breakfast. Cable TV. Pool. Tennis court. No pets. No kids under 12. No smoking. | 1110 Verona Rd. | 616/789–1992 | fax 616/781–4723 | rosehill@internet1.net | www.rose-hill-inn.com | 6 rooms | $99–$145 | MC, V.

Joy House Bed and Breakfast. A large square tower dominates the front of this 1844 home in the historic district, two blocks from downtown. Rooms are antique-filled and two porches overlook the surrounding gardens. Complimentary breakfast. No room phones, no TV in some rooms, TV in common area. No pets. No smoking. | 224 N. Kalamazoo Ave. | 616/789–1323 | fax 616/789–1308 | www.kephart.com/joyhouse | 3 rooms | $80–$100 | AE, MC, V.

MENOMINEE

MAP 9, B4

(Nearby towns also listed: Escanaba, Iron Mountain)

The name of the Upper Peninsula's southernmost city means "wild rice," and was given by Native Americans who once farmed here. Today, the former fur-trading post ranks as the state's largest dairy producer. (*Note:* Area codes in this vicinity are scheduled to change to 989 beginning April 7, 2001.)

Information: Menominee Area Chamber of Commerce | 1005 10th Ave., Menominee 49858 | 906/863–2679.

Attractions

First Street Historic District. Specialty shops line this historic neighborhood full of vintage 19th-century residences. Parks, restaurants, galleries, and a marina also are here. | 906/774–5480 | www.uptravel.com | Free | Daily.

Henes Park. A tiny zoo, nature trails, a beach, and picnic areas fill this small but popular park. Two mi northwest of Menominee. | 906/863–2656 | Free | Daily dawn to dusk.

J. W. Wells State Park. An abundance of waterfront campsites and rustic cabins on Green Bay attract outdoor enthusiasts to this 700-acre state park, with 3 mi of shoreline. You can go hiking or biking through an old-growth forest with a 7-mi network of trails. | M–35 | 906/863–9747 or 800/447–2757 | www.dnr.state.mi.us/camping | $4 per car, per day | Daily dawn to dusk.

Menominee Marina. Boaters find this site among the best small-craft marinas on the Great Lakes. It has a beach and is close to restaurants. | Doyle Dr. | 906/863–8498 or 906/863–5101 | fax 906/863–5218 | www.menomineemarina.com | May–Oct., daily.

North Pier Light. You can walk out to this Lake Michigan lighthouse at the mouth of the Menominee River. The present 1927 steel and concrete tower replaced an 1877 structure.

Stephenson Island. This island park in the Menominee River is at the entry to the U.P. from Menominee's sister city of Marinette, Wisconsin. Picnic and playground areas and a historical museum with a variety of local artifacts and displays are highlights. | 906/774–5480 | Free | Daily.

ON THE CALENDAR
JUNE: *Art for All*. Held on the Sunday of the last full weekend in June, this festival at Great Lakes Memorial Marina Park has a juried art sale, food, and live jazz. | 906/863–2679.
AUG.: *Waterfront Festival*. Menominee's scenic marina is the site of this annual event celebrating the life and lore of the lakes. Includes arts and crafts, boat tours, food booths, and kids' activities. | 906/863–2679.

Dining
Landing Restaurant. American. On the water at Green Bay, the restaurant showcases nautical maps, oars, models of ships, and an anchor. Try the Jack Daniel's steak or fresh whitefish. | 450 1st St. | 906/863–8034 | No lunch Sat., closed on Sun. Open seasonally | $10–$17 | AE, D, DC, MC, V.

Lodging
Gehrke's Gasthaus. Some of the antique-filled rooms in this 1880 home have water views; the hot tub has a view of Green Bay. A fireplace, grand piano, and pump organ are in the living room. Complimentary breakfast. Some kitchenettes, no room phones, no TV in some rooms. Beach. No pets. No smoking. | 320 1st St. | 906/863–2295 or 906/863–9005 | fax 906/863–6837 | nagehrke@yahoo.com | 5 rooms | $68–$88 | Closed Oct.–May 1 | MC, V.

MIDLAND

MAP 9, E6

(Nearby towns also listed: Alma, Bay City, Clare, Flint, Frankenmuth, Mt. Pleasant, Saginaw)

Once dependent on the lumber industry, this mid-Michigan town was given a second chance when H. H. Dow founded Dow Chemical here in 1897, largely because of the large salt brine deposits under the city's soil. The company is still based here and still employs the majority of the town's 38,000 residents. The city is also home to the well-known Dow Gardens, developed by Herbert H. Dow to reforest the city's neighborhoods and surrounding area. (*Note:* Area codes in this vicinity are scheduled to change to 989 beginning April 7, 2001.)

Information: Midland County Convention and Visitors Bureau | 300 Rodd St., Midland 48640 | 517/839–9901 or 888/4–MIDLAND | www.midlandcvb.org.

Attractions
Architectural Tour. Self-guided walking and driving tours take in the city's wide range of architectural styles, including the Frank Lloyd Wright-inspired designs of Herbert Dow's son Alden, who studied with the master at Taliesin in Wisconsin. Dow designed more than 40 buildings in Midland, including his own house and studio (the suggested starting point

for tours), the Whitman House, Stein House, and area churches. Most structures are closed to the public. | 315 Post St. | 800/464–3526.

Chippewa Nature Center. Woods, fields, ponds, rivers, and wetlands fill this preserve. There are 12 mi of hiking and cross-country ski trails, a museum with a restored 19th-century farm and log schoolhouse, and an arboretum of Michigan trees and shrubs. | 400 S. Badour Rd. | 517/631–0830 | Free | Weekdays 8–5, Sat. 9–5, Sun. 1–5.

Dow Gardens. Besides being a prolific inventor, Dow was an avid gardener, who believed that the bare woods surrounding Midland could be returned to their 19th-century lushness. He also believed in beautifying downtown streets and individual gardens. Today, his contributions include more than 600 species of flowers and shrubs on 100 landscaped acres. | Eastman Ave. at W. St. Andrews | 517/631–2677 | www.dowgardens.org | $3 | Daily.

Herbert H. Dow Historical Museum. Midland owes its modern existence to the founder of Dow Chemical. The historical museum tracing the life and times of founder Herbert H. Dow is housed in a former gristmill near the site where Dow once conducted experiments. Inside, you can see Dow's first office, his father's workshop, and a videotape explaining Dow's important contributions to the world of chemistry. | 3200 Cook Rd. | 517/832–5319 | $2 | Wed.–Sat. 10–4, Sun. 1–5.

Midland Center for the Arts. Alden Dow, Herbert's son and a protégé of Frank Lloyd Wright, designed the building that houses this center, home to a science, technology, art, and history museum and a stage for concerts, plays, and musicals. The Midland Historical Society displays changing exhibits and its permanent collection here. Guided tours are available. | 1801 W. St. Andrews | 517/631–5930 | $4 | Daily 10–6.

Rail Trail. A 22-mi stretch of railroad track is now a hiking and biking trail between Ashman Street and Coleman.

ON THE CALENDAR

MAR.: *Maple Syrup Festival.* Syrup demonstrations, maple candy making and tasting, kids' events, and more celebrate the coming of spring to the forests near Midland. Activities take place at the nature center and sugar house. | 517/631–0830.
MAY–JUNE: *Matrix: Midland Festival.* A two-month-long festival celebrates mid-Michigan's ever-growing art scene with music, theater, and dance performances. Venues are all over town. | 517/631–8250.
JUNE, JULY, SEPT.: *Michigan Antique and Collectibles Festival.* On the first weekend in June and the last weekends in July and September, more than 800 antique vendors market their wares here. See folk and craft arts, books, auto parts, and a car show at the Midland County Fairgrounds. | 6905 Eastman Ave. | 517/687–9001.
OCT.: *Fall Festival.* Annual family fun the second weekend of October emphasizes the fall harvest, with pumpkin carving, nature walks, and kids' activities. | 517/631–0830.

Dining

Cafe Edward. Continental. A soothing pastel interior and a creative menu featuring elegant and ever-changing entrées make this one of Midland's most romantic and popular eateries. Don't miss the delectable desserts prepared on the premises. | 5010 Bay City Rd. | 517/496–3351 | Closed Sun. No lunch | $21–$48 | AE, MC, V.

Crossways Restaurant. American. The menu here lists prime steaks, corn chowder, perch, and chicken. There's a lounge with lighter fare and a fireplace and terrace. | 111 W. Main St. | 517/839–0500 | $13–$28 | MC, V.

Nicole's. Continental. A stone fountain, skylights, and courtyard views set the mood in the dining room here. On the menu are grilled flank steak, rainbow trout in a bacon and shrimp sauce, and T-bone steaks in garlic butter. Breakfast is also available. | 5221 Bay City Rd. | 517/496–3130 | No lunch | $12–$19 | AE, D, DC, MC, V.

Lodging

Ashman Court Hotel. This bustling downtown hotel near the riverfront and the Tridge Bridge is a favorite of both business travelers and families. Restaurant, room service. In-room data ports, some in-room hot tubs (in suites). Cable TV. Indoor pool. Health club. Sauna. Airport shuttle. | 111 W. Main St. | 517/839–0500 | fax 517/837–6000 | www.marriothotels.com | 103 rooms, 7 suites | $79–$104, $105–$125 suites | AE, D, DC, MC, V.

Best Western Valley Plaza. This popular chain hotel is a favorite of business travelers mid-week and families on weekends. Restaurant, room service. In-room data ports. Cable TV. Indoor pool, lake, wading pool. Beach. Game room. Airport shuttle. Some pets allowed. | 5221 Bay City Rd. | 517/496–2700 | fax 517/496–9233 | www.bestwestern.com | 162 rooms | $62–$82 | AE, D, DC, MC, V.

Bramble House Bed and Breakfast. In a quiet, residential neighborhood, this 1977 brick house with black shutters is within walking distance of many city attractions. Some rooms have four-poster beds, and there are three fireplaces in common areas. Complimentary breakfast. In-room data ports. Cable TV. Library. No pets. No smoking. | 4309 Brambleridge Ln. | 517/832–5082 | www.bbhost.com/bramblehousebb | 3 rooms (2 with private bath) | $95–$125 | D, DC, MC, V.

Hampton Inn. The comfortable accommodations here are across from Midland Mall. Complimentary Continental breakfast. Cable TV. Indoor pool. Hot tub. Gym. Business services. | 6701 Eastman Ave. | 517/837–4000 | fax 517/837–7241 | www.hampton-inn.com | 87 rooms | $59–$99 | AE, D, DC, MC, V.

Holiday Inn. Downtown Midland and the Soaring Eagle Casino aren't far from this chain hotel. Restaurant, bar (with entertainment), room service. In-room data ports, minibars. Cable TV. Indoor pool. Hot tub. Exercise equipment. Game room. Business services, airport shuttle. Some pets allowed. | 1500 W. Wackerly St. | 517/631–4220 or 800/465–4329 | fax 517/631–3776 | www.basshotels.com/holiday-inn | 236 rooms | $79–$140 | AE, D, DC, MC, V.

Ramada Inn Midland. In Midland's business district, this two-story chain hotel is north of U.S. 10 and 5 mi from Valley Plaza Convention Center. Restaurant, bar, complimentary Continental breakfast. In-room data ports, in-room safes, some in-room hot tubs. Cable TV. Pool. Gym. Laundry service. Business services. Pets allowed. | 1815 S. Saginaw Rd. | 517/631–0570 or 800/298–2054 | fax 517/631–0920 | www.ramada.com | 80 rooms | $55–$72 | AE, D, DC, MC, V.

MONROE

MAP 9, E8

(Nearby towns also listed: Dearborn, Detroit, Ypsilanti)

The seat of Monroe County in Michigan's southeast corner, Monroe was once called Frenchtown because of its 18th-century Gallic heritage. One of the oldest communities in the state, it was founded in 1780 by the French on the site of a Native American village. The River Raisin, which runs through town, was named for the grapes that once grew abundantly along its banks. The river was the site of a bloody 1813 massacre, part of the War of 1812. The city is also known as the birthplace of Gen. George Armstrong Custer, who lived here for many years before his army service.

Information: Monroe County Chamber of Commerce | 106 W. Front St., Monroe 48161 | 734/457–1030 | www.monroeinfo.com.

Attractions

La-Z-Boy Museum. You need an appointment to visit this 1927 La-Z-Boy factory. Here you can see old photos, examples of early chairs, and the tools used to make chairs in the early 20th century. | 1284 Telegraph Rd. | 734/242–1444 | Free.

Monroe County Historical Museum. The city's former post office now houses historical displays, including one on the family of native son and colorful figure Gen. George Armstrong Custer. Exhibits also include Victorian furnishings and Native American and French pioneer artifacts. | 126 S. Monroe St. | 734/240–7780 | Free.

River Raisin Battlefield Visitor Center. The Battle of the River Raisin in January 1813 was a turning point and one of the largest battles of the War of 1812. A thousand U.S. soldiers were pitted against British, Native American, and Canadian forces. Only 33 Americans remained free afterwards; the rest were either killed or taken as prisoners of war. A 10-min. presentation explains the war's background and importance. Displays include dioramas, maps, and costumed mannequins. | 1402 Elm Ave. | 734/243–7136 | Free | Memorial Day–Labor Day, daily 10–5; Labor Day–Memorial Day, weekends 10–5.

Sterling State Park. The only Michigan state park on Lake Erie, Sterling has swimming, boating, and fishing areas. You can sight a variety of wildlife in the park's marshes and lagoons. | Off N. Dixie Hwy. | 734/289–2715 or 800/447–2757 | www.dnr.state.mi.us/camping | $4 per car, per day | Daily dawn to dusk.

ON THE CALENDAR

JULY–AUG.: *Monroe County Fair.* This southeastern Michigan county fair includes midway rides, food displays and booths, and 4-H agricultural and livestock exhibitions. Held at the Monroe County Fairgrounds. | 734/241–5775.

AUG.: *Old French Town Days.* The city celebrates its Gallic heritage and historic events at this annual festival. Reenactments, food booths, and children's crafts are some of the activities. | 734/243–7137.

OCT.: *Old Mill Harvest Festival.* At the Old Mill Museum in Dundee, an 1850s gristmill, you can browse craft shows, taste cider and doughnuts, and see pumpkin carving demonstrations. | 242 Toledo St., Dundee | 734/529–2650.

Dining

Colonial House. Continental. Elegant chandeliers and white tablecloths dominate the dining room of this restaurant opened in 1970. House specials include Italian, French, and American dishes. | 14900 S. Dixie Hwy. | 734/241–9292 | Closed Sun. | $17–$25 | AE, D, DC, MC, V.

Joe's French-Italian Inn. Continental. This family-oriented eatery, established in 1930, has handmade windowpanes, old photographs, and memorabilia. It serves fresh local perch, steaks, pasta, lasagna, frog legs, and escargot. Two miles east of I–75. | 2896 N. Dixie Hwy. | 734/289–2800 | No lunch Sat.–Mon. | $10–$15 | AE, MC, V.

Lodging

Amerihost Inn. Rooms and suites are available at this chain hotel on a busy commercial strip near downtown. Complimentary Continental breakfast. Some refrigerators, in-room hot tubs (in suites). Cable TV. Indoor pool. Hot tub, sauna. | 14774 LaPlaisance Rd. | 734/384–1600 | fax 734/384–1180 | www.amerihostinn.com | 63 rooms, 7 suites | $70–$85, $89–$149 suites | AE, D, DC, MC, V.

Comfort Inn. This three-floor chain hotel, west off I–75 N, Exit 11, is next door to Horizon Outlet Mall. Complimentary Continental breakfast. In-room data ports, microwaves, refrigerators, some in-room hot tubs. Cable TV. Pool. Hot tub. Laundry service. Business services. Pets allowed. | 6500 E. Albain Rd. | 734/384–1500 | fax 734/384–1515 | www.choicehotels.com | 65 rooms | $74–$134 | AE, D, DC, MC, V.

Days Inn. Basic accommodations are available at this chain motor inn off I–75 near downtown and the Horizon Outlet Mall. Restaurant, bar, room service. In-room data ports. Cable TV. Indoor pool. Hot tub, sauna. Business services. Some pets allowed. | 1440 N. Dixie Hwy. (Rte. 50) | 734/289–4000 | fax 734/289–4262. www.choicehotels.com | 115 rooms | $53–$65 | AE, D, DC, MC, V.

Holiday Inn. Native son Gen. George Custer is honored in the rustic look and vintage Western photos of this hostelry. Restaurant, bar (with entertainment), room service. In-room data ports. Cable TV. Indoor pool. Hot tub, sauna. Game room. Some pets allowed. | 1225 N. Dixie Hwy. | 734/242–6000 | fax 734/242–0555 | www.basshotels.com/holiday-inn | 127 rooms | $69–$89 | AE, D, DC, MC, V.

Lotus Bed and Breakfast. Five miles west of Lake Erie, this 1870 Italiante, with its bed of lotus flowers, is in a historic neighborhood and within walking distance of downtown. Choose from rooms with a wood-burning fireplace, hot tub, or the suites with kitchenettes. Complimentary Continental breakfast. Some microwaves, refrigerators. Cable TV. No pets. No kids under 10. No smoking. | 324 Washington St. | 734/384–9914 | 5 rooms | $95 | MC, V.

MONTAGUE (SEE WHITEHALL AND MONTAGUE)

MT. CLEMENS

MAP 10, F2

(Nearby towns also listed: Detroit, St. Clair, Warren)

This northeastern Detroit suburb on the banks of the Clinton River is the site of Metro Beach, a popular Detroit-area MetroPark with swimming, a nature center, and an 18-hole golf course. The town once was famous for its mineral baths.

Information: Central Macomb County Chamber of Commerce | 58 S. Gratiot Ave., Mt. Clemens 48043 | 810/463–1528 | www.central-macomb.com.

Attractions

Crocker House. This residence was once home to the city's first two mayors and is now the headquarters of the Macomb Historical Society. Period rooms and furnishings and changing exhibits attract visitors. | 15 Union St. | 810/465–2488 | $2 | Mar.–Dec., Tues.–Thurs. 1–5.

Michigan Transit Museum. Built in 1859, this station was where Thomas Edison held a job and became familiar with telegraphing. You also can see the rail travel exhibits. | 200 Grand St. | 810/463–1863 | Free | Sat.–Sun. 1–4.

Metro Beach Metropark. One of nine Huron-Clinton Metroparks, Metro Beach, some 22 mi northeast of Detroit, fronts the St. Clair River and has boating, swimming, volleyball and shuffleboard courts, nature trails, and more. The busy ¾-mi beach, golf course, and nature center are the top summertime attractions. In winter ice fishing, ice skating, and cross-country skiing are equally popular. The park covers more than 770 acres. *(See also Detroit.)* | 31300 Metro Pkwy., Mt. Clemens | 810/463–4581 or 800/477–3172 | www.metroparks.com | $3 | Daily dawn to dusk.

ON THE CALENDAR

AUG.: *Bath City Festival.* The town celebrates the area's former renown for its mineral baths at this downtown event. There are historical displays, live music, and carnival rides, and arts and crafts, antiques, and collectibles vendors selling their wares. | 810/469–4168.

Dining

Paul's Riverhouse. American. Sit under a vaulted ceiling of knotty pine and watch the Clinton River at this eatery. A house special is the honey pecan pickerel. | 24240 North River Rd. | 810/465–5111 | No lunch Sun. | $10–$18 | AE, D, DC, MC, V.

Lodging

Comfort Inn. Lakeside, one of metro Detroit's largest shopping malls, is 1 mi from this chain hotel. Complimentary Continental breakfast. In-room data ports. Cable TV. Laundry facilities. Business services, airport shuttle. | 11401 Hall Rd., Utica | 810/739–7111 | fax 810/739–1041 | www.comfortinn.com | 104 rooms | $69–$79 | AE, D, DC, MC, V.

Roseville Microtel Inn and Suites. Opened in 1999, this three-floor hotel is 5 mi south of Mt. Clemens and is west of I–94, Exit 232, a couple of blocks south of Macomb Mall. Complimentary Continental breakfast. Microwaves, refrigerators. Cable TV. Pool. Gym. Laundry service. Business services. No pets. | 20313 E. 13 Mile Rd., Roseville | 810/415–1000 | fax 810/859–1414 | 98 rooms | $64–$79 | AE, D, DC, MC, V.

MT. PLEASANT

MAP 9, D6

(Nearby towns also listed: Alma, Big Rapids, Clare, Midland)

Originally known as Ojibway Besse, central Mt. Pleasant was once a fertile hunting ground of the state's Chippewa Indians. Later, it became known for its pine and hardwood forests and as a major lumber center. Today's city is best known as the home of Central Michigan University and seat of Isabella County. The Saginaw Chippewa Indian tribe has a reservation and a popular casino here; the casino is a top tourist attraction. (*Note:* Area codes in this vicinity are scheduled to change to 989 beginning April 7, 2001.)

Information: **Mt. Pleasant Area Convention and Visitors Bureau** | 111 E. Broadway St., Mt. Pleasant 48858 | 517/772–4433 or 800/772–4433 | www.mt-pleasant.net.

Attractions

Central Michigan University. The university's sprawling campus dominates the town. The school enrolls more than 16,000 students. | 517/774–4000 | www.cmich.edu | Free | Daily.

On CMU's campus, the **Center for Cultural and Natural History** has more than 40 exhibit areas exploring local geology and history, including displays on lumbering, the Civil War, and Native American art. Highlights are the Michigan wildlife displays and the skeletal remains of an American mastodon. | 517/774–3829 | www.cmich.edu | Free | Sept.–Apr., weekdays 8–noon and 1–5, Sat. 1–4.

Rare documents relating to the Northwest Territory attract scholars to the **Clarke Historical Library.** It also has a children's library, changing exhibits during the school year, and other historic artifacts and manuscripts. | 517/774–3352 | www.cmich.edu | Free | Mon.–Thurs. 8 AM–midnight, Fri. 8 AM–10 PM, Sat. 9 AM–10 PM, Sun. noon–midnight.

Loafers Glory-Antique Village. In late 1800s, this building was a hardware store. It's now home to Victorian antiques, craft goods, and a sandwich/soup shop. Next door is Auntie's House, a 19th-century home with antiques for sale. The shop is 15 mi southwest of Mt. Pleasant. | 431 Main St., Blanchard | 517/561–2020 | Free | Daily 9–5.

Soaring Eagle Casino and Resort. Mid-Michigan's answer to Las Vegas is the largest casino in the Midwest. Open 24 hours a day and operated by local Native Americans, it includes a hotel, a restaurant, and every kind of gaming imaginable. | 6800 Soaring Eagle Blvd. | 888/732–4537. www.soaringeaglecasino.com | Free | Daily.

ON THE CALENDAR

APR.: *Maple Syrup Festival.* Maple syrup and sugar making and tasting dominate this event held in nearby Shepherd the last weekend in April. Carnival rides, pancake breakfasts, and train rides round out the activities. | 517/828–6486.

JUNE: *J Bar J Rodeo.* Each summer this professional traveling rodeo visits the Isabella County Fair grounds. The dates vary from year to year, so check ahead of time. | 517/386–2442.

AUG.: *Little Elk's Retreat Powwow.* The Saginaw Chippewa campground is a show-place of native culture the first weekend of August. You can watch a dance competition, see Native American crafts, and sample the foods. | 517/775–4695 | www.sagchip.com.

OCT.: *Apple Fest.* The fall harvest is the focus of this popular event, usually held the first weekend of the month at Macintosh Orchard on W. M–20. You can take part in apple picking, apple crafts, apple baked goods, cider making, and other family fun. | 517/773–3028.

Dining

Embers. American. Candlelight and white linen, makes it romantic, but it's still somewhat casual. Huge 16-oz pork chops, king crab, prime rib, and a tangy Caesar salad lead the list of favorites at this casual eatery 1 mi north of Central Michigan University and the casino. The menu also includes seafood and pasta dishes. Kids' menu. Sun. brunch. | 1217 S. Mission St. | 517/773–5007 | No lunch Mon.–Sat. | $24–$39 | AE, D, DC, MC, V.

Maxfield's. American. A doll collection and original art adorn the walls of this 1959 restaurant 15 mi southwest of Mt. Pleasant. Prime rib is served Tuesday through Saturday. Wednesday there's a surf and turf buffet. | 11228 N. Wyman Rd., Blanchard | 517/427–5889 or 800/550–5630 | Closed Mon. | $14–$23 | AE, D, MC, V.

Sinikaung Steak and Chop House. Steak. Part of the Soaring Eagle Casino and Resort, the restaurant name means "Place of Stone." The two-level dining room has many booths, gleaming wood tables, and a wrought-iron balustrade. The menu has filet mignon, salmon, and lamb chops. | 6800 Soaring Eagle Blvd. | 517/775–5106 | Reservations not accepted | $15–$22 | AE, D, MC, V.

Water Lilly. Contemporary. A large stone fireplace is the centerpiece of this restaurant at the Soaring Eagle Casino and Resort. Try filet mignon topped with foie gras on a bed of potato and zucchini cake with baby vegetables, or sturgeon with a short rib of beef in a butter sauce. Breakfast is also available. | 6800 Soaring Eagle Blvd. | 517/775–5496 | Reservations essential | Coat and tie required | $18–$36 | AE, D, MC, V.

Lodging

Baymont Inn. In-room coffeemakers are one of the nice things about this economy hotel close to the Soaring Eagle Casino and just off the freeway. Complimentary Continental breakfast. Some refrigerators, cable TV. Business services. | 5858 E. Pickhard Ave. | 517/775–5555 or 800/789–4103 | fax 517/775–5566 | www.baymontinns.com | 103 rooms | $46–$96 | AE, D, DC, MC, V.

Comfort Inn University Park. This comfortable facility next to Central Michigan University is also across the street to the Soaring Eagle Casino. It's within walking distance of restuarants. Complimentary Continental breakfast. In-room data ports. Cable TV, in-room VCRs (and movies). Indoor pool. Game room. Laundry facilities. Business services. Some pets allowed. | 2424 S. Mission St. | 517/772–4000 | fax 517/773–6052 | www.comfortinn.com | 138 rooms, 12 suites | $59–$150, $99–$195 suites | AE, D, DC, MC, V.

Fairfield Inn. Central Michigan University is across the street and the Soaring Eagle Casino is 4 mi from this hotel on parklike, well-landscaped grounds. Complimentary Continental breakfast. In-room data ports. Cable TV. Indoor pool. Game room. Laundry facilities. Business services. Some pets allowed. | 2525 University Park | 517/775–5000 | fax 517/773–1371 | www.labellemanagement.com | 74 rooms | $55–$90 | AE, D, DC, MC, V.

Green Suites. Built in 1995, this hotel is at Holiday Greens Golf Course of the Holiday Inn resort. There are some three-bedroom units available. In-room data ports. Cable TV. No pets. | 1900 Summerton Rd. | 517/772–1703 or 800/292–8891 | fax 517/772–1721 | 42 rooms | $59–$425 | AE, D, DC, MC, V.

Holiday Inn. A wide range of facilities are available at this modern chain hotel that's 4 mi to Central Michigan University and a mile to the Soaring Eagle Casino. Restaurants, bar (with entertainment), room service. In-room data ports, some minibars, refrigerators, in-room hot tubs. Cable TV. 2 pools (1 indoor). Hot tub. Driving range, 36-hole golf course, putting green, tennis. Exercise equipment. Playground. Laundry facilities. Business services, airport shuttle. Some pets allowed. | 5665 E. Pickard Rd. | 517/772–2905 | fax 517/772–4952. www.highresort.com | 184 rooms | $65–$150 | AE, D, DC, MC, V.

Mt. Pleasant Best Western. East of U.S. 27, this one-floor hotel is 1 mi west of Soaring Eagle Casino and Resort, 2 mi south of the airport. Complimentary Continental breakfast. In-room data ports. Cable TV. Pool. Hot tub, sauna. No pets. | 5770 E. Pickard St./M–20 | 517/772–1101 or 800/780–7234 | fax 517/772–8986 | www.bestwestern.com | 51 rooms | $59–$79 | AE, D, DC, MC, V.

Roycroft Inn Bed and Breakfast. On a 20-acre property, this 1877 farmhouse is 1½ mi from downtown. Rooms have 19th-century oak and ash furnishings. The home is 4,000 square ft, with three living rooms. Skiing trails lead to the Chippewa River. Complimentary breakfast. No room phones, TV in common area. Hiking. Cross-country skiing. No pets. No smoking. | 2265 W. Broomfield Rd. | 517/772–3298 or 800/864–3253 | jrf2amf@aol.com | 6 rooms | $69–$125 | D, MC, V.

Soaring Eagle Casino and Resort. Glitzy (for mid-Michigan), this 200,000-square-ft casino and resort hotel is one of the state's first and most popular Native American-run gaming areas. Restaurant, bar (with entertainment). Some refrigerators. Cable TV. Indoor pool. Business services. | 6800 Soaring Eagle Dr. | 517/775–7777 | fax 517/775–5383 | www.soaringeaglecasino.com | 512 rooms | $129–$299 | AE, D, DC, MC, V.

Super 8. Basic, no-frills accommodations are available at this motel just off U.S. 27. Complimentary Continental breakfast. Some refrigerators. Cable TV. Business services. Some pets allowed. | 2323 S. Mission | 517/773–8888 or 800/800–8000 | fax 517/772–5371 | www.super8motels.com | 143 rooms | $49–$90 | AE, D, DC, MC, V.

MUNISING

MAP 9, B2

(Nearby towns also listed: Gladstone, Grand Marais, Manistique, Marquette, Newberry)

Waterfalls, Pictured Rocks National Lakeshore, and Hiawatha National Forest (*see Escanaba*) bring scores of visitors to this Upper Peninsula town. Multicolored sandstone cliffs along Lake Superior rise as high as 200 ft. (*Note:* Area codes in this vicinity are scheduled to change to 989 beginning April 7, 2001.)

Information: **Alger County Chamber of Commerce** | 422 E. Munising Ave., Munising 49862 | 906/387–2138 | www.algercounty.com/chamber.

Attractions

Alger County Heritage Center. Displays and exhibits trace the area's history. Also, there's a gift shop. | Washington St. | 906/387–4308 | Free | Tue.–Sat. 10–4.

Pictured Rocks Boat Cruises. Two-hour trips skirt the colorful rock formations that rise sharply from Lake Superior and tower almost 200 ft overhead. Trips leave from the City Dock. | leaves from City Dock, Box 355 | 906/387–2379 | $25 | June–early Oct., daily.

Pictured Rocks National Lakeshore. (*See also* Grand Marais.) Named for the spectacular sandstone cliffs that rise above Lake Superior, Pictured Rocks National Lakeshore extends 15 mi from Munising to Grand Marais in the Upper Peninsula. | 906/387–2607 | www.nps.gov/piro | Free | Daily.

JUNE: *Pictured Rocks Road Race.* An annual road race and walk through the scenic Pictured Rocks National Lakeshore attracts thousands to this U.P. park along a 15-mi section of Lake Superior shoreline. Usually held the last weekend of June. | 906/387–3387.
DEC.: *Trail Lunch.* Held between Christmas and New Year, this annual celebration is on snowmobile trail 8, at Highway 13. Free coffee, hot chocolate, and hot dogs are available. | 906/387–4143.

Dining

Bear Trap Restaurant. American. Pine paneling and stuffed animals adorn the walls of this restaurant 7 mi east of Munising at the highway entrance to Pictured Rocks National Lakeshore. On Friday night try the fresh whitefish and trout, deep-fried or broiled. | N7294 H–58/Hwy. 15, Shingleton | 906/452–6364. | $7–$9 | MC, V.

Brownstone Inn. American. The 1946 stone lodge housing this restaurant has a fieldstone fireplace, pine-paneled walls, and mahogany wainscoting. Talk to anyone in town about restaurants and this is the place they'll recommend. House specials are hand-cut steaks, burgers, and fresh whitefish. Desserts include homemade cheesecakes, pies, and a rich fudge cake. | E4635 M–28, Au Train | 906/892–8332 | fax 906/892–8337 | www.destinationmichigan.com/index | Labor Day to Memorial Day, closed Mon. | $6–$14 | AE, D, MC, V.

Dog Patch Restaurant. American. "Li'l Abner" cartoon portraits hang on the walls here. The menu has burgers, steaks, and a "monster" salad bar. | 325 E Superior St. | 906/387–9948 | $10–$17 | MC, V.

Sydney's. Seafood. This casual hangout is known for just-caught fish, Saturday all-you-can-eat buffets, and huge steaks, including 24-oz T-bones. Salad bar. Sun. brunch. | Rte. 28 | 906/387–4067 | $18–$25 | AE, DC, MC, V.

Lodging

Alger Falls. Cozy, independently owned lodgings sit back from the road, surrounded by evergreens and trees. Picnic area. Cable TV. Snowmobiling. Some pets allowed. | E9427 M–28 | 906/387–3536 | fax 906/387–3537 | www.algersfallsmotel.com | 17 rooms | $35–$64 | D, MC, V.

Best Western. Comfortable accommodations and on-site groomed snowmobile trails attract snowmobilers. Nearby cross-country ski trails include the Valley Spur ski area (5 mi). The motor inn is 4 mi out of town and surrounded by forest. Restaurant, bar, picnic area. Some refrigerators. Indoor pool. Hot tub, sauna. Snowmobiling. Business services. Some pets allowed. | M–28, Box 310 | 906/387–4864 or 800/780–7234 | fax 906/387–2038 | www.bestwestern.com | 80 rooms | $55–$85 | AE, D, DC, MC, V.

Comfort Inn. Pictured Rock cruises and highways are near this chain hotel. Complimentary Continental breakfast. Cable TV, in-room VCRs (and movies). Indoor pool. Hot tub. Exercise equipment. Cross-country skiing. Laundry facilities. Business services. Some pets allowed. | M–28, Box 276 | 906/387–5292 or 800/228–5150 | fax 906/387–3753 | www.choicehotels.com | 61 rooms | $55–$85 | AE, D, DC, MC, V.

Days Inn. Pictured Rocks cruises and downtown are 5 blocks from this chain hotel with basic accommodations. Cable TV, in-room VCRs (and movies). Indoor pool. Hot tub, sauna. Business services. | M–28 E | 906/387–2493 or 800/388–7829 | fax 906/387–5214 | www.daysinn.com | 66 rooms | $50–$94 | AE, D, DC, MC, V.

Homestead Bed and Breakfast. This four-story 1890 house is on 25 wooded acres. The interior has Alaskan photos, masks, Russian dolls, and walrus ivory ornaments. A spacious porch overlooks the lawn and gardens. Breakfast is fresh fruit, bagels, and homemade muffins. Complimentary Continental breakfast. No TV in some rooms, TV in common area. Snowmobiling. Pets allowed. No smoking. | 713 Prospect St. | 906/387–2542 | 6 rooms (3 with private bath) | $65–$90 | MC, V.

Pinewood Lodge Bed and Breakfast. Pines and oaks surround this log house 9 mi east of Munising. Log furniture and antiques fill the rooms. The log beds are handmade and have custom-made mattresses. Complimentary breakfast. In-room VCRs. Beach. No smoking. | E4836 M-28, Au Train | 906/892–8300 | fax 906/892–8510 | pinewood@tds.net | www.michigantraveler.com/pinewood.html | 6 rooms | $120–$140 | D, MC, V.

Sunset Resort. This simple motel on Lake Superior is a favorite of families. Picnic area. No air-conditioning, some kitchenettes. Cable TV. Lake. Dock. Playground. Some pets allowed. | 1315 Bay St. | 906/387–4574 | 16 rooms, 5 suites | $35–$49, $55–$75 suites | Closed late Oct.–Apr. | MC, V.

Super 8. Cross-country skiing and snowmobile trails connect the street from these no-frills chain accommodations. Complimentary Continental breakfast. Some refrigerators. Cable TV. Hot tub, sauna. | M–28 | 906/387–2466 or 800/800–8000 | fax 906/387–2355 | www.super8motels.com | 29 rooms | $68–$74 | AE, D, DC, MC, V.

Terrace Motel. Snowmobile trails begin at this motel two blocks from M–28, four blocks from Pictured Rocks Golf Course. Accommodations include one, two, and three-bedroom units. You can use a recreation room with billiards, a kitchen, and a sauna. Cable TV. Sauna. Pets allowed. | 420 Prospect St. | 906/387–2735 | fax 906/387–2754 | 18 rooms | $40–$52 | D, MC, V.

MUSKEGON

MAP 9, C6

(Nearby towns also listed: Coopersville, Grand Haven, Grand Rapids, Holland, Whitehall/Montague)

Once known as the Lumber Queen of the World, Muskegon today is the largest city on Lake Michigan's eastern shore, with a diversified economy based on industry, tourism, and recreation. More than 80 mi of lakefront attract sun seekers and fishermen intent on hooking the area's famed coho, chinook salmon, lake trout, perch, and walleye. (*Note:* Area codes in this vicinity are scheduled to change to 989 beginning April 7, 2001.)

Information: Muskegon County Convention and Visitors Bureau | 610 W. Western Ave., Muskegon 49440 | 800/235–3866 | www.visitmuskegon.org.

Attractions

Hackley and Hume Historic Site. These adjacent Queen Anne and Victorian-style mansions have elaborate interiors, with pieces of stained glass, intricately carved woodwork, tiled fireplaces, and stenciled walls. | 72 and 484 W. Webster | 231/722–7578 | www.visitmuskegon.org | $3 | Wed.–Sun. 12–4.

Michigan's Adventure Amusement Park. The state's only amusement park has more than 20 kid-pleasing rides, including three scream machines and a huge Ferris wheel. A wave pool, slides, water cannons, and a man-made river provide watery fun at the on-site Wild Water Adventure water park. | 4750 Whitehall Rd. | 231/766–3377 | www.visitmuskegon.org | $20 | Daily 10–10.

Muskegon County Museum. Learn about the lumber industry, mastodons and dinosaurs, and the mechanics of the human body here. | 430 W. Clay Ave. | 231/722–0278 | www.visitmuskegon.org | Free | Weekdays 9:30–4:30, weekends 12:30–4:30.

Muskegon Museum of Art. Noted American artists Winslow Homer, Edward Hopper, and John McNeill Whistler are among the many masters whose works are displayed by this downtown museum. The European holdings include works by Rembrandt and the French

Impressionists, including Degas and Pissarro. | 296 W. Webster Ave. | 231/722–2600 | www.visitmuskegon.org | Free | Tues.–Sat. 10–5, Sun. 12–5.

Muskegon State Park. With 2 mi of Lake Michigan shoreline and 1 mi on Muskegon Lake, this park provides the best of both Great Lakes and inland recreation in summer, including swimming, fishing, and boating. One of only four luge runs in the country and 12 mi of lighted cross-country trails provide winter fun. The park has one of the largest dunes along Lake Michigan, as well as picnic areas and play equipment. | 3560 Memorial Dr. | 231/744–3480 or 800/447–2757 | www.dnr.state.mi.us/camping | $4 per car, per day | Daily dawn to dusk.

Muskegon Trolley Company. Historic red trolleys take you along three routes past historic sites, downtown beaches, and Michigan's Adventure Amusement Park. | 231/724–6420 | 25¢ | Memorial Day–Labor Day, daily.

P. J. Hoffmaster State Park. The 2 mi of sandy shoreline along Lake Michigan and towering sand dunes are the main attractions at this West Michigan state park. Here you can swim, picnic, camp, and hike along 10 mi of trails. It's 5 mi north of Grand Haven off U.S. 131. | 6585 Lake Harbor Rd. | 800/44–PARKS or 230/798–3711 | www.dnr.state.mi.us/camping | $4 per car, per day | Daily dawn to dusk.

Gillette Visitor Center. Interpretive programs, hands-on displays, and nature programs tell the story of Michigan's sand dunes. Sledding, snowshoeing, and cross-country skiing are available here in winter. | 6585 Lake Harbor Rd. | 231/798–3573 | Free | Daily.

USS *Silversides*. Docked on the south side of the channel, this renowned World War II submarine served in the Pacific along the coast of Japan and received many honors. Guided tours take would-be sailors through the compartments and show what life was like 20,000 leagues beneath the sea | Pier Marquette Beach | 231/755–1230 | $4 | June–Aug., weekdays 1–5:30, weekends 10–5:30; Apr., May, Sept., and Oct., weekends 10–5:30.

ON THE CALENDAR
JUNE–JULY: *Muskegon Summer Celebration*. Big-name music, entertainment, carnival rides, and an art fair on the waterfront are part of this event that usually starts the last Thursday in June and runs 11 days. | 231/722–6520 | www.visitmuskegon.org.
JULY: *AVP Volleyball Tournament*. Professional players from around the world gather the second weekend of the month on the Muskegon waterfront at Père Marquette Beach to battle their way to trophies. | 800/250–WAVE | www.visitmuskegon.org.
JULY: *Muskegon Air Fair*. This event held at the Muskegon County Airport includes flight demonstrations, vintage and fighter plane exhibitions, aerial demonstrations, and rides. Usually the third weekend in July. | 231/798–4596 | www.visitmuskegon.org.

Dining
House of Chan. Chinese. Pagoda-like booths impress visitors expecting a lackluster interior. A popular Chinese-American lunch buffet is served three days a week (Tuesday, Thursday, and Sunday); if you miss it, try entrées off the regular menu such as seafood wo buy (bok choy with shrimp, scallops, and lobster) or crispy Beijing shrimp. Buffet. Kids' menu. Sun. brunch. Wine only. | 375 Gin Chan Ave. | 231/733–9624 | Closed Mon. No lunch Sun. | $15–$19 | AE, MC, V.

Rafferty's Dockside. Continental. Waterfront dining and dramatic harbor views characterize this casual restaurant specializing in seafood, steaks, and prime rib. Open-air dining in season. Kids' menu. | 601 Terrahe Point Blvd. | 231/722–4461 | No dinner Sun. | $21–$32 | AE, D, MC, V.

Station Grill. American. A corvette, split down the middle, hangs from the wall at this local favorite. Choose from burgers, burritos, buffalo wings, and salads. | 910 W. Broadway | 231/759–0633 | $3–$8 | D, MC, V.

Tony's Club. Greek. An authentic Greek menu brings diners from all across western Michigan. The chef makes a weekly trip to Chicago for the freshest Greek supplies and the results are seen in dishes such as Greek-style lamb chops or whitefish. The restaurant also serves huge 14 oz prime ribsteaks and "Sam's Famous Bar Cheese." Kids' menu, early bird suppers. | 785 W. Broadway | 231/739–7196 | Closed Sun. No lunch Sat. | $19–$28 | AE, D, MC, V.

Lodging

Bel-Aire Motel. Anglers, boaters, and snowmobilers stop regularly at this older motel 8 mi southeast of downtown. The 1957 one-story motel is in a quiet residential area. Cable TV. | 4240 Airline Rd. | 231/733–2196 | fax 231/733–2196 | 16 rooms | $39–$68 | AE, D, MC, V.

Best Western Park Plaza. This full-service hotel in the heart of Muskegon is just off U.S. 31 and minutes from the amusement park, beaches, and downtown. The interior has contemporary furnishings. Restaurant, bar (with entertainment), room service. Cable TV. Indoor pool. Sauna. Game room. Business services, airport shuttle. | 2967 Henry St. | 231/733–2651 or 800/780–7234 | fax 231/733–5202 | www.bestwestern.com | 108 rooms | $53–$109 | AE, D, DC, MC, V.

Days Inn. Easy access to the amusement park makes this chain hotel a popular family choice. Complimentary Continental breakfast. Cable TV. Pool. Hot tub. Laundry facilities. Business services. | 3450 Hoyt St. | 231/733–2601 or 800/368–4571 | www.daysinn.com | 107 rooms | $45–$85 | AE, D, DC, MC, V.

Hackley–Holt House Bed and Breakfast. Michigan's Lieutenant Governor Henry Holt called this 1857 Italianate house with wraparound porch home. Rooms have Victorian antiques, lace curtains, and floral-patterned wallpaper. The inn is two blocks from Muskegon Lake, adjacent to Hackley and Hume Historic Site. Complimentary breakfast. Cable TV, some room phones. Bicycles. No pets. No smoking. | 523 W. Clay Ave. | 231/725–7303 or 888/271–5609 | hhhbb@gte.net | 4 rooms | $89 | AE, D, MC, V.

Holiday Inn–Muskegon Harbor. A great harborfront location distinguishes this otherwise undistinguished chain hotel. You can walk to plays, museums, marinas, and beach. Restaurant, bar, room service. Cable TV. Indoor pool. Hot tub. Exercise equipment. Business services, airport shuttle. | 939 3rd St. | 231/722–0100 or 800/465–4329 | fax 231/722–5118 | www.basshotels.com/holiday-inn | 201 rooms | $75–$85 | AE, D, DC, MC, V.

Port City Victorian Inn Bed and Breakfast. You can see Muskegon Lake through the leaded glass windows in this 1877 Queen Anne home. Anastasia's Room has floral-patterned wallpaper, drapes, and coverlet. The Captain's Room has nautical accents. Two suites have whirlpools and lake views. Complimentary breakfast. In-room data ports, some in-room hot tubs. Cable TV, in-room VCRs. Business services. No pets. No smoking. | 1259 Lakeshore Dr. | 231/759–0205 or 800/274–3574 | fax 231/759–0205 | www.portcityinn.com | 2 suites, 3 rooms | $80–$150 | AE, D, DC, MC, V.

Super 8. This modern chain motel just outside of town overlooks Lake Michigan. It's 5 mi from downtown Muskegan, and within walking distance of some chain restaurants. Cable TV. Business services. | 3380 Hoyt St. | 231/733–0088 or 800/800–8000 | fax 231/733–0088 | www.super8motels.com | 62 rooms | $46–$62 | AE, D, DC, MC, V.

NEWBERRY

MAP 9, C2

(Nearby towns also listed: Brevort, Grand Marais, Manistique, Munising, Paradise)

This former Upper Peninsula lumber town celebrates its heritage each August during its Lumberjack Days festival. Nearby 95,000-acre Seney National Wildlife Refuge and

KODAK'S TIPS FOR PHOTOGRAPHING LANDSCAPES AND SCENERY

Landscape
- Tell a story
- Isolate the essence of a place
- Exploit mood, weather, and lighting

Panoramas
- Use panoramic cameras for sweeping vistas
- Don't restrict yourself to horizontal shots
- Keep the horizon level

Panorama Assemblage
- Use a wide-angle or normal lens
- Let edges of pictures overlap
- Keep exposure even
- Use a tripod

Placing the Horizon
- Use low horizon placement to accent sky or clouds
- Use high placement to emphasize distance and accent foreground elements
- Try eliminating the horizon

Mountain Scenery: Scale
- Include objects of known size
- Frame distant peaks with nearby objects
- Compress space with long lenses

Mountain Scenery: Lighting
- Shoot early or late; avoid midday
- Watch for dramatic color changes
- Use exposure compensation

Tropical Beaches
- Capture expansive views
- Don't let bright sand fool your meter
- Include people

Rocky Shorelines
- Vary shutter speeds to freeze or blur wave action
- Don't overlook sea life in tidal pools
- Protect your gear from sand and sea

In the Desert
- Look for shapes and textures
- Try visiting during peak bloom periods
- Don't forget safety

Canyons
- Research the natural and social history of a locale
- Focus on a theme or geologic feature
- Budget your shooting time

Rain Forests and the Tropics
- Go for mystique with close-ups and detail shots
- Battle low light with fast films and camera supports
- Protect cameras and film from moisture and humidity

Rivers and Waterfalls
- Use slow film and long shutter speeds to blur water
- When needed, use a neutral-density filter over the lens
- Shoot from water level to heighten drama

Autumn Colors
- Plan trips for peak foliage periods
- Mix wide and close views for visual variety
- Use lighting that accents colors or creates moods

Moonlit Landscapes
- Include the moon or use only its illumination
- Exaggerate the moon's relative size with long telephoto lenses
- Expose landscapes several seconds or longer

Close-Ups
- Look for interesting details
- Use macro lenses or close-up filters
- Minimize camera shake with fast films and high shutter speeds

Caves and Caverns
- Shoot with ISO 1000+ films
- Use existing light in tourist caves
- Paint with flash in wilderness caves

From *Kodak Guide to Shooting Great Travel Pictures* © 2000 by Fodor's Travel Publications

Tahquamenon Falls State Park attract nature lovers. (*Note:* Area codes in this vicinity are scheduled to change to 989 beginning April 7, 2001.)

Information: Newberry Area Chamber of Commerce | Box 308, Newberry 49868 | 906/293–5562 | www.exploringthenorth.com/newbchamb/main.html.

Attractions

Luce County Historical Museum. In this 19th-century Queen Anne-style museum, which was once the town jail, the still-intact cells are among the most popular displays (yes, they're open to the public). The rest of the museum holds artifacts and antiques relating to the history of this Upper Peninsula county. | 411 W. Harriet St. | 906/293–5946 | Free | June–Aug. Tues.–Thurs. 1–5, Sept.–May, weekends 1–5.

Seney National Wildlife Refuge. At 95,000 acres, Seney is the largest nature preserve east of the Mississippi River. Among the many species spotted here are bald eagles, deer, loons, beavers, otters, ducks, and sandhill cranes. Although you can use the refuge any time of the year, it's accessible by canoe, mountain bike, or self-guided auto tours from May to October only. Two- and four-hour canoe trips on the Manistique River are available through a number of area outfitters, including **Northland Outfitters** in Germfask (906/586–9801 | www.northoutfitters.com). Cyclists can enjoy more than 100 mi of mountain-bike trails. An on-site visitor center has an interpretive program with films, displays, nearby nature trails. Fishing is allowed in the area. | 8174 M–77 | 906/586–9801 | Free | Daily dawn to dusk.

Tahquamenon Logging Museum. Michigan's lumbering heritage is the theme of this museum on 29 acres 1.5 mi north of Newberry. You can explore an authentic cook shack, original C.C.C. (Civilian Conservation Corps) building, a family home, and a museum filled with artifacts. You can also hike a nature trail, take the boardwalk to the Tahquamenon River, and picnic here. | M–123 | 906/293–3700 or 800/831–7292 | www.exploringthenorth.com/newbchamb/calend.html | $3 | Memorial Day–Labor Day, daily 9–5.

Tahquamenon Falls State Park. The River Unit near Paradise has a scenic campground and a launch site for boaters and canoers. | M–123 | 906/492–3415 or 800/447–2757 | www.dnr.state.mi.us/camping | $4 per car, per day | Daily dawn to dusk.

Toonerville Trolley and Riverboat Trip to Tahquamenon Falls. You can catch this popular excursion to Tahquamenon Falls at Soo Junction, 2 mi off M–28, 12 mi east of Newberry. A narrow-gauge railroad takes you through 5½ mi of wilderness to the Tahquamenon River, where you board a riverboat, built especially for sight-seeing, for the 21 mi journey to the Upper Tahquamenon Falls. Narrators on both legs of the trip provide passengers with a history of the area and other points of interest. There's one 6½-hour trip daily in season, or you can take the 1¾-hour train ride. | 906/876–2311 or 888/778–7246 | www.destinationmichigan.com/toonerville-trolley.html | $22, $11 train only | June–Oct., daily at 10:30.

ON THE CALENDAR

AUG.: *Luce-West Mackinac County Fair.* Rides, games, and food are all to be had at this popular U.P. county fair. Held the second week in August at the Luce County Fairgrounds, 3 mi east of Newberry. | 800/831–7292.

AUG.: *Lumberjack Days.* The Upper Peninsula's long and colorful ties to logging are commemorated during this annual event featuring logging displays, demonstrations, food booths, and children's activities. Held the fourth weekend of August at the Tahquamenon Logging Museum, 1 mi north of Newberry on M–123. | 800/831–7292.

Dining

Edge of Paradise. American. Here, about 4 mi east of Soo Junction, you can eat a good and hearty home-style meal, complete with homemade bread and pies. The cook says her specialties are lasagna and Swedish meatballs, but New York strip steak and a few pasta dishes are also on the menu. This is the only place for miles around where you can get take-out pizza. | 2551 S. M–123, Eckerman | 906/274–5555 | $4.50–$10 | AE, D, DC, MC, V.

Timber Charlies Food and Spirits. American. Wood paneling, wood tables, and a stuffed bear and otter give this eatery, a favorite of snowmobilers and skiers, outdoor appeal. House specials are barbecued ribs slathered with a homemade sauce and burritos. | 110 S. Newberry Ave. | 906/293–3363 | $7–$15 | AE, MC, V.

Zellar's. American. Stained-wood wainscoting and wood tables distinguish the dining room here in Zellar's Village Inn. Try the homemade pasties (meat-stuffed pastries), steaks, burgers, or whitefish. You can also eat in the lounge, which serves more than 20 kinds of beer. Breakfast also available. | Newberry Ave./M–123 | 906/293–5114 | $6–$12 | AE, D, DC, MC, V.

Lodging

Comfort Inn. Tahquamenon Falls State Park, snowmobile trails, and Manistique Lake are near this comfortable chain hotel. Some in-room hot tubs. Cable TV. Game room. Laundry facilities. Business services. | M–28 & M–123 | 906/293–3218 | fax 906/293–3435 | www.choicehotels.com | 54 rooms | $56–$70 | AE, D, DC, MC, V.

Days Inn. Close to the Upper and Lower Tahquamenon Falls, this chain hotel is 2.5 mi from downtown Newberry. Complimentary Continental breakfast. Some refrigerators. Cable TV. Indoor pool. Hot tub, sauna. Cross-country skiing. Game room. Laundry facilities. Business services. | M–28, Box 680 | 906/293–4000 or 800/388–7829 | fax 906/293–4005 | www.daysinn.com | 66 rooms | $45–$76 | AE, D, DC, MC, V.

Gateway Motel. Less than 1 mi from downtown Newberry, this small motel is popular with snowmobilers and cross-country skiers. Cable TV, no room phones. Cross-country skiing. | 980 S. M–123 | 906/293–5651 or 800/791–9485 | 11 rooms | $38–$65 | D, MC, V.

Macleod House. Nicknamed "The Painted Lady" for its dark red, green, purple, and tan exterior, this 1898 Queen Anne house in Newberry sits on 120 acres of a former farm. The interior has a parquet floor, oak staircase, and a fireplace made of copper. Bedroom walls are covered with Victorian wallpaper. The bed and breakfast is 1 mi south of Newberry and 30 mi from Tahquamenon Falls. Complimentary breakfast. Some in-room hot tubs, TV in common area. No pets. No smoking. | 943 County Rd. 402 | 906/293–3841 | fax 906/293–3841 | fcicala@up.net | www.macleodhouse.com | 3 with baths | $65–$89 | MC, V.

Rainbow Lodge. Surrounded by state forests, this lodge, ¼ mi from Lake Superior, is popular with hunters and snowmobilers. The cafe is open during snowmobiling season. Restaurant. Some kitchenettes, some refrigerators. No room phones, no TV. Cross-country skiing. Pets allowed. | County Rd. 423 | 906/658–3357 | 10 rooms, 2 cabins | $40–$80 | MC, V.

Zellar's Village Inn. Taquamenon Falls State Park is 30 mi from this small, independently owned motel right in the center of town. Restaurant, bar, room service. In-room data ports. Cable TV. Game room. Business services. Some pets allowed. | 7552 S. Newberry Ave. | 906/293–5114 | fax 906/293–5116 | 20 rooms | $50–$65 | AE, D, DC, MC, V.

NEW BUFFALO

MAP 9, B8

(Nearby towns also listed: Niles, Paw Paw, St. Joseph)

A year-round resort community near the Indiana border, New Buffalo is popular with vacationers from nearby Chicago and Detroit, who come to enjoy Lake Michigan.

Information: Harbor Country Chamber of Commerce | 530 S. Whitaker St., New Buffalo 49117 | 616/469–5409 | info@harborcountry.org | www.harborcountryguide.com.

Attractions

New Buffalo Beach. It's a short walk from downtown to this large, sandy Lake Michigan beach adjacent to the marina and harbor, where you can swim and sunbathe. Restrooms and a playground. | 616/469–5409 | info@harborcountry.org | www.harborcountryguide.com.

Red Arrow Highway. This scenic two-lane highway cuts through much of the southwest Michigan area known as Harbor Country and is lined with restaurants, antiques shops, and unusual boutiques. | 800/362–7251 | www.harborcountryguide.com | Free | Daily.

ON THE CALENDAR

AUG.: *Ship and Shore Festival.* On the first full weekend of August, activities stretch from the downtown to the beach. There's live entertainment, food vendors, craft booths, games, fireworks, and a lighted boat parade. | 616/469–5409 | www.harborcountry.org.

Dining

Miller's Country House. Contemporary. Gourmets who want to watch their food being prepared ask for tables near the small exhibition kitchen in this homey, antiques-filled restaurant in Union Pier near New Buffalo. Other highlights include the herb-filled garden, which supplies most of the flavor in the entrées such as rack of lamb or tournedos of tuna. Kids' menu. | 16409 Red Arrow Hwy., Union Pier | 616/469–5950 | Closed Sept.–May and Tues. | $22–$34 | AE, D, MC, V.

Redamak's. American. For more than two decades, huge build-your-own burgers and Friday night frogs' legs have drawn a casual, fun-loving crowd of locals and vacationers to this Harbor Country institution. Open-air dining. Kids' menu. | 616 E. Buffalo | 616/469–4522 | Closed mid-Nov.–mid-Mar. | $13–$19 | No credit cards.

Lodging

Comfort Inn. A pleasant breakfast room overlooks the courtyard of this chain hotel near beaches and shopping. Restaurant. Some in-room hot tubs. Cable TV. Gym. Game room. Laundry facilities. Business services. Some pets allowed. | 11539 O'Brien Ct. | 616/469–4440 | fax 616/469–5972 | www.choicehotels.com | 96 rooms | $59–$115 | AE, D, DC, MC, V.

Garden Grove Bed and Breakfast. This 1925 home surrounded by gardens is less than a mile from the sandy beaches of Lake Michigan. The Violet Room has a vaulted ceiling, French doors, private balcony, and claw-foot bathtub. Two rooms have fireplaces and hot tubs. Complimentary breakfast. Some in-room hot tubs. Cable TV, in-room VCRs. Outdoor hot tub. Bicycles. Library. No pets. No smoking. | 9549 Union Pier Rd., Union Pier | 616/469–6346 or 800/613–2872 | fax 616/469–3419 | gardenbnb@triton.net | www.gardengrove.net | 4 rooms | $120–$160 | AE, D, MC, V.

Harbor Grand Hotel. This hotel sits on the shore of Lake Michigan and commands a view of the impressive New Buffalo harbor. Public areas and guest rooms are designed in the Mission style, with attention to detail a hallmark. Restaurant, bar, complimentary Continental breakfast, room service. Some in-room hot tubs. Cable TV. Indoor pool. Hot tub. Gym. Cross-country skiing. Business services. | 111 W. Water St. | 616/469–7700 | fax 616/469–7386 | 55 rooms | $100–$190 | AE, DC, MC, V.

Sans Souci Euro Inn. A relaxing retreat in a busy resort area is provided by this charming European-style bed and breakfast inn. Accommodations are in a historic home amidst 50 acres of pines, springfed lakes, and wildflower fields when in season. Refrigerators, some in-room hot tubs. Beach. | 19265 S. Lakeside Rd. | 616/756–3141 | fax 616/756–5511 | 6 rooms | $110–$255 | AE, D, MC, V.

Tall Oaks Inn. On four wooded acres west of New Buffalo, this 1914 lodge is less than a 5-minute walk from Lake Michigan. Eight rooms have hot tubs, six have private decks, and four have private fireplaces. The Texas Blue Bonnet room has cowboy accents, and the Wild

Rose is Victorian. Home-baked cookies are always available. Complimentary breakfast. Some in-room hot tubs. No room phones, no TV. Bicycles. Cross-country skiing. No pets. No smoking. | 19400 Ravine Dr. | 616/469–0097 or 800/936–0034 | fax 616/469–0629 | talloaks@triton.net | www.harborcountry.com/guide/talloaks | 12 rooms | $75–$230 | AE, MC, V.

NILES

(Nearby towns also listed: New Buffalo, St. Joseph, Three Rivers)

English, French, Spanish, and American flags have all flown over this city, once a stage-coach stop on the Detroit–Chicago road (now Route 12) in the southwestern corner of the state, not far from I–94. Among the city's native sons are Montgomery Ward and the Dodge brothers of automotive fame.

Information: **Four Flags Council on Tourism** | 321 E. Main St., Niles 49120 | 616/683–3720 | www.michigan.org/mi/fourflagsarea.

Attractions

Fernwood Botanic Gardens. More than 100 acres await botanists and nature lovers at this bucolic preserve. Gardens, woodland trails, and a restored prairie entice visitors; there's also a visitor center with a gift shop and frequent special events. | 13988 Range Line Rd. | 616/695–6491 | landtrust.org/fernwood/fernwood.htm | $3 | Tues.–Sun. 10–6.

Fort St. Joseph Museum. The carriage house of an 1882 home contains an unlikely and fascinating 10,000-item collection, including relics and art of the Sioux and Potawatomi tribes, pictographs of Indian chief Sitting Bull, and remnants and memorabilia from the now-gone fort. The collection is considered to be one of the top five Sioux art collections in the nation. | 508 E. Main St. | 616/683–4702 | Free | Wed.–Sat. 10–4.

Niles Depot. This 1892 sandstone Neo-Romanesque- style building was constructed for train travelers on their way to Chicago. It was used in the movies *Midnight Run* and *Continental Divide.* | N. 5th St. and Dey St.

ON THE CALENDAR

AUG.: *Niles River Festival.* Everyone becomes a mariner the first weekend in August when they enter the "Anything-That-Can-Float Raft Race" and the "Dragon Boat Race." Craft booths, food vendors, and live entertainment round out the event. | 616/684–0172.
SEPT.: *Four Flags Area Apple Festival.* The apple harvest is celebrated with apple picking, cider making, baked goods, and crafts. | 616/684–7444.

ONTONAGON

(Nearby towns also listed: Calumet, Hancock, Houghton, Ironwood, Wakefield)

Once a stopping point for the 17th-century Jesuits and voyageurs, this U.P. town was renowned for a huge copper boulder once reported here; its discovery sparked the copper rush. Porcupine Mountains Wilderness State Park attracts nature lovers. (*Note:* Area codes in this vicinity are scheduled to change to 989 beginning April 7, 2001.)

Information: **Ontonagon County Chamber of Commerce** | Box 266, Ontonagon 49953 | 906/884–4735 | www.ontonagonmi.com.

Attractions

Adventure Mine. You can descend 300 ft into an abandoned copper mine, or take a tour of the surface. Tours are 45 minutes or more than an hour. | 200 Adventure Rd. | 906/883–3371 | $10–$15 | Daily.

Porcupine Mountains Wilderness State Park. Stop at the visitor center 3 mi west of Silver City to get a handle on this sprawling park and its many recreation options. With more than 60,000 acres on the shores of Lake Superior in the U.P., "the Porkies" has towering old-growth forests, cliff-top scenic vistas, waterfalls, and four lakes, including the famed Lake of the Clouds. You can hike on more than 90 mi of trails in summer, and cross-country ski on 26 mi of trails in winter. The downhill ski area has 15 runs—the longest is 6,000 ft—along a 641-ft vertical drop. Spend the night camping in a backcountry or modern campsite, or rent one of 16 rustic cabins. The Presque Isle Unit north of Wakefield includes camping, waterfalls, cascades, and the rapids of the Presque Isle River. | 412 S. Boundary Rd. | 906/885–5275 or 800/447–2757 | www.porkies.com/porkies/ or www.dnr.state.mi.us/camping | Daily dawn to dusk.

ON THE CALENDAR

SEPT.: *Labor Day Festival.* You can join in the fun all weekend long. Saturday and Sunday nights there's dancing. Sunday there's a big parade with floats and bands. A kids' parade is on Monday. You can also enjoy a pig roast and a picnic. | 906/884–4196.

Dining

Syl's Café. American. The walls here are covered with area photographs you can purchase after your meal. Try the homemade pasties (meat pies), trout, fried chicken, and homemade desserts. Breakfast is also available. | 713 River St. | 906/884–2522 | $4.25–$6.25 | No credit cards.

Lodging

Best Western Porcupine Mountains Lodge. Porcupine Mountains State Park and ski resorts are a short drive away from this chain hotel. Restaurant, bar, picnic area, complimentary Continental breakfast. Cable TV. Indoor pool. Hot tub, sauna. Beach. Cross-country and downhill skiing. Game room. Business services, airport shuttle. | 120 Lincoln Ave. | 906/885–5311 or 800/780–7234 | fax 906/885–5847 | www.bestwesternmichigan.com | 71 rooms | $52–$78 | AE, D, DC, MC, V.

Lambert's Chalet Cottages. These cozy cottages on the Lake Superior shore are near area hiking and ski trails. Picnic area. No air-conditioning. Cable TV. Lake. Beach. Cross-country and downhill skiing. Airport shuttle. | 287 Lakeshore Rd. | 906/884–4230 | 15 cottages | $60–$215 | AE, D, MC, V.

Northern Light Inn. From this 19th-century home a block from Lake Superior, you can walk to shops and restaurants. The inn's furnished for comfort with large pillows and cushions. Relax in the living room in front of a fireplace. Three rooms have hot tubs. Complimentary breakfast. No room phones, no TV in some rooms, TV in common area. No pets. No smoking. | 701 Houghton St. | 906/884–4290 or 800/238–0018 | fax 906/884–6470 | 5 rooms | $75–$150 | D, MC, V.

OSCODA

MAP 9, E5

(Nearby towns also listed: Alpena, Roscommon, Tawas City/East Tawas)

Oscoda was a major logging center in the late 1800s. Today, it's better known for its fishing and canoeing on the Au Sable River. (*Note:* Area codes in this vicinity are scheduled to change to 989 beginning April 7, 2001.)

Information: **Oscoda-Au Sable Chamber of Commerce** | 4440 U.S 23 N, Oscoda 48750 | 517/739–7322 or 800/235–4625 | www.oscoda.com.

Attractions

Paddle Wheeler boat trips. The Au Sable River provides the scenery for paddle-wheel riverboat trips on the *Queen of Oscoda*. Summer and fall foliage trips on the glass-enclosed boat take two hours and cover 19 mi of historic and scenic attractions. | Oscoda | 517/739–7351 | $8.50 | Memorial Day–Oct.

River Road. From this 25-mi byway along the Au Sable River you can see panoramic vistas, largo Springs, and a memorial to canoers.

ON THE CALENDAR

JUNE: *Art on the Beach.* More than 200 vendors sell their crafts and fine art here at Oscoda Beach Park on Lake Huron during the third weekend in June. | 517/739–7322.
JULY: *Weyerhaeuser Au Sable River Canoe Marathon and Festival.* The week-long Grayling-to-Oscoda canoe race kicks off with a lively race through downtown Grayling. A bed race and 10K run are for those who prefer to race ashore. A parade, fine arts and crafts sales, food booths, children's activities, an antique car show, and street dancing round out the events. | 800/937–8837 | www.ausaublerivercanoemarahton.org.

Dining

Pack House. Contemporary. Family heirlooms and Victorian antiques furnish this onetime lumber baron's home that dates from the 1870s. The menu ranges from casual burgers and sandwiches to a more formal charbroiled herb chicken or tasty vegetables topped with dill and feta and baked in parchment. Kids' menu. | 5014 U.S. 23 N | 517/739–2096 | Closed Dec.–Apr. and Sun. | $22–$38 | AE, MC, V.

Wiltsie's Brew Pub and Family Restaurant. American. Quaff a pint of the restaurant's tasty home-brewed ales and lagers while deciding on something from the menu. Choices include chicken and steaks cut to order as well as sandwiches, salads, and more. Desserts and baked goods are homemade. Kids' menu. | 5606 U.S. 41 N | 517/739–2231 | $17–$24 | MC, V.

Lodging

Huron House Bed and Breakfast. Many rooms at this inn on a secluded, sandy beach 2 mi south of Oscoda have views of Lake Huron. All rooms have private hot tubs, either inside or outside on private decks. There's a perennial garden in the courtyard. Complimentary breakfast. Some microwaves, refrigerators, some in-room hot tubs. Cable TV, no room phones. Beach. No pets. No smoking. | 3124 N. U.S. 23 | 517/739–9255 | www.huronhouse.com | 15 rooms | $115–$175 | AE, D, MC, V.

Lake Trail Resort. The 300 ft of beach on Lake Huron and choice of accommodations draw vacationers to this year-round resort near downtown. Picnic area, complimentary Continental breakfast. Some refrigerators. Cable TV. Lake. Tennis. Beach, boating. Airport shuttle. | 5400 U.S. 23 N | 517/739–2096 or 800/843–6007 | fax 517/739–2565 | www.lakeresort.com | 42 rooms, 20 suites, 2 cottages | $60–$90 rooms, $120–$130 suites, $90 cottages | D, MC, V.

Redwood Motor Lodge. You can rent either rooms or cottages at this quiet hostelry. Bar, picnic area. Cable TV. Indoor pool. Hot tub, sauna. Game room. Playground. | 3111 U.S. 23 N | 517/739–2021 | fax 517/739–1121 | 37 rooms, 9 cottages | $50–$65 rooms, $80–$85 cottages | AE, D, DC, MC, V.

OWOSSO

MAP 9, E6

(Nearby towns also listed: Flint, Lansing/East Lansing)

Owosso is an industrial and trading center on the Shiawassee River, and the birthplace of naturalist-author James Oliver Curwood, Impressionist-style painter Frederick Carl Frieseke, and Thomas E. Dewey, onetime governor of New York.

Information: **Owosso–Corunna Area Chamber of Commerce** | 215 N. Water St., Owosso 48867 | 517/723–5149 | chamber1@shianet.org | www.shianet.org/chamber.

Attractions

Curwood Castle. James Oliver Curwood, author of many well-known wilderness novels and a prominent conservationist, once lived in this Norman castle replica, the only residence of its kind in the state. Today, it's open to the public. | 224 Curwood Castle Dr. | 517/725–0597 | www.shianet.org/chamber | Free | Tues.–Sun. 12–5.

Durand Union Station and Michigan Railroad History Museum. Built in 1903, this Chateau Romanesque depot was once the second largest in the state. Today, it's one of the most photographed train stations in America and a railroad museum. Also an Amtrak station, it's 11 mi southeast of Owosso. | 200 Railroad St., Durand | 517/288–3561 | dusi@shianet.org | www.durandstation.org | Free | Tues.–Sun. 1–5.

Shiawasee Art Center. Two impressionist pieces by native son Fredrick Carl Frieseke are on permanent exhibit here beside works from local artists. | 206 Curwood Castle Dr. | 517/723–8354 | Free | Tues.–Sun. 1–5.

ON THE CALENDAR

JUNE: *Curwood Festival.* This fun-filled event honors local writer-naturalist James Oliver Curwood, whose Norman castle replica is one of the area's top attractions. The event includes river rafting, bed and canoe races, pioneer demonstrations and displays, a fun run, and an art show. Held the first full weekend of the month. | 224 Curwood Castle Dr. | 517/723–8844 | www.shianet.org/community/curwood/.

AUG.: *Shiawassee County Fair.* The county fairgrounds in Corunna host agricultural and livestock displays, midway rides, and 4-H exhibits to make this fair an area favorite. Held the second week in August. | 517/743–2223.

SEPT.: *Historic Home Tour.* On the fourth Saturday of September, tour historic homes, Curwood Castle, churches, and the farmers market. | 517/723–8354.

Dining

Eddie O'Flynns. American. The walls of this casual eatery are made of barn siding. A fireplace and 1920s memorabilia add to its rustic charm. Steaks, seafood, and sandwiches are on the menu. Kids' menu. | 2280 M–21 W | 517/723–6741 | $19–$23 | AE, D, MC, V.

Lodging

Cobb House Bed and Breakfast. Period antiques fill this 1880 Victorian, which is on the National Register of Historic Places. On weekends a full breakfast is served. Complimentary Continental breakfast. No room phones, no TV. No pets. No smoking. | 115 W. 2nd St. | 517/625–7443 | fax 517/625–7443 | twillson@voyager.net | 3 rooms (1 room with private bath) | $70–$95 | MC, V.

PARADISE

(Nearby towns also listed: Grand Marais, Newberry, Sault Ste. Marie)

When one of the town's founder's described the spot in the 1920s as a "regular paradise," the name stuck. Today, the small resort town's biggest claim to fame is a large festival celebrating the town's blueberry crop and the national forests that surround the village, favorites of snowmobilers and cross-country skiers. (*Note:* Area codes in this vicinity are scheduled to change to 989 beginning April 7, 2001.)

Information: Paradise Tourism Council | Box 64, Paradise 49768 | 906/492–3310 | fax 906/492–3943 | www.paradisemi.com.

Attractions

Tahquamenon Falls State Park. The park is a hiker's paradise, with 25 mi of forest trails that wind through 40,000 acres of wilderness. The Upper Falls are its best-known natural feature and rank among the largest in the country, with a drop of 50 ft and a width of 200 ft. Near the shore of Whitefish Bay on Lake Superior, there's also swimming, boating, fishing, snowmobiling, cross-country and downhill skiing, and camping. | 906/492–3415 or 800/447–2757 | www.dnr.state.mi.us/camping | $4 per car, per day | Daily dawn to dusk.

Whitefish Point Bird Observatory. Across the parking lot from the Great Lakes Shipwreck Museum, this interpretive center emphasizes education and the preservation of Great Lakes birds, especially loons, cedar waxwings, and kingfishers. | 16914 N. Whitefish Point Rd. | 906/492–3596 | Free | Mid-Apr.–mid-Oct., daily 10–6; grounds open all year.

Whitefish Point/Great Lakes Shipwreck Museum. A spit of land jutting into Lake Superior is the site of this fascinating shipwreck museum and the area's first lighthouse. The museum, run by the Great Lakes Shipwreck Historical Society, has displays on the 1816 wreck of the schooner *Invincible* and on the *Edmund Fitzgerald,* which sank in 1975. Whitefish Point, on the Lake Superior's Whitefish Bay, is known as the "Graveyard of the Great Lakes." Scuba divers can dive here. | 18335 N. Whitefish Point | 906/635–1742 | www.shipwreck-museum.com | $7 | Mid-May–mid-Oct., daily 10–6.

ON THE CALENDAR

AUG.: *Blueberry Festival.* Blueberry picking, blueberry pancakes, blueberry muffins; lots and lots of blueberries are to be had at this event. | 906/492–3219.

Dining

Tahquamenon Falls Brewery and Pub. American. This rustic restaurant within the Tahquamenon Falls State Park has wood-paneled walls, a fieldstone fireplace, and red chairs at stained-wood tables. Try the fresh whitefish and homemade pasties. Twelve beers are brewed here, and there are four on tap at any given time. | M–123 | 906/492–3300 | Closed Dec.—third week in Apr. | $9–$17 | AE, D, DC, MC, V.

Lodging

Howard Johnson Paradise. Woods surround this two-story motel not far from the center of Paradise. You can drive a snowmobile from your door. It's at the junction of Hwy. M–123 and Whitefish Point Rd. Complimentary Continental breakfast. Some microwaves, some refrigerators. Cable TV. Laundry facilities. Business services. No pets. | Whitefish Point Rd. | 906/492–3940 | fax 906/492–3943 | gm@paradiseinnmich.com | www.paradiseinn-mich.com | 36 rooms | $52–$115 | AE, D, DC, MC, V.

PAW PAW

MAP 9, C7

(Nearby towns also listed: Battle Creek, Kalamazoo, St. Joseph, South Haven, Three Rivers)

Paw Paw was named for the nearby river of the same name and the papaw trees that once grew along its banks. It's the Van Buren County seat and the center of Michigan's grape-growing region, part of the area's vast and fertile fruit belt. St. Julian Winery, the state's largest vineyard, is here and is a popular stop on tours of the region.

Information: Greater Paw Paw Chamber of Commerce | 111 E. Michigan Ave., Paw Paw 49079 | 616/657–5395 | ppccdd@btc-bci.com | www.pawpaw.net.

Attractions

Maple Lake. On an island 1 mi north of town, this small park area was created at the turn of the century when the Paw Paw River was dammed to generate electric power. Swimming, boating, and picnic areas are available. | 616/456–8557 | www.wmta.org | Free | Daily dawn to dusk.

Van Buren County Courthouse. The copper dome and clock-tower complement the stone facade and columns of this stately, 19th-century courthouse in the center of town. | 212 Paw Paw St. | 616/657–8218.

Winery tours. Gentle winds off Lake Michigan and rich, fertile soil make the southwest part of the state well suited to grape-growing, and vineyards are a common sight along area highways.

The **St. Julian Wine Co.** is both the state's largest and oldest winery. Tours and tastings are every 30 minutes daily. | 716 S. Kalamazoo St. | 616/657–5568 | www.stjulian.com | Free | Mon.–Sat. 10–5, Sun. 12–5.

A smaller vineyard best known for its sparkling wines and juices, **Warner Vineyards** gives tours of its champagne cellar and an introduction to ages-old French wine-making methods. The on-site restaurant is a great place to take a break after a tour. | 706 S. Kalamazoo St. | 616/657–3165 | www.warnervineyards.com | Free | Mon.–Sat. 10–5, Sun. 12–5.

ON THE CALENDAR

SEPT.: *Wine and Harvest Festival.* Downtown Paw Paw hosts this annual event the second weekend of the month that honors the fruits of some of Michigan's best vineyards. Wine tastings, food, and vineyard tours make it one of the state's most popular fall events. Carnival rides, a parade, live music, and a grape-stomping competition round out the activities. | 616/657–5395 | www.pawpaw.net.

Dining

La Cantina Ristorante. Italian. Eat outside on patios overlooking Maple Lake at this family-owned restaurant. Cedar plank walleye, steaks, and rack of lamb with spicy sauce served with pesto pasta top the menu. The restaurant was stablished in 1937. | 139 W. Michigan Ave. | 616/657–7033 | $11–$21 | AE, MC, V.

Lodging

Castle in the Country Bed and Breakfast. Five acres of gardens and fields surround this 1912 Victorian inn 15 mi north of Paw Paw and 6 mi south of Allegan. Hardwood floors, period wallpaper, hand-painted furniture, and unique antique pieces adorn the interior. You can choose from rooms with fireplaces and whirlpools, or the Rose Gazebo room inside the turret. Complimentary breakfast. Some in-room hot tubs. Some in-room VCRs. Hiking. No smoking. | 340 M–40 S, Allegan | 616/673–8054 or 888/673–8054 | fax 616/686–0058 | www.castleinthecountry.com | 5 rooms | $85–$185 | AE, MC, V.

Quality Inn and Suites. Comfortable accommodations are at this two-story chain hotel built downtown in 1997. Some in-room hot tubs. Cable TV. Gym. Cross-country skiing. Game room. Laundry facilities. Business services. Some pets allowed. | 153 Ampey Rd. | 616/655–0303 or 800/228–5151 | fax 616/657–1015 | www.qualityinn.com | 49 rooms, 16 suites | $55–$100 | AE, D, DC, MC, V.

PETOSKEY

MAP 9, D3

(Nearby towns also listed: Boyne City, Charlevoix, Harbor Springs, Indian River)

This longtime resort center on Little Traverse Bay was once the summer home of writer Ernest Hemingway. Petoskey's gaslight shopping district is one of northern Michigan's most popular attractions, and nearby Petoskey State Park is a great place to hunt for the fossilized coral that is the state stone. (*Note:* Area codes in this vicinity are scheduled to change to 989 beginning April 7, 2001.)

Information: **Petoskey–Harbor Springs–Boyne County Visitors Bureau** | 401 Mitchell St., Petoskey 49770 | 231/348–2775 or 800/845–2828 | fax 231/348–1810 | info@boynecounty.com | www.boynecounty.com.

Attractions

Crooked Tree Art Center. Housed in an historic church, this art center showcases the works of local artists and Native Americans. | 461 E Mitchell St. | 231/347–4337 | www.crookedtree.org | Free | Mon.–Fri. 10—5, Sat. 11–4.

Gaslight District. Stroll through a 19th-century downtown neighborhood filled with galleries, restaurants, a chemist's shop, Ernest Hemingway's former residence, and the city's oldest structure, a Catholic church.

Little Traverse History Museum. Displays that trace writer Ernest Hemingway's connections to the Petoskey area (he had a cottage nearby) are among the most popular at this museum on the bay. Other exhibits in the restored 1892 cover the area's Odawa Indian, pioneer, and Victorian-era past and a the city's long history as a resort colony. There's also a section on native son and writer Bruce Catton, a Civil War historian. | 100 Depot Ct. | 231/347–2620 | $1 | Memorial Day–Labor Day, Mon.–Sat. 10–4; Labor Day–Nov., Tues.–Sat. 1–4.

Petoskey State Park. Spread out across 2 mi of Little Traverse Bay, this popular 300-acre state park is a favorite of rock hunters who flock here to search for Michigan's Petoskey stones. Facilities include a wide sandy beach, a bath house, shaded campsites, and hiking and cross-country ski trails. | 231/347–2311 or 800/447–2757 | www.dnr.state.mi.us/camping | $4 per car, per day | Daily dawn to dusk.

ON THE CALENDAR
JUNE: *Crooked Tree House Tour.* On the third Monday of the month, the finest residences of Petoskey and nearby Bay View open their doors to visitors during this popular summer event. | 231/347–4150.
JULY: *Petoskey Antiques Festival.* Thousands of antiques enthusiasts from across the state meet the last weekend of July at the fairgrounds for one of northern Michigan's finest antiques fairs. | 231/347–4150.

Dining

Andante. Contemporary. A quiet, understated dining room in a former home at the edge of the city's Gaslight District is accented with Impressionist-style art and classical music. The restaurant is considered to be among northern Michigan's best. A changing menu often features dishes as varied as Louisiana crab cakes with chipotle mayonnaise or grilled venison and spaetzle. No smoking. | 321 Bay St. | 231/348–3321 | Closed Sun. and Mon. Oct.–May. No lunch | $24–$39 | AE, MC, V.

1893 Walloon Lake Inn. French. While dining you can see across the lake to a tree-lined coast, 7 mi south of Petoskey. Items on the extensive menu include steak filet with morel mushrooms, braised lamb shanks, and rainbow trout Hemingway, which is sautéed with shallots, garlic, cognac, and mushrooms. Top off dinner with creme caramel. | Windsor St., Walloon Lake | 231/535–2999 | www.walloonlakeinn.com | No lunch | $19–$29 | MC, V.

Roast and Toast. American. A great place to stop while shopping the city's Gaslight District, this spot is equal parts coffee roaster and restaurant. Step back through the coffee paraphernalia and you'll see a few simple tables in the back, where during lunch and dinner the owners serve up some of the freshest fare, including chicken Caesar salads, a number of changing daily soups, and hearty quiches. Of course, the coffee and desserts are excellent, too. Entertainment. | 309 E. Lake St. | 231/347–7767 | $8–$17 | No credit cards.

© Artville

HEMINGWAY IN MICHIGAN

Ernest Hemingway once said that all American literature up to his time came from Mark Twain. In turn, every American writer since Hemingway owes a literary debt to him. Certainly few writers have ever practiced Hemingway's own dictum as scrupulously as he did: Write what you know. Hemingway knew and wrote about Italy, Spain, France, Africa, and Cuba.

But—apart from his hometown of Oak Park, Illinois—the first place Hemingway knew really well and wrote vividly about was Michigan.

His father, a doctor, loved nature and the outdoors, hunting and fishing, and the family had a cabin in the wooded area of northern Michigan east of Lake Michigan. This retreat quickly became Ernest's favorite place when he was growing up. Named Windermere by Ernest's mother, it stood on the shore of Walloon Lake near the little town of Horton Bay. There Ernest learned hunting and fishing from his father, together with a profound respect for nature itself. Once, when Ernest and a friend shot a porcupine that had been fighting with a dog, his father used the episode as a harsh lesson. Insisting that the boys should never kill anything they didn't intend to eat, he instructed them to cook and eat the porcupine.

While Ernest was still a boy, the family bought a 40-acre farm across the lake from the cabin and named it Longfield Farm. His father planted hardwood and fruit trees there and his mother built a small hilltop cottage as a private retreat.

Through his teen years, Ernest spent the summers and as much time as possible at Windermere and Longfield Farm, selling vegetables to the hotels springing up on Walloon Lake, hiking in the woods, sleeping outdoors, and developing the sense of self-reliance and endurance that would shape all his later writing. He made friends there who would change his life too. Through one friend, who later married John Dos Passos, he met his first wife, Hadley Richardson, and he used some local people as characters in his stories. But most of all, the woods and lakes of Michigan, where he often carried a notebook on hikes to jot down observations and story ideas, formed a sturdy and long-lasting foundation for the great novels of his adult life.

Stafford's Bay View Inn. Contemporary. This classic, white-clapboard Victorian inn has excellent views of Little Traverse Bay as well as charming dining and accommodations. Local whitefish, cold cherry soup, seared beef tenderloin medallions served with port and dried cherries, and a variety of fresh pastas are among the menu staples. The Sunday brunch is an area tradition, with four tables filled with hot and cold meats, breakfast items, salads, and sweets. Don't miss the signature cherry French toast at breakfast or the cherry pepper steak at dinner. Sun. brunch. BYOB. | 2011 Woodland Ave. | 231/347–2771 | $21–$36 | AE, MC, V.

Terrace Inn. American. Light from the dining room's many windows illuminates the wood details of tables, ceilings, and walls. The menu has broiled whitefish, filet mignon, and barbecued baby back ribs. | 1539 Glendale Ave. | 231/347–2410 or 800/530–9898 | www.theterraceinn.com | $11–$18 | Closed Sun.–Mon. | AE, MC, V.

Villa Ristorante Italiano. Italian. A local favorite, this tiny Italian-style trattoria has the expected checked tablecloths and Chianti bottles hanging from the ceiling. The food is equally comfort-inducing, including tangy pizzas and a wide variety of homemade pastas as well as thin veal and thick steaks. Try the veal scallopini or seafood fettuccine Alfredo. Salad bar. Kids' menu. | 887 Spring St. (U.S. 131) | 231/347–1440 | No lunch | $18–$30 | AE, MC, V.

Lodging

Apple Tree Inn. This cheerful motel is on U.S. 131, outside of downtown. The Victorian-inspired rooms all have queen- or king-size beds. Complimentary Continental breakfast. Refrigerators, some in-room hot tubs. Cable TV. Indoor pool. Hot tub. Exercise equipment. Game room. Playground. Business services. | 915 Spring St. (U.S. 131) | 231/348–2900 | fax 231/348–9748 | www.appletreeinn.com | 40 rooms | $59–$106, $105–$145 suites | AE, D, DC, MC, V.

Baywinds Inn. A fireplace and antiques in the lobby welcome you to this cozy, independently owned motel. The attractive guest rooms are Victorian-inspired. The area's largest indoor pool is here. Complimentary Continental breakfast. Refrigerators, some in-room hot tubs. Cable TV. Indoor pool. Hot tub. Exercise equipment. Game room. | 909 Spring St. (U.S. 131) | 231/347–4193 or 800/204–1748 | fax 231/347–5927 | wwwbaywindsinn.com | 48 rooms | $55–$128 | AE, D, DC, MC, V.

Econo Lodge. Comfortable lodgings are provided by this chain hotel on the outskirts of town near the junction of routes 31 and 131. Complimentary Continental breakfast. Cable TV. Indoor pool. Hot tub. Business services. Some pets allowed. | 1858 U.S. 131 S | 231/348–3324 or 800/553–2666 | fax 231/348–3521 | www.econolodge.com | 60 rooms | $41–$110 | AE, D, DC, MC, V.

1893 Walloon Lake Inn. An original inn, the building sits directly on Lake Walloon, a quarter block from the marina in the tiny village of Walloon Lake, 7 mi south of Petoskey. Two rooms have views of the lake. A common area upstairs has a balcony where you can enjoy water views. Complimentary Continental breakfast. No room phones, no TV. Dock, boating, fishing. No pets. | Windsor St., Walloon Lake | 231/535–2999 or 800/956–4665 | wli@walloonlakeinn.com | www.walloonlakeinn.com | 5 rooms | $75 | MC, V.

Holiday Inn. You can see downtown Petoskey and Little Traverse Bay from this hilltop full-service chain hotel. Restaurant, bar (with entertainment), room service. Cable TV. Indoor pool. Hot tub. Exercise equipment. Game room. Playground. Laundry facilities. Business services. | 1444 U.S. 131 S | 231/347–6041 or 800/465–4329 | fax 231/347–6041 | www.basshotels.com/holiday-inn | 144 rooms | $70–$95 | AE, D, DC, MC, V.

Serenity Bed and Breakfast. Rooms in this 1890 Victorian in the Gaslight District have lace, four-poster beds, or white brass beds. Hand-painted walls add extra charm, as do views of Little Traverse Bay. Afternoon snacks, sodas, and bottled water are complimentary. Complimentary breakfast. No room phones, no TV. No pets. No kids under 12. No smoking. | 504 Rush St. | 231/347–6171 or 877/347–6171 | 3 rooms | $105–$125 | MC, V.

Stafford's Bay View. Public and guest rooms are filled with antiques and reproductions. Restaurant, picnic area, complimentary breakfast. Bicycles. Cross-country and downhill skiing, sleigh rides. Business services. | 613 Woodland Ave. | 231/347–2400 | fax 231/347–3413 | 52 rooms | $80–$96 | AE, MC, V.

Stafford's Perry. One of the city's finest and oldest hotels occupies a vintage 1899 brick structure in the Gaslight District near restaurants and shopping. Ernest Hemingway and other luminaries once stayed here. Restaurant, bar. Cable TV. Hot tub. Exercise equipment. Business services. | Bay and Lewis Sts. | 231/347–4000 or 800/456–1917 | fax 231/347–0636 | 81 rooms | $75–$200 | AE, MC, V.

Terrace Inn. Original furniture fills the house and rooms of this 1911 Victorian inn. The spacious property, 1½ mi east of Petoskey, has cross-country skiing trails and its own private beach. Restaurant, complimentary Continental breakfast. No room phones, TV in common area. Tennis court. Hiking. Beach, dock, bicycles. Cross-country skiing. | 1549 Glendale Ave. | 231/347–2410 or 800/530–9898 | fax 231/347–2407 | info@theterraceinn.com | www.theterraceinn.com | 43 rooms | $77–$159 | AE, MC, V.

PLYMOUTH

MAP 10, A4

(Nearby towns also listed: Ann Arbor, Dearborn, Detroit, Farmington/Farmington Hills)

This western Detroit suburb of about 9,000 residents has a charming downtown full of 19th century-style shops and restaurants. The city is also home to a popular winter ice-carving festival held each January. In 1967, in celebration of the town's centennial, the mayor of Plymouth, England, presented the town a piece of Plymouth Rock, which you can see on south Main Street.

Information: **Plymouth Chamber of Commerce** | 386 S. Main St., Plymouth 48170 | 734/453–1540 | www.plymouthmi.org.

Attractions
Historic Plymouth. Surrounding the tree-filled Kellogg Park Square and its fountain, the historic neighborhood has restaurants, coffee houses, and shops. There's even an old movie theater that still draws a crowd. | Farmer St.

ON THE CALENDAR
JAN.: *Ice-Sculpture Spectacular.* Hundreds of intricate ice masterpieces line downtown streets and attract thousands of spectators during this annual event during the third weekend of the month. Kellogg Park is the site of professional and student chef ice-carving competitions, demonstrations, and other chilly events. | 734/453–1540.
SPRING, SUMMER, FALL: *Farmer's Market.* Every Saturday in spring, summer, and fall, the market draws local craftspeople and farmers to the Gathering Downtown Pavilion to sell their wares and produce. | 734/453–1540.

Dining
Café Bon Homme. Contemporary. This European-style bistro has a charming location in downtown Plymouth and an accomplished, if small, menu, with standouts that include seafood bisque and southern French lamb pie. Specials change daily. | 844 Penniman | 734/453–6260 | Closed Sun. | $23–$29 | AE, DC, MC, V.

Ernesto's. Italian. Fireplaces in separate dining rooms lend a cozy air to this Italian-style country inn, with food that's hearty and traditional. Standouts include pasta with fresh tomatoes and basil, beef tenderloin with chianti gravy, chicken piccata, and the pollo da Vinci, consisting of fettuccine with chicken and artichokes in cream sauce. Open-air dining in season. Pianist Tues.–Sat., strolling minstrels Mon.–Thurs. | 41661 Plymouth Rd. | 734/453–2002 | $16–$25 | AE, D, DC, MC, V.

Station 885. American. Eat in a restored freight house next to the railroad tracks, where miniature trains chug above you around the ceilings. Choose from prime rib, seafood, pasta dishes, and pizza. The "Veal 885" is topped with gulf shrimp in a beurre blanc sauce, the chicken picatta has sauteed artichokes and mushrooms. Live jazz music Wednesday through Saturday nights. | 885 Starkweather St. | 734/459–0885 | Sun. brunch | $10–$20 | AE, D, DC, MC, V.

Lodging

Fairfield Inn by Marriott. This chain hotel with its signature blue-and-white exterior is just off I–275 and near a large shopping mall. Restaurant, complimentary Continental breakfast. Cable TV. Pool. Business services. | 5700 Haggerty Rd., Canton | 734/981–2440, ext. 709 | fax 734/981–2440 | www.fairfieldinn.com | 133 rooms | $44–$79 | AE, D, DC, MC, V.

932 Penniman: A Bed and Breakfast. One block from Kellogg Park Square, this 1903 home has bay windows, a glass-enclosed wraparound porch, oak stairs, and oak wood details. The Rose Room has rose-colored wallpaper and carpet; Linnea's Garden has floral-patterned wallpaper and a Shaker bed. Complimentary breakfast. In-room data ports, some in-room hot tubs. Cable TV, in-room VCRs. No pets. No smoking. | 932 Penniman Ave. | 734/414–7444 or 888/548–4887 | fax 734/414–7445 | www.bbonline.com/mi/penniman/index/html | 4 rooms | $109–$175 | AE, D, MC, V.

Quality Inn. Many rooms in this modern chain hotel have a cozy recliner. Complimentary Continental breakfast. In-room data ports. Cable TV. Pool. Business services. | 40455 Ann Arbor Rd. | 734/455–8100 or 800/228–5151 | fax 734/455–5711 | www.qualityinn.com | 123 rooms | $80–$96 | AE, D, DC, MC, V.

Red Roof Inn. Basic budget lodgings are available at this chain hotel near restaurants and shopping. In-room data ports. Cable TV. Some pets allowed. | 39700 Ann Arbor Rd. | 734/459–3300 or 800/733–7663 | fax 734/459–3072 | 109 rooms | $43–$63 | www.redroof.com | AE, D, DC, MC, V.

Willow Brook Inn Bed and Breakfast. An acre of woods, gardens, and a brook surround this 1929 arts and crafts home. Breakfast, made to order and at the time you want, is served on a deck in summer, in the garden room in winter, or in your room. A guest area has a computer, microwave, and refrigerator with complimentary snacks and sodas. Complimentary breakfast. Some in-room hot tubs, in-room VCRs. Pets allowed. No smoking. | 44255 Warren Rd., Canton | 734/454–0019 or 888/454–1919 | fax 734/451–1126 | wbibnb@earthlink.net | www.bbonline.com/mi/willow/index/html | 3 suites | $95–$125 | AE, MC, V.

PONTIAC

MAP 9, E7

(Nearby towns also listed: Birmingham, Bloomfield Hills, Detroit, Holly, Troy, Warren)

A northern Detroit suburb and seat of Oakland County, Pontiac is the former stomping grounds of Ottawa chief Pontiac and headquarters for General Motors' Pontiac division. Almost a dozen parks and natural lakes are nearby.

Information: Greater Detroit Chamber of Commerce, Oakland County Division | 1760 S. Telegraph Rd., Bloomfield Hills 48302 | 248/456–8600.

Metropolitan Detroit Convention and Visitors Bureau | 211 W. Fort St., Ste. 1000, Detroit 48226 | 800/DETROIT or 313/202–1800 | www.visitdetroit.com.

Attractions

Alpine Valley Ski Resort. This often crowded metro Detroit ski hill, 12 mi from Pontiac, has 25 runs. The longest run is ⅓ mi and has a vertical drop of 320 ft. | 6775 E. Highland Rd., White Lake | 248/887–2180 or 248/887–4183 (snow conditions) | Nov.–Mar., daily.

Highland Recreation Area. Glacial movement left this area with many ponds, marshes, fields, and rolling hills covered with dense forests. Today, trails for horseback riding, hiking, and cross-country skiing wind through the park's 5,000 wooded acres. You can also swim, boat, and hunt here, as well as picnic and camp. | 5200 E. Highland Rd., White Lake | 248/685–2433 | www.dnr.state.mi.us/camping | $4 per car, per day | Daily 8 AM–10 PM.

Pontiac Lake Recreation Area. No matter the season, you can enjoy outdoor sports at this 3,000-acre park. You can water ski, swim, boat, and fish on the lake. On land you can horseback ride, hunt, or practice your skills at an archery range. In winter, downhill skiing is just one sport you can do here. The park also has picnic areas, a playground, and camping sites. | 780 Gale Rd., Waterford | 248/666–1020 or 800/447–2757 | www.dnr.state.mi.us/camping | $4 per car, per day | Daily 8 AM–10 PM.

Pontiac Silverdome. Home to the Detroit Lions, the stadium seats 80,000 and is also used for carnivals, tractor pulls, off-road races, and concerts. | 1200 Featherstone Ave. | 248/858–7358.

ON THE CALENDAR

SEPT.: *Chrysler Arts, Beats, and Eats Festival.* Held each Labor Day Weekend, the event draws nearly a million people to art exhibits, music acts, and food booths (sponsored by local restaurants). | 248/335–9600.

Dining

Great American Grill. American. Eat in the five-story atrium of the Hilton Suites Auburn Hills, adjacent to a fountain. The menu has Jamaican jerk chicken, blackened swordfish, shrimp, steaks, and pasta. | 2300 Featherstone Rd., Auburn Hills | 248/334–2222 | $10–$20 | AE, D, DC, MC, V.

Muskies Irvin Pier. American. This popular bar across from the Palace of Auburn Hills (home to the Detroit Pistons) is known for barbecued ribs, a New York strip smothered in Jack Daniels sauce, and tasty, casual cuisine. Kids' menu. | 3880 Lapeer Rd., Auburn Hills | 248/373–7330 | Closed Sun. No lunch Sat. | $17–$34 | AE, D, DC, MC, V.

Pike Street. Contemporary. An eclectic menu characterizes this popular downtown Pontiac eatery. Catering to a variety of tastes, the changing menu ranges from soft-shelled crabs in a medley of fresh veggies and sauces to an Asian-influenced vegetable sushi to a more traditionally inspired filet mignon with sautéed foie gras. Entertainment Thurs.–Sat. | 18 W. Pike St. | 248/334–7878 | $33–$47 | AE, D, DC, MC, V.

Lodging

Best Western Concorde Inn. Southwest of the Oakland/Pontiac Airport and east of Pontiac Lake, this white, three-floor hotel is 7 mi west of Pontiac. Most of the rooms have hot tubs. Complimentary Continental breakfast. Some refrigerators. Cable TV. Pool. Gym. Shops. Laundry facilities. Business services. No pets. | 7076 Highland Rd. | 248/666–8555 or 800/WESTERN | fax 248/666–8573 | www.bestwestern.com | 111 rooms | $89–$179 | AE, D, DC, MC, V.

Courtyard by Marriott. These chain accommodations are arranged around a central courtyard. The hotel is close to the Palace of Auburn Hills, Birmingham shopping, and restaurants. Bar. In-room data ports, minibars, some refrigerators. Cable TV. Indoor pool. Hot tub. Exercise equipment. Laundry facilities. Business services. | 1296 Opdyke Rd., Auburn Hills | 248/373–4100 | fax 248/373–1885 | www.courtyard.com | 148 rooms, 10 suites | $69–$129, $149 suites | AE, D, DC, MC, V.

Fairfield Inn by Marriott. The Palace of Auburn Hills, Great Lakes Crossing outlet mall, the Silverdome, and Pine Knob Music Theatre are near this chain hotel. Complimentary Continental breakfast. In-room data ports. Cable TV. Pool. | 1294 Opdyke Rd., Auburn Hills | 248/373–2228 | fax 248/373–2228 | www.fairfieldinn.com | 134 rooms | $53–$70 | AE, D, DC, MC, V.

Hampton Inn. You're near of the Palace, the Silverdome, Pine Knob, and the Great Lakes Crossing outlet mall at this chain hotel. Complimentary Continental breakfast. In-room data ports. Cable TV. Pool. Exercise equipment. | 1461 N. Opdyke Rd., Auburn Hills | 248/370–0044 | fax 248/370–9590 | www.hampton-inn.com | 124 rooms | $79–$95 | AE, D, DC, MC, V.

Hilton Suites. Roomy, suite-size accommodations are handy for business travelers and families. The hotel is near Daimler-Chrysler headquarters, the Silverdome, the Palace, and other Oakland County attractions. Restaurant, bar, complimentary breakfast, room service. In-room data ports, refrigerators. Cable TV, in-room VCRs (and movies). Indoor pool. Hot tub. Exercise equipment. Game room. Laundry facilities. Business services. Some pets allowed. | 2300 Featherstone Rd., Auburn Hills | 248/334–2222 | fax 248/334–2922 | www.hilton.com | 224 suites | $129–$149 suites | AE, D, DC, MC, V.

Holiday Inn Select Detroit–Auburn Hills. Daimler–Chrysler world headquarters and the Pontiac Silverdome are within 1 mi of this eight-floor hotel, 2 mi northeast of Pontiac and west of I–75 at Exit 79. Restaurant, bar, room service. Some refrigerators. Cable TV. Pool. Hot tub, sauna. Gym. Laundry facilities, laundry service. Business services. No pets. | 1500 N. Opdyke Rd., Auburn Hills | 248/373–4550 or 800/465–4329 | fax 248/373–8220 | www.basshotels.com/holiday-inn | 190 rooms | $160–$195 | AE, D, DC, MC, V.

PORT AUSTIN

INTRO
ATTRACTIONS
DINING
LODGING

PORT AUSTIN

MAP 9, F5

(Nearby towns also listed: Bay City, Port Huron, Saginaw)

This small fishing village at the northern tip of Michigan's "thumb" is home to a preserved Victorian village and a 1,000-acre state park on Saginaw Bay. Named for P. C. Austin, who erected a beckoning makeshift lighthouse on the boat dock he built in 1839, it's renowned for both its vivid sunsets and abundance of charter fishing. (*Note:* Area codes in this vicinity are scheduled to change to 989 beginning April 7, 2001.)

Information: Greater Port Huron Area Chamber of Commerce | 920 Pine Grove Ave., Port Huron 48060 | 810/985–7101 | fax 810/985–7101 | www.porthuron-chamber.org.

Attractions

Albert E. Sleeper State Park. This 1,000-acre park, 25 mi east of Caseville, has a ½-mi beach of fine sand on Lake Huron, 4 mi of marked nature trails that traverse old dune ridges, and 280 modern campsites. In winter, you can go skiing and snowmobiling. A playground and picnic areas are other niceties. | 6573 State Park Rd., Caseville | 517/856–4411 or 800/447–2757 | www.dnr.state.mi.us/camping | $4 per car, per day | Daily dawn to dusk.

Huron City Museums. Horrible forest fires destroyed Huron City, a once thriving village midway between Port Austin and Port Hope, twice in the late 1800s. The area was abandoned for good after wells dried up near the turn of the century. In the 1960s a group of local preservationists restored nine buildings on the site as a museum dedicated to the original town. Included are a general store, a church, a log cabin, a carriage shed, an inn, a U.S. Life-Saving Station, and an 1881 Victorian mansion with original furnishings, once the home of lumberman Langdon Hubbard, the village's founder. | 7930 Huron City Rd. | 517/428–4123 | www.tour-michigan.com/~hcmus | $10 | July–Labor Day, daily except Tues.–Wed. 10-5.

Port Austin Breakwall. Walk along the city breakwall for a wonderful view of the harbor. It's a perfect spot to see the sunset.

ON THE CALENDAR

OCT.: *Scarecrow Days*. The last week in October, you can join in a scavenger hunt, dance at a masquerade ball, shop for sales, and watch a juried show of the city's best scarecrows. The festival takes place throughout the town. | 517/738–7111 or 800/35–THUMB | www.huroncounty.com.

Dining

Garfield Inn. Contemporary. An elegant mansion from the 1830s, the Garfield is two blocks from Lake Huron. It's on both the state and national historic registers and is furnished with antiques. The chef is known for using fresh ingredients and creative techniques in his frequently changing menu. The seafood and steaks are what keep folks coming back. The Inn also has a "pub" that serves liqueurs and wines from around the world. No smoking. | 8544 Lake St. | 517/738–5254 | fax 517/738–6384 | www.bbonline.com/mi/garfield | Closed Jan. | $25–$32 | AE, MC, V.

Lodging

Garfield Inn. This elegant B&B two blocks from Lake Huron in the heart of Port Austin has cozy rooms in an 1830s residence. It's on the state and national historic registers. The French Second Empire architecture includes bay windows overlooking the garden. Rooms have unique themes, such as a pink color scheme and sunflower motif. Restaurant (*see* Garfield Inn), complimentary Continental breakfast. | 8544 Lake St. | 517/738–5254 | fax 517/738–6384 | www.bbonline.com/mi/garfield | 6 rooms | $90–$110 | AE, D, MC, V.

Lakeside Motor Lodge. In downtown, this motel sits directly on Lake Huron. The cottages have full kitchens, and rooms have views of the water. Some kitchenettes, some microwaves, some refrigerators. Cable TV. Pool. Boating, fishing. Playground. Pets allowed. | 8654 Lake St. | 517/738–5201 | 35 rooms, 15 cottages | $40–$90 | AE, MC, V.

PORT HURON

MAP 9, F6

(Nearby towns also listed: Flint, Port Austin, St. Clair)

This town is the boyhood home of Thomas Edison and political seat of St. Clair County. Linked to Sarnia, Ontario, by the Blue Water Bridge, it's one of the state's oldest settlements, originally a 17th-century French fur-trading post.

Information: **Greater Port Huron Area Chamber of Commerce** | 920 Pine Grove Ave., Port Huron 48060 | 810/985–7101 | www.porthuron-chamber.org.

Attractions

Fort Gratiot Lighthouse. You'll need reservations to tour this 1823 brick lighthouse at the U.S. Coast Guard Station. | 2800 Omar St. | 810/982–3659 | By appointment.

Lakeport State Park. This southeast Michigan park boasts 580 acres, including a 1-mi-long beach along Lake Huron, a large modern campground, water skiing, boating, perch fishing, picnicking, and a playground. | 7605 Lakeshore Rd., Lakeport | 810/327–6224 or 800/447–2757 | www.dnr.state.mi.us/camping | $4 per car, per day | Daily dawn to dusk.

Museum of Arts and History. This vintage building holds more than 300 years of local history behind its doors. Displays include Native American relics, marine artifacts, a full-size pioneer log house, and mementos related to Thomas Edison, who lived here as a boy and worked on the steam trains between Port Huron and Detroit. Also at the site is the Lightship Museum. | 1115 6th St. | 810/982–0891. | $2 | Wed.–Sun. 1–4:30.

Lightship Museum. Pine Grove Park is the permanent resting place of the *Huron,* a decommissioned 1920s lightship. The floating lighthouse guided ships safely into shore and out to sea as late as the early 1970s. You can tour the ship and learn about how its beacon worked. | 1115 6th St. | 810/982–0891 | $2 | June–Sept., Wed.–Sun. 1–4:30.

ON THE CALENDAR

JAN.: *Silver Stick Hockey.* Watch a competition among 150 teams from across the U.S. and Canada, held over the last three weekends in January. Most events take place at McMorran Place (701 McMorran Blvd.). | 810/985–6166.

MAY: *Feast of the Ste. Claire.* Pine Grove Park goes back to the 18th century on Memorial Day weekend when military units reenact battles of the French and Indian and other early American wars. Fur traders demonstrate their occupation as do period craftspersons and musicians. | 810/985–7101.

JULY: *Blue Water Festival/Mackinac Race.* This harborfront festival coincides with the Port Huron-to-Mackinac sailboat races, one of the state's most colorful events. It also includes sailing demonstrations, food, entertainment, and other family-focused events. | 810/985–7101.

Dining

Fogcutter. Continental. At this restaurant in the Port Huron Office Center, you can enjoy panoramic views of the Blue Water Bridge, the St. Clair River, and Canada. On the menu, there's prime rib and sampler platters with shrimp, scallops, and frog legs. A rooftop dining room has the best views. Kids' menu. | 511 Fort St. | 810/987–3300 | fax 810/987–3306 | www.bwb.net/fogcutter/ | $22–$31 | AE, D, DC, MC, V.

Victorian Inn. Continental. The Victorian Inn has just two dinner seatings in an elegantly restored turn-of-the-century mansion furnished with lots of oak and antiques. It's known for entrées such as prime rib and rack of lamb. Accommodations are available and there's an English-style pub in the basement. Entertainment. | 1229 7th St. | 810/984–1437 | fax 810/984–5777 | marv-sue@victorianinn-mi.com | www.victorianinn-mi.com | Reservations essential | Closed Sun.–Mon. | $28–$52 | AE, D, DC, MC, V.

Lodging

Comfort Inn. Near area attractions like the Blue Water Bridge and the Museum of Arts and History, both within 3 mi, this two-story chain hotel is off I–94 on the east side of Port Huron. Complimentary Continental breakfast. In-room data ports, some refrigerators. Cable TV. Indoor pool. Hot tub. Exercise equipment. Video games. Laundry facilities. | 1700 Yeager St. | 810/982–5500 | fax 810/982–7199 | www.comfortinn.com | 80 rooms | $60–$99. | AE, D, DC, MC, V.

Davidson House Bed and Breakfast. Butternut and oak details, jewel-glass windows, Victorian antiques, and seven fireplaces are only some of this 1888 B&B's charms. The first electrified house in the city, it's south of town at Business 69 and Military St. Two rooms have fireplaces. Complimentary breakfast. Some in-room hot tubs. Cable TV, no room phones. No pets. No kids under 10. No smoking. | 1707 Military St. | 810/987–3922 | www.davidsonhouse.com | 4 rooms | $80–$150 | No credit cards.

Fairfield Inn by Marriott. This three-story chain property is surrounded by restaurants. It is 3 mi from the Museum of Arts and History and 4 mi from the beach and a golf course. All the rooms have work desks. Complimentary Continental breakfast. Some refrigerators, cable TV. Indoor pool. | 1635 Yeager St. | 810/982–8500 | fax 810/982–4114 | www.fairfieldinn.com | 63 rooms | $55–$94. | AE, D, DC, MC, V.

Thomas Edison Inn. Antiques and reproductions fill the rooms in this modern, Tudor-style three-story hotel beneath the Blue Water Bridge. Restaurant, bar, room service. Cable TV. Indoor pool. Hot tub. Gym. Business services. | 500 Thomas Edison Pkwy. | 810/984–8000 or 800/451–7991 | fax 810/984–3230 | tei@thomasedisoninn.com | www.thomasedis-oninn.com | 141 rooms, 8 suites | $89–$124 rooms, $165–$305 suites | AE, D, DC, MC, V.

Victorian Inn. The Victorian wallpaper and antiques lend romance to this 1896 home down-town. Two rooms have double beds and a shared bathroom with a claw-foot tub. An embroidered headboard and tapestry bed is the centerpiece of another room. Restaurant, bar. Some in-room hot tubs. No room phones, no TV. No pets. No kids under 13. No smok-ing. | 1229 7th St. | 810/984–1437 | fax 810/984–5777 | marv-sue@victorianinn-mi.com | www.victorianinn-mi.com | 4 rooms (2 with private bath) | $100–$150 | AE, D, DC, MC, V.

PRESQUE ISLE

MAP 9, E3

(Nearby towns also listed: Alpena, Cheboygan)

Presque Isle, a village with a post office, a chapel, and a small general store, is not an all-seasons town—come October, the shutters go up. Starting each May, it springs back into action. Two 19th-century lighthouses preserve the town's history, while state-oper-ated Presque Isle Harbor attracts personal boaters and holds a wooden boat festival each June. (*Note:* Area codes in this vicinity are scheduled to change to 989 beginning April 7, 2001.)

Information: **Presque Isle Area Commerce Committee** | Box 74, Presque Isle 49777 | 517/595–5095 or 800/968–2858 | www.presqueisle.com.

Attractions

New Presque Isle Lighthouse. This 113-ft lighthouse, built in 1871, is the younger of the area's two lighthouses. It's still operated by the U.S. Coast Guard. You can relax in the outdoor pavilion, hike, and tour the lighthouse. | Grand Lake Rd. | 517/595–9917 | $2 | May 15–Oct. 15, daily 9–6.

Old Presque Isle Lighthouse. Built in 1840, this retired elder brother of the New Presque Isle Lighthouse is accessible by land and open for public exploration. There's a hands-on museum for kids. | Grand Lake Rd. | 517/595–6979 | $2 | May 15–Oct. 15, daily 9–6.

Thompson's Harbor State Park. This park 12 mi southeast of Rogers City is a good place to come if you're interested in wildflowers. The 5,000 undeveloped acres, crossed by 6 mi of trails, is noted for its assortment of endangered wildflowers as well as for its rugged beauty. | U.S. 23, next to harbor, Rogers City | 517/734–2543 or 800/447–2757 | www.dnr.state.mi.us/camping | All year.

Dining

Fireside Inn Resort. American. The family-style meals here are home-cooked and hearty—strictly meat and potatoes. | 18730 Fireside Hwy. | 517/595–6970 | Closed Nov.–Apr. | $7–$8 | No credit cards.

Portage Restaurant. Seafood. At the turn into the 20th century, residents cut ice from the Lake Huron and stored it in sawdust in this former icehouse with an expansive view of Presque Isle Harbor. Locals appreciate the whitefish dinner—it's fresh and well-prepared—but you can also get pasta and stir-fried dishes. | 5549 E. Grand Lake Rd. | 517/595–6051 | Closed Nov.–Apr. | $9–$22 | MC, V.

Lodging

Fireside Inn Resort. Breakfasts and dinners, along with use of the inn's kayaks, canoes, and rowboats, are included in the rates at this 17-acre resort. Stay in the rustic main lodge, built in 1908, or in cabins constructed between the 1920s and the 1940s. On the property, you can play tennis on a clay court, shuffleboard, tetherball, volleyball, bocce ball, or 9-hole disk golf course, where you aim disks at targets instead of hitting balls toward holes. Golf course. | 18730 Fireside Hwy. | 517/595–6970 | 17 cabins, 15 rooms | $300 per week | Closed Nov.–Apr. | No credit cards.

Northwood Shores Cabin Resort. These housekeeping cottages on the east shore of Grand Lake are 5 mi from Lake Huron. Some are no-smoking. No air conditioning. No room phones. Boating. Pets allowed. | 8844 E. Grand Lake Rd. | 989/595–6429 | pettalia@freeway.net | www.oweb.com/upnorth/northwood | 6 cabins, 3 two-level | $420–$520 per week | Closed Nov.–Apr. | V, MC.

ROCHESTER

(Nearby towns also listed: Pontiac, Southfield, Warren)

Settled in 1817 by James Graham and his family, but not formally incorporated until 1869, Rochester and the adjoining Rochester Hills today are mostly residential communities. Some 80,000 residents call the towns just north of M–59 home. Rochester's downtown, looking as if it could have come straight from a Norman Rockwell painting, showcases myriad architectural styles.

Information: Rochester Chamber of Commerce | 71 Walnut St., Ste. 110, Rochester 48307 | 248/651–6100 | fax 248/651–5270 | rchamber@ees.eesc.com | www.rochester-chamber.com.

Attractions

Oakland University. On wooded and hilly land acquired by auto tycoon John Dodge and his wife Matilda Dodge Wilson, the university, founded in 1957, is now one of the state's largest, with more than 12,000 students. It is also the site of the Meadow Brook Music Festival, held from late June to early September, and the summer home of the Detroit Symphony Orchestra. | Walton Blvd. and Squirrel Rd. | 248/370–2100 | www.oakland.edu | Free | Daily.

The palatial **Meadow Brook Hall** was built for the automotive pioneer Dodge family between 1926 and 1929 at a cost of more than $4 million. Matilda Dodge Wilson culled mansions all over Great Britain for architectural elements—even whole rooms—to create the 100-room Tudor Revival mansion. The house has a two-story ballroom, 24 fireplaces, hand-carved paneling, and a sculptured dining room ceiling. Knole Cottage is a six-room mini-Meadow Brook that's furnished in the same vein and served as a playhouse. Today, the estate holds special events and is open for tours. | Walton Blvd. and S. Squirrel Rd. | 248/370–3140 | wheeler@oakland.edu | www.meadowbrook.org | $8 | Tours Mon.–Sat. 1:30, Sun. 1:30 and 3:30).

The **Meadow Brook Theatre** is a respected university-run theater that puts on a wide variety of classic and modern plays. | Walton Blvd. and Squirrel Rd. | 248/377–3300 | www.oakland.edu | Early Oct.–mid-May.

ON THE CALENDAR

JUNE–AUG.: *Meadow Brook Music Festival.* This open-air concert series on the grounds of Oakland University's Meadow Brook attracts big-name entertainment, from pop to classical. The venue is the summer home of the Detroit Symphony Orchestra. | 248/567–6000 | www.palacenet.com.

Dining

Andiamo's Osteria. Italian. Here you're entertained by strolling musicians Monday and Tuesday, sax jazz Wednesday, and Rochester's answer to Frank Sinatra on Thursday. The rich Italian sauces and robust pasta dishes draw locals and visitors alike. | 401 W. Main St.

| 248/601–9300 | fax 248/601–2406 | ljump@andiamoitalia.com | www.andiamoitalia.com/aor.htm | No lunch Sat. or Sun. | $11–$27 | AE, MC, V.

Knapp's Dairy Bar. American. Knapp's doesn't get any fancier than a burger and a shake. The Formica-topped tables date from the 1950s at this eatery that's a favorite of Rochester families. | 304 Main St. | 248/651–4545 | No breakfast Sun. | $8–$12 | No credit cards.

Rochester Chop House. American. This classic restaurant has an enthusiastic local following. Try the grilled salmon Lawrence with lobster, shrimp, asparagus, and saffron cream sauce. Live piano Wed.–Sat. | 306 Main St. | 248/651–2266 | $10–$23 | AE, D, MC, V.

Lodging

Spartan Motel. Built in the 1950s, this two-story brown brick motel is the only motel in Rochester. Five blocks from downtown, it fronts Paint Creek Trail, a footpath used by local hikers and bicyclists. Cable TV. | 1100 N. Main | 248/651–8100 | fax 248/651–2741 | 46 rooms, 2 one-bedroom apartments | $48–$57 rooms, $70 1–bedroom apartments | AE, D, MC, V.

ROMULUS

MAP 10, B6

(Nearby town also listed: Ann Arbor, Dearborn, Detroit, Monroe, Plymouth, Ypsilanti)

Romulus, a west side suburb of Detroit that straddles I–94, is filled with chain hotels and fast-food restaurants. It's also home to Detroit Metropolitan–Wayne County Airport, one of the country's busiest.

Information: **Detroit Metro Convention and Visitors Bureau** | 211 W. Fort St., Ste. 1000, Detroit 48226 | 313/202–1800 or 800/DETROIT | rmonfort@visitdetroit.com. | www.visitdetroit.com.

Attractions

Belleville Area Museum. The museum was built in 1875 and was originally used as the Town Hall. It showcases artifacts, quilts, and old photos relating to the city's history, and is 7 mi east of Romulus. | 405 Main St., Belleville | 734/699–1944 | Free | Tues.–Sat. noon–4.

Dining

Amelia's. American. Savor the ribs in a Jack Daniel's sauce, spinach lasagna, or chicken baked with almonds and pineapple at this restaurant in the Doubletree Detroit Airport hotel. You also can choose from steak and pasta dishes. In the lounge you can watch a large-screen TV while eating lighter fare like burgers and sandwiches. Breakfast is also available. | 31500 Wick Rd. | 734/467–8000 | fax 734/721–8870 | www.hilton.com/doubletree/ | $10–$18 | AE, D, DC, MC, V.

Belleville Grille. American. In summer you can dock your boat at one of the five slips here, eat on the patio, and enjoy live entertainment while viewing Belleville Lake. Try coconut shrimp, Mesquite-grilled ribs, porterhouse steaks, or pasta del mar with shrimp, scallops, swordfish, marlin, and mussels. The restaurant is 7 mi east of Romulus. | 146 High St., Belleville | 734/699–1777 | Sun. brunch | $9–$22 | AE, D, DC, MC, V.

Salvatore Scallopini Italian Ristorante. Italian. The flower and fruit tablecloths add a homey touch to the dining room of this restaurant 14 mi east of Romulus. Specials are traditional favorites like osso buco, pasta, and lasagna. | 13499 Dix/Toledo Rd., Southgate | 734/246–5900 | $7–$13 | AE, MC, V.

Teasers. American. The second-largest brew pub in the state, 10 mi north of Romulus, brews seven beers on the premises. Check out the golf clubs and other golf paraphernalia on the walls while eating buffalo wings, sandwiches, meat loaf, steaks, or ribs. | 6677 N. Wayne Rd., Westland | 734/595–1988 | $10–$15 | AE, D, MC, V.

Lodging

Baymont Inn Detroit Airport. Less than a mi from Detroit Metro Airport, this three-floor hotel is north of I–94, off Exit 198. Complimentary Continental breakfast. In-room data ports, some microwaves, some refrigerators. Cable TV. Business services. Airport shuttle. Pets allowed. | 9000 Wickham Rd. | 734/722–6000 | fax 734/722–4737 | feedback@baymontinns.com | www.baymontinns.com | 81 rooms | $89–$99 | AE, D, DC, MC, V.

Comfort Inn–Metro Airport. This three-story hotel is north of Detroit Metro Airport, off I–94 at Exit 198. Restaurant, bar, complimentary Continental breakfast, room service. In-room data ports, some refrigerators, some in-room hot tubs. Cable TV. Laundry facilities, laundry service. Business services, airport shuttle. No pets. | 31800 Wick Rd. | 734/326–2100 or 800/228–5150 | fax 734/326–9020 | www.comfortinn.com | 123 rooms | $69–$199 | AE, D, DC, MC, V.

Courtyard by Marriott. This three-story hotel is near the airport and fast-food restaurants. Its signature courtyard makes for pleasant lobby and gazebo areas. Restaurant, bar. In-room data ports, some refrigerators. Cable TV. Indoor pool. Hot tub. Exercise equipment. Laundry facilities. Business services, airport shuttle, parking (fee). | 30653 Flynn Dr. | 734/721–3200 or 800/321–2211 | fax 734/721–1304 | www.courtyard.com | 146 rooms | $64–$124 | AE, D, DC, MC, V.

Crowne Plaza. Its upscale accommodations and proximity to the airport are this hotel's two best selling points. Its welcoming lobby and dramatic, 11-story atrium, which some rooms overlook, are also big pluses. It's 2 mi north of Detroit Metro Airport in a commercial area. Restaurant, bar. In-room data ports, cable TV. Indoor pool. Hot tub. Exercise equipment. Business services, airport shuttle. Some pets allowed. | 8000 Merriman Rd. | 734/729–2600 or 800/227–6963 | fax 734/729–9414 | detroitcrown@cs.com | www.holidayinn.com.ru/crowneplaza | 365 rooms | $130–$150. | AE, D, DC, MC, V.

Days Inn. This three-story hotel is your basic budget hotel. It's close to the airport and nearby eateries. Restaurant, complimentary Continental breakfast. Cable TV. Airport shuttle. | 9501 Middlebelt Rd. | 734/946–4300 | fax 734/946–7787 | www.daysinn.com | 127 rooms | $69–$99 | AE, D, DC, MC, V.

Doubletree Detroit Airport. Polished cherry pillars and beams stand in the entranceway of this four-story hotel north of I–94 at Exit 197. It's less than a mile from the airport. Restaurant, bar, room service. In-room data ports. Cable TV. Pool. Hot tub. Gym. Shops. Laundry service. Business services, airport shuttle. No pets. | 31500 Wick Rd. | 734/467–8000 | fax 734/721–8870 | www.hilton.com/doubletree/ | 263 rooms | $119–$159 | AE, D, DC, MC, V.

Hampton Inn. This three-story hotel is an economy choice near the airport. This property in a bustling commercial area is surprisingly quiet despite overhead air traffic. Complimentary Continental breakfast. In-room data ports. Cable TV. Pool. Business services, airport shuttle. | 30847 Flynn Dr. | 734/721–1100 | fax 734/721–9915 | internethamp@hiltonres.com. | www.hampton-inn.com | 136 rooms | $68–$109 | AE, D, DC, MC, V.

Hilton Suites. The Detroit airport area's only suite hotel has two-room suites with living areas and work spaces. Some suites have balconies. This hotel is less than 1 mi from the airport and restaurants. Complimentary cocktails every evening during the 5:30–7 manager's reception. Restaurant, bar, complimentary breakfast. In-room data ports, refrigerators. Cable TV, in-room VCRs (and movies). Indoor-outdoor pool. Hot tub. Exercise equipment. Laundry facilities. Business services, airport shuttle. | 8600 Wickham Rd. | 734/728–9200 | fax 734/728–9278 | www.hilton.com | 151 suites | $139–$179 | AE, D, DC, MC, V.

Marriott. This four-story hotel in a commercial area is near the airport, making it a favorite with airline travelers and personnel. Restaurant, bar. In-room data ports, minibars, some refrigerators. Cable TV. Indoor pool. Hot tub. Exercise equipment. Business services, airport shuttle. | 30559 Flynn Dr. | 734/729–7555 | fax 734/729–8634 | www.marriotthotels.com | 245 rooms | $159–$194 | AE, D, DC, MC, V.

Quality Inn. This single-story motel on the west side of town is near restaurants and car-rental agencies, and serves as a basic overnight stop near the airport. Bar, complimentary Continental breakfast. In-room data ports. Cable TV. Laundry facilities. Business services, airport shuttle. | 7600 Merriman Rd. | 734/728–2430 or 800/228–5151 | fax 734/728–3756 | www.qualityinn.com | 140 rooms | $59–$69 | AE, D, DC, MC, V.

Ramada Inn. This four-story hotel is close to the highways and restaurants. Restaurant, bar, room service. Cable TV. Indoor pool. Exercise equipment. Playground. Business services, airport shuttle. | 8270 Wickham Rd. | 734/729–6300 or 800/298–2054 | fax 734/722–8740 | www.ramada.com | 243 rooms | $79–$89 | AE, D, DC, MC, V.

ROSCOMMON

MAP 9, D5

(Nearby towns also listed: Gaylord, Grayling, Houghton Lake)

Roscommon is on the banks of the Au Sable River, only miles from crystal-clear pine-edged Higgins Lake. This area is rich in natural resources–you can canoe, hike, and go trout fishing. (*Note:* Area codes in this vicinity are scheduled to change to 989 beginning April 7, 2001.)

Information: **Roscommon Chamber of Commerce** | 701 Lake St., Roscommon 48653 | 517/275–2160 | fax 517/275–2029 | info@hlrcc.com | www.hlrcc.com.

Attractions

North Higgins Lake State Park. You can glimpse Michigan history at a Civilian Conservation Corps museum here, and a self-guided nature trail takes you through a state forest nursery dating back to 1903. The park also has a shallow swimming area and boat rentals. | 11252 N. Higgins Lake Dr. | 517/821–6125 or 800/447–2757 | dnr-suggestion-box@state.mi.us | www.dnr.state.mi.us/camping | $4 per car, per day | No camping Jan.–mid-Apr.

South Higgins Lake State Park. You can rent boats, hike, fish, and go scuba diving here. The swimming area has a gentle, gradual slope. The trails are good for walking in summer and cross-country skiing in snowy weather. | 106 State Park Dr. | 517/821–6374 or 800/447–2757 | dnr-suggestion-box@state.mi.us | www.dnr.state.mi.us/camping | $4 per car, per day | No camping Jan.–mid-Apr.

Dining

Fifth Street Grill. American. The menu changes weekly at this spot, but usually includes lamb, pork, and seafood. You can see the work of contemporary artists on the walls. | 104 N. 5th St. | 517/275–1515 | $16–$23 | AE, D, MC, V.

Tee Pee Restaurant. American. This rustic, family-style establishment serves everything from hot dogs to Mexican dishes to steaks. | 333 W. Federal Hwy. | 517/275–5203 or 800/420–5948 | $3–$9 | No credit cards.

Lodging

North Winds Motor Lodge. This cedar-sided motel has both standard rooms and a cabin that sleeps six. | 9123 N. Cut Rd. | 517/821–6972 | 14 rooms, 1 cabin | $35–$45, $250 per week for cabin | AE, D, MC, V.

ROYAL OAK

(Nearby towns also listed: Birmingham, Farmington/Farmington Hills, Detroit, Southfield, Troy)

Once a sleepy northern suburb of Detroit, Royal Oak is now known for its trendy restaurants, night spots, galleries, and boutiques. Royal Oak also is where you'll find the Detroit Zoo. There's a sizable antiques trade here, mostly along and just off Main Street.

Information: Royal Oak Chamber of Commerce | 200 S. Washington St., Royal Oak 48067 | 248/547–4000 | fax 248/547–0504 | info@virtualroyaloak.com | www.virtualroyaloak.com.

Attractions
Detroit Zoological Park. One of the first zoos in the country to incorporate barless exhibits, the Detroit Zoo is in suburban Royal Oak. More than 100 acres are filled with animals from around the world, including the 4-acre Chimps of Harambee and great ape exhibit, a penguinarium, a free-flight aviary, and a butterfly house/wildlife gallery. | 8450 W. Ten Mile Rd., Royal Oak | 248/399–7001 | www.detroitzoo.org | $7.50 | Apr.–Oct., daily 10–5; Nov.–Apr., daily 10–4.

ON THE CALENDAR
JULY: *Antique and Garage Sale.* The second weekend in July, the antiques and collectibles sale attracts nearly 340 vendors and 40,000 people to the Center Street Parking Structure. | 248/547–4000.
JULY: *Art in the Park.* Art lovers flock to this juried show of fine art, paintings, ceramics, and sculpture. It's held the first weekend in July at Memorial Park. | 13 Mile Rd. and Woodward Ave. | 248/547–4000.

Dining
Memphis Smoke. Barbecue. This relaxed restaurant serves up a slice of New Orleans with a Cajun flair. Known for its smoked pork ribs and pulled pork, it's a loud, brassy hot spot with tangy barbecue and blues entertainment Tuesday through Sunday. Southern-style ribs, beef brisket, and other meats slow-cooked over wood coals are among the menu highlights. Made-from-scratch desserts are a good topper. Kids' menu. | 100 S. Main St. | 248/543–4300 | $8–$15 | AE, D, DC, MC, V.

Lodging
Quality Inn Hazel Park. Two miles southeast of Royal Oak, this nine-floor hotel is off I–75 at the 9 Mile Road exit in Hazel Park. Some rooms have balconies overlooking the city. Restaurant, bar, room service. Some in-room hot tubs. Cable TV. Business services. Pets allowed. | 1 W. 9 Mile Rd., Hazel Park | 248/399–5800 | fax 248/399–2602 | www.qualityinn.com | 184 rooms | $66–$89 | AE, MC, V.

SAGINAW

(Nearby towns also listed: Bay City, Flint, Frankenmuth, Midland, Port Austin)

Once the lumber capital of the world, Saginaw now relies on the bumper crops of sugar beets and beans from its surrounding fields. Nearby General Motors plants have helped diversify the local economy and attract other industry. (*Note:* Area codes in this vicinity are scheduled to change to 989 beginning April 7, 2001.)

Information: **Saginaw County Convention and Visitors Bureau** | 1 Tuscola St., Ste. 101, Saginaw 48607 | 517/752–7164 or 800/444–9979 | info@saginawcvb.org | www.saginawcvb.org.

Attractions

Andersen Water Park and Wave Pool. Splash in this park's wave pool, zoom down its double water slide, and enjoy all its other watery attractions. | M–46 at Saginaw River off Fordney St. | 517/759–1386 | $5 | Memorial Day–Labor Day, daily 10–10.

Children's Zoo. This zoo is home to more than 20 species spread out over 8 acres. Timber wolves, red-tailed hawks, and train and pony rides are among the family favorites, as is the small petting area. | 1730 S. Washington Ave. | 517/771–4966 | $3.50 | Memorial Day–Labor Day, daily 10–5; Labor Day–Nov., weekends 10–5.

Heritage Theater at the Saginaw Civic Center. Built in the early 1970s, the theater hosts dramatic performances, dance, and musical concerts. | 303 Johnson St. | 517/759–1320 | $15–$40.

Historical Society of Saginaw County. A post office occupied the Society's French chateau-style building, known as the Castle, when it was built in 1897. Today, it houses both permanent and changing exhibits that trace the area's history from its founding by French explorers (hence the architectural style) to its modern reliance on the sugar-beet, bean, and automotive industries. | 500 Federal Ave. | 517/752–2861 | $1 | Tues.–Sat. 10–4:30, Sun. 1–4:30, closed Mon.

Japanese Cultural Center and Tea House. Saginaw's close ties to its sister city of Tokushima, Japan, helped to create this cultural center and friendship garden, the only one in the state. You can wander the serene gardens on Lake Linden, enjoy a traditional tea and snack, and tour several authentic Japanese buildings designed by architect Yataro Suzue. | 527 Ezra Rust Dr. | 517/759–1648 | Gardens free, tea house tour $3 | June–Sept., Tues.–Sat. 9–8; Apr.–May, Oct.–Nov., Tues.–Sat. 9–4.

Saginaw Art Museum. A Georgian Revival mansion from the turn of the century serves as the home to a collection that includes 19th- and 20th-century American art, Asian art, landscapes, contemporary prints, and textiles. A surrounding landscaped garden has been restored to its 1904 design. | 1126 N. Michigan Ave. | 517/754–2491 | saginawartmuseum@usa.net | www.members.xoom.com/saginawart | Free | Tues.–Sat. 10–5, Sun. 1–5.

Saginaw Railway Museum. This museum is in a train yard and 1906 depot. You can see a 1932 caboose, 3 diesel locomotives, and some boxcars, artifacts, and old pictures of the railroad. | 900 Maple St. | 517/793–6005 | $1 | Second and fourth Sun. of every month or by appointment 24 hours ahead.

Saginaw Valley State University. Some 8,600 undergraduate students attend this public university founded in 1963 and located in a semi-rural setting. The Detroit Lions hold their summer training camp here. | 7400 Bay Rd. | 517/790–4000 | www.svsu.edu | Free | Daily.

   Marshall M. Fredericks Sculpture Gallery. Works by this prolific Michigan sculptor are here and there throughout the state, most notably in Detroit, where his *Spirit of Detroit* stands in front of the City-County Building. This gallery on the campus of Saginaw Valley State University includes more than 200 original plaster models as well as freestanding sculptures and photographs of large pieces from around the world. | 2250 Pierce Rd. | 517/790–5667 | panhorst@svsc.edu | www.svsu.edu/mfsm | Free | Tues.–Sun. 1–5, closed Mon.

ON THE CALENDAR

JUNE–AUG.: *Saginaw Harness Raceway.* High-spirited horse-racing attracts equine enthusiasts during the warm months. | 2701 E. Genesee Ave. | 517/755–3451 | www.saginawraceway.com.

JUNE: *Greek Festival.* Spicy food and lots of lively dancing lead the list of attractions at this annual ethnic event at St. Demetrios Church. | 800/444–9979.

JULY–AUG.: *Friday Night Live Series.* On six consecutive Friday nights, hear free live performances of Motown, country, and classic rock at Morley Plaza on Washington Avenue. See a complimentary movie at the Temple Theater next door. | 517/771–2409.

SEPT.: *Saginaw County Fair.* This classic 4-day country fair at the Saginaw fairgrounds includes food, midway rides, and agricultural and livestock displays. | 800/444–9979.

Dining

Café Suz. American. Burgundy, gold, and navy blue accents surround you while you choose from prime rib, whitefish, salmon, and walleye. The spinach quesadillas are a hit. | 6099 Gratiot Rd. | 517/791–2343 | Closed Mon. | $5–$29 | D, MC, V.

Montague Inn. Contemporary. Chandeliers and white linen add elegance to the dining room of this 1929 brick mansion. Ask for the bay window table for views of the Saginaw River while you dine on filet mignon, lobster tail stuffed with salmon mousse, or pork tenderloin beneath walnuts and red currant demi glace. | 1581 S. Washington Ave. | 517/752–3939 | montagueinn@aol.com | www.montagueinn.com | No lunch Sun.–Mon., no dinner Sun. | $16–$24 | AE, MC, V.

Lodging

Cousins Bed and Breakfast. This inn sits on a landscaped acre filled with wildflowers and pine trees. The two suites have Victorian furnishings and original fine art. Breakfast is served on a glass-enclosed sun porch. Complimentary breakfast. Some refrigerators. Some in-room VCRs, no TV in some rooms. Business services. No pets. No smoking. | 4694 Brockway Rd. | 517/790–1728 | fax 517/790–3440 | www.rodeodesigns.com/cousins | 2 suites | $125–$150 | D, MC, V.

Four Points by Sheraton. Country French describes this six-story hotel is ¾ mi from the Fashion Square Mall. Restaurant, bar, room service. Cable TV. Indoor-outdoor pool. Hot tub, sauna. Business services, airport shuttle. Some pets allowed. | 4960 Towne Centre Rd. | 517/790–5050 | fax 517/790–1466 | www.fourpoints.com | 156 rooms | $99–$129 | AE, D, DC, MC, V.

Hampton Inn. On the north side of Saginaw, this two-story property is 1 mi from the Fashion Square Mall. Some of the rooms have sofas, easy chairs, and desks. Complimentary Continental breakfast. Cable TV. Pool. | 2222 Tittabawassee Rd. | 517/792–7666 | fax 517/792–3213 | www.hampton-inn.com | 120 rooms | $63–$74 | AE, D, DC, MC, V.

Montague. Antiques, Oriental rugs, and a library distinguish this inn from the competition. The 1929 Victorian-style mansion sits on 6½ acres of landscaped grounds that slope gracefully to Lake Linden. Dining room, complimentary Continental breakfast. Cable TV. Lake. | 1581 S. Washington Ave. | 517/752–3939 | fax 517/752–3159 | montagueinn@aol.com | www.montagueinn.com | 18 rooms (two with shared bath) | $55–$160 | AE, MC, V.

Saginaw Comfort Suites. A half mile west of I–675 at Exit 6, this three-story hotel is two blocks from the Fashion Square Mall. Complimentary Continental breakfast. In-room data ports, microwaves, refrigerators. Cable TV. Pool. Hot tub. Laundry service. Business services. No pets. | 5180 Fashion Square Blvd. | 517/797–8000 | fax 517/797–8000 | www.comfort-suites.com | 66 rooms | $60–$131 | AE, D, DC, MC, V.

Super 8. This three-story budget motel is 2 blocks from the Fashion Square Mall. Cable TV. Some pets allowed. | 4848 Town Centre Rd. | 517/791–3003 | fax 517/791–3003 | www.super8.com | 62 rooms | $38–$52 | AE, D, DC, MC, V.

ST. CLAIR

MAP 9, F7

(Nearby town also listed: Detroit, Port Huron, Warren)

Settled by the British in the 1700s, this lovely town on the St. Clair River was once, like many other towns in 19th-century Michigan, a lumbering center. Today, it's a place to stroll along the boardwalk and watch freighter traffic on the river or shop in a variety of antiques and specialty shops.

Information: **St. Clair Chamber of Commerce** | 505 N. Riverside Ave., St. Clair 48079 | 810/329–2962 | www.stclairchamber.com.

Attractions

Boardwalk. At 1,500 ft, the longest freshwater boardwalk in America stretches along the St. Clair River and is a popular recreational venue for bikers, walkers, and fishermen, day and night. From this vantage point you can watch ocean-going freighters passing to and from Lakes Huron and Erie. Enter the park through Palmer Park, on Riverside Ave., across the street from downtown shopping in Riverside Plaza. | 810/329–2962 | www.stclair-chamber.com | Free | Daily.

St. Clair Historical Museum. Once an old Baptist church, the museum has photographs of ships built in the city, textiles and clothing, period toys, and other artifacts. See dioramas of 19th-century kitchens and bedrooms. | 308 S. 4th St. | 810/329–6888 | Free | Tues. 9:30–noon, weekends 1:30–4:30.

ON THE CALENDAR

JUNE: *St. Clair Art Fair.* Face painting, caricature drawing, and live music accompany this juried art show in Palmer Park and Riverview Plaza the last weekend in June. | 810/329–9576 | www.stclairart.org.

Dining

Pepper Joe's. Steak. Eat in a booth inside or on a deck overlooking the Pine River. Wood trim, ceramic tile floor, and coarse rugs create a southwestern look. Choose from steaks, ribs with six different homemade sauces, Italian dishes, or fried perch with bay scallops and shrimp served over angel hair pasta. Dock your boat here. | 119 Clinton Ave. | 810/326–1710 | $5–$29 | AE, MC, V.

River Crab. Seafood. This casual, nautically themed restaurant is a favorite of boaters. Entrées include the classic Charley's Chowder and loads of fresh fish—such as the trademark potato-encrusted whitefish—all served with tasty homemade rolls. The Sunday brunch has everything from cold shrimp and smoked fish to hot quiche, omelets, and apple dumplings. An enclosed porch and deck seat about 100. Entertainment includes live jazz during Sunday brunch, and in summer, music out on the deck Wednesdays to Fridays. Kids' menu. Early bird suppers. | 1337 N. River Rd. | 810/329–2261 | rivercrab@muer.com | www.muer.com/rivercrab.html | $14–$39 | AE, D, DC, MC, V.

St. Clair Inn. Continental. A Michigan landmark since 1926, this elegant, English Tudor-inspired inn on the St. Clair River is known for gracious waterfront dining and for its prime rib, pastas, and porterhouse steak. Adventurous diners might like the pecan-crusted chicken breast with raspberry sauce. Top it all off with a piece of key lime pie, a menu favorite. There are views of the river from every table. Accommodations are available. Friday and Saturday evenings you can dine to the sound of live piano music. Kids' menu. | 500 N. Riverside Ave. | 810/329–2222 | stclairinn@firststep.net | www.stclairinn.com | $25–$32 | AE, D, DC, MC, V.

Lodging

River Crab Blue Water Inn. This three-story hostelry on the St. Clair River, next door to the River Crab Restaurant, is popular with boaters. You can also spend time fishing at the boat dock in front of the hotel. All the rooms overlook the river and are done in distinctive motifs, including Colonial, marine, and there's an Asian room with an oriental cherrywood canopy bed. The inn, built in the 1950s, is tucked into a residential neighborhood. Restaurant (*see* River Crab Restaurant), bar, complimentary Continental breakfast. Refrigerators. Cable TV. Pool. Business services. | 1337 N. River Rd. | 810/329–2236 or 800/468–3727 | fax 810/329–6056 | dbauer@muer.com. | www.muer.com | 21 rooms | $75–$92 | AE, D, DC, MC, V.

St. Clair Inn. It's a short walk to the boardwalk and restaurants from this Tudor-style hostelry. This inn, constructed in 1926, has panoramic waterfront views of the St. Clair River and Canada. Restaurant, bar (with entertainment), room service. Cable TV. Indoor pool. Hot tub. | 500 N. Riverside Ave. | 810/329–2222 or 800/482–8327 | fax 810/329–2348 | stclairinn@first-step.net | www.stclairinn.com. | 96 rooms | $75–$140 | AE, D, DC, MC, V.

William Hopkins Manor. This stately 1876 mansion stands across the street from the St. Clair River. The first floor has two parlors with fireplaces, a sun room, and a game room. Rooms are individually appointed with period antiques and some have river views. Walk to area restaurants. Complimentary breakfast. No room phones, no TV. Massage. No pets. No smoking. | 613 N. Riverside Ave. | 810/329–0188 | fax 810/329–6239 | whmanor@aol.com | www.laketolake.com/whmanor/ | 5 rooms | $80–$100 | MC, V.

ST. IGNACE

MAP 9, D3

(Nearby towns also listed: Brevort, Mackinaw City, Mackinac Island, Sault Ste. Marie)

ST. IGNACE

INTRO
ATTRACTIONS
DINING
LODGING

On the Straits of Mackinac, St. Ignace is the gateway to the Upper Peninsula. During the course of its rich history, it has been home to Native Americans, French fur traders, and British soldiers. Today, it is a vacation destination and departure point for ferries to Mackinac Island from the Upper Peninsula. (*Note:* Area codes in this vicinity are scheduled to change to 989 beginning April 7, 2001.)

Information: **St. Ignace Area Chamber of Commerce** | 560 N. State St., St. Ignace 49781 | 906/643–8717 or 800/338–6660 | www.stignace.com.

Attractions

Castle Rock. This ancient lookout of the Ojibwa Indians, often referred to as Pontiac's lookout, rises 195.8 ft above water level and provides panoramic views of the forests and waters of the Mackinac region. It's just 3 mi north of downtown St. Ignace. | I–75, Exit 348 | 906/643–8268 | www.stignace.com/attractions | May–Oct.

Father Marquette National Memorial and Museum. This park 2 mi northwest of the Mackinac Bridge includes a small museum honoring the life and work of Jacques Marquette, the Jesuit explorer and missionary. On display are artifacts from Marquette's journeys, Native American articles (including a longhouse and a canoe), and educational programs on Marquette and area history. | 720 Church St. | 906/643–9394 | www.sos.state.mi.us/history/museum/musemarq | $4 per car, per day | Mid-June–late Sept., daily 9:30–8.

Fort deBuade Indian Museum. Native American and Colonial artifacts from the 18th-century and before are here in this 1681 fort. There's military paraphernalia, clothing, trade goods, and an art gallery of paintings, etchings, and photographs. | 334 N. State St. | 906/643–6642 | www.avwd.com/debuade | $2.50 | May 30–Oct. 1, daily 9–9.

Mackinac Island Ferries. These three family-run ferries run regular 15–20-min. trips to Mackinac Island from St. Ignace: **Arnold Transit Company** | 906/847–3351 or 800/847–3892 | fax 906/847–3892 | tonyfrazier@portup.com | www.arnoldline.com | $14.50 round-trip | May–Dec., daily.

    Shepler's Mackinac Island Ferry | 231/436–5023 or 800/828–6157 | fax 231/436–7521 | sheplers@freeway.net | $14.50 round-trip | Early May–Oct., daily.

    Star Line Ferry | 590 N. State St., St. Ignace | 231/436–5045 or 800/638–9892 | fax 906/643–9856 | www.mackinacferry.com | $14.50 round-trip | May–Oct., daily.

Marquette Mission Park and Museum of Ojibwa Culture. Believed by many to be the final resting place of Marquette, the park includes a statue honoring him, information about his life, and a restored Victorian-style garden. An adjacent 19th-century Jesuit church contains art and artifacts relating to Ojibway culture, including objects of this Native American people dating back as far as 6000 BC. | 500 N. State St. | 906/643–9161 | www.stignace.com/attractions/ojibwa | $2 | Memorial Day–June, Mon.–Sat. 11–5, Sun. 1–5; July–Labor Day, daily 10–8.

Mystery Spot. This popular site 5 mi west of U.S. 2 and the Mackinac Bridge is about 300 ft in diameter. It was discovered by three surveyors from California in the 1950s who experienced unusual optical and sensory illusions only within the confines of the site, thus its name. You can experience these illusions—and gravity seemingly gone haywire—for yourself. | 150 Martin Lake Rd. | 906/643–8322 | www.stignace.com/attractions | $5 | Mid-May–June, 9–8, June–Labor Day, 8AM–9PM, Labor Day–Oct., 9–7; closed Nov.–mid-May.

ON THE CALENDAR
JULY: *French Heritage Days.* Actors portray upper Great Lakes 18th-century pioneers through encampments, demonstrations, dance, and music. | 800/338–6660 | www.sos.state.mi.us/history/museum/musemarq/.

Dining
Dockside Restaurant. American. You can see a panoramic view of Lake Huron from here, and the Best Western Georgian House is next door. Live Maine lobster, whitefish, and prime rib are house specialties. | 1101 N. State St. | 906/643–7911 | $10–$24 | AE, D, MC, V.

The Galley. American. Thick steaks, Cajun-style catfish, and other hearty favorites have made this an area favorite for more than a half century. This casual dining spot on the shores of Lake Huron has excellent views of the straits. The Galley is best known for its whitefish and roasted prime rib. | 241 N. State St. | 906/643–7960 | Open 24 hours | Closed Oct.–Apr. | $8–$26. | D, MC, V.

Little Bob's New Frontier. American. A covered wagon sits atop the roof of this restaurant. The dining room has Old West memorabilia. Home-cooked fried chicken, buffalo steaks, barbecue ribs, prime rib, perch, and pasta are specialties. Breakfast is also available. | 3021 Mackinac Trail | 906/643–3512 | $7.50–$13 | AE, D, DC, MC, V.

Mackinac Grille. American. This restaurant at Star Line Ferry Dock has unobstructed views of Mackinac Island and the surrounding waters of Lake Huron. Choose from pasta, ribs, steaks, and lake whitefish. Breakfast is also available. | 251 S. State St. | 906/643–7482 | $8–$16 | AE, MC, V.

Taste of the Upper Peninsula. American. Pasties and fudge are the two "Yooper" specialties here. Try the seasonal fudge flavors, vanilla and chocolate amaretto, or chocolate and butter pecan. Pasties are filled with meat (turkey or beef) or vegetables. | 914 U.S. 2 W | 906/643–9734 | kmassey@portup.com | www.stignace.com/business/tasteUP/ | $3–$5 | D, MC, V.

Lodging
Aurora Borealis. This two-story hotel near I–75 caters to senior citizens with special rates. It's 2 blocks from the ferry landing, and there's a restaurant next door. Many rooms have views of the water. Cable TV, room phones. | 635 U.S. 2 W | 906/643–7488 or 800/462–6783 | 56 rooms | $49–$89 | Closed Nov.–Apr. | D, MC, V.

Bay View Beachfront Resort. This single-story motel in a commercial area has a garden and views of Lake Huron. It was built in the 1940s. Picnic area. Cable TV. Beach. Airport shuttle. | 1133 N. State St. | 906/643–9444 | 23 rooms | $28–$60 | Closed Nov.–Apr. | D, MC, V.

Best Western Georgian House. This full-service chain hotel has lots to occupy families heading for Mackinac Island. Picnic area. In-room data ports. Cable TV. Indoor pool. Hot tub. Miniature golf. Playground. Laundry facilities. Business services. | 1131 N. State St. | 906/643–8411 or 800/780–7234 | fax 906/643-8924 | www.bestwesternmichigan.com | 85 rooms in 2 buildings | $54–$148 | AE, D, DC, MC, V.

Boardwalk Inn. Built in 1928, this hotel across the street from the boardwalk is the city's oldest. Some rooms have views of Mackinac Island, quilts, and hand-painted floral decorations on the walls. Complimentary Continental breakfast. Cable TV, no room phones. No pets. No smoking. | 316 N. State St. | 906/643–7500 or 800/254–5408 | info@boardwalkinn.com | www.boardwalkinn.com | 12 rooms | $54–$119 | AE, D, MC, V.

Budget Host Golden Anchor. This hotel is 1 mi north of the Mackinac Bridge and a block from the ferries. Some rooms have private balconies or decks with stunning views of Lake Huron. The Huron boardwalk is within walking distance, as are shops, restaurants, the beach, and a museum. In-room data ports, some refrigerators, in-room hot tubs. Cable TV. Indoor pool. Hot tub. Playground. Business services. Some pets allowed. | 700 N. State St. | 906/643–9666 | fax 906/643–9126 or 800/872–7057 | stay@stignacebudgethost.com | www.stignacebudgethost.com | 56 rooms | $55–$170 (suites) | AE, D, DC, MC, V.

Colonial House Bed and Breakfast. A yellow 1840 Victorian, this home has been a B&B since 1940. The inn sits across from the boardwalk and Arnold Ferry in downtown St. Ignace. You can see the Mackinac Straits from the wraparound porch and second floor veranda. Four-poster beds and antiques, some dating to the 18th-century, add a special charm. A simpler motel-style section is next door. Complimentary breakfast. Cable TV, no room phones. No pets. No smoking. | 90 N. State St. | 906/643–6900 | chi@30below.com | www.colonial-house-inn.com | 6 rooms in B&B; 11 rooms in motel | $79–$119 for B&B; $49–$59 for motel | D, MC, V.

Comfort Inn. Many of this beachfront hotel's rooms have lake views. It's about ½ mi to the Mackinac Bridge and Mackinac Island ferries. Picnic area, complimentary Continental breakfast. Refrigerators. Cable TV. Indoor pool. Hot tub. Exercise equipment. Beach. Playground. Laundry facilities. Business services. | 927 N. State St. | 906/643–7733 or 800/228–5150 | fax 906/643–6420 | www.comfortsuites.com | 100 rooms | $128–$168 | AE, D, DC, MC, V.

Days Inn and Suites. You can view Lake Huron and Mackinac Island from this chain hotel that's within walking distance of downtown St. Ignace. There's free shuttle service to Mackinac Island ferries and the Kewadin Casino in Sault Ste. Marie. Complimentary Continental breakfast. Cable TV. 2 indoor pools. Hot tub, sauna. Video games. Laundry facilities. | 1067 N. State St. | 906/643–8008 or 800/388–7829 | fax 906/643–9400 | www.daysinn.com | 110 rooms | $44–$149 (suites) | AE, D, DC, MC, V.

Harbour Pointe. Nightly bonfires on this motor inn's 800-ft beach are a highlight of a stay here. In the morning you can walk to the ferry. Picnic area, complimentary Continental breakfast. Some refrigerators. Cable TV. 2 pools (1 indoor). 3 hot tubs. Beach. Playground. Laundry facilities. Business services, airport shuttle. | 797 N. State St. | 906/643–9882 or 800/642–3318 | fax 906/643–6946 | sales@harbourpointe.com | www.harbourpointe.com | 123 rooms | $110–$198 | AE, D, MC, V.

Holiday Inn Express. Many rooms at this hotel on Lake Huron have water views. In winter you can snowmobile from the property. Complimentary Continental breakfast. Some in-room hot tubs. Cable TV. Pool. Spa. Beach. Laundry service. No pets. | 965 N. State St. | 906/643–0200 or 800/906–0201 | www.basshotels.com/holiday-inn | 35 rooms | $88–$135 | AE, D, DC, MC, V.

Howard Johnson Express. This two-story hotel on the southwest side of St. Ignace is ½ mi from the ferries and has a 24-hour shuttle to the Kewadin Casino in Sault Ste. Marie. You can rent one of the hotel's snowmobiles in winter. Complimentary Continental breakfast. Cable TV. Indoor pool. Hot tub. Video games. Laundry facilities. Some pets allowed. | 913 Boulevard Dr. | 906/643–9700 | fax 906/643–6762 | helmera@up.net | www.hojoexpress.net | 57 rooms | $89–$129 | AE, D, DC, MC, V.

K Royale Motor Inn. You can relax on a nice deck and beach at this three-story property on the north side of town in a commercial area. Picnic area, complimentary Continental breakfast. Refrigerators. Cable TV. Indoor pool. Hot tub. Video games. Beach. Playground. Laundry facilities. Airport shuttle. | 1037 N. State St. | 906/643–7737 or 800/882–7122 | fax 906/643–8556 | cmuscott@portup.com | www.stignace.com/lodging/kroyale | 95 rooms | $39–$79 | Closed Nov.–Mar. | D, MC, V.

Kewadin Inn. This single-story property motel on the north side of town has a free shuttle to the Kewadin Casino in Sault Ste. Marie. Picnic area. Cable TV. Pool. Playground. | 1140 N. State St. | 906/643–9141 | fax 906/643–9141 | 71 rooms | $49–$65 | AE, D, DC, MC, V.

Northern Host Inn. This basic two-story motel was built in the 1950s and is 1 mi north of the downtown shops. Picnic area. In-room data ports, some refrigerators. Cable TV. Indoor pool. Hot tub. Playground. | 1030 N. State St. | 906/643–8060 or 800/752–3454 | fax 906/643–7251 | 58 rooms | $42–$92 | Closed Nov.–Apr. | AE, D, DC, MC, V.

Rodeway Inn. Off I–75 at Exit 344A, the hotel is at the Mackinac Bridge. Some rooms open onto the pool. Complimentary Continental breakfast. Some microwaves, some refrigerators, some in-room hot tubs. Cable TV. Pool. Hot tub. No pets. | 750 U.S. 2 W | 906/643–8511 | fax 906/643–6358 | rodeway@northernway.net | www.rodeway.com/hotel/mi713 | 42 rooms | $59–$125 | AE, D, MC, V.

Tradewinds. This motel overlooking Lake Huron has a beautifully landscaped courtyard. It's 3 mi from the Mackinac Bridge and the Kewadin Casino, and the Mackinac County Airport is 500 ft away. Picnic area. Cable TV, no room phones. Pool. Playground. Airport shuttle. | 1190 N. State St. | 906/643–9388 or 800/677–8162 | fax 906/643–7253 | www.stignace.com/lodging/tradewinds | 25 rooms | $36–$56 | Closed Nov.–Apr. | MC, V.

ST. JOSEPH

MAP 9, B8

(Nearby towns also listed: Douglas, Kalamazoo, New Buffalo, Niles, Paw Paw, Saugatuck, South Haven)

Formerly a way station for travelers between Detroit and Chicago, this town in the state's southwest corner lies on the St. Joseph River and Lake Michigan. Specialty stores attract shoppers to downtown, and nearby Warren Dunes State Park draws nature lovers.

CAR RENTAL TIPS

- ❑ Review auto insurance policy to find out what it covers when you're away from home.
- ❑ Know the local traffic laws.
- ❑ Jot down make, model, color, and license plate number of rental car and carry the information with you.
- ❑ Locate gas tank—make sure gas cap is on and can be opened.
- ❑ Check trunk for spare and jack.
- ❑ Test the ignition—make sure you know how to remove the key.
- ❑ Test the horn, headlights, blinkers, and windshield wipers.

*Excerpted from *Fodor's: How to Pack: Experts Share Their Secrets*
© 1997, by Fodor's Travel Publications

Information: Cornerstone Alliance | 38 W. Wall St., Benton Harbor 49022 | 616/925–6100 | fax 616/925–4471 | gvaughn@cstonealliance.org | www.cstonealliance.org/.

Attractions

Curious Kids Museum. One of the best children's museums in the state despite its small size, this colorful museum with murals by a local artist lets kids serve customers in a mock diner, pick apples from simulated trees, type their names in braille, and listen to a Teddy bear's heartbeat. | 415 Lake Blvd. | 616/983–2543 | www.curiouskidsmuseum.org | $3.75 | Wed.–Sat. 10–5, Sun. 12–5.

Krasl Art Center. This lakeside attraction displays works by regional artists, folk art and crafts, and up to 10 traveling exhibits a year from across the country. The permanent Krasl collection consists of outdoor sculptures. | 707 Lake Blvd. | 616/983–0271 | info@krasl.org | www.krasl.org | Free | Mon.–Fri., Sun. 1–4, Sat. 10–4.

Warren Dunes State Park. Winding streams, old forests, and meadows blanketed by wildflowers make this 1,952-acre preserve an unforgettable outdoor experience. One of southwest Michigan's most visited parks, it has more than 2 mi of shoreline and sand dunes towering more than 200 ft above Lake Michigan. You can go swimming or hiking, use the picnic areas and playground, or visit the concession stand. Nearby Warren Woods has 200 acres of virgin forest. | 12032 Red Arrow Hwy. | 616/426–4013 or 800/447–2757 | fax 616/426–7829 | www.dnr.state.mi.us/camping | $4 per car, per day | Daily dawn to dusk.

ON THE CALENDAR

MAY: *Blossomtime Festival.* Western Michigan salutes spring with this early May event in and around St. Joseph. A blessing of the blossoms, a blossom ball, a grand floral parade, and other horticultural events make up the festivities. | 616/925–6301 | www.blossomtimefestival.org/.
JULY: *Lake Bluff Art Fair.* St. Joseph's Lake Bluff Park, on downtown's Lake Boulevard, attracts hundreds of exhibitors and thousands of art lovers for this two-day event in mid-July. | 616/925–6301 | www.krasl.org/.
JULY: *Venetian Festival.* Lighted boat parades, fireworks, concerts, land and water competitions, and other family fun will beckon you to downtown St. Joseph during the third weekend in July. There also are sand-castle competitions, food booths, and art exhibits. | 616/925–6301 | www.venetian.org.
SEPT.: *Tri-State Regatta.* This race that draws more than 200 sailors starts in Chicago on Friday night of Labor Day weekend and ends its first leg in St. Joseph. Here a festival celebrates the sailors' arrival with arts and crafts booths, a farmers market, and live music. | 616/982–0032 | www.stjoesailing.com.

Dining

Grand Mere Inn. Contemporary. Stunning sunsets over Lake Michigan and an antiques-filled dining room set this eatery apart from the crowd. The bar area houses the owner's quirky collection of Michigan-related memorabilia. The food is equally impressive. Choose from lake perch or barbecued ribs on the menu or one of the daily specials. Entertainment. | 5800 Red Arrow Hwy., Stevensville | 616/429–3591 | Closed Sun. | $10–$16 | AE, DC, MC, V.

Port Authority. American. Nearby Lake Michigan is the inspiration for the nautical motif at this friendly, family-style dining establishment. Don't miss the open-hearth specialties or the delectable house salad. Kids' menu. Sun. brunch. Karaoke Wed.–Sat. | 105 Main St. | 616/983–2334 | $12–$23 | AE, D, MC, V.

Schuler's of Stevensville. American. Established in 1908, Schuler's has a long history of catering to Michigan families. Regulars come for the appetizers like the barbecued meatballs, mushroom soup, and the famous soft-spread bar cheese. Other highlights include the whitefish and prime rib. Kids' menu. Sun. brunch. | 5000 Red Arrow Hwy., Stevensville | 616/429–3273 | info@schulersrest.com | www.schulersrest.com | $23–$34 | AE, D, DC, MC, V.

Tabor Hill Winery. Contemporary. The winery's restaurant is on a hill overlooking the vineyards. In winter ask for a seat near the fieldstone fireplace. Try raspberry chicken with pecans, mesquite-grilled shrimp, salmon baked in grape leaves served with a Hollandaise sauce, or rabbit. The winery has 10 to 20 wines, depending on the year. | 185 Mt. Tabor Rd., Buchanan | 800/283–3363 | fax 616/422–2787 | info@taborhill.com | www.taborhill.com | May–Nov. closed Mon.–Tues., Dec.–Apr. closed Mon.–Thurs. | $15–$20 | AE, D, MC, V.

Tossi's. Italian. Established in 1948, this restaurant with wooden chandeliers and exposed beams is in a large house surrounded by landscaped gardens. Choose from brick-oven pizza, eggplant manicotti, lasagna with wild mushrooms, charcoal-grilled steaks, or salmon in a tomato and basil sauce. | 4337 Ridge Rd., Stevensville | 616/429–3689 or 800/218–7745 | No lunch weekends; Nov.–Mar. no lunch | $15–$30 | AE, D, MC, V.

Lodging

Benton Hotel and Suites. In a commercial area off I-94, this hotel is 4 mi from the Krasl Art Center and beaches. Restaurant, bar, room service. Cable TV. Indoor-outdoor pool. Hot tub. Exercise equipment. Business services. | 2860 Rte. 139 S, Benton Harbor | 616/925–3234 | fax 616/925–6131 | 150 rooms | $40–$90 | AE, D, DC, MC, V.

Boulevard All Suite. You'll be near downtown parks and beaches at this seven-story, all-suite lakefront hotel. It's 4 blocks from Lake Michigan and 1 block from the Curious Kids Museum and Krasl Art Center. You'll find attractive, stylistic touches in the guest and public rooms. Restaurant, bar. Refrigerators. Cable TV. Business services. | 521 Lake Blvd. | 616/983–6600 or 800/875–6600 | fax 616/983–0520 | 85 suites | $145–$205 | AE, D, MC, V.

Chestnut House Bed and Breakfast. Gardens surround this 1924 Craftsman house on a bluff overlooking Lake Michigan. Rooms have antiques, four-poster beds, and oak floors. Eat breakfast in the solarium, and on Saturday evenings, sample appetizers by the parlor fireplace. Complimentary breakfast. Some in-room hot tubs. Cable TV. Pool. No pets. No smoking. | 1911 Lake Shore Dr. | 616/983–7413 | fax 616/983–2122 | flcare@aol.com | www.bbonline.com/mi/chestnut | 5 rooms | $105–$130 | D, MC, V.

Comfort Inn. This single-story chain motel is off I-94 in downtown Benton Harbor. Complimentary Continental breakfast. Some refrigerators. Cable TV. Indoor pool. Hot tub. Business services. Some pets allowed. | 1598 Mall Dr., Benton Harbor | 616/925–1880 | comfortinn@portup.com | www.comfortinn.com | 52 rooms | $73–$113. | AE, D, DC, MC, V.

Courtyard by Marriott. This two-story chain hotel encircles an attractive courtyard. It's on the outskirts of Benton Harbor near I-94. Picnic area. In-room data ports. Cable TV. Indoor-outdoor pool. Exercise equipment. Business services. Free parking. | 1592 Mall Dr., Benton Harbor | 616/925–3000 | fax 616/925–8796 | www.courtyard.com/ | 98 rooms | $79–$129 | AE, D, DC, MC, V.

Days Inn. Lake Michigan fishing charter boats and golfing are 5 mi away from this two-story chain hotel. Its 50-ft heated pool is an added bonus. Complimentary Continental breakfast, room service. Some refrigerators. Cable TV. Indoor pool. Hot tub. Laundry facilities. Business services. | 2699 Rte. 139 S., Benton Harbor | 616/925–7021 | fax 616/925–7115 | www.daysinn.com/ | 120 rooms | $49–$99 | AE, D, DC, MC, V.

Holiday Inn Express. Just off I-94 at Exit 29, this three-floor chain hotel is 3 mi southeast of St. Joseph and 1 mi from Lake Michigan College. Complimentary Continental breakfast. In-room data ports, some kitchenettes, some refrigerators, some in-room hot tubs. Cable TV. Pool. Spa. Laundry service. No pets. | 2276 Pipestone Rd., Benton Harbor | 616/927–4599 | fax 616/927–4699 | www.basshotels.com/holiday-inn | 79 rooms | $89–$129 | AE, D, DC, MC, V.

St. Joseph Golden Link Lodge. At this single-story hostelry you'll be close to Lake Michigan as well as to a bustling commercial area. Complimentary Continental breakfast. Some refrigerators. Cable TV. Pool. | 2723 Niles Ave. | 616/983–6321 | fax 616/983–7630 | 36 rooms | $31–$62 | AE, D, DC, MC, V.

South Cliff Inn Bed and Breakfast. This cottage-like B&B, in a residential neighborhood 1 mi south of downtown, has antique and contemporary furnishings. Some rooms have whirlpools, fireplaces, and balconies with lake views. See the sunset from the gardens and decks. Complimentary breakfast. Some refrigerators. Cable TV. No pets. No smoking. | 1900 Lake Shore Dr. | 616/983–4881 | fax 616/983–7391 | www.southcliffinn.com | 7 rooms | $85–$195 | AE, D, MC, V.

Super 8. There's no-frills lodging at this three-story chain hotel on the outskirts of Benton Harbor. It's near Lake Michigan and I–94. Cable TV. Business services. Some pets allowed. | 1950 E. Napier Ave., Benton Harbor | 616/926–1371 | fax 616/926–1371, ext. 169 | 62 rooms | $39–$46 | AE, D, DC, MC, V.

SAUGATUCK

(Nearby towns also listed: Douglas, Grand Haven, Holland, St. Joseph, South Haven)

Saugatuck is a well-known art colony at the mouth of the Kalamazoo River that attracts visitors from Detroit and Chicago, including a sizable gay population. Among its charms are more than 35 bed and breakfast inns, a 19th-century downtown area, and nearby state parks with dunes and abundant beaches.

Information: Saugatuck-Douglas Visitors and Convention Bureau | 1902 Blue Star Hwy., Douglas 49406 | 616/857–1701 | fax 616/857–2319 | www.saugatuck.com.

Attractions

Fenn Valley Vineyards and Wine Cellar. This small, family-owned winery sits in the rolling hills of southwestern Michigan. Self-guided tours let you learn about the wine-making process and view the cellars. A picnic area is the perfect spot for a tasting. | 6130 122nd Ave. | 616/561–2396 | www.fennvalley.com | Free | Mon.–Sat. 10–5, Sun. 1–5.

***Keewatin* Marine Museum.** This restored passenger steamer once plied the Great Lakes for the Canadian Pacific Railroad. Today, it serves as a marine museum with everything from the ornate cabins and furnishings to the meticulously kept engine room on display. | 219 Union St. | 616/857–2464 | $4 | Memorial Day–Labor Day, daily 10:30–4:30.

Saugatuck Dune Rides. Your driver will no doubt yell "I lost the brakes," but it's all in a day's fun on these rides over the breathtaking Saugatuck dunes. | Blue Star Hwy., ½mi west of I–196, Exit 41 | 616/857–2253. | $11.50 | May–mid-Sept., Mon.–Sat. 10–5, Sun. 12–5; mid-Sept.–mid-Oct., weekends only 12–5.

Star of Saugatuck. You embark on 60- or 90-minute narrated tour on this 82-passenger sternwheeler, which travels the Kalamazoo River to Lake Michigan. | 716 Water St. | 616/857–4261 | $9 | Memorial Day–Labor Day, daily cruises at 11, 1, 3, 5, and 8.

Wicks Park. You can view the harbor while picnicking here under the Victorian gazebo. | Water St. and Mary St.

ON THE CALENDAR

APR.–SEPT.: *Allegan Antiques Market.* More than 300 exhibitors from around the country sell their goods on Sundays at the Allegan County fairgrounds. | 616/453–8780 | Sun. 7:30–4.

JULY: *Harbor Days/Venetian Nights.* A lighted boat parade, fireworks at dusk, and other waterfront fun attract locals and visitors on the last Sunday in July at the harbor. | 616/857–8851.

AUG.: *Taste of Saugatuck*. The city's best restaurants gather for a street festival on Water Street, the last Sunday in August, running from noon to 7 PM. Food booths, open-air entertainment, and more are on tap. | 616/857–1701.

OCT.: *Annual Goose Festival*. This townwide celebration includes arts and crafts, free entertainment, a parade, and a wildlife art show. | 616/561–5550.

OCT.: *Gallery Stroll*. Participating galleries in downtown Saugatuck and nearby Douglas open their doors on the first weekend of the month to packs of roving art enthusiasts. There are refreshments and music by area performers. | 616/857–1557.

Dining

Belvedere Restaurant. Contemporary. Hardwood floors, chandeliers, and fireplaces grace three dining rooms in this 1913 mansion. Begin your dinner with sautéed brie with almonds and honey, then choose roast duck, pork chops, filet mignon, or ravioli stuffed with duck, pecan, and ricotta as your entrée. | 3656 63rd St. | 616/857–5777 or 877/858–5777 | fax 616/857–7557 | www.thebelvedereinn.com | June–Labor Day closed Sun.–Tues.; Labor Day–May closed Sun.–Wed. | $16–$24 | MC, V.

Chequers. English. This pub/restaurant in downtown Saugatuck has dark paneling and British sporting paraphernalia on the walls. Its fare includes fish and chips, the ploughman's platter with a selection of cheeses accompanied by bread and English pickle relishes, and classic shepherd's pie. Not surprisingly, the bar stocks the area's largest selection of British brews. | 220 Culver St. | 616/857–1868 | Reservations not accepted | $10–$20 | AE, DC, MC, V.

Loaf and Mug. American. Grab a few tasty sandwiches for an impromptu picnic on the beach or sit a spell in one of two charming dining areas, one inside and one out. Soups and pastas are served in round homemade bread bowls. The eatery also is known for its ribbon sandwich, which layers egg and tuna salad sandwiches on top of each other, and BBQ. The garden patio seats up to 70. Entertainment June to August. Kids' menu. | 236 Culver St. | 616/857–2974 | No supper Sun.–Thurs. | $13–$21 | AE, D, MC, V.

Restaurant Toulouse. French. Enjoy a bit of sunny Provence in western Michigan. Named after artist Henri Toulouse-Lautrec, the restaurant takes its inspiration from both his work and homeland. Whitewashed walls lined with art and cozy tables for two in front of a roaring fireplace make it a romantic favorite. Menu staples include wild mushrooms duxelles with saffron cream sauce and a casserole of beef, lamb, pork, duck, and white beans. There's a summer patio, where you can enjoy your meal under umbrellas. | 248 Culver St. | 616/857–1561 | Closed Jan. and Feb., Mon.–Wed. | $25–$40 | AE, D, DC, MC, V.

Lodging

Bay Side Inn. A renovated 1927 boathouse in downtown on the Kalamazoo River, the inn has rooms with contemporary furniture and private balconies facing the city or water. Four rooms are efficiencies with fireplaces. Eat breakfast on a patio overlooking the river. Complimentary Continental breakfast. Some kitchenettes. Cable TV. Spa. No pets. No smoking. | 618 Water St. | 616/857–4321 or 800/548–1870 | fax 616/857–1870 | www.bbonline.com/mi/bayside | 10 rooms | $95–$235 | AE, D, MC, V.

Belvedere Inn. This 1913 stone mansion sits on five acres of landscaped grounds and gardens. Hardwood floors, armoires, and four-poster beds fill the rooms, all of which have views of the grounds. Restaurant, complimentary breakfast. TV in common area. Pond. No pets. No smoking. | 3656 63rd St. | 616/857–5777 or 877/858–5777 | fax 616/857–7557 | www.thebelvedereinn.com | 10 rooms | $160–$295 | MC, V.

Holiday Inn Express Saugatuck. Some of the larger rooms here have king-sized beds, fireplaces, and views of the woods. One mile from I-196, Exit 41, this two-floor hotel is next to a golf course and 1/2 mi from Saugatuck Dune Rides. Complimentary Continental breakfast. In-room data ports, refrigerators, some in-room hot tubs. Cable TV. Pool. Hot tub. Gym. Laundry service. Business services. No pets. | 3457 Blue Star Hwy. | 616/857–7178 | fax 616/857–7169 | www.holidayinn.com.ru/ | 38 rooms, 14 suites | $149–$169 | AE, D, DC, MC, V.

Lake Shore Resort. At this single-story hostelry 3 mi south of Saugatuck you can hike nature trails in a wooded area or bicycle. If you prefer, you can enjoy the lake on the resort's private beach. Cable TV. Pool. lake. Beach. | 2885 Lake Shore Dr. | 616/857–7121. | fax 616/857–4656 | 30 rooms | $75–$140 | Closed Nov.–Apr. | MC, V.

Maplewood Hotel. Upscale traditional touches, including many antiques, adorn this three-story Greek Revival hotel in downtown. Complimentary breakfast. Cable TV. Pool. No smoking. | 428 Butler St. | 616/857–1771 or 800/650–9790 | fax 616/857–1773 | info@maplewoodhotel.com | www.virtualcities.com/ons/mi/ | 15 rooms (11 with shower only) | $130–$185 | AE, MC, V.

Park House. The Greek Revival-style house that's this hostelry's main building was built in 1857 and is the oldest residence in Saugatuck. Pine floors and stenciled walls give the place a distinctly New England appearance. Relax by the fireplaces in some rooms or on the screened porch. Picnic area, complimentary breakfast. Some room phones, TV in some rooms, TV in common area. Business services. | 888 Holland St. | 616/857–4535 or 800/321–4535 | fax 616/857–1065 | info@parkhouseinn.com. | www.parkhouseinn.com | 9 rooms, 3 suites, 4 cottages | $95–$165, $165 suites, $125–$225 cottages | AE, D, MC, V.

Rosemont Inn Bed and Breakfast. This romantic Victorian retreat was built in the early 1900s. Gas fireplaces, antiques, and country-style accents adorn the rooms. A long veranda and gazebo allow you to relax and take in the Lake Michigan views. The grounds are beautifully landscaped with a waterfall garden. Complimentary breakfast. In-room data ports. Cable TV. Pool. Hot tub, sauna. Beach. Business services. No kids allowed. No smoking. | 83 Lake Shore Dr. | 616/857–2637 or 800/721–2637. | www.saugatuck.com | 14 rooms | $125–$305 | AE, D, MC, V.

Shangrai-La. You can stroll through the landscaped grounds of this single-story motel built in the mid-1950s. Though it's in a wooded country area, it's only 3 mi to area restaurants and shopping. Picnic area. In-room VCRs (and movies). Pool. | 6190 Blue Star Hwy. (U.S. 2 A) | 616/857–1453 or 800/877–1453 | fax 616/857–5905 | www.saugatuck.com/sbonline/shangraila | 20 rooms | $90–$145 | Closed Jan. | AE, D, MC, V.

Sherwood Forest. This red, Victorian-style B&B, built in the early 1900s, is in a tranquil, wooded area a half block from the beach. Don't miss the pool during the warm months. At the bottom of the pool there's a mural of a sunken ship surrounded by a rainbow of tropical fish. The innkeepers occasionally stage Monopoly tournaments. Picnic area, complimentary breakfast. In-room VCRs (and movies), no room phones, no TV in some rooms, TV in common area. Pool. Hot tub. Bicycles. No smoking. | 938 Center St. | 616/857–1246 or 800/838–1246 | fax 616/857–1996 | sherwoodforest@hayburn.com | www.sherwoodforestbandb.com | 5 rooms, 1 cottage | $90–$125, $165 cottage | D, MC, V.

Timberline Motel. You can enjoy a stroll and other recreation at this motel on several wooded acres 1 mi north of downtown. Picnic area. Some in-room hot tubs. Cable TV. Pool. Hot tub. Volleyball. Playground. | 3353 Blue Star Hwy. (U.S. 2A) | 616/857–2147 or 800/257–2147 | timberlinemotel@softhouse.com | www.timberlinemotel.com | 29 rooms | $50–$95 | AE, D, MC, V.

Twin Gables Country Inn. A long front porch catches your eye when you see this B&B overlooking Kalamazoo Lake. You'll find a spacious common room with large wood-burning fireplaces, a reading area and cable TV with a VCR. Additionally, the Twin Gables has 2 beautifully landscaped acres for strolling and a pond. Picnic area, complimentary breakfast. No room phones, no TV in rooms, TV in common area. Pool. Hot tub. Business services. Airport shuttle. | 900 Lake St. | 616/857–4346 or 800/231–2185 | fax 616/857–1092 | 14 rooms, 3 cottages | $68–$165, $125–$200 cottages | AE, D, MC, V.

Wickwood Country Inn. Cookbook author Julee Rosso-Miller (*The Silver Palate*) and her husband, Bill, have bedecked the common areas of their bed and breakfast with their favorite things, such as French and English antiques, oriental rugs, overstuffed chairs, flowers, and original art and sculptures. Guest rooms in the two-story house, built in 1925, are eclectically furnished. All have private baths and many have fireplaces. Breakfast or brunch is served in the Garden Room. You'll also get to sample Julee's snacks and hors d'oeuvres. Complimentary breakfast. No room phones. Library. Business services. | 510 Butler St. | 616/857–1465 or 800/385–1174 | fax 616/857–1552 | innkeeper@wickwoodinn.com | www.wickwoodinn.com | 11 rooms | $195–$305 | MC, V.

SAULT STE. MARIE

MAP 9, D2

(Nearby towns also listed: Newberry, Paradise, St. Ignace)

Settled in the 1620s, the Upper Peninsula's Sault Ste. Marie (better known simply as "the Soo") is the state's oldest town. It's home to the Soo Locks, one of the greatest engineering feats in the United States, as well as to railways, highways, and bridges linking the city with its Canadian twin of the same name. (*Note:* Area codes in this vicinity are scheduled to change to 989 beginning April 7, 2001.)

Information: Sault Ste. Marie Convention and Visitors Bureau | 2581 I–75 Bus. Spur, Sault Ste. Marie, 49783 | 906/632–3301 or 800/MI–SAULT | info@saultstemarie.com. | www.saultstemarie.com.

Attractions

Brimley State Park. The Upper Peninsula's oldest park includes a 270-site campground with large, grassy sites, mini-cabin rentals, and a swimming beach on Lake Superior's Whitefish Bay. Brimley has the warmest swimming water of any state park on Lake Superior and is popular with anglers in search of northern pike and walleye. There's a spectacular view of the Canadian highlands from Six Mile Road, 1 mi east of Brimley. | 9200 W. Six Mile Rd., Brimley | 906/248–3422 or 800/447–2757 | www.dnr.state.mi.us/camping | $4 per car, per day | Daily dawn to dusk.

Kewadin Casino. One of the state's first casinos run by Native Americans, Kewadin Casino continues to be the largest casino in northern Michigan, with over 2,300 slots, and an attached restaurant, hotel and convention center. | 2186 Shunk Rd. | 800/539–2346 or 906/632–0530 | Free | Daily, 24 hrs.

Lake Superior State University. On a hill overlooking the city, this pretty, 3,000-student campus includes many buildings that were once part of Fort Brady. The library's Marine Collection is considered one of the best on Great Lakes shipping. | 650 W. Easterday Ave. | 906/632–6841 | fax 906/635–2111 | www.lssu.edu | Free | Daily.

Museum Ship *Valley Camp* and Great Lakes Maritime Museum. This retired 11-ton freighter was launched in 1917 in Ohio and logged 3 million mi before being taken out of service in 1966. Today, it's the world's largest maritime museum, with three levels and 100 exhibits that explore life—and death—at sea. Other highlights include a marine hall of fame, six aquariums, and a display on the wreck of the *Edmund Fitzgerald*. | 501 E. Water St. | 906/632–3658 | fax 906/632–9344 | shipstore@sault.com | www.soohistoricinc.sault.com/valleycomp.htm | $6.50 | July–Aug., daily 9–9; May–June, Sept.–Oct., daily 10–6.

Soo Locks. A true man-made wonder, the Soo Locks make up the largest waterway traffic system on Earth. A series of three locks—MacArthur, Poe, and Davis—provides huge ships with passage around the rapids of the St. Mary's River, where water falls more than 20 ft from Lake Superior to the lower lakes. On-site there's a visitor center with a working model of a locks, films on the locks' history, and other exhibits. | Soo Locks Ave. | 906/632–2394 | www.huron.lre.usace.army.mil/SOO/soohmpg.html | Free | Daily.

Soo Locks Boat Tours. These two-hour narrated excursions take you through the locks alongside massive ocean-going freighters. You'll hear tales of the locks and colorful Soo-area history. Dinner cruises also are available. | Dock #1, 1157 E. Portage Ave.; dock #2, 515 E. Portage Ave. | 906/632–6301 or 800/432–6301 | fax 906/632–1811 | sales@soolocks.com | www.soolocks.com. | $15 | Mid-May–mid-Oct.

Soo Locks Tour Trains. Take a one-hour train ride, originating across from the Corps of Engineers Park, through the Soo and over the International Bridge. Stops along the way include the 21-story Tower of History and the museum ship *Valley Camp*. | 315 W. Portage Ave. | 800/387–6200 | $5.25 1-hr. tour, $9.75 for 2-hr. tour | Memorial Day–mid-Oct., daily.

Tower of History. Panoramic views of the locks, the St. Mary's River, and the city's historical sites are three good reasons to ride the express elevator to the top of this 21-story downtown structure. Artifacts and a videotape in the tower's lower level show the history of the Soo and the Great Lakes. | 326 E. Portage St. | 906/632–3658 | www.soohistoricinc.sault.com/towerofhistory.html | $3.25 | Mid-May–Oct., daily 10–6.

ON THE CALENDAR
JUNE–JULY: *Soo Locks Festival.* Celebrate Canada Day (July 1), Independence Day, and Engineers' Day (the last Friday in June) when the locks are opened to the public. Enjoy live performances, parades, and activities from the last week in June through the first week in July. | 906/632–3301 | www.soolocksfestival.com.

AUG.: *Chippewa County Fair.* Primarily an agricultural fair with livestock competitions, tractor pulls, and antique tractor and car shows, this fair also has a full midway, a demolition derby, mud runs, an arts and crafts exhibit, and lots of delicious homemade foods. The fair begins the second week in August and continues through Labor Day at the Chippewa County Fairgrounds, 15 mi south of Salt Ste. Marie. | 906/495–5915.

SAULT STE. MARIE

INTRO
ATTRACTIONS
DINING
LODGING

Dining
Abner's. American. For 25 years this local favorite 1 mi south of downtown has been known for its hand-cut steaks and all-you-can-eat backwoods buffet of baked whitefish and prime rib. You can also get a variety of sandwiches and burgers all day. | 2865 I–75 Bus. Spur | 906/632–4221 | Breakfast also available | $6–$20 | AE, MC, V.

The Antler's. American. Antlers are just one of the wildlife-themed accents in this rustic lodge-like bar. Housed in a building dating from the 1800s, it also displays full-size stuffed animals, fishing gear, and other outdoor paraphernalia. Besides its well-known burgers— try the Paul Bunyan—the menu is packed with Mexican specialties as well as homemade breads and desserts. Kids' menu. | 804 E. Portage Ave. | 906/632–3571 | $9–$19 | AE, D, MC, V.

Cup of the Day. Café. A popular downtown specialty coffee shop, it also has panini sandwiches, pitas, and wraps. | 406 Ashmun St. | 906/635–7272 | fax 906/632–1621 | www.cupofthe-day.com/local.html | $4–$5.50 | MC, V.

Dream Catchers Restaurant. Seafood. On the "trail" at Kewadin Casino between the hotel and Bawating Gallery of Woodland Native art, this restaurant has escargot, shrimp pizza, whitefish, and salmon. A seafood buffet is available on Friday and Saturday nights, or you can order sandwiches, burgers, pasta, steaks, or barbecued ribs. Breakfast is also available. | 2186 Shunk Rd. | 906/635–1400 | www.kewadin.com | $8–$20 | AE, D, DC, MC, V.

Freighters. Continental. Watching enormous freighters from all over the world navigate the Soo Locks is the top entertainment at this eatery in the Ojibway Hotel. The dining room has fresh flowers, white tablecloths, and a menu studded with lots of fresh fish, including an excellent whitefish. Though this place is known for seafood and prime rib, the Louisiana chicken and sausage gumbo is worth a try. Kids' menu. Sun. brunch. | 240 W. Portage St. | 906/632–4211 | $25–$31 | AE, D, DC, MC, V.

La Señorita. Mexican. With three locations in northern Michigan, La Señorita is a lively Mexican cantina with colorful Latin art. While south-of-the-border fare such as enchiladas, tacos, and chimichangas are the stars, there also are a few American entrées. Kids' menu. | 4478 I–75 Bus. Spur | 906/632–1114 | www.michiweb.com/lasenorita | $16–$22 | AE, D, DC, MC, V.

Mancino's Pizza and Grinders. Pizza. The chefs make their own crusts and sauces here. Specials of the house are pizza, grinders, and salads. The Italian combo is a grinder with sausage, ham, salami, veggies, and cheese. | 4422 I–75 Bus. Spur | 906/635–8000 | $6–$9 | No credit cards.

Studebaker's. American. Pictures of cars line the walls here. The menu has Italian and Mexican as well as American dishes, but the lake whitefish and weekend buffets are the most popular choices. | 3583 I–75 Bus. Spur | 906/632–4262 | $9–$18 | AE, D, MC, V.

Lodging

Bambi Motel. Two miles from Exit 392 off I–75, this motel is 1 mi south of the Soo Locks. Picnic area. Some refrigerators. Cable TV. Pool. Playground. Pets allowed. | 1801 Ashmun St. | 906/632–7881 or 800/289–0864 | www.saultstemarie.com/accom/bambi/bambi.html | 25 rooms | $39–$65 | MC, V.

Best Western Colonial Inns. This chain hotel is 2½ mi from downtown, off I–75. The hotel has tickets for Soo Locks boat tours and the train to Agawa Canyon. There's a free casino shuttle. Complimentary Continental breakfast. In-room data ports, refrigerators. Cable TV. Indoor pool. Sauna. Video games. Laundry facilities. Business services. | 4281 I–75 Bus. Spur | 906/632–2170 or 800/297–2858 | fax 906/632–7877 | www.bestwestern.com | 112 rooms | $79–$99 | AE, D, DC, MC, V.

Budget Host Crestview Inns. You'll be close to attractions, restaurants, and shopping at this single-story motel downtown. In-room data ports. Cable TV. Some pets allowed. | 1200 Ashmun St. | 906/635–5213 or 800/955–5213 | fax 906/635–9672 | www.saultstemarie. com/accom/crestv/ | 44 rooms | $39–$59 | AE, D, DC, MC, V.

Comfort Inn. This two-story chain hotel is just off I–75. Complimentary Continental breakfast. Cable TV. Pool. | 4404 I–75 Bus. Spur | 906/635–1118 or 800/228–5150 | fax 906/635–1119 | 86 rooms | $64–$94 | www.comfortinn.com | AE, D, DC, MC, V.

Days Inn. This two-story chain hotel is a favorite of business and vacation travelers. It's close to the Soo Locks and Lake Superior State University. In-room data ports. Cable TV. Indoor pool. Hot tub. Video games. Laundry facilities. | 3651 I–75 Bus. Spur | 906/635–5200 or 800/ 388–7829 | fax 906/635–9750 | days@sault.com | www.daysinn.com | 84 rooms | $69–$140 | AE, D, DC, MC, V.

Doral Motel. The Soo Locks and the *Valley Camp* Museum Ship are across the street from this small, two-story motel. Picnic area. Cable TV. Pool. Hot tub, sauna. Video games. | 518 E. Portage Ave. | 906/632–6621 or 800/998–6720 | fax 906/632–8214 | 20 rooms | $62–$70 | Closed Nov.–Apr. | D, MC, V.

Hampton Inn Sault Ste. Marie. This chain hotel is 1 mi north of I–75 at Exit 392, 2 mi south of the Soo Locks. Complimentary Continental breakfast. In-room data ports, refrigerators, some in-room hot tubs. Cable TV. Pool. Hot tub. Business services. No pets. | 3295 I–75 Bus. Spur | 906/635–3000 | fax 906/635–0034 | www.hampton-inn.com | 82 rooms | $79–$89 | AE, D, DC, MC, V.

Holiday Inn Express Sault Ste. Marie. Rooms here have views of the St. Mary's River and the bridge connecting the U.S. to Canada. The hotel is at I–75, Exit 394. Complimentary Continental breakfast. In-room data ports, some kitchenettes, some in-room hot tubs. Cable TV. Pool. Hot tub. Gym. Laundry service. Business services. No pets. | 1171 Riverview Way | 906/632–3999 or 800/592–7879 | fax 906/632–9633 | www.basshotels.com/holiday-inn | 97 rooms | $89–$109 | AE, D, DC, MC, V.

Kewadin Casino Hotel. This six-floor hotel is connected to the casino. The Bawating Gallery of Native American art is also here. Some rooms have whirlpools in the bedrooms. The three-room suites have whirlpools in the baths. Restaurant, bar, room service. Some microwaves, some refrigerators, some in-room hot tubs. Cable TV. Pool. Hot tub, sauna. Gym. Shops. Business services. No pets. | 2186 Shunk Rd. | 906/635–1400 or 800/KEWADIN | www.kewadin.com | 320 rooms | $79–$119 | AE, D, DC, MC, V.

Lawson Motel. This two-story motel is in a commercial area and 4 mi from the Kewadin Casino. Some refrigerators, cable TV. Airport shuttle. | 2049 Ashmun St. | 906/632–3322 or 800/457–8536 | fax 906/632–4234 | www.saultstemarie.com/accom/lawson | 16 rooms | $36–$68 | AE, D, MC, V.

Quality Inn. The Soo Locks are 2 mi away, and the Soo Shopping Plaza is next door to this two-story chain hotel. Restaurant, bar, room service. Cable TV. Indoor pool. Hot tub. Exercise equipment. Playground. Business services. | 3290 I–75 Bus. Spur | 906/635–1523 or 899/228–5151 | fax 906/635–2941 | www.qualityinn.com | 130 rooms | $65–$99 | AE, D, DC, MC, V.

Ramada Plaza Ojibway. Period pieces furnish this hotel dating from 1928 that overlooks the Soo Locks. The six-story property attracts both business and pleasure travelers. Restaurant, bar. In-room data ports, some in-room hot tubs. Cable TV. Indoor pool. Hot tub, sauna. Business services. | 240 W. Portage St. | 906/632–4100 or 800/654–2929 (Mich. only) | fax 906/632–6050 | RamadaPlaza@ojibwayhotel.com | www.ojibwayhotel.com | 71 rooms | $139–$155 | AE, D, DC, MC, V.

Super 8. Budget-minded travelers frequent this two-story hotel. In a commercial area, it's 3 mi to the Soo Locks, and 2 mi to the casino. Complimentary Continental breakfast. Cable TV. Laundry facilities. Some pets allowed. | 3826 I–75 Bus. Spur | 906/632–8882 or 800/800–8000 | fax 906/632–3766 | www.super8motels.com | 61 rooms | $40–$68 | AE, D, DC, MC, V.

SOUTHFIELD

MAP 10, C4

SOUTHFIELD

INTRO
ATTRACTIONS
DINING
LODGING

(Nearby towns also listed: Dearborn, Detroit, Farmington/Farmington Hills, Pontiac, Warren)

A northwest Detroit suburb, Southfield is among the state's largest business centers, with local headquarters for IBM and other Fortune 500 companies as well as four universities. Northland Center, the nation's first regional shopping mall, is also here.

Information: Southfield Chamber of Commerce | 17515 W. 9 Mile Rd., Ste. 750, Southfield 48075 | 248/557–6661 | fax 248/557–3931 | info@southfieldchamber.com | www.southfieldchamber.com.

Attractions

Cranbrook Institute of Science. Laser-light shows, a large rock and mineral collection, and Native American artifacts are the big draws at this popular science museum. Besides the planetarium, there are also an observatory, a physics hall, and national touring exhibits, many from the Smithsonian. It's on the campus of the Cranbrook Educational Community. There you can also see an art academy and museum, as well as an English Manor with gardens. (*See also* Bloomfield Hills.) | 39221 N. Woodward | 248/645–3200 | www.cranbrookscience.org | $7. | Sun.–Thurs., Fri. 10–10, Sat. 10–5.

ON THE CALENDAR

JUNE: *Jazz Festival.* On the first Saturday and Sunday of the month hear live jazz performed on the front lawn of the Southfield Municipal Complex. Tickets are required. | 26000 Evergreen Rd. | 248/354–1000.

Dining

Beans and Cornbread. Soul. Lined with *Life* magazine photos of notable African-Americans, the restaurant serves up meaty chicken wings, spicy catfish, savory greens, and tangy ribs. There also are upscale dishes such as shrimp and wild mushroom fritters with tomato sauce, and escargots in puff pastry. Kids' menu. | 29508 Northwestern Hwy. | 248/208–1680 | $11–$18 | D, MC, V.

Golden Mushroom. Continental. Excellent food, expert service, and an extensive wine cellar are the hallmarks of this local institution. Menu stalwarts include Dover sole, a velvety mushroom soup, game dishes, and fettuccine with truffles. Downstairs is the more relaxed—and less expensive—Mushroom Cellar. Here you'll find lighter fare such as burgers and pastas. Parking (fee). | 18100 W. 10 Mile Rd. | 248/559–4230 | Closed Sun. No lunch Sat. | $35–$55 | AE, D, DC, MC, V.

Le Metro. Continental. Traditional bistro-style cooking characterizes this delightful spot in an otherwise undistinguished strip mall. There's often a wait even if you have reservations. Signature dishes include the potato-crusted whitefish and pan-seared salmon. Entertainment Wed. and Thurs. Early bird suppers. | 29855 Northwestern Hwy. | 248/353–2757 | $15–$22 | AE, D, DC, MC, V.

Morton's of Chicago. Steak. The Windy City meets the Motor City in this classic, Chicago-style steak house. The white tablecloths and a dimly lit dining room set the right tone. Everything here seems oversized, from the huge baked potatoes and the giant cigars in private humidors to the gargantuan steaks. If you get tired of red meat, the menu includes fresh seafood. | 1 Town Sq. | 248/354–6006 | No lunch | $20–$33 | AE, DC, MC, V.

Musashi Japanese Cuisine. Japanese. This upscale restaurant is committed to providing an authentic experience of Japanese food and culture. You can dine sitting Japanese- or Western-style, while the kimono-wearing staff serve specialties such as filet mignon teriyaki, shrimp tempura, the sushi and sashimi-filled bento box, or the delicacy Wagyu beef, which is cooked tableside. The restaurant is in the center of the town's Fortune 500 district. | 2000 Town Center, Ste. 98 | 248/358–1911 or 888/358–1911 | fax 248/358–2530 | No lunch weekends | $12.50–$25 | AE, DC, MC, V.

Sweet Lorraine's Cafe. Contemporary. Almost always crowded, this bistro has colorful walls with vintage posters and a globally inspired menu. Daily specials might include a Spanish paella, French pot pie, or spicy Texas pork loin. Other options are the pecan chicken, shrimp Creole, and the vegetarian meat loaf. | 29101 Greenfield Rd. | 248/559–5985 | $14–$23 | AE, D, DC, MC, V.

Tom's Oyster Bar. Seafood. As the name suggests, Tom's is an area favorite for its extensive oyster selection. Don't miss the spicy crawfish bisque, the many fresh fish dishes, and lobster fest on Tuesday nights. The walls are done in dark paneling covered by lots of old *New Yorker* covers. There's open-air dining on a flower-filled patio. Live piano bar Monday to Thursday, live jazz Fridays and Saturdays. Kids' menu. | 29106 Franklin Rd. | 248/356–8881 | $15–$27 | AE, D, DC, MC, V.

Lodging

Candlewood Suites. You'll have use of many little extras at this downtown hotel, which is within walking distance of all central businesses. The generously sized rooms, with white, maroon, and blue color schemes, include a CD player and clock-radio, two phone lines, and complimentary use of the washers and dryers. In-room data ports, some kitchenettes. Cable TV, in-room VCRs. Exercise equipment. Shops. Laundry facilities. no pets. | 26655 Lois La. | 248/945–0010 | fax 248/945–0115 | www.candlewoodsuites.com | 121 rooms, suites | $69–$114 rooms, $89–$135 suites | AE, D, DC, MC, V.

Courtyard by Marriott. This three-story chain hotel surrounds an extensively landscaped courtyard. It's in the heart of busy Southfield, and there's a Hertz rental car office right next door. Restaurant. In-room data ports. Cable TV. Indoor pool. Hot tub. Exercise equipment. Laundry facilities. Business services. | 27027 Northwestern Hwy. | 248/358–1222 or 800/321–2211 | fax 248/354–3820 | www.courtyard.com/ | 147 rooms | $69–$124 | AE, D, DC, MC, V.

Hampton Inn. This two-story chain hotel on busy Northwestern Highway is surrounded by corporate headquarters. The Tel-Twelve Mall is 1 mi away, as are several restaurants. Picnic area, complimentary Continental breakfast. In-room data ports. Cable TV. Indoor pool. Hot tub. Exercise equipment. Laundry facilities. Business services. | 27500 Northwestern Hwy. | 248/356–5500 | fax 248/356–2083 | www.hampton-inn.com | 153 rooms | $79–$89 | AE, D, DC, MC, V.

Hilton Garden Inn. A business traveler's first choice, this 6-story hotel with nice amenities is off busy I–696 and the Lodge Freeway (U.S. 10). There are private sitting areas in the lobby, and a garden lounge, as well as a sun deck. The rooms have multiple phone lines. Restaurant, bar. In-room data ports. Cable TV. Indoor pool. Hot tub. Exercise equipment. Business services. Some pets allowed. | 26000 American Dr. | 248/357–1100 or 800/445–8667 | fax 248/799–7030 | www.hilton.com | 197 rooms | $120–$170 | AE, D, DC, MC, V.

Holiday Inn. This 16-story chain hotel in a circular glass tower is popular with business travelers. It has a Holidome recreation center, and is 2 mi from a shopping mall, 5 mi from the Detroit Zoo, and 15 mi from the Henry Ford Museum. Restaurant, bar, room service. Cable TV. Indoor pool. Beauty salon, hot tub. Video games. Laundry facilities. Some pets allowed. | 26555 Telegraph Rd. | 248/353–7700 | fax 248/353–8377 | gm201@:columbiasussex.com | www.basshotels.com/holiday-inn | 415 rooms | $75–$99 | AE, D, DC, MC, V.

Marriott. In the heart of the Southfield business district, minutes from downtown, this six-story hotel has seven meeting rooms, which makes it popular with corporate travelers. Restaurant, bar. In-room data ports, refrigerators. Cable TV. Indoor pool. Hot tub. Exercise equipment. Business services. | 27033 Northwestern Hwy. | 248/356–7400 or 800/228–9290 | fax 248/356–5501 | www.marriothotels.com | 226 rooms | $115–$165 | AE, D, DC, MC, V.

Marvins Garden Inn. This 2-story hotel built in 1985 is known for its spacious guest rooms and reasonable rates. Restaurants and area attractions are 5–15 mi. Complimentary Continental breakfast. Cable TV. | 27650 Northwestern Hwy. | 248/353–6777 | fax 248/353–2944 | 110 rooms | $45–$56 | AE, D, DC, MC, V.

Ramada Inn. Rooms here have either a king-size bed or two doubles, a redwood desk and table, and dark green carpeting. The chain hotel is across the street from IBM, FOX 2 News, and a health club, which is complimentary for Ramada guests. Restaurant, bar, room service. In-room data ports, some in-room hot tubs. Cable TV. Pool. Exercise equipment. no pets. | 17017 W. Nine Mile Rd. | 248/552–7777 or 800/298–2054 | fax 248/552–7778 | www.ramada.com | 221 | $102–$112 | AE, D, MC, V.

Westin Southfield–Detroit. At this 12-story hotel in the heart of the Fortune 500 district, you'll sleep on the popular "heavenly" bed, a high-quality mattress with a layered mattress cover, down comforter, and five pillows. Rooms also have an oversized desk and lounge chair. The contemporary furnishings include dark red velvety curtains and moss green, red, and beige hues accenting the bedding and carpeting. Restaurant, bar, room service. In-room data ports, some in-room hot tubs. Cable TV. Indoor pool. Hot tub, sauna. Health club. Baby-sitting, children's programs (0–12). | 1500 Prudential Town Ctr. | 248/827–4000 | fax 248/827–1364 | www.westin.com | 388 rooms | $139–$20 | AE, D, DC, MC, V.

SOUTH HAVEN

MAP 9, B7

(Nearby towns also listed: Douglas, Holland, Kalamazoo, Paw Paw, Saugatuck, St. Joseph)

Beachfront and blueberries make South Haven a well-known spot to the denizens of southwest Michigan and northeastern Illinois. The town was once a major port for the 19th-century steamships from Chicago that brought summer vacationers seeking relief from the heat. This history and more can be seen in the city's Michigan Maritime Museum. If you visit during August, stop by the National Blueberry Festival. Any other time of year, check out The Blueberry Store in town, which sells sweet treats.

Information: **South Haven Lakeshore Convention and Visitors Bureau** | 415 Phoenix St., South Haven 49090 | 616/637–5252 | fax 616/637–8710 | info@southhaven.org | www.southhavenmi.com.

Attractions

Liberty Hyde Bailey Birthsite Museum. The former home of horticulturist Dr. Liberty Hyde Bailey now contains family-related memorabilia and farmstead artifacts. One of the earliest houses in South Haven, it is a National Historic Site. | 903 S. Bailey Ave. | 616/637–3251 | Free | Tues., Fri., Sun. 2–4:30, Sat. 10–4.

Michigan Maritime Museum. One of the state's largest maritime museums, this South Haven attraction brings to life the stories of the people who built and sailed boats on the Michigan's Great Lakes and waterways. Displays include accounts from passenger steamers that once crossed Lake Michigan, maps, artifacts, marine art, and a U.S. Coast Guard exhibit. | 260 Dyckman Ave. | 616/637–8078 | fax 616/637–1594 | mmmuseum@accn.org | www.michiganmaritimemuseum.org | $2.50 | May–Oct., Tues.–Sat. 10–5, Sun. 12–5, closed Mon.

Van Buren State Park. This 407-acre park has almost 1 mi of Lake Michigan frontage. It is 6 mi from the Kal-Haven Trail State Park, a rails-to-trails route between Kalamazoo and South Haven that is a favorite of cyclists and cross-country skiers. Picnic areas, a playground, sand dunes, swimming, and camping also are available. | 23960 Ruggles Rd. | 616/637–2788 or 800/447–2757 | www.dnr.state.mi.us/camping | $4 per car, per day | Daily dawn to dusk.

ON THE CALENDAR

FEB.: *Ice Breaker.* On the second full weekend in February, ice sculptors carve big blocks of ice all over town in this annual competition. A chili cook-off helps keep things warm. | 616/637–5252.

JUNE: *Harborfest.* This family-focused event on the harbor has dragon boat races, music, a children's carnival, and arts and crafts. | 616/637–5171.

AUG.: *National Blueberry Festival.* The area's berries take center stage during this four-day bash on the Lake Michigan shore, the second week of the month. South Haven, the country's blueberry capital, salutes its top industry with blueberry treats, a sand sculpting contest, beach volleyball, parades, children's contests, and other fun. | 616/637–5171 | www.blueberryfestival.com.

Dining

Clementine's. Continental. Once a bank built at the turn of the century, this South Haven building still has exposed brick walls, teller windows, and safes. Vintage photographs depicting Great Lakes shipping and the ornately carved bar salvaged from a long-gone steamship give it a nautical flair as well. Menu choices range from prime rib with grilled mushrooms, onions, and roasted red peppers to simpler fare such as sandwiches and salads. Kids' menu. | 500 Phoenix St. | 616/637–4755 | $25–$33 | AE, D, MC, V.

Idler Riverboat–Magnolia Grille. Continental. The riverboat home of this eatery was built as a private steamer at the turn of the century. It's docked beside the Old Harbor Inn on the Black River. The staterooms, with dark wood paneling and views of the harbor, now are dining rooms. The menu emphasizes fresh seafood, thick cuts of beef, and Cajun-inspired dishes, but also includes sandwiches for lighter appetites. Open-air dining. Kids' menu. | 515 Williams St. | 616/637–8435 | Closed Oct.–mid-Apr. | $29–$37 | AE, D, DC, MC, V.

Tello's Trattoria and Cabaret. Italian. This elegant yet welcoming restaurant 2 mi north of town has white linen and lamp lights—and brown paper and crayons for kids. Old-style Italian scenes and photos of jazz and blues singers cover the walls. One of the specialties is blackened seafood pasta, a linguini dish with sauteed crab, shrimp, leeks, garlic, and pancetta blackened with squid ink and topped with fresh basil and smoked salmon. Homemade cannoli, tiramisu, and cheesecake are for dessert. On Saturday evenings you can hear the Star and Charlie duet perform old favorites like Sinatra used to sing. | 1701 N. Shore Dr. | 616/639–9898 | www.tellostrattoria.com | $7.95–$15.95 | D, MC, V.

Lodging

Econo Lodge. A standard budget motel, this single-story, red-trimmed property is 1 mi from downtown South Haven. Bar. Cable TV. Indoor pool. Gym. Playground. Laundry facilities. Some pets allowed. | 09817 Rte. 140 | 616/637–5141 | fax 616/637–1109 | 60 rooms | $55–$120 | AE, D, DC, MC, V.

Inn at HawksHead. This elegant white 1930s lodge is on the Black River, 5 mi west of town. Some rooms have a fireplace, and some have a handsome window seat where you can look out over the golf course, the river, or the woods. Breakfast is brought to your room. The restaurant serves lunch and dinner in a large dining room with lots of windows and a beautiful fireplace. Restaurant, bar, complimentary breakfast. Driving range, 18-hole golf course, putting green. No pets. | 6959 105th Ave. | 616/639–2146 | fax 616/637–2324 | www.hawksheadlinks.com. | 9 rooms with baths | $120–$170 | AE, D, MC, V.

Lake Bluff Motel. The name says it all; this three-story motel sits on a bluff overlooking Lake Michigan. The property, 1½ mi from downtown, is close to beaches and area attractions. Picnic area. Some kitchenettes. Pool, lake, wading pool. Hot tub, sauna. Business services. | 76648 11th Ave. | 616/637–8531 or 800/686–1305 (Great Lakes states) | fax 616/637–8532 | lakebluffmotel@btc.bci.com | www.lakebluffmotel.com | 49 rooms | $44–$74 | AE, D, DC, MC, V.

Will O'Glenn Irish Bed and Breakfast. This 1920s farmhouse is on 17 well-cared-for acres 10 mi north of town. Here you'll experience hospitality and charm. Imported Irish meats are served for the full breakfast, and Irish soda bread and Irish tea are served at tea time. Cozy sitting areas are near wood-burning fires. Authentic Irish art, including Celtic metalwork, musical instruments, and many photos and posters of the homeland cover the walls. Some guest rooms have a canopy bed and a fireplace. Complimentary breakfast. Some in-room hot tubs. Cross-country skiing. No pets. | 1286 64th St. | 616/227–3045 or 888/237–3009 | fax 616/227–3045 | shamrock@irish-inn.com | www.irish-inn.com | 4 rooms with baths | $89–$165 | MC, V.

Yelton Manor. A mansion built in 1890 is home to this charming Victorian B&B furnished with antiques and reproductions. It overlooks Lake Michigan and is within walking distance of shops, parks, and restaurants. Some rooms have jetted tubs and views of the garden. Complimentary breakfast. Cable TV, no room phones. Business services. No smoking. | 140 N. Shore Dr. | 616/637–5220 | fax 616/637–4957 | elaine@yeltonmanor.com | www.yeltonmanor.com | 17 rooms | $135–$210 | AE, MC, V.

SUTTONS BAY

MAP 9, C4

(Nearby towns also listed: Empire, Glen Arbor, Leland, Traverse City)

Harry C. Sutton established a lumber camp here in 1854 to supply fuel to wood-burning steamboats. Today, the town, surrounded by vineyards and cooled by the north arm of the Grand Traverse Bay, is a bustling summer resort on the Leelanau Peninsula. Specialty shops, restaurants, and the waterfront draw vacationers. (*Note:* Area codes in this vicinity are scheduled to change to 989 beginning April 7, 2001.)

Information: Suttons Bay Area Chamber of Commerce | Box 46, Suttons Bay 49682 | 231/271–5017 | www.suttonsbayarea.com.

Attractions

Leelanau Sands Casino. This glitzy, Las Vegas–style gaming facility, with a restaurant and adjacent hotel, is run by local Native Americans. | 2521 NW Bayshore Dr. | 231/271–4104 or 800/922–2946 | tbcr@casino2win.com | www.casino2win.com | Free | Mon.–Thurs. 8 AM–2 AM, Fri., Sat. 8 AM–3 AM, Sun. 9 AM–2 AM.

L. Mawby Vineyards and Winery. One of the many wineries in the Traverse City area, L. Mawby's is a good place to stop for a tasting and guided tours. It's off Rte. 22 north of Traverse City. | 4519 S. Elm Valley Rd. | 231/271–3522 | fax 231/271–2927 | larry@lmawby.com | www.lmawby.com/ | Free | May–Oct., Thurs.–Sat. by appointment only.

The Leelanau Trail. Hikers, mountain bikers, and cross-country skiers are welcome to use this beautiful trail on a former railbed. The trail stretches for 15 mi from Suttons Bay to Traverse City, winding through woods, open pastures, across several creeks, and beside a small lake. You can in-line skate on the 3 mi near Traverse City that are paved. Entrance to the trail is next to the Town Depot. | Cedar St. | 231/883–8278 | Free.

ON THE CALENDAR

JULY: *Jazz Fest.* Professional musicians perform at this day of classic jazz that draws more than 2000 fans to the Suttons Bay Marina Park. The great music starts at noon on the fourth Saturday of month. Delicious local food and wines are available. | 231/271–4444 | www.leelanau.com/jazzfest/.

AUG.: *Suttons Bay Art Fair.* Artists gather in the city's waterfront Marina Park to exhibit and sell their wares. This art exposition one of the most competitive juried art shows in northern Michigan. Also available are food booths, kids' events, and entertainment. | 231/271–5077.

Dining

Boone's. American. This pub attracts both locals and vacationers with its family-style dining and daily lunch specials. Cozy booths and the wood-and-stone interior add to its rustic appeal. Favorites include whitefish, steaks, and sandwiches. Kids' menu. | 102 St. Joseph St. | 231/271–6688 | $15–$22 | MC, V.

Eagle's Ridge Fine Dining. American. The menu at this restaurant 4 mi north of town focuses on Native American fare, but there are more common dishes as well. One of the most popular specials is Indian tacos, made with fried unleavened bread, ground beef, native vegetables, and a special seasoning. Also, try the Indian corn soup and fried cabbage and bacon. The dining area has Native American artwork, stained glass windows, an arched window in front, and nicely finished wood tables with wood-accent trim. Breakfast is also served. | 2511 N. West Bay Shore Dr. | 231/271–7166 | $4–$19 | MC, V.

Hattie's. Continental. Artwork from local artists accents the spare, elegant interior of this upscale restaurant. You can choose the morel ravioli or Thai-style scallops from the innovative menu. Don't miss the sinful chocolate paradise with raspberries for dessert. | 111 St. Joseph St. | 231/271–6222 | $27–$42 | AE, D, MC, V.

Lodging

Fig Leaf Bed and Breakfast. The owner of this 1900 farmhouse has created a unique, romantic place to spend the night. The house, which is filled with original artwork, is in town, within walking distance of all shops and restaurants. The waterfall and stream with colorful ducks add charm to the grounds outside. You can sit on the deck or in the common room, but you won't find a single television here. Complimentary Continental breakfast. No smoking. | 112 W Race St. | 231/271–3995 | figleafbnb@mindspring.com | www.leelanau.com/figleaf | 4 (2 with shared baths) | $105–$145 | D, MC, V.

Stone Schoolhouse Bed and Breakfast. This 1906 schoolhouse converted into a bed and breakfast is just one block from downtown shopping. The two guest suites are uniquely appointed with art and music memorabilia, respectively. The common room resembles a 1950s-style cafe with a soda fountain and the added modern comforts of a wide-screen TV, pool table, and darts. Complimentary breakfast. Cable TV, in room VCRs (and movies), TV in common area, room phones. No pets. No smoking. | 513 St. Mary's Ave. | 231/271–2738 | 2 suites | $120 | No credit cards.

TAWAS CITY AND EAST TAWAS

(Nearby towns also listed: Alpena, Bay City, Houghton Lake, Oscoda)

The Iosco County seat, Tawas City boasts great fishing and bike trails. Nearby East Tawas is home to the district ranger's office for Huron-Manistee National Forest and the Perchville USA Festival, held each February. (*Note:* Area codes in this vicinity are scheduled to change to 989 beginning April 7, 2001.)

Information: **Tawas Area Chamber of Commerce** | 402 E. Lake St., Box 608, Tawas City 48764 | 517/362–8643 or 800/55–TAWAS | www.tawas.com.

Attractions

Tawas Point State Park. This point of land separates Tawas Bay from Lake Huron, creating a 2-mi sandy beach. Boating, sailing, fishing, and swimming are popular here. You can also hike, bike, or ski around the point on a 1½-mi trail and find the bird sanctuary, where you can see loons, cormorants, and piping plovers. The Au Sable River also runs close by, giving avid canoeists a challenging ride. | 686 Tawas Beach Rd., East Tawas | 517/362–5041 | www.llbean.com/park | $4 per car, per day | Daily, dawn to dusk.

You can tour the 71-ft-tall **Tawas Point Lighthouse** on the second weekend of June during the Tawas Point Celebration Days. The original lighthouse was built in 1853, but due to shifting sands was moved 1 mi inland in 1875 to its current site. The lighthouse resumed operation in 1876 with special lenses made in France. The lenses in its white and red lights still concentrate the light. On a clear night you can see the lighthouse from Port Austin, which is 20 mi away. | Tawas State Park, U.S. 23, East Tawas | 517/362–8643 | www.tawas.com | $4 per day, per car | Daily.

ON THE CALENDAR

FEB.: *Perchville USA.* This 3-day fishy festival's highlights include a parade, contests for area anglers, a softball tournament, ice sculptures, and other wintry fun. Held in early February in East Tawas. | 800/55–TAWAS | www.michiganadventure.com/.
JULY: *Iosco County Fair.* During the last week of July this agricultural fair in Hale brings in the crowds. Livestock competitions, carnival rides, a rodeo, contests in arts and crafts, fine arts, and baked and canned goods are some of the yearly attractions. | 517/728–3566.
AUG.: *Tawas Bay Waterfront Art Show.* Browsers and buyers from around the state gather to admire the works of more than 200 professional and amateur artists in this juried show on the first weekend of the month. Held on the waterfront in East Tawas. | 800/55–TAWAS.

Dining

Genii's Fine Foods. American. A great location on Lake Huron makes this a favorite hangout for both locals and vacationers. Popular dishes include sweet and sour chicken and almond boneless chicken. Salad bar. Kids' menu. | 601 W. Bay St., East Tawas | 517/362–5913 | $14–$27 | D, MC, V.

Whitetail Cafe. American. Omelettes, pancakes, burgers, and hot sandwiches are the popular fare here. Pictures of deer and wood-paneled wainscoting cover the walls. The restaurant is in town, two blocks from the water. | 221 Newman St., East Tawas | 517/362–1090 | No dinner | $3.50–$6.50 | MC, V.

Lodging

Aaron's Wooded Acres Resort. The homey cottages at this resort 4 mi north of town on Lake Huron have full kitchens, a sitting area with a fireplace, one, two, or three bedrooms, and are privately spaced around the 2½-acre grounds. You can go swimming in the lake

TAWAS CITY AND
EAST TAWAS

INTRO
ATTRACTIONS
DINING
LODGING

or play darts and billiards in the game room. Picnic area. Some in-room hot tubs. Beach. Boating, fishing. Pets allowed. | 968 N. U.S. 23, East Tawas | 517/362–5188 | www.aaronswood-edacresresort.com | 11 cottages | $75–$95 | D, MC, V.

Dale Motel. You get lake views at this standard one-story motel off U.S. 23. Rooms have floral decorations, and windows are placed high up for privacy. Cable TV. No pets. No smoking. | 1086 U.S. 23 S, Tawas City | 517/362–6153 | fax 517/362–6154 | 16 rooms | $45–$65 | AE, D, DC, MC, V.

East Tawas Junction Bed and Breakfast. This country Victorian on an estate-sized lot shaded with stately oak trees overlooks beautiful Tawas Bay. It's steps from the beach and about four blocks south of the town's shops and restaurants. Guest rooms have water views. You can relax in the many peaceful common areas—the glassed-in furnished porch, two decks facing the bay, a parlor with a collector's piano, a library, and a family room. Complimentary breakfast. TV in common area. No pets. No smoking. | 514 W. Bay St., East Tawas | 517/362–8006 | fax 517/362–9060 | info@east-tawas.com | www.east-tawas.com | 5 rooms with baths | $99–$149 | D, MC, V.

Huron House Bed and Breakfast. Everything about this contemporary adult getaway on the shores of Lake Huron is designed for your privacy. Most rooms have fireplaces and views of Lake Huron. Many rooms have private decks and private outdoor hot tubs. And Continental breakfast is brought to your room each morning. Complimentary Continental breakfast. Some microwaves, some refrigerators, some in-room hot tubs. Cable TV, in-room VCRs (and movies), room phones. No pets. No kids under 18. No smoking. | 3124 N. U.S. 23, Oscoda | 517/739–9255 | www.huronhouse.com | 11 rooms | $125–$185 | MC, V.

Tawas Bay Holiday Inn Resort. This two-story chain hotel is on the Lake Huron waterfront in downtown East Tawas. Restaurant, bar, room service. In-room data ports. Cable TV. Indoor pool. Hot tub, sauna. Exercise equipment. Beach, water sports. Video games. Kids' programs, playground. Laundry facilities. Business services. | 300 E. Bay St., East Tawas | 517/362–8601 or 800/336–8601 | fax 517/362–5111 | www.tawasholidayinn.com/ | 103 rooms | $79–$159 | AE, D, DC, MC, V.

Tawas Motel. This single-story motel is a good bet for budget-minded travelers. You'll find an inviting sun room and enclosed walkways. Refrigerators, some in-room hot tubs. Cable TV. Pool. Hot tub, sauna. Video games. Playground. | 1124 U.S. 23 S, Tawas City | 517/362–3822 | fax 517/362–3822 | tawasmotel@wazzumail.com | 21 rooms | $55–$70 | AE, D, DC, MC, V.

THREE RIVERS

MAP 9, C8

(Nearby towns also listed: Battle Creek, Coldwater, Kalamazoo, Marshall, Niles)

Three Rivers, settled in the 1830s at the intersection of the St. Joseph, Portage, and Rocky rivers, grew with the development of local water power and a railroad in the 1850s. Its downtown is on national and state historic registers because of the many 1870s to turn-of-the-century buildings. The local ski area is one of the few in southwestern Michigan. The town is roughly halfway between Detroit and Chicago.

Information: Three Rivers Chamber of Commerce | 103 Portage Ave., Three Rivers 49093 | 616/278–8193 | fax 616/273–1751 | www.trchamber.com.

Attractions

Carnegie Center for the Arts. Built in 1904, this distinctive pink granite building is one of the few remaining original Carnegie libraries built by Andrew Carnegie in the early 20th century. Today, it houses three exhibit galleries for fine arts and hosts annual concert series and dance recitals and educational art programs. | 107 N. Main St. | 616/273–8882 | www.rivercountry.com/attractions | Free | Daily.

Hidden Marsh Sanctuary. A beautiful nature trail leads you through this 38-acre conservation area, where you can see and hear many types of water birds. The trail leads you to the Portage River and back. Drive about 1 mi north of town and look for a very large parking lot on the east side of the road. | 1501 Portage Rd. | 616/324–1600 | Free.

Historic Downtown Three Rivers. The downtown commercial district of Three Rivers is one of the best-preserved Victorian streetscapes in southwestern Michigan. Key attractions of downtown include the Mural Mall on North Main St. (three murals depicting the history and wildlife of the town), the Carnegie Center for the Arts, the W. R. Monroe Museum, and the Silliman House Museum. Many antique shops, restaurants, art galleries, artists studios, as well as a book and children's store occupy the restored buildings. | Main St. | 616/278–8193 | www.rivercountry.com | Free | Daily.

Swiss Valley Ski Area. This ski area is the closest one to Chicago (103 mi) and to Indiana (approx. 20 mi). Eleven runs cover varied terrain. The longest run is 1,800 ft and has a vertical drop of 225 ft. | Rte. 1, Jones | 616/244–5635 or 616/244–8016 (snow conditions) | skiswiss@skiswissvalley.com | www.skiswissvalley.com | Dec.–Mar.

ON THE CALENDAR

JUNE: *Three Rivers Water Festival.* Many of the events of this annual festival held the third weekend take place in Scidmore Park. The ox roast dates back to the original "water carnival" in 1957, when a parade of floats went down the Rocky River. Today, an antique and classic car show, entertainment, arts and crafts, fireworks in Memory Isle Park, and kids activities also are part of the fun. | 616/278–8193 | www.trchamber.com/waterfest.html.

SEPT.: *St. Joseph County Grange Fair.* Since the 1850s this fair has been entertaining the area locals with livestock, crafts, and other exhibits. A parade, harness racing, tractor pulls, and a large midway provide fun at this fair that happens the third full week of September. | 616/467–8935, tickets 888/873–0550 | www.2mm.com/info/fair.

Dining

Christmere House Inn. American. You can dine on seafood or steak on the enclosed Victorian porch or in any of three dining rooms on the main floor of this Queen Anne-style brick mansion. Choose from dishes such as crab stuffed shrimp, seafood Newburg, lamb chops, and cornish game hen. | 110 Pleasant St., Sturgis | 616/651–8303 | Reservations essential | $8–$18 | AE, D, MC, V.

Paisano's Pizzeria. Italian. This in-town, casual dining spot has linen tablecloths, dim drop lighting, and pictures of local areas and of Italy on the walls. Try the locally famous Paisano's Pride, a pizza with everything you can imagine on it, including sausage, pepperoni, ham, and vegetables. Pasta dishes are on the menu, too. Have cheesecake or spumoni for dessert. | 16 N. Main St. | 616/278–8525 | Closed Mon. | $8–$15 | AE, D, MC, V.

Lodging

Christmere House Inn. This Queen Anne-style Victorian brick mansion served as the first hospital in Sturgis in 1869. Many of the rooms and suites have fireplaces, and all uniquely reflect the Victorian origins of the home. It's just ¼ block off Chicago Rd. (U.S. 12), near shopping and art galleries, and about 20 mi southeast of downtown Three Rivers. Complimentary breakfast. In-room data ports, some in-room hot tubs. Cable TV, room phones. No pets. No smoking. | 110 Pleasant St., Sturgis | 616/651–8303 | www.rivercountry.com | 2 rooms, 5 suites | $80 rooms, $125–$140 suites | AE, D, MC, V.

Holiday Inn Express Hotel and Suites. Rooms and suites in this two-story chain hotel, 1 mi southwest of town, are white, maroon, and hunter green and have work desks and ample lighting. A cozy sitting area with a fireplace is in the lobby. Complimentary breakfast. In-room data ports, some kitchenettes. Cable TV. Indoor pool. Hot tub, spa. Exercise equipment. No pets. | 58656 Corey Lake Rd. | 616/244–5620 or 800/465–4329 | fax 616/244–9084 | www.basshotels.com/holiday-inn | 56 rooms, 20 suites | $69–$89 | AE, D, DC, MC, V.

Mendon Country Inn. Originally built in 1843, the Wakeman House, overlooking the St. Joseph River, has served stagecoach, train, and car travelers. A walnut spiral staircase is the focal point of the lobby. Rooms, such as the Rooftop Garden, are furnished in a manner that reflects their names. Breakfast is served in the Puddleburg Room. You can also choose to stay in the Innkeepers Cottage or Creekside Lodge, which are separate accommodations. Picnic area, complimentary Continental breakfast. Some refrigerators, no room phones, no TV in rooms, TV in common area. Boating, bicycles. Business services. No kids under 12. No smoking. | 440 W. Main St., Mendon | 616/496–8132 or 800/304–3366 | fax 616/496–8403 | www.rivercountry.com/mci/index.html | 18 rooms with private baths, 1 cottage (with 2 suites), 1 lodge (with 5 suites) | $69–$159 | AE, D, MC, V.

Sanctuary at Wildwood. On 95 acres of wooded land, this double-level B&B, built in 1973, is a peaceful retreat. Suites are furnished with queen-size beds, fireplaces, and jetted tubs. All have private balconies or decks. Complimentary breakfast. No room phones. Pond. No smoking. | 58138 Rte. 40, Jones | 616/244–5910 or 800/249–5910 | fax 616/244–9022 | wildwoodinns@rivercountry.com | www.rivercountry.com/saw/index.html | 11 rooms | $139–$179 | AE, D, MC, V.

Sturgis Hampton Inn. Just off I–80/90 Exit 121, this chain hotel is 4 mi south of downtown Sturgis and 20 mi southeast of downtown Three Rivers. Complimentary Continental breakfast. In-room data ports, some microwaves, some refrigerators. Cable TV, room phones, TV in common area. Indoor pool. Hot tub. No pets. | 71451 S. Centreville Rd., Sturgis | 616/651–4210 | www.hampton-inn.com | 60 rooms | $69–$89 | AE, D, DC, MC, V.

TRAVERSE CITY

MAP 9, C4

(Nearby towns also listed: Bellaire, Beulah, Empire, Glen Arbor, Leland, Suttons Bay)

Once a major lumbering center, Traverse City is now the hub of a flourishing cherry-growing community and northern Michigan's unofficial capital. Its charming downtown is filled with restaurants and shops selling resort wear and antiques.

More than 30 golf courses, good sailing, fishing, nearby downhill skiing, and more make this town, which is blessed with a strategic location at the mouth of scenic Grand Traverse Bay, a busy year-round destination. The drive along Rte. 37 through the Old Mission Peninsula, which splits the bay into two long, narrow arms, is spectacular in spring and fall. Traverse City hosts the National Cherry Festival each July, one of the state's largest and best-attended events. (*Note:* Area codes in this vicinity are scheduled to change to 989 beginning April 7, 2001.)

Information: Traverse City Convention and Visitors Bureau | 101 W. Grandview Pkwy., Traverse City 49615 | 231/947–1120 or 800/TRAVERS. | www.tcvisitor.com.

Attractions

Amon Orchards. From July through October you can feed and pet goats, pigs, chickens, and rabbits at this family owned and operated orchard. In summer, staff will take you on a trolley ride and explain why and how each kind of produce grows. You can also purchase baked goods, jams, and jellies made on the premises. The orchard is 10–15 mi north of downtown Traverse City. | 7404 U.S. 31 N, Acme | 231/938–1644 or 800/937–1644 | fax 231/938–9145 | info@amonorchards.com | www.amonorchards.com | Free | June–Nov., daily 10–5.

City Opera House. A classic example of Victorian theatre architecture, the opera house opened three years before Traverse City received its city charter and has played an integral part in the city's history from that time on. For more than 100 years, it has hosted plays, concerts, recitals, lectures, conventions, political benefits, community and arts events—but never a true opera. | 106–112 ½ E. Front St. | 231/941–8082.

Clinch Park. A small downtown park on Grand Traverse Bay, Clinch is best known for its tiny zoo with animals that are native to the woods and fields of northern Michigan. The star attractions include wolves, bears, foxes, and even a pair of playful beavers. An aquarium displays native fish. There's also a steam train that tours the park from Memorial Day through Labor Day. | 400 Boardman Ave. | 231/922–4904 | $4 (includes train) | Memorial Day–Labor Day, daily 9–5:30; mid-Apr.–Memorial Day, Labor Day–Oct., daily 10–4.

You can see changing exhibits on the natural and social history of the region at the **Con Foster Historical Museum.** The downtown museum on the grounds of the Clinch Park Zoo focuses on the cultural heritage of the pioneers and Native Americans. | 181 E. Grandview Pkwy. | 231/922–4905 | www.traverse.net/traversecity/services/museum.html | Memorial Day–Labor Day, daily 10–4.

The **Schooner Madeline** is a 56-ft replica of a 19th-century schooner dates from the 1840s. It's docked in the marina from May through October. If conditions aren't right for tours, you can still view the vessel at its dock site. | 232 E. Front St. | 231/946–2647 | Free (donation welcome) | May–Oct., tours daily 8 AM–9 PM.

Dennos Museum Center. You can see visual and performing arts exhibits here in a range of media and on all sorts of subjects. Displays range from historical art to contemporary works by artists of statewide, national, and international stature. The museum's permanent display of sculpture, prints, and drawings by the Inuit artists of the Canadian Arctic is one of the largest and most historically complete collections anywhere. There are also a hands-on kid's gallery and a gift shop. | Northwestern Michigan College, 1701 E. Front St. | 231/922–1055 or 800/748–0566 | fax 231/995–1597 | www.dmc.nmc.edu/ | $2 | Mon.–Sat. 10–5, Sun. 1–5.

Interlochen Center for the Arts. This arts academy and camp has more than 1,000 students ranging in age from 8 to 18. They come to study theater, dance, music, and the visual arts and to present many exhibits and productions throughout the year. The school is also host to a large and well-known summer performance program, which includes nightly concerts by famous musicians as well as by academy students. | 4000 Rte. 137, Interlochen | 231/276–6230 | www.interlochen.org | Free | Sept.–May.

Interlochen State Park. One of Michigan's few remaining stands of virgin pine is in Interlochen's 187 acres. The park has swimming, boating, fishing and picnic areas. Campsites also are available. The park is adjacent to the Interlochen Center for the Arts. | Rte. 137, Inter-

TRAVERSE CITY CHERRIES

Cherry butter, cherry salsa, even cherry-pecan sausage; it's clear after a visit to Traverse City that there isn't a dish that can't be complemented with that little red fruit.

Traverse City is the Cherry Capital of the World. Orchards are scattered along the area's 250 mi of Lake Michigan shoreline. The area's bounty yields up to one-third of the nation's tart cherry crop. The Old Mission Peninsula, just northeast of downtown, claims to have the world's largest concentration of cherry trees.

While cherry confections are sold throughout downtown, you can go right to the source at Amon Orchards near Acme, Cherry Republic near Glen Arbor, or Pleva's Meats in Cedar. There you can pick up some cherry pasta sauce or a few pounds of cherry hamburger to take home. | 231/947–1120 or 800/TRAVERS. | www.tcvisitor.com.

© Artville

lochen | 231/276–9511 or 800/447–2757 | www.dnr.state.mi.us/camping | $4 | Daily dawn to dusk.

The Music House. Not your ordinary museum, the Music House in nearby Acme is a former farm filled with rare early phonographs, music boxes, nickelodeons, pipe organs, and more. | 7377 U.S. 31 N, Acme | 231/938–9300 | fax 231/938–3650 | www.musichouse.org | $7 | May–Oct., Mon.–Sat. 10–4, Sun. 12–4.

Sugar Loaf Resort Ski Area. On the bucolic Leelanau Peninsula, this northern Michigan resort has some of the best skiing in Middle America. There are 23 trails spread out over some 80 acres. The longest run is 1 mi. Snowboarding, NASTAR racing, and night skiing are available. In summer the resort's two 18-hole golf courses and a shuttle to the Leelanau Sands Casino in Suttons Bay keep you busy. | 4500 Sugar Loaf Mountain Rd., Cedar | 231/228–5461 | fax 231/228–6545 | Weekdays $27, weekends $35 | Nov.–Mar.

Tall Ships *Westwind* and *Manitou*. Sailing onto Grand Traverse Bay from downtown, the tall ship *Westwind* embarks on two daily cruises and a sunset picnic sail. For folks looking for a longer itinerary, its sister ship *Manitou* makes three- and six-day excursions from Northport on the Leelanau Peninsula. | 13390 SW Bayshore Dr. | 231/941–2000 or 800/678–0383 | www.traverse.net/tallship/home.html | Westwind $25–$38, Manitou $399–$619 | May–Oct.

ON THE CALENDAR

JAN.: *Winterfest*. This family event in nearby Kalkaska on the last weekend of the month includes dogsled races, a volleyball tournament, a snowman-building contest, a pancake breakfast, kids' games, and a spicy chili cookoff. | 231/258–9103 | www.kalkaska-county.com/rec.htm.

MAY: *Mesick Mushroom Festival*. The forests in Mesick, near Traverse City, attract thousands of fungi fans hunting for the elusive morel, which grows abundantly here. Mushroom cuisine, a carnival, a rodeo, baseball and horseshoe tournaments, and a Saturday parade attract all ages during the second week of the month. | 231/885–2679 | www.mesick-mushroomfest.org/.

JUNE–SEPT.: *Interlochen Arts Camp*. Students and their guests participate in a variety of music, dance, and other arts. Nationally known entertainers perform during its summer-long season. The camp is 14 mi southwest of Traverse City at 4000 Rte. 137 at Interlochen. | 231/276–6230 | www.interlochen.org.

JULY: *National Cherry Festival*. The country's cherry capital celebrates its harvest the second week of the month with more than 120 events, including three parades, concerts, fireworks, an air show, a Native American powwow, crafts, a rubber ducky race, and family activities. One of northern Michigan's top events. | 231/947–4230 | www.cherryfestival.org/.

AUG.: *Northwestern Michigan Fair*. Fun for the whole family includes exhibits, animals, a carnival, harness racing, grandstand events, and free entertainment, in early August. | 231/943–4150.

NOV.: *Northwoods Festival of Lights*. A fantasy forest complete with woodland creatures, fairies, elves, and a gingerbread house light up Grand Traverse Resort in Acme for four weeks, starting in mid-November. | 231/938–2100.

Dining

Apache Trout Grill. American. You can really experience Northern Michigan at this popular spot named for a fish rescued from the endangered species list. Stuffed fish and wood carvings adorn the walls, unique lamps are carved in the shape of bears and fishing poles, and there's a great view of the lake in front. On the menu are fresh-grilled or sauteed fish, steaks, barbecued ribs, and several pastas. | 13671 S. West Bay Shore Dr. | 231/947–7079 | $12–$20 | AE, D, DC, MC, V.

Auntie Pasta's. Italian. This trattoria has two distinct dining areas. The more casual space presents pizzas, calzones, and sandwiches. In the formal dining room you can order homemade pastas and signature entrées such as pesto chicken. | 2030 S. Airport Rd. | 231/941–8147 | $16–$29 | AE, D, MC, V.

Boat House Blue Water Bistro. Contemporary. You may think you're at your cottage when you dine at this quaint restaurant on the Old Mission Peninsula. It's right on the water 10 mi north of town. Entrées include chicken, steak, seafood, and vegetable specialties. | 14039 Peninsula Dr. | 231/223–4030 | Closed Mon.–Tues. No lunch Wed.–Thur. | $12–$18 | AE, MC, V.

Bowers Harbor Inn. Continental. You get a striking view of Grand Traverse Bay from this elegant restaurant on the Old Mission Peninsula. Try the fish in a bag and the macadamia nut–encrusted whitefish. Its more casual area, Bowery, which serves ribs, steaks, and chicken dishes, is in the residence's old servants' quarters. Kids' menu. | 13512 Peninsula Dr. | 231/223–4222 | Reservations essential | No lunch | $22–$49 | AE, D, MC, V.

La Cuisine Amical Café. French. Plants, statuettes, and wall-hangings adorn this little in-town bistro that has a patio for summer dining. Braised lamb shank and exquisite French pastries keep customers coming back, but you also have a choice of sandwiches, soups, salads, and pastas. | 229 E. Front St. | 231/941–8888 | Mon.–Sat. 11–10, Sun. 9–3 | $12–$20 | AE, MC, V.

La Señorita. Mexican. Bright, eye-catching fixtures complement the zesty fare. It's one of the few places in Traverse City you'll find burritos, chimichangas, and fajitas as well as a fine selection of mesquite-grilled dishes. Other favorites include the linguini and any of the eight signature burgers. Kids' menu. | 1245 S. Garfield St. | 231/947–8820 | www.lasenorita.net/ | $6–$15 | AE, D, MC, V.

Minerva's. Continental. Just because this dining room's in the Park Place Hotel—and the food's elegant—doesn't mean you have to dress up. The soft lighting and bare wood tables are meant to be welcoming and comfortable. Barbecued ribs and filet mignon are the more popular entrées, but tortellini chicken breast carbonara, in a delicate herbed cream sauce, is a close runner-up. Top off dinner with death by chocolate, bananas Foster, or tiramisu for dessert. The hotel and restaurant are in the historic district of town. | 300 E. State St. | 231/946–5093 | fax 231/946–2772 | Breakfast also available | $9.95–$18.95 | AE, D, DC, MC, V.

Reflections. Continental. Stylish fare and an expansive view of East Grand Traverse Bay and Old Mission Peninsula make this fourth-floor restaurant in the Waterfront Inn a standout. In addition to the classic prime rib, pecan walleye, and Atlantic char-grilled salmon, you can try one of many sandwiches and entrée-size salads. Try the thick, creamy chowder with rice, corn, and shrimp or the apple chutney chicken. For dessert, sample the Black Forest cheesecake with tangy Traverse City cherries. Entertainment Fri.–Sat. Kids' menu. Sun. brunch. | 2061 U.S. 31 N | 231/938–2321 | $15–$27 | AE, D, DC, MC, V.

Schelde's. Continental. Geared to families, Schelde's has a country-style flair with oak booths and tables and a wide range of adult- and kid-pleasing entrées. Good bets include the large soup and salad bar with homemade breads, sandwiches, chicken, and stir-fry dishes. Kids' menu. | 714 Munson Ave. | 231/946–0981 | $18–$27 | AE, D, MC, V.

Sleder's Family Restaurant. American. This family-run business in the center of town has been in operation since the 1880s. Deer and elk heads and a bearskin line the wood-paneled walls, and an antique chandelier hangs over green tablecloths. Dinner specials include steak, burgers, and Mexican-style dishes. There's outdoor dining in summer. | 717 Randolph St. | 231/947–9213 | www.sleders.com/ | $7.95–$13.95 | D, MC, V.

Windows. Continental. Readers of *Traverse Magazine* regularly vote this their favorite restaurant. With views of the bay from every table and a menu that emphasizes both old favorites and artful, new cuisine, it does indeed serve up a memorable dining experience. Try the firecracker pork on bow-tie pasta with cashews, veal Winn Dixie, which is veal sautéed with shrimp, artichokes, and mushrooms, and duck and sausage gumbo. Sinful desserts include chocolate pâté and chocolate mousse Olivia. Windows also is known for an extensive wine list. Kids' menu. No smoking. | 7677 W. Bay Shore Dr. | 231/941–0100 | Closed Nov.–May, Sun.– Mon. | $22–$32 | DC, MC, V.

Lodging

Anchor Inn. You may feel nostalgic when you see the knotty pine furniture and quilts and dust ruffles on the beds in the rooms and cottages here. The one, two, and three-bedroom cottages have fireplaces and kitchens. Bring your own boat; there's plenty of parking. Enjoy the 100-ft water frontage on west Grand Traverse Bay. The inn is 2½ mi north of town. Picnic area. Some kitchenettes. Cable TV, room phones. Lake. Volleyball. Beach. Playground. Pets allowed. | 11998 S. West Bay Shore Dr. | 231/946–7442 | fax 231/929–2589 | anchorinn@aol.com | www.anchorinn.net | 6 rooms, 8 cottages | $59–$102 rooms, $118–$176 cottages | AE, D, MC, V.

Bayshore Resort. This three-story Victorian-theme hotel is 1 mi from downtown Traverse City. You can view the sandy beaches of Lake Michigan's West Grand Traverse Bay from your room's private balcony or patio. Complimentary Continental breakfast. Cable TV. Indoor pool. Hot tub. Exercise equipment. Beach. Video games. Laundry facilities. Business services, airport shuttle. No smoking. | 833 E. Front St. | 231/935–4400 or 800/634–4401 | fax 231/935–0262 | bayshore@bayshore-resort.com | www.bayshore-resort.com | 120 rooms | $75–$220 | AE, D, DC, MC, V.

Beach Condos. These upscale condos are on 350 ft of sandy beach. Private balconies face the East Bay. Accommodations sleep four. Kitchenettes, in-room hot tubs. Cable TV. Pool. Hot tub. Beach. Business services. | 1995 U.S. 31 N. | 231/938–2228 | fax 231/938–9774 | 30 1-bedroom condos | $299 per week | AE, D, MC, V.

Beach Haus Resort. Private patios overlook 200 ft of beach at this two-story East Bay motel. Picnic area, complimentary Continental breakfast. Refrigerators. Cable TV. Beach, dock. Laundry facilities. Business services, airport shuttle. | 1489 U.S. 31 N. | 231/947–3560 | fax 231/947–0199 | 29 rooms | $75–$215 | Closed Dec.–Apr. | MC, V.

Best Western Four Seasons. This chain hotel is at the base of Old Mission Peninsula. Rooms are spread out over four two-story buildings. Some refrigerators, in-room hot tubs, cable TV. 2 pools (1 indoor). Hot tub. Business services. | 305 Munson Ave. (U.S. 31) | 231/946–8424 or 800/780–7234 | fax 231/946–1971 | www.bestwestern.com/ | 111 rooms | $79–$109 | AE, D, DC, MC, V.

Cider House Bed and Breakfast. Perched high on a hill, this two-story colonial farmhouse, 1 mi west of town, overlooks a 10-acre apple orchard. The homey rooms are named for varieties of apples; the Macintosh Room has blue hues and wicker furniture. You can stroll around the lovely grounds on a well-kept path circling the orchard. Be sure to stop and watch the goldfish in the pond and admire the vegetable and flower gardens. Complimentary breakfast. Some in-room hot tubs. Cable TV. Hiking. Tobogganing. No pets. No smoking. | 5515 Bamey Rd. | 231/947–2833 | fax 231/947–2833 | ciderhsebb@aol.com | www.bbonline.com/mi/cider/ | 5 with baths | $85–$90 | No credit cards.

Crystal Mountain Resort. Golfers flock to this resort for its 36 holes, a 10-acre practice center, and instruction supervised by pro Brad Dean. Accommodations include resort hotel rooms, suites, condos, and homes. In addition to the golf, this four-season resort is known for excellent skiing in the winter. Bar, dining room, picnic area. No air-conditioning in some rooms, some kitchenettes, some refrigerators. Cable TV. 2 pools (1 indoor). Hot tub. Driving range, 2 golf courses, tennis. Exercise equipment, hiking. Bicycles. Cross-country skiing, downhill skiing, sleigh rides. Children's programs (infants–17), playground. Laundry facilities. | 12500 Crystal Mountain Dr., Thompsonville | 231/378–2000 or 800/968–7686 | fax 231/378–4594 | info@crystalmtn.com | www.crystalmtn.com. | 81 rooms, 90 apartments | $58–$140; $122–$317 apartments | AE, D, DC, MC, V.

Days Inn. An appealing atrium greets you as you enter the lobby of this two-story chain hotel. If you have your family along, you might want to get one of the two suites with a living room and dining room. Complimentary Continental breakfast. Some in-room hot tubs. Cable TV. Indoor pool. Hot tub. Playground. Laundry facilities. Business services, airport shuttle. | 420 Munson Ave. (U.S. 31) | 231/941–0208 or 800/388–7829 | fax 231/941–7521

| info@tcdaysinn.com | www.daysinn.com | 183 rooms, 2 suites | $110–$135 rooms, $148–$165 suites | AE, D, DC, MC, V.

Grainery Bed and Breakfast. Just 3 mi south of downtown, this 1892 gentleman's farm on 10 acres was converted into a bed and breakfast in 1990. Rooms in the house are uniquely appointed with antiques and country furnishings; all have private baths. Rooms in the carriage house have fireplaces, while the cottage has a private deck and sitting area. The breakfast room overlooks a pond with swans, ducks, and wild turkeys. Any time of day you can snack on goodies from the dessert and fruit table, or relax and sip on lemonade or iced tea while lounging in the two-person hammock. You can practice your golf swing on 2 golf greens with provided clubs and balls. Complimentary breakfast. Some in-room hot tubs, TV in common area. Driving range. No pets. | 2951 Hartman Rd. | 231/946–8325 | www.bbhost.com/thegrainery/ | 4 rooms, 1 cottage | $85 rooms, $115 cottage, $139 carriage house rooms | AE, MC, V.

Grand Beach Resort Hotel. A 300-ft sugar sand beach beckons from this three-story hotel on West Grand Traverse Bay. There are eight styles of rooms. Complimentary Continental breakfast. Refrigerators. Cable TV, in-room VCRs (and movies). Indoor pool. Hot tub. Exercise equipment. Beach. Video games. Laundry facilities. Business services. | 1683 U.S. 31 N. | 231/938–4455 or 800/968–1992 | fax 231/938–4435 | gbeach@ptway.com | www.grand-beach.com/ | 95 rooms | $159–$199 | AE, D, DC, MC, V.

Grand Traverse Resort. This top-shelf resort in Acme is on 1,400 acres along the shores of Lake Michigan's East Grand Traverse Bay. It's the area's largest four-season resort hotel, known for its 54 golf holes, including The Bear, which was designed by Jack Nicklaus. Winter getaway packages are available. For a little relaxation check out the resort's 7,000-sq-ft spa complex. Within the complex you can take advantage of the state-of-the-art workout facilities and tennis center. Bar, dining room, room service. Cable TV, in-room VCRs. 4 pools (2 indoor). Hot tub. Driving range, 3 golf courses, putting green, tennis. Gym. Beach, water sports. Ice-skating, cross-country skiing, downhill skiing, sleigh rides, tobogganing. Children's programs (6–12). Laundry facilities. Business services, airport shuttle. | 100 Grand Traverse Village Rd., Acme | 231/938–2100 or 800/748–0303 | fax 231/938–5494 | info@grandtraverseresort.com | www.grandtraverseresort.com/ | 426 rooms, 250 apartments | $129–$179, $95–$325 apartments | AE, D, DC, MC, V.

Hampton Inn. This four-story chain hotel is 3 mi from downtown and across the street from a public beach. Miniature golf is right next door. Complimentary Continental breakfast. In-room data ports, some refrigerators. Cable TV. Indoor pool. Hot tub. Exercise equipment. Business services, airport shuttle. | 1000 U.S. 31 N | 231/946–8900 | fax 231/946–2817 | tvclm01@hi-hotel.com | www.hampton-inn.com/ | 127 rooms | $129–$139 | AE, D, DC, MC, V.

Heritage Inn. The city's only heart-shaped spas make this older two-story Colonial-style motel popular with honeymooners. Picnic area. Some in-room hot tubs. Cable TV, in-room VCRs (and movies). Pool. Exercise equipment. Video games. | 417 Munson Ave. (U.S. 31) | 231/947–9520 or 800/968–0105 | fax 231/947–9523 | 39 rooms | $129–$139 | AE, D, DC, MC, V.

Historic Victoriana 1898. The authentic details here allow this house to live up to its name, for it's full of rare delights of a bygone era. The outside is painted in a pale yellow with dark green and white trim. The beautifully landscaped grounds include a terrace for sitting. Inside there are antiques, family heirlooms and photos, old quilts on the walls, and even a rare wreath made of hair, according to the whimsy of the era. Breakfast is one of the highlights also, with homemade breads and muffins, fresh fruit, and a hot entrée. You're steps from the west Grand Traverse Bay at this bed and breakfast in town. Complimentary breakfast. TV in common area. | 622 Washington St. | 231/929–1009 | fax 231/929–2966 | rscherme@traverse.net | www.historicvictoriana.org | 3 with baths | $65–$95.

Holiday Inn. On West Grand Traverse Bay, this four-story chain hotel has a private marina and beach. It's 1-½ blocks from downtown. Restaurant, bar, room service. Some refrigera-

tors. Cable TV. Indoor pool. Hot tub. Exercise equipment. Video games. Business services, airport shuttle. Some pets allowed. | 615 E. Front St. | 231/947–3700 | fax 231/947–0361 | sales@traverse-holidayinn.com | www.basshotels.com/holiday-inn | 179 rooms | $80–$142 | AE, D, DC, MC, V.

Linden Lea on Long Lake. An eclectic mix of northern Michigan handmade items, antiques, and twig furniture furnish the rooms at this bed and breakfast 10 mi west of town. Window seats have extra special views of the lake. Complimentary breakfast. Beach, boating. | 279 Long Lake Rd. | 231/943–9182 | lindenlea@aol.com | www.lindenleabb.com | 2 rooms with baths | $90–$110 | No credit cards.

Main Street Inn. All rooms are on the street level at this motel close to a park, the beach on scenic Front Street, and the downtown area. Kitchenettes. Cable TV. Pool. Putting green. Laundry facilities. Business services. Some pets allowed. | 618 E. Front St. | 231/929–0410 or 800/255–7180 | fax 231/929–0489 | www.mainstreetinnsusa.com | 95 rooms | $40–$90 | AE, D, DC, MC, V.

Neahtawanta Inn. Known as a waterfront hotel since 1906, this inn, painted pale yellow with white trim and with a lovely front porch, is steps from a 325-ft beach on Grand Traverse Bay. Rooms have older country-style furniture. The suite has two bedrooms, a bath, and a living room. The Neahtawanta Center, where you can take a yoga class, is also on the premises. The inn is 12 mi north of town. Complimentary breakfast. Sauna. Beach. No pets. No smoking. | 1308 Neahtawanta Rd. | 231/223–7315 | inn@oldmission.com | www.old-mission.com/inn | 4 rooms (2 with shared bath), 1 suite | $85–$140.

North Shore Inn. One- and two-bedroom condos are available in this New England-style, three-story hotel. There's 200 ft of sandy beach. Cable TV. Pool. Some refrigerators. Laundry facilities. No smoking. | 2305 U.S. 31 N. | 231/938–2365 or 800/938–2365 | fax 231/938–2368 | www.northshoreinn.net | 26 condos (9 with shower only) | $69–$229 | AE, D, MC, V.

Park Place Hotel. In 1930, the completion of the 10-story tower made the Park Place Hotel Traverse City's tallest building. The penthouse-level Beacon Lounge at the "Top of the Park" has spectacular views. Restaurant, bar. Refrigerators. Cable TV. Indoor pool. Hot tub. Exercise equipment. Business services, airport shuttle. | 300 E. State St. | 231/946–5000 or 800/748–0133 | fax 231/946–2772 | hotel@aliens.com | www.park-place-hotel.com | 140 rooms and suites | $85–$150 | AE, D, DC, MC, V.

Pine Crest Motel. This family owned and operated motel has an in-town location at the foot of the peninsula. There's a café next door. Complimentary Continental breakfast. Refrigerators. Cable TV, in-room VCRs (and movies). Pool. Hot tub. | 360 Munson Ave. | 231/947–8900 or 800/223–4433 | fax 231/947–8900 | 35 rooms | $36–$95 | AE, D, DC, MC, V.

Pinestead Reef Resort. This all-suites hotel is right on Grand Traverse Bay, 3 mi east of town. Studio and one- or two-bedroom suites have balconies with water views. You can lounge on the 700-ft sandy beach or rent a boat here. In-room data ports, kitchenettes. Cable TV, in-room VCRs. Indoor pool. Hot tub, sauna. Beach, boating. Laundry facilities. | 1265 U.S. 31 N | 231/947–4010 | fax 231/947–0255 | pinestead@gtii.com | www.pinestead.com | 46 suites | $69–$155 studio, $99–$199 2 bedrooms | AE, D, MC, V.

Pointes North Inn. All the suite-like rooms at this three-story hotel overlook East Grand Traverse Bay. Beautifully landscaped grounds include a 300-ft sandy beach. Complimentary Continental breakfast. Microwaves, refrigerators, some in-room hot tubs. Cable TV. Pool. Beach. | 2211 U.S. 31 N. | 231/938–9191 or 800/968–3422 | fax 231/938–0070 | getaway@pointes-north.com | www.pointesnorth.com | 52 rooms | $65–$155 | AE, MC, V.

Sugar Beach Resort Hotel. On the East Bay, this three-story hotel has beachfront rooms with private balconies and family suites. Complimentary Continental breakfast. Cable TV. Indoor pool. Hot tub. Exercise equipment. Video games. Laundry facilities. Business services. | 1773 U.S. 31 N. | 231/938–0100 or 800/509–1995 | fax 231/938–0200 | sbeach@ptway.com | www.sugarbeach.com | 85 rooms, 11 suites | $149–$199 rooms, $189–$299 suites | AE, D, DC, MC, V.

Sugar Loaf Resort. This resort has some of the Midwest's best snowboarding and skiing terrain and a championship golf course. The lodge has rooms and suites; townhouses with four-bedroom apartments and condos with one- to two-bedroom apartments also are available. If you're winging it, there's also a 3,500-ft paved airstrip. Bar, dining room. Some refrigerators, cable TV. 3 pools (1 indoor). Hot tub. Driving range, golf courses, putting green, tennis. Exercise equipment. Bicycles. Cross-country, downhill skiing. Game room. Children's programs. Business services. | 4500 Sugar Loaf Mountain Rd., Cedar | 231/228–5461 | fax 231/228–6545 | 150 lodge rooms, 69 bedrooms total in townhouses and condos | $125–$170, $170–$300 1– to 2–bedroom apartments, $500 4–bedroom apartments | Closed Apr. and Nov. | AE, D, DC, MC, V.

Traverse Bay Inn. One- and two-bedroom suites and studios are available at this small motel minutes from downtown. You can use one of the motel's bicycles to ride on the adjoining Traverse Area Recreational Bike Trail. Picnic area. Some refrigerators. Cable TV. Pool. Hot tub. Bicycles. Video games. Playground. Laundry facilities. Business services. Some pets allowed. | 2300 U.S. 31 N. | 231/938–2646 or 800/968–2646 | fax 231/938–5845 | fun@traversebay.com | www.traversebay.com | 24 rooms | $79 studios, $149–$209 suites | AE, D, MC, V.

Warwickshire Inn. This 1902 restored white farmhouse, 2 mi west of town, is across the street from a golf course and close to the Interlochen Center for the Arts. You can enjoy the outdoors on the deck or in the garden hammock. The interior has some lovely antiques, queen-size beds, and a common room. The pancake and bacon breakfast is a big hit. No pets. | 5037 Barney Rd. | 231/946–7176 | www.inn.warwick.org | 3 with baths | $75 | No credit cards.

TROY

MAP 10, D2

(Nearby towns also listed: Detroit, Pontiac, Royal Oak, Southfield, Warren)

Established by early land grants, this northern Detroit suburb was a center of trade between Detroit and Pontiac by the 19th century. Today, it's the suburb of choice for many well-known corporations (including Kmart) that have followed the city's residents north along I–75. It's also the site of the tony Somerset Collection, a mall with designer shops and high-end department stores.

Information: Troy Chamber of Commerce | 4555 Investment Dr. #300, Troy 48098 | 248/641–8151 | fax 248/641–0545 | theteam@troychamber.com | www.troychamber.com.

Attractions

Cranbrook Academy and Art Museum. Here you can view painting, photography, and sculpture, from the past to today, including works done by Cranbrook's own Academy of Art students. You can also tour the Cranbrook Institute of Science and an English manor and gardens while on the campus of the Cranbrook Educational Community. (*See also* Bloomfield Hills.) | 39221 Woodward Ave., Bloomfield Hills | 248/645–3320 | fax 248/646–0046 | www.cranbrook.edu | $5 | Sept.–May, Tues.–Sun. 11–5, Thurs. 11–8; June–Aug., Tues.–Sun. 11–5, Fri. 11–10; closed Mon.

Stony Creek Metropark. (*See also* Detroit.) One of the excellent Huron-Clinton Metroparks in the Detroit area, Stony Creek is known for its fine sandy beach and trails for both hikers and cross-country skiers. You can also go swimming, fishing, boating, biking, picnicking, and golfing. | 4300 Main Park Rd., Shelby Township | 810/781–4242 or 800/477–7756 | www.metroparks.com | $3, free Wed. | Daily dawn to dusk.

Troy Museum and Historical Village. Much of suburban Troy has become a concrete jungle, thanks to the influx of many Fortune 500 companies. This museum recalls the city's more rural days, with displays that include furnishings and other artifacts, an 1820s log cabin, a house built in the 1830s, and much more. | 60 W. Wattles Rd. | 248/524–3570 | www.city-oftroy.com | Free | Tues.–Sat. 9–5:30, Sun. 1–5, closed Mon.

ON THE CALENDAR

SEPT.: *Troy Daze.* Area businesses have booths at this annual community fair, which takes place at Boulan Park on the third full weekend of the month. You can expect plenty of food, arts and crafts, music, and carnival rides. | 248/528–1515 | www.ci.troy.mi.us/departments/parks/TroyDaze/TroyDaze.html.

Dining

Capital Grille. Continental. A see-and-be-seen favorite of Michigan politicos and local CEOs, this dim, clubby restaurant with booths and tables made of mahogany is in the upscale Somerset Collection shopping mecca. While steaks are king, the crab and lobster cakes and calamari are prepared with equal skill. You might drool over the strawberries drizzled with port and Grand Marnier. It's also known for dry-aged steak on display in a glass-fronted locker. Cigar-friendly section. | 2800 W. Big Beaver Rd. | 248/649–5300 | fax 248/554–9284 | smurdock@loho.com | www.capitalgrille.com | $30–$50 | AE, D, MC, V.

Champps. Contemporary. This is the place to go for sports entertainment. With 20 television sets, you can't miss the game. There's a circular bar and stadium-style seating, as well as a more quiet enclosed room for dining. Steaks, burgers, and Tex-Mex dishes are all on the menu. | 301 W. Big Beaver Rd. | 248/526–0333 | fax 248/526–0156 | $7.95–$15.95 | AE, MC, V.

Charley's Crab. Seafood. Opened in 1976, this chain restaurant has been given a face-lift, evident both in its interior design and menu. It's still known for seafood, although entrées now include global touches such as yellowfin tuna sashimi or poblano peppers stuffed with rock shrimp and Monterey Jack cheese. Other favorites include whitefish, lobster, crab, halibut Oscar, and crab cakes. Kids' menu. | 5498 Crooks Rd. | 248/879–2060 | fax 248/879–7472 | www.meur.com | $20–$49 | AE, D, DC, MC, V.

Joe Kool's. American. This homey sports bar has pool tables, arcade games, television sets, and four areas for dining, separated by lots of old junkyard treasures and crates. Old advertisements cover the brick walls. The menu's a sports fan's delight, with steaks, burgers, pizza, and pasta. | 1835 E. Big Beaver Rd. | 248/526–KOOL | $4.99–$9.99 | AE, D, DC, MC, V.

Mon Jin Lau. Pan-Asian. This longtime favorite with its high, peaked ceilings, palms, and a soothing color scheme is the dressiest Asian restaurant in the metro Detroit area. The menu includes staples such as moo shu pork and General Tso's chicken. Other choices include the inventive Singapore noodles—chicken, shrimp, chiles, and curry on angel-hair pasta—and seared sea scallops with corn chile sauce. Also worth trying are the ginger garlic eggplant and coconut shrimp. Kids' menu. | 1515 E. Maple Rd. | 248/689–2332 | fax 248/689–6709 | No lunch weekends | $22–$31 | AE, DC, MC, V.

Picano's. Italian. Quaint old scenes of the motherland hang from the walls, and on the tables are white linen and votive candles at this relaxed yet elegant in-town spot. Specialties include homemade ravioli, lasagna, and several veal dishes. | 3775 Rochester Rd. | 248/689–8050 | fax 248/689–4360 | $11.95–$35.95 | AE, MC, V.

Priya. Indian. Hard-to-find southern Indian cuisine reigns in this stylish and serene Troy eatery. The menu lists seven kinds of dosas (crepes with different lentil flours) and little bowls of mint, coconut, and tomato. Try tandoori chicken, ginger chicken, or spicy ginger shrimp. Buffet. No smoking. | 72 W. Maple Rd. | 248/269–0100 | fax 248/269–9358 | $10–$16 | AE, D, DC, MC, V.

Lodging

Candlewood Suites. Especially accommodating for business travelers, this in-town hotel provides extended-stay discounts, oversized work desks, full kitchens, same-day dry cleaning, and complimentary fax/copy services. You can choose a one bedroom with a sleep-sofa in the sitting area or a studio with an oversized recliner. All rooms have a maroon, dark teal, and off-white color scheme. Food's available 24 hrs a day in the Candlewood Cupboard. Restaurant. In-room data ports, kitchenettes. Cable TV, in-room VCRs (and movies). Exercise equipment. no pets. | 2550 Troy Center Dr. | 248/269–6600 | fax 248/269–8449 | www.candlewoodsuites.com | 118 suites | $129–$149 | AE, D, DC, MC, V.

Courtyard by Marriott. This three-story chain hotel is on the west side of the city in a residential area. The rooms are pleasantly designed. The property is near corporate parks and the Somerset Collection. In-room data ports, some refrigerators. Cable TV. Indoor pool. Hot tub. Exercise equipment. Laundry facilities. Business services. | 1525 E. Maple Rd. | 248/528–2800 | fax 248/528–0963 or 800/321–2211 | www.courtyard.com | 161 rooms | $69–$124 | AE, D, DC, MC, V.

Drury Inn. The Somerset Collection and Kmart headquarters are near this four-story chain hotel. It's a favorite of business travelers. Complimentary Continental breakfast. In-room data ports. Cable TV. Pool. Some pets allowed. | 575 W. Big Beaver Rd. | 248/528–3330 | fax 248/528–3330 | www.drury-inn.com | 153 rooms | $91–$108 | AE, D, DC, MC, V.

Embassy Suites. The suites in this in-town hotel have many attractive features, such as a living room with a sleep sofa, king-size beds, a wet bar, and two televisions. You'll be close to a busy corporate park, the Somerset Collection, and the Palace of Auburn Hills when you stay at this eight-story, all-suite hotel just off I–75. Restaurant, bar. In-room data ports, minibars, refrigerators. Cable TV. Indoor pool. Hot tub. Exercise equipment. No pets. | 850 Tower Dr. | 248/879–7500 | fax 248/879–9139 | www.embassysuites.com | 251 suites | $125–$145 suites | AE, D, DC, MC, V.

Fairfield Inn by Marriott. This three-story blue-and-white budget hotel has a handy location off busy I–75, making it convenient for both Detroit and northern suburban stays. Not far from the Detroit Zoo, shopping, and Royal Oak restaurants. Complimentary Continental breakfast. Cable TV. Pool. | 32800 Stephenson Hwy., Madison Heights | 248/588–3388 | fax 248/588–3388 | www.fairfieldinn.com | 134 rooms | $49–$65 | AE, D, DC, MC, V.

Hamilton Hotel. There are terry-cloth robes, Starbuck's coffee, and a Nintendo video game waiting for you in these elegant beige, burgundy, and hunter green rooms. Choose a king, queen, or two double-size beds. The hotel is 1 mi north of town. Complimentary breakfast, room service. In-room data ports. Cable TV. Exercise equipment. No pets. | 35270 Woodward Ave. | 248/642–6200 | fax 248/642–6567 | www.hamiltonhotel.com | 64 rooms | $109–$155 | AE, D, DC, MC, V.

Hampton Inn. This chain hotel is in an upscale part of Madison Heights, and has four stories. Complimentary Continental breakfast. In-room data ports. Cable TV. Exercise equipment. Some pets allowed. | 32420 Stephenson Hwy., Madison Heights | 248/585–8881 | fax 248/585–9446 | www.hampton-inn.com | 124 rooms | $68–$85 | AE, D, DC, MC, V.

Holiday Inn. This four-story hotel is in southwest Troy just off I–75. It's close to shopping, restaurants, and the city's corporate parks. Restaurant, bar, room service. In-room data ports. Cable TV. Pool. Exercise equipment. Some pets allowed. | 2537 Rochester Ct. | 248/689–7500 or 800/465–4329 | fax 248/689–9015 | www.basshotels.com/holiday-inn | 153 rooms | $69–$119 | AE, D, DC, MC, V.

Kingsley Hotel and Suites. With its location 5 mi west of town and 2 mi from I–75, this hotel is close to local art galleries, antiques shops, and clothing stores. Breakfast is available. 2 restaurants, room service. In-room data ports. Cable TV. Indoor pool. Exercise equipment. No pets. | 1475 N. Woodward Ave. | 248/644–1400 | fax 248/644–5449 | www.whghotels.com/kingsley | 150 rooms, 8 suites | $109–$169 | AE, D, DC, MC, V.

Marriott. A large atrium lobby and stylish rooms distinguish this 17-story hotel on Troy's west side. It is convenient to Troy corporate parks, restaurants, and shopping. Restaurant, bar. In-room data ports. Cable TV. Indoor pool. Hot tub. Exercise equipment. Business services. Some pets allowed. | 200 W. Big Beaver Rd. | 248/680–9797 or 800/228–9290 | fax 248/680–9774 | www.marriott.com | 350 rooms | $84–$174 | AE, D, DC, MC, V.

Northfield Hilton. This full-service hotel is off I–75 and near Somerset Collection, office parks, and restaurants. Restaurant, bar (with jazz entertainment, cigar bar), room service. In-room data ports, some refrigerators. Cable TV. Indoor pool. Sauna. Business services. Some pets allowed. | 5500 Crooks Rd. | 248/879–2100 or 800/445–8667 | fax 248/879–6054 | www.hilton.com | 191 rooms | $79–$159 | AE, D, DC, MC, V.

Red Roof Inn. This budget-minded, two-story chain hotel is on Troy's southwest side near Oakland University, site of the Meadow Brook Music Festival. In-room data ports. Cable TV. Some pets allowed. | 2350 Rochester Ct. | 248/689–4391 or 800/733–7663 | fax 248/689–4397 | www.redroof.com | 109 rooms | $51–$77 | AE, D, DC, MC, V.

Residence Inn by Marriott. Business travelers prefer this two-story, all-suite hotel just off I–75 because it's near many corporate complexes. Picnic area, complimentary Continental breakfast. In-room data ports, kitchenettes. Cable TV. Pool. Hot tub. Laundry facilities. Some pets allowed. | 2600 Livernois Rd. | 248/689–6856 | fax 248/689–3788 | www.marriothotels.com | 152 suites | $129–$179 | AE, D, DC, MC, V.

Somerset Inn. The Somerset Collection is next door and Kmart headquarters is a ½ block from this 14-story hotel. You'll find contemporary designs inside, with marble, light woods, and attractive guest rooms. Restaurant, bar, room service. In-room data ports. Cable TV. Pool. Business services. | 2601 W. Big Beaver Rd. | 248/643–7800 or 800/228–8769 | fax 248/643–2296 | 250 rooms | $139–$159 | AE, D, DC, MC, V.

WAKEFIELD

MAP 9, E2

(Nearby towns also listed: Iron River, Ironwood, Ontonagon)

This Upper Peninsula town is in Gogebic County. "Gogebic" translates as "where trout rising make small rings upon the surface." On the peninsula's far western end, the county is best known for its recreational possibilities, with 100 waterfalls, nearby Lake Superior, inland fishing, and ski resorts. It's part of "Big Snow Country," a Midwestern snow belt that receives as much as 300 inches a year. (*Note:* Area codes in this vicinity are scheduled to change to 989 beginning April 7, 2001.)

Information: Wakefield Chamber of Commerce | Box 93, Wakefield 49968 | 906/224–2222 or 800/522–5651 | jbekkala@mail.portup.com | www2.fwdwakefield.org.

Attractions

Eddy Park. This pleasant park on Sunday Lake has a beach where you can picnic or join the ducks for a swim. A campground is less than a ¼ mi from the picnic area. | Lakeshore Dr., off U.S. 2 | 906/229–5131 | fax 906/229–5331 | Free | May–Sept.

Indianhead Mountain Resort. Nineteen runs with a vertical drop of 638 ft make this a good destination for beginner and intermediate schussers. You can also ski at night, snowboard, snowshoe, and snow tube here. Dogsled and horse-drawn sleigh rides are available too. | 500 Indianhead Rd. | 906/229–5920 or 800/346–3426 | fax 906/229–5920 | info@indianheadmtn.com | www.indianheadmtn.com | $30–$36 | Nov.–mid-Apr., daily.

Lake Gogebic. The biggest lake in the U.P. spans two counties and two time zones. There's great fishing on the 13,380-acre lake that's about 20 mi from Wakefield. You can also snowmobile, hunt, ski, bike, and camp in the area. | 906/575–3265 | info@lakegogebic.com | www.lakegogebic.com.

ON THE CALENDAR

FEB.: *Wakefield Historical Society Chili Feed.* You can join a walking tour of town and feast on hot chili afterwards during this event. Other food and door prizes are also on the agenda at the Society's Museum. | 906/224–8151.

Dining

Club 28 Inc. American. There's a popular fish fry on Fridays at this family-style restaurant in the heart of town, near Sunday Lake. Shrimp dinners, sandwiches, and pizza are also served. | 203 Sunday Lake St. | 906/224–8781 | Open daily | $5.75–$9 | No credit cards.

Lodging

Indianhead Mountain Resort. Several types of accommodations are available at this resort on 185 acres. You can stay in the main lodge, or rent a condo or a trailside chalet. Bar (with entertainment), dining room. Cable TV. Indoor pool. Hot tub. 9-hole golf course, tennis. Exercise equipment, hiking. Bicycles. Downhill skiing, sleigh rides. Children's programs (infants–17), playground. Business services. Some pets allowed. | 500 Indianhead Rd. | 906/229–5920 or 800/346–3426 | fax 906/229–5920 | info@indianheadmtn.com | www.indianheadmtn.com/lodging.html | 40 rooms, 60 condos, 43 chalets | $90–$164, $72–$152 condos, $122–$256 chalets | Closed mid-Apr.–June, Oct.–mid-Nov. | AE, D, MC, V.

Northwoods Motel. This no-frills place is right on the main highway, 2 mi west of town. The rooms are quiet and have two double beds. Some pets allowed. | 912 W. U.S. 2 | 906/224–8631 | 16 | $35–$42 | D, MC, V.

Regal Country Inn. Rooms in this motel have Victorian, country, and historic themes. A 1950s-style ice cream parlor and soda fountain on the premises are a delightful treat. Complimentary Continental breakfast. Cable TV. Sauna. | 1602 U.S. 2 E | 906/229–5122 | regalinn@partup.com | 18 rooms | $30–$68 | AE, D, MC, V.

WARREN

MAP 9, F7

(Nearby towns also listed: Detroit, Madison Heights, Mt. Clemens)

Now the third-largest city in the state, this northern Detroit suburb owes its growth to the General Motors Tech Center. The center was designed by noted architect Eero Saarinen and has attracted a number of car-related industries, restaurants, and hotels.

Information: **Warren, Center Line, Sterling Heights Chamber of Commerce** | 30500 Van Dyke Ave., Warren 48093 | 810/751–3939 | cmoskal@wcschamber.com | www.wcschamber.com.

Attractions

Norman J. Halmich Park. Whatever your game, you can probably do it here, at the largest of the 24 city parks. There are six soccer fields, four volleyball courts, two basketball courts, four tennis courts, and horseshoe pits. In winter you can glide on a natural ice-skating rink. You can also stroll on six walking paths, picnic in shelters, and listen to music in the two concert pavilions. | Ryan Rd. and Thirteen Mile Rd. | 810/268–8400 | Free | Daily, dawn to dusk.

ON THE CALENDAR

MAY–AUG.: *Summer Concert Series.* From Memorial Day to the last week of August, Halmich Park hosts concerts every weekend. A military band, the Warren Symphony Orchestra, and other local talents entertain. | 810/264–0959.

DEC.: *Warren Christmas Tree Lighting and Sing-Along.* This holiday celebration is held on the first Saturday of the month at Warren City Hall, 29500 Van Dyke Ave. between Twelve Mile Rd. and Thirteen Mile Rd. Festivities include the lighting of a Christmas tree, hayrides, Christmas carols, and the arrival of Santa by helicopter. Hot chocolate is served. | 810/574–4500 | www.cityofwarren.org.

Dining

Albion's. Continental. A varied menu and a spacious dining room, with comfortable booths, makes this restaurant a great place for parties and families. You can choose from Italian and Greek dishes, as well as from such staples as New York steak and meat loaf. Kids' menu. Breakfast is also available. | 2270 E. Ten Mile Rd. | 810/758–2727 | $6–$12 | MC, V.

All American Restaurant. American. Traditional booths and counter seating go right along with the traditional fare this diner serves. Popular dinners include pork chops and New York strip steak. | 21403 Van Dyke Ave. | 810/754–4436 | Breakfast also available | $4–$7 | No credit cards.

Andiamo Italia. Italian. This east side eatery has Mediterranean appeal and an upscale menu. Start your meal with the tender calamari or portobello al forno, a hefty mushroom in a rich chicken and veal stock. The light-as-air veal dishes are truly inspired (try the osso buco), as are the homemade pastas, including the farfalle noodles with chicken, mushrooms, cannelloni, spinach, tomatoes, and asiago cheese. Entertainment Wed.–Sat. | 7096 14 Mile Rd. | 810/268–3200 | fax 810/268–5707 | No lunch weekends | $13–$22 | AE, MC, V.

Chinese Village Inn. Chinese. Contemporary Chinese pictures on the walls and soft lighting set the mood at this large restaurant. Here you can eat carefully prepared favorites like sweet and sour chicken, shrimp fried rice, and vegetable lo mein. | 28740 Ryan Rd. | 810/574–1560 | Closed Tues. | $6–$10 | AE, D, DC, MC, V.

Costanzo's Victorian Room. Italian. Lasagna and baked ziti, as well as filet mignon and fresh fish, are on the menu at this lovely little Victorian-style restaurant. For dessert, try the homemade tiramisu, cannoli, or zuppe inglese, a five-flavored brandy sponge cake. | 3601 E. Twelve Mile Rd. | 810/751–6880 | $8.95–$20.95 | AE, D, DC, MC, V.

Stevie's End Zone. American. This sports bar in the Ramada Inn has a love for the singer Stevie Nicks. Lots of posters and mementos of her adorn the walls. Grilled dinners include burgers, steaks, and chicken. Pastas and salads are also available. | 30000 Van Dyke Ave. | 810/573–7600 | fax 810/573–7356 | $6.95–$12.95 | AE, MC, V.

Lodging

Best Western Sterling Inn. This chain hotel 3 mi from the GM Tech Center caters to business travelers. An on-site restaurant, the Loon River Café, emphasizes regional cuisine, including northern Michigan fish and game. Restaurant, bar, room service. In-room data ports, refrigerators, some in-room hot tubs. Cable TV. Indoor pool. Hot tub. Exercise equipment. Business services. | 34911 Van Dyke Ave., Sterling Heights | 810/979–1400 or 800/780–7234 | fax 810/979–0430 | www.sterlinginn.com | 160 rooms | $79–$129 | AE, D, DC, MC, V.

Candlewood Suites. Two blocks north of the GM Tech Center, this all-suites hotel makes it easy for you to cook in with a 24-hr food shop on the premises. Suites are furnished in maroon and beige. In-room data ports, kitchenettes. Cable TV, in-room VCRs (and movies). Exercise equipment. No pets. | 7010 Convention Blvd. | 810/978–1261 | fax 810/978–1701 | www.candlewoodsuites.com | 122 suites | $95–$115 | AE, D, DC, MC, V.

Courtyard by Marriott. This three-story hotel built in 2000 is popular with those doing business at the GM Tech Center across the street. In-room data ports, some kitchenettes, some refrigerators, cable TV. Indoor pool. Hot tub. Exercise equipment. Laundry facilities. | 30190 Van Dyke Ave. | 810/751–5777 or 800/321–2211 | fax 810/751–4463 | www.courtyard.com | 161 rooms | $64–$114 | AE, D, DC, MC, V.

Fairfield Inn by Marriott. Marriott's answer to the budget hotel, this property sports the signature blue-and-white exterior and has reliable, basic rooms. The three-story hotel, built in the early 1990s, is on the north side of Warren. Complimentary Continental breakfast.

In-room data ports. Cable TV. Pool. | 7454 Convention Blvd. | 810/939–1700 | fax 810/939–1700 | www.fairfieldinn.com | 132 rooms | $64–$88 | AE, D, DC, MC, V.

Georgian Inn. Despite being along the busy Gratiot strip, this two-story hotel in Roseville has a quiet location and a peaceful courtyard. It's 6 mi from Warren. Restaurant, bar, room service. In-room data ports, some in-room hot tubs. Cable TV. Pool. Exercise equipment. Laundry facilities. Business services. Some pets allowed. | 31327 Gratiot Ave., Roseville | 810/294–0400 or 800/477–1466 | fax 810/294–1020 | www.thegeorgianinn.com | 111 rooms | $70–$76. | AE, D, DC, MC, V.

Hampton Inn. The GM Tech Center is 2 blocks from this three-story chain hotel on the north side of Warren. Complimentary Continental breakfast. In-room data ports, some refrigerators. Cable TV. | 7447 Convention Blvd. | 810/977–7270 | fax 810/977–3889 | www.hampton-inn.com | 124 rooms | $69–$89 | AE, D, DC, MC, V.

Holiday Inn Express. A handy location off I–696 and special amenities for business travelers, such as extra large desks and webTV Internet access, distinguish this contemporary two-story inn. It's tucked away in a residential area on the east side of Warren. Complimentary Continental breakfast. In-room data ports. Cable TV. Pool. Business services. | 11500 11 Mile Rd. | 810/754–9700 or 800/465–4329 | fax 810/754–0376 | www.basshotels.com/holiday-inn | 125 rooms | $79–$109 | AE, D, DC, MC, V.

Homewood Suites. Apartment-style rooms are designed to make business travelers feel at home. This three-story hotel is 17 mi north of downtown Detroit. Complimentary Continental breakfast. In-room data ports, kitchenettes. Cable TV, in-room VCRs (and movies). Pool. Hot tub. Exercise equipment. Laundry facilities. Business services. Some pets allowed (fee). | 30180 N. Civic Center Dr. | 810/558–7870 or 800/225–5466 | fax 810/558–8072 | www.homewood-suites.com | 76 suites | $89–$169 | AE, D, DC, MC, V.

Motel 6. Rooms have either one king or two double-size beds in this motel in the heart of the business district. In-room data ports. Some pets allowed. | 8300 Chicago Rd. | 810/826–9300 | fax 810/979–4525 | 115 rooms | $42.95 | AE, D, DC, MC, V.

Ramada Inn. Some rooms in this well-equipped in-town hotel have work desks and recliner chairs. Restaurant, bar. In-room data ports, some microwaves, some refrigerators. Indoor pool. Hot tub. No pets. | 30000 Van Dyke Ave. | 810/573–7600 or 800/298–2054 | fax 810/573–7356 | www.ramada.com | 156 rooms | $74–$79 | AE, D, DC, MC, V.

Red Roof Inn. This no-frills chain hotel just off I–696 at Exit 20 has location going for it. It's 4 mi to the Detroit Zoo, 5 mi to the Michigan State Fairgrounds, and 20 mi to the Pontiac Silverdome and the Palace of Auburn Hills. In-room data ports. Cable TV. Business services. Some pets allowed. | 26300 Dequindre Rd. | 810/573–4300 | fax 810/573–6157 | www.redroof.com | 136 rooms | $45–$60 | AE, D, DC, MC, V.

Residence Inn by Marriott. One- and two-bedroom suites make this three-story hotel popular with business travelers. It's on the east side of Warren. Picnic area, complimentary Continental breakfast. In-room data ports, kitchenettes. Cable TV, in-room VCRs (and movies). Pool. Hot tub. Exercise equipment. Laundry facilities. Some pets allowed (fee). | 30120 Civic Center Dr. | 810/558–8050 | fax 810/558–8214 | www.marriotthotels.com | 133 suites | $79–$129 | AE, D, DC, MC, V.

Van Dyke Park Hotel and Conference Center. Rooms here are forest green with floral patterns on the bedding and draperies. Each room comes with a work desk and either two double beds or one king-size bed. The hotel is in the heart of the business district. Restaurant, complimentary Continental breakfast. Indoor pool. Hot tub, sauna. Health club. No pets. | 31800 Van Dyke Ave. | 810/939–2860 | 235 rooms | $99–$115 | AE, D, DC, MC, V.

WHITEHALL AND MONTAGUE

MAP 9, C6

(Nearby towns also listed: Grand Haven, Holland, Ludington)

The twin cities of Whitehall and Montague are distinguished by the presence of both the White River Lighthouse and a 4,300-pound, 48-ft weather vane mentioned in the *Guinness Book of Records*. The area is a busy summer resort, with a Lake Michigan shoreline and a number of inland lakes nearby. (*Note:* Area codes in this vicinity are scheduled to change to 989 beginning April 7, 2001.)

Information: **White Lake Area Chamber of Commerce** | 124 W. Hanson St., Whitehall 49461 | 231/893–4585 or 800/879–9702 | fax 231/893–0914 | info@whitelake.org | www.whitelake.org.

Attractions

Hart-Montague Trail. Michigan's first linear state park, this 22½-mi paved trail runs north to Hart through fields, orchards, and woods. Purchase a pass from the gas station near the Montague entrance or at the Chamber of Commerce. The trail is at least 30 ft wide, perfect for in-line skating, biking, hiking, or snowmobiles. | 31 Water St. | 231/893–4585 | www.whitelake.org | $2 | Daily.

Montague City Museum. This local historical museum traces the past and present of the twin cities of Whitehall and Montague, including their ties to the lumber and shipping industries. You'll also see a section devoted to Nancy Ann Fleming, a native daughter who was voted Miss America in 1961. | Church and Meade St. | 231/894–6813 | Free | June–Sept., Sat. and Sun 1–5.

White River Light Station Museum. This lighthouse dating from 1875 displays photographs, paintings, and marine artifacts drawn from a time when this western Michigan area was known as the "Lumber Queen of the World." You can climb the spiral stairs in the light's tower to see the original Fresnel lens and view Lake Michigan and White Lake. | 6199 Murray Rd., Whitehall | 231/894–8265 | $2 | June–Aug., Tues.–Fri. 11–5, Sat. and Sun. 12–6; Sept., weekends only. Tours by appointment.

World's Largest Weathervane. You can see this 48-ft-tall weather vane listed in the *Guinness Book of Records* on the north shore of White Lake. A replica of a 19th-century schooner tops the hand-formed structure, which weighs more than two tons, and a working weather station is in the base. Whitehall Metal Studios donated the weather vane to the city. | Bus. Rte. 31, Montague | 231/894–8265 | Free | Daily.

ON THE CALENDAR

JUNE–AUG.: *Summer Concerts.* The White Lake Music Shell welcomes a variety of local performers during its summer-long, open-air concert season. | Dowling St. | 231/893–4585 | www.whitelake.org.
AUG.: *White Lake Maritime Festival.* A Venetian parade, a sailing regatta, and a water-ski show skim over White Lake in Whitehall at this event during the third weekend of August. Kids' shows, arts and crafts, sporting events, a food tent, and live entertainment also are part of the fun. | 231/893–4585 | www.whitelake.org.

Dining

Outer Edge Restaurant. American. In the Ramada Inn, this spot has everything you expect to find in a sports bar—televisions and pool tables around the room, plus burgers, chicken and shrimp baskets, sandwiches, and pizza on the menu. There are separate dining and lounge areas. | 2685 Colby Rd., Whitehall | 231/893–3030 | fax 231/893–3030 | $3.50–$10 | AE, D, DC, MC, V.

Lodging

Ramada Inn Whitehall. Michigan Adventure Amusement Park is 5 mi and five golf courses are within 10 mi of this chain hotel. Restaurant, bar, room service. Some kitchenettes, some in-room hot tubs. Cable TV. Pool. Hot tub, sauna. Exercise equipment. | 2865 Colby Rd., Whitehall | 231/893–3030 or 800/298–2054 | www.ramada.com | 66 rooms.

White Swan Inn. An 1884 Queen Anne Victorian, this in-town bed and breakfast has a screened-in porch and is surrounded by mature maples and lily-of-the-valley beds. Rooms are well-furnished with antiques, wicker furniture, iron beds, desks, and some claw-foot tubs. The house is across the street from the summer theater and within walking distance of the lake, shops, and restaurants. Complimentary breakfast. Cable TV. No pets. No smoking. | 303 S. Mears Ave., Whitehall | 231/894–5169 or 888/WHT–SWAN | fax 231/894–5169 | info@whiteswanninn.com | www.whiteswanninn.com | 3 rooms with baths | $65–$85 | AE, MC, V.

YPSILANTI

(Nearby towns also listed: Ann Arbor, Dearborn, Detroit, Monroe, Plymouth)

Ypsilanti, named after a Greek patriot, is on the Huron River near Ann Arbor. A home to industry and Eastern Michigan University, its downtown still retains many fine examples of Greek Revival architecture.

Information: Ypsilanti Area Convention and Visitors Bureau | 106 W. Michigan Ave., Ypsilanti 48197 | 734/483–4444 or 800/265–9045 | fax 734/483–0400 | info@ypsilanti.org | www.ypsilanti.org.

Attractions

Eastern Michigan University. This state university dating from 1849 has more than 25,000 students. Tours beginning at Starkweather Hall take in sites such as the Quirk Dramatic Arts Theater, Pease Auditorium, Bowen Field House, Rynearson Stadium, and the Ford Art Gallery. | 734/487–1849 or 734/487–INFO | fax 734/487–6559 | www.emich.edu | Free | Daily.

Ford Lake Park. This 98-acre city park has something for everyone—boating, tennis, picnicking, fishing, volleyball, and more. | 9075 S. Huron River Dr. | 734/544–3800. | $4 per vehicle | Daily dawn to dusk.

Me 'N' My Sister's Country Store. A former freight station on the Huron River houses this unique shop in the Depot Town Shopping area. Here you can find one-of-a-kind craft items, Warren Kimball prints, Pat Richter lamps and pictures, a full line of Boyds collectibles, Heritage lace, ornaments, vases, birdhouses and garden supplies, as well as many other specialty items. | 13 E. Cross St. | 734/487–0503 | fax 734/487–0860 | www.me-n-my-sisters.com | Mon.–Wed. 10-6; Thurs.–Fri. 10-8; Sat. 9-5; Sun. 12-5.

Yankee Air Museum. Milestones of Southeastern Michigan aviation history are on display in a particular hangar at Willow Run Airport. The hangar played a major role in producing the famous four-engine B-24 bombers during World War II. The museum is off I–275, Exit 20, or I–94, Exit 190, 5 mi south of downtown. | Willow Run Airport, Beck Rd. | 734/483–4030 | fax 734/483–5076 | www.yankeeairmuseum.org | $5 | Tues.–Sat. 10–4, Sun. 12–4.

Ypsilanti Automotive Heritage Museum. You can learn about the unusual role Ypsilanti and its pioneers played in the history of the American automobile, see vintage vehicles, and study the signs and records of early auto dealers here. | 112 E. Cross St. | 734/482–5200 | Free | Weekdays 1:30–5:30, Sat. 9–5, Sun. 12–5.

Ypsilanti Historical Museum. Life in 19th-century Ypsilanti is the focus of this museum housed in a building that dates from the 1860s. The rooms, which contain the furnishings of the era, display historical information, rotating exhibits, and the city's archives. | 220 N. Huron St. | 734/482–4990 | Free | Thurs.–Sun. 2–4, closed Mon.–Wed.

ON THE CALENDAR

JUNE: *Frog Island Jazz/Blues Festival.* A lively host of bands—including jazz, blues, zydeco, gospel, and world beat—gather at Frog Island Park, off Rice Street, along the banks of the Huron River. This festival showcases the diverse styles and talents of local and national performers. | 734/761–1800 | www.a2ark.org.

JUNE: *Ypsilanti Orphan Car Show.* Cars, trucks, and motor scooters that are no longer produced are the stars of this one-day event in early June at Riverside Park. You learn about the vehicles on display—with nameplates such as Sunset, Cushman, Hudson, Tucker, and Gotfredson—from noted automobile historians during a drive-by narration. | Cross and Huron Sts. | 734/482–5200 | www.ypsilanti.org.

AUG.: *Ypsilanti Heritage Festival.* Dioramas of early American life, arts and crafts, and entertainment along the river are all part of this shindig in Ypsilanti's Depot Town neighborhood the third weekend of the month. | 734/483–4444 | www.ypsilanti.org.

OCT.: *Ypsilanti Farmers' Market Fall Fair.* This colorful month-long harvest festival at Wiard's Farm, 5565 Merrit Road, has live music, a petting zoo, pony rides, a cider mill, and you can pick apples and pumpkins. | 734/483–1480.

Dining

Cady's Grill. American. Grilled or sautéed fresh fish and charbroiled steaks and burgers are the favorites at this restaurant in a former railroad station at the Depot Town shopping area. Pictures of the town's old buildings are on the walls. | 36 E. Cross St. | 734/483–2800 | $6.95–$12.95 | AE, MC, V.

Haab's. Steak. An area favorite since the 1930s, Haab's is known for its simple food and ample servings. Homemade bread starts off a stick-to-your-ribs selection of dishes that includes pan-fried chicken, prime rib, juicy steaks, and smoked pork. The interior is steak-house classic—dark paneling, Tiffany-style lamps, and tin ceilings—in a building that dates from the 19th century. Kids' menu. | 18 W. Michigan Ave. | 734/483–8200 | www.annarbor.org/pages/haabs.html | $19–$29 | AE, D, DC, MC, V.

© Artville

MADE IN MICHIGAN

Michigan is known for goodies such as American Spoon Foods and Mackinac Island fudge. However, few visitors are aware of some of its other delights: the delicate, one-of-a-kind earrings by Zoe Elle of Ypsilanti, malted pancake and waffle mix from F. S. Carbon of Buchanan, or hand-cut scented soaps by Homesong of Williamston.

Once upon a time you had to traverse the state to find these more unusual offerings. For the past decade, however, they've been as close as Michigania's 20-page catalog.

Jan Hayhow, company president of Michigania, said too many "Michigan" gifts are made in the Far East and simply stamped with the state's name. Her company has made a niche by selling quality Michigan-made goods in its stores in Lansing and Birmingham and through its catalog. While popular with state residents, Michigania also peddles unique souvenirs for anyone who wants to take home a piece of the Great Lakes State. | 800/533–9553 | www.michigania.com.

Pickle Barrel Inn. American. A restored building from the 1870s is home to this cozy local tavern furnished with antiques. The staff serves up old-fashioned favorites including prime rib, Alaskan cod, homemade pickle chips, and soups. Kids' menu. Salad bar. | 10256 Willis Rd. | 734/461–2391 | $14–$19 | MC, V.

Lodging

Parish House Inn. A former parsonage on a pretty lot overlooking the Huron River, this Queen Anne Victorian is painted dusty rose with cream trim and maroon accents. Rooms have antique furnishings and wallpaper. Some have fireplaces, and one has a hot tub. You're welcome to relax on the patio and in the rose garden, or by the parlor fireplace. Complimentary breakfast. In-room data ports. In-room VCRs (and movies). | 103 S. Huron St. | 734/480–4800 or 800/480–4866 | fax 734/480–7472 | info@parishhouseinn.com | www.parish-houseinn.com | 9 rooms with baths | $79–$124 | AE, MC, V.

Ypsilanti Marriott at Eagle Crest. This eight-story conference resort hotel overlooking Ford Lake has 130 rooms specially equipped for business travelers. It's the only hotel in southeastern Michigan with an 18-hole championship golf course on the premises. It's 1 mi north of downtown, off I–94 exit 153. 2 restaurants, 2 bars. In-room data ports, some minibars, some in-room refrigerators. Cable TV, room phones, TV in common area. Indoor pool, lake. Hot tub, sauna. 18-hole golf course, 2 tennis courts. Health club. Shops. Baby-sitting. Laundry services. Business services. No pets. | 1275 S. Huron St. | 734/487–2000 or 800/228–9290 | fax 734/487–0773 | www.marriott.com | 236 rooms, 8 suites | $159, $250 suites | AE, D, DC, MC, V.

Ohio

A New Yorker or Nebraskan who's never been to Ohio likely conjures up an image with plenty of barn silos, a dairy cow in every backyard, and perhaps a smoky skyline or two. That's not surprising, given that for centuries Ohio has been known as the "Gateway to the West." In truth the Buckeye State, which has reinvented itself over the last 40 years, is a beautifully balanced blend of not only everything Midwestern but also everything American.

Ohio folks might spend a summer Saturday at a county fair sampling peach preserves—and then head downtown in time for dinner and the symphony. They live in bustling cities such as Akron, Cleveland, Cincinnati, Columbus, Dayton, and Toledo as well as sleepy small towns that awaken to host spirited seasonal festivals celebrating everything from tomatoes and strawberries to twins and underwear. Thanks to this diversity, you'll find urban and rural, physical and intellectual activities from which to choose.

No matter what the season, Ohioans—and their visitors—spend plenty of time outdoors. A national forest, one of 73 state parks, or a metro park is never more than a buckeye's throw away. (Out-of-staters note: A buckeye is a horse chestnut.)

Ohio's eastern landscape is distinguished by steep hills and rocky soil. In fact, the edges of the Appalachian Mountains reach into eastern Ohio. Coal is found primarily in the southeast; Ohio also produces plenty of lime, clay, salt, sand, gravel, and stone.

To the west, on Ohio's flat plains, is the state's richest, most fertile soil, in which soybeans, corn, wheat, and tomatoes are grown. (Ohio produces more tomato juice than any other state in the country.) Ohio farms also provide us with hay, cattle, hogs, and dairy products.

Today most farms in the state are run as a sideline by people with other jobs, and only about one-fourth of Ohio's population lives in rural areas. But that's okay: Most Ohioans are never far from a produce stand or two that sells fresh-picked corn, tomatoes, and beans as soon as the weather turns warm.

CAPITAL: COLUMBUS	POPULATION: 11,186,331	AREA: 44,828 SQ MI
BORDERS: PA, WV, KY, IN, MI, AND LAKE ERIE	TIME ZONE: EASTERN	POSTAL ABBREVIATION: OH
WEB SITE: OHIOTOURISM.COM OR TRAVELOHIO.COM OR OHIOHISTORY.ORG		

Lake Erie is the state's largest body of water and attracts fishermen—and women—from far and near. Vineyards and peach and cherry orchards dot the lush land along its banks. Spanning much of southeastern and southern Ohio is Wayne National Forest, the only national forest in the state, offering plenty of activities for outdoor and sports enthusiasts. And no matter where you are in Ohio, you may see a white-tailed deer; the state animal grazes in all 88 counties.

Ohio has traditionally manufactured coal, iron, steel, rubber, and glass, but today it produces that and more. While still a manufacturing mecca—known for products such as transportation equipment, jet engines, computers, chemicals, soap, processed food, plastic and paper products, machines and machine tools, metal products, and auto parts—the state is now a high-tech hotbed too. Some several hundred scientific and technology companies have moved in. You'll also find headquarters for corporate giants such as the Kroger Co., Procter and Gamble Co., and NCR Corp. They've been here for years, and they're still thriving. Ohio the Rust Belt? Not anymore.

Ohio's biggest city, Columbus, just keeps getting bigger. Today it is the nation's 16th largest city. Also in Columbus is Ohio State University, the nation's largest single-university campus, founded in 1870. The state's next-largest city is Cleveland. Forget that old joke about "the mistake on the lake"; the city is now famous for its Rock and Roll Hall of Fame and Museum and much more.

Ohio has had its share of inventors over the years. The Wright Brothers invented and then perfected powered flight in Dayton; Thomas A. Edison of Milan dreamed up the incandescent light bulb, the phonograph, and early motion-picture cameras; Charles F. Kettering of Dayton gave us self-starting automobiles; and thanks to W. F. Semple of Mt. Vernon, we have chewing gum.

Throughout the state monuments and memorials honor Ohio's most noteworthy sons and daughters, among them astronaut Neil Armstrong, John Glenn, sharpshooter Annie Oakley, African-American poet laureate Paul Dunbar, and eight U.S. presidents: William Henry Harrison, Ulysses S. Grant, Rutherford B. Hayes, James A. Garfield, Benjamin Harrison, William McKinley, William Howard Taft, and Warren G. Harding.

History

Retreating glaciers during the last Ice Age around 12,000 BC created the landform now known as Ohio. The earliest inhabitants of the state were likely hunters of mastodon, mammoths, and giant beaver. Around 1000 BC, they were followed by people known as Mound Builders—native Americans of the Adena, Hopewell, Cole, Fort Ancient, and Erie tribes. They buried their dead, along with pottery, tools, ornaments, and weapons, in earthen mounds, which can still be seen in some Ohio state parks.

In the late 1600s, the English and French struggled for control of the land that included Ohio country. In the meantime, Indian groups, including the Erie, Huron (Wyandot), Ottawa, Tuscarora, Mingo, Delaware, Shawnee, and Miami, made their own claims to the land. (Many Ohio counties later were named after these tribes.) Conflicts and battles

OH Timeline

1669	1754–63	1775–83	1787
French explorers Adrien Jolliet and Rene-Robert Cavelier Sieur de La Salle explore the Ohio Valley, claiming it for the French.	French and British battle for control of the Ohio River; British are victors, winning Ohio country.	The American Revolution. The Treaty of Paris awards Ohio country to the United States rather than Great Britain.	Ohio becomes part of the Northwest Territory.

INTRODUCTION
HISTORY
REGIONS
WHEN TO VISIT
STATE'S GREATS
RULES OF THE ROAD
DRIVING TOURS

erupted. It wasn't until after the American Revolution, in 1783, that Ohio country was firmly in the hands of the United States.

On March 1, 1803, several months after a state convention in Chillicothe, Ohio became the 17th state in the Union. After the War of 1812, Gen. William Henry Harrison of Ohio was recognized as a war hero; he went on to win the U.S. presidential election in 1840.

In the first half of the 19th century, Ohio focused on building canals as a way of getting the state's goods to market year-round. Construction of the Ohio-Erie Canal began in 1825; the Miami-Erie Canal was completed in 1845. But the need for canals was short-lived, thanks to the railroads, which grew rapidly, beginning in the 1850s.

The Civil War strengthened and expanded Ohio's iron and steel manufacturing industries. In the late 19th century, Akron grew up around rubber manufacturing, and Toledo around glass manufacturing. The state economy seemed unstoppable—until the Great Depression, when more than a million Ohioans lost their jobs. World War II and the development of the aluminum and chemical industries in the 1950s and 1960s revitalized the state economy until the country-wide downturn in manufacturing in the 1970s.

By the 1980s and 1990s, Ohio's economy had diversified to include new high-tech and service industries, Japanese auto manufacturing plants, and industrial research and development. Today the state enjoys great economic prosperity.

Regions

1. NORTHWESTERN REGION

Rural lifestyles, serene small towns, and historic sites contribute to the flavor of northwestern Ohio, which is bordered by Michigan to the north and Indiana to the west. Farmland here is some of Ohio's most fertile; there are also a few thriving industrial areas. You'll find restored 19th-century buildings and mansions, tree-lined streets, and historic museums and villages. The Maumee, Ottawa, and Blanchard rivers also flow through this part of the state.

Towns listed: Bowling Green, Defiance, Findlay, Lima, Van Wert, Wauseon

2. NORTHERN REGION

Ready for white beaches and resorts? Northern Ohio is where you want to be. The focal points are Lake Erie, the Sandusky River, and several magical islands where you can forget your troubles during leisurely strolls and cruises, while eating ice-cream cones and looking out over the water.

Highlights of the region include a cavern, more than a handful of museums, quaint specialty shops, New England architecture, restored homes, and historic and Native American sites. You'll also find harbors, public parks, wineries, and plenty of fishing.

1788	1790s	1794	1795	1798
Marietta, in Ohio country, is the territory's first permanent American settlement.	Native Americans battle fiercely with settlers.	U.S. Army Maj. Gen. Anthony Wayne defeats Shawnee Chief Blue Jacket at the Battle of Fallen Timbers.	Greenville Treaty allows permanent settlement in Ohio.	Zane's Trace, an early road in Ohio country, opens.

At the mouth of the Maumee River is Toledo, the big-city anchor for northern Ohio. When you're tired of resort towns and rural scenery, hit Toledo for culture.

Towns listed: Bellevue, Elyria, Fremont, Kelleys Island, Lorain, Marblehead, Milan, Oberlin, Port Clinton, Put-in-Bay, Sandusky, Tiffin, Toledo, Vermilion

3. NORTHEASTERN REGION

Northeastern Ohio, with Lake Erie to the north and Pennsylvania to the east, is a perfect slice of everything Ohio. There are harbors and rounded hills, cities and suburbs, modern industry and still-fertile farms, theme parks and state parks, crafts and Amish culture, history and sports, horticultural parks and waterfront resorts, museums and manmade lakes.

Northeastern Ohio recalls days gone by, when Native Americans, New England pioneers, presidents, and canal-towing mules lived here. In addition to historical sites, you can try cross-country skiing in winter and, the rest of the year, boat and fish, go swimming, and raft the region's rivers, including the Mahoning, Ashtabula, Grand, and Cuyahoga. When evening falls, you can queue up for a luxurious dining cruise.

Towns listed: Akron, Alliance, Ashtabula, Aurora, Beachwood, Brecksville, Canton, Chardon, Cleveland, Conneaut, Eastlake, East Liverpool, Geneva-on-the-Lake, Kent, Massillon, Mentor, Painesville, Strongsville, Warren, Youngstown

4. NORTH CENTRAL REGION

While the western portion of north-central Ohio is flat, especially the counties of Hardin, Wyandot, Marion, and Crawford, it's slightly hillier in the region's eastern half, where the Appalachian foothills begin. Dairy farming, popcorn production, and agricultural research and development are big here, as is manufacturing. Of particular interest are a pioneer log blockhouse, colonial architecture, sheep farms, Amish enclaves, and a garden with 500 varieties of roses.

Towns listed: Mansfield, Marion, Mount Gilead, Mount Vernon, Wooster

5. WESTERN REGION

Farming is at its best in rural western Ohio, which has some of the flattest, most tillable soil in the state. But Ohio's highest point, Campbell Hill (1,550 ft above sea level) is also here, near Bellefontaine. Other area high points include Ohio's largest inland manmade lake, Grand Lake, which shelters a state park, weekend getaway homes, and great fishing; one of the state's most popular ski resorts; and an air and space museum that bears the name of Wapakoneta native son Neil Armstrong. Several unique historical areas focus on prehistoric times, Indian lore and villages, the Revolutionary War, and canal days. The Great Miami and Stillwater rivers run through Western Ohio, which is home to several hundred diverse industries.

Towns listed: Bellefontaine, Celina, Piqua, Sidney, Wapakoneta

March 1, 1803	1811	1812–15	1816	1825
Chillicothe is made the capital of Ohio, now the 17th state and the first from the Northwest Territory.	Ohio settlers defeat Shawnee chief Tecumseh at the Battle of Tippecanoe.	The War of 1812. Ohioans are victorious against the British at Fort Meigs, Fort Stephenson, and at the Battle of Lake Erie.	Columbus becomes the permanent state capital.	The state legislature approves canal building.

6. CENTRAL REGION

This is both the geographical and the emotional heart of the state. Here you'll find Columbus, the capital city, known for its entrepreneurs and its universities, including the daddy of them all, Ohio State University. Farms are in outlying areas of the "big city" and historical buildings and sites—including a large group of prehistoric burial mounds—are scattered throughout the region. This part of Ohio is crisscrossed by the Scioto, Olentangy, and Licking rivers and dotted by several manmade lakes, including the Delaware, Alum Creek, Madison, Deer Creek, and Buckeye. There is a huge array of cultural, intellectual, and physical activities, from race tracks to opera, spectacular malls and symphony orchestra concerts.

Towns listed: Columbus, Delaware, Granville, Lancaster, Newark, Washington Court House

7. EASTERN REGION

Bordering eastern Ohio is the beautiful Ohio River and the scenic hills of West Virginia. But make no mistake: There are plenty of steep hills, deep valleys, and winding streams on the Ohio side, too. Filled with coal and clay, the soil here is generally unsuitable for farming. Nevertheless, eastern Ohio has always made the most of its natural resources, producing plenty of pottery and glass over the last several hundred years.

Holmes and Tuscarawas counties are Amish country, home to delightful tree-lined towns. Throughout the region are reminders of those who've gone before: German-Swiss religious pilgrims from Pennsylvania, Delaware Indians, Hopalong Cassidy—even Johnny Appleseed, who planted orchards here.

Towns listed: Berlin, Cambridge, Coshocton, Dover, Gnadenhutten, New Philadelphia, St. Clairsville, Steubenville, Sugarcreek, Zanesville, Zoar

8. SOUTHEASTERN REGION

Wayne National Forest is the major geographical attraction of Ohio's southeastern region; West Virginia lies to the east. Important rivers are the Muskingum, Licking, and the Ohio. The region lies in the Appalachian foothills; the steep hills and deep valleys of eastern Ohio continue in the southeast. Manufacturing firms and some high-tech companies do business in this area. The town of Marietta, Ohio's oldest settlement, named in honor of Queen of France Marie Antoinette, is here. So is Athens, which grew up around Ohio University. State parks, ancient Indian mounds, and scenic highways are other local highlights.

Towns listed: Athens, Logan, Marietta

9. SOUTHERN REGION

The biggest part of Wayne National Forest is in southern Ohio; in fact, virtually all of Lawrence County is forestland. Gaze south, across the Ohio River, and you'll see the states of Kentucky and West Virginia. But look closer: Southern Ohio is actually an indus-

INTRODUCTION
HISTORY
REGIONS
WHEN TO VISIT
STATE'S GREATS
RULES OF THE ROAD
DRIVING TOURS

1832	1837	1838	1845	1851
Ohio-Erie Canal completed.	Significant railroad and industrial development begins.	National Road is completed, paving the way for overland transportation.	Miami-Erie Canal completed.	State's major cities are connected via railroad, slowly replacing canals.

trial landscape fueled by paper mills, iron, brick, plastic, and furniture manufacturing. Plenty of railroads remain.

Southern Ohio includes Chillicothe, Ohio's first capital. Mount Logan, the inspiration for the state seal, is also here. You're likely to stumble upon Greek Revival architecture, restored buildings, and antiques and specialty shops. You can also enjoy pleasant drives down the region's many state and U.S. highways.

Towns listed: Chillicothe, Gallipolis, Ironton, Portsmouth

10. SOUTHWESTERN REGION

Bordering southwestern Ohio are Kentucky and the Ohio River to the south, and Indiana to the west. Farming and industry, some of it high-tech, mix well here. But the southwestern Ohio landscape can change in a minute. Drive through Cincinnati and Hamilton County, and you'll switch into low gear more times than you can count on the hilly, curvy backroads. But head up Interstate 75, the major north-south route through western Ohio, and you'll find the terrain plenty flat.

Want to dine on the riverfront? No problem in Cincinnati, southwestern Ohio's most cosmopolitan city. Curious about the Wright Brothers? Hit Dayton's Aviation Trail. Interested in the Shakers? Stop in Lebanon. Want a wild ride? Hop on a roller coaster at Paramount's Kings Island in Mason. Outdoor playlands abound, thanks to the many state and metropolitan parks. In Cleveland's green spaces—part of a 100-mile chain called the "Emerald Necklace"—you can try any activity from water sports in summer to tobogganing in winter.

Towns listed: Cincinnati, Dayton, Hamilton, Lebanon, Mason, Miamisburg, Middletown, Oxford, Springfield, Vandalia, Waynesville, Wilmington, Yellow Springs

When to Visit

The four seasons in Ohio are quite distinct. Spring can be cloudy, chilly, and rainy with occasional teases of summerlike weather. Summer can get warm and extremely humid, making it feel 100 degrees-plus when it's only 85. Autumn can be beautiful, perfect for a fall-foliage tour. Winters are cold, with temperatures in the 20s and 30s. Expect at least a couple surprise snowstorms or ice storms, most of them in January. The farther north you go in winter, the colder, windier, and snowier it gets, thanks to Lake Erie.

In spite of summer's humidity, there's more to do in Ohio in summer than during any other season. (Ohioans, having been snowed in during winter and rained out in spring, are usually ready to be outdoors by summer.) Expect the hottest weather during the dog days of August, when temperatures are frequently in the 90s. Autumn is a good time for outdoor activities; the weather is usually fairly decent, and occasionally quite warm, through October.

The record high temperature for the state is 113°F, which was recorded in Centerville on July 21, 1934. The record low is -39 °F, which was recorded in Milligan on Feb.

1861–65	1870		Late 1880s	1902
Manufacturing boom, including iron and steel production, begins with the onset of the Civil War.	Benjamin F. Goodrich begins rubber manufacturing in Akron after opening a fire-hose production factory; by the turn of the century, Akron is the world's rubber capital. Billionaire-to-be	John D. Rockefeller creates the Standard Oil Company in Cleveland, now part of Cleveland-based British Petroleum America.	Natural gas is discovered near Toledo, leading to decades of glass manufacturing.	State flag adopted.

INTRODUCTION
HISTORY
REGIONS
WHEN TO VISIT
STATE'S GREATS
RULES OF THE ROAD
DRIVING TOURS

10, 1899. Steubenville holds the record for snowfall at 36 inches, which was recorded in November 1950, and a record 9.54 inches of rain fell in an eight-hour period in Sandusky on July 12, 1966. The average annual precipitation is usually around 30 to 40 inches, but the northeastern part of the state can see more than 40 inches annually.

CLIMATE CHART
Average Temperatures (°F) and Monthly Precipitation (in inches)

	JAN.	FEB.	MAR.	APR.	MAY	JUNE
CLEVELAND	32/18	35/19	46/28	58/37	69/47	78/57
	2.0	2.2	2.9	3.1	3.5	3.7
	JULY	AUG.	SEPT.	OCT.	NOV.	DEC.
	82/61	81/60	74/54	62/44	50/35	37/25
	3.5	3.4	3.4	2.5	3.2	3.1
	JAN.	FEB.	MAR.	APR.	MAY	JUNE
COLUMBUS	34/19	38/21	51/31	62/40	72/50	80/58
	2.2	2.2	3.3	3.2	3.9	4.0
	JULY	AUG.	SEPT.	OCT.	NOV.	DEC.
	84/63	82/61	76/55	65/43	51/34	39/25
	4.3	3.7	3.0	2.2	3.2	2.9

FESTIVALS AND SEASONAL EVENTS
WINTER

Dec. **Annual Historic Lebanon Christmas Festival and Horsedrawn Carriage Parades.** This free family event draws 50,000 people to Lebanon each year for live entertainment, costumed characters, food and crafts booths, and pictures with Mr. and Mrs. Claus. A daytime parade showcases Victorian costumes and antique carriages; the evening parade is for romantics. Expect lots of Christmas carols and candlelight. | 513/932–1100.

SPRING

Mar. **Cincinnati Home and Garden Show.** The Cincinnati Convention Center showcases everything new for the home and garden, including fine furnishings and products and services related to building and remodeling, gardening, and outdoor living. | 513/281–0022.

May **Cincinnati May Festival.** The annual celebration of choral and orchestral music encompasses five performances over two weekends and presents an unusual choral repertoire. The first festival was in 1873; it became an annual event in 1967. It's

---

1913
Miami River Valley suffers a devastating flood; a landmark flood-control system, the Miami Conservancy District, is built.

1929
The Great Depression hurts Ohio farms and industries; more than a million Ohioans lose their jobs.

1941–45
U.S. involvement in World War II. Ohio, engaged in the war effort, enjoys great prosperity.

1950s and 1960s
Ohio develops aluminum and chemical industries.

1967
The first black mayor of a major American city is Carl Stokes, elected in Cleveland.

said to be the longest continuously held music festival in North America. | 513/381–3300.

SUMMER

June **Crosby Festival of the Arts.** Ohio's oldest and largest outdoor juried art show is held at the Toledo Botanical Garden. More than 200 fine artists from across the country display and sell their works. Entertainment, food, and kids' art activities are part of the festivities. | 419/936–2986.

July **United States Air and Trade Show.** World aerobatic champs, aerobatic teams, wingwalkers, and barnstormers perform breathtaking maneuvers in this nationally acclaimed air show at Dayton International Airport in Vandalia. U.S. aircraft demos and displays, parachuting, pyrotechnics, and vintage aircraft are also on display. The U.S. Air Force Thunderbirds and the U.S. Navy Blue Angels perform on an alternating schedule; one group appears one year, the other the next. | 937/898–5901.

AUTUMN

Sept. **Ohio Heritage Days.** One of Ohio's largest free outdoor crafts festivals takes place each year at Malabar Farm State Park, west of Mansfield in Lucas. Skilled artisans practice crafts of yester-year; musicians perform vintage music. Steam-powered and vintage tractors and the Malabar Farm sawmill can be seen in operation, and massive steel steam engines and draft horses are on display. There's also Civil War and fur trappers encampments, a Saturday-evening barn dance to live music, and square dancing for novices and experts alike. | 419/892–2784.

Oct. **Circleville Pumpkin Show.** Nearly half a million people from around the world descend on this small Ohio town for the state's oldest, largest festival. Big pumpkins are the name of the game—beginning with the water tower, which is in the shape of a pumpkin. Pumpkin shows up at many a food stand as well. The setting is downtown Circleville, about 20 mi north of Chillicothe. | 740/474–7000.

1970s and 1980s	Mid-1980s	Late 1980s–1990s
A severe downturn in Ohio's auto, steel, and coal industries threatens the state's industrial base and economic vitality.	Akron, once an important center for rubber manufacturing, ceases rubber-product production. Other industrial plants are modernized; high-tech industries open.	Japanese auto manufacturers, new service industries, and industrial research and development contribute significantly to Ohio's economy.

State's Greats

Travel and tourism is a $9.9 billion industry in this state, and with good reason. From college and pro sports to ballet and theater, Ohio's got a lot to entice folks from out of town. There are history, science, art, and children's museums; and water parks north and south. There are gardens sheltering colorful butterflies and hundreds of varieties of roses. Food lovers relish the many ethnic eateries. Indoor and outdoor concerts pull in the biggest names around, while riverboats and dining cruises entertain you with games of chance and stage shows. Natural attractions and outdoor activities can be found in parks and along lakes and rivers throughout the state. Across the state each year, nearly 100 county and independent fairs and festivals make for even more fun.

Culture, Education, and History

The Ohio story is an interesting one, and the **Ohio Historical Society** is the organization charged to keep it alive for thousands of visitors annually. You'll find more than 60 historical landmarks and museums throughout the state.

A good way to approach a historical tour of Ohio is to focus on one or more "gateways" to state history: major sites organized according to theme, including American Indian heritage, settlement and transportation, military history, African-American heritage, leadership, social and economic history, and natural history. There are many gateway sites, but the following are especially interesting. **Fort Ancient,** a National Historic Landmark in Lebanon, is the largest, best-preserved prehistoric Indian hilltop enclosure in North America. The **Campus Martius Museum** in Marietta focuses on early settlement and migration into the Northwest Territory. **Fort Meigs,** on the Maumee River in Perrysburg, south of Toledo, was a supply post and staging area during the War of 1812; today the site contains one of the largest log forts in the country, blockhouses, and other war-related artifacts. The **Hayes Presidential Center** in Fremont includes the restored mansion of U.S. President Rutherford B. Hayes, the first presidential library, a museum, and the tomb of the president and his wife. You'll learn about Ohio's agricultural history at Zoar's **Zoar Village,** which features an early 19th-century German communal settlement, and at the **Piqua Historical Area,** where you also can take a ride on a restored section of the Miami-Erie Canal. At the 400-acre **Cedar Bog Nature Preserve** near Springfield, you'll learn about plants and animals of prehistoric times, after the last Ice Age.

Ohio cities and towns, both large and small, have many cultural attractions. For the best of the best, get tickets to the **Cleveland Orchestra,** known worldwide for its superb performances. If you want to get in the mood with sounds of the Big Band era, then the **Jazz Arts Group's Columbus Jazz Orchestra** is a must-hear. For theater entertainment riverboat-style, board the *Showboat Majestic* at the Public Landing on the Cincinnati riverfront.

Museums

Devote an entire day to Cincinnati's **Museum Center at Union Terminal,** an Art Deco train station that houses the **Cincinnati History Museum** and the **Museum of Natural History and Science.** The **Center of Science and Industry (COSI)** in Columbus delights kids and adults alike with its hands-on exhibits exploring health and life, history and the earth, and physical science and technology. Cleveland's star attraction is also its newest one, the **Rock and Roll Hall of Fame and Museum.** One of the state's greatest free attractions is the **U.S. Air Force Museum,** near Dayton, where you can learn military aviation history at the world's largest and oldest military aviation museum. (Be sure to walk inside the vintage aircraft on display.)

Beyond Ohio's larger cities are a number of other intriguing museums. Canton has two of particular note: the **Canton Classic Car Museum** and the **Pro Football Hall of**

Fame. The state's native sons are honored at the **Neil Armstrong Air and Space Museum** in Wapakoneta, and **Edison Birthplace Museum** in Milan. Ohio's contributions to the world are on display, too. The state's claim to being the "popcorn capital of the country" is proven at the **Wyandot Popcorn Museum** in Marion, and the remarkable intricate woodworkings of master carver David Warther are on display at **Warther Carvings** in Dover.

Parks, Natural Areas, and Outdoor Recreation

Cedar, pine, and hardwood trees line **Wayne National Forest,** which covers a remarkable 229,000 acres in southern and southeastern Ohio. You can hike, backpack, camp, and ride horses through this wilderness. It's likely you'll see songbirds, wild turkeys, and, of course, white-tailed deer, here. Ohio also has 19 state forests; all but one are in east-central and southeastern Ohio. You'll also find more than 100 **wildlife areas** operated by the state, and 77 nature preserves.

There are 73 **state parks,** scattered throughout Ohio, many near manmade lakes. Summer activities include boating, picnicking, bicycling, hiking, swimming, and camping; some parks have bikes, jet skis, and pedal boats for rent. State park campgrounds fill quickly, so if you plan on camping you should arrive early or call for reservations. In winter, the parks are great places to try cross-country skiing and snowmobiling. Many parks also host interpretive programs and contain restored historical structures.

Maumee Bay State Park, near Toledo, offers a comfortable and modern lodge/hotel and spacious, furnished cottages. For excellent trout fishing, head to the **Clear Fork River** in Mohican State Park. Many of Ohio's larger cities have superbly groomed **metroparks.** Among them is the **Cuyahoga Valley National Recreation Area,** which spans 33,000 acres between Cleveland and Akron, giving city dwellers and visitors the chance to enjoy nature, culture, and history. Thanks to **Lake Erie** and Ohio's many **rivers,** fishing and boating are almost always close at hand.

If it's beaches you want, then the shores of **Lake Erie** are where you need to be. From **Port Clinton** you can take a ferry to lovely **Put-in-Bay** or scenic **Kelleys Island.** Further south, try a beach on one of Ohio's manmade lakes, such as **Indian Lake** or **Grand Lake.** These beaches are sandy, too, though the sand is not quite as white as that along Lake Erie.

If you're ready for some serious bicycling, hook up with 3,000 other riders on the **Great Ohio Bicycle Adventure,** a week-long tour in June. (A recent tour covered Ashland, Orrville, New Philadelphia, Coshocton, Mount Vernon, and Galion.) If you prefer to ride or hike on your own, try one of the abandoned railroads now converted into biking and hiking trails by **Ohio's Rails To Trails Conservancy.** | 614/841–1075 | fax 614/841–9857 | www.rtcohio@transact.org.

In winter, you can ski at more than a handful of Ohio resorts. Try **Mad River Mountain** in Bellefontaine, which has 15 runs and an "avalanche" snow-tubing park.

Spectator Sports

Ohio has a full complement of professional sports squads: the **Cincinnati Reds** and **Cleveland Indians** baseball teams, the **Cleveland Cavaliers** basketball team, and the **Cincinnati Bengals** and the **Cleveland Browns** football teams. (The Browns, back in Cleveland after a four-year absence, got a brand-new stadium in 1999.) The National Hockey League's expansion team, the **Columbus Blue Jackets,** took to the ice for the first time in 2000 at their brand new Nationwide Arena.

And of course, there's the state's beloved college football team, the **Ohio State Buckeyes,** who play at the **Ohio State University Stadium** in Columbus. If you're lucky

INTRODUCTION
HISTORY
REGIONS
WHEN TO VISIT
STATE'S GREATS
RULES OF THE ROAD
DRIVING TOURS

enough to know somebody who knows somebody who can get tickets, by all means go, even if you don't understand the game that well. Buckeye fever is contagious, so you're sure to have a great time.

Ohio has lots more for sports lovers of all stripes. The **Columbus Crew** plays major-league soccer in Columbus Crew Stadium, and there's harness racing at **Scioto Downs,** near Columbus. Golf lovers won't want to miss the annual PGA Kroger Senior Classic golf tournament at the **Golf Center at Kings Island** in Mason, which takes place in September. Those who prefer to hit the links themselves can do it here as well.

Other Points of Interest

Thrill seekers won't want to miss **Cedar Point** in Sandusky, continually rated Ohio's best amusement/theme park. (You'll go upside down six times on the inverted Raptor roller coaster.) The **Soak City** water park and **Challenge Park,** featuring race cars and miniature golf courses, are both next to Cedar Point.

Ohio Caverns, near Bellefontaine, is considered one of the most colorful caves in the country with its wonderful white formations and mysterious murals.

The **Toledo Zoo** is home to more than 500 species of mammals, birds, and reptiles—even a "hippoaquarium." For something truly out of the ordinary, go on safari at the largest wildlife conservation facility in North America, **The Wilds,** near Cambridge in Muskingum County. You'll see many free-roaming, exotic animals.

Rules of the Road

License requirements: 16 and 17 year olds who have completed drivers' education classes can obtain licenses; otherwise, drivers must be 18.

Right turn on red: Unless posted otherwise, it is legal to make a right turn at a red light after a full stop.

Seat belt and helmet laws: Drivers and front-seat passengers must wear seat belts. Kids under age 4 or less than 40 pounds must use a child-safety restraint. Motorcyclists under age 18 or with less than one-year's driving experience must wear helmets.

Speed limits: Speed limits are 25 to 35 mph in most cities and towns; 55 mph on township, county, and state roads; and 55 to 65 mph on expressways and the Ohio Turnpike.

For more information: Call the Ohio Bureau of Motor Vehicles: 800/589–TAGS.

Southern Ohio Tour

FROM NEW RICHMOND ALONG THE OHIO RIVER AND NORTH TO LEBANON, WAYNESVILLE, SPRINGFIELD, AND BELLEFONTAINE

Distance: 130 mi (210 km)   Time: 3–4 days

Breaks: Spend the first night in Lebanon, preferably at Ohio's oldest inn. Springfield is a convenient place to stay a second night, and a third, if you want to spend another day enjoying Buck Creek State Park.

Southern Ohio's hot spots, like Paramount's Kings Island theme park, are fairly well-known. This tour covers the southern Ohio that not as many people venture out to see. It begins with a scenic drive along the Ohio River and then proceeds north through several interesting and historic villages and towns.

❶ Start in **New Richmond** and take a scenic drive north along the Ohio River on U.S. 52.

❷ **Lebanon** (40 mi northwest of New Richmond; follow I–275 north to I–71 exit 32) makes a good base for the first day. Begin by exploring **Fort Ancient State Memorial,** an Ohio Historical Society museum that chronicles the state's Native American history. Also here is a 100-acre Native-American burial site and the nation's second largest earth-work. Return to Lebanon and stroll through the downtown area, which is lined with antiques shops and specialty stores. You might want to take a ride aboard the **Turtle Creek Valley Railroad.** A restored steam locomotive takes passengers through the rural countryside of southern Ohio on the old Indiana and Ohio Railroad tracks. The **Golden Lamb Inn,** Ohio's oldest inn (1803), is a destination in its own right, and a great place to stop for the night. Eighteen guest rooms are decorated with antique Shaker furnishings; the restaurant serves bountiful American fare. (Lebanon has a few other, less expensive, lodging spots as well.)

❸ The next morning, drive to **Waynesville** (about 20 mi north on U.S. 42), which bills itself as "The Antiques Capital of the Midwest." More than two dozen antiques stores line the streets of the downtown area. If you are in Waynesville on a fall weekend, be sure to check out the **Ohio Renaissance Festival.** Main Street is taken over for three days by the **Ohio Sauerkraut Festival** in October.

❹ In **Springfield** (follow U.S. 42 north to Xenia, then follow U.S. 68 north for 25 mi) you can try a variety of outdoor activities like hiking, fishing, boating, and camping at **Buck Creek State Park.** Then spend the night in Springfield.

❺ In **Bellefontaine** (34 mi north on U.S. 68), two of the main attractions are underground. The **Ohio Caverns,** among the most colorful in the country, feature magnificent white stalactites and mysterious cave murals. At **Zane Shawnee Caverns,** tour guides lead you through a maze of chambers and corridors hewn by nature over thousands of years. After exploring the caves, be sure to check out **Campbell Hill**—the tallest point in Ohio. For the most direct route back to New Richmond, follow U.S. 68 south for 60 mi to Xenia, then take Rte. 42 south for about 40 mi to I–275, and I–275 south for about 20 mi to the junction with Route 52. Follow Route 52 south for about 15 mi into New Richmond.

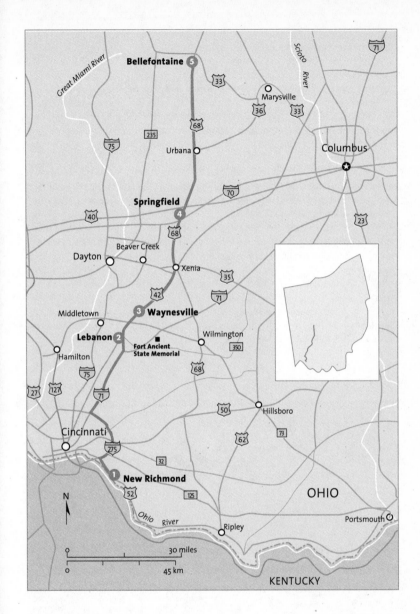

North Loop Cities Tour

FROM CANTON TO AKRON, CLEVELAND, ELYRIA, SANDUSKY, AND PORT CLINTON

Distance: 135 mi (218 km)   Time: 5–6 days

Breaks: There's lots to see and do at every stop along this route, so plan on staying overnight in Akron, Cleveland, Sandusky, and Port Clinton.

This tour highlights the bustling cities of Northern Ohio. The drive begins in the Akron-Canton area, continues to the rocking city of Cleveland, and concludes with a jaunt to the more serene Port Clinton peninsula.

❶ **Canton** is home to the **National Football League Hall of Fame.** The gridiron's greatest players are enshrined at this tribute to football. Highlights include interactive exhibits, memorabilia, and a two-story movie theater. Another fun stop in Canton is the **Harry London Candies.** At this factory, you can watch as chocolate candy is made, packaged, prepared, and shipped out. The factory also has a candy store and a "Chocolate Hall of Fame" exhibit.

❷ In **Akron** (20 mi north on I–77), if your timing is right, take a narrated cruise around 4,963-acre **Portage Lakes** on the **Portage Princess,** a rustic paddlewheeler. Return to downtown Akron and cap off the day with a visit to **Quaker Square.** Akron is the home of the Quaker Oats Company, the first company to register a cereal trademark and the first to nationally advertise food. The original Quaker Oats mills have been converted into a shopping, restaurant, and entertainment complex. The silos, which once housed foodstuffs for a nation, now house travelers; they are part of the 173-room **Hilton Quaker Square** hotel. Spend an evening in the entertainment area before heading off to sleep in a silo.

❸ **Cleveland** (30 mi north on I-77) is home to the **Rock and Roll Hall of Fame and Museum,** which exhibits memorabilia from some of rock's greatest stars. If you're in Cleveland

during basketball or baseball season, try to get tickets to see the Cavaliers or Indians. The Cavs take to the basketball court at **Gund Arena** and the Indians play baseball at **Jacob's Field.** Plan to stay overnight in Cleveland.

❹ In **Elyria** (25 mi west on I–90) check out the **Hickories Museum,** in a 1894 Tudor home built by inventor Arthur Garford, the man who brought us the padded bicycle seat. The **Elyria Civil War Monument,** dedicated in 1888, commemorates local residents who died in the War Between the States.

❺ **Sandusky** (40 mi west on Route 2) is most famous for its **Cedar Point** amusement park, one of the largest in the country. It has everything from thrilling roller coasters to trains for tiny tots. Plan to check into a nearby hotel after a long day of speeding and twirling.

❻ **Port Clinton** is the final stop, a good spot to kick back and relax for a day or two, after three days of sightseeing. Here you'll find the breathtaking city of Port Clinton, which has the oldest lighthouse on the Great Lakes and plenty of gorgeous scenery. **Kelleys Island** and **Put-In-Bay** are just north of Port Clinton and are accessible by ferry. These two scenic, agricultural areas are nice places to relax and wind down. If you're returning to Canton, take Route 53 south to I–80/90 east. Proceed east for about 90 mi to Exit 12 and head south on I–77 for about 35 mi.

AKRON

(Nearby towns listed: Aurora, Brecksville, Canton, Kent, Massillon)

Prior to the 19th century, the area of northern Ohio that would become Akron was primarily pioneer country. But once the 1800s hit, accessibility became the region's primary goal. By 1825, the region had its first canal under construction. Soon the Ohio and Erie canals were carrying goods and people in and out of the area and providing water power that fueled mills and industry. After the Civil War, orders for all types of merchandise poured in and Akron grew rapidly. The burgeoning city attracted a number of innovative and ambitious people, among them Ferdinand Schumacher, the Quaker Oatmeal King; Ohio C. Barber, who started the Diamond Match Company; and Dr. Benjamin Franklin Goodrich, who began Akron's most important industry—the manufacture of rubber.

Today nearly 1,500 of the country's most important manufacturers make the Akron area home, including more than 150 Fortune 500 companies with facilities in the Greater Akron area. Akron's contributions to the world have included oatmeal and fried chicken, gold-medal athletes, and national champion coaches. Its products have flown around the world and to the moon. Quaker Square, at the site of the Quaker Oats Co., Inventure Place, and the Stan Hywet Hall and Gardens are some of the major attractions here.

Information: Akron/Summit Convention and Visitors Bureau | 77 E. Mill St., 44308 | 330/374–7560 or 800/245–4254 | www.visitakron-summit.org.

Attractions

Akron Art Museum. It may not be the biggest art museum in the state, but it has a lovely home in the restored Old Akron Post Office, an Italianate Renaissance structure. Its three floors of galleries present one of the largest collections of contemporary paintings and photography in Ohio. | 70 E. Market St. | 330/376–9185 | www.akronartmuseum.org | Free | Daily 11–5.

Akron Civic Theatre. Some of Akron's best non-professional actors and actresses make up this community troupe. Shows are performed throughout the year in various venues in the city. | 182 S. Main St. | 330/535–3179 or 330/535–3178 (recording) | www.akroncivic.com | Ticket prices vary | Weekdays 11–5:30.

Akron Zoological Park. Favorite attractions at this zoo in Perkins Woods include Monkey Island, River Otters, and the Ohio Farmyard. There are Sumatran tigers, sun bears, and a treehouse and train in the Tiger Valley exhibit. The zoo has a number of endangered species, including red pandas, bald eagles, and Chinese alligators. | 500 Edgewood Ave. | 330/375–2525 or 330/375–2550 | www.akronzoo.com | $7.50 | Jan.–Apr., daily 11–4; May–Dec., Mon.–Sat. 10–5, Sun. 10–6.

© Artville

AKRON, AURORA, AND CLEVELAND

Variety can make a vacation—and its absence is sure to break it. With this in mind, consider a trip inland to Akron, Cleveland, and Aurora. Each city offers experiences that are a bit out of the ordinary. And best of all (parents take note), they all feature no-fail, kid-pleasing places that are lots of fun for grown-ups, too.

Ohio has produced more than its share of inventors (Thomas Edison among them) and Akron's Inventure Place lets you follow in the footsteps of the state's finest. Hands-on, interactive exhibits and experiments make it possible for everyone to become an inventor. Don't miss the National Inventors Hall of Fame.

After expending all that mental energy, take a stroll through Akron's Quaker Square, a shopping and recreation complex set in the former Quaker Oats Company mills. Eat in one of the restaurants, then browse the specialty shops and boutiques. An overnight stay in the Akron Hilton at Quaker Square offers another unique experience—the rooms are built in former oats silos.

By now the kids are begging for action, so take them to Sea World Adventure Park in Aurora, a 90-acre marine life park. It'll be hard to decide where to begin—a penguin encounter? the World of the Sea Aquarium?—so study the "Shamu Adventure Guide" carefully. Nighttime laser displays, fireworks, and other shows are presented daily June through August.

Another area attraction allows folks to enjoy nature in a more, well, natural setting. The 33,000–acre Cuyahoga Valley National Recreation Area follows the Cuyahoga River for 22 mi between Cleveland and Akron. Here you'll see nature at its most pristine: streams, creeks, forested land, plateaus, and scenic overlooks. Pack a picnic before you go and enjoy your lunch alfresco at one of the area's four visitor centers. Then hike along the Ohio and Erie Canal Towpath Trail. In the winter, pack your sled, ice skates, or skis.

Top off your vacation with a trip to the place that continues to make Cleveland world-famous: the Rock and Roll Hall of Fame and Museum. You might want to return a second day; there's lots to see, do, and listen to here. This is one place that parents may enjoy even more than their Backstreet Boys–adoring offspring.

Towns listed: Akron, Aurora, Cleveland.

Boston Mills/Brandywine Ski Resort. Ski by day or night on the sister ski resorts' 19 slopes 10 mi north of Akron. Both resorts accept the same lift tickets and passes. Ski and snowboard equipment rentals are available; there's also snow tubing here. | 7100 Riverview Rd., Peninsula | 330/657–2334 or 330/655–6703 (snow conditions) or 800/875–4241 | fax 330/657–2660 | www.bmbw.com | Dec.–mid-Mar.

Cuyahoga Valley National Recreation Area. The 33,000-acre recreation area sprawls along 22 mi of the Cuyahoga River between Cleveland and Akron. You can take part in fishing, biking, camping, winter sports, horseback riding, and more. The 19.5-mi-long Ohio and Erie Canal Towpath Trail takes about 10 hours to hike and about 2.5 hours to bike. There are five visitor facilities; The Hunt Farm center is the closest to Akron. | Bolanz Rd. between Riverview and Akron-Peninsula Rds. | 216/524–1497 | www.nps.gov/cuva/home.htm | Free | Daily, dawn–dusk.

Dover Lake Waterpark. Get soaked at this water park in Sagamore Hills just outside the Cuyahoga Valley National Recreation Area. Seven water slides, three inner-tube rides, a wave pool, a water whirl ride, and two speed slides are among the wet attractions that await. | 1150 W. Highland Rd., Sagamore Hills | 330/467–7946 | fax 330/467–1422 | www.dover-lake.com | $11–$13, parking $3 | June–Aug.

F. A. Seiberling Naturealm Visitors Center. The 100-acre Metro Parks nature center and arboretum is named in honor of F. A. Seiberling, founder of The Goodyear Tire and Rubber Company. Seiberling, an early member of the Board of Park Commissioners, donated more than 400 acres to help establish Sand Run Metro Park, of which the Naturealm is a part. There is a 16-acre arboretum, a Rock & Herb Garden, observation decks, three ponds, hiking trails including a suspension bridge, and a tallgrass prairie demonstration area. | 1828 Smith Rd. | 330/865–8065 | www.summitmetroparks.org | Free | Mon.–Sat. 10–5, Sun. noon–5.

Goodyear World of Rubber. In this interactive museum across the street from Goodyear headquarters, you'll learn about the history and versatility of rubber. Highlights include an Indy race car, an artificial heart, and a plethora of Goodyear products. | Goodyear Hall, 4th floor, 1201 E. Market St. | 330/796–7117 | Free | Weekdays 8–4:30.

Hale Farm and Village. The buildings on this farmstead north of Akron are original structures, more than 170 years old. They've been moved here from various other locations over the past century and a half. The original farm was founded by pioneer Jonathan Hale during the canal years in Ohio. Crafters, such as a glass blower, candle maker, potter, and blacksmith, demonstrate the industries of the mid-1800s. On spring weekends, there are maple sugar festivities. | 2686 Oak Hill Rd., Bath | 330/666–3711 or 800/589–9703 | www.wrhs.org | $9.50 | May–Oct., Tues.–Sat. 10–5; Sun. noon–5.

Hower House. Built in 1871, this mansard-roofed home in the Second Empire Italianate style was continuously lived in for 102 years by three generations of the Hower family. The lavish furnishings from around the world were collected by John Hower, a leading Akron industrialist. It's listed on the National Register of Historic Places. Tours are available by reservation; with a visit to the Cellar Door Store, you'll need to allow 1 ½ hours. | 60 Fir Hill | 330/972–6909 | www.uakron.edu/howerhse | $5 | Feb.–Dec., Wed.–Sat. 12–3:30, Sun. 1–4.

Inventure Place. Exhibits at The National Inventor's Hall of Fame celebrate the creative and entrepreneurial spirit of great inventors who have been inducted into this organization since its founding in 1973, from Thomas Edison to Apple Computer's Steve Wozniak. In addition, water play, a K'NEX table and other hands-on attractions let you explore your own creativity. | 221 S. Broadway St. | 330/762–4463 or 800/968–IDEA | www.invent.org | $7.50 | Tues.–Sat. 9–5, Sun. noon–5.

John Brown Home. The fight to free slaves ruled abolitionist John Brown's life. Trace the life of the famous Akron resident from his days in this 1830s home to the 1859 raid on Harper's Ferry. The house displays photographs from the late antebellum period, a reconstruction of a canal boat captain's quarters, and changing temporary exhibits. The Summit County Historical Society has offices here and gives tours that include this home and the Perkins

AKRON

INTRO
ATTRACTIONS
DINING
LODGING

Mansion, just across the street. | 514 Diagonal Rd. | 330/535–1120 | www.akronschs.org | $5 for John Brown Home and Perkins Mansion | Mar.–Dec., second and fourth weeks of the month, Wed.–Sun. 1–4.

Perkins Mansion. Built in the 1830s by Col. Simon Perkins Jr., son of Akron's founder Gen. Simon Perkins, this mansion is one of the finest examples of Greek Revival architecture in Ohio. The Perkins family lived for more than 100 years in this grand home, which is filled with early and late Victorian furnishings. The home is just across the street from the John Brown Home; a tour includes both houses. | 550 Copley Rd. | 330/535–1120 | www.akronschs.org | $5 for Perkins Mansion and John Brown Home | Mar.–Dec., second and fourth weeks of the month, Wed.–Sun. 1–4.

Portage Lakes State Park. You can swim, camp, hike, fish, boat, and enjoy the great outdoors at this 4,963-acre lake area. Its wetlands attract waterfowl and shorebirds. | 5031 Manchester Rd. | 330/644–2220 | www.dnr.state.oh.us/odnr/parks/directory/PORTAGE.htm | Free | Daily.

© Artville

FROM THE AMAZON TO AKRON

When entrepreneurs in the outside world first saw those balls of raw rubber, darkened by the smoke in which they were cured, they knew there had to be a good use for the stuff. But what? It was waterproof, certainly, but what could be done to keep it from becoming rock-hard in cold weather and melting in hot weather?

Enter an American named Charles Goodyear. Caught up in the "rubber fever" of the 1830s, he became obsessed with rubber, determined to master its mysteries. It took him five years but, in 1839, he finally hit on a way to make rubber weatherproof as well as waterproof, a process we know as vulcanization. Alas, Goodyear was a terrible businessman and spent the rest of his life making bad deals, missing opportunities, and trying to defend his legal rights. He was once represented in court by no less a figure than then Secretary of State Daniel Webster, but it was all in vain. He died in 1860, $200,000 in debt.

Instead, it was a Dr. Benjamin Franklin Goodrich who, almost literally, put rubber on the map, and especially on the map of Ohio. In 1871, he and 23 Akron businessmen began manufacturing rubber tires to take advantage of the new craze for bicycles. It wasn't until 1898 that the Goodyear Tire & Rubber Company (which had no connection to Charles Goodyear and merely honored him with its name) also began turning out bicycle tires.

These two companies, and other rubber manufacturers who also located here (Firestone, General, Sun, Mohawk, and Seiberling), reigned supreme in Akron for nearly a century. In an exercise of enlightened self-interest, they encouraged the paving of roads, the installation of directional signs, and the widespread use of the automobile in general. Goodrich began publishing maps and guidebooks. In 1927, Charles Lindbergh's "Spirit of St. Louis" was equipped with Goodrich Silvertown tires. The company also made the first pressurized flight suit for pioneer aviator Wiley Post and went on to develop space suits for Mercury astronauts. Goodyear, meanwhile, became famous for its blimps.

But times change. Most of the rubber industry has left Akron now and moved south, leaving behind chemical and technical industries spun off from the rubber business, and leaving behind too names like Goodyear Heights and Firestone Park, and the history of an American heyday.

Portage Princess Cruise. You can take a narrated cruise aboard a majestic paddle wheeler and absorb the sights and sounds of the Portage Lakes area. | 357 W. Turkey Foot Lake Rd. | 330/499–6891 | $11–$15 | May–mid-Oct., daily.

Quaker Square. Originally the Ferdinand Schumacher Milling Company, the Quaker Oats Company became the first company to register a cereal trademark and the first to nationally advertise food. The Quaker Oats mills, built in 1854, have been converted into a shopping, restaurant, and entertainment complex. | 135 S. Broadway | 330/253–5970 | Free | Mon.–Sat. 10–9, Sun. 11–6.

Stan Hywet Hall and Gardens. Built on a stone quarry, this English Tudor mansion was the home of the Seiberling family—the founders of the Goodyear Tire and Rubber Company. It has 23 fireplaces and a number of concealed telephones. | 714 N. Portage Path | 330/836–5533 | www.stanhywet.org | $8 | Apr.–Dec., daily 9–6 (tours 10–4:30); Feb.–Mar., Tues.–Sat. 10–4, Sun. 1–4.

Summit Mall. This is probably the biggest mall in the area, with stores like Abercrombie, American Eagle, Gap, and Brookstone. In addition there's a large food court, live entertainment (even a circus), and two department stores, Dillard's and Kaufmans. | 3265 W. Market St. | 330/867–1555 | Mon.–Sat. 10–9, Sun. 11–6.

University of Akron. Founded in 1870, this university is one of the 50 largest in the nation, with 25,000 students and a 170-acre campus. Its Knight Chemical Laboratory is internationally known. Campus tours for small groups, led by student guides, are available weekdays and Saturdays. Tours leave the Office of Admissions weekdays at 10 and 2, and Saturday at 10. | 302 E. Buchtel Common | 330/972–7111 or 330/972–7100 | www.uakron.edu | Free | Daily.

The Winery at Wolf Creek. The forest view from the tasting room is as invigorating as the wine. Bring dinner or a picnic lunch or arrange to eat either meal with the aptly named owner, Hart Wineberg. Wine and snack baskets are sold in the gift shop. Allow 45 minutes for the winery tour. | 2637 S. Cleveland-Massillon Rd., Norton | 330/666–9285 | Free | Oct.–May, Wed.–Thurs. noon–8, Fri.–Sat. noon–10, Sun. 1–8; June–Sept. Wed.–Thurs. noon–9, Fri.–Sat. noon–10, Sun. 1–9.

ON THE CALENDAR

FEB.–NOV.: *Ohio Ballet.* Some of the most popular ballets are performed by this professional troupe, which dances at E. J. Thomas Hall on the University of Akron campus. | 198 Hill St. | 330/972–7900.

MAY–SEPT.: *Blossom Music Center.* This venue hosts everything from symphonies to pop acts and from heavy metal to rap. | 1145 W. Steels Corners Rd., Cuyahoga Falls | 330/920–8040.

JULY: *All-American Soap Box Derby.* Held since 1934, this race attracts more than 100 teams of kids from throughout the region. | Soap Box Derby International Race Track, 789 Derby Downs Dr. | 330/733–8723.

AUG.: *NEC "World Series of Golf."* Some of the best local, regional, and national golfers participate in this tournament at the Firestone Country Club. | 452 E. Warner Rd. | 330/644–2299.

SEPT.–MAY: *Akron Symphony Orchestra.* This professional orchestra performs pops, classical, and orchestral concerts throughout the year at E. J. Thomas Hall, on the University of Akron campus. | 198 Hill St. | 330/535–8131.

OCT.: *Maps Air Museum Pancake Breakfast.* Take the family to this day-long event at the old National Guard Armory and Akron Canton Airport, 12 mi from downtown Akron. Start out with a plate of pancakes, and then learn about World War II military aircraft. | 5359 Massillon Rd. | 330/896–6332.

OCT.: *Harvest Festival.* During this annual fall festival at Hale Farm and Village you can take part in cider pressing, apple-butter making, grain threshing, and more. | 2686 Oak Hill Rd. | 330/666–3711 or 800/589–9703.

OCT.: *Wonderful World of Ohio Mart.* You'll find anything and everything to do with Ohio at this annual mega flea market at Stan Hywet Hall. | 714 N. Portage Path | 330/836–5533.

Dining

Art's Place. American/Casual. This laid-back restaurant has a menu featuring steaks, pasta dishes, chicken, barbecued ribs, and sandwiches. Locals rave about the ribs and Art's Salad, a bed of greens topped with seasonal vegetables, cheese, and the house sweet-and-sour dressing. Kids' menu. | 2225 State Rd., Cuyahoga Falls | 330/928–2188 | No lunch Sat. | $7–$14 | AE, D, MC, V.

House of Hunan. Chinese. Large portions of standard Oriental dishes, with a focus on Hunan and Szechuan recipes, are the hallmark of this strip-mall eatery. Japanese entrées and sushi are also available. | 2717 W. Market St., Fairlawn | 330/864–8215 | $8–$24 | AE, D, DC, MC, V.

Ken Stewart's Grille. Contemporary. This art-filled restaurant has a sophisticated Southwestern theme and attracts near-capacity crowds just about every night of the week. It's known for steaks, fresh lobster, and 10 or more imaginative daily specials, ranging from the latest trends to variations on old favorites. Chicken breast in phyllo with a light pepper-cream sauce, grilled pork tenderloin, potato-crusted halibut, and penne pasta with artichoke hearts, sun-dried tomatoes, and garlic are just a few examples. Kids' menu. | 1970 W. Market St. | 330/867–2555 | Reservations essential | Closed Sun. | $14–$25 | AE, D, DC, MC, V.

Lanning's. Steak. Dim lighting, windows with a view of a nearby wooded creek, and an open-flame grill in the intimate dining room make this a popular spot for special occasions. The delicious Lanning's Secret Sauce (the owner refuses to divulge the ingredients) is brushed onto all steaks prior to cooking. The restaurant also serves a variety of seafood dishes ranging from shrimp scampi to filet of salmon. Pianist Sat. | 826 N. Cleveland-Massillon Rd. | 330/666–1159 | www.lannings-restaurant.com | Closed Sun. No lunch | $18–$28 | AE, D, DC, MC, V.

Liberty Street Brewing Company. Cajun/Creole. Crawfish is flown in daily and it pops up all over the menu: sautéed as an appetizer, tossed into a salad—even laid onto pizza. Just about everything has a spicy kick, but if it isn't enough, there are bottles of hot sauce on every table. Even the desserts have a Louisiana flair—the New Orleans bread pudding is topped with Jack Daniels whiskey sauce. Memorabilia from Akron's historic moments, old photos, and newspaper clippings decorate the walls of this brew pub. A huge English oak bar dominates the lounge area. | 1238 Weathervane La. | 330/869–2337 | Closed Mon. No lunch Tues.–Fri. | $10–$22 | AE, D, DC, MC, V.

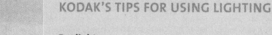

KODAK'S TIPS FOR USING LIGHTING

Daylight
- Use the changing color of daylight to establish mood
- Use light direction to enhance subjects' properties
- Match light quality to specific subjects

Dramatic Lighting
- Anticipate dramatic lighting events
- Explore before and after storms

Sunrise, Sunset, and Afterglow
- Include a simple foreground
- Exclude the sun when setting your exposure
- After sunset, wait for the afterglow to color the sky

From Kodak Guide to Shooting Great Travel Pictures © 2000 by Fodor's Travel Publications

Mustard Seed Market Cafe. Eclectic. Gourmet health-food appetizers, salads, and sandwiches pack the menu at this deli cafe on a mezzanine overlooking the market. Influences range from Asian (peanut Thai shrimp) to Mexican (bean quesadillas). Daily specials can be more substantial, like almond-crusted sea bass with a pesto pierogi filled with garlic mashed potatoes. Known for healthful and creative combinations of grains, beans, and vegetables and macrobiotic fare. Entertainment Fri.–Sun. Sun. brunch. No smoking. | 3885 W. Market St. | 330/666–7333 | No supper Sun. | $10–$19 | MC, V.

Tangier. Middle Eastern. With a 3,000-pound, 50-ft-tall blue fiberglass dome outside and a circular dining room with ceiling-high vases of palm fronds inside, dining at the Tangier is like a visit to a kasbah. The kitchen turns out classic American dinner selections—surf and turf, chicken, veal, and pasta— as well as Middle Eastern fare such as stuffed grape leaves and beef shish kebab. The yogurt sauce that accompanies many entrées is a delight. You can tour the kitchen, too, which is every bit as impressive as the Las Vegas–style floor shows presented out front in the nightclub. Entertainment. Kids' menu. | 532 W. Market St. | 330/376–7171 | www.tangier.com | Closed Sun. | $20–$40 | AE, D, DC, MC, V.

Triple Crown. American. Standard American fare is served in a handsomely decorated dining room with a fireplace. Pictures of some winning racehorses adorn the walls, and others are commemorated in brass sculpture throughout the dining area. The menu is dominated by steaks and prime rib, but pasta dishes, like seafood pasta pesto and chicken broccoli Alfredo, also merit consideration. Pianist on weekends. Kids' menu. Sun. brunch. | 335 S. Main, Munroe Falls | 330/633–5325 | www.triplecrownrestaurant.com | No lunch Sat. | $9–$24 | AE, D, MC, V.

Lodging

Best Western Executive Inn. Built in the mid-1960s, this two-story brick motel occupies an industrial park about 7 mi from downtown Akron. Guest rooms are done in the modern-modular style you might expect from a mid-range chain property, and there are several popular fast-food establishments within walking distance. Restaurant, bar, room service. Cable TV. Pool. Exercise equipment. Business services. Free parking. | 2677 Gilchrist Rd. | 330/794–1050 or 800/528–1234 | fax 330/794–8495 | www.bestwestern.com | 120 rooms, 1 suite | $55, suites $150 | AE, D, DC, MC, V.

Comfort Inn West. Occupying a hill in the Montrose suburb 7 mi east of Akron, this two-story motel caters primarily to business travelers. There are plenty of fast-food and sit-down dining options within a mile or so of the motel itself. Complimentary Continental breakfast. In-room data ports, some refrigerators. Cable TV. Indoor pool. Hot tub. Laundry facilities. Business services. Free parking. | 130 Montrose West Ave. | 330/666–5050 or 800/228–5150 | fax 330/668–2550 | www.comfortinn.com | 132 rooms | $79–$129 | AE, D, DC, MC, V.

Hilton Inn-West. With two swimming pools, a shopping mall across the street, and downtown Akron just 5 mi away, this hotel might be an option if you're traveling with the family. Guest rooms are spare and furnished with unassuming wood-veneer pieces. Restaurant, bar, room service. In-room data ports, some refrigerators. Cable TV. 2 pools (1 indoor). Exercise equipment. Laundry facilities. Business services. Airport shuttle. Free parking. Some pets allowed. | 3180 W. Market St. | 330/867–5000 or 800/445–8667 | fax 330/867–1648 | awhilton@aol.com | www.hilton.com | 204 rooms | $109 | AE, D, DC, MC, V.

Hilton Quaker Square. In the early 1930s, the structure that now houses travelers housed grain for the Quaker Oats Company. The eight-story building occupies several grain storage silos that were converted into unique, round hotel rooms in the 1980s. Don't expect to wake up with oat hulls in your hair, however. Guest rooms are modern in every way and betray little of the structure's original purpose. The hotel is a historic site; it has hand-sculpted wall murals and history displays. It's part of downtown Akron's shopping, restaurant, and entertainment complex. Restaurant. Cable TV. Indoor pool. Exercise equipment. Business services. | 135 S. Broadway | 330/253–5970 or 800/445–8667 | fax 330/253–2574 | www.hilton.com | 185 rooms | $145 | AE, D, DC, MC, V.

Holiday Inn Akron/Fairlawn. This hotel's location off I–77, 12 mi north of downtown Akron, makes it a likely suspect if you're just passing through the area and don't want to deal with city traffic. It's in Akron's quiet Fairlawn suburb. There are numerous restaurants and shopping complexes within a mile or two of the hotel. Restaurant, room service. In-room data ports. Cable TV. Pool. Exercise equipment. Laundry facilities. Business services. Free parking. | 4073 Medina Rd., Fairlawn | 330/666–4131 or 800/465–4329 | fax 330/666–7190 | www.holiday-inn.com | 166 rooms | $89 | AE, D, DC, MC, V.

Holiday Inn-South. This two-story stucco lodging 8 mi from downtown Akron was built in 1973 and has been renovated several times since. There's nightly entertainment in the hotel bar if you don't feel like venturing out into the city. Restaurant, bar, complimentary Continental breakfast. Cable TV. Pool. Business services. Airport shuttle. Free parking. Some pets allowed. | 2940 Chenoweth Rd. | 330/644–7126 or 800/465–4329 | fax 330/644–1776 | www.holiday-inn.com | 131 rooms | $79–$89, hot tub rooms $109 | AE, D, DC, MC, V.

O'Neil House. This two-story brick Tudor home was built in 1930 for the founder of the General Tire Company. All the rooms are distinctive, with their cherry wood; one has a sleigh bed. Wake up to a cozy breakfast in the sunroom porch. This bed-and-breakfast is 10 mi west of downtown Akron and 3 mi from I–77. Complimentary breakfast. Cable TV. No smoking. | 1290 W. Exchange St. | 330/867–2650 | 4 rooms | $100–$150 | D, MC, V.

Red Roof Inn. Restaurants and shops surround this two-story suburban motel roughly 10 mi south of downtown Akron. The exterior is stucco on a brick foundation, and guest rooms are simply furnished with basic wood-veneer pieces. Cable TV. Some pets allowed. | 99 Rothrock Rd. | 330/666–0566 or 800/843–7663 | fax 330/666–6874 | www.redroof.com | 108 rooms | $39–$49 | AE, D, DC, MC, V.

ALLIANCE

MAP 14, F3

(Nearby towns listed: Akron, Canton, Youngstown)

Alliance, in the northeast part of the state, was formed when the three villages of Williamsport, Liberty, and Freedom merged in 1854. The new village was given its name by Gen. J. S. Robinson, a railroad official from Pittsburgh; it refers to the inter-section of the Cleveland and Wellsville and the Ohio and Pennsylvania railroads here. In 1889, Alliance was incorporated as a city. Two years later, Mount Union Village was annexed.

Many famous people have passed through Alliance over the years, including Abra-ham Lincoln, who visited just before his inauguration. In 1867, Civil War generals Grant, Sherman, and Sheridan stopped at the Sourbeck Dining Hall at the Union Depot Station. President-to-be William McKinley made his first-ever political speech at Henry Martin's wagon shop in Mount Union during his campaign for prosecuting attorney. James A. Garfield, the 20th president, frequently spoke at the old College Hall in Mount Union.

Today, Alliance is a college town. Mount Union College, in the heart of downtown, has a wealth of cultural and recreational activities and facilities. As in many northern cities, a revitalization of the downtown area is underway and is targeted to attract professional, retail, and commercial ventures to the area.

Information: **Alliance Area Chamber of Commerce** | 210 E. Main St., 44601 | 330/823–6260 | fax 330/823–4434 | www.rodman.lib.oh.us/chamber.

Attractions

Firehouse Theatre. This downtown theater stages performances year-round. | 450 E. Mar-ket | 330/821–8712 | $6–$8.

Glamorgan Castle. Akron businessman Col. William Henry Morgan built this "castle" as his home at the turn of the century. It now houses administrative offices for the Akron City Schools system. The castle's rooms are decorated in a variety of styles, including Italian Renaissance, French Empire, Louis XV, Elizabethan, and Japanese. | 200 Glamorgan St. | 330/821–2100 | www.rodman.lib.oh.us/chamber/castle.htm | $3 | Weekdays 1–3.

Mabel Hartzell Museum. This house was built in 1867 for Matthew Early, a well-known politician and businessman, and his wife Mary Edwards Early. The museum is named for their adopted daughter, Mabel. Hartzell was a prominent educator in Alliance and a woman's suffrage leader in Northeast Ohio. Her election to the Alliance Board of Education in 1909 and her leadership in the community helped pave the way for other women to become active participants in the community and in city government. | 840 N. Park Ave. | 330/823–1677 or 330/823–4115 | $2 | Weekdays by appointment.

Mount Union College. This private liberal arts college of 1,500 students is affiliated with the United Methodist Church. Its campus, which spans 72 scenic acres, is distinguished by both contemporary and traditional architecture, including two buildings that are listed in the National Register of Historic Places. | 1972 Clark Ave. | 330/821–5320 | www.muc.edu | Free | Daily.

ON THE CALENDAR

JULY: *Hot Stove League.* Junior league baseball tournaments go on at the Butler Rodman Park. There are always plenty of out-of-towners stopping by to catch a glimpse. | 2100 W. State Ave. | 330/821–4589.

AUG.: *Carnation Festival.* The streets of downtown Alliance are filled with residents and visitors during this week-long summer celebration. There are live music performances, hot air balloons, and a ribs cook-off. | Various locations in Alliance | 330/823–6260.

Dining

Hartville Kitchen. American. A variety of soups and salads are available, as are hot sandwiches served with mashed potatoes and gravy. On Tuesday, the lunch special is meatloaf; on Friday it's turkey. Kids' menu. No smoking. It's in Hartville, about 12 mi northwest of Alliance. | 788 Edison St., Hartville | 330/877–9353 | Reservations not accepted | Closed Wed., Sun. | $8–$10 | No credit cards.

Taster's Choice Cafe. American. This cafe serves satisfying, home-cooked fare for breakfast, lunch, and dinner. For dessert, try the homemade carrot cake. Beer and wine are available. Kids' menu. | 1908 S. Union Ave. | 330/821–6666 | No dinner Sun. and Mon. | $7–$9 | D, MC, V.

Lodging

Comfort Inn. Adjacent to an Alliance's small downtown shopping mall, this five-story lodging was built in 1989 and is popular with parents who are in town to visit students at Mount Union. Guest rooms are basic and uncluttered with the usual modular-type furniture. There are several sit-down, family-style restaurants in the adjacent mall, as well as within a few blocks of the hotel. Complimentary Continental breakfast. Cable TV. Indoor pool. Hot tub. Exercise equipment. Laundry facilities. Business services. Some pets allowed (fee). | 2500 W. State St. | 330/821–5555 or 800/228–5150 | fax 330/821–4919 | www.comfortinn.com | 113 rooms | $99 | AE, D, DC, MC, V.

ASHTABULA

MAP 14, F2

(Nearby towns listed: Conneaut, Geneva-on-the-Lake)

Ashtabula sits on the southern shore of Lake Erie, about halfway between Cleveland, Ohio, and Erie, Pennsylvania. After its harbor was discovered in 1796 by Moses Cleave-

ASHTABULA

INTRO
ATTRACTIONS
DINING
LODGING

land, it became a major port for coal and iron. Today, it's a resort area and a center of manufacturing.

Ashtabula County is a water-lovers paradise, with everything from sailing and fishing to wading along the beach, jet skiing, and wind surfing. Easy access to Lake Erie is available from four public beaches and a number of area marinas. The town has an interesting marine museum and a home that was a final stop on the Underground Railroad.

Information: **Ashtabula Area Chamber of Commerce Bureau** | 4536 Main Ave., 44004 | 440/998–6998 | www.ashtabulacounty.com.

Attractions

Ashtabula Arts Center. This busy arts venue hosts many music, dance, theater, and visual arts events throughout the year, including performances of *The Nutcracker* in December. In the summer months, productions move outdoors to a covered, open-air theater; most of these shows are musicals. | 2928 W. 13th St. | 440/964–3396.

Great Lakes Marine and U.S. Coast Guard Memorial Museum. Situated in the former home of a lighthouse operator, this museum has marine artifacts, ship models, and art that chronicles the lives and times of sailors who navigated the waters of the Great Lakes during the past two centuries. | 1071-73 Walnut Blvd. | 440/964–6847 | $2–$8 | Memorial Day–Labor Day, Fri.–Sun. noon–6; after Labor Day–Oct., Fri.–Sun. 1–5.

Hubbard House Underground Railroad Museum. This 1841 house turned museum on Lake Erie once served as the endpoint of the Underground Railroad. Period furnishings and Civil War artifacts specific to Ashtabula are on display here. Runaway slaves would wait in its barn until a ship could come to take them to Canada. | Walnut Blvd. and Lake Ave. | 440/964–8168 | $3 | Memorial Day–Labor Day, Fri.–Sun. noon–6. After Labor Day–Sept. Fri.–Sun. 1–5.

ON THE CALENDAR

AUG.: *Ashtabula County Fair.* Games, rides, food, and livestock shows are all part of this traditional agricultural fair at the Ashtabula County Fairgrounds in Jefferson, south of Ashtabula. | Poplar St. | 440/998–6998.

OCT.: *Ashtabula County Covered Bridge Festival.* A tour of 15 covered bridges is the highlight of this festival, which celebrates Ashtabula County's claim to fame as the covered bridge capital of the world. | 440/998–6998.

Dining

Casa Capelli. Eclectic. There are Italian, American, and Mexican options—including seafood and steaks—on the menu at this former bank, which has stained glass and a beautiful arched skylight. The bank vault is now a private dining room. Kids' menu. | 4641 Main Ave. | 440/992–3700 | No lunch Sat. until 2 | $8–$28 | AE, D, MC, V.

El Grande. Steak. Despite the guns and holsters on the walls, the black leather tablecloths, and the photos of old-time cowboys like Gene Autry and Roy Rogers, the menu here is more Midwestern than Western. The steaks are cowboy-sized, and there are plenty of seafood, pasta, and chicken dishes and sandwiches to round out the menu. | 2145 W. Prospect St. | 440/998–2228 | Closed Sun. and Mon. No lunch Sat. | $7–$16 | AE, D, MC, V.

Lodging

Cahill Bed and Breakfast. This 1880 Stick style, late Victorian home on the National Register of Historic Places sits in the harbor district, two blocks from Walnut Beach. Rooms, which have views of Lake Erie, are furnished in the Victorian period, with accents like Jenny Lind beds. It's 5 mi from I–90. Complimentary breakfast. TV in common room. | 1106 Walnut Blvd. | 440/964–8449 | cahill@apk.net | www.bedandbreakfast.com | 4 rooms | $65–$75 | No credit cards.

Cedars Motel. This single-story wood motel was built in 1935 and has been renovated a number of times since then. You can park right in front of your room, and downtown Ashtabula is only a mile and a half away. Cable TV. Business services. | 2015 W. Prospect Rd. (U.S. 20) | 440/992–5406 or 800/458–2015 | fax 440/992–5943 | 17 rooms | $60–$70 | AE, D, DC, MC, V.

Comfort Inn. Occupying a section of commercial strip off I-90, this motel is a single-story, brown-brick affair about 6 mi from downtown Ashtabula. There are a number of fast-food and mid-range chain restaurants nearby. Restaurant, bar, room service. In-room data ports. Cable TV. Pool. Laundry facilities. Business services. | 1860 Austinburg Rd. | 440/275–2711 or 800/228–5150 | fax 440/275–7314 | www.comfortinn.com | 119 rooms | $89 | AE, D, DC, MC, V.

Peggy's Bed and Breakfast. This B&B, which opened in 2000, gives you more privacy than most. Accommodations are in a cottage nestled in the woods 100 yards from the main house. The cottage has a gas fireplace and a kitchen; with its loft, it sleeps four. You can enjoy breakfast on your private porch, with a view of a small ravine. Stuffed ham and cheese french toast with broiled apples, cheese, and sausage grits are a good way to start the day. Peggy's is 2 mi from I-90. | 8721 Munson Hill Rd. | 440/969–1996. Complimentary breakfast. Kitchenette. In-room VCR (and movies). No smoking. | fax 440/964–5767 | peggy@peggysbedandbreakfast.com | www.peggysbedandbreakfast.com | 1 cottage | $80 | MC, V.

Travelodge. With easy access by car to a nearby golf course, several restaurants, and a winery or two, this two-story blue-and-white stucco motel is not a bad choice if you're more interested in exploring the Ashtabula surrounds than spending time in a motel room. Downtown Ashtabula is about 12 mi away, and Lake Erie is 50. Complimentary Continental breakfast. Cable TV. Pool. Exercise equipment. Business services. | 2352 Rte. 45, Austinburg | 440/275–2011 or 800/255–3050 | fax 440/275–1253 | www.travelodge.com | 47 rooms | $75 | AE, D, DC, MC, V.

ATHENS

MAP 14, D6

(Nearby towns listed: Lancaster, Logan, Marietta)

Although it's in the rolling foothills of the Appalachian Mountains, the town of Athens actually has its roots in the city of Boston, Massachusetts. In 1786, 11 Bostonians organized the Ohio Company, which the next year contracted to buy 740,000 acres of land north and west of the Ohio River. From this beginning arose the Ordinance of 1787, which provided for the continuation of an organized survey of land and the extension of individual rights and freedoms to the settlers moving west. The provision also declared that "schools and the means of education shall forever be encouraged." Ohio University (chartered by the state of Ohio in Athens in 1804), which now has an enrollment of more than 19,000 students, became the first college founded in the Northwest Territory. Shortly after the city was founded, it was named Athens after the Greek center of learning. In 1805, the city was dubbed the county seat of Athens County. Today, Ohio University remains the city's largest employer, although Athens is also home to a number of businesses and industrial facilities.

Information: Athens Area Chamber of Commerce | 5 N. Court St., 45701 | 740/594–2251 | www.athenschamber.com.

Attractions

Burr Oak State Park. Nature programs, hunting, biking, fishing, and bridle paths are among the features that draw visitors to the 3,200-acre park about 14 mi north of Athens. You can boat and fish on Burr Oak Lake. | 10220 Burr Oak Lodge Rd., Glouster | 740/767–

3570 (park office) or 740/767–2112 | www.ohioparks.net/burroak/index.htm | Free, camping $11 per night | Daily.

Dairy Barn Cultural Center. Once a functioning dairy barn, this venue now houses an array of eclectic art exhibitions and special events, ranging from an international quilt show to a display on the Vietnam War. | 8000 Dairy La. | 740/592–4981 | www.dairybarn.org | $4 | Open only during exhibitions: Tues.–Sun. 11–5, Thurs. 11–8.

Lake Hope State Park. Camping facilities are a highlight of this 3,000-plus-acre park about 15 mi west of Athens. It also has facilities for hiking, swimming, boating, and fishing. | 27331 Rte. 278, McArthur | 740/596–5253 | www.dnr.state.oh.us | Free | Daily.

Ohio University. Ohio University was chartered by the state of Ohio in 1804 and is the oldest university in the Northwest Territory. In the scenic Appalachian foothills of southeastern Ohio, its classic residential campus is one of the most attractive in the nation. The charm of tree-lined brick walkways on the university's College Green makes you feel as if you are at a small college rather than a large university. You can phone the admissions office for a guided tour. | Court St. | 740/593–4100 | www.ohiou.edu/welcome.html | Free | Daily.

Strouds Run State Park. Camping and hiking, along with fishing and boating on Dow Lake are among the activities that can be enjoyed at this 2,600-acre park 8 mi northeast of Athens. | 1161 State Park Rd. | 740/592–2302 | Free | Daily.

Wayne National Forest. This forest covers approximately 229,000 acres and stretches across southeast Ohio. On a map, it appears in three "patches"—one at the southern tip of Ohio, the other two flanking the city of Athens. The forest has facilities for boating, hiking, camping, and more. *(See also* Ironton.) | Supervisor's Office and Athens Ranger District, 219 Columbus Rd. | 740/592–0200 | fax 740/593–5974 | www.fs.fed.us/r9/wayne | Free | Daily.

ON THE CALENDAR

APR.: *Kid's Fest.* The campus of Ohio University gets invaded by children during this annual festival of games and rides. | 331 Richland Ave. | 740/592–3061.

JUNE: *International Street Fair.* Forty international and community organizations celebrate the countries of the world with music, food, and cultural displays. It's held in downtown Athens on a Saturday. | Court St. | 740/593–4330.

AUG.: *Athens County Fair.* This weeklong central Ohio fair, a summer tradition, has prize-winning farm animals, rides, and games. It's held at the Athens County Fairgrounds. | 740/592–1532.

Dining

Seven Sauces. Contemporary. This tiny bistro is hip enough to seem a little out of place in the hills of southeastern Ohio. Nestled among college bars and other businesses that cater to the Ohio University students, Seven Sauces serves up all kinds of innovative fare, such as garlicky shrimp and artichoke linguine, Tuscan gumbo, and cashew trout. There are also thick lamb chops, Oriental steamed dumplings, and many vegetarian entrées. | 66 N. Court St. | 740/592–5555 | No lunch | $9–$17 | AE, D, MC, V.

Sylvia's. Italian. Sylvia's walks the line between being a fun, casual place for students to dine with friends and a nice spot for dinner with the parents or a date. The menu combines traditional renditions of pasta favorites like lasagna and manicotti with creative entrées like the scampi Florentine (shrimp and angel-hair pasta with a shallot white sauce). There's also a low-carbohydrate menu. You can dine inside or at an umbrella-shaded table outdoors. Kids' menu. | 4 Depot St. | 740/594–3484 | No lunch Sat. Closed Sun. | $9–$14 | AE, MC, V.

Union Street Cafe. American. Students from Ohio University come here for breakfast around the clock. The omelets are famous, and there are plenty of desserts and savory entrées. It's open 24 hours a day, except on Sunday, when it closes at 5 PM for a rest until Monday morning. | 102 W. Union St. | 740/594–6007 | $6–$9 | D, MC, V.

Lodging

Amerihost Inn. This two-story brick motel houses lots of out-of-towners during college sporting events. Downtown Athens' bars and restaurants are only about 3 mi away, and there's more dining and shopping within a mile of the motel. It's just off U.S. 33. Complimentary Continental breakfast. Cable TV. Indoor pool. Hot tub. Exercise equipment. | 20 Home St. | 740/594–3000 or 800/434–5800 | fax 740/594–5546 | www.amerihostinn.com | 014@amerihostinn.com | 100 rooms, 9 suites | $76–$89, suites $120–$200 | AE, D, DC, MC, V.

Burr Oak Resort. Most cabins at this wooded resort in Burr Oak State Park, 14 mi north of Athens, have window walls affording a magnificent view of Burr Oak Lake. Guest rooms have rough-hewn walls, chandeliers, and rustic-elegant sofas and chairs. The resort has various activities, ranging from fishing and boating to basketball and volleyball. Lodge guests can access any state park facility. Dining room, bar. Kitchenettes (in cottages). Cable TV. Indoor pool. Tennis. Playground. Business services. It's right off Route 78. | 10660 Burr Oak Lodge Rd., Glouster | 740/767–2112 | fax 740/767–4878 | www.burroakresort.com | 60 rooms, 30 cottages | $90–$107, cottages $130–$155 | AE, DC, MC, V.

Days Inn. This motel's rural location, just off Route 78 about 4 mi from the downtown area, affords pleasant views from the guest rooms and a quiet respite from urban distractions. A nearby driving range and putting course make it a favorite of golfers. Complimentary Continental breakfast. Cable TV. Business services. | 330 Columbus Rd. | 740/592–4000 or 800/325–2525 | fax 740/593–7687 | www.daysinn.com | 60 rooms | $75 | AE, D, DC, MC, V.

Highlander Motel. One mile from downtown in a commercial district, this is a simple, moderately priced hostelry. Rooms are spacious and pleasantly furnished but there are no frills. Cable TV. | 420 W. Union St. | 740/593–6449 | fax 740/593–6449 | 20 rooms | $49–$60 | AE, D, MC, V.

Ohio University Inn. Just four blocks from the heart of Ohio University's main campus, this hotel consists of three connected brick buildings and a pair of restaurants. The University Inn is very popular among visitors to the school, and tends to be booked solid for sporting and academic events, so call well in advance. Restaurant, bar, room service. Cable TV. Pool. Gym. Business services. | 331 Richland Ave. | 740/593–6661 | fax 740/592–5139 | www.ouinn.athens.oh.us | 143 rooms | $99–$169 | AE, D, DC, MC, V.

Woodspirit Getaway. This cabin in the woods, built in March 1999, has Adirondack furniture and high loft ceilings. It sleeps four (two upstairs and two down), and the screened-in porch has a hot tub. This cabin 6 mi south of downtown Athens, makes a great weekend getaway for couples or families who need a little privacy. Kitchen. Direct TV. Hot tub. No smoking. | 6170 N. Coolville Ridge Rd. | 740/593–5628 or 877/593–5628 | btsix@frognet.net | www.travelohio.com/woodspiritgetaway | 1 cabin | $150 | MC, V.

AURORA

(Nearby towns listed: Akron, Brecksville, Kent, Warren, Youngstown)

Aurora is a city steeped in tradition. Established nearly 200 years ago by Revolutionary War veterans, it grew from a small Ohio farming town considered the nation's cheese-making capital to a metropolitan American city with a population of about 12,000. The city also has expensive private residential communities, many with golf courses; the Barrington Golf Club Community, with a Jack Nicklaus–designed course, is one example. Nearby attractions like Sea World and Six Flags Ohio bring thousands of visitors to the area each year.

Information: Aurora Chamber of Commerce | 173 S. Chillicothe Rd., Aurora 44202 | 330/562–3355 or 800/648–6342.

Attractions

Aurora Premium Outlets. Many people shop for hours at this enormous outlet mall, snatching up labels like Polo Ralph Lauren, Tommy Hilfiger, Saks Fifth Ave., Gap, Levis and more. It's 5 mi north of I–80 on Route 43. | 549 Chillicothe Rd. | 330/562–2000 | Mon.–Sat. 10–9, Sun. 10–6.

Sea World. Explore the wonders of the ocean in the middle of Ohio. Sea World, 3 mi west of Aurora, is home to aquatic creatures, including such famous residents as Shamu, the killer whale. Popular attractions include encounters with sharks and penguins, a sea lion show, an interactive bottlenose dolphin exhibit, and a 4-D high-tech movie. The newest attraction is "Mission: Bermuda Triangle," a flight simulation adventure ride. The park also schedules shows like "All Star Mutts," "Shamu Adventure," and "Intensity Games." There's great evening entertainment with lasers, fountains, and fireworks. | 1100 Sea World Dr. | 330/995–2135 or 800/637–4268 | www.seaworld.com | $28–$36 | Memorial Day weekend–Labor Day, daily from 10 AM; closing times vary. May–Labor Day, daily; May and Sept., weekends, hrs vary.

Six Flags Ohio. You'll find thrills and tamer family fun at this mega theme park; Six Flags invested over $40 million in Aurora's old Geauga Lake amusement park, built 20 rides and reopened it under the Six Flags label. Thrills include four cutting-edge roller coasters, including the Superman Ultimate Escape, which gives riders with dangling feet a free-fall experience; the floorless Batman Knight Flight; a classic giant wooden coaster; and a Roadrunner-themed family coaster. Looney Tunes Boom Town is a large, themed children's play area. Broadway-style musical productions, a stunt show, and a Looney Toons production starring Bugs Bunny are on the entertainment schedule. There's a water park on the property. | 1060 N. Aurora Rd. | 330/562–8303 | www.sixflags.com | $18–$35 | Memorial Day–Labor Day, daily; May and Oct., weekends.

On hot days, you can cool off at Six Flag's **Hurricane Harbor,** a water park with a 25,000-square-ft wave pool, a relaxing "lazy river," a tube slide complex and high-speed, plummeting wet slides. Turtle Beach is a water playground just for younger kids; Hook's Lagoon is a family attraction with a five-story treehouse, special-effects lagoons, water gadgets and water slides. | 1060 N. Aurora Rd. | 330/562–8303 | www.sixflags.com | Free with Six Flags Ohio admission | Memorial Day–Labor Day, daily 11–7. Weekends in May, weather permitting.

ON THE CALENDAR

MAY: *Memorial Day Parade.* This typical small town parade is usually held on the Monday of Memorial Day weekend. High school marching bands and other participants walk from Aurora Road to Pioneer Trail. | 330/562–7274 or 800/648–6342.

Dining

Reggie's. Italian. Once a house, Reggie's is now a lively family Italian restaurant with open-air dining in summer. The pasta is exceptionally good. Beer and wine are available. Kids' menu. | 4 New Hudson Rd. | 330/562–4924 | No lunch | $5–$14 | MC, V.

Vito's Italian Grille. Italian. This restaurant occupies a turn-of-the-last-century building that has done time as a farmhouse, a winery, and a tavern. The main dining area now incorporates all these historical elements into a unique melange. Menu suggestions include a number of pasta dishes, pizza with handmade crust and tangy tomato sauce, as well as steaks and a few seafood dishes. | 395 N. Aurora Rd. | 330/562–6010 | No lunch | $7–$19 | MC, V.

Lodging

Aurora Inn. This three-story downtown hostelry has been around since 1965. Rooms are done in burgundy, forest green, and tan, as in a New England country house, with needlepoint hangings on the walls. Restaurant, bar, room service. In-room data ports. Cable TV. Two pools (one indoor). Hot tub, sauna. Tennis courts. Exercise equipment. Laundry facilities. Business services. | 30 E. Garfield Rd. | 330/562–6121 | fax 330/562–5249 | www.places-tostay.com | 69 rooms | $149–$199 | AE, D, DC, MC, V.

Six Flags Hotel. This two-story brick lodging was built in the early 70s; now it's under the wing of the Six Flags Ohio management. The hotel is popular with families that are in town to visit nearby Sea World and Six Flags Ohio. There's free shuttle service to the parks. Downtown Aurora is about 2 mi away. Restaurant, bar, room service. Cable TV. Indoor pool. Hot tub. Video games. Laundry facilities. Business services. | 800 N. Aurora Rd. (Rte. 43) | 330/562–9151 or 800/877–7849 | fax 330/562–5701 | www.sixflagsohio.com | 139 rooms, 6 suites | $185–$200, suites $175–$295 | AE, D, DC, MC, V.

BEACHWOOD

(Nearby towns listed: Aurora, Brecksville, Chardon, Cleveland, Eastlake)

Once part of Warrensville Township in the northeastern part of the state, Beachwood was incorporated as a village in 1915. Named for the trees that once covered the majority of the city, Beachwood is primarily a small, quiet residential town, though it's close enough to Cleveland (about 15 mi west) to benefit from that city's cultural life. The town covers an area of about 6 square mi and has a population of more than 12,000.

Information: Beachwood Chamber of Commerce | 24500 Chagrin Blvd. #110, 44122 | 216/831–0003 | www.beachwood.org.

Attractions

Nature Center at Shaker Lakes. This nature center east of Beachwood has walking trails and wildlife programs as well as a variety of botanical displays. | 2600 S. Park Blvd., Shaker Heights | 216/321–5935 | www.naturecenter£shakerlakes.org | Free | Nature Center: Mon.–Sat. 10–5, Sun. 1–5. Trails: Daily dawn–dusk.

Thistledown Racing Club. The horses race here throughout the summer and fall and on weekends in spring at this track south of Beachwood. There are live races every day but Tuesday and Thursday. Every day the track is open, you can bet on the simulcast races. | Northfield and Emery Rd., North Randall | 216/662–8600 | www.thistledown.com | $1 | Apr.–Dec., daily, 12:55–5; Mar., weekends 12:55–5.

Dining

Benihana Japanese Steak House. Japanese. Delicate paper screens and austere black-lacquered tables set the scene in the dining room at Benihana. The menu presents a fairly standard selection of steak and seafood, playing second fiddle to the show put on by the experienced chefs, who slice, dice, and cook your meal tableside. The chicken-and-shrimp combo is popular. Also try the flambéed shrimp, the teppanyaki filet mignon, or the sirloin steak. Kids' menu. | 23611 Chagrin Blvd. | 216/464–7575 | www.benihana.com | No lunch Sun. | $13–$28 | AE, D, DC, MC, V.

Charley's Crab. Seafood. Sea critters are the stars at this comfortable East Coast-style crabhouse with wall-sized seascape murals, mahogany framed windows, and white linen tablecloths. In addition to the seafood entrées, there are several pasta dishes (most include seafood in the sauce) as well as filet mignon, roast rack of lamb, and grilled chicken breast. Kids' menu. | 25765 Chagrin Blvd. | 216/831–8222 | www.muer.com | No lunch Sun. | $15–$38 | AE, D, DC, MC, V.

Lion and Lamb. American. Stained- and leaded-glass windows, large wooden booths, and dim lighting give this casually intimate spot an almost reverent feel. The chef prepares several different beef entrées, plus pasta and specialty veal entrées. Entertainment Tues. to Sat. | 30519 Pine Tree Rd., Pepper Pike | 216/831–1213 | No lunch Sun. | $13–$27 | AE, D, DC, MC, V.

Ristorante Giovanni. Italian. Though jeans and sneakers are not allowed here, the overall warm demeanor of this small Northern Italian restaurant makes you feel as though the owners have invited you into their home for dinner. A Cleveland institution since the late 1970s, Ristorante Giovanni can be counted on to serve dependably good pastas. The seafood dishes, including Maryland crabcakes and sweetwater prawns with asparagus, are noteworthy as well. | 25550 Chagrin Blvd. | 216/831–8625 | Reservations essential | Closed Sun. No lunch Sat. | $18–$42 | AE, D, DC, MC, V.

Shuhei. Japanese. The dining area here is spare, uncluttered, and stylish, and the waitstaff sweep quietly from table to table dressed in traditional kimono. Shuhei's artfully presented tempura and sushi are among the best in town, and the house specialty—the somewhat dauntingly titled Spider Maki—is a whole softshell crab drizzled with spicy mayonnaise. Traditional Japanese noodle and seafood dishes are also available. | 23360 Chagrin Blvd. | 216/464–1720 | No lunch Sun. | $13–$30 | AE, D, DC, MC, V.

Lodging

Courtyard by Marriott. A modern, four-story hotel in the suburbs outside Beachwood, this Courtyard is used largely by business travelers. The area surrounding the hotel is thick with popular chain restaurants, and downtown is a short drive away. Restaurant, bar, room service. Some refrigerators. Cable TV. Pool. Business services. Free parking. | 3695 Orange Pl. | 216/765–1900 or 800/321–2211 | fax 216/765–1841 | www.courtyard.com | 109 rooms, 4 suites | $139, $169 suites | AE, D, DC, MC, V.

Embassy Suites. This all-suites hotel occupies a section of a suburban commercial strip lined with other lodgings, independent and chain restaurants, and dozens of shops. Restaurant, bar, complimentary breakfast. In-room data ports, refrigerators. Cable TV. Indoor pool. Hot tub. Exercise equipment. Video games. Laundry facilities. Business services. | 3775 Park East Dr. | 216/765–8066 or 800/362–2779 | fax 216/765–0930 | www.embassysuites.com | 216 suites | $189 | AE, D, DC, MC, V.

Holiday Inn-Beachwood. This four-story hotel in a largely commercial area just outside downtown Beachwood is surrounded by restaurants and other lodgings. Restaurant, bar, room service. In-room data ports. Cable TV. Indoor-outdoor pool. Sauna. Exercise equipment. Laundry facilities. Business services. | 3750 Orange Pl. | 216/831–3300 or 800/465–4329 | fax 216/831–0486 | www.holiday-inn.com | 172 rooms | $105–$130 | AE, D, DC, MC, V.

Hilton Cleveland-East. This large hotel, a Marriott-turned-Hilton at U.S. 422 and 1–272, has equipped all its rooms with Sony Playstations and the Movie Channel. Restaurant, bar, room service. Some refrigerators. Cable TV. Indoor-outdoor pool. Hot tub, sauna. Exercise equipment. Video games. Laundry facilities. Business services. Some pets allowed (fee). | 3663 Park East Dr. | 216/464–5950 or 800/445–8667 | fax 216/464–6539 | www.hilton.com | 403 rooms | $109–$159 | AE, D, DC, MC, V.

Radisson Hotel Beachwood. This full-service hotel has a gift shop and a barber shop on-site. It's at the junction of I–271 and U.S. 422. Restaurant, lounge, room service. In-room data ports. Pool. Exercise equipment. Laundry facilities. Business services. Free parking. | 26300 Chagrin Blvd. | 216/831–5150 or 800/333–3333 | www.radisson.com | 191 rooms, 5 hot tub suites | $119, suites $200 | AE, D, DC, MC, V.

Residence Inn By Marriott–Cleveland-Beachwood. This four-story brick hostelry in the Beachwood business district is comfortable for a longer stay; it's an all-suites property with studios and one- and two-bedroom units. Complimentary Continental breakfast. In-room data ports, refrigerators, microwaves. Cable TV. Pool. Tennis court. Exercise equipment. Video games. Laundry service, laundry facility. Pets allowed (fee). | 3628 Park East Dr. | 216/831–3030 or 800/331–3333 | fax 216/831–3232 | www.marriot.com | 174 rooms, 46 two-bedroom units | Studios $149, one–bedroom units $159, two–bedroom units, $205 | AE, D, DC, MC, V.

Super 8 Hotel. A number of restaurants and retail stores are within walking distance of this two-story motel in Beachwood's business district. A sizeable shopping mall is 2 mi away.

Complimentary Continental breakfast. Some refrigerators. Cable TV. Business services. Airport shuttle. | 3795 Orange Pl. | 216/831–7200 or 800/848–8888 | fax 216/831–0616 | www.super8motels.com | 128 rooms | $99 | AE, D, DC, MC, V.

BELLEFONTAINE

(Nearby towns listed: Sidney, Wapakoneta)

Bellefontaine was founded at the turn of the 19th century by Canadian traders, who gave it the French name for "beautiful fountains," referring to the natural springs which run through the area. In the west-central section of Ohio at the highest point in the state (1,550 ft), the city's in the midst of broad fertile forests; there are lowlands near the Miami River. Like many Ohio cities, Bellefontaine prospered during the 1920s and 1930s, thanks to significant railroad traffic.

Despite the positive effect of trains on the local economy, some in the city had better ideas on how to get around. For years, pharmacist George Bartholomew experimented with a compound that could be formed into a hard surface for roads and buildings. The result: In 1891, Bellefontaine became the first city in the world to have a concrete street. A statue of Bartholomew stands near the street—Court St.—he laid. You can also check out 32-ft-long McKinley Street, the shortest street in the world. It's geography gives the area its chief attractions: caverns and ski slopes.

Information: Logan County Area Chamber of Commerce | 100 S. Main St., 43311 | 937/599–5121 or or 888/564–2626 | fax 937/599–2411 | www.logancountyohio.com.

Attractions

Indian Lake State Park. A full-service campground on over 600 acres, 16 mi northwest of Bellefontaine, serves boaters, fishermen, hikers, and other lovers of the outdoors. | 12774 Rte. 235 N, Lakeview | 937/843–2717 | www.dnr.state.oh.us/odnr/parks/directory/indianlk.htm | Free | Daily.

Mad River Mountain Ski Resort. Winter sports fans can opt for everything from downhill skiing to sledding at this winter playground 5 mi east of Bellefontaine. It's Ohio's highest skiing elevation (about 1,400 ft) and the site of Ohio's longest ski run, one of 15 trails on more than 120 acres. | 1000 Snow Valley Rd., Zanesfield | 937/599–1015 | www.skimadriver.com | Adult lift ticket $36 | Dec.–Mar., daily.

Ohio Caverns. Some of America's most colorful caverns are beneath West Liberty, 8 mi south of Bellefontaine. The underground caves have magnificent white stalactites and mysterious cave murals. | 2210 Rte. 245, West Liberty | 937/465–4017 | www.cavern.com/ohiocaverns | $8.50 | Apr.–Oct., daily 9–5; Nov.–Mar., daily 9–4.

Piatt Castles. Nestled in the lush countryside 10 mi south of Bellefontaine, these two European-style chateaux were constructed at the turn of the century as private residences. They are now open to the public for tours of the collections of original furnishings, Native American art, and firearms. | 10051 Rd. 47, West Liberty | 937/465–2821 | $7 | Apr.–May and Sept.–Oct., daily noon–4; June–Aug., daily 11–5.

Shadybowl Speedway. Racing buffs gather every Saturday night at the speedway southwest of Bellefontaine, one of the world's fastest ³⁄₁₀-mi asphalt ovals. | 9872 Flowing Wells Rd., DeGraff | 937/585–9456 | www.shadybowl.com | $12 | Sat.

Zane Shawnee Caverns. Guides lead you on a one-hour tour through chambers and tunnels carved out over millennia. A museum on the site has a scale model of a Shawnee village and Native American artifacts. | 7092 Rte. 540 | 937/592–9592 | www.zaneshawneecaverns.org | $7 | Apr.–Oct., daily 10–5; Nov.–Mar., Wed.–Sun. 10–5.

MAY: *Logan Hills Festival.* Held annually on Memorial Day weekend, this event attracts thousands to the Bellefontaine suburb of Logan Hills. Local bands play; there's also a cooking competition and a pizza-eating contest. | 937/599–3389.

JULY: *Logan County Fair.* Logan County's annual mid-summer bash features livestock shows, games, food, and rides at the Logan County Fairgrounds. | 301 E. Lake Ave. | 937/599–4178.

Dining
Palmer Farms/Fox's Pizza Den. Italian. This large, family place 3 mi from downtown Bellefontaine is a combination bakery, deli, pizza parlor, and smokehouse, serving everything from strombolis to smokehouse ribs. Smokehouse items include pulled pork, turkey, Cornish hens, and brisket. No alcohol is served. | 936 E. Sandusky Ave. | 937/592–3697 | $4–$7 | No credit cards.

Lodging
Comfort Inn. The two-story motel was built in 1989 and is about 2 mi from the downtown area. A dozen or so restaurants are within a 5 mi radius of the motel, as are ski slopes and golf courses. Bar with entertainment, complimentary Continental breakfast. In-room data ports, microwaves, some refrigerators. Cable TV. Pool. Exercise equipment. Laundry facilities. Some pets allowed (fee). | 260 Northview Dr. | 937/599–6666 or 800/228–5150 | fax 937/599–2300 | www.comfortinn.com | 80 rooms | $71–$115 | AE, D, DC, MC, V.

Whitmore House. This inn 4 mi west of Bellefontaine anchors four acres of lawn and garden in a peaceful, rural setting. The house is an 1875 Victorian furnished in period antiques specific to each of the three garden theme rooms. The owners frequently set up day trips to see the regional sights, and won't let you leave without a bag lunch. Restaurant, complimentary breakfast. No room phones, no TV. Library. | 3985 Rte. 47 W | 937/592–4290 | fax 937/592–6963 | 3 rooms | $55 | No credit cards.

BELLEVUE

MAP 14, C3

(Nearby towns listed: Sandusky, Tiffin, Vermilion)

Bellevue came into existence mainly because of the Mad River and Lake Erie Railroad Company, which was given $200,000 by the state to build a railroad from Tiffin to Sandusky. Several businessmen purchased land around the route and named their town after the railroad project engineer, James H. Bell. By the time the railroad was in place in 1837, the town was already prospering. Since then, it has become known as the home of the Seneca Caverns and the Mad River and NKP Railroad Society Museum.

Information: **Bellevue Area Tourism and Visitors Bureau** | Box 63, 44811 | 419/483–5359 or 800/562–6978.

Attractions
Historic Lyme Village. On a 2½-hour guided tour, you'll see restored 19th century buildings, including barns, a schoolhouse, a general store, a log church, a post office, and shops. The centerpiece of this village is the Wright Mansion, built in 1880 and furnished with Victorian antiques. | 5001 Rte. 4 | 419/483–4949 or 419/483–6052 | www.onebellevue.com/lymevillage | $7 | June–Aug., Tues.–Sun. 1–5; May and Sept., Sun. 1–5.

Mad River and NKP Railroad Society Museum. The largest train museum in Ohio chronicles Bellevue's history as a railroad center. Outdoors, you'll see the first domed railcar, dining cars, converted troop carriers, diesels, and other restored railroad cars. Inside, there are lanterns, uniforms, china, model railroads, and other memorabilia. | 253 S. West St. | 419/

483–2222 | www.onebellevue.com/madriver | $3 | June–Aug., Tues.–Sun. 1–5; May, Sept.–Oct., weekends 1–5.

Seneca Caverns. The caverns are billed as "Ohio's greatest natural underground adventure." On a one-hour guided tour, you'll go 110 ft beneath the surface into seven "rooms," the largest one being 250 ft long. The crystal-clear stream that runs underground here left behind fossilized fish, shells, and coral. | 15248 E. Thomson Township Rd. | 419/483–6711 | www.seneca-cavernsohio.com | $8 | June–Aug., daily 9–7; May, Sept.–Oct., weekends 10–5.

Sorrowful Mother Shrine. This Marian shrine sits on 120 acres of unspoiled woods and is the oldest pilgrimage site in the Midwest devoted to the Virgin Mary. It has lovely grottos and statues and a chapel, where mass is held each day at 11 and 4:30. | 4106 Rte. 269 | 419/483–3435 | www.sanduskyohio.com/funspots | Free | Daily 9–5.

ON THE CALENDAR
SEPT.: *Pioneer Days.* Held in the Historic Lyme Village complex, this event illustrates and celebrates the lives and times of early area settlers. | 5001 Rte. 4 | 419/483–4949.

Dining

American Bean Bag Cafe. American/Casual. This breakfast and lunch spot serves a lot of croissants and bagels in addition to sausage and egg breakfasts. For lunch try the quiche and/or one of the kitchen's own soups. Another big hit, the ciabatta sandwich, is stuffed with ham, salami, pepperoni, and provolone. | 120 E. Main St. | 419/484–3020 | No dinner. Closed Sun. | $3.50–$5 | AE, MC, V.

McClain's. American. A rustic, old-fashioned saloon with mounted elk and deer heads and exposed brick walls, McClain's is right in the center of town. The secret-recipe barbecue sauce that the locals love is drizzled over everything from ribs to chicken to shrimp. Down-home side dishes like home fries with onions and gravy complement the beef, chicken, and pork entrées. Kids' menu. | 137-139 Main St. | 419/483–2727 | Closed Sun. | $9–$29 | MC, V.

Lodging

Best Western Bellevue Inn. One of the few motels in Bellevue, this two-story brick affair is situated in a mostly industrial area; you can see a pair of plastic factories from the parking lot. Inside, it has spacious rooms and large indoor and outdoor pools. There are some Jacuzzi rooms. Restaurant, bar. Refrigerators. Cable TV. 2 pools (1 indoor). Laundry facilities. | 1120 E. Main St. | 419/483–5740 or 800/528–1234 | fax 419/483–5740 | www.rutahotels.com | 83 rooms | $94 | AE, D, DC, MC, V.

Relax Inn. This tiny roadside motel is in the commercial district of Bellevue, surrounded by fast-food joints, a half mile from downtown. Room service. Cable TV. | 620 W. Main St. | 419/483–6630 | 15 rooms | $49–$69 | AE, D, MC, V.

BERLIN

MAP 14, E4

(Nearby towns listed: Canton, Dover, East Liverpool, Gnadenhutten, New Philadelphia, Sugarcreek, Zoar)

Berlin (pronounced BER-lin by the locals) was named for the original settlers' hometown in Germany and is the center of Amish Country. Downtown Berlin stretches along Route 39 and is perhaps the most commercialized strip in Ohio's Amish Country, home to the nation's largest settlement (35,000 in three counties) of Amish. It's also the best place to browse the many blocks of shops selling crafts, clothing, baked goods, and furniture made by nearby Amish residents. You'll run into a lot of other tourists on Friday and Saturday.

Information: **Holmes County Chamber of Commerce and Tourism Bureau** | 35 N. Monroe St., Millersburg, 44654 | 330/674–3975 | www.visitamishcountry.com.

Attractions

Behalt at the Mennonite Information Center. A 265-ft mural painted on the walls of a circular room tells the story of the Anabaptist movement in 17th-century Europe and how it led to the Amish settlement in Ohio. You'll also find books, videos, and other resources about the Amish, Mennonite, and Hutterite faiths. | 5798 Rte. 77 | 330/893–3192 | www.behalt@sssnet.com | $5.50 | June–Oct., Mon.–Thurs. 9–5, Fri.–Sat. 9–8; Nov.–May, Mon.–Sat. 9–5.

Helping Hands Quilt Museum and Shop. Handmade Amish quilts (both antique and new) are on display and for sale. Amish women give quilting demonstrations, and videos describe the history and details of Amish quilt patterns. If you're a quilter or aspiring quilter, you can buy fabric, stencils, and other supplies. If you're an admirer, you can order a custom-made quilt. | 4826 Main St. (Rte. 39) | 330/893–2233 | Free | Mon.–Sat. 9–5.

Kidron Auction. Every Thursday morning, Amish farmers from all around the area come to the livestock sale at Kidron, about 10 mi north of Berlin. It's been going on since 1923 and is now a place to get a taste of true Amish life as well as a chance to buy authentic Amish-made goods. Hay and straw are the first to go on the block. | 4885 Kidron Rd. | 330/857–2641 | Thurs. from 10 AM.

Schrock's Amish Farm and Home. The guides here (many of whom are Amish) lead you through a typical Amish home and explain how they live without electricity or telephones. Afterwards, you can pet the farm animals and take a buggy ride. | 4363 Rte. 39 | 330/893–3232 | fax 330/893–3158 | www.amish-r-us.com | $7 | Apr.–Oct., Mon.–Fri. 10–5, Sat. 10–6.

Dining

Boyd and Wurthmann Restaurant. American. This diner with booths and a counter draws some regulars for both breakfast and lunch. The daily specials are hearty homestyle dishes, such as meatloaf and chicken and noodles. | E. Main St. | 330/893–3287 | $4–$8 | Closed Sun. | No credit cards.

Der Dutchman. American. Generous portions of tasty comfort food and reasonable prices keep patrons coming back to this Holmes County restaurant just east of Berlin, one of seven in a locally owned chain. Salad bar. Family-style service. Kids' menu. No smoking. | 4967 Walnut St., Walnut Creek | 330/893–2981 | Closed Sun. | $7–$10 | D, MC, V.

Dutch Harvest Restaurant. American. Traditional Amish dishes such as roast beef, baked ham, and roast turkey are all served up in a dining room that could easily double for one in an Amish home except it's much bigger. All entrées come with sides like mashed potatoes or corn. Pie varieties change daily but usually include seasonal fruits. Breakfast is served; it's also one of the few area restaurants that's open on Sunday. | 5330 County Rd. 201 | 330/893–3333 | $4–$8 | D, MC, V.

Lodging

Donna's Premier Lodging. Just off the shopping strip on Berlin's Main Street, Donna's has cottages, chalets, and bed-and-breakfast rooms, decorated with lace and ruffles. Complimentary evening snack, complimentary breakfast (full or Continental, depending on your room type). Some kitchenettes, some minibars, some microwaves, some refrigerators, some in-room hot-tubs. Cable TV, some in-room VCRs. No pets. No smoking. | 309 East St. | 330/893–3068 or 800/320–3338 | fax 330/893–0037 | www.donnasb-b.com | 13 rooms | Bed–and–breakfast rooms, $55–$85; villas and chalets, $199–$249, cottages, $149–$179 | DC, MC, V.

Inn at Honey Run. Secluded in the woods, this inn's main building is a wooden lodge furnished with overstuffed chairs and homemade quilts. The honeycomb building is on the side of a hill so that it's practically underground and barely visible. Dining room, complimentary Continental breakfast. Some kitchenettes, some minibars, some microwaves, some refrigerators, some in-room hot-tubs. Cable TV, some in-room VCRs. Some laundry facilities. | 6920 County Rd. 203 | 330/674–0011 or 800/468–6639 | fax 330/674–2623 | www.innathoneyrun.com | 37 rooms, 3 cottages | Inn rooms $65–$150; honeycombs, $99–$160; cottages, $150–$280 | AE, D, MC, V.

BOWLING GREEN

(Nearby towns listed: Findlay, Fremont, Toledo, Wauseon)

From Bowling Green's unique vantage point along the I–75 corridor, you can virtually hear the Great Lakes freighters in Toledo hauling their cargoes of steel for England, lumber for Japan, grain for Russia, and coal for River Rouge. Served by road and rail, Bowling Green's northwest Ohio location translates into fast deliveries and lower freight costs. The city is also home to Bowling Green State University, a highly respected educational institution. Just 30 minutes to the north is Toledo Express Airport, with national and international passenger connections; Wood County Airport is also nearby.

Information: Bowling Green Convention and Visitors Bureau | 163 N. Main St., 43402 | 419/353–7945 or 800/866–0046 | www.bgcvb@dacor.net.

Attractions

Bowling Green State University. Founded in 1914 as a teacher-training college, this is now a university with more than 19,000 students and 200 degree programs. Tours of the 200-acre campus are given daily during the school year. | 1001 E. Wooster St. | 419/372–2531 | www.bgsu.edu | Free | Daily.

The university's **Educational Memorabilia Center** is in a one-room schoolhouse that was built in 1875 in Huron County and moved to the BGSU campus 100 years later. The tiny red-brick building is now a history museum. | 1001 E. Wooster St. | 419/372–7405 | Free | Daily.

Mary Jane Thurston State Park. You can fish, boat, swim, hike, and more at this 550-acre park about 12 mi west of Bowling Green. | 1466 Rte. 65 | 419/832–7662 | Free | Daily, dawn–dusk.

Wood County Historical Museum. The former Wood County Infirmary once served as respite for anyone who had fallen upon hard times–orphans, the mentally ill, sick children, etc. Today, the 60-room Victorian main building is furnished to reflect styles from the 19th and 20th centuries, and memorabilia from area residents fill the military room, the business room, and other themed areas. On the 54-acre property is an ice house, horse and hog barns, a pauper's cemetery, and an herb garden, as well as a hospital for the violently insane, known as the Lunatic House. Guided tours are available on weekends. | 13660 County Home Rd. | 419/352–0967 | $2 | Apr.–Oct., Tues.–Fri. 9:30–4:30, weekends 1–4.

ON THE CALENDAR

AUG.: *Wood County Fair.* Livestock, games, and live entertainment are the chief attractions at this annual festival at the Wood County Fairgrounds. | 13800 W. Poe Rd. | 419/352–0441.

Dining

Aztec. Mexican. At this traditional spot, Tacos Alambres are popular, with grilled meat, sautéed veggies, and Swiss cheese melted over the top. Or try the quesadillas and tamales. Work by local artists embellishes the walls. Kids' menu. | 101 S. Main St. | 419/353–2505 | $3–$16 | AE, D, MC, V.

Junction Bar and Grill. American. The rooftop patio gets crowded on warm, sunny afternoons and breezy summer evenings, when both the locals and students from Bowling Green

University come to enjoy alfresco dining and drinking. Chicken, steak, and vegetable fajita dinners, fettuccine Alfredo, barbecued ribs, and many vegetarian entrées are top picks. Kids' menu. | 110 N. Main St. | 419/352–9222 | $7–$16 | AE, D, MC, V.

Kaufman's Steakhouse. Steak. Behind Kaufman's rustic, roadhouse exterior is a lounge, a sports bar, and a dimly-lit sit-down dining area with a pair of aquariums and a big fireplace that crackles to life in colder months. You can order hearty, down-home steaks or grilled chicken dishes off the menu, or plunder the extensive salad bar. Many regulars have made a habit out of Kaufman's monster onion rings, lightly battered and fried to golden crispiness. Kids' menu. | 163 S. Main St. | 419/352–2595 | Closed Sun. | $10–$30 | AE, D, DC, MC, V.

Lodging

Days Inn. Just off I–75 and within spitting distance of Bowling Green State University, this motel is usually swarming with people in town to visit students or attend university events. The two-story brick structure also has easy access to nearby restaurants and shopping, most of which are within a 3 mi radius. Complimentary Continental breakfast. Cable TV. | 1550 E. Wooster St. | 419/352–5211 or 800/325–2525 | fax 419/354–8030 | www.daysinn.com | 100 rooms | $85 | AE, D, MC, V.

Quality Inn. This two-story motel has spacious but simple rooms and is opposite the campus of Bowling Green State University and just 2 mi from downtown. Restaurant. In-room data ports. Cable TV. Indoor pool. Hot tub. Video games. | 1630 E. Wooster St. | 419/352–2521 or 800/228–5151 | fax 419/353–5975 | www.qualityinn.com | 86 rooms, 15 suites | $55–$75; suites $129 | AE, D, DC, MC, V.

BRECKSVILLE

MAP 14, E3

(Nearby towns listed: Aurora, Beachwood, Cleveland, Strongsville)

Although it is just 15 mi south of Cleveland, Brecksville maintains a small-town charm and rural flavor. One-third of the city's 20 square mi are occupied by the Metroparks' Brecksville Reservation and the Cuyahoga Valley National Recreation Area (See Akron.) The city's growth has been carefully monitored to maintain a balance of residential, retail, and light manufacturing areas.

Information: **Brecksville Chamber of Commerce** | 10107 Brecksville Rd., 44141 | 440/526–7350.

Attractions

Squire Rich House Museum. Squire B. Rich and his wife, Anne Jane Rich, were among the early settlers in Brecksville, and built this modest salt-box home in 1835. You can see the house, the barn and tool shed, and then cross an eerie bridge that leads to the cemetery where Benjamin Waites, a war hero of the American Revolution, is buried. | 9367 Brecksville Rd. | 440/526–7156 | Free | Mid-May–mid-Oct., Sun. 2–5.

ON THE CALENDAR

JULY: *Home Days.* Local music of all genres, food vendors, and rides make this fair a small-town 4th of July carnival. | Rte. 21, at Rte. 82 | 440/526–4351.

Dining

Eddie's Creekside Restaurant. American. Windows overlook the Chippewa Creek at this peaceful family place, known for flavorful dishes like penne Sorrento and New Orleans shrimp with pasta. The menu favors beef, but there's also a huge selection of other dishes, like barbecued ribs, honey walnut chicken, specialty salads, Portobello burgers, and fish. For brunch on Saturday and Sunday, there are homemade Belgian waffles. | 8803 Brecksville Rd. | 440/546–AE–0555 | $10–$20 | AE, D, DC, MC, V.

Marco Polo's. Italian. The building that houses Marco Polo's has seen action as both a retail space and a dance hall. The dining area retains some of the structure's original charm, with high ceilings and big windows. The menu's strong on traditional Italian fare, like fettuccine Alfredo and chicken parmigiana. Entertainment Fri. and Sat. | 8188 Brecksville Rd. | 440/526–6130 | www.polo8188.com | Reservations essential | No lunch Sat. | $13–$22 | AE, D, DC, MC, V.

Lodging

Days Inn Cleveland South. A mile and a half from downtown Brecksville, this ranch-style motel is right in the business area and within walking distance of a restaurant or two. Rooms are modest and pleasant. In-room data ports. Cable TV. Pool. | 4501 E. Royalton Rd. | 440/526–0640 or 800/325–2525 | fax 440/526–5542 | www.daysinn.com | 108 rooms | $50–$80 | AE, D, DC, MC, V.

Hilton Cleveland South. Comfortably removed from the bustle and hurry of Cleveland proper, this two-story hotel's exterior is reminiscent of the English countryside's exposed-timber cottages. Downtown Cleveland is about 12 mi away, or you can go the other direction and explore Brecksville. Restaurant, room service. In-room data ports. Cable TV. Indoor-outdoor pool. Tennis. Exercise equipment. Playground. Business services. Airport shuttle. Some pets allowed. | 6200 Quarry La., Independence | 216/447–1300 or 800/445–8667 | fax 440/642–9334 | www.hilton.com | 195 rooms | $105 | AE, D, DC, MC, V.

Holiday Inn-Independence. Just off I–77 and about 5 mi north of Brecksville, this large five-story brick hotel is surrounded by a wide range of fast-food and family dining options. Restaurant, bar with entertainment, room service. In-room data ports. Cable TV. Indoor pool. Sauna. Laundry facilities. Business services. Airport shuttle. | 6001 Rockside Rd., Independence | 216/524–8050 or 800/465–4329 | fax 440/524–9280 | www.holiday-inn.com | 363 rooms | $89 | AE, D, DC, MC, V.

Pilgrim Inn. Built in 1957, this two-story motel with an impressive front lawn is in the center of the business district. It has a homey place, with a friendly front desk and a variety of accommodations from singles to efficiencies. Extended stays are available. In-room data ports. Cable TV. Laundry facilities. | 8757 Brecksville Rd. | 440/526–4621 | 67 rooms | $47–$67 | AE, D, MC, V.

CAMBRIDGE

MAP 14, E5

(Nearby towns listed: Coshocton, Zanesville)

In 1796, Ebenezer Zane received funds from the federal government to cut a road from Ohio to Kentucky. He set to work, naming one of his first settlements Cambridge in honor of his hometown in Maryland. Another group of settlers, from the Isle of Guernsey in the British Channel, pitched camp in Cambridge in 1806. Central to the history of the area was the building of the national road through Cambridge in 1827. Many bridges were built in that era, including the first bridge authorized in the Northwest Territory. Since then, Cambridge has become known for its glass industry. Several glass companies have museums, shops, and factories in the city, and many give tours to the public.

Information: **Cambridge Area Chamber of Commerce** | 918 Wheeling Ave., Cambridge 43725 | 740/439–6688 | www.visitguernseycounty.com.

Attractions

Boyd's Crystal Art Glass. See skilled glass artisans at work in their shops making hand-blown and machine-crafted reproductions of antique glass. | 1203 Morton Ave. | 740/439–2077 | Free | Weekdays 10–4.

The Cambridge Glass Museum. Thousands of elegant works in glass made between 1906 and 1958 are on display in this gem of a museum, which is considered to be the largest private collection of Cambridge glass in the nation. | 812 Jefferson Ave. | 740/432–3045 | $2 | June–Nov., Mon.–Sat. 1–4.

Degenhart Paperweight and Glass Museum. Exhibits illustrating and explaining the different types of glass produced in the Cambridge area are on display at this museum. You'll see Midwestern pattern glass, cruets, and Degenhart glass and paperweights. Also on hand is an extensive collection of works by local and regional glass artists. | 65323 Highland Hills Rd. | 740/432–2626 | $1.50 | Apr.–Dec., Mon.–Sat. 9–5; Jan.–Mar., weekdays 10–5.

Mosser Glass. One of Cambridge's famous glass factories gives free one-hour tours of its operation. | U.S. 22 E | 740/439–1827 | Free | Weekdays, 8–4; closed first two weeks in July.

Muskingum Watershed Conservancy District and Senecaville Lake Park. Activities like boating, swimming, hiking, and fishing are also available in this 7,600-acre park southeast of Cambridge. Nature programs are presented here. | 22172 Park Rd. | 740/685–6013 | $2 per vehicle Mon.–Thurs., $5 Fri.–Sun. | Daily, dawn–dusk.

Salt Fork State Park. This 20,000-acre park 7 mi northeast of Cambridge has stables, a marina, hiking trails, and bicycles to rent. There's an 18-hole golf course, which belongs to the Salt Fork Resort and Conference Center, a state-of-the-art hotel that's in the state park. | 740/439–3521 | www.amfac.com | Free | Daily, dawn–dusk.

ON THE CALENDAR

APR.: *Hopalong Cassidy Festival.* The Wild West comes to Cambridge at this annual tribute to native son William Boyd, better known as Hopalong Cassidy. Highlights include Western entertainment and visits from Hollywood stars. It's held at the Pritchard Laughlin Civic Center, the first weekend of May. | 7033 Glenn Hwy. | 740/432–2022 or 800/933–5480.

JUNE–SEPT.: *Living Word Outdoor Drama.* Ohio's only outdoor passion play dramatizes the life of Jesus Christ. The 2½-hour show is performed in a natural amphitheater. Reservations are a good idea. | 6010 College Hill Rd. | 740/439–2761.

AUG.: *Salt Fork Arts and Crafts Festival.* Thousands of people attend this annual show at Cambridge City Park, the second weekend of August, to see the latest creations of local and regional artists. | N. 8th St. | 740/432–2022.

OCT.: *Oktoberfest.* Local residents and visitors gather in downtown Cambridge the first weekend of October to celebrate the city's German heritage with music, dance, games, and food. | Wheeling Ave. | 740/439–6688.

Dining

Theo's Coney Island. Eclectic. At this family-owned, diner-style restaurant, American, Greek, Italian, and Asian flavors make up the menu. There's homemade pasta, bread, and many desserts to sample, as well as Coney Island hot dogs. Try the Greek salad or the chicken stir fry. Local art brightens the dining room. Kids' menu. | 630 Wheeling Ave. | 740/432–3878 | Closed Sun. | $5–$10 | AE, D, MC, V.

The Forum. Eclectic. This tavern-style restaurant just a mile from the center of town is a good place to take children. The wide-ranging menu includes a Greek sampler and a Greek salad, Mexican burritos and fajitas, as well as pizza, pastas, steak, and terrific hamburgers. Olympic chicken fettuccine comes with artichokes, broccoli, and a mushroom and garlic sauce. Kids' menu. | 2205 Southgate Pkwy. | 740/439–2777 | $7–$14 | AE, D, MC, V.

Lodging

Best Western. Right off I–70, this motel is just minutes away from the Cambridge Glass Museum and Salt Fork State Park. The two-story brick building is in a largely commercial area that includes a score of restaurants, a large discount store, and several small shopping plazas. Bar. Cable TV. Pool. Business services. Some pets allowed. | 1945 Southgate Pkwy. | 740/439–3581 or 800/528–1234 | fax 740/439–1824 | www.bestwestern.com | 95 rooms | $65 | AE, D, DC, MC, V.

Colonel Joseph B. Taylor Inn Bed and Breakfast. This three-story 1878 painted lady home is furnished with Victorian antiques. Plush robes, fresh roses, a fireplace in the room, and the lavish breakfast are nice touches. Complimentary breakfast. No room phones. TV in common area. Hot tub. Library. Business services. | 633 Upland Rd. | 740/432–7802 | fax 740/435–3152 | www.coltaylorinnbb.com | 4 rooms | $115–$125 | D, MC, V.

Holiday Inn. Strategically located at the junction of I–70 and I–77, this hotel is a pretty good bet if you're just passing through the area. There's a multiscreen movie theater right across the street, and two major shopping malls within 30 minutes of the hotel. If you've come to explore, downtown Cambridge is only 2 mi away. Restaurant, bar, room service. Cable TV. Pool. Laundry facilities. Business services. Some pets allowed. | 2248 Southgate Pkwy. | 740/432–7313 | fax 740/432–2337 | www.holiday-inn.com | 109 rooms | $69–$99 | AE, D, DC, MC, V.

Misty Meadow Farm Bed and Breakfast. This 1910 farmhouse and guest cottage are on 150 trail-crossed acres with a spring-fed pond, a French garden, and an orchard. A fresh peach and glass of champagne is delivered to your room, and the breakfast runs to three courses. Complimentary breakfast. No room phones. TV in common area. Pool. Sauna, hot tub. No kids. No smoking. | 64878 Slaughter Hill Rd. | 740/439–5135 | misty@cambridgeoh.com | www.mistymeadow.com | 3 rooms, 1 cottage | Rooms $130, cottage $190 | MC, V.

Salt Fork Resort and Conference Center. Opened in 1972, this four-story wooden lodge serves as the main accommodation for the Salt Fork State Park. The lodge's exterior and the guest rooms have a rustic, rough-hewn flavor with lots of windows and wood paneling. A number of private cottages dot the property and allow for more privacy amid the trees. Next to peaceful relaxation, fishing is the most popular park activity; canoes, motorboats, rowboats, and sailboats are available to guests. Bar, dining room, picnic area. Some refrigerators. Cable TV. In cottages: Kitchenettes. No air-conditioning. No room phones. Some hot tubs and fireplaces. 2 pools (1 indoor), wading pool. Some hot tubs and fireplaces. Eighteen-hole golf course, tennis. Exercise equipment, hiking. Marina, boating. Video games. Playground. Laundry facilities. Business services. | U.S. 22 E | 740/439–2751 or 800/282–7275 | fax 740/432–6615 | www.saltforkresort.com | 148 rooms, 54 cottages | Rooms $118–$160, 2-bedroom cottages $145–$180 | AE, D, DC, MC, V.

Travelodge. Built in 1968 at the intersection of I–70 and I–77, this no-frills motel is about 1 mi outside of downtown Cambridge and occupies a mostly commercial district of small businesses and chain restaurants. Cable TV. Pool. Sauna. Business services. | 8777 Georgetown Rd. | 740/432–7375 or 800/255–3050 | fax 740/432–5808 | www.travelodge.com | 48 rooms | $75 | AE, D, DC, MC, V.

CANTON

MAP 14, E3

(Nearby towns listed: Akron, Alliance, Massillon, New Philadelphia)

In 1806 Bezaleel Wells, a surveyor from Steubenville, laid out the plots for what would become Canton, the first town to be settled in Stark County in northeast Ohio. It was incorporated as a village in 1815 and by 1854 became a city. Some attribute Canton's orderliness to the Swiss and German watchmakers who had a part in city planning.

Today, Canton is a city of diversified industries: more than 1,500 different products are manufactured here. Agriculture also plays a strong role as Canton is home to nationally known dairy products and poultry farms. Stark County was the home of President William McKinley, and you can see a large national memorial erected to his memory in Canton. It's also the home of the Pro Football Hall of Fame.

Information: Canton/Stark County Convention and Visitors' Bureau | 229 Wells Ave. NW, 44703 | 330/454–1439 or 800/533–4302 | fax 330/452–7786 | www.visitcantonohio.com.

Attractions

Canton Classic Car Museum. More than 35 classic automobiles are displayed here, among them cars featured in movies and vehicles once owned by celebrities. The museum is housed in the first Ford dealership in Ohio; cars are displayed along with advertisements and fashions from their time period. | 555 Market Ave. SW | 330/455–3603 | www.cantonclassiccar.org | $6 | Daily 10–5.

Harry London Candies. Watch chocolate candy being made from cocoa beans, and see how it is packaged, prepared, and shipped out on a 45-minute factory tour, that also includes a visit to the "Chocolate Hall of Fame." You'll get to taste samples, and then head to the candy store on the premises. Reservations are essential. | 5353 Lauby Rd. | 330/494–0833 or 800/321–0444 | fax 330/499–6902 | www.londoncandies.com | $2 | Mon.–Sat. 9–4, Sun. 12–3:30.

Hoover Historical Center. One of only two vacuum cleaner museums in the world, the center chronicles how the suction cleaner developed during the past century. The museum is in the boyhood home of William Henry Hoover, founder of the Hoover Company. A variety of early vacuum cleaners are on display, including a 1910 model that users had to pump with their feet. | 1875 Easton St. NW, North Canton | 330/499–0287 | www.hoover.com | Free | Tues.–Sun. 1–5.

McKinley National Memorial. This national landmark is dedicated to the 25th president. This is the burial site of President William McKinley (1843–1901) and his wife and children. An adjacent museum chronicles McKinley's life and times. | 800 McKinley Monument Dr. NW | 330/455–7043 | www.mckinleymuseum.org | $6 | Mon.–Sat. 9–5, Sun. noon–5.

The interactive history and science exhibits at the **McKinley Museum of History, Science and Industry** encourage people of all ages to explore fossils, dinosaurs, and the life of early man. You can hunt for baby Maisaurus dinos, meet Alice the robotic Allosaurus, check out chinchillas in their simulated mountain habitat, and learn about stars at the Hoover-Price Planetarium. The history exhibits include the Street of Shops, lined with a pioneer house, general stores, print store and more. | 800 McKinley Monument Dr. NW | 330/455–7043 | www.mckinleymuseum.org | $6 | Museum: Mon.–Sat. 9–5, Sun. noon–5. Planetarium shows: Sat. 2, Sun. 2, 3.

Pro Football Hall of Fame. The gridiron's greatest players are honored at this shrine to professional football. There are interactive exhibits, players' memorabilia, profiles of teams and their stars, and a two-story movie theater. This is also the site of Fawcett Stadium, home of the annual Hall of Fame Game. | 2121 George Halas Dr. NW | 330/456–8207 | www.profootballhof.com | $10 | Memorial Day–Labor Day, daily 9–8; Labor Day–Memorial Day, daily 9–5.

Stadium Park. This park next to the Pro Football Hall of Fame has a softball complex, a playground, 68 acres of nature and picnic areas, a duck pond, the John F. Kennedy Memorial Fountain, and a 1.5-mi rubberized walking track with exercise stations. | 1615 Stadium Park Dr. NW | 330/456–7022 | Free | Weekdays 7:30–3.

Waterworks Park. This portion of Canton Park, next to the McKinley National Memorial, has picnic tables and play areas. | 100 Washington Blvd. | 330/489–3015 | Free | Daily.

JULY–AUG.: *Hall of Fame Festival.* Some of the greatest football players in the history of the sport gather at the Pro Football Hall of Fame for the annual induction of new members. Year 2000 inductees included Joe Montana. A week of football-related activities leads up to the event. | 2121 George Halas Dr. NW | 330/456–8207 | www.profootball-hoffestival.com.

Dining

John's Grille. American. If you're looking for cheap eats and an informal, relaxed, and friendly bar, this is the spot. The super-size burgers, fresh-cut fries, and hearty steaks draw praise from locals. The minimal furnishings include wooden tables and booths and sports pictures scattered across the walls; there's also a sunny "garden" dining room with windows and plants. | 2749 Cleveland Ave. | 330/454–1259 | Closed Sun. | $9–$17 | AE, D, MC, V.

Lolli's. Italian. At this restaurant you can dine by candlelight at intimate booths. Popular dishes include garlic chicken and angel-hair pasta topped with smoked salmon and shrimp in a dill cream sauce. Also on the menu are seafood and veal medallions. Early bird dinners. | 4801 Dressler Rd. NW | 330/492–6846 | Closed Sun., Mon. | $9–$20 | AE, D, MC, V.

Spread Eagle Tavern and Inn. Continental. Built as an inn in 1837, this restaurant 20 mi east of Canton contains several romantic, candlelit dining rooms, including the Barn Room, with a large stone fireplace, the Patriot's Room, decorated with Civil War–era memorabilia, and the Barbara Bush Room, filled with pictures and memorabilia of the former First Lady. The menu offers fresh fish, smoked rack of lamb, and beef and chicken entrées as well as lobster and Maryland-style crab cakes. Meats are smoked in the restaurant's own smokehouse. Entertainment Sat. Kids' menu. No smoking. | 10150 Plymouth St., Hanoverton | 330/223–1583 | $16–$25 | AE, D, MC, V.

Lodging

Comfort Inn Canton. This solid motel, housed in a three-story redbrick building, is near I–77, one exit north of the Pro Football Hall of Fame, surrounded by restaurants and stores. Complimentary Continental breakfast. In-room data ports. Cable TV. Pool. Business services. Free parking. | 5345 Broadmoor Circle NW | 330/492–1331 or 800/228–5150 | fax 330/492–9093 | www.comfortinn.com | 124 rooms | $89 | AE, D, DC, MC, V.

Four Points by Sheraton. This Sheraton is right off I–77, 10 minutes away from the Pro Football Hall of Fame and in the center of the Beldon Village shopping district. The six-story white stucco hotel was built in the 1970s and in 2000 underwent a $2 million renovation. Restaurant, bar, room service. Some refrigerators. Cable TV. Indoor-outdoor pool. Exercise equipment. Video games. Business services. Airport shuttle. Free parking. | 4375 Metro Circle NW | 330/494–6494 or 800/325–3535 | fax 330/494–7129 | www.fourpointscanton.com | 152 rooms | $115 | AE, D, DC, MC, V.

Hampton Inn. A variety of restaurants and retail stores surround this four-story hotel, which is off I–77. The hotel is also close to the Pro Football Hall of Fame. Complimentary Continental breakfast. In-room data ports. Cable TV. In-room video games. Free parking. | 5335 Broadmoor Circle NW | 330/492–0151 or 800/426–7866 | fax 330/492–7523 | www.hamptoninn.com | 107 rooms | $85 | AE, D, DC, MC, V.

Hilton Canton. This eight-story downtown hotel has a plush lobby with wood walls and burgundy furnishings and spacious rooms. Restaurant, bar, room service. Cable TV. Indoor pool. Sauna, hot tub. Exercise equipment. Video games. Business services. Airport shuttle. | 320 Market Ave. S | 330/454–5000 or 800/742–0379 | fax 330/454–5494 | www.hilton.com | 170 rooms, 3 suites | $119 | AE, D, DC, MC, V.

Holiday Inn-North Canton. This newly renovated member of the familiar hotel chain is across the street from the Beldon Village Mall, a popular shopping area, and is less than a quarter mile from I–77. Restaurant, bar with entertainment, room service. In-room data ports. Cable TV. Pool. Business services. Airport shuttle. Some pets allowed. | 4520 Everhard Rd.

NW | 330/494–2770 or 800/465–4329 | fax 330/494–6473 | www.holiday-inn.com | 194 rooms | $149 | AE, D, DC, MC, V.

CELINA

MAP 14, A4

(Nearby towns listed: Van Wert, Wapakoneta)

Celina, with a population of 10,000, is the county seat of Mercer County. The Main Street historic district is lined with grandiose turn-of-the-century homes. This small city has five city parks and a number of sporting complexes, as well as a bike path that runs to nearby Coldwater. Celina's Grand Lake is a popular spot for fishing and boating.

Information: **Celina-Mercer County Chamber of Commerce** | 226 N. Main St., 45822 | 419/586–2219 | Weekdays 11–7.

Attractions

Bicycle Museum of America. On display are more than 5,000 pieces of bicycle memorabilia and 200 bikes, dating from 1816 to the present. It's about 12 mi southeast of Celina. | 7 W. Monroe St., New Bremen | 419/629–9249 | www.bicyclemuseum.com | $3 | Weekdays 11–5, Sat. 11–2.

Grand Lake–St. Mary's State Park. At 15,000 acres, this is Ohio's largest inland lake. It was constructed between 1837 to 1841 to serve as a federal reservoir for the Miami-Erie Canal System. Tours of the lake and canals are available. You can bicycle on the designated bike path, hike, swim, and boat here. | 834 Edge Water Dr. | 419/394–2774 | Free | Daily, dawn–dusk.

Mercer County Historical Museum. This museum chronicles the past 200 years of Mercer County life. Also known as the Riley House, the museum contains genealogical materials and many books on local history. It's within easy walking distance of downtown. | 130 E. Market St. | 419/586–6065 | Free | Oct.–Apr., Wed.–Fri. 8:30–4, Sun. 1–4; May–Sept., Wed.–Fri. 8:30–4.

National Marian Shrine of the Holy Relics. This shrine contains approximately 500 relics of the saints and is the second largest collection of its kind in the United States. Built in 1890, the shrine and the adjacent former convent building were placed on the National Register of Historic Places in 1976. It is owned and operated by the Sisters of the Precious Blood. | 2291 St. John's Rd. | 419/925–4532 | $2 suggested | Tues.–Sun. 9:30–4:30.

ON THE CALENDAR

JULY: *Celina Lake Festival.* Begun in 1936, this summer celebration is a Celina institution. Three days of games, food, and rides are topped off with a fireworks display over Grand Lake. It's usually held the last full weekend of July, along Main Street in Celina, at the park and the lake. | Grand Lake, 834 Edge Water Dr. | 419/586–2219.

AUG.: *Governor's Cup Regatta.* Boats in six different classes compete in races on Grand Lake St. Mary's, Ohio's largest inland lake. Some boats reach speeds of 150 mph. | 834 Edge Water Dr. | 419/586–2219.

Dining

Welch's Restaurant. American. This nautical steak and seafood place overlooks Grand Lake, either from the porch or through huge windows. Try the filet mignon, the surf and turf, or the eggplant parmesan. For dessert don't miss the homemade coconut cream pie. You can also order lighter fare, like sandwiches, pasta or taco salads, priced from about $7. It's 1 mi from Route 127. Sun. brunch. Kids' menu. | 1081 W. Bank Rd. | 419/586–2579 | No dinner Sat. | $10–$24 | AE, D, DC, MC, V.

Lodging

Comfort Inn-Celina. Outoor hallways offer a spectacular view of neighboring Grand Lake at this small hotel 1 mi east of Celina. Complimentary Continental breakfast. Cable TV. | 1421 Rte. 703 E | 419/586–4656 or 228–5150 | fax 419/586–4152 | www.comfortinn.com | 40 rooms | $75 | AE, D, DC, MC, V.

Holiday Inn Express-Celina. This motel on the outskirts of town is 2 mi from Route 127 and a ½ mi from Grand Lake. A fishing pond is on the property. Complimentary Continental breakfast. In-room data ports. Cable TV. Indoor pool. Hot tub. Exercise equipment. Laundry facilities. | 2020 Holiday Dr. | 419/586–4919 or 800/465–4329 | fax 419/586–4919 | www.holiday-inn.com | 52 rooms | $84 | AE, D, DC, MC, V.

CHARDON

(Nearby towns listed: Beachwood, Cleveland, Mentor, Painesville)

Chardon is a tiny village about 25 mi east of Cleveland. The town was named after Bostonian Peter Chardon Brooks and was established as a county seat in 1808. Sixty years later, the entire business district was destroyed by a fire which began in a saddle and harness shop. The town center was rebuilt, and the resulting Chardon Village is architecturally striking. Today about 5,000 people call the village home.

Information: Chardon Area Chamber of Commerce | 112 E. Park St., 44024 | 440/285–9050 | www.geaugalink.com.

Attractions

Alpine Valley. This ski resort about 5 mi southwest of Chardon has something for everyone. There's downhill skiing—day and night—on 10 trails;, snowboarding in Xtreme Park, which has a half pipe with its own lift; and a long snowtubing hill, also with its own lift. | 10620 Mayfield Rd., Chesterland | 440/729–9775 | www.alpinevalleyohio.com | Adult lift ticket, $36 | Dec.–Mar., depending on conditions.

Century Village. The home of Thomas and Lydia Umberfield, two of the county's first residents who settled in 1798, is a focal point of this restored Western Reserve village, which is run by the Geauga County Historical Society. You take a tour "through 100 years of history," hence the name, and see a 1798 log cabin, an 1846 church, five furnished historic homes, vintage barns, an early schoolhouse and a 1878 train station. There is also a 9,000 piece toy-soldier display. The village is about 9 mi southeast of Chardon. | 14653 E. Park St., Burton | 440/834–1492 | fax 440/834–4012 | www.geaugalink.com/homefrm.html | $5 | May–mid-Nov., Tues.–Fri., tours at 10:30, 1 and 3; weekends, tours at 1 and 3.

Chardon Village. The long row of white clapboard buildings that originally lined Chardon's Main Street were destroyed by fire in 1868. When the Village Square was rebuilt, it was in the High Victorian Italianate style, with arched windows, entrance columns and lots of ornamentation. You can walk around this historic town center today; its buildings are occupied by businesses, shops, and restaurants and it's bordered by a park. | On the Square in Chardon, between Main St. and E. Park St. | Free | Daily.

Fowler's Mill Golf Course. This 27-hole Pete Dye masterpiece, about 5 mi southwest of Chardon, was voted one of the top public golf courses in Ohio by *Golf Magazine*. You should reserve a tee time two weeks in advance. Greens fees include golf cart. | 13095 Rockhaven Rd., Chesterland | 440/286–9545 | www.cdsalesman.com/golfersweb/fowlers.htm | $42–$52 | Daily.

Punderson State Park. With 1,000 lush acres of forest, this park is a great place for boating, hiking, and camping. The park has a lodge, cabins, and a golf course. It's 7 mi of Chardon on Route 87. | 11577 Kinsman Rd., Newbury | 440/564–2279 | Free | Daily.

MAR.–APR.: *Geauga County Maple Festival.* This festival celebrating maple sugar season is held every year on the first weekend after Easter on the square in Chardon Village. There are rides, food, maple syrup displays, parades, bath tub races, quilts, and entertainment. | Between Main St. and E. Park St. | 216/286–3007.

Dining

Bass Lake Taverne. American/Casual. Situated along a pastoral road, this tavern in the woods has hand-hewn beams and brickwork. The menu includes large cuts of meat, hearty burgers, and fresh catch from nearby Lake Erie. Open-air dining in a courtyard that seats about 40. Entertainment Fri. and Sat. | 426 South St. | 440/285–3100 | $14–$25 | AE, D, DC, MC, V.

The Inn at Fowlers Mill. Continental. Go for a window table and you'll have a view of the nearby Alpine Valley ski resort. The sterling salmon in butter sauce flavored with lemon, white wine, and dill is a popular selection, as are the prime rib and the creative pastas. There's open-air dining on an outdoor deck and a Sunday brunch. Kids' menu. The restaurant is about 4.5 mi south of Chardon. | 10700 Mayfield Rd. | 440/286–3111 | No dinner Sun. Closed Mon. | $14–$25 | AE, D, DC, MC, V.

Mark's Maple Leaf Restaurant. American. This small-town family eatery is in Maple Leaf Plaza, 1 mi from Chardon's town center. Breakfast is served all day; there's also a Sunday brunch buffet with home-baked goodies. | 540 Water St. | 440/286–5151 | $7–$9 | MC, V.

Lodging

Avalon Gardens. This 1870s Victorian farmhouse with bay windows is on the grounds of a working nursery, and that's what you see when you look out of your antiques-filled bedroom. You can eat your hearty breakfast in the sunny parlor and drink your tea on the spacious patio, where there's an outdoor fireplace. The inn is within viewing distance of Alpine Valley ski resort. Complimentary breakfast. No room phones. TV in common area. Shared bath. | 12511 Fowlers Mill Rd. | 440/286–2126 or 888/485–0734 | fax 440/729–3240 | www.avalongardensinn.com | 2 rooms | $115 | MC, V.

CHILLICOTHE

MAP 14, C6

(Nearby towns listed: Columbus, Washington Court House)

In 1796, Nathaniel Massie founded a town that he called Chillicothe, a name derived from the Shawnee Indian word meaning "principal town." The following year, Massie offered free lots to the first 100 settlers. The lots went quickly and subsequently the town grew and prospered. When Ohio entered the union in 1832, Chillicothe became the state's first capital. The construction of the Ohio-Erie Canal in 1831 made Chillicothe a major port, allowing local farmers to transport their crops to market. The canal, combined with the construction of the Marietta and Cincinnati Railroad, attracted many new settlers from Pennsylvania, Delaware, and Maryland.

Today Chillicothe is an industrial city, surrounded by one of the most productive agricultural areas in the state. Its attractions include mansions with period furnishings, numerous state parks, and Native American burial mounds and an intriguing serpent effigy on a hillside.

Information: Chillicothe-Ross Chamber of Commerce | 165 S. Paint St., 45601 | 740/702–2722. .

Attractions

Adena State Memorial. Built in 1807, this refurbished 20-room Georgian mansion was the home of one of Ohio's early governors, Thomas Worthington, and contains many antiques from that time period. It was built by Benjamin Latrobe, who went on to oversee the rebuilding of the Capitol in Washington, D.C., after it burned. From the overlook, you can see the hills that are pictured on the state seal. | Adena Rd. | 740/772–1500 or 800/319–7248 | $5 | Memorial Day–Labor Day, Wed.–Sat. 9:30–5, Sun. noon–5; Sept.–Oct., Sat. 9:30–5, Sun. noon–5.

Hopewell Culture National Historical Park. Operated by the National Park Service, this monument protects 23 prehistoric burial mounds that were erected by the Hopewell Indians, who lived in this area from about 200 BC to AD 500. There is an orientation film and exhibits at the visitor center. It's 3 mi north of Chillicothe. | 16062 Rte. 104 | 740/774–1125 | www.nps.gov | $2 | Grounds: daily, dawn–dusk. Visitor Center: 8:30–5:00, with extended summer hours. Closed Dec.–Feb., Mon. and Tues.

James M. Thomas Telecommunication Museum. This museum in the phone company's building displays telephone equipment and related paraphernalia dating back to 1895. | 68 E. Main St. | 740/772–8200 | www.horizontel.com | Free | Mon.–Fri. 8:30–4:30.

Paint Creek State Park. A pioneer farm, nature programs, and bridle trails are within this 10,000-acre state park, about 20 mi west of Chillicothe. There's also camping, boating, hiking and riding trails | 14265 U.S. 50 | 937/365–1401 | www.nps.gov | Free | Daily.

Ross County Historical Society Museum. Here you'll find exhibits on early Chillicothe and Ohio, the Civil War, World War I, and the Mound Builders. There's a Conestoga Wagon and hands-on exhibits for children. The tour includes a visit to the adjacent Knoles Log House, a pioneer home from the early 1800s. | 45 W. 5th St. | 740/772–1936 | www.rosscountyhistorical.org | $4 | Apr.–Aug., Tues.–Sun. 1–5; Sept.–Dec., weekends 1–5; Jan.–Mar. by appointment.

The Ross County Historical Society also operates **Franklin House,** a turn-of-the-century prairie-style building, which houses a collection of 19th- and 20th-century textiles, clothing, furniture, and decorative arts. | 80 S. Paint St. | 740/772–1936 | www.rosscountyhistorical.org | $4 | Apr.–Aug., Tues.–Sun. 1–5; Sept.–Dec., weekends 1–5; Jan.–Mar. by appointment.

Seip Mound State Memorial. This site about 15 mi southwest of Chillicothe contains the 30-ft-high central burial mound of a group of Hopewell Indian earthworks. A pavilion area in the middle of this earthwork allows you to see the entire structure at once. | U.S. 50, Bainbridge | No phone | Free | Daily, dawn–dusk.

Serpent Mound Park. This manmade embankment of earth nearly a quarter-mile long resembles a snake. It is the largest and finest Native American serpent effigy in North America. Through carbon-dating, it's been attributed to the Fort Ancient culture, one of three Native American groups who lived in this area thousands of years ago. The Serpent Mound Museum contains exhibits illustrating various interpretations of the effigy's form, the processes of constructing the effigy, and the culture of the native people who lived in this area. The site is about 35 mi southwest of Chillicothe. | 380 Rte. 73, Locust Grove | 937/587–2796 | www.ohiohistory.org | $5 per car | Park: June–Aug., daily 9:30–8; Sept.–May, 10–5. Museum: June–Aug., daily 9:30–5; Apr.–May, Sept.–Oct. 10–5.

Seven Caves. Three self-guided nature trails lead to seven illuminated caves with sidewalks and handrails. Push buttons light up different formations such as cliffs, waterfalls, and more than 300 different species of plants. There's also a designated picnic area. Wear comfortable shoes; you'll have to climb a lot of stairs. | 7660 Cave Rd., Bainbridge | 937/365–1283 | www.7caves£webtv.net | $10 | Daily 9–dusk.

Splashdown. This waterpark includes a raft ride, two thrill slides, a 13,000-square-ft, 3½-ft-deep activity pool with lily pads and nets, go-carts, and miniature golf. There's also year-round camping and log cabin rentals here, about 25 mi southeast of Chillicothe. | 6173 Rte. 327, Jackson | 740/384–5113 or 888/775–2741 | www.splashdownohio.com | $14.95 | Memorial Day–Labor Day, Mon.–Sat. 10–7, Sun. noon–7.

Tar Hollow State Park. Twisting roads pass through deep ravines and dense woodlands at this state park just east of Chillicothe. Growing on the ridge are shortleaf and pitch pines, which were the source of pine tar for early settlers. You can picnic, hike, and camp here. | 16396 Tar Hollow Rd., Laurelville | 740/887–4818 | Free | Daily.

ON THE CALENDAR

JUNE–SEPT.: *Chillicothe Paints Baseball.* The Single-A Frontier League's games combine the excitement of professional baseball with a small-town atmosphere. | Veterans Stadium, 17273 Rte. 104 | 740/773–TEAM | www.chillicothepaints.com.

JUNE–SEPT.: *"Tecumseh!"* The story of the Shawnee Indian leader is brought to life Monday to Saturday evenings at 8 in a grand outdoor staging at the Sugarloaf Mountain Amphitheater. Tickets are required. | Delano Rd. off Rte. 159 | 740/775–0700 (Mar.–Sept.).

AUG.: *Ross County Fair.* The fair has all the traditional attractions: livestock shows, rides, games, and live entertainment. It's at the Ross County Fairgrounds, 5 mi north of Chillicothe. | 344 Fairgrounds Rd. | 740/775–5083.

OCT.: *Circleville Pumpkin Show.* More than 400,000 visitors come from across the country and around the world to see world-class giant pumpkins (some more than 500 pounds) at this popular event, which bills itself as Ohio's oldest and largest festival. Food, arts and crafts, bands, and parades add to the fun, and a large selection of pumpkins and gourds are sold. Don't miss the pumpkin-shaped water tower. It's held in downtown Circleville, about 20 mi north of Chillicothe. | 740/474–7000.

OCT.: *Fall Festival of Leaves.* The blazing red and orange autumn foliage of southwest Ohio is celebrated with games, demonstrations, and a large flea market on the third weekend of October. The festival occupies all of the tiny town of Bainbridge, 11 mi north of Chillicothe. | 740/634–2085.

Dining

Damon's. American/Casual. This sports-themed restaurant has a bar with wall-size big-screen televisions, local sports team memorabilia, and electronic trivia games. Barbecued ribs and chicken are the specialties, but just as popular is the onion loaf appetizer, a tasty tangle of thin onion pieces that are breaded and deep-fried. Kids' menu. | 10 N. Plaza Blvd. | 740/775–8383 | $8.50–$20 | AE, D, DC, MC, V.

New York New York of Chillicothe. Contemporary. Soft jazz plays and murals of New York City line walls of this restaurant. Menu highlights include onion and lemon seeded chicken breast, braised Colorado lamb shank, and a grilled salmon BLT sandwich. Try the Godiva chocolate crème brûlèe. | 200 N. Plaza Blvd. | 740/773–2100 | Closed Sun. | $9–$22 | AE, D, DC, MC, V.

Lodging

Chillicothe Bed and Breakfast. Antiques and collectibles fill this 1864 Italianate house downtown where rooms overlook a large garden. The owner is an artist whose printmaking studio is on the property. Complimentary breakfast. No room phones, TV in common room. | 202 S. Paint St. | 740/772–6848 or 877/484–4510 | www.bestinns.net/usa/oh/chil.html | 4 rooms | $60–$70 | AE, MC, V.

Comfort Inn. This Comfort Inn, just 1 mi north of Chillicothe, is close to the Hopewell Culture National Historic Park. Weekends are hopping at the hotel bar, where bands perform on Friday and Saturday nights. Bar with entertainment, complimentary Continental breakfast. Cable TV. Pool. Some pets allowed. Business services. | 20 N. Plaza Blvd. | 740/775–3500 | fax 740/775–3588 | 106 rooms, 8 suites | $80, $95 suites | AE, D, DC, MC, V.

Country Hearth Inn. A standard red brick hotel is at the east end of town in a residential area near a golf course and the Ross County Historical Museum. Spacious rooms range from single to triples, and there are some fast-food restaurants nearby. Complimentary Continental breakfast. Cable TV. Pool. Business services. | 1135 E. Main St. | 740/775–2500 | fax 740/775–2500 | www.countryhearth.com | 58 rooms, 1 suite | $62 rooms, $67 suite | AE, D, DC, MC, V.

Days Inn. This standard hotel is on the north edge of Chillicothe, close to the Adena State Memorial and the Franklin House. Cable TV. Pool. Business services. Some pets allowed. | 1250 N. Bridge St. | 740/775–7000 | fax 740/773–1622 | www.daysinn.com | 42 rooms | $59 | AE, D, DC, MC, V.

CINCINNATI

(Nearby towns also listed: Mason, Middletown, Hamilton)

Over the past 200 years, Cincinnati has captured the fancy of many renown individuals. Winston Churchill dubbed it "The most beautiful inland city in the union." Charles Dickens called it "thriving and animated," and Longfellow labeled it the "Queen City."

The first settlers came to Cincinnati in 1798. Pioneer life was uneventful until the advent of the steam-powered riverboat. At the height of the steamboat craze, Cincinnati's location on the Ohio River lured ship-building companies. The city's economy grew even more when the Miami-Erie Canal was finally connected to the Ohio River in 1829. By 1835, the city added another source of economic development to its cache as it became the nation's largest pork producer, a title that would later pass to Chicago and St. Louis.

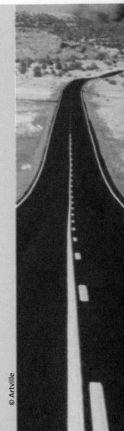

CINCINNATI BRIDGES: A PRIMER

In most cities, bridges are called by their official names—the ones that appear on the road signs and are printed on the local maps. But in Cincinnati things are a bit more complicated. Travelers need to be aware of what the city's bridges are really called around town before attempting to drive in the Queen City. Commit this list to memory—or keep it close at hand. Your map won't help you here.

The proper name of the bridge that connects the eastern portion of Cincinnati with Northern Kentucky is the Combs-Hehl Bridge. Among locals, however, it's simply the "275 Bridge," because it is part of the I–275 highway system.

The Daniel Beard Bridge crosses the Ohio River from Cincinnati to Northern Kentucky and is part of the I–471 system. But local motorists refer to it as the "Big Mac Bridge," because of its yellow arches.

The double-decker Brent Spence Bridge connects Cincinnati and Covington. Both I–75 and I–71 cross over it. Many locals call it the I–75 bridge or the "Car Strangled Banner."

Two exceptions to this rule are the L&N Bridge and the Taylor Southgate Bridge. The L&N Bridge connects Pete Rose Way in Cincinnati to Northern Kentucky and is so named because the L&N railroad tracks also run on it. The Taylor Southgate Bridge, which connects Newport, Kentucky, to Cincinnati is a fairly new bridge that's also called by its proper name—for now. Give Cincinnatians some time to think about it.

© Artville

During the 1840s, thousands of Irish and German immigrants flocked to Cincinnati, and people of those ethnic backgrounds make up a sizable portion of the population to this day. Cincinnati hit a growth spurt in the late 1870s when businesses like the 5/3 Bank, The Cincinnati Reds, and The Kroger Co. came to town. For the next 40 years, Cincinnati continued to grow. But in 1937, disaster struck. The Ohio River rose to 80 ft—some 25 ft above flood stage—and left most of the downtown area under water. When the flood waters subsided, Cincinnatians gritted their teeth and rebuilt. During that time, some of the city's most notable buildings were constructed, including Dixie Terminal, the Carew Tower, and Union Terminal.

From 1930 to 1950, the city put away its construction tools only to pick them up again in 1965, when two large riverfront arenas were built, as well as the city's trademark Fountain Square. During the 1970s, the city rallied around its hometown baseball team, the Reds. Better known as the "Big Red Machine," the team dominated the major leagues with stars like Pete Rose, Johnny Bench, and Tony Perez. The 1980s produced major ups and downs for the city. In 1985, Cincinnati set off the nation's worst savings and loan disaster after a local bank, Home State Savings, was caught making bad investments. The tide turned in 1988 when the city celebrated its 200th birthday by dedicating a 22-acre park along the riverfront. Today, the park, known as Bicentennial Commons, is a favorite hangout of locals and visitors alike. In 1999, the city kicked off another capital campaign. Construction on a new football stadium, Paul Brown Stadium, began on the riverfront, and a major highway and downtown renovation project got underway in an attempt to better link the city to its riverfront.

Cincinnati's rapidly growing downtown area—with its museums, entertainment and restaurant districts, and sporting venues—offer plenty of diversions. In downtown Cincinnati, you can take in everything from professional football, baseball, and hockey games to the Cincinnati Symphony and ballet performances. There are also a variety of museums—the largest of which is Union Terminal, a former railroad station that's now the home of the Cincinnati Museum of Natural History and Science and the Cincinnati Children's Museum.

Information: **Greater Cincinnati Convention and Visitors Bureau** | 300 W. 6th St., 45202 | 513/621–2142 or 800/344–3445 | fax 513/621–5020 | www.cincyusa.com.

NEIGHBORHOODS

Covington/Newport

These two cities on the other side of the Ohio River in Kentucky serve as one of Cincinnati's main entertainment districts. A number of bars, restaurants, and nightclubs line the riverfront. The Newport Aquarium is also here.

Clifton Heights/Corryville

This north Cincinnati neighborhood is home to the University of Cincinnati and "Pill Hill," the city's hospital district. It also is the site of a number of nightclubs and bars frequented by fun-seeking college students.

Hyde Park

On Cincinnati's east side, bordered in the north by Lunken Airport, Hyde Park is among the most desirable places to live. The neighborhood is home to chic clothing stores and upscale restaurants and is a magnet for those wanting to see and be seen.

Indian Hill

In the northeast part of town, bordered by I–275 and I–71, Indian Hills is Cincinnati's version of Bel-Air. This area is home to the city's wealthiest citizens, including Karl Lindner, owner of Chiquita Banana, and Cincinnati Red's owner Marge Schott.

Mount Adams

On a hill overlooking downtown Cincinnati, Mount Adams' bars are open into the wee hours of the morning. If you plan to hit this hot spot, it's best to take a cab. Mount

Adams' narrow streets and a lack of parking lots make driving here a frustrating experience.

Over-the-Rhine
This neighborhood in the eastern part of downtown Cincinnati was once the site of the city's most beautiful buildings—and is slowly on its way to recapturing those days. At present, however, it's a high crime area, best avoided at night. A daytime trip to the neighborhood's farmer's market, Findlay Market, is worthwhile.

TRANSPORTATION
Air: Cincinnati/Northern Kentucky International Airport | Box 752000, Cincinnati | 606/767–3151. This airport has commercial, private, and charter flights, and is a major Delta hub.
Bus: Metro Bus System | 120 E. 4th St. # 1, Cincinnati | 513/621–4455.
Rail: Amtrak | Cincinnati Union Terminal, 1301 Western Ave., Cincinnati | 513/651–3337 or 800/872–7245.

DRIVING AROUND TOWN
I–71 and I–75 are the major thoroughfares into the city. I–71 comes from the east and I–75 approaches from the west. Downtown, one-way streets are common and the area is congested with pedestrians and vehicles, as is the riverfront, especially during rush hours, between 7 and 8:30 in the morning and from 5 to 6:30 in the evening. Metered parking is available but it's often hard to find a spot. Illegally parked vehicles are quickly ticketed. Parking garages are plentiful and parking for a whole day costs $7 to $12. If you plan to stay downtown, park your car and leave it. The area is very walkable and the city Metro operates a downtown loop bus.

Attractions
ART AND ARCHITECTURE
Carew Tower. Cincinnati's 49th-floor version of the Empire State Building gives you a breathtaking view of the Queen City. The Art Deco building was built in 1930 and is home to dozens of shops and restaurants. | 441 Vine St., at 5th St. | 513/241–3888 or 513/579–9735 | $2 | Mon.–Thurs. 9:30–5:30, Fri.–Sat. 9:30–9, Sun. 11–5.

City Hall. In the heart of downtown, this colossal structure houses the city council and the mayor's office. It also hosts an occasional musical series. | 801 Plum St. | 513/352–3000 | Free | Weekdays 8–5.

Dixie Terminal. This was the Cincinnati terminal for Kentucky streetcars when it was built in 1921. The Neoclassical Revival landmark is known for its marble arcade and Rookwood pottery details. | 41–53 E. 4th St. | 513/621–2142 or 800/344–3445 | Free | Daily.

Fountain Square. This Queen City landmark, right in the middle of downtown, is a popular hangout for locals by day. The centerpiece of the square is the Tyler Davidson Fountain, which was cast in 1867 at the Royal Bavarian Foundry in Munich, Germany. It is also the site of the city's annual Oktoberfest ceremony. | 5th and Vine Sts. | 513/621–2142 or 800/ 344–3445 | Free | Daily.

Hamilton County Courthouse. This Gothic-style structure, built in 1911, was the site of the infamous "People vs. Larry Flynt" trials. | 1000 Main St. | 513/946–6464 | Free | Weekdays 8–4.

Union Terminal. The Amtrak station is in a handsome, restored Art Deco building with large mosaic tile murals dating from the 1930s. It also houses the Museum Center which contains the OMNIMAX Theatre, the Museum of Natural History, the Cincinnati History Museum, and the Cinergy Children's Museum. | 1301 Western Ave. | 513/287–7000 or 800/ 733–2077 | www.cincymuseum.com.

CULTURE, EDUCATION, AND HISTORY

Cincinnati Playhouse in the Park. One of Cincinnati's top-notch performing-arts organizations stages productions year-round at this theater in Eden Park. Local and national actors are featured. | 962 Mount Adams Circle | 513/421–3888 | www.cincyplay.com | $29–$41.

Harriet Beecher Stowe Memorial. *Uncle Tom's Cabin* author Harriet Beecher Stowe lived here in the 1830s. You can view her journal, along with exhibits on the abolitionist movement and African-American history. | 2950 Gilbert Ave. | 513/632–5120 | Free | Tues.–Thurs. 10–4.

Heritage Village Museum. Restored 19th-century buildings were brought here from southwest Ohio to re-create a village of the times. There's a log house with period furnishings, a doctor's office with Civil War medical and pharmaceutical equipment, plus an icehouse, smokehouse, and a barn. The village is about 15 mi north of downtown Cincinnati. | 11450 Lebanon Pike, Sharonville | 513/563–9484 | www.thinkhistory.org | $5 | May–Oct., Wed.–Sun. noon–4.

Music Hall. A two-ton brass and hand-cut crystal chandelier crowns the main auditorium of this modified and modernized Gothic structure built in 1878. The site of the 1880 Democratic Convention, it is now home to the Cincinnati Symphony Orchestra, the opera, and the ballet. Tours are available. | 1243 Elm St. | 513/621–1919 | w3.one.net/~spmh.

Showboat Majestic. Among the last of the old showboats, the Majestic has floated on the Cincinnati riverfront for more than 30 years. Operation of this 75-year old showboat was assumed by the Cincinnati Recreation Commission in 1990 and it's now a riverboat theater. | Riverfront Public Landing below Mehring Way entrance | 513/241–6550 | Ticket prices vary | Closed in winter.

Skirbal Museum. Jewish history and culture is thoroughly explored at this museum on the campus of Hebrew Union College—Jewish Institute of Religion. Exhibits explore immigration, Jewish life-cycle events, the Holocaust, the Torah, and more. | 3101 Clifton Ave. | 513/221–1875 | Free | Mon.–Thurs. 11–4, Sun. 2–5.

University of Cincinnati. This university, with an enrollment of 33,000 students, is the home of the Bearcats and 17 different Division I athletic teams. The University of Cincinnati traces its origins to 1819 when the Cincinnati College and the Medical College of Ohio were founded. In 1870, the city established the University of Cincinnati, which absorbed the earlier institutions. Self-guided tour maps and brochures of the campus and surrounding area are available. Some of Cincinnati's best music venues surround the campus. | 2624 Clifton Ave. | 513/556–6000 or 513/556–4183 | www.uc.edu/about.html | Free | Mon.–Sat. 8–5.

William Howard Taft National Historic Site. This Greek Revival home was the birthplace and boyhood home of Taft (1857–1930), the 27th U.S. president and a chief justice of the Supreme Court. Some rooms are furnished as they were during Taft's residence; others hold exhibits about the president's family and career. | 2038 Auburn Ave. | 513/684–3262 | www.nps.com | Free | Daily 8–4.

Xavier University. The university, in a rustic neighborhood in the scenic hills of northern Cincinnati, has an enrollment of 6,500 students. Tour guides will take you on a stroll through the small campus, free of charge. | 3800 Victory Pkwy. | 513/745–3201 | www.xu.edu | Free | Daily.

MUSEUMS

American Classical Music Hall of Fame. This national museum and institute celebrates American musicians, from performers to composers, conductors to educators. A timeline clarifies significant events and there are two listening centers. Some of the many musicians honored are Duke Ellington, Scott Joplin, Marian Anderson, and Beverly Sills. | 4 W. Fourth St. | 513/621–3263 | www.classicalhall.org | Free | Weekdays 10–4.

Cincinnati Art Museum. The museum, opened in 1881, explores 5,000 years of art through paintings, sculpture, decorative arts, and special exhibitions from around the world. Frank Duveneck, perhaps Cincinnati's best-known artist, bequeathed his collection to the museum in 1919, which included his masterpiece, "The Whistling Boy." The museum hosts frequent lectures and special events, including a monthly "Thank van Gogh It's Friday" party. It's in Eden Park. | 953 Eden Park Dr. | 513/721–5204 or 877/472–4226 | www.cincinnatiart-museum.org | $5 | Tues.–Sat. 10–5, Sun. noon–6.

Cincinnati Fire Museum. Exhibitions tell the story of the nation's first professional fire department (it began operating in 1788). There are many hands-on attractions for the kids. | 315 W. Court St. | 513/621–5553 | www.cincyfiremuseum.com | $4.50 | Weekdays 10–4, weekends noon–4.

Contemporary Arts Center. This unique downtown museum in the Mercantile Center attracts eclectic, sometimes interactive exhibitions of paintings, sculpture, and photography. It's free on Monday. | 115 East 5th St. | 513/721–0390 | $3.50 | Mon.–Sat. 10–6, Sun. noon–5.

John Hauck House Museum. This 1800s Italianate townhouse, former home of a prominent brewer, sits on Cincinnati's "Millionaire's Row." Its restored first floor is furnished with family heirlooms and Victorian-era antiques. | 812 Dayton St. | 513/721–3570 | www.thinkhistory.org | $3 | Fri. noon–4, and the last two Sat. of each month.

Museum Center at Union Terminal. Four of Cincinnati's best museums call this restored Art Deco train station home. There's a children's museum, a natural history and science museum, an OMNIMAX theater and a history museum. You can buy individual tickets or a combination ticket that gives you entry to all three museums and the theater. | 1301 Western Ave. | 513/287–7000 or 800/733–2077 | www.cincymuseum.org | Combination ticket, $15 | Mon.–Sat. 10–5, Sun. 11–6.

Cincinnati's golden years are recalled at the **Cincinnati History Museum** in the Museum Center at Union Terminal. You can walk down a re-creation of a city street from the early 1900s and view dozens of Queen City artifacts, along with vintage automobiles and a 1920s streetcar. | 1301 Western Ave. | 513/287–7000 or 800/733–2077 | www.cincymuseum.org | $6.50 | Mon.–Sat. 10–5, Sun. 11–6.

At the **Cinergy Children's Museum** in the Museum Center at Union Terminal, kids can climb, crawl, and explore the world around them. Play areas include a forest with a two-story treehouse, a construction site, an energy zone with pedals and pulleys, and a water-works with small boats and a series of locks. For kids from infants to 10 years of age. | 1301 Western Ave. | 513/287–7000 or 800/733–2077 | www.cincymuseum.org | $6.50 | Mon.–Sat. 10–5, Sun. 11–6.

You can get a close up look at whales, volcanoes, Mt. Everest or whatever wonders are on the schedule at the **Linder Family OMNIMAX Theater.** Movies, which are shown on a five-story, 72-ft-wide domed screen, start the top of the hour. | 1301 Western Ave. | 513/287–7000 or 800/733–2077 | www.cincymuseum.org | $6.50 | June–Aug., daily from 11. Sept.–May, weekdays from 1, weekends from 11. Evening schedule varies.

Exhibits at the **Museum of Natural History and Science** in the Museum Center at Union Terminal take you on a journey back in time to various eras, including the age of the dinosaurs, the English Renaissance, and the Wild West. There's a colony of bats and underground water-falls in a replica of a limestone cave. | 513/287–7000 or 800/733–2077 | www.cincymuseum.org | $6.50 | Mon.–Sat. 10–5, Sun. 11–6.

Taft Museum of Art. Works by artists from around the globe are displayed in this Federal period mansion, which is famous at the site where William Howard Taft accepted his presidential nomination. The collection includes paintings by Rembrandt, Gainsborough, and Corot; Chinese porcelains; 19th-century American furniture; French Renaissance enameled plaques; jewelry and watches. There's a formal garden on the property. | 316 Pike St. | 513/241–0343 | $4, free Wed. and Sun. | Mon.–Sat. 10–5, Sun. 1–5.

PARKS, NATURAL AREAS, AND OUTDOOR RECREATION

Bicentennial Commons at Sawyer Point Park. The 22-acre riverfront park, opened in celebration of the city's 200th birthday in 1988, has hiking and biking trails, jogging paths, and great picnic spots. Tall Stacks, a riverboat festival, takes place here every four years; the next one is in 2003. | 705 E. Pete Rose Way | 513/352–6180 | Free, $2 parking | Daily.

Burnet Woods. Southwest Ohio's native birds and other wildlife are routinely spotted at the park next to the University of Cincinnati, which has hiking trails and a small lake. The Trailside Nature Center also contains the Wolff Planetarium, the second-oldest planetarium west of the Allegheny mountains; reservations are required. | Brookline Ave., at intersection of Ludlow and Jefferson Sts. | 513/751–3679 | Free | Park: daily 7 AM–10 PM. Nature center and planetarium: weekdays 9–5; 3rd weekend of each month, weekends noon–4.

Cincinnati Nature Center. East of Cincinnati, near Milford, is a 790-acre nature preserve with 14 mi of trails. Hikers of all fitness levels are accommodated through trails with varying degrees of difficulty. Several ponds and lakes are also great for a picnic or rest. There's also a gift shop, bookstore, nature exhibits, and a bird-viewing area in the Nature Center. | 4949 Tealtown Rd. | 513/831–1711 | $5 | Grounds: Daily, 8–dusk. Nature center: Mon.–Sat. 9–5, Sun. 1–5.

Civic Garden Center of Greater Cincinnati. A butterfly garden is one of the highlights here. There are also herb gardens, perennial gardens, and a variety of trees. The center also houses the Hoffman Library, which contains over 2,000 books on horticulture. | 2715 Reading Rd. | 513/221–0981 | Free | Weekdays 9–4, Sat. 9–3.

East Fork State Park. Some 10,580 acres of land have been set aside for camping, fishing, boating, and other outdoor activities. The park is about 25 mi east Cincinnati, near the town of Bethel. | 2505 Williamsburg Bantam Rd. | 513/734–4323 | Free | Daily.

Eden Park. Cincinnati is known for its grand and sumptuous parks, and this aptly named green space is the best of them all. Overlooking downtown Cincinnati, it has a brilliant reflecting pool, gardens, and playing fields. The park is also the site of the Cincinnati Art Museum, the Cincinnati Playhouse in the Park, and the Krohn Conservatory. | Off Gilbert Ave., between Elsinore and Morris Rds. | 513/621–2142 or 800/344–3445 | Free | Daily.

Krohn Conservatory. This huge greenhouse in Eden Park is divided into various environments, including a desert with cactus plants and a tropical rain forest. The palm trees and indoor waterfalls are a welcome sight in the middle of a Cincinnati winter. Seasonal exhibits include a Christmas show with pointsettias and model trains and a summer show with live butterflies and the plants that attract them. | 1501 Eden Park Dr. | 513/352–4086 | Free | Daily 10–5.

Mount Airy Forest and Arboretum. It's heavenly here in spring, when the lilacs, azaleas and trees on the 120-acre grounds are in bloom. You can hike through the 1,400 acres. Reservations are required for guided tours. | 5080 Colerain Ave. | 513/541–8176 | cinci-park.org | Free | Daily 6 AM–10 PM.

SHOPPING

Findlay Market. This open-air market in the Over-the-Rhine neighborhood is famous for its fresh meats and local produce. You can find exotic herbs, grilled ribs, and bakery items as well. | Race and Elder Sts. | 513/352–6364 | Wed. and Fri. 7–6, Sun. 6–6.

Mount Adams. This trendy, hillside neighborhood overlooking downtown is the place to be on the weekend. Nightclubs and restaurants line the streets and are open into the wee hours of the morning. Parking is difficult; consider taking a cab. | 513/621–2142 or 800/344–3445 | Free | Daily.

SPECTATOR SPORTS

Cincinnati Bengals. Cincinnati's National Football League team, play in the new state-of-the-art Paul Brown Stadium on the riverfront. | 1 Paul Brown Stadium | 513/621–3550 | www.bengals.com | Tickets $35–$50.

Cincinnati Reds. This National League team is the oldest team in baseball and the 1990 World Champions. They play home games at Cinergy Field from April through October. | 100 Cinergy Field | 513/421–4510 | www.cincinnatireds.com | Tickets $5–$21.

OTHER POINTS OF INTEREST

Cincinnati Zoo and Botanical Garden. This is one of the country's most respected zoological institutions. In 1999, it was one of three facilities outside of Florida to be allowed to take in Florida manatees; the mammals can be observed at the Manatee Springs exhibit. The zoo is also home to walruses, lowland gorillas, polar bears, Bengal tigers and hundreds of other species. In the summer, there are animal shows and camel and train rides. The zoo is open evenings from late November to early January for its annual Festival of Lights. | 3400 Vine St. | 513/281–4701 (recording) or 513/281–4700 | www.cincyzoo.org | $11, parking $5 | Daily 9–5.

Meier's Wine Cellars. Ohio's oldest winery is more than a century old. It's in Silverton, about 11 mi northeast of downtown. Tours depart hourly; afterward, you can sample the wines. | 6955 Plainfield Rd., Silverton | 513/891–2900 or 800/346–2942 | www.meierswinecellars.com | Free | June–Oct., Mon.–Sat. 9–5.

Newport Aquarium. This aquarium opened in May 1999 in Newport, Kentucky, on the banks of the Ohio River, just a two minute drive from downtown Cincinnati. The fish are visible through clear, seamless tunnels, so you can get up close and personal—in fact, 25 sharks swim around you, separated by only 2.5 inches of acrylic. Highlights include a large open-air shark viewing area, a King Penguin habitat, Gator Bayou, Jellyfish Gallery, and the Bizarre and Beautiful, where you'll see poison frogs and pufferfish. | One Aquarium Way, Newport, KY | 859/261–7444 | www.newportaquarium.com | $14.95, parking $3 | Memorial Day–Labor Day, daily 9–7; Labor Day–Memorial Day, daily 10–6.

SIGHTSEEING TOURS

Delta Queen, Mississippi Queen,* and *American Queen. Three of the world's largest paddle-wheel steamships make regular stops in Cincinnati. The Delta Queen Steamboat Company offers 3 to 14 night cruises. Prices include lodging, lavish meals, entertainment, and nightly dancing. Three night minimum. | Cincinnati Riverfront at the Public Landing | 800/543–1949 | www.deltaqueen.com | $500–$1,070 | (office hours) weekdays 8–8, weekends 9–5.

BB Riverboats. Hop aboard the *Funliner, Mark Twain,* or *Becky Thatcher* for a cruise down the Ohio River past Cincinnati and Northern Kentucky. | 1 Madison Ave. Covington, KY | 606/261–8500 | www.bbriverboats.com | $10–$42 | Daily 9 AM–7 PM.

WALKING-AND-DRIVING TOUR

Park downtown near Fountain Square, at the intersection of Fifth and Vine streets. Take a look at the Tyler Davidson Fountain and then cross the street to Carew Tower. You can get a wonderful view of the city from the 48th-floor observation deck. Double back on Fifth Street past Fountain Square until you come to the Contemporary Arts Center, which presents the work of cutting-edge artists. Continue east on Fifth Street for about four blocks until you come to Pike Street; turn right and you'll soon arrive at the Taft Museum of Art, famous for its Chinese porcelains. Next walk south to E. Pete Rose Way and Eggleston Avenue. Here you'll find the Bicentennial Commons at Sawyer Point; monuments at this riverfront park tell the story of Cincinnati's origins as a river town. Walk back and retrieve your car; follow Seventh Street to Gilbert Avenue; drive north until you see Eden Park, a grand greensward overlooking downtown. Here you'll find the Cincinnati Art Museum, known for its collection of works by Cincinnati's own Frank Duveneck, and the Krohn Conservatory, where plants from all over the world are exhibited in natural settings. After relaxing for a bit in the park, get back in your car and take Gilbert Avenue to Central Parkway, turning right on Elm Street. Continue on Elm until you come to the Music Hall, which was built in 1878 and is the home of the

Cincinnati Symphony Orchestra. Back in your car, the next stop is the Museum Center at Union Terminal, west of the Music Hall, off I–75 at Ezzard Charles Drive. This historic former train station houses the Cinergy Children's Museum, an imaginative place filled with interactive exhibits; the Museum of Natural History and Science, which has a cave with real bats; the Cincinnati History Museum; and an OMNIMAX Theatre.

ON THE CALENDAR

FEB.–MAR.: *Cincinnati Home and Garden Show.* This show at the Cincinnati Convention Center exhibits fine furnishings and products and services related to building and remodeling, gardening, and outdoor living. | 525 Elm St. | 513/281–0022.

APR.–SEPT.: *River Downs Race Track.* The stakes are high at this track on the banks of the Ohio River. Live horse races take place from late April to early November. Simulcast races are featured daily the rest of the year. | 6301 Kellogg Ave. | 513/232–8000 | www.riverdowns.com.

MAY: *May Festival.* The oldest choral and orchestral festival in the country is presented in a series of concerts with the Cincinnati Symphony Orchestra. Guest soloists are featured. | Cincinnati Music Hall, 1241 Elm St. | 513/381–3300 | www.cincinnatisymphony.org.

MAY: *Cincinnati Flying Pig Marathon.* This 26.2 mi race, created to raise money for local charities, attracts fit runners from all over. | 513/721–7447.

JUNE–JULY: *Cincinnati Opera.* The opera, the nation's second oldest, was started in 1920. It performs in the Cincinnati Music Hall, a theater that's listed as a National Historic Landmark. | 1241 Elm St. | 513/241–ARIA | www.cincinnatiopera.com.

SEPT.: *Riverfest.* Cincinnati bids farewell to summer with this Labor Day weekend party on the banks of the Ohio River. Hundreds of thousands of people come to see the water skiing, sky diving, and air shows. A highlight is the 30-minute fireworks display choreographed with music broadcast live on a local radio station. | 513/621–2142 or 800/344–3445 | www.cincyusa.com.

SEPT.: *Oktoberfest-Zinzinnati.* This three-day celebration of the city's German heritage takes place in mid-September. A six-block area around Fountain Square is turned into a German biergarten, with music, dancing—and beer. | Fountain Square, 5th and Vine Sts. | 513/579–3191.

SEPT.–MAY: *Cincinnati Symphony Orchestra.* Under the direction of maestro Jesus Lopez-Cobos, the orchestra is among the most respected in the world. | Music Hall, 1241 Elm St. | 513/381–3300.

SEPT., DEC.–MAR.: *Turfway Park Race Course.* This track, about 10 mi southwest of downtown Cincinnati, is home to the Kentucky Derby prep race, Spiral Stakes. Daily matinee and night races are held in season. | 7500 Turfway Rd., Florence | 859/371–0200 or 800/733–0200.

OCT.–MAY: *Cincinnati Ballet.* This world-renowned professional ballet company performs classical and contemporary works. | 1555 Central Pkwy. | 513/621–5219 | www.cincinnatiballet.com.

Dining

INEXPENSIVE

Aglamesis Bros. Cafe. Since 1913, the Greek immigrant Aglamesis brothers have been serving up homemade chocolates and ice cream in this small ice-cream parlor and confectionery in Oakley Square. The interior has checkered tile floors, marble-topped tables, and cushioned chairs; the marble soda fountains and Tiffany-style lamps are the original fixtures. The legendary opera creams, rectangular cream-filled dark chocolate candy, remain a secret family recipe. A deli also serves a limited sandwich menu. | 3046 Madison Rd. | 513/531–5196 | www.aglamesis.com | $5–$10 | MC, V.

Atlanta Bread Company. American. Fresh baked bread makes for great sandwiches at this popular downtown lunch spot for locals. Try the homemade soup of the day and indulge in a pastry for dessert. | 100 E. 4th St. | 513/621–2410 | Closed weekends | $3–$6 | MC, V.

First Watch Restaurant. American. Breakfast and brunch are satisfying at this restaurant in downtown Cincinnati; try banana crunch or raisin walnut pancakes. The lunch menu is creative as well, and entrées such as pecan dijon salad draw kudos from all. | 700 Walnut St. | 513/721–4744 | No dinner | $4–$7 | AE, D, DC, MC, V.

LeBoxx Cafe. American/Casual. This fun, casual downtown lunch spot with pillars and multicolored tablecloths serves up light entrées to a mostly business crowd. Entrées include quesadillias, burgers, salads, Caribbean chicken, and deli sandwiches. | 819 Vine St. | 513/721–5638 | Closed weekends. No dinner weekdays | $4.50–$6.50 | AE, D, DC, MC, V.

Lenhardt's and Christy's. German. This Clifton Heights restaurant is in a beautifully restored Victorian home with artwork on the ceiling. The chef prepares a wide selection of German and Hungarian dishes. There's spaetzle, chicken paprika, roast duck, hot slaw, potato pancakes, and mashed potatoes. | 151 W. McMillan St. | 513/281–3600 | Closed first week of Aug., 1 week at Christmas | $4.50–$9 | AE, D, MC, V.

Red Fox Grill. American. The chef cooks up good omelets at this downtown breakfast and lunch place, surrounded by office buildings. For lunch, try a double-decker club sandwich. | 232 E. 6th St. | 513/621–7924 | Closed Sat. and Sun. No dinner | $3.50–$4.50 | No credit cards.

The Simmering Pot. American. A true Midwest eatery, this restaurant in a downtown Cincinnati Holiday Inn is known for its chicken pot pies and pot roasts. Dinner is more formal, with soft lighting. Try the homemade pies and cakes. | 800 8th St. | 513/241–8660 | No lunch | $6–$18 | AE, D, DC, MC, V.

Tandoor India. Indian. Decorative objects scattered around this low-key Market Place

PASS THE TABASCO

If you order chili in a Cincinnati restaurant, be prepared for the following question: "Wanna three-way, four-way, or five-way?" Cincinnati is known for its chili, which is different from any other kind of chili in the world. Much different. Cincinnati chili is more a topping than a stew; it's a meaty ground beef and plenty-of-secret-spices sauce ladled over a hefty plate of—are you ready for this?—spaghetti. But back to your waitress's question: When chili is served on spaghetti with mounds of shredded cheddar it is called a "three-way." Each additional topping ups the number a notch. Request onions and it's a "four-way"; add beans to that and it's a "five-way." Don't want the spaghetti? Ask for a "cheese coney"—a hot dog in a bun topped with mustard, a small ladle of chili, and cheese. (Plain coneys, without cheese, don't quite cut it.)

The original Cincinnati chili is said to have been concocted by two Greek immigrants, Tom and John Kiradjieff, more than 75 years ago. The brothers served it up at the Empress chili parlor on Vine Street downtown. Cincinnatians took to the new-fangled dish quite enthusiastically, and soon other folks opened chili parlors with their own versions of the recipe. (The original Empress recipe is still under lock and key.)

Today Cincinnati is the Chili Capital of America, with more than 100 chili parlors in the metro area. The most popular are Skyline Chili and Goldstar Chili. When you stop by one of them, the people who work there will be more than happy to help you to select a chili dish that suits you—and order it by the correct name.

© Artville

restaurant—brass objects and large paintings—are as traditional as the Northern Indian cuisine. There are many vegetarian selections on the menu; the palakpanner (creamed spinach) is popular. The lunch buffet is a real steal. There's open-air patio dining with garden view. Salad bar. | 8702 Market Place La. | 513/793–7484 | www.tandoor.com | Closed Sun. | $7–$13 | AE, DC, MC, V.

MODERATE

American Pie Cafe. American. Usually filled with business people at lunch and families at supper time, this restaurant in Harper's Point offers a menu that includes vegetarian mushroom pie and Black Angus beef. Try the homemade key lime or apple pie. Kids' menu. | 11371 Montgomery Rd. | 513/469–6400 | $9–$20 | AE, D, DC, MC, V.

Black Forest. German. This restaurant captures the look of a Bavarian chalet. The menu includes wild game dishes like sautéed venison medallions with mushroom- brandy sauce; side dishes include potato salad and steaming platter of smoked mettwurst and apple fritters. The signature appetizer is sauerkraut balls—the German version of eggrolls—served with beer cheese dip and breaded mushrooms. Kids' menu. Live entertainment Fri. and Sat. | 8675 Cincinnati-Columbus Rd., Westchester | 513/777–7600 | www.theblackforest.com | No lunch weekends | $10–$22 | AE, MC, V.

Chateau Pomije Cafe. Continental. A neighborhood cafe in the artsy Obryonville area, it specializes in creative variations of standard chicken, beef, and seafood dishes. You can choose a bottle from the wine shop to drink with dinner. Try Chateau chicken or fresh salmon. There's a seasonal open-air dining area enclosed in ivy-covered brick walls. Beer and wine only. | 2019 Madison Rd. | 513/871–8788 | Closed Sun. | $12–$25 | D, MC, V.

Cherrington's. Continental. Housed in an intimate century-old building, this restaurant next to Eden Park is known for its creative comfort food. Mashed-potato rolls, tangy chicken Dijon, and Hungarian mushroom soup are flavorful favorites. For dessert, the homemade banana coconut cream pie lives up to its outstanding reputation. There's open-air courtyard dining and classical music on weekends. | 950 Pavilion St. | 513/579–0131 | Closed Mon. | $10–$24 | AE, D, DC, MC, V.

China Gourmet. Chinese. The setting at this restaurant in Hyde Park is more upscale than most Chinese restaurants and the fare is also more of a Chinese haute cuisine. Cantonese and Szechuan specialties include seafood and pan-fried noodles, Confucius chicken—breast of chicken with vegetables covered in brown sauce with shrimp and pork. There are also Chinese preparations of Lake Erie walleye, a regional speciality. | 3340 Erie Ave. | 513/871–6612 | Closed Sun. | $11–$28 | AE, D, DC, MC, V.

Desha's American Tavern. American. This airy California-style eatery in the middle of a shopping center in Montgomery has a large stone fireplace. Steaks and chops are marinated in a pineapple barbecue sauce and cooked on a wood grill. One of the regional favorites on the menu is the Kentucky Hot Brown—rotisserie turkey, Canadian bacon, cheddar cheese, tomato, bacon bits, and cream sauce on a French biscuit. Open-air dining is available on a deck overlooking a manmade lake. Kids' menu. Sun. brunch buffet. | 11320 Montgomery Rd. | 513/247–9933 | www.deshas.com | $9–$22 | AE, D, DC, MC, V.

The Diner on Sycamore. American/Casual. Stainless steel and neon set the scene for this eatery that caters to the hip Generation Xers who frequent the nearby Main Street club district. The Blue Plate Special is pork chops with a barbecue sauce made with Jack Daniels and Coca-Cola. A martini bar mixes more than 18 varieties of the cocktail, both shaken and stirred. Try a blue cheese salad, crab cake sandwich, or the house specialty, the Caribbean white crab chili. Open-air patio dining is available. Kids' menu. Sun. brunch. | 1203 Sycamore St. | 513/721–1212 | $12–$15 | AE, D, DC, MC, V.

Fore and Aft. Seafood. This double-decker riverboat-era paddlewheel boat has been floating for more than 30 years; now it's docked on the Ohio River in Saylor Park. After cocktails on the upper open-air deck, dine on beef and seafood combination plates at wood tables with decorative candles. The house specialty is Alaskan king crab legs served with drawn butter. You can also dine outdoors on a covered deck with a view of the Ohio River. Raw bar. Kids' menu. | 7449 Forbes Rd. | 513/941–8400 | No lunch Sat. | $12–$17 | AE, MC, V.

Forest View Gardens. German. Built in 1939, the restaurant in Monfort Heights resembles a chalet and serves up different types of schnitzel and a thick prime rib. Singing servers, voice students from the nearby conservatory, bring heaping plates of traditional and Americanized Bavarian cuisine to your table. If tableside entertainment isn't your stein of beer, sit in the Edelweiss room, where the waiters just talk. Open-air patio dining in a garden setting. Kids' menu. | 4508 North Bend Rd. | 513/661–6434 | www.forestviewgardens.com | No lunch weekends | $12–$19 | AE, D, DC, MC, V.

Grand Finale. Continental. Mismatched antique wooden tables and chairs fill the charming Victorian dining rooms. The bread—homemade dark-rye mini loaves and sweet wheat rounds—make for a grand beginning to a meal. Chicken, lamb, steak, and seafood comes with sauces and garnishes at dinner. Don't miss the Sunday brunch buffet's specialty crepes, served with a variety of fillings. Open-air dining is available. Kids' menu. No smoking. | 3 East Sharon Ave. | 513/771–5925 | Closed Mon. No dinner Sun. | $10–$34 | AE, D, DC, MC, V.

House of Tam. Chinese. The strip mall location belies the welcoming interior of this family-owned restaurant, with its traditional Chinese decor. Try the salmon with ginger and scallions, or lemon shrimp with walnuts, pine nuts chicken. No smoking. | 889 W. Galbraith Rd. | 513/729–5566 | Closed Sun. | $9–$18 | AE, MC, V.

Iron Horse Inn. American. There are two levels at this restaurant in the suburb of Sharonville: upstairs has live jazz twice a week and is casual, while downstairs is more formal, with linen tablecloths. Entrées range from pasta to Panko fried lobster tail with Japanese flavorings and wasabi. Sun. brunch. | 40 Village Sq., Sharonville | 513/771–4787 | No lunch Sat. No dinner Sun. | $10–$27 | AE, D, DC, MC, V.

Mecklenburg Gardens. German. At one time a gathering place for opera stars and singing societies, this German tavern in Clifton/Corryville closed in 1982 and reopened as an updated version of its old self. Grapevines stretch over the biergarten, and the mahogany bar is always well-stocked. Traditional German dishes such as sausages, noodles, and soups are on the menu; for dessert, there's coffee-toffee black bottom pecan pie. There's open-air dining in the grape-arbored garden. Entertainment Wed.–Sat. nights. Kids' menu. | 302 E. University Ave. | 513/221–5353 | No lunch weekends | $11–$19 | AE, D, DC, MC, V.

Montgomery Inn. Barbecue. Cincinnati's northeastern suburb of Montgomery is the original location of this sports-themed restaurant rib joint. The menu is so dominated by ribs that even the few poultry and seafood items are barbecued themselves or served as a combo with ribs. There are several sandwiches and salads on the lunch menu. Also known for Boathouse crab cakes, onion straws, and Saratoga chips (potatoes sliced and fried). Kids' menu. | 9440 Montgomery Rd., Montgomery | 513/791–3482 | www.montgomeryinn.com or www.ribsking.com | No lunch Sun. | $11–$25 | AE, D, DC, MC, V.

Montgomery Inn at the Boathouse. Barbecue. The sister location of the original, this downtown restaurant has views of the Ohio River and the Cincinnati skyline. It has two floors and several dining areas, all brimming with unique sports memorabilia and serving tender, finger-licking rib dishes. You can dine outdoors on the balcony. Kids' menu. | 925 Eastern Ave. | 513/721–7427 | www.montgomeryinn.com or www.ribsking.com | No lunch weekends | $12–$22 | AE, D, MC, V.

National Exemplar. American. This restaurant in Mariemont is in a charming Tudor-style hostelry with a fireplace and exposed beams. On the dinner menu, prime rib and poached salmon with dill sauce are highlights. Kids' menu. | 6880 Wooster Pike, Mariemont | 513/271–2103 | Breakfast also served | $12–$20 | AE, D, DC, MC, V.

Pacific Moon. Pan-Asian. This upscale restaurant in the suburb of Montgomery serves such creative dishes as Thai-grilled chicken, sesame chicken marinated in a slightly spicy ginger soy peanut dressing, and Siam-steamed pike. Check out the ancient kimonos on display in glass cases. Open-air patio dining is complete with a little pond in the front. Entertainment Sat. | 8300 Market Place La., Montgomery | 513/891–0091 | www.pacificmooncafe.com | $12–$19 | AE, D, DC, MC, V.

Promontory Bar and Grill. American/Casual. Dine in a casual setting at this restaurant in Mount Adams and choose from menu items that include chicken, sea bass and a variety of salads and pastas. There's also an extensive wine list. There's jazz on Friday and Saturday evenings from 10 to 1:30. | 1111 St. Gregory St. | 513/651–4777 | Closed Sun. | $10–$22 | AE, D, DC, MC, V.

Rookwood Pottery. American/Casual. Cincinnati is well-known among antiques collectors as the home of the famous Rookwood art pottery, and this restaurant, in what was once the Rookwood factory in Mount Adams, has achieved its own level of local fame. The dining area is situated in the old kiln room. Menu favorites include burgers and the seafood-stuffed, Cajun-spiced mushroom appetizer. Best bets among entrées are poached salmon with light lemon cucumber sauce and linguine, and Oriental stir-fried turkey. Kids' menu. | 1077 Celestial St. | 513/721–5456 | $9–$19 | AE, DC, MC, V.

Seafood 32. Seafood. This revolving restaurant is on the 32nd floor of the Millennium Hotel, right next to Convention Hall downtown. It's a popular choice for anniversaries and other special occasions. The menu is predominately seafood, although rack of lamb, prime rib, New York strip steak, pasta, and chicken dishes are also on the menu. Entertainment Fri. and Sat. | 150 W. 5th St. | 513/352–2160 | Closed Sun. and Mon. No lunch | $9–$29 | AE, D, DC, MC, V.

Teak. Thai. This casual restaurant in Montgomery specializes in crispy duck. The entrées run the gamut from mild to kick-in-the-pants hot. There's open-air patio dining. | 1049 St. Gregory St. | 513/665–9800 | No lunch weekends | $10–$21 | AE, D, DC, MC, V.

EXPENSIVE

Chester's Road House. Contemporary. This restaurant, housed in a 19th-century red farmhouse in the suburb of Montgomery, is a popular special-occasion spot. On spring weekends it fills up fast with prom-goers. The main dining room has a glass greenhouse ceiling, which allows in plenty of light for the large Floridian silk oak tree growing inside. Several dining rooms have been added to the original house. The menu includes Northern Italian specialties, California-style gourmet pizzas, prime rib, rack of lamb, and a salad bar. | 9678 Montgomery Rd., Montgomery | 513/793–8700 | www.chestersroadhouse.com | No lunch weekends | $13–$25 | AE, D, DC, MC, V.

Germano's. Italian. The location in a busy suburban shopping district allows for plenty of people-watching from window tables. Executive Chef Domenico Germano, born in Italy, creates authentic dishes including extra-creamy fettuccine Alfredo, and daily fish and shellfish specials. No smoking. | 9415 Montgomery Rd., Montgomery | 513/794–1155 | Closed Sun. | $14–$34 | AE, D, MC, V.

The Grille at the Palm Court. Continental. This downtown restaurant in the Carew Tower's Omni Netherland Plaza echoes the elegant, Art Deco of the hotel. Look up and you'll see murals on the restaurant's 30-ft ceilings. Many of the beautifully presented dishes feature Ohio's bounty, for example, the Lake Erie walleye with a lobster and carrot fricassee. On weekend evenings, there's live jazz. Sun. breakfast. Valet parking. Discounted parking rates for restaurant patrons. | 35 W. 5th St. | 513/564–6465 | $14–$38 | AE, D, DC, MC, V.

The Heritage Restaurant. Contemporary. Cajun and Southwestern cuisine is prepared with a sophisticated touch and served in an 1827 early-American style building with wood-panelled dining rooms. Ohio-produced pasta and pork items are menu highlights—especially notable are the barbecued baby-back ribs. In summer, produce comes from nearby Hillsboro and the herbs are grown on-site. Try the Cajun barbecued shrimp or pecan

Pack an easy way to reach the world.

123 456 7891 2345
J.D. SMITH

Wherever you travel, the MCI WorldCom Card℠ is the easiest way to stay in touch. You can use it to call to and from more than 125 countries worldwide. And you can earn bonus miles every time you use your card. So go ahead, travel the world. MCI WorldCom℠ makes it even more rewarding. For additional access codes, visit **www.wcom.com/worldphone**.

EASY TO CALL WORLDWIDE

1. Just dial the WorldPhone® access number of the country you're calling from.
2. Dial or give the operator your MCI WorldCom Card number.
3. Dial or give the number you're calling.

Canada	1-800-888-8000
Mexico	01-800-021-8000
United States	1-800-888-8000

EARN FREQUENT FLIER MILES

6 "I'm thirsty"s, 9 "Are we there yet"s, 3 "I don't feel good"s,
1 car class upgrade.
At least something's going your way.

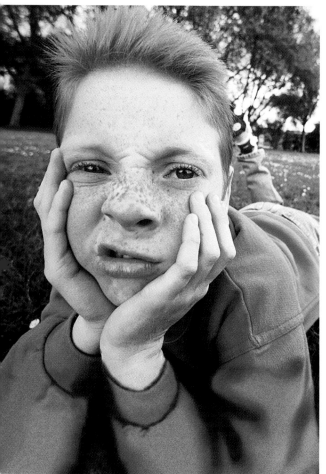

Hertz rents Fords and other fine cars. ® REG. U.S. PAT. OFF. © HERTZ SYSTEM INC., 2000/005-00

Make your next road trip more comfortable with a free one-class upgrade from Hertz.

Let's face it, a long road trip isn't always sunshine and roses. But with Hertz, you get a free one car class upgrade to make things a little more bearable. You'll also choose from a variety of vehicles with child seats, Optional Protection Plans, 24-Hour Emergency Roadside Assistance, and the convenience of NeverLost, the in-car navigation system that provides visual and audio prompts to give you turn-by-turn guidance to your destination. In a word: it's everything you need for your next road trip. Call your travel agent or Hertz at **1-800-654-2210** and mention PC# **906404** or check us out at **hertz.com** or AOL Keyword: **hertz**. Peace of mind. Another reason nobody does it exactly like Hertz.

Hertz
exactly.®

chicken with Dijon mustard sauce. Open-air patio dining is available. Kids' menu. Sun. brunch. | 7664 Wooster Pike (U.S. 50), Mariemont | 513/561–9300 | www.theheritage.com | No lunch | $16–$27 | AE, D, DC, MC, V.

Nicola's Ristorante. Italian. Antique clock faces decorate the walls of this sophisticated Northern Italian restaurant in Over-the-Rhine, which serves such favorites as bruschetta, calamari, osso bucco, and panna cotta. A formal dress code takes effect for dinner; no jeans or tennis shoes allowed. There's seasonal open-air dining in a courtyard with umbrellaed tables. | 1420 Sycamore St. | 513/721–6200 | No lunch Sat. Closed Sun. | $13–$32 | AE, D, DC, MC, V.

Primavista. Italian. You'll have a spectacular panoramic view of the city from this restaurant perched on top of Price Hill, a well-known high point in the city. Interesting antiques from old wine boxes to odd sculptures are displayed throughout. The menu emphasizes classic Northern and Southern Italian dishes, and there are savory choices in each category—antipasti, pasta, veal, beef, lamb, poultry, and seafood. Try the salmon basted in a light butter sauce. | 810 Matson Pl. | 513/251–6467 | www.pvista.com | No lunch | $15–$29 | AE, D, DC, MC, V.

VERY EXPENSIVE

★ **The Celestial.** Eclectic. You can dine on caviar and foie gras in luxurious gilt-and-mirrored surroundings in this Mount Adams restaurant with a spectacular view. You can order such classic French fare as as veal medallions and Dover sole sautéed in lemon butter; some dishes come with a Caribbean twist. The "trim cuisine" is prepared without sauces, oil, or salt. Jazz Tues.–Sat. | 1071 Celestial St. | 513/241–4455 | Jacket required | Closed Sun. and Mon. | $33–$37 | AE, DC, MC, V.

Maisonette. French. Paintings by famous Cincinnati artists hang throughout this downtown restaurant, which has three formal dining rooms. A self-portrait of well-known local artist Frank Duvanek is over the bar. Chef Jean-Robert de Cavel blends classical and modern fare, such as escalopes de foie gras. The menu changes daily but always includes beef tenderloin, sea scallops, and rack of lamb. | 114 E. 6th St. | 513/721–2260 | www.maisonette-group.com | Reservations essential | Jacket required | Closed Sun. No lunch Mon. and Sat. | $33–$44 | AE, D, DC, MC, V.

The Palace Restaurant. Continental. Appearance is almost as important as flavor at this lavish Art Deco restaurant in the landmark Cincinnatian Hotel downtown. Frederick Pissaro, great-grandson of the celebrated Impressionist painter, created artwork exclusively for the Palace. The menu changes seasonally, but there is always salmon, sea bass, and tenderloin entrées; they may be French, Italian, Australian, or German, but are always creative and beautifully presented. The dessert cart is amazing. Sunday brunch is served from Labor Day to Mother's Day. | 601 Vine St. | 513/381–6006 | Reservations essential | Jacket required | $28–$35 | AE, D, DC, MC, V.

La Normandie Taverne and Chophouse. Steak. Rough-hewn beams and heavy draperies give this 65-year-old downtown chophouse the look of an Olde English cellar. The traditional shrimp cocktail is good for starters, followed by a creamy yellow squash and asparagus soup. Menu highlights include the Cajun filet mignon, blackened and topped with a jalapeno butter swirl, and the broiled New Zealand rack of lamb. | 118 E. Sixth St. | 513/721–2761 | www.lanormandy.com | No lunch weekends. Closed Sun. | $18–$30 | AE, D, DC, MC, V.

The Precinct. Steak. At this restaurant, servers introduce you to your food before you order it. They'll show off, for example, the 28-day-aged Colorado Angus steak and the gigantic South African lobster tail that's part of the surf and turf combo. Entrées include all the oven-baked bread you can eat and a tangy Greek salad or Kentucky hot slaw. The noisy, crowded dining rooms are good places to sight visiting celebrities and notable locals. Raw bar. | 311 Delta Ave. | 513/321–5454 | www.theprecinctinc.com | Reservations essential | $27–$33 | AE, D, DC, MC, V.

Lodging
INEXPENSIVE

Cross Country Inn. A variety of restaurants and shopping centers are just a stone's throw away from this hostelry in a suburb about 20 mi north of Cincinnati. The hotel has two separate buildings, one for smoking and the other for no-smoking guests. Cable TV. Pool. Business services. Free parking. | 330 Glensprings Dr., Springdale | 513/671–0556 or 800/621–1429 | fax 513/671–4953 | www.crosscountryinn.com | 120 rooms | $57 | AE, D, DC, MC, V.

Cross Country Inn-Clermont. This standard hotel is off I–275 just north of Cincinnati. There are separate buildings for smoking and no-smoking guests. Cable TV. Pool. Business services. Free parking. | 4004 Williams Dr. | 513/528–7702 or 800/621–1429 | www.cross-countryinn.com | fax 513/528–1246 | 128 rooms | $58 | AE, D, DC, MC, V.

Fairfield Inn by Marriott. Surrounded by Sharonville's shopping district and set next to I–75, this business hotel includes amenities such as a well-lit work desk, data port phones, fax service, free local calls, and a card-key security system. It's 15 mi north of the city. Complimentary Continental breakfast. In-room data ports. Cable TV. Pool. Business services. Free parking. | 11171 Dowlin Dr., Sharonville | 513/772–4114 or 800/288–2800 | fax 513/772–4114 | www.fairfieldinn.com | 135 rooms | $67 | AE, D, DC, MC, V.

Hampshire House Hotel. This hotel is in the suburb of Springdale, just off I–275 about 20 mi north of downtown Cincinnati. Shops and strip malls are within walking distance, as well as bowling and movie theatres. Beds are either king or double and rooms are spacious and modern. In-room data ports. Cable TV. Indoor pool, sauna, exercise room. Business services. | 30 Tri-County Pkwy., Springdale | 513/772–5440 or 800/543–4211 | fax 513/772–1611 | info@hampshirehousehotel.com | www.hampshirehousehotel.com | 150 rooms | $69–$79 | AE, D, DC, MC, V.

Imperial House. This brown brick hotel contains Victorian furnishings and has relaxing amenities, including a steam room and sauna. It's northwest of downtown Cincinnati, at exit 11 of I–74. Restaurant, bar with entertainment. In-room data ports, some kitchenettes. Cable TV. Pool, sauna, steam room. Laundry facilities. Business services. | 5510 Rybolt Rd., Dent | 513/574–6000 or 800/543–3018 | fax 513/574–6566 | 196 rooms, 2 suites | $72, $135 suites | AE, D, DC, MC, V.

Red Roof Inn. This two-story hotel in Sharonville, about 15 mi north of downtown Cincinnati, is easily identified by the chain's signature red roof. The king rooms have large-screen TVs. Cable TV. Business services. Free parking. Some pets allowed. | 11345 Chester Rd., Sharonville | 513/771–5141 or 800/843–7663 | fax 513/771–0812 | www.redroofsharonville.com | 108 rooms | $64 | AE, D, DC, MC, V.

MODERATE

Best Western Mariemont Inn. The Old English Tudor-style building which houses this Best Western Inn was built in 1926. Some rooms have handcarved oak headboards and tapestries. It's in the little village of Mariemont on Route 50 near the city's antiques district and minutes away from major shopping centers and restaurants. Restaurant, bar, room service. In-room data ports. Cable TV. Laundry facilities. Business services. Free parking. | 6880 Wooster Pike | 513/271–2100 or 800/528–1234 | fax 513/271–1057 | www.bestwestern.com | 60 rooms | $80 | AE, D, DC, MC, V.

Best Western-Springdale. This hotel and convention center is a 10-story contemporary highrise. It's north of Cincinnati in Springdale, along I–275. Restaurant, bar with entertainment, room service. In-room data ports. Cable TV. Indoor pool, hot tub. Exercise equipment. Video games. Laundry facilities. Business services. | 11911 Sheraton La., Springdale | 513/671–6600 or 800/528–1234 | fax 513/671–0507 | www.bestwestern.com | 267 rooms, 25 suites | $89, $99–$179 suites | AE, D, DC, MC, V.

Comfort Suites. This all-suites hotel is nestled in the quiet and upscale suburb of Blue Ash, northeast of Cincinnati. The colonial brick exterior belies the New Orleans French-style interior. There are plenty of plants in the courtyard lobby, which get natural sunlight from the skyroof above. Restaurant, bar, complimentary Continental breakfast. Refrigerators. Cable TV. Pool. Exercise equipment. Business services. Free parking. | 11349 Reed-Hartman Hwy., Blue Ash | 513/530–5999 or 800/221–2222 | fax 513/530–0179 | www.choicehotels.com | 50 suites | $99 suites | AE, D, DC, MC, V.

Four Points by Sheraton. This hotel has a full slate of facilities and a sunny gazebo. It's off I–71, northeast of downtown Cincinnatti, across the street from the Kenwood Towne Centre mall, Cincinnati's most popular shopping center. Restaurant, bar, room service. Cable TV. 2 pools (1 indoor), hot tub. Tennis. Exercise equipment. Business services. | 8020 Montgomery Rd., Kenwood | 513/793–4300 or 800/325–3535 | fax 513/793–1413 | www.starwood.com | 152 rooms | $89 | AE, D, DC, MC, V.

Hampton Inn-Cincinnati North. This four-story hotel in Sharonville, just south of I–275, is removed from the crowds of downtown while still being convenient to the city's attractions. A golf driving range is next door. Complimentary Continental breakfast. In-room data ports. Cable TV. Pool. Video games, billiards. Business services. | 10900 Crowne Point Dr., Sharonville | 513/771–6888 or 800/426–7866 | fax 513/771–5768 | www.hampton-inn.com | 130 rooms | $95 | AE, D, DC, MC, V.

Parker House Bed and Breakfast. This restored 1878 Victorian mansion, near the University of Cincinnati, has a music parlor, antique furnishings, reproduction wall coverings, and murals of Beethoven and Mozart handpainted on the ceiling. Guests can use the kitchen. Complimentary breakfast. No room phones. No TV. | 2323 Ohio Ave. | 513/579–8236 or 877/411–0148 | www.bbhost.com/parkerhsebbcinohio | 4 rooms | $90–$110 | MC, V.

Quality Hotel and Suites Central. This eight-story property is just a few blocks away from Xavier University and 7 mi north of downtown Cincinnati. It's attached to a popular seafood restaurant. Restaurant, bar, room service, picnic area, complimentary Continental breakfast. In-room data ports, some microwaves, some refrigerators. Cable TV. Pool. Business services. Airport shuttle. Some pets allowed. | 4747 Montgomery Rd., Norwood | 513/351–6000 or 800/292–2079 | fax 513/351–0215 | www.qualityinn.com | 148 rooms, 14 suites | $95, $110 suites | AE, D, DC, MC, V.

Radisson Hotel Cincinnati. This business-friendly hotel with an attractive atrium lobby has spacious rooms with king-size beds. It's off exit 15 of I–75, just 1½ mi from the Tri-County Mall. Restaurant, bars, room service. in-room data ports. 2 pools (1 indoor), hot tub, gym. Laundry service. Business services. Free parking. | 11320 Chester Rd., Sharonville | 513/772–1720 or 800/333–3333 | fax 513/772–4347 | www.radissoncincinnati.com | 350 rooms | $99–$159 | AE, D, DC, MC, V.

Residence Inn by Marriott. All rooms are suites in this two-story hostelry designed for extended stays. It's made up of several two-story buildings, each with eight units ranging from studios to penthouse apartments; each has a fireplace. It's in Sharonville, one of the fastest-growing suburbs of Cincinnati, next to the Tri-County Mall. Picnic area, complimentary Continental breakfast. Kitchenettes, microwaves. Cable TV. Pool, hot tub. Laundry facilities. Business services. Free parking. Some pets allowed (fee). | 11689 Chester Rd., Sharonville | 513/771–2525 or 800/331–3131 | fax 513/771–3444 | www.marriott.com | 144 suites | $99–$149 | AE, D, DC, MC, V.

Super 8 Motel. This two-story, red-brick budget motel is a short walk from the popular Tri-County Mall. It is also close to the Sharonville Convention Center. Complimentary Continental breakfast. Cable TV. Pool. Laundry facilities. Free parking. Business services. Some pets allowed. | 11335 Chester Rd., Sharonville | 513/772–3140 or 800/800–8000 | fax 513/772–1931 | www.super8motels.com | 144 rooms | $81 | AE, D, DC, MC, V.

Wingate Inn. This four-story hotel with larger-than-average rooms is 15 mi northeast of downtown Cincinnati in Blue Ash. Rooms are equipped with large desks, lounge chairs, cordless, two-line speaker phones, and Nintendo. There's a 24-hour self-service business center in the lobby. Complimentary Continental breakfast, room service. In-room data ports, in-room safes, refrigerator, microwave. Cable TV, in-room movies. Indoor pool, sauna, exercise room. Laundry services. Business services. | 4320 Glendale-Milford Rd., Blue Ash | 513/733–1142 or 800/993–7232 | www.wingateinn.com | 85 rooms | $79 | AE, D, DC, MC, V.

Woodfield Suites. Just off I–75 in Sharonville, this all-suites hotel has spacious rooms and attractive cherry furnishings. Complimentary cocktails are served in the evening. Restaurants, a shopping mall, the Cincinnati Zoo, and the Riverfront Stadium are within 10 mi of the property. Complimentary Continental breakfast. In-room data ports, some kitchenettes, microwaves, refrigerators, in-room hot tubs (in some suites). Cable TV. Indoor pool, hot tub. Exercise equipment. Playground. Laundry facilities. Business services. Free parking. Some pets allowed. | 11029 Dowlin Dr., Sharonville | 513/771–0300 or 800/338–0008 | fax 513/771–6411 | www.woodfieldsuites.com | 151 suites | $99–$189 | AE, D, DC, MC, V.

EXPENSIVE

Amerisuites. Spacious rooms and an array of business amenities are featured at this six-story hotel 15 mi northeast of downtown Cincinnati. Complimentary Continental breakfast. In-room data ports, refrigerators, microwaves. Cable TV, in-room VCRs. Pool. Exercise equipment. Laundry facilities. Business services. Free parking. Some pets allowed. | 11435 Reed-Hartman Hwy., Blue Ash | 513/489–3666 or 800/833–1516 | fax 513/489–4187 | www.amerisuites.com | 127 suites | $149 | AE, D, DC, MC, V.

★ **Cincinnatian Hotel.** The most luxurious property in the Queen City may well be this elegant, restored landmark hotel built in 1882 downtown. The marble-and-walnut staircase is original, and ornate furniture and fine linens fill the spacious rooms. You can have afternoon tea or dine in its top-notch Palace Restaurant. Restaurant, bar with entertainment, room service. In-room safes, minibars. Cable TV. Sauna. Exercise equipment. Business services. | 601 Vine St. | 513/381–3000 or 800/942–9000 | fax 513/651–0256 | info@cincinnatianhotel.com | www.cincinnatianhotel.com | 147 rooms, 8 suites | $255, $350–$1,500 suites | AE, D, DC, MC, V.

Courtyard by Marriott. This three-story hotel, which caters mainly to business visitors, has a pleasant outside courtyard. It's just 15 minutes northeast of downtown Cincinnati in Blue Ash. Restaurant, bar. In-room data ports. Cable TV, in-room movies. Indoor pool, hot tub. Exercise equipment. Laundry facilities. Business services. Free parking. | 4625 Lake Forest Dr., Blue Ash | 513/733–4334 or 800/321–2211 | fax 513/733–5711 | www.courtyard.com | 149 rooms, 11 suites | $109 | AE, D, DC, MC, V.

Crowne Plaza. This high-rise hotel is downtown. The eighth-floor terrace has a city view and a garden. The elegant suites are spacious. Restaurant, bar. Refrigerators. Cable TV. Beauty salon. Exercise equipment. Business services. Parking is $17 per day. | 15 W. Sixth St. | 513/381–4000 or 888/279–8260 | fax 513/354–5158 | www.crowneplaza.com | 321 rooms, 44 suites | $159, $209–$259 suites | AE, D, DC, MC, V.

Embassy Suites Blue Ash. This modern all-suites hotel right off I–71 in northeastern Cincinnati has balcony suites and spacious accommodations. Restaurant, complimentary breakfast, and evening cocktails. Microwaves, refrigerators, cable TV. Indoor pool, hot tub. Exercise equipment. Laundry facilities. Business services. | 4554 Lake Forest Dr., Blue Ash | 513/733–8900 or 800/362–2779 | fax 513/733–3720 | cybga@aol.com | www.embassysuites.com | 235 suites | $149 suites | AE, D, DC, MC, V.

Garfield Suites Hotel. This contemporary hotel with a glass greenhouse lobby is across the street from Piatt Park. Many of its suites have balconies. It's three blocks from the center of town. Restaurant, bar, room service. Kitchenettes, microwaves, in-room safes. Cable TV. Exercise equipment. Laundry facilities. Business services. Some pets allowed (fee). Parking $5 per day, $17 per valet. | 2 Garfield Pl. | 513/421–3355 or 800/367–2155 | fax 513/421–3729 | 150 suites | $165–$185 suites, $175–$200 2–bedroom suites, $425–$1,200 penthouse suites | AE, D, DC, MC, V.

Holiday Inn Cincinnati-Eastgate. This member of the familiar chain is on the east side of Cincinnati, where Route 275 intersects with Route 32. The white stone exterior contains an Italian-themed lobby, with various rooms named after Italian cities. Shopping areas are nearby. Restaurant, bar. Microwaves (in suites), in-room hot tubs (in suites), cable TV. Indoor pool, hot tub. Exercise equipment. Business services. | 4501 Eastgate Blvd., Eastgate | 513/752–4400 or 800/465–4329 | fax 513/753–3178 | www.holiday-inn.com | 247 rooms, 6 suites | $109, $200–$250 suites | AE, D, DC, MC, V.

Homewood Suites by Hilton. This three-story hotel caters to business travelers. Suites are exceptionally large, modern, and pleasantly furnished in dark wood furniture; some have fireplaces. The hotel is 15 mi north of Cincinnati in Sharonville, a ¼ mi from Exit 44 of I-275. Complimentary Continental breakfast. In-room data ports, some kitchenettes. Cable TV. Pool. Exercise room. Laundry service. Business services. Some pets allowed (fee). | 2670 E. Kemper Rd., Sharonville | 513/772–8888 | fax 513/772–8737 | www.homewood/suites.com | 111 suites | $109–$149 | AE, D, DC, MC, V.

Hyatt Regency. One of the largest hotels in Cincinnati, this downtown landmark has an atrium lobby with glass walls and ceiling, contemporary rooms, and first-rate service. It is also the site of downtown Cincinnati's largest ballroom. Two restaurants, bar. Some refrigerators. Cable TV. Indoor pool, hot tub. Exercise equipment. Shops. Business services. Parking $16/day. | 151 W. Fifth St. | 513/579–1234 or 800/233–1234 | fax 513/354–4299 | www.hyatt.com | 488 rooms, 11 suites | $155–$230, $400–$700 suites | AE, D, DC, MC, V.

Millennium Hotel. This huge 32-story hotel downtown has a revolving rooftop restaurant, Seafood 32, with spectacular city views. It's opposite Convention Hall. 2 restaurants, 2 bars. In-room data ports, cable TV. Pool. Business services. | 150 W. Fifth St. | 513/352–2100 or 800/876–2100 | fax 513/352–2148 | 872 rooms | $119 | AE, D, DC, MC, V.

Mount Adams Bed and Breakfast. This three-story bed and breakfast next to Eden Park has a cozy sitting room with a fireplace, a private garden, a bistro patio, and a living room with a 60-inch TV screen. In the Hemingway Suite, there's a spiral staircase to a loft study and a Jacuzzi bathroom. Both rooms have remote-controlled gas log fireplaces. The Plantation Suite has a private deck and Victorian accents. Breakfast is served next door in Cherrington's Restaurant. Complimentary breakfast. Hot tub. Business services. | 1107 Belvedere St. | 513/651–4449 or 888/233–8770 | fax 513/421–4442 | www.cincinnati-bed-and-breakfast.com | 2 rooms | $155–$165 | AE, D, MC, V.

Omni Netherland Plaza. The Art Deco architecture is exceptional at this historic hotel downtown, one block from Fountain Square. Built in 1929, it occupies 29 floors of the Carew Tower, which has shops and restaurants. Room sizes vary considerably—see the room before you commit to it so you don't get stuck with small quarters for the same rate as a bigger space. The hotel's Continental restaurant, The Grille at the Palm Court, is top-notch. Restaurant, bar with entertainment. Cable TV. Indoor pool, hot tub, sauna. Business services. | 35 W. Fifth St. | 513/421–9100 | fax 513/421–4291 | www.omnihotels.com | 607 rooms, 5 suites | $160, $450 suites | AE, D, DC, MC, V.

Vernon Manor Hotel. This 1924 hotel, modeled after an English manor, is dignified and traditional. It's just 2 mi from downtown, though it seems farther away; it's tucked away on the hills of Clifton overlooking the city. Restaurant, bar. In-room data ports, some refrigerators. Cable TV. Barbershop, beauty parlor. Exercise equipment. Laundry facilities. Business services. | 400 Oak St. | 513/281–3300 or 800/543–3999 | fax 513/281–8933 | www.vernon-manor.com | 177 rooms, 60 suites | $160, $200–$700 suites | AE, D, DC, MC, V.

Westin Hotel. In the heart of Cincinnati's hotel district, the Westin overlooks the city's most popular landmark, the Tyler Davidson Fountain on Fountain Square. The building, designed in the Classic Renaissance style, was once the Albee Theater. It's also just a short stroll away from the Carew Tower Mall. 2 restaurants, piano bar, room service. In-room data ports, mini-bars. Cable TV. Indoor pool, hot tub, massage. Exercise equipment. Business services. | 21 E. Fifth St. | 513/621–7700 or 800/937–8461 | fax 513/852–5670 | www.westin.com | 450 rooms and 25 suites | $120, $350–$1,500, suites | AE, D, DC, MC, V.

CLEVELAND

(Nearby towns also listed: Beachwood, Brecksville, Eastlake, Elyria, Lorain, Mentor, Painesville, Strongsville)

Moses Cleaveland and his Connecticut Land Company founded the city of Cleveland in 1796. (The "a" was dropped from Cleaveland's name so it could fit across a news-paper banner heading.) Located right on Lake Erie, Cleveland grew into a metropolis during the 19th century; its first major role was as a shipbuilding city. During the War of 1812 two of Commodore Oliver Perry's ships, the *Porcupine* and the *Portage,* were built here on the Cuyahoga River. Following the opening of the Ohio-Erie Canal in 1832 and the Miami-Erie Canal in 1845, Cleveland became an important shipping and trade center; the canals granted Cleveland access to almost all Eastern cities by water, which was the easiest way to travel at the time. The canals were soon replaced by railroads, and Cleveland, centrally located between New York and Chicago, became an even bigger trade center. The city later became an industrial hub, thanks to the abundance of iron ore, coal, and limestone found in the area.

A number of well-known business tycoons and inventors emerged from Cleveland in the 1800s. John D. Rockefeller founded Standard Oil Company here in 1870. Jeptha Wade put together 13 telegraph companies to form Western Union. And, in 1879, Charles Brush invented the arc light, which was used for street lamps. But by 1900 down-town Cleveland began to decay. Tom Johnson, the mayor at that time, brought in the famous architect Daniel Burnham to revamp the city's downtown area. Burnham recommended the construction of several new buildings, among them the Terminal Tower (now a 42-story building, the tallest in Cleveland). A building boom started in 1910, but was cut short in 1930 by the Great Depression.

The end of World War II brought servicemen back to the country, most of whom bought houses in the suburbs of major cities. This trend hit Cleveland particularly hard,

CLEVELAND VS. CINCINNATI

Although they are at opposite ends of the state, Cleveland and Cincinnati have always had it in for each other. Since the two cities became the largest in the state, they have been desperately trying to outdo each other.

"Competition" is putting it mildly. When Cleveland got the Rock-and-Roll Hall of Fame city residents gloated—loudly. When the Cincinnati Reds won the World Series in 1990, Cleveland felt the taunts from 250 mi away.

No one's sure how the rivalry got started, but one thing is certain—it's not going to stop anytime soon. Not now that the Cincinnati Reds and Cleveland Indi-ans baseball teams are playing against each other in inter-league play. And with the resurrection of the Cleveland Browns, the archenemies of the Cincinnati Ben-gals, things could even get more intense—on and off the football field.

© Artville

drawing both businesses and residents away from the downtown area. By the 1960s downtown Cleveland was once again in need of revitalization, and the Erieview Plan was born. Like architect Daniel Burnham's plan of the early 1900s, it called for the construction of several new buildings. By 1964 a new 40-story office building, a 32-story federal building, and two large apartment buildings had been constructed. Despite these additions, however, much of the downtown area was still left unused. Cleveland slowly began to rebuild until the term of Mayor Dennis Kucinich, when the city went bankrupt over an unrealized sale of the city-owned electric company to a private utility company. As a result, the city was unable to make good on millions of dollars in bank loans and became the first major American city to default on its obligations since the Depression. It emerged from default in 1987.

Today the city is still in the process of rebuilding itself. Recent projects include renovations to the Terminal Tower and construction of Jacobs Field (for the Cleveland Indians) and Gund Arena (for the Cleveland Cavaliers). In 1995, Cleveland was chosen as the home for the Rock and Roll Hall of Fame and Museum, and the Cleveland Browns Stadium opened for the 1999–2000 football season.

Information: Convention and Visitors Bureau of Greater Cleveland | 3100 Terminal Tower, 50 Public Square, 44113 | 216/621–5555 or 800/321–1001 | travelcleveland.com.

NEIGHBORHOODS

Buckeye Shaker. The Buckeye Shaker neighborhood is bordered by East 72nd Street on the west, Woodland on the north, East 140th Street on the east, and Kinsman on the south. Originally part of Newburgh and Shaker Townships and annexed to Cleveland in 1913 and 1915, the Buckeye-Shaker neighborhood developed between 1900 and 1930. During these decades the Buckeye Road area attracted the largest Hungarian population outside of Hungary and became known as Cleveland's Little Hungary. From the 1930s to the early '90s the neighborhood was in decline. The development of a 120,000-square-ft shopping center near East 116th and Buckeye streets in the early 1990s and a more recent upturn in storefront renovation have led to renewed optimism for the neighborhood's future.

Fairfax. Fairfax, centered around West 65th Street and Detroit Avenue on Cleveland's west side, is home to three nationally recognized institutions. The foremost of these is the Cleveland Clinic, established in 1921 and now Cleveland's largest private employer, with a staff of almost 8,000. To the west, at East 86th and Euclid streets, is the Cleveland Play House, an architectural and cultural landmark. The third is the Karamu House, a multicultural theater arts center that dates from 1915. Continuing expansion of the Cleveland Clinic and the completion of the Church Square shopping center along the neighborhood's northern border are helping to encourage private development in Fairfax.

The Flats. The Flats is the name for the lowlands near the mouth of the Cuyahoga River. Cleveland's earliest settlers chose this area as the site for their cabins, but this swampy environment caused so much illness that most soon migrated to higher ground. The Flats ultimately were abandoned to commerce and industry; shipping and steel production took over the area during the 1900s. In the 1970s and 1980s the area enjoyed a new vitality as nightclubs and restaurants sprouted up. The nonprofit Flats Oxbow Association was organized in 1978 to promote the economic well-being of the area. Today the Flats is Cleveland's entertainment district, with more than 60 restaurants and nightclubs, an outdoor amphitheater and boardwalks and patios along the riverfront.

Forest Hills. The Forest Hills neighborhood, once part of Glenville Village, began as a resort complex developed by John D. Rockefeller in 1873. Although the resort lasted only a year, the estate served as the Rockefeller family's summer home until 1917. The estate was later developed as a residential subdivision, parcels of which now lie in the cities of Cleveland, Cleveland Heights, and East Cleveland. The neighborhood is west of Lee Road and south of Euclid Avenue on Cleveland's east side.

Mt. Pleasant. Mt. Pleasant is a vital residential community in southeast Cleveland bounded by Milverton and Griffing streets on the north, Martin Luther King Boulevard on the west, East 155th Street on the east, and Harvard Street on the south, with Kinsman as the main thoroughfare. The first residents of the area were Manx farmers who migrated in 1826. Today it has many African-American homeowners.

Ohio City. This neighborhood, just across the Cuyahoga River from downtown, is known for its ethnic diversity and the huge indoor/outdoor West Side Market. This area has been home to a succession of ethnic groups, beginning with the Irish and German settlers of the 19th century and the later immigrants from Italy and Romania. In more recent years these groups were joined by Hispanics and migrant workers from Appalachia. Residents began to move out of the area in large numbers in the 1980s, and the neighborhood began to decline. Recent revitalization efforts have included the renovation of the Gordon Square Arcade (West 65th and Detroit streets) and the addition of an outdoor recreation complex at the Zone Recreation Center. You'll find antiques shops on Lorain Avenue, and renovated Victorian-era homes, along with some noteworthy restaurants.

Tremont. Young professionals are moving into Tremont's affordable homes and making it the new hot spot; its original tenants were Eastern European, Appalachians, Greek, Polish, and African-American. This newly rejuvenated neighborhood is centered around Lincoln Park. You'll find a lot of options for entertainment, dining, and shopping.

University. The University neighborhood includes both the University Circle and Little Italy areas. The area's name refers to Case Western Reserve University, which is in this neighborhood. Four miles east of downtown, University Circle is just 1 square mi in size, but it's packed with cultural and performing arts institutions, including the Cleveland Museum of Art, the Cleveland Museum of Natural History, the Western Reserve Historical Society and Severance Hall, the Cleveland Orchestra's winter home. The adjacent Little Italy was settled by Italian artisans in the 19th century; it has a large number of art galleries and shops and fine Italian restaurants. The neighborhood's largest annual event is the four-day celebration of the Feast of the Assumption, which attracts crowds of up to 100,000 on a single August night.

Warehouse District. Cleveland's first neighborhood and downtown's oldest commercial district is a National Historic Landmark. Originally a residential area, the district became the hub of Cleveland commercial life in the post-Civil War years. Between downtown's Public Square and the east bank of the Flats, the Warehouse District encompasses 43 acres and contains more than 70 historic buildings. Some of the finest examples of Victorian commercial architecture (circa 1850–1920) in the United States, the structures were built to house wholesale grocers, dry goods merchants, hardware distributors, garment manufacturers, and chandleries. Within walking distance of the Gateway District (the area around Jacobs Field and Gund Arena), Tower City (a shopping complex), and the Rock and Roll Hall of Fame, the Warehouse District is fast becoming one of Cleveland's premier destinations. It's loaded with trendy restaurants, jazz and blues clubs, coffee shops, specialty shops, and galleries.

TRANSPORTATION INFORMATION

Air: Cleveland Hopkins International Airport is served by major carriers and is a hub for Continental Airlines. A light-rail line connects the airport with downtown. | 5300 Riverside Dr., Cleveland | 216/265–6000.

Bus: Greater Cleveland Regional Transit Authority (RTA) operates buses and three light-rail lines throughout the metro area. | 615 Superior Ave. NW, Cleveland, | 216/566–5100.

Rail: Amtrak trains connect Cleveland with Chicago, Washington, and New York. | 200 Cleveland Memorial St., Cleveland | 216/696–5115.

DRIVING AROUND TOWN

I–71, I–77, I–90, and Route 2 are the major thoroughfares into downtown. I–77 can be quite busy throughout the day, and traffic can be heavy during morning and evening rush hours. All roads and highways are well signed and there are not too many narrow or one-way streets. Downtown, streets are consecutively numbered; in the University Circle area, the other main tourist center, roads are curvy and it can be challenging to stay on track. A good option is to park downtown and ride the Rapid Transit Authority's red line to University Circle. Metered parking is available but it is often hard to find a spot. Parking garages are plentiful downtown. Depending on how early you arrive, you can pay between $5 and $10 for a full day. If you do find parking on the street, be sure to put sufficient money in the meter; meter maids are efficient.

Attractions

ART AND ARCHITECTURE

City Hall. *The Spirit of '76*, the famous fife-and-drum painting by Archibald Willard, is on display at City Hall, which overlooks Lake Erie. | 601 Lakeside Ave. E at E. 6th St. | 216/664–2000 | Free | Weekdays 8–5.

Terminal Tower. Take a ride to the 42nd floor observation deck for a splendid view of Cleveland and Lake Erie. The tower was completed in 1930 and rises 52 stories tall. Pick up tickets at the Tower City Center visitor center in Public Square. | 50 Public Square | 216/621–7981 | $1 | May–Sept., weekends 11–4:30; Oct.–Apr., weekends 11–3:30.

CULTURE, EDUCATION, AND HISTORY

Beck Center for the Arts. This visual- and performing arts center in Lakewood, west of downtown Cleveland, has a contemporary theater, art galleries, recitals, and other arts events. | 17801 Detroit Ave., Lakewood | 216/521–2540 | www.beckcenter.org | Art gallery: free. Shows: $18 | Mon.–Sat. 9–8, Sun. 11:30–8.

Case Western Reserve University. A combination of two schools, Case Institute of Technology and Western Reserve University, Case Western Reserve University is one of the leading independent research universities in the country. Its students hail from all 50 states and 97 different countries. The 550-acre parklike campus is at the center of the University neighborhood. | 10900 Euclid Ave. | 216/368–2000 | www.cwru.edu | Free | Daily.

Cleveland Institute of Music. Students at this respected music school in University Circle frequently give recitals on Wednesday evenings and weekends; many of the concerts are free. A variety of genres of music are represented at the institute's annual concert series. It also hosts tributes to the city's most renowned musicians, Sergei Babayan and Margarita Shevchenko. | 11021 East Blvd. | 216/791–5000 | Free | Daily 7:15 AM–9 PM or later.

Cleveland Play House. The oldest regional theater in America, founded in 1915, is an architectural landmark. A 1983 addition, designed by architect Phillip Johnson, incorporate four performance spaces under one roof. Throughout the year, there are productions of musicals, comedies, and classic and contemporary dramas. | 8500 Euclid Ave. | 216/795–7000 | www.clevelandplayhouse.com.

Cleveland State University. The 85-acre, 35-building campus was established in 1964. Call the admissions office to arrange a guided tour. | Euclid Ave., at E. 24th St. | 216/687–2000 | www.csuohio.edu | Free | Daily.

Dunham Tavern Museum. Once a stagecoach stop on the old Buffalo-Cleveland-Detroit post road, this is the oldest building still standing on its original site in Cleveland. The museum is filled with artifacts from the Dunham family, the original residents. | 6709 Euclid Ave. | 216/431–1060 | Free | Wed., Sun. 1–4.

John Carroll University. John Carroll University, one of 28 colleges and universities operated in the United States by the Society of Jesus, was founded as St. Ignatius College in

1886. Tours of the campus are available. | Warrensville Center and Fairmount Blvd. | 216/397–1886 | www.jcu.edu | Free | Daily.

Lake View Cemetery. A monument to Ohio native and former President James A. Garfield stands at his tomb in Lake View Cemetery. Some of Cleveland's most renowned citizens, including oil tycoon John D. Rockefeller and John Hay, President William McKinley's secretary of state, are buried in here. | 12316 Euclid Ave. | 216/421–2665 | Free | Apr.–mid-Nov., daily 9–4.

Playhouse Square Center. Cleveland's "home for the performing arts" has four beautifully restored, landmark theaters: the Ohio Theater, the State Theater, the legendary Palace Theater, and the historic Allen Theater. The center hosts the Cleveland Opera, dance companies, pop performers, and several theater series. | 1501 Euclid Ave. | 216/241–6000 or 800/766–6048.

USS *COD*. This World War II submarine once sank enemy boats. Now it's docked on the banks of Lake Erie. Tours are available; the guides are often Navy submarine veterans. | N. Marginal Rd. | 216/566–8770 | $5 | May–Sept., daily 10–5.

MUSEUMS

Cleveland Institute of Art. Paintings, sculptures, and prints by local, regional, and national artists are displayed. The museum focuses on contemporary art, but exhibits of all eras rotate through regularly. | 11141 East Blvd. | 216/421–7000 | Free | Sept.–May, daily 9–5; June–Aug., weekdays 9–5.

Cleveland Museum of Art. In its 70 galleries, the museum presents art chronologically, from the ancient Mediterranean times to the present. The museum is known for its medieval European, Asian, and pre-Columbian collections. Its holdings include works by Picasso, Michelangelo, Monet, and Van Gogh. Other popular exhibits feature mummies, African masks, and weapons. | 11150 East Blvd. | 216/421–7340 or 888/262–0033 | www.clemusart.com | Free | Tues., Thurs., and weekends 10–5, Wed. and Fri. 10–8.

Cleveland Museum of Natural History. A 70-ft-long dinosaur skeleton and the world's oldest human fossil—"Lucy"— are among the treasures housed here. The collection contains artifacts and environmental samples from nearly 1,700 sites and documents more than 10,000 years of prehistoric life in Ohio. The largest specimen is the 3,600-year-old Ringler dugout, one of the oldest watercraft found in North America. The museum is also known for its 1,500-piece collection of rare gems. There's also a planetarium. | 1 Oval Wade Dr., at University Circle | 216/231–4600 | $6.50 | Mon.–Sat. 10–5, Sun. noon–5.

The 4.9-meter copper Hanna Star Dome at the **Ralph Mueller Planetarium** displays 12 skies—one for each month. The dome, built in 1936, is illuminated by one lamp, with stars displayed by the use of fiber optics. | 1 Wade Oval Dr., at University Circle | 216/231–4600 | $1.50, in addition to museum admission | Mon.–Sat. 10–5, Sun. noon–5; stargazing Sept.–May, Wed. 8:30–10 PM.

Dittrick Museum of Medical History. The largest medical technology museum in the United States has a collection of items related to the history of surgery. Housed on the third floor of the Allen Memorial Medical Library, it also has a rare book collection that includes works by Charles Darwin and Sigmund Freud. | 11000 Euclid Ave. | 216/368–3648 | Free | Mon.–Sat. 8:30–5.

Great Lakes Science Center. There are more than 300 interactive exhibits and daily demonstrations at this indoor/outdoor educational center. Science and technology displays include a bridge of fire, an indoor tornado, and an especially good area that focuses on the environment of the Great Lakes region. There's a six-story OMNIMAX theater on the premises. | 601 Erieside Ave. | 216/694–2000 | Exhibits or OMNIMAX, $7.95; combination ticket, $10.95 | Sun.–Thurs. 9:30–5:30, Fri. 9:30–5:45, Sat. 9:30–6:45.

The Health Museum of Cleveland. This museum, the first of its kind in the Western Hemisphere, is dedicated to health and living well, and has a total of 150 hands-on exhibits. Juno, a jumbo, transparent, 40-year-old woman who talks, is a bit of a folk legend in Cleveland. Another exhibit, Body Stops, addresses the reproductive, muscular, skeletal, and cardiovascular systems. You may enjoy the sperm game, where the object is to get marbles past various obstacles to fertilize the egg. | 8911 Euclid Ave. | 216/231–5010 | fax 216/231–5129 | www.healthmuseum.org | $5 | Weekdays 9–5, Sat. 10–5, Sun. 12–5.

Lake Erie Nature and Science Center. Exhibits and hands-on activities provides a glimpse into the depths of Lake Erie. | 28728 Wolf Rd. | 440/871–2900 | Free | Daily 9–5.

★ **Rock and Roll Hall of Fame and Museum.** This museum honors musicians and music-industry figures who have contributed to the energy and evolution of rock music. To be eligible for inclusion, musicians and bands must have released a record at least 25 years ago. In the Hall of Fame area, you can listen to the songs these artists recorded, while film clips and photographs are flashed on 20-ft-tall screens. There's also a retrospective of MTV music videos and occasional concerts. | 1 Key Plaza | 216/781–ROCK or 888/764–7625 | www.rockhall.com | $15 | Daily 10–5:30, Wed. until 9.

Steamship *William G. Mather* Museum. Housed on a 1925 freighter once used to carry coal on the Great Lakes, this museum displays an engine room, sleeping quarters, a brass and oak pilothouse, and an extravagant dining room. | 1001 E. 9th St. | 216/574–6262 | little. nhlink.net/wgm/wgmqf.html | $5 | May 1–Memorial Day and Labor Day–Oct., Fri.–Sat. 10–5, Sun. noon–5; Memorial Day–Labor Day, Mon.–Sat. 10–5, Sun. noon–5.

Temple Museum of Religious Art. This gallery in Temple Tifereth Israel, near University Circle, houses a large collection of Jewish art, artifacts, and archives. | 1855 Ansel Rd. | 216/831–3233 | Free | By appointment.

Western Reserve Historical Society Museum and Library. This museum, which resides in two Italian Renaissance-style mansions, is considered to be Cleveland's oldest cultural institution. It chronicles the history of the Western Reserve, a tract of land on the south shore of Lake Erie in Northeast Ohio, and houses a library and a topnotch auto and aviation collection. One admission fee covers all the properties. | 10825 East Blvd. | 216/721–5722 | www.wrhs.org | $7.50 for all three | Mon.–Sat. 10–5, Sun. noon–5.

You can see how the rich—and their servants—lived at the **History Museum** in the Western Reserve Historical Society complex. The museum includes the Chisholm Halle Costume Wing, one of the nation's top-ranked collections, with garments from the late 1700s to the present. Tours of the Hay-McKinney Mansion are given every day between noon and 5. | 10825 East Blvd. | 216/721–5722 | www.wrhs.org | $7.50 | Mon.–Sat. 10–5, Sun. noon–5.

Car Collectors magazine has called the **Crawford Auto-Aviation Museum** one of the top 10 collections in the nation. This museum in the Western Reserve Historical Society complex showcases nearly 200 antique, vintage, and classic automobiles, from Model T's and the first enclosed automobile to late-model Jaguars. There are models dating to 1895, when Cleveland was a center of car manufacturing. The aviation collection includes a 1912 Curtiss Hydroaeroplane. | 10825 East Blvd. | 216/721–5722 | www.wrhs.org | $7.50 | Mon.–Sat. 10–5, Sun. noon–5.

The **Library of the Western Reserve Historical Society** has over six million items, including prints and photographs, manuscripts and newspapers, focusing primarily on Ohio's history. The library's vast collection of genealogical materials has made it one of the largest family history research centers in the country. | 10825 East Blvd. | 216/721–5722 | www.wrhs.org | $7.50 | Tues.–Sat. 9–5, Wed. until 9 PM, Sun. noon–5.

PARKS, NATURAL AREAS, AND OUTDOOR RECREATION

Edgewater State Park. The upper and lower areas of the park are connected by paved bike trails and a fitness course. The statue of Conrad Mizar, the oldest monument in Cleveland, is near the pavilion in the upper portion of the park. The lower part of the park has a swimming beach, boat ramps, a fishing pier, concessions stand, and picnic shelters. | 8000 W. Memorial Shoreway | 216/881–8141 | www.ohiostatepark.org | Free | Daily 6 AM–11 PM.

Gordon Park. Part of the 14-mi-long Cleveland Lakefront State Park on Lake Erie, this scenic place is at the tip of Martin Luther King Drive near University Circle. | E. 72nd St. and Cleveland Memorial Shoreway | 216/881–8141 | Free | Daily dawn–dusk.

Rockefeller Park. This 250-acre park is the last remnant of the estate of John E. Rockefeller. It includes a 3-acre turn-of-the-century greenhouse that houses exotic flowers and plants, and 4 acres of outdoor gardens, including a Japanese and a peace garden. | 750 E. 88th St. | 216/664–3103 | Free | Park: daily dawn–dusk. Greenhouses: daily 10–4.

Wildwood Park. Part of Cleveland Lakefront State Park on Lake Erie, this open space has a variety of amusements, including beaches, slides, paddle boats, and miniature golf. | Lakeshore Blvd. and Neff Rd. | 216/881–8141 | Free | June–Sept., daily dawn–dusk.

SHOPPING

Tower City Center. This renovated train terminal houses an upscale, indoor shopping mall with over 120 shops and restaurants and an 11-screen movie theater. It's a beautiful space, with a glass domed ceiling, marble staircases, and brass storefronts. The Terminal Tower building, which was the tallest building in the Midwest in 1930, is attached. | 50 Public Sq. | 216/621–7981 | Free | Mon.–Sat. 10–8, Sun. noon–6.

West Side Market. In existence for over 85 years, the market is the place to sample local fare and get in some excellent people watching, perhaps the best in the city. Over 68 vendors sell anything from lamb chops to cigars in two buildings and an outdoor arcade, which is covered with tarps for the winter. The Grand Market Hall is over 241 ft long with vaulted ceilings 44 ft high. | 1979 W. 25th St. | 216/644–3386 | Free | Mon. and Wed. 7–4, Fri. and Sat. 7–6.

SIGHTSEEING TOURS

Goodtime III. This 1,000-passenger cruise ship operates daily tours on the Cuyahoga River and along the Cleveland lakefront. | 825 E. 9th St. Pier, North Coast Harbor | 216/861–5110 | www.goodtimeiii.com | $12.50 | Daily, cruise times vary.

Lolly the Trolley Tours of Cleveland. Vintage trolley cars with narrators wind through the streets of downtown and beyond. | Elm St. and Winslow Ave. | 216/771–4484 or 800/848–0173 | www.lollytrolley.com | $9 | June 15–Sept., daily, times vary.

Nautica Queen. You can eat—and eat some more—while cruising Lake Erie on this boat with two buffet dining decks and an open-air observation deck. The boat is docked at the west bank of the Flats. | 1153 Main St. | 216/696–8888 or 800/837–0604 | $22 lunch, $39–$45 dinner | Easter–Dec., daily, times vary.

SPECTATOR SPORTS

Cleveland Browns. Cleveland's NFL team plays football from September to December at the Cleveland Browns Stadium, which opened in the fall of 1999. Tickets are quite scarce, but any remaining ones are put on sale on Wednesday the week of the game. | 1085 W. Third St. | 440/891–5050 or 888/891–1999 | www.clevelandbrowns.com | $20–$67 | Ticket office: Weekdays 9–5.

Cleveland Cavaliers. Cleveland's pro basketball team battles its NBA Eastern Conference rivals at Gund Arena. | 1 Center Ct. | 216/420–2000 | www.cavs.com | $10–$65 | Ticket office: Nov.–May, Mon.–Sat. 9:30–6.

Cleveland Indians. The Indians, Cleveland's boys of summer, meet their American League opponents at Jacobs Field, a downtown ballpark, every April through October. | 2401 Ontario St. | 216/420–4200 | www.clevelandindians.com | $6–$36 | Ticket office: Apr.–Oct., Mon.–Sat. 9:30–6.

OTHER POINTS OF INTEREST

Cleveland Metroparks Zoo and Rainforest. This zoo is home to 3,300 animals who live in naturalistic habitats—giraffes and zebras roam in the African Plains Savanna, kangaroos hop around in the Australian children's area, and gray wolves and beavers in the Wolf Wilderness. | 3900 Brookside Park Dr. | 216/661–6500 | www.clemetzoo.com | Zoo and Rainforest, $8 | Memorial Day–Labor Day, weekdays 10–5, Labor Day–Memorial Day, daily 9–5.

There's a thunderstorm every 15 minutes in **The Rainforest,** a simulated tropical habitat with waterfalls, rainforest animals, and plants from jungles around the world. | 3900 Brookside Park Dr. | 216/661–6500 | www.clemetzoo.com | Rainforest and Zoo, $8 | Memorial Day–Labor Day, weekdays 10–5 (until 9 Wed.), weekends, 10–7; Labor Day–Memorial Day, daily 10–5, Wed. until 9.

Great Lakes Brewery. The six buildings that make up the brewery were stables and a warehouse for the Schlather Brewing Company at the turn of the century. The buildings have been restored to expose the grandeur of the gabled roofs and cork walls. The two-story brew house has full glass walls so you can see the brewmasters at work. Tours leave every half hour. | 2516 Market Ave. | 216/771–4404 | www.greatlakesbrewing.com | Free | Fri. 5 PM–9 PM, Sat. 2–8.

NASA Glenn Visitor Center. A moon rock and space suits worn by astronauts who orbited the Earth are displayed at this out-of-this-world attraction. It also has a microgravity science laboratory and spacecraft replicas. NASA renamed it after John Glenn in March 1999. It's west of the airport. | 21000 Brookpark Rd. | 216/433–2000 | Free | Weekdays 9–4, Sat. 10–3, Sun. 1–5.

WALKING TOUR

Begin at the Tower City Center, just off the Public Square at the intersection of Ontario Street and Euclid Avenue. This is the city's central landmark and home to the historic Terminal Tower; its 42nd-floor observation deck offers a splendid view of Cleveland and Lake Erie. One block east of the Public Square, between Superior and Euclid avenues, is America's first indoor shopping mall, the Cleveland Arcade—built in 1890 and still filled with shops. From here, move south of the Public Square down Ontario Street. You'll soon be able to see Gund Arena, home of the National Basketball Association's Cleveland Cavaliers. Next door is the Cleveland Indians' Jacobs Field, a trapezoidal baseball park that looks at once old-fashioned and brand new. Now head back on Ontario Avenue to the Tower City Center. Board the RTA's Waterfront Line and travel north on East 9th Street as far as the North Coast Harbor stop. Minutes away, on Erieside Avenue, you'll find the Great Lakes Science Center, with interactive exhibits and an OMNIMAX theater. Adjacent is the Rock and Roll Hall of Fame and Museum. Use the RTA to return to the Tower City Center and pick up RTA's Red Line to University Circle, 4 mi to the east. The centerpiece of University Circle is the Cleveland Museum of Art on East Boulevard, renowned for its medieval European collection and Egyptian art. Across the street is the Cleveland Institute of Art, which is strong on contemporary art, and Severance Hall, home of the Cleveland Orchestra. Next follow East Boulevard north to the Western Reserve Historical Society's complex. The society's History Museum, set in a mansion, chronicles the history of northeast Ohio. Connected to the Historical Society is the Crawford Auto-Aviation Museum, which showcases nearly 200 antique, vintage, and classic automobiles and aircraft. Continue on East Boulevard until you come to East 108th Street/Wade Oval. Go south and you will soon be at the Cleveland Museum of Natural History, which features an observatory and planetarium.

ON THE CALENDAR

APR.: *Tri-C Jazzfest.* Thousands of people line the streets of downtown Cleveland to listen to some of jazz's top musicians perform in concert. The 10-day series, sponsored by Cuyahoga County Community College, is held at various locations throughout the city. | 216/987–4444.

JULY–AUG.: *Blossom Music Festival.* The orchestra's summer series runs from July 4th through Labor Day at the open-air Blossom Music Center in Cuyahoga Falls, a half-hour's drive south of Cleveland. | 1145 W. Steels Corners Rd. | 216/231–1111 or 800/686–1141 | www.clevelandorchestra.com.

AUG.: *Cuyahoga County Fair.* This agriculture-oriented event, one of the largest in Ohio, has all the usual fair fare—games, rides, exhibits and more. It's held in Berea, southwest of downtown Cleveland. | 57th St., at Fleet St. | 440/243–0090.

AUG.: *Slavic Village Harvest Festival.* This ethnic street fair takes place the last week-end in August on 10 blocks in Slavic Village, a historic Polish neighborhood. | E. 55th Fleet St.–E. 65th Fleet St. | 216/271–5591.

SEPT.: *Cleveland National Air Show.* One of the premier airshows in the country draws more than 40 military and civilian aircraft to the Burke Lakefront Airport in downtown Cleveland for the three-day Labor Day weekend. | 1501 N. Marginal Rd. | 216/781–0747.

SEPT.–MAY: *The Cleveland Orchestra.* Beginning in mid-September, the orchestra per-forms works by contemporary and classical composers at Severance Hall in the Univer-sity Circle neighborhood. | 11001 Euclid Ave. | 216/231–1111 or 800/686–1141 | www.clevelandorchestra.com.

SEPT.: *German Village Oktoberfest.* The Brewer's Yard development hosts this three-day extravaganza. There's music on three stages, including everything from polka to hard rock, as well as German food, and arts and crafts. | 614/224–4300.

Dining
MODERATE

Alvies Gateway Grille. American. This downtown diner with a counter and bar stools is popular for breakfast and lunch. Specialties include the corned beef sandwich with potato pancakes, homemade soups that change daily, and omelets. | 2033 Ontario St. | 216/771–5322 | No dinner. Closed weekends | $10–$17 | AE, MC, V.

Fulton Bar and Grill. Contemporary. Word of mouth spread quickly and steadily about this spot in Ohio City. Vintage photographs of local bars decorate the walls of the second-floor dining room, and serving pieces and flatware are mix-and-match. There's nothing boring coming out to the open kitchen, either—check out the typically innovative pasta-crusted salmon in yellow pepper béarnaise sauce, which is served with roasted asparagus and goat cheese salad. | 1835 Fulton Ave. | 216/694–2122 | No lunch | $7–$25 | AE, MC, V.

Great Lakes Brewing Co. American. The traditional grub at this pub southwest of down-town in Ohio City includes calamari, the sausage sampler, chili, black-bean ravioli, and ribs. A specialty is the brewmaster's pie—hot and mild Italian sausage, spinach, mozzarella and ricotta cheeses, baked in a flaky pie crust and served on a bed of marinara sauce. Wash it down with one of varieties of beer brewed here. Open-air dining is available in a court-yard with 25 tables. Kids' menu. | 2516 Market St. | 216/771–4404 | $10–$20 | AE, DC, MC, V.

Heck's Cafe. American. Pub-like and in the historic Warehouse District, this eatery has an open kitchen and glass garden atrium filled with plants. It's known for its bouillabaisse and extensive burger menu. You can dine at tables or in booths. | 2927 Bridge Ave. | 216/861–5464 | $12–$20 | AE, D, MC, V.

HI & DRY. Contemporary. High ceilings, exposed brick walls, full-story glass windows, and an open kitchen distinguish the dining room of this restaurant in Cleveland's Tremont neigh-borhood, and Venetian glass lamps hang over the bar. You might want to start with the orange-and-vanilla bean martini (tastes like a Creamsicle). Main-course flavors are teamed in equally unusual combinations, exemplified by the blackened snapper with black bean hummus and tequila-spiked corn salad. There is outside seating. | 2207 W. 11th | 216/621–6166 | Closed Sun. | $8–$16 | MC, V.

La Dolce Vita. Italian. Besides its food, this Little Italy neighborhood restaurant is known for its eclectic choice of musicians, including strolling mariachis and live opera performers. On Monday nights, there's an eight-course meal; on other days, specials include veal, seafood, and pizzas. They line up for the pesto pasta and the rotating risotto dishes. | 12112 Mayfield Rd. | 216/721–8155 | No lunch | $12–$20 | AE, MC, V.

Lemon Grass. Thai. Dine in the casual sunroom or the more formal front room at this restaurant in a suburb east of Cleveland. The menu includes lemongrass soup, a Thai hot-and-sour shrimp soup, steamed shellfish with chili powder, curry duck, and pad Thai. The seafood *choo chee* is a medley of shrimp, squid, and scallops with curry and vegetables. Open-air dining is available on a patio surrounded by a brick fence. | 2179 Lee Rd., Cleveland Heights | 216/321–0210 | Closed Sun. No lunch Sat. | $9–$20 | AE, DC, MC, V.

Luchita's. Mexican. With authentic cuisine, generous portions, good margaritas, and friendly service, it's no wonder that this place on Cleveland's western border is jammed on weekends. The menu changes every three months. Paintings in the style of Mexican muralist Diego Rivera cover the yellow sponged walls. | 3456 W. 117th St. | 216/252–1169 | No lunch Sun. Closed Mon. | $11–$13 | AE, MC, V.

New York Spaghetti House. Italian. This downtown/Gateway District institution with paintings of New York and Italy covering the walls has been serving classic Italian fare for more than 70 years. Its proximity to the Gateway sports complex brings diners for pre- and post-game meals. The menu includes lasagna, veal parmesan, and pasta with seafood. | 2173 E. 9th St. | 216/696–6624 | $9–$18 | AE, D, DC, MC, V.

Sweetwater's Cafe Sausalito. Mediterranean. A popular spot before the theater, this bright downtown restaurant has lots of windows and a large mural of a San Francisco bar scene. The wine selection covers a wall. The emphasis on the menu is on seafood and pasta; there's lobster and potato pierogi with caramelized onions and saffron cream and Hungarian-style chicken breast with noodles. A pianist performs Friday and Saturday nights. | 1301 E. 9th St. | 216/696–2233 | Closed Sun. | $12–$16 | AE, D, DC, MC, V.

EXPENSIVE

The Century. Continental. A railroad theme prevails in this traditionally furnished dining room in the Ritz-Carlton Hotel. Shrimp, scallops, roast pork chops, and pastas fill the menu. On Friday evenings international fare is the highlight; a different country or region is showcased each month. There's also a sushi bar and a Sunday brunch. Breakfast, lunch, and dinner are served daily. Kids' menu. | 1515 W. Third St. | 216/623–1300 | Reservations essential | $17–$20 | AE, D, DC, MC, V.

Don's Lighthouse Grille. Seafood. Known for its legendary happy hours, this west end eatery across from Eden Park is in a 1929 building with a steeple. The dining room has large windows, a high ceiling, chandeliers, and nautical murals. The catch of the day may be scrod, tuna, or salmon; you'll always find jumbo sea scallops, halibut, and sea scallop ravioli. | 8905 Lake Ave. | 216/961–6700 | www.donslighthouse.com | No lunch weekends | $16–$28 | AE, D, DC, MC, V.

Guarino's. Italian. Owned by the same family for more than 80 years, this cozy restaurant in the Little Italy section of the University neighborhood serves classic Italian fare including many varieties of pasta as well as seafood and beef dishes. Open-air dining is available weather permitting. Kids' menu. | 12309 Mayfield Rd. | 216/231–3100 | Reservations essential | $14–$30 | AE, D, DC, MC, V.

Johnny's Bar. Italian. Mammoth portions of veal, pasta, and seafood draw diners to this small Art Deco hot spot in a 1917 building in Ohio City. A specialty is the red bell pepper pasta tossed with shrimp and a cayenne-spiked cream sauce. You can eat inside on white linen or, in good weather, have a meal outside on the backyard patio. The place fills up quickly on weekends. | 3164 Fulton Rd. | 216/281–0055 | Reservations essential | Closed Sun. | $17–$35 | AE, DC, MC, V.

Lola. Contemporary. Chef-owner Michael Simon has received national attention from food and wine critics for the creations he describes as "urban comfort food"—homey classics with a novel twist. Best-sellers on the winter menu at this restaurant in Tremont are lobster pierogi and macaroni and cheese with fresh rosemary, goat cheese, and roasted chicken. Specialties include fish and game, and desserts such as molten chocolate cake. | 900 Literary Rd. | 216/771–5652 | Closed Mon. No lunch | $13–$22 | AE, D, DC, MC, V.

Metropolitan Cafe. Seafood. This restaurant is in a 100-year-old building in the historic Warehouse District; floor-to-ceiling windows provide a great view of the Cleveland skyline. The cafe specializes in seafood cooked on a wood-enhanced grill. Pasta, steak, and chicken dishes are also available. | 1352 W. 6th St. | 216/241–1300 | $14–$35 | AE, D, DC, MC, V.

★ **Moxie.** American. In the upscale town of Beachwood, 20 minutes southeast of downtown Cleveland by car, this trendy newcomer is a must. It's unassuming from the outside, but once you step into the large, bright room and taste the creatively prepared American fare with a nouvelle twist, you'll understand why they named it Moxie. | 3355 Richmond Rd., off I–271, Beachwood | 216/831–5599 | $18–$28.50 | AE, D, MC, V.

The Palazzo. Italian. The two granddaughters of the original owner prepare and serve northern Italian cuisine just three nights a week in this romantic hideaway just west of downtown in the Cudell-Edgewater neighborhood. Whether turning out updated versions of her recipes or new dishes inspired by annual trips back to Italy, they do their grandma proud. | 10031 Detroit Ave. | 216/651–3900 | Closed Sun.–Wed. No lunch | $14–$22 | AE, MC, V.

Pier W. Seafood. Shaped like a ship, this restaurant in Lakewood, about 5 mi east of downtown Cleveland, juts out over Lake Erie, offering a good view of the city skyline and the

© Corbis

ROCK 'N' ROLL HISTORY

Cleveland, once known as the city whose river was so polluted that it caught fire, is now much better known as the home of the Rock and Roll Hall of Fame and Museum. And that seems only right. Clevelanders were the first ever to hear not just the music but the actual term, "rock 'n' roll" coming from their radios in the voice of legendary DJ Alan Freed.

Freed was born in Johnstown, Pennsylvania, but when he first began broadcasting on Cleveland radio station WJW in 1951, he quickly changed history. Using the name Moondog, playing rhythm 'n' blues records by black artists, and leaving his microphone open while he sang along with the songs and beat time on a telephone book, he conveyed to listeners his own genuine excitement for the music he called rock 'n' roll.

The Moondog Rock 'n' Roll Party, as he called his show, quickly attracted young listeners. In 1952, Freed hosted the Moondog Coronation Ball at the Cleveland Arena, now credited as the first rock 'n' roll concert. In 1954, Freed headed to radio station WINS in New York and to even greater national fame, but he, Cleveland, and Clevelanders had already changed the history of American popular culture. And when the Rock and Roll Hall of Fame began inducting honorees in 1986, Alan Freed was on the very first list.

Ohio has given the music world many of its most influential artists. Akron nurtured Pere Ubu, Devo, and Chrissie Hynde. The Moonglows and Screamin' Jay Hawkins came to fame in Cleveland. The Isley Brothers and Bootsy Collins came from Cincinnati, and it was there in the 1960s that King Records recorded the Platters, Bill "Honky Tonk" Doggett, and many of James Brown's classic hits.

Still, it may well be that Ohio's, and Cleveland's, most famous moment in rock history is when the band Spinal Tap, in Rob Reiner's *This is Spinal Tap*, burst through a doorway in the (non-existent) Xanadu Star Theatre and shouted to no one at all, "Hello, Cleveland!"

water. The menu includes seafood dishes, fresh catch from Lake Erie, and beef and chicken entrées. There's entertainment on Friday and Saturday nights. Sunday brunch. | 12700 Lake Ave., Lakewood | 216/228–2250 | No lunch Sat. | $17–$55 | AE, D, DC, MC, V.

Sans Souci. Mediterranean. This French countryside-style restaurant in the Renaissance Cleveland Hotel has bright murals on the walls and a massive stone hearth. Earthy foods—especially seafood—from the coasts of Spain, Morocco, Italy, and France are highlights. Entrées include sautéed snapper, grilled salmon, grilled tuna steak, Black Angus strip steak, and veal saltimbocca. Lobster dishes are featured in October and November. The carrot soup with leeks and apples is a specialty. | 24 Public Square | 216/696–5600 | Reservations essential | No lunch weekends | $14–$28 | AE, D, DC, MC, V.

That Place on Bellflower. Contemporary. Cozy nook-and-cranny dining rooms are filled with modern art at this restaurant in a 1890 building in University Circle. The place is known for its seafood and pasta, but popular dishes also include beef Wellington, fresh Great Lake walleye, chicken breast in a champagne cream sauce with almonds, and salads. Open-air dining is available on the back patio. Kids' menu. | 11401 Bellflower Rd. | 216/231–4469 | No lunch Sun. No dinner Mon. | $13–$27 | AE, DC, MC, V.

Watermark. Seafood. A waterside location in a restored warehouse in the Flats provides a view of river traffic. The menu changes daily and emphasizes exotic seafood such as ahi and sailfish. Steak, chicken, and pasta dishes are also available. Desserts include fresh strawberry zabaglione. Open-air dining is available on the riverfront patio. Kids' menu. | 1250 Old River Rd. | 216/241–1600 | $16–$55 | AE, D, DC, MC, V.

VERY EXPENSIVE

Baricelli Inn. Contemporary. Housed in a 19th-century mansion that's now a seven-room bed and breakfast inn, this restaurant in University Circle is known for its veal and fresh fish, but the house specialty is the boneless rack of lamb. The European menu includes salmon with rosemary pesto, scallops with couscous, and veal tenderloin with a muscat reduction sauce and golden chanterelle mushrooms. Herbs come from the inn's garden. There's an extensive wine list. Open-air dining is available on the front patio. | 2203 Cornell Rd. | 216/791–6500 | Closed Sun. | $23–$35 | AE, DC, MC, V.

John Q's Steakhouse. Steak. The hardwood floors, cherrywood, brass, and sports memorabilia complement the prime cuts of beef at this downtown chain restaurant known for its pepper strip steak and fresh vegetable sides. It's across the street from the Renaissance Cleveland Hotel. Open-air dining is available on the front patio. | 55 Public Square | 216/861–0900 | No lunch weekends | $24–$41 | AE, D, DC, MC, V.

Morton's of Chicago. Steak. The downtown Cleveland branch of the well-known chain in the Tower City Center has its trademark formal mahogany interior with white tablecloths. Large portions of choice cuts of beef and seafood are accompanied by baked or mashed potatoes, salad, and fresh vegetables. | 1600 W. Second St. | 216/621–6200 | No lunch weekends | $68–$78 | AE, DC, MC, V.

Parker's. French. White tablecloths and a warm fireplace dominate this French bistro in Ohio City. Local ingredients are used extensively, so the menu changes with the harvest and the season. Whenever possible, organically grown vegetables are selected. Popular dishes include free-range chicken, pork tenderloin, grilled filet of beef, and roasted salmon. For dessert, try the lemon soufflé. No smoking. | 2801 Bridge Ave. | 216/771–7130 | Closed Mon. Lunch on Fri. only | $21–$47 | AE, D, MC, V.

Players on Madison. Italian. Patrons create their own gourmet pizzas at this neighborhood trattoria-style restaurant in Lakewood, about 5 mi west of downtown Cleveland. More than 50 toppings are available. The menu also includes innovative pasta dishes, like ravioli filled with acorn squash, ricotta and pine nuts, and free-range poultry dishes. | 14523 Madison Ave., Lakewood | 216/226–5200 | Closed Sun. No lunch | $19–$28 | AE, D, DC, MC, V.

Sushi Rock. Pan-Asian. This lively pink-and-purple hot spot is in the downtown Warehouse District. The illuminated pictures of New York may add to your general confusion as you try to categorize the cuisine: Crab-lobster tater tots keep company with the house-famous dragon roll (a tumble of shrimp tempura, surimi, cucumber, avocado, and eel) as appetizers, and entrées range from spice-rubbed pork to roasted sea scallops, served with tomato, cucumber, onion, and ginger salad. | 1276 W. 6th St. | 216/623–1212 | fax 216/623–1218 | Closed Sun. No lunch on Sat. | $21–$30 | AE, MC, V.

Lodging
INEXPENSIVE

Red Roof Inn. The three-story stucco motel built in 1980 is 4 mi from the airport. The bright rooms with slate gray carpet have lounge chairs. Several restaurants and stores are nearby. Cable TV. Some pets allowed. Free parking. | 17555 Bagley Rd., Middleburg Heights | 440/243–2441 or 800/843–7663 | fax 440/243–2474 | www.redroof.com | 117 rooms | $65 | AE, D, DC, MC, V.

MODERATE

Clarion Hotel-West. The hotel in a two-story stucco building is 5 mi from the airport and 10 mi from downtown. The bright rooms are furnished with desks. Restaurant, bar with entertainment, room service. In-room data ports. Cable TV. 2 pools (1 indoor), wading pool. Sauna. Laundry facilities. Business services. Airport shuttle. Free parking. | 17000 Bagley Rd., Middleburg Heights | 440/243–5200 or 800/252–7466 | fax 440/243–5240 | www.clarion.com | 238 rooms | $99 | AE, D, DC, MC, V.

Clifford House Bed and Breakfast. This two-story, Tuscan-style brick home, built in 1868, is in the downtown neighborhood known as Ohio City. The urban, residential neighborhood is just five minutes from the more rowdy nightlife of The Flats. The uncluttered, cozy rooms are painted in warm tones; have restored pine-plank, cherry, dark walnut, or maple floors; and quilt-covered beds. Most of the upstairs rooms have vaulted ceilings. Some rooms share a bath. Complimentary Continental breakfast. In-room refrigerators, some in-room VCRs. Business services. | 1810 W. 28th St. | 216/589–9432 | www.cliffordhouse.com | 3 rooms | $95–$135 | AE, D, MC, V.

Comfort Inn-Cleveland Airport. This four-story brick hotel is off I–71, near restaurants and stores. It was a Choice Hotels Gold Award winner from 1994-1999. Complimentary breakfast. Cable TV, in-room movies. Pool. Business services. Airport shuttle. Some pets allowed. Free parking. | 17550 Rosbough Dr., Middleburg Heights | 440/234–3131 or 800/228–5150 | fax 440/234–6111 | www.comfortinn.com | 136 rooms | $108 | AE, D, DC, MC, V.

Edgewater Estates I and II. This 1920s English Tudor is directly across the street from Edgewater State Park, a three-minute drive from downtown. The guest rooms, furnished with period antiques, look out on either the gardens of the estate or Lake Erie. There are two kitchens (one for you to share with the rest of the guests) and two dining rooms. Complimentary breakfast. Some microwaves, some refrigerators. Hiking. Beach, dock, swimming and water sports, boating, fishing. Laundry facilities. Airport shuttle. Pets allowed. | 9803–5 Lake Ave. | 216/961–1764 | fax 216/961–7043 | lopezgayle@hotmail.com | www.bedandbreakfast.com/bbc/p616727.asp | 5 rooms | $110–$135 | AE, D, MC, V.

Fairfield Inn by Marriott-Brook Park. This three-story motel built in 1987 is 1 mi from the airport. Rooms have beige walls and dark brown carpet. Each has a work desk and two double beds or a king-size bed. Complimentary Continental breakfast. Cable TV. Pool. Business services. Airport shuttle. Free parking. | 16644 Snow Rd., Brook Park | 216/676–5200 or 800/288–2800 | fax 216/676–5200, ext. 709 | www.fairfieldinn.com | 135 rooms | $79 | AE, D, DC, MC, V.

Hampton Inn Cleveland–Downtown. In the heart of the city is this hotel suited for the business traveler and tourist alike. The business center has audiovisual equipment. All guests have complimentary access to the swimming pool and exercise equipment across the street. Complimentary Continental breakfast. In-room data ports. Laundry service. Business services. | 1460 E. 9th St. | 216/241–6600 or 800/426–7866 | fax 216/241–8811 | www.hampton-inn.com | 194 rooms | $119 | AE, D, DC, MC, V.

Hilton Garden Inn-Cleveland Airport. This seven-story hotel is 1 mi north of the airport, just off I–480, and 12 mi south of downtown. It has an extensive business center. Restaurant, room service. In-room data ports, microwaves, refrigerators. Indoor pool. Hot tub. Exercise equipment. Laundry facilities. Business services. Airport shuttle. | 4900 Emerald Ct. SW | 216/898–1898 or 800/774–1500 | fax 216/898–1498 | www.hilton.com | 168 rooms | $99–$109 | AE, D, DC, MC, V.

Radisson Inn Cleveland Airport. This six-story brick hotel is 4 mi west of the airport next to the Great Northern Mall. All rooms have a sitting area with a love seat. Suites have a separate bedroom and a living room with a wet bar and a sofa bed. Business class rooms and Jacuzzi suites are available. Restaurant, bar. In-room data ports, some refrigerators. Cable TV. Indoor pool. Hot tub. Exercise equipment. Business services. Airport shuttle. Free parking. | 25070 Country Club Blvd., North Olmsted | 440/734–5060 or 800/333–3333 | fax 440/734–5471 | www.radisson.com | 139 rooms, 7 suites | $109, $160 suites | AE, D, DC, MC, V.

Residence Inn-Cleveland Airport. Some rooms have fireplaces at this all-suites, three-story hotel built in 1992. All rooms have a desk and one or two queen-sized beds. It's 4 mi from the airport. Picnic area, complimentary full breakfast. Kitchenettes, microwaves. Cable TV. Pool. Hot tub. Exercise equipment. Laundry facilities. Business services. Airport shuttle. Some pets allowed (fee). Free parking. | 17525 Rosbough Dr., Middleburg Heights | 440/234–6688 | fax 440/234–3459 | www.residenceinn.com | 158 suites | $79, $179 suites | AE, D, DC, MC, V.

EXPENSIVE

Baricelli Inn. This bed and breakfast is in a three-story brownstone mansion, dating from 1896. Each of the spacious guest rooms has lovely antique furnishings and modern amenities. It's in the University Circle neighborhood, 15 minutes from downtown. Guests get passes to a local fitness center. Dining room, complimentary Continental breakfast. Cable TV. Business services. Free parking. | 2203 Cornell Rd. | 216/791–6500 | fax 216/791–9131 | www.baricelli.com | 7 rooms | $150–$175 | AE, MC, V.

The Brownstone Inn–Downtown. This four-story guest house, built in 1874, is on the National Register of Historic Places; it's downtown between Playhouse Square and University Circle. You can't miss its peacock blue double-entrance doors atop a short set of stone steps. Inside are numerous period details, such as pocket doors, a marble fireplace, and French wallpaper. The bridal suite has a four-poster bed. You can cap off your day with a complimentary glass of sherry or port. Weather permitting, breakfast is served on the back deck. Complimentary breakfast. Some kitchenettes. In-room VCRs. | 3649 Prospect Ave. | 216/426–1753 | ryates@lopener.net | www.brownstoneinndowntown.com | 5 rooms | $85–$215 | AE, MC, V.

Cleveland Airport Marriott. Almost half of the rooms at this nine-story hotel are designed for business travelers and have work stations. Guests in concierge rooms have access to a private lounge. It's 2 mi from the airport and 7 mi from downtown. Restaurant, bar. In-room data ports. Cable TV. Indoor pool. Hot tub. Exercise equipment. Laundry facilities. Business services. Airport shuttle. Some pets allowed (fee). Free parking. | 4277 W. 150th St. | 216/252–5333 or 800/228–9290 | fax 216/251–1508 | www.marriott.com | 371 rooms, 4 suites in 2 buildings | $139–$159 | AE, D, DC, MC, V.

Embassy Suites. This all-suites hotel in a 13-story, brick-and-stone, early 1900s building is in downtown's Reserve Square. The two-room suites have a bedroom with two double beds or a king-sized bed, and a living room with a sofa bed. Connecting units are available. Restaurant, bar, complimentary breakfast. In-room data ports, minibars, microwaves. Cable TV. Indoor pool. Tennis. Exercise equipment. Laundry facilities. Some pets allowed. | 1701 E. 12th

St. | 216/523–8000 or 800/362–2779 | fax 216/523–1698 | www.embassysuites.com | 268 suites | $129–$199 | AE, D, DC, MC, V.

Hilton Cleveland-South. This five-story hotel, 10 mi east of the airport, is at the intersection of I–77 and I–480, off Rockside Road. Standard rooms, executive rooms, and suites are available. The pool is half indoors, half outdoors, and one of Don Shula's steak houses, Shula's Steak 2, is on the premises. Restaurant, bar, room service. In-room data ports. Indoor-outdoor pool. Hot tub. Gym. Business services. Airport shuttle. | 6200 Quarry La., Independence | 216/447–1300 or 800/774–1500 | fax 216/642–9334 | www.hilton.com | 191 rooms | $159 | AE, D, DC, MC, V.

Marriott Downtown at Key Center. This 25-story hotel is on the northeast corner of Public Square downtown, less than 1 mi from Cleveland Browns Stadium. Some rooms have work stations. Guests in concierge level rooms have access to a private lounge. Restaurant, bar. In-room data ports. Cable TV. Indoor pool. Hot tub. Sauna. Exercise equipment. Laundry facilities. Business services. | 127 Public Sq. | 216/696–9200 or 800/228–9290 | fax 216/696–0966 | www.marriott.com | 400 rooms, 15 suites | $160, $219–$299 suites | AE, D, DC, MC, V.

Renaissance Cleveland. This grand 14-story hotel built in 1851 is within walking distance of the Cleveland Convention Center, the Flats, the Theater District, and the Rock & Roll Hall of Fame and Museum. Each tastefully furnished room has one or two queen-sized beds or a king-sized bed, a dark wood entertainment center, plush sitting chair with ottoman, and work desk. Jacuzzi suites are available. The lobby area has a towering atrium and the (see Sans Souci) restaurant. 2 restaurants, bar with entertainment. In-room data ports, refrigerators. Cable TV. Indoor pool. Gym. Business services. | 24 Public Sq. | 216/696–5600 or 800/228–9290 | fax 216/696–0432 | www.renaissancehotels.com | 491 rooms, 50 suites | $149, $249 suites | AE, D, DC, MC, V.

★ **The Ritz-Carlton, Cleveland.** This seven-story grand luxury hotel in the Tower City Center blends modern elegance with a touch of Victorian charm. The bright guest rooms have work desks and marble baths. It opened in 1991. Tea is served in the lobby in the afternoon. Restaurant (see Riverview Room), bar with entertainment, room service. In-room data ports. Cable TV. Indoor pool. Hot tub, massage. Exercise equipment. Business services. Some pets allowed. | 1515 W. Third St. | 216/623–1300 or 800/241–3333 | fax 216/623–0515 | www.ritzcarlton.com | 208 rooms, 21 suites | $209, $339 suites | AE, D, DC, MC, V.

Sheraton City Centre. Most of the rooms in this 22-story brick hotel opposite the Cleveland Convention Center have a view of Lake Erie and the Cleveland lakefront. The downtown hotel opened in 1995 and is near the Galleria. Restaurant, bar. In-room data ports. Cable TV. Exercise equipment. Business services. Airport shuttle. | 777 St. Clair Ave. | 216/771–7600 or 800/325–3535 | fax 216/566–0736 | www.sheraton.com | 470 rooms, 24 suites | $119, $154 suites | AE, D, DC, MC, V.

Wyndham Hotel at Playhouse Square. This 14-story glass hotel built in 1995 is in the heart of Cleveland's theater district. Rooms are bright with beige carpet. Restaurant, bar. Cable TV. Indoor pool. Hot tub. Exercise equipment. Business services. Free parking. | 1260 Euclid Ave. | 216/615–7500 or 800/996–3426 | fax 216/615–3355 | www.wyndham.com | 205 rooms | $129–$249 | AE, D, DC, MC, V.

COLUMBUS

MAP 14, C5

(Nearby towns also listed: Chillicothe, Delaware, Lancaster, Newark, Springfield, Washington Court House)

Named after discoverer Christopher Columbus, Ohio's capital city encompasses a six-county metropolitan area and covers 3,142 square mi. The city is home to Ohio State

University, the largest academic institution in the state, with more than 50,000 students. Another well-known local institution is the Columbus Zoo, one of the nation's most acclaimed. Among the city's other highlights are the Ohio Historical Center, The Wexner Center for the Arts, the Columbus Museum of Art, and the popular COSI Columbus (Columbus' Museum of Science and Industry).

Transportation to Columbus and its attractions is easy; I–70 runs east–west, I–71 runs north–south and I–270 circles the metro area. I–670 runs from downtown to the Port Columbus International Airport, which handles more than 400 domestic and international arrivals and departures each day.

In 1816 the Ohio Legislature moved the state capital to Columbus from nearby Chillicothe. Columbus prospered thanks to its location on the banks of the Scioto River, which attracted money, visitors, and settlers. Major railroads came next. Following damaging floods in 1913, the Scioto River was widened and levees, retaining wall, and bridges were built, which allowed for riverfront development.

Even when the rest of Ohio began to suffer industrial decline in the second half of the 20th century, Columbus grew, primarily because its economy is based on state government, education, finance and insurance, and light industry. This continued prosperity has made Columbus an attractive place to live and visit.

Information: Greater Columbus Convention and Visitors Bureau | 90 N. High St., 43215 | 614/221–6623 or 800/345–4386 | fax 614/221–5618 | www.surpriseitscolumbus.com.

TRANSPORTATION INFORMATION

Air: Port Columbus International Airport. The airport is 7 mi east of downtown. | 4600 International Gateway, Columbus | 614/239–4000.

Bus. COTA: The buses of the Central Ohio Transit Authority provide transportation throughout the city and suburbs. | 177 S. High St., Columbus | 614/228–1776.

DRIVING AROUND TOWN

Two major interstates, east–west I–70 and north–south I–71, intersect near downtown. I–670 connects the airport to downtown, and I–270 loops around the outer boundaries of the city. I–70, I–71, and I–670 headed toward downtown are congested in the morning; in the evening, the roads are clogged in the opposite direction. The Short North area and High Street are also very busy. Traffic usually flows smoothly in outlying suburbs (you do need a car in these areas because bus service is infrequent). Downtown, metered parking is available but difficult to find. If you find a spot, be sure to put sufficient money in the meter; meter maids are efficient here. Parking garages are plentiful in this area and near the Ohio State University campus. Parking for an entire day costs between $6 and $10.

NEIGHBORHOODS

Brewery District. The warehouses that once marked Columbus's industrial area at the turn of the century have been converted into condos, restaurants, and bars, now teeming with young professionals. The district is bounded by Livingston Avenue, S. High, S. Front, and Whittier streets.

German Village. This 233-acre downtown district, six blocks south of the Ohio Statehouse, had its roots in an 1814 addition to Columbus's south side. It really developed in the 1840s as Germans fled villages in the Palatinate and Baden-Wurttemburg to escape wars, famine, and poor living conditions; World War I aviation pioneer Eddie Rickenbacker was born on Pearl Alley in 1890. Protected as a historic area since the 1960s and listed on the National Register of Historic Places since 1975, its brick streets are lined with charming old homes, gardens, and shops. There's a lively Oktoberfest and Shakespeare in Schiller Park in summer. Boundaries are Livingston Avenue on the north, Nursery Lane on the south, and Pearl Street on the west; the eastern boundary is jagged but becomes apparent as you stroll about. Local information is available at the German Village Society headquarters at 588 S. 3rd Street.

Short North. This arts district is just north of downtown and south of the Ohio State University campus, off High Street between Nationwide Boulevard and King Avenue. In the 1860s, Goodale Boulevard, toward the southern end of Short North, was the quiet northern edge of Columbus. By 1920 High Street was a thriving urban area, and today it's a lively, trendy neighborhood, full of excellent restaurants, bars, boutiques, and unique shops. Try to catch the Gallery Hop, held on the first Saturday night of each month; crowds congregate to stroll from gallery to gallery.

Attractions
ART AND ARCHITECTURE

City Hall. A tour includes a stroll through city council chambers and the mayor's office. City Hall also houses the Columbus Hall of Fame, honoring noteworthy city natives like Jack Nicklaus and Archie Griffin. | N. Front, W. Gay, W. Broad Sts. and Marconi Blvd. | 376/544–9000 | Free | Daily 9–5.

McKinley Memorial. This statue of Ohio native and President William McKinley stands prominently at the entrance to the grounds of the Ohio Capitol. It was sculpted by John Massey-Rhind in 1917. | 40 N. Main St. | 330/652–1704 | Free | Daily.

Ohio Statehouse. This 1861 Greek Revival building is the home of the Ohio Legislature. The dome of the rotunda is painted with the state seal; the building also has portraits of Ohio's

© Corbis

THE OHIO STATE BUCKEYES, SLOOPY, AND THE TBDBITL

As any Ohioan proudly proclaims, the state is the home of The Best Damn Band in the Land.

That's TBDBITL (pronounced ti-bittle), for short, and we're not talking about an orchestra here. We're talking about a marching band, THE marching band—the Ohio State University Marching Band.

Over the years, Ohio State's band has been recognized nationally and internationally for its performances, traditions, and innovations. Hearing TBDBITL break into Ohio State's fight songs ("Buckeye Battle Cry" and "Across The Field") is sure to evoke a swell of pride in each and every Buckeye fan and Ohio State alum.

Many say TBDBITL's most spectacular achievement is a formation known as "Script Ohio." The 192 band members march onto the field single file, creating the perfectly formed letters "O-h-i-o". Script Ohio, first performed in 1936, is now the band's trademark.

Another high spot in the band's history was its discovery of a little ditty called "Hang on Sloopy." Since about 1965, the song has become a hymn of sorts for Ohio State football fans. Expect to hear it during time-outs, at the end of the third quarter, and at any intense moments during a game. (Sometimes, hearing 95,000 fans sing and sway to "Sloopy" in Ohio Stadium is just what the Bucks need to "win this game today.")

The "Sloopy" phenomenon even captured the Ohio legislature; it became the official state rock song in 1985.

governors and presidents and historical documents. You can take a self-guided tour of the Senate chamber when it's not in session. Building tours are given every 30 minutes weekdays from 9:30–3, weekends at 11:15, 12:30, 2, and 3. | Capitol Square on U.S. 23 | 614/752–6350 | Free | Weekdays 7–7, weekends 10–4.

CULTURE, EDUCATION, AND HISTORY

Camp Chase Confederate Cemetery. This large cemetery is the final resting place of 2,260 Confederate soldiers who died in Civil War battles. | 2900 Sullivant Ave. | 614/276–3630 | Free | Daily.

Martha Kinney Cooper Ohioana Library. Only books about Ohio or Ohioans, or written by Ohioans, can be found in this library. | Ohio Departments Building, 65 S. Front St., Room 1105 | 614/466–3831 | Free | Weekdays 8:30–4:30, 1st Sat. of each month, 9–12.

Ohio Historical Center. This two-building complex, just past the Ohio State Fairgrounds, houses a museum, a state archives, and a replica of an 1800s village where docents dress in period clothes. The museum presents the history of the Buckeye State in collections ranging from Native American fossils to papers written by Ohio political leaders. | 1982 Velma Ave. | 614/297–2300 | www.ohiohistory.org/places/ohc | museum $2.50; Ohio Village and museum $5 | Mon.–Sat. 9–5, Sun. 10–5.

The reconstructed **Ohio Village** re-creates a rural county seat of the mid-19th century. Sixteen buildings, connected by a wooden boardwalk, house 22 craft shops, residences, and offices, in which costumed interpreters talk about life in Ohio during the Civil War. Also on site are period gardens, a Gothic Revival-style church and the Colonel Crawford Inn, a period restaurant where you can sample authentic Colonial recipes. | 1982 Velma Ave. | 614/297–2300 | www.ohiohistory.org/places/ohvillag | $5, includes Ohio Historical Center | Apr.–Nov., Wed.–Sun. 10–4; Dec., Wed.–Sun. 11:30–8:30; Jan.–Mar., weekends 9–5.

Ohio State University. This leading teaching and research university offers an extensive range of academic programs in the liberal arts, the sciences, and the professions. The Oval, the heart of the Columbus campus, is beautifully landscaped with 115 varieties of trees and surrounded by stately buildings including historic Orton Hall, the Main Library, and University Hall. There are guided tours weekdays at 10 and 2. Call for reservations. | N. High St., between 11th and Lane Aves. | 614/292–3980 | Daily.

The on-campus **Chadwick Arboretum** has local and regional trees and plants. | 2120 Fyffe Rd. | Free | Apr.–Oct., daily.

Contemporary art—including performance art and mixed-media works—is the focus of the **Wexner Center for the Arts.** | N. High St. and 15th Ave. | 614/292–3535 | www.wexarts.org/home.shtml | $3 | Tues.–Sun. 10–6, also Thurs. 6–9 PM.

Santa Maria **Replica.** This is an authentic full-size reproduction of the 15th-century lead ship that Christopher Columbus used on his journey to the New World. Costumed docents lead 45-minute tours. | 90 W. Broad St. | 614/645–8760 | www.santamaria.org/index.html | $3 | Memorial Day–Labor Day, Wed.–Fri. 10–5, weekends 11:30–6; mid-Apr.–Memorial Day and Labor Day–Oct., Wed.–Fri. 10–3, weekends, noon–5.

MUSEUMS

Columbus Museum of Art. The collection includes Old Masters, early Modernist paintings, modern American paintings, Impressionist and Expressionist works. Outdoors is a sculpture garden. A café and a gift shop are on the premises. | 480 E. Broad St. | 614/221–6801 | $4 | Tues.–Sun. 10–5:30, Thurs. until 8:30.

COSI Columbus. More than 1 million visitors have come through COSI's doors since it opened in 1964. Interactive exhibits at this first-class science center allow you to explore underwater shipwrecks and discover hidden treasures or join an archeological dig. The "i/o" room teaches you about the technology of video games and lets you grab a joystick and play a few. You'll also be able to time travel in "Progress," leaping from 1889 to 1962 in the blink of an eye. | 333 W. Broad St. | 614/228–2674 | $12 | Museum: Daily 10–5. Theaters and shops: Sun.–Thurs. 10–5; Fri.–Sat. 10–9.

Riffe Gallery. In the Vern Riffe Center for the Government and the Arts, directly across from the State House, is this gallery that features works by Ohio artists as well as items from the collections of the state's museums. Exhibits in the big open gallery space change approximately every three months. | 77 S. High St. | 614/644–9624 | www.oac.state.oh.us/riffegallery | Free | Mon.–Tues. 10–4, Wed.–Fri. 10–8, Sat. noon–8, Sun. noon–4.

PARKS, NATURAL AREAS, AND OUTDOOR RECREATION

Hoover Reservoir Area. This large manmade body of water, about 20 mi north of downtown Columbus, is open for boating, fishing, swimming, and other outdoor activities. There's also a picnic area on the grounds. | 7701 Sunbury Rd., Westerville | 614/645–3350 | Free | Daily, dawn–dusk.

Wyandot Lake Adventure Park. Though there are water rides and amusement rides, the former is the main focus at this park about 25 minutes northwest of downtown. Slip down the water slides and frolic in the wave pool at the water park, then head over to the amusement park for roller coasters, carousels, and other rides. | 10101 Riverside Dr. | 614/889–9283 or 800/328–9283 | $19.99 | Memorial Day–Labor Day, daily 10–8.

SHOPPING

City Center Mall. This mall in the downtown shopping district is anchored by Jacobsons and Marshall Field's. A bridge over High Street connects the mall to the Lazarus department store, the flagship store of this Ohio chain. | 111 S. Third St. | 614/221–4900 | Mon.–Sat. 10–9, Sun. noon–6.

The North Market. The North Market sits on what was once the North Graveyard, and though tales of hauntings continue to this day, the market has remained in its present spot since 1876. Vendors sell produce, fish, meat, and breads. There are several ethnic food booths. Frank's Diner is a stuff-your-face, sit-down restaurant right at the entrance. Only some vendors come on Mondays, so if you want the complete olfactory and gastronomic experience, come another day. | 59 Spruce St. | 614/463–9664 | Free | Mon. 9–5, Tues.–Fri. 9–7, Sat. 8–5, Sun. 12–5.

SPECTATOR SPORTS

Columbus Bluejackets. This brand-new National Hockey League team made their debut in fall 2000. Their 18,000-seat arena is the only one in the nation with an adjacent practice stadium. They take to the ice from October to April. | Nationwide Blvd., at Front St. | 614/246–4625 | www.columbusbluejackets.com | $16–$134.

OTHER POINTS OF INTEREST

Columbus Zoo. Made famous by its director, Jack Hanna, the zoo is home to a 100,000-gallon coral reef exhibit and one of the largest reptile collections in the United States. A children's petting zoo has small nurse sharks you can pet. | 9990 Riverside Dr. | 614/645–3550 | www.germanvillage.org | $7 | Daily 9–5.

Topiary Garden. Instead of stippled paint, the medium is shrubbery for the one-of-a-kind topiary replica of Georges Seurat's post-Impressionist masterpiece, *A Sunday on the Island of La Grande Jatte,* in this garden. There are also 54 people, eight boats, three dogs, a monkey, and a cat, who look to a creek instead of the ocean. The tallest figure stands 12 ft high. | 480 E. Town St. | 614/645–0197 | fax 614/645–0172 | Free | Daily, dawn to dusk.

WALKING TOUR

Start just south of downtown in the German Village district between Livingston and Nursery Lane; the area is full of 19th-century brick homes and gardens. To the west is the Brewery District, where old breweries have been turned into restaurants and bars.

After walking through these two neighborhoods, stroll north on High Street until you come to Broad Street. At the intersection is the Ohio Statehouse, a domeless Greek Revival capitol building. Across the street in the Vern Riffe Center for Government and the Arts is the Riffe Gallery, which showcases works in various mediums by Ohio artists. Go west on Broad Street across the Scioto River to COSI Columbus; kids love the fascinating interactive exhibits here. Walk east on Broad as far as High Street. Head north for approximately 15 minutes to the Short North arts district on your left, filled with excellent restaurants and art galleries. Just north of Short North is the expansive Ohio State University campus. The biggest attraction on campus is the Wexner Center for the Arts, which displays contemporary art in a building designed by Peter Eisenmann. At this point, you can either take a bus back to the downtown area or walk back along High Street. At Broad Street, head east to the Columbus Museum of Art, where there's an outstanding collection of works by Impressionists, Cubists, and contemporary artists.

ON THE CALENDAR

MAY–SEPT.: *Harness Racing at Scioto Downs.* Races are held daily in season. | 6000 S. High St. | 614/491–2515.

JUNE: *Greater Columbus Arts Festival.* The best artists in the Columbus area display their works at this annual three-day street festival and show along the riverfront in downtown Columbus. | 614/221–6623.

AUG.: *Ohio State Fair.* The largest junior fair in the nation is a highlight, with its agricultural displays and children's contests. There are also rodeos, tractor pulls, nationally known musical acts, and laser light shows. | Expo Center, between 11th Ave. and 17th Ave. | 614/221–6623 or 800/345–4386.

SEPT.–APR.: *BalletMet.* Columbus's professional ballet company performs a range of dances, from classic to contemporary at the Ohio Theater. | 55 E. State St. | 614/229–4848.

SEPT.: *German Village Oktoberfest.* The Brewer's Yard development hosts this three-day extravaganza, with three stages of music including everything from polka to hard rock, German food, arts and crafts, and a kinderplatz area with kids' programming. | 614/224–4300.

SEPT.–MAY: *Thoroughbred Racing at Beulah Park Jockey Club.* Horse-racing fans try their luck at this track in Grove City. | 3664 Grant Ave. | 614/871–9600.

OCT.–APR.: *Opera/Columbus.* Some of the country's greatest opera performers make their way to the city during the Columbus opera season at the Palace Theater. | 34 W. Broad St. | 614/461–0022.

NOV.–MAY: *Columbus Symphony Orchestra.* The orchestra presents concerts on Friday and Saturday evenings, and some Sunday afternoons, in the Ohio, Palace, and Southern theaters downtown. | 55 E. State St. | 614/228–8600 or 614/228–9600 | www.columbussymphony.org.

Dining
INEXPENSIVE

Cap City Diner. Contemporary. Downhome favorites are modified for urban tastes at this '90s-style stainless-steel diner in Grandview with Formica tabletops, vinyl-covered benches, and neon lights. Fresh seafood, pork chops with chutney toppings, and four-cheese macaroni are favorites. Garlic mashed potatoes accompany almost everything. The menu also includes sandwiches and meat loaf, and there's a raw bar. Entertainment Sunday and Tuesday. Kids' menu. | 1299 Olentangy River Rd. | 614/291–3663 | $6–$19 | AE, D, DC, MC, V.

China Dynasty. Chinese. This casual strip-mall restaurant in Upper Arlington, east of downtown, serves large portions of Hunan, Szechuan, and Mandarin dishes. The General Tso chicken is popular. There's also a buffet. Sunday brunch. | 1677 W. Lane Ave. | 614/486–7126 | $7–$16 | AE, D, DC, MC, V.

Katzinger's. Delicatessen. The menu is printed on chalkboards at this New York-style downtown deli known for its reuben sandwiches. Open-air dining is available. Kids' menu. No smoking. | 475 S. 3rd St. | 614/228–3354 | $5–$10 | AE, D, MC, V.

Mac's Cafe. American/Casual. Golf items cover the walls at this Short North neighborhood bar with a Scottish theme. The bar stocks nearly 50 types of Scotch whiskies. The menu includes cottage and steak pies, burgers and sandwiches, and heaping plates of fries and onion rings. A pianist performs Friday and Saturday evenings. | 693 N. High St. | 614/221–6227 | $4–$17 | AE, DC, MC, V.

Olde Mohawk. American. One of German Village's first German pubs, this eatery in a 1933 building is famous for its horseshoe-shaped bar. Pictures of staff and customers cover the walls. The Thursday night special is all-you-can-eat quesadillas; there are specials on other nights, too. The roast beef sandwich with chicken salad on top is popular, as is the beef stew served in a hollowed-out round of bread. | 821 Mohawk St. | 614/444–7204 | $8–$11 | AE, D, DC, MC, V.

Schmidt's Sausage Haus. German. Accordion players serenade and servers are decked out in Bavarian costumes at this popular two-level, beer hall-style restaurant in a 1880 brick building in German Village. The signature dish is the Bahama Mama, a giant bratwurst served with your choice of toppings, such as sauerkraut and mustard. The dessert menu includes cream puffs. Kids' menu. | 240 E. Kossuth St. | 614/444–6808 | www.schmidt-house.com | $6–$12 | AE, D, DC, MC, V.

MODERATE

Ann and Tony's. Italian. The menu at this fancy restaurant with tablecloths includes home-style classics such as six-layer lasagna, rigatoni with meatballs, veal or chicken parmesan, and beef ravioli. New York strip and a fisherman's platter are also available. Kids' menu. It's about a half hour drive west of downtown. | 211 E. Main St., West Jefferson | 614/879–8897 | Reservations not accepted | Closed Mon. and week of July 4. No dinner Sun. | $12–$22 | D, MC, V.

Bravo! Italian Kitchen. Italian. Popular with a diverse crowd of young professionals and families, this restaurant in the northwestern suburb of Dublin is one in a growing chain. There's pizza with creative toppings, wood-grilled meats, and northern Italian pasta selections including lasagna bolognese, chicken scallopini, and fettuccine Alfredo. The interior has a Roman ruin motif with columns and tapestries. Open-air dining is available out front on marble tables with wicker chairs. Kids' menu. | 3000 Hayden Rd., Dublin | 614/791–1245 | Mon.–Sun. 11–10 | $10–$19 | AE, D, DC, MC, V.

The Clarmont. American. Famous for playing host to the power breakfasts of the city's elite, this German Village restaurant with white tablecloths is known for its steak and seafood and its famous chicken in a clay pot. Adjacent is the Round Bar, a lounge in a small circular building. | 684 S. High St. | 614/443–1125 | No breakfast or lunch Sun. | $12–$22 | AE, DC, MC, V.

Cooker Bar and Grille. American. Baskets of biscuits are served with the entrées at this family-style chain restaurant north of downtown near Westerville. The menu includes pot roast, chicken Monterey, and large dinner salads. Kids' menu. Sun. brunch. | 6193 Cleveland Ave. | 614/899–7000 | $9–$15 | AE, D, DC, MC, V.

Engine House No. 5. Seafood. This Columbus cousin of Charley's Crab is in a 100-year-old firehouse with a fire pole in German Village. Steamed lobster, buckets of mussels, and oysters on the half-shell are favorites. Pasta dishes are served downstairs. A pianist performs Friday and Saturday. Kids' menu, early bird dinners. | 121 Thurman Ave. | 614/443–4877 | www.meur.com | Reservations essential | No lunch on weekends | $11–$32 | AE, D, DC, MC, V.

Hunan House. Chinese. Marble lions and statues dominate this restaurant northwest of downtown that's been open since 1982. Eggplant Szechuan, Hunan chicken, and moo shu pork are popular dishes. | 2350 E. Dublin-Granville Rd. | 614/895–3330 | $9–$14 | AE, DC, MC, V.

K2u. Mediterranean. Updated Greek and Italian dishes have been served since 1989 at this trendy Gen-X hangout in the arty Short North district. Walls are covered with murals of Columbus history, starring figures from European history and illuminated by track lighting. The menu includes hand-cut steaks and chops, pizza, moussaka, calamari, and bruschetta. There's live entertainment Mon., Thurs., and Fri. | 641 N. High St. | 614/461–4766 | Closed Sun. | $12–$25 | AE, D, DC, MC, V.

EXPENSIVE

Bexley's Monk. American. Skylights and candles cast light on the tables at this Bexley restaurant that draws a lively crowd for weekday business lunches and weekend dinners. The menu includes wood-fired pizza, pasta, rack of lamb, and seafood dishes. The chef makes great desserts. There's live music seven days a week. | 2232 East Main St. | 614/239–6665 | www.bexleymonk.com | No lunch weekends | $15–$35 | AE, D, DC, MC, V.

Lindey's. Contemporary. The walls are covered with artwork at this popular New York-style bistro in a mid-1800s building in German Village. A specialty of the house is the shrimp and angel hair pasta with a Cajun sauce. The menu also includes steak, rack of lamb, and seared peppered tuna tournedos. The signature dessert is a homemade fudge brownie served with coffee ice cream and a Kahlua hot fudge sauce. There's entertainment Thurs. and Sun. Sun. brunch. | 169 E. Beck St. | 614/228–4343 | $16–$28 | AE, D, DC, MC, V.

Rigsby's Cuisine Volatile. Mediterranean. Chefs are visible behind a large marble counter at this trendy restaurant in Short North where tables have a view of the busy sidewalk. Specialties might be the veal medallions with port, Roquefort, and green peppercorn sauce. The menu also includes salmon, shrimp, steak, and chicken entrées. There's entertainment Wed. and Thurs. | 698 N. High St. | 614/461–7888 | Reservations essential | Closed Sun. | $16–$44 | AE, D, DC, MC, V.

Seven Stars Dining Room. American. The specialties at this antiques-filled dining room in the historic Worthington Inn are the New Zealand rack of lamb and the grilled salmon. The menu also includes chicken, steak, seafood, and vegetarian selections. Open-air dining is available on the front porch with cast iron furniture. There's entertainment Fri. and Sat. | 649 High St., Worthington | 614/885–2600 | www.worthingtoninn.com | $16–$25 | AE, D, DC, MC, V.

The Top. Steak. This 45-year-old Columbus institution with wood paneling and leather booths is in Bexley. It's known for its steak, seafood, and barbecued ribs; the filet mignon and the porterhouse are popular. | 2891 E. Main St. | 614/231–8238 | No lunch | $14–$29 | AE, D, DC, MC, V.

VERY EXPENSIVE

Cameron's. Contemporary. This Bexley restaurant is done in vibrant colors and lively patterns. The portobello mushroom with caramelized onions is a good starter. Entrées are updated versions of American favorites and include roasted double-cut pork chops, walnut-crusted salmon and beef tenderloin and mushroom farfalle, and Lake Erie walleye in cream sauce. Kids' menu. | 2894 E. Main St. | 614/235–3662 | No lunch | $20–$33 | AE, D, DC, MC, V.

Handke's Cuisine. Contemporary. Seasonal ingredients are the focus at this Brewery District restaurant in a converted 1820s beer cellar with stone vaulted ceilings and green chairs. The menu might include Caesar salad garnished with fresh salmon and served in a baked parmesan cheese shell, New York strip, and herb-crusted lamb. | 520 S. Front St. | 614/621–2500 | Reservations essential | No lunch. Closed Sun. | $32–$44 | AE, D, MC, V.

Hyde Park Grille. Steak. The cozy dining rooms have dark wood and fireplaces at this restaurant where steaks are named after famous Ohio sports figures, such as Ohio State coach John Cooper, auto racing star Bobby Rahal, and former Browns quarterback Bernie Kosar. The Kosar, a filet mignon topped with lobster and béarnaise sauce, is the most popular dish. There's live entertainment Wed.–Sun. | 1615 Old Henderson Rd., Upper Arlington | 614/442–3310 | No lunch | $20–$45 | AE, D, DC, MC, V.

L'Antibes. French. This candlelit Short North restaurant serves classic French dishes with a twist. The menu changes every six weeks to take advantage of in-season produce, exemplified by the Cornish hen with dried cherries, salmon with horseradish sauce, and veal loin medallions with Brie sauce. | 772 N. High St. | 614/291–1666 | users.all.com/lantibes | Reservations essential | No lunch. Closed Sun. and Mon. | $19–$29 | AE, D, DC, MC, V.

Morton's of Chicago. Steak. The downtown Columbus branch of the well-known chain has its trademark formal mahogany interior with white tablecloths. Large portions of choice cuts of beef and seafood are accompanied by baked or mashed potatoes, salad, and fresh vegetables. The bar has an extensive wine list. | 280 N. High Street Nationwide Plaza | 614/464–4442 | www.mortons.com | Reservations essential | No lunch | $25–$40 | AE, D, DC, MC, V.

Refectory. French. This restaurant is northwest of downtown in a restored church dating from the 1850s, with exposed brick walls and wooden tables. The seasonally changing menu might include rack of lamb, beef tenderloin medallions, and fresh seafood dishes. Creme brûlé is a popular dessert. Open-air dining is available in a courtyard. | 1092 Bethel Rd. | 614/451–9774 | www.therefectoryrestaurant.com | Reservations essential | Closed Sun. No lunch | $24–$28 | AE, D, DC, MC, V.

Tapatio. Mexican. The pasta and beef entrées are interesting takes on familiar Mexican-influenced fare at this colorful restaurant with a lively bar and white tablecloth-swathed dining room. The menu includes Atlantic salmon, the black bean hummus, and crab cakes in red pepper sauce, as well as some Caribbean and South American dishes. Open-air dining is available weather permitting. It's across from North Market. | 491 N. Park St. | 614/221–1085 | No lunch Sun. | $18–$33 | AE, D, DC, MC, V.

Tony's Italian Ristorante. Italian. This fancy German Village restaurant has a bright dining room with pink and beige walls and linens. There is an extensive antipasti menu. Entrées might include several varieties of fresh grilled fish, roasted stuffed veal chop or braised short ribs. A pianist performs on Saturday evenings. | 16 W. Beck St. | 614/224–8669 | No lunch Sat. Closed Sun. | $30–$50 | AE, DC, MC, V.

Lodging
INEXPENSIVE

Best Western-East. This motel was built in 1980 and is 15 minutes from the Columbus airport and 20 minutes east of downtown. Restaurant, bar, room service. In-room data ports. Cable TV. Pool. Business services. Airport shuttle. Free parking. Some pets allowed. | 2100 Brice Rd., Reynoldsburg | 614/864–1280 or 800/528–1234 | fax 614/864–1280, ext. 388 | www.bestwestern.com | 143 rooms | $61 | AE, D, DC, MC, V.

Best Western-North. This two-story brick motel built in the late 1960s and renovated in 1999 is 8 mi from downtown. Rooms have two double beds. There's a full health club on the premises, with jogging track, Cybex machines and aerobics classes. Restaurant, bar, complimentary Continental breakfast, room service. Cable TV. 2 pools (1 indoor). Hot tub, sauna. Health club. Laundry facilities. Business services. Free parking. | 888 E. Dublin-Granville Rd. | 614/888–8230 or 800/528–1234 | fax 614/888–8223 | www.bestwestern.com | 180 rooms | $75 | AE, D, DC, MC, V.

Cross Country Inn-Sinclair. This regional chain's two-level stucco motel, built in 1984, is 6 mi north downtown off I–71 at exit 116. Rooms have two doubles or a king-size bed. Cable TV. Pool. Business services. Free parking. | 4875 Sinclair Rd. | 614/431–3670 or 800/621–1429 | fax 614/431–7261 | 136 rooms | $56 | AE, D, DC, MC, V.

Fairfield Inn by Marriott. This three-story brick motel built in 1989 has beautiful landscaping and comfortable rooms furnished with desks. It is within walking distance of Northland Mall and 8 mi north of downtown. Complimentary Continental breakfast. In-room data ports. Cable TV. Pool. Business services. Free parking. | 887 Morse Rd. | 614/262–4000 or 288–2800 | fax 614/262–4000 | www.fairfieldinn.com | 135 rooms | $56 | AE, D, DC, MC, V.

German Village Inn. Friendly service and low rates distinguish this two-story, no-frills German Village hotel near downtown. Rooms are decorated in jewel tones, with pictures of pastoral scenes. The entire hotel was remodeled in June 2000. Cable TV. | 920 S. High St. | 614/443–6506 | fax 614/443–5663 | 44 rooms | $69 | AE, D, DC, MC, V.

Lenox Inn. All rooms have double beds at this two-story motor hotel that opened in 1975. It's 20 minutes east of downtown. Restaurant, bar, room service. In-room data ports. Cable TV. Pool. Business services. Airport shuttle. Free parking. Some pets allowed (fee). | I–70E at Rte. 256, Reynoldsburg | 614/861–7800 or 800/821–0007 | fax 614/759–9059 | 151 rooms | $71 | AE, D, DC, MC, V.

157 on the Park Bed and Breakfast. This brick German cottage is in the heart of German Village, directly across the street from Schiller Park. Though the home has not been restored to period, the detailed woodwork and stained-glass windows hearken to days gone by. One of the rooms accommodates up to six people and takes up the entire third floor. All rooms are individually appointed. Complimentary breakfast. Cable TV. | 157 E. Deshler Ave. | 614/443–6935 | 3 rooms | $65 | No credit cards.

Red Roof Inn-Columbus North. This two-story early '70s brick motel is within walking distance of Sam's Diner and 8 mi north of downtown. Rooms are basic. Cable TV. Business services. Some pets allowed. Free parking. | 750 Morse Rd. | 614/846–8520 or 800/843–7663 | fax 614/846–8526 | www.redroof.com | 107 rooms | $58 | AE, D, DC, MC, V.

MODERATE

Best Western Clarmont Inn & Suites. This four-story motel in German Village is 1½-mi from City Center and within walking distance of shopping and dining. It was torn down and rebuilt in 1998; the large rooms have cherrywood furnishings and queen-sized beds. The mini-suites have refrigerators, microwave, and pull-out bed. Restaurant. Some refrigerators, some microwaves. Cable TV. Pool. Free parking. | 650 S. High St. | 614/228–6511 or 800/528–1234 | www.bestwestern.com | 48 rooms, 12 suites | $79, $99 suites | AE, D, DC, MC, V.

Concourse Hotel. You can't get any closer to the airport than this. This two-level hotel, which opened in 1985, is on the grounds of Port Columbus International Airport. The marble and mahogany lobby has Palladium windows. The rooms have nice touches, too, like plush bathrobes, fresh flowers, and a 5-inch color TV in the bathroom. Guests have free access to an athletic club. Restaurants, bar, room service. In-room data ports. Cable TV. 2 pools (1 indoor). Hot tub. Exercise equipment. Business services. Airport shuttle. Free parking. | 4300 International Gateway | 614/237–2515 or 800/541–4574 | fax 614/237–6134 | www.theconcoursehotel.com | 147 rooms | $88 | AE, D, DC, MC, V.

Hampton Inn Columbus Airport. All standard rooms have two double beds in this four-story 1997 motor inn within walking distance of the airport and 5 mi from downtown. Studios have a king-size bed, a sofa bed, and a desk. Complimentary Continental breakfast. In-room data ports, some in-room hot tubs. Cable TV. Pool. Business services. Airport shuttle. | 4280 International Gateway | 614/235–0717 or 800/426–7866 | fax 614/231–0886 | www.hamptoninn.com | 129 rooms | $88–$98 | AE, D, DC, MC, V.

Holiday Inn-Airport. You'll think you're already in the tropics in the atrium lobby of this three-story airport motel, with tropical plants and a resident parrot. The glass-enclosed indoor recreation center is a big draw. It's 2 mi from the Columbus airport and 5 mi from downtown. Restaurant, bar, room service. In-room data ports. Cable TV. Indoor pool. Hot tub. Exercise equipment. Laundry facilities. Business services. Airport shuttle. Some pets allowed. | 750 Stelzer Rd. | 614/237–6360 or 800/465–4329 | fax 614/237–2978 | www.holiday-inn.com | 236 rooms in 3 buildings | $89 | AE, D, DC, MC, V.

The House of 7 Goebels. This home, built in 1977, is a reproduction of a 1780 Connecticut river valley farmhouse. It was constructed with Colonial materials and methods, such as square nails, hand-split Shaker roofing, and exterior handmade doors with wooden latches and Indian bars. Weather permitting, you can sample the house-famous Belgian waffles on the stone patio. The two-acre yard has a creek, rock garden, flower beds, and croquet court. It's northwest of downtown, between Dublin and Hilliard. Complimentary breakfast. No room phones. No TV. | 4975 Hayden Run Rd. | 614/761–9595 | fax 614/761–9595 | fgoebel@colmbus.rr.com | www.bbhost.com/7goebels | 2 rooms | $90 | MC, V.

La Grande Flora Bed and Breakfast. A mile east of the City Center Mall in Olde Town is this 1903 Victorian home. The hand-painted, gold-trimmed fireplace tiles, the oak woodwork, carved oak mantels, shuttered windows, and beveled leaded-glass windows recall another era, but conveniences are up to date. Some rooms have brass beds and marble-topped washstands. Upstairs, the French Garden Room is where you can enjoy your afternoon snack. Complimentary Continental breakfast. In-room data ports, microwaves, refrigerators. Cable TV, in-room VCRs. | 820 Bryden Rd. | 614/251–0262 or 800/251–2588 | fax 614/252–7693 | www.bbonline.com/oh/flora | 2 rooms | $75–$100 | AE, D, DC, MC, V.

Ramada Plaza. This six-story brick-faced hotel built in 1970 was totally remodeled in 2000. The restaurant serves American regional cuisine; the lounge has a DJ and dancing. Restaurant, bar with entertainment. In-room data ports. Cable TV. 2 pools (1 indoor), wading pool. Hot tub. Exercise equipment. Video games. Business services. Airport shuttle. Free parking. Some pets allowed. | 4900 Sinclair Rd. | 614/846–0300 or 800/272–6232 | fax 614/ 847–1022 | www.ramadaplaza.com | 268 rooms | $99 | AE, D, DC, MC, V.

Signature Inn-Columbus North. This two-story chain property is at exit 27 N of I–270, 15 minutes north of downtown. The hotel offers free access to a well-stocked business center and complimentary popcorn and cookies each evening. Guests have privileges at a local fitness center. Complimentary Continental breakfast. In-room data ports, microwaves, refrigerators. Cable TV. Pool. Business services. Free parking. | 6767 Schrock Hill Court | 614/ 890–8111 or 800/822–5252 | fax 614/890–8111 | www.signatureinns.com | 125 rooms | $76 | AE, D, DC, MC, V.

Trueman Club Hotel. Each evening, there's a manager's reception with complimentary hors d'oeuvres at this hotel, which is 12 mi north of downtown. Bar, complimentary Continental breakfast. Some refrigerators. Cable TV. Indoor pool. Hot tub. Exercise equipment. Laundry facilities. Business services. Airport shuttle. Pets allowed. | 900 E. Dublin-Granville Rd. | 614/888–7440 or 800/477–7888 | fax 614/888–7879 | redroof.com | 182 rooms, 16 suites | $91, $129 suites | AE, D, DC, MC, V.

EXPENSIVE

Adam's Mark. This sleek 21-story downtown hotel is within walking distance of the Cleveland Convention Center, the Capitol, and shopping. The rooms are done in muted tones and have hardwood furnishings and large closets. The hotel has a sports bar, a health club, and round-the-clock room service. Restaurant, bar, room service. In-room data ports. Cable TV. Pool. Hot tub, sauna. Exercise equipment. Laundry facilities. Business services. | 50 N. Third St. | 614/228–5050 or 800/444–2326 | fax 614/228–2525 | www.adamsmark.com | 415 rooms, 3 suites | $129, $800 suites | AE, D, DC, MC, V.

Amerisuites. This six-story all-suites property built in 1994 has a lovely lobby with a polished marble floor. It's 20 minutes north of downtown at the junction of I–270 and Route 23 N, at the border of Worthington. Complimentary Continental breakfast. In-room data ports, microwaves, refrigerators. Cable TV, in-room VCR. Pool. Exercise equipment. Laundry facilities. Business services. Airport shuttle. Free parking. Some pets allowed. | 7490 Vantage Dr. | 614/846–4355 or 800/833–1516 | fax 614/846–4493 | www.amerisuites.com | 126 suites | $109 suites | AE, D, DC, MC, V.

Columbus Marriott-North. This nine-story brick hotel is in the suburbs 20 minutes north of downtown at I–71 Exit 117. A number of rooms are specially equipped for business travelers; a full business center is in the lobby. Restaurant, bar, room service. In-room data ports. Cable TV. Indoor-outdoor pool. Hot tub. Exercise equipment. Game room. Laundry facilities. Business services. Airport shuttle. Free parking. Pets allowed (fee). | 6500 Doubletree Ave. | 614/885–1885 or 800/228–9290 | fax 614/885–7222 | www.marriott.com | 300 rooms, 7 suites | $139, $275 suites | AE, D, DC, MC, V.

Courtyard by Marriott-Worthington. Rooms in this suburban business hotel are equipped with a work desk and lamp. The hotel is 15 mi north of downtown; local restaurants deliver dinner to your room. Restaurant, bar, complimentary breakfast. In-room data ports, refrigerators (in suites). Cable TV, in-room movies. Indoor pool. Hot tub. Exercise equipment. Laundry facilities. Business services. Free parking. | 7411 Vantage Dr., Worthington | 614/436–7070 or 800/321–2211 | fax 614/436–4970 | www.courtyard.com | 145 rooms, 12 suites | $114, $129 suites | AE, D, DC, MC, V.

Doubletree Guest Suites–Columbus. This 10-story stone-faced hotel is on the river, within walking distance of the Convention Center. The well-appointed one-bedroom suites have wet bars; some have river views. Restaurant, bar. In-room data ports, refrigerators, wet bars. Cable TV. Business services. Some pets allowed (fee). | 50 S. Front St. | 614/228–4600 or 800/528–0444 | fax 614/228–0297 | www.doubletree.com | 194 suites | $119–$139 | AE, D, DC, MC, V.

Embassy Suites. This eight-story all-suites hotel with an atrium lobby opened in 1975. The spacious units have a separate bedroom, a living area with a queen-size sofa bed, a table and chairs, and a wet bar. It's 15 minutes north of downtown and 12 mi from the Columbus airport. Restaurant, bar, complimentary breakfast. In-room data ports, kitchenettes, microwaves, refrigerators. Cable TV, in-room VCRs. Indoor-outdoor pool. Hot tub. Exercise equipment. Video games. Business services. Airport shuttle. | 2700 Corporate Exchange Dr. | 614/890–8600 or 800/362–2779 | fax 614/890–8626 | www.embassysuites.com | 221 suites | $139 suites | AE, D, DC, MC, V.

50 Lincoln Inn. This restored 1917 brick townhouse in the Italian Village neighborhood is a bed-and-breakfast with an artistic theme. Each room is named for an artist—Ansel Adams, Degas, Picasso, and the like—and furnished with both antique and modern furnishings. The downstairs gallery features the works of local artists. The cobblestone patio off the rear of the house is a fine place to sit and ponder whether life really does imitate art. In-room data ports. Laundry facilities. No smoking. | 50 E. Lincoln St. | 614/299–5050 | fax 614/291–4924 | 8 rooms | $99–$129 | AE, D, DC, MC, V.

Harrison House Bed and Breakfast. This turquoise-and-cream 1890 Queen Anne is a perfect fit in its Victorian Village surroundings. Open for business since 1989, the inn has a reputation for impeccable service, and guests rave about the candlelit breakfast. Rooms are individually styled but maintain a scheme of mauves and creams. It's easy to imagine yourself in another century as you lounge in a wicker chair on the bright blue front porch. A fully stocked apartment designed for short stays is also available. Complimentary breakfast. Cable TV. | 313 W. 5th Ave. | 614/421–2202 or 800/827–4203 | www.columbus-bed-breakfast.com | 4 rooms | $109 | AE, D, MC, V.

Holiday Inn-Columbus/Worthington Area. This six-story hotel, built in 1988, has an atrium lobby with a classical Italian theme. If you're in town on business, you can request a room with a desk and a second phone line. It's 10 mi north of downtown on the I–270 beltway, near Worthington's restaurants and retail stores. Restaurant, bar, room service. In-room data ports, refrigerators (in suites). Cable TV. Indoor pool. Exercise equipment. Laundry facilities. Business services. Airport shuttle. Free parking. Some pets allowed. | 175 Hutchinson Ave. | 614/885–3334 or 800/465–4329 | fax 614/846–4353 | www.holiday-inn.com | 316 rooms, 6 suites | $109, $205 suites | AE, D, DC, MC, V.

Holiday Inn-City Center. This chain's 12-story downtown Columbus property is a few blocks from the Capitol and the City Center Mall. Rooms have desks and beds with wooden headboards. Restaurant, bar. Cable TV. Pool. Business services. Airport shuttle. Some pets allowed (fee). | 175 E. Town St. | 614/221–3281 or 800/465–4329 | fax 614/221–2667 | www.holiday-inn.com | 240 rooms | $145 | AE, D, DC, MC, V.

Holiday Inn-East. This 12-story brick hotel dating from the 1970s is near I–70 Exit 107. It's 8 mi from the Columbus airport and 8 mi from downtown. Some guest rooms have a sleeper sofa. Restaurant, bar. In-room data ports. Cable TV. Indoor pool, wading pool. Exercise equipment. Playground. Business services. Airport shuttle. Pets allowed. | 4560 Hilton Corporate Dr. | 614/868–1380 or 800/465–4329 | fax 614/863–3210 | www.holiday-inn.com | 278 rooms | $99–$129 | AE, D, DC, MC, V.

Wyndham Dublin. The rooms in this three-story stucco hotel are spacious; they have a large work area and a long phone cord, making it easy to get your work done. Some rooms have skylights and balconies. It's 25 minutes northwest of downtown. 2 restaurants, bar. In-room data ports, room service. Cable TV. Indoor pool. Sauna. Business services. Free parking. Some pets allowed (fee). | 600 Metro Place N, Dublin | 614/764–2200 or 800/996–3426 | fax 614/764–1213 | www.wyndham.com | 217 rooms, 5 suites | $129, $349 suites | AE, D, DC, MC, V.

VERY EXPENSIVE

Crowne Plaza. This 12-story brick-faced hotel, built in 1988, is connected to the Columbus Convention Center and 1 mi from German Village. There's 8,000 square ft of meeting space here, and a car rental desk in the lobby. You'll be in the midst of all the hustle-bustle, but also in the middle of downtown's attractions. 3 restaurants, bar. In-room data ports. Cable TV. Indoor pool. Exercise equipment. Laundry facilities. Business services. Parking (fee). | 33 E. Nationwide Blvd. | 614/461–4100 or 800/338–4462 | fax 614/461–5828 | www.crowne-plaza.com | 423 rooms, 7 suites | $149, $200–$300 suites | AE, D, DC, MC, V.

Hyatt on Capitol Square. In the heart of downtown near the state capitol, this posh 22-story hotel is next to the City Center Mall. Its large rooms are tastefully decorated with cherry-veneer furniture. Restaurant, bar with entertainment. In-room data ports. Cable TV. Massage. Exercise equipment. Business services. | 75 E. State St. | 614/228–1234 or 800/233–1234 | fax 614/469–9664 | www.hyatt.com | 400 rooms, 12 suites | $209, $325 suites | AE, D, DC, MC, V.

Hyatt Regency. Connected to the Columbus Convention Center, Columbus's first and bigger Hyatt caters to business travelers. Business-class rooms have a desk and a fax machine. The 20-story glass-and-concrete structure was built in 1975. 2 restaurants, bar with entertainment, room service. In-room data ports. Cable TV. Indoor pool. Business services. | 350 N. High St. | 614/463–1234 or 800/233–1234 | fax 614/280–3046 | www.hyatt.com | 631 rooms, 16 suites | $179, $205–$650 suites | AE, D, DC, MC, V.

★ **The Lofts Hotel.** The Lofts is in an old warehouse building dating from 1882 and across from the Columbus Convention Center. The room fixtures and decor are a mixture of IKEA and Ralph Lauren. The bathroom tiles came from New York City subway stations. The rooms have tan-and-gray checked carpeting, sleek headboards, exposed bricks and beams, arched doorways, and floor-to-ceiling windows. The second floor is connected to the Crowne Plaza Hotel. A valet service will take you anywhere within a 1 mi radius of the hotel. Restaurant, complimentary Continental breakfast, room service. In-room data ports, in-room safes. Cable TV. Indoor pool. Sauna. Exercise equipment. Business services. | 55 Nationwide Blvd. | 614/461–2663 or 800/735–6387 | fax 614/461–2630 | contact@55lofts.com | www.55lofts.com | 44 rooms | $149–$200 | AE, D, DC, MC, V.

Radisson Airport Hotel and Conference Center. This large six-story hotel with a brick facade has a lovely fountain in its lobby. The hotel is 1 mi from the Columbus airport and 4 mi from downtown. Restaurant, bar. In-room data ports, some refrigerators, some in-room hot tubs. Cable TV. Indoor pool. Hot tub, sauna. Exercise equipment. Laundry facilities. Business services. Airport shuttle. Free parking. | 1375 N. Cassady Ave. | 614/475–7551 or 800/333–3333 | fax 614/476–1476 | www.radisson.com | 247 rooms, 4 suites | $139, $239 suites | AE, D, DC, MC, V.

Sheraton Suites–Columbus. Rooms have plenty of work space and large bathrooms at this nine-story all-suites hotel built in 1981. It's 15 minutes north of downtown. Restaurant, bar. In-room data ports, microwaves, refrigerators. Cable TV, in-room VCR. 2 pools (1 indoor). Hot tub. Exercise equipment. Laundry facilities. Business services. Airport shuttle. | 201 Hutchinson Ave. | 614/436–0004 or 800/325–3535 | fax 614/436–0926 | www.sheraton.com | 261 suites | $189 suites | AE, D, DC, MC, V.

★ **The Westin Great Southern Columbus.** Author James Thurber used to live in this downtown hotel, which was built in 1897. The elaborate public spaces of this Victorian building are decorated with art exhibits, including some prints by Thurber. Rooms have marble baths, high ceilings, and Queen Ann furnishings—and modern conveniences. Some of the rooms are small. Restaurant, bar, room service. In-room data ports, in-room safes, minibars. Cable TV. Health club. Business services. Parking (fee). | 310 S. High St. | 614/228–3800 or 800/937–8461 | fax 614/228–7666 | www.westin.com | 196 rooms, 32 suites | $109–$210, $159–$260 suites | AE, D, DC, MC, V.

Woodfin Suites. This two-story, all-suites brick-faced complex opened in 1990. Many of the one- and two-bedroom suites have fireplaces. You can rent a video from the hotel's library to watch in your room. It's 20 minutes from downtown. Complimentary breakfast. In-room data ports, kitchenettes, microwaves. Cable TV, in-room VCRs, and movies. Pool. Hot tub. Laundry facilities. Business services. Free parking. Some pets allowed (fee). | 4130 Tuller Rd., Dublin | 614/766–7762 or 800/237–8811 | fax 614/761–1906 | www.woodfinsuiteshotels.com | 88 suites | $150–$189 | AE, D, DC, MC, V.

The Worthington Inn. This three-story, 1831-era inn, 13 mi north of downtown, is filled with authentic American antiques. Some rooms have canopy beds; all have fluffy robes and fine toiletries. No two rooms are alike. The four suites, which are in a separate building, have sitting rooms with fireplaces. The innkeepers serve complimentary cocktails at sunset. Restaurant (*see* Seven Stars Dining Room), bar, complimentary breakfast, room service. Cable TV, in-room VCRs. Business services. | 649 High St., Worthington | 614/885–2600 | fax 614/885–1283 | www.worthingtoninn.com | 26 rooms, 4 suites | $175, $215 suites | AE, D, MC, V.

CONNEAUT

(Nearby towns listed: Ashtabula, Geneva-on-the-Lake)

Situated along Lake Erie's shoreline in the northeast corner of Ashtabula County, Conneaut was originally a farming and shipping town. The name means "where snows remain later" in the language of the Seneca Indians. To visitors, Conneaut offers a number of historic and cultural attractions as well as beautiful natural surroundings. The railroad depot, built in 1900, houses a railroad museum. The community center, once a Finnish meeting house, hosts concerts, exhibits, and other special events. Along the expansive shoreline of this city of 13,000 people are a number of beaches and picturesque parks; Conneaut Harbor has marinas and restaurants; and Conneaut Creek is a favorite of anglers. There are several golf courses and campgrounds in the area, along with three wineries offering tastings and tours.

Information: Conneaut Area Chamber of Commerce | 235 Main St., Box 722, 44030 | 440/593–2402.

Attractions

Conneaut Historical Railroad Museum. This museum is housed in the town's old railroad depot, which was built in 1900. This tribute to the locomotive includes a steam engine and railroad cars. | 342 Depot St. | 440/599–7878 | Free | Memorial Day–Labor Day, daily noon–5.

Lodging

Conneaut Days Inn. This no-frills chain is within minutes of Lake Erie. The two-story stucco building, erected in 1975, is off Highway 90 at exit 241. Restaurant, complimentary Continental breakfast. Some microwaves, some refrigerators. Cable TV. Pool. Pets allowed. | 600 Days Blvd. | 440/593–6000 or 800/325–2525 | fax 440/593–6416 | www.daysinn.com | 104 rooms | $85–$150 | AE, D, DC, V.

COSHOCTON

MAP 14, E4

(Nearby towns listed: Cambridge, Gnadenhutten, Newark)

Located near the center of a triangle formed by Columbus, Cleveland, and Wheeling, Coshocton sits in an unspoiled valley, surrounded by wooded hills and lush forests. Indian mound builders were the first people to settle on this spot, where the Tuscarwas and Walhonding rivers meet to form the Muskingum River. The town itself was laid out in 1802; originally called Tuscarwas, in 1811 it was renamed Coshocton, an Indian word meaning "black bear." At first, the town's economy was based on agriculture, but by 1834 coal was being mined in the area, and when the Ohio-Erie Canal opened, Coshocton became an important shipping town. Today 35,000 people call it home.

Information: Coshocton County Chamber of Commerce | 124 Chestnut St., 43812 | 740/622–5411.

Attractions

Pomerene Center for the Arts. The five galleries in the center host rotating exhibits, showing works of individual artists and some juried shows. The center was built in 1836 and is one of Ohio's finest examples of Greek Revival architecture. | 317 Mulberry St. | 740/622–0326 | Free | Tues.–Fri. 1–4, Sun. 1–4.

Historic Roscoe Village. This restored village was once a port on the Ohio and Erie canal; it has shops, historic houses, restaurants, and an inn. The agricultural town sits on the banks of the Walhonding River, which served as the major artery in connecting Roscoe with the outside world, especially Cleveland. In the Living History Tour actors and actresses portray village residents and craftsmen give demonstrations, illustrating life in the 1800s. Other highlights include canal boat tours and the Johnson-Humrickhouse Museum. | 381 Hill St. | 740/622–9310 or 800/877–1830 | www.roscoevillage.com | Free, tour $8.95 | Daily 10–5; tours daily 10–3.

The **Johnson-Humrickhouse Museum** is renowned for its Native-American art collection. The exhibition includes basketry, carvings, pottery, and cloisonne. | 300 N. Whitewoman St. | 740/622–8710 | $2 | May–Oct., daily noon–5; Nov.–Apr., Tues.–Sun. 1–4:30.

You can take a horse-drawn canal boat ride on the *Monticello III.* The 45-minute trip leaves from a spot a half mile north of Roscoe Village. | 740/622–7528 | $6 | Memorial Day–Labor Day, daily 1–5; Labor Day–mid-Oct., weekends 1–5.

ON THE CALENDAR

MAY: *Dulcimer Days.* The Mid-Eastern Regional Dulcimer Championships are held at Historic Roscoe Village during this festival, which also includes exhibits, workshops, and entertainment. | 381 Hill St. | 740/622–9310 or 800/877–1830.
JUNE: *Hot Air Balloon Festival.* Dozens of hot-air balloons land in Coshocton for this colorful event. The highlight is the "night balloon glow," during which all the balloons are lit up at once. | Coshocton County Fairgrounds, 707 Kenilworth Ave. | 740/622–2385.
AUG.: *Coshocton Canal Festival.* This celebration of the city's waterway at Historic Roscoe Village includes horse-drawn canal ride on the *Monticello III.* | 381 Hill St. | 740/622–9310 or 800/877–1830.

OCT.: *Apple Butter Stirrin'.* Large kettles of apple butter simmer over open fires during this fall festival at Historic Roscoe Village. Other ingredients include entertainment, craft shows, and more seasonal fare. | 381 Hill St. | 740/622–9310 or 800/877–1830.

OCT.: *Coshocton County Fair.* The old-fashioned summer celebration at the county fairgrounds includes livestock shows, games, rides, and live entertainment. | 707 Kenilworth Ave. | 740/622–2385.

DEC.: *Christmas Candle Lightings.* Experience all the warmth and charm of a 19th-century country Christmas at Historic Roscoe Village. The festivities take place during three weekends in December. | 381 Hill St. | 740/622–9310 or 800/877–1830.

Dining

Robson's Restaurant. American. Open all day, this family spot right by the river can quell just about any craving you may have. The breakfast skillets are served with toast or a biscuit. Dinner favorites are a juicy steak or seafood fettuccine, served with Robson's famous hand-tossed salads, made tableside. Save room for Kentucky pie, a chocolate chip cookie baked in a pie pan and served warm with a mound of whipped cream. | 442 Main St. | 740/622–8262 | $10–$19 | AE, D, DC, MC, V.

The Warehouse. American. Waitresses in gingham aprons and full-skirted dresses serve you at wooden tables and booths at this family-style restaurant in an 1800s-era feedmill. Popular dishes include liver, chicken, and all-you-can-eat fish. Also on the menu are big deli sandwiches on croissants, burgers, meat loaf, and chicken dinners. Kids' menu. | 400 N. Whitewoman St. | 740/622–4001 | $7–$11 | AE, D, DC, MC, V.

Lodging

Apple Butter Inn. This 1840 home in the heart of Roscoe Village has views overlooking Lake Erie. You can stay in the main house, the two-bedroom carriage house, or the three-bedroom home across the street. The carriage house is the most plush and is geared to an uninterrupted stay–breakfast is even delivered to your door. All rooms have antique furnishings and some rooms have fireplaces. Complimentary breakfast. Some minibars, some refrigerators, some in-room hot tubs. Some room phones. | 455 Hill St. | 740/622–1329 | www.spiker.net/apple butter/ | 9 rooms | $69–$125 | AE, D, MC, V.

Inn at Roscoe Village. This 1980s-era, four-story brick inn is on the grounds of historic Roscoe Village. Furnishings are Shaker-style. Fireside dining is available in the Centennial Room. Restaurant, bar with entertainment. Cable TV. Business services. | 200 N. Whitewoman St. | 740/622–2222 or 800/237–7397 | fax 740/623–6568 | www.roscoevillage.com. | 51 rooms | $89 | AE, D, DC, MC, V.

DAYTON

MAP 14, B5

(Nearby towns listed: Miamisburg, Vandalia)

Dayton, located in southwest Ohio, is a city literally at the crossroads of America. Incorporated in 1803, it was a thriving town by 1812, complete with a new brick courthouse, five new taverns, grist and sawmills, and frame houses springing up to replace log cabins. A nail factory, dyeing plant, weaving mill, and tannery were all in operation.

The city is best known as the birthplace of Orville and Wilbur Wright. Their boyhood home and the bicycle shop where they started toying with the notion of flying are both open to visitors. Aviation aficionados visit the United States Air Force Museum at Wright-Patterson Air Force Base, just outside the city limits.

Dayton has continued to grow in industrial power and has blossomed as a center of high technology, research and information services, and as a service and distribution hub. Today the metro area is home to almost 1 million people. The city has many historic sites, noteworthy museums, an array of recreational activities, and natural areas ranging from prairies to wetlands.

Information: Dayton Area Chamber of Commerce | 1 Chamber Plaza #200, 45402 | 937/226–1444 | www.daytonchamber.org.

Attractions

Carillon Historical Park. The 65-acre park, presided over by the Deeds Carillon, is the repository for a number of city treasures, particularly those that document the area's transportation history. The 1905 Wright Flyer III, one of the brothers' first planes is in the Wright Hall. There's also the 1796 Newcom Tavern, a lock of the Miami Erie Canal, and a 1924 Sun Oil gas station, as well as locally made cars, bicycles, and a rail parlor car. | 2001 S. Patterson Blvd. | 937/293–2841 | $2 | Apr.–Oct., Tues.–Sat. 9:30–5, Sun. noon–5.

The park is named for the **Deeds Carillon,** a 151-ft bell tower with 57 bells, the largest in the state. In the summer, you can hear the bells ring at weekend Carillon concerts. | 2001 S. Patterson Blvd. | 937/293–2841 | $2 | Concerts, Apr.–May, Sun. at 3 PM; June–Aug., weekends at 3 PM.

Dayton Art Institute. Dayton's best-known landmark, this Italian Renaissance-style structure founded in 1919, overlooks the Great Miami River. The encyclopedic collection includes more than 12,000 art objects spanning 5,000 years of history and covering diverse cultures, from American and European to African and Asian. You'll see paintings, photography, sculpture, furniture, and decorative arts. Experiencenter, a hands-on children's center, is a popular attraction. | 456 Belmont Park N | 937/223–5277 or 800/296–4426 | www.daytonartinstitute.org | Free | Daily 10–5, Thurs. until 9.

Throughout the year the **Dayton Art Institute Concert Series** hosts local and nationally known artists. | 456 Belmont Park N | 937/223–5277 or 800/296–4426.

Dayton Museum of Discovery. There are interactive exhibits for all ages, including "That Kids' Playce," an activity area for children up to age 6. | 2600 DeWeese Pkwy. | 937/275–7431 | $7 | Mon.–Sat. 9–5, Sun. noon–5.

Dayton Visual Arts Center. Founded in 1991, the center aims to promote awareness of Dayton's contemporary visual artists. Eight major exhibitions are held here every year. | 40 W. 4th St. | 937/224–3822 | www.sinclair.edu/community/dvac | Free | Weekdays 10–4, Sat. 1–4.

Eastwood Lake. If you're looking to catch some fish—or just some rays—this peaceful lake on Dayton's west side has fishing, swimming, boating, and picnic areas. | Harshman Rd., Rte. 4 | 937/275–PARK | Free | Daily, dawn–dusk.

Oregon Historic District. Dayton's oldest neighborhood now serves as the city's liveliest entertainment district. The downtown streets are lined with bustling restaurants and nightclubs housed in restored buildings. | E. 5th St. between Wayne Ave. and Patterson Blvd. | 937/223–0838 | Free | Daily.

Paul Laurence Dunbar State Memorial. Dunbar (1872–1906) was a noted African-American poet, playwright, novelist, and civil rights activist. He published more than 400 poems. Many of the writer's belongings can be viewed in this restored house, which was his last before he died in 1906. | 219 Paul Laurence Dunbar St. | 937/224–7061 | $3 | Nov.–May, weekdays 9:30–4:30; June–Aug., Wed.–Sat. 9:30–4:30, Sun. noon–4:30; Sept.–Oct., Sat. 9:30–4:30, Sun. 12:30–4:30.

Sunwatch Prehistoric Indian Village. This is a reconstruction of an 800-year-old village that belonged to the Fort Ancient Indians, who had a unique sun-based system of charting time. It is built on a site excavated by the Dayton Museum of Natural History. Watch a Native-American ceremony and the making of authentic weapons and pottery. | 2301 W. River Rd. | 937/268–8199 | $5 | Tues.–Sat. 9–5, Sun. noon–5.

University of Dayton. The university is one of the Midwest's premier small universities, with 9,000 students and an emphasis on programs in the humanities. The campus is open to tours and visits daily. Student theater groups present a variety of productions throughout the year. | 300 College Park Ave. | 937/229–4114 | Free | Daily.

Woodland Cemetery and Arboretum. Several of Dayton's most famous citizens, including the Wright brothers and writer Erma Bombeck, are buried in this picturesque cemetery. | 118 Woodland Ave. | 937/222–1431 | Free | Daily, dawn–dusk.

Wegerzyn Gardens MetroPark. These are formal gardens: there are Victorian, English, and Federal theme gardens, as well as rose, shade, and children's gardens. You can walk on a boardwalk through a wetland woods or along a nature trail. The Stillwater River runs through the park. | 1301 E. Siebenthaler Ave. | 937/277–6545 | Free | Daily, 8–dusk.

Wright Cycle Company Shop. This printing and bicycle store was operated by brothers Orville and Wilbur Wright from 1895 to 1897. The re-created shop now contains bicycles and machinery of the late 1800s. | 22 S. Williams St. | 937/225–7705 | Free | Memorial Day–Labor Day, Mon.–Sat. 8:30–4:30, Sun. 11–4:30; Sept.–May, Wed.–Sat. 8:30-4:30, Sun. 11:30–4:30.

Wright-Patterson Air Force Base. The base is home to one of the U.S. Air Force's largest and most relied-upon arsenals of military aircraft. | Springfield St. | 937/255–3284 | Free | Daily 9–5.

The **National Aviation Hall of Fame** honors America's greatest pilots and astronauts like the Mercury 7 astronauts and the first men on the moon. | 1100 Spatz St. | 937/256–0944 | Free | Daily 9–5.

The **United States Air Force Museum** is the oldest and largest military aviation museum in the world, with 300 airplanes and thousands of aviation artifacts, including missiles used during the Persian Gulf War. The newest exhibit is the Air Force One jet used to transport the body of President John F. Kennedy back to Washington after his assassination in 1963. It joins a collection which includes other presidential aircraft, from as far back as Franklin D. Roosevelt. | 1100 Spatz St. | 937/255–3284 | Daily 9–5 | Free.

The **Wright Brothers Memorial** is a tribute to the brothers who achieved the dream of flight in 1903 at Kitty Hawk, N.C. The site overlooks the field where the men perfected their flying machine, created the world's first airport, and ran a flight school. | Kauffman and National Rds. | Free | Daily 8–8.

Wright State University. Named for Dayton's aviation pioneers, Orville and Wilbur Wright, the university serves nearly 16,000 students with programs leading to more than 100 undergraduate and 40 graduate degrees. Concerts are held at the Nutter Center | 3640 Col. Glenn Hwy. | 937/775–3333 | www.wright.edu/aboutwsu | Free | Daily.

The **Irvin J. Nutter Center,** on the Wright State University campus, is Dayton's principal concert and entertainment venue. | 3640 Col. Glenn Hwy. | 937/775–3498 | www.nuttercenter.com.

ON THE CALENDAR

MAR.: *Dayton Home and Garden Show.* Check out the latest trends in home fashion and garden accessories at this annual four-day event that occupies the Dayton Convention Center. | 22 E. 5th St. | 937/333–4700.

JUNE: *CITYFOLK Festival.* Well-known national acts from across the country perform in this celebration of folk music, held the third weekend in June (in 2003, it'll be July 4th weekend). The events, which are held indoors and out, are focused along Main Street in downtown Dayton, from First to Fourth Sts. | 937/223–3655.

SEPT.: *Montgomery County Fair.* More than 50,000 people flock to the Montgomery County Fairgrounds for the week-long activities, with livestock shows, games, rides. The fun begins the Wednesday before Labor Day. | 143 S. Main St. | 937/224–1619.

OCT.: *Oktoberfest.* The Dayton Art Institute celebrates all things German. The festivities take place at the institute's lavish building overlooking downtown Dayton. | 456 Belmonte Park N | 937/223–5277 or 800/296–4426.

Dining

Amar India. Indian. Pictures of India cover the walls of this suburban restaurant, about 10 mi south of downtown Dayton, known for its northern Indian cuisine and lunch buffet. The menu includes many vegetarian dishes, curry chicken, and the Mattu Special—a bowl of chicken tandoori with spices and onions stuffed in a pastry shell and deep fried. | 2759 Miamisburg-Centerville Rd., Centerville | 937/439–9005 | $7–$14 | AE, D, DC, MC, V.

Anticoli's. Italian. This restaurant has been serving up classic Italian fare since 1951. The menu includes chicken juliano, veal parmesan, lasagna, and New York Tuscany steak. The place is dark with Italian statues and paintings. Kids' menu. | 3045 Salem Ave. (Rte. 49) | 937/277–2264 | Closed Mon. | $12–$18 | AE, D, DC, MC, V.

Barnsider. Steak. This casual steak house with a dark rustic interior has been serving since 1975. The menu includes New York strip steak, filet mignon, prime rib, and lamb chops. Kids' menu. | 5202 N. Main St. | 937/277–1332 | No lunch. Open Sun. at noon | $10–$20 | AE, MC, V.

Bravo! Italian Kitchen. Italian. Rich sauces and large portions are the draws of this Columbus-based restaurant chain known for its wood-grilled Tuscan cuisine and pizza. Kids' menu. It's in Centerville, about 10 mi south of downtown Dayton. | 2418 Centerville Rd., Centerville | 937/439–1294 | $19–$32 | AE, D, DC, MC, V.

China Cottage. Chinese. Fresh seafood, chicken, beef, and pork dishes prepared in the Szechuan and Mandarin traditions are served in large portions at this restaurant with cathedral ceilings. A popular dish is the walnut chicken. | 6290 Far Hills Ave. (Rte. 48) | 937/434–2622 | $7–$10 | AE, DC, MC, V.

Elinor's Amber Rose. Eastern European. Traditional German, Russian, and Eastern European dishes are the specialties at this eatery with an old general store motif. The menu includes home-style versions of German sauerbraten, Russian beef stroganoff, cabbage rolls, and schnitzels. Pastas and filet mignon round out the menu. | 1400 Valley St. | 937/228–2511 | Closed Sun. No dinner Mon. and Tues. | $9–$23 | AE, D, DC, MC, V.

Elsa's Mexican Restaurant. Mexican. This restaurant is famous for its house-special drinks, the Bad Juan, with top-secret ingredients, and the Gringo, for the more meek. A few drinks

A FLOOD—AND A RAINBOW

The flood that swept over Dayton and the Miami Valley in March 1913 took the region by surprise. The waters rose dramatically, killed more than 300 people, and destroyed more than 1,000 homes.

When the flood waters receded, area residents faced an even greater problem than the mud, filth, and devastation. Preventing another such catastrophe meant raising $2 million—immediately. Dayton had just lost $100 million in land and buildings, and people were plenty poor in spirit. But in a little over a month, not $2 million, but $2.15 million had been contributed to the flood prevention fund. Leading the effort was John H. Patterson, co-founder of the National Cash Register Co. in Dayton, now corporate giant NCR Corp. With the money in hand, Patterson and his committee promptly hired Moran Engineering Company of Memphis to design an extensive flood-control system in the Miami Valley to prevent future disasters. The project involved moving some 13 million cubic yards of dirt. By 1922, five giant earthen dams were operating throughout the Miami Valley region. Today, the dams not only keep Dayton and the surrounding region safe from floods, but they're also the sites of popular parks and recreation areas, offering walking trails, biking, picnicking, and other outdoor activities.

© Corbis

and a totally stuffed burrito with your choice of meat filling will have you throwing your sombrero to your amigo and doing the cha-cha. | 3618 Linden Ave. | 937/252–9635 | $7–$12 | AE, D, DC, MC, V.

J. Alexander's. American/Casual. This popular chain in the suburbs about 10 mi south of downtown Dayton serves prime rib in a dimly lit dining room with lots of dark woodwork and a stone floor. The menu includes beef, pork, seafood, and chicken dishes including Delmonico steak and barbecue ribs. Kids' menu. | 7970 Washington Village Dr., Centerville | 937/435–4441 | $8–$22 | AE, D, DC, MC, V.

Jay's Seafood. Seafood. This restaurant in a renovated 1850s gristmill has wooden tables, floors, and beams; velvet upholstered chairs; and an antique mahogany bar. The seafood combo appetizer is enough oysters Rockefeller and clams casino for two. Menu highlights include Alaskan king salmon, sole stuffed with crab and topped with lobster sauce, and swordfish. Kids' menu. | 225 E. 6th St. | 937/222–2892 | No lunch | $14–$32 | AE, D, DC, MC, V.

L'Auberge. French. Original art adorns the inside of this sophisticated French eatery known for pâté, imported fresh seafood, and game. Some popular dishes include chateaubriand, roasted rack of lamb, sautéed John Dory (a type of fish) and sea bass. There's live entertainment. L'Auberge is in a suburb about 5 mi south of downtown Dayton. | 4120 Far Hills Ave., Kettering | 937/299–5536 | Jacket required | Closed Sun. | $30–$45 | AE, DC, MC, V.

Lincoln Park Grille. American. The large front patio offers diners a view of the entertainment in the nearby Fraze Pavilion while they eat. The menu has an Italian accent and includes grilled pork chops with chipotle apple glaze, New York strip, and barbecued duck with bacon-wrapped scallops and corn coulis. Live entertainment every night but Wed. | 580 Lincoln Park Blvd. | 937/293–6293 | No lunch Sat. Closed Sun. | $12–$30 | AE, D, DC, MC, V.

Oakwood Club. Contemporary. This dark suburban eatery with tableclothed tables, Tiffany glass, and original artwork serves first-rate steaks and prime rib. The lobster tails and potato-crusted sea bass are also noteworthy. It's in Oakwood, about 4 mi south of downtown Dayton. | 2414 Far Hills Ave., Oakwood | 937/293–6973 | Closed Sun. | $18–$25 | AE, DC, MC, V.

Olivia's. Contemporary. Works of local artists cover the walls and white linens cover the tables at this dining spot in the Kettering Tower. The menu includes roast pepper duck, pike, salmon, pork, beef, and veal. | 40 N. Main St. | 937/222–6771 | Closed Sun. and Mon. No lunch Sat. | $18–$24 | AE, D, DC, MC, V.

Peasant Stock on the River. French. Dine in a small atrium at the front of this restaurant on the Great Miami River. The interior has wood beams and stained-glass detailing. The menu includes chicken cordon bleu, filet of beef cordon bleu, prime rib, and steaks. There's live entertainment nightly. | 424 E. Stroop Rd. | 937/224–0535 | Closed Sun. No lunch Sat. | $21–$36 | AE, D, DC, MC, V.

Pine Club. Steak. This is a busy steak and chops house; prepare for a wait. Among the choice cuts is a 36-ounce porterhouse for two. | 1926 Brown St. | 937/228–7463 | Reservations not accepted | Closed Sun. No lunch | $15–$35 | No credit cards.

Steve Kao's. Chinese. Popular dishes at this casual restaurant are Iceland crab fish, red snapper, walleye, Szechuan chicken, Cantonese-style chicken, and Peking duck. The menu also includes stir-fry and noodle dishes. | 8270 Springboro Pike | 937/435–5261 | $8–$13 | AE, D, DC, MC, V.

Sweeny's Seafood. Seafood. In the heart of old Centerville, just 10 mi south of Dayton, is this celebration of the fruits of the sea. While you dine, you can watch the saltwater fish swimming in the 1,000-gallon tank. Dinner selections include grilled salmon in horseradish crust or grilled tilapia with a lemon parmesan crust. If you aren't feeling fishy, there are sandwiches, pastas, and burgers, too. | 28 W. Franklin, Centerville | 937/291–3474 | Closed Mon. No lunch on weekends | $8–$18 | AE, D, MC, V.

Thomato's. Mediterranean. The menu changes with the season at this restaurant with a New York motif. Chicken, salmon, and steak dishes are always available, but prepared with ingredients in season and complimentary sauces. One dessert, the Rattlesnake Club pressed chocolate cake (named for the Rattlesnake Club in Chicago where it was first served) is a permanent fixture. The restaurant has the most wines by the glass in Dayton. | 110 N. Main St. | 937/228–3333 | Closed Sun. | $21–$28 | AE, D, DC, MC, V.

Welton's. Contemporary. Beef is the big draw at this New York-style bistro with lots of windows, lanterns on the tables, and black wrought iron. Filet mignon, sirloin, and ribs are popular, but the menu also includes fresh fish. There's an extensive wine list and cigar smoking at the bar. | 4614 Wilmington Pike | 937/293–2233 | Closed Sun. | $14–$20 | AE, D, MC, V.

Lodging

Best Western Executive Hotel. This two-story chain is 5 mi southeast of the airport, right off I–75. Lush greenery covers the lobby, which has an overhead skylight. Rooms range from standard rooms with twin beds to executive whirlpool suites. Kids under 12 stay free. Restaurant, bar. In-room data ports, some microwaves, some refrigerators, some in-room hot tubs. Cable TV. Indoor pool. Sauna. Gym. Laundry facilities, laundry service. Business services. Airport shuttle. Some pets allowed. | 2401 Needmore Rd. | 937/278–5711 or 800/528–1234 | fax 937/278–6048 | www.bestwestern.com | 231 rooms | $79–$119 | AE, D, DC, MC, V.

Comfort Inn. This small two-story motel is in the north part of the metro area, 6 mi from downtown. Rooms have two doubles or a king-size bed. Complimentary Continental breakfast. In-room data ports, microwaves (in suites), refrigerators (in suites), in-room hot tubs. Cable TV. Hot tub. Exercise equipment. Free parking. | 7907 Brandt Pike, Huber Heights | 937/237–7477 or 800/228–5150 | fax 937/237–5187 | www.comfortinn.com | 53 rooms, 6 suites | $75, $120 suites | AE, D, DC, MC, V.

Comfort Inn-Dayton North. This hotel is just off I–75, 7 mi north of downtown Dayton, in a cluster of other hotels and chain restaurants. Rooms come with two queen beds, one king, or a suite with a king bed and queen sofa bed. Complimentary Continental breakfast. In-room data ports, some microwaves, some refrigerators. Indoor pool. Hot tub. | 7125 Miller La. | 937/890–9995 or 800/ 228–5150 | fax 937/890–9995 | www.comfortinn.com | 56 rooms | $79–$100 | AE, D, DC, MC, V.

Cross Country Inn. The regional chain's Dayton two-story property, built in 1988, is 15 mi north of downtown, near restaurants and shops. Rooms have two doubles or a king-size bed. Cable TV. Pool. Business services. | 9325 N. Main St., Englewood | 937/836–8339 or 800/ 621–1429 | fax 937/836–1772 | www.crosscountryinns.com | 120 rooms | $53 | AE, D, DC, MC, V.

Crowne Plaza Dayton. Connected to the downtown Dayton Convention Center, this 14-story hotel has bright rooms with wood desks and armoires. Each has two doubles or a king-size bed. Restaurant, bar with entertainment, room service. Cable TV. Pool. Hot tub. Exercise equipment. Business services. Some pets allowed. | 33 E. 5th St. | 937/224–0800 or 800/ 227–6963 | fax 937/224–3913 | www.crowneplaza.com | 284 rooms | $99, $249–$349 suites | AE, D, DC, MC, V.

Dayton Days Inn Wright-Patterson A.F.B./Museum. This two-story chain, right off Route 4, is almost a bed-and-breakfast, with a Bob Evans restaurant right outside your door. One room is fully handicapped-accessible. Smoking and no-smoking rooms are available. In-room data ports, some microwaves, some refrigerators. Laundry facilities. Pets allowed. | 1891 Hersham Rd. | 937/236–8083 or 800/325–2525 | fax 937/236–8083 | www.daysinn.com | 47 rooms | $56 | AE, D, DC, MC, V.

Fairfield Inn by Marriott–Dayton North. This three-story motel built in 1989 is 15 minutes from downtown. Complimentary Continental breakfast. In-room data ports. Cable TV. Pool. Business services. | 6960 Miller La. | 937/898–1120 or 800/288–2800 | fax 937/898–1120 | www.fairfieldinn.com | 135 rooms | $75 | AE, D, DC, MC, V.

Hampton Inn. This three-story brick motel built in 1995 is 25 minutes east of downtown, off I–675. Complimentary Continental breakfast. In-room data ports, refrigerators (in suites). Cable TV. Indoor pool. Hot tub. Business services. Free parking. Some pets allowed.

| 2550 Paramount Pl., Fairborn | 937/429–5505 or 800/426–7866 | fax 937/429–6828 | www.hampton-inn.com | 63 rooms, 8 suites | $84, $93 suites | AE, D, DC, MC, V.

Hampton Inn-Dayton South. This four-story concrete motel is 10 mi from downtown and five minutes from the Dayton Mall. Complimentary Continental breakfast. Cable TV. Pool. Exercise equipment. Business services. | 8099 Old Yankee St. | 937/436–3700 or 800/426–7866 | fax 937/436–2995 | www.hampton-inn.com | 130 rooms | $80 | AE, D, DC, MC, V.

Holiday Inn I–675 Conference Center. This six-story brick hotel built in 1987 is 15 mi from downtown in a suburban area. Rooms have a work desk and one or two doubles or a king-sized bed. Restaurant, bar with entertainment, room service. Cable TV. Indoor pool. Hot tub. Exercise equipment. Business services. Airport shuttle. Free parking. | 2800 Presidential Dr., Fairborn | 937/426–7800 or 800/465–4329 | fax 937/426–1284 | www.holiday-inn.com | 204 rooms | $109 | AE, D, DC, MC, V.

Homewood Suites Fairborn. The roomy suites at this Hilton-owned property, 1 mi from Wright Patterson Air Force Base, have kitchens and separate living areas and bedrooms. Some have fireplaces. The two- and three-story buildings were built in 1990. It's 20 minutes from downtown. Picnic area, complimentary Continental breakfast. In-room data ports, microwaves, refrigerators. Cable TV, in-room VCRs, and movies. Pool. Hot tub. Exercise equipment. Laundry facilities. Business services. Free parking. Some pets allowed. | 2750 Presidential Dr., Fairborn | 937/429–0600 or 800/225–5466 | fax 937/429–6311 | www.home-woodsuites.com | 128 suites in 3 buildings | $119 suites | AE, D, DC, MC, V.

Howard Johnson. This two-story hacienda-style motor inn is 6 mi north of downtown and 5 mi south of the airport. Rooms have two doubles or a king-size bed. Bar, complimentary Continental breakfast. Cable TV. Pool. Laundry facilities. Business services. Airport shuttle. Free parking. Some pets allowed (fee). | 7575 Poe Ave. | 937/454–0550 or 800/654–4656 | fax 937/454–5566 | www.hojo.com | 121 rooms | $60–$70 | AE, D, DC, MC, V.

Marriott. This hotel five minutes from downtown is one of Dayton's largest lodging properties. Rooms have two doubles or a king-sized bed. Guests in concierge rooms have access to a private lounge. The six-story white concrete building opened in 1982. Restaurant, bar with entertainment, room service. In-room data ports. Cable TV. Indoor-outdoor pool. Hot tub. Exercise equipment. Laundry facilities. Business services. Free parking. Some pets allowed. | 1414 S. Patterson Blvd. | 937/223–1000 or 800/228–9290 | fax 937/223–7853 | www.marriott.com | 399 rooms | $129 | AE, D, DC, MC, V.

Quality Inn-Dayton South. This two-story brick motel is 9 mi south of downtown Dayton and 1 mi east of the Dayton Mall. Complimentary Continental breakfast. Some kitchenettes, some refrigerators. Cable TV. Pool. Business services. Free parking. | 1944 Miamisburg-Centerville Rd. | 937/435–1550 or 800/228–5151 | fax 937/438–1878 | www.qualityinn.com | 72 rooms in 2 buildings | $58 | AE, D, DC, MC, V.

Ramada Inn–North Airport. This two-story accommodation is 20 minutes north of Dayton, directly off I–75. The area is rich with restaurants. Complimentary Continental breakfast, restaurant, room service. In-room data ports, some refrigerators. Pool. Laundry facilities, laundry service. Business services. Airport shuttle. Small pets allowed. | 4079 Little York Rd. | 937/890–9500 or 800/228-2828 | fax 937/890–8525 | www.ramada.com/ramada.html | 136 rooms | $65–$135 | AE, D, DC, MC, V.

Red Roof Inn-North. This two-story motel built in the mid-'70s is 7 mi from downtown. Cable TV. Business services. Some pets allowed. | 7370 Miller La. | 937/898–1054 or 800/843–7663 | fax 937/898–1059 | www.redroof.com | 109 rooms | $55 | AE, D, DC, MC, V.

Yesterday Bed and Breakfast. This two-story taupe-and-beige Victorian home, built in 1882, is 10 mi south of downtown Dayton. You can find solace on the wraparound porch or on the brick patio in back. The double house is shared with the innkeepers, who try to keep the place old-fashioned, as its name suggests. Inside, the home reflects its Victorian roots with period antiques, collectibles, lacy curtains, and frilly rooms. Downstairs has the old hardwood floors but the upstairs rooms are carpeted. Complimentary breakfast. No room phones, no TV. No kids under 12. | 39 S. Main St., Centerville | 937/433–0785 | 3 rooms | $75–$85 | No credit cards.

DEFIANCE

MAP 14, A3

(Nearby towns listed: Van Wert, Wauseon)

French missionaries were the first Europeans to wander among the Native American tribes who lived in the area between 1672 and 1712. In 1793 the most famous council of the Indian tribes in North America was held at an Indian trading center, which the French had named Grand Glaize. This was at the confluence of the Maumee and Auglaize Rivers, the eventual site of the city of Defiance.

Defiance, 55 mi southwest of Toledo, was named after Fort Defiance, which was built in 1794 by General "Mad" Anthony Wayne, who had been sent to subdue the Native Americans and put an end to British influence in this area. Fort Defiance become known as the strongest fort ever built by Wayne in his military campaigns. He defeated the Indians during the Battle of Fallen Timbers, and later Fort Defiance was abandoned. In the Peace Treaty of 1795 the Native Americans gave up their Ohio lands. Today the city has a population of 18,000.

Information: Defiance Area Chamber of Commerce | 615 W. 3rd St., 43512 | 419/782–7946 or 800/686–4382 | defiancechamber.com.

Attractions

Auglaize Village. Seventeen new and restored buildings make up this re-created 19th-century village and farm museum. Restored buildings (circa 1860-1920) include a cider mill, sawmill, doctor's office, blacksmith shop, and one-room schoolhouse. A number of festivals are held here throughout the year. | 12296 Krouse Rd. | 419/784–0107 or 419/782–7255 | www.defiance-online.comçauglaize | $2 | June–Labor Day, weekends 11–4.

Fort Defiance Park. This city park was the site of Fort Defiance, built by General Anthony Wayne in 1794. It has a scenic view of the confluence of the Maumee and Auglaize Rivers. | Fort St. and Washington Ave. | 419/354–6223 | Free | Daily, dawn–dusk.

Independence Dam State Park. This 600-acre park 4 mi east of Defiance has boating, fishing, camping, and hiking. | Rte. 424 | 419/784–3263 | Free | Daily.

ON THE CALENDAR

SEPT.: *Johnny Appleseed Festival.* Auglaize Village hosts this annual fall festival. Highlights include apple butter and cider making and harvest demonstrations. | 12296 Krouse Rd. | 419/393–2662.

Dining

Bud's. American. No matter what you choose to eat at this family place across from the courthouse, save room for a slice of homemade pie. This soup-to-nuts place makes nearly 50 different kinds every day. Beforehand, you will find daily specials and a menu that appeals to meat eaters with its burgers, Swiss steak, cheesesteak, ham, veal, and liver and onions, all served with a choice of slaw, applesauce, cottage cheese, or a house salad. | 505 W. 2nd St. | 419/782–9101 | Closed Sun. | $5–$8 | No credit cards.

Kissner's. American. This Victorian building and bustling business has remained in the Kissner family for some three-quarters of a century. The building, which was built in 1888 and opened as a tavern in 1901, has its original tin ceilings and a 12-by-28-ft back bar. In the wee hours, Kissner's caters to both farmers and businessmen, with coffee and donuts and biscuits and gravy. Lunch includes chef salads and plate lunches, such as Swiss steak and dressing or beef and noodles. The dinner menu ranges from lobster and king crab to chicken strips and fries. Kids' menu. | 524 Clinton St. | 419/782–1116 | Closed Sun. | $8–$13 | MC, V.

Lester's Diner. American. Pink neon, stainless steel, and chrome give this family-style diner a 1950s look, although it was built in the '60s. The menu includes baked chicken, Swiss steak, barbecued spare ribs, and meat-loaf sandwiches. It's in Bryan, about 15 mi north-west of Defiance. Kids' menu. | 223 S. Main St., Bryan | 419/636–1818 | Reservations not accepted | $5–$10 | MC, V.

Lodging

Comfort Inn. This two-story brick-and-concrete motel is ½ mi from downtown. It opened in 1992. Rooms have two doubles or a king-sized bed. Complimentary Continental breakfast. In-room data ports, some refrigerators. Cable TV. Indoor pool. Hot tub. Laundry facilities. | 1900 N. Clinton St. | 419/784–4900 or 800/228–5150 | fax 419/784–5555 | www.comfortinn.com | 72 rooms | $72 | AE, D, DC, MC, V.

Days Inn. This two-story chain motel was built in the early '60s and is 1½-mi from downtown. Restaurant, bar, room service. Cable TV. Indoor pool. | 1835 N. Clinton St. | 419/782–5555 or 800/325–2525 | fax 419/782–8085 | www.daysinn.com | 121 rooms | $66 | AE, D, DC, MC, V.

Defiance Super 8 Motel. Just off Route 25 is this two-story motel. Opt for a Jacuzzi suite and you can go from a hot soak right into bed. Complimentary Continental breakfast. Some in-room hot tubs. Laundry service. Business services. | 1902 N. Clinton St. | 419/782–8000 or 800/848–8888 | fax 419/782–4645 | www.super8.com | 50 rooms | $43–$75 | MC, V.

Frank Baker Inn. Frank Baker, a prominent Defiance citizen, built this modified Queen Anne downtown in 1908. Its doors opened as a bed-and-breakfast in 1996. Great care has been taken to restore the original treasures of the home, such as the leaded-glass windows and intricate woodwork, and the home is filled with period-appropriate antiques. Two parlors provide reading materials, and fresh cookies are baked every day. Rooms have antique beds, Victorian needlepoint cushions, old family photographs, and walnut and elm furniture. Complimentary breakfast. TV in common area. | 821 S. Clinton St. | 419/784–5027 | 3 rooms | $65 | No credit cards.

DELAWARE

MAP 14, C4

(Nearby towns listed: Columbus, Marion, Mount Gilead, Mount Vernon)

Once part of the Northwest Territory, Delaware is 27 mi north of Columbus, in approximately the center of the state. The Olentangy Indian Caverns and Ohio Frontierland are popular sites, as is Perkins Observatory, the only observatory in Ohio state.

Information: **Delaware Area Chamber of Commerce** | 46 E. Winter St., 43015 | 740/369–6221 | www.delaware.org.

Attractions

Alum Creek State Park. Alum Creek is 9,000 acres of reservoir fields, and woodlands, just 22 mi north of Columbus. A 7½ mi hiking trail curving in and out from the shoreline begins at the New Galena Road boat launch on the east side of the reservoir. Boating and camping are permitted. | 3615 S. Old State Rd. | 740/548–4631 | Free | Daily.

Delaware County Historical Society Museum. This two-building complex offers the 1876 Nash House, with mid- to late-19th-century appointments, including hand-carved furniture made in the county, and the Museum Annex, with local Indian artifacts and a historical and genealogical library. | 157 E. William St. | 740/369-3831 | Free | Mid-Mar.–mid-Nov., Wed., Thurs., Sat., Sun., 2–4:30.

Oakhaven Golf Course. This 18-hole, par-72, championship course designed by Mike Zimmerman has a clubhouse, banquet facilities, and a pro shop. Lessons are available. Because the course is open year-round, there are 33 covered tees. On weekends, you must play 18 holes. | 2871 U.S. 23 N | 740/548-5636 or 800/504-6281 | fax 740/363-9900 | $38 with a cart | Daily.

Ohio Wesleyan University. Nestled in a forest of 55 acres, this 150-year-old college is home to 1,800 students. You can call to arrange a guided tour weekdays from September through May. | 61 S. Sandusky | 740/369-4431 or 740/368-2000 | fax 740/368-3299 | Free | Daily.

Olentangy Indian Caverns and Ohio Frontierland. These caverns were formed millions of years ago by the force of an underground river cutting through solid limestone rock. The Wyandot Indians found shelter here; today you can take a tour through their winding passages which descend 105 ft below ground. Also at the site is Ohio Frontierland, a replica of a Western town and an Indian village geared toward young explorers. | 1779 Home Rd. | 740/548-7917 | $8 | Apr. 1–Oct. 31, daily 9:30–5.

Perkins Observatory. Admission gets you a tour of the observatory, an astronomy lecture, and a peek at the universe through a high-powered telescope. Call ahead to get tickets. | 3199 Columbus Pike/U.S. 23 | 740/363-1257 | fax 740/363-1258 | www.perkins-observatory.org | $5 | May–Aug., weekends at 9 PM; Sept.–May, weekends at 8 PM.

ON THE CALENDAR

AUG.: *Highland Folk Festival.* More than two dozen bands get together for this two-day festival at Cashman's Cattle Farm. A variety of folk music is performed, including Irish, Scottish, and Appalachian. | Rte. 42 N | 740/363-6073.

SEPT.: *Delaware County Fair.* Five days of Grand Circuit harness racing on the world's fastest half-mile track climax with The Little Brown Jug, the largest attended harness race in the world, run on the third Thursday after Labor Day. The fair begins the Saturday before that race. Other crowd favorites are the demolition derby and concerts by nationally known performers. | 236 Pennsylvania Ave. | 740/362-3851.

Dining

Branding Iron. American. Ten miles south of town, you can spot the hitching posts and redwood facade that mark this eatery. Grilled steaks, ribs, fish, and kabobs are popular here. Kids' menu. Sunday brunch. | 1400 Stratford Rd. | 740/363-1846 | Closed Mon. and first 2 weeks in Aug. No lunch | $8–$15 | D, MC, V.

The Brown Jug. American. Delaware native Curly Smart won the first Brown Jug harness race, and this two-story brick family restaurant was named in his honor. The menu has a lot of modified Italian favorites, such as spaghetti and meatballs, and tons of subs stuffed with veal, stromboli ingredients, and the Ohio treasure, buffalo chicken. | 13–15 W. William St. | 740/369-3471 | Closed Sun. | $5–$15 | MC, V.

Bun's of Delaware. American. You get family-style service in Bun's three dining rooms in this 1864 Victorian building. There's roast turkey with dressing as an entrée and chocolate fudge cake and apple dumplings for dessert. Kids' menu. | 6 W. Winter St. | 740/363-3731 | Closed Mon. | $12–$20 | AE, D, MC, V.

Michael Oliver's. Contemporary. Familiar dishes are served with a Creole kick at this small dining room in the Best Western Delaware Hotel. Entrées include pork roulade, seafood jambalaya, and blackened New York strip steak. Kids' menu. Early bird dinners. Sun. brunch. | 351 S. Sandusky St. | 740/363-1262 or 800/837-1262 | $8–$26 | AE, D, MC, V.

Lodging

Days Inn. This hotel, which is 16 mi east of Delaware, gives guests free access to a nearby community pool and fitness center. Picnic area, complimentary Continental breakfast. In-room data ports, some kitchenettes, some in-room hot tubs. Cable TV. Business services. Some pets allowed. | 16510 Square Dr., Marysville | 937/644–8821 or 877/644–8821 | www.travelweb.com/daysinn.html | 74 rooms | $69–$99 | AE, D, DC, MC, V.

Travelodge. This hotel is in front of the Delaware County Fairgrounds on State Route 23N Restaurant. Cable TV. Business services. Some pets allowed (fee). | 1001 U.S. 23N | 740/369–4421 or 800/255–3050 | fax 740/362–9090 | www.travelodge.com | 35 rooms | $52 | AE, D, DC, MC, V.

Welcome Home Inn Bed and Breakfast. This Southern-style farm home is nestled on six wooded acres about 10 mi southwest of Delaware. You can rock in a wicker rocker on the wraparound front porch and enjoy the woodland critters. Some rooms have private decks, two rooms have private baths, and oak antique accent pieces are scattered throughout the home. The dining room has a grand piano and leaded stained-glass windows. Your arrival is met with homemade sugar cookies. Weather permitting, breakfast is served on the screened-in porch. Ask for a slice of poppy bread for breakfast. Complimentary breakfast. No room phones. Basketball court. | 6640 Home Rd. | 740/881–6588 or 800/381–0364 | www.bbonline.com/oh/welcomehome | 4 rooms | $75–$110 | AE, D, MC, V.

DOVER

(Nearby towns listed: Berlin, Canton, Gnadenhutten, New Philadelphia, Sugarcreek, Zoar)

Dover was founded by two brothers-in-law who took a horseback trip from Baltimore, Maryland, in 1802 and liked the fertile plateau they found at the confluence of the Tuscarawas River and Sugarcreek. Dover soon grew from a grist mill at the Tuscarawas River ford to a canal town and then an industrial center along the railroad. The city was always called Dover, but the post office was called Canal Dover for many years because of other Dover, Ohio, post offices that were later abolished.

Information: Tuscarawas County Convention and Visitors Bureau | 125 McDonalds Dr. SW, New Philadelphia, 44663 | 330/339–5453 | www.neohiotravel.com or www.doverohio.com.

Attractions

J.E. Reeves Victorian Home and Museum. This 19th-century farmhouse, remodeled by a Dover industrialist in 1900, has a leaded-glass front door and a carved oak stairway that testify to the wealth of the former owner. Seventeen rooms and a third-floor ballroom are restored and furnished with antiques, chandeliers, and fine china pieces from the era and from the family's estate. | 325 E. Iron Ave. | 330/343–7040 | $5 | May–Sept., Tues.–Sun. 10–4. Off-season hours by appointment.

Warther Carvings. This museum shows the amazing work of master carver Ernest Warther, who took up carving as a hobby and built his workshop in 1912. His highly intricate wooden carvings of models of steam locomotives, done only with a knife and files, document the history of trains from 250 B.C. to the present. On a guided tour you can see a model of an 18th-century steel mill and his Tree of Pliers, more than 500 pairs of pliers carved out of one piece of wood. There's also an exhibit of his wife's collection of 73,000 buttons. The Swiss-style flower gardens are a nice place to stroll. The last tour begins an hour before closing. | 331 Karl Ave. | 330/343–7513 | www.warthers.com | $7 | Mar.–Nov., daily 9–5; Dec.–Feb., daily 10–4.

Dining

Dover Station. American. Meat loaf and mashed potatoes, chicken, pork chops, and other traditional dishes are on the menu. Old-fashioned wooden tables and chairs evoke the early

19th-century canal era. | 221 W. Third St. | 330/364–9951 | No dinner Sun. | $5–$15 | No credit cards.

Goshen Dairy. Deli. The family-owned Goshen Dairy has been in business for more than 100 years making ice cream, butter, whipping cream, and chip dips. All are for sale at this convenience store and deli in one. Subs, sandwiches, coffee drinks, nuts, candies, and cakes are also available. | 320 N. Wooster Ave. | 330/343–8515 | Closed Christmas | $1.30–$5 | No credit cards.

Lodging

Comfort Inn. Just off I–77, this reliable chain is close to Amish Country and the Pro Football Hall of Fame. Room phones, cable TV. Indoor pool. | 2024 Rte. 39 NW | 330/364–7724 or 800/762–6474 | fax 330/364–7728 | www.comfortinn.com | 100 rooms | $50–$75 | AE, D, MC, V.

Hospitality Inn. This medium-sized, independently owned motel is next to two restaurants and the Warther Museum. Cable TV. Pool. Exercise equipment. | 889 Commercial Pkwy. | 330/364–7724 or 800/762–6474 | fax 330/364–7728 | 100 rooms | $60 | AE, D, MC, V.

Olde World Bed & Breakfast. Antiques, linens, and decorations give each room a different theme, from Victorian to Mediterranean. The Amish country-style breakfasts are made with ingredients from the garden. A tea room is open Tuesday and Wednesday. Complimentary breakfast. TV in common area, outdoor hot tub. No kids. | 2982 Rte. 516 NW | 330/343–1333 or 800/447–1273 | fax 330/364–8022 | www.oldeworldbb.com | 5 rooms | $60–$105 | MC, V.

EASTLAKE

MAP 14, E2

(Nearby towns listed: Beachwood, Cleveland, Mentor, Painesville)

Eastlake has only been a city since 1951, but people have lived in this northeastern part of Ohio for more than three centuries. The Erie Indians had a village near what is now Lakeshore Boulevard and Reeves Road over 300 years ago. A French trading post, Charlton (in present-day Eastlake), was established at the mouth of the Chagrin River in 1750. In 1830–40, settlers came here from New York State, having purchased land from the Connecticut Land Company for $7 to $10 per acre. A streetcar line was brought to the region in 1897 and the Eastlake area began to grow and prosper. Agriculture was the main source of income at first, but retail and industrial development soon followed.

Information: Eastlake Chamber of Commerce | 35150 Lake Shore Blvd., 44095 | 440/951–3600.

Attractions

Chagrin River Park. This 101-acre park has something for everyone. You can take one of the winding hiking trails, have a picnic, visit the playground, or play a game of volleyball. Fishing and bird-watching are popular activities. Look for great blue herons, kingfishers, bank swallows, sandpipers, and blue-winged teal. | Off Reeves Rd., near Lost Nation Rd. | 216/639–7275 | www.lprca.on.ca/chgrnrv.htm | Free | Daily, dawn–dusk.

ON THE CALENDAR

AUG.: *National Ribfest Classic.* Contestants from all over the country vie for rib-making honors at this event, held outdoors under a tent in Eastlake. The ribs, and the sauces, are for sale. There's also entertainment. | Erie Rd. and Lakeshore Blvd. | 440/951–1416.

Dining

Ice Breakers on the River. American. The dining room has a nautical feel with buoys and fishing nets strewn about. In warmer weather, you can sit outside under a big blue-and-white umbrella, and enjoy the sunshine and the activity on the Chagrin River, and enjoy the sunshine. The potato-flake-breaded walleye is a hit, as is the sausage sandwich, both of which are accompanied by a fried pickle. There is a selection of salads, including the standard Cobb as well as a shrimp spinach salad. Kids' menu. | 35901 Lakeshore Blvd. | 440/951–5373 | Closed Mon. | $6–$17 | AE, D, DC, MC, V.

Lodging

Radisson Hotel and Conference–Cleveland Eastlake. The $4 million renovation project, completed in 1998, makes this five-story deluxe accommodation, just 14 mi east of downtown Cleveland, all the more appealing. Rooms have cherrywood furniture and a mauve, purple, and tan color scheme. Kids stay free. Restaurant, bar, room service. In-room data ports, some microwaves, some refrigerators. Indoor pool. Gym. Laundry service. Business services. | 35000 Curtis Blvd. | 440/953–8000 or 800/333–3333 | fax 440/953–1706 | www.radisson.com | 126 rooms | $119–$129 | AE, D, DC, MC, V.

EAST LIVERPOOL

MAP 14, F4

(Nearby towns listed: Alliance, Steubenville)

On the Ohio River in Columbiana County, East Liverpool lies where the states of Ohio, Pennsylvania, and West Virginia meet. Eastern Indian tribes occupied the land before it was purchased under the Land Act of 1796. The town was originally called St. Clair, but it got its present name from English potters who migrated here in 1834. Soon after their arrival, the city became known as the pottery capital of the country. Today, East Liverpool and the surrounding area still produce pottery, which can be seen and purchased at a number of shops and museums in town.

Information: East Liverpool Area Chamber of Commerce | 529 Market St., 43920 | 330/385–0845 | www.elchamber.com.

Attractions

Beaver Creek State Park. This 5,000-acre park has camping, mountain biking, hiking, horseback riding, and boating. In the winter there's sledding and ice-skating. | 12021 Echo Dell Rd. | 330/385–3091 | Free | Daily.

Museum of Ceramics. Modern and antique pottery, earthenware, and porcelain items are displayed here, along with photographs and life-size dioramas explaining the industry's impact on the area. | 400 E. 5th St. | 330/386–6001 | $5 | Mar.–Nov., Wed.–Sat. 9:30–5, Sun. 12–5. By appointment Dec.– Feb.

Pottery City Antique Mall. More than 200 dealers display their glassware, pottery, books, antiques, and collectibles in a spacious 40,000-square-ft building. | 409 Washington St. | 330/385–6933 | Free | Mon.–Sat., 10–6, Sun. noon-6.

ON THE CALENDAR

JUNE: *Tri-State Pottery Festival.* Potters from around the region gather on the streets of downtown East Liverpool on the third weekend of June to show off their wares. | 4th and Broadway | 330/386–6060.

OCT.: *Beaver Creek State Park Pioneer Craft Days.* Craft vendors, some in period garb, demonstrate canning, weaving, looming, black-smithing, and candle making at this event held the second full weekend in October. Crafts are for sale; a shuttle bus transports you from the parking field to the heart of the festival. | 12021 Echo Dell Rd. | 330/385–3091.

Dining

Landora. Cafe. This four-story Victorian home was built in 1900 across the street from the Ceramic, a local night spot, and connected by an underground tunnel. The garden room, with skylight, running fountain, ivy-coated walls, and iron gate, is a relaxing spot for lunch. Specialties include the stacked ham and turkey on marbled bread; mesquite turkey with muenster cheese, artichoke hearts, and roasted red peppers on French bread, or anything on the homemade croissants. All sandwich specials come with soup or salad. Don't miss the tiramisu for dessert. | 117 E. 4th St. | 330/382–0239 | Lunch, Tues.–Sat. No dinner | $3–$7 | AE, MC, V.

Lodging

The Sturgis House. This restored Victorian mansion, a former funeral parlor right in the middle of town, is where Charles Arthur "Pretty Boy" Floyd, Public Enemy No. 1, was embalmed. There is a collection of memorabilia and photos of the event on the lower level of the three-story brick home. The home has period furnishings, Victorian revival wallpaper, cherry furniture, and wood-parquet floors. Rooms are ornate–lots of pinks and lace–and each room comes with cozy robes. There is a covered front porch with wicker furniture where you can relax and watch the townsfolk. Complimentary Continental breakfast. Some refrigerators. Cable TV. | 122 W. 5th St. | 330/385–0194 | fax 330/385–1163 | info@sturgishouse.com | www.sturgishouse.com | 6 rooms | $80–$90 | AE, MC, V.

ELYRIA

MAP 14, D3

(Nearby towns listed: Cleveland, Lorain, Oberlin, Strongsville)

In northern Ohio, Elyria is 25 mi west of Cleveland and 7 mi south of Lake Erie. The town is named for its founder, Herman Ely, son of Justin Ely, a well-to-do merchant, land developer, and heavy investor in the northeast Ohio (Western Reserve) lands of the Connecticut Land Company. The Township of Elyria, originally comprising present-day Elyria and Carlisle Townships, was created in 1819. Elyria became an independent town in 1833.

Information: Lorain County Chamber of Commerce | 6100 S. Broadway #201, Lorain, 44053 | 440/233–6500 or 800/334–1673 | www.eshores.com.

Attractions

The Hickories Museum. This 1895 mansion, surrounded by hickory trees, was built by inventor and Elyria native Arthur Garford. Among the museum's major collections are Victorian-era clothing and furniture. Exhibits include brilliant glassware and early woodworking tools. | 509 Washington Ave. | 440/322–3341 | $3.50 | Tues.–Fri. 9:30–4; tours at 1 and 2:30.

Lorain County Courthouse. This 1880 Gothic, sandstone courthouse is the county's oldest building. It is on the National Register of Historic Places. | 348 2nd St. | 440/284–6631 | Free | Daily, 8–4.

ON THE CALENDAR

SEPT.: *Apple Festival.* Cider and apple-butter making, hayrides, and parades are staples of this annual tribute to the apple on the streets of downtown Elyria. | On the Square, at Court St. | 440/233–6500.

NOV.: *Fall Home Spun.* The Field House at Loraine County Community College is host to this two-day crafts show with over 120 artists, which is held on the second weekend of November. There is a small entry fee. | 1005 Abbe Rd. N | 440/933–0693.

Dining

Grassie's Wayside Inn. American/Casual. The surf and turf dinners, seafood Alfredo, and Grassie burgers—a double patty with cheese, lettuce, tomato, and mayo sauce–bring wedding parties, construction workers, and everyone in between to this restaurant. Family-style service. Kids' menu. | 447 Oberlin Rd. | 440/322–0690 | Closed Sun. | $8–$33 | AE, D, MC, V.

Hometown Buffet. American. This good hearty slice of America, complete with a Norman Rockwell–themed dining room, is on Route 57, just 10 minutes from central Elyria. There's a salad bar, a hot food bar, and a beverage and dessert bar, all with unlimited trips. The two homemade soups, chicken noodle and creamy clam chowder, rotate daily. The 40 hot food items include fried chicken. | 1565 W. River Rd. N | 440/324–2177 | $8 | D, MC, V.

Jade Palace. Chinese. This popular and economical family spot is northeast of Elyria in North Ridgeville. The house special, Mongolian beef, keeps locals sliding into booths in this elongated dining room, which is covered with photographs of tourist destinations in China. | 38903 Center Ridge Rd., North Ridgeville | 440/327–2442 | $6–$11 | AE, D, MC, V.

Jumbo Buffet. Chinese. This relative newcomer, which opened in 1999, is so popular you may have to wait a bit before you are seated. There are 80 selections on the hot food bar, including chicken with broccoli, fried shrimp, dumplings, pepper steak, and fried rice. American selections include macaroni and cheese and chicken wings. There is a cold American salad bar that includes sushi. Three soups rotate daily. The lunch buffet is $5.50; dinner is $8.50. On Sunday, dinner is served all day. | 451 Griswold Rd. | 440/324–1228 | $5.50–$8.50 | D, DC, MC.

Pasquale's. Italian. Imagine a menu that includes spaghetti, lasagna, and wedding soup; Louis Prima crooning through the air; and generations of Pasquale photographs covering the wall. The Italian recipes are supplemented by a chef with a decidedly Hungarian hand; while one of you eats eggplant parmigiana, the other can have chicken paprikash. If you don't like spumoni, you are out of luck; it's the only dessert. | 301 Broad St. | 440/322–8611 | Closed Sun. No lunch Sat. | $6–$10 | AE, D, MC, V.

YOUR CAR'S FIRST-AID KIT

- ❏ Bungee cords or rope to tie down trunk if necessary
- ❏ Club soda to remove stains from upholstery
- ❏ Cooler with bottled water
- ❏ Extra coolant
- ❏ Extra windshield-washer fluid
- ❏ Flares and/or reflectors
- ❏ Flashlight and extra batteries
- ❏ Hand wipes to clean hands after roadside repair
- ❏ Hose tape

- ❏ Jack and fully inflated spare
- ❏ Jumper cables
- ❏ Lug wrench
- ❏ Owner's manual
- ❏ Plastic poncho—in case you need to do roadside repairs in the rain
- ❏ Quart of oil and quart of transmission fluid
- ❏ Spare fan belts
- ❏ Spare fuses
- ❏ Tire-pressure gauge

*Excerpted from *Fodor's: How to Pack: Experts Share Their Secrets*
© 1997, by Fodor's Travel Publications

Lodging

Camelot Inn. This low-budget, no-frills mom-and-pop hotel, right off Route 57, has been under new management since 1999. Rooms come with two twin beds or one queen bed. Some pets allowed. | 550 Griswold Rd. | 440/324–3232 | fax 440/324–3232, ext. 103 | 27 rooms | $40 | AE, D, DC, MC.

Cleveland North Ridgeville Super 8. This two-story chain motel is 7 mi northeast of Elyria, accessible by both I–80 and Route 10. Cable TV. Laundry facilities. | 32801 Lorain Rd. | 440/327–0500 or 800/848–8888 | fax 440/327–0500, ext. 300 | www.super8.com | 55 rooms | $40–$70 | AE, D, DC, MC, V.

Comfort Inn. This two-story hotel on the north side of town is opposite the Midway Mall. Complimentary Continental breakfast. Some microwaves, some refrigerators, some in-room hot tubs. Cable TV. Laundry facilities, laundry service. Pets allowed (fee). | 739 Leona St. | 440/324–7676 or 800/228–5150 | fax 440/324–4046 | www.comfortinn.com | 66 rooms, 9 suites | $79 | AE, D, DC, MC, V.

Days Inn. Both I–90 and I–80 are accessible from this hotel, which has spacious rooms and three stories. Complimentary Continental breakfast. In-room data ports. Cable TV. Indoor pool. Sauna. Exercise equipment. Video games. Laundry facilities. Business services. | 621 Midway Blvd. | 440/324–4444 or 800/325–2525 | fax 440/324–2065 | www.daysinn.com | 101 rooms, 30 suites | $79 | AE, D, DC, MC, V.

Econo Lodge. A strip of retail stores and restaurants surrounds this hotel on either side. Pool. Cable TV. | 523 Griswold Rd. | 440/324–3911 or 800/553–2666 | fax 440/324–3911 | www.econolodge.com | 116 rooms | $69–$99 | AE, D, DC, MC, V.

Holiday Inn. This is a full-service hotel only 3 mi from the Midway Mall. Restaurant, bar, complimentary Continental breakfast, room service. In-room data ports. Cable TV. Pool. Exercise equipment. Laundry facilities. Business services. Airport shuttle. | 1825 Lorain Blvd. | 440/324–5411 or 800/465–4329 | fax 440/324–2785 | www.holiday-inn.com | 250 rooms | $99–$119 | AE, D, DC, MC, V.

Howard Johnson. This motel, 5 mi from downtown Elyria, has a fast-food restaurant open for dinner only. Restaurant, complimentary Continental breakfast. Cable TV. | 1724 Lorain Blvd. | 440/323–1515 or 800/654–4656 | fax 440/322–8763 | www.hojo.com | 38 rooms | $79 | AE, D, DC, MC, V.

FINDLAY

MAP 14, B3

(Nearby towns listed: Bowling Green, Fremont, Tiffin)

Colonel James Findlay built Fort Findlay in the northeast section of Ohio during The War of 1812. The village bearing the colonel's name was incorporated in 1826. Later, it became a stop on the Underground Railroad. It is the home of the University of Findlay, which was established 60 years later. The first classes at the university were held in the building known today as "Old Main."

Information: Findlay Hancock County Chamber of Commerce | 123 E. Main Cross St., 45840 | 419/422–4594 or 800/424–3315 | www.findlayhancockchamber.com.

Attractions

Hancock Historical Museum. Findlay Glass tableware and an original log cabin dating from the 1800s are displayed here. | 422 W. Sandusky St. | 419/423–4433 | Free | Wed.–Fri. and Sun. 1–4; tours by appointment.

Litzenberg Memorial Woods. This 227-acre preserve is rich with recreational activities; it has wetlands, hiking trails, waterfowl and small game hunting, playgrounds, and sheltered areas for picnicking. An old farmhouse has exhibits of Findlay's farming history. The park is 5 mi west of Findlay on Route 224. | 6100 State Rte. 224 W | 419/425–PARK | fax 419/423–5811 | www.hancockparks.com | Daily, dawn–dusk.

Mazza Collection Galleria. The Virginia B. Gardner Fine Arts Pavilion on the University of Findlay Campus houses this gallery known for its large collection of original art by children's book illustrators. The over 18,000 holdings include original illustrations from Cinderella and drawings by Robert J. Caldecott. A taped tour is available. | 1000 N. Main St. | 419/424–4560 | Free | Wed.–Fri. 12–5, Sun. 1–4.

ON THE CALENDAR

AUG.: *Gus Macker 3 on 3 Basketball Tournament.* This slam-dunking festival, held the second weekend in August, will make any basketball fan drool. Main Street is blocked off so that the over 600 teams, ranging in ages from wee ball players to senior citizens, can compete. There are also free-throw contests, concessions, and other related activities. | Main St. | 419/422–4594 or 800/424–3315 | www.gusmacker.com.

Dining

Bistro on Main. American. A former gambling parlor has been reborn as a bistro, where you can dine on dishes like tangy pecan chicken and Creole shrimp. | 407 S. Main St. | 419/425–4900 | Closed Sun. No lunch Sat. | $14–$23 | AE, DC, MC, V.

Japan West. Japanese. Locals come for the beef tenderloins, teppanyaki, sushi, and sashimi. You can dine at the teppanyaki tables or the sushi bar. | 406 S. Main St. | 419/424–1007 | Reservations essential | Closed Sun. | $15–$32 | AE, D, MC, V.

Lodging

Cross Country Inn. You can find this two-story motel off I–75, 3 mi from town. Cable TV. Pool. | 1951 Broad Ave. | 419/424–0466 or 800/621–1429 | fax 419/424–0466 | www. cross-countryinns.com | 120 rooms | $55 | AE, D, DC, MC, V.

Fairfield Inn by Marriott. This three-story hotel 3 mi from downtown Findlay has contemporary decor and lobby that was remodeled in 2000. It's one block from the mall and surrounded by several restaurants. Complimentary Continental breakfast. Some refrigerators. Cable TV. Indoor pool. Hot tub. Business services. | 2000 Tiffin Ave. | 419/424–9940 or 800/288–2800 | fax 419/424–9940 | www.fairfieldinn.com | 57 rooms | $67 | AE, D, DC, MC, V.

Findlay Inn and Conference Center. This circular hotel in downtown Findlay is locally owned and operated. Personalized voice mail and free local transportation are available. Restaurant, bar, complimentary Continental breakfast, room service. In-room data ports. Cable TV. Indoor pool. Hot tub. Exercise equipment. Laundry service. Business services. | 200 E. Main Cross St. | 419/422–5682 or 800/825–1455 | fax 419/422–5581 | 80 rooms, 12 suites | $105, $95–$130 suites | AE, D, DC, MC, V.

Ramada Inn Findlay. This two-story chain, with outside room access, is just 3 mi from the University of Findlay, right off Interstate 75, exit 159. There are three meeting rooms on-site. Restaurant, room service. Pool. Laundry service. Business services. Pets allowed (fee). | 820 Trenton Ave. | 419/423–8212 or 800/228–2828 | fax 419/423–8217 | www.ramada.com/ramada.html | 140 rooms | $55–$71 | AE, D, DC, MC, V.

Rose Gate Cottage Bed and Breakfast. This two-story, rose stucco Victorian home, built in 1899, has a music room, two porches, a rear deck, and a pool table. Rooms are uniquely appointed: The Garden Villa Room has a four-poster, queen-size wheat bed; the Tea Rose Room has tea rose wall covering and a cherry bed; the Azur Vineyard Room has blue rose wallpaper and an oak high-back double bed; and Mary's Room has twin pinecone poster beds. The adjacent carriage house is available for business meetings. Complimentary breakfast, TV in common area. Business services. | 423 Western Ave. | 419/424–1940 | rosegate@rosegateinn.com | www.rosegateinn.com | 4 rooms | $55–$75 | AE, MC, V.

FREMONT

(Nearby towns listed: Bellevue, Bowling Green, Findlay, Sandusky, Tiffin, Toledo)

Fremont lies on the banks of the Sandusky River in the north central part of the state on land that was once home to the Seneca, Crawford, Wyandotte, and Ottawa Indians. Settled in the mid- to late-1600s, Fremont was officially named a city in 1849. Most of Fremont's growth during the 1800s came from river commerce. In the 1900s, much of the river traffic was diverted to Cleveland and Toledo because of their canals, so Fremont looked to the railroads to regain its momentum. Today, Fremont has a central location along a number of major roadways. It's best known as the home of former president Rutherford B. Hayes.

Information: Chamber of Commerce of Sandusky County | 101 S. Front St., 43420 | 419/332–1591 or 800/255–8070 | www.scchamber.org.

Attractions

Hayes Presidential Center. This 33-room mansion on 25 acres was the home of Rutherford B. Hayes (1822–93), the 19th president of the United States. The Victorian mansion is on a site known as Spiegel Grove. The iron gates at the property entrances are the same ones that stood in front of the White House during Hayes's presidency. Also on site is the first official presidential museum, which contains the president's books and family mementos. | 1337 Hayes Ave. | 419/332–2081 or 800/998–7737 | www.rbhayes.org | $8.50 | Mon.–Sat. 9–5, Sun. 12–5.

Walsh Park. A brick fountain greets you as you enter this 49-acre park, right along the Sandusky River. The memorial tree garden has been planted by locals to honor their loved ones. There are paved and more rugged hiking trails as well as a sheltered area and playground. | 610 Morrison St. | 419/334–5906 | Free | Daily, dawn–dusk.

ON THE CALENDAR

JUNE–JULY: *Medieval Fantasy Faire.* This riotous event takes you back to the days of ladies in waiting, minstrels, and gladiators. There are tons of activities on the 30-acre lot: full-armor jousting, live shows, comedy, a fencing arena, and knighting ceremonies. At the King's Feast Banquet buffet, you dine with the king, queen, and courtiers and eat off silver platters—after bowing to the king. The fair takes place for five consecutive weekends, beginning at the end of June. | 1313 Tiffin St. | 419/334–7774 or 419/333–2450 | www.medievalfantasy.net.

OCT.: *Civil War Encampment and President Hayes Birthday Reunion.* The city of Fremont hosts a yearly birthday party in honor of its most famous son, U.S. president Rutherford B. Hayes. Civil War reenactments are the highlight of the event, held the first full weekend in October at the Hayes Presidential Center. | 1337 Hayes Ave. | 419/332–2081 or 800/998–7737.

Dining

818 Club. Continental. This hard-to-classify restaurant has a St. Patrick's theme with one wall dedicated to the owner's beer stein collection, and a menu that includes Mexican specials along with a variety of standbys for the meat eater. The steak-and-shrimp combo is a popular choice. | 818 Croghan St. | 419/334–9122 | Closed Sun. | $7–$18 | AE, D, MC, V.

Lodging

Days Inn. This two-story hotel is ¼ mile off the Ohio Turnpike and about 20-minute drive from Lake Erie. Restaurant, bar, room service. Cable TV. Pool. Video games. Playground. Laundry facilities. | 3701 N. Rte. 53 | 419/334–9551 or 800/325–2525 | fax 419/334–9551 | www.daysinn.com | 105 rooms, 2 suites | $105–$125 | AE, D, DC, MC, V.

Fremont Travelodge. This two-story motel is 4 mi south of the Ohio Turnpike. There are a surprising number of amenities, considering the low rates, including recliner chairs in every room. In-room data ports, some microwaves, some refrigerators. Cable TV. Pool. Pets allowed. | 1750 Cedar St. | 419/334–9517 or 800/255–3030 | fax 419/334–9517 | www.travelodge.com | 50 rooms | $39–$71 | D, DC, MC, V.

GALLIPOLIS

(Nearby towns listed: Athens, Ironton)

Gallipolis, meaning "City of the Gauls," began as a speculation project of the Scioto Company, which in 1803 encouraged French investors to purchase lands in Ohio. Hundreds of members of the French middle class invested money, hoping to find prosperity in America. But when they arrived, they found their deeds worthless. They petitioned both Congress and President Washington for aid, and as a result, the Scioto Company sent a group of woodsmen from Marietta to build a settlement in southeast Ohio near present-day Gallipolis. The French settlers arrived on Oct. 17, 1790, surprised by the hardships of frontier life. Eventually, however, they established a thriving river trade town. Today, evidence of Gallipolis's French heritage is throughout the city. If you're interested in the history of Gallipolis, you can tour the French Art Colony and the Our House Museum.

Information: Gallia County Chamber of Commerce | 16 State St., 45631 | 740/446–0596 | www.galliachamber.org.

Attractions

Ariel Theatre. Originally constructed in 1895 for the Ariel Lodge of Oddfellows, the building also served as the Ariel Opera House, Gallipolis Opera House, and Gallipolis Theatre. Though its oak entrance doors were closed for 25 years, it has been re-established as the home stage for the Ohio Valley Symphony and the Ariel Players. The acoustics are bell-clear, and the ceiling stencil has been restored to its original state. Tours are available. | 426 2nd Ave. | 740/446–ARTS.

Bob Evans Farm. This working farm about 10 mi northwest of Gallipolis belongs to native son Bob Evans, who started the chain of more than 400 restaurants that bears his name. The farm has a log cabin village, small animal barnyard, and farm museum. Canoeing, horseback riding and hay rides are available for a fee. | 10854 Rte. 588, Rio Grande | 740/245–5305 or 800/994–FARM | www.bobevans.com | Farm, free | Memorial Day–Labor Day, daily 8:30–5.

French Art Colony. Housed in Riverby, an 1855 Greek Revival house, this arts center has gallery exhibits that change every six weeks. | 530 1st Ave. | 740/446–3834 | Free | Tues.–Fri. 10–3, Sun. 1–5.

Our House Museum. Between 1819 and 1865 guests such as the Marquis de Lafayette were entertained in this 19th-century tavern and inn along the river. Today, it's a museum with period furnishings. Tours describing travel in frontier America and a one-day Civil War camp for children are available. | 432 1st Ave. | 740/446–0586 | $3 | Memorial Day–Labor Day, Wed.–Sat. 10–4, Sun. 1–4; May, Sept.–Oct., Sat. 10–4, Sun. 1–4.

ON THE CALENDAR

JULY: *Fourth of July River Recreation Festival.* The festival is held in Riverside Park on the banks of the Ohio River and includes boat races, kids' games, music, a youth talent show, and a rock-climbing wall. Other events include a parade and a display of fireworks. | McManness Ave. | 419/422–4594 or 800/424–3315.

OCT.: *Bob Evans Farm Festival.* This annual fair is held at the very first Bob Evans Restaurant, on the Bob Evan's Farm in Rio Grande, about 10 mi northwest of Gallipolis. There are farm demonstrations, hayrides, and craft exhibits. Over 1,000 people attend each year. | 10854 Rte. 588, Rio Grande | 740/245–5305 or 800/994–FARM.

Dining

Bob Evans. American/Casual. This is No. 1 in a chain of 447 restaurants founded by Bob Evans, a native of Gallipolis. Evans and his family lived on the farm next to the restaurant. Today you can order wholesome, homestyle dishes like meat loaf, chicken pot pie, turkey and dressing, and country-fried steak. There are hearty breakfasts and tasty desserts like caramel apple dumplings and coconut cream pie. Kids under 10 eat for $1.99. | 10854 Rte. 588, Rio Grande | 740/245–5324 | Daily, 6 AM–9 PM | $7–$12 | AE, MC, V.

The Down Under. Continental. Don't expect kangaroo or Aboriginal art. This dining room's name describes its location, which is in the basement of the Lafayette Mall, across from the city park. Tables are dressed with mauve cloths and white linen napkins and marked by a single candle. One wall displays a collection of model ships. The prime rib and filet mignon are the specialties of the house. Pasta, chicken, and seafood are also available. | 300 2nd Ave. | 740/446–2345 | Closed Sun. | $12–$25 | AE, D, MC, V.

Lodging

Holiday Inn Gallipolis-Point Pleasant. Just 10 mi east of the Bob Evans Farm at the junction of Ohio Route 7 and U.S. 35 stands this two-story chain. The guest rooms include a desk, reclining chair, and entertainment center. There is a 2,000-square-ft meeting room, which can be divided into three parts. Restaurant. In-room data ports. Pool. Business services. Pets allowed. | 577 Rte. 7 N | 740/446–0090 or 800/465–4329 | fax 740/446–0090 | kilgore@zoomnet.net | www.basshotels.com | 100 rooms | $69 | AE, D, DC, MC, V.

William Ann Motel. Three-quarters of a mile from downtown, this is one of the few motels in Gallipolis. It's privately owned; you'll get donuts and coffee in the morning. Some microwaves, some refrigerators. Cable TV. Business services. Some pets allowed. | 918 2nd Ave. | 740/446–3373 | fax 740/446–1337 | 50 rooms | $45 | AE, MC, V.

GENEVA-ON-THE-LAKE

MAP 14, F2

(Nearby towns listed: Ashtabula, Chardon, Conneaut, Mentor, Painesville)

Ohio's first summer resort, aptly called Geneva-on-the-Lake, is just north of the town of Geneva on the shores of Lake Erie in northern Ohio. Since 1869, this town has been a favorite spot for vacationers. Many families return year after year to rent cottages, fish, swim, sunbathe, and enjoy "The Strip," a mile-long collection of arcades, fun houses, restaurants, miniature golf courses, and dance halls. There's also an amusement park with bumper boats, go-carts, and water slides.

Information: Geneva-on-the-Lake Chamber of Commerce | 5536 Lake Rd. E., Geneva, 44041 | 440/466–8600.

Attractions

Erieview Park. On Geneva-on-the-Lake's "Strip," this park has water slides and classic rides, such as bumper cars. | 5483 Lake Rd. | 440/466–8650 | Park, free. Ride prices vary | May–Sept., daily. Water slide, noon–9. Amusement rides, 2–10.

Geneva State Park. This park on the shores of Lake Erie has a beach, a 400-ft fishing pier, and 350-slip marina. You can camp, boat, fish, or picnic here. | 429 Padanarum Rd. | 440/466–8400 | Free | Apr.–Nov., daily.

Jennie Munger Gregory Museum. The museum, home of the Ashtabula County Historical Society, is housed in an 1823 Federal farmhouse, the first clapboard house on the lake. It has exhibits of artifacts from the Geneva-on-the-Lake area, including ship memorabilia and items used by sailors on Lake Erie. | Lake Rd. between Putnam Dr. and Grandview Dr. | 440/466–7337 | $3 | Memorial Day–Labor Day, Tues.–Fri. 12–4, and by appointment.

Old Firehouse Winery. This unique Ohio winery, host to a Tex-Mex restaurant and a slew of annual events, overlooks Lake Erie. For groups, tours of the winery can be arranged; otherwise, one of the amiable staff members probably show you the production room and let you look around the facilities. Each of the 20 wines, including cherry, sweet concord, spice apple, red raspberry, frosty peach, and more premium wines like spumante champagne, is available for sale by the bottle. If it's a nice day, you can order the sample tray and sit under the gazebo, enjoying the view and the wine. | 5499 Lake Rd. | 440/466–9300 | fax 440/466–8011 | Free | June–Aug., daily noon–midnight; late-Apr.–May and Sept.–Dec., Sun.–Thurs. noon–7, weekends noon–midnight; Jan.–late-Apr., Fri.–Sun. noon–7.

ON THE CALENDAR
JUNE: *Northeast Ohio Polka Festival.* The second weekend of June, the Old Firehouse Winery hosts a number of bands, specializing in Slovenian, Chicago-style, and Polish polka for a hopping, swinging, oom-pa-pa weekend. The outside covered stage has 175 seats for you to sit while you catch your breath. The restaurant expands its menu for the event and includes more ethnic-befitting choices like sausages and pierogies. | 5499 Lake Rd. | 440/466–9300.
SEPT.: *Geneva Grape Jamboree.* The streets of Geneva, 5 mi south of Geneva-on-the-Lake, are alive with games, food, and parades during this annual celebration the last full weekend of September. It marks Ohio's status as the nation's third-large grape-growing region, behind California and New York. | Main St. and Broadway, Geneva | 440/466–5262.

Dining
Old Firehouse Winery. Tex-Mex. This restaurant, in a former firehouse and attached to a winery, has a south-of-the-border flair. Though the menu includes enchiladas, tacos fajitas, and burritos, the favorite entrée is the spicy, tender ribs. Half slabs are also available. Each of the vineyard's 20 wines is available for dinner. You can eat inside or out, and there is nightly live entertainment. Kids' menu. | 5499 Lake Rd. | 440/466–9300 | fax 440/466–8011 | Open weekends only, Oct.–Dec. Closed Jan.–Apr. | $6–$16 | AE, D, MC, V.

Lodging
Charlman Bed and Breakfast. Just west of the Geneva State Park campground is this cozy spot. Rooms have brass beds, skylights, and antique furnishings. The homey atmosphere is accentuated by oversized towels and a homemade nightcap. TV in common area. | 6739 Lake Rd. W | 440/466–3646 | 2 rooms | $105–$125 | Closed Sept.–June | No credit cards.

GNADENHUTTEN

MAP 14, E4

(Nearby towns listed: Berlin, Coshocton, Dover, New Philadelphia, Sugarcreek)

Gnadenhutten is a small village (pop. 1,300) in south central Tuscarawas County in the west central part of the state. It lies in a valley partly surrounded by hills; the Tuscarawas River forms its southwest border. The city's beginnings can be traced to 1798, when John Heckewelder returned to the area 16 years after the brutal massacre of 90 Native Americans by U.S. troops in 1782. In the years that followed, many Moravian families from eastern Pennsylvania came to the area to live.

Information: **Twin City Chamber of Commerce** | 325 E. 2nd St., Uhrichsville, 44683 | 740/922–5623.

Attractions

Clendening Lake Marina. On 6,500-acre Clendening Lake, about 20 mi southeast of Gnadenhutten, you can rent a boat or jet ski, gas up, and buy snacks at this marina. | 79100 Bose Rd., Rte. 2, Freeport | 740/658–3691 | Free | May–Oct., daily 8–6.

Gnadenhutten Museum. This museum was built in the 1930s by the state of Ohio, using stones that resemble the ones in the Ohio Canal locks. Inside the museum, you'll find a collection of Native American artifacts, Moravian books and bibles, and implements from the original Gnadenhutten village. A videotape explains the town's significance in Ohio's history. The museum has a gift shop. | 352 S. Cherry St. | 740/254–4143 | fax 740/254–4986 | $1 | May–Sept., Mon.–Sat. 10–5, Sun. 12–5; Sept.–Oct., Sat. 10–5, Sun. 12–5.

Tappan Lake Park. This roughly 5,000-acre park east of Gnadenhutten is a popular place to fish, boat, hike, camp, and swim. Boats are available for rental. | 84000 Mallernee Rd., Deersville | 740/922–3649 | $5 per car | Memorial Day–Labor Day, daily, 8 AM–9 PM.

ON THE CALENDAR

AUG.: *Native American Gathering.* The fourth weekend in August, the Gnadenhutten Historical Park, in front of the Gnadenhutten Museum, hosts Native American tribes who share their history with the community. Many tribal members dress in traditional clothing. The Historical Society sells fry bread, beef stew, and cornbread. | 352 S. Cherry St. | 740/254–4143.

Dining

Ike's Family Restaurant. American. The all-you-can-eat fried fish special (on Friday nights) and the hot apple dumplings are favorites at this casual spot in Uhrichsville, 8 mi east of Gnadenhutten. Ike's also serves T-bone steaks, spaghetti, and pies in every flavor. Breakfast is served every day, all day. On weekends, Ike's is open all night. Kids' menu. | 101 McCauley Dr., Uhrichsville | 740/922–0092 | $5–$8 | AE, D, DC, MC, V.

Lodging

Best Western Country Inn. The Country Inn has efficiency suites and double rooms, each in an Early American style. It is 8 mi east of Gnadenhutten, just off Route 250 and right behind Ike's Family Restaurant. There is a laundromat in the strip mall across the street. Kids under 18 stay free. Complimentary Continental breakfast. In-room data ports, some kitchenettes. Business services. Pets allowed (fee). | 111 McCauley Dr., Uhrichsville | 740/922–0774 or 800/528–1234 | fax 740/922–2270 | www.bestwestern.com | 48 rooms | $75–$82 | AE, D, DC, MC, V.

GRANVILLE

MAP 14, D5

(Nearby towns listed: Columbus, Coshocton, Mount Vernon, Newark)

Settled by a group of pioneers from Granville, Massachussetts, who named their new Ohio home after their original one in New England, Granville has changed little since its founding in the mid-19th century. Its downtown shops aren't touristy trinket shops, but working village stores such as a hardware shop and a butcher. Nearly the entire town of 4,000 is on the National Register of Historic Places. Granville is also home to Denison University, a well-known and highly regarded private liberal arts college.

Information: **Licking County Convention and Visitors Bureau** | P.O. Box 702, Newark, 43055 | 740/345–8224 or 800/589–8224 | www.granville.oh.us or www.lccvb.com.

Attractions

Denison University. This private liberal arts college is routinely on *U.S. News and World Report's* list of best colleges. The architecture is reminiscent of New England, and the tree-lined quads add to the charm of the campus. You can take a free tour of the campus. | 100 South Rd. | 740/587–0810 or 800/DENISON | www.denison.edu | Free | Daily.

Granville Life-Styles Museum. This Vicorian Italianate house built in 1870-71 was the home of H. D. Robinson. You can take tours and attend lectures on period clothing and furnishings. The gardens are tended by volunteers and are open to the public. | 121 S. Main St. | 740/587–0373 | $1.50 | Apr.–Oct., Sun. 1:30–4 and by appointment.

Robbins Hunter Museum. Granville's museum, in the 1842 Avery-Downer House, has several rooms with mid-19th-century American, European, and Asian furnishings, including Oriental carpets, musical instruments, sculpture, and china. Tours of the Greek Revival style home and the historic district around it are available. | 221 E. Broadway | 740/587–0430 | Free | May–Oct., Wed.–Sun. 1–4 and by appointment.

ON THE CALENDAR

OCT.: *Olde Granville Antiques Fair.* This antiques fair in mid-October is an annual tradition in the village of Granville, which was founded in 1805. American and European furniture are featured, along with china, glassware, decorative items, country pieces, quilts, jewelry, and collectibles. | Broadway St. | 740/345–9757.

Dining

Buxton Inn. Contemporary. Simple dishes, like grilled ham steak with a baked potato, as well as complex recipes, like pork loin roasted over apples with a raspberry and pine-nut stuffing, fill the menu. Try the roast duckling with cranberry-orange sauce and the gingerbread with lemon sauce for dessert. Open-air dining is available in an attractive courtyard as well as a greenhouse. Family-style service. Kids' menu. Sun. brunch. | 313 E. Broadway | 740/587–0001 | $8–$23 | Closed Mon. | AE, D, MC, V.

Granville Inn. Continental. Prime rib, roasted duckling, and flounder Belle Franklin, a filet of white fish covered in rich butter-cream sauce, are popular choices at this century-old mansion that was once home to one of the town's wealthiest citizens. For dessert, try the fluffy pumpkin cake or a hearty slice of walnut pie. All meals are served with fresh-baked and iced raisin bread. In summer, you can dine al fresco on the patio. Kids' menu, early bird dinners. No smoking. | 314 E. Broadway | 740/587–3333 | Reservations essential | Closed Sun. | $18–$30 | AE, D, MC, V.

Lodging

Buxton Inn. A renovated Sears catalog house from the early 20th century is the main house, and there are five adjacent buildings. Rooms are decorated to reflect the period of the buildings with antiques, linens, and artwork. At breakfast, you can spread your toast with the inn's homemade raspberry, apricot, and strawberry preserves. The buildings are rumored to be haunted. Restaurant, bar, complimentary Continental breakfast. Refrigerators. Cable TV. | 313 E. Broadway | 740/587–0001 | fax 740/587–1460 | www.buxtoninn.com | 25 rooms in five buildings | $70–$90 | AE, D, MC, V.

Granville Inn. The inn was built in the 1920s by wealthy industrialist John Suthpin Jones to entertain his friends. With expensive touches such as carved oak paneling, tapestries, and upholstered walnut and mahogany furniture, the place looks more like a palatial home than an inn. Restaurant, complimentary Continental breakfast. In-room data ports. Cable TV, some in-room VCRs. | 314 E. Broadway | 740/587–3333 | www.granvilleinn.com | 27 rooms, three suites | $84–$100 rooms, $115–$150 suites | AE, D, MC, V.

HAMILTON

(Nearby towns listed: Cincinnati, Dayton, Lebanon, Mason, Middletown, Oxford)

In 1791, a small brigade of U.S. soldiers established Fort Hamilton, a remote frontier outpost along the shores of the Great Miami River. The fort supplied American troops with sundries and ammunition for five years before it was abandoned. The pioneers who settled in the fort's vicinity, however, stayed on even after it closed. Later, after the Miami and Erie Canal brought industry to the area, Irish and German immigrants settled here to find jobs.

Today, the once-lonely riverfront military outpost is the city of Hamilton (pop. 80,000), just 20 mi from downtown Cincinnati and 35 mi from downtown Dayton. In the past few years, more than a half-dozen international companies have moved to the Hamilton area, giving the economy a boost. Hamilton has three districts—Rossville, Dayton Lane, and German Village– where historic houses and commercial buildings are clustered, and Pyramid Hill, the nation's only drive-through sculpture park.

Information: Hamilton Chamber of Commerce | 201 Dayton St., 45011 | 513/844–1500.

Attractions

Butler County Historical Museum. The museum is housed in the 1861 Benninghofen House, which has Victorian furnishings. Exhibits include antique dolls, tolls, clocks, and American Indian artifacts. | 327 N. 2nd St. | 513/896–9930 | $1 | Tues.–Sun. 1–4.

Jungle Jim's International Farmer's Market. In front of this market 10 mi south of Hamilton are giant statues of wild animals. You'll find acres of produce from area farms, fresh seafood, a great bakery and more. While you shop for food and beverages from around the world, you'll be entertained by mechanical puppets. | 5440 Dixie Hwy., Fairfield | 513/829–1919 | Free | Daily, 8 AM–10 PM.

Lane-Hooven House. This octagonal 1863 home in the Gothic Revival style has an unusual spiral staircase that winds to the third-floor turret and a beautiful stained glass entrance and detailed woodwork. The house is partially furnished in period pieces. It is the working office of the Hamilton Community Foundation, and tours are available during office hours. | 319 N. 3rd St. | 513/863–1389 | Free | Weekdays 8:30–4:30.

Pyramid Hill Sculpture Park & Museum. Ohio's only sculpture park—and the only drive-through sculpture park in the nation—is set on 265 wooded acres just south of the Hamilton city limits. There are 40 large, contemporary sculptures intermingled among gardens and lakes. You can drive through on a one-way road with a map and a description of the art in hand. Hiking is also allowed. | Rte. 128, (Hamilton-Cleves Rd.) | 513/868–8336 | $4 weekends, $3 weekdays | Apr.–Oct., Tues.–Sun. 10–6; Nov.–Mar., weekends 10–5.

Soldiers, Sailors, and Pioneers Monument. This monument was built to honor the men and women who first settled Butler County and also to "perpetuate the memory of all the soldiers and sailors of Butler County." The neoclassical monument building on the site of Fort Hamilton stands 100 ft tall and 40 ft square; it's topped by a statue of a Civil War soldier. The names of Ohioans who served in the Civil War and World War I are recorded in the library inside the monument. | High Street Bridge and Monument Ave. | 513/867–5823 | Free | Monument, daily. Library, weekdays 10–4, Sat. 11–3.

Trader's World. This flea market, 10 mi west of Hamilton, is one of the largest flea markets in the Midwest, with over 600 dealers spread out over 2 mi. | 601 Union Rd., Monroe | 513/424–5708 | $0.75 | Weekends 9–5.

JULY: *Fourth at the Fort.* Hamilton turns back the clock to its days as a frontier fort at this annual July 4th celebration at Courthouse Square. Exhibits, demonstrations, and entertainment recall life in the mid-1800s. | High and 2nd Sts. | 513/844–8080.

JULY: *Antique Car Parade.* Antique automobiles from every era motor through town on the fourth Saturday of the month. Afterwards, they're displayed for a few hours at Courthouse Square. | High and 2nd Sts. | 513/844–8080.

JULY: *Butler County Fair.* This is one of the largest county fairs in Ohio. Close to 100,000 people attend each year on the last full week of July to see more than 75 livestock shows, watch five nights of demolition derby, and try their luck at the many games of chance at the Butler County fairgrounds, | Fairgrove Ave. and Rte. 4 | 513/892–1423.

SEPT.: *Dam Fest.* The Great Miami River becomes a playground for the best water-skiers in the country at the Dam Fest. Athletes perform flips, jumps, and twists for the crowds. You can watch the fun at the riverfront in downtown Hamilton. | Neilan Blvd. | 513/867–2282 or 800/311–5353.

Dining

Academy. Eclectic. You can have seafood and steak, or vegetarian dishes such as Italian peasant stew, and be entertained by a pianist Wednesday–Saturday at Academy. | 343 N. 3rd St. | 513/868–7171 | Reservations essential | Closed Sun. | $10–$22 | AE, MC, V.

Alexander's Grill. Continental. People come to this restaurant in the Hamiltonian hotel, done in burgundy and dark green, for the beef, and lots of it. If you can't make up your mind, you can order the combination platters, such as prime rib and salmon or grilled turkey chop and filet mignon. Also popular is the roast pork Florentine, served with a dijon cream sauce, artichoke hearts, and grilled mushroom caps. A cozy hearth warms the dining room. | 1 Riverfront Plaza | 513/896–6200 | $14–$18 | AE, D, DC, MC, V.

Lodging

The Hamiltonian. This six-story hotel is on Great Miami River in downtown Hamilton. There's a concierge level with extra amenities. It houses a popular restaurant, Alexander's Grill, and a sports lounge. Guests can use the nearby fitness club. Restaurant, bar, room service. In-room data ports. Cable TV, in-room movies. Pool. Business services. Some pets allowed. | 1 Riverfront Plaza | 513/896–6200 or 800/522–5570 | fax 513/896–9463 | www.brilyn.com | 120 rooms, 4 suites | $81–$89, $149 suites | AE, D, DC, MC, V.

White Rose Bed and Breakfast. Built in 1905, this two-story home is in Hamilton's historic German Village. There are flood marks on the second floor from the 1913 flooding of the Miami River. The home's proximity to the river affords many scenic views. You can borrow bikes, and after a long day of touring, you can relax in the outdoor Jacuzzi on the back porch. Rooms blend antiques with more modern furnishings. All rooms have private baths, though one upstairs bedroom has a downstairs bath. A full breakfast is served on week-ends, and a Continental breakfast on weekdays. Some room phones, TV in common area. Outdoor hot tub. No kids under 12. Small pets allowed. | 116 Buckeye St. | 513/863–6818 | wrose@fuse.net | www.bbonline.com/oh/whiterose | 3 rooms | $65–$75 | No credit cards.

IRONTON

MAP 14, D7

(Nearby town listed: Gallipolis)

Ironton, the seat of Lawrence County, is on the Ohio River in the middle of what was once known as the Hanging Rock Iron Region. The city was founded after commercial deposits of coal and iron were discovered in the region in the mid-1800s. These find-ings led to the establishment of highly successful iron furnaces, which were the primary source of employment in Ironton for the next 50 years. After that, Ironton focused its attention on coal, supplying it to areas across southwest Ohio and Kentucky via the Ohio River.

Ironton is known for its covered bridges, which graced the city for nearly a century. Only one remains in operation—the Scottown Bridge over the Indian Guygon Creek. Ironton's primary attraction, however, is nearby Wayne National Forest. Thousands of people come here every year to hike and camp in the area and to take on the waters of Lake Vesuvius.

Information: Greater Lawrence County Area Chamber of Commerce | 1733 Winchester Ave., Ashland 41101 | 740/377–4550 or 800/408–1334 | www.lawrencecountyohio.org.

Attractions

Lawrence County Museum. In what was once Colonel George N. Gray's home, an Italian villa most notable for its tower with portholes and a truncated roof with wrought-iron cresting, are historical displays of Lawrence County and Civil War memorabilia. There is also an ongoing lecture series. | 506 S. 6th St. | 740/532–1222 | $2 | Apr.–Dec., Fri.–Sun. 1–5.

Wayne National Forest. The forest, named for Gen. Anthony Wayne, a Revolutionary War hero, covers over 200,000 acres in southeastern Ohio. On a map, the forest appears in three "patches"—two flanking the city of Athens and one stretching across the southernmost tip of Ohio. The entrance to this third patch, which covers about 29,000 acres, is 7 mi north of Ironton. Lake Vesuvius is a favorite spot for swimming, boating, and fishing. There are hiking trails, and camping is permitted. *(See* also Athens.) | 6518 Rte. 93, Pedro | 740/534–6500 | fax 740/534–6565 | www.fs.fed.us/r9/wayne | Free | Daily.

ON THE CALENDAR

MAY: *Ironton Memorial Day Parade.* This parade, which dates from around 1865, is one of the longest-running ones in the country. The 2½-hour trek down 3rd Street to Quincy Street includes school bands, a grand marshal and floats depicting Ironton's history. | 740/377–4550.

JUNE–AUG.: *Tri-State Fair and Regatta.* The main attraction here is the regatta, in which the country's best boat drivers race hydroplanes on the Ohio River at speeds of up to 180 mph. | 740/377–4550.

JULY: *Lawrence County Fair.* The best produce and livestock grown in this farming community are displayed at this weeklong fair at the county fairgrounds. There are games, food, rides, and performances by nationally known artists. | Rte. 7 and 243, Proctorville | 740/377–4550.

Dining

C.R. Thomas. American. This restaurant is often referred to as the "old place" because of all the collectibles—old license plates, movie memorabilia, Tiffany lamps—and the original tin ceiling. There are several sampler trays, including the snack-attack appetizer and the backyard barbecue, which includes house favorites, such as mushrooms stuffed with Alouette cheese and lip-smacking ribs. The burgers and sandwiches are also a hit. Top off your meal with a piece of homemade Snickers pie. | 124 S. 2nd St. | 740/532–8500 | $9–$14 | AE, D, DC, MC, V.

Lodging

Sheridan House Bed and Breakfast. This 1890 Victorian home on a quarter-acre residential lot is gray with white trim. If you stay in the Sheridan room, you will occupy part of the turret. Another room has a private sun porch. All rooms have antique furnishings, one of which is a 7-ft headboard. You won't want to oversleep if the house specialty, almond French toast, is served for breakfast. It's 10 minutes from Lake Vesuvius. Complimentary breakfast. Cable TV. No pets. No smoking. | 703 Park Ave. | 740/532–2038 | 3 rooms | $65–$70 | AE, D, DC, MC, V.

KELLEYS ISLAND

(Nearby towns listed: Marblehead, Port Clinton, Put-in-Bay, Sandusky)

Kelleys Island is the largest freshwater island in Lake Erie. It's a few miles south of the Canadian border, and only 4 mi north of Marblehead on the Ohio mainland. The island was formed by giant glaciers that moved across the lake centuries ago. Before the Europeans arrived, it was inhabited by Native Americans, primarily the Erie, Ottawa, and Huron tribes, who hunted here 300 to 400 years ago.

Today the island is a favorite vacation and day-trip destination for Ohioans and out-of-staters alike. Water sports of all kinds, from jet skiing and boating to snorkeling and scuba diving, are popular, and most equipment can be rented at local shops. The island is known as the "Walleye Capital of the World," and perch, catfish, smallmouth, and white bass are caught in quantity here. Waterfowl are also abundant, including heron, egrets, and an occasional osprey or eagle. The island's 800 acres of parkland have miles of nature and hiking trails, and downtown, you can browse in the gift and clothing shops, or play miniature golf. No cars are permitted on the island. Ferry service is available from Marblehead year-round, as long as there are no fierce winds or ice on the lake. You can also fly from Port Clinton and Sandusky.

Information: Kelleys Island Chamber of Commerce | 130 Division St., 43438 | 419/746–2360 | www.kelleysisland.com.

KELLEYS ISLAND

INTRO
ATTRACTIONS
DINING
LODGING

Attractions

Kelleys Island State Park. There are miles of hiking trails in this park on the northern edge of the island. There's also a sandy beach along the North Bay, a stone pier for fishing, a free double boat launching ramp, trailer parking, and 129 shaded camping sites. The park is open year-round, but the water is shut off in late October and the boat docks are pulled in the winter. | 733 Division St., North Shore | 419/746–2546 (Memorial Day–Labor Day), 419/797–4530 (off season) | Free | Daily.

You can see the world's largest examples of glacial grooves at the aptly named **Glacial Grooves State Memorial,** an international study site in the state park. These gashes in the native limestone bedrock were caused by the advancement of the Wisconsin glacier 30,000 years ago; scientists come to study the fossilized marine life which is embedded here. The largest groove is 400 ft deep and 35 ft wide. | 733 Division St. | 419/797–4530 | Free | Daily.

Inscription Rock State Memorial. Pictographs of men, birds, and animals can be seen at the flat-topped limestone boulder that was carved by the Erie Indians 300 to 400 years ago. | 733 Division St. | 419/746–2546 | Free | Daily.

Prince Shipwreck. The Prince, a 1911 shipwreck submerged 18 ft under water, is visible from the surface. It lies 100 ft off the east shore of the island and can be reached by boat or by swimming. Snorkeling and scuba gear are available at North Coast Scuba in Marblehead. | Eastern shore | 419/798–5557 | Free | Daily.

ON THE CALENDAR

MAY: *Nest with the Birds Week.* The Audubon Society hosts this weeklong event, which begins on Mother's Day. There are daily nature programs, guided bird walks and on Saturday, a bird banding program. | St. Michael's Hall, 219 Chappel St. | 419/746–2258.

Dining

Island Cafe and Brew Pub. American/Casual. The island's only brew pub has indoor and outdoor dining with a view of Lake Erie. The relaxed family dining is popular locally for its Lake Erie walleye and perch, reuben sandwiches, and cheeseburgers. Plants, rocks, and tiki torches add an island touch. | At the top of the Kelleys Island ferry dock | 419/746–2314 | Closed mid-Nov.–mid-Apr. Closed Mon.–Wed. | $9–$16 | AE, MC, V.

Lodging

Himmelblau. This 100-year-old Queen Anne Victorian B&B has its own panoramic view of Lake Erie. The large, enclosed porch faces east, making it the best place to watch the sunrise on the island. The rooms are eclectic, with antique furnishings. Complimentary breakfast. TV with VCR. Laundry facilities. | 337 Shannon Rd. | 419/746–2200 | 3 rooms | $85–$95 | Closed Dec.–Mar. | DC, MC, V.

KENT

MAP 14, E3

(Nearby towns listed: Akron, Alliance, Aurora, Youngstown)

In 1805, John Haymaker ventured westward to the newly formed state of Ohio and settled with his family on the banks of the Cuyahoga River. Taking advantage of the power from by a nearby waterfall, Haymaker erected a gristmill operation. This marked the beginning of a village later to become known as Kent. Thanks to its location on stagecoach routes, the village prospered. Today, the city of Kent hosts a wide range of businesses, including national and international corporations. It's also home to Kent State University, which has over 32,000 students enrolled, more than the number of residents in the town itself.

Information: Kent Area Chamber of Commerce | 155 E. Main St., 44240 | 330/673–9855 | www.kentbiz.com.

Attractions

Kent State University. Kent State University's 20,000 students have more than 150 undergraduate and 50 postgraduate programs from which to choose. In a wooded area overlooking the University Commons is the May 4th Memorial, which commemorates the May 4, 1970, student protest against the Vietnam War, when National Guard troops killed four students and wounded nine others. Guided tours of the campus are available free of charge. | E. Main St. | 330/672–2727 | www.kent.edu | Free | Tours Wed.–Sun.

A fashion arts collection of 18th, 19th, and 20th century costumes and clothes by contemporary designers are the highlight of the **Kent State University Museum.** The nine galleries also display Ohio pottery, glass, ivory, and decorative arts from the 1700s to the present. | Rockwell Hall, E. Main St. | 330/672–3450 | $5 | Wed., Fri., Sat. 10–4:45; Thurs. 10–8:45; Sun. 12–4:45.

West Branch State Park. This park 12 mi east of Kent encompasses more than 8,000 acres. You can hike, boat, fish, camp, and mountain bike here. | 5708 Esworthy Rd., Ravenna | 330/296–3239 | Free | Daily.

ON THE CALENDAR

JULY: *Kent Heritage Festival.* This day-long celebration, held the first Saturday in July, occupies all of downtown Kent. There's a 10K race, musical entertainment, crafts, food, a car show, and fireworks. | Main and Water Sts. | 330/673–9855.

Dining

Mike's Place. American/Casual. The menu is as eclectic as the memorabilia at this restaurant. The main dining room has old license plates and x-wing memorabilia strewn about; the private party room looks like a castle and is decorated with armor and swords. Attached to the restaurant is an old twin coach bus (these were made in Kent), which has tables for dining. On the menu: stir fry, quesadillas, and 60 different sandwiches. A specialty is the 12-inch-long Sumo Class Sandwich. | 1700 S. Water St. | 330/673–6501 | $6–$13 | D, MC, V.

Pufferbelly Ltd. American/Casual. The former Atlantic and Great Western train station has been reborn as a family dining spot with antiques lining the walls. Patrons flock here for beef, sandwiches, and the chicken Pufferbelly, a panfried chicken breast over fettuccine primavera. Kids' menu. Sunday brunch. | 152 Franklin Ave. | 330/673–1771 | $8–$15 | AE, D, MC, V.

Lodging

Days Inn. This two-story hotel is 5 mi south of downtown Kent, but is still surrounded by restaurants and shops. Complimentary Continental breakfast. Cable TV. Pool. Business services. | 4422 Edson Rd., Brimfield | 330/677–9400 or 800/325–2525 | fax 330/677–9456 | www.daysinn.com | 67 rooms | $76 | AE, D, DC, MC, V.

Holiday Inn. It's 3 mi to Kent State University and golfing from this hotel. In season, you can enjoy the pool and hot tub with a cabana bar. Restaurant, bar, room service. Cable TV. Pool. Hot tub. Exercise equipment. Video games. Laundry facilities, laundry service. Business services. Some pets allowed. | 4363 Rte. 43 | 330/678–0101 or 800/465–4329 | fax 330/677–5001 | www.holiday-inn.com | 150 rooms | $79–$119 | AE, D, DC, MC, V.

Inn of Kent. This Kent motel has been housing parents for over 25 years. It's two blocks from the Kent State University and downtown Kent. About half of the rooms have kitchenettes. Restaurant, bar, room service. Some kitchenettes. Cable TV. Indoor pool. Laundry facilities. Business services. | 303 E. Main St. | 330/673–3411 | fax 330/673–9878 | 57 rooms | $75 | AE, D, DC, MC, V.

University Inn. This independently owned hotel is one block from downtown Kent and three blocks from the University. It offers a few family rooms with balconies and full-size kitchens. Restaurant. In-room data ports, some refrigerators. Cable TV. Pool. Laundry facilities. Business services. | 540 S. Water St. | 330/678–0123 | fax 330/678–7356 | www.kentuniversityinn.com | 107 rooms | $85 | AE, D, DC, MC, V.

LANCASTER

MAP 14, D5

(Nearby towns listed: Athens, Chillicothe, Columbus, Washington Court House)

Lancaster was founded in 1800 by Colonel Ebenezer Zane, the famous merchant, trailblazer, pioneer, and soldier from Wheeling, West Virginia. He designed the city with four public squares, three of them parks, reminiscent of William Penn's design for Philadelphia. Although the city grew steadily in its first three decades, it received a huge boost in 1836, when the Lancaster Lateral Canal opened to commerce. The canal brought new markets and wealth to Lancaster. Its economic impact still can be seen in the city's many massive 19th-century homes, which are clustered around an area called Square 13. Among Lancaster's famous sons are General William T. Sherman and eight Ohio governors. Today, Buckeye Lake State Park and Mount Pleasant are the city's main attractions, bringing in thousands of visitors each year.

Information: Lancaster-Fairfield County Chamber of Commerce | 109 N. Broad St., 43130 | 740/653–8251 | www.lancoc.org.

Attractions

Buckeye Lake State Park. You can boat, fish, and picnic at this 3,557 acre park, in the heart of Ohio, 15 mi north of Lancaster. | Liebs Island Rd., Rte. 13, Millersport | 740/467–2690 | Free | Daily.

Decorative Arts Center of Ohio. This arts center opened in September 2000 in the Reese Peters House, an 1834 Federal-style mansion next door to the Sherman House. There are frequently changing exhibits of decorative arts, ranging from glass to quilts, as well as an artist-in-residence program and art classes. | 145 E. Main St. | 740/681–1423 | www.decartsohio.org | Free | Tues., Wed., Fri., Sat. 11–4; Thurs. 11–8, Sun. noon–4.

The Georgian. Period furnishings, largely from Fairfield County, and an early glass collection adorn this 19th-century brick Federal-style home. You can buy a combination ticket that includes admission to the Sherman House. | 105 E. Wheeling St. | 740/654–9923 | $2.50, combination ticket $4 | Apr.–mid-Dec., Tues.–Sun. 1–4.

Mount Pleasant. You can follow a trail to the top of Mount Pleasant, a 250-ft-tall sandstone rock formation that was formed by glaciers. The flat top was once used by American Indians and settlers as an observation point and fortress; today, you can see all the way to Columbus, 40 mi away, on a clear day. Some people say the south side projections resemble the profile of an American Indian. | Rising Park, N. High St., north of Fair Ave. | Free | Daily.

Sherman House. This museum displays antiques and Civil War artifacts that belonged to General William T. Sherman and his brother, John Sherman, author of the Sherman Anti-Trust Act. You can buy a combination ticket that includes admission to The Georgian. | 137 E. Main St. | 740/687–5891 or 740/654–9923 | $2.50, combination ticket $4 | Apr.–mid-Dec., Tues.–Sun. 1–4.

Square 13. Architectural historians have said this square, a National Register Historic District, has one of the finest collections of 19th century homes in a concentrated area. You can pick up a free audiocassette for a self-guided tour weekdays, 8–5, at the Convention and Visitors Bureau, 1 N. Broad St., or weekends at Shaw's Restaurant, 123 N. Broad St. Allow about an hour for your walk. | 1 N. Broad St. | 740/653–8251 | www.visitfairfieldcountyoh.org | Free | Daily.

ON THE CALENDAR

MAY: *Pilgrimage of Homes.* Each year, on the first weekend of May, Lancaster's most luxurious private homes are open to the public for tours. | 740/654–9923.

JUNE: *Spring Old Car Festival.* Antique automobiles dating back to the 1920s are always on hand, as are models from the '50s and '60s, at this festival the first week of June at the Fairfield County Fairgrounds. | 157 E. Fair Ave. | 740/653–8251 or 800/626–1296.

AUG.: *Zane Square Arts and Crafts Festival.* This longtime Lancaster tradition reflects the city's fondness for handmade goods with a juried craft show and live entertainment. It occupies much of the downtown area. | Main and Broad Sts. | 740/687–6651.

SEPT.: *Millersport Sweetcorn Festival.* Ohio's most important crop is the centerpiece of this four-day festival held the Wednesday to Saturday before Labor Day in the village of Millersport, 15 mi north of Lancaster. You can try dozens of foods made from sweetcorn. | Rte. 204, just east of Rte. 37 | 740/467–3943.

OCT.: *Fairfield County Fair.* This weeklong festival draws more than 75,000 people each year to the Fairfield County Fairgrounds with national music acts, rides, and a petting zoo. It's held the second full week in October. | 157 E. Fair Ave. | 740/653–3041 or 800/626–1296.

DEC.: *Christmas Candlelight Tour.* On the second Saturday in December, you can take a candlelit tour of homes and businesses decked for the season. At tour's end, participants can sip hot chocolate and sing carols. | 740/654–9923 or 800/626–1296.

Dining

Four Reasons Bakery and Deli. American/Casual. This restored warehouse with high ceilings and tile floors is downtown's artsiest hangout. At lunchtime, it's the busiest; the courthouse is just a block away. Try the locally famed sandwich, Ryckman's Reuben. The menu also features pasta salads, tossed salads, and deli sandwiches. It's open for breakfast daily. | 135 W. Main St. | 740/654–2253 | No dinner weekends | $4.40–$5.50 | AE, D, DC, MC, V.

Shaw's Restaurant. American. An extensive wine list and microbrewed beers complement a menu of steak and seafood. Prime rib, lamb chops, and barbecued ribs are also served in this Victorian dining room, which shares an address with *(see* Shaw's Inn). Breakfast is served daily. Sunday brunch. Kids' menu. | 123 N. Broad St. | 740/654–1842 | $15–$18 | MC, V.

Lodging

Amerihost Inn. This two-story hotel next to the River Valley Mall is at the north end of Lancaster, about 3 mi from downtown. You'll get a free newspaper in the morning with your breakfast. Complimentary Continental breakfast. Cable TV. Indoor pool. Hot tub. Exercise equipment. | 1721 River Valley Circle N | 740/654–5111 or 800/434–5800 | fax 740/654–5108 | www.amerihostinn.com | 60 rooms, 2 suites | $80, $159 suites | AE, D, DC, MC, V.

Best Western. The River Valley Mall is directly across the street from this hotel. Free passes to the local YMCA fitness center are available. Restaurant, bar, room service. Some refrigerators. Cable TV. Pool. Putting green. Laundry facilities, laundry service. Business services. Airport shuttle. Some pets allowed. | 1858 N. Memorial Dr. | 740/653–3040 or 800/528–1234 | fax 740/653–1172 | www.bestwestern.com | 168 rooms | $65 | AE, D, DC, MC, V.

Hampton Inn of Lancaster. This modern, three-story hotel, 3 mi from downtown Lancaster and 30 mi southeast of Columbus on Rte. 33, has a number of spacious king study rooms. Complimentary Continental breakfast. In-room data ports, some refrigerators, some microwaves, some in-room hot tubs. Cable TV. Indoor pool. Hot tub. Exercise equipment and gym. Laundry facilities, laundry service. | 2041 Schorrway Dr. | 740/654–2999 or 800/426–7866 | www.hampton-inn.com | 75 rooms | $71 | AE, D, DC, MC, V.

Knights Inn. You can park right at the door at this one-story motel a mile from the River Valley Mall. Complimentary Continental breakfast. Some kitchenettes. Cable TV. Business services. Some pets allowed. | 1327 River Valley Blvd. | 740/687–4823 or 800/843–5644 | fax 740/687–4823 | www.knightsinn.com | 60 rooms | $62 | AE, D, DC, MC, V.

Shaw's Inn. This six-story B&B in downtown Lancaster was built in the Federalist style in 1939. Each of the eclectically furnished rooms is done in a different theme, ranging from Caribbean island to southwestern. The inn is across the street from the Georgian and one block away from the Decorative Arts Center of Ohio. Restaurant, complimentary breakfast. Some kitchenettes, some microwaves, some in-room hot tubs. Cable TV, some in-room VCRs. Library. Laundry service. | 123 N. Broad St. | 740/653–5522 or 800/654–2477 | 22 rooms | $70 | MC, V.

LEBANON

MAP 14, B6

(Nearby towns listed: Mason, Cincinnati, Middletown, Waynesville, Wilmington)

Lebanon, the seat of Warren County in southwestern Ohio, was settled by early pioneers after the American Revolution. In 1802, a surveyor laid out the community, with Broadway and Main Streets intersecting at the center of town. Since that time, Lebanon has become the cultural and business hub of a lucrative agricultural area of the Miami Valley. Just 30 mi from Cincinnati and Dayton, Lebanon (pop. 11,000) spreads over 10½ square mi. It incorporates four major retail centers and two industrial parks. The city's main attraction is the Golden Lamb Inn, Ohio's oldest hotel, dating from 1803. The downtown area, with its tree-lined streets and antiques shops, has a Colonial air.

Information: **Lebanon Chamber of Commerce** | 25 W. Mulberry St., 45306 | 513/932–1100.

Attractions

Fort Ancient State Memorial. The Hopewell Indians built this prehistoric earthwork mound, the nation's second largest, on a plateau about 6 mi east of Lebanon. The site includes circular mounds which were used as a calendar and a museum that documents the religion and customs of this prehistoric period. | 6123 Rte. 350, Oregonia | 513/932–4421 | www.ohiohistory.org | $5 | Memorial Day–Labor Day, daily 10–8; Mar.–May and Sept.–Nov., Wed.–Sun. 10–5.

Glendower State Memorial. This 1840 Greek Revival home has period furnishings and artifacts that illustrate the home life of the times. | 105 Cincinnati Ave. (U.S. 42) | 513/932–1817 or 513/932–5366 | $3 | June–Labor Day, Wed.–Sat. noon–4, Sun. 1–4; Labor Day–Oct., Sat. noon–4, Sun. 1–4.

Golden Lamb Inn–Shaker Museum. Established in 1803, Ohio's oldest inn still accommodates travelers in its 18 guest rooms. The house has a great collection of antique Shaker furniture and toys. | 27 S. Broadway | 513/932–5065 | www.goldenlamb.com | Free | Daily 10:30–9.

Turtle Creek Valley Railway. A restored steam locomotive takes passengers through the countryside of Southern Ohio on the old Indiana and Ohio Railroad tracks. Special events include murder mystery train rides and rides with Santa during the holiday season. | 198 S. Broadway | 513/398–8584 or 513/933–8014 | $10 | Apr.–Dec.

Valley Vineyards Winery. Self-guided tours at this Southern Ohio winery just 8 mi east of Lebanon include wine-tasting and cheese samples. The winery hosts cook-it-yourself steak cookouts on weekends. | 2276 E. U.S. Rtes. 22 & 3, Morrow | 513/899–2485 | Free | Mon.–Thurs. 11–8, Fri.–Sat. 11–9:30, Sun. 1–6.

Warren County Historical Society Museum. The Shaker furniture collection is the highlight of this museum, whose holdings range from prehistoric artifacts to contemporary objects. There's also a life-size replica of a mid- to late-19th-century village green, complete with shops. | 105 S. Broadway | 513/932–1817 | $3 | Tues.–Sat. 9–4, Sun. 12–4.

ON THE CALENDAR

JULY: *Warren County Fair.* Warren County is one of the fastest-growing counties in Ohio, so events and attractions are always being added to the line-up. Nationally known acts take the stage every year the third week of July at the Warren County Fairgrounds. | 665 N. Broadway | 513/932–2636.
SEPT.: *Applefest.* You can take part in the pie-eating contest or simply watch the parade go by. | Downtown Lebanon | 513/932–1100.
SEPT.–MAY: *Lebanon Raceway.* Southwest Ohio's most daring drivers battle it out on this harness racing track. The drivers, dubbed "weekend warriors," are doctors, lawyers, mechanics, and such during the rest of the week. | 665. N. Broadway | 513/932–4936.
DEC.: *Annual Historic Christmas Festival and Horsedrawn Carriage Parade.* This is a family event that draws 50,000 people to Lebanon each year. The daytime parade shows off Victorian costumes and antique carriages. Other highlights include live entertainment, pictures with Mr. and Mrs. Claus, and an evening parade. | Downtown Lebanon | 513/932–1100 | Free.

Dining

The Best Cafe. Eastern European. Knotty pine, high booths, and dim lighting give this 150-year-old cafe a pub-like coziness. Bohemian fare includes cabbage strudel, schnitzel sandwiches, goulash, and vegetarian quiche. Six beers are on tap. | 17 E. Mulberry St. | 513/932–4400 | Closed Sun. | $6–$17 | AE, D, MC, V.

Golden Lamb Inn. American. You can get the likes of lamb shanks, turkey and mashed potatoes, and Sister Lizzy's Shaker Sugar Pie at this restaurant which dates back to 1803. Kids' menu, early bird suppers. | 27 S. Broadway | 513/932–5065 | $15–$30 | AE, D, DC, MC, V.

Village Cellars. Delicatessen. Sandwiches are the specialty at this popular lunchtime destination in downtown Lebanon. Choose from ham, turkey, and many other toppings. The two big, laid-back rooms are done in hunter green and maroon. You can stop in for a light dinner every night until 7:30. | 42 E. Mulberry St. | 513/932–5355 | Reservations not accepted | $3.50–$5 | MC, V.

Lodging

Budget Inn. This tiny, modern motel with cherry furnishings is in downtown Lebanon, 10 mi from I–75. Take exit 29. Cable TV. | 115 N. Broadway | 513/932–1966 or 800/283–4678 | 16 rooms | $60 | AE, MC, V.

Burl Manor. This Victorian B&B, built in 1847, has brick walls throughout, Victorian furnishings and canopy beds. It's two blocks south of downtown Lebanon's antique shopping district. Dining room. Complimentary breakfast. In-room VCRs. Pool. Library. No kids under 2. | 230 S. Mechanic St. | 513/934–0400 or 800/450–0401 | 4 rooms | $85 | MC, V.

Golden Lamb Inn. Established in 1803 as a stage coach stop, the Golden Lamb is Ohio's oldest inn. Its rooms are furnished with antiques dating back to the 1850s. The hotel has a gift shop as well as "The Black Horse Tavern," a popular spot for a drink. Restaurant (see Golden Lamb Inn), bar, complimentary Continental breakfast. Cable TV. Business services. | 27 S. Broadway | 513/932–5065 | fax 513/934–3049 | www.goldenlamb.com | 18 rooms | $103 | AE, D, DC, MC, V.

Knights Inn. There's a friendly staff and coffee in the lobby at this one-story wood-frame motel next to the Colony Square Shopping Plaza. Some kitchenettes, some microwaves. Cable TV. Pool. Business services. | 725 E. Main St. | 513/932–3034 or 800/843–5644 | fax 513/932–3034 | www.knightsinn.com | 58 rooms | $65 | AE, D, DC, MC, V.

Shaker Inn. This small, one-story motel is family owned and operated and has spotless rooms. It's a half mile out of town. Refrigerators. Cable TV. Pool. | 600 Cincinnati Ave. (U.S. 42S) | 513/932–7575 or 800/752–6151 | www.lebanon-ohio.com/shaker-inn.html | 20 rooms, 4 two-bedroom units | $52–$72 | AE, D, MC, V.

LIMA

MAP 14, B4

(Nearby towns listed: Celina, Findlay, Van Wert, Wapakoneta)

In 1831, Lima got its name rather simply—several pioneers put names into a hat and drew one. Lima, a quinine bark used for the treatment of swamp fever or malaria at the time, was chosen. In northwest Ohio, Lima grew quickly. Locomotives brought people and money to the city in the 1850s, and the area economy got an added boost when a train manufacturing company, The Lima Locomotive Works, began operations here in 1870. Lima was thrust onto the national financial scene when oil was discovered in 1870. For two years following the discovery, the city was known as the oil capital of the world.

Today, the fruit of that era can be seen in the city's Golden Block area, where the sprawling mansions built by oil barons still stand. Lima and the surrounding region continue to thrive. Local manufacturers produce such diverse products as the M1-A2 Abrams Tank, automotive engines, and NFL footballs.

Information: Lima/Allen County Chamber of Commerce | 147 N. Main St., 45801 | 419/222–6045 and 888/222–6075 | www.laccoc.com.

Attractions

Allen County Museum. This museum has quite an eclectic collection. Antique automobiles and bicycles, steam and electric railroad items, and musical instruments are on display. There's also a re-created barber's shop, doctor's office, and country store, as well as a log house with exhibits on pioneer life. A 10-by-15-ft model of Mount Vernon is "furnished" with period pieces. During summer afternoons, a hands-on museum for children is open. | 620 W. Market St. | 419/222–9426 | Free | June–Aug., Tues.–Sat. 10–5, Sun. 1–5; Sept.–May, Tues.–Sun. 1–5.

ArtSpace/Lima. Lima's premier arts center features a gallery with changing photography, clay, pottery, glass, and textile exhibits. Works by nationally and internationally known artists are displayed; Ohio artists are emphasized. | 65–67 Town Square | 419/222–1721 | Free | Weekdays 10–5, Sat. 12–3, Sun 2–4; extended summer hours: Mon. 10–8.

Lincoln Park Railway Exhibit. A steam-engine (the last one built in Lima) and a railcar and caboose are on outdoor display in Lincoln Park. There's also a 1895 country railroad station. | E. Elm St. | 419/222–9426 | Free | Daily.

ON THE CALENDAR

MAR.: *Greater Limaland Blues Festival.* Nationally known artists such as Billy Branch, Lonnie Brooks, and Sweet Alice Hoskins help make this event a sell-out every year. It's held the first weekend of the month at Allen County Memorial Hall. | W. Elm St. | 419/222–1721.
AUG.: *Square Fair/Summer Community Arts Festival.* Music, dance, fine arts exhibits, and children's activities fill the Lima Town Square for this celebration the first weekend of the month. | Town Square | 419/222–1096.
AUG.: *Allen County Fair.* For the past century and a half, local residents have flocked to this nine-day fair for livestock shows, games, and rides. The nine-day fair concludes the Saturday before Labor Day weekend. | 2750 Harding Hwy. | 419/228–7141.

Dining

Kewpee Hamburgers. American/Casual. With a neon facade and a giant plastic kewpee doll above the doorway, this diner has been serving malts, hamburgers, fries, chili, and fresh baked pies since 1928. Breakfast is served ever day but Sunday. | 111 N. Elizabeth St. | 419/228–1778 | Reservations not accepted | No lunch Sun. | $4–$8 | No credit cards.

Tudor's. American/Casual. You can get steak, chicken, ribs, and pastas here, plus desserts such as Kentucky Derby pie, a combination of pecan pie and warm chocolate chip cookie. Salad bar. Kids' menu, early bird suppers. | 2383 Elida Rd. | 419/331–2220 | $10–$20 | AE, MC, V.

Lodging

Fairfield Inn by Marriott. This three-story hotel is 2 mi northwest of downtown Lima and within one block of the Lima Mall. Complimentary Continental breakfast. Some microwaves, some refrigerators. Cable TV. Indoor pool. Laundry service. | 2179 Elida Rd. | 419/224–8496 or 800/288–2800 | www.marriott.com | 64 rooms | $65–$95 | AE, D, DC, MC, V.

Holiday Inn Lima. The hotel has an interior, four-story, glass-enclosed tropical atrium, with a pool and hot tub. You can ask for a room with an outside view or one with a balcony overlooking the atrium. It's 5 mi from downtown Lima and 3 mi from the Allen County Fairgrounds, at I–75 and Route 309. Restaurant, bar with entertainment, room service. In-room data ports. Cable TV. Indoor pool. Hot tub, sauna. Exercise equipment. Video games. Playground. Laundry facilities. Business services. Some pets allowed. | 1920 Roschman Ave. | 419/222–0004 or 800/465–4329 | fax 419/222–2176 | www.holiday-inn.com | 150 rooms | $110 | AE, D, DC, MC, V.

LOGAN

(Nearby towns listed: Athens, Columbus, Chillicothe, Lancaster)

A quaint town in its own right, with a 19th-century town square and lots of shops, Logan is nevertheless best known as the entryway to the Hocking Hills region. An area untouched by the glaciers that flattened much of the rest of Ohio, Hocking Hills is filled with rock formations, waterfalls, caves, and deep woods that more closely resemble the mountainous areas of neighboring West Virginia. Many artists and other creative types live here because of the proximity to the natural beauty, and there are some unique shops in which to buy their wares. You'll find good hiking and canoeing, too.

Information: Hocking County Tourism Association | 13178 Rte. 664, 43138 | 740/385–9706 | www.hockinghills.com.

Attractions

Hocking Hills State Park. Scattered in pieces over Hocking County, the 2,348-acre state park in the Hocking State Forest has six must-see attractions, including gorges, a sandstone cave, cascading waterfalls, and unusual rock formations. Over 100 kinds of birds nest in the park, and most species of wildlife native to the Midwest can be seen here. The park, which is south and west of Logan, is a great place for challenging hikes. | 20160 Rte. 664 | 740/385–6841 | www.dnr.state.oh.us/odnr/parks/directory/hocking.htm | Free | Dawn–dusk.

At **Conkles Hollow,** named for W. J. Conkle, who carved his name and the year 1797 in a tree, you can hike around the top of the cliffs on the Rim Trail or into the deep gorge, which ends at a cave and waterfalls. It's 14 mi southwest of Logan. | Rte. 374 | 740/385–6841 | Free | Dawn–dusk.

The 80-acre sandstone **Ash Cave,** 15 mi south of Logan, is a huge recess in a rock. A 90-ft waterfall drops from the rock's top. | Rte. 56 | 740/385–6841 | Free | Dawn–dusk.

About 2 mi north of Ash Cave and 13 mi south of Logan is **Cedar Falls,** named for the hemlock trees that early explorers mistook for cedars. It's another cascading waterfall at the back of a gorge. A 3 mi trail connects it to Old Man's Cave. | Rte. 374 | 740/385–6841 | Free | Dawn–dusk.

After the Civil War, a hermit lived in **Old Man's Cave,** an area distinguished by interesting rock formations, two caves, waterfalls, and a wooded ravine. It 12 mi southwest of Logan, and connected to Cedar Falls by a 3 mi path. | State Rt. 664 | 740/385–6841 | Free | Dawn–dusk.

According to rumor, thieves once roosted in **Rock House,** an eroded rock formation in the face of a steep cliff 12 mi west of Logan. | Rte. 374 | 740/385–6841 | Free | Dawn–dusk.

You can make the steep hike up the jutting rocks of **Cantwell Cliffs,** 12 mi west of Logan. In the fall, the view of the trees below is breathtaking. | Rte. 374 | 740/385–6841 | Free | Dawn–dusk.

Hocking House. The area's best-known artist, Jean Magdich, makes and sells her porcelainware and other ceramic pieces here. Prices on seconds (with only minor, sometimes unnoticeable flaws) can be as much as half off the regular price. | Rte. 664 and Big Pine Rd. | 740/385–4166 | Free | Memorial Day–Labor Day, Tues.–Sun., noon–5; Sept.–May, weekends noon–5.

Hocking Valley Scenic Railway. The depot is in Nelsonville, about 12 mi southeast of Logan on Route 33. The locomotive takes riders through the Wayne National Forest and the surrounding areas as guides recount the local history. You can take the noon train to Haydenville (13 mi round trip) or a 2:30 excursion to Logan (25 mi round trip). Trains make a stop at Robbins Crossings, a re-creation of a settlers' village from the 1860s. During the first three weekends of December, you can take the special Santa Train to Logan. | 33 E. Canal St., Nelsonville | 740/753–9531 | $8–$11 | Memorial Day–Nov., weekends.

JAN.: *Winter Hike.* More than 5,000 hikers show up on the third Saturday in January to walk the 5 mi from Cedar Falls to Ash Cave and see the forest covered in snow and ice. Bean soup is served at the end of the hike. This is the biggest event of the year in Hocking Hills. | 20160 Rte. 664 | 740/385–6841.

Dining
Great Expectations. Delicatessen. This small cafe is tucked in a side room of a renovated Victorian house that's also a bookstore. Culinary students at nearby Hocking Technical College make panini sandwiches, pasta salads, and other side dishes, as well as cakes and pies. Breakfast is also served. The college is renowned statewide for its cooking program. | 179 S. Market St. | 740/380–9177 | No dinner weekends | $3–$8 | MC, V.

Inn at Cedar Falls. Contemporary. The chef cooks up lavish meals using fresh vegetables and herbs grown in the inn's garden. The menu rarely repeats itself, but typical entrées include pork tenderloin with bordelaise, beef medallions, and herbed chicken breast. Call ahead for reservations as eary as possible if you're not staying at the inn. Dinners are fixed price. | 21190 Rte. 374 | 740/385–7489 or 800/65–FALLS | No lunch | Reservations essential | Sun.–Thurs. $21, Fri.–Sat. $30 | AE, D, MC, V.

Jack's Steakhouse. Steak. T-bones and ribeyes are the specialty here, both served with oversized baked potatoes. Sunday through Wednesday the dinner special lets you buy one steak dinner and pay half price for the other. | 35770 Hocking Dr. | 740/385–9909 | $10–$15 | MC, V.

Lodging
AmeriHost Inn. Just off Route 33 in the heart of Hocking Hills region, this motel is close to the state park and to downtown. Restaurant. Cable TV. Indoor pool. | 12819 Rte. 664 | 740/385–1700 or 800/459–4678 | fax 740/385–9288 | www.amerihostinn.com | 60 rooms | $69–$129 | AE, D, MC, V.

Inn at Cedar Falls. You can stay in the lodge, a refurbished barn whose rooms are furnished with primitive antiques, or in one of the 19th-century cabins, which sleep up to four. Each cabin was moved from other parts of the country and decorated with antiques picked personally by the innkeeper. Homemade granola is always served; other breakfast fare includes omelets, french toast, and crepes. Dining room, complimentary breakfast. Some kitchenettes, some in-room hot tubs. No room phones. No TV. Some pets allowed. No smoking. | 21190 Rte. 374 | 740/385–7489 or 800/65–FALLS | fax 740/385–0820 | 8 rooms, 5 cabins | Lodge, $65–$100; cabins, up to $240 | AE, D, MC, V.

Old Man's Cave Chalets. These cabins, 11 mi south of Logan, are tucked in the woods and have private porches, hot tubs, and full kitchens. They range in size from two-person A-frame cottages to large lodges that can sleep up to 20 people or more. Kitchenettes, microwaves, refrigerators. In-room hot tubs. Cable TV, in-room VCRs. Pool. Tennis. Some pets allowed. | 18905 Rte. 664 S | 470/385–6517 or 800/762–9396 | www.oldmanscavechalets.com | 30 cabins, 4 lodges | Cabins and suites, $99–$205; lodges, $399–$775 | AE, D, MC, V.

LORAIN

MAP 14, D2

(Nearby towns listed: Cleveland, Elyria, Oberlin, Strongsville, Vermilion)

Incorporated in 1874, the city of Lorain is in northeastern Ohio on the shore of Lake Erie. It is the 10th largest city in the state with a population of 69,800. Lorain has an international port with access to world markets via the St. Lawrence Seaway. There are public beaches along the lake, shoreline restaurants and shops, fishing charters, and marinas. Wind surfing, scuba diving, fishing, and boating are popular recreational activities here. The Lorain Palace Civic Center, in downtown, is a 1,600-seat facility on the National Register of Historic Places; it hosts a variety of musical and cultural events year-round. The city holds a number of annual celebrations, including the International Festival, which celebrates Lorain's multicultural heritage—people of more than 70 ethnic backgrounds reside here.

Information: Lorain County Chamber of Commerce | 6100 S. Broadway, #201, 44053 | 440/233–6500 or 800/334–1673 | www.lcvb.org.

Attractions

Black River Historical Society. This museum, in the restored home of former mayor Leonard Moore, depicts the history and industries of Lorain. Artifacts, photographs, and documents date from the early 1800s to the present. Industry exhibit includes items from Lorain's early steel-making days, the first automatic revolving steam shovel works, wooden and steel ship-building companies, lake freighters, stove manufacturing, and early telephone systems. Domestic exhibit includes clothing, tools, maps, clocks, time-saving devices, entertainment, toys, and jewelry. | 309 W. 5th St. | 440/245–2563 | $2 | Wed., Sun., 1–4; Fri. 10–1.

Lakeview Park. This park facing Lake Erie offers facilities for numerous recreational activities, include swimming, tennis, baseball, basketball, volleyball, lawn bowling, windsurfing, and ice skating. There's a sand beach, picnic areas, a formal rose garden, a playground, fountains, and a gazebo. Summer concerts are held here. | W. Erie Ave., between Broadway and Leavitt Rd. | 440/244–9000 | Free | Daily, dawn–dusk.

Lorain Palace Civic Center. This restored Gothic theater, built as a "movie palace" in 1928, now hosts professional dance, music, and drama productions. | 617 Broadway | 440/245–2323 | Prices vary.

ON THE CALENDAR

JUNE: *International Festival Week.* Food, dancing, and music from around the world are all part of this tribute to global diversity held the third week of June at the Sheffield Shopping Center. | 222 Sheffield Ctr. | 440/233–6500 or 800/334–1673.
JULY: *Port and Lighthouse Fest.* Waterfront events and activities are the highlights of this late July festival. On the schedule are entertainment, food, crafts, and lighthouse displays. | 110 Alabama Ave. | 440/233–6500 or 800/334–1673.

Dining

The Golden Crown. Chinese. This casual restaurant with chandeliers and shell paintings is known locally for its sweet and sour chicken. Cantonese and Mandarin fare is served. | 449 W. 4th St. | 440/246–6816 | Reservations not accepted | $6–$15 | MC, V.

Lodging

Spitzer Plaza Hotel. This stately hotel in downtown Lorain, built in the 1920s, was an office building until its reincarnation in the late 1980s. Grand pillars, graceful chandeliers, and period furnishings have been retained. It's within walking distance of the marina. Restaurant, bar, room service. Some in-room data ports, in-room safes, kitchenettes, minibars, refrigerators. Cable TV. Indoor pool. Sauna, hot tub. Video games. | 301 Broadway Ave. | 440/246–5767 or 800/446–7452 | 69 rooms | $92–$97 | AE, D, DC, MC, V.

MANSFIELD

INTRO
ATTRACTIONS
DINING
LODGING

MANSFIELD

MAP 14, D4

(Nearby towns listed: Mount Gilead, Mount Vernon, Wooster)

Mansfield, in the north central portion of Ohio, is the county seat of Richland County. The city was founded in 1813 and named after Colonel Jared Mansfield, who was the

United States Surveyor General at the time. Mansfield was the site of several Revolutionary War skirmishes between pioneer settlers and Native Americans who were aligned with the British. During the War of 1812, settlers constructed two large block houses in the public square to protect themselves from Indian raids. One of the structures still stands in the South Park area. Today, Mansfield is known as the home of the popular Clear Fork Ski Area and the beautiful gardens of the Kingwood Center.

Information: **Mansfield-Richland Area Chamber of Commerce** | 55 N. Mulberry St., 44902 | 419/522–3211 | www.mansfieldtourism.org.

Attractions

Charles Mill Lake Park. You'll find plants and wildlife in numerous species at this park, which is part of the Muskingum Watershed Conservancy District. Facilities include swimming (beach and pool), boating (canoes and pontoon boats), and camping. | 1271 Rte. 430 | 419/368–6885 | Free | Daily.

Charles Mill Marina. The manmade lake features a marina and a campground. You can rent boats or embark on a cruise boat with a captain. | 1277 Rte. 430 | 419/884–0166 | Free | Daily.

Clear Fork Ski Area. You can ski all day and all night at this Central Ohio ski area, 15 mi south of Mansfield, and then head into the lodge for apres-ski fun. There are nine trails, serviced by six lifts, winding through elevations of 1,100 to 2,400 ft. The vertical drop is 300 ft. Rental equipment is available. | 341 Resort Dr. | 419/883–2000 or 800/237–5673 (snow conditions) | Lift tickets, $32 day on weekends | Nov.–Mar., Mon. noon–10, Tues.–Fri. 10–10, weekends 9–10.

Kingwood Center. Over 40 acres of beautiful gardens, woods, and ponds surround the former estate of Charles K. King. Several greenhouses shelter seasonal displays of tulips and other flowers. You can also take a self-guided tour of Kingwood Hall, a circa 1926 French Provincial mansion with period furnishings. | 900 Park Ave. W | 419/522–0211 | Free | Gardens: Apr.–Oct., daily 8–dusk; Nov.–Mar., daily 8–5. Kingwood Hall: Tues.–Sat. 9–5. Also open Sun. 1–5 Apr.–Oct. and Dec.

Malabar Farm State Park. The brainchild of Pulitzer Prize-winning writer Louis Bromfield, this working farm allows you to experience rural life. Highlights include tractor-drawn wagon tours and tours of the 32-room farmhouse. The park is in Lucas, about 10 mi west of Mansfield | 4050 Bromfield Rd., Lucas | 419/892–2784 | www.malabarfarm.org | Grounds free, $3 for house tour | Daily 10–5.

Mohican State Park. The Clear Fork River and the Clear Fork Gorge run through this state park in Loudonville, southeast of Mansfield. The river is stocked with brown trout and is a prime fishing spot. A trail runs through the 1,000-ft-wide by 300-ft-deep gorge past waterfalls and beautiful scenery. | Rte. 97, Loudonville | 419/994–4290 | Free | Daily 8 AM–9 PM.

Oak Hill Cottage. Built in the 1840s and restored several times since, this Victorian Gothic house with seven gables has a well-maintained collection of original furnishings. | 310 Springmill St. | 419/524–1765 | www.mansfieldtourism.org/pages/members/oakhill.html | $3 | Apr.–Dec., Sun. 2–5.

Richland Carousel Park. This heated pavilion in Mansfield's Carousel District houses a beautiful, all-wood, hand-carved carousel designed and made in Ohio, the first one built since the early 1930s. | W. 4th St., at Main St. | 419/522–4223 | Free | Memorial Day–Labor Day, daily 10–5, until 8 on Wed.; Labor Day–Memorial Day, daily 11–5, until 8 on Wed.

Richland County Museum. Memorabilia illustrating the county's history is displayed in an 1850 schoolhouse in Lexington, a few miles south of Mansfield. The collection includes tools, clothing, children's toys and furniture and paintings. | 51 W. Church St., Lexington | 419/756–9960 | Free | May–Oct., weekends 1:30–4:30.

FEB.: *Ohio Winter Ski Carnival.* This annual heart-of-winter event at the Snow Trails Ski Resort in Mansfield includes ski and snowboard races, kids' games, a costume contest, and a ski patrol cookout. Lift ticket prices and ski equipment rental rates are lowered on the last weekend in February for the occasion. | Snow Trails Ski Resort, 3100 Possum Run Rd. | 419/774–9818 or 800/OHIOSKI.

MAY–OCT.: *Auto Racing at the Mid-Ohio Sports Car Course.* They may not be Jeff Gordon or Dale Earnhardt, but the drivers who race at this Lexington course, a few miles south of Mansfield, are just as entertaining to watch. Amateur and professional drivers compete in modified cars; races are held on weekends. | 7721 Steam Corners Rd., Lexington | 419/884–4000 or 800/MID–OHIO.

AUG.: *Richland County Fair.* Almost everyone knows everyone else at this hometown county fair, but out-of-towners are welcomed with open arms. Take in some of the livestock shows, sample the food, and by all means hit a few of the thrill rides. | 750 N. Home Rd. | 419/747–3717.

SEPT.: *Ohio Heritage Days.* Actors and actresses portray Native Americans and pioneer settlers during this annual celebration of Ohio's history, held in Lucas, about 10 mi west of Mansfield. One of Ohio's largest free outdoor crafts fairs is part of the event, as are live musical performances, a barn dance, demonstrations of vintage tractors, and the Malabar Farm sawmill. There's also a Civil War and fur trappers encampment, and exhibits about state historical events. | Malabar Farm State Park, 4050 Bromfield Rd., Lucas | 419/892–2784.

Dining

Brunches Restaurant. Cafe. This eatery in the heart of the Carousel District attracts many business people on weekdays with its breakfast specials and light lunch fare. The menu includes daily quiche variations, specialty deli sandwiches, creative salads, and gourmet coffee. Known for breakfast specials and light lunch fare. Kids' menu. No smoking. | 103 N. Main St. | 419/526–2233 | No dinner | $5–$8 | D, MC, V.

Mama's Touch of Italy. Italian. This Northern Italian restaurant, festooned with greenery and done in reds, is cozy and very relaxed. The lasagna and baked ziti are favorites. | 275 Park Ave. W | 419/526–5099 | Closed Sun. No lunch Sat. | $9–$14 | AE, D, DC, MC, V.

Skyway East. Steak. With its 1950s supper-club style, complete with dim lighting and white linen tablecloths, Skyway East has been a favorite among locals for 30 years. After you treat yourself to oysters Rockefeller, you can dine on big portions of steak, prime rib, fresh fish, and shellfish (jumbo shrimp is popular). Known for filet mignon, prepared several different ways. | 2461 Emma La. | 419/589–9929 | Closed Sun. No lunch | $10–$30 | AE, D, DC, MC, V.

Lodging

Best Value Inn. Right off I–71 and Route 30, this chain property is close to several restaurants and stores. Restaurant, bar, room service. Cable TV. Pool. Business services. Some pets allowed. | 880 Laver Rd. | 419/589–2200 | fax 419/589–5624 | 101 rooms | $75 | AE, D, DC, MC, V.

Comfort Inn North. On the north side of Mansfield in the Carousel District, this property is about 20 minutes away from the Clear Fork Ski Area. A restaurant is next door. Bar, complimentary Continental breakfast, room service. In-room data ports, refrigerators (in suites). Cable TV. Indoor pool. Hot tub, sauna. Laundry facilities. Business services. Some pets allowed. | 500 N. Trimble Rd. | 419/529–1000 or 800/918–9189 | fax 419/529–2953 | www.christopherhotels.com | 114 rooms, 22 suites | $70, $79 suites | AE, D, DC, MC, V.

Holiday Inn Hotel and Suites. Just minutes away from the Clear Fork Ski Area, this six-story hotel is packed with skiers in the winter. Restaurant, bar, room service. In-room data ports, some refrigerators. Cable TV. Indoor pool. Hot tub. Exercise equipment. Business services. | 116 Park Ave. W | 419/525–6000 or 800/465–4329 | fax 419/525–0197 | www.holidayinn.com | 158 rooms | $89 | AE, D, DC, MC, V.

Knights Inn. Rooms are in four buildings at this one-story motel next to a restaurant and near area shopping. Complimentary Continental breakfast, room service. Cable TV, in-room VCRs and movies. Pool. Laundry service. Business services. Some pets allowed. | 555 N. Trimble Rd. | 419/529–2100 or 800/843–5644 | fax 419/529–6679 | www.christopherhotels.com | 110 rooms | $50 | AE, D, DC, MC, V.

Mansfield/Ontario Hampton Inn. This hotel is 3 to 4 mi from Kingwood Center, the Carousel District, and downtown Mansfield; 8 mi west of I–71 on Route 30. Complimentary Continental breakfast. Some microwaves, some refrigerators. Cable TV, in-room movies. Indoor pool. Hot tub. Pets allowed in some rooms. | 1051 N. Lexington Spring Mill Rd. | 419/747–5353 or 800/426–7866 | www.hampton-inn.com | 62 rooms | $69 | AE, D, DC, MC, V.

The Olde Stone Bed and Breakfast. This 1826 Greek Revival sandstone house is a few minutes' drive from the Mid-Ohio auto racing track, the Kingwood Center gardens, and downtown Mansfield. Settle in for a medieval experience: the interior looks like a castle, with handpainted stone walls, wrought iron accessories, and handmade log beds. Take Route 39 off I–71. Kitchen and patio. Complimentary breakfast. Room service. Cable TV, in-room VCRs. Pool. | 291 N. Stewart Rd. | 419/589–9662 | 2 rooms | $70 | No credit cards.

Travelodge. Right at the entrance to the Clear Fork Ski Area, this hotel is for skiers who like to be near the slopes. There's a 24-hour restaurant next door. Complimentary Continental breakfast. Some microwaves, some refrigerators. Cable TV. Pool. Business services. Some pets allowed (fee). | 90 Hanley Rd. | 419/756–7600 or 800/255–3050 | www.travelodge.com | 46 rooms | $75 | AE, D, MC, V.

MARBLEHEAD

MAP 14, D2

(Nearby towns listed: Kelleys Island, Port Clinton, Sandusky)

Settled because of the huge limestone quarry that sits in the middle of the Marblehead peninsula, Marblehead the town is actually on the easternmost tip of the peninsula and is now more of a tourist hub than anything else. Visitors come to see the lighthouse, take in the views of Lake Erie and boat, fish, and relax. Ocean-size waves lap the rocky shoreline here in the summer, and gale-force winds can blow through in the winter.

Information: **Peninsula Chamber of Commerce** | Box 268, 43440 | 419/798–9777 | www.lake-erie.com.

Attractions

Marblehead Lighthouse. The oldest continuously operating lighthouse on the Great Lakes dates from 1821; it one of the most photographed scenes in the state. Visitors may climb 87 spiral steps to the top of the lighthouse on the second Saturday of each month from June to October. | off Bayshore Rd. | 419/734–4386 or 800/441–1271 | Free | Daily.

Prehistoric Forest Park. When the park opened in 1959, families came to ride through the forest in small carts and shoot toy machine guns at dinosaur statues. Now, it's a walk-through park, with attractions including a volcano inhabited by skeletons, full-size dinosaur statues, live animals, and an archaeological dig, where you can uncover fossils. Mystery Hill is a gravity-defying fun house where water seems to run uphill and chairs stand on only two legs. There's miniature golf here, too. | 8232 E. Harbor Rd. | 419/798–5230 | www.mysteryhill.com | $6.95 | May and Sept., weekends 10–7, June–Aug., daly 10–7.

Dining

Big Boppers. American. Bar food, such as the locally famous island-heat chili, barbecue chicken, hot wings, and sandwiches are popular choices. | 7581 E. Harbor Rd. | 419/734–4458 | $5–$12 | AE, D, MC, V.

Mariner's Retreat Restaurant & Mopey Dick's Lounge. American. Here you can have a fancy dinner or a casual bite with a great view of the beautiful East Harbor and marina activity. Daily specials including a wide variety of entrées, including steaks, ribs, and fresh seafood. You can dock for free if you arrive by water. | 6801 E. Harbor Rd. | 419/732–2587 | fax 419/734–3280 | Open mid-Apr.–mid-Oct., Sun.–Thurs. 11–8, Fri.–Sat. 11–9, stays open one hour later June–Aug. Closed Tues. | $10–$20 | MC, V.

Lodging

Lake Point Motel. Most of the rooms in this reasonably priced hotel literally steps from the shore have lake views. You can stroll on the beach or go boating. Picnic area. Some kitchenettes, some microwaves, refrigerators, some in-room hot tubs. Cable TV. | 908 E. Main St. | 419/798–4684 | www.lakepointmotel.com | 14 rooms | $45–$88 | MC, V.

Marblehead Inn. Just down the road from the Marblehead Lighthouse, the inn faces a rocky shoreline and a view of such local attractions as Cedar Point Amusement park and Kelleys Island, not to mention a parade of passing boats. Some kitchenettes, some microwaves, some refrigerators, some in-room hot tubs. Cable TV, some in-room VCRs. | 614 E. Main St. | 419/798–8184 or 877/H2O–VIEW | www.marbleheadinnohio.com | 61 rooms, 7 suites | $99, suites $130–$400 | AE, D, MC, V.

Old Stonehouse Bed & Breakfast. This is the largest bed and breakfast in Marblehead. The rooms have pastel quilted bedspreads and antiques, as well as claw-foot bathtubs and potbelly stoves. All rooms have lake views. Dining room, complimentary breakfast. Some in-room hot tubs. Lake, fishing. No kids under 10. | 133 Clemons St. | 419/798–5922 | www.oldstonehousebandb.com | 11 rooms | $99–$149 | D, MC, V.

MARIETTA

MAP 14, E6

(Nearby towns listed: Athens, Zanesville)

Founded in 1788 at the junction of the Ohio and Muskingum rivers and named after French Queen Marie Antoinette, Marietta is officially considered to be the first organized settlement in the Northwest Territory. Boat building was one of the early industries in Marietta; even ocean-going vessels were constructed here and sailed down river to the Mississippi and on to the Gulf of Mexico. Other important industries included brick factories and sawmills that supplied materials for area homes and public buildings, an iron mill, and several foundries that provided rails for the railroad industry.

Today, Marietta is a city (pop. 15,026) with an appealing small-town atmosphere. The red brick streets and cobblestone levy are indicative of the city's rich history, as are the extravagant Victorian homes adorned with leaded glass windows that line the streets of downtown. In addition to interesting history and architecture, the city shows off a smorgasbord of arts venues, the Fenton Art Glass Company, and several collectible doll factories. The *Valley Gem* sternwheeler has daily tours down the Ohio River, and the *Delta Queen, Mississippi Queen,* and *American Queen* riverboats make regular stops here. A number of seasonal festivals are held downtown.

Information: Marietta/Washington County Chamber of Commerce and Convention and Visitors Bureau | 316 3rd St., 45750 | 740/373–5176 (Chamber) or 800/288–2577, and 740/373–5178 (Visitors Center) | www.mariettaohio.org.

Attractions

Campus Martius Museum of the Northwest Territory. The Campus Martius fort was home to the pioneers who established Marietta as the first organized settlement in the

Northwest Territory. The museum houses the Rufus Putnam house, part of the original fort, plus Native American and pioneer artifacts. Many of the exhibits focus on the city's Appalachian roots. | 601 2nd St. | 740/373–3750 or 800/860–0145 | www.ohiohistory.org/places/campus | $4 | Mar.–Apr., Oct.–Nov., Wed.–Sun. 9–5; May–Sept., daily 9–5.

Fenton Art Glass Co. A factory tour and museum show off the artistry of the Fenton Art Glass Co., the nation's largest producer of handmade colored glass. On the tour, you'll see skilled artisans transform fiery glass into exquisite pieces of art and equally skilled painters add color to the pieces. The museum exhibits art glass made by the company since its founding in 1905, including its iridescent "Carnival" glass, which is a popular collectible today. The factory is in West Virginia, just across the Ohio River from Marietta. | 420 Caroline Ave., Williamstown, WV | 304/375–7772 or 800/319–7793 | www.fentonartglass.com | Free | Weekdays 8–8; Sat., 8–5; Sun. 12:15–5. No evening hrs Jan.–Mar.

Muskingum Park. This scenic city park provides a breathtaking view of the Muskingum River. | Front St. | 740/373–5178 | Free | Daily.

Ohio River Museum. You can learn everything you ever wanted to know about the Ohio River here. One exhibit documents the river's natural history, while another celebrates the golden age of the steamboat (in the late 19th century) with scale models of riverboats and a full-size calliope. One of the most interesting attractions is the *W.P. Snyder Jr.* steam-powered, stern-wheeled towboat, the last of its kind, which is moored in the Muskingum River alongside the museum. | 601 Front St., at Washington St. | 740/373–3750 or 800/860–0145 | www.ohiohistory.org/places/ohriver | $5 | May–Sept., Mon.–Sat. 9:30–5, Sun. noon–5; Mar.–Apr., Oct.–Nov., Wed.–Sat. 9:30–5, Sun. noon–5.

Rossi Pasta. One of the country's most noted pasta manufacturers shows you how it creates its mushroom, calamari, chocolate, and other flavored pastas. | 114 Greene St. | 740/376–2065 or 800/227–6774 | www.rossipasta.com | Free | Mon.–Sat. 9–7; Sun. noon–5.

Trolley Tours. Tour Marietta on an old-fashioned trolley. This is a particularly pleasant way to enjoy the colorful fall foliage. Tours last one hour; reservations suggested. | 127 Ohio St. | 740/374–2233 | $7.50 | Apr.–mid-June, Sept.–Oct., weekends; mid-June–late-June, Wed.–Sun.; July–Aug., Tues.–Sun.

Valley Gem. You can board this 300-passenger replica of a stern-wheeler riverboat for a scenic excursion on the Ohio River. | Front and Washington Sts. | 740/373–7862 | $5.50 | June–Aug., Tues.–Sun.; May and Sept., weekends only.

Wayne National Forest. This 63,075-acre forest has 73.9 mi of foot trails and a large area for hunting grouse, deer, turkey, and squirrel. The fishing is especially good for muskie, large mouth bass, crappie, catfish, rockbass, and small mouth bass. You can pick up a map at the office on Route 7 in Reno, 5 mi SE of Marietta. | Access points on Rte. 26, 4 mi NE of Marietta | 740/373–9055 | Free | Office: weekdays 8–4:30.

ON THE CALENDAR

MAR.: *River City Blues Festival.* An annual three-day music festival that draws blues lovers from all over America. | 101 Front St. | 740/373–6640 or 800/288–2577.
SEPT.: *Ohio River Sternwheel Festival.* More than two dozen sternwheelers converge on Marietta on the weekend after Labor Day for entertainment and games. Highlights include sternwheeler races and fireworks. | Ohio Riverfront Park, Ohio St. | 740/373–5178 or 800/288–2577.

Dining

The Gun Room. American. This restaurant has a Victorian riverboat theme with pilot wheels, bells, and a collection of antique longrifles dating back to 1795. It's in the historic Lafayette Hotel, which overlooks the confluence of the Muskingum and Ohio rivers. Diners are lured by the filet mignon, ranch pork chops, and crab cakes, as well as the early bird suppers. Popular appetizers include crab-stuffed mushrooms with hollandaise sauce and the shrimp cocktail. Sunday brunch is served. | 101 Front St. | 740/373–5522 | $20–$40 | AE, D, DC, MC, V.

Levee House Cafe. American. It still feels like a 19th-century saloon at this former dry goods store and tavern built in 1826. The menu changes monthly, but generally includes a selection of seafood, beef, and chicken entrées, such as filet mignon and chicken and pea fettuccine with cream sauce. The outdoor cafe has views of the Ohio River. Kids' menu. No smoking. | 127 Ohio St. | 740/374–2233 | Closed Sun. | $8–$26 | D, MC, V.

Marietta Brewing Co. American. The front of this restaurant is three stories high and houses the brewing equipment, while the rest of the space is reserved for dining. The dining room has exposed brick walls with murals depicting each of the home brews, a copper-topped bar with solid wood and mirrors behind it, and wooden tables and chairs. Fresh seafood entrées, steaks, specialty pizzas, sandwiches, and salads fill the menu, and the barbecued ribs are always popular. There are a number of low-fat, low-calorie items as well. Wash down your order with a fresh-brewed lager, ale, or root beer. Salad bar. Live entertainment Saturday nights. | 167 Front St. | 740/373–2739 | $9–$15 | D, DC, MC, V.

Lodging

Best Western. The hotel is on the banks of the Muskingum River, and you can enjoy a picnic overlooking the water. Picnic area, complimentary Continental breakfast. Refrigerators. Cable TV. Dock. Laundry service. Business services. Some pets (fee). | 279 Muskingum Dr. | 740/374–7211 or 800/528–1234 | www.bestwestern.com | 47 rooms | $72 | AE, D, DC, MC, V.

Econo Lodge. Some rooms at this two-story hotel, situated right behind a public golf course, have river views. You can drive right up to your room. Picnic area, complimentary Continental breakfast. Cable TV. Pool. Pets allowed (fee). | 702 Pike St. | 740/374–8481 or 800/446–6900 | www.hotelchoice.com | 48 rooms | $60 | AE, D, MC, V.

Holiday Inn. This hotel near the river has a restaurant and a picnic area in a landscaped courtyard. Restaurant, bar, picnic area, room service. In-room data ports. Cable TV. Pool, wading pool. Exercise equipment. Laundry service. Business services. | 701 Pike St. | 740/374–9660 or 800/465–4329 | fax 740/373–1762 | www.holidayinn.com | 109 rooms | $69 | AE, D, DC, MC, V.

Knights Inn. The convenient location off I–77, front-door parking, and a restaurant next door that delivers directly to your room make this a good stopping point. In-room data ports, some kitchenettes. Cable TV. Pool. Business services. Pets allowed (fee). | 506 Pike St. | 740/373–7373 or 800/526–5947 | fax 740/374–9466 | www.christopherhotels.com | 111 rooms | $65–$95 | AE, D, DC, MC, V.

Lafayette Hotel. One of the Historic Hotels of America, the Lafayette sits on the Ohio River Levee, giving you a spectacular view of the water. Opened in 1918 on the site of a hotel that burned in 1916, this building has a unique pie-shaped, almost flat-iron structure. The furnishings are largely reproduction antiques. The hotel has a popular restaurant, The Gun Room, and a full-service spa, Natural Remedies, which draws many of its guests. Restaurant (see The Gun Room), bar, room service. Cable TV. Spa. Laundry facilities, laundry service. Business services. Airport shuttle. | 101 Front St. | 740/373–5522 or 800/331–9336 | fax 740/373–4684 | www.lafayettehotel.com | 79 rooms, 8 suites | $85, $150 suites | AE, D, DC, MC, V.

Super 8. A modern three-story motel 1.5 mi from downtown Marietta. The Becky Thatcher Dinner Theater is nearby. In-room picnic table. In-room data ports, in-room safes, some microwaves, some refrigerators. Cable TV and in-room movies. | 46 Acme St., Washington Center | 740/374–8888 or 800/848–8888 | www.super8motels.com | 52 rooms | $57 | AE, D, DC, MC, V.

The Twin Doors. This 1872 Italianate Colonial bed and breakfast stands out with its poppy red shutters and trim against brown clapboard. Its two rooms are the Quilt & Hearth Room and the Victorian Garden Suite. The lush property is surrounded by a wrought iron fence and includes a brick courtyard and patio, and a water garden. It's in downtown Marietta, two blocks from the Campus Martius Museum and three blocks from the Muskingum River. Dining room, picnic area. Complimentary breakfast. One in-room hot tub. Laundry facilities. | 611 4th St. | 740/373–9443, 888/762–6922 | 2 rooms | $70–$80 | No credit cards.

MARION

MAP 14, C4

(Nearby towns listed: Delaware, Mount Gilead)

Marion's main claim to fame is as the former residence of Warren G. Harding, the 29th president of the United States, who was for years editor of the *Marion Star*. The Harding Home was occupied by the Hardings until they left for Washington in 1921. It was from this Victorian home that Harding, then a U.S. senator, conducted his famous "front porch campaign" in 1920. It is now a museum.

Founded in 1820, Marion was named after General Francis Marion, an outstanding Revolutionary War patriot and guerilla fighter from South Carolina. It experienced a population boost in the early 1820s when settlers, many of them veterans of the War of 1812, came to town. During its early days, there was practically no manufacturing in Marion; in 1846, its only industries were one sawmill and one carding mill. Today, as the largest producer of corn-based snacks, Marion (pop. 34,075) is known as the "World's Popcorn Capital."

Information: Marion Area Chamber of Commerce | 206 S. Prospect St., 43302 | 740/ 382–2181 | www.mariononline.com.

Attractions

Harding Home and Museum. This 1891 house was occupied by U.S. Senator Warren G. Harding and his wife, Florence Kling, until they left for the White House in 1921. On display are the home's original furnishings, along with possessions of the 29th president, including the podium used at his inauguration. The adjacent press house, used during the 1920 campaign, is a museum dedicated to the lives of President and Mrs. Harding. | 380 Mt. Vernon Ave. | 740/387–9630 or 800/600–6894 | www.ohiohistory.org/places/harding | $3 | June–Aug., Wed.–Sat. 9:30–5, Sun. noon–5; Sept.–Oct., Sat. 9:30–5, Sun. noon–5; Nov.-May, weekends by appointment.

Heritage Hall. The Marion County Historical Society presents two entertaining museums under one roof. One depicts the county's history and economic development through permanent and temporary exhibits. The Warren G. Harding Presidential Collections are housed here, along with three galleries devoted to the Harding presidency. The Wyandot Popcorn Museum houses the world's largest single collection of restored popcorn wagons and popcorn vending machines, like those you would have seen at the circus or in a movie theater lobby in days of old. | 169 E. Church St. | 740/387–4255 | $2 (suggested) | May–Oct., Wed.–Sun. 1–4; Nov.–Apr., weekends 1–4.

Stengel True Museum. This 1868 Victorian-style brick home is known for its beautiful white Italian marble fireplaces. It's a showcase for guns from the Revolutionary and Civil Wars and unique collections of primitive lighting fixtures, clocks, and antique toys. | 504 S. State St. | 740/387–6140 or 740/382–2826 | Free | Weekends 1–4:30, or by appointment.

ON THE CALENDAR

JULY: *Marion County Fair.* There are more than 40 county fairs in Ohio each year, and each one is special. The Marion County Fair, held the first week of July, has pony rides, midway games, livestock shows—and a friendly, hometown atmosphere. | 220 E. Fairground St. | 740/382–2558.

SEPT.: *Popcorn Festival.* Marion closes off its downtown area each year to celebrate its status as the nation's popcorn capital with music and dance. Nationally known entertainers perform; tours of the Wyandot Popcorn Museum are available. The event is held the weekend after Labor Day. | Downtown Marion | 740/387–3378.

SEPT.-OCT.: *Buckeye Country Corn Maze.* A 10-acre corn maze in the countryside 10 mi south of Marion also has hay rides, a straw fort, a piglet pen, and a country store. An antique tractor show, an animal petting zoo, a hog roast, farm tours, bonfires, a night maze, and a Pumpkin Fest are also on the schedule, which runs weekends (including Friday nights) in September and October. | 4 mi north of Waldo on Rte. 98 | 740/389–3696 or 740/389–1033.

Dining

Warehouse: An Italian Grill and Bar. Italian. The spaghetti is the all-time favorite at this converted railroad station. Cement floors, open ceilings, glazed brick interior and exterior, and antique furnishings lend a warehouse casualness. The ravioli and the veal parmesan are popular too. | 320 W. Center St. | 740/387–8124 | Closed Sun. No dinner Mon. | $6–$12 | AE, D, DC, MC, V.

Lodging

Comfort Inn. This hotel near the Harding Home entices you with an indoor heated pool and hot tub. It's in a prime business and shopping area and within walking distance of three restaurants. Complimentary Continental breakfast. Refrigerators (in suites). Cable TV. Indoor pool. Hot tub. Laundry service. Some pets allowed. | 256 James Way | 740/389–5552 or 800/228–5150 | www.comfortinn.com | 56 rooms, 4 suites | $67, $76 suites | AE, D, DC, MC, V.

Super 8. The many amenities at this modern motel on the edge of downtown Marion make it a popular place to stay. Complimentary Continental breakfast. In-room data ports. Some microwaves, some refrigerators, some in-room hot tubs. Cable TV, in-room movies. Indoor pool. Hot tub, gym. Laundry facilities. Business services. | 2117 Marion-Mount Gilead Rd. | 740/389–1998 or 800/848–8888 | www.super8motels.com | 53 rooms | $61 | AE, D, DC, MC, V.

Travelodge. The first-floor rooms of this two-story hostelry next to Route 23 have outside access; you enter second-floor rooms through the lobby. A restaurant is next door. Complimentary Continental breakfast. In-room data ports. Cable TV. Pool. Business services. Some pets allowed. | 1952 Marion-Mount Gilead Rd. | 740/389–4671 or 800/578–7878 | www.travelodge.com | 46 rooms | $54 | AE, D, DC, MC, V.

MASON

MAP 14, B6

(Nearby towns listed: Cincinnati, Hamilton, Lebanon, Middletown, Oxford)

Originally known as the village of Palmyra, Mason was founded in 1915 by Major William Mason, a Revolutionary War hero. Twenty years later, the community's name was changed in honor of its founder. Prior to the early 1990s, Mason was primarily a farming town, but in the past decade it has attracted a number of corporations. Centrally located along U.S. 42 and between I–71 and I–75, Mason is a convenient drive from anywhere in southwest Ohio. Popular attractions in the area include Paramount's Kings Island and The Beach Waterpark. Mason is also the home of the annual PGA Kroger Senior Classic golf tournament.

Information: Mason Chamber of Commerce | 316 W. Main St., 45040 | 513/398–2188.

Attractions

The Beach Waterpark. It's the place to be on a hot summer day. Popular water rides include the Aztec Adventure water coaster, the Thunder Beach wave pool, and the five-story free-fall slide, The Cliff. | 2590 Waterpark Dr. | 513/398–7946 or 800/886–7946 | www.thebeachwaterpark.com | $11.95–$22.95 | Memorial Day–Labor Day, 10–9.

Chateau Larouche. In 1929, the late Harry D. Andrews began building a castle in Loveland on the north bank of the Little Miami River, using river rock as his construction stones. His castle was a full-scale replica of a medieval Normanesque castle in southwest France, Château Laroche, where he was stationed during World War I. Loveland's castle became his life's work; over the next 50 years, he built 17 rooms, including a great hall, banquet hall, armory, ballroom, chapel, small work office, and dungeon. The castle, which is about 10 mi southeast of Mason, is surrounded by beautiful gardens with exceptional plants and flowers. | 12025 Shore Dr., Loveland | 513/683–4686 | www.lovelandcastle.org | $2 | Apr.–Sept., daily 11–5, Labor Day–Mar., weekends 11–5.

The Dude Ranch. Although it's just 20 minutes from downtown Cincinnati, this ranch would be right at home in the Wild, Wild West. There are horse rides through the woods and cattle drives where you can round up Texas Longhorns. | 3205 Waynesville Rd. | 513/899–DUDE | www.theduderanch.com | Daily 9–5:30.

Golf Center at Kings Island. The PGA's Kroger Senior Classic takes place at this Jack Nicklaus-designed golf course each August. All 36 holes are open to the public. | 6042 Fairway Dr. | 513/398–7700 (tee reservations) or 513/398–5200 (office) | www.thegolfcenter.com | $30–$65 per person | May.–Aug., daily 7 AM–8 PM; Sept.–Apr., daily 9–5.

Paramount's Kings Island. One of the Midwest's largest amusement parks is home to more than a dozen roller coasters including Son of Beast, the world's first wooden looping roller coaster, and Face/Off, a face-to-face inverted roller coaster. The park also has water rides, a Nickelodeon stage show, nightly fireworks, and a kids' area called Hanna-Barbera Land, starring well-known cartoon characters. | 6300 Kings Island Dr. | 513/754–5800 | www.pki.com | $39.99 | Memorial Day–Labor Day, Mon.–Fri. and Sun., 9 AM–10 PM; Sat. 9 AM–11 PM.

ON THE CALENDAR

AUG.: *Tennis Masters Series Cincinnati.* Tennis' top names play in this late-summer hard-court competition. Andre Agassi, Pete Sampras, Monica Seles, and Steffi Graf have all appeared here. | ATP Tennis Center, 6140 Fairway Dr. | 513/651–0303.
SEPT.: *Kroger Senior Classic.* The biggest names in golf tee off for close to $1 million in prize money at the Golf Center at Kings Island. Past participants include Arnold Palmer and Ben Hogan. | 6042 Fairway Dr. | 513/398–5742.

WHAT TO PACK IN THE TOY TOTE FOR KIDS

❏ Audiotapes

❏ Books

❏ Clipboard

❏ Coloring/activity books

❏ Doll with outfits

❏ Hand-held games

❏ Magnet games

❏ Notepad

❏ One-piece toys

❏ Pencils, colored pencils

❏ Portable stereo with earphones

❏ Sliding puzzles

❏ Travel toys

Dining

Carrabba's. Italian. Italian overtones are found in the grapevines, mosaic tables, terra cotta floor, and the open kitchen here. The Northern Italian cuisine has a Sicilian blend. Don't miss the popular Chicken Polla Rosa Maria–two breasts grilled over hickory and pecan wood, filleted and stuffed with prosciutto, lemon sauce, and mushrooms. | 5152 Merten Dr. | 513/339–0900 | $7–$18 | No lunch | AE, D, DC, MC, V.

Courseview Restaurant. Contemporary. Sit by the fireplace and enjoy Amish chicken, pasta gambretti, salmon oriental or the fresh catch of the day while listening to live entertainment and getting a view of the course at the Golf Center at Kings Island. Golf memorabilia is scattered throughout. On Friday nights in the summer, the large brick patio becomes the site of a pig roast, and guests dine next to the putting green. Live music Wed.–Sat. | 6042 Fairway Dr. | 513/573–3321 | $11–$17 | No dinner Nov.–Feb., Sun.–Tues. | AE, D, DC, MC, V.

Houston Inn. American. An attractive cedar and stone facade greets patrons of this antiques-filled restaurant. Frog legs are the specialty; more than 1,500 deep-fried legs are served each week. Another highlight is the 32-item salad bar; it's the largest in the area, with all kinds of greens, slaws, vegetables, and fresh fruit. Other favorites are slow-cooked prime rib, broiled pork chops, and lamb chops with mint jelly. Don't fail to try a side of the mashed potato salad. | 4026 U.S. 42 | 513/398–7377 | Closed Mon. | $10–$17 | AE, D, DC, MC, V.

Lodging

Best Western Inn & Suites. This modern hotel, furnished in oak, was built in 1999. It's right off I–71 at exit 25, just 5 mi from Kings Island Beach Waterpark and Paramount's Kings Island amusement park. Complimentary Continental breakfast. Some in-room data ports, some in-room hot tubs, microwaves, refrigerators. Cable TV. Indoor pool. Hot tub. Exercise equipment. Video games. Laundry facilities, laundry service. | 2793 Water Park Dr. | 513/754–1166 or 800/528–1234 | www.bestwestern.com | 56 rooms, 14 suites | $99–$119, suite $129 | AE, D, DC, MC, V.

Comfort Inn–Northeast. This three-story hotel, just minutes south of Paramount's Kings Island amusement park, gives you easy access to the theme park while charging much lower rates than hostelries that are closer. Complimentary Continental breakfast. Cable TV. Pool. Business services. Free parking. | 9011 Fields Ertel Rd. | 513/683–9700 or 800/228–5150 | fax 513/683–1284 | www.choicehotels.com | 116 rooms | $99 | AE, D, DC, MC, V.

Comfort Suites—Kings Island. The queen-size suites in this all-suites hotel can sleep up to six people, making it ideal for families who want to visit the Kings Island Beach Waterpark and Paramount's Kings Island amusement park, which are less than a mile away. Complimentary Continental breakfast. In-room data ports, in-room safes, refrigerators. Cable TV. Indoor pool. Laundry service. Business services. | 5457 Kings Center Dr. | 513/336–9000 or 800/228–5150 | www.comfortinn.com | 79 suites | $65–$125 | AE, D, DC, MC, V.

Days Inn Kings Island. Just minutes away from Paramount's Kings Island and The Beach Waterpark, this establishment is popular with families visiting the area. Complimentary Continental breakfast. Cable TV. Pool. Video games. Playground. Business services. Some pets allowed. | 9735 Mason-Montgomery Rd. | 513/398–3297 or 800/325–2525 | www.travelweb.com/daysinn.html | 124 rooms | $109 | AE, D, DC, MC, V.

Houston Motel. This small motel is family-owned by folks who have been in the business for over 30 years. They also have the popular Houston Inn restaurant across the street. The motel is 2 mi from Paramount's Kings Island and in close proximity to three golf courses, restaurants, and retail stores. Cable TV. Pool. | 4026 State Rte. 42 | 513/398–7277 or 800/732–4741 | 42 rooms, 6 suites | $70 | AE, D, DC, MC, V.

Kings Island Resort and Conference Center. The top lodging spot in Mason, this resort provides a complimentary shuttle to the amusement park. It's usually fully booked all summer, so make reservations well in advance. Restaurant, bar with entertainment, room service. In-room data ports. Cable TV. 2 pools (1 indoor). Hot tub. Tennis, basketball, volleyball. Fishing. Video games. Playground. Laundry facilities, laundry service. Business services. | 5691 Kings Island Dr. | 513/398–0115 or 800/727–3050 | fax 513/398–1095 | 288 rooms | $119 | AE, D, DC, MC, V.

Marriott-Northeast. This hotel has a red brick exterior and a dark wood interior. Plants and a fountain fill the attractive lobby. It's a popular choice for those visiting nearby Paramount's Kings Island. Restaurant, bar. In-room data ports, refrigerators (in suites). Cable TV. 2 pools (1 indoor). Exercise equipment. Business services. Free parking. | 9664 Mason-Montgomery Rd. | 513/459–9800 or 800/228–9290 | fax 513/459–9808 | www.marriott.com | 302 rooms, 7 suites | $145, $225 suites | AE, D, DC, MC, V.

Quality Inn-Kings Island. Just off I–71, this hotel offers easy-off, easy-on access to the interstate. Plus it's just minutes away from Paramount's Kings Island and the Beach Waterpark. A Chinese restaurant is on the premises. Restaurant, complimentary Continental breakfast, room service. In-room data ports. Cable TV. Pool. Playground. Business services. Some pets allowed. | 9845 Escort Dr. | 513/398–8015 or 800/228–5151 | fax 513/398–0822 | www.qualityinn.com | 104 rooms | $99 | AE, D, DC, MC, V.

Red Roof Inn. Its proximity to Paramount's Kings Island keeps this property filled most of the summer. This hotel is within walking distance of 30 restaurants. Make reservations well in advance. Some kitchenettes. Cable TV. Pool. Playground. Business services. | 9847 Escort Dr. | 513/398–3633 or 800/843–7663 | www.redroof.com | 124 rooms | $89 | AE, D, DC, MC, V.

Signature Inn. This two-story hotel, designed for the business traveler, has reasonable rates. It's also good for families, who want to go to the Kings Island amusement park, which is just a five-minute drive away. Hotel guests have free access to a nearby health club. There are two restaurants just outside the hotel. Complimentary Continental breakfast. In-room data ports, refrigerators, microwaves. Pool. Business services. | 8870 Governor's Hill Dr. | 513/683–3086 or 800/822–5252 | fax 513/683–3086, ext. 500 | www.signature-inn.com | cincyne@signature-inn.com | 99 rooms | $99 | AE, D, DC, MC, V.

MASSILLON

MAP 14, E3

(Nearby towns listed: Akron, Canton, Wooster, Zoar)

Massillon's strategic location in northeastern Ohio on the Tuscarawas River, the Ohio & Erie Canal and at the hub of the railroads has colored its history and ensured its prosperity. Once the boundary line between the French and English settlers, the Tuscarawas River was established as the boundary between the Indians and the Territory of the United States by the Fort McIntosh Treaty of 1785. When the Ohio & Erie Canal opened in 1828, Massillon was a bustling port; Ohio farmers brought their grain here to be loaded onto the canal barges. Later, when the railroads came to town, Massillon became a center of steam engine manufacturing and steel production. Massillon's attractions include a history museum that honors native son P.T. Barnum and another that documents Massillon's heyday as a canal port.

Information: **Massillon Area Chamber of Commerce** | 137 Lincoln Way E., 44646 | 330/833–3146 | www.massillonohchamber.com.

Attractions

Canal Fulton Heritage Society. A group of attractions 7 mi north of Massillon give you a taste of life during the "old canal days." The Old Canal Days Museum presents Ohio & Erie Canal memorabilia and local history displays. The salt-box-style Oberlin House, built in 1847, is decorated with period furnishings. Admission includes a narrated ride on the *St. Helena*

III Canal Boat, a replica of a 19th-century horse-drawn canal freighter. | 103 Tuscarawas, Canal Fulton | 330/854–3808 or 800/435–3623 | $6.50 | June–Aug., daily 10–4; mid-May–late May, early Sept.–mid-Sept., weekends 1–4.

Massillon Museum. The history of Massillon is the focus here. Among the items on display are memorabilia from native son P.T. Barnum, including Barnum's cane and Tom Thumb's clothing. | 121 Lincoln Way E | 330/833–4061 | Free | Tues.–Sat. 9:30–5, Sun. 2–5.

Spring Hill. Built in the 1820s, this rural home was once a stop on the Underground Railroad. It's now dressed up with a fine display of antiques and old-fashioned gardens. | 1401 Spring Hill Lane NE, Rte. 241 | 330/833–6749 | $3 | June–Aug., Wed., Thurs., Sun. 1–4; Apr.–May, Sept.–Oct., by appointment.

ON THE CALENDAR
JUNE: *Cruise On In and Dance Party.* Annual car show and dance attracts 80,000 people on the Saturday before Father's Day. Free live entertainment starts at 11 AM and continues until 11 PM. | Downtown Massillon | 330/833–3146.
SEPT.: *Yankee Peddler Festival.* Crafts, games, and amusement park rides are featured at this annual fall event at Clay's Park Resort in Canal Fulton. | 800/535–5634.

Dining
Smiley's Italian Restaurant. Italian. In this cozy place with red booths, black and white tile floor, and an open kitchen, your food is sautéed in front of you. Try the chicken parmesan, the linguine, or the shrimp Alfredo. | 27 Lincoln Way E | 330/832–3388 | $8–$11 | MC, V.

Lodging
Hampton Inn. This hotel in downtown Massillon, 7 mi off I–77 on State Route 21, opened in 2000. Complimentary Continental breakfast. In-room data ports. Cable TV. | 44 1st St. SW | 330/834–1144 or 800/426–7866 | www.hampton-inn.com | 74 rooms | $69–$79 | AE, D, DC, MC, V.

MENTOR

MAP 14, E2

(Nearby towns listed: Chardon, Cleveland, Eastlake, Painesville)

Mentor is northeast of Cleveland near Lake Erie, in an area known as Ohio's Lake County. The community, founded by white settlers in 1797, was incorporated as a township in 1815 and as a city in 1963. Named for Hiram Mentor, an early settler, Mentor was mostly rural until the 1960s, when it grew as a suburb of Cleveland and a center of light manufacturing. Among the products made here are fork lifts and electronic components and equipment. The city (pop. 8,271) is the site of Lawnfield, the home-turned-museum of former U.S. President James A. Garfield.

Information: **Mentor Area Chamber of Commerce** | 7547 Mentor Ave., #302, 44060 | 440/946–2625 | www.mentorchamber.org.

Attractions
Great Lakes Mall. This monster of a mall with nearly 150 stores, including J.C. Penney, Kaufmann's, and Dillards, has a hefty schedule of events as well as a movie theater and plenty of fast food. | Mentor Ave., at Plaza Blvd. | 440/255–6900 | www.shopsimon.com | Mon.–Sat. 10–9, Sun. 11–6.

Headlands Beach State Park. Swimming, fishing, and hiking are among the pastimes possible on over 100 acres along Lake Erie. | 9601 Headlands Rd. | 216/881–8141 | Free | June–Sept., daily.

Holden Arboretum. Walking trails weave through more than 3,000 acres of natural woodlands and lush gardens at this arboretum 5 mi southeast of Mentor. There's a visitor center and picnic area on the grounds. | 9500 Sperry Rd., Kirtland | 440/946–4400 | $4 | Tues.–Sun. 10–5.

Lake Metroparks. This 26-park system along Lake Erie includes Lake Farmpark, a farm designed to show kids that milk doesn't come from the grocery store; two golf courses; a one-room schoolhouse open by appointment; Penitentiary Glen Reservation, a nature park with a wildlife rehabilitation area and nature center; Fairport Harbor Lakefront Park; and many nature parks. Lake Farmpark is the most popular attraction; it's in Kirtland, just south of Mentor. | 880 Chardon Rd. | 440/639–7275 or 800/366–3276 | www.lakemetroparks.com | Free | Hours vary for different attractions.

Lawnfield (James A. Garfield National Historic Site). James A. Garfield (1831–81), the 20th president of the United States, once lived in this Victorian mansion, which still displays its original furnishings. Lawnfield is the home of the first presidential memorial library. Displays include the wreath Queen Victoria sent when Garfield was assassinated in Washington, D.C. | 8095 Mentor Ave., U.S. 20 | 440/255–8722 | www.nps.gov/jaga | $6 | Mon.–Sat. 10–5, Sun. noon–5.

ON THE CALENDAR
SEPT.: *It's Better in Mentor Days.* The highlights of this annual festival are the rides, entertainment, 5K race, and the chili cook-off. | 440/946–2625.

Dining

Molinari's. Contemporary. There's a California air to both the dining room and the menu, which includes a wide range of entrées, among them crab cakes, filet mignon stuffed with gorgonzola and walnut pesto, beef tips in red wine sauce, pasta puttanesca (here made with chicken, sausage, mushrooms, and asiago cheese), and veal four seasons (with roasted red peppers, prosciutto, portobello mushrooms, and artichoke hearts in vodka cream sauce). Jazz Fri. and Sat. | 8900 Mentor Ave. | 440/974–2750 | Closed Sun. No dinner Mon. | $15–$25 | AE, D, DC, MC, V.

Potpourri Fondue. Continental. Mood lighting and wine racks make this a romantic place for dinner, although dress is casual and guests of all ages eat here. The extensive fondue menu includes cheeses, beef, shrimp, chicken, and chocolate. Steaks and pasta are also served. | 8885 Mentor Ave. | 440/255–4334 | No lunch | $10–$17 | D, DC, MC, V.

Lodging

Courtyard by Marriott. An attractive, modern hotel south of Mentor in Willoughby. Restaurant, Complimentary Continental breakfast. In-room data ports, some microwaves, some in-room hot tubs. Cable TV. Video games. Indoor pool, gym. Laundry facilities. | 35103 Maple Grove Rd., Willoughby | 440/530–1100 or 800/288–9290 | www.marriott.com | 90 rooms | $114 | AE, D, DC, MC, V.

Fairfield Inn by Marriott-Willoughby. This three-story hotel is south of Mentor in Willoughby; it's 4 mi from the Great Lakes Mall and James A. Garfield's home. Complimentary Continental breakfast. Cable TV, in-room movies. Pool. Laundry facilities. Business services. | 35110 Maple Grove Rd., Willoughby | 440/975–9922 or 800/288–2800 | fax 440/942–9928 | www.marriott.com | 134 rooms | $85 | AE, D, DC, MC, V.

Holiday Inn Express at La Malfa Centre. This amply furnished hotel built in 1998 is close to shopping and restaurants. The modern interior is done in bold, contrasting colors. It's 30 minutes from downtown Cleveland. Complimentary Continental breakfast. In-room data ports. Some in-room kitchenettes, minibars, microwaves, refrigerators. Cable TV, in-room VCRs. Hot tubs. Gym. Laundry facilities, laundry service. | 5785 Heisley Rd. | 440/357–9333 or 800/465–4329 | www.holidayinn.com | 79 rooms | $78–$135 | AE, D, DC, MC, V.

Ramada Inn. This upscale hotel in Willoughby, about 5 mi south of Mentor, has two pools and a picnic area complete with a cabana. Restaurant, bar, picnic area, room service. In-room data ports, some refrigerators. Cable TV. 2 pools (1 indoor), wading pool. Sauna. 2 tennis courts. Exercise equipment. Video games. Laundry facilities, laundry service. Business services. Pets allowed (fee). | 6051 SOM Center Rd., Willoughby | 440/944–4300 or 800/228–2828 | fax 440/944–5344 | www.ramada.com/ramada.html | 146 rooms | $99 | AE, D, DC, MC, V.

MIAMISBURG

MAP 14, A5

(Nearby towns listed: Dayton, Middletown, Vandalia)

The Anglo-American settlement of Miamisburg began with the arrival of Virginian Zachariah Hole and his family in 1797. The small community was named "Hole's Station" in his honor, until years later when it was renamed Miamisburg, combining "Miamis" (for the Miami Indian tribe that resided in the area before Hole arrived) with "burg," which denotes a borough or town. On Feb. 20, 1818, four men from Pennsylvania—Emanuel Gebhart, Jacob Kercher, Dr. John Treon, and Dr. Peter Treon—auctioned off 90 one-fifth-of-an-acre lots in this newly christened town. There were many takers from Pennsylvania who arrived over the next several years.

Today, Miamisburg is a small town (pop. 18,000) that enjoys the big-city resources of Cincinnati (45 mi south) and nearby Dayton (9 mi north). In fact, the Dayton Mall is in Miamisburg. Market Square, the original core of the city, is surrounded by 19th-century homes of various architectural styles. The city's 23 parks cover 245 acres and offer a full range of recreational opportunities.

Information: South Metro Regional Chamber of Commerce | 1414B Miamisburg Centerville Rd., Dayton 45459 | 937/433–2032 | www.smcoc.org.

MIAMISBURG

INTRO
ATTRACTIONS
DINING
LODGING

Attractions

JB Ranch. This is a great place for a family outing. The ranch holds daily pony rides and mutton-bustin'. There's also a petting zoo. Professional rodeos are held here from time to time. | 7491 Farmington Rd. | 937/865–0961 | www.jbranchandrodeo.com | $12 | Daily 9–5.

Miamisburg Mount State Memorial. This burial mound is believed to be the work of the prehistoric Adena Indians, who lived in this area from about 800 BC to AD 100. Considered the largest conical burial mound in the state, and maybe the eastern U.S., it's 877 ft in circumference. You can climb the 116 steps from the base to the 100-ft bluff for a view of the surrounding area, which includes a park. | Mound Ave., 1 mi south of Rte. 725 | 614/297–2300 | Free | Daily dawn–dusk.

ON THE CALENDAR

SEPT.: *Starving Artist's Show.* Hundreds of artists and craft makers converge at this mid-September fair to display and sell their work, which includes paintings, ceramics, woodworking, floral wreaths and arrangements, stained glass, jewelry and country home accessories. Most are less than $50. Other highlights include an ironsmith and tinsmith, glass blowers, potters, and woodworkers. | Library Park, 426 Central Ave. | 937/433–2032.

Dining

Bullwinkle's Top Hat Bistro. Barbecue. This pleasantly noisy eatery, in a two-story brick building built in the late 1800s, is a nice place to enjoy a heaping plate of ribs. Steak, chops, and chicken dinners are also popular. There is also an outdoor sidewalk cafe and an indoor grill-your-own barbecue area. Entertainment Sat. Kids' menu. | 19 N. Main St. | 937/859–7677 | Closed Sun. | $11–$19 | AE, D, DC, MC, V.

Hunan House. Chinese. The small, casual dining room in a shopping center has fast service for both eat-in and carry-out. The most popular dish on the Hunan menu is the General Tso's chicken. | 1228 E. Central Ave. | 937/847–1900 | $4–$10 | MC, V.

Peerless Mill Inn. American. This old lumber mill, once a part of The Great Peerless Mills, has six dining rooms on three levels. Are all dressed up with wagon wheels, antiques, and wooden beams. Patrons come here for hearty country meals that include chowders, aged steaks, roasts, chops, and seafood flown in fresh from Boston. Pianist on weekends. Kids' menu. Sun. brunch. | 319 S. 2nd St. | 937/866–5968 | Closed Mon. No lunch | $13–$20 | AE, DC, MC, V.

Lodging

Best Western Continental Inn. A basic, modern hotel 1 mi from the Dayton Mall. A quarter mile off I–75 on Exit 44. Restaurant, bar, complimentary Continental breakfast, room service. In-room data ports. Cable TV. TV in common area. | 155 Monarch La. | 937/866–5500 or 800/528–1234 | www.bestwestern.com | 60 rooms | $63 | AE, D, DC, MC, V.

Courtyard by Marriott. Most rooms at this large hotel have balconies which overlook the courtyard. You can enjoy an indoor pool and hot tub and easy access to the Dayton Mall across the street. Restaurant, bar, complimentary Continental breakfast. In-room data ports, refrigerators (in suites). Cable TV. Indoor pool. Hot tub. Exercise equipment. Laundry facilities. Business services. | 100 Prestige Pl. | 937/433–3131 or 800/228–9290 | fax 937/433–0285 | www.marriott.com | 146 rooms, 12 suites | $90–$109, $104–$119 suites | AE, D, DC, MC, V.

Doubletree Guest Suites. Each suite in this three-story, all-suites stone property has a separate living room with a sofabed and a bedroom with two doubles or a king-size bed. Restaurant, bar. Refrigerators. Cable TV. Indoor-outdoor pool, wading pool, hot tub. Exercise equipment. Video games. Laundry facilities. Business services. Free parking. | 300 Prestige Pl. | 937/436–2400 or 800/528–0444 | fax 937/436–2886 | www.doubletree.com | 138 suites | $140 | AE, D, DC, MC, V.

English Manor. The rooms of this restored 1924 Tudor-style mansion are adorned with antiques dating back to the mid-1800s. Complimentary breakfast. No room phones. No TV in rooms, TV in sitting room. No smoking. | 505 E. Linden Ave. | 937/866–2288 or 800/676–9456 (reservations) | 5 rooms, 2 with shared bath | $95 | AE, D, DC, MC, V.

Holiday Inn-Dayton Mall. This full-service hotel across the street from Dayton's popular mall is within walking distance of dozens of restaurants and stores. There's a sports bar on the premises; the game room also has pool and ping pong tables. Restaurant, bar with entertainment, room service. In-room data ports. Cable TV. 2 pools (1 indoor), wading pool. Putting green. Exercise equipment. Video games. Laundry facilities. Business services, airport shuttle. | 31 Prestige Plaza Dr. | 937/434–8030 or 800/465–4329 | fax 937/434–6452 | www.holidayinn.com | 195 rooms | $87 | AE, D, DC, MC, V.

Homewood Suites Hotel by Hilton. The interior of this all-suite hotel, built in 1999, is indeed homey. It's 10 minutes from downtown Dayton and across the road from the Dayton Mall. Take Exit 44 off I–75, or Exit 2 off I–675. Complimentary Continental breakfast. In-room data ports, kitchenettes, microwaves, refrigerators. Cable TV, free VCRs. Pool. Gym. Balls, board games. Gift/snack shop, video games. Laundry facilities, laundry service. Business services. Pets allowed (fee). | 3100 Contemporary La. | 937/432–0000 or 800/225–5466 | www.welcomehomewood.com | 96 rooms in 2 towers | $135 | AE, D, DC, MC, V.

Knights Inn. A 24-hour restaurant just steps away is one of the conveniences available at this budget hotel. Complimentary Continental breakfast. Some kitchenettes, some refrigerators. Cable TV. Pool. Some pets allowed. | 185 Byers Rd. | 937/859–8797 or 800/843–5644 | fax 937/859–5254 | www.christopherhotels.com | 100 rooms | $56 | AE, D, DC, MC, V.

Red Roof Inn-Dayton South. Proximity to I–75, two family-style eateries just steps away and nearby stores make this a popular place to stay. In-room data ports, some refrigerators. Cable TV. Business services. Pets allowed. | 222 Byers Rd. | 937/866–0705 or 800/843–7663 | fax 937/866–0700 | www.redroof.com | 107 rooms | $55 | AE, D, DC, MC, V.

Residence Inn by Marriott. Roomy accommodations are the hallmark of this all-suites hotel. Some rooms have fireplaces. The hotel hosts a complimentary social hour weeknights with snacks and beverages pool-side during the summer. You can use the sport court, complete with tennis and basketball. Picnic area, complimentary Continental breakfast. In-room data ports. Cable TV. Pool. Hot tub. Tennis, basketball. Laundry facilities, laundry service. Business services. Some pets allowed. | 155 Prestige Pl. | 937/434–7881 or 800/331–3131 | fax 937/434–9308 | www.marriott.com | 96 suites | $97–$125 1–bedroom suites, $120–$150 2–bedroom suites | AE, D, DC, MC, V.

Signature Inn Dayton. Downtown Miamisburg is 2 mi away from this modern chain hotel; the Wright Patterson Airforce Base and the U.S. Air Force Museum are also nearby. Take Exit 44 off I–75. Complimentary Continental breakfast. In-room data ports, microwaves, refrigerators, some in-room hot tubs. Cable TV. Pool. Business services. | 250 Byers Rd. | 937/865–0077 or 800/822–5252 | www.signature-inns.com | 125 rooms | $71 | AE, D, DC, MC, V.

MIDDLETOWN

MAP 14, A6

(Nearby towns listed: Cincinnati, Dayton, Hamilton, Lebanon, Oxford, Mason, Miamisburg)

Some time in 1791, Daniel Doty reached the Great Miami River and constructed a rough log cabin on its east bank. Soon other settlers followed suit, and the town of Middleton was born. It was named for its position midway (almost) between Dayton (20 mi north) and Cincinnati (about 35 mi south). The town experienced a growth spurt in the late 1800s, with the advent of the railroad and Miami Canal. In the 1900s, the city found its true calling: steel. Two major steel companies set up headquarters in the town in 1899 and have been there ever since; today the biggest employer in town is AK Steel. The town's history is on display at the Canal Museum.

Information: Mid-Miami Valley Chamber of Commerce | 1500 Central Ave., 45042 | 513/422–4551.

Attractions

Canal Museum. This downtown museum exhibits a reproduction of a typical locktender's house from the days when locktenders kept watch over the Miami Erie Canal as it flowed through Middletown. The collection of the Middletown Historical Society is also housed here. | In Smith Park, off Tytus Ave. | 513/422–3030 or 888/664–3353 | Donation | Apr.–Oct., Sun. 2–4.

Miami University Middletown. The regional campus of Miami University, which offers two- and four-year programs, is here. There is a weekly "tour and talk" you can join to see the campus. | 4200 E. University Blvd. | 513/727–3200 | www.mid.muohio.edu | Free | Tues. 10 and 6.

Sorg Opera Company. One of the few small-town opera companies left, the Sorg Opera puts on three productions per year and brings in performers from around the country. | 65 S. Main St. | 513/425–0180 | www.sorgopera.com.

ON THE CALENDAR

JULY: *All American Weekend*. Fireworks, a hot air balloon festival, rides, games, and a craft show distinguish this free annual three-day celebration of America's independence. | Downtown Middletown | 513/422–3030 or 888/664–3353.

Dining

Bamboo Garden. Chinese. Wall mirrors, flowers, and a maroon interior lend a bright elegance to this restaurant. Mandarin, Szechuan, and Hunan cuisine are all represented on the menu. General Tso's Chicken is popular, as is the seafood. The hot and sour soup is renowned. | 3446 Village Dr. | 513/422–7920 | $6–$14 | AE, D, DC, MC, V.

Damon's. American. A great place to watch the game. Damon's has local sports team memorabilia, electronic trivia games, and enough wall-size big-screen television sets give you a great view from any table. Wings and barbecue ribs and chicken are the specialties, but just as popular is the onion loaf appetizer, a tasty tangle of thin onion straws that are breaded and deep fried. Kids' menu. | 4750 Roosevelt Blvd. | 513/423–8805 | $10–$26 | AE, D, DC, MC, V.

Lodging

Best Western. A modern motel, 7 mi from downtown Middletown and 20 mi from King's Island Theme Park. A mini-golf park is within walking distance. Located right off I–75 at Exit 32. Complimentary Continental breakfast. In-room data ports, some in-room hot tubs. Cable TV. Indoor pool. | 3510 Commerce Dr. | 513/727–0440 or 800/528–1234 | www.bestwestern.com | 51 rooms | $75–$83 | AM, D, DC, MC, V.

Fairfield Inn by Marriott. This hotel just off I–75 is within walking distance of a major mall and more than two dozen restaurants, movie theaters, and stores. Restaurant, complimentary Continental breakfast, room service. Cable TV, in-room VCRs. Indoor pool. Hot tub. Laundry service. Business services. | 6750 Roosevelt Pkwy. | 513/424–5444 or 800/228–2800 | fax 513/424–5444 | www.marriott.com | 65 rooms | $75 | AE, D, DC, MC, V.

Manchester Inn and Conference Center. This hostelry in downtown Middletown hosts most of the city's banquets and receptions. Restaurant, bar with entertainment, room service. In-room data ports, some refrigerators. Cable TV, some in-room VCRs. Laundry service. Business services. Some pets allowed. | 1027 Manchester Ave. | 513/422–5481 or 800/523–9126 (reservations) | fax 513/422–4615 | www.manchesterinn.com | 78 rooms | $80–$133 | AE, D, DC, MC, V.

MILAN

MAP 14, D3

(Nearby towns listed: Bellevue, Oberlin, Sandusky, Vermilion)

Milan was founded in 1816 as Merry's Mill, named after Ebenezer Merry, who settled here and built a flour and sawmill. In 1839, the completion of the canal linking Milan to the Huron River launched a trade boom. But canal usage was eventually replaced by the railroad, and when a flood destroyed the dam, the canal was never rebuilt. Milan's history also includes an era of shipbuilding; 75 schooners up to 125 ft long were built between 1841 and 1867. During the same period, the town served as the formation site of wagon trains headed West.

In 1885 Milan's largest potato farmer, Isaac Hoover, invented and manufactured the "Hoover Potato Digger." But the town's other inventor is far more famous. Thomas Alva Edison was born in Milan on February 11, 1847, and spent his early childhood here. Edison's former home is now open to the public.

Information: Milan Chamber of Commerce | 11001 U.S. 250 N, 44846 | 419/499–4909.

ATTRACTIONS

Edison's Birthplace Museum. Thomas Edison's inventions (including the phonograph, stock ticker, and incandescent bulb) and related items are displayed in this seven-room house, where the famous inventor was born in 1847. | 9 Edison Dr. | 419/499–2135 | $5 | June–

Aug., Tues.–Sat. 10–5, Sun. 1–5; Apr.–May, Sept.–Oct., Tues.–Sun. 1–4; Nov.–Mar. by appointment.

Milan Historical Museum. Items from Milan's past keep company with a collection of 300 dolls, pressed glass, and china. The collection is exhibited in an 1846 house; other buildings in the complex include a general store and blacksmith house. | 10 Edison Dr. | 419/499–2968 | $2 (suggested) | Apr.–May, Sept.–Oct., Tues.–Sun. 1–5; June–Aug., Tues.–Sat. 10–5, Sun. 1–5.

Dining

Homestead Inn. American. Beef, chicken, and seafood entrées give a modern twist to this restaurant in a late-19th-century Italianate building. Filet of tenderloin and Lake Erie perch are popular. Downstairs in the Rathskeller, additional snacks and a salad bar are available in addition to the offerings on the regular menu. Try the seafood salad with creamy avocado dressing. Salad bar. Kids' menu. | 12018 U.S. 250 | 419/499–4271 | $13–$17 | AE, D, DC, MC, V.

Invention Family Restaurant. American/Casual. The fresh Lake Erie perch stands out at this local diner. The antiques and memorabilia remind you that you're in the hometown of Thomas Edison. Try the elderberry pie. | 15 Main St. N, on the Square | 419/499–2661 | No dinner Sun. | $5–$7 | No credit cards.

Lodging

Colonial Inn South. A modern hotel on Route 250, 15 minutes from Cedar Point Amusement Park. Restaurant. Pool. | 12211 Milan Rd. (Rte. 250) | 419/499–3403 or 800/886–9010 | 60 rooms in two buildings | $49–$89 | AE, D, MC, V.

Comfort Inn. The hotel is close to many restaurants and stores, and you can choose to relax in either the indoor or outdoor pool. Complimentary Continental breakfast. Cable TV. 2 pools (1 indoor). Hot tubs, sauna. Laundry facilities. | 11020 Milan Rd. (Rte. 250) | 419/499–4681 or 800/228–5150 | fax 419/499–3159 | www.comfortinn.com | 102 rooms | $79 | AE, D, DC, MC, V.

Ramada Limited. This two-story hotel is on U.S. 250. Complimentary Continental breakfast. Cable TV. Indoor pool. Hot tub, sauna. Laundry facilities. Business services. | 11303 Milan Rd. (Rte. 250) | 419/499–4347 or 800/228–2828 | www.ramada.com/ramada.html | 56 rooms | $99–$119 | AE, D, MC, V.

Super 8. Right on the business strip of U.S. 250, this hotel is surrounded by restaurants and stores. Restaurant, complimentary Continental breakfast. Some refrigerators. Cable TV. Pool. Video games. Laundry facilities. | 11313 Milan Rd. (Rte. 250) | 419/499–4671 or 800/848–8888 | www.super8.com | 69 rooms, 9 suites | $79, $139 suites | AE, D, DC, MC, V.

MOUNT GILEAD

MAP 14, C4

(Nearby towns listed: Delaware, Mansfield, Marion, Mount Vernon)

In 1824, settler Jacob Young came to the area around Mount Gilead to plot out a town he called Whetsom. Young and other settlers cleared the land and the town thrived on farming. Its name was changed to Mount Gilead in 1832 by a public vote, and in 1851, the Cleveland, Columbus, Cincinnati Railroad came through town and brought a large number of new settlers to the area. During World War I, the citizens of surrounding Morrow County purchased more War Bonds per capita than any other county in the nation; they were honored with a gift from the federal government: the Victory Shaft monument, which still sits in the middle of Mount Gilead's north public square. Today, Mount Gilead serves as a trade and service center for the surrounding agricultural area, providing the most of the shopping and health care facilities, as well as commercial and industrial employment for Morrow County residents.

Information: **Morrow County Chamber of Commerce** | 17½ W. High St., 43338 | 419/946–2821 | www.mountgilead.net.

Attractions

Mount Gilead State Park. Small but pleasant, the 300-acre state park has facilities for boating, hiking, fishing, and camping. | 4119 Rte. 95 | 419/946–1961 | Free | Daily.

Pine Lakes Golf Club. This 18-hole public golf course has a restaurant on the premises. | 901 E. High St. | 419/946–1856.

ON THE CALENDAR

OCT.: *The Ohio Gourd Show.* This annual festival, held in mid-October, centers around the local specialty, the gourd. Displays, entertainment, a Gourd Queen, and workshops are among the highlights. | 195 S. Main St. | 419/946–2821.

Dining

Cornerstone Restaurant. American. The desserts are especially popular at this old-fashioned mom and pop diner. | 11 N. Main St. | 419/947–1446 | Closed Sun. | Under $5 | No credit cards.

Lodging

Best Western Executive Inn. This modern motel is right off I–71, 6 mi southeast of downtown Mount Gilead. Complimentary Continental breakfast. Some in-room microwaves, some refrigerators, some in-room hot tubs. Cable TV. Pool. Exercise equipment. Video games. | 3391 County Rd. 172 | 419/768–2378 or 800/528–1234 | www.bestwestern.com | 33 rooms | $60–$70 | AM, D, DC, MC, V.

MOUNT VERNON

MAP 14, D4

(Nearby towns listed: Delaware, Mansfield, Mount Gilead)

The settlement of Mount Vernon, a farming community, was established in 1805; among its early inhabitants was Johnny Appleseed (John Chapman), who is credited with planting apple trees across the country. Mount Vernon remains mostly a residential and farming community with pleasant, tree-lined streets, historic homes, and a high quality of life.

A highlight of this pioneer city is the 1865 Woodward Opera House, where Mount Vernon's most famous son, Daniel Decatur Emmett, made his farewell appearance. Emmett was the author and composer of "Dixie," the beloved song of the South during the Civil War. Once a venue for local entertainment, traveling performers, and vaudeville acts, the opera house now hosts an occasional function or show. At the center of town is the public square, with a monument honoring local soldiers who died in the Civil War.

Information: **Knox County Convention and Visitors Bureau** | 7 East Ohio Ave., 43050 | 740/392–6102.

Attractions

Kenyon College. Private, four-year liberal arts college with programs in the arts, humanities, natural sciences, and social sciences is 5 mi east of Mount Vernon. The admission office can arrange a tour. | 103 Chase Ave., Gambier 43022 | 740/427–5147 or 800/KEN–YONC | Free.

AUG.: *Dan Emmett Music and Arts Festival.* Mount Vernon's native son, Dan Emmett, composer of the song *Dixie,* is honored with an annual festival on the second full weekend of August. The event includes music, food, arts, crafts, car show, entertainment, fine arts, and sidewalk sales. | Public Square, S. Main St. | 740/392–6102 | Free.

Dining

Uncle Dan's Playhouse and Tavern. American. The 1870s-style tavern in the Dan Emmet House Hotel serves steak, ribs, and chicken. Meat loaf, burgers, and sweet potato chips are favorites, as are barbecued ribs and strip steak. Open-air dining is available on a patio complete with views of the river and a professional volleyball court. Entertainment most weekends. Kids' menu. | 150 Howard St. | 740/392–6886 | $10–$15 | AE, D, DC, MC, V.

Lodging

Dan Emmett House Hotel. Built in 1996, this modern hotel in downtown Mount Vernon is close to many antique stores and a bike trail. Restaurant, bar, picnic area, complimentary full breakfast on weekdays, complimentary Continental breakfast on weekends. In-room data ports, kitchenettes, microwaves, refrigerators, hot tubs in some rooms. Cable TV. Indoor pool. Exercise bike. Laundry facilities. Pets allowed (fee). | 150 Howard St. | 740/392–6886 or 800/480–8221 | 59 rooms | $65 | AE, D, DC, MC, V.

White Oak Inn. This country inn on 14 acres in the heart of Amish country provides lodging in two buildings: a farmhouse built in 1915 and a restored chicken barn. You can relax in the common room and enjoy a selection of books and magazines from the library. A generous breakfast is included; a fixed-price dinner is served with advance reservations. It's about 12 mi east of Mount Vernon. Complimentary breakfast. No smoking. No kids under 12. Business services. | 29683 Walhonding Rd., Danville | 740/599–6107 | www.whiteoakinn.com | 10 rooms | $90–$130 | AE, D, MC, V.

NEWARK

MAP 14, D5

(Nearby towns listed: Columbus, Granville, Lancaster, Mount Vernon, Zanesville)

Newark's first settlers were Native Americans, who lived here along the Licking River in central Ohio east of Columbus more than 200 years ago. When the tribes left the area in the early 1700s, they left behind some of the most elegant earthworks in the region. Two of the mounds are preserved today at the Moundbuilders and Octagon Earthworks; these memorials are visited by thousands of tourists each year.

The city was settled in 1802; it received a boost in 1825, when the Ohio Canal was built between Lake Erie and the Ohio River. Later, Newark's growth was sustained by the railroads that went through town. Now it is one of the fastest-growing areas in Ohio. The city offers a number of museums and historic districts, in addition to the nearby Native American mounds.

Information: Newark and Licking County Chamber of Commerce | 50 W. Locust St., 43055 | 740/345–9757 | www.newarkchamber.com.

Attractions

Blackhand Gorge State Nature Preserve. A 970-acre wooded area whose highlight is an inspiring gorge. The park includes a 4.3 mi bike trail, old locks of the Ohio and Erie Canal, and the tunnel of the Interurban Railway. Hiking, bird-watching, and canoeing are possible. | 5213 Rock Haven Road SE | 740/763–4411 | Free | Daily, dawn–dusk.

Buckeye Lake State Park. At 3,557 acres, Buckeye Lake is one of the largest fishing and boating spots in Ohio. You can enjoy a relaxed picnic in the warmer months and snowmobiling and ice booting in the winter. It's about 10 mi south of Newark. | 2905 Leibes Island Rd., Millersport | 740/467–2690 | Free | Daily.

Dawes Arboretum. You can stroll around the 1,100-plus acres, which are naturally land-scaped with a Japanese garden, a collection of oak and beech trees from around the world, a manmade lake populated with waterfowl, and Ohio buckeye trees planted in the shape of the number 17 (Ohio was the 17th state in the union). | 7770 Jacksontown Rd. SE | 740/323–2355 | www.dawesarb.org | Free | Mon.–Sat. 8–5, Sun. 1–5.

Flint Ridge State Memorial. The memorial, which is operated by the Ohio Historical Soci-ety, has picnic tables, hiking trails, a museum, and a nature preserve. The museum dis-plays an interesting three-dimensional layout of the topography of the area. Indian tools and artifacts are also on display. | 7091 Brownsville Rd. | 740/787–2476 or 800/600–7174 | $5 per vehicle | Memorial Day–Labor Day, Wed.–Sat. 9:30–5, Sun. noon–5; Sept.–Oct., Sat. 9:30–5, Sun. noon–5.

Highwater Orchard. Pick apples, pears, and grapes at this orchard 1 mi off State Route 661. | 2010 Lundys La. | 740/587–1711 or 800/220–9233 | $1 | Mon.–Sat. 10–6, Sun. 1–5.

Moundbuilders State Memorial. The memorial, which spans 66 acres, preserves the Great Circle earthwork, a part of the Newark Earthworks, the largest system of connected geo-metric earthworks in the world. These prehistoric mounds were built by the Hopewell Indi-ans approximately 2,000 years ago as their ceremonial center. The circle is nearly 1,200 ft in diameter; its grass-covered earthen walls are 14 ft high in places. On the memorial grounds is the Ohio Indian Art Museum. | 99 Cooper Ave. | 740/344–1920 | Memorial free, museum $3 | Apr.–Oct., daily 8–7.

National Heisey Glass Museum. Hundreds of patterns of Heisey glass—the full range of etched and engraved glassware produced by A.H. Heisey & Co. from 1896 to 1957—are on display, including experimental colors and production techniques. The collection of over 5,000 pieces is housed in part in the King House, an 1831 Greek Revival style home. | 169 W. Church St. | 740/345–2932 | www.heiseymuseum.org | $2 | Tues.–Sat. 10–4, Sun. 1–4.

Octagon Earthworks. These octagon-shaped mounds, which are thousands of years old, were built by the Hopewell Indians. The earthworks are thought to have had spiritual sig-nificance to these native peoples. The site is difficult to find without a guide. Inquiries should be addressed to the office at the Moundbuilders site. You'll also need a guide to find the Newark and Wright earthworks, which are in the vicinity. | 99 Cooper Ave. | 740/344–1920 | Free.

Sherwood-Davidson House Museum. Victorian, Civil War, and Indian artifacts are exhib-ited in this circa 1815 structure. The house has a front fan doorway and a two-story side gallery. | N. 6th St. at W. Main St. | 740/345–6525 | Free | Tues.–Sun. 1–4 and by appointment.

Webb House Museum. Built in 1907 by Frank Camden Webb for his bride, this arts-and-crafts style house is full of early-20th-century family heirlooms. | 303 Granville St. | 740/345–8540 | Free | Apr.–Dec, Thurs., Fri., Sun. 1–4 and by appointment.

Dining

Cherry Valley Lodge. American. French tapestries, a gazebo, a stone fireplace, and candlelit tables make this restaurant cozy and rustic. Wood-fired venison, lamb, steak, poultry, pork, and seafood entrées keep patrons coming back again and again. Try almond rainbow trout or pork chops with apple chutney. There's open-air dining on a patio overlooking the courtyard and a pond. Kids' menu. Sunday brunch. No smoking. | 2299 Cherry Valley Rd. | 740/788–1200 or 800/788–8008 | Reservations essential | $18–$25 | AE, D, DC, MC, V.

Damon's. American. Lots of big-screen televisions make this a great place to enjoy a big plate of the specialty barbecued ribs while you watch the game. Also popular are wings, chicken, and the onion loaf appetizer, a tasty tangle of thin onion straws that are breaded and deep fried. Kids' menu. | 1486 Granville St. | 740/349–7427 | $10–$26 | AE, D, DC, MC, V.

Natoma. American. It's a locally loved neighborhood joint that serves basic, hearty meals. Try veal parmesan over spaghetti or ground beefsteak with tomatoes, mushrooms, and onions. Also popular are seafood and ribs. | 10 N. Park Pl. | 740/345–7260 | $10–$21 | AE, D, DC, MC, V.

Lodging

Cherry Valley Lodge. A real family inn, a lake, well-tended acreage, and lots of extras put this lodge at the top of the list of area hostelries. The hotel has complimentary bikes and has 22 mi of paths. If that's not enough activity, there's volleyball, shuffleboard, basketball, and croquet. Restaurant (*see* Cherry Valley Lodge), bar, room service. In-room data ports. Cable TV, in-room VCRs and movies. 2 pools (1 indoor), lake. Hot tub. Basketball, exercise equipment, volleyball, bicycles. Baby-sitting, playground. Laundry service. Business services. Pets allowed (fee). | 2299 Cherry Valley Rd. | 740/788–1200 or 800/788–8008 | fax 740/788–8800 | www.cherryvalleylodge.com | 200 rooms | $149–$159 | AE, D, DC, MC, V.

NEW PHILADELPHIA

MAP 14, E4

(Nearby towns listed: Berlin, Canton, Dover, East Liverpool, Gnadenhutten, Sugarcreek, Zoar)

On October 23, 1804, John Heckewelder sold John Knisely 3,554 acres for the sum of $5,454.33. The land comprises most of the present-day city of New Philadelphia. Knisely plotted his new community with great care. Instead of permitting it to grow haphazardly, as so many pioneer settlements did, he had a surveyor lay out the entire town on a checkerboard plan, similar to that of the city of Philadelphia. In fact, many of the streets were named after those in the Pennsylvanian capital. New Philadelphia was incorporated on February 12, 1833.

Information: Tuscarawas County Chamber of Commerce | 1323 4th St. NW, 44663 | 330/343–4474 or 800/527–3387 | www.neohiotravel.com.

Attractions

Atwood Lake Park. More than 4,500 acres await you at this family fun spot east of New Philadelphia, part of the Muskingum Watershed Conservancy District. Nature programs are held daily, as are hikes and bird-watching tours. | 49–56 Shop Rd. | 330/343–6780 | Free | Daily.

Fernwood State Forest. A 3 mi hiking trail loops around the largest tract of this 3,023-acre forest. Picnic tables are clustered throughout. Two scenic vistas overlook the surrounding countryside. The forest, which has many ponds scattered about, is open to public fishing and hunting. There are three shooting ranges. | 2205 Reiser Ave. SE | 330/339–2205 | Free | Daily, 6 AM–11 PM.

Leesville Lake. The lake east of New Philadelphia has 3,500 acres and a plethora of recreational activities, including swimming, boating, and hiking. It's part of the Muskingum Watershed Conservancy District. | 5 mi south of Carrollton, off Rte. 332 | 330/627–4270 | Free | Apr.–mid-Nov., daily dawn to dusk.

Schoenbrunn Village State Memorial. Founded in 1772 as a Moravian mission, this memorial appears as it did over 200 years ago. It consists of 17 reconstructed log buildings, the original cemetery, and over 2 acres of planted fields. A recorded tour is available in both English and German. The village also includes a museum, a video orientation program, a gift shop, and picnic facilities. | 1984 E. High Avenue Rd. | 330/339–3636 or 800/752–2711 | Daily.

ON THE CALENDAR

AUG.: *Tuscarawas County Italian American Festival.* An annual celebration of Italian heritage enlivens the Tuscarawas Valley the second week in August. Highlights include a mayor's breakfast, live entertainment, Italian dancers, a commemorative plate auction, Italian & American food, rides, arts and crafts booths, a beverage garden, 5K run, and spaghetti sauce, wine, and pizza eating contests. | On the Square, Downtown New Philadelphia | 330/339–6405 | Free.

Dining

Alpine Alpa. Swiss. Homestyle Amish and Swiss meals are served in this restaurant in a Swiss village market in the heart of Amish country about 10 mi northwest of New Philadelphia. It's worth a stop just to see the 23-ft-tall cuckoo clock, considered to be the world's tallest. A house specialty is the Der Deutscher, a spicy German wurst accompanied by warm potato salad. Buffet Sunday, family-style service. Kids' menu. No smoking. | 1504 U.S. 62, Wilmot | 330/359–5454 | $10–$15 | AE, D, MC, V.

Amish Door. American. This eatery in the Amish countryside 10 mi northwest of New Philadelphia serves hearty, homestyle fare. Try the broasted chicken dinner and one of the 19 varieties of pie for dessert. Family-style service. Kids' menu. No smoking. | 1210 Winesburg St. (U.S. 62), Wilmot | 330/359–5464 | Closed Sun. | $7–$10 | D, MC, V.

Lodging

Atwood Lake Resort. Walls of glass at this hillside resort lend a spectacular view of the lake, which covers over 1,500 acres. Motorboats, sailboats, canoes, and rowboats are available. There's sledding on the grounds in winter. The resort is about 10 mi east of New Philadelphia. Box lunches may be arranged. Bar, dining room, picnic area, room service. Kitchenettes (in cottages). Cable TV. 2 pools (1 indoor). Hot tub. Driving range, golf courses, putting green, tennis. Exercise equipment. Boating, bicycles, cross-country skiing. Business services. Airport shuttle. | 2650 Lodge Road, Dellroy | 330/735–2211 or 800/362–6406 | fax 330/735–2562 | www.atwoodlakeresort.com | 104 rooms, 17 cottages | $119, $900 4–bedroom cottages (7–day stay) | AE, D, DC, MC, V.

Days Inn. This hotel close to downtown New Philadelphia has spacious rooms. It's right off I–77 at Exit 81. Bar, patio. Complimentary Continental breakfast. In-room data ports, in-room safes, some microwaves, refrigerators, in-room hot tubs. Cable TV. Indoor pool. Video games. | 1281 W. High Ave. | 330/339–6644 or 800/528–1234 | www.bestwestern.com | 104 rooms | $69 | AE, D, DC, MC, V.

Holiday Inn. This two-story hotel, off I–77, was built in 1996. Restaurant, bar. Some refrigerators, some in-room hot tubs. Cable TV. 2 pools (1 indoor). Hot tub. Exercise equipment. Business services. Some pets allowed. | 131 Bluebell Dr. | 330/339–7731 or 800/465–4329 | fax 330/339–1565 | www.holidayinn.com | 107 rooms | $79 | AE, D, DC, MC, V.

Schoenbrunn Inn. Amish quilts decorate the beds and locally made pieces fill the rooms in this modern motel done in Amish country style. It's 1½ mi from downtown, off I–77 Exit 81. Suites with kitchenettes are across the street. Bar. Complimentary Continental breakfast. In-room data ports. Some microwaves, some refrigerators, some in-room hot tubs. Cable TV. Indoor pool. Hot tub. Exercise equipment. Laundry facilities. Pets allowed (fee). | 1186 W. High Ave. | 330/339–4334 or 800/929–7799 | 60 rooms, 6 suites | $72–$80 | AM, D, DC, MC, V.

Travelodge. Off I–77, this is a convenient place to call it a day while traveling through northern Ohio. Cable TV. Pool. Business services. | 1256 W. High Ave. | 330/339–6671 or 800/255–3050 | www.travelodge.com | 62 rooms | $39 | AE, D, DC, MC, V.

OBERLIN

(Nearby towns listed: Elyria, Milan, Norwalk, Strongsville)

Founded in 1833, Oberlin has a history of social leadership. Oberlin College, founded in 1833, was the first in the country to admit women, and was an early leader in the education of African-Americans. The city was also an important stop on the Underground Railroad in the years before the Civil War. Today, Oberlin is a residential community with commercial interests, featuring a number of museums and homes dedicated to the preservation of its heritage.

Information: **Oberlin Area Chamber of Commerce** | 20 E. College St., 44074 | 440/774–6262 | www.oberlin.org.

ATTRACTIONS

Allen Memorial Art Museum. The museum, which includes a wing designed by architect Robert Venturi, is a showcase for contemporary American art, Japanese prints, 17th-century Dutch and Flemish paintings, and European art of the early 20th century. On the premises is a 1949 house designed by Frank Lloyd Wright, which is open for tours by reservation the first Saturday and third Sunday of the month. | 87 N. Main St. | 440/775–8665 | Free | Museum, Tues.–Sat. 10–5, Sun. 1–5. Closed Mon.

First Church in Oberlin. The Oberlin Anti-Slavery Society met in this church, built in 1842. The funeral for a 4-year-old fugitive slave child, buried in Westwood Cemetery, was held here. So was the memorial service for John Copeland and Sheilds Green, who were hanged for their participation in John Brown's Raid on Harpers Ferry. | Lorain and Main Sts. | 440/775–1711 or 800/334–1673 | Free | Weekdays 8–5.

Oberlin College. Oberlin was the first college in the country to admit women, and an early leader in the education of African-Americans. Guided tours of the campus are available. You can arrange one Monday through Saturday at the admissions office in the Carnegie Building. | N. Professor St. | 440/775–8121 or 800/622–6243 | Free | Daily.

ON THE CALENDAR

JUNE–AUG.: *Summer Music Festival.* Free weekly outdoor concerts, starting Friday nights at 7, feature big bands, jazz, and garage bands. The series runs from the last week in June through August in downtown Oberlin. | Tappan Square | 440/774–6262.

Dining

Black River Cafe. French. The minimalist interior has kitsch accents, including unique salt and pepper shaker sets on each table. The menu is contemporary and focuses on pasta and seafood. Try the herb polenta napoleon with portobello stuffing. | 15 S. Main St. | 440/775–3663 | Breakfast also available. No dinner Sun. and Mon. | $11–$15 | D, MC, V.

Lodging

Ivy Tree Inn. This Colonial Revival cottage in downtown Oberlin was built in the 1860s and evokes Cape Cod with its black shutters against a white exterior. The extensive gardens include a winding perennial bed and fountains. Inside, the furnishings are eclectic and antique. Complimentary breakfast. Cable TV, phone. Books in common room. No kids under 8. | 195 Professor St. | 440/774–4510 | 4 rooms | $79–$99 | MC, V.

Oberlin Inn. This hostelry on the Oberlin College campus is always packed with school visitors. Restaurant, room service. Cable TV. Business services. Airport shuttle. Free parking. | 7 N. Main St. | 440/775–1111 | fax 440/775–0676 | 76 rooms | $89 | AE, D, DC, MC, V.

OXFORD

MAP 14, A6

(Nearby towns listed: Cincinnati, Hamilton, Mason, Middletown)

In 1792, President George Washington signed an act of Congress mandating that one complete township of the John Cleves Symmes purchase (a plot of land in southwest Ohio) be set aside in support of higher education. In 1809, the Ohio General Assembly established Oxford Township, which was to be the site of Miami University. The university opened its doors in 1824, and the village of Oxford was incorporated in 1830. Now primarily a college town—as it was then—Oxford stands out for both its architecture and its landscape. The campus of Miami University is considered one of the loveliest in the nation. The "Old Mile Square" is filled with 19th-century homes in New England and Southern styles.

Information: **Oxford Visitor's Bureau** | 118 W. High St., 45056 | 513/523–8687 | www.oxford-chamber.org.

Attractions

Hueston Woods State Park. Popular with Miami University students, this park 5 mi north of Oxford features boating, hiking, and fishing. A resort with hotel rooms and cabins is also here. | Rte. 732 | 513/523–6347 | www.oberlin.edu/~allenart/general-info.html | Free | Daily, dawn-11 PM.

Miami University. Miami University was founded in 1809 and is the seventh oldest state-assisted university in the nation. The university offers nearly 100 bachelors degrees, more than 50 masters degrees, and nine doctoral programs. Zoology, art, and geology museums are on campus. | 500 E. High St. | 513/529–1809 | Free | Daily.

The **McGuffey Museum,** the 19th-century home of William McGuffey, the author of the McGuffey Reader books, is also on campus. | Spring and Oak Sts. | 513/529–2232 | www.lib.muohio.edu/mcguffey/introduction.php | Free | Tues.–Fri. 10–5, weekends noon–5, closed Mon.

Miami University Art Museum. The five galleries here display changing exhibits and a permanent collection of 16,000 works. Exhibits feature historical and contemporary art, decorative arts, and represent diverse cultures. The museum is surrounded by a three-acre sculpture park. | Patterson Ave. (U.S. 27) | 513/529–2232 | www.muohio.edu/artmuseum | Free | Tues.–Fri. 10–5, weekends 12–5.

Pioneer Farm House Museum. This 19th-century farm house and barn features furniture, clothing, and toys that were typical of a three-generational pioneer family of the era. | Doty and Brown Rds | 513/523–8005 | Free | Memorial Day–Labor Day, weekdays noon–4, weekends 9–5.

ON THE CALENDAR

JUNE–JULY: *Outdoor Summer Music Festival.* Uptown Oxford is transformed into a giant outdoor dance club during this annual event. Local and regional entertainers jam on an outdoor stage erected in Martin Luther King Park. The music ranges from rock to blues to contemporary Christian to pop. | 513/523–8687.

SEPT.–DEC.: *Miami University Football.* The Redhawks struggled for years to gain national attention; in 1997 they landed a trip to one of the most prestigious bowl games in the country. See them in action on their home field throughout the fall. | Yager Stadium | 513/529–1809.

OCT.–MAR.: *Miami University Basketball.* The Redhawks, in the MAC conference, gained the respect of basketball fans by going to the Elite 8 NCAA tournament in 1999. Home games are played in Millet Hall, a 12,000-seat convocation center. | North end of campus | 513/529–1809.

OCT.: *Red Brick Rally Car Show.* Antique cars and street rods rumble into this popular annual event each fall. Car enthusiasts won't want to miss the festival's special events like engine exhibits and product demonstrations. | At Uptown Park, on High St. | 513/523–8687.

Dining

Mary Jo's Cuisine. French. This intimate bistro is run by one woman. Favorites include spring lamb stew with organically grown local vegetables and chicken breast with preserved lemon, pistachios, bulgur wheat, and roasted Moroccan red pepper. No smoking. | 308 S. Campus Ave. | 513/523–2653 | Reservations essential | Closed Mon. No dinner weekdays, no lunch Sat. | $23–$25 | AE, D, DC, MC, V.

Lodging

Alexander House Historic Inn and Restaurant. This Federalist style B&B in downtown Oxford was built in 1869 and is on the Registry of Historic Places. Restaurant, bar, outdoor dining area. Complimentary breakfast. TV in common area. | 22 N. College Ave. | 513/523–1200 or 877/792–9854 | 5 rooms | $85–$125 | D, MC, V.

Hampton Inn. Some of the rooms here are equipped with hot tubs and refrigerators. Complimentary Continental breakfast. In-room data ports, some refrigerators, some in-room hot tubs. Cable TV. Indoor pool. Hot tub. Exercise equipment. Business services. | 5056 College Corner Pike | 513/524–0114 or 800/426–7866 | fax 513/524–1147 | www.hampton-inn.com | 66 rooms | $69 | AE, D, DC, MC, V.

Hueston Woods Resort. This resort overlooking a lake is the gateway to Hueston Woods State Park. It has spacious rooms and cabins, and guests enjoy all the activities at the state park. The lobby features a large fireplace and Native American furnishings. Restaurant, bar. Some kitchenettes, microwaves (in cabins). Cable TV. 2 pools (1 indoor), wading pool. 18-hole golf course, tennis. Exercise equipment. Cross-country skiing. Video games. Kids' programs, playground. Business services. | RR 1, College Corner | 513/523–6381 or 800/282–7275 | fax 513/523–1522 | www.amfac.com | 94 rooms, 35 cabins | $109 rooms, cabin prices vary | AE, D, DC, MC, V.

PAINESVILLE

MAP 14, E2

(Nearby towns listed: Chardon, Eastlake, Mentor, Geneva-on-the-Lake)

Painesville had its beginning in two settlements on the banks of the Grand River in the early years of the 19th century. The first settlement, known as New Market, was laid out in 1803; the second, called Champion, was established 2 mi to the south two years later. The community was later renamed Painesville in honor of General Edward Paine, a representative to the Northwest Territorial Legislature. Today, Painesville is primarily a small residential town 30 mi south of Cleveland's many attractions.

Information: Painesville Area Chamber of Commerce | 391 W. Washington St., #15, 44077 | 440/357–7572 or 800/368–LAKE | www.lakevisit.com.

Attractions

Fairport Harbor Lighthouse and Marine Museum. The museum, just north of Painesville on Lake Erie, features maps, charts, and a large ship wheel. The main attraction is the working lighthouse that overlooks the lake. | 129 2nd St., in Fairport Harbor | 440/354–4825 | $2 | Wed.–Sun. dawn to dusk.

ON THE CALENDAR

JULY: *Mardi Gras.* This tiny lakeside village, 10 minutes from Painesville, hosts an annual July 4th celebration with games, rides, and vendors. | Fairport Harbor Lakefront Park | 440/352–3620 or 800/368–LAKE.

AUG.: *Lake County Fair.* This typical county fair draws thousands of people each year to the Lake County Fairgrounds. | 1301 Mentor Ave. | 440/357–7572 or 800/368–LAKE.

Dining

Dinner Bell Diner. American. George's world-famous ribs and the complimentary sticky buns are menu favorites. The walls are adorned with photos of celebrities who've eaten here. Kids' menu. | 1155 Bank St. | 440/354–3708 | Closed Mon. | $7–$20 | AE, D, MC, V.

Rider's Inn. Continental. Set in a stagecoach stop built in 1812, the inn serves food adapted from recipes used in the 19th century. Rider Rib, a slow-roasted Angus prime rib, is a house specialty. Open-air dining, small deck with picnic tables. Entertainment Friday and Saturday. Kids' menu. Sun. brunch. | 792 Mentor Ave. | 440/942–2742 | $21–$41 | AE, D, MC, V.

Lodging

Quail Hollow Resort and Country Club. Those who love the outdoors enjoy this resort a five minutes' drive east of Painesville. You have access to tennis courts and golf courses. Bar with entertainment, dining, snack bar, room service. Cable TV. 2 pools (1 indoor). Hot tub. Driving range, golf course, putting green, tennis. Exercise equipment. Playground. Business services. | 11080 Concord-Hambden Rd., Concord | 440/352–6201 or 800/792–0258 | fax 440/350–3504 | 169 rooms | $119 | AE, D, DC, MC, V.

Rider's 1812 Inn. The inn, built in 1812, was originally a resting point for stagecoaches passing through; it was later part of the Underground Railroad. Rooms are furnished with some 19th-century antiques. Restaurant *(see* Rider's Inn), complimentary breakfast, room service. Cable TV. Business services. Airport shuttle. Some pets allowed. | 792 Mentor Ave. | 440/354–8200 | 10 rooms | $109 | AE, D, MC, V.

PIQUA

MAP 14, B5

(Nearby towns listed: Dayton, Sidney, Vandalia)

Piqua's development can be traced to the earliest Paleo-Indian bands that hunted mastodon and bison in the upper Miami Valley. During the following centuries, Adena and Hopewell Indians made their way into the area, leaving behind earthworks, burial sites, and villages. The Miami and Shawnee Indian tribes dominated the area during the 16th and 17th centuries; their influence is still evident in the many Indian place names throughout the region. The cremation myth of the Shawnee Indians is the source of the name Piqua, which means "man who rose from the ashes." European settlers first arrived in Piqua in 1797. Industrial growth prospered during World War I and II. The opening of I–75 in 1958 also contributed to the town's prosperity, as businesses popped up near the interstate.

Piqua (pop. 20,612) is home to more than 100 medium to small industrial firms, and farming is still an important industry. The town's history is preserved at a number of historical sites, including the Historic Indian Museum and the Piqua Historical Area.

Information: Piqua Chamber of Commerce | 326 N. Main St., 45356 | 937/773–2765 | www.wnet.com.

Attractions

Piqua Historical Area State Memorial. The culture of the Eastern Indian Woodlands, Ohio's canal history, and life on the early Ohio frontier are presented here. The 174-acre farmstead was the home of John Johnston, a federal Indian agent and commissioner of the Ohio Canal. Costumed guides lead tours of the 1815 home, summer kitchen, cider house, and barn, and you can see demonstrations of pioneer crafts. Also on the grounds is a Native American museum that has artifacts from the Hopewell, Miami, and Adena tribes. Admission includes a mule-drawn canalboat ride on the Miami-Erie Canal. | 9845 N. Hardin Rd. | 937/773–2522 or 800/752–2619 | $5 | June–Aug., Wed.–Sat. 9:30–5, Sun. noon–5; Sept.-Oct., Sat. 9:30–5, Sun. noon–5.

Piqua Historical Museum. This former grocery in the Caldwell Historic District was built in 1890 and now chronicles Piqua area history through exhibits on the prehistoric age to the 20th century. The second floor of the museum contains an extensive fine arts exhibit. | 509 N. Main St. | 937/773–2307 | www.tdn-net.com/miamivcb/icore_group4.html | Donation | Apr.–Oct., Thurs., Sat., Sun. 12:30–4:30; or by appointment.

ON THE CALENDAR
MAY: *Taste of the Arts.* At this annual festival, held in conjunction with the Miami Valley Fine Arts Exhibition, artists demonstrate mediums from watercolors to pottery, charcoal to stained glass. Area restaurants serve samples of their most popular menu items. This free event is held the third Saturday of May from 3 to 9 PM. | 326 N. Main St. | 937/773–2765.
SEPT.: *Heritage Festival.* Dubbed "Ohio's Wilderness Frontier Festival," this annual event on Labor Day weekend is held at the Piqua Historical Area State Memorial. | 9845 N. Hardin Rd. | 937/773–2765.

Dining
El Sombrero. Mexican. This Mexican restaurant is reminiscent of a fiesta, with sombreros, blankets, and Mexican paintings on the walls, and colorful flowers. Favorites are the enchiladas and burritos. | 902 Scot Dr. | 937/778–2100 | $4–$11 | D, MC, V.

Lodging
Comfort Inn. Restaurants and stores surround this motel. Complimentary Continental breakfast. Pool. Hot tub. Exercise equipment. Business services. | 987 E. Ash St. | 937/778–8100 or 800/228–5150 | fax 937/778–9573 | www.comfortinn.com | 124 rooms | $69 | AE, D, DC, MC, V.

Ramada Inn Limited. This modern motel is across the road from the Miami Valley Center Mall and next to the Hollow Park, which has a stream, trail, and softball field. It's off I–75 Exit 82. Complimentary Continental breakfast. In-room data ports, some refrigerators, some microwaves, some in-room hot tubs. Cable TV, in-room movies. Indoor pool. Spa. Laundry facilities. Business services. Pets allowed (fee). | 950 E. Ash St. | 937/615–0140 or 800/228–2828 | www.ramada.com/ramada.html | 70 rooms | $64–$70 | AE, D, DC, MC, V.

PORT CLINTON

MAP 14, C2

(Nearby towns listed: Kelleys Island, Marblehead, Put-in-Bay, Sandusky)

In 1827, Ezekiel Smith Haines bought 1,212 acres in Sandusky County in northwest Ohio for $4,000. Built on its status as a lakefront community, tourism and shipping were early factors in the town's economic base. Port Clinton is now one of Ohio's most distinctive lakeshore communities. Its proximity to Midwest, East Coast, and Canadian markets and easy access to truck, rail, and air transportation systems provide businesses with an opportunity to reach nearly two-thirds of the U.S. population. Several parks and wildlife preserves dot the area.

Information: Port Clinton Chamber of Commerce | 304 Madison St., #3, 43452 | 419/734–5503 or 800/441–1271.

Attractions

African Safari Wildlife Park. More than 400 wild animals wander freely as you drive through this 100-acre park. | 4½ mi east of Port Clinton, on Lagtner Rd. | 419/732–3606 | $11 | May–Sept., daily 9–5.

Catawba Island State Park. This small park along Lake Erie, 6 mi north of Port Clinton has camping, fishing, and boating. | Off Rte. 53 | 419/797–4530 | Free | Daily.

Magee Marsh Wildlife Area. This 2,000-acre wildlife refuge about 15 mi west of Port Clinton has a half mile of pristine Lake Erie Beach. There is also a half-mile-long bird watching trail. The Sportsman's Migratory Bird Center displays exhibits on animal life, Native American history, the fur trade, and duck hunting. | 13229 W. State Rte. 2, Oak Harbor | 419/898–0960 | Free | Daily, dawn to dusk.

Ottawa County Historical Museum. Fossils, Indian artifacts, and the military history of Ohio are among the topics covered at this northern Ohio museum. | W. 3rd and Monroe Sts. | 419/732–2237 | Free | June–Aug., Mon.–Sat. 9–5; Sept.–May, Tues.–Thurs. 9–5, or by appointment.

Ottawa National Wildlife Refuge. More than 9 mi of pathways and an observation deck give you a bird's-eye view of the migratory birds that make this their stop on the journey south for the winter and north for the summer. In February and October, thousands of birds stop over here. The refuge is near the Magee Marsh and 15 mi west of Port Clinton. | 1400 W. Rte. 2 | 419/898–0014 | Free | Daily, dawn to dusk.

ON THE CALENDAR

JULY–AUG.: *National Matches.* Shooters of all ages take part in this national rifle competition, which includes rifle and pistol contests. | Camp Perry, between Port Clinton and Oak Harbor | 419/635–2141 or 800/441–1271.

SEPT.: *Harvest Fest.* This annual festival in late September has live entertainment, a craft fair, and children's events. | Downtown Port Clinton | 419/734–4386 or 800/441–1271.

Dining

Garden at the Lighthouse. Continental. The main dining room has floor-to-ceiling windows and a view of Lake Erie. Seafood dishes dominate the menu. Try the *poulet d'elegance,* a chicken breast stuffed with lobster tail and Swiss cheese and baked in a puff-pastry shell. Open-air dining is available from Memorial Day to Labor Day. Kids' menu. | 226 E. Perry St. (Rte. 163) | 419/732–2151 | Closed Sun., Sept.–May | $10–$38 | AE, D, DC, MC, V.

Mon Ami Restaurant and Winery. Contemporary. Antique chandeliers and dark wood detailing give the dining room an elegant feel. You can also dine in the more casual chalet, which has a round fireplace in the center of the room. Seafood, ribs, chicken, steaks, and chops are served; each menu listing includes a recommended wine. The winery produces some of the most highly regarded varieties in Ohio. Open-air dining on patio. Entertainment Fri. and Sat. Kids' menu. Sun. brunch. | 3845 E. Wine Cellar Rd. | 419/797–4445 or 800/777–4266 | $12–$25 | AE, D, MC, V.

Lodging

Country Hearth Inn. This modern hotel on the shores of Lake Erie is off State Route 2, 10 minutes from Clinton Bay and 20 minutes from Cedar Point Amusement Park. Complimentary Continental breakfast. In-room data ports, in-room safes, some in-room microwaves and refrigerators. Cable TV. Pool. Laundry facilities. Pets allowed. | 1815 E. Perry St. | 419/732–2111 or 800/282–5711 | 66 rooms | $106 | AE, D, DC, MC, V.

Fairfield Inn by Marriott. You can dine at the hotel's restaurant and bar or head out to one of several establishments nearby. Complimentary Continental breakfast. Some refrigerators. Cable TV. Airport shuttle. | 3760 E. State Rd. | 419/732–2434 or 800/288–2800 | www.marriott.com | 64 rooms | $99 | AE, D, DC, MC, V.

PORTSMOUTH

(Nearby towns listed: Ironton, Gallipolis)

The history of the city dates to the discovery of the Ohio Valley by the French in 1749. In 1803, Henry Massie founded the settlement, naming it after Portsmouth, New Hampshire, the hometown of a good friend. Set on the Ohio River, Portsmouth became the terminus for the Ohio-Erie Canal.

Today, Portsmouth still serves as a major hub to railways and water transportation. It is the gateway to three states—Ohio, Kentucky, and West Virginia, and lies within 100 mi of many major metropolitan markets, including Cincinnati, Columbus, and Louisville. Set in an agricultural area, Portsmouth (pop. 25,000) is an industrial city, and home to forestry and agricultural concerns. The hub of the cultural life here is the Southern Ohio Museum and Cultural Center. Also noteworthy is the Floodwall Murals Project; begun in 1993 along the Front Street floodwall, the ongoing endeavor includes more than 20 murals, including one depicting cowboy Roy Rogers, one of Portsmouth's most famous native sons.

Information: Portsmouth Area Chamber of Commerce | Box 509, 45662-0509 | 740/ 353–7647 | www.portsmouth.org.

Attractions

Shawnee State Forest. This 1,100-acre park about 8 mi west of Portsmouth has nature programs and a variety of recreational activities. | 13291 U.S. Highway 52 | 740/858–6685 | Free | Daily.

Shawnee State University. On the banks of the Ohio River, the campus of Ohio's newest public university covers 52 acres. | 940 2nd St. | 740/355–2221 or 800/959–2778 | www.shawnee. edu | Free | Daily.

Southern Ohio Museum and Cultural Center. History exhibits focus on Southern Ohio people and events; you'll also see art works by prominent Portsmouth artists. | 825 Gallia St. | 740/354–5629 | $1 | Tues.–Fri. 10–5, weekends 1–5.

ON THE CALENDAR

MAR.: *First Moon of Spring Ceremony.* This Pow-wow, held at the Tallige Cherokee Nation in West Portsmouth, celebrates the coming of spring. | 740/858–4227 or 740/ 354–9752.

APR.: *Trout Derby.* This festival at Turkey Creek Lake in Shawnee State Forest celebrates the start of the fishing season. | 13291 U.S. Highway 52 | 614/858–6652.

JUNE: *Charity Horse Show.* Horses of all sizes compete in several classes on the first weekend in June. The show extends over a three-day period. | Lucasville County Fairgrounds, 1193 Fairground Rd. | 740/353–3698 or 740/259–2726.

JUNE: *Roy Rogers Festival.* Roy Rogers enthusiasts gather for a weekend filled with memorabilia, celebrities, and Western fun. A high point is a visit to Rogers' boyhood home. | Ramada Inn, 711 2nd St. | 740/353–0900.

AUG.: *Scioto County Fair.* Livestock shows, games, rides, and musical acts make this fair a must on any visitor's list. | Scioto County Fairgrounds | 740/353–3698.

SEPT.: *River Days Festival.* The family-oriented event has rides, arts and crafts, and entertainment. | Court Street Landing | 740/354–6419.

Dining

A Touch of Italian. Italian. Specialties, like grilled panini sandwiches and pasta, are served at this restaurant in the Best Western Inn, which also has traditional American dishes for breakfast, lunch, and dinner. | 3762 U.S. 23 | 740/354–2851 | $8–$12 | AE, D, MC, V.

Scioto Ribber. Barbecue. Chefs cook up ribs, chicken, and steaks on a huge outdoor hickory grill all year round. | 1026 Gallia St. | 740/353–9329 | Closed Mon. | $11–$33 | AE, MC, V.

Lodging

Best Western Inn. This two-story chain motel is just 2 mi north of downtown and five minutes from golf, fitness center, and tours. Restaurant, bar, complimentary Continental breakfast, room service. Some in-room data ports, some refrigerators. Cable TV. Pool. Laundry facilities. Pets allowed. | 3762 U.S. 23 | 740/354–2851 or 800/528–1234 | fax 740/354–2851 | www.bestwestern.com | 100 rooms | $53–$75 | AE, D, DC, MC, V.

Ramada Inn. Near downtown Portsmouth, this motel is accessible to area attractions. Restaurant, complimentary Continental breakfast, room service. Some refrigerators. Cable TV. Indoor pool, wading pool. Hot tub. Business services. Some pets allowed. | 711 2nd St. | 740/354–7711 or 800/228–2828 | fax 740/353–1539 | www.ramada.com/ramada.html | 119 rooms | $89 | AE, D, DC, MC, V.

PUT-IN-BAY

MAP 14, D2

(Nearby towns listed: Kelleys Island, Marblehead, Port Clinton, Sandusky)

Surrounded by the deep blue waters of Lake Erie, Put-in-Bay is a small resort town on South Bass Island. Iroquois Indians were the first inhabitants of the area. Cook settled here in the 1800s. It became a vacation destination when the Victory Hotel was built in early 1800s. Visitors enjoy fishing, boat charters, great nightlife, shopping, historical attractions, wineries, and exceptional places to stay. Attractions include Perry's Victory and International Peace Memorial, which commemorates the Battle of Lake Erie and the peace following the War of 1812. You can catch the ferry to Put-in-Bay from Catawba Island from April through November.

Information: Put-in-Bay Chamber of Commerce | Box 250, 43456 | 419/285–2832 | www.put-in-bay.com.

Attractions

Beer Barrel Saloon. Since 1989, the *Guiness Book of World Records* has crowned the saloon with the title of "the longest bar." It measures in at 405 ft, 10 inches. | 116 Delaware Ave. | 419/285–2337 | www.beerbarrelpib.com | Free | May–Oct., daily 1 PM–12:30 AM.

Crystal Cave. Thousands of visitors are drawn to the underground confines every year. Guided tours are available. | 798 Catawba Ave. | 419/285–2811 | $7.50 | Daily 9–5.

Lake Erie Island State Park. The park overlooking Lake Erie has boating, fishing, camping, and other outdoor activities. | 441 Catawba Ave. | 419/797–4530 | Free, campsite fees vary by location | Daily.

Perry's Cave. General Perry hid his arsenal of ammunition in this cave during the battle of Lake Erie. Now it's open to the public for tours. | Catawba Ave. | 419/285–2405 | www.perryscave.com | $4.50 | June–Aug., daily 9–5; April–May, Sept.–Oct., weekends 11–sunset.

Perry's Victory and International Peace Memorial. The memorial commemorates the War of 1812's Battle of Lake Erie, when Commodore Oliver Hazard Perry and his American fleet defeated the British, who controlled the lake. That's when Perry uttered his famous message: "We have met the enemy and they are ours." The 352-ft-tall memorial also commemorates the years of peace that followed the war. | 93 Delaware Ave. | 419/285–2184 | Free, $3 for the observation deck | Mid-June–Labor Day, daily 10–8; late Apr.–mid-June, Labor Day–mid-Oct., 10–5.

Put-In-Bay Tour Train. Trains depart every 30 minutes for an hour-long narrated tour of South Bass Island. You can get off and reboard at any point. | Downtown Depot | 419/285–4855 | $8 | May–mid-Sept., daily 10:15–4:15.

MAY: *Island Bird-a-Thon.* Sponsored by the Chamber of Commerce, this weeklong festival features competitions, birding seminars, and nature talks. | 419/285–2832.
AUG.: *Bay Week and Regatta.* It's seven days of sailing and special events, among them the three-day regatta. | Lakefront | 419/285–2832.

Dining
The Boardwalk. Seafood. This restaurant features seafood, from fresh Maine lobster to Lake Erie perch. Every table has a good view of the marina, where you can enjoy the sunset. The restaurant also has live entertainment and offers free boat dockage. | Bay View Ave. | 419/285–3695 | www.the-boardwalk.com | Closed Oct.–Apr. | $5–$27 | MC, V.

Lodging
Park Hotel. A restored Victorian hotel with individually decorated rooms has a large front porch. It's next to DeRiviera Park and the harbor. There are no private baths; communal bathrooms are on each floor. Cable TV. Laundry services. | 234 Delaware Ave. | 419/285–3581 | 25 rooms | $60–$100 | Closed Nov.–Apr. | AE, D, MC, V.

ST. CLAIRSVILLE

MAP 14, F5

(Nearby towns listed: Cambridge, Steubenville)

Originally named Newellstown after its founder, David Newell, in 1796, this southeast Ohio town was renamed seven years later in honor of Newell's cousin, General Arthur St. Clair, the first governor of the Northwest Territory.

Today, St. Clairsville (pop. 5,100) is a picturesque hilltop community, nestled in a rural setting near Wheeling, West Virginia. The town's sidewalks, lighting, and building fronts have been renovated to re-create the community's early 19th-century appearance. The downtown area is on the National Register of Historic Districts.

Information: St. Clairsville Chamber of Commerce | 116 W Main St., 43950 | 740/695–9623 | www.stchamber.com.

Attractions
CannonballMotor Speedway. This clay race track is ³⁄₈ mi long and has late model, modified, street stock, and pure stock car racing. | Off I–70, at exits 208/213 | 740/676–5444 | www.cannonballspeedway.com | $10.

JULY: *Jamboree in the Hills.* Local and regional country and rock acts perform at this annual music festival in the hills of St. Clairsville. | Off I–70, at exits 208/213 | 304/232–1170 or 800/624–5456.
SEPT.: *Belmont County Fair.* This fair, which begins the Wednesday after Labor Day, features carnival rides, exhibits, games, and 4H and Boy Scout exhibitions. | 102 Fair St. | 740/695–9623.

Dining
Mehlman Cafeteria. American. Sunday dinner-type food is the order of the day. Plentiful portions of roasted turkey with mashed potatoes, meat loaf, and fried chicken are the favorites.

Breads and pies are baked on the premises. Cafeteria service. | 51800 National Rd. | 740/695–1000 | Reservations not accepted | Closed Mon. | $5–$7 | No credit cards.

Undo's. Italian. This family restaurant is known for its pizza bread and chicken and veal parmesan. Low-cholesterol entrées are available. Open-air tent dining is available, with views of the Ohio valley. Early bird dinners. Sun. brunch. | 51130 National Rd. | 740/695–8888 | $10–$20 | AE, D, MC, V.

Lodging

Days Inn-West. This two-story hotel, at the junction of I–70 and State Route 214 is convenient for those who want to avoid city traffic. Restaurant, bar, complimentary Continental breakfast. Cable TV. Pool. Business services. | 52601 Holiday Dr. | 740/695–0100 or 800/325–2525 | fax 740/695–4135 | www.daysinn.com | 138 rooms | $89 | AE, D, DC, MC, V.

Knights Inn. A few of the rooms in this motel, which is near local restaurants, are equipped with hot tubs. In-room data ports, some kitchenettes, some microwaves, some in-room hot tubs. Cable TV. Pool. Business services. Some pets allowed. | 51260 National Rd. | 740/695–5038 or 800/835–9628 | fax 740/695–3014 | www.christopherhotels.com | 104 rooms | $69 | AE, D, DC, MC, V.

Super 8. This three-story chain motel is downtown off Route 70 near several restaurants. Cable TV. Pets allowed. | 68400 Matthew Dr. | 740/695–1994 or 800/848–8888 | www.super8motels.com | 62 rooms | $35–$60 | AE, D, MC, V.

SANDUSKY

MAP 14, C2

(Nearby towns listed: Kelleys Island, Marblehead, Port Clinton, Put-in-Bay, Vermilion)

In the late 17th century, Indian colonies lined the fertile banks of the Sandusky River in north-central Ohio. The peaceful Wyandot tribe chose the name "Sandusky," meaning "at the cold water" for the riverside plot of land on which the present-day town now stands. After the first white settlers arrived in 1775, a trade route was paved from the eastern states up to Detroit, opening up a steady flow of migration, industry, and commerce. Today, agriculture, education, health services, and industry are the mainstays of a county that serves 62,000 people. Tourists are attracted to its lakeside location as well as to Cedar Point Amusement Park.

Information: Sandusky Visitors and Convention Bureau | 4424 Milan Road, Suite A, 44870 | 419/625–2984 or 800/255–ERIE | www.buckeyenorth.com.

Attractions

Battery Park. This park has a breathtaking view of Sandusky Bay. The best times to check it out are at sunrise and sunset. | 701 E. Water St. | 419/625–6142 | Free | Daily.

Cedar Point. One of the country's largest and most thrilling amusement parks, Cedar Point opened in 1870. It's thoroughly modern though; it has record-breaking roller coasters (14 in all, thought to be the world's largest collection). Perhaps its best coaster is Millennium Force, at 310 ft, it's billed as the world's "tallest, fastest and steepest." There are also kiddie rides, a PEANUTS family area, an IMAX theater, live entertainment, the Soak City waterpark, and a sandy stretch of Lake Erie beach. Next door is Challenge Park, featuring race cars and miniature golf courses. | 1 Cedar Point Rd. | 419/627–2350 | $10–$38, multiple day and combination tickets available | Mid-May–Labor Day, daily from 10 AM, closing hrs vary; after Labor Day–mid-Oct., weekends only.

Follett House Museum. At this research center in the home of Oran Follet, one of the founders of the Republican Party, you can view artifacts and drawings from Johnson's Island Prison, which housed captured Confederate officers during the Civil War. Built in the 1830s, this

Greek Revival house has a widow's walk that overlooks Sandusky. | 404 Wayne St. | 419/627–9608 | www.sandusky.lib.oh.us | Free | June–Aug., Tues.–Sat. 12–4; Sept.–Dec., weekends 12–4.

Lake Erie Circle Tour. This 200 mi driving tour around the Lake Erie shore, along scenic routes 6 and 2, shows off the attractions along the way as well. To get the tour map, call or visit the Web site, and then plot your route. | 419/625–2984 or 800/255–3743 | www.circle-erie.com.

Merry-Go-Round Museum. Carnival memorabilia is displayed in this colorful gallery. The tour gives you the chance to watch craftsmen carve carousel horses. Top off your visit with a ride on a 1930s carousel. | W. Washington and Jackson Sts. | 419/626–6111 | $4 | Wed.–Sun. 9–5.

MV *Pelee Islander.* Take a scenic afternoon or evening cruise on Sandusky Bay or out on Lake Erie aboard this yacht. | Foot of Jackson St. | 519/724–2115 | $10 | Daily.

Neuman Boat Line. This tour boat takes you on scenic trips on Sandusky Bay and Lake Erie. | 101 E. Shoreline Dr. | 419/626–5557 | $10 | June–Oct., daily.

Old Woman Creek National Estuarine Research Reserve. Scientists and educational institutions conduct research here. The reserve's forest and tributaries are also open to the public. | 25-4 Cleveland Rd., off Rte. 14 | 419/433–4601 | Free | Jan.–Mar., weekdays 9–5; Apr.–Dec., Wed.–Sun. 9–5.

ON THE CALENDAR

AUG.: *Erie County Fair.* Games, food, rides, and live entertainment are all part of the fun at this annual county fair. Livestock shows are the main events here. | Erie County Fairgrounds, 3110 Columbus Ave. | 419/625–2984 or 800/255–3743.

SEPT.: *Millennium Mania at Cedar Point.* In the fall, Cedar Point amusement park opens its doors (at a reduced admission) for parkgoers who just want to ride their famous rollercoasters. Experience the Millenium Force, Magnum XL-200, Raptor, Mantis and Power Tower, some of the fastest and most terrifying rollercoasters in America. Attendance is limited; the $19 tickets must be purchased by the end of August. | 419/627–2350.

DEC.: *Tour of Homes.* Some of the most beautiful private homes in Sandusky are open to the public for tours during this annual holiday event. | 419/625–2984 or 800/255–3743.

Dining

Bay Harbor Inn. American. The restaurant just outside Cedar Point amusement park is a favorite of park visitors. Seafood dominates the menu, but there's also filet mignon and New York strip steak. Kids' menu. No smoking. | Cedar Point Marina, on Causeway Dr. | 419/625–6373 | No lunch | $20–$50 | AE, D, MC, V.

Damon's at Battery Park. American/Casual. This sports bar chain has wall-sized big-screen televisions, local sports team memorabilia, and electronic trivia games. Try the popular onion loaf appetizer, a tasty tangle of thin onion straws that are breaded and deep fried. Dock space. | 701 E. Water St. | 419/627–2424 | $10–$26 | AE, D, MC, V.

DeMore's Fish Den. Seafood. The fish, sold as dinners or by the pound, comes fresh from DeMore's wholesale distributorship, the largest for yellow perch in the Midwest. Known for Great Lakes fish and clam chowder. Open-air dining. Cafeteria service. Kids' menu. | 302 W. Perkins Ave. | 419/626–8861 | $6–$11 | MC, V.

Lodging

Best Western-Cedar Point. After a day of frolicking at Cedar Point amusement park, many families crash at this clean and comfortable motel. Restaurant. Cable TV. Pool. Video games. Laundry facilities. | 1530 Cleveland Rd. | 419/625–9234 or 800/528–1234 | fax 419/625–9971 | www.bestwestern.com | 105 rooms | $109 | AE, D, DC, MC, V.

Breakers Express. Independent, three-story motel with two queen-size beds in each room. Take a swim in the pool shaped like Snoopy. Cable TV. Outdoor pool. Video games. Laundry facilities. | 1 Cedar Point Dr. | 419/627–2109 | fax 419/627–2267 | www.cedarpoint.com | 350 rooms | $59–$79 | mid-Oct.–Apr. | D, MC, V.

Clarion Inn. This hotel is across the street from the Sandusky Mall and within minutes of the area's tourist major attractions. Restaurant, bar with entertainment, room service. In-room data ports. Cable TV. Indoor pool. Hot tub. Exercise equipment. Video games. Business services. Some pets allowed. | 1119 Sandusky Mall Blvd. | 419/625–6280 or 800/252–7466 | www.clarioninn.com | fax 419/625–9080 | 143 rooms | $109 | AE, D, DC, MC, V.

Clarion Inn-Twine House. This hotel is on the shores of Lake Erie in Huron, about 20 minutes east of Sandusky. Restaurant, bar with entertainment, picnic area. Some in-room hot tubs, room service. Cable TV. Indoor pool. Hot tub. Exercise equipment. Beach. Video games. Laundry facilities. Business services. | 132 N. Main St., Huron (20 mins from Sandusky) | 419/433–8000 or 800/252–7466 | fax 419/433–8552 | www.clarioninn.com | 65 rooms | $109 | AE, D, DC, MC, V.

Fairfield Inn by Marriott. A sauna and indoor pool are highlights at this motel, which is close to dining and shopping. Complimentary Continental breakfast. Some in-room hot tubs. Cable TV. Indoor pool. Sauna. Laundry facilities. Business services. | 6220 Milan Rd. | 419/621–9500 or 800/288–2800 | www.marriott.com | 63 rooms | $99 | AE, D, DC, MC, V.

Holiday Inn. In its well-equipped Holidome, the Holiday Inn offers recreation for families who still have some energy left after a day at Cedar Point amusement park. Restaurant, bar, room service. In-room data ports, some in-room hot tubs. Cable TV. 2 pools (1 indoor). Hot tub. Miniature golf, tennis. Exercise equipment. Video games. Free laundry service. Business services. | 5513 Milan Rd. | 419/626–6671 or 800/465–4329 | fax 419/626–9780 | www.holidayinn.com | 175 rooms, 15 suites | $99, $169–$219 suites | AE, D, DC, MC, V.

★ **Hotel Breakers.** Every room has a balcony—most have a view of Lake Erie—at this hotel with a rotunda that has a waterfall. Kids like the Peanuts floor, where the rooms have Peanuts characters on the walls, as well as Beaches and Cream, a 1950's-style ice cream parlor. Restaurant. Cable TV. Indoor-outdoor pool. Outdoor hot tub. Spa. Beach. Shops, video games. Laundry facilities. | 1 Cedar Point Dr. | 419/627–2109 | www.cedarpoint.com | 650 rooms | $140–$170 | mid-Oct.–Apr. | D, MC, V.

Radisson Harbour Inn. Most of the rooms at this hotel have breathtaking views of the waterfront of Sandusky Bay. Restaurant, bar with entertainment, room service. In-room data ports. Cable TV. Indoor pool. Hot tub. Exercise equipment. Video games. Kids' programs. Laundry facilities. Business services. Airport shuttle. Some pets allowed. | 2001 Cleveland Rd. | 419/627–2500 or 800/333–3333 | fax 419/627–0745 | www.radisson.com | 237 rooms, 49 suites | $135, $189–$209 suites | AE, D, DC, MC, V.

Sandcastle Suites Hotel. Every room is a suite at this lakefront hotel, which is within walking distance of restaurants and shopping. Some microwaves, refrigerators. Cable TV. Pool. Spa. Tennis. Beach. | 1 Cedar Point Dr. | 419/627–2109 | www.cedarpoint.com | 187 rooms | $135–$205 | mid-Oct.–Apr. | D, MC, V.

SIDNEY

MAP 14, B4

(Nearby towns listed: Bellefontaine, Piqua, Vandalia)

The city of Sidney was settled in 1819. The town's growth was aided by the construction of the Miami-Erie Canal, which connected Sidney with Ohio's major trade centers. As the influence of the canal declined, railroads took over. In the 1950s, I–75, which connects

Sidney with Canada to the north and Florida to the south, played a significant role in the city's development.

Today Sidney is a working class industrial city. Its downtown features the People's Savings and Loan building, designed by noted architect Louis Sullivan; the Monumental Building, and the Shelby County Courthouse. The courthouse is on Court Square, which was named one of the "Great American Public Places" by The Lyndhurst Foundation of Chattanooga, TN; this is also the site of farmers market on Saturday mornings in the summer.

Information: **Sidney–Shelby Chamber of Commerce** | 100 S. Main Ave., 45365 | 937/492–9122 | www.sidneyshelbychamber.com.

Attractions
Holiday Bowl and Family Fun Center. Fun and games for the entire family; activities range from bowling to laser tag, video games to karaoke. | 1400 W. Michigan St. | 937/492–9141 | Prices vary | Mon.–Thurs. 11–11, Fri. 7:30 AM–2:30 AM, Sat. 8:30 AM–2:30 AM, Sun. noon–9.

ON THE CALENDAR
JULY: *Country Concert at Hickory Hill Lakes.* The biggest names in country music travel to Fort Loramie, about 8 mi west of Sidney, for a four-day outdoor concert the weekend after July 4. | 7103 Rte. 66 | 937/295–3000.

SEPT.: *Lake Loramie Fall Festival.* Set around the waters of Lake Loramie in the state park, this end-of-summer festival features games, rides, and entertainment. The lake is also open for boating, fishing, and other water activities. The park is about 8 mi west of Sidney. | Off Rte. 66 | 937/492–9122.

SEPT.–OCT.: *Great Sidney Farmers Market.* This lively downtown festival occurs every Saturday morning and features antiques and vintage cars. | Court Square, downtown Sidney | 937/492–9122.

Dining
Fairington. American. Meals are elegant affairs here, complete with blue-velvet chairs, a baby grand piano, and between-course sorbet. Black Forest steak, chicken Oscar, and stuffed orange roughy are specialties. Pianist Fri. and Sat. Kids' menu, early bird dinners. | 1103 Fairington Dr. | 937/492–6186 | Closed Sun., no lunch Sat. | $15–$55 | AE, D, DC, MC, V.

Michael Anthony's Pasta and Grill. Italian. Wrought-iron birdcages, candlelit tables, grapevines, and a mural of the Mediterranean give this restaurant an elegant, Old World atmosphere. Veal dishes, pastas, and chicken marsala are served, along with steaks, chops, and fish from a wood-fired grill. | 420 Folkerth Ave. | 937/497–9732 | $8–$25 | AE, D, MC, V.

Lodging
Comfort Inn. This motel off I–75 is a good choice for motorists. Complimentary Continental breakfast. Microwaves and refrigerators in suites, some in-room hot tubs. Cable TV. Pool. Business services. | 1959 W. Michigan St. | 937/492–3001 or 800/228–5150 | fax 937/497–8150 | www.comfortinn.com | 88 rooms | $69 | AE, D, DC, MC, V.

Greatstone Castle Bed and Breakfast. This mansion has been an Ohio landmark for 100 years. Constructed of 18-inch-thick Bedford Indiana limestone, it features a wraparound porch supported by intricate stone columns, and has three turrets. The interior has stained glass and imported hardwoods, elaborately carved. Complimentary Continental breakfast. Spa. Library. No pets. No smoking. | 429 N. Ohio Ave. | 937/498–4728 | fax 937/498–9950 | www.greatstonecastle.com | 5 rooms | $85–$125 | AE, MC, V.

Holiday Inn. A pool and restaurant make this a good stopping point for families with young children. Restaurant, bar, room service. In-room data ports, microwaves (in suites). Cable TV. Pool. Exercise equipment. Laundry facilities. Business services. Some pets allowed. | 400

Folkerth Ave. | 937/492–1131 or 800/465–4329 | fax 937/498–4655 | www.holidayinn.com | 134 rooms, 5 suites | $69, $74 suites | AE, D, DC, MC, V.

SPRINGFIELD

MAP 14, B5

(Nearby towns listed: Columbus, Dayton, Vandalia, Yellow Springs)

Named for the abundance of springs and lakes in the area, Springfield owes its successful development to the locomotive; by the turn of the century, more than 50 trains arrived daily. Later, businesses like International Harvester Co. and the Crowell-Collier Publishing Co. came to town. Among the city's most noteworthy sons are William Whitley, who invented the self-raking reaper and mower in 1856, and A.B. Graham, who in 1902 organized a local boys and girls organization that became the 4-H Club. Since its inception, Springfield has grown from a rural settlement to an urban zone; more than 147,200 people now live in the city and its environs. Whitenberg University, a leading educational institution with 2,000 students, is here. The Springfield Antique Show and Flea Market is held one weekend a month, as is the Summer Arts Festival.

Information: Springfield–Clark County Chamber of Commerce | 333 N. Limestone St., Suite 201, 45503-4292 | 937/325–7621 | www.springfieldnet.com.

Attractions

Buck Creek State Park. This park covers more than 4,000 acres and has boating, fishing, and camping. | 1901 Buck Creek La. | 937/322–5284 | Free | Daily.

Cedar Bog Nature Preserve. The 428-acre preserve about 15 mi north of Springfield is a remnant of a vast wetland that covered much of the valley prior to settlement. You can walk on a bridge over the bog. | 980 Woodburn Rd., Urbana | 937/484–3744 | $3 | Apr.–Sept., Wed.–Sun. 9–4:30; Oct.–Mar. by appointment.

John Bryan State Park. This small park is a nice spot for a quiet day of fishing or hiking. | 3790 Rte. 370 | 937/767–1274 | Free | Daily.

Springfield Antique Show and Flea Market. About 500 dealers display their wares at this huge monthly show at the Clark County Fairgrounds. It's held the third weekend of every month, except in December, when it's the second weekend. | 4401 S. Charleston Pke. State Rte. 41 | 937/325–0053 | $2 | Sat. 8–4, Sun. 9–4.

Springfield Museum of Art. European and American artwork from the 19th and 20th centuries is on display here. | 107 Cliff Park Rd. | 937/325–4673 | Free | Tues., Thurs., Fri. 9–5; Wed. 9–9, Sat. 9–3, Sun. 2–4. Closed Mon.

ON THE CALENDAR

JUNE–JULY: *Springfield Arts Festival.* The summer concert series features some of the biggest names in music. All types of music—rhythm and blues, rock, jazz, country—are performed. | In Veterans Park, off Fountain Ave. | 937/324–2712.

JULY: *Clark County Fair.* Look for a petting zoo, demolition derby, rides, and games at this local fair, held the last week of July at the Clark County Fairgrounds. | 4401 S. Charleston Pike, Rte. 41 | 937/323–3090.

Dining

Casey's. American. Sandwiches, burgers, and chargrilled steaks and chicken are the staples here. Family-style service. Entertainment Fri. and Sat. | 2205 Park Rd. | 937/322–0397 | Closed Sun. No lunch | $9–$18 | AE, DC, MC, V.

Klosterman's Derr Road Inn. Continental. The rustic surroundings are comfortable and the fare is good and hearty. Sautéed salmon with shrimp cream sauce is a specialty. Kids' menu. | 4343 Derr Rd. | 937/399–0822 | No lunch weekends | $14–$21 | AE, D, DC, MC, V.

Lodging

Fairfield Inn by Marriott. Spacious rooms and a full set of facilities and services await you at this establishment. Complimentary Continental breakfast. Some microwaves, some refrigerators. Cable TV. Indoor pool. Hot tub. Business services. | 1870 W. 1st St. | 937/323–9554 or 800/288–2800 | www.marriott.com | 63 rooms | $74–$80 | AE, D, DC, MC, V.

Hampton Inn. This four-story chain motel is off I-70 near downtown. Complimentary Continental breakfast. Cable TV. Indoor pool. Spa. Exercise room. Laundry service. | 101 W. Leffel | 937/325–8480 or 800/426–7866 | fax 937/325–8634 | www.hampton-inn.com | 100 rooms | $84 | AE, MC, V.

Springfield Inn. This hotel is in downtown Springfield; balconies overlook the town. Restaurant, bar. Cable TV. Business services. | 100 S. Fountain Ave. | 937/322–3600 or 800/234–3611 | fax 937/322–0462 | 124 rooms | $64 | AE, D, DC, MC, V.

STEUBENVILLE

MAP 14, F4

(Nearby towns listed: East Liverpool, St. Clairsville)

The seat of Jefferson County in eastern Ohio, Steubenville is one of the state's oldest cities. The site was settled temporarily as early as 1776; in 1786, Fort Steuben, named for Baron von Steuben, soldier and patriot of the American Revolution, was built here. Next to the Ohio River, one of the nation's principal waterways, and in an area rich in coal and clay, the city became an important manufacturing and commercial center. In the period after the War of 1812, the manufacture of textiles became the city's most important industry.

Today, Steubenville's economy is focused on the production of steel, chemicals, dinnerware, brick and tile, heaters, stoves, electrical equipment, paperboard, and ferro alloy metals. The Welsh Classic Car Museum and the Creegan Animation Factory are popular attractions.

Information: Steubenville Chamber of Commerce | 630 Market St., 43952-2808 | 614/282–6226.

Attractions

Creegan Animation Factory. You can watch the nation's largest manufacturer of animated and costume characters at work here. The company's credits include costumes for the Exxon Tiger and the Rutgers University mascot, along with animations for the Hershey Co. Avoid stopping by at lunch, when work pretty much comes to a halt. | 510 Washington St. | 740/283–3708 | Free | Weekdays 10–4.

Franciscan University of Steubenville. Franciscan University of Steubenville has been recognized as one of the best Catholic universities in the country by *U.S. News and World Report,* the Templeton Foundation, *Barron's, National Review,* and the *National Catholic Register.* The campus is open year-round for self-guided tours. | 100 Franciscan Way | 740/283–6276 | Free | Daily.

Jefferson County Historical Association Museum and Genealogical Library. Set in a Victorian mansion, the museum and library chronicle Steubenville's steamboat and river history. | 426 Franklin Ave. | 740/283–1133 | Free | Tues.–Fri. 10–3.

Welsh Classic Car Museum. Cool, classic cars are on display here; the collection is focused on Jacquars, though other favorites, like the Ford Model A, are also showcased. | 501 Washington St. | 740/282–8649 or 800/875–5247 | $1 | Wed.–Sun. noon–6.

ON THE CALENDAR

JUNE: *Dean Martin Festival.* This film festival celebrates Steubenville's favorite son and features live and silent auctions of memorabilia. | 740/283–4935 or 800/510–4442.

Dining

Jaggin' Around Restaurant and Pub. American/Casual. Housed in the refurbished 1936 Ohio Power building, this landmark retains many of the Art Deco details from the original building. Known for tremendous deli sandwiches. Kids' menu. Sun. brunch. | 501 Washington St. | 740/282–1010 | $12–$26 | AE, D, MC, V.

Lodging

Hilltop Haven Bed and Breakfast. This ranch-style home has a kitchen that's always open for a quick snack. There are genealogy records for Jefferson County here and wildlife walks start right outside the back door. It's just 9 mi south of town. Complimentary breakfast. TV in common area. Pond. No pets. No smoking. | 228 High Haven Dr., Toronto | 740/537–1250 or 877/466–8722 | fax 740/537–3878 | 2 rooms | $55–$65 | D, MC, V.

Holiday Inn. A number of restaurants and shops are within minutes of this hotel. Restaurant, bar, room service. In-room data ports. Cable TV. Pool. Laundry facilities. Business services. Some pets allowed. | 1401 University Blvd. | 740/282–0901 or 800/465–4329 | fax 740/282–9540 | www.holidayinn.com | 120 rooms | $79 | AE, D, DC, MC, V.

STRONGSVILLE

MAP 14, D3

(Nearby towns listed: Brecksville, Cleveland, Elyria, Oberlin)

Strongsville was founded by John S. Strong, a native New Englander, in 1816. It has progressed from a farming community to one of the fastest-growing Cleveland suburbs, and a prime location for industry and business. Among the town's landmarks are Cleveland Metroparks, Gardenview Horticultural Park, and the Strongsville Historical Village.

Information: **Strongsville Chamber of Commerce** | 18829 Royalton Rd., 44136-5130 | 440/238–3366 | www.strongsville-ohio.com.

Attractions

Gardenview Horticultural Park. Hundreds of different species of flowers and trees flourish here in English cottage garden settings. A 10-acre arboretum has more than 2,500 unusual trees. | 16711 Pearl Rd. | 440/238–6653 | $5 | Apr.–mid-Oct., weekends noon–6.

Strongsville Historical Village. This collection of re-created homes and buildings, dating from 1822 to 1904, show the development of the community of Strongsville. An old schoolhouse and general store are among the quaint buildings at the village, and antique farm tools and other artifacts fill the grounds. | 13305 Pearl Rd. | 440/572–0057 | Free | Apr.–Nov. Wed., Sat., Sun. 1–4.

ON THE CALENDAR

OCT.: *Annual All Nations Festival.* Held at the Strongsville Recreation and Senior Complex, this festival features live entertainment and a sampling of international cuisine. | 18100 Royalton Rd. | 440/238–7111.

Dining

Simmering Pot. American. This home-style restaurant in the Holiday Inn Select serves up pot roast, beef stew, chicken pot pie and other comfort cooking. Breakfast is available. | 15471 Royalton Rd. | 440/238–8800 | $8–$23 | D, MC, V.

Lodging

Holiday Inn Select. In the heart of the city, this Holiday Inn features an Executive Club Level with private access and upgraded amenities. Restaurant, bar, room service. In-room data ports. Cable TV. Indoor pool. Hot tub, sauna. Exercise room. Laundry services. No pets. | 15471 Royalton Rd. | 440/238–8800 or 800/465–4329 | fax 440/238–0273 | www.holidayinn.com | 304 rooms | $69–$139 | AE, D, MC, V.

SUGARCREEK

MAP 14, E4

(Nearby towns listed: Berlin, Canton, Dover, East Liverpool, Gnadenhutten, New Philadelphia, Zoar)

Known throughout the state as the "Little Switzerland of Ohio" because of its Swiss founders and thriving Swiss cheese-making industry, Sugarcreek is also in the midst of Ohio's Amish Country, which is home to one of the largest concentrations of Amish in the country.

Information: Tuscarawas County Convention and Visitors Bureau | 125 McDonald Dr. SW, New Philadelphia, 44663 | 330/339–5453 | www.neohiotravel.com or www.sugarcreekohio.org.

Attractions

Alpine Hills Historical Museum. See replicas of an old cheese house and an Amish kitchen. The on-site tourist resource center provides sightseeing brochures of the area. | 106 W. Main St. | 330/852–4113 or 888/609–7592 | $1 suggested | Apr.–Sat. after Thanksgiving, Mon.–Sat. 10–4:30.

Ohio Central Railroad. Ride in coaches pulled by vintage steam and diesel locomotives on an hour-long narrated train trip through Amish Country. The tiny depot in Sugarcreek dates from 1915. | 111 Factory St. | 330/852–4676 | $7 | May 2-last Sat. in Oct.: Mon.–Sat. 11, 12:30, 2, 3:30 departures. July, Aug., and Oct: extra trains on Sat. at 9:30 and 5.

ON THE CALENDAR

OCT.: Ohio Swiss Festival. On the fourth Friday and Saturday after Labor Day, the German-Swiss heritage of the area is celebrated with Swiss cheese exhibits, a parade, contests for the best Swiss costumes, yodeling, and live polka bands. | Follow signs from Rte. 32 | 330/852–4113.

Dining

Beachy's Country Chalet. American. This "all-you-care-to-eat" restaurant features roast beef, turkey, ham, mashed potatoes, vegetables, fresh bread, and, for dessert, 18 varieties of pie. Wooden bench-style seats and Amish quilts are homey touches. Family-style service. Kids' menu. No smoking. | 115 Andreas Dr. | 330/852–4644 | Closed Sun. | $6–$10 | MC, V.

The Swiss Hat. American. All-you-can-eat buffets, Swiss steak, Wiener schnitzel, and Friday fish fry, plus homemade pies and apple dumplings for dessert make this a popular spot. | 108 E. Main St. | 330/852–2821 | $7–$15 | D, MC, V.

Lodging

Bed and Breakfast Barn. Originally a cheese house built in 1858, this inn was transformed into a bed and breakfast in 1988. The beams and flooring are original, with some detailing in century-old oak. Dining room, complimentary breakfast. Some kitchenettes, some microwaves, some refrigerators. Cable TV. Spa. No smoking. | 560 E. Sugarcreek St. | 330/852–BEDS or 888/334–2436 | web.tusco.net/bedbarn | 12 rooms, 10 cabins | $60–$120 | D, MC, V.

Swiss Village Inn. The rooms have floral curtains and bedspreads and Amish-style oak furnishings. You're within walking distance from many shops and restaurants in the commercial district of Sugarcreek. Dining room, complimentary Continental breakfast. Some refrigerators. Cable TV. No smoking. | 206 S. Factory St. | 330/852–3121 or 800/792–6822 | 10 rooms | $45–$75 | MC, V.

TIFFIN

MAP 14, C3

(Nearby towns listed: Bellevue, Findlay, Fremont)

On the Sandusky River 42 mi southeast of Toledo, Tiffin is in one of the most fertile agricultural regions in Ohio. The city was born in 1820 when Joniah Hedges bought a piece of land on the south bank of the river; he named his new village in honor of the first governor of Ohio. Tiffin was incorporated as a city in 1835, but it began to grow in 1886, when oil was discovered in the area. Tiffin is now a prosperous industrial city, home to Allied Signal, National Machinery, and American Standard. Some 62,000 people live here. A museum and annual event celebrate the area's history of fine glassmaking.

Information: Tiffin Area Chamber of Commerce | 62 S. Washington St., 44883 | 419/447–4141 | www.tiffinohio.com/chamber.

Attractions

Glass Heritage Gallery. This museum showcases the area's long history of fine craftsmanship in glassmaking, which began when natural gas was discovered near Toledo. In the late 19th and early 20th centuries, several glass manufacturers set up shop in this area west of Tiffin. | 109 N. Main St., Fostoria | 419/435–5077 | Free | Tues.–Sat. 10–4.

Seneca County Museum. Elegant Tiffin glass adorns this mid-19th-century house, now a museum devoted to the history of Seneca County. | 28 Clay St. | 419/447–5955 | Free | June–Aug., Tues.–Thurs., Sun. 2–5; Sept.–May, Wed., Sun. 2–5; and by appointment.

ON THE CALENDAR

JULY: *Glass Heritage Festival.* Glassmaking, long an important industry in this town, is celebrated with this three-day festival. There are crafts, games, rides, and live music. | 21 N. Main St. | 419/435–0486.

AUG.: *Sandusky River Valley Doll Show.* Antique, modern, and collectable dolls are showcased and sold here at the Seneca County Fairgrounds. Collectors can enter the doll competition in several categories. | 100 Hopewell Ave. | 419/937–2645.

SEPT.: *Tiffin-Seneca Heritage Festival.* The history of the city of Tiffin and Seneca County are the focus of this celebration, which includes storytelling, crafts, and music. | Downtown Tiffin and Hedges Boyer Park, with shuttle service running between the two locations | 419/447–5866 or 888/SENECA–1.

Dining

Black Cat. Steak. Traditional steakhouse fare is on the menu, including beef tenderloin with garlic cottage cheese, and homemade onion rings at this restaurant about 10 mi west of Tiffin. Kids' menu, early bird dinners. | 820 Sandusky St., Fostoria | 419/435–2685 | Reservations essential | $18–$31 | AE, D, MC, V.

Pioneer Mill. American. Antique mill machinery and wagon-wheel lamps give this place an old-fashioned, rustic feel. Diners enjoy sizeable steaks and a wide array of shellfish and fish dinners, including Lake Erie walleye. Try Old Faithful, a grilled bologna sandwich with your choice of toppings. Kids' menu, early bird dinners. Sun. brunch. No smoking. | 255 Riverside Dr. | 419/448-0100 | $14–$37 | D, MC, V.

Lodging

Quality Inn. This riverfront hotel in the downtown area is surrounded by historical homes and close to hiking, golf, tennis, and the Tiffin Mall. Room service. In-room data ports, some microwaves, some refrigerators. Cable TV. Outdoor pool. Laundry facilities. | 1927 S. SR. 53 | 419/447-6313 or 800/228-5151 | www.qualityinn.com | 72 rooms | $75–$110 | AE, D, MC, V.

TOLEDO

MAP 14, C2

(Nearby towns listed: Bowling Green, Fremont, Wauseon)

The Maumee River, along which Toledo is built, is the largest river flowing into the Great Lakes; for ages it has served as a natural highway. The land was Erie Indian territory, but in 1668, it was claimed by French explorer Rene-Robert Cavelier Sieur de LaSalle in the name of Louis XIV. French rule gave way to British at the end of the French and Indian War. In 1774, the area was annexed to the Canadian province of Quebec; in 1783, Britain gave the land to the United States and Toledo became a part of the Northwest Territory. Toledo was opened to settlement after the Battle of Fallen Timbers in 1794. Several small villages developed in the area following a series of treaties with the Native Americans in the area. Two villages, Port Lawrence (1817) and Vistula (1832) consolidated in 1833 to form Toledo, named after Toledo, Spain, and incorporated in 1837.

Since that time, Toledo has grown into one of the largest cities in the state. More than 3,500 businesses, producing everything from glass and plastics to fabricated metal products and automotive parts, make their home in Toledo. Its parks, cultural activities, and vibrant economy continue to draw new residents and visitors. Popular attractions include COSI Toledo and Fort Meigs State Memorial.

Information: Toledo Chamber of Commerce | 300 Madison Ave., Suite 200, 43604-1575 | 419/243-8191 | www.toledochamber.com.

Attractions

COSI Toledo. The Center of Science and Industry has hands-on exhibits and demonstrations on topics ranging from the brain to sports. You can test the laws of physics when you ride a bicycle on a high wire above the atrium or design a roller coaster. | 1 Discovery Way, at Summit and Adams Sts. | 419/244-2674 | $7.50 | Mon.–Sat. 10–5, Sun. noon–5.

Crane Creek State Park. This 80-acre park east of Toledo on the shores of Lake Erie has fishing, swimming, hiking, camping and picnic areas. | 1/2 mi NW of Locust Point | 419/898-2495 or 419/836-7758 | Free | Daily, dawn till dusk.

Detwiler/Bay View Park. This community park has a great view of Maumee Bay. | 4001 N. Summit St. | 419/726-9353 | Free | Daily, dawn to dusk.

Fort Meigs State Memorial. Fort Meigs, south of Toledo, served as a security post for the Western frontier during the War of 1812. You can tour the reconstructed fort, which includes seven blockhouses and the actual cannons used in the war against the British. | W. River Rd. (Rte. 65), Perrysburg | 419/874-4121 | $5 | Memorial Day–Labor Day, Wed.–Sat. 9:30–5, Sun. noon–5; Labor Day–Oct., Sat. 9:30–5, Sun. noon–5.

Maumee Bay State Park. This 1,300-acre park 8 mi east of Toledo, has boating, fishing, and camping. | 3 mi north off Rte. 2, Oregon | 419/836–7758 (park administration), 419/836–1466 or 800/282–7275 (lodge and cabin reservations) | Free | Daily.

Port of Toledo. It's fun to watch the boats come into port from their journeys on Lake Erie. | Cherry St. and Summit St. | 419/243–8251 | Free | Daily.

SS *Willis B. Boyer* Museum Ship. When this ship was launched in 1911, it was the biggest and most modern of its day. It's now been refurbished as a museum with exhibits focusing on life on Lake Erie. See artifacts and memorabilia from sailors who have traveled the lake on freighters over the past 200 years. | East side of river at International Park | 419/936–3070 | $5 | May–Sept., Mon.–Sat. 10–5, Sun. noon–5; Oct.–Apr., Wed.–Sun. 10–5.

Toledo Botanical Garden. Fifty-seven acres of gardens and meadows, lined with roses, wildflowers, and herbs, make this a serene spot in a bustling city. A replica of a pioneer homestead is on the property. | 5403 Elmer Dr. | 419/936–2986 | Free | Daily, 8–dusk.

KODAK'S TIPS FOR PHOTOGRAPHING THE CITY

Streets
- Take a bus or walking tour to get acclimated
- Explore markets, streets, and parks
- Travel light so you can shoot quickly

City Vistas
- Find high vantage points to reveal city views
- Shoot early or late in the day, for best light
- At twilight, use fast films and bracket exposures

Formal Gardens
- Exploit high angles to show garden design
- Use wide-angle lenses to exaggerate depth and distance
- Arrive early to beat crowds

Landmarks and Monuments
- Review postcard racks for traditional views
- Seek out distant or unusual views
- Look for interesting vignettes or details

Museums
- Call in advance regarding photo restrictions
- Match film to light source when color is critical
- Bring several lenses or a zoom

Houses of Worship
- Shoot exteriors from nearby with a wide-angle lens
- Move away and include surroundings
- Switch to a very fast film indoors

Stained-Glass Windows
- Bright indirect sunlight yields saturated colors
- Expose for the glass not the surroundings
- Switch off flash to avoid glare

Architectural Details
- Move close to isolate details
- For distant vignettes, use a telephoto lens
- Use side light to accent form and texture

In the Marketplace
- Get up early to catch peak activity
- Search out colorful displays and colorful characters
- Don't scrimp on film

Stage Shows and Events
- Never use flash
- Shoot with fast (ISO 400 to 1000) film
- Use telephoto lenses
- Focus manually if necessary

From *Kodak Guide to Shooting Great Travel Pictures* © 2000 by Fodor's Travel Publications

Toledo Firefighters Museum. Located in the old No. 18 Firehouse, this museum has over 150 years of fire fighting history on display, including Toledo's first fire pump, "1837 Neptune." | 918 Sylvania Ave. | 419/478–3473 | Free | Weekends 12–4.

Toledo Museum of Art. Works by contemporary and classical artists, including treasures from Egypt, Greece, and Rome and works by Matisse, Rembrandt, and Hopper, are housed here in a lovely Grecian-style marble building. The collection also includes books, glass, sculpture, medieval ivories and tapestries. | 2445 Monroe St. | 419/255–8000 | Free, $1 parking | Tues.–Thurs., Sat. 10–4, Fri. 10–10, Sun. 11–5, Closed Mon.

Toledo Storm. Watch the Toledo affiliate of the Detroit Red Wings play ice hockey at the Toledo Sports Arena from October to April. | 1 Main St. | 419/691–0200 | fax 419/698–8998 | www.thestorm.com | $8–$25.

Toledo Zoo. The highlight of this medium-sized zoo is the world's first Hippoquarium, which allows you to watch hippos as they move under water. The zoo has a large meadow for its gorillas, fresh and saltwater aquariums, and all the usual lions and tigers and bears. | 2700 Broadway | 419/385–5721 | $6 | Apr.–Sept., daily 10–5; Oct.–Mar., daily 10–4.

University of Toledo. Founded in 1872 by Jessup Scott, the school is in an attractive residential section on the western edge of Toledo. It is easily reached via I–75 or the Ohio Turnpike (I-80/90). A guided tour of the campus not only includes beautiful architecture, but also a visit to Ritter Planetarium. | W. Bancroft St. | 419/530–8888 or 800/586–5336 | Free | Oct.–June.

Ritter Planetarium. This 40-ft domed auditorium seats 92. Its Spitz A3P central star projector is capable of reproducing the sky as seen from anywhere on Earth at any time. There are weekend planetarium shows followed by observatory sessions. | W. Bancroft St. | 419/530–4037 | $3 | Fri. and Sat. 7:30 PM.

Wolcott House Museum Complex. The site in Maumee, southwest of Toledo, includes the original 1836 Federal-style home of James and Mary Wolcott, which has period antiques and American Indian artifacts. A log cabin, saltbox farmhouse, 19th century churb and railroad depot make up this tribute to 1800s life in the Maumee Valley. | 1031 River Rd., Maumee | 419/893–9602 | $3.50 | Apr.–Dec., Wed.–Sun. 1–4.

ON THE CALENDAR

MAR.–NOV.: *Horse Racing at Toledo Raceway Park.* Both matinee and night races are held at this track. | 5700 Telegraph Rd. | 419/476–7751.

JUNE: *Crosby Festival of the Arts.* More than 200 artists participate at this downtown Toledo festival. Entertainment, food, and children's art activities are all part of the picture. | Toledo Botanical Garden, 5403 Elmer Dr. | 419/936–2986.

AUG.: *Northwest Ohio Rib-Off.* Barbecue venders from around the state and region compete to see who can concoct the best recipes. This is one of the more popular events in Ohio. | In Promenade Park off Summit St. | 419/321–6404 or 800/243–4667.

OCT.: *Autumn Fest of Crafts.* A wide selection of unusual handmade crafts is displayed at this juried show. | Stranahan Theatre, 4645 Heatherdowns Blvd. | 419/895–0615.

Dining

Cousino's Navy Bistro. American. You may have to wait up to two hours for a table on weekends, but as regulars tell you, the food is worth the wait. It's on the Maumee River, so there's a great view. Selections range from Reuben sandwiches to filet mignon. Kids' menu. | International Park, 30 Main St. | 419/697–6289 | Reservations not accepted | $12–$30 | AE, D, MC, V.

Fifi's. Continental. In this formal restaurant, favorite dishes include clam chowder with sour cream and bacon and the *boeuf au fromage,* medallions of tenderloin topped with a Parmesan and Roquefort glace. Pianist Fri. and Sat. | 1423 Bernath Pkwy. | 419/866–6777 | Reservations essential | Closed Sun. | $29–$43 | AE, D, DC, MC, V.

Georgio's Cafe International. Seafood. This family-owned restaurant serves fresh seafood in a romantic setting with mirrored walls and a brass and marble bar. | 426 N. Superior St. | 419/242–2424 | Reservations essential | $15–$24 | AE, D, MC, V.

Mancy's. Steak. Run by the Mancy family for more than 70 years, this is arguably the most popular steak restaurant in Northwest Ohio. Locals rave about the huge portions, the fresh seafood, and attentive service. Kids' menu. | 953 Phillips Ave. | 419/476–4154 | Reservations essential | Closed Sun. | $20–$40 | AE, D, DC, MC, V.

Maumee Bay Brewing Company. American. This microbrewery on the water is in the oldest standing building in Toledo and serves an array of seafood and wood-oven pizzas. A vegetarian menu is available, as is patio dining (summer months only). Brewery tours are available by appointment. | 27 Broadway | 419/241–1253 | $6–$20 | D, MC, V.

Smedlap's Smithy. American. The old-time feel is worth the scenic (less than 10 mi) drive south of Toledo to Waterville. Burgers, chicken, and steak are served. Kids' menu. | 205 Farmsworth Rd., Waterville | 419/878–0261 | Closed Sun. | $10–$25 | AE, D, MC, V.

Tony Packo's Cafe. Hungarian. Autographed hot dog buns from celebrities ranging from Tip O'Neill to Tracy Ullman adorn the walls. The spicy Hungarian hot dogs, loaded with chili and other toppings, are delicacies in this town. Jazz band Fri. and Sat. evenings. Kids' menu. | 1902 Front St. | 419/691–6054 | $7–$12 | AE, D, MC, V.

Lodging

Clarion Westgate. A landscaped enclosed courtyard keeps this hotel's lobby open and airy. Restaurant, bar, room service. In-room data ports. Cable TV. Indoor pool. Hot tub. Exercise equipment. Video games. Business services. Free parking. Some pets allowed. | 3536 Secor Rd. | 419/535–7070 or 800/252–7466 | fax 419/536–4836 | www.clarioninn.com | 305 rooms | $99 | AE, D, DC, MC, V.

Comfort Inn Westgate. This two-story motel off I-475 in Toledo is smaller and less expensive than the Clarion Westgate next door, though you can use that hotel's indoor pool. Picnic area, complimentary Continental breakfast. Cable TV. Some pets allowed. | 3560 Secor Rd. | 419/531–2666 or 800/228–5150 | fax 419/531–4757 | www.comfortinn.com | 70 rooms | $89 | AE, D, DC, MC, V.

Courtyard by Marriott. The rooms in this motel are spacious and have comfortable sitting areas. It's just west of Toledo in Holland. Restaurant, bar. In-room data ports, microwaves and refrigerators (in suites). Cable TV. Indoor pool. Hot tub. Exercise equipment. Laundry facilities. Airport shuttle. Free parking. | 1435 E. Mall Dr., Holland | 419/866–1001 or 800/321–2211 | fax 419/866–9869 | www.courtyard.com | 149 rooms, 12 suites | $99, $169 suites | AE, D, DC, MC, V.

Crown Inn. This small, locally owned motel has a pool and a restaurant. Restaurant, complimentary Continental breakfast. Some refrigerators. Cable TV. Pool. | 1727 W. Alexis Rd. | 419/473–1485 | www.crowninn.com | 40 rooms | $70 | AE, D, DC, MC, V.

Days Inn. A number of restaurants and stores surround this motel, which is just off I-80/90 in Maumee, about 10 mi southwest of Toledo. Complimentary Continental breakfast. Some kitchenettes, some microwaves, some refrigerators. Cable TV. Pool. Business services. Free parking. Some pets allowed. | 150 Dussel Dr., Maumee | 419/893–9960 or 800/325–2525 | fax 419/893–9559 | www.daysinn.com | 120 rooms, 6 suites | $89 | AE, D, DC, MC, V.

Hampton Inn-South. A pool and a health center are pluses here. Complimentary Continental breakfast. Cable TV. Pool. Gym. Airport shuttle. Free parking. | 1409 Reynolds Rd., Maumee | 419/893–1004 or 800/426–7866 | fax 419/893–4613 | www.hampton-inn.com | 129 rooms | $79 | AE, D, DC, MC, V.

Hilton Toledo. Among the property's many amenities is a tennis court. Shopping and dining are nearby. Restaurant, bar. In-room data ports. Cable TV. Indoor pool. Hot tub, sauna. 3 lighted tennis courts. Business services. Airport shuttle. | 3100 Glendale Ave. | 419/381–6800 or 800/445–8667 | fax 419/389–9716 | www.hilton.com | 213 rooms | $109 | AE, D, DC, MC, V.

Holiday Inn. This is a full-service hotel with indoor pool, restaurant, and beauty salon among the on-site conveniences. Restaurant, bar, room service. In-room data ports. Cable TV. Indoor pool. Beauty salon. Exercise equipment. Business services. Airport shuttle. Some pets allowed. | 2340 S. Reynolds Rd. | 419/865–1361 or 800/465–4329 | fax 419/865–6177 | www.holidayinn.com | 218 rooms | $89 | AE, D, DC, MC, V.

Quality Hotel. The Olympic-size indoor pool, hot tub, and playground are appealing to families with children. Business travelers like the business services, modem links, and airport shuttle. Restaurant, bar. In-room data ports. Cable TV. Indoor pool. Hot tub. Playground. Business services. Airport shuttle. Free parking. Some pets allowed. | 2429 S. Reynolds Rd. | 419/381–8765 | fax 419/381–0129 | 246 rooms | $69–$89 | AE, D, DC, MC, V.

Maumee Bay Resort. This large resort hotel has a prime spot on Lake Erie; it's in the Maumee Bay State Park, a 1,300 acre park about 8 mi east of Toledo. Guest rooms have balconies overlooking the lake; the lobby is made cozy with a stone fireplace. There are an abundance of recreational activities available on-site. Restaurant, bar. Refrigerators. Cable TV. Indoor and outdoor pool. Hot tubs. Exercise room. 18-hole golf course, tennis courts. Volleyball. Beach, boating, fishing. Nature center. Video games. Playground. Business services. | 1750 Park Rd. #2, Oregon | 419/836–1466 or 800/282–7275 | www.maumeebayresort.com | 120 rooms, 20 cottages | $140, 2–bedroom cabin $225, 4–bedroom $275 | MC, V, AE, DC, D.

Radisson Hotel Toledo. This 15-story hotel is connected to the Seagate Convention Center, and all rooms have views of the river. Restaurant, bar, room service. In-room data ports. Cable TV. Sauna. health club. Laundry facilities. Pets allowed. | 101 N. Summit St. | 419/241–3000 or 800/333–3333 | www.radisson.com | 399 rooms | $109–$149 | AE, D, MC, V.

Studio Plus-Toledo. This hotel is a home away from home, with a complete kitchen and even a barbecue pit for each unit. It's 12 mi from the downtown area and 8 mi from the airport. In-room data ports. Cable TV. Pool. Exercise room. Laundry service. Pets allowed (fee). | 540 W. Dussell Dr. | 419/244–5676 | 73 rooms | $59 | AE, D, MC, V.

Toledo Hawthorne Hotel & Suites. This 19-story hotel has a restaurant and bar on the top floor, overlooking the city. It's connected to the SeaGate Convention Center. Complimentary Continental breakfast. In-room data ports, some refrigerators. Cable TV. Indoor pool. Business services. Pets allowed. | 141 N. Summit St. | 419/242–8885 or 800/527–1133 | 168 rooms, 30 suites | $89–$130 | D, MC, V.

Wyndham Toledo. A professional staff takes good care of you at this 12-story hotel downtown on the Maumee River. Restaurant, bar, room service. In-room data ports. Cable TV. Indoor pool. Hot tub. Video games, pool table. Exercise equipment. Business services. Parking costs $13 per day. No pets. | 2 Seagate | 419/241–1411 or 800/996–3426 | fax 419/241–8161 | www.travelweb.com | 241 rooms | $84–$129 | AE, D, DC, MC, V.

VANDALIA

(Nearby towns listed: Dayton, Miamisburg, Piqua, Springfield)

In 1838, Benjamin Wilhelm founded and laid out the village of Vandalia, named by a group of westward-bound settlers who stopped in the area on their way to Vandalia, Illinois. In early days, stagecoach lines helped the new community's two taverns do a flourishing business. Later, the construction of Dixie Highway as a main north–south route aided in the area's growth. Since then, the community (pop. 14,000) has continued to grow. Vandalia, a short distance north of downtown Dayton, is now home to Dayton International Airport, which is served by the major airlines and is the hub for Emery Worldwide air freight. The headquarters of KitchenAid, Shopsmith, Lucas Ledex Inc., and the Lighting Systems Divisions of General Motors are here.

Information: **Vandalia-Butler Chamber of Commerce** | 76 Fordway Dr., #4 | 937/898–5351 | www.coax.net/vandalia.

Attractions

Aullwood Audubon Center and Farm. Known as the Miami Valley's first educational farm, this 350-acre wildlife sanctuary has 6 mi of trails winding through prairie, woods, ponds, and meadows. | 1000 Aullwood Rd. | 937/890–7360 | www.audubon.org/local/sanctuary/aullwood | $4 | Mon.–Sat. 9–5, Sun. 1–5.

Crossroads of America. The intersection of what is still Dixie Highway and National Road was used in the late 19th-century by settlers traveling throughout the Midwest and for the passage of freights. National Road, which runs east to west, stayed intact through the 1913 flood and was the principal way of escape for settlers during Ohio's cholera epidemic of 1849. The modern day "Crossroads of America" would now be considered I–70 and I–75 | Dixie Hwy. and National Rd. | 937/898–5351 | www.ci.vandalia.oh.us | Free | Daily.

Trapshooting Hall of Fame and Museum. The world's best trapshooters are enshrined in this gallery. A collection of antique guns, shells, and trapshooting targets is displayed. | 601 W. National Rd. | 937/898–4638 | Free | Weekdays 8–4:30.

ON THE CALENDAR

JULY: *United States Air and Trade Show.* World aerobatic champs, aerobatic teams, wingwalkers, and barnstormers perform breathtaking maneuvers in this nationally acclaimed air show. U.S. aircraft demos and displays, parachuting, pyrotechnics, and vintage aircraft are also on display. The U.S. Air Force Thunderbirds and the U.S. Navy Blue Angels perform on an alternating schedule; one group appears one year, the other the next. | Dayton International Airport, 1501 N. Marginal Rd. | 937/898–5901.

AUG.: *Grand American World Trapshooting Tournament.* The Amateur Trapshooting Association of America sponsors this annual event at the Trapshooting Hall of Fame Museum. | 601 W. National Rd. | 937/898–4638.

Dining

Original Rib House. American. This restaurant is a 20-year-old Vandalia institution famous for rotisserie-cooked baby-back and boneless ribs, served with anything from salads or vegetables to onion rings. | 275 E. National Rd. | 937/898–4601 | No lunch | $5–$20 | D, MC, V.

Lodging

Cross Country Inn. A variety of restaurants and stores surround this three-story hotel, which offers guests drive-through check-in and check-out. Cable TV. Pool. Business services. | 550 E. National Rd. (U.S. 40) | 937/898–7636 or 800/621–1429 | fax 937/898–0630 | 94 rooms | $54 | AE, D, DC, MC, V.

Park Inn International. This single-story inn is directly across from the Dayton International Airport, a half mile from the center of Vandalia. Complimentary Continental breakfast. Some kitchenettes, some microwaves, some refrigerators. Cable TV. Pool. Gym. Laundry facilities. Pets allowed (fee). Airport shuttle. | 75 Corporate Center Dr. | 937/898–8321 or 800/437–7275 | fax 937/898–6334 | www.parkinn.com | 97 rooms | $60 | AE, D, DC, MC, V.

VAN WERT

MAP 14, A3

(Nearby towns listed: Celina, Lima)

Van Wert and Van Wert County were named in honor of Isaac Van Wert, one of three patriots who captured British spy Major John Andre during the Revolutionary War. The town was founded in 1834, when Peter Aughenbaugh, George Marsh, and James

Watson Riley bought 240 acres of land in the center of Van Wert County in northwest Ohio. Completed in 1876, the Van Wert County Courthouse is now on the National Register of Historic Places; sketches of the classical structure are on display in the Smithsonian Institution in Washington, D.C. Van Wert is also the site of Brumback Library, the nation's first public county library.

The agriculture-based economy has yielded to small- and medium-sized business, but the relatively small town is still predominantly residential.

Information: Van Wert Area Chamber of Commerce | 118 W. Main St., 45891 | 419/238–4390 or 877/989–2282 | www.vanwert.com.

Attractions

Van Wert Historical Society. Founded by local attorney William Fosnaught in 1953, this society holds a wealth of information about Van Wert's history in its two buildings, one of which is a Victorian home built circa 1896. You can see old photographs of Van Wert and wartime pictures inside. The society also organizes a historical walking tour that brings you by several Native American artifacts. | 602 N. Washington St. | 419/238–5297 | www.geocities.com/vanwertmuseum | Free | Mar.–Nov., Sun. 2–4:30 and by appointment.

Wassenberg Art Center. Visit the former home of Charles Wassenberg, a nationally known peony farmer. The house and grounds were bequeathed to the town to promote Van Wert as an art center and to develop local art talent. Exhibits vary throughout the year. | 643 S. Washington St. | 419/238–6828 | Free | Tues.–Sun. 1–5.

ON THE CALENDAR

SEPT.: *Van Wert County Fair.* Rides, games, and a variety of farm animals are all part of this annual summer bash at the Van Wert County Fairgrounds. | Fox Rd. | 419/238–3131.
OCT.: *Apple Festival.* Sample the wares of local orchard owners, from raw produce to gourmet specialty foods made from the latest harvests, and wander between booths displaying handmade furnishings, clothing, and arts and crafts for sale. This event is held annually on the third weekend of Oct. at the Van Wert County Fairgrounds. | Fox Rd. | 419/238–4390.

Dining

Balyeat's Coffee Shop. American. Even though it's called a coffee shop, it's more like a home-style restaurant. You can watch the cooks slicing ham or pork from big fresh roasts. Try the Tuesday special, knocker (knockwurst) and kraut. | 133 E. Main St. | 419/238–1580 | Reservations not accepted | Closed Mon. | $4–$8 | No credit cards.

Lodging

Holiday Inn Express Van Wert. Rooms in this two-story hotel are spacious and decorated in burgundy and hunter green. You'll find both a breakfast bar and a lobby furnished with armchairs and loveseats. The hotel is 1 mi north of downtown, and two family restaurants are nearby. Complimentary Continental breakfast. In-room data ports, some microwaves, some refrigerators, some in-room hot tubs. Cable TV. Pool. Hot tub, sauna. Gym. No pets. | 840 N. Washington St. | 419/232–6040 or 800/465–4329 | fax 419/232–6210 | www.hiexpress.com | 53 rooms, 4 suites | $64, $89 suites | AE, MC, V.

VERMILION

MAP 14, D2

(Nearby towns listed: Elyria, Lorain, Milan, Oberlin, Sandusky)

This quaint town on northeastern Ohio's Vermilion River was once a bustling ship-building, fishing, lumbering, and farming center. Harbor Town 1837, Vermilion's downtown district, features sandy beaches along Lake Erie, charming shops, and restored 19th-century homes. The city also offers Lake Erie's most beautiful small boat harbor, sailing and yacht races, boat rides on the Vermilion River, a sandy beach, fishing charters, marinas, public docks, and a public boat ramp. There are also beautiful parks, several museums, and many fine restaurants.

Information: **Vermilion Chamber of Commerce** | 5495 Liberty Ave., 44089 | 440/967–4477.

Attractions

Harbour Town 1837. Browse through quaint antiques and curio shops in this restored section of Vermilion. The town also has a sandy beach along Lake Erie, and restored 19th-century homes. | Downtown Vermilion | Free | Daily.

Inland Seas Maritime Museum. This museum tells the story of the Great Lakes with photographs, ship instruments, a steam engine, and a 1905 pilot house. The highlights are the lighthouse and timbers from Gen. Perry's ship. | 480 Main St. (U.S. 6) | 440/967–3467 | $5 | Daily 10–4.

Mystic Belle Boat Cruise. Take a relaxed cruise of the Vermilion River and Lagoons on an old paddlewheeler, which holds about 30 people. | 5150 Liberty Ave. | 440/967–5025 | $6 | Daily.

ON THE CALENDAR

JUNE: *Festival of the Fish.* Crafts, food, fish dinners, kids' games, crazy craft races, nightly entertainment, a lighted boat parade, a sand castle contest, a father/grandfather essay contest, a parade, and children's rides all add up to a lot of fun during this annual Father's Day weekend event at Victory Park. | Ohio and Main Sts. | 440/967–4477.
AUG.: *Boat Regatta.* Powerful boats race on the Vermilion waterways. Residents and guests set up picnics along the shoreline. | 5416 Liberty Ave. | 440/967–4477.

Dining

Chez Francois. French. The original brick floors remain, but the walls of this old sail loft are now adorned with paintings of the French countryside. The kitchen prepares classic French seafood, beef, and chicken dishes. Open-air dining. Live entertainment Tues., Thur., Sun. No smoking. | 555 Main St. | 440/967–0630 | Reservations essential | Jacket required | Closed Jan.–mid-Mar. and Mon. No lunch | $25–$50 | AE, MC, V.

Old Prague Restaurant. Czech. Feast on homestyle ethnic cooking. Popular Czech favorites include roast duck and chicken paprikash. Known for Wiener schnitzel, central European foods. Kids' menu, early bird dinners. | 5586 Liberty Ave. | 440/967–7182 | $14–$22 | D, MC, V.

Lodging

Vermilion Holiday Inn Express. Rooms are decorated in peach and green at this hotel built in 1997; those in the back overlook a cornfield. It's 1½ mi south of downtown. Complimentary Continental breakfast. In-room data ports, some in-room hot tubs. Cable TV. Pool. Hot tub. Gym. Pets allowed. | 2417 Rte. 60 | 440/967–8770 or 800/465–4329 | fax 440/967–8772 | www.hiexpress.com | 50 rooms, 16 suites | $139, $159 suites | AE, D, DC, MC, V.

WAPAKONETA

MAP 14, B4

(Nearby towns listed: Bellefontaine, Celina, Lima, Van Wert)

Wapakoneta, the county seat of Auglaize County in west central Ohio, was originally the site of a Native American village established by the Shawnee Indians after their expulsion from Piqua in 1780.

Now a thriving agricultural town of 10,000 people, Wapakoneta raised one of the most noted Americans of the 20th century: Neil Armstrong grew up here. The city's primary tourist attraction is the Neil Armstrong Air and Space Museum, which features aircraft flown by Armstrong and suits worn during his space missions.

Information: Wapakoneta Chamber of Commerce | 16 E. Auglaize St., 45895 | 419/738–2911 | www.wapakoneta.com.

Attractions

Auglaize County Courthouse. The heart of Wapakoneta, this courthouse was built in the late 19th-century, and has been serving the community since 1894. You can stop into this working courthouse to admire the stained glass skylights, murals, light fixtures and other original architectural details. | 201 S. Willipie St. | 419/738–2911 | Free | Weekdays 8–4:30.

Neil Armstrong Air and Space Museum. Take one small step into this museum and learn about the life and times of the first person on the moon, who grew up right here in Wapakoneta. You'll see a Jupiter rocket engine, model airplanes, and the Gemini 8 capsule in which Armstrong rode into space. Simulations include a domed theatre that creates the feeling of a moon voyage and the infinity cube, that lets you imagine how it feels being projected into space. | 500 S. Apollo Dr. | 419/738–8811 | $5 | Mar.–Nov., Mon.–Sat. 9:30–5, Sun. noon-5:00.

ON THE CALENDAR

JULY: *Festival of Flight.* Held on the grounds of the Neil Armstrong Museum, this festival celebrates flight and the first moon landing in 1969. Some of Armstrong's aircraft, as well as flight-related exhibits, are displayed. | 500 S. Apollo Dr. | 419/738–8811.
AUG.: *Auglaize County Fair.* People from across the state attend this mid-summer bash at the Auglaize County Fairgrounds, 10 blocks from downtown Wapakoneta. | 1001 Fairview Dr. | 419/738–2515.
SEPT.: *Wapakoneta Indian Summer Festival.* The banks of the Auglaize River fill with local residents during this "so long to summer" celebration at the Auglaize County Fairgrounds, 10 blocks from downtown Wapakoneta. | 1001 Fairview Dr. | 419/738–2911.

Dining

The Chalet Inn. American. The main dining room at this Swiss chalet-style restaurant is a lovely setting for a formal meal; customers come to the Chalet for the best cuts of steak, as well as chicken and seafood dishes. Try the prime rib or the shrimp fettucine. You can also enjoy lighter fare in the coffee shop. You'll find this restaurant off I–75, 3 mi west of downtown. | 1530 Saturn Dr. | 419/738–6414 | Breakfast also available | $10–$17 | AE, D, MC, V.

Lodging

Budget Host Inn. Rooms are spacious at this motel about 7 mi south of Wapakoneta. Restaurant, bar, complimentary Continental breakfast. Some kitchenettes, microwaves (in kitchenette units). Cable TV. Pool. Tennis. Laundry facilities. Business services. | 505 State St., Botkins | 937/693–6911 | fax 937/693–8200 | 50 rooms | $51 | AE, D, MC, V.

Holiday Inn. This hotel next to the Neil Armstrong Museum is a convenient place to cap off a day of space exploration. Restaurant, bar, complimentary Continental breakfast, room service. In-room data ports. Cable TV. Pool. Exercise equipment. Laundry facilities. Business services. Some pets allowed. | 1510 Saturn Dr. | 419/738–8181 or 800/465–4329 | fax 419/738–6478 | www.holidayinn.com | 99 rooms | $69 | AE, D, DC, MC, V.

Holiday Inn Express Wapakoneta. Open since August 2000, this hotel has large, forest-green rooms as well as a great room with a fireplace, overstuffed chairs and a sofa. It's in a commercial area 1 mi east of downtown, off I–75 at exit 111. Complimentary Continental breakfast. In-room data ports. In-room safes, some microwaves, some refrigerators, some in-room hot tubs. Cable TV, TV in common area. Pool. Hot tub. No pets. | 1008 Lunar Dr. | 419/738–2050 or 800/465–4329 | fax 419/738–2050 | www.hiexpress.com | 45 rooms, 10 suites | $69–$85, $120 suites | AE, D, MC, V.

WARREN

MAP 14, F3

(Nearby towns listed: Aurora, Youngstown)

Founded in 1799 and named for surveyor Moses Warren, this northeast Ohio city is the seat of Trumbull County. The Packard brothers, who later manufactured the Packard automobile in Detroit, established a company in Warren in the late 19th century that made electrical products and incandescent lamps. (Warren was the first city to light its streets with these bulbs.) Stephen Foster wrote the song "Jeannie With The Light Brown Hair" here.

Today Warren County's businesses produce everything from iron and steel and transportation equipment to electrical machinery, automobile parts, and dairy products.

Information: Youngstown/Warren Regional Chamber of Commerce. | 160 E. Market St., #225, 44482 | 330/393–2565 or 330/744–2131 | www.regionalchamber.com.

Attractions

Mosquito Lake State Park. Bridle trails, boating, hiking, and camping are just a few of the draws of this park 10 mi north of Warren. | 1439 Rte. 305, in Cortland | 330/637–2856 | Free | Daily.

National Packard Museum. Learn about the Packard family and Packard automobiles (manufactured from 1903 to 1958) at this local museum, where you can see such automotive gems as a 1910 Model 30 Touring, a 1926 Roadster, and a 1958 Hawk. The museum is 2 ½ mi north of downtown, and 2 mi from the Route 82 bypass. | 1899 Mahoning Ave. NW | 330/394–1899 | www.packardmuseum.org | $5 | Tues.–Sat. 12–5, Sun. 1–5.

Dining

Cafe 422. Italian. An extensive array of fine Italian dishes, steaks, chops, and lobster, along with some heart-healthy choices, are served in a pleasant Mediterranean surrounding. Family-style service. Kids' menu. | 4422 Youngstown Rd. | 330/369–2422 | $12–$30 | AE, D, DC, MC, V.

Central Cafe. American. This downtown jazz café specializes in fried chicken. You can get over 40 different sauces on your wings plus pizza, burgers, and six different kinds of french fries. There's entertainment here every night of the week: live jazz performers play every Saturday night, and there are DJs or karaoke the rest of the week. | 480 E. Market St. | 330/395–4051 | No dinner Sun. Breakfast available weekdays | $3–$8 | AE, MC, V.

Lodging

Avalon Inn. This resort-type motor hotel has a wide range of facilities. Restaurant, bar, snack bar, room service. Some refrigerators. Cable TV. Indoor pool. Hot tub. Driving range, 18-hole golf courses, putting green, tennis. Exercise equipment. | 9519 E. Market St. | 330/856–1900, 800/828–2566 (OH), or 800/221–1549 (outside OH) | fax 330/856–2248 | 144 rooms | $74 | AE, D, DC, MC, V.

Best Western-Downtown. In the heart of downtown, this motel is within minutes of Warren attractions and points of interests. Complimentary Continental breakfast. Some refrigerators. Cable TV. Pool. Business services. Some pets allowed. | 777 Mahoning Ave. | 330/392–2515 or 800/528–1234 | fax 330/392–7099 | www.bestwestern.com | 73 rooms | $99 | AE, D, DC, MC, V.

Fairfield Inn. This three-story, brick hotel has a pleasant, blue-carpeted lobby with armchairs and a sofa. It's on Route 46 about 7 mi south of downtown Warren. The Eastwood Mall and many restaurants are nearby. Complimentary Continental breakfast. Cable TV, TV in common area. Pool. Spa. No pets. | 1860 Niles-Cortland Rd. SE, Niles | 330/544–5774 or 800/228–2800 | fax 330/544–5774 | www.fairfieldinn.com | 64 rooms | $71–$85 | AE, D, DC, MC, V.

Holiday Inn Express. Plants decorate every room in this hostelry, which opened in 2000. An in-house masseuse is available, and the huge Eastwood Mall is across the street with some 150 shops and restaurants and a movie theater; over 60 restaurants are within 2 mi. Complimentary Continental breakfast. In-room data ports. Cable TV, TV in common area. Pool, spa. Gym. No pets. | 135 Highland Terrace Blvd., Niles | 330/544–8807 or 800/465–4329 | fax 330/544–8965 | www.hiexpress.com | 78 rooms, 29 suites | $119, $129–$149 suites | AE, D, DC, MC, V.

Park Hotel. This family-run motel is set in a late 19th-century brick building and has clean and comfortable rooms. Families with children are welcome. Restaurant. Cable TV. Business services. Airport shuttle. Some pets allowed. | 136 N. Park Ave. | 330/393–1200 or 800/397–7275 | fax 330/399–2875 | 66 rooms | $77–$109 | AE, D, DC, MC, V.

WASHINGTON COURT HOUSE

MAP 14, C6

(Nearby towns listed: Chillicothe, Columbus, Wilmington)

Settled in 1819 as "Washington, Ohio" in honor of George Washington, the town was always referred to as Washington Court House because it was the county seat. The name was made official around 1830. Today, the town (pop. 13,100) is the center of a primarily agricultural county. Its proximity to I-71 has made it a common stop for travelers making their way between Cincinnati and Columbus.

Information: **Fayette County Chamber of Commerce** | 101 E. East St., 43160 | 740/335–0761 or 740/335–8008 or 800/479–7797 | www.fayettecountyohio.com.

Attractions

Archibald Willard Murals at the Court House. Three 10-by-14-ft murals by this Ohio-born painter artist, famous for his painting *Spirit of '76*, adorn the second floor of the county court house. They're entitled *Spirit of Electricity, Spirit of the U.S. Mail,* and *Spirit of the Telegraph.* | 220 Park Ave. | 740/335–8008 | Free.

Oak Creek Farms. Fayette County is known as the birthplace of trotters and pacers. Tours are given by appointment at this large breeding farm. | 1270 U.S. Rte. 62 SW | 740/335–2079.

Prime Outlets at Jeffersonville I and II. Shop for clothes from labels such as Nike and Ralph Lauren, housewares from Rubbermaid and Mikasa, as well as shoes, books, CDs, and appliances at the factory outlets. Prices can be as much as half off regular retail prices. The outlets are about 10 mi west of Washington Court House. | I-71 at exits 65 and 69, Jeffersonville | 740/948–9090 or 800/746–7644 | www.primeoutlets.com | Mon.–Sat. 10–9, Sun. noon–6.

Dining

Cider Mill Restaurant. American. Wooden tables and chairs and ruffled curtains lend a country home atmosphere. You can dine on homestyle meals of roasted chicken, pork chops with gravy, pork tenderloin, hamloaf, catfish, and chicken and noodles served with sides from mashed potatoes to in-season vegetables. | 827 E. Market St. | 740/333–6455 | $6.50–$9 | No credit cards.

Lodging

Amerihost Inn. This chain is a good place to stop if you're planning on shopping; it's just off I-71 near the Prime Outlets, about 10 mi west of Washington Court House. Complimentary Continental breakfast. Cable TV. Indoor pool. Sauna, whirlpool. | 11431 Allen Rd. NW, Jeffersonville | 740/948–2104 | fax 740/948–2110 | 60 rooms | $78–$125 | AE, D, MC,V.

Knights Inn. This motel is just off U.S. 62 near Washington Square Shopping Plaza. Cable TV. Some pets allowed. | 1820 Columbus Ave. | 740/335–9133 or 800/843–5644 | fax 740/333–7938 | 56 rooms | $48–$56 | AE, D, MC, V.

WAUSEON

MAP 14, B2

(Nearby towns listed: Bowling Green, Defiance, Toledo)

Established in 1850, Fulton County was one of the last Ohio counties to be organized. It is composed of land taken from Henry, Lucas, and Williams counties. Prior to the arrival of European settlers, this area was inhabited by Ottawa, Potowatami, and Miami Indians. The name honors Chief Wa-se-on, a leader of the Ottawa tribe. Today, Wauseon (pop. 6,322) remains primarily an agricultural area. Corn and soybeans are the main cash crops; livestock is also raised. Many areas of Fulton County currently are experiencing rapid development and growth, due in part to the westward migration of Lucas County residents and businesses.

Information: Wauseon Chamber of Commerce | 115 N. Fulton St., Box 217, 43567 | 419/335–9966 | www.wauseonchamber.com.

ON THE CALENDAR

JULY: *Carp Festival.* Back in the late 1800s, the Tiffin River flooded into the streets of Archbold; local historians swear there were carp swimming through town. The event is commemorated every July with a downtown festival with games, rides, and plenty of food. It's 12 mi west of Wauseon. | 419/445–2222.

Dining

White Lattice Cafe. American. Named for its white latticework inside, this family restaurant serves home-cooked meals to locals who always return for more. The homemade soups are classic here, as are the roasted chicken and the ham and beans. Then choose a slice from one of 15 different homemade pies. Breakfast is served every day. | 1290 N. Shoop Ave. | 419/337–3331 | $5–$13 | D, MC, V.

Lodging

Best Western Del Mar. This single-story hotel was refurbished in 2000; you can borrow a video from their library to watch in your room. A variety of restaurants and stores surround this property, which is a mile north of downtown Wauseon. Complimentary Continental breakfast. Refrigerators. Cable TV. Pool. Playground. Some pets allowed. | 8319 U.S. 108 | 419/335–1565 or 800/528–1234 | fax 419/335–1828 | www.bestwestern.com | 39 rooms, 9 suites | $75 | AE, D, DC, MC, V.

Wauseon Holiday Inn Express. You'll find this modern, brick, three-story hotel surrounded by farmland about 3 mi from Wauseon. Several restaurants are within 2 mi of the hotel. Inside, rooms have both king- and queen-size beds, and there's a lobby with a fireplace and a sofa. Complimentary Continental breakfast. In-room data ports, some in-room hot tubs. Cable TV, TV in common area. Pool. Hot tub, sauna. Laundry facilities. No pets. | 8135 Rte. 108 | 419/335–1177 or 800/465–4329 | fax 419/335–2299 | www.hiexpress.com | 61 rooms, 2 suites | $75–$85, $99–$105 suites | AE, D, DC, MC, V.

WAYNESVILLE

(Nearby towns listed: Dayton, Lebanon, Miamisburg, Middletown, Wilmington)

Samuel Heighway founded Waynesville in 1797. The town was laid out like an English village with formal parks and squares surrounding a central public square. Early industry centered around farming. Today, the city has assumed a new role as antique capital of the midwest, with many small shops and a large gallery with some 200 vendors.

Information: Waynesville Area Chamber of Commerce | P.O. Box 281, 45068 | 513/897–8855 | www.waynesvilleohio.com.

Attractions

Caesar Creek Flea Market. You are sure to find your heart's desire at this year-round weekend flea market. Browse through countless vendor stands of antiques and collectibles. It's held on the outskirts of Caesar Creek State Park. | 7763 Rte. 73 | 937/382–1669 | $1 per car | Weekends 9–5.

Caesar Creek State Park. The park, 5 mi east of Waynesville, has a 2,400-acre lake, a nature preserve and wildlife area, Pioneer Village, and a visitor center where American Indian artifacts are displayed. | 8570 E. Rte. 73 | 513/897–3055 | Free | Daily, dawn–dusk.

The park is also home to **Pioneer Village,** a re-creation of a 19th-century settlement, including a Quaker meetinghouse. The village is open usually one weekend a month for a special event, like a maple syrup festival or a 19th-century market fair. | 3999 Pioneer Village Rd. | 513/897–1120 | $5.

Little Miami State Park. This linear, 50-mi-long path is known for its elegant bridletrails. You can also hike or bike the paved path from Milford to Xenia. There are entrances along the trail; there's one in Corwin, just east of Waynesville. | 513/897–3055 | Free | Daily, dawn–dusk.

Main Street Downtown District. Visit shops that were once home to prominent citizens in this five-block-long area indowntown Waynesville, which is dressed up with copper street lamps, brick sidewalks, and flower boxes. An old stagecoach stop, the Hammel House Inn, now provides a place to lunch and relax. The town is also home to Waynesville's famous antiques shops. | Main St. | 513/897–8855 | Daily 9–5.

ON THE CALENDAR

AUG.–OCT.: *Ohio Renaissance Festival.* Enjoy the jousting and pageantry, then indulge in some "olde" food and drink at this re-creation of merry old England. The festival is held on weekends from late August to mid-October. | Harveysburg, 5 mi east of Waynesville | 513/897–7000.

OCT.: *Ohio Sauerkraut Festival.* More than 20,000 pounds of sauerkraut are consumed at this three-day annual tribute to the cabbage. Waynesville's downtown district is closed off for 400 arts and craft exhibitors and lots of visitors for this event, which is held the second full weekend of October. | 513/897–8855.

Dining

Hammel House Restaurant. American. At this cozy, country-decorated lunch place, you can tuck into fresh quiches, homemade soups, sandwiches, and salads. Don't miss the famous Hammel Reuben sandwich or one of the salads served with home-baked muffins. | 121 S. Main St. | 513/897–3779 | No dinner. Closed Mon. | $5–$6 | AE, D, MC, V.

Lodging

Hammel House Inn. You'll find this B&B in a fully restored house from 1822 in the middle of town. It's within a few blocks of several antique and gift stores. The breakfast room has exposed-brick walls, and guest rooms three and four are spacious with shining cherry-wood furniture. Restaurant, complimentary breakfast. No room phones. No pets. No kids. No smoking. | 121 S. Main St. | 513/897–3779 | 5 rooms | $85–$90 | AE, D, MC, V.

WILMINGTON

MAP 14, B6

(Nearby towns listed: Cincinnati, Dayton, Lebanon, Mason, Washington Court House, Waynesville)

In the southwest portion of the state, Wilmington is set in a region that is home to both agriculture and business. Wilmington's early residents were from Virginia, Kentucky, North Carolina, and Pennsylvania. The town was founded in 1810 and relied on farming as the mainstay of the economy. Many of the settlers from Pennsylvania were Quakers, who established Wilmington College in 1870.

Wilmington is still mainly a farming community, producing corn, soybeans, and hogs. *Cincinnati Magazine* has called Wilmington the "most livable city" in the Cincinnati area; it has also been named the best small town in Ohio, and one of the 100 best small towns in America by Norman Crampton in his book, *The 100 Best Small Towns in America* (1995).

Information: Wilmington/Clinton Co. Chamber of Commerce | 40 N. South St., 45177 | 937/382–2737 or 937/382–1965 | www.wccchamber.com.

Attractions

Cowan Lake State Park. A favorite of cyclists, this park has 1,775 acres to pedal through. The large lake is ideal for boating and fishing. It's 5 mi south of Wilmington. | 729 Beechwood Rd. | 937/289–2105 | Free | Daily, dawn–dusk.

Rombach Place. The museum of the Clinton County Historical Society presents exhibits and artifacts that take you through the county's 200-year history. | 149 E. Locust St. | 937/382–4684 | Free | Mar.–Dec., Wed.–Fri. 1–4:30.

Wilmington College. Founded in the 1870s by the Religious Society of Friends (Quakers) in Wilmington, Ohio, the college is about an hour from Cincinnati, Dayton, and Columbus. | 251 Ludovic St. | 937/382–6661 | Free | Daily.

ON THE CALENDAR

JUNE: *Banana Split Festival*. Wilmington kicks off summer (the second weekend of June) with this traditional festival; J.W. Denver Park park is filled with games, rides, and musical performances. | 937/382–2737.

SEPT.: *Clinton County Corn Festival*. The city starts the summer with banana splits and ends it with corn at this festival held the weekend after Labor Day at the Clinton County Fairgrounds. | 851 W. Main St. | 937/382–2737.

Dining

Damon's. American. Wings, barbecue ribs, and chicken are the specialties at this sports bar chain. Catch the games on one of the big-screen televisions. Begin with the onion loaf appetizer, a tasty tangle of thin onion straws that are breaded and deep fried. Kids' menu. | 1045 Eastside Dr. | 937/383–1400 | $10–$26 | AE, D, DC, MC, V.

El Dorado Mexican Restaurant. Tex-Mex. This restaurant, festively decorated in reds and greens, is the local favorite for south-of-the-border fare like chimichangas and tacos. Try the spicy chicken fajitas or the beef tacos. | 1362 Rombach Ave. | 937/383–3763 | $6–$8 | AE, D, MC, V.

Lodging

Amerihost Inn. Suites are equipped with refrigerators and hot tubs. There are restaurants nearby. Complimentary Continental breakfast. In-room data ports, microwaves (in suites), refrigerators (in suites), in-room hot tubs (in suites). Cable TV. Indoor pool. Hot tub. Exercise equipment. Business services. | 201 Carrie Dr. | 937/383–3950 | fax 937/383–1693 | www.amerihost.com | 61 rooms, 5 suites | $65, $105–$120 suites | AE, D, DC, MC, V.

Cedar Hill Bed & Breakfast. Guest rooms are in the carriage house of this 10-acre estate and thus have private entrances. There's a common room with a fireplace and a VCR, and you'll also find walking trails on the property. Complimentary breakfast, kitchenettes, refrigerators, TV in common area. No pets. No kids under 12. No smoking. | 4003 Rte. 73 | 937/383–2525 or 877/722–2525 | www.ohiobba.com/cedarhill.htm | 3 rooms | $80–$90 | AE, D, MC, V.

Wilmington Inn. Queen Anne cherrywood furnishings fill this rustic, two-story stone and wood hotel in a residential area off I–73 west of town. You can use the recreational facilities at the nearby YMCA. Complimentary Continental breakfast. Cable TV. Business services. | 909 Fife Ave. | 937/382–6000 | fax 937/382–6655 | 51 rooms, 2 suites | $65, $85 suites | AE, DC, MC, V.

Yesterday Again Bed & Breakfast. This farmhouse, originally built in 1823 from hand-hewn lumber and cinderblock, is perched on 22 acres of hayfields and rolling hills. You'll find picnic areas, sand volleyball courts, and walking trails on the property. The B&B is off I–71, at exit 50, about 2 mi from downtown. In-room VCRs, no room phones. TV in common area. Pool. Hot tub. Hiking, volleyball. No pets. No smoking. | 3556 Rte. 68 N | 937/382–0472 or 800/382–0472 | www.yesterdayagain.com | 5 rooms | $80 | AE, D, MC, V.

WOOSTER

MAP 14, D3

(Nearby towns listed: Akron, Berlin, Mansfield, Massillon)

Wooster is in northcentral Ohio in Wayne County. The area's first settlers established a farming-based community here in 1808, naming the new town in honor of David Wooster, Brigadier General of the Revolutionary War.

Today Wooster enjoys a healthy economy with a solid, diversified manufacturing base and a steadily increasing population (pop. 22,191 at last count). It has well-kept homes, tree-lined streets, and an attractive downtown.

Information: Wooster Area Chamber of Commerce | 377 W. Liberty St., 44691 | 330/262–5735 | www.wooster-wayne.com.

Attractions

College of Wooster. Wooster was founded in the 1860s by Presbyterians. The campus is particularly pretty in the late fall, when the foliage is at its brightest. Self-guided tours are available. | East University St. and Beall Ave. | 216/263–2000 or 216/263–2345 | Free | Daily.

Ohio Agricultural Research and Development Center. Considered the top agricultural research center in the country, this facility is credited with inventing crop dusting and vitamin D–enriched milk. Tours are available. | 1 mi south of Wooster, on Madisonberg Rd. | 216/263–3779 | Free | Weekdays, tours by appointment.

Quailcrest Farm. Herbs, perennials, and flowers grow on this farm's 100 acres, 7 mi north of downtown. You can also visit the restored 19th-century schoolhouse on the premises and purchase farm products from the gift store. | 2810 Armstrong Rd. | 330/345–6722 | www.quailcrest.com | Free | Mar.–Dec., Tues.–Sat. 10–5, Sun. 1–5. Extended spring and Christmas hrs.

Wayne County Historical Society Museum. The museum is housed in the 1815 Beall House, and shows furniture, porcelains, American Indian artifacts, mounted animals, firearms, and clothing. On the grounds are a late 1800s log cabin and schoolhouse with period furnishings, an old general store, and a carpenter shop with pioneer tools. | 546 E. Bowman St. | 330/264–8856 | $3 | Wed.–Sun. 2–4:30 and by appointment.

ON THE CALENDAR

SEPT.: *Herb Festival.* Besides fresh herbs, you can purchase antiques, stoneware, baskets, and more crafts at this festival held annually on the Saturday after Labor Day at Quailcrest Farm, one of the largest herb growers in northeast Ohio. | 2810 Armstrong Rd. | 330/345–6722.

SEPT.: *Wayne County Fair.* Thousands of area folks take part in games, rides, and livestock shows at this county fair. | 199 Vanover St. | 330/264–1800 or 800/362–6474.

Dining

The Granery at The Pine Tree Barn. American. This gourmet luncheonette overlooks a private lake and a Christmas tree farm. You can order homemade soups, specialty sandwiches, and salads. Top your meal off with a lemon crumb muffin or a slice of sour cream fruit pie. | 4374 Shreve Rd., off Rte. 350 | 330/264–1014 | No dinner | $5–$8 | D, MC, V.

TJ's. American. You get two options in one here. Upstairs, TJ's serves veal, steak, prime rib, and seafood in five dressy but cozy dining rooms with wood, marble, and antiques, including a bistro room. Downstairs, C.W. Burgerstein's is a sports bar where you can watch the game while you munch burgers, wings, and specialty sandwiches. Kids' menu, early bird dinners. | 359 W. Liberty St. | 330/264–6263 | Closed Sun. | $8–$22 | AE, D, DC, MC, V.

Lodging

Best Western Wooster Plaza. This two-story hotel and convention center is right in downtown Wooster, just east of the square. Restaurant, bar, room service. Cable TV, in-room VCRs and movies. Pool. Beauty salon. Business services. | 243 E. Liberty St. | 330/264–7750 or 800/528–1234 | fax 330/262–5840 | www.bestwestern.com | 100 rooms | $79 | AE, D, DC, MC, V.

Econo Lodge. An indoor pool, hot tub, and picnic tables are nice features for families. Picnic area, complimentary Continental breakfast. Cable TV. Indoor pool. Hot tub. Laundry facilities. Business services. Some pets allowed. | 2137 Lincoln Way E | 330/264–8883 or 800/248–8341 | fax 330/264–8883, ext. 301 | www.hotelchoice.com | 98 rooms | $84 | AE, D, DC, MC, V.

Overholt Bed & Breakfast. This stick-style Victorian house is next to the College of Wooster campus. It has a flying staircase (one with no visible means of support) as well as two parlors with fireplaces and a deck. Most rooms have private baths, and the two that share are usually reserved as a suite. Complimentary Continental breakfast. Cable TV. Hot tub. No pets. No smoking. | 1473 Beall Ave. | 330/263–6300 | www.bbonline.com/oh/overholt | 4 rooms | $75, $140 suite | AE, D, MC, V.

Wooster Inn. The College of Wooster owns this hotel on the school's campus. Restaurant, picnic area. Cable TV. Driving range, nine-hole golf course, putting green. Business services. Some pets allowed. | 801 E. Wayne Ave. | 330/264–2341 | fax 330/264–9951 | 15 rooms | $99 | Closed Jan. 2–9, Dec. 25, 26 | AE, D, DC, MC, V.

Wooster Super 8. This single-story motel is surrounded by shops, restaurants, and nightlife venues a half mile south of downtown. The Metroplex Convention Center is also nearby. Complimentary Continental breakfast. In-room data ports. Cable TV. Pets allowed (fee). | 969 Timken Rd. | 330/264–6211 or 800/800–8000 | fax 330/264–6211 | www.super8.com | 43 rooms | $48–$60 | AE, D, DC, MC, V.

YELLOW SPRINGS

(Nearby towns listed: Columbus, Dayton, Springfield, Vandalia)

Named for the iron-tinged yellow water in the nearby mineral springs, the town was first a health spa with a resort hotel. Now it's a college town with a population of 4,000 and a reputation for liberal thinking.

Information: **Yellow Springs Chamber of Commerce** | 108 Dayton St., 45387 | 937/767–2686 | www.yellowsprings.com.

Attractions

Clifton Gorge State Nature Preserve/John Bryan State Park. The 130-ft gorge here was carved out by the Little Miami River. It is now designated a State and National Scenic River. | 3790 Rte. 370 | 937/767–1274 | Free | Daily, dawn–dusk.

Glen Helen. The mineral springs that gave the town its name are here on this 1,000-acre nature preserve. You can hike the trails and bird-watch. | 405 Corry St. | 937/767–7375 | Free | Daily, dawn–dusk.

Antioch College. This famously liberal arts college founded in the 1850s is known for its progressive ideas, such as the ask-at-each-step sexual relationship policy. The town and college are so interlinked, there isn't any town-and-gown conflict. You can get a tour of the campus for free. | 795 Livermore St. | 937/754–5100 | www.antioch-college.edu | Free | Weekdays 8–5.

Dining

Clifton Mill. American. This restaurant 3 mi east of Yellow Springs inhabits the nation's largest remaining water-powered grist mill that's still in operation. The mill grinds flour that's used in the restaurant's famous pancakes. Take a tour and get a free bag of flour. The mill is lighted with more than a million lights at Christmastime. | 75 Water St., Clifton | 937/767–5501 | www.cliftonmill.com | No dinner | $3–$10 | MC, V.

The Winds Cafe. Contemporary. Unexpected combinations of ingredients make for unusual cuisine here. The menu changes monthly. Recent entrées included pan-fried trout with lemon caper cream, squash lasagna with shallot cream sauce, and grilled steak with roasted peppers in tomato sauce. Meals are complemented by one of the 60 rotating wines from the cellar next door. Open air dining. Kids' menu. Sun. brunch. No smoking. | 215 Xenia Ave. | 937/767–1144 | Reservations essential | No dinner Sun. Closed Mon. | $16–$24 | AE, D, DC, MC, V.

Young's Jersey Dairy. Ice Cream. Locals know Young's for their ultra-rich ice cream: it's 14 percent butterfat and made with fresh milk from the cows out back. Sandwiches are also served and children are allowed to pet the animals in the barn. | 6880 Springfield Xenia Rd. | 937/325–0629 | Open 24 hours, every day except Christmas | $1–$8 | No credit cards.

Lodging

Morgan House Bed & Breakfast. Works by local artists fill this art gallery and bed and breakfast in the former home of an Antioch College president. Complimentary breakfast. TV in common area, no room phones. No pets. | 120 W. Limestone St. | 937/767–7509 | 6 rooms | $58 | MC, V.

YOUNGSTOWN

(Nearby towns listed: Akron, Alliance, Kent, Warren)

In 1797, John Young purchased 15,560 acres in the Mahoning Valley from the Connecticut Land Company. During the next century, Youngstown grew rapidly, thanks in part to the coal, railroad, and metal industries. Beginning in the mid-1900s, however, the city suffered through several recessions and other setbacks. In the early 1980s, Youngstown began to turn itself around; over the past two decades, a number of new businesses have come to the city, including giants such as Delphi Packard Electric Systems and General Motors, and some 10,000 new jobs have been created. Local attractions include the Arms Family Museum of Local History and the Butler Institute of American Art.

Information: Youngstown/Warren Regional Chamber of Commerce | 50 Federal Plaza E, 44503 | 330/744-2131 | www.regionalchamber.com.

Attractions

Arms Family Museum of Local History. The first floor of this arts-and-crafts style home of the early 1900s has period rooms; upstairs is an extensive collection of documents and books relating to the history of Youngstown can be found here. | 648 Wick Ave. | 330/743-2589 | $3 | Tues.–Fri. 1–4, weekends 1:30–5.

Butler Institute of American Art. This gallery is a showcase of American art from Colonial times to present, including major works by Mary Cassatt, Thomas Eakins, and Winslow Homer. It also features a children's gallery and an American sports gallery. | 524 Wick Ave. | 330/743-1107 or 330/743-1711 | Free | Tues.–Sat. 11–4, Wed. 11–8, Sun. noon–4.

Mill Creek Metro Park's Fellows Riverside Gardens. Bequeathed by the late Elizabeth A. Fellows, wife to a local industrialist also deceased, these gardens cover eight well-tended acres. Walk among rhododendrons, azaleas, tulips, chrysanthemums, and many different varieties of roses. Flagstone terraces, a Victorian gazebo, and a reflecting pool and fountain complete the picture. One end of the garden presents a view of Lake Glacier, the other a view of the city. | 123 McKinley Ave. | 330/740-7116 | Free | Weekdays 10–5, weekends 12–5.

Youngstown Historical Center of Industry and Labor. The history of the iron and steel industry is documented in this tribute to labor. The center is set up like a series of typical mill rooms. | 151 W. Wood St. | 330/743-5934 | $5 | Wed.–Sat. 9–5, Sun. noon–5.

Youngstown Playhouse. This community theater has main-stage productions, summer musicals, and youth performances. | 600 Playhouse La. | 330/788-8739 | Prices vary | Sept.–June, weekends.

Youngstown State University. Eleven baccalaureate degrees and 110 major programs from traditional arts and sciences to high-technology and healthcare fields are offered here. Student-led one-hour tours of the campus are available. | One University Plaza | 330/742-1400 | Free | Daily. Established in 1991 on the campus of Youngstown State University, the **McDonough Museum of Art** museum showcases the work of regional artists as well as that of YSU faculty and students. | One University Plaza | 330/742-1400 | Free | Tues., Thurs. 11–4, Wed. 11–8, Fri.–Sun. 11–4.

Youngstown Symphony Center. This is the home of the Youngstown Youth Symphony Orchestra, which performs both pops and symphonic concerts throughout the year. | 260 Federal Plaza W | 330/744-0246.

ON THE CALENDAR

OCT.: *San Francisco Western Opera Theater.* See the touring branch of the San Francisco Opera perform at the Youngstown Symphony Center, in the Edward Powers

Auditorium, every year during the week before Halloween. | 260 Federal Plaza W | 330/744-4269.

Dining

Alberini's. Italian. The main dining room is adorned with original murals; there's also a less formal sunroom with the same menu. Seafood and many varieties of pasta are served. Kids' menu. | 1201 Youngstown Warren Rd. | 330/652-5895 | Closed Sun. | $12-$30 | AE, D, DC, MC, V.

Anthony's on the River. Italian. Locals flock here for the homemade sauces and cavatelli. In the center of downtown in the Spring Commons area, it overlooks the Mahoning River. | 15 Oak Hill Rd. | 330/744-7888 | Closed Sun. and Mon. No lunch Sat. | $7-$16 | AE, D, MC, V.

Crystal's. American. Unique appetizers, like the filet gorgonzola (medallions of tenderloin wrapped around blue cheese), are the specialties at this steak-and-seafood restaurant. Try the porterhouse or the braised veal shank. Crystal's superb fish dishes include sole with lemon-cream sauce, Florida snapper with toasted almonds, and yellowfin tuna. | 1931 Belmont Ave. | 330/743-5381 | No lunch Sat. Closed Sun. | $13-$25 | AE, MC, V.

Rachel's Steak and Seafood. Steak. You'll get certified Angus beef in this upscale steakhouse 10 mi south of Youngstown. Order the porterhouse or the filet mignon. If you don't want steak, try the Alaskan king crab, the whole lobster, or one of the tasty pasta dishes. For dessert, have the tiramisu, the chocolate volcano, or the strawberry cheesecake, all made on the premises. | 8586 South Ave., Boardman | 330/799-2800 | No lunch Fri. or Sat. Closed Sun. | $13-$42 | AE, MC, V.

Lodging

Best Western Meander Inn. Several restaurants and stores surround the motel. More than a dozen businesses are within walking distance. Restaurant, bar. Complimentary Continental breakfast, room service. Cable TV. Pool. Laundry facilities. Some pets allowed. | 870 N. Canfield-Niles Rd. | 330/544-2378 or 800/528-1234 | fax 330/544-7926 | www.bestwestern.com | 57 rooms | $89 | AE, D, DC, MC, V.

Comfort Inn. You'll find standard accommodations near local dining and shopping in this six-story hotel in northern Youngstown. Restaurant, bar, complimentary Continental breakfast, room service. In-room data ports, some refrigerators. Cable TV. Indoor pool. Video games. Business services. Airport shuttle. | 4055 Belmont Ave. | 330/759-3180 or 800/228-5150 | fax 330/759-7713 | www.comfortinn.com | 144 rooms | $79 | AE, D, DC, MC, V.

Days Inn. This single-story motel is 6 ½ mi south of downtown, off I-76. A business and shopping district surrounds the motel; nearby you'll find Canfield Fair, the largest county fair in Ohio, Youngstown State University, and several different major league sports venues. Complimentary Continental breakfast. Cable TV, TV in common area. Pool. | 8392 Market St., Boardman | 330/758-2371 or 800/544-8313 | fax 330/758-2371 | www.daysinn.com | 49 rooms | $55 | AE, D, DC, MC, V.

Holiday Inn. Contemporary cherrywood furniture graces the guest rooms in this six-story hotel. The pool is roofed with plate-glass skylights, and the lobby is carpeted and softly lit. The hotel is popular among business travelers; there are 10 conference and meeting rooms on-site. Restaurant, bar. In-room data ports, some refrigerators, room service. Cable TV. Pool. Laundry facilities. Business services. | 7410 South Ave., Boardman | 330/726-1611 or 800/465-4329 | fax 330/726-0717 | www.holidayinn.com | 126 rooms | $84 | AE, D, DC, MC, V.

Holiday Inn–Airport Metroplex. Just off I-80, this bright-white, four-story, concrete hotel has a large plate-glass atrium over the lobby and a covered drive. Restaurant, bar, room service. Cable TV. Pool. Exercise equipment. Business services. Airport shuttle. | 1620 Motor Inn Dr., Girard | 330/759-0606 or 800/465-4329 | fax 330/759-7632 | www.holidayinn.com | 136 rooms | $89 | AE, D, DC, MC, V.

Motel 6. You can park right in front of your room at this modest, exterior-corridor motel. The surrounding area is thick with popular chain restaurants and mini-malls and you are within 10 mi of two major malls. Cable TV. Pool. Business services. | 5431 Seventy-Six Dr. | 330/793–9305 or 800/466–8356 | hotelnikko.com | fax 330/793–2584 | 79 rooms | $59 | AE, D, MC, V.

Ramada Inn. This mid-range hotel, off I–80 at exit 229, is surrounded by chain restaurants and discount stores. Downtown Youngstown is a 15-minute drive. Restaurant, bar with entertainment, room service. Cable TV. Indoor pool. Beauty salon. Exercise equipment. Laundry service. Business services, airport shuttle. | 4255 Belmont Ave. | 330/759–7850 or 800/228–2828 | fax 330/759–8147 | www.ramada.com/ramada.html | 130 rooms | $84 | AE, D, DC, MC, V.

Youngstown Boardman Hampton Inn. In a business district 8 mi south of downtown, this bustling hotel is surrounded by lively family restaurants. The Southern Park mall is a mile up the road. You'll find only king- and queen-size beds in the rooms, as well as a chair and ottoman, a work desk, and an entertainment center. Complimentary Continental breakfast. In-room data ports, some microwaves, some refrigerators. Cable TV, TV in common area. Pool. Hot tub. Business services. No pets. | 7395 Tiffany S | 330/758–5191 or 800/426–7866 | www.hamptoninn.com | 58 rooms, 6 suites | $80, $120 suites | AE, D, DC, MC, V.

ZANESVILLE

MAP 14, E5

(Nearby towns listed: Cambridge, Columbus, Newark)

In the 1790s, a settlement was established at the confluence of the Licking and Muskingum rivers as Colonel Ebenzer Zane and his son-in-law, John McIntire, blazed Zane's Trace, the original pioneer trail into the old Northwest Territory. A town laid out by McIntire, called Westbourne, quickly grew out of the settlement, and in 1801, it was renamed Zanesville in honor of Colonel Zane. The city, in the central part of the state, served as capital of Ohio from 1810 to 1812. Transportation played a key role in its history and development; Zane's Trace later became the National Road, while the Muskingum River transported steamboats and barges up from the Ohio River. Today, the community of some 84,000 people is composed of a thriving central city, well-groomed residential areas, rural rolling hills, and picturesque villages.

Information: **Zanesville-Muskingum County Chamber of Commerce** | 205 N. 5th St., 43701 | 740/455–8282 | www.zanesville-ohio.com.

Attractions

Blue Rock State Park. There are 101 non-electric campsites available for tent or trailer camping in two separate areas near the lake. Boating, fishing, and hunting are also allowed. | 79-24 Cutler Lake Rd. | 740/674–4794 | Free | Daily.

Dr. Increase Mathews House Museum. Built in 1805, this house is the oldest in town. You can see 19th-century room settings with vintage quilts and coverlets, as well as a Muskingum River display and a military exhibit. | 304 Woodlawn Ave. | 740/454–9500 | Free | June–Aug., Sat. 12–4, or by appointment.

Ohio Ceramic Center. Five buildings display and sell various types of ceramics, including art pottery, bricks, and gardenware. | 7327 Ceramic Rd. | 740/697–7021 | $2 | May–Oct., Wed.–Sat. 9:30–5.

Putnam Manse. This private home, built in 1849, is available to tour by reservation only. You'll see extensive collections of 19th-century clothing, Victorian dolls, and antiques on display inside. | 425 Woodlawn Ave. | 740/455–8282 or 800/743–2303 | $3 | By appointment only.

Putnam Presbyterian Church. The first minister of this church was William Beecher, brother of Harriet Beecher Stowe. Stained glass windows, and one Tiffany window, make this church a popular Zanesville site to visit. | 467 Woodlawn Ave. | 740/452–2445 | Free | Daily.

Robinson-Ransbottom Pottery Co. See bowls, pots, vases, and other forms of pottery being made by skilled artisans at this well-known company. | 5545 3rd St. | 740/697–7355 | Free | Weekdays 9–2.

***The Lorena* Sternwheeler.** The classic riverboat takes passengers on a one-hour scenic cruise down the Muskingum River. Dinner cruises are available. | Zane's Landing Park, west end of Market St. on the Muskingum River | 740/455–8883 or 800/246–6303 | www.zanesville.com/lorena | $5 | June–Aug., daily 1, 2:30, 4; Sept.–Oct., weekends 1, 2:30, 4.

Zanesville Art Center. The center takes great pride in its glass and ceramic collections of Zanesville-area glass and ceramics. Paintings and sculptures from Asia, Africa, and Europe are on display, along with works by contemporary Ohio artists. | 620 Military Rd. | 740/452–0741 | Free | Tues., Wed., Fri. 10–5; Thurs. 10–8:30; weekends 1–5.

ON THE CALENDAR
JUNE: *Muskingum River Lock Festival.* Take a unique look at the operations of a river dam. Festival highlights include lock demonstrations, scuba diving, and mussel displays. | On the riverfront at the Rokeby Lock | 740/674–4794.
JULY: *A Taste of Zanesville.* The city's top restaurants whip up their best dishes downtown. | 740/455–8282.
AUG.: *Muskingum County Blue Ribbon Fair.* Livestock shows, rides, and entertainment—this traditional county fair at the Muskingum County Fairgrounds has it all. | 1300 Pershing Rd. | 740/872–3912.

Dining
Howard House. Continental. With antiques from the owner's own collection as well as other period furnishings, the place 20 mi south of Zanesville looks much as it did in the mid-1800s. Tenderloin Roquefort (beef medallions with sautéed mushrooms and onions) and Maryland crab cakes with tangy Creole mustard sauce are two specialties. Sunday brunch. | 507 E. Main St., McConnelsville | 740/962–5861 | Closed Mon. | $12–$30 | AE, D, DC, MC, V.

Maria Adornetto Restaurant. American. The head chef, a Culinary Institute of America graduate, serves up steaks and seafood in addition to pasta dishes and Italian specialties. Entertainment in the piano bar. Kids' menu, early bird suppers. | 953 Market St. | 740/453–0643 | No lunch Sat. Closed Sun. | $8.50–$35 | AE, D, DC, MC, V.

Old Market House Inn. American. The setting evokes King Arthur's court, thanks to giant wooden tables and wood-beamed ceilings–there's even a suit of armor. For dinner, oversized salads with freshly cracked pepper and juicy steaks are popular choices. | 424 Market St. | 740/454–2555 | Closed Sun. | $13–$26 | AE, D, DC, MC, V.

Tom's Ice Cream Bowl. Cafe. Linoleum floors and counter help who wear folded paper hats give this shop an old-time feel. Even the ice cream, served in cereal bowls with dripping sauce and marshmallow topping, is reminiscent of an earlier era. Sandwiches are also available. | 532 McIntire Ave. | 740/452–5267 | Reservations not accepted | Closed Mon. | $7–$10 | No credit cards.

Zak's Restaurant. Mexican. The high ceilings, exposed support beams, and plaster details in the three dining rooms are left over from the days when the building was a warehouse. The menu has the Mexican-American standards as well as fancier entrées such as Mexican shrimp Jalisco with crab quesadillas. Buffet on Thurs. Kids' menu. | 32 N. 3rd St. | 740/453–2227 | $10–$15 | AE, D, DC, MC, V.

Lodging

Comfort Inn. The suites at this two-story hotel near restaurants and pottery shops has nice suites with whirlpools and refrigerators. Complimentary Continental breakfast. Cable TV. Indoor pool. Hot tub. Exercise equipment. Laundry facilities. Business services. Pets allowed (fee). | 500 Monroe St. | 740/454–4144 or 800/228–5150 | www.comfortinn.com | 93 rooms, 20 suites | $69 | AE, D, DC, MC, V.

Days Inn. This two-story stucco-finished building is in a largely commerical area. The surrounding blocks are home to a dozen or so popular chain and family-style restaurants. Complimentary Continental breakfast. Cable TV. Indoor pool. | 4925 East Pike | 740/453–3400 or 800/325–2525 | fax 740/453–9715 | www.travelweb.com/daysinn.html | 60 rooms | $74 | AE, D, DC, MC, V.

Fairfield Inn by Marriott. In-room easy chairs and big work desks make this three-story hotel comfortable for business travelers, and the large indoor pool is a hit with families and kids. The downtown historical district is only a mile away, and restaurants abound on the adjacent blocks. Complimentary Continental breakfast. Some refrigerators. Cable TV. Indoor pool. Business services. | 725 Zane St. | 740/453–8770 or 800/288–2800 | www.marriott.com | 63 rooms | $75 | AE, D, DC, MC, V.

Flint Ridge Vineyard B&B. This 100 year-old B&B on a secluded rural farm has its own five-acre vineyard, 80 acres of birding and walking trails, and is removed from road traffic. Every September the owners host a picking party in the vineyard. It's in Hopewell, 10 mi west of Zanesville, on Route 40, off I–70. Dining room, picnic area. Complimentary breakfast. Pond with fishing, poles available. Library with wood stove, stereo. Laundry facilities. | 3890 Pert Hill Rd., Hopewell | 740/787–2103 | 1 room | $50 | No credit cards.

Hampton Inn Zanesville. This hotel is on the northern tip of downtown off I–70, at exit 155. The Zanesville airport is 5 mi away and the Colony Square Mall is 3 mi away. Riverside Park is a mile and a half southeast. Complimentary Continental breakfast. Cable TV, TV in common area. Pool. | 1009 Spring St. | 740/453–6511 or 800/426–7866 | fax 740/450–2899 | www.hamptoninn.com | 64 rooms | $80 | AE, D, DC, MC, V.

Holiday Inn Conference Center. This motel is off I–70 in a quiet, rural area, 5 mi from Zanesville Restaurant, bar, room service. In-room data ports. Cable TV. Indoor pool. Hot tub. Exercise equipment. Playground. Laundry facilities. Business services. Some pets allowed. | 4645 E. Pike | 740/453–0771 or 800/465–4329 | www.holidayinn.com | 130 rooms, 4 suites | $69 | AE, D, DC, MC, V.

Super 8 Zanesville. This hotel is in a gleaming white, three-story building, reminiscent of the Tudor style, right off I–70 at exit 152. Downtown Zanesville is 2 mi away and Dillon Lake is 8 mi away. Complimentary Continental breakfast. Cable TV. Pets allowed. | 2440 National Rd. | 740/455–3124 or 800/800–8000 | www.super8.com | 62 rooms | $45–$65 | AE, D, DC, MC, V.

ZOAR

MAP 14, E4

(Nearby towns listed: Berlin, Canton, Massillon, New Philadelphia, Sugarcreek)

Settled in 1817 by a group of German religious dissenters, this former communal society lasted until 1898 when Society of Separatists of Zoar disbanded. The historic village where the commune lived is still intact, and the rest of Zoar retains a sense of history with its shady streets and German-style buildings.

Information: **Tuscarawas County Convention and Visitors Bureau** | 125 McDonald Dr. SW, New Philadelphia, 44663 | 330/339–5453 | www.neohiotravel.com.

Attractions

Fort Laurens State Memorial and Museum. The Fort Laurens Memorial, about 3 mi north of Zoar, commemorates the only fort built by the American Continental Army in what is now Ohio. The tomb of Ohio's unknown patriot, a memorial to the heroes of the American Revolution, is here. The fort has been restored and is open for tours. Revolutionary War re-enactments are held on weekends. The museum has displays on the Revolutionary War. | 5 mi west of junction of I-77 and Rte. 212, Bolivar | 330/874-2059 | Memorial free, museum $3 | Memorial: Apr.-Oct., daily 9:30-dusk. Museum: June-Aug., Wed.-Sat. 9:30-5, Sun. noon-5; Apr.-May, and Sept.-Oct., Sat. 9:30-5, Sun. noon-5.

Zoar Village. This 12-block district includes original 19th-century homes, shops, and businesses from a utopian community that comprised 75 families. You can experience the life of the agrarian Separatists by visiting the 10 restored buildings (Number One House, Kitchen/Magazine Complex, Bimeler Museum, Garden House, Bakery, Tinshop, Dairy, Wagon Shop, Blacksmith Shop, and Zoar Store), which are staffed with costumed interpreters and furnished with items made or used by the Separatists. Though the historic buildings are closed from November to March, shops and restaurants stay open year-round. | 198 Main St. | 330/874-3011 or 800/262-6195 | www.zca.org | $5 | Memorial Day-Labor Day, Wed.-Sat., 9:30-5, Sun. 12-5; Apr.-May, Sept.-Oct., Sat. 9:30-5, Sun. 12-5.

ON THE CALENDAR

AUG.: *Zoar Harvest Festival.* The year's harvest is celebrated at Zoar Village with food, games, parades, and live entertainment. | 198 Main St. | 330/874-2100.
DEC.: *Christmas in Zoar.* Holiday festivities at Zoar Village include parades, holiday music, and arts and crafts. An appearance by Santa Claus is the high point for kids. | 198 Main St. | 330/874-3011.

Dining

Inn on the River. American. This 1831 Canal Inn is rumored to be haunted. It's a good special-occasion spot, right on Tuscarawas River. The menu features chicken, fish, steak, and pasta dishes. | 8806 Towpath Rd. NE | 330/874-3770 | No dinner Sun. and Mon. | $12-$40 | MC, V.

Zoar Tavern and Inn. American. In addition to sandwiches and entrées of chicken, pasta, and seafood, you can get German fare such as spaetzle and cabbage, schnitzel and sausages, and bread puddding for dessert. | 162 Main St. | 330/874-2170 or 888/874-2170 | www.zoar-tavern-inn.com | $8-$20 | AE, D, MC, V.

Lodging

Cowger House #9. Rooms are in an 1817 log cabin, a 1833 post-and-beam building, and a modern Amish-style bed and breakfast building. The cabin is the most rustic and historic. Restaurant, complimentary breakfast. | 197 4th St. | 330/874-3542 or 800/874-3542 | www.zoarvillage.com | 10 in 3 buildings | $70-$159 | AE, D, MC, V.

Zoar Tavern and Inn. Hand-hewn beams, brick and stone walls, and antique furnishings lend a historic feel to these rooms in this home, which once belonged to the village doctor and is right in the center of town. Restaurant, lounge. Cable TV. No smoking. | 162 Main St. | 330/874-2170 or 888/874-2170 | www.zoar-tavern-inn.com | 5 rooms | $70-$95 | AE, D, MC, V.

West Virginia

West Virginians take their state motto to heart: *Montani Semper Liberi,* or "Mountaineers Are Always Free." It's a spirit born during settlement in the early 18th century and fostered over nearly 300 years of wars and peace, depression and prosperity.

The people here have endured centuries of conflict—the French and Indian War and the American Revolution in the 1700s, the Civil War in the 1800s, and labor strife in the 1900s—to emerge as a strong-willed people able to adapt to changing times. Those who have called West Virginia home have been a fiercely independent breed— a nature shaped as much by the state's history as by its physical features.

Dominated by the craggy peaks of the Allegheny Mountains, part of the Appalachian chain, West Virginia has a varied landscape: The gentle hills of the Eastern Panhandle give way to the rugged mountains of the Potomac Highlands and Mountaineer Country, which then slope into the lush Greenbrier and New River valleys and the scenic Mountain Lakes region. Moving west toward the Ohio River, the rolling terrain fades into the populous swath of the Metro and Mid-Ohio valleys and the Northern Panhandle.

A statewide economy based on coal and lumber has broadened to include the chemical and manufacturing industries and, increasingly, tourism. Ski resorts, caverns, hot springs, and unparalleled natural scenery draw visitors to the Mountain State. Some of the best white-water rafting in the nation is less than an hour from the Metro Valley. The Monongahela National Forest, popular with hikers, anglers, hunters, and rock climbers, covers more than 900,000 acres along the eastern border. Historic sites—from 2,000-year-old Native American burial mounds to Civil War battle fields—are found throughout the state, many just a day trip from metropolitan Pittsburgh or Washington, D.C.

History

Small groups of nomadic Paleo-Indians lived in the Kanawha and Ohio valleys as early as 11,000 BC, hunting mammoth and mastodon with crude stone weapons. When most

CAPITAL: CHARLESTON	POPULATION: 1,816,000 (1997)	AREA: 24,282 SQUARE MI
BORDERS: KY, MD, OH, PA, AND VA	TIME ZONE: EASTERN	POSTAL ABBREVIATION: WV
WEB SITE: WWW.WESTVIRGINIA.COM		

of the large game became extinct, the early hunters either died out or adapted to different ways of getting food, such as hunting small game, gathering edible plants, and harvesting shellfish from the Kanawha River.

The Adena culture emerged around 1000 BC in the Northern Panhandle and lower Kanawha Valley, where they settled in villages and grew crops. They were the first Native Americans known to build burial mounds, most likely to honor chiefs, shamans, or great warriors. These massive dirt structures—the tallest rising more than 60 ft high—can still be seen today in Moundsville and South Charleston.

Various Native American tribes occupied present-day West Virginia by the time the Europeans arrived in the latter part of 17th century. The Iroquois, Delaware, and Shawnee were firmly established here; Cherokee, Ottawa, and Mingo also had a presence. They lived in small villages, hunting, fishing, and growing crops such as corn, beans, and squash. Trade with the Europeans proved beneficial, though white settlement threatened their way of life.

Although tradition credits Welshman Morgan Morgan as the first white settler in West Virginia, it was more likely that Germans from Pennsylvania established the first settlement here, founding Mecklenburg (now Shepherdstown) in 1727. By the late 1700s, the Eastern Panhandle supported a number of growing towns; land disputes and conflicts with Native Americans slowed settlement of the western regions.

In 1746 the King of England granted all land in western Virginia up to the North Branch of the Potomac River to Lord Fairfax, who hired a team of surveyors (including young George Washington) to help clear the way for white settlement. Within 3 years, the first European settlement west of the Alleghenies was established in present-day Marlinton.

England made other large land grants, particularly in the Ohio Valley. The French also laid claim to these lands, as did the powerful Iroquois Confederacy, an alliance of Native American tribes. This three-way rivalry for the Ohio Valley eventually led to armed conflict and the outbreak in 1756 of the French and Indian War, much of which was fought in West Virginia. Although the war officially ended with the Treaty of Paris in 1763, clashes with Native Americans continued through the late 1700s, primarily at white settlements along the Ohio River.

The 1800s brought a different tension, this time over slavery and the power of the federal government. On October 16, 1859, abolitionist John Brown led a raid on the U.S. Arsenal in Harpers Ferry in hopes of supplying weapons for a slave rebellion. His attempt failed, and Brown was tried and hanged for treason. His actions helped spark the Civil War; the first land battle of the war was fought on June 3, 1861, in Philippi. When Virginia seceded from the Union in 1861, the disenfranchised western counties voted overwhelmingly to form a new state. In 1863 President Abraham Lincoln proclaimed West Virginia the 35th state in the Union.

The beginning of the 20th century was marked by the rise of the coal industry, and with it, the labor movement. Dangerous working conditions and frequent mining accidents claimed many hundreds of lives. In 1907 explosions at a coal mine in Monongah killed 362 men and boys, the worst mining disaster in U.S. history. A series of labor strikes and riots became known collectively as the Mine Wars.

WV Timeline

ca. 11,000 BC		ca. 1,000 BC– AD 1600	
Paleo-Indians, early nomadic hunters from Asia, arrive in the Kanawha and Ohio valleys, hunting mammoths, mastodons, and buffalo. Their stone weapons have been uncovered in	present-day Wood and Upshur counties.	The Adena people emerge in the Northern Panhandle and the lower Kanawha Valley, building ceremonial burial mounds, the most famous of which are the Grave Creek Mound in	Moundsville and the Criel Mound in South Charleston.

INTRODUCTION
HISTORY
REGIONS
WHEN TO VISIT
STATE'S GREATS
RULES OF THE ROAD
DRIVING TOURS

Repeated attempts to unionize workers were met with intimidation by mining companies, triggering the arrival of many national labor leaders, including Mary Harris "Mother" Jones. In 1920–21, the Mine Wars culminated in the Matewan Massacre. Federal troops were called in to stop the fighting, a bloody 4-day gunfight that left 10 dead.

Reforms helped to change mine conditions, yet even today tension still exists between many West Virginians and the coal industry—though in the 21st century, it is environmental concerns that shape the debate.

Regions

1. METRO VALLEY

The most populated region in West Virginia, the Metro Valley lies in the southwestern part of the state and includes its two largest cities—Huntington, on the Ohio River, and Charleston, the capital, on the Kanawha River. The metropolitan corridor along Interstate 64 is a thriving center of government, commerce, and culture. Small towns, state forests, and wildlife areas dot the surrounding counties.

Towns listed: Barboursville, Charleston, Huntington, Nitro, Point Pleasant, Williamson

2. MID-OHIO VALLEY

The rolling hills and valleys along the Ohio River have seen many changes over the centuries. Military forts sprang up along the river during early settlement. Later, as the land was peopled, the Ohio River became a major transportation and shipping route. Railroads connected the state to distant markets. Many of the towns here were built on the oil, natural gas, and glass industries, and boom times brought great wealth to the region.

Towns listed: Mineralwells, Parkersburg, Ripley

3. NORTHERN PANHANDLE

The narrow strip of West Virginia that lies between Ohio and Pennsylvania is a intriguing mix of industry and recreation, where mighty steel mills give way to expansive parks, Victorian homes, and historical landmarks. Wheeling, the state's third-largest city, is steeped in history: it is here that the last battle of the American Revolution was fought and the western regions of Virginia declared their independence during the Civil War.

Towns listed: Bethany, Sistersville, Weirton, Wheeling

4. MOUNTAINEER COUNTRY

Like many parts of the state, Mountaineer Country prospered from the coal and timber industries. In the late 1800s there was an influx of foreign immigrants to the region,

---

1669
King Charles II of England grants land patents, including some for eastern parts of present-day West Virginia, to his supporters.
John Lederer, a German physician employed by

Colonial Governor William Berkeley, leads an expedition to the crest of the Blue Ridge Mountains; he and his group are apparently the first Europeans to see the region.

1671
Englishmen Thomas Batts and Robert Fallam lead an expedition into the New River Valley and claim for the king all land drained by the New River and its tributaries.

1719
Thomas, Lord Fairfax, finishes consolidating his claims, and after winning a dispute in 1746 with Virginia, is granted all the land to the North Branch of the Potomac River.

1727
White settlement of present-day West Virginia likely begins with German pioneers at Mecklenburg (Shepherdstown). However, tradition credits Welshman Morgan Morgan,

coming to work as laborers; vestiges of these European roots are still evident. West Virginia University, the state's largest institution of higher learning, is located here. The region is also known for its fishing, white-water rafting, and fall foliage.

Towns listed: Aurora, Bridgeport, Clarksburg, Fairmont, Grafton, Morgantown, Philippi, Salem

5. MOUNTAIN LAKES

The heartland of West Virginia is a sparsely populated region filled with lakes, rivers, unspoiled woodlands, state parks, and small towns. The area is a natural destination for outdoor enthusiasts, from white-water rafters and hunters to water-skiers and naturalists.

Towns listed: Buckhannon, Glenville, Richwood, Summersville, Sutton, Webster Springs, Weston

6. NEW RIVER/GREENBRIER VALLEY

White-water rafting on the New River has earned this region a national reputation among rafting enthusiasts. This lush valley in the southernmost part of the state is also known for its hunting, fishing, and hiking. Like elsewhere in the state, history and mountain culture are strong here—the world famous Greenbrier Resort in White Sulphur Springs has hosted presidents and royalty. Beckley, the area's largest city, is home to Tamarack, a showcase for the state's arts, crafts, and cuisine.

Towns listed: Ansted, Beckley, Bluefield, Fayetteville, Gauley Bridge, Hinton, Lewisburg, Princeton, White Sulphur Springs

7. POTOMAC HIGHLANDS

Running north to south along the spine of the Allegheny Mountains, the Potomac Highlands is the center of the state's outdoor tourist industry. Ski resorts, hiking trails, caves, and rivers dot the region, which is dominated by the Monongahela National Forest. Spruce Knob, the highest point in West Virginia (4,861 ft) is located here, in Spruce Knob National Recreation Center.

Towns listed: Davis, Elkins, Franklin, Hillsboro, Marlinton, Moorefield, Petersburg

8. EASTERN PANHANDLE

At the northeastern tip of the state, the Eastern Panhandle is just an hour from the Washington, DC, area and 2 hours from Baltimore. The first white settlers here established towns along the Potomac River, and George Washington slept here. The historic events that shaped the course of the country are commemorated at Harpers Ferry National Historical Park. In recent years, bedroom communities have sprung up among the area's small historic towns.

1731	**1747**	**1749**	**1756–63**
who arrived in the Eastern Panhandle in 1726, with being the first European settler in the region.	Morgan Morgan establishes the first permanent settlement in what is now Berkeley County.	George Washington surveys land in western Virginia for Lord Fairfax.	Jacob Marlin and Stephen Sewell establish the first recorded settlement west of the Alleghenies, near what now is Marlinton.	French and Indian War.

Towns listed: Berkeley Springs, Charles Town, Harpers Ferry, Martinsburg, Shepherds-town

INTRODUCTION
HISTORY
REGIONS
WHEN TO VISIT
STATE'S GREATS
RULES OF THE ROAD
DRIVING TOURS

When to Visit

West Virginia's climate varies from region to region. In low-lying areas, such as the Eastern Panhandle and the Mid-Ohio and Metro valleys, winters are mild and summers are warm and pleasant. Towns along the Ohio River tend to be extremely humid in summer. In the central and mountainous regions, winters are colder and often harsh, but summers are mild with low humidity.

The state's record low of 37°F was set in the eastern mountains at Lewisburg in 1917; the high of 112°F occurred in Martinsburg in the Eastern Panhandle in 1936. Average rainfall ranges from 45 to 50 inches, with some areas of the Allegheny Mountains receiving well above that. Snowfall averages about 35 inches, although snowpacks of more than 150 inches have been recorded on the highest peaks.

CLIMATE CHART

Average High/Low Temperatures (°F) and Monthly Precipitation (in inches)

	JAN.	FEB.	MAR.	APR.	MAY	JUNE
BECKLEY	38/20	41/23	52/32	62/40	70/49	76/56
	2.9	2.9	3.4	3.4	4	3.8

	JULY	AUG.	SEPT.	OCT.	NOV.	DEC.
	79/60	78/59	72/53	63/42	52/34	42/25
	4.7	3.4	3.3	2.9	3	3.2

	JAN.	FEB.	MAR.	APR.	MAY	JUNE
CHARLESTON	41/23	45/26	57/35	67/43	76/52	83/60
	2.9	3	3.6	3.3	3.4	3.6

	JULY	AUG.	SEPT.	OCT.	NOV.	DEC.
	86/64	84/63	79/57	68/44	57/36	46/28
	5	4	3.2	2.9	3.6	3.4

	JAN.	FEB.	MAR.	APR.	MAY	JUNE
ELKINS	38/16	41/18	52/27	62/35	71/44	78/52
	3	3	3.8	3.8	4.1	4.5

	JULY	AUG.	SEPT.	OCT.	NOV.	DEC.
	80/57	79/56	64/37	64/37	53/30	43/21
	4.5	4.4	3	3	3.33	3.5

1763
The Treaty of Paris ends the French and Indian War, giving the British claim to virtually all territory east of the Mississippi River.

1768
The Iroquois and Cherokee tribes release claim on the territory between the Ohio River and Allegheny Mountains, clearing the way for white settlement.

1774
Settlers murder the family of Mingo chieftain Tah-gah-jute (Logan), an advocate for peace. The trajedy spurs him to kill 13 white settlers, then justify his action in a famous letter.

Governor John Murray of Virginia sends 2,500 troops into the Ohio Valley, and they clash with the 1,200 men of Shawnee chief Keigh-tugh-qua (Cornstalk) in present-day Point Pleasant. After both

sides suffer considerable losses, the Shawnee retreat. In the Treaty of Camp Charlotte, the Delaware, Mingo, and Shawnee tribes relinquish claims to all land south of the Ohio River.

FESTIVALS AND SEASONAL EVENTS
WINTER

Nov.–Dec.	**Christmas in Shepherdstown.** Strolling carolers in turn-of-the-century garb, carriage rides, and house tours highlight this month-long celebration.	304/876–9388.
Nov.–Jan.	**Festival of Lights in Oglebay Park.** Miles of glittering lights illuminate a 1,500-acre park in Wheeling, with architectural and landscape displays and a Fantasy in Light parade.	304/243–4010.
Mar.	**Governor's Cup Ski Race.** The oldest ski race in the South, this 2-day downhill event is held at the Timberline Four Seasons Resort Canaan Valley. Prizes are awarded in all age categories, with the overall winner receiving the trophy cup.	800/782–2775.

SPRING

Apr.	**International Feast of the Ramson.** The ramson, known locally as the ramp, is a wild leek harvested for only a short time each spring; it is served in dozens of different ways at this annual feast in Richwood.	304/846–6790.
May	**Bluefield Mountain Festival.** Gospel music, carnival rides, and road races—including a 1-mi Fun Run, a 5K race, and a 10K race—are some of the activities at this Bluefield event.	304/327–7184.
	Rendezvous on the Island. Mountain men and muzzle loaders re-create the frontier era at Blennerhassett Island Historical State Park near Parkersburg.	304/420–4800.
	Three Rivers Festival. Commemorating Civil War history, men in period costumes stage a battle on a bridge that actually saw action during the war; the performance is in Fairmont and includes a parade, a carnival, live entertainment, and a golf tournament.	304/363–2625.
	Vandalia Gathering. Old-time music, clogging, and traditional Appalachian arts from throughout the state are showcased in this festival at the Capitol Complex in Charleston.	304/558–0220.
	Webster County Woodchopping Festival. Lumberjacks from around the world gather for a championship contest. There's also a turkey-calling competition, dancing, and parades.	304/847–2454.

1805
On what is now Blennerhassett Island near Parkersburg, Harman Blennerhassett and Aaron Burr allegedly plot to conquer territory in the Southwest.

1859
John Brown and his followers raid the federal arsenal in Harpers Ferry. Brown is convicted of treason and hanged at Charles Town.

1861
Despite opposition from the western counties, Virginia secedes from the Union on May 23. The first land battle of the Civil War is fought June 3 at Philippi. On October 24, voters in the western counties overwhelmingly support the formation of a new state.

1863
West Virginia is admitted as the 35th state to the Union.

INTRODUCTION
HISTORY
REGIONS
WHEN TO VISIT
STATE'S GREATS
RULES OF THE ROAD
DRIVING TOURS

West Virginia Strawberry Festival. This family event in downtown Buckhannon has strawberry pie-eating contests, strawberry cook-offs, a kids' strawberry blond contest, street parties each night, and three parades. | 304/472–1722.

June

West Virginia State Folk Festival. Banjo and fiddle music has people square dancing in the streets of Glenville. Since 1948 this event has been showcasing the finest Appalachian musicians, dancers, and storytellers. | 304/462–8427.

Blue and Gray Reunion Civil War Reenactment. A mustering of troops in Philippi commemorates the first land battle of the Civil War, which took place there in 1861. | 304/457–4625.

SUMMER

June–Aug.

Theatre West Virginia. Musical dramas are performed under the stars at the Cliffside Amphitheatre at Grandview, part of the New River Gorge National River near Beckley. | 304/256–6800 or 800/666–9142.

June and Sept.

Mountain Heritage Arts and Crafts Festival. Bluegrass and country music as well as artisans from across the country contribute to this nationally known festival held in Charles Town. | 304/725–2055.

July

Mountain State Art and Craft Fair. From weaving to wood-carving, more than 200 craftspeople demonstrate and sell their wares at this juried event in Ripley. | 304/372–2260 or 304/372–2034.

Pioneer Days in Pocahontas County. Square dancing, fiddle music, and handmade crafts evoke olden times at this festival of mountain culture in Marlinton. | 304/799–6569.

Tri-State Fair and Regatta. Jet-ski races on the Ohio River highlight this riverfront event in Huntington, with ethnic foods, games for kids, and nightly concerts. | 304/525–7333 or 800/635–6329.

West Virginia Interstate Fair and Exposition. The state's largest county fair draws crowds to Mineral Wells for carnival rides, livestock exhibits, concerts, and more. | 304/489–1301.

July–Aug.

Augusta Heritage Center. From blues to bluegrass, this 5-week workshop at Davis and Elkins College in Elkins covers all types of traditional music, dance, folklore, and crafts. Weekly public concerts and dances are also staged here. | 304/637–1209.

1865
Two months before the end of the Civil War, Governor Arthur I. Boreman approves an act abolishing slavery.

1870
The world's first brick street is laid in Charleston.

1873
The 6,000-ft-long Big Bend Tunnel opens near Talcott. Legend has it that John Henry, thought to be a freed slave, beat a steam-powered drill during the tunnel's construction, only to die in the effort.

1880
Governor Henry M. Mathews sends militia to Hawks Nest to stop the state's first major coal strike.

Aug.   **West Virginia State Water Festival.** Boatmen poling flat-bot-
tomed bateaux take you on rides along the New River at this
recreation of pre-Civil War days in Hinton, west of Lewisburg,
with frontier camps, blacksmithing, and candle making. | 304/
466–5420.

Appalachian Arts and Crafts Festival. Southern West Virginia's
largest quilt exhibit, along with woodcarving, pottery, and
other mountain crafts, are the focus of this 3-day juried show
in Beckley. | 304/252–7328.

State Fair of West Virginia. Draft horse pulls, pig racing, and
bass fishing demonstrations are some of the events at the
state fairgrounds in Fairlea, along with livestock and agricultural exhibits, a carnival midway, fireworks, and headline acts
in the grandstand. | Lewisburg | 304/645–1090.

Aug.–Sept.   **Charleston Sternwheel Regatta Festival.** Paddleboats churning across the Kanawha River are the highlight of this 5-day
riverfront celebration, with towboat contests, deckhand com-
petitions, rubber ducky races, nightly concerts, and more. |
304/344–5075 or 800/733–5469.

FALL

Sept.   **Autumn Harvest Festival and Roadkill Cook-Off.** Venison
steaks or rattlesnake stew may take the top prize in this wild-
game cooking contest in Marlinton. | 800/336–7009.

Treasure Mountain Festival. Storytellers weave tales of buried
treasure at this event hosted by the town of Franklin. Beard
and mustache contests, dancing, and food are also part of the
celebration. | 304/249–5422.

Chilifest. Sanctioned by the International Chili Society, the
state's championship chili cook-off and hot-pepper-eating
contest is held in downtown Huntington. | 304/529–4857.

West Virginia Honey Festival. Beekeeping demonstrations,
beeswax candle making, a honey baking contest—and even a
man wearing a beard of live bees—will grab your attention at
this yearly event in Parkersburg. | 304/428–1130.

West Virginia Italian Heritage Festival. There's dancing in the
streets and plenty of food at this celebration of Italian ances-
try in Clarksburg. A creative arts program for kids, a parade,
and big-name entertainment are also part of the activities. |
304/622–7314.

1882	**1896**	**1897**	**1907**	**1908**
When Johnse Hat-field attempts to elope with Rosanna McCoy, Ellison Hat-field is shot, setting off the Hatfield-McCoy feud.	The first rural free mail delivery in the United States begins in Charles Town.	Mary Harris Jones (Mother Jones) is sent to West Vir-ginia to organize miners.	In the worst mine disaster in U.S. his-tory, 362 men and boys are killed in Marion County.	The first official Mother's Day ser-vice is held in Grafton, six years before it's declared a national holiday.

INTRODUCTION
HISTORY
REGIONS
WHEN TO VISIT
STATE'S GREATS
RULES OF THE ROAD
DRIVING TOURS

Oct. **Apple Butter Festival.** You can see apple butter cooking in open kettles—and buy some to take home—at this family festival in historic Berkeley Springs. Hog-calling contests and turtle races are highlights, along with 200 arts and crafts booths. | 304/258–3738.

Bridge Day. Parachutists leap from the New River Gorge Bridge, the nation's second-highest, at this daredevil event near Fayetteville. | 304/465–0508.

Election Day 1860. The Civil War era comes to life with a mustering of troops and military encampments at Harpers Ferry National Historical Park. | 304/535–6748.

Mountaineer Balloon Festival. Hot-air balloons fill the skies over Morgantown during this weekend rally with five different balloon races and rides for the public. | 304/292–5081 or 800/458–7373.

Mountain State Forest Festival. Started in 1936, this Elkins event is the state's oldest festival, presenting gospel and country music, arts andcrafts, and even motorcycle and all-terrain-vehicle races. | 304/636–1824.

State's Greats

Aside from a handful of smallish cities (the largest being Charleston with a population of 57,300), West Virginia is a state of small towns scattered among the forested mountains and river valleys. Two-thirds of West Virginians live in rural areas. With more than 226,500 acres of state parks, forests, and recreation areas, and more than a million acres of federal lands, West Virginia offers a quick escape from the urban centers of Baltimore, Philadelphia, Pittsburgh, and Washington, DC.

Art and Architecture

Appalachian Mountain crafts, music, and dance are celebrated throughout the state, particularly at local festivals and fairs. The **State Capitol Complex** in Charleston hosts the annual Vandalia Gathering every Memorial Day, as well as performances, lectures, and films in the **Cultural Center Theater.** The **Huntington Museum of Art** has a collection of Appalachian folk art, along with a range of exhibits—from pre-Columbian artifacts to Oriental prayer rugs and European paintings.

Culture, Education, and History

Historic sites are found in all corners of the state, from the Eastern Panhandle towns of Harpers Ferry and Berkeley Springs on the Potomac River, to Point Pleasant on the Ohio, where the **Point Pleasant Battle Monument** commemorates the first battle of

1912–13	1920		1920–21	
Paint Creek–Cabin Creek strike in the state's first and worst mine war.	Ten people die in the deadliest shoot-out in U.S. history after Matewan police chief Sid Hatfield tries to arrest detectives hired by coal operators to evict fired union members from	company housing. Hatfield, who becomes a folk hero, is shot and killed the next year in retaliation for the Matewan Massacre.	Fights between miners and company guards, police, and federal troops escalate to the point that the National Guard brings in planes to drop bombs during the battle of Blair	Mountain. Federal troops eventually are sent in to end the riots.

the Revolutionary War. In Wheeling, **West Virginia Independence Hall–Custom House,** the site of West Virginia's secession from Virginia, displays exhibits relating to the state's cultural heritage. The **West Virginia State Museum** in Charleston traces the state's history from early mound-building Native Americans through the coal mining industry and oil booms of later centuries.

Parks, Natural Areas, and Outdoor Recreation

West Virginia boasts some of the nation's most beautiful scenery, much of it federally managed. The **Monongahela National Forest** in the Allegheny Mountains of the Potomac Highlands region covers more than 900,000 acres, with everything from skiing to spelunking, trout fishing to rock climbing. The **New River Gorge National River** is a rugged river canyon with Class V rapids. **Harpers Ferry National Historical Park** takes you back in time—to the colonial period, when George Washington frequented the region, through the Civil War, when John Brown was tried and hung for treason here.

But perhaps the real jewel in West Virginia's tourism crown is its nearly 50 state parks and forests. Hunters can find quiet havens in the largely undeveloped **Camp Creek** and **Calvin Price** state forests, while hikers and mountain bikers find plenty of challenges on the trails of **Coopers Rock** and **Kanawha.** If you're interested in camping, most all state forests have campsites, and some, such as **Greenbrier, Seneca,** and **Cabwaylingo,** have cabins, as do many state parks.

For lodge accommodations, you can visit West Virginia's resort state parks, which have a wealth of recreational activities. You can ski the snow-packed slopes in **Canaan Valley Resort State Park,** hit 18 holes of golf at **Twin Falls,** or ride an aerial tramway at **Hawks Nest.** If you simply want the peace and tranquility of nature—with plenty to see and do—there's **Watoga, Lost River, Holly River,** and **Babcock** state parks, to name just a few.

West Virginia's great outdoors draws all manner of recreationalists and adventurers. The **New River,** the **Cheat,** and the **Gauley** are renowned for their roiling white-water rapids, and dozens of outfitters guide boatloads of people down these raging rivers each year. The **Appalachian National Scenic Trail** traverses the state on its way from Georgia to Maine. Hikers also tread the **Greenbrier River Trail** and **North Bend Rail Trail** as well as the many hundreds of miles of hiking and biking trails that lace the state's forests and parks.

Canaan Valley, Snowshoe Mountain Resort, and **Winterplace** are popular winter destinations for downhill and cross-country skiers and snowboarders. Rock climbers scale the vertical faces of **Seneca Rocks National Recreation Area.** Lakes throughout the state draw boaters and anglers; hunting, and even trapping, is permitted in most state parks, forests, and recreation areas.

1928	**1962**	**1972**	**1977**	**1992**
Minnie Buckingham Harper of Welch is appointed to succeed her husband in the House of Delegates, becoming the first black woman in the United States to serve as a legislator.	The world's largest movable radio telescope begins regular operations at Green Bank, Pocahontas County. It collapses in 1988.	A flood kills 118 people in Logan County after a coal-waste dam collapses at Buffalo Creek.	The New River Gorge Bridge, the world's longest steel-arch span, opens near Fayetteville.	It is revealed that, for the past three decades, a huge two-story bunker has existed under the Greenbrier resort in White Sulphur Springs. The bunker was built to house the entire

Rules of the Road

License requirements: You must be at least 16 years old and have a valid driver's license to drive in West Virginia; 15 with a restricted license. Residents of Canada and most other countries can drive here with valid licenses from their home countries.

Seat Belt and Helmet Laws: Seat belts are required for all front-seat occupants and backseat passengers under 18; child restraints are required for kids under 2. Helmets are mandatory for both motorcycle drivers and passengers.

Speed Limits: The speed limit on interstate highways is 70 mph and 55 mph on most major state routes. Be sure to check locally posted signs.

For More Information: Contact the **West Virginia Department of Public Safety** | 304/746–2100.

Midland Trail Driving Tour Along U.S. 60

A SOUTHERN SWING THROUGH THE STATE

Distance: 119 mi   Time: 2 days

Breaks: Consider stopping at Hawks Nest State Park, near the halfway point of the tour, where the lodge and aerial tramway offer spectacular views of the New River Gorge.

Once the route of early Native Americans and westward-bound pioneers, the Midland Trail traverses the southern part of the state, winding westward through the Allegheny Mountains and forested valleys and past the rim of the New River Gorge before following the Kanawha River on the way to historic Charleston. As summer days give way to crisp autumn nights, the lush mountain foliage slowly transforms the landscape into a patchwork of color. Take extreme caution driving this route in winter or at night, since it follows a winding, two-lane highway for much the way.

❶ Begin in **White Sulphur Springs,** where **The Greenbrier** resort has attracted the rich and mighty to its mineral springs since the early 1800s. A National Historic Landmark, the grand hotel sits on 6,500 acres in a scenic mountain valley. You can even tour a cavernous, once-secret bunker built during the Cold War to house Congress in the event of nuclear war.

❷ Leaving White Sulphur Springs, head west on U.S. 60 for 10 mi, driving through forested hills and farmlands until you reach **Lewisburg.** Antiques shops, art galleries, and small

2000

Congress for 40 days in case of nuclear attack.

Middle East peace talks are held in Shepherdstown.

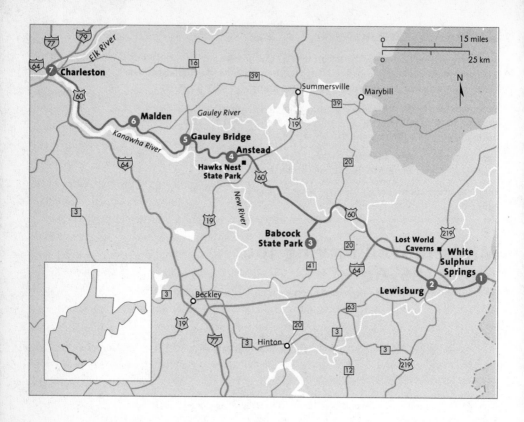

cafés—serving everything from country cooking to health food—are housed in the 18th- and 19th-century buildings of the town's **National Historic District.** North of Lewisburg on U.S. 219, **Lost World Caverns,** with a gigantic main room and impressive stalagmites and stalactites, provide a look at the region's vast underground network of caves.

❸ Take U.S. 60 to Route 41 (approximately 35 mi) and turn south, following the signs to **Babcock State Park.** Famous for its working gristmill, the park has miles of hiking trails, a lake, a pool, campsites, and log cabins. Near the rim of the New River Gorge, it is also just minutes from challenging rock-climbing walls.

❹ Return to U.S. 60 and head west for approxiately 15 mi to Mile 73 and the town of **Ansted.** Here, along a winding section of the Midland Trail, **Hawks Nest State Park** offers a bird's-eye view of the New River Gorge National River canyon. An aerial tramway runs 446 ft from the rim lodge to Hawks Nest Lake in the gorge, where you can rent paddleboats at the marina.

❺ Continue west on U.S. 60 to Mile 80 and **Gauley Bridge.** The toll bridge for which the town was named saw heavy fighting during the Civil War and was destroyed during a Confederate retreat in 1861. Here the Gauley and New rivers join to create the Kanawha River, which flows on to the Ohio. A renovated train depot here has a museum that traces the area's history.

INTRODUCTION
HISTORY
REGIONS
WHEN TO VISIT
STATE'S GREATS
RULES OF THE ROAD
DRIVING TOURS

6 Your next stop is the small town of Malden, at Mile 114. Famed educator Booker T. Washington grew up in Malden, where he worked in the salt furnaces during the early 1800s. The salt industry brought boom times to the Kanawha Valley, which was dotted with 30 salt furnaces and employed more than 3,000 people; by 1876 only one furnace remained. Stop at the information center at the **Cabin Creek Quilts Cooperative,** and listen to the artisans relate the history of the salt industry as they stitch the co-op's world-famous quilts.

7 Keep heading west on U.S. 60, traveling approximately 30 mi to **Charleston,** the state capital and the end of this driving tour. Chartered in 1794 when the region's economy was being spurred on by the salt industry, Charleston is now the state's business and cultural center as well as the seat of government. Noted architect Cass Gilbert designed the Italian Renaissance–style **Capitol Building** (at E. Kanawha Boulevard between Greenbrier Street and California Avenue) with its gold-leaf dome; the building was completed in 1932. The **State Capitol Complex** also includes the Cultural Center and the Governor's Mansion. Just to the west lies the **East End Historic District,** a neighborhood with an eclectic mix of architectural styles—Colonial, Greek Revival, Victorian, Georgian, Spanish Colonial, Italianate, and Renaissance. Overlooking the city and housed in two historic mansions, **Sunrise Museum** has art galleries, a planetarium, and a nature trail.

River Cities Historical Tour Along Route 2

LIFE ALONG THE MIGHTY OHIO

Distance: 193 mi   Time: 2 days
Breaks: Parkersburg, near the halfway point of the tour, has shopping, dining, lodging, and a historic state park on an island in the Ohio River reached by a stern-wheel paddleboat.

Meandering along the Ohio River, this tour travels south on Route 2 from Wheeling in the Northern Panhandle to Huntington in the Metro Valley. This stretch of land, the battleground of many wars, was among the last areas of West Virginia to be settled. It is an area steeped in history: Early Native Americans built massive burial sites here, and Revolutionary, French and Indian, and Civil War battles were fought here. With the rise of industry, coal and oil barons left an architectural legacy of stately homes and extensive gardens. Early October is an ideal time to visit.

1 The tour begins in **Wheeling.** A frontier town that witnessed the last battle of the American Revolution, Wheeling was a Union stronghold during the Civil War, served twice as state capital, and later boomed with industrial growth. Industrialist Earl W. Oglebay bequeathed the city's 1,500-acre **Oglebay Resort Park,** with gardens, greenhouses, and fountains; today it also includes a children's zoo, a miniature golf course, and restaurants. During the 19th century Wheeling was famous for manufacturing glass and china, and the **Carriage House Glass Museum** showcases glassware produced from 1817 to 1939.

2 Nine miles farther south in **Moundsville,** you can view the region's distant past at **Grave Creek Mound State Park.** Built more than 2,000 years ago by Adena Indians, this ceremonial burial mound is the largest of several mounds that dot the Ohio and Kanawha valleys. On the grounds, the **Delf Norona Museum and Culture Center** displays artifacts from the Adena period (about 1000 BC to AD 1).

❸ Continue south on Route 2 for approximately 32 mi to Mile 51 and the small town of **Sistersville.** With the discovery of oil on a nearby farm in 1889, this quiet community experienced a 26-year boom. Oil rigs sprouted on the hillsides, and oil barons built hand-some mansions along **Wells Street.** Pick up a map for the self-guided walking tour at the Wells Inn and stroll along the former business district to see an impressive vari-ety of architectural styles.

❹ Following the Ohio River south along Route 2, drive approximately 45 mi to **Parkers-burg.** The city's location at the confluence of the Ohio and the Little Kanawha rivers was instrumental to the economic growth of the area, described at the **Oil, Gas and**

Industrial Historical Museum, a turn-of-the-century building with displays of rigs, pumps, tools, and other industrial artifacts. A few miles downriver, and reached by sternwheel paddleboat, **Blennerhassett Island Historical State Park** is the site of the palatial home and landscaped grounds of Harman Blennerhassett, who allegedly conspired with Aaron Burr in 1805 join the western part of the United States with Spanish territory to form a new empire. You can tour the 7,000-square-ft mansion, picnic in the extensive gardens, or take a horse-drawn wagon ride around the island, which is open May through November.

❺ From Parkersburg, Route 2 joins I-77 for approximately 30 mi. Exit the interstate at Ravenswood (Exit 146) and follow the signs for Route 2. Continue about 30 mi more to **Point Pleasant.** At the confluence of the Ohio and Kanawha rivers, an 84-ft-high granite shaft at **Point Pleasant Battle Monument State Park** commemorates the first battle of the Revolutionary War, which was fought here on October 10, 1774. Each October, the 2-day **Battle Days Celebration** showcases military reenactments, an ox roast, period demonstrations, and a Colonial Ball.

❻ Leaving Point Pleasant, Route 2 once again snakes along the Ohio River, continuing south for about 43 mi to the city of **Huntington,** the final destination on this tour. Founded in 1871 by Collis P. Huntington, president of the Chesapeake and Ohio Railroad, the city has always been closely linked to the railroads. The refurbished warehouses and boxcars of **Heritage Village** house an array of shops and restaurants; a statue of Collis P. Huntington stands nearby. The brick streets of the **9th Street West Historic District** are lined with stately turn-of-the-century houses and cast-iron fences. Just southeast of the district is the **Huntington Museum of Art,** the largest museum in West Virginia, displaying collections of Ohio Valley glass, firearms, 19th- and 20th-century artwork, and exhibits specifically for children. There is an observatory and marked nature trails on the 52-acre grounds.

ANSTED

INTRO
ATTRACTIONS
DINING
LODGING

ANSTED

MAP 17, C6

(Nearby towns also listed: Fayetteville, Gauley Bridge)

First settled by Baptists in 1790, the town was later named in honor of geologist David T. Ansted, who interested investors in digging coal mines nearby during the 1830s. Today the economy has shifted from coal to tourism. The town of 1,600 is 2 mi from Hawks Nest State Park, with its panoramic views of the New River and the surrounding mountains.

Information: Southern West Virginia Convention and Visitors Bureau | Box 1799, Beckley 25802 | 304/252-2244 or 800/VISIT-WV | travel@visitwv.co | www.visitwv.org.

Attractions
Hawks Nest State Park. On the rim of the New River, this 276-acre park overlooks the placid waters of Hawks Nest Lake, with views of the narrow river canyon farther upstream. An aerial tramway drops 500 vertical ft to the lake, where paddleboats and jetboat rides are available. A log cabin museum displays pioneer and Native American artifacts, and there are hiking trails, a swimming pool, and a lodge. On Rte. 60 in the center of Ansted. | Rte. 60 | 304/658-5212 | Free | Daily 6 AM-10 PM.

Lodging
Hawks Nest Lodge. Built in 1967, this three-story brick lodge in Hawks Nest State Park overlooks Hawks Nest Lake and the New River Gorge. Dining room. Cable TV. Pool. Tennis. Busi-

ness services. | Rte. 60 W, Box 857 | 304/658–5212 | fax 304/658–4549 | 31 rooms, 5 suites | $67–$71 rooms, $82–$98 suites | AE, DC, MC, V.

AURORA

(Nearby town also listed: Grafton)

Founded in 1787, Aurora was one of first settlements in Preston County and claims the oldest Lutheran church in the Alleghenies. This small town, a farming community of 150, sits at the edge of Cathedral State Park, one of the few stands of virgin forest in the state.

Information: **Preston County Convention and Visitors Bureau** | Box 860, Arthurdale 26520 | 304/864–4601 or 800/571–0912 | prestoncvb@prestoncounty.com | www.prestoncounty.com.

Attractions

Alpine Lake Resort and Conference Center. You can fish in a 148-acre stocked lake, play 18 holes of golf, or cross-country ski through forest trails at this year-round recreational community, which also has hiking, biking, tennis, a beach, and an indoor pool. | 700 W. Alpine Dr., Terra Alta | 304/789–2481 or 800/752–7179 | fax 304/789–3026 | www.alpinelake.com | Free | Daily.

Cathedral State Park. Towering stands of virgin hardwood and hemlock trees—the oldest more than 500 years old—have earned this 132-acre park a listing in the National Register for Natural History Landmarks. Hiking and cross-country ski trails wind through the forest, which is 1 mi east of Aurora on Route 50. | Rte. 50 | 304/735–3771 | www.wvparks.com/cathedral | Free | Daily.

St. Paul's Lutheran Church. Built in 1889, this church, with an interior of hand-hewn chestnut and cherry wood, is the third building to house the oldest Lutheran church in the Alleghenies, established in 1787. | HC 82, ½ mi from Hwy. 50; box 15 | 304/735–3709 | Free | Daily.

Lodging

Alpine Lake Resort. The restaurant and pool are in a building separate from this two-story lodging. Both are part of the resort on Alpine Lake about 14 mi north of town. Restaurant, complimentary Continental breakfast. Cable TV. Pool. Boating, fishing. No pets. | 700 W. Alpine Dr., Terra Alta | 304/789–2481 | fax 304/789–3026 | 35 rooms | $45–$54 | AE, D, DC, MV, V.

Brookside Inn. Directly across the road from Cathedral State Park, this rustic red-shingle inn, built in 1899, is an example of early Arts and Craft architecture, with two porches and a large living room filling nearly the entire first floor. Dinner is included in the room rate. The inn is across the street from Cathedral State Park, on U.S. Route 50. Complimentary breakfast. No in-room TV. | Rte. 50 | 304/735–6344 | fax 304/735–3563 | 4 rooms (3 with shared bath) | $135–$145 | MC, V.

BARBOURSVILLE

(Nearby town also listed: Huntington)

Once a crossroads for Shawnee Indians who hunted game and mined salt in the area, the town of Barboursville was established in 1813 and served as the county seat until 1888. Today this town of 2,774 is home to the Huntington Mall, the state's largest shopping center.

Information: Cabell/Huntington Convention and Visitors Bureau | 739 3rd Ave., Huntington 25708 | 304/525–7333 or 800/635–6329 | htgncvb@marshall.edu | www.wvvisit.org.

Huntington Mall. Shop yourself to exhaustion at the largest mall in the state. You'll find five department stores and over 150 specialty shops filling over 1 million square ft plus a fountain and a food court under skylights. | Mall Rd., Rte. 60 | 304/733–0492 | Free | Mon.–Sat. 10–9, Sun. 12–6.

BECKLEY

MAP 17, C6

(Nearby town also listed: Hinton)

Founded in 1838, Beckley is the "smokeless coal" capital of the world, centrally located among hundreds of small coal mining communities that produce bituminous (smokeless) coal. A city of 18,300, Beckley serves as the economic and cultural center of the southern coalfield region, and is home to the College of West Virginia and the Tamarack crafts center.

Information: Southern West Virginia Convention and Visitors Bureau | Box 1799, 25802 | 304/252–2244 or 800/VISIT–WV | travel@visitwv.com | www.visitwv.org.

Attractions

Babcock State Park. You'll get great views of the New River Gorge from the Island in the Sky Trail, one of the 20 mi of trails that thread through this 4,127-acre park. There's also a working grist mill, horseback riding, fishing, boating, cross-country skiing, cabins, and campgrounds. The park is 35 mi northeast of Beckley on Route 41 South. | Route 41 S | 304/438–3003 or 800/CALL–WVA | www.babcocksp.com | Free | Daily dawn to dusk.

Beckley Exhibition Coal Mine. Riding in a remodeled mine car, you'll traverse 1,500 ft of underground passages on a guided tour through this former working coal mine, which also has a museum, a turn-of-the-century company house, and a restored mine superintendent's home. In New River City Park. | 513 Ewart Ave. | 304/256–1747 | $8.50 | Apr.–Oct., daily 10–6.

Grandview. With bird's-eye views of the New River Gorge and Horseshoe Bend, this 900-acre former state park is now part of the New River Gorge National River, with overlook hiking trails. Theatre West Virginia presents outdoor performances here during the summer. The park is 10 mi south of Beckley, off the Grandview Rd. exit on I–64 | 4700 Grandview Rd. | 304/763–3715 | fax 304/763–3792 | Free | Daily dawn to dusk.

Lake Stephens. This 2,700-acre recreation area has a beach, a water slide, fishing, and boat rentals, as well as a general store, 46 tent sites, and 100 trailer hookups. It's 9 mi west of Beckley, off Route 3. | 350 Lake Stephens Rd. | 304/934–5323 | $3 boat launch (Apr.–Oct.) | Daily, dawn to dusk.

Plum Orchard Lake Wildlife Management Area. Deer and small game abound here, and you can fish for bass and bluegill in a 200-acre lake. Boat rentals, a rifle range, hiking, and camping are also available. It's 5 mi from I–77, off the Mossy (southbound) or Pax (northbound) exits. | Plum Orchard Lake Rd. | 304/469–9905 | Free | Daily.

Tamarack. Quilters, wood carvers, glass blowers, potters, and other artisans demonstrate their skills at this emporium for West Virginia–made products. There's also a 200-seat theater, an art gallery, and herb and sculpture gardens. | 1 Tamarack Park | 304/256–6843 or 888/262–7225 | www.tamarackwv.com | Free | Daily 8–8.

Twin Falls Resort State Park. A restored pioneer homestead provides a glimpse of life in the 1830s, when this area was first settled. The 3,776-acre park also has an 18-hole golf course, hiking, swimming, camping, cottages, and a mountaintop lodge. The park is 23 mi southwest of Beckley. | Rte. 97, Mullens | 304/294–4000 or 800/CALL–WVA | Free | Daily.

Winterplace Ski Resort. Some 27 trails cover 600 vertical ft at this ski area, which also has night skiing and snowboarding and snow-tubing parks. The resort is 15 mi south of Beckley. | 100 Old Flat Top Mountain Rd., Ghent | 304/787–3221 or 800/607–SNOW | fax 304/787–9885 | www.winterplace.com | Dec.–Apr.

Youth Museum of Southern West Virginia. Including a one-room schoolhouse, a blacksmith shop, a country store, and moonshine, this museum entertains kids with hands-on activities that highlight the region's history and culture. There's also interactive science exhibits and a planetarium. In New River City Park. | 511 Ewart Ave. | 304/252–3730 | $2 | May–Labor Day, daily 10–5; Labor Day–Apr., Tues.–Sat. 10–5, closed Mon.

COAL COUNTRY

Even if you think you know nothing about the history of the coal mining industry in West Virginia, you might know more than you think. You certainly do if you've seen the 1987 film, Matewan, written and directed by John Sayles.

Matewan recounts, in almost documentary fashion, the most dramatic episode in the story of West Virginia coal mining. In 1921, the Stone Mt. Coal Co. suddenly announced that it was cutting the wages of miners. The miners, who worked under nearly intolerable conditions—risking everything from explosions and collapses to black lung disease—took up arms, enlisted other people in their cause, and rebelled. The confrontation literally came to a showdown with guns blazing in the main street of the town. The film was actually shot in the nearly abandoned town of Thurmond which, like the original locale, has a railroad track running down the center of its one street.

Coal has long been both a blessing and a curse for West Virginia since it was first discovered in 1917 in the Kanawha Valley. For most of the 20th century, the state ranked second in coal production. But, while it's brought jobs and business to the state, the price has been high. Accidents have cost thousands of lives and black lung disease has claimed many more.

Visitors to West Virginia today see the legacy of coal mining in a different way. Modern mining companies favor the complete removal of a mountaintop as the best means of mining surface coal. The result, as reported by the *Charleston Gazette*, is that "an untold amount of the state has been flattened, and hundreds of miles of streams have been buried." (The valueless rubble from the mountain is dumped into the surrounding valleys by earth-moving machines as tall as 20 stories.) Bullpush Mountain, for example, which straddles the line of Fayette and Kanawha Counties, is now a flat, grassy meadow.

In October 1999, a federal judge ruled that strip mining and mountaintop removal had to be limited, but the struggle continues among mine operators, employees, local residents, state and local agencies, and the federal courts.

JUNE–AUG.: *Theatre West Virginia.* The Hatfields and McCoys continue their family feud—this time set to music—in "Honey in the Rock," a musical about the state's separation from Virginia during the Civil War. The performance is held in the open-air amphitheater at Grandview in the New River Gorge National River. | 304/256–6800 or 800/666–9142.

AUG.: *Appalachian Arts and Crafts Festival.* Drawing crowds since 1964, this 3-day juried event at the Raleigh County Armory showcases weaving, wood carving, and blacksmithing, as well as southern West Virginia's largest quilt exhibit. | 304/252–7328.

Dining

Char. Contemporary. Popular with locals and tourists, this family-owned restaurant has been serving steaks, seafood, and pasta since 1965. The dining room, with linen tablecloths and a fireplace, overlooks a pond on 12 acres. | 100 Char Dr. | 304/253–1760 | Reservations not accepted | Closed Jan. and Sun. No lunch | $9–$38 | AE, D, DC, MC, V.

Lodging

Best Western Four Seasons Inn. One-half mile from I–77 Exit 44 (Harper Rd. exit), this two-story motel is 1 mi from the Tamarack craft center. Cable TV. Sauna, spa. Some pets allowed. | 1939 Harper Rd. (Rte. 3) | 304/252–0671 | fax 304/252–3951 | 80 rooms | $59–$64 | AE, D, DC, MC, V.

Comfort Inn. This Tudor-style chain is ¾ mi from downtown Beckley and ¾ mi from the Tamarack craft center. Complimentary Continental breakfast. Microwaves, refrigerators. Cable TV. Exercise equipment, health club. Laundry facilities. Business services. Some pets allowed. | 1909 Harper Rd. (Rte. 3) | 304/255–2161 | fax 304/255–2161 | www.comfortinn.com | 130 rooms in 2 buildings | $49–$109 | AE, D, DC, MC, V.

Country Inn and Suites. Built in 1997, this three-story building is 2 mi from the Tamarack craft center and 4 mi from downtown Beckley. The cozy lobby has wood floors, cushy chairs and couches, a fireplace, and ivy stenciling along the walls; rooms are decked in harvest colors of green, brown, and maroon. Complimentary Continental breakfast. In-room data ports. 2 pools (1 indoor). Laundry facilities. | 2120 Harper Rd. (Rte. 3) | 304/252–5100 | fax 304/252–3135 | www.countryinn.com | 157 rooms, 78 suites | $85–$95, $97 suites | AE, D, DC, MC, V.

Hampton Inn. This five-story chain is 2 mi from Tamarack and 5 mi from downtown Beckley. Complimentary Continental breakfast. Cable TV. Pool. Business services. | 110 Harper Park Dr. | 304/252–2121 | fax 304/252–2121 | 108 rooms | $64–$90 | AE, D, DC, MC, V.

Holiday Inn. This three-story chain is ⅓ mi from I–77 Exit 44 (Harper Rd. exit), 2 mi from the Tamarack craft center, and 5 mi from downtown Beckley. Restaurant, bar, room service. In-room data ports, some microwaves, some refrigerators. Cable TV. Pool. Exercise equipment. Laundry facilities. Business services. | 1924 Harper Rd. (Rte. 3) | 304/255–1511 | fax 304/256–0526 | www.holiday-inn.com | 105 rooms | $70–$109 | AE, D, DC, MC, V.

BERKELEY SPRINGS

MAP 17, E2

(Nearby town also listed: Martinsburg)

Hot mineral waters have drawn people to Berkeley Springs for centuries. Native Americans traveled here for the healing powers of the "medicine waters," and wealthy colonials discovered the area later. George Washington helped establish the town as a health resort in 1776 and owned property nearby. The town of 700 still caters to visitors who come to enjoy the 74°F. spring waters. Prospect Peak, a popular vantage point overlooking the Potomac River, is 3 mi west of the city.

Information: **Travel Berkeley Springs** | 304 Fairfax St., 25411 | 304/258–9147 or 800/447–8797 | tbs@intrepid.net | www.berkeleysprings.com.

Attractions

Berkeley Springs State Park. This four-acre park near the center of town has a spring-fed pool and hosts the famous mineral baths, which have been used by the public since 1776. The historic Roman Bath House still stands from 1815, and you can choose from a variety of spa treatments, from massages to mineral baths. Reservations for baths and massages are recommended. | 121 S. Washington St. | 304/258–2711 or 800/225–5982 | www.wvparks.com/berkeleysprings | Park admission free; baths and massages, $10–$65 | Park: daily dawn–10 PM; baths: daily 10–4:30.

★ **Cacapon Resort State Park.** At 2,300 ft, Cacapon Mountain dominates this narrow 6,000-acre park, which is laced with 27 mi of hiking and bridle trails. The 18-hole Robert Trent Jones golf course surrounds a nearby lodge, 10 mi south of Berkeley Springs off U.S. 522. | Hwy. 522 | 304/258–1022 or 800/CALL–WVA | www.cacaponresort.com | Free | Daily.

Sleepy Creek Wildlife Management Area. Wild turkey, squirrel, and deer roam this forested 22,000-acre area, which has hunting, a rifle range, and a 200-acre lake for boating and fishing. It has approximately 70 mi of hiking trails and 75 primitive campsites. | Jones Spring Rd.; 6 mi west of I–81 off Rte. 9 | 304/822–3551 | Free | Daily.

ON THE CALENDAR

OCT.: Apple Butter Festival. You can watch apple butter cooking in open kettles—and buy some to take home—at this Columbus Day weekend festival, which also has kids' contests and more than 200 arts and crafts booths. | 304/258–3738.

Lodging

Cacapon Lodge. The "new" lodge in Cacapon Resort State Park was completed in 1956 and has 48 rooms filled with locally made oak furniture; the black-walnut paneled main lounge has a wood-burning fireplace. The 11-room Old Inn, with hand-hewn log beams and stone chimneys, was built in the 1930s by the Civilian Conservation Corps. There are also 44 cabins, 13 of which are deluxe, with fireplaces, furnaces, and kitchenettes, and available year-round. Cable TV is available in some rooms. The lodge is 10 mi south of Berkeley Springs on U.S. 522, in Cacapon Resort State Park. Dining room, picnic area. Some kitchenettes. Driving range, 18-hole golf course, putting green, tennis. | Hwy. 522 | 304/258–1022 or 800/225–5982 | fax 304/258–5323 | www.cacaponresort.com | 59 rooms, 44 cabins | $51–$65, $60–$146 cabins (7–day minimum stay in summer) | AE, DC, MC, V.

★ **Coolfont Resort.** On 1,350 wooded acres, this rustic resort, complete with rocking chairs and hanging quilts, emphasizes recreation and activities—from chamber concerts to watercolor workshops. Rooms are in the stately 1912 Manor House, are individually decorated, and have fireplaces. The A-frame chalet-style cottages are nestled in pine groves throughout the resort grounds. The resort is 4 mi west on Route 9. Bar (with entertainment), dining room, picnic area. Some refrigerators. Indoor pool. Hot tub, massage. Tennis. Exercise equipment, hiking. Beach, boating. Sleigh rides. Kids' programs, playground. Laundry facilities. | 1777 Cold Run Valley Rd. | 304/258–4500 or 800/888–8768 (outside WV) | fax 304/258–5499 | www.coolfont.com | 22 rooms, 34 cottages | $272, $328 cottages | AE, D, MC, V.

The Country Inn and Renaissance Spa. The white-columned front porch, colonial furnishings, and English garden at this inn will transport you back to another era; the spa facility will make you want to never leave. Lavish rooms are filled with antiques, and many have four-poster canopy beds. One block from downtown Berkeley Springs. Dining room. Cable TV. Massage, spa. Business services. | 207 S. Washington St. | 304/258–2210 or 800/822–6630 | fax 304/258–3986 | www.countryinnwv.com | 67 rooms (13 with shared bath) | $39–$165 | AE, D, DC, MC, V.

Highlawn Inn. Built in the 1890s by Algernon Unger as a gift for his bride, this restored home later served as a boarding house. The interior has ornate fireplaces and period furnishings. Rooms are furnished with antiques, and most have either a fireplace or hot tub. Complimentary snacks are served in the afternoon. Complimentary breakfast. Some in-room hot tubs. Cable TV, no room phones. No kids. | 304 Market St. | 304/258–5700 or 888/290–4163 | www.virtualcities.com | 12 rooms in 4 buildings, 2 cottages | $85–$140, $180–$300 cottages | MC, V.

BETHANY

MAP 17, C3

(Nearby towns also listed: Weirton, Wheeling)

Bethany was founded in 1815 by Alexander Campbell, a leader in religious and educational reform. In 1840 he chartered Bethany College, which remains the focal point of this town of 1,000. A walking tour of the historic district goes past homes dating back 200 years; tour maps are available at the Historic Bethany Center, on campus.

Information: Historic Bethany | Historic Bethany, Delta Tau Delta Founder's House, Main St. (Rte. 67) 26032 | historic@mail.bethanywv.edu | www.bethanywv.edu | 304/829–7285.

Attractions

Bethany College. A four-year private liberal arts college affiliated with the Disciples of Christ, the 1,600-acre campus is home to 750 students from more than 33 states and 24 countries. You can take a self-guided tour of the campus or arrange a guided tour through the Historic Bethany Center. | Main St. (Rte. 67) | 304/829–7000 or 800/922–7611 | www.bethanywv.edu | Free | Daily.

The Campbell Mansion. This national landmark home was built by Irish immigrant and founder of Bethany College, Alexander Campbell, between 1792 and 1840. Eighteen of the 24 rooms—including a hexagonal study and a schoolroom—are furnished with period antiques. You'll even find wallpaper from 1840 in the guest wing. | ³⁄₄ mi east of Bethany College on Hwy. 67 | 304/829–7285 | $4 | Apr.–Oct., Tues.–Sat. 10–12 and 1–4, Sun. 2–4, closed Mon.; Nov.–Mar. by appt. only.

Historic Bethany. Housed in the historic 1858 Federal-style Delta Tau Delta Founder's House, this organization offers tours to the seven major historic sites in Bethany, which include: the 1858 Gothic-style Bethany College building, Old Main; the 1832 Campbell Study (outside the Campbell Mansion); God's Acre, the Campbell family graveyard; an old church meeting house circa 1852; and the 1910 Oglebay Gates, which guard the entrance to the Bethany College Campus. | 304/829–7285 | www.bethanywv.edu | $4 | Tours Apr.–Oct., Tues.–Sat. 10 and 4; Nov.–Mar. by appt. only.

Castlemans Run Lake Wildlife Management Area. You can cast your line into a 22-acre fishing lake or go hunting or trapping at this wildlife area, approximately 3 mi south of Bethany on County Route 32. | County Rte. 32 | 304/367–2720 | Free | Daily dawn to dusk.

Lodging

Gresham House. Affiliated with Bethany College, this facility less than 1 mi from campus is used for academic conferences and is open to guests. You'll have access to the college recreation center, which includes an indoor pool, racquetball courts, and a weight room. Cable TV. No smoking. | Rtes. 67 and 88 at the Leadership Center—Bethany College | 304/829–4343 | fax 304/829–7626 | 40 rooms | $63 | AE, D, DC, MC, V.

BLUEFIELD

MAP 17, B7

(Nearby town also listed: Princeton)

Founded in 1889 as the regional headquarters of the Norfolk and Western Railway, Bluefield was named for the chicory flowers growing on the surrounding hillsides. The city of 11,500, which straddles the border between West Virginia and Virginia, draws baseball enthusiasts in summer when the Bluefield Orioles play at Bowen Field.

Information: Mercer County Convention and Visitors Bureau | 500 Bland St., 24701 | 304/325–8438 or 800/221–3206 | staff@mccvb.com | www.mccvb.com.

Attractions

Bowen Field. Built in City Park in 1939, the field is home to the Bluefield Orioles, a minor league baseball team that's a farm team to the Baltimore Orioles. | On Stadium Dr. | 540/326–1326 | Admission varies per event | June–Aug.; call for hrs.

Bramwell Walking Tour. Nine miles north of Bluefield on U.S. 52, Bramwell (population 600) was once considered the richest town in the world, counting 14 millionaires among its residents. You can take a self-guided tour of its stately mansions; tour maps are available at the Bramwell Town Hall. | 100 Symmons Ave., Bramwell | 304/248–7114 | Free | Weekdays 8–5, closed weekends.

Eastern Regional Coal Archives. The collection chronicles coal mining history through artifacts, old mining equipment, films, and diaries. | Craft Memorial Library, 600 Commerce St. | 304/325–3943 | Free | Exhibits Mon.–Thurs. 9:30–8, Fri.–Sat. 9:30–5, closed Sun.; access to archives by appointment only.

Panther State Forest. Hikers tread where mountain lions once roamed in this rugged 7,810-acre woodland, which offers fishing, hunting, picnicking, concessions, and a swimming pool. The forest is about 50 mi west of Bluefield off U.S. 52. | Rte. 3/2, Panther Creek Rd., Panther | 304/938–2252 or 800/CALL–WVA | www.wvparks.com/panther | Free | Daily 6 AM–10 PM.

Pinnacle Rock State Park. A towering sandstone pillar is the namesake of this 250-acre park, which has a seasonally stocked 15-acre lake, picnic shelters, and hiking trails. The park is about 10 mi west of Bluefield on U.S. 52. | 304/589–5307 | www.wvparks.com/pinnaclerock | Free | Daily 6 AM–10 PM.

ON THE CALENDAR

MAY: *Bluefield Mountain Festival.* Carnival rides, national headline acts, and road races—including a 1-mi fun run, a 5K race, and a 10K race—highlight this springtime celebration. | 304/327–7184.

Lodging

Country Chalet. In a secluded rural setting with mountain views, this three-story, shake cedar A-frame has floor-to-ceiling windows, a deck, and a stone fireplace. The chalet is off I–77 at Exit 1 (Bluefield ext.). Permission is required to bring kids under 12. Complimentary breakfast. Some pets allowed. No smoking. | New Hope Rd., Box 176B | 304/487–2120 | www.countrychalet.com | 2 rooms | $40–$70 | No credit cards.

Holiday Inn. Seven miles off I–77 Exit 1 (Bluefield exit), this two-story motel has mountain views, a stone fireplace in the lobby, and a "picture window" skylight in the cafe. Restaurant. In-room data ports. Cable TV. Pool. Sauna. Some pets allowed. | U.S. 460/52 Bypass | 304/325–6170 | fax 304/323–2451 | www.holiday-inn.com | 118 rooms | $79 | AE, D, DC, MC, V.

Ramada Inn. Approximately 6 mi off I–77 Exit 1 (Bluefield exit), this two-story motel has a view of the scenic East River Mountain. Restaurant, bar (with entertainment), room service. Some refrigerators. Cable TV. Indoor pool. Hot tub. Exercise equipment. Business services. | 3175 E. Cumberland Rd. | 304/325–5421 | fax 304/325–6045 | 98 rooms | $75 | AE, D, DC, V.

BRIDGEPORT

MAP 17, D4

(Nearby towns also listed: Clarksburg, Fairmont, Grafton)

Founded as a trading post in 1764, Bridgeport was chartered in 1816 and incorporated in 1887. Two miles east of Clarksburg on U.S. 50, it still draws travelers, who stop here for food, fuel, or shopping in the town's antique shops. With 8,000 residents, Bridgeport retains a small-town atmosphere while supporting light industry and small businesses.

Information: Bridgeport/Clarksburg Convention and Visitors Bureau | 109 Platinum Dr., Ste. B, East Point Business Park 26330 | 304/842–7272 or 800/368–4324 | www.bridgeport-clarksburg.com.

Lodging
Days Inn. One-half mile off I–79 Exit 119 (Clarksburg/Bridgeport exit), this two-story motel is within both the Bridgeport and Clarksburg city limits. Restaurant, bar (with entertainment), complimentary breakfast. Cable TV. Indoor pool. Hot tub. Business services. | 112 Tolley Dr. | 304/842–7371 | fax 304/842–3904 | 62 rooms | $43–$70 | AE, D, DC, MC, V.

BUCKHANNON

MAP 17, D4

(Nearby towns also listed: Elkins, Philippi, Weston)

The first Europeans to settle here were John and Samuel Pringle, who deserted Fort Pitt during the French and Indian War and took up residence in the hollow of a sycamore tree. After learning that a peace treaty had ended the war, they left their hiding place but pledged to return. In 1768, Samuel came back to establish a permanent settlement, the first west of the Allegheny Mountains between Pittsburgh and the Gulf of Mexico. Today, the town of 6,820 is county seat and the economic hub of Upshur County.

Information: Buckhannon Convention and Visitors Bureau | 16 S. Kanawha St. 26201 | 304/472–1722 | justin@wvlink.com | www.wvlink.com/upshur.

ON THE CALENDAR
MAY: *West Virginia Strawberry Festival.* This family event in downtown Buckhannon has strawberry pie–eating contests, strawberry cook-offs, a kids' strawberry blond contest, street parties every night, and three parades. | 304/472–1722.

Attractions
Audra State Park. Camp along the banks of the Middle Fork River in this 355-acre park, which has a riverside beach and bathhouse as well as hiking, picnicking, camping, and a playground. The park is about 15 mi northeast of Buckhannon off Route 33; take Talbott Road exit to Audra Park Road | Audra Park Rd. | 304/457–1162 | www.wvparks.com/audra | Free | Daily 6 AM–10 PM.

BUCKHANNON

INTRO
ATTRACTIONS
DINING
LODGING

West Virginia State Wildlife Center. You can see nearly 50 species of native wildlife—from bald eagles to black bears—living in their natural habitat. There's also a trout pond and picnic area. The center is 12 mi south of Buckhannon on Route 20 South. | Rte. 20 S at French Creek | 304/924–6211 | $2 | May–Oct. daily; Apr. and Nov. weekends and holidays only; Dec.–Mar. hrs vary.

West Virginia Wesleyan College. Founded in 1890 as a liberal arts college closely related to the Methodist Church, the school has an enrollment of 1,600. | 59 College Ave. | 304/473–8000 | www.wvwc.edu | Free | Daily.

Wesley Chapel. Built as part of the mid-20th-century expansion efforts of college president Dr. Stanley H. Martin, this typical Georgian brick chapel with columns is the largest in the state. | Center of campus, off Camden Ave. | 304/473–8007 | Free | Tours available weekdays 8–4, open daily 7–10.

Lodging

Bicentennial Motel. Two blocks from West Virginian Wesleyan College, this two-story brick hostelry is next door to an antique mall. Rooms are standard sized and individually decorated with the usual modular motel furniture. Restaurant, bar, picnic area, room service. Some refrigerators. Cable TV. Pool, wading pool. Playground. Business services. | 90 E. Main St. | 304/472–5000 or 800/762–5137 | fax 304/472–9159 | 55 rooms | $58 | AE, D, DC, MC, V.

Centennial Motel. This one-story brick motel in downtown Buckhannon has views of the nearby mountains. The motel is within 1 block of several restaurants, on the city's main commercial strip. Some refrigerators, cable TV. Some pets allowed. | 22 N. Locust St. | 304/472–4100 | fax 304/472–9158 | 26 rooms | $53 | AE, D, DC, MC, V.

Deer Park Inn and Lodge. Four miles east of town on 100 acres with a pond, a meadow, and mountain views, this inn is a turn-of-the-century log farmhouse. Antiques and period furniture fill the interior; there is also a Victorian-style wing. Complimentary Continental breakfast. Cable TV. Library. No smoking. | Heavner Grove Rd. | 304/472–8400 or 800/296–8430 | fax 304/472–5363 | www.deerparkcountryinn.com | 4 rooms, 2 suites | $100–$110, $100–$210 suites | AE, D, DC, MC, V.

A Governor's Inn. Daniel Farnsworth, the state's second governor, built this brick Victorian mansion in 1863; today, the house is a bread-and-breakfast with a landscaped courtyard and a wraparound veranda in downtown Buckhannon. Some in-room hot tubs. Cable TV, in-room VCRs. Baby-sitting. Some pets allowed. No smoking. | 76 E. Main St. | 304/472–2516 | fax 304/472–1613 | 6 rooms (1 with shared bath) | $69–$125 | AE, MC, V.

CHARLESTON

MAP 17, B6

(Suburb also listed: Nitro)

Founded in 1794, Charleston became the state capital in 1885 after a political tug-of-war with Wheeling. Wheeling served as capital from 1863, when West Virginia attained statehood, until 1870, when the state legislature voted to move the capital to Charleston. A boat floated officials and state records down the Ohio and Kanawha rivers to Charleston. Five years later a new legislature moved the capital back to Wheeling. In 1877 yet another legislature decided to let the citizens vote on the issue (surprisingly, Wheeling wasn't one of the choices), and in 1885 the capital was permanently moved back to Charleston. Today, the gold-leaf dome of the State Capitol dominates the city's skyline.

As West Virginia's largest city, Charleston has a population of 57,300 and is the state's political, cultural, and business center. Natural resources—such as coal, oil, natural gas, and salt—have contributed significantly to the region's economy and development, as has the manufacturing of glass and chemicals. At the confluence of the Kanawha and Elk rivers, and at the intersection of three interstate highways (I–64, I–77, and I–79), Charleston plays an important role in the state's trade, commerce, and banking. Museums, historic neighborhoods, academic institutions, shopping districts, and a riverfront location all add to Charleston's urban character.

Information: Charleston Convention and Visitors Bureau | 200 Civic Center Dr. 25301 | 304/344–5075 or 800/733–5469 | cwalker@intelos.net | www.charlestonwv.com.

NEIGHBORHOODS

East End. An eclectic mix of architectural styles, from Victorian to Spanish Colonial, has earned this quiet residential neighborhood a designation as a historical district. The area extends from downtown east to the Capitol Complex and from the Kanawha River to Interstate 77/64.

West End. To the west of downtown Charleston, the West End extends from I–64 to Patrick Street and from the Kanawha River into the hills overlooking the city. The neighborhood is a mix of residential buildings and small, locally owned businesses near the riverfront, while the hills to the north are crisscrossed with steep, narrow streets lined with quaint bungalows and opulent mansions.

South Hills. Across the Kanawha River, this neighborhood is home to many of the city's elite. Although there are some modest houses and a few specialty shops here, the area is known for its elegant older homes and million-dollar estates perched on hilltops overlooking the city.

Kanawha City. This community spreads out over the flat plain across the river from the State Capitol, and is dissected by MacCorkle Avenue, a busy thoroughfare. A few blocks to either side of MacCorkle, the commercial area gives way to tree-lined residential streets.

WALKING TOUR

A Stroll Through Downtown Charleston (approx. 4 hours, 45 minutes)
This walking tour starts near the corner of Greenbrier Street and Kanawha Boulevard, in front of the **State Capitol,** which was designed in the classic Italian-Renaissance style. Guided tours are available. From the capitol, turn left and walk ½ block on Kanawha Boulevard to the **Governor's Mansion,** a Georgian Colonial building that has been home to the state's chief executive since 1925.

Continue west along tree-lined Kanawha Boulevard for 10 blocks. The grand homes on the right side of the street are a testament to the fortunes made in coal, oil, and natural gas during the late 19th and early 20th centuries. On the left, pleasure boats and the occasional turn-of-the-century stern-wheeler ply the waters of the **Kanawha River,** where you might also see a string of barges hauling coal and chemical products to distant markets.

The **Union Building,** the state's first skyscraper built in 1911, stands at the intersection of Kanawha Boulevard and Capitol Street. Turn right on **Capitol Street,** the heart of the city's downtown. Continue on Capitol to the **Victorian Block,** a group of restored buildings, some dating back to 1887, between Virginia and Quarrier streets.

Walking along Capitol Street, you will pass old brick buildings housing specialty shops, ethnic restaurants, bookstores, and coffee houses—a good place to stop for a latte or a bite to eat. Now double back on Capitol Street to Quarrier Street, turn left, and go four blocks to the corner of Broad Street, where the impressive steeple and pointed arches of **St. John's Episcopal Church** combine elements of Gothic and Romanesque architecture.

Stay on Quarrier Street, which traverses the heart of the **East End Historical District.** Most of the homes here were built between 1895 and 1925 and reflect an array of architectural styles—Victorian, Colonial, Georgian, Spanish, Greek Revival, and Renaissance.

Quarrier ends at Greenbrier Street. Cross Greenbrier to the **Cultural Center,** where you can visit the state history museum. The tour ends here, near where you started, on the grounds of the **State Capitol Complex,** which includes the Cultural Center, the State Capitol, the Governor's Mansion, and landscaped grounds with statues and fountains.

TRANSPORTATION

Airport: Yeager Airport, 3 mi from downtown off I-64 Exit 99 (Greenbrier St. exit), has daily non-stop flights to Atlanta, Charlotte, Chicago, Cincinnati, Cleveland, Detroit, Philadelphia, Pittsburgh, Roanoke, and Washington, DC | 304/345–0661.

Amtrak: Passenger rail service is available three times a week on the *Cardinal,* traveling from Washington, DC through the Midwest. | 350 MacCorkle Ave., 25304 | 304/342–6766.

Bus Lines: Greyhound has bus transportation to cities across the country. | 300 Reynolds St. | 304/357–0056.

Intra-Area Transportation: Kanawha Regional Transit Authority (KRT) has bus service for Charleston and points throughout Kanawha Valley. | 1550 4th Ave. | 304/343–7586.

Attractions

ART AND ARCHITECTURE

State Capitol. The city's most prominent architectural feature, the 23-karat gold-leaf dome of the Capitol towers 293 ft above street level and is 5 ft taller than the U.S. Capitol. Designed by Cass Gilbert, architect of the U.S. Supreme Court, the buff limestone building took eight years to complete and has 14 acres of floor space. Dedicated in 1932, it is considered one of the finest 20th-century examples of classic Italian-Renaissance architecture in the U.S. A 10,000-piece hand-cut crystal chandelier hangs in the rotunda. Guided tours are available. | 1900 Kanawha Blvd. E | 304/558–4839 or 800/225–5982 | Free | Weekdays 9–3, Sat. 1–5, closed Sun.

Governor's Mansion. A redbrick building with a white columned portico distinguishes this 30-room Georgian Colonial mansion, which sits on the Capitol Complex grounds overlooking the Kanawha River. Official state rooms occupy the first floor; the second floor serves as private residence for the governor and his family. | 1716 Kanawha Blvd. E | 304/558–3588 | Free | Tours Thurs. and Fri. by appointment.

CULTURE, EDUCATION, AND HISTORY

The Cultural Center. This vast multipurpose building houses the state archives, a reference library, the state history museum, and a 500-seat theater used for films, concerts, lectures, theatrical performances, and radio broadcasts. | 1900 Kanawha Blvd. E | 304/558–0220 | www.wvdch@wvculture.org. | Free | Weekdays 9–5, weekends 1–5.

Broadcast from the **Cultural Center Theater** and heard on 130 stations nationwide, *Mountain Stage* is a live public-radio show presenting internationally known musicians playing blues, jazz, folk, and rock. Plays, movies and other theatrical events are also staged in this 450-seat oak-lined theater. | 1900 Kanawha Blvd. E | 304/342–5757 or 342/556–4900 | www.wvpubrad.org | $9 | Sun. 6 PM; other performance times vary.

Tracing the state's history from prehistoric Native American tribes through the Civil War and the oil and coal mining booms of the early 20th century, the **West Virginia State Museum** is a 23,000-square-ft exhibit space in the Cultural Center. A gallery displays works by West Virginia artists. | 1900 Kanawha Blvd. E | 304/558–0220 | Free | Weekdays 9–5, weekends 1–5.

West Virginia State College. Founded in 1891 as a land-grant college for black students, WVSC voluntarily desegregated in 1954, attracting a culturally diverse student body and staff. It still serves as a center of African-American culture. With 5,000 students, it is the largest college in the Kanawha Valley. The campus is 9 mi west of Charleston on I–64. | Barron Dr., Institute | 304/766–3221 or 800/987–2112 | www.wvsc.edu | Free | Daily.

MUSEUMS

Sunrise Museum. Built in 1905 by William A. MacCorkle, the ninth governor of West Virginia, the 36-room Sunrise Mansion now contains a planetarium and hands-on science and technology exhibits. Torquilstone, a mansion built by MacCorkle's son in 1928, exhibits 19th- and 20th-century American artworks. The two buildings are surrounded by landscaped gardens and nature trails on 16 wooded acres overlooking the Kanawha River. The museum is across South Side Bridge from downtown Charleston. | 746 Myrtle Rd. | 304/344–8035 | www.sunrisemuseum.org | $4 | Wed.–Sat. 11–5, Sun. 12–5, closed Mon.–Tues.

PARKS, NATURAL AREAS, AND OUTDOOR RECREATION

Coonskin Park. This park has a lake, an 18-hole golf course, putt-putt golf, a swimming pool, tennis courts, nature trails, and a restaurant, all 5 mi north of downtown Charleston off Route 114. | 2000 Coonskin Dr. | 304/341–8000 | Free | Daily.

Elk River Scenic Drive. From Charleston, Route 4 winds along the Elk River 20 mi north to Clendenin, where you can drive a particularly scenic stretch another 26 mi north to the town of Clay. The route follows the Elk River through mountain valleys filled with evergreen forests. | 800/225–5982.

Kanawha State Forest. The 9,300-acre forest has hiking and cross-country ski trails, horseback riding, fishing, hunting, swimming, playgrounds, and campsites. The forest is 7 mi south of Charleston. | 304/558–3500 | Kanawha Forest Dr. | www.wvparks.com/kanawha | Free | Daily 6 AM–10 PM.

SHOPPING

Cabin Creek Quilts Cooperative. A living cottage industry, all the quilts and other quilted items sold in this shop, are completed in local quilters' homes. You'll often find the shopkeepers quilting as they run the store. | 4208 Malden Dr., Malden | 304/925–9499 | Free | Mon.–Sat. 10–5, Sun. 1–4.

Capitol Market. Inside this Italian-style marketplace, you'll find stores specializing in wine, cheese, fresh seafood, meats, and coffes. Outside, local farmers sell their seasonal produce: tomatoes and zucchini in summer, pumpkins in fall, and holiday trees in winter. | 800 Smith St. | 304/344–1905 | Free | Mon.–Sat. 9–6, Sun. 12–5.

Charleston Town Center. A three-story waterfall in the center court anchors this shopper's heaven. With over 100 stores spread over 1 million sq. ft., the Charleston Town Center is one of the largest downtown malls in the country. | 3000 Charleston Town Center | 304/345–9535 | Free | Mon.–Sat. 10–9, Sun. 12:30–6.

SPECTATOR SPORTS

Charleston Alley Cats. This class-A minor league baseball team affiliated with the Toronto Blue Jays plays every day during the season, either at home in Whatt Powell Park, or away. | 3403 MacCorkle Ave. | 304/344–2287 | www.charlestonalleycats.com | $5–$7 | Daily Apr.–Sept.

ON THE CALENDAR

MAY: *Vandalia Gathering.* A celebration of folk life, this Memorial Day weekend festival at the Capitol Complex includes mountain crafts, storytellers, a liar's contest, clogging, and traditional dance, as well as fiddle, banjo, and dulcimer competitions. | 304/558–0220.

AUG.–SEPT.: *Stern-wheel Regatta Festival.* Paddleboats churning across the Kanawha River are the highlight of this riverfront celebration, with towboat contests, deckhand competitions, rubber ducky races, nightly entertainment, and more. | 304/344–5075 or 800/733–5469 | www.charlestonwv.com.

Dining

INEXPENSIVE

Blossom Deli. Contemporary. Deli by day, restaurant by night, this eatery caters to locals and downtown business people. Try the spicy Thai shrimp, peppercorn steaks, or walnut-encrusted salmon. | 904 Quarrier St. | 304/345–2233 | Closed Sun. No dinner Mon. | $9–$20 | AE, D, DC, MC, V.

MODERATE

Cagney's. Continental. Etched glass and brass give a turn-of-the-century feel to this multiroomed restaurant. Specialities include the prime rib and the Cajun chicken pasta. Kids' menu available. | 400 Court St. | 304/345–3463 | $12–$18 | AE, D, DC, MC, V.

Chef Dan's. Italian. Bright Tuscan artwork and statuary fill three large dining areas in a casual, bistro-like setting. Try the pizza, the fresh pasta, or the shrimp pesto ravioli. Kids' menu available. Beer and wine only. No smoking. | 222 Broad St. | 304/344–2433 | Reservations not accepted | Closed Mon. and Sun. No lunch Sat. | $8–$13 | AE, D, DC, MC, V.

Joe Fazio's. Italian. Try the veal dishes, the chicken cacciatore, or the large Italian sampler platters; you won't leave hungry. Candle-lit tables fill several softly lit dining areas; photos of presidents and celebrities who have dined here adorn the walls. | 1008 Bullitt St. | 304/344–3071 | Closed Mon. No lunch | $10–$21 | AE, DC, MC, V.

Laury's. Continental. High ceilings, chandeliers, and white linen tablecloths create an elegant setting in this renovated train depot overlooking the Kanawha River and the Charleston skyline. Specialities include rack of veal, chateaubriand, and filet mignon stuffed with crabmeat. | 350 MacCorkle Ave. SE | 304/343–0055 | Closed Sun. No lunch Sat. | $13–$35 | AE, D, DC, MC, V.

Tarragon Room. Continental. This formal restaurant in the downtown Marriott is several steps above most hotel dining rooms: Guest chefs from around the world visit regularly, preparing special menus during their stay. The regular menu has a selection of meat, seafood, and pasta dishes. | 200 Lee St. | 304/353–3636 | Closed Sun. No lunch | $15–$24 | AE, D, DC, MC, V.

Tidewater Grill. Seafood. A mesquite-wood grill, an open kitchen, and a large dining room and bar make this restaurant a lively place. Fresh seafood is flown in every other day; try the crab cakes in mustard sauce or the surf and turf combos. Steaks, pasta, and sandwiches are also on the menu. Open-air dining. | 1060 Charleston Town Ctr. | 304/345–2620 | $14–$22 | AE, D, DC, MC, V.

Lodging

INEXPENSIVE

Red Roof Inn. This chain is 5 mi from the State Capitol Complex off I–64 Exit 95 (MacCorkle Ave. exit) in Kanawha City. Cable TV. Business services. Some pets allowed. | 6305 MacCorkle Ave. SE | 304/925–6953 | fax 304/925–8111 | i0059@redroof.com | www.redroof.com | 108 rooms | $43 | AE, D, DC, MC, V.

MODERATE

Brass Pineapple Bed and Breakfast. You can eat breakfast on the veranda at this 1910 Victorian home in Charleston's historic district. It's one block from the river and 2 mi from downtown. The small, Romantic-era rooms are outfitted with antiques, designer comforters and robes, and elaborate hanging lamps or ceiling fans. Complimentary Continental breakfast. In-room data ports, cable TV, in-room VCRs. | 1611 Virginia St. E | 304/344–0748 | fax 304/344–0748 | 6 rooms | $89–$129 | www.bbonline.com/wv/brasspineapple | AE, DC, MC, V.

Hampton Inn. Off I–64 at Exit 58 (westbound, Civic Center/Washington Ave. exit; eastbound, Virginia St. exit), this five-story motel is one block from the Charleston Civic Center and 2 mi from the State Capitol Complex. Complimentary Continental breakfast. Cable TV. Pool. Business services. Airport shuttle. | 1 Virginia St. W | 304/343–9300 | fax 304/342–9393 | 112 rooms | $84 | www.hamptoninn.com | AE, D, DC, MC, V.

Hampton Inn—Southridge. This six-story hostelry is 5 mi southeast of downtown in a commercial area next to three major shopping centers. The hotel is off I–64 at Exit 58A (Oakwood Rd. exit). Complimentary Continental breakfast. In-room data ports, some kitchenettes, some microwaves, some refrigerators, some in-room hot tubs. Cable TV. Indoor pool. Hot tub. Exercise equipment. Laundry facilities. Business services, airport shuttle. | 1 Preferred Pl. | 304/746–4646 | fax 304/746–4665 | www.hamptoninn.com | 104 rooms | $83 | AE, D, DC, MC, V.

Kanawha City Motor Lodge. This motel is 3 mi from downtown in a commercial area across the river from the State Capitol Complex. Rooms are spare and no-frills; the motel across the street from the Charleston Area Medical Center and 1 mi west of the University of Charleston. Refrigerators, cable TV. Business services. | 3103 MacCorkle Ave. SE | 304/344–2461 | fax 304/345–1419 | 50 rooms | $61 | AE, D, DC, MC, V.

EXPENSIVE

Embassy Suites. Only two blocks from three major interstates (I–64, I–77, and I–79), the Embassy is in downtown Charleston. The nine-story atrium is landscaped with greenery, waterfalls, and babbling brooks. Restaurant, bar, complimentary breakfast, room service. Indoor pool. Hot tub, spa. Gym. Business services. | 300 Court St. | 304/347–8700 | fax 304/347–8737 | www.embassysuites.com | 253 suites | $99–$169 | AE, D, DC, MC, V.

Holiday Inn—Charleston House. In the downtown business district and 5 mi from the airport, this 12-story hostelry has a restaurant and bar on the top floor with views of the city. Restaurant, bar, dining room. In-room data ports. Cable TV. Pool. Beauty salon. Exercise equipment. Business services, airport shuttle. Some pets allowed. | 600 Kanawha Blvd. | 304/344–4092 | fax 304/345–4847 | www.holiday-inn.com | 256 rooms | $99–$125 | AE, D, DC, MC, V.

Holiday Inn—Civic Center. This six-story chain is next to the civic center, Charleston's main entertainment and concert venue, in the central downtown area. Restaurant, bar. Some refrigerators, room service. In-room data ports. Cable TV. Pool. Laundry facilities. Business services, airport shuttle, free parking. | 100 Civic Center Dr. | 304/345–0600 | fax 304/343–1322 | www.holiday-inn.com | 197 rooms | $99 | AE, D, DC, MC, V.

VERY EXPENSIVE

Marriott Town Center. Two miles from the State Capitol Complex in central downtown Charleston, this 12-story high-rise with attached parking facility is across from the Town Center. The formal restaurant (*see* Tarragon Room) is popular. Restaurant, in-room data ports, bar, dining room. Some refrigerators. Cable TV. Indoor pool. Hot tub. Exercise equipment. Laundry facilities. Business services. | 200 Lee St. E | 304/345–6500 | fax 304/353–3722 | www.charlestonmarriott.com | 352 rooms | $109–$275 | AE, D, DC, MC, V.

CHARLES TOWN

MAP 17, F2

(Nearby towns also listed: Harpers Ferry, Shepherdstown)

Named after George Washington's youngest brother, who platted the town in 1786 and named several streets after family members, Charles Town is rich in history. Abolitionist John Brown was tried for treason and hanged here. The town of 3,100 is the county seat of Jefferson County, known for its fruit orchards and beef and dairy cattle as well as industries such as textiles and quarrying.

Information: Jefferson County Chamber of Commerce | 201 Frontage Rd., Box 426, 25414 | 304/725–2055 or 800/624–0577 | www.jeffersoncounty.com/chamber.

Attractions

Charles Town Races. Horse racing here dates back to the 18th century. There's thorough-bred racing day and night, as well as video gambling on 1,500 machines. The races are 1 mi east of town on U.S. 340 N. | Flowing Springs Rd. | 304/725–7001 or 800/795–7001 | www.ctownraces.com | Free | Thurs.–Sat. 7:15 PM, Sun. 1, closed Mon.–Wed.

Jefferson County Courthouse. John Brown's trial was held here in October 1859. He was convicted of treason and sentenced to death for raiding the U.S. Arsenal in Harpers Ferry. | 100 E. Washington St. | 304/725–9761 or 800/848–TOUR | Free | Tours Mon.–Sat. 10–4, closed Sun.

Jefferson County Museum. John Brown's gun and the wagon that carried him to his execution are displayed here, along with Washington family memorabilia and Civil War artifacts. | 200 E. Washington St. | 304/725–8628 | Free | Tours Apr.–Nov., Mon.–Sat. 10–4, closed Sun.

Site of the John Brown Gallows. During John Brown's hanging in December 1859, some 1,500 troops surrounded the scaffold erected next to the courthouse. The site is marked by stones reportedly taken from his jail cell. | 635 S. Samuel St. | 304/725–9761 | Free | Daily.

Zion Episcopal Church. This church housed Union troops during the Civil War. The cemetery, a National Historic Landmark, contains the graves of 75 members of George Washington's family. | 300 E. Congress St. | 304/725–5312 | Free | By appointment only.

ON THE CALENDAR
JUNE, SEPT.: *Mountain Heritage Arts and Crafts Festival.* Held each spring and fall, this festival showcases artisans from across the country as well as nationally known country and bluegrass musicians. | 304/725–2055.
AUG.: *Jefferson County Fair.* This is a traditional county fair with livestock shows, carnival rides, and entertainment. | 304/725–2055.

Lodging

Hillbrook. In a rural setting 6 mi southwest of Charles Town, this rambling wood-and-stone Tudor-style country inn is surrounded by terraced gardens. You are required to have dinner there (which comes in seven courses) at least one night during your stay. Dining room, bar, complimentary breakfast. Some refrigerators, some in-room hot tubs, some TVs. Library. Business services. | Summit Point Rd. | 304/725–4223 or 800/304–4223 | fax 304/725–4455 | www.hillbrookinn.com | 11 rooms | $250–$325 | AE, D, MC, V.

Towne House. This two-story motel is across from the Charles Town Races, 1 mi east of downtown. Rooms are standard-sized, with basic decor; the motel is in a commercial area within 5 blocks of several fast-food restaurants. Restaurant. Refrigerators. Cable TV. Pool. Business services. | 549 E. Washington St. | 304/725–8441 or 800/227–2339 | fax 304/725–5484 | 115 rooms | $38–$50 | AE, DC, D, MC, V.

Turf. Originally built in 1955, this two-story brick motel is next to the Charles Town Races racetrack, and 5 mi east of Harper's Ferry. Although basic, rooms are ultra-clean, and have framed fabric wall-hangings. Restaurant, bar, room service. Some refrigerators, some in-room hot tubs. Cable TV. Pool. Business services. Some pets allowed (fee). | 608 E. Washington St. | 304/725–2081 or 800/422–8873 | fax 304/728–7605 | 46 rooms, 3 suites | $66, $80–$155 suites | AE, D, DC, MC, V.

Washington House Inn. This 1899 Victorian residence was built by descendants of George Washington's brothers, John Augustine and Samuel, and is filled with period furnishings and fireplaces with carved oak mantles. Extra niceties like fresh flowers and terry-cloth robes make the Victorian-style guest rooms homey. The inn is in the center of colonial Charles Town, and is 8 blocks from Charleston Gaming, 3 blocks from the Old Opera House, and 2 blocks from the Jefferson County Court House. Afternoon snacks are complimentary. Complimentary breakfast. In-room data ports, cable TV. Business services, airport shuttle. No pets. No smoking. | 216 S. George St. | 304/725–7923 or 800/297–6957 | fax 304/728–5150 | www.washingtonhouseinnwv.com | 6 rooms (shower only) | $125 | AE, D, MC, V.

CLARKSBURG

(Nearby towns also listed: Grafton, Philippi)

Founded in 1785, Clarksburg is the birthplace of Gen. Thomas J. "Stonewall" Jackson, born here in 1824. Jackson's parents died shortly after he was born and he was raised in Weston by his uncle. The town served as an important supply depot for Union troops. After the war, immigrant laborers moved to the area for factory jobs. Clarksburg, population 18,000, is also home to the new FBI Criminal Justice Information facility (closed to the public).

Information: Bridgeport/Clarksburg Convention and Visitors Bureau | 109 Platinum Dr., Ste. B, East Point Business Park 26330 | 304/842–7272 or 800/368–4324 | www.bridgeport-clarksburg.com.

Attractions
North Bend Rail Trail. Suitable for hiking, biking, and horseback riding, the trail follows the old B & O Railroad bed 72 mi to Parkersburg. You can pick up the trailhead in Wolf Summit, approximately 10 mi west of Clarksburg off U.S. 50. | 304/643–2500 or 800/899–6278 | Free | Daily.

Fort New Salem. A frontier village of 20 log buildings—relocated here from sites throughout the state—brings pioneer history to life; costumed interpreters present folklore and craft demonstrations. The village is near the Salem-Teikyo campus, 12 mi west of Clarksburg off U.S. 50, on Rte 23. | Rte. 23 | 304/782–5245 | $4 | Memorial Day–Labor Day, Wed.–Sun. 10–5, closed Mon.–Tues.

Stealey-Goff-Vance House. Built in 1807, the city's oldest house has been restored as a museum with period furniture, antique tools, and Native American artifacts. | 123 W. Main St. | 304/627–2236 | Free | May.–Sept., Fri. by appointment only, closed Sun.–Thurs., Sat.

Watters Smith Memorial State Park. A restored 18th-century homestead includes a log cabin museum with displays of antique farm implements. There are also hiking trails, picnic areas, and a playground in the 500-acre park, approx. 18 mi south of Clarksburg; take I–79 10 mi south to the Lost Creek exit, and follow directional signs 7 mi to park entrance. | Off I–79 at Lost Creek Exit | 304/745–3081 | Free | Park mid-Apr.–mid-Oct., daily; Museum Memorial Day–Labor Day, daily 11–7.

ON THE CALENDAR
SEPT.: *West Virginia Italian Heritage Festival.* There's dancing in the streets, a pasta cook-off and sauce competition, a parade, and entertainment at this celebration of the town's Italian immigrant history. | 304/622–7314.

Dining
Jim Reid's. Continental. Candles illuminate linen-topped tables in a restaurant inspired by the Scottish heritage of owner Jim Reid. Dishes include black angus steaks, prime rib, and a variety of chicken dishes. Kids' menu available. | 1422 Buckhannon Pike, Nutter Fort | 304/623–4909 | Closed Mon. | $15–$20 | AE, MC, V.

Lodging

Greenbrier Motel. This colonial-style motel is ¾ mi off U.S. 50 and 12 mi east of historic Fort New Salem in a commercial area just outside downtown Clarksburg. Standard-sized rooms are clean and comfortable, and the inn is within 3 blocks of several restaurants. Restaurant. Room service. Cable TV, in-room VCRs. Hot tub, sauna. Some pets allowed. | 200 Buckhannon Pike | 304/624–5518 | fax 304/624–5510 | 50 rooms | $49 | AE, D, DC, MC, V.

Holiday Inn of Clarksburg and Bridgeport. This two-story motel is in a commercial area at the junction of I–79 and U.S. 50. Restaurant, room service. In-room data ports. Cable TV. Pool, wading pool. Business services, airport shuttle. | 100 Lodgeville Rd., Bridgeport | 304/842–5411 | fax 304/842–7258 | 160 rooms | $79 | AE, D, DC, MC, V.

DAVIS

MAP 17, E4

(Nearby town also listed: Elkins)

Founded in 1883, Davis is the product of a lumber boom. At the northern end of the Monongahela National Forest, the town of 800 is a popular stopover for skiers, mountain bikers, and white-water rafters.

Information: Tucker County Convention and Visitors Bureau | Box 565, William Ave. 26260 | 304/259–5315 or 800/782–2775 | tccvb@access.mountain.net | www.canaan-valley.org.

Attractions

Blackwater Falls State Park. Three miles southwest of Davis off Route 32, this densely wooded park is crowned by Blackwater Falls, a 50-ft-high waterfall on the Blackwater River. The park includes a 55-room lodge at the canyon rim, 25 cabins, and a 65-site campground. | 304/259–5216 or 800/CALL–WVA | County Rte. 29, 26260 | www.blackwater-falls.com | Free | Daily.

Skiing. Downhill and cross-country skiing are available at several resorts near Davis, including Canaan Valley, Timberline Four Seasons Resort, and White Grass Ski Touring Center. | 800/CALL–WVA.

Thirty-four slopes and a vertical drop of 850 ft make **Canaan Valley** a popular winter destination, with snowboarding, snow tubing, night skiing, ice skating, and 18 mi of cross-country ski trails. The resort is 10 mi south of Davis off Route 32. | Rte. 32 | 304/866–4121 or 800/622–4121 | www.canaanresort.com | $43 | Dec.–Mar.

One of the longest ski trails south of New England, the 2-mi Salamander Run is one the highlights at the **Timberline Four Seasons Resort,** a 55-acre resort with 35 slopes, a 1,000-ft vertical drop, and 150 inches of snow per year. Ten miles south of Davis, the resort also has snowboarding, night skiing, and cross-country trails. | 488 Timberline Rd. | 304/866–4801 or 800/SNO–WING | www.timberlineresort.com | $39 (day only) | Dec.–Mar.

White Grass Ski Touring Center has 30 mi of cross-country skiing on 45 trails, as well as telemark glades and snowshoeing. The ski area is 8 mi south of Davis, off Route 32 South. | Freeland Run Rd. | 304/866–4114 | www.whitegrass.com | $15 | Dec.–Mar.

White-water Rafting. Intermediate to advanced white-water rafters can take on the challenge of Class III–V rapids on the Cheat River. | Blackwater Outdoor Adventures, Rte. 1, St. George 26290 | 304/478–3775 or 800/225–5982 | www.raftboc.com | $42–$65 | Wed.–Sat. 10–5, closed Sun.–Tues.

MAR.: *Governor's Cup Ski Race.* Watch top skiers compete in what is the oldest ski race in the South. The 2-day downhill event is at the Timberline Four Seasons Resort, 10 mi south of Davis. | 800/782–2775.

Lodging

Best Western Alpine Lodge. This two-story wood-and-brick motel is 1 mi from the entrance to Blackwater Falls State Park and approximately 10 mi north of both Canaan Valley and Timberline ski resorts. Restaurant. Some refrigerators. Cable TV. Pool. Hot tub. Laundry facilities. Business services. | Rte. 32 | 304/259–5 | fax 304/259–5168 | 46 rooms | $62 | AE, D, DC, MC, V.

Blackwater Lodge. This stone and wood lodge is in Blackwater Falls State Park, 3 mi southwest of Davis off Route 32. The lodge sits in a pine-studded rim of Blackwater Canyon; rooms in the front of the hotel overlook the canyon. The inn is 12 mi north of Canaan Valley Resort. Dining room, picnic area. Some kitchenettes. Cable TV. Lake. Tennis. Cross-country skiing. Playground. Laundry facilities. Business services. | County Rte. 29 | 304/259–5216 | fax 304/259–5881 | 55 rooms, 25 cabins | $67–$85, $90 cabins (7-day minimum June–Aug.) | AE, DC, MC, V.

Canaan Valley Resort and Conference Center. This state-run recreational resort is in a 6,000-acre wooded area in the Allegheny Mountains; golfing, skiing, and hiking are all within 2 mi of the lodge. The inn is 10 mi south of Davis on Route 32. Dining room, picnic area. Some refrigerators. Cable TV. 2 pools (1 indoor). Hot tub. Driving range, 18-hole golf course, miniature golf, putting green, tennis. Exercise equipment. Bicycles. Cross-country skiing, downhill skiing. Kids' programs, playground. Laundry facilities. Business services. | Rte. 32 | 304/866–4121 or 800/622–4121 | fax 304/866–2172 | 250 rooms, 23 cabins | $64–$105, $151–$234 cabins | AE, D, DC, MC, V.

ELKINS

MAP 17, D5

(Nearby towns also listed: Davis, Philippi)

Founded in 1890, Elkins became a center for coal, timber, and railroad operations. At the edge of the sprawling Monongahela National Forest and within driving distance of the state's tallest mountains, the town of 7,400 also caters to visitors who come here to ski, hike, bike, and take in the natural beauty of the Allegheny Mountains.

Information: Randolph County Convention and Visitors Bureau | 200 Executive Plaza 26241 | 304/636–2717 or 800/422–3304 | tourism@randophcountywv.com | www.randolphcountywv.com.

Attractions

Bowden Fish Hatchery. Brook, brown, and rainbow trout are raised at this hatchery 10 mi east of Elkins on U.S. 33. Reservations are required for tours. | Rte. 1, Box 80 | 304/637–0238 | Free | Daily 10–6.

Monongahela National Forest. Covering 909,000 acres in the heart of the Allegheny Mountains, the Monongahela has countless scenic and recreational attractions, including the state's tallest mountain (Spruce Knob, elev. 4,861 ft), rock formations (Seneca Rocks), five wilderness areas, and hiking trails (including 124 mi of the Appalachian Trail); you can go hunting, fishing, rock climbing, spelunking, skiing, boating, swimming, camping, and more. Northern and southern plant zones meet here, resulting in an abundance of tree, plant, and flower species; bear, deer, and wild turkey roam the woodlands. Elkins park headquarters is east of town on U.S. 33. | 200 Sycamore St. | 304/636–1800 | www.fs.fed.us/r9/mnf | Free | Daily.

The Old Mill. Listed on the National Register of Historic Places, this working gristmill still grinds corn, wheat, buckwheat, and rye. There is also a museum and an outlet for local crafts people. The mill is 25 mi east of Elkins off U.S. 33. | Rte. 32 N, Harman | 304/227–4598 | Free, donations accepted | Memorial Day–Labor Day, daily 10–5.

ON THE CALENDAR

JULY–AUG.: *Augusta Heritage Center.* Every year, the Davis and Elkins College hosts a five-week workshop that focuses on all types of traditional arts—from Appalachian to Cajun—through music, dance, crafts, and folklore. | 304/637–1209.

SEPT.–OCT.: *Mountain State Forest Festival.* Gospel and country music, motorcycle races, and arts and crafts draw people to the state's oldest festival in Elkins. | 304/636–1824.

Dining

Cheat River Lodge and Inn. American. Audubon-inspired bird prints adorn this rustic inn, known for its fresh rainbow trout and farm-raised fish entrées. Outdoor deck seating overlooks the Cheat River. | Rte. 1, Box 115 | 304/636–6265 | Closed Mon. No lunch | $12–$20 | MC, V.

Lodging

Budget Host. This two-story chain in two buildings is less than 1 mi east of downtown Elkins on the Beverly Pike. Rooms are standard-sized; the motel is in a commercial area on the outskirts of town. Cable TV. Business services. | Rte. 219 | 304/636–7711 or 800/BUD–HOST | fax 304/636–5419 | 63 rooms | $52–$59 | AE, D, DC, MC, V.

Econo Lodge. This two-story brick motel is in a commercial area 1½ mi from Elkins and Davis College, 2 mi from a movie theater, and within 1 mi of restaurants and shopping. Picnic area, complimentary Continental breakfast. Cable TV. Indoor pool. Hot tub. Laundry facilities. Business services. | Rte. 33 E | 304/636–5311 or 800/797–0014 | www.econolodge.com | 72 rooms | $65–$68 | AE, D, DC, MC, V.

Elkins Super 8. This two-story motel is 5 mi from Monongahela National Forest. Rooms in the back of the motel are quiet, and have views of a wooded area; front rooms face the highway. On the southern edge of Elkins, ½ mi from a shopping plaza and restaurants. Some microwaves, some refrigerators, cable TV. Business services. | 350 Beverly Pike | 304/636–6500 | fax 304/636–6500 | 44 rooms | $53 | AE, D, DC, V.

Four Seasons Motel. A two-story stone building, this 1960s-style, family-owned motel—a favorite with longtime customers—is in a commercial district ½ mi from downtown Elkins, 1 mi from Elkins and Davis College, and within 8 blocks of several restaurants. Cable TV, microwaves, refrigerators. | 1091 Harrison Ave. | 304/636–1990 or 800/367–7130 | 18 rooms | $44 | AE, D, MC, V.

FAIRMONT

MAP 17, D4

(Nearby towns also listed: Clarksburg, Morgantown)

Founded in 1793, Fairmont—originally two towns—sprang up on the steep hills on either side of the Monongahela River. Ferries transported people and goods across the river until a suspension bridge was built in 1852; Confederate troops destroyed it during an attack on the town in 1863. After the war, coal mining became the mainstay of the region, and it still contributes to the economy, along with manufacturing. More recently, high-tech software development has come to this town of 20,000.

Information: **Marion County Convention and Visitors Bureau** | 110 Adams St., Box 58, 26555 | 304/368–1123 or 800/834–7365 | cvb@marioncvb.com | www.marioncvb.com.

Attractions

Fairmont State College. On 30 acres overlooking the city, Fairmont State College was founded in 1865 as a teachers' training school. A one-room school museum recalls the college's first years. | 1201 Locust Ave. | 304/367–4141 | www.fscwv.edu | Free | Daily.

Marion County Historical Museum. The museum's five furnished rooms represent different periods in U.S. history, from 1776 to the 1920s. The museum is next to the Marion County Courthouse, an 1897 building that is considered one of the finest examples of Beaux Arts classicism in the state. | 200 Adams St. | 304/367–5398 | Free | Memorial Day–Labor Day, Mon.–Sat. 10–2, closed Sun.; Labor Day–Memorial Day, weekdays 10–2, closed weekends.

Pricketts Fort State Park. The log fort here was reconstructed to resemble the one pioneers built in 1774 as protection against Native Americans. Costumed interpreters reenact colonial life in a compound that includes 16 cabins, a storehouse, and a meeting hall; there's also an amphitheater, a picnic area, and a boat ramp with access to the Monongahela River. The park is 2 mi west of I–79 at exit 139. | Rte. 3, Box 407, 26554 | 800/225–5982 or 304/363–3030 | fax 304/363–3857 | www.dmssoft.com/pfork | $5 | May–Oct., Mon.–Sat. 10–5, Sun. noon–5.

ON THE CALENDAR

MAY: *Three Rivers Festival*. People wearing period costumes reenact the Civil War battle on a bridge over the Monongahela River with a parade, a carnival, entertainment, and a golf tournament. | 304/363–2625.

Dining

Tiffany's Continental Key Club. Continental. The beef Wellington, veal parmigiana, or whole Maine lobster all come highly recommended at this semi-formal restaurant. The light is low, and tables are widely-spaced and draped with linens. Kids' menu. | N. Bellview Blvd. | 304/363–7859 | Closed Sun. | $10–$18 | AE, D, DC, MC, V.

Lodging

Comfort Inn and Suites. This two-story chain is approximately 10 mi from downtown Fairmont. The motel, in a business district on the northern outskirts of town, attracts a corporate crowd, and is within 4 blocks of several restaurants. Prickett's Fork State Park is 1 mi north. Complimentary Continental breakfast. Cable TV. Pool. Business services. | 1185 Airport Rd. | 304/367–1370 | fax 304/367–1806 | 98 rooms | $125 | AE, D, DC, MC, V.

Holiday Inn. With a scenic hilltop view, this family-friendly motel, where kids eat and stay for free, is ⅓ mi from downtown Fairmont. Restaurant, room service. In-room data ports. Cable TV. Pool. Business services. | 930 Old Grafton Rd. | 304/366–5500 | fax 304/363–3975 | www.holiday-inn.com | 106 rooms | $72–$149 | AE, D, DC, MC, V.

Red Roof Inn. Easy to spot with its trademark red roof, this two-story motel is off I–79 Exit 132 (South Fairmont exit), about 5 mi from downtown. The motel is in a commercial area, across the street from a shopping plaza, within 3 blocks of several restaurants, and 1½ mi from Morris Park. Cable TV. Business services. Pets allowed. | 50 Middletown Rd. | 304/366–6800 | fax 304/366–6812 | www.redroof.com | 108 rooms | $46–$66 | AE, D, DC, MC, V.

FAYETTEVILLE

MAP 17, C6

(Nearby towns also listed: Ansted, Gauley Bridge)

Founded in 1818 and named for the Marquis de Lafayette, Fayetteville, population 2,200, owes its rise to coal and lumber. While mines are slowly disappearing, the logging continues, and the new growth industry is recreation. At the edge of the New

River, Fayetteville has a village-like setting, with galleries, diners, and sport shops—a popular draw for the white-water enthusiasts who come to raft the rapids of the New and Gauley rivers.

Information: Southern West Virginia Convention and Visitors Bureau | Box 1799, Beckley 25802 | 304/252–2244 or 800/VISIT–WV | travel@visitwv.com | www.visitwv.org.

Attractions

New River Gorge Bridge. The longest single-arch, steel-span bridge in the world and the second-highest bridge in the United States, this 876-ft-high structure was completed in 1977. The National Park Service operates a visitor center, with a boardwalk and overlook, on U.S. 19, 1 mi north of Fayetteville. | U.S. 19 N, Lansing | 304/574–2115 | Free | Visitor center open daily 9–5.

New and Gauley Rivers. You'll find some of the best whitewater rafting east of the Mississippi on these rivers with class IV and V whitewater rapids which even run through town. Several local companies arrange guided trips. One of them, Raft West Virginia, is 4 mi north of downtown Fayetteville. | 304/252–2244 or 800/782–7238 | www.raftwvinfo.com | Call for information and rates | Daily.

ON THE CALENDAR

OCT.: *Bridge Day.* Parachutists leap off the New River Gorge Bridge during this 1-day event, when the bridge is open to pedestrians. | 304/465–0508.

Dining

Sedona Grill. Eclectic. Southwestern selections are prevalent—try the fajitas or the black bean burritos—but the menu encompasses a world of dishes, from Tex-Mex and Italian to Greek and Thai. Vividly painted walls give this cozy bar and grill a festive feel. | 106 E. Maple Ave. | 304/574–3411 | Reservations not accepted | Closed Wed. | $12–$15 | AE, D, DC, MC, V.

FRANKLIN

MAP 17, E5

(Nearby town also listed: Elkins)

On the South Branch of the Potomac River, Franklin was settled in 1794 and now serves as the seat of Pendleton County. The town of 900 sits right in the middle of caving country, and spelunkers travel here to explore caves both large and small.

Information: Pendleton County Visitors Commission | Box 602, 26807 | 304/358–7573 | www.visitpendleton.com.

Attractions

Seneca Caverns. Spectacular stalactite and stalagmite formations adorn this 165-ft-deep cave, the state's largest. Seneca Indians took refuge from winter storms here, and legend has it that Princess Snow Bird married a young brave in the Grand Ballroom, a subterranean chamber 60 ft long, 30 ft wide, and 70 ft high. Guided tours are available. Go 17 mi on U.S. 33 to Riverton, then drive 3 mi east. | On Rte. 9 | 304/567–2691 | www.senecacaverns.com | $8 | Daily.

ON THE CALENDAR

SEPT.: *Treasure Mountain Festival.* Storytellers weave tales of buried treasure during this fall festival; you'll also find square dancing, clogging, mountain music, and beard and mustache contests. | 304/249–5422.

GAULEY BRIDGE

(Nearby towns also listed: Ansted, Fayetteville)

Named for the bridge over Gauley River that was destroyed in 1861 amid retreating Confederate troops, this tiny town of 700 bore witness to ferocious military action during the Civil War. Today, Gauley Bridge largely supports itself from the white-water rafting industry that has sprung up here and in nearby river towns.

Information: Gauley Bridge Tourist Craft Center | U.S. Rte. 60 at Gauley Bridge, 25080 | 304/632–1284.

Attractions

Contentment Museum Complex. Purchased in 1872 by Colonel George Imboden, who served under Gen. Robert E. Lee during the Civil War, this house is now part of a museum complex operated by the Fayette County Historical Society. Displays include period furnishings and artifacts. The complex is 7 mi east of Gauley Bridge on U.S. Rte. 60. | U.S. Rte. 60, Lover's Leap | 304/658–5695 | $2 | Tours June–Sept., daily 10–4; Oct.–May. by appointment.

Gauley Bridge Railroad Station and Town Hall. Built in 1893, the Gauley Bridge Company Passenger Station is a good example of the prefabricated "company trademark" railroad stations prevalent in small communities in early 19th- and late 20th-century America. It is now the town hall; explore to your heart's content. | 278 Railroad St. | 304/632–2504 | Weekdays 8–4, closed weekends | Free.

White-water Rafting. Rafting excursions are offered on the New, Cheat, and Gauley rivers by more than a dozen white-water outfitters. Every year, more than 100,000 people raft the New River and the more challenging Gauley. There's a wide variation in prices, depending upon outfitter, the length of trip, and the rapids level. Put-in points vary with companies. | 800/927–0263 or 800/CALL–WVA | www.newrivercvb.com/whitewater.htm | Call individual outfitters for hours and fees.

ON THE CALENDAR

OCT.: *Annual Anniversary Celebration.* Food, music, and dancing bring the residents of Gauley Bridge out every October to celebrate their town's founding. Arts and crafts commemorating the occasion are for sale. | 304/632–2505.

Dining

Gino's Pizza and Spaghetti House. Italian. Pictures of the New River Gorge, Gauley Bridge, and Venice fill the walls of this bistro, where you can spin some tunes on the jukebox while waiting for your meal. The house specialities are homestyle spaghetti Bolognese and "pubwiches," which include ham and cheese sandwiches made with pizza dough. | 6 Main St. | 304/632–1742 | $5–$10 | MC, V.

Lodging

Bavarian Gasthaus Bed & Breakfast. This Victorian house was built around 1900 for the mayor of Beckley; you can still see part of the Underground Railroad, a secret passage inside the wall that was once used to hide slaves. Rooms are filled with period antiques. The inn is 18 mi outside of Gauley Bridge. The bed and breakfast is in downtown Beckley, 1 mi from New River City Park and 2 mi from Tamarack. Complimentary breakfast. Cable TV. | 109 Beckley Ave., Beckley | 304/253–1140 | fax 304/253–5591 | 5 rooms | $45–$65 | D, MC, V.

Glen Ferris Bed and Breakfast. A simple, elegant style characterizes this B&B. Built in 1850 of brick and stucco, it's an excellent example of Federal architecture. Guest rooms command panoramic views of the Appalachian Mountains and Kkanawah Falls and are furnished with a blend of antique and contemporary pieces ranging in style from Victorian to Shaker. The inn is less than ¼ mi from Gauley Bridge. Cable TV. Library. Business services. | Rte. 60, Glen Ferris | 304/632–1111 | fax 304/632–1502 | 15 rooms, 3 suites | $60–$75, $130 suites | www.emoney.net/glenferris | AE, D, MC, V.

GLENVILLE

MAP 17, C5

(Nearby towns also listed: Buckhannon, Weston)

Although it is small, this town of 1,800 is home to Glenville State College and was the birthplace of Ellen King and H.A. Engle's "The West Virginia Hills." The town has weathered several name changes as well, starting out as Stewart's Creek and changing to Hartford before finally settling on its current moniker. Glenville was incorporated in 1871; today its economy centers largely on the college.

Information: **Glenville City Hall** | 20 N. Court St., Glenville 26351 | 304/462–8040.

Attractions

Glenville State College. Built in the early 1800s, this college is perched on a hill overlooking the town. You can walk around the grounds and explore the many buildings, including the famous Arbuckle House. All buildings are open to the public. | 200 High St. | 304/462–7361 | Free.

ON THE CALENDAR
JUNE: *West Virginia State Folk Festival.* This event celebrates popular music written before 1930 with jam sessions in the street, competitions, and a turkey calling contest. | 304/462–8427.
OCT.: *OctoberFest.* A celebration of Autumn, this festival has arts and crafts, a Halloween parade, food, carnival rides, and karaoke. The celebration is held on Glenville's Main Street. | 304/462–8040.

Dining

Common Place. American. Housed in a brick building in the center of town, this restaurant takes the "meat and potatoes" approach to dining. The rib-eye steak and the roast beef sandwich are popular, as are the many different desserts. | 19 E. Main St. | 304/462–7454 | Breakfast also available | $5–$10 | MC, V.

Lodging

Conrad Motel. This two-story family-owned brick hostelry is off Main Street, behind the United National Bank, and sits on the bank of the Little Kanawha River; some of the rooms have limited river views. The motel is 3 blocks from Glenville State College. Cable TV. No pets. | 100 Conrad Ct. | 304/462–7316 | 38 rooms | $45 | AE, DC, MC, V.

GRAFTON

MAP 17, D4

(Nearby towns also listed: Clarksburg, Fairmont)

Named after John Grafton, a civil engineer who played a pivotal role in routing the Baltimore and Ohio rail lines across West Virginia, this town of 5,814 was chartered in 1856. Grafton is also the hometown of Anna Jarvis, who is best known as the founder of Mother's Day.

Information: **Grafton-Taylor County Convention and Visitors Bureau** | Box 355, Grafton 26354 | 304/265–0164.

Attractions

Grafton National Cemetery. Dedicated in 1867, Grafton National Cemetery is one of only two national cemeteries in the state. It contains the grave of the first Union soldier killed by the Confederate Army. The cemetery is on the Civil War Discovery Trail. | 431 Walnut St. | 304/265–2044 | Free | Daily.

International Mother's Day Shrine. Built in 1873, this two-story brick church, formerly Andrews Methodist Church, was the site of the first Mother's Day celebration on May 10, 1908. | 11 E. Main St. | 304/265–1589 or 304/265–1177 | Free | Mid-Apr.–mid-Oct., weekdays 9–3:30, closed weekends.

Tygart Lake State Park. The lake shoreline stretches 11 mi, offering boating, swimming, and scuba diving. Park facilities include a 20-room lodge, a restaurant, 10 cabins, and 40 camp-sites. | From downtown Grafton, take Rte. 50 to South Grafton and follow the signs to the park | Off Rte. 50, South Grafton | 304/265–3383 | www.tygartlake.com | Free | Daily 6 AM–10 PM.

ON THE CALENDAR

AUG.: *The Foot of the Dam Jam.* This music and food festival is held every third week-end in August at the Grafton City Park; the park has picnic and camping facilities. | 304/265–3938.

JULY: *Taylor County Fair.* This fair includes crafts, carnival rides, livestock exhibits, and food. | 304/265–3938.

Dining

Four Corners Restaurant. American. This is a casual, blue jeans and T-shirt restaurant less than 1 mi from downtown Grafton. Try the steak or roast turkey, topped off with fruit pie for dessert. You can eat outdoors on the deck while gazing into the fish pond. Inside, there is counter-style eating and tables. Weekend breakfast buffet available. | 1 Blueville Dr. | 304/265–3810 | $5–$11 | AE, DC, MC, V.

Lodging

Acacia House Bed & Breakfast. Fifteen miles north of Grafton in Fairmont, this B&B was built in 1917. A four-story brown brick home with oak floors, handsome furnishings, and six decorative fireplaces, the Acacia also has a glass-enclosed porch and a lower-level TV room warmed by a woodburning stove. The rooms are appointed with antiques and collectibles, some of which are tagged for sale. A gift shop is on premises. Complimentary breakfast. No pets. | 158 Locust Ave. | 304/367–1000 or 888/269–9541 | fax 304/367–1000 | acacia@acaciahousewv.com | www.acaciahousewv.com | 4 rooms | $45–$70 | AE, D, DC, MC, V.

Crislip Motor Lodge. Within 5 mi of both Tygart Lake State Park and Grafton's Mother's Day Shrine, this L-shaped brick motor lodge is ³/₄ mi from downtown Grafton. The basic motel rooms are average-sized; there is a pool table and TV in the lobby area. Cable TV. Pool. Business services. | 300 Moritz Ave. | 304/265–2100 | fax 304/265–2017 | 40 rooms | $40–$55 | AE, D, DC, MC, V.

Tygart Lake State Park Lodge. The 10 deluxe cabins that make up the bulk of this property were built on the lakeshore in 1957. All have fireplaces, electric heat, modern kitchens and bathrooms, and a supply of cooking utensils and bed and bath linens. In 1964, the State Park built a rustic-deluxe chalet-like lodge overlooking the water and boat docks; the cozy, wood-paneled guest rooms all have views of the lake. Between June and Labor Day, cabins are rented by the week only. Restaurant, picnic area. Cable TV. Boating, fishing. Kids' programs. | From downtown Grafton, take Rte. 50 to South Grafton and follow the signs to the park | Rte. 1,

Box 260 | 304/265–6148 or 800/225–5982 | 20 rooms in the lodge, 10 individual cabins | $62–$74 rooms, $73–$95 cabins (during fall and spring) | Closed Jan.–Apr. | AE, MC, DC V.

HARPERS FERRY

MAP 17, F2

(Nearby towns also listed: Charles Town, Shepherdstown)

This tiny town is best known as the site of abolitionist John Brown's 1859 raid on the federal arsenal. Situated at the junction of the Potomac and Shenandoah rivers, Harpers Ferry was also a strategic hot spot during the Civil War. Most of the town and its 300 residents is encompassed by the Harpers Ferry National Historical Park, making it a popular tourist destination and augmenting the community's economy.

Information: Jefferson County Convention and Visitors Bureau | Box A, 25425 | 304/535–2627 or 800/848–TOUR | visitors@jeffersoncountycvb.com | www.jefferson-county.com/cvb.

Attractions

Appalachian National Scenic Trail. Two-and-one-half miles of this 2,150-mi footpath, which runs from Georgia to Maine, are in West Virginia and extend through lower Harpers Ferry, following the Stone Steps and crossing the footbridge over the Potomac River. | Shenandoah St. and High St. | 304/535–6298 | Free | Daily.

Chesapeake and Ohio Canal National Historic Park. The canal runs 185 mi from Washington, D.C., to Cumberland, Maryland, stretching along the Potomac River from Harpers Ferry to Paw Paw in West Virginia. Visitors may hike or bike the former tow path along the canal, or camp, fish, and boat in designated areas. | Sections of the canal can be reached via I–495, I–70, and I–68. For directions to specific sites, call the Visitor Center | 301/739–4200.

Harpers Ferry Ghost Tours. Wander the streets of Harpers Ferry by lantern light to gain a unique look at the town's history. Guide Shirley Dougherty will take you to meet the spirits from John Brown's raid. Tours meet on the patio of Hot Dog Haven, across from the railroad station. | Potomac St. | 304/725–8019 | $3 | Apr., Sat. at 8 PM; May–mid-Nov., Fri.–Sun. at 8 PM.

Harpers Ferry National Historical Park. This 2,300-acre park includes land in West Virginia, Virginia, and Maryland. Six major historical themes relating to the area's past are illuminated here through museum exhibits and scheduled activities: the natural environment, industry, John Brown, the Civil War, African-American history, and transportation. The park, which is West Virginia's most-visited attraction, is also part of the Civil War Discovery Trail. | Rte. 340 | 304/535–6298 | www.nps.gov/hafe | $3; cars $5 | May–Oct daily 8–6, Nov.–Apr. daily 8–5.

A gap in the Blue Ridge Mountains, the scenic overlook known as **The Point** provides a panoramic view of the town and surrounding area. You'll find it in Harpers Ferry National Historical Park at the southeast corner of town, at the convergence of the Potomac and Shenandoah rivers. | Just off Shenandoah and Potomac Streets | Free | Daily.

Now a brick firehouse in Arsenal Square, **John Brown's Fort** was the site of the famed abolitionist's capture. The structure was dismantled in the early 1890s and shipped to the World's Columbian Exposition in Chicago. It now stands near its original site on Harpers Ferry park grounds. | Arsenal Sq. | 304/535–6298 | www.nps.gov/hafe | Free | Daily 8–5.

Also part of the Historical Park, the **John Brown Museum** has exhibits and artifacts from the abolitionist's 1859 raid of the U.S. Arsenal. | Shenandoah St. | 304/535–6298 | www.nps.gov/hafe | Admission included in price of admission to park | Daily.

Accessible from stone steps leading from High Street, the 1782 **Harper House** is one of the oldest surviving structures in the town, part of the Harpers Ferry park grounds. | Route 340 | Public Way | 304/535–6298 | www.nps.gov/hafe | Admission included in price of admission to park | Daily 8–5.

The Harper House is part of **Marmion Row,** a line of stone structures that date from the late 1700s to the early 1800s and can be viewed from High Street. | Public Way; off Route 340 | 304/535–6298 | Free | Daily 8–5.

At the edge of Harpers Ferry National Historical Park and by the Appalachian Trail lie the ruins of **St. John's Episcopal Church,** which was used as a hospital during the Civil War. Stone walls and an interpretive marker are all that remain. | Church St. | Free | Daily.

From a vantage point in the Harpers Ferry park known as **Jefferson's Rock,** Thomas Jefferson sat in 1783 and observed West Virginia, Virginia, and Maryland. He wrote: "This view is well worth a trip across the Atlantic." | Off Route 340 | Free | Daily.

The **Lockwood House** served as the armory official's quarters until 1861, when it was used and nearly destroyed by soldiers. The house now serves as offices for the Harpers Ferry National Historical Park and is not open to the public. | Fillmore St., 25425 | 304/535–6298.

Another Harpers Ferry park attraction is the **John Brown Wax Museum,** a privately-owned facility which presents life-sized figures depicting the life of abolitionist John Brown. | 168 High St. | 304/535–6342 | $2.50 | Daily 9:30–4:30.

White-water Rafting. Blue Ridge Outfitters offers excursions on Class II–III rapids past Harpers Ferry on the Potomac River. | Frontage Rd., Box 750 | 800/225–5982 or 304/725–3444 | $43–$68 | Apr.–Oct.

ON THE CALENDAR

JULY: *Freedom's Birth.* Come to see the Fourth of July fireworks bonanza at Harpers Ferry National Historical Park, one of the best shows around. Live music at this free event augments the powerful display of pyrotechnics. | 304/535–2627.

OCT.: *Election Day 1860.* The festivities during this event include encampments, music, exhibits, and Civil War–era militia muster. | 304/535–6748.

DEC.: *Old Tyme Christmas.* Concerts, caroling, and ghost tours are held throughout town and in the Harpers Ferry National Historical Park. | 304/725–8019 or 304/535–2511.

Dining

The Anvil Restaurant. Contemporary. The main themes of the menu are seafood and steak; a host of cheesecakes and pies stand ready for dessert. For a less formal experience, eat in the pub; the drafts are only 50 cents during happy hour. | 1270 Washington St. | 304/535–2582 | Closed Mon.–Tues. | $10 | AE, MC, V.

Lodging

Comfort Inn. One mile from Harpers Ferry National Historical Park and the downtown area, some rooms in this two-story chain have excellent views of the mountains. Complimentary Continental breakfast. Cable TV. Business services. | Corner of Union St. and Rte. 340, Box 980 | 304/535–6391 | fax 304/535–6395 | 50 rooms | $55–$100 | AE, D, DC, MC, V.

Harpers Ferry Guest House. This building is intended to conform to the Federal architecture of Harpers Ferry. The main guest rooms each have a four-poster queen bed and high sloping ceilings with fans. The front porch has a wisteria vine, rocking chairs, and a swing; a small private parking lot and flower gardens are out back. Complimentary breakfast. No air-conditioning. No pets. No kids under 10. | 800 Washington St. | 304/535–6955 | www.harpersferry-wv.com/BandB/ | 3 rooms | $65–$95 | No credit cards.

HILLSBORO

MAP 17, D6

(Nearby town also listed: Marlinton)

The story of this tiny town's genesis reads like a folk legend: In 1765, a man named John McNeil fled into the woods after a boxing match during which he believed he had killed his opponent. Some months later, two brothers exploring the area discovered McNeil in hiding, told him that his opponent had recovered, and tried to persuade him to return to civilization. But McNeil refused to return; instead, he convinced the brothers to stay and help him found a settlement. Today, that settlement is home to about 200 people and is the birthplace of the celebrated author Pearl S. Buck.

Information: **Pocahontas County Tourism Commission** | Box 275, Marlinton 24954 | 304/799–4636 or 800/336–7009 | pctc@neumedia.net | www.pocahontas.org.

Attractions

Beartown State Park. Near Droop Mountain Battlefield, this rugged park contains huge rocks and boulders strewn across a dense forest. Beartown's name comes from local legend, which claims that colonies of black bears once inhabited the house-sized rock formations. | 7 mi south of Hillsboro on Beartown Rd. | 304/653–4254 | Free | Daily.

Droop Mountain Battlefield State Park. This 287-acre park marks the location of the largest Civil War battle in West Virginia. Part of the 1863 battlefield is marked for visitors, and a museum contains Civil War artifacts. | Bordering Hwy. 219 5 mi. south of Hillsboro | 304/653–4254 | Free | Daily.

Locust Creek Covered Bridge. Built in 1888, this 130-ft, postcard-worthy structure is the lone survivor of Pocahontas County's covered bridges. The bridge is 3 mi from Route 219 on Locust Creek Road, 6 mi out of Hillsboro. The architecture of the interior is mostly of the Howes type construction. | Locust Creek Rd. | Free | Daily.

Pearl S. Buck Birthplace Museum. This restored home 1/4 mi north of Hillsboro is the birthplace of the only female author to win both the Nobel and Pulitzer prizes; it is furnished with some period pieces and contains items from Buck's life. The boyhood home of Buck's father, Absalom Sydenstricker, is right next door. | Rte. 219 | 304/653–4430 | $4 | Tours May.–Oct., Mon.–Sat. 9–4:30, Sun. 1–4:30.

Watoga State Park. A sprawling wooded area laced with hiking and horseback-riding trails, the park also has swimming, 33 rental cabins, and two campgrounds. The park is 10 mi east of Hillsboro off Route 219. | Rte. 27, Marlinton | 304/799–4087 | www.wvparks/watoga | Free | Daily 6 AM–10 PM.

Calvin Price State Forest. This 9,842-acre park is next to Watoga State Park. Here you can hike, fish, and hunt. The park is also 10 mi east of Hillsboro off Route 219. | Rte. 27, Marlinton | 304/799–4087 | www.wvparks.com/calvinprice | Free | Daily.

ON THE CALENDAR

JUNE: *Pearl Buck Birthday Celebration.* Held at the Pearl S. Buck Birthplace Museum, this festival includes arts and crafts, free birthday cake, and historical tours. | 304/653–4430.

Dining

The Country Roads Cafe. American. This bistro has antiques on display, but its most distinguishing attribute is the book-packed shelves lining the walls. The menu runs the gamut, from sandwiches, marinated chicken breast, rib-eye steak, and pork tenderloin, to crab cakes, shrimp, and seafood linguine. You can eat al fresco on the front lawn. | HC 64, Rte. 219 | 304/653–4697 | $9–$15 | AE, D, DC, MC, V.

Lodging

Cranberry Mountain Lodge. Perched at 4,000 ft on top of Cranberry Mountain, the lodge adjoins nearly a million acres of the Monongahela National Forest; you can see more than 40 mi of it from the deck. The adjacent Cranberry Black Bear Sanctuary is one of the largest east of the Mississippi. You'll stay in secluded luxury, since the seven-room home must be rented as a whole. Outdoor hot tub. Hiking. Bicycles. Cross country skiing, downhill skiing. | John Wimer Road | 304/242–6070, or 800/CAL–LWVA | cmlodge@hgo.net |

www.cranberrymountainlodge.com | 7 rooms | $650 for 2 nights (2–night minimum), $120 for each additional night | D.

The Current Bed and Breakfast. Built on the Greenbrier River Trail in 1905, this cozy farmhouse with a 4-acre pasture can accommodate both you and your horses. Country-style antiques fill the guest rooms, and beds are draped with handmade quilts. Kids allowed by permission. The inn is 5 mi southeast of Hillsboro, off Denmar Rd. Cable TV, no room phones. Hot tub. Some pets allowed. | Beard Post Office Rd. | 304/653–4722 | www.currentbnb.com | 6 rooms (some with private baths) | $60–$85 | MC, V.

HINTON

(Nearby towns also listed: Beckley, Lewisburg)

Hinton grew up around the Chesapeake and Ohio rail lines in the 1870s and is a center for rail trade even today. The town supports 3,433 residents, boasts a vibrant historic district with more than 200 buildings executed in many different architectural styles, and is conveniently located close to the Pipestem Resort State Park, New River Gorge National River, and Bluestone Lake.

Information: Summers County Convention and Visitors Bureau | 206 Temple St., Hinton 25951 | 304/466–5420.

Attractions

Bluestone State Park. Bordering Bluestone Lake, this 2,155-acre park offers cabins, camping areas, boat-launching facilities, fishing, water skiing, and hiking trails. The park is 5 mi south of Hinton off Route 20 South | Bluestone State Park Rd. | 304/466–2805 | www.wvparks.com/bluestone | Free | Daily.

New River Gorge National River. Stretching 52 mi along the New River, this park winds through the gorge from Hinton to the New River Gorge Bridge near Fayetteville. Despite its name, the New River is thought to be one of the oldest rivers in North America, and unlike most rivers, the New flows north. Its swift rapids make it popular among white-water rafters and fishing enthusiasts. You can reach the river from the Canyon Rim Visitors Center, 3 mi north of Fayetteville on Route 19. | Box 246, Glen Jean | 304/465–0508 | www.nps.gov/neri | Free | Visitor center daily 9–5.

Pipestem Resort State Park and Equestrian Center. Perched on the Bluestone Gorge, this 4,023-acre park has two lodges, golf courses, swimming pools, restaurants, camping sites, and horseback riding. The park is 12 mi south of Hinton on Route 20 South. | Rte. 20 S, Pipestem | 304/466–1800 | www.pipestemresort.com | Free | Daily.

ON THE CALENDAR
AUG.: *West Virginia State Water Festival.* Boat races, a pageant and ball, a car show, food booths, and an arts and crafts exhibit are all part of this water festival. | 304/466–5420.

Dining

Bluestone Dining Room. American. The daily buffet offerings and open-air dining with breathtaking views of Pipestem Resort State Park draw both locals and tourists to this casual restaurant. Plate-glass windows on three sides of the dining room open onto wooded vistas of the Pipestem Resort State Park. You can order off the menu or take advantage of the ever-changing buffet, including seafood and prime rib. Sun. brunch and kids' menu available. | In Pipestem State Park Lodge off Rte. 20 | 304/466–1800, ext. 368 | Reservations not accepted | Breakfast also available | $10–$15 | DC, MC, V.

Kirk's. American. A covered open-air veranda with wrought-iron railings commanding views of the New River and Bluestone State Park is the hallmark at Kirk's. The juicy home-cooked pork chops is a favorite among locals and tourists alike. The restaurant is on the eastern edge of town, on New River. | Rte. 20 | 304/466–4600 | Breakfast also available | $6–$12 | No credit cards.

Mountain Creek. Eclectic. Tucked at the base of the Pipestem Resort State Park gorge, this restaurant is accessible via the aerial tram that goes down into the canyon. Once you reach the bottom, try the tender oven-roasted free-range chicken or fresh seafood. Kids' menu available. | In Pipestem Resort State Park, Pipestem Resort, Pipestem on Rte. 20 | 304/466–1800, ext. 387 | Continental breakfast also available | $18–$25 | DC, MC, V.

Oak Supper Club. American. An old-school supper club reminiscent of a farmhouse, the Oak is popular among locals and visitors alike. It's known for the barbecued pork, fresh mountain trout, and lamb. Kids' menu available. The restaurant is 12 mi south of Hinton, off Route 20 | Pipestem Knob Rd. | 304/466–4800 | Open Fri.–Sat. only, Feb.–Apr., Nov., and Dec.; May–Oct. Tues.–Sat.; Closed Jan. No lunch | $20 | MC, V.

Lodging

Mt. Creek Lodge. Hidden away at the bottom of the 1,000-ft-deep Bluestone Canyon, this remote lodge and convention complex boasts some of the most beautiful scenery and wildlife-watching opportunities around. Most guest rooms have mountain views, and the lodge itself is accessible only via the canyon's aerial tramway. 3 restaurants, bar, picnic area. Some kitchenettes. Cable TV. 2 pools (1 indoor), wading pool. Sauna. Exercise equipment. 18-hole golf course, tennis. Cross-country skiing, sleigh rides, tobogganing. Playground. Business services. | In Pipestem Resort State Park on Rte. 20, Pipestem | 304/466–1800 or 800/225–5982 | fax 304/466–5679 | 173 rooms in 2 buildings; 25 cottages | $74, $117 cottages | AE, DC, MC, V.

Pence Springs Hotel. Built in 1918 for guests who came to "take the waters" of Pence Springs, this hotel has seen a lot of action since. It was closed in 1935 because of Depression-era financial woes, then in 1947 was turned into a women's prison, which closed in 1985. The restored structure retains elements of a rambling country house, including a sun-

© Corbis

THE LEGEND OF JOHN HENRY

Myth or Herculean man? John Henry lives today in song and folklore, but did the Steel Driving Man really exist, or was he the creation of people in need of a hero? Though no one knows for sure, research indicates that a man fitting Henry's description did live near Talcott, Summers County, during the early 1870s.

Building the 6,500-ft Big Bend Tunnel through a West Virginia mountain was an incredible feat that required the skills and endurance of some incredible men. Legend has it that one of those men was a certain John Henry, a strong African-American laboring to help take the C&O Railroad through the mountain.

His job involved driving steel drills into solid rock. One day when the foreman brought a new steam drill to test, a contest ensued to determine whether man or machine was stronger. The story has it that Henry proved he could outperform the device, but the strain killed him.

Today a statue along Route 3 near Talcott stands as testament to John Henry, and you can peer into the tunnel where Henry is said to have hidden. Meanwhile, the search for clues that support the legend continues.

room, a portico, and a gallery. The hotel is 18 mi east of Hinton on Route 3. Bar, dining room, picnic area, complimentary breakfast. No room phones, no TV in some rooms. Business services. | Rte. 3, Pence Springs | 304/445–2606 or 800/826–1829 | fax 304/445–2204 | 15 rooms, 2 cottages | $75–$110, $300–$500 cottages | AE, D, DC, MC, V.

HUNTINGTON

(Nearby town also listed: Barboursville)

Nestled between a range of low rolling hills and the Ohio River, Huntington is the second-largest city in West Virginia. Founded in 1871 by Collis P. Huntington, president of the Chesapeake and Ohio Railroad, the city is the largest metropolitan area in the state and has long served as a center for industry and trade.

Cobblestone boulevards and ornate wrought-iron detailing characterize the Old Central City. Home to the city's nationally recognized rose garden, beautiful Ritter Park flanks Four Pole Creek and extends into Park Hills.

Huntington claims the main campus of Marshall University, which, with more than 15,000 students, is West Virginia's second-largest institution of higher education.

Information: Cabell/Huntington Convention and Visitors Bureau | 739 3rd Ave., Box 347, Huntington 25708 | 304/525–7333 or 800/635–6329 | htgncvb@marshall.edu | www.wvvisit.org.

Attractions

Beech Fork State Park. Camping and fishing are the primary attractions at this 3,981-acre park outside of Huntington. The park has 275 campsites, hiking trails, picnic areas, and seasonal naturalist programs. | 5601 Long Branch Rd., Barboursville | 304/522–0303 | www.wvparks.com/beechfork | Free | Daily.

Benjy's Harley-Davidson Motorcycle Museum. Housed in a single large display room, the exhibits of vintage motorcycles and motorcycle-related art pay homage to an American classic. Visit the gift store on the ground floor for bandanas, Zippo lighters, books, and other souvenirs. | 408 4th St. | 304/523–1340 | www.benjy'shd@aol.com | Free | Mon.–Thurs. 10–6, Fri. 10–9, Sat. 10–2:30, closed Sun.

Blenko Glass Visitor Center and Factory Outlet. You can view glassblowers at work here from the observation booth. The adjacent Blenko Historical Museum contains glassware, glass-making equipment, military uniforms, and historic documents. The center is 25 mi east of Huntington off I-64, Fairground Road exit. | Fairground Rd., Milton; 2 mi off Exit 28 | 304/743–9081 | www.blenkoglass.com | Free | Mon.–Sat. 8–4, Sun. 12–4; closed late July, late Dec.

Camden Park. The state's only amusement park, Camden Park opened in 1903. The 26-acre park includes rides, picnic areas, and stern-wheeler riverboat cruises on the Ohio River. Fireworks and big-name entertainment are featured on many holidays. | U.S. 60 E | 304/429–4321 | $1; rides $1 or $12.95 all-day ride pass | Mid-May–late Sept., Tues.–Fri. noon–10, weekends 11–10, closed Mon.

East Lynn Lake and Wildlife Management Area. The 1,005-acre lake here is ideal for boating and fishing, while the adjacent 24,821 acres of public land provide hunting for deer, waterfowl, and small game. | 35 mi from Huntington on Route 37, Wayne | 304/849–2355 | Free | Daily.

Harris Riverfront Park. Along the river behind the Huntington Civic Arena, this park has a boat dock and playgrounds. | Veterans Blvd. (2nd Ave.) and 10th St. | 304/696–5990 | Free | Daily.

Heritage Village. A former railway yard houses shops and restaurants in restored warehouses and boxcars. A statue of city founder Collis P. Huntington stands nearby. | 11th St. and Veterans Memorial Blvd. | 304/696–5954 | Free | Daily 11–5.

Huntington Museum of Art. A large collection of firearms, silver, glass, Islamic prayer rugs, and 19th- and 20th-century American and European paintings and prints fills this museum, which resides on 54 acres. Art classes and workshops are available to all ages. | 2033 McCoy Rd. | 304/529–2701 | Donations accepted | Tue. 10–9, Wed.–Sat. 10–5, Sun. 12–5, closed Mon.

Old Central City. Antiques stores, florist shops, and a café fill what was the old downtown, centered around a gazebo. | 555 W. 14th St. | 304/525–1500 | Free | Mon.–Sat. 10–5, closed Sun.

Pilgrim Glass Corp. Pilgrim Glass is one of the world's largest manufacturers of cranberry and cameo glass. You can watch glassmaking from an observation room during the 30-minute tour. The factory is 5 mi east of Huntington off I-64, exit 1 (Kenova exit). | Airport Rd., Ceredo | 304/453–3553 | www.pilgrimglass.com | Free | Mon.–Sat. 9–5, Sun. 1–5.

Ritter Park. Ballfields, tennis courts, an outdoor public pool, picnic areas, an amphitheater, and a playground named one of the ten best in the country by *Child* magazine fill this downtown park. | 8th–12th Sts., 13th Ave. | 304/696–5954 | Free | Daily.

Rose Garden. Since 1934, this municipal garden has been nationally recognized for its 1,000 different plant varieties and its All-American Rose Selections, which include 87 varieties of roses. | Ritter Park, 8th St. Hill | 304/696–5954 | Free | Daily.

ON THE CALENDAR

JULY: *Summerfest.* This riverfront celebration includes a carnival, lots of food, live entertainment, and boat races. | 304/525–7333.

SEPT.: *Chilifest.* The West Virginia Chili Championship is sanctioned by the International Chili Society and offers music, street performances, a hot-pepper-eating contest, and a chili cook-off. | 304/529–4857.

SEPT.: *Hilltop Festival.* Held at the Huntington Museum of Art, this annual celebration caters to kids and adults. Youngsters can feed the sheep at the petting zoo while Mom and Dad peruse the book fair. Food, live entertainment, and craft displays round out the events. | 304/529–2701.

Dining

Chili Willi's Mexican Cantina. Southwestern. A festive, bright, and noisy cantina, Chili Willi's has exposed brick walls, mismatched dishes, and an explosion of colorful wall hangings. Try the smoked chicken nachos, blue corn relleno, mesclun salad, queso fundito, or broiled chevre with salsa fresca. | 841 4th Ave. | 304/529–4857 | $6–$15 | AE, D, DC, MC, V.

Rebels and Redcoats Tavern. Continental. A quiet, romantic spot with the feel of a Colonial-era pub, the tavern is a popular spot where locals often gather after work for a bite to eat. Try the chateaubriand for two, or perhaps the chicken divan. | 412 W. 7th Ave. | 304/523–8829 | $9–$19 | AE, D, DC, MC, V.

Rocco's Ristorante. Italian. Candlelit tables occupy every corner of this small, romantic hideout. You can sample a variety of Italian specialties while soft music plays in the background. Specialties include the crab-stuffed beef filet and the lobster ravioli. | 252 Main St., Ceredo | 304/453–3000 | No lunch. Closed Mon. | $10–$27 | AE, D, DC, MC, V.

The Station at Heritage Village. Contemporary. Restored to its original 19th-century grandeur, the station has kept its original ornate oak bar intact. You can eat indoors beneath polished-wood ceiling fans as a miniature train periodically circumnavigates the dining area, or outside under an old-fashioned awning. The Station is popular among its well-heeled clientele for its savory baby back ribs and rich pasta dishes. | 11th St. and Veterans Memorial Blvd. | 304/523–6373 | Closed Sun. | $6–$23 | AE, D, MC, V.

Lodging

Best Western—Gateway. This two-story chain is in the suburbs of Huntington, 2 mi from the Huntington Mall, West Virginia's largest mall. It's also 8 mi east of the downtown area. Restaurant, bar, complimentary breakfast. Cable TV. Indoor pool. Beauty salon. Video games. Playground. Laundry facilities. Business services, free parking. | 6007 U.S. 60 E, Barboursville | 304/736–8974 | fax 304/736–8974 | gateway@ezwv.com | 174 rooms | $69 | D, DC, MC, V.

The Cedar House Bed and Breakfast. This tri-level home was custom-designed for maximum privacy and noise control, with lots of open space and breezes in the warmer months. Surrounded by 5½ acres of wooded property, the B&B also has a lofty back deck, high ceilings, and panoramic views of the surrounding countryside. It's 20 mi east of Huntington. Complimentary breakfast. Cable TV. Game room. | 92 Trenol Heights, Milton | 304/743–5516 or 888/743–5516 | www.bbonline.com/wv/cedarhouse | 3 rooms | $65–$75 | AE, D, MC, V.

Colonial Inn. Family owned and operated, this motel is 4 mi from downtown Huntington in a busy commercial area. Although there are no food facilities or services on the premises, there is a diner/omelette shop next door, and many other restaurants and shops within 5 blocks. The inn is 8 mi from the Huntington Mall. Cable TV. | 4644 U.S. Rte. 60 E | 304/736–3466 | 40 rooms | $35 | AE, D, DC, MC, V.

Days Inn. This two-story chain has a huge outdoor pool, a patio, and picnic areas. It is 10 mi northwest of downtown Huntington, and all of the rooms have outdoor access. Complimentary Continental breakfast. In-room data ports. Cable TV. Outdoor pool. Laundry facilities. | 5196 U.S. Rte. 60 E | 304/733–4477 or 800/694–8999 | www.daysinn.com | 139 rooms | $70–$90 | AE, D, DC, MC, V.

Hampton Inn. The hostelry is adjacent to the Huntington Mall, the largest mall in West Virginia. The accommodations are 5 mi from the Barboursville business area, less than 1 mi out of downtown Huntington. Complimentary Continental breakfast. In-room data ports, some microwaves, some refrigerators, some in-room hot tubs. Cable TV. Outdoor Pool. Exercise equipment. Laundry services. | 1 Cracker Barrel Dr. | 304/733–5300 or 800/HAMPTON | fax 304/733–3700 | www.hamptoninn.com | 90 rooms | $70 | AE, D, DC, MC, V.

Radisson. This high-rise chain is strategically situated in the heart of downtown Huntington, two blocks from the civic area and one block from the Harris Riverfront Park. Restaurant, bar. In-room data ports. Cable TV. Pool. Exercise equipment. Business services, airport shuttle, free parking. | 1001 3rd Ave. | 304/525–1001 | fax 304/525–1048 | 202 rooms, 6 suites | $109, $160–$400 suites | AE, D, DC, MC, V.

Red Roof Inn. Five miles from the Huntington Mall, the Civic Center, and the Blenko Glass Factory, and not far from nearly all of Huntington's major tourist attractions, this two-story white stucco motel is between Huntington and Barboursville near I–64. Cable TV. Business services. Some pets allowed. | 5190 U.S. 60 E | 304/733–3737 | fax 304/733–3786 | www.redroof.com | 108 rooms | $55 | AE, D, DC, MC, V.

Stone Lodge. Downtown Huntington is 7 mi away from this three-story brick building with copper roof trim. The inn is on a commercial strip right off the highway; it's 4 mi from Huntington Mall and 12 mi from Blenko Glass Factory, but many chain shops and restaurants are less than 5 blocks away. Restaurant, complimentary Continental breakfast. Cable TV. Pool. Business services. | 5600 U.S. 60 E | 304/736–3451 | fax 304/736–3451 | 120 rooms | $46–$65 | AE, D, DC, MC, V.

Travelodge Uptowner Inn. In the heart of downtown Huntington, next to Marshall University, this concrete and stucco building has an enclosed central corridor lined with smoked glass. Restaurant, bar, room service. In-room data ports. Cable TV. Pool, wading pool. Exercise equipment. Business services. Some pets allowed. | 1415 4th Ave. | 304/525–7741 or 800/828–9016 (reservations) | fax 304/525–5599 | 138 rooms | $65 | AE, D, DC, MC, V.

LEWISBURG

(Nearby town also listed: White Sulphur Springs)

Lewisburg, seat of Greenbrier County, is in the heart of the bluegrass country long known as the Big Levels. Originally called Camp Union, Fort Union, and Fort Savannah, the town was renamed in honor of General Andrew Lewis, who led Virginia militiamen in the battle of Point Pleasant in 1774. Lewisburg itself was the site of a battle on May 23, 1862, when Confederate and Union forces clashed; although the Union won the battle, Lewisburg remained a Confederate outpost for most of the war. The town still shows scars from the Civil War today.

Lewisburg is an ideal place to stay while exploring the surrounding countryside or shopping the local stores, and is justly famous for its wealth of antique stores. A large part of the town is designated a National Register Historic District, where you'll find more than 60 18th-century buildings, many made of native limestone or brick. At night, gas lamps flicker on the quaint storefronts and signs.

Information: **Lewisburg Visitors Center** | 105 Church St. 24901 | 304/645–1000 or 800/833–2068.

Attractions

Carnegie Hall. Built in 1902 as a classroom building and an auditorium for the Lewisburg Female Institute, this three-story brick building today serves as a center for educational and cultural activities. The auditorium hosts drama, music, dancing, pottery making, and weaving classes and recitals. Carnegie Hall is home to the Chamber of Commerce and the Visitors Center. | 105 Church St. | 304/645–1000 | Free | Daily.

Confederate Cemetery. Ninety-five unknown Confederate soldiers, casualties of the 1862 Battle of Lewisburg, are buried in this mass grave. You can pick up at brochure at the Carnegie Hall Visitor Center. | McElhenney Rd., off Church St. behind Carnegie Hall | 304/645–1000 | Free | Daily, dawn to dusk.

KODAK'S TIPS FOR PHOTOGRAPHING WEATHER

Rainbows
- Find rainbows by facing away from the sun after a storm
- Use your auto-exposure mode
- With a SLR, use a polarizing filter to deepen colors

Fog and Mist
- Use bold shapes as focal points
- Add extra exposure manually or use exposure compensation
- Choose long lenses to heighten fog and mist effects

In the Rain
- Look for abstract designs in puddles and wet pavement
- Control rain-streaking with shutter speed
- Protect cameras with plastic bags or waterproof housings

Lightning
- Photograph from a safe location
- In daylight, expose for existing light
- At night, leave the shutter open during several flashes

From Kodak Guide to Shooting Great Travel Pictures © 2000 by Fodor's Travel Publications

Lewisburg Historic District. Sixty homes and other buildings from the 18th and 19th centuries make up the 235-acre historic district in Lewisburg which centers around the Old Stone Church and Carnegie Hall. | 304/645–1000 | Daily.

Lost World Caverns. Discovered in 1942, the caverns contain several large rooms with stalactite, stalagmite, and flowstone formations. The main room is 1,000 ft long and nearly 75 ft wide; one rock formation is more than 40 ft high and has a circumference of 25 ft. | HC34 Fairview Rd.; Route 60, 2 mi west of Lewisburg | 304/645–6677 | $8 | Mid-May–Labor Day, daily 9–7; Labor Day–mid-May, daily 9–5.

North House Museum. This restored 1820 house has antiques and artifacts dating from the early 1700s to the late 1800s; there is also a library filled with antiques from the same period. | 301 Washington St. | 304/645–3398 | www.greenbrierhistorical.org | $3 | Mon.–Sat. 10–4, closed Sun.

Old Stone Church. Home to one of the earliest Presbyterian congregations in the state, the Old Stone Church was founded in 1796 by Scots-Irish settlers. They built the church with native limestone blocks; it is believed that women from the congregation carried the blocks on horseback from the Greenbrier River, 4 mi away. Today, the church retains its original slave balcony and hand-hewn woodwork. | 200 Church St. | 304/645–2676 | Free | Daily 9–4.

ON THE CALENDAR

AUG.: *State Fair of West Virginia.* This two-week celebration includes a circus, a carnival, fireworks, performers, and exhibits; each day there are livestock shows, harness racing, and crafts displays. The fair is 3 mi south of I–64 on Route 219. | 304/645–1090.
OCT.: *T.O.O.T.* The T.O.O.T. (Taste Of Our Towns) festival lets you sample dishes prepared by local restaurants and residents; live entertainment plays in the background as you embark upon your culinary journey. | 304/645–1000.

Dining
Food and Friends. Eclectic. American, Italian, and Mexican cuisine have found a place on the menu here. The house signature dish is the Applejack chicken, a sautéed chicken breast topped with wild mushrooms and caramelized pears flamed with applejack brandy. For dessert, the cappuccino eclair cake makes a decadent selection. There are two open rooms with many single-table nooks and crannies; dried flowers, fresh flowers, and artwork adorn the tables and walls. You can also eat outside on the patio. | 213 W. Washington St. | 304/645–4548 | Closed Sun. | $6–$15 | AE, D, DC, MC, V.

The General Lewis Country Inn and Restaurant. Continental. Expect elegant dining at this 1843 country inn, surrounded by broad lawns, flowering gardens, and tall trees; don't miss the huge, hand-hewn beams in the entryway. The fresh veal, Southern fried chicken, roast duckling, filet mignon, lamb, and fresh mountain trout all vie for attention, but the inn also serves other Southern-style dishes and homemade bread and desserts. Before or after your meal, you'll sense those rocking chairs on the veranda beckoning. | 301 E. Washington St. | 304/645–2600 or 800/628–4454 | Reservations essential | $10–$20 | AE, D, MC, V.

Washington Street Inn. Italian. Built in 1800, the Washington Street Inn became a restaurant in 1999. The menu is varied and changes frequently; marinated shrimp, mussels with penne pasta, and the filet of beef highlight the menu. Dine in the main room, decorated with a vast collection of antiques and Civil War memorabilia, or on the porch. | 208 W. Washington St. | 304/645–1744 | Closed Sun., Mon. | $10–$24 | AE, D, DC, MC, V.

Lodging
Brier Inn. Directly off I–64 Exit 169 (Roenceverte exit), this hostelry is not fancy; parking is available for 18-wheel trucks. Restaurant, bar (with entertainment), room service. In-room data ports. Cable TV. Pool. Business services. Some pets allowed (fee). | 540 N. Jefferson St. | 304/645–7722 | fax 304/645–7865 | 162 rooms | $47 | AE, D, DC, MC, V.

Days Inn. This one-story chain is only ½ mi from downtown restaurants. Because of its hilltop location above I–64, every room has scenic views. Cable TV. Business services, airport shuttle. Some pets allowed (fee). | 635 N. Jefferson St. | 304/645–2345 or 800/325–2525 | fax 304/645–5501 | 26 rooms | $110 | AE, D, DC, MC, V.

Embassy Inn. This two-story brick building is in downtown Lewisburg; rooms have wood paneling and flowered bedspreads. There is a private outdoor patio, and the inn is surrounded by restaurants. Complimentary Continental breakfast. In-room data ports. Microwaves, refrigerators. Cable TV. Outdoor hot tub. Laundry facilities. Pets allowed (fee). | 107 West Fair St. | 304/645–7070 or 800/260–8641 | fax 304/645–3383 | www.embassyinn.com | 32 rooms | $40—$55 | MC, V.

Fort Savannah Inn. This three-story hostelry is in the heart of historic Lewisburg. The inn is on a quiet street, 1 block from several historic sites, and 3 mi from Lost World Caverns. Restaurant, room service. Cable TV. Pool. Business services, airport shuttle. Some pets allowed (fee). | 204 N. Jefferson St. | 304/645–3055 or 800/678–3055 | 67 rooms | $70 | AE, D, DC, MC, V.

★ **The General Lewis Country Inn and Restaurant.** The brick building is furnished with 19th-century pieces and antiques collected in the area. Every room has china, glass, prints, and other memorabilia; you can be sure the bed you sleep in is at least a century old. Downstairs is the popular restaurant; historical sites are three blocks away. Restaurant, bar, dining room, room service. Cable TV. No smoking. | 301 E. Washington St. | 304/645–2600 or 800/628–4454 | fax 304/645–2600 | www.generallewisinn.com | 24 rooms, 2 suites | $82–$123, $107–$140 suites | AE, D, MC, V.

The Minnie Manor Inn. From the back terrace of this circa-1830s, two-story brick house on a hill, you can take in views of Lewisburg. Fireplaces and floral Laura Ashley furnishings enhance the accommodations. Complimentary breakfast. Cable TV. Outdoor hot tub. No pets. | 403 E. Washington St. | 304/647–4096 | 8 rooms | $65–$70 | No credit cards.

MARLINTON

MAP 17, D6

(Nearby town also listed: Richwood)

Marlinton is known as "the birthplace of rivers" because eight major rivers—the Cheat, Cranberry, Elk, Greenbrier, Shaver's Fork, Williams, Tygart, and Gauley—all begin there.

The first settlers were Stephen Sewell and Jacob Marlin, for whom the town was named. The two men came here in 1749 and built themselves a log cabin, thus establishing the first English settlement west of the Alleghenies. One night they had a serious quarrel, apparently over a religious question, and Sewell stormed out of the cabin and took up temporary residence in a hollow tree that stood near the railroad station until 1930.

Information: **Pocahontas County Tourism Commission** | 700 4th Ave. 24954 | 304/799–4636 or 800/336–7009 | pccvb@pocahontascountywv.com | www.pocahontas-countywv.com.

Attractions

Cass Scenic Railroad State Park. This state park encompasses an authentic turn-of-the-century lumber-company town and offers you a ride up to the second-highest peak in West Virginia in open railcars once used to haul logs off the mountain. Trains are drawn by geared Shay steam locomotives, built at the turn of the century to negotiate steep terrain. Both 2-hr and 5-hr trips are available. | Off Rte. 92, on Rte. 66, Main St. | 304/456–4300 | www.neumedia.net/~cassrr | $14–$19 | Mid-May–Oct., daily, weekends only after Labor Day; fall schedule varies.

Cranberry Mountain Nature Center—Monongahela National Forest. This popular center exhibits plants and animals of the region. | Rte. 150, on Rtes. 39 and 55, 14 mi west of Marlinton | 304/653–4826 or 304/846–2695 | Free | Apr.–Nov., daily 9–5.

The largest bogs in West Virginia are 14 mi west of Marlinton at the **Cranberry Glades Botanical Area,** and include plant and animal species that are common to the tundra but rare in Appalachia. A ½-mi boardwalk winds through parts of 35,600 acres. | Rte. 150 | 304/653–4826 | Apr.–Nov., daily.

Edray Trout Hatchery. Here you'll see rainbow, brook, brown, and golden trout. You may be lucky enough to feed the larger fish in their natural habitat. | 17 Edray Rd. | 304/799–6461 | Free | Daily 9–4.

Elk River Touring Center (Skiing). Off-road mountain bike and cross-country ski tours include the Greenbrier River Trail, Cranberry Glades, and Cass Scenic Railroad State Park. Multiday tours, instruction, rentals, a snowshoe resort, fly fishing, and equipment are available. | U.S. 219, Slatyfork | 304/572–3771 | www.ertc.com | Admissino price varies | Daily.

Greenbrier River Trail. This hiking, biking, and skiing trail follows the Chesapeake and Ohio Railroad. The trail passes over 35 bridges and through two tunnels from just south of Cass to south of White Sulphur Springs. | County Road 21, Beaver Creek Road, off Rte. 9 | 304/799–4087 | www.wvparks.com/greenbrierrivertrail.com | Free | Daily.

★ **National Radio Astronomy Observatory.** Jutting from the landscape 25 mi north of Marlinton proper, huge radio telescopes listen for life in outer space. The Green Bank Telescope, completed in 1998, is the largest telescope of its kind in the world. | Rte. 28/92, Green Bank | 304/456–2209 | www.gb.nrao.edu | Free | Daily 9–4; tours by appointment on the hour.

The Pocahontas County Courthouse. This municipal building was built in 1893; the two-story, brick Victorian Romanesque structure fills a full city block. Visit the jail at the back of the courthouse to learn about its once infamous residents. | 900 10th Ave. | 304/799–6063 | Free | Weekdays 9–4:30, closed weekends.

The Pocahontas County Historical Museum. Operated by the Pocahontas County Historical Society, this small museum has documents, vintage photographs, and artifacts detailing the county's history. The building itself dates back to 1904. One item of special interest is a Swiss music box that plays 36 songs. | U.S. 219 S | 304/799–6659 | $2 | June–Labor Day, Mon.–Sat. 11–5, Sun. 1–5.

Seneca State Forest. The 11,684-acre state forest is West Virginia's oldest. It has rental cabins, hiking trails, and a small lake for fishing. | Rte. 28, 4 mi south of Dunmore | 304/799–6213 | www.wvparks.com | senecasf@neumedia.net | Free | Daily.

Snowshoe/Silver Creek Mountain Resort (Skiing). This resort has the state's largest developed skiing and snowboarding operation, with 53 slopes and trails. It has 125 mountain bike trails, a golf course, tennis courts, and swimming for year-round recreation. | 10 Snowshoe Dr., Rte. 66 | 304/572–1000 or 304/572–4636 | www.snowshoemtn.com | Free | Daily.

ON THE CALENDAR

JULY: *Pioneer Days in Pocahontas County.* This celebration of mountain culture showcases bluegrass, fiddle, and banjo contests; square dances; parades; and crafts displays. The festival is held on 2nd Avenue. | 304/799–4315.

SEPT.: *Autumn Harvest Festival and Roadkill Cook-Off.* An annual festival that includes a wild-game cooking contest, music, and arts and crafts. | 800/336–7009.

Dining

The River Place. American. This eatery is family owned and operated, and serves homestyle desserts. Daily specials include the rainbow trout served with potatoes, salad, and

MARLINTON

INTRO
ATTRACTIONS
DINING
LODGING

dinner rolls. The dining room displays local artwork, honey and syrup containers, weavings, candles, and other handcrafted gifts. You can eat at the Amish oak tables, or sit outside on a deck overlooking the Greenbrier River. | 814 1st Ave. | 304/799–7233 | fax 304/799–4465 | Breakfast also available | $6–$15 | AE, MC, V.

Lodging
Marlinton Motor Inn. This property, composed of two brick buildings in a rural area just outside Marlington, is nestled in the Allegheny Mountains, and surrounded by fields and woods. There are restaurants ½ mi away. Restaurant, bar, room service. Outdoor pool. Some pets allowed. | HC 69, Box 25; Rte. 219, 4 mi north of Marlinton | 304/799–4711 | 70 rooms in 2 buildings | $59 | AE, D, DC, MC, V.

The River Place. Built in 1994, this hostlery is on the edge of town on the banks of the Greenbrier River. In addition to the five rooms upstairs, there is a three-bedroom cottage with a full kitchen that is available to guests. Rooms have contemporary furnishings. Cable TV. No pets. | 814 1st Ave. | 304/799–7233 | fax 304/799–4465 | melriver@neumedia.net | www.neumedia.net/~melriver | 8 rooms | $30–$90 | AE, MC, V.

MARTINSBURG

MAP 17, F2

(Nearby town also listed: Shepherdstown)

General Adam Stephen laid out Martinsburg in 1773, and the town was incorporated in 1778. Quaint and picturesque, full of historic attractions, Martinsburg can be said to be showing its age. With the arrival of the railroad, it became an important rail and shipping point. In the 19th century, orchards were planted around Martinsburg, transforming it into a distribution center for apples and peaches. Today you can watch fruit being prepared for shipment at the Jefferson Orchards in Kearneysville, about 10 mi southeast of the city.

Martinsburg was the home of Belle Boyd, the most celebrated female spy of the Civil War, known to her many admirers as "La Belle Rebelle." When only 17, she shot a Union soldier in her parents' house after he threatened her mother.

Information: **Martinsburg/Berkeley County Convention and Visitors Bureau** | 208 S. Queen St. 25401 | 304/264–8801 or 800/4WVA–FUN | www.travelwv.com.

Attractions
The Belle Boyd House. Home of the famous Confederate spy Belle Boyd, this house was built in 1853 in Greek Revival style. Today it houses Civil War antiquities and an archives department with a focus on local history. There is period clothing on display in the Corning Room. | 126 E. Race St. | 304/267–4713 | Free | Wed.–Sat. 10–4, closed Sun.–Tues.

General Adam Stephen House. The house was built of limestone between 1772 and 1789 by General Adam Stephen, a Revolutionary War officer and the founder of Martinsburg (he named the town for a friend, Colonel Thomas B. Martin). | 309 E. John St. | 304/267–4434 | www.travelwv.com/adam.htm | Free | May–Oct., Wed. and Fri. 10–2:30, weekends 2–5; tours by appointment; closed Mon., Tues., Thurs.

Located on the grounds of the General Adam Stephen House, the 1876 **Triple Brick Museum** gets its name from the fact that it was built in three sections. It's now a museum devoted to local history. | 313 E. John St. | 304/267–4434 | www.travelwv.com/triple.htm | Free | May–Oct., Daily 10–2:30, weekends 2–5; tours by appointment.

Jefferson Orchards. You can pick your own pumpkin in the fall, or buy fresh-picked apples or baked goods at this 500-acre orchard. | Rte. 9; 7 mi east of Martinsburg | 304/725–9149 | Free | Daily 8–4:30.

MAY: *West Virginia Wine & Arts Festival.* Held on the lawn of the Boydville Inn during Memorial Day weekend, this is a gathering of vintners and artists. Live jazz and contemporary music, magicians, dance, and food highlight the scheduled events. Tickets are $10 if you're tasting wine and $5 if you're not. | 304/263–0224.

Dining

Cracker Barrel Old Country Store. Southern. Filled with artifacts, genuine antiques, memorabilia, and old farm equipment, the Cracker Barrel chain serves big helpings of Southern fare such as chicken and dumplings, sugar-cured ham, farm-raised catfish filet, grilled pork chops, and breaded fried okra. | 725 Foxcroft Ave. | 304/262–3660 | Breakfast also available | $7–$10 | AE, D, DC, MC, V.

El Ranchero. Mexican. Serving traditional fare like fajitas and enchiladas, this eatery is in one of Martinsburg's larger shopping malls. The interior is decorated with authentic Mexican ornaments. | North Mall Plaza, on Foxcroft Dr. | 304/262–4053 | $10–$15 | AE, D, DC, MC, V.

Fazoli's. Italian. Italian music plays in the background all day long at this casual eatery in downtown Martinsburg. While squares of lasagne are served by the dozen, patrons also favor the spaghetti, fettucine, ravioli, and pizza. Vintage pictures of Italy line the walls. | 775 Foxcroft Ave. | 304/262–2822 | $5–$10 | MC, V.

Heatherfield's Restaurant. American. In downtown Martinsburg, this restaurant has linen tablecloths, fresh flowers, and local artwork on the walls. The most popular dishes are the prime rib and the grilled chicken. Kids menu and weekend buffet available. | 301 Foxcroft Ave. | 304/267–8311 | Closed Sun. No lunch | $10–$15 | AE, D, DC, MC, V.

Historic Boomtown Restaurant. American. Housed in a restored Victorian, this restaurant has four dining rooms filled with period antiques; the walls are lined with Civil War–era paintings. Outdoor seating is available on the patio in the garden. Choose from salads, steak, and pasta; the homemade crab cakes are popular. | 522 W. King St. | 304/263–8840. | Closed Sun. | $15–$20 | AE, D, MC, V.

Lodging

Boydville—the Inn at Martinsburg. Built in 1812, this manor house is on 10 wooded acres; 19th-century notables such as Stonewall Jackson and Henry Clay both stayed here. French chandeliers light the front parlors, and murals adorn the guest rooms. The shops and restaurants of Martinsburg are a 5-minute drive away. | 601 S. Queen St. | 304/263–1448 | lfrye@intrepid.net | Closed Aug. | 7 rooms | $100–$125 | MC, V.

Comfort Inn. This four-story chain is in a commercial area 1½ mi outside town off I-81 Exit 16E (Queen St. exit). The hostelry is 2 mi from the Belle Boyd House and the Triple Brick Museum, and within 6 blocks of several restaurants. Complimentary Continental breakfast. In-room data ports, some minibars, some microwaves, some refrigerators. Cable TV. Pool. Gym. Laundry facilities. Business services. | 1872 Edwin Miller Blvd. | 304/263–6200 | fax 304/267–0095 | wvweb.com/www/comfort_inn_mtsbg.html | 110 rooms, 15 suites | $69, $125 suites | AE, D, DC, MC, V.

Comfort Suites. In an isolated residential area 5 mi south of Martinsburg, this three-story chain is built in a modern adobe style. It is 5 mi from Martinsburg Mall, and 10 mi from the C & O Canal. Harpers Ferry National Park and Antietam Park are 15 mi away. Complimentary Continental breakfast. Microwaves, refrigerators. Cable TV. Pool. Hot tub. Exercise equipment. Laundry facilities. Business services. | U.S. 9 E and Short Rd. | 304/263–8888 | fax 304/263–1540 | wvweb.com/www/comfort_suites | 76 rooms | $65–$75 | AE, D, DC, MC, V.

Farmhouse on Tomahawk Run. About 10 mi west of Martinsburg, this large Civil War–era farmhouse is beside the Tomahawk Run stream. It is surrounded by walking paths that wind through 280 acres of woods, hills, and meadows. Rooms are furnished with period antiques and have private balconies. Relax in one of the rocking chairs on the wraparound porch. Complimentary breakfast. TV in common area. Outdoor hot tub. No pets. | 1828 Tomahawk Run Rd. | 304/754–7350 or 888/266–9516 | tomahawk@intrepid.net | www.tomahawkrun.com | 5 rooms | $95–$165 | AE, D, DC, V.

Holiday Inn. About ½ mi off I–81 exit 13 (King St. exit) near downtown Martinsburg, this five-story brick hotel is in a commercial area 1½ mi from War Memorial Park. The Victorian-style interior was renovated in 2000. Restaurant. In-room data ports, some refrigerators. Cable TV. 2 pools (1 indoor). Hot tub. Tennis. Gym. Business services. Some pets allowed. | 301 Foxcroft Ave. | 304/267–5500 | fax 304/264–9157 | 120 rooms | $79–$89 | AE, D, DC, MC, V.

Knights Inn. In a commercial area ¼ mi from Martinsburg, this hostelry is on 1 acre surrounded by trees and flowers. The motel is 10 mi from Antietam Battlefield, and Harpers Ferry is approximately 20 mi away. Some kitchenettes, microwaves, refrigerators. Cable TV. Business services. Some pets allowed. | 1599 Edwin Miller Blvd. | 304/267–2211 | fax 304/267–9606 | 59 rooms | $50 | AE, D, DC, MC, V.

Pulpit & Palette. This 1870 Victorian villa is in the middle of town. The rooms are furnished in a combination of wicker and period antiques. Afternoon tea, drinks, and evening snacks are complimentary. Lounge on the upstairs veranda or in the TV room. Complimentary breakfast. No pets. | 516 W. John St. | 304/263–7012 | www.pulpitandpalette.com | 2 rooms | $65–80 | Closed Jan. | MC, V.

Super 8. This three-story chain is in a commercial area in Martinsburg off I–81 Exit 16 E(Queen St. exit). The inn is 1 block from a steak house, within 5 blocks of several other restaurants, and 2 mi from the Martinsburg Mall. Complimentary Continental breakfast. Cable TV. Some pets allowed. | 1602 Edwin Miller Blvd. | 304/263–0801 | 43 rooms | $56 | AE, D, DC, MC, V.

The Woods Resort and Conference Center. You'll find rustic furnishings and a rural setting at this mountain resort, surrounded by 1,800 acres, mountain views, and a golf course. The resort is 12 mi off I–81 Exit 16 West (Hedgesville/Berkeley Springs exit). Bar (with entertainment), dining room. Some kitchenettes, refrigerators, some in-room hot tubs. Cable TV. 3 pools (1 indoor), wading pools. Hot tub. Tennis. Exercise equipment. Children's programs. Laundry facilities. Business services. | Mountain Lake Rd., Hedgesville | 304/754–7977 or 800/248–2222 | fax 304/754–8146 | www.thewoodsresort.com | 60 rooms in 3 lodges; 14 cabins | $108, $159 cabins (2–night minimum stay on weekends) | AE, D, DC, MC, V.

MINERALWELLS

MAP 17, B4

(Nearby town also listed: Parkersburg)

The British seized this region in 1763, right at the end of the French and Indian War. Settlement of the area didn't begin in earnest until oil was discovered in the area in 1860.

The spelling of this Wood County community's name—one word or two—is debated as much as its unwillingness to incorporate. Southwest of Parkersburg off I–77, Mineralwells is among the fastest growing areas in the state.

Information: Parkersburg/Wood County Convention and Visitors Bureau | 350 7th St., Parkersburg 26101 | 304/428–1130 or 800/752–4982 | www.parkersburgcdb.org.

JULY: *West Virginia Interstate Fair and Exposition.* The state's largest county fair draws crowds from near and wide; there are performers, a carnival, livestock, arts and crafts, and food. You'll find the fair at the 4-H Campgrounds on Butcher Bend Road. | 304/489–1301.

SEPT.: *West Virginia Honey Festival.* The festival offers a honey-bake contest, a bee beard demonstration, and a honey run, at the 4-H Campgrounds on Butcher Bend Road. | 304/428–1130.

Dining

Colonnade Grille. Seafood/Steak. Steak and seafood selections dominate the menu at this restaurant in central Mineralwells, next to the Woodridge Plantation Golf Course. The building was constructed in 1992, although the traditional wood-paneled dining room looks much older. Early American and Colonial-era prints of the area line the walls. | 301 Woodridge Dr. | 304/489–3990 | Closed Sun., Mon. No lunch | $14–$22 | AE, D, DC, MC, V.

Lodging

Hampton Inn Hotel. This three-story hotel is 3 mi from several golf courses. The inn is off the interstate on the main commerical strip in Mineralwells, surrounded by restaurants, convenience stores and gas stations. Microwaves, refrigerators. Cable TV. Outdoor Pool. Hot Tub. Exercise equipment. Laundry facilities. No pets. | I–77 and Rte. 14 | 304/489–2900 or 800/426–7866 | fax 304/489–2920 | www.hamptoninn.com | 68 rooms | $68–$90 | AE, D, DC, V.

MOOREFIELD

MAP 17, E4

(Nearby town also listed: Petersburg)

Moorefield, with a population of 2,148, is listed on the National Register of Historic Places. It was established in 1777 and named after Conrad Moore, who owned the land on which the town was laid out. The historic district includes the Dr. William B. Bowen House, the McCoy-McMechen Theatre and Museum, and the Old Stone Tavern.

Information: **Potomac Highlands Travel Council** | Box 1456, Elkins 26241 | 304/636–8400 | www.mountainhighlands.com.

Attractions

Dr. Bowen House. In 1887, about the time Dr. Bowen bought this 1801 home, which had previously been used as a tavern, it was divided into two buildings by an alleyway. Today the Hardy County Historical Society owns it; the collection of local artifacts is showcased. | 135 N. Main St. | 304/538–2974 | Donations accepted | By appointment only.

Lost River State Park and Stables. Part of this 3,712-acre park remains virgin forest. The park offers swimming, fishing, hiking, horseback riding, and rental cabins. | 4 mi west of Rte. 259, on Rte. 12 | 304/897–5372 or 800/CALL–WVA | www.wvparks.com/lostriver | Free | Daily 6 AM–10 PM.

McCoy-McMechen Theatre Museum. Eunice McCoy built this theater in 1928 and showed plays and movies there until her death in the 1980s, when she left most of her estate to the community to renovate the theater. Today, two museum rooms display items from her estate, and the 248-seat theater resembles its old Roaring-Twenties self. Theatrical and musical groups perform here throughout the year; call the library for current information. | 111 N. Main St. | 304/538–6560 | $10 | Tour by appointment only.

Nan & Pap's Flea Market. This small, family-run flea market is a picker's palace of secondhand goods, antiques, and other collectibles. | 59 Jenkins Run Rd. | 304/538–6505 | Mon.–Sat. 8–6 | Sun.

Old Stone Tavern. The first section of this, the oldest home in town, was built in 1788, and two more sections were built in the mid-nineteenth century and at the turn of the century. Dark woodwork and leaded-glass bay window accent the most recent section of the house. On the National Register of Historic Places, the home is currently occupied but open to the public during Heritage Weekend, held on the last weekend in September. | 117 S. Main St. | 304/636–8400 | Free | Private residence; open to public last weekend in Sept.

ON THE CALENDAR

JULY: *West Virginia Poultry Convention and Festival.* Watch a reenactment of the Civil War or hunker down with some barbecued chicken at this summer festival. Events are scattered throughout the community for one week every July. | 304/538–2725.

SEPT.: *Hardy County Heritage and Harvest Weekend.* Held the last weekend of the month, this annual event gives locals and visitors alike the opportunity to tour historic buildings (including the Old Stone Tavern and Bowen House). The weekend festival also features walking tours, a parade, a Civil War encampment, and an antique auto show. | 304/538–6560.

Dining

Colts Restaurant & Pizza Park Eatery. American. The country cooking at this restaurant is its signature—from grilled steaks and pizzas to homemade cobblers, apple dumplings, and pies. The eclectic dining room, covered in flowered wallpaper and hung with taxidermied deer heads and paintings by the owner's daughter, draws locals and tourists alike. It's just outside of Moorefield. | 425 S. Main St. | 304/538–2523 | $5–$14 | No credit cards.

Lodging

Evans' Motel. Originally built in the 1950s, this one-story motel is in a commercial area on the north side of town. The motel is 25 mi from Seneca Rocks and Smoke Hole Caverns. In-room data ports. Cable TV. | 508 N. Main St. | 304/538–7771 | 12 rooms | $40–$45 | AE, DC, MC, V.

South Branch Inn. This inn has suites with hot tubs and living areas, as well as a conference facility. It is next to a Ponderosa Steak House restaurant and ½ mi from the town park. Complimentary Continental breakfast. In-room data ports, some microwaves, some refrigerators. Cable TV. Hot tubs. Laundry service. No pets. | Route 220 N | 800/856–9167 | 54 rooms, 2 suites | $50–$70 rooms, $99 suites | AE, DC, D, MC, V.

MORGANTOWN

MAP 17, D3

(Nearby towns also listed: Clarksburg, Fairmont)

Morgan Morgan of Wales is usually credited as being the first European settler in what is now West Virginia. It was his son Zackquill Morgan who founded Morgantown, in 1766–68, on the east bank of the Monongahela River. When the Baltimore and Ohio Railroad company wanted to lay a track through the town, residents protested the plans of the "soulless corporation," claiming the "screeching locomotives would affect wagon traffic, reduce the price of horse feed, set our haystacks on fire, and frighten to death our hogs and wives." The rail line was diverted to nearby Fairmont, which soon prospered.

All was not lost, however; today Morgantown is a university town and is best known as the home of West Virginia University and its athletic teams, the Mountaineers.

The university is the economic hub of the city, and its medical center draws people from around the state.

Information: Greater Morgantown Convention and Visitors Bureau | 709 Beechurst Ave. 26505 | 304/292–5081 or 800/458–7373 | www.tourmorgantown.com.

Attractions

Coopers Rock State Forest. Woods, rock formations, and hiking and cross-country skiing trails cover 12,713 forested acres off I–68. The Henry Clay Iron Furnace, built in the 19th century, and a spectacular view of the Cheat River Valley are among the highlights here. | I–68, | 304/594–1561 | www.wvparks.com/coopersrock | Free | Daily, dawn to dusk. Closed mid-Dec.–Mar.

Chestnut Ridge Park. Located just outside Morgantown, the park provides camping, reunion facilities, picnic areas, swimming, and trails for sledding and cross-country skiing. | Off I–68, Exit 15, 7 mi from Morgantown | 304/594–1773 | Free | Daily.

West Virginia University. Founded in 1867, this is the state's largest institution of higher learning. Through its 13 colleges and schools, WVU offers 166 bachelor's, master's, doctoral, and professional degrees; its annual operating budget is $461 million. | Woodburn Hall, University Ave. | 800/344–9881 | www.wvu.edu | Free | Daily.

A replica of a 19th-century pharmacy, the **Cook-Hayman Pharmacy Museum** is housed in the West Virginia University Medical Center. | Health Sciences Center North, Room 1132 Medical Center Dr. | 304/293–5101 | Free | Tours by appointment.

The 50-acre **Core Arboretum** contains hundreds of species of trees, shrubs, and native wildflowers, and 3½ mi of trails. It serves as a research facility and classroom for the university. | Monongahela Blvd. | 304/293–5201 | Free | Daily.

The university's mass-transit system, **Personal Rapid Transit System (PRT),** connects the downtown and Evansdale campuses. Guided tours are available by reservation. The route connects WVU campuses and downtown Morgantown. | 99 8th St. | 304/293–5011 | www.wvu.edu | 50¢ | Fall/spring hours are same as university hours; summer hours vary.

Originally the site of a female seminary, the three buildings that make up **Woodburn Circle** became the core of the university in 1867. Woodburn Hall was finished in 1893; two wings were added by 1911. It now houses administrative offices and classrooms. | University Ave., | 304/293–4611 | www.wvu.edu | Weekdays during school hrs.

White-water Rafting. Several white-water outfitters, including **Appalachian Wildwater** (800/4RAFTIN), **Cheat River Outfitters** (888/99–RIVER), and **Laurel Highlands River Tours** (304/329–2024. www.laurelhighlands.com), offer rafting on the Cheat River. | 800/CALL–WVA | www.cheatriveroutfitters.com | Admission prices vary | Call individual outfitters for times and hours.

ON THE CALENDAR

SEPT.: Mason-Dixon Festival. The dividing line between North and South is commemorated with a river regatta, cruises, crew races, and arts and crafts. | 304/599–1104.
SEPT.–DEC.: Mountaineer Football. Few college football programs have as loyal a fan base as the West Virginia Mountaineers. Each home game brings upward of 70,000 people to Mountaineer Field, 3 mi south of downtown Morgantown. The tailgate parties before the gridiron contests are legendary. | 800/WVU–GAME.
OCT.: Mountaineer Balloon Festival. Hot-air balloonists, races, and rides are the highlights of this annual balloon festival. | 304/296–8356.

Dining

Back Bay. American. The large wooden deck that marks the entryway to this seafood restaurant is hung with nautical flags and stuffed fish; inside, the marine motif continues. You can choose from a wide selection of seafood dishes, including the Surf and Turf (a strip steak or prime rib served with your choice of seafood), or the enormous

Admiral's Feast Platter, which offers a mound of lobster, scallops, stuffed shrimp, crab legs, and a catch of the day. | 1869 Mileground | 304/296–3027 | No lunch Sat. | $12–$20 | AE, D, MC, V.

Glasshouse Grille. Contemporary. Fresh seafood, steaks, original pasta combinations, and salads are the staples of the Mediterranean-influenced menu at this small bistro. Beer and liquor is served, along with a large selection of wines. | 709 Beechurst Ave., Seneca Center | 304/296–8460 | Closed Sun. No lunch | AE, D, DC, MC, V.

La Casa Mexican Grill. Mexican. Burritos, tacos, chimichangas, and tamales are available at this bar and grill, which is in a 19th-century warehouse. You can sit on the deck overlooking the Monongahela River. There is a long list of imported Mexican beers. | 156 Clay St. | 304/292–6701. | $7–$18 | AE, D, MC, V.

Mountain People's Kitchen. Vegetarian. The Fakin' Fajita and the Philly Cheese Steak are two of the more popular seitan (a beef substitute) selections made at this vegan deli and market. Hummus, house salads, beans, tofu, and soy products round out the menu. The dinner specials are influenced by Native American tradition. Sunday brunch available. | 1400 University Ave. | 304/291–6131 | $3–$5 | D, MC, V.

Tiberio's Italian Restaurant. Italian. This local favorite can be found in the Cheat Lake area, and is known for its large selection of entrées, including pasta, steaks, seafood, chicken, and veal. Locals come for the homemade red sauce and the coconut cream pie. | 857 Pierpont Rd. | 304/594–0832 | Closed Mon. | $7–$16 | AE, DC, MC, V.

Lodging

Almost Heaven Bed & Breakfast. Hundreds of books can be seen in the parlor as you enter this Queen Anne Victorian structure built in 1989. Rooms have feather beds, ceiling fans, and early-20th-century antiques. The veranda affords a panoramic view of the mountains. Dining room, complimentary breakfast. Cable TV. No kids. No pets. | 91 Scott Ave. | 304/296–4007 | www.sbccom.com/vid/almostheaven | 5 rooms | $75–$150 | AE, DC, D, MC, V.

Applewood Bed & Breakfast. This post-and-beam house was built on the second highest peak in Monongahela County. You can explore the 35 acres of grounds or warm up by the huge stone fireplace. Cherrywood furnishings are in the common areas and the guest rooms. The inn is 4 mi outside of Morgantown. Complimentary breakfast. Cable TV, VCR. Outdoor pool. Hot tub. Pets allowed. | 1749 Smithtown Rd. | 304/296–2607 | www.appelwood.com | 3 rooms | $55–$75 | MC, V.

Comfort Inn. This motel is near I–68 in a commercial area 3 mi south of Star City. It is close to WVU, the WVU Mountaineer Stadium, and a shopping mall. Complimentary Continental breakfast. Cable TV. Pool. Hot tub. Exercise equipment. Business services. | 225 Comfort Inn Dr. | 304/296–9364 | fax 304/296–0469 | 81 rooms | $68 | AE, D, DC, MC, V.

Days Inn. This three-story chain is in a commercial area close to WVU, the WVU Mountaineer Stadium, a shopping mall, and I–79. Restaurant, bar (with entertainment), complimentary breakfast, room service. Cable TV. Indoor pool. Hot tub. Exercise equipment. Laundry facilities. Business services. | 366 Boyers Ave., Star City | 304/598–2120 | fax 304/598–3272 | 102 rooms | $70 | AE, D, DC, MC, V.

Econo Lodge. Close to a shopping center, WVU, and the WVU Mountaineer Stadium, this two-story chain is in a suburb less than 2 mi west of Morgantown. Cable TV. Business services. | 15 Commerce Dr., Westover | 304/296–8774 | 81 rooms | $52–$58 | AE, D, DC, MC, V.

Econo Lodge—Coliseum. This two-story chain is in a commercial area 1 mi outside of Morgantown in Star City, next to the WVU Coliseum and the WVU Evansdale Campus. Complimentary Continental breakfast. Cable TV. Business services. Some pets allowed. | 3506 Monongahela Blvd. | 304/599–8181 | fax 304/599–8187 | 72 rooms | $66 | AE, D, DC, MC, V.

Fieldcrest Manor Bed & Breakfast. This fieldstone house built in 1915 is situated on five manicured acres of 100-year-old maples and evergreens. The guest rooms are filled with antiques and have wood floors and large windows overlooking the property. You can sit out on the front veranda and watch the mountain sunset. Complimentary breakfast. In-room data ports. Cable TV. No pets. No kids. | 1440 Stewartstown Rd. | 304/599–2686 or 800/765–0569 | fax 304/599–2853 | innkeeper@fieldcrestmanor.com | www.fieldcrestmanor.com | 6 rooms | $75–$115 | AE, MC, V.

Friends Inn. This inn is in a rural area, close to the WVU stadium and within view of the WVU Medical Center. Cable TV. Business services. Some pets allowed. | 452 Country Club Rd. | 304/599–4850 or 888/811–4850 | fax 304/599–4866 | www.friendsinn.com | 42 rooms in 2 buildings | $53 | AE, D, MC, V.

Hampton Inn. This five-story hostelry is directly across the street from Mountaineer Field and 3 mi south of downtown Morgantown. Complimentary Continental breakfast. Cable TV. No pets. | 1053 Van Voorhis Rd. | 304/599–1200 | fax 304/598–7331 | www.hamptoninn.com | 108 rooms | $64–$89 | AE, DC, D, MC, V.

Holiday Inn. This chain is 4 mi from Morgantown Mall and the WVU campus, and 1 mi from the WVU Medical Center. Restaurant, bar, room service. Cable TV. Pool. Business services. Some pets allowed. | 1400 Saratoga Ave. | 304/599–1680 | fax 304/598–0989 | 147 rooms | $79 | AE, D, DC, MC, V.

★ **Lakeview Resort and Conference Center.** Ten miles east of Morgantown, this country club turned resort is in a secluded forest area with breathtaking views of Cheat Lake. The standard motel rooms are accessed by a warren of halls and stairways. The resort provides conference rooms for special occasions. Bar (with entertainment), dining rooms. Some refrigerators. Cable TV. 4 pools (2 indoor), wading pool. Hot tub, massage. 2 18-hole golf courses, tennis. Gym. Business services, airport shuttle. | 1 Lakeview Dr. | 304/594–1111 | fax 304/594–9472 | www.lakeviewscanticon.com | 187 rooms | $175 | AE, D, DC, MC, V.

Ramada Inn. On a hilltop near I–68 and I–79, this Colonial-style facility only 1 mi south of Morgantown has views of the Appalachian Mountains. Executive suites are available, as are rooms with Jacuzzis. Restaurant. In-room data ports. Cable TV. Pool. Exercise equipment. Business services, airport shuttle. | U.S. 119 S, at the junction of I–68 and I–79 | 304/296–3431 | 163 rooms | $75 | AE, D, DC, MC, V.

NITRO

MAP 17, B5

(Nearby town also listed: Charleston)

In 1918 the federal government built the enormous Explosive Plant C to produce smokeless powder for the American Expeditionary Force and the Allies. In that way the city of Nitro came into being. Located in western Kanawha County, Nitro "boomed" to 35,000 residents almost overnight. When World War I ended, the plant was sold to a group of bankers who hoped to attract private industry to the empty buildings, but it didn't work. Many of the buildings were scrapped, and the houses were sold to coal companies and shipped down river.

Today Nitro, which has dropped to 6,737 residents, is a major producer of chemicals in the Metro Valley.

Information: **Charleston Regional Chamber of Commerce and Development** | 106 Capitol St., Rte. 100, Charleston 25301 | 304/345–0770.

Attractions

Ridnour Park and Lake. Nitro is rarely buzzing with activity, so take advantage of the serenity. This town park is prime picnic country and has a lake for fishing and a playground. | 21st St.

Tri-State Greyhound Park. The year-round dog track includes a 3,000-seat climate-controlled grandstand, a 700-seat clubhouse, and 600 video lottery slot machines. | 1 Greyhound Dr., Crosslanes | 304/776–1000 | Free | Sun.–Thurs. 11 AM–2:30 AM, Fri. and Sat. 11 AM–3 AM.

Waves of Fun. West Virginia's largest wave pool and water park, with an aqua tube, three water slides, a concession area, a fitness trail, sandlot volleyball, and picnic areas. | 1 Valley Park Dr., Hurricane | 304/562–0518 | fax 304/562–5375 | $6.75 | Memorial Day–July, Mon.–Sat. 11–7, Sun. noon–7; Aug.–Labor Day, weekends only, Sat. 11–6, Sun. noon–7.

ON THE CALENDAR
MAR.: *Civil War Encampment and Battle Reenactment.* The reenactments are performed by the 1st West Virginia Light Artillery. | 304/562–5896.
NOV.–DEC.: *The Festival of Lights.* This is one of the largest displays of lights on the east coast. In Saint Auburn, right across the Kanawha River from Nitro, the electricity flows freely to celebrate the holiday season. See unique displays put on by area residents. | 304/727–2971.

Dining

Biscuit World. American. This chain restaurant is a West Virginia institution. Baked steak, roast beef, and fried chicken make up the Southern selections. | 4113 1st Ave. | 304/755–2001 | Open 24 hrs | $5–$8 | No credit cards.

Diehl's. American. An old-style restaurant founded in 1916, Diehl's has kept its original decor; the hearty fare is made from scratch. A variety of specials are made daily, although the signature dish is the roast beef. | 152 Main Ave. | 304/755–9353 | $5–$6 | D, MC, V.

Lodging

Best Western Motor Inn. This traditional-style chain hotel is located 12½ mi outside of town. Its two buildings are surrounded by trees in an industrial area just off I–64; fast-food restaurants are nearby. Cable TV. Business services. | 4115 1st Ave. | 304/755–8341 | fax 304/755–2933 | 42 rooms | $45 | AE, D, DC, MC, V.

Comfort Inn. This two-story chain hotel is on a quiet hilltop in ½ mi from the Tri-State Greyhound Park and a little more than 9 mi northwest of Nitro in the suburb of Cross Lanes. Bar, complimentary Continental breakfast. Cable TV. Pool. Hot tub. Business services. | 102 Racer Dr., Cross Lanes | 304/776–8070 | fax 304/776–6460 | 112 rooms | $59–$69 | AE, D, DC, MC, V.

Ramada Limited. In a rural community, this Victorian-style chain is about 30 mi from both Huntington and Charleston, off I–64 Exit 34 (Hurricane exit). Picnic area, complimentary Continental breakfast. Some refrigerators. Cable TV. Pool. Business services. Some pets allowed (fee). | 419 Hurricane Creek Rd., Hurricane | 304/562–3346 | fax 304/562–7408 | 147 rooms | $49–$64 | AE, D, DC, MC, V.

PARKERSBURG

MAP 17, B4

(Nearby town also listed: Mineralwells)

Located at the confluence of the Little Kanawha and Ohio rivers, Parkersburg was once a Native American hunting ground. In 1770 George Washington passed through on his way to lands awarded him by Governor Dinwiddie of Virginia for military service. Three years later, Robert Thornton made a claim to part of the site, but in 1783 he sold out (for $50) to Alexander Parker of Pittsburgh. The city's position made it a key center of supply and shipping for the state's first oil fields, which were drilled nearby in 1860. The numerous natural gas fields became a major source of fuel for industries, helping to propel the city's economic growth. Today more than 100 companies produce chemicals, glass, metals, plastics, and other products in the Mid-Ohio Valley.

Parkersburg, which was incorporated in 1910 by the state legislature, is West Virginia's fourth-largest city.

Information: Parkersburg/Wood County Convention and Visitors Bureau | 350 7th St. 26101 | 304/428–1130 or 800/752–4982 | info@parkersburgcdb.org.

Attractions

Actors Guild Playhouse. The group offers a variety of musical, comedic, and dramatic productions throughout the year at the Cultural Center of Fine Arts. | 724 Market St. | 304/485–1300 | Performance times vary; tours by appointment.

Blennerhassett Island Historical State Park. In 1800 Harman Blennerhassett built a mansion on an island in the Ohio River, where he allegedly plotted with Aaron Burr to establish an empire in the American Southwest. After both men were arrested, Blennerhassett fled the island, never to return. The mansion burned down in 1811, but has been reconstructed. You can reach the island via a stern-wheeler shuttle from Point Park in downtown Parkersburg. | 137 Juliana St. | 304/420–4800 | Free; mansion tour $3; wagon ride around island $4 | May–Labor Day, Tues.–Sun. 10–5:30, closed Mon.; Labor Day–Oct., Thurs.–Sun. 10–4:30, closed Mon.–Wed.

Blennerhassett Museum. The museum has three floors of archaeological and historical displays. | 137 Juliana St. | 304/420–4800 or 800/225–5982 | $1 | Tours May–Oct., Tues.–Sat. 9–5:30, Sun. noon–5:30, closed Mon.; Nov.–Apr., Sat. 11–5, Sun. 1–5, or by appointment; closed weekdays.

City Park. This large municipal park has a swimming pool, playgrounds, baseball fields, picnic areas and shelters, basketball courts, paddleboats, and the Henry Cooper Log House, a two-story cabin built in 1804 in Mineral Wells and moved to the park in 1910. | Park Ave. and 23rd St. | 304/424–8572 | Free | Daily.

Cook House. One of the few remaining buildings from Wood County's settlement period, this Federal-style structure was built in 1925–29. Inside you'll find several hands-on exhibits. | 1301 Murdoch Ave. | 304/422–6961 | Free | Tours by appointment.

Mountwood Park. Located near Parkersburg, the 2,600-acre park offers camping, hiking, picnic areas, game parks, swimming, fishing, playgrounds, and a large lake. | Rte. 2 (Box 56), Waverly | 304/679–3611 | Free | Daily.

North Bend State Park. The cabin area of this 1,405-acre park offers a playground, tennis courts, miniature golf, and swimming. | Rte. 1, Box 221, Cairo | 304/643–2931 or 800/CALL–WVA | www.wvparks.com/northbend | Free | Daily 6 AM–10 PM.

Oil & Gas Museum. Engines, oil drills, tanks, documents, and photographs illustrate the history of the oil and gas industry, and especially its role in the Civil War. | 119 3rd St. | 304/485–5446 | $2 | Weekdays, Sun. 12–5, Sat. 10–5.

Parkersburg Art Center. The cultural center offers touring exhibitions and shows of local and regional artists. | 220 8th St. | 304/485–3859 | $1 | Tues.–Fri. 10–4, weekends 1–4, closed Mon.

TOURS

Fenton Art Glass Co. With about 350 full-time employees, Fenton is world-famous for its glassware. Guided tours take you through the glassmaking process, from the furnace to the finished product. The Fenton Glass Museum displays early Ohio Valley glass. | 700 Elizabeth St., Williamstown; Rte. 114, 1½ mi off I–77 | 304/375–7772 or 800/319–7793 | www.fentonartglass.com | Free | Tours weekdays 8–4:50, closed weekends; closed 1st 2 weeks in July and national holidays.

Ruble's Stern-wheelers Riverboat Cruises. Authentic stern-wheelers shuttle passengers to and from Blennerhassett Island. Boats leave from the foot of 2nd St. in Point Pleasant's lush Point Park. The last shuttle leaves the island at 5:30 PM. | 2nd St. in Point Park | 740/423-7268 | $6 | May–Labor Day, daily 10–5:30; Labor Day–Oct., Thurs.–Sat. 10–4:30, Sun. noon–4:30, closed Mon.–Wed.

ON THE CALENDAR
MAY: *Rendezvous on the Island.* Muzzle loaders and mountainmen recreate frontier life at the Blennerhassett Island Historical State Park. | 304/420-4800.
AUG.: *Parkersburg Homecoming.* Parkersburg celebrates its homecoming with performers, ski and boating events, fireworks, and a half marathon. | 304/422-3588.
SEPT.: *Volcano Days.* This festival commemorates the 1890s oil boomtown of Volcano with steam engines, equipment, and food. | 304/679-3611.

Dining
Columbo's. Italian. In the middle of Parkersburg, this trattoria serves all the standards: lasagne, pizza, pasta, veal parmigiana, and sandwiches. The prime rib is the most popular item on the menu. The walls are lined with photographs of patrons and pictures of Parkersburg. | 1236 7th St. | 304/428-5472 | Closed Mon. No lunch | $9–$12 | AE, D, DC, MC, V.

Point of View. Continental. The wall-to-wall windows in the dining room offer wonderful views of Blennerhassett Island. From the candlelit tables you can watch meals being prepared at an open-hearth grill. The crab and lobster bisque soup is good for starters. House specials include rotisserie chicken, prime rib, and pepper steak. Kids' menu available. | 548 Blennerhassett Heights Rd. | 304/863-3366 | No lunch Fri.–Sun. | $10–$20 | AE, D, DC, MC, V.

Third Street Deli. Casual. By day, this is a New York–style deli that serves sandwiches, soups, salads, and desserts; by night, the "After Five" dinner menu expands to include grilled steaks, seafood, pasta dishes, and gourmet pizzas. Inside you will find black-and-white tiled floors, linen tablecloths, and pictures by local artists; outside there is a heated patio for outdoor dining year-round. | 430 3rd St. | 304/422-0003 | Closed Sun. | $9–$23 | AE, D, DC, MC, V.

Lodging
AmeriHost Inn Parkersburg North. In the center of Parkersburg, this two-story brick building is adjacent to the Grand Central Mall and close to a handful of restaurants. The rooms are all furnished in oak. Complimentary Continental breakfast. In-room data ports. Cable TV. Indoor Pool. Hot tub, sauna. Exercise equipment. No pets. | 401 37th St. | 304/424-5300 or 800/434-5800 | www.amerihostinn.com | 79 rooms | $85 | AE, D, DC, MC, V.

The Avery-Savage House. This restored Victorian home was built in 1880 for Thomas S. Savage, owner of Parkersburg Ice and Coal. It's full of antiques, and is on the National Register of Historic Places. Rooms are quaint, decked out in Victorian-era reproductions. The inn is 6 blocks from the Parkersburg Art Center and the Actor's Guild Playhouse, and 1 mi from Blennerhassett Island. Dining room, complimentary breakfast. | 420 13th St. | 304/422-9820 or 800/315-7121 | fax 304/485-1911 | 4 rooms | $65–$85 | AE, D, MC, V.

Clarion Carriage House Inn—Blennerhassett. More than a century old, this historic hotel in the middle of town has a rustic, Victorian style; there are antique furnishings on all five floors. Restaurant, bar. In-room data ports. Cable TV. Business services, airport shuttle. | 320 Market St. | 304/422-3131 | fax 304/485-0267 | 104 rooms | $100–$125 | AE, D, DC, MC, V.

Holiday Inn. This chain property is located in the commercial part of town, only 5 mi from historic Blennerhassett Island. Restaurant, bar (with entertainment), room service. Some refrigerators. Cable TV. Indoor pool. Hot tub, sauna. Laundry facilities. Business services. | Rte. 50 and I–77 | 304/485-6200 | fax 304/485-6200, ext. 350 | 148 rooms | $74 | AE, D, DC, MC, V.

North Bend Lodge. State owned and operated, this lodge is 4 mi outside of town on the Hughes River. It has an especially good view of the Appalachian Mountains; the scenery includes a bridge overlooking a valley and a river. All rooms have solid oak furniture that was handmade in West Virginia; the cabins are on secluded hilltops. The inn is 25 mi east of Parkersburg Restaurant, picnic area. Cable TV. Pool. Tennis. Kids' programs. Business services. | Rte. 1, Box 221, Cairo | 304/643–2931 or 800/225–5982 | fax 304/643–2970 | www.wvweb.com/www/north_bend | nbpark@ruralnet.org | 29 rooms, 8 cabins | $61, $86–$101, cabins | AE, MC, V.

Williams House Bed & Breakfast. Less than 5 mi north of Parkersburg, this early-1900s four-square brick house is on an acre of grassy land. The rooms are filled with antiques from the early 1900s and family memorabilia. Fireplaces warm the rooms. Kids may stay with prior permission. Complimentary breakfast. Cable TV. Outdoor pool. No pets. | 5406 Grand Central Ave., Vienna | 304/295–7212 | willhous@wirefire.com | 5 rooms | $69 | MC, V.

PETERSBURG

(Nearby town also listed: Moorefield)

German colonists settled Petersburg in 1745; it was named for Jacob Peterson, who opened the first store. Because of its location on the South Branch of the Potomac River, the town served as a Union outpost during the Civil War. Today, Petersburg is a convenient gateway to the Monongahela National Forest, Spruce Knob–Seneca Rocks National Recreation Area, and Petersburg Gap.

Information: Potomac Highlands Travel Council | 1200 Harrison Ave., Elkins 26241 | 304/636–8400 | www.potomachighlands.org.

Attractions

Country Store Opry. Petersburg hails itself as the "Country Music Capital of the Potomac Highlands." The opry, formerly a country store, is home to a nine-piece country music band that has been playing since 1967. The store is 6 mi south of Petersburg on U.S. 220. | Rte. 220 | 304/257–1743 | $3 | Apr.–Dec., every 1st, 3rd, and 5th Saturday night, at 7 PM.

Petersburg Gap On U.S. 220 and Route 55, Petersburg Gap rises to 800 ft, creating the Pictured Rocks, where figures of a fox and an ox, or buffalo, appear to have been carved into the cliffs. The trout fishing and canoeing between the tall rock walls draw people from all over the East Coast. | 304/636–8400 | Free | Daily.

Smoke Hole Caverns. Reportedly used by native tribes to smoke meat and by early white settlers to make moonshine, the caverns feature several unusual rock formations, including one of the world's longest ribbon stalactites. | Rtes. 25 N and 55 E | 304/257–4442 | www.smokehole.com | $7.50 | Daily.

Spruce Knob–Seneca Rocks National Recreation Area. These 100,000 acres of the Monongahela National Forest, with rock climbing and mountain views, 40 mi south of town were the first National Recreation Area, so designated in 1965. Information at the Seneca Rocks Visitor Center. | Jct. of Hwy 28 and Hwy 33, Seneca Rocks | 304/567–2827 | Free | Park open daily; Visitor Center hours Apr.–Oct. daily 9–5:30; Nov.–Mar. weekends 9–4:30, closed weekdays.

ON THE CALENDAR

APR.: *Spring Mountain Festival.* Trout fishing contests, a catch and fry, a trout supper, local music, gospel singing, a pancake supper, cloggers, wine tasting, antique cars, a 10k run, a parade, turkey calling, and owl hooting contests are among the many events at this country extravaganza. | 304/257–2722.

Dining

Foxes Pizza Den. Casual. Serving pizza, sandwiches, and salads, this is one of the town's oldest eateries. The house special is the Chester chicken, breaded and served with potatoes and vegetables. A huge painting of a fox is the only indication of this restaurant's namesake. | 508 Keyser Ave. | 304/257–4342 | $7 | No credit cards.

Sites Restaurant. American. Established in 1915, the eatery serves the gamut from grilled cheese sandwiches to T-bone steaks; the peanut-butter pie is a popular dessert. A portrait of "Grandaddy" Dennis Sites, the restaurant's founder, peers over the cash register. | 35 S. Main St. | 304/257–1088 | Breakfast also available | $5–10 | No credit cards.

Lodging

Hermitage Motor Inn. There's a crafts shop and bookstore in this 1840s inn, which melds Victorian furnishings with modern facilities. The inn is in a commercial area, surrounded by several popular chain restaurants and shopping options. Restaurant. In-room data ports. Cable TV. Pool. Hot tub. Business services. | 203 Virginia Ave. | 304/257–1711 or 800/437–6482 | fax 304/257–4330 | 38 rooms | $45–$51 | AE, D, DC, MC, V.

Homestead Inn Motel. On the edge of the city limits, this two-story brick motel has a 6-acre cattle and sheep farm out back; check out the arts and crafts gift shop for a souvenir. All rooms are accessible from outdoors, and each one has its own wall-length hand-painted mural. The inn is approximately 1 mi west of Petersburg and 20 mi east of Seneca Rocks. Complimentary Continental breakfast. Cable TV. Refrigerators. | Rtes. 55 and 28 | 304/257–1049 | 12 rooms | $45–$55 | AE, D, DC, MC, V.

North Fork Mountain Inn. A rustic log inn nestled on a hilltop 15 mi west of Petersburg, the North Fork and its adjoining cottage are in the mountains, with scenic wilderness views. Complimentary breakfast. Some in-room hot tubs. No room phones. | Off Rte. 55, Box 114 | 304/257–1108 | 6 rooms, 1 cottage | $85–$105, $135 cottage | MC, V.

Smoke Hole Caverns Motel. Next to Smoke Hole Caverns, just outside Petersburg, the motel and cabins are made of logs, and the beautiful wood finish is visible from both the inside and out. Some rooms have fireplaces and hot tubs. Some refrigerators, some in-room hot tubs. Cable TV. Pool. Playground. | Rtes. 28 N and 55 E, HC 59, Seneca Rocks | 304/257–4442 or 800/828–8478 | fax 304/257–2745 | 13 rooms, 25 cabins, 18 log cabins | $49–$59, $99–$129 cabins, $129–$149 log cabins | AE, D, MC, V.

Smoke Hole Lodge Bed & Breakfast. A remote 1,500-acre tract in West Virginia's famed Smoke Hole Gorge is home to this lodge, which prides itself on being a wilderness retreat. The grounds are made up of several different farmholdings, and each of the guest rooms is unique, though all have a rustic country appeal, with antiques, handmade quilts, and some four-poster beds. Complimentary breakfast. Cable TV. Pets allowed. | Rte. 28 S | 304/242–8377 or 304/257–1539 | 7 rooms | $90–$165 | No credit cards.

PHILIPPI

MAP 17, D4

(Nearby towns also listed: Buckhannon, Grafton)

The first land battle of the Civil War took place at Philippi on June 3, 1861, when Colonel B. F. Kelley's detachment of Union troops surprised and drove off newly recruited Confederate soldiers led by Colonel George Alexander Porterfield. The battle was known as the "Philippi races" because of the speed with which the Confederate forces left the field.

Philippi is also home to Alderson-Broaddus College, which overlooks the city of 3,132.

Information: **City of Philippi Convention and Visitors Bureau** | 108 N. Main St. 26416 | 304/457–3700, ext. 211.

Attractions

Barbour County Historical Museum. On the site of the first battle of the Civil War, this museum in a B & O Railroad station has reenactments of the battle and displays a drum played while General Lee surrendered to General Grant, ending the Civil War. You can also tour a collection of mummies embalmed by a local mortician in 1888. | 200 N. Main St. | 304/457–4846 | Free; mummy tour $1 | Late June–late Oct., Mon.–Sat. 11–4, Sun. 1–4; closed Nov.–mid-June.

Covered Bridge. Confederate and Union troops used this covered bridge to cross the Tygart River during the Civil War. Originally built in 1852, the bridge burned in 1989; it has been completely restored. This is the longest two-lane covered bridge still in use on a federal highway. | 304/457–4846 | Free | Daily.

ON THE CALENDAR
JUNE: *Blue and Gray Reunion Civil War Reenactment.* The mustering of troops commemorates a Civil War battle, with concerts, food, arts, and crafts on Main Street. | 304/457–4625.
AUG.: *Barbour County Fair.* Held the last week of August before Labor Day, this fair has a carnival, entertainment, arts and crafts, and food. | 304/457–3254.

Dining

Medallion Restaurant. American. Pictures of Philippi's famous covered bridge line the walls and fresh flowers decorate the tables at this joint across from the courthouse. Choose from a menu of steak, meatloaf, chicken dinners, and hamburgers. | 75 Main St. | 304/457–3463 | No dinner Sun. Breakfast also served | $5–$10 | AE, D, DC, MC, V.

Lodging

Super 8. This two-story brick chain is in a quiet, rural setting. The motel is 3 mi south of Parkersburg, and the Barbour County Historical Museum. Some refrigerators. Cable TV. Business services. | Rte. 2, U.S. 250 | 304/457–5888 | 40 rooms | $36–$81 | AE, D, DC, MC, V.

Tygart Valley Star B&B. Tall trees shade this three-story bed-and-breakfast, which is in a residential neighborhood four blocks from the business district. Complimentary breakfast. Cable TV, no room phones. No pets. No smoking. | 14 N. Walnut St. | 304/457–1890 | 4 rooms | $65 | MC, V.

POINT PLEASANT

MAP 17, A5

(Nearby town also listed: Ripley)

George Washington surveyed the area in the 1740s, camped there in 1770, and referred to the confluence of the Kanawha and Ohio rivers as "Pleasant Point." In 1774 it was the site of a bloody battle between Native Americans and white settlers and is the burial place of Cornstalk, the chief of the Shawnees, and Ann Bailey, a celebrated frontierswoman. Today the city of 5,000 is the seat of government for Mason County.

Information: **Mason County Office of Tourism** | 305 Main St. 25550 | 304/675–8799.

Attractions

Country Cottage. You can peruse crafts by local artists, including handmade candles, wreaths, and yard art in this local shop. | 1215 Viand St. | 304/675–8030 | Free | Mon.–Sat. 10–6, closed Sun.

Krodel Park and Lake. Inside the park is a reconstruction of Fort Randolph; there are also campsites, a playground, facilities for miniature golf, and fishing. | Rtes. 2 and 62 | 304/675–1068 | Free | Daily dawn to dusk.

POINT PLEASANT

INTRO
ATTRACTIONS
DINING
LODGING

McClintic Wildlife Station/Management Area. This 3,066-acre region 6 ½ mi north of Point Pleasant provides varied habitat for deer and small game. Trapping, fishing, and camping are available in some sections. | Rte. 1, just off Rte. 62 | 304/675–0871 | Free | Weekdays 8:30–4:30, closed weekends.

Old Town Camp Ground. An 18-hole golf course, a fishing pond, an outdoor pool, a playground, and hiking trails fill this 118-acre campground 5 mi east of town. | Sandhill Rd. and Rte. 1, Box 527E | 304/675–3095 | $2 pool fee | Closed Dec.–Mar.

Point Pleasant Battle Monument State Park. A monument marks the site of the battle that took place on Oct. 10, 1774, pitting 1,100 frontiersmen under Andrew Lewis against Chief Cornstalk's 1,000 warriors. The battle of Point Pleasant broke the power of the Native Americans in the Ohio Valley; it was the crowning event in what has come to be known as Lord Dunmore's War. | 1 Main St. | 304/675–0869 | www.wvparks.com/pointpleasant | Free | Mon.–Sat. 10–4:30, Sun. 1–4:30.

Mansion House. Built in the late 18th century as a public inn, this house contains local colonial furniture and relics from the battle of Point Pleasant. | 1 Main St. | 304/675–0869 | Free | May–Oct., Mon.–Sat. 10–4:30, Sun. 1–4:30, closed Nov.–Apr.

West Virginia State Farm Museum. The 50-acre museum contains 19th-century pioneer artifacts and buildings, including log cabins built in the early 1800s, a replica of an old Lutheran church, a one-room schoolhouse, a chapel, and a barn. Picnic areas are available. | Rte. 1, Box 479, on Fairground Rd. | 304/675–5737 | Donations accepted | Tours Apr.–Nov., Tues.–Sat. 9–5, Sun. 1–5, closed Mon.; closed Dec.–Mar.

ON THE CALENDAR

AUG.: *Mason County Fair.* The fair offers a carnival, entertainment, arts and crafts, and food. | 304/675–5463.

OCT.: *Point Pleasant Battle Days.* Reenactments in period clothing at the Point Pleasant Battle Monument Park the first full weekend of the month commemorate the first battle of the American Revolution. | 304/675–8799.

Dining

Melinda's Restaurant. American. You won't find anything deep-fried on the menu, but you will find "comfort foods" like macaroni and cheese, meatloaf, mashed potatoes, and homemade coconut cream pie. The dining room's country decor includes pictures of chickens, old photographs, and kitchen paraphernalia, and the restaurant is popular with locals and tourists alike. | 509 Main St. | 304/675–7201 | Breakfast also served | $8–$10 | No credit cards.

Lodging

Lowe Hotel. In the heart of downtown Point Pleasant just one block from local shops and restaurants, this four-story, family-operated hotel has been operating since 1901. Rooms are filled with period antiques, some dating to the early 1900s. Some refrigerators. Cable TV. Business services. | 401 Main St. | 304/675–2260 | 30 rooms | $42 | AE, D, DC, MC, V.

Stone Manor Bed and Breakfast. Built in 1885 on the bank of the Great Canal River, this B&B has views of the river and Point Pleasant Battle Monument State Park across the way. The house is filled with period antiques—one bedroom has a Civil War–era Victorian Renaissance Revival walnut bedroom set. Dining room, complimentary breakfast. No room phones, no TV in some rooms, TV in common area. Laundry facilities. No smoking. | 12 Main St. | 304/675–3442, 304/675–7323 | 2 rooms, 1 suite | $50–$60 | No credit cards.

PRINCETON

(Nearby towns also listed: Beckley, Bluefield)

Princeton is the seat of government for Mercer County and was named in honor of General Hugh Mercer, an officer in the Revolutionary War; Princeton was the name of the New Jersey battle in which Mercer was killed. In 1860 it was a village with just 40 houses; today, it is a thriving town of 7,000 and a favorite destination of auto-racing fans. Thrill-seekers flock to the Princeton Speedway to cheer their drivers on to victory on the ³/₈-mi dirt track. Basketball enthusiasts may know Princeton as the birthplace of Rod Thorn, who scored 2,180 points in 1961–63 for the West Virginia University Mountaineers.

Information: Mercer County Convention and Visitors Bureau | 500 Bland St., Box 4088, Bluefield 24701 | 304/325–8438 or 800/221–3206 | staff@mccvb.com | www.mccvb.com.

Attractions

Camp Creek State Park. This recently designated state park offers camping, hiking, and fishing; an adjacent forest has more than 5,300 acres for hiking, hunting, and fishing. | Camp Creek Rd., Exit 20, 2 mi off I-77 | 304/425–9481 | www.wvparks.com/campcreek | Free | Apr.–Oct., daily 6 AM–10 PM, closed Nov.–Mar.

Princeton Speedway. Four varieties of stock cars, including mini-stock and street stock, as well as modified and late model cars, race on this ³/₈-mi dirt track. | 177 Racetrack Rd. | 304/425–9429 | Prices vary per event | Closed Dec.–Mar.

ON THE CALENDAR
JUNE: *Princeton Summerfest.* This outdoor festival includes a firefighters' muster, a chili cook-off, a spaghetti-eating contest, a volleyball tournament, and a karaoke contest. | 304/487–1502.
JUNE–SEPT.: *Princeton Devil Rays Baseball.* This minor league baseball team is affiliated with the major league Tampa Bay Devil Rays; they play on Hunnicutt Field on Old Bluefield Road. Check their web site or call ahead for schedules and ticket prices. | 304/487–2000 | www.princetondevilrays.com.

Dining

East & West. Eclectic. Egg rolls, fried rice, and lo mein share the menu with hamburgers and steaks in this sports-memorabilia-filled restaurant in the business district. | 108 Douglas St. | 304/425–5851 | Casual | Closed Sun. No lunch | $7–$12 | No credit cards.

Johnston's Inn. Continental. Founded in 1960, this restaurant has kept some of its '60s decor on the walls. The steak and lobster platters are popular here. Salad bar and kids' menu available. | Old Oak Vale Rd. | 304/425–7591 | Breakfast also available | $8–$30 | AE, D, DC, MC, V.

Lodging

Comfort Inn. Only 2 blocks from shopping and restaurants, this chain hotel is 3 mi east of I-77 Exit 9 (Princeton exit). Complimentary Continental breakfast. Cable TV. Hot tub. Business services. | U.S. 460 and Ambrose La. | 304/487–6101 | fax 304/425–7002 | 51 rooms | $64 | AE, D, DC, MC, V.

Days Inn. In a commercial area between Bluefield and Beckley and surrounded by trees and flowers, this two-story chain is 19 mi from the Winterplace Ski Resort. Complimentary Continental breakfast. Cable TV. Indoor pool. Hot tub. Business services. Some pets allowed. | 347 Meadowfield La. | 304/425–8100 | fax 304/487–1734 | 122 rooms | $69 | AE, D, DC, MC, V.

PRINCETON

INTRO
ATTRACTIONS
DINING
LODGING

Hampton Inn. Four miles from downtown Princeton and 10 mi west of the Mercer County Airport, this five-story hostelry is just off I–77 Exit 9 (Princeton Exit). 2 restaurants. Cable TV. Outdoor pool. Laundry services. Business services. No pets. | 27 Meadowfield La. | 304/431–2580 | fax 304/431–2366 | 115 rooms | $65–$105 | AE, D, DC, MC, V.

Ramada Limited. Off I–77 Exit 9 (Princeton exit), this no-frills two-story chain is 2 mi from downtown. Picnic area, complimentary Continental breakfast. Cable TV. Outdoor pool. Business services, airport shuttle, free parking. No pets. | 1115 Oakville Rd. | 304/425–8711 | fax 304/487–9785 | 97 rooms | $38–$63 | AE, D, DC, MC, V.

Sleep Inn. This three-story hotel is off I–77 Exit 9 (Princeton exit). It is 2 mi from downtown and 15 mi southeast of the Mercer County Airport. Complimentary Continental breakfast. In-room data ports. Cable TV, room phones. Indoor pool. Hot tub. Pets allowed. | 1015 Oakvale Rd. | 304/431–2800 | fax 304/425–7693 | 81 rooms | $45–$95 | AE, D, DC, MC, V.

RICHWOOD

MAP 17, C6

(Nearby town also listed: Summersville)

Richwood got its name from the area's wealth of natural resources, primarily coal and timber. While those resources were long a mainstay of Richwood's economy, they have slowly given way to tourism and recreation; the Cherry Hill Country Club is just minutes from the city, as is the Monongahela National Forest. Like many towns in the region, Richwood celebrates its mountain heritage with several festivals throughout the year. It is also famous as the ramp capital of the world, a vegetable the town celebrates with a festival every April.

Information: **Richwood Area Chamber of Commerce** | 50 Oakwood Ave. 26261 | 304/846–6790.

Attractions
Highland Scenic Highway. You can see panoramas of the Monongahela National Forest on Route 150, which begins off Route 55 at the Cranberry Mountain Visitor's Center 25 mi west of town. | Rte. 150 | 304/653–4826 | Free | Daily.

Cherry Hill Country Club. On Hinkel Mountain, this nine-hole golf course has panoramic views of the surrouding area. Follow Cranberry River Rd. north from the east side of town, turn right at the top of Hinkel Mountain. | 36 B Ave. | 304/846–9876 | $20 | Apr.–Nov., closed Dec.–Mar.

ON THE CALENDAR
APR.: *International Feast of the Ramson.* The pungent wild leeks called ramps are celebrated with a dinner, old-time music, and activities. | 304/846–6790.

APR.: *Ramp Dinner.* Literally a ton of locally-grown ramps—onion-like vegetables—are cooked in bacon fat and served with fried potates, brown beans, and ham to over a thousand people. The dinner takes places in the high school. | 304/846–6790.

AUG.: *Cherry River Festival.* Fireman parade down Main Street, local kids do water tricks in the public pool, and there are bed races and a talent show in this festival the first full week of the month. | 304/846–6790.

OCT.: *Heritage Festival.* An art show of local artists' paintings, sculpture, and blown glass in City Hall is the centerpiece of this festival the first week of the month. | 304/846–6790.

Dining
Anthony's Gateway Restaurant and Lounge. American. Railroad lanterns and pictures of trains share the walls with faux grapevines in this downtown dining room, where the reg-

ulars, local senior citizens, order spaghetti and ribeye steak. The restaurant is ¼ mi east of downtown. | Marlinton Rd. (Rte. 39/Rte. 55) | 304/846–4494 | $5–$11 | AE, D, MC, V.

Lodging

Four Seasons Lodge. Overlooking Rudolph Falls and at the edge of the Monongahela National Forest, this two-story motel has rooms with wooded views. The innkeepers can help you arrange mountain biking, fishing, cross-country skiing, or kayaking trips during your stay. The motel is 1 mi east of downtown. Complimentary Continental breakfast. Cable TV. Bicycles. Pets allowed. | Marlinton Rd. (Rte. 39/Rte. 55) | 800/829–4605 | fax 304/846–2170 | 27 rooms, 2 suites | $50–$76 rooms, $125 suites | AE, D, DC, MC, V.

Watergate Inn. If you bring your own pole and tackle, you can fish in the Cherry River just a few feet from the door of this no-frills motel, 1 mi west of downtown. Sparse rooms in neutral tones overlook the trout stream. Complimentary Continental breakfast, some microwaves, some refrigerators, cable TV. Fishing. No pets. No smoking. | 1 Bridge Ave., at Rte. 55 W | 304/846–2632 | 25 rooms | $65–$80 | AE, D, DC, MC, V.

RIPLEY

(Nearby towns also listed: Charleston, Point Pleasant)

Settled in 1768 and chartered in 1832, the city was named in honor of Harry Ripley, a minister who drowned in Big Mill Creek in 1830. The Jackson County seat, Ripley is best known for the Mountaineer State Art and Craft Fair, held each July at Cedar Lakes.

Information: **Ripley City Hall** | 113 S. Church St. 25271 | 304/372–3482.

Attractions

Cedar Lakes Craft Center. There are workshops in stained glass, pottery, painting, jewelry making and other crafts at this center, which hosts the annual Mountaineer State Art and Craft Fair. To get there, take Exit 132 (Rte. 21) off I–77 and follow the signs 3½ mi to the Center. | Cedar Lakes Dr. | 304/372–7860 | $5 | Daily 8 AM–9 PM.

Washington's Lands Museum and Park. The museum traces the region's pioneer and river history. The park offers picnic areas and boat-launching facilities. | 208 N. Church St. | 304/372–5343 | Free | Daily.

ON THE CALENDAR

JULY: *Jackson County Fair.* The largest livestock sale in the state is the highlight at this fair, which also has carnival rides, live music, games, and food. The fair is at the Jackson County Fairground on Mill Creek, 5 mi northwest of town. | 304/372–9292.
JULY: *Mountaineer State Art and Craft Fair.* More than 200 juried craftspeople demonstrate and sell wares at the Cedar Lakes Conference Center. | 304/372–8159 or 304/340–3145.
OCT.: *West Virginia Black Walnut Festival.* This fall festival includes a majorette and band festival, arts and crafts, an auto show, and a walnut sale. | 304/927–1780.

Dining

Calamity Jane's Steakhouse & Saloon. Continental. Chandeliers and white starched table linens set the stage for steak and lobster tails and chateaubriand at this two-story restaurant overlooking a golf course 3 mi northeast of town. In summer you can eat on the patio. To get there take I–77 North, Exit 132 and drive 4 mi to Sycamore Creek Rd. | Sycamore Creek Rd.; Golf Club at Sycamore Creek, north of Rte. 21 | 304/372–1800 | Closed Sun., Mon. No lunch | $13–$50 | MC, V.

Lodging

Best Western McCoys Inn and Conference Center. Some of the suites have fireplaces in this downtown hotel, which also has a courtyard where you can play horseshoes. Restaurant, bar, complimentary Continental breakfast. In-room data ports, some minibars, some refrigerators, some in-room hot tubs. Cable TV, some in-room VCRs. Outdoor pool. Exercise equipment. Children's programs. Laundry facilities. Business services. No pets. | 701 W. Main St. | 304/372–9122 | fax 304/372–4400 | 120 rooms, 22 suites | $70 rooms, $150 suites | AE, MC, V.

Holiday Inn Express. This two-story motel is off I–77 at Exit 138, in a commercial area about halfway between Charleston and Parkersburg. Area attractions include the Theater Lakes Conference Center, which is 3 mi southeast of the hotel, and the Ohio River, which is 10 mi west of the hotel. Complimentary Continental breakfast. Cable TV. Business services. | 1 Hospitality Dr. | 304/372–5000 | fax 304/372–5600 | 65 rooms | $72 | AE, D, DC, MC, V.

SALEM

(Nearby town also listed: Clarksburg)

Founded in 1792 and chartered two years later as New Salem, the town came into being as the final home for a group of Seventh Day Baptist families; they named it after the town in New Jersey where they had started their journey. At the turn of the century, the coal, oil, and gas industry brought wave after wave of European immigrants to the area, creating a rich cultural history. Today, visitors to Salem can enjoy hiking, horseback riding, or biking on the 66-mi North Bend Rail Trail, which winds past downtown Salem.

Information: **Salem Area Chamber of Commerce** | Box 352, Mill and Valley, Box 191, 26426 | 304/782–1318.

Attractions

Fort New Salem. Eighteen original 19th-century log cabins, including a printshop, blacksmith shop, and several homes, recreate what rural life was like over 100 years ago. The fort is less than 1/8 mi south of U.S. 50. From U.S. 50 go south on Route 23 to University Dr. Extension. | University Dr. Exit, 1/4 mi south of U.S. 50 on Rte. 23 | 304/782–5245 | $4 | Memorial Day–Oct. Wed.–Sun. 10–5, closed Mon.–Tues.; Apr.–May and Nov.–Dec. weekdays 10–5, closed weekends.

Salem-Teikyo University. Founded in 1888 as Salem Academy, the private college has a partnership with Teikyo University in Tokyo, Japan. More than 700 students attend classes here, taking one course at a time in an academic year divided into 12 four-week modules. The 100-acre campus is 12 mi west of town off U.S. 50. | 223 W. Main, Salem | 304/782–5011 or 800/283–4562 | www.salem-teikyo.wvnet.edu | Free | Daily.

ON THE CALENDAR
AUGUST: *Annual Fort New Salem Dulcimer Weekend.* Held on the second week of August, dulcimer demonstrations, workshops, and concerts celebrate this stringed folk instrument. | 304/782–5245.

OCT.: *Salem Apple Butter Festival.* Apple-butter making, quilt and apple-butter judging, an auto show, and a petting zoo are the highlights of this fall festival. | 304/782–3565 | www.salemwv.com/applebutterfestival.

Dining

Cottage Corner, Too. American. Meatloaf with mashed potatoes and gravy, steak, and chili are on the menu. Inside, pictures of angels fill the walls; there's a view of the soccer field across the street. To get there, take Route 1 about 2 mi west of town. | Rte. 1 (Old Rte. 50) | 304/782–3228 | Breakfast also served | $5–$8 | MC, V.

Lodging
Old Salem Bed & Breakfast. The president of Salem-Teikyo University (then known as Salem College) built this two-story downtown building in 1889. The university is two blocks away. There are several restaurants within a few blocks of the B&B. Dining room, complimentary breakfast. Cable TV. Pets allowed. No smoking. | 117 W. Main St. | 304/782–1227 | 5 rooms | $50 | AE, D, MC, V.

SHEPHERDSTOWN

MAP 17, F2

(Nearby towns also listed: Charles Town, Harpers Ferry, Martinsburg)

Originally named Mecklenburg, Shepherdstown claims to be the oldest continuously settled community in the state, and it was probably the first white settlement in present-day West Virginia. Thomas Shepherd purchased the grant to the land in 1732. In 1790 George Washington considered it as site for the national capital. The town's greatest crisis occurred on September 17, 1862, when hundreds of wounded Confederate soldiers from the battle of Antietam flooded in, instantly transforming every building into a field hospital.

Shepherd College, founded in 1872, is the core of the community's economy, earning Shepherdstown the nickname "Georgetown West." Today Shepherdstown's quaint wooden storefronts and tree-lined brick streets form the framework for a collection of specialty shops, small inns, and restaurants that lure city folk from the Washington-Baltimore area.

Information: Shepherdstown Visitors Center | 102 E. German St. 25442 | 304/876–2786.

Attractions
Historic Shepherdstown Museum. Housed in the three-story Entler Hotel (1786), the museum displays muzzle-loading rifles, locks, quilts, and various antiques. | 304/876–0910 | Free | Tours Apr.–Oct., weekends 8–4, closed weekdays.

Historic Shepherdstown. The museum arranges guided walking tours through the town, which was used as a vast hospital during the battle of Antietam. Historic buildings include Shepherd College, built in 1872, and the Entler Hotel, built in 1786. | E. German St. at Princess St. | 304/876–0910 | Free | By appointment only.

ON THE CALENDAR
JULY: *Contemporary American Theatre.* The state's only professional theater company stages four contemporary American plays in repertory for the month of July as part of a festival which also includes month-long exhibits of artwork, puppet shows, music, and dance at the Frank Center Stage and the Sara Cree Studio Theater on the Shepherd College campus. | 800/999–2283, 304/876–3473.
SEPT.–OCT: *Appalachian Heritage Festival.* Story-telling, dance, and live music celebrate the state's oldest town and its Appalachian roots. The festival is held on the last weekend in September or the first weekend in October. | 304/876–5113.
NOV.: *Christmas in Shepherdstown.* Strolling carolers in turn-of-the-century garb, a town bonfire, street peddlers, carriage rides, and tours are features of this festival. | 304/876–4553 or 304/876–9388.

Dining

Amy's Los Amigos. Mexican. Choose from burritos, burgers, and other Mexican fare at this restaurant decorated with lanterns, sombreros, and stained glass south-of-the-border scenes on the walls. The restaurant is 1 mi from downtown Shepherdstown. | 120 E. German St. | 304/876–1008 | $5–$13 | AE, D, MC, V.

Bavarian Inn and Lodge. German. The servers' authentic German dress adds to the Bavarian mood at this award-winning inn, which has several dining rooms overlooking the Potomac River. The signature dish is filet mignon and crab cakes, but the menu extends to wild pheasant, venison, and boar. Entertainment. Kids' menu available. The inn is two blocks north of downtown. | Rte. 480 | 304/876–2551 | No lunch Sun. | $13–$25 | AE, D, DC, MC, V.

Old Pharmacy Cafe. Contemporary. Original equipment is featured in this turn-of-the-century building, including a traditional soda fountain. The sandwiches, vegetarian dishes, and soups are all popular. Kids' menu available. Beer and wine only. | 138 E. German St. | 304/876–2085 | $14–$17 | D, DC, MC, V.

Yellow Brick Bank and Little Inn. Continental. New American and northern Italian specials are served in this restored inn, which also offers lodging. The most popular dishes are the pasta, steak, and seafood. Sun. brunch available. | 201 E. German St. | 304/876–2208 | $14–$23 | DC, MC, V.

Lodging

Bavarian Inn and Lodge. Above the Potomac, this inn includes a greystone main lodge with antique German decor and separate chalets reminiscent of old Bavarian inns. It was built as a home in 1930, was changed into a country inn in 1962, and was completely renovated in 1977. There are five buildings; the luxurious guest rooms have canopy beds. The inn is two blocks north of downtown. Bar, dining room. In-room data ports, in-room hot tubs, cable TV. Pool. Putting green, tennis. Exercise equipment. Business services. | Rte. 480 | 304/876–2551 | fax 304/876–9355 | www.bavarianinnwv.com | 73 rooms | $115–$275 | AE, D, DC, MC, V.

Clarion Hotel and Suites. A four-story hotel in a rural area that caters to convention visitors, the Clarion has exterior-entrance rooms on the ground floor. The hotel is ⅓ mi south of downtown Shepherdstown's antique stores. Other nearby attractions include the Antietam Battlefield 5 mi north, historic Harper's Ferry 15 mi east, and the Charlestown Racetrack 15 mi northeast of the hotel. Restaurant, bar, complimentary breakfast. Cable TV. Outdoor pool. Hot tub, spa. Golf. Health club. Business services. No pets. | 17 Lowe Dr. | 800/252–7466, 304/876–7000 | 159 rooms, 8 suites | $79–$149 rooms, $129 jr. suites, $249 suites | AE, D, DC, MC, V.

Mecklenberg Inn. Each room in this Revolutionary War–era downtown inn (built while George Washington was president) has a theme. The Lincoln room, for example, has a fireplace and is filled with Victorian furniture; the country room has an antique bed with a rope box spring. There is live entertainment in the English-style pub. Bar, complimentary breakfast. No TV in some rooms. Pets allowed. No smoking. | 128 E. German St. | 304/876–2126 | 4 rooms, 1 suite | $75 rooms, $130 suite | MC, V.

Thomas Shepherd Inn. This Federal-style house built in 1868 is in the historical downtown area on land originally owned by town founder Thomas Shepherd. Originally built as a Lutheran parsonage, it was expanded in 1937 and made into an inn in 1984. The rooms have polished floors and Oriental rugs; the furnishings are all American antiques. Antietam is 5 mi north; Harpers Ferry is 10 mi south. Complimentary breakfast. TV in common area. Business services. No kids under 8. No smoking. | 300 W. German St. at Duke St. | 304/876–3715 or 888/889–8952 (reservations) | fax 304/876–3313 | www.thomasshepherdinn.com | 6 rooms | $85–$135 | AE, MC, V.

SISTERSVILLE

(Nearby towns also listed: Clarksburg, Parkersburg)

The father of 22 children, Charles Wells settled Sisterville in 1802; he named the town after Sarah and Deliah, his 18th and 19th daughters. (Evidently running short of names, he called child 20 and 21 Twenty and Plenty, but got back to names for his last child, Beth.) The town was incorporated in 1839 and was a quiet farming community until 1889, when oil was discovered, transforming it into a major drilling center. The discovery brought with it both unsightly rigs and rich oil barons, who built the magnificent homes that still stand here today a century after the end of the oil boom.

Information: **The Wells Inn** | 316 Charles St. 26175 | 304/652–1312.

Attractions
Self-Guided Tours. A brochure is available outlining a tour past the city's historic buildings. | Wells Inn, 316 Charles St. | 304/652–1312 | fax 304/652–1354 | Free | Daily.

ON THE CALENDAR
SEPT.: *West Virginia Oil and Gas Festival.* The city celebrates the oil boom of the 1890s with food, a gas engine show, a crafts fair, fiddling contests, and rides on the Ohio River's last remaining ferry. | 304/652–2939.

Dining
The Birch Tree. Eclectic. Contemporary Russian oil paintings, white table linens, and jazz music fill this bistro, which serves such specialties as rosemary pork cutlets, linguine with shrimp and crabmeat in white wine sauce, and cashew chicken. | 717 Wells St. | 304/652–1337 | fax 304/652–1447 | No lunch | $10–$15 | AE, D, DC, MC, V.

Murph's Restaurant. American. Meatloaf and mashed potatoes, fried chicken, steaks, and hamburgers make up the hearty fare at this downtown place. Try a slice of homemade coconut cream, lemon chocolate, or butterscotch pie for dessert. | 701 N. Wells St. | 304/652–1780 | Breakfast also available. No dinner | $5–$11 | AE, D, DC, MC, V.

Lodging
The Historic Wells Inn. Built in 1894 by the grandson of the town's founder, this brick inn across from the Ohio River is listed on the National Register of Historic Places. Pool table and dartboards available. Within a three block radius of the inn there's the Gaslight Theater, the old Coke factory which has been converted into a weekend flea market, the Townhouse Art Gallery, and antique stores. Restaurant, bar, complimentary breakfast. Cable TV. Indoor pool. Massage. Exercise equipment. | 316 Charles St. | 304/652–1312 | fax 304/652–1354 | www.tylercounty.net/wellsinn | 32 rooms | $75–$150 | AE, DC, MC, V.

SUMMERSVILLE

(Nearby town also listed: Richwood)

Summersville was burned in July 1861 when the 20-year-old Confederate spy Nancy Hart (known as Peggy by soldiers in both armies) led an attack on the town. In September of the same year, Union troops under William S. Rosecrans ran into a Confederate force under John B. Floyd. The battle is commemorated with reenactments each September at the Carnifex Ferry Battlefield State Park. U.S. 19 provides easy access to the Summersville Lake and Wildlife Management Area.

Information: **Summersville Area Chamber of Commerce** | 411 Old Main Dr., Box 567, 26651 | 304/872–1588.

Attractions

Carnifex Ferry Battlefield State Park. The 156-acre park is on the site of a Civil War battle fought September 10, 1861. The park museum displays relics from the battle; reenactments of the engagement usually take place the Sunday after Labor Day. | Rte. 2 at Carnifex | 304/872–0825 | www.wvparks.com/carnifexferrybattlefield | Free | May–Labor Day, daily.

Gauley River National Recreation Area. The area encompasses 25 mi of the Gauley River and 6 mi of the Meadow River and offers white-water rafting, kayaking, hunting, fishing, and trapping. | 104 Main St., Glen Jean | 304/465–0508 | www.nps.gov/neri | Free | Daily 9–5.

Kirkwood Winery. You can tour, taste, and shop at this family-owned Appalachian winery 3 mi north of town. | Phillips Run Rd., off Rte. 19 | 888/498–9463 | www.kirkwood-wine.com | Free | Weekdays 9–7, weekends 1–7.

Snowshoe Mountain Resort. You can ski down one of 53 trails—the longest is 1½ mi—from the 4,848-ft summit of Snowshow Mountain. Each year the mountain gets 180 inches of natural and man-made snow. The resort is about 30 mi north of Summersville, off Rte. 219. | 10 Snowshoe Dr., off Rte. 66, Snowshoe | 304/572–1000 | $55 | Nov.–Apr., closed May–Oct.

Summersville Lake and Wildlife Management Area. The state's largest lake draws visitors interested in fishing, boating, water skiing, and scuba diving. | 304/872–5809 | Free | May–Oct., daily, closed Nov.–Apr.

ON THE CALENDAR

MAY: *Cork Poppin' Chilifest and Homecoming Celebration.* A chili cook-off, live music, and children's activities make up this festival the third weekend of the month at 1350 Phillips Run Rd. | 888/498–3463.

JULY: *Nicholas County Fair.* Horse shows, exhibits, live music, arts and crafts, and food are the highlights of this summer fair. | 304/872–1454.

SEPT.: *Kirkwood Grape Stomping Festival.* Professional grape-stompers, a blacksmith, and a gunsmith demonstrate their talents at the Kirkwood Winery the third weekend of the month. | 888/498–9463.

SEPT.: *Nicholas County Potato Festival.* Celebrate the spud with a parade, a car show, a 5K walk/run, potato judging, and an auction. | 304/872–3722.

Dining

Mamma Jarroll's Country Road Inn. Italian. Antique and contemporary furnishings fill the interior of this restaurant 8 mi west of Summersville. The multi-course meals include antipasto, garden salad, homemade pasta and meat dishes such as lasagna, eggplant parmigiana, chicken scallopini, Italian sausages, and homemade desserts. The price includes all courses. The sample platter of all main dishes is popular. Kids' menu available. | Country Rd., off Rte. 39 | 304/872–1620 or 800/439–8852 (WV) | No lunch | $15–$24 | AE, D, MC, V.

Lodging

Best Western Summersville Lake. This three-story chain in a commercial area is 2 mi from Summersville Lake and 4 mi from the airport. Restaurant, bar, complimentary Continental breakfast, room service. Cable TV. Business services. Some pets allowed. | 1203 Broad St. off Rte. 19 | 304/872–6900 | fax 304/872–6908 | 59 rooms | $47–$53 | AE, D, DC, MC, V.

Hampton Inn. This three-story chain is in a commercial area 3 mi from Summersville Lake, and 3 mi from sky-diving facilities. Complimentary Continental breakfast. Cable TV. Outdoor pool. Exercise equipment. Business services. No pets. | 5400 Webster Rd. | 304/872–7100 | fax 304/872–7101 | 76 rooms | $50–$70 | AE, D, DC, MC, V.

Sleep Inn Summersville. This two-story hotel is in a shopping complex on the east side of town, near a medical clinic and several restaurants. Restaurant, picnic area, complimentary Continental breakfast. In-room data ports, cable TV, in-room VCRs (and movies). Outdoor pool. Kids' programs, playground. Laundry facilities. Business services. Pets allowed. | 701 Professional Park Dr. | 304/872–4500 | fax 304/872–0288 | 97 rooms | $79–$199 | AE, D, DC, MC, V.

SUTTON

(Nearby town also listed: Summersville)

Settled by John D. Sutton in 1810 and incorporated in 1883, this town of under 1,000 is in the center of the Mountain Lakes region and is close to lakes, state parks, and wildlife management areas. Fishing, swimming, boating, and hunting are popular in the area.

Information: Braxton County Convention and Visitors Bureau | 245 Skidmore La., 26601 | 304/765–3300 | www.braxtonwv.org.

Attractions

Elk River Wildlife Management Area. You can hunt small game or fish for catfish, trout, bass, and walleye in the Elk River and Sutton Lake on this 18,000-acre wildlife management area 3½ mi southeast of town. | Access from Rte. 15, or Rte. 17 | 304/765–7837 | Free | Dawn to dusk.

Sutton Lake. The lake, which is known for bass, muskie, pike, and trout fishing, offers 1,500 surface acres and a marina for boat rentals. | Rte. 15 | 304/765–2705 | Free | May–Dec., daily, closed Jan.–Apr.

ON THE CALENDAR

SEPT.: *Annual Mule and Donkey Show.* Tractor rides, mule and donkey rides, and a pig roast make up this Central West Virginia Riding Club festival, in which several classes of donkeys and mules compete. Labor Day weekend. | 304/364–8364.

Dining

BJ's Place. American. A 20-ft-wide fireplace is the centerpiece at this dining room full of oak tables that's popular with local residents. Order from a menu of steak, ribs, and grilled or deep-fried seafood. The restaurant is in a commerical area across from the Flatwood Factory Outlet Mall, off I–79. | 2250 Sutton La. | 304/765–2766 | Breakfast also served | $5–$10 | No credit cards.

Lodging

Days Inn. This chain motel is within 2 mi of Sutton Lake. Some rooms have private balconies with scenic views of the valley and mountains. Restaurant, bar. In-room data ports. Cable TV. Indoor pool. Exercise equipment. Business services. | 2000 Sutton La. | 304/765–5055 | fax 304/765–2067 | 200 rooms | $59–$160 | AE, D, DC, MC, V.

Stone Farm Bed & Breakfast. In a school house on 170 acres of rolling hills, this bed-and-breakfast is on a working farm established in 1910 19 mi north of town. The rooms have a birdhouse and quilt theme, and there's a brass fireplace with the original oak mantel piece. You can keep your horse in the stable. Complimentary breakfast. No room phones. Outdoor hot tub. Hiking, horseback riding. No pets. No smoking. | Rte. 1 | 304/452–8477 | sfbb@msys.net | www.msys.net/sfbb | 3 rooms | $40–$60 | AE, D, MC, V.

Sutton Lane. This no-frills motel is in a commercial area 5 mi outside of town. Restaurant. Cable TV. | 2120 Sutton La. | 304/765–7351 | fax 304/765–2067 | 31 rooms | $43 | AE, DC, MC, V.

WEBSTER SPRINGS

(Nearby towns also listed: Richwood, Summersville)

Webster Springs was incorporated in 1892 as Addison, named for Addison McLaughlin, upon whose land it was built; it was later renamed after Daniel Webster. The town of 1,509 has two natural features of particular interest: the world's largest sycamore tree, located on the Back Fork of the Elk River; and one of only two patches of running buffalo clover believed to remain in the United States (the other is in Fayette County).

Information: **Webster Springs Chamber of Commerce** | 110 Main St., Box 4, 26288 | 304/847–7666.

Attractions

Baker's Island. A central park with a baseball diamond, picnic shelters, public pool, and many trees is on this island between the Elk and Back Fork of Elk River. | Rte. 20 and Bakers St. | 304/847–7291 | Free | Daily 6 AM–11 PM.

Buffalo Clover Patch. A stone fountain and memorial mark the place on Point Mountain, 5 mi south of town, where the last buffalo in the state was killed. | Rte. 15 | 304/847–7291 | Free | Daily.

Holly River State Park. The remoteness of this 8,292-acre state park draws visitors for hiking and trout fishing. Cabins and campsites are available. To get there, take I–79 to Route 33 to Route 22; the entrance is 22 mi north of downtown Webster Springs. | Rte. 20 | 304/493–6353 | www.wvparks.com/hollyriver | Free | Daily 6 AM–10 PM.

Kumbrabow State Forest. This 9,474-acre wooded area offers rental cabins, campsites, fishing, hiking trails, and picnic areas. | Rtes. 219 and 16 | 304/335–2219 | www.wvparks.com/kumbrabow | Free | Daily 6 AM–10 PM.

Sycamore Tree. The oldest and largest sycamore in the world is on the Back Fork of Elk River, 2 mi northeast of town. Cross a swinging bridge over the river to get to the tree, a park with picnic tables, and a 1-mi-long hiking trail to the Big Falls on the river. | Back Fork Rd. | 304/847–7291 | Free | Daily.

ON THE CALENDAR

MAY: *Webster County Woodchopping Festival.* This Memorial Day weekend world championship woodchopping contest draws lumberjacks from around the world; there's also a turkey-calling contest, parades, and dancing. | 304/847–7666 or 304/847–2454.

SEPT.: *Webster County Fair.* Held every Labor Day weekend, the fair has live music, a carnival, arts and crafts, exhibits, and food. | 304/226–3888.

OCT.: *Burgoo Cook-Off.* A combination of at least three meats, fish, or fowl—excluding bacon and salt pork, which are allowed only for seasoning—make up burgoo stew, the centerpiece of this cooking competition the first weekend of the month on Baker's Island. | 304/847–7291.

NOV.: *Veteran's Day Parade.* A ceremony at the Veteran's Memorial on Court Square, a parade down Main Street, live music, and a pig roast commemorate the nation's veterans on this national holiday. | 304/847–7291.

Dining

The Salt Sulphur Café. Italian. In this octagonal-shape building with 18-ft ceilings you'll dine on Americanized spaghetti and meatballs, chicken Parmesan, pizza, steak, and burgers. You can gaze at the shelves of bottles of Italian olive oils and photos of area attractions such as Whittaker Falls (12 mi southeast of the restaurant) and aerial views of town.

The restaurant has its own label of red and white Chianti, which it sells by the bottle. Adjacent to the restaurant you can rejuvenate in the black walnut-walled public mineral salt bath house; the basalt lava rock tubs are filled with therapeutic mineral water. | 3 Spring St. | 304/847–5109 | $8–$15 | D, DC, MC, V.

Lodging

Brass Tea Pot Bed and Breakfast. There is an authentic Murphy bed with a feather mattress in the downstairs bedroom of this 1910 two-story home. You'll find the B&B on 1½ acres 13 mi northeast of town. Complimentary breakfast. Cable TV, no room phones. Outdoor hot tub. No pets. No smoking. | 60 Summit Ave., Cowen | 304/226–0687 | fax 304/226–5333 | 4 rooms | $55–$65 | MC, V.

Mineral Springs Motel. You'll have scenic views from any room in this two-story motel near the Elk River, high in the Appalachians. Get a room in the front and you'll have a view of mountains; get one in the back and you'll have one of the mountains and the river too. Air-conditioning, cable TV. Pets allowed (fee). | 1 Spring St. | 304/847–5305 | 23 rooms | $42 | AE, D, DC, MC, V.

WEIRTON

MAP 17, C2

(Nearby town also listed: Bethany)

Founded in 1909 by steel giant Ernest T. Weir, the city began with 25 mill company houses built on a hillside. Weirton, with a population of 22,124, remains a true steel town, with Weirton Steel Corp. as a primary center of industry. *Reckless*, a 1984 film about alienated youth starring Daryl Hannah and Aidan Quinn, was filmed here.

Information: Weirton Area Chamber of Commerce | 3200 Main St. 26062 | 304/748–7212.

Attractions

Mountaineer Racetrack and Resort. The resort has a video lottery, thoroughbred racing, and three restaurants. Next to the racetrack is the Mountaineer Lodge, with a golf course and swimming pools. To get there, take I–22 15 mi north of Weirton. | Rte. 2, off I–22, Chester | 304/387–2400 | www.mtrgaming.com | Free | Racetrack: Fri.–Tues. 7 PM–10 PM; gaming: Mon.–Sat. 9 AM–3 AM, Sun. 1 PM–3 AM; golf: Apr.–Nov. 7 AM–dark.

Tomlinson Run State Park. The park's 1,398 acres provide opportunities for fishing, swimming, camping, tennis, and miniature golf. The park is 19 mi north of Weirton. | Hwy. 2, off Hwy. 8 | 304/564–3651 | www.wvparks.com/tomlinsonrun | Free | Daily 6 AM–10 PM.

Woodview Golf Course. The green price includes a golf cart at this 18-hole public course; there's also a snack bar and a pro shop. The course is 5 mi north of Weirton. | RR 4, off Rte. 2, New Cumberland | 304/564–5765 | Mar.–Dec., closed Jan.–Feb.

Weirton Steel Corp. and Half Moon Industrial Park. Founded in 1905, Weirton Steel Corp. is the eighth-largest producer of integrated steel in the nation. With 4,800 workers, the company is West Virginia's largest industrial employer. Tours of the facilities and the chemical companies of the neighboring Half Moon Industrial Park can be arranged by appointment. | 400 Three Spring Dr. | 304/748–7212 | www.weirton.com | Free | Tours by appointment.

ON THE CALENDAR
JULY: *Greek Bazaar.* This festival in downtown Weirton celebrates Greek heritage with music, entertainment, and food. | 304/797–9884 or 304/797–1725.

Dining

Marino's Italian Restaurant. Italian. Checkered cloths and fresh flowers brighten the tables, and pictures of Italy line the walls of this trattoria on a country road 4 mi from town. Portions of pasta, chicken, and veal Parmesan standards are extra-large. To get there, take Route 2 North 4 mi from downtown Weirton. | Wiley Ridge Rd., off Searingen Hill Rd., New Cumberland | 304/748–3147 | $5–$10 | MC, V.

Lodging

Weirton Holiday Inn. This five-story chain in a commercial area is 2 mi east of downtown Weirton and about 20 mi east of Oglebay Park. Restaurant, bar, room service. Air-conditioning, some microwaves, some refrigerators, cable TV, room phones, TV in common area, outdoor pool. Gym. Children's programs, business services, no pets. | 350 Three Springs Dr. | 304/723–5522 | fax 304/723–1608 | 114 rooms, 2 suites | $89 rooms, $149–$169 suites | AE, D, DC, MC, V.

WESTON

MAP 17, C4

(Nearby towns also listed: Buckhannon, Elkins)

A city of 4,926 in the Mountain Lakes region, Weston is a center of agriculture and features unusual blends of architecture, from Victorian to Art Deco, including the former Weston State Hospital and the Citizens Bank Building.

Information: Lewis County Convention and Visitors Bureau | 345 Center Ave., Box 379, 26452 | 304/269–7328.

Attractions

Cedar Creek State Park. The 2,443-acre outdoor area offers a restaurant, campsites, swimming, fishing, and hiking and horseback trails. | 119 Cedar Creek Rd., off Rte. 33 | 304/462–7158 | www.wvparks.com/cedarcreek | Free | Daily 6 AM–10 PM.

Citizens Bank Building. The 54-ft-tall Citizens Bank Building, designed in the classic Art Deco style, is believed to be the tallest single-story structure in the United States. | 201 Main St. | 304/269–2862 | Free | Mon.–Thurs. 8:30–3, Fri. 8:30–5:30, closed weekends.

Jackson's Mill Historic Area/Museum. The original five acres of Stonewall Jackson's boyhood home feature two 1700s log cabins and a working gristmill. | Rte. 1 | 304/269–4588, 304/269–5100, or 800/287–8206 | $4 | Memorial Day–Labor Day, Tues.–Sun. 10–5, closed Mon. and Labor Day–Memorial Day.

Jackson's Mill State 4-H Conference Center. This 523-acre facility was the nation's first 4-H camp. The grounds include livestock pavilions, flower gardens, tennis courts, and a swimming pool. It is the site of the Stonewall Jackson Heritage Arts and Crafts Jubilee on Labor Day weekend. | Rte. 1 | 304/269–5100 | Free | Daily.

Louis Bennett House (Public Library). The 17-room mansion, built around 1875, is an example of High Victorian Italianate architecture. The house, which contains the Louis Bennett Public Library, retains some of its original furnishings. | 148 Court Ave. | 304/269–5151 | Free | Weekdays 10–6, Sat. 10–2, closed Sun.

Stonewall Jackson Lake State Park and Wildlife Management Area. The 3,800-acre park surrounds the state's second-largest lake and is next to an 18,346-acre wildlife management area. The areas have fishing, boating, hunting, camping, and a visitor center. The entrance is 2½ mi south of Exit 91, off I–79. | Rte. 19 | 304/269–0523 | www.wvparks.com/stonewalljacksonlake | $1 per car | Daily dawn to dusk.

Weston State Hospital Building. Three-and-a-half acres of roof cover the 9½ acres inside this four-story antebellum building, one of the largest hand-cut stone buildings in the country. It was a state psychiatric hospital, and is currently unoccupied and not open to public, but warrants a drive-by peek. | W. 2nd St. | 304/269–7328.

SEPT.: *Stonewall Jackson Heritage Arts and Crafts Jubilee.* On Labor Day weekend, the Civil War general's birthplace hosts arts and crafts, music, and battle reenactments. At Jackson's Mill State 4-H Conference Center on Route 1. | 304/269–1863.
OCT.: *Storytelling Festival Voices of the Mountains.* Nationally known and West Virginia storytellers spin yarns of Appalachia at Jackson's Mill Historic Area Museum. | 304/472–4218.

Dining

Coke & Float. American. A jukebox plays 1950s classics and black-and-white photos of performers line the walls at this downtown soda shop, where you can order a milkshake, hamburger, and fries from the counter or in a booth. | 624 W. Second St. | 304/269–7420 | Breakfast also served | $5–$8 | AE, D, MC, V.

Lodging

Comfort Inn. Right off Exit 99 on I–79 and 3 mi east of town, this two-story hostelry is near shopping and 4 mi north of Stonewall Jackson Lake State Park. The hotel is renovated every winter. Restaurant, bar. Cable TV. Pool. Some pets allowed. | I–79 and U.S. 33 E | 304/269–7000 | 60 rooms | $59–$61 | AE, D, DC, MC, V.

Super 8 Motel. This two-story chain is 3 mi east of downtown Webster Springs; area attractions include Jackson's Mill State 4-H Conference Center, 4 mi north of the motel, and Stonewall Jackson Lake State Park and Wildlife Management Area, which is 6 mi south of the motel. All rooms have interior entrances. Cable TV, some in-room VCRs. No pets. | 12 Market Pl. | 304/269–1086 | fax 304/269–1086 | www.super8.com | 62 rooms | $50–$70 | AE, D, DC, MC, V.

WHEELING

MAP 17, C3

(Nearby towns also listed: Bethany, Weirton)

The site of the last battle of the American Revolution, Wheeling was the capital of the "Restored Government of Virginia" and twice was capital of West Virginia, finally losing in a political tug-of-war with Charleston. The state's third-largest city, Wheeling is perhaps best known for the 900-ft-long Wheeling Suspension Bridge and Oglebay Resort Park, a 1,500-acre recreation area on the northern edge of the city.

Information: **Wheeling Convention and Visitors Bureau** | 1401 Main St., Heritage Sq. 26003 | 304/233–7709 or 800/828–3097 | info@wheelingcvb.com | www.wheelingcvb.com.

Attractions

The Artisan Center. This restored historic industrial building contains the Nail City Brewing Company and Restaurant, the Wymers General Store/Museum, and Industrial Heritage exhibits. Working artisans provide demonstrations and sell crafts. | 1400 Main St., Heritage Sq. | 304/232–1810 | Free | Mon.–Thur. 11–7; Fri.–Sat. 11–9, closed Sun.

Grave Creek Mound State Park. This park first opened in 1838. The prehistoric burial mound here was built in 250–150 BC by the Adena Indians and is the largest in the world—69 ft high and 295 ft in diameter. Next to the mound and also part of the park is the Delf Norona Museum and Cultural Center. | 801 Jefferson Ave., Moundsville | 304/843–4128 | www.wvparks.com | $3 | Daily 6 AM–10 PM; museum Mon.–Sat. 10–4:30, Sun. 1–5.

Oglebay Resort Park. In this 1,500-acre municipal park you'll find gardens, greenhouses, restaurants, golf courses, and cross-country skiing. Popular events at Oglebay include a fireworks display the first weekend of October and the Festival of Lights from early November through late January. | Rte. 88 N | 304/243–4000 or 800/624–6988 | www. oglebayresort.com | $10.60 all-day pass | Daily.

Located in the park, the **Carriage House Glass Museum** presents an extensive collection of glassware produced from 1817 to 1939. Working artisans give demonstrations of glass blowing. | 304/243–4058 | $2 | Call for hours.

The **Mansion Museum** is filled with items from early life in the Ohio Valley. Changing exhibits are featured. | 304/242–7272 | $5 | Apr.–Dec. daily 10–5; Jan.–Mar. Fri.–Sun. 10–5, closed Mon.–Thurs.; special holiday hours.

Home to more than 250 North American species, **Oglebay's Good Zoo** has a children's farm, a deer contact area, and a natural science theater. A 1863 train tours the grounds. | 304/243–4030 | www.oglebay_resort.com | $4.50 | Weekdays 11–5, weekends 10–6.

Site of Fort Henry. The last battle of the Revolutionary War was fought here September 11–13, 1782, when 40 British soldiers and 260 Native Americans attacked the fort. Ebenezer and Silas Zane, who founded Wheeling in 1769, led the defenders. The site is marked by a memorial stone on Main Street. | Main St. | Free | Daily.

West Virginia Independence Hall–Custom House. Built in 1859 as the Wheeling Custom House, the building housed the loyalists' government for the restored state of Virginia and the conventions that declared West Virginia's independence from the commonwealth. Guided and self-guided tours are available; you'll need reservations for the guided tours. | 1528 Market St. | 304/238–1300 | Free | Mar.–Dec., daily 10–4; Jan. and Feb., Mon.–Sat. 10–4, closed Sun.

West Virginia State Penitentiary. Tours of West Virginia's first territorial prison include the Alamo Cell Block, where the worst inmates were housed. The prison was built in 1866. | 818 Jefferson Ave. | 304/845–6200 | www.wvpentours.com | $7 | Tours Apr.–Dec., Tues.–Sun. 10–4, closed Mon.; Jan.–Mar. tours by appointment only.

Wheeling Park. Choose from paddleboating, ice skating, indoor and outdoor tennis courts, a miniature golf course, a nine-hole golf course, and a swimming pool and water slide at this 406-acre park. | 1801 National Rd. | 304/242–3770 | $7 | Daily.

THE MOUND BUILDERS

They are America's answer to the Great Pyramids, burial mounds throughout the valleys of the Mississippi and Ohio rivers. Built by the Adena Indians, who lived from 800 BC to AD 100, the mounds measure about 70 ft high and 200 ft across. One of the largest is Grave Creek Mound near Moundsville in West Virginia's Northern Panhandle. In the 1830s, people who had no anthropological expertise opened the mound. Inside they found human remains, beads, shells, and copper bracelets. But it was a stone inscribed with markings similar to Viking runes that created the most excitement. Was it evidence of written communication by this ancient civilization? That's the subject of extensive debate. While many scholars have spent considerable time trying to translate the stone, archaeologists at the National Museum in Washington, DC, believe it was placed in the excavation as a hoax. Some people hoping to unlock the mystery to a lost civilization aren't convinced.

© Corbis

Wheeling Suspension Bridge. Opened in 1849, this 1010-ft suspension bridge, the longest in the world, was the first bridge to cross the Ohio River. It collapsed in 1854, was rebuilt in 1860 and restored again in 1990. | 10th St., at Main St. | 304/233–7709 | Free | Daily.

ON THE CALENDAR

JULY–AUG.: *Jamboree USA.* Home of WWVA radio's "Jamboree USA," the Capitol Music Hall has live performances by country music greats and two big-name jamborees. | 304/234–0050 or 800/624–5456 | www.jamboreeusa.com.

OCT.: *Oglebayfest.* This park celebration in downtown Wheeling has dancing, a country fair, and a juried arts and crafts show. | 304/243–4000.

NOV.–JAN.: *City of Lights Festival.* This festival includes miles of light displays, a Fantasy in Light parade, Victorian house tours, and specialty shops. | 304/243–4010.

Dining

Cork 'N' Bottle. Continental. A variety of American and Continental favorites are served at this restaurant. The fresh seafood specials are worth a try. Entertainment. Kids' menu available. | 39 12th St. | 304/232–4400 | Closed Sun. | $10–$15 | AE, D, DC, MC, V.

Ernie's Esquire. Continental. Choose from several elegant, individually decorated rooms at this restaurant that's known for its fresh seafood, beef, veal, and pasta dishes; a particular favorite is the chicken romano. Entertainment on weekends. Kids' menu available. Sun. brunch. | 1 W. Bethlehem Blvd. | 304/242–2800 | $10–$20 | AE, D, DC, MC, V.

Lodging

Best Western Wheeling Inn. This chain hotel is two blocks south of the Victorian section of Wheeling. Local attractions such as the Wheeling Suspension Bridge and the Capital City Music Hall are within walking distance. The Wheeling Downs Racetrack and Gaming Center is 1 mi west. Restaurant, bar. Complimentary Continental breakfast. Cable TV. Hot tub. Exercise equipment. Business services. | 949 Main St. | 304/233–8500 | fax 304/233–8500, ext. 345 | 80 rooms | $67–$77 | AE, D, DC, MC, V.

Days Inn. Just to make a point, there's an 18-wheeler truck in the lobby of this chain motel 5 mi west of downtown Wheeling, off I–70 Exit 11 (Dallas Pike). The hotel is near a commercial area. Bar, complimentary Continental breakfast. Some in-room hot tubs. Cable TV. Pool. Business services. Some pets allowed. | Exit 11 and I-70, Triadelphia | 304/547–0610 | fax 304/547–9029 | 106 rooms | $47–$55 | AE, D, DC, MC, V.

Hampton Inn. Just off I–70 Exit 2A and 2 mi west of Wheeling, this is the closest hotel to Oglebay Resort. It has five floors and is in the residential part of town. Complimentary Continental breakfast, room service. In-room data ports, some refrigerators. Cable TV. Exercise equipment. Business services. | 795 National Rd. | 304/233–0440 | fax 304/233–2198 | 104 rooms, 2 suites | $74, $84 suites | AE, D, DC, MC, V.

Holiday Inn Express. There are mountain views from some of the rooms at this two-story motel 8 mi east of town. Complimentary Continental breakfast. In-room data ports, some in-room hot tubs. Cable TV. Outdoor pool. Laundry facilities, laundry service. Business services, free parking. Pets allowed (fee). | Rte. 1 | 304/547–1380 or 800/422–7829 | fax 304/547–9270 | 116 rooms, 1 suite | $70 rooms, $109 suite | AE, D, DC, MC, V.

Oglebay's Wilson Lodge. This resort in the hills surrounding the city is 3 mi from I–70 Exit 2A. In addition to a two-story lodge, the property has cabins and chalets. You can rent a paddleboat to use on Schenk Lake. There's also a children's zoo. Dining room, picnic area, room service. In-room data ports, some kitchenettes. Cable TV. 2 pools (1 indoor), lake, wading pool. Hot tub. Driving range, 2 18-hole golf courses, miniature golf, 11 tennis courts. Gym, horseback riding. Boating, fishing. Kids' programs, playground. Business services. | Rte. 88 N, off Exit 2A | 304/243–4000 or 800/624–6988 | fax 304/243–4070 | www.oglebay-resort.com | 212 rooms in 2-story lodge; 49 cabins; 4 chalets | $75–$155, $315–$1042 cabins (7–day minimum stay), $420–$1395 chalets (2–day minimum weekend stay) | AE, D, DC, MC, V.

★ **Stratford Springs.** The inn, next to Oglebay Resort Park, is listed on the National Register of Historic Places. The inn is composed of two turn-of-the-century houses and stands on 30 wooded, secluded acres. Rooms are Colonial in style with cherry furniture. Restaurants, pool, exercise room. | 100 Kensington Dr. | 304/233–5100 | 3 rooms | $95–$115 | AE, MC, V.

WHITE SULPHUR SPRINGS

MAP 17, D6

(Nearby town also listed: Lewisburg)

The mineral springs for which White Sulphur Springs was named were attracting attention for their avowed curative powers as early as 1772. By 1778 White Sulphur Springs was considered a fashionable health resort. The site of the original spring is on the grounds of the Greenbrier resort. The hotel was used an internment facility for Axis diplomats stationed in Washington, DC, from the time the United States entered World War II until July 1942, when they were exchanged for American diplomats held in Germany and Italy. The resort also served as a soldiers' hospital during the war. Today, the outdoor baths are gone, although guests to the Greenbrier can enjoy a soak in the indoor spa.

Information: **White Sulphur Springs Convention and Visitors Bureau** | 34 W. Main St. 24986 | 304/536–3590 or 800/284–9440.

Attractions

1884 Oakhurst Links. Sheep graze this nine-hole course built by Russell Montague in 1884, the oldest golf club in the country. A tour of the property's history and optional period costumes are included in the green fee. | 1 Montague Dr. | 304/536–1884 | www.oakhurstlinks.com | May–Oct., daily 8–5, closed Nov.–Apr.

The Coal House. Blocks of coal shaped with hatchets and joined with black mortar form this gift shop 2 mi east of downtown. The shop is one of the three remaining coal structures in the world. | U.S. 60 | 304/536–3288 | Free | Mar.–Dec. weekdays 9–5, weekends 9–6; closed Jan.–Feb.

Greenbrier State Forest. Just minutes from I–64 and White Sulphur Springs, this outdoor area has 5,130 acres for hiking, hunting, camping, and swimming. Rental cabins are available. Take Exit 175 off I–65 East/West. | Old Rte. 60 | 304/536–1944 | www.greenbriersf.com or www.wvparks.com | Free | Daily 6 AM–10 PM.

Memorial Park. The municipal park offers swimming, game fields, picnic areas, and tennis and basketball courts. | Greenbrier Ave. and Memorial St. | 304/536–1454 | Free | Daily.

National Fish Hatchery. The hatchery propagates rainbow and brook trout for distribution into streams of the Monongahela State Forest. The visitor center has aquariums and displays of the facility's activities. You can observe spawning December through January and June through September. | 400 E. Main St. | 304/536–1361 | Free | Daily.

ON THE CALENDAR

MAY: *Show-Me-Hike.* You can view wildflowers in the Greenbrier State Forest and along the Greenbrier River Trail on hikes hosted by the White Sulphur Springs Garden Club all month. | 304/536–1944, 304/536–2500.
MAY: *West Virginia Dandelion Festival.* Come to this celebration to taste the greens and wine made from this yellow flower and to browse through locally made arts and crafts. | 304/536–4007.

Dining

The Greenbrier Main Dining Room. Continental. The dining is formal in a large, elegantly appointed hall with crystal chandeliers and exquisite artwork and drapery. Specialty dishes include veal medallions with creamed morels, roast Long Island duckling, or fresh North Carolina seafood. All meals are five courses prix fixe, excluding wine and tax. The restaurant is next to the Greenbrier lodge. Kids' menu available. | 300 W. Main St. | 304/536–1110, ext. 7112 | Reservations essential | Jacket and tie | Breakfast also available | $67 | AE, D, DC, MC, V.

The Tavern Room. Continental. This comfortably elegant dining area resembling an intimate old English tavern has live piano music and an extensive international wine list. You can choose from fresh lobster, veal, rack of lamb, or certified Angus steaks. Pictures of French wine labels grace the walls. All meals are five courses prix fixe, excluding tax and beverages. | 300 W. Main St. | 304/536–1110 | Reservations essential | Jacket and tie | No lunch | $90 | AE, D, DC, MC, V.

Trails Inn Restaurant. American. Pull up and honk in the parking lot to signal you're ready to order at this '50s-style restaurant. Daily country specials are delivered right to your car, where you eat off of trays hooked to the car window. Regular specials include pan-fried chicken, country-fried steak, spaghetti, meat loaf, and baked fish. If you're feeling more conventional, you can eat inside at oblong family-style tables. The Trails Inn is 12 mi north of town. | Rte. 92, Neola | 304/536–1900 | Breakfast also available | $4–$11 | No credit cards.

Lodging

★ **The Greenbrier.** The Greenbrier was built in 1780; extensive renovations and additions have been constructed over the years to make this one of the leading resorts in the country. Surrounded by 6,500 acres, the resort has a grand turn-of-the-century style: massive white columns rise six stories against a white facade, and nine lobbies offer vast, chandeliered common areas. Every guest room is different and decorated in Dorothy Draper pastel prints. For outdoor enthusiasts, there's canoeing, rafting, horseback riding, a hunt club and game preserve, facilities for trap- and skeet-shooting, and a regulation croquet court. 4 dining rooms, room service. In-room data ports, some refrigerators. Cable TV, 2 pools (1 indoor), wading pool. Hot tub, spa. Driving range, 3 18-hole golf courses, 2 putting greens, 20 tennis courts. Bowling, gym, horseback riding. Boating, bicycles. Ice skating, sleigh rides. Kids' programs, playground. Business services, airport shuttle. | 300 W. Main St. | 304/536–1110 or 800/624–6070 | fax 304/536–7854 | tjkbrier@aol.com | www.greenbrier.com | 443 rooms, 32 suites, 67 cottages, 4 estate houses | $203–$361 rooms, $286–$439 cottages, $387–$465 estate houses | AE, D, DC, MC, V.

Lillian's Antique Shop and B&B. All the antiques in this 1905 bed-and-breakfast are for sale. One guest room is in the servant's outbuilding. Dining room, complimentary breakfast. Cable TV. No pets. No smoking. | 204 W. Main St. | 877/536–1048, 304/536–1048 | lillian@brier.net | 4 rooms | $75–$135 | AE, MC, V.

Old White. Off I–64, this motel is ½ mi east of town and 1½ mi east of the Greenbrier. To get there traveling on I–64 West, take Exit 181 to I–60 West ¼ mi from the exit; traveling I–64 East, take Exit 175 to I–60 East 4½ mi from the exit. Cable TV. Pool. Some pets allowed. | 865 E. Main St. (Rte. 60) | 304/536–2441 or 800/867–2441 | fax 304/536–1836 | 26 rooms | $45 | AE, D, DC, MC, V.

WILLIAMSON

MAP 17, A7

(Nearby towns also listed: Charleston, Huntington)

Located at the heart of what was once called the "Billion Dollar Coal Field," Williamson is the business center for the coalfields of the Tug Valley and is rich in mining and labor history, including a chamber of commerce building that's made from locally mined coal.

Information: Tug Valley Chamber of Commerce | 2nd Ave. and Court St., Box 376, 25661 | 304/235–5240.

Attractions

Cabwaylingo State Forest. Named for Cabell, Wayne, Lincoln, and Mingo counties, this 8,123-acre state forest has rental cabins, camping, swimming, hunting, hiking, and picnic areas. | Rte. 1, Dunlow | 304/385–4255 | www.wvparks.com/cabwaylingo | Free | Daily 6 AM–10 PM.

Tug Valley Chamber of Commerce Building. The home to Williamson's chamber of commerce is also known as the Coal House; it was built in 1933 from 65 tons of locally mined coal. | 2nd Ave. and Court St. | 304/235–5240 | Free | Weekdays 9–5.

Historic Matewan. The site of the 1920 Matewan Massacre, this town of 600, 11 mi southeast of Williamson, played a pivotal role in the state's mining history and the national labor movement. United Mine Workers of America's efforts to unionize coal miners led to the bloodiest gunfight in U.S. history; 10 people were killed after the sheriff and townspeople clashed with agents hired by the coal company. The infamous Hatfield and McCoy feud began in 1882 not far from Matewan and lasted for nearly eight years. Self-guided walking tours begin at the McCoy Building and continue through the town's historic streets. Guide brochures are available. | 8 Mate St., off Rte. 49 | 304/426–4239 | Free | Daily.

Williamson Public Library. You can rent videos, music, and books at this courthouse library located downtown behind the Court House Annex. | Logan St. | 304/235–6029 | Free | Weekdays 10–5, closed weekends.

ON THE CALENDAR

JUNE: *Hatfield & McCoy Reunion Festival.* Since 1863, the McCoy and Hatfield families have perpetuated one of the most notorious feuds in U.S. history. The families put aside differences to hold the annual reunion, reviving the feud with a tug-of-war, a pig roast, softball and bowling tournaments, mussel-loading competitions, and a unifying church service. | 304/235–5240 or 606/353–9719.

SEPT.: *King Coal Festival.* Pageants, a parade, gospel music, bluegrass, street dancing, and an arts and crafts fair are organized every year in this celebration of coal. | 304/235–5560.

Dining

Brass Tree Restaurant. Continental. In the Sycamore Inn (*below*), this restaurant has a lounge for evening drinks, two banquet rooms, and a gift shop, which sells everything from books about West Virginia to animal figurines. You can order steak and baked potato or scallops in a sun-dried tomato and wine sauce. | 101 Prichard St. | 304/235–0811 | Jacket and tie | No lunch | $10–$20 | AE, D, DC, MC, V.

Lodging

Sycamore Inn. Centrally located in downtown Williamson, this three-story contemporary hotel is 13 mi from Historic Matewan, in the middle of Hatfield/McCoy Feud country, and approximately 5 mi from a Hatfield/McCoy recreational trail head. Restaurant, bar, complimentary Continental breakfast. Some in-room data ports. Cable TV. Business services. No pets. | 201 W. 2nd Ave. | 304/235–3656 or 800/446–6865 | fax 304/235–4609 | sycamoreinn@cyberriver.com | www.sycamoreinn.com | 47 rooms | $64 | AE, D, DC, MC, V.

Index

Detroit Zoological Park (Royal Oak, MI), 497

Detwiler/Bay View Park (Toledo, OH), 711

Devou Park (Covington (Cincinnati Airport Area), KY), 206

Dewey Lake (Prestonsburg, KY), 291

Dewolf-Allerdice House (Indianapolis, IN), 91

Dexter-Huron (Ann Arbor, MI), 333

Diamond Caverns (Cave City, KY), 201

Diamond Caverns Resort and Golf Club (Cave City, KY), 201

Diehl's (Nitro, WV), 794

Different Drummer (Greencastle, IN), 70

Dig's Diner (Warsaw, IN), 163

The Diner on Sycamore (Cincinnati, OH), 596

Dinner Bell (Berea, KY), 191

Dinner Bell Diner (Painesville, OH), 696

Dinosaur Gardens Prehistoric Zoo (Alpena, MI), 330

Dittrick Museum of Medical History (Cleveland, OH), 608

Diguid House B&B (Murray, KY), 279

Dixie Belle Riverboat Tours (Harrodsburg, KY), 230

Dixie Terminal (Cincinnati, OH), 589

Dobbs Park and Nature Center (Terre Haute, IN), 153

Doc Pierce's (Mishawaka, IN), 120

Dockside Restaurant (St. Ignace, MI), 502

Doctor's Office Exhibit (New Harmony, IN), 132

Dodge Fountain (Detroit, MI), 373

Doe Run Inn (Brandenburg, KY), 195

Dog Patch Restaurant (Munising, MI), 469

Dogtown Tavern (Evansville, IN), 55

Doherty Hotel (Clare, MI), 358

Don Hall's Guesthouse (Fort Wayne, IN), 62

Don Hall's–The Factory Steakhouse (Fort Wayne, IN), 61

Don's Lighthouse Grille (Cleveland, OH), 613

Donna's Premier Lodging (Berlin, OH), 574

Door Prairie Museum (Laporte, IN), 106

Doral Motel (Sault Ste. Marie, MI), 512

Dormitory No. 2 (New Harmony, IN), 133

Dossin Great Lakes Museum (Detroit, MI), 370

Doubletree (Farmington/Farmington Hills, MI), 381

Doubletree Detroit Airport (Romulus, MI), 495

Doubletree Guest Suites (Miamisburg, OH), 684

Doubletree Guest Suites–Columbus (Columbus, OH), 629

Doubletree Guest Suites–Indianapolis and Carmel (Indianapolis, IN), 91

Dover Lake Waterpark (Akron, OH), 557

Dover Station (Dover, OH), 643

Dow Gardens (Midland, MI), 462

The Down Under (Gallipolis, OH), 652

Downtown Historic District (Shelbyville, KY), 296

Downtown shopping district (Birmingham, MI), 344

Downtown shopping district (Clare, MI), 357

Dr. Bowen House (Moorefield, WV), 789

Dr. Increase Mathews House Museum (Zanesville, OH), 730

Dr. Ted's Musical Marvels (Santa Claus, IN), 145

Dr. Thomas Walker State Historic Site (Barbourville, KY), 186

Dr. William Hutchings Hospital Museum (Madison, IN), 109

Dragon Palace (Ashland, KY), 184

Drawbridge Inn (Covington (Cincinnati Airport Area), KY), 208

Dream Catchers Restaurant (Sault Ste. Marie, MI), 511

Driving around Town (Indianapolis, IN), 88

Droop Mountain Battlefield State Park (Hillsboro, WV), 776

Drury Inn (Frankenmuth, MI), 386

Drury Inn (Paducah, KY), 285

Drury Inn (Troy, MI), 531

Drury Inn–Evansville North (Evansville, IN), 56

Druther's (Campbellsville, KY), 198

Duba's (Grand Rapids, MI), 398

Dubois County Courthouse (Jasper, IN), 95

The Dude Ranch (Mason, OH), 678

Dudley's (Lexington, KY), 247

Duncan House Museum and Art Gallery (Greenville, KY), 229

Duncan Tavern Historic Shrine (Paris, KY), 287

Dune Ridge Winery (Valparaiso, IN), 155

Duneland Beach Inn (Michigan City, IN), 118

Dunham Tavern Museum (Cleveland, OH), 607

Dupont Lodge (Corbin, KY), 204

Durand Union Station and Michigan Railroad History Museum (Owosso, MI), 480

Dutch Colonial Inn (Holland, MI), 411

Dutch Harvest Restaurant (Berlin, OH), 574

Dutch Village (Holland, MI), 409

E. G. Hill Memorial Rose Garden (Richmond, IN), 141

E. P. "Tom" Sawyer State Park (Louisville, KY), 256

Eagle Creek Park and Nature Preserve (Indianapolis, IN), 82

Eagle Pointe Golf Resort (Bloomington, IN), 40

Eagle's Ridge Fine Dining (Suttons Bay, MI), 518

Earle (Ann Arbor, MI), 335

Earlham College (Richmond, IN), 140

Early American (Gilbertsville, KY), 226

Early West Street Log Structures (New Harmony, IN), 132

Easley's Winery (Indianapolis, IN), 87

East & West (Princeton, WV), 801

East Bank Emporium (South Bend, IN), 150

East Fork State Park (Cincinnati, OH), 592

East Indiana Section–National Road National Scenic Byway (Richmond, IN), 139

East Lansing Marriott University Place (Lansing and East Lansing, MI), 438

East Lynn Lake and Wildlife Management Area (Huntington, WV), 779

East Race Waterway (South Bend, IN), 150

East Tawas Junction B&B (Tawas City and East Tawas, MI), 520

Eastern Market (Detroit, MI), 371

Eastern Michigan University (Ypsilanti, MI), 537

Eastern Regional Coal Archives (Bluefield, WV), 756

Eastwood Lake (Dayton, OH), 634

Echo Valley (Kalamazoo, MI), 428

Econo Lodge (Cadillac, MI), 350

Econo Lodge (Coldwater, MI), 360

Econo Lodge (Elkhart, IN), 53

Econo Lodge (Elkins, WV), 768

Econo Lodge (Elyria, OH), 648

Econo Lodge (Escanaba, MI), 380

Econo Lodge (Grayling, MI), 404

Econo Lodge (Manistique, MI), 455

Econo Lodge (Marietta, OH), 675

Econo Lodge (Morgantown, WV), 792

Econo Lodge (Mount Vernon, KY), 278

Econo Lodge (Petoskey, MI), 485

Econo Lodge (Richmond, KY), 294

Econo Lodge (Richmond, KY), 294

Econo Lodge (South Haven, MI), 517

Econo Lodge (Wooster, OH), 726

Econo Lodge–Coliseum (Morgantown, WV), 792

Econolodge (South Bend, IN), 151

EconoLodge at the Bridge (Mackinaw City, MI), 450

Ed and Fred's Desert Moon Restaurant (Lexington, KY), 247

Eddie O'Flynns (Owosso, MI), 480

Eddie's Creekside Restaurant (Brecksville, OH), 576

Eddy Park (Wakefield, MI), 532

Eden Park (Cincinnati, OH), 592

Edge of Paradise (Newberry, MI), 474

Edgewater Estate I and II (Cleveland, OH), 616

Edgewater Inn (Charlevoix, MI), 353

Edgewater Resort Country Log Cabins (Iron Mountain, MI), 419

Edgewater State Park (Cleveland, OH), 609

Atlas

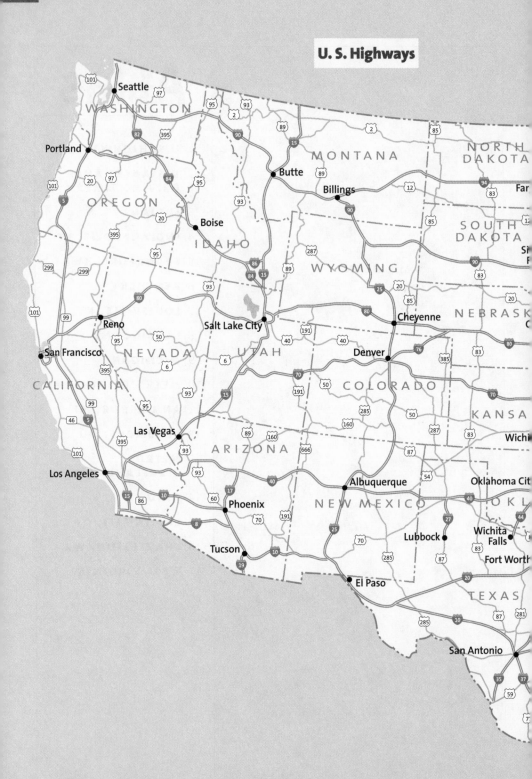

U. S. Highways

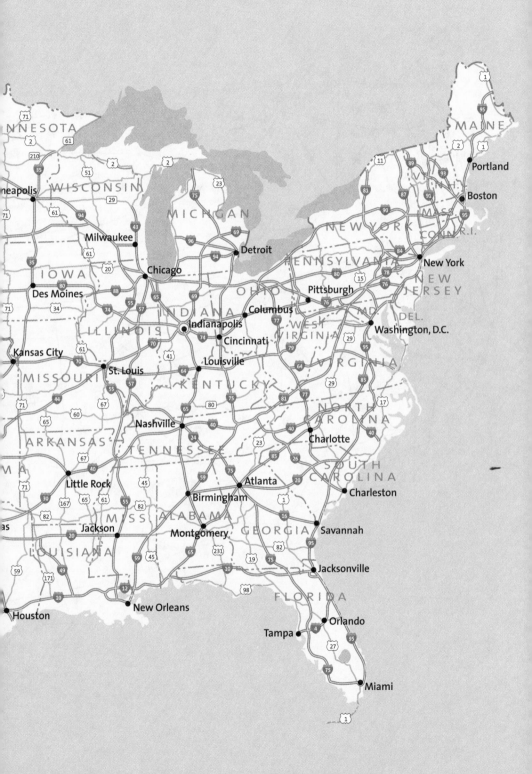

Distances and Driving Times

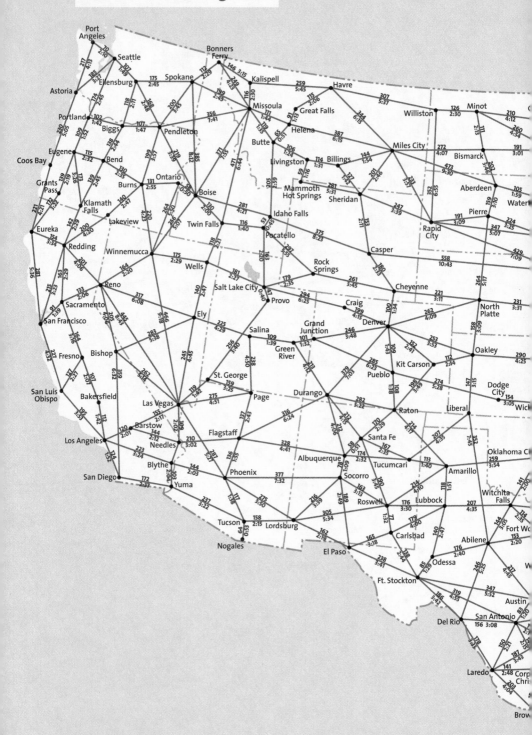

Indiana – Cities and Towns

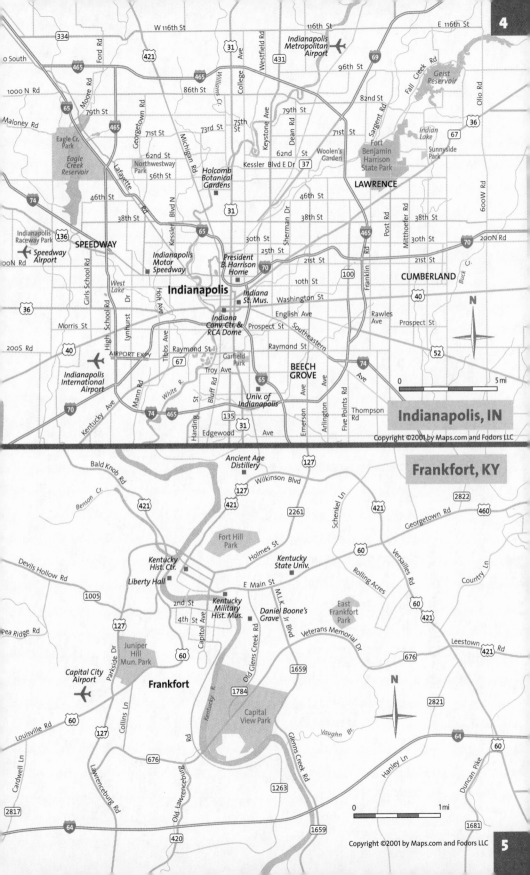

Indianapolis, IN

Copyright ©2001 by Maps.com and Fodors LLC

Frankfort, KY

Copyright ©2001 by Maps.com and Fodors LLC

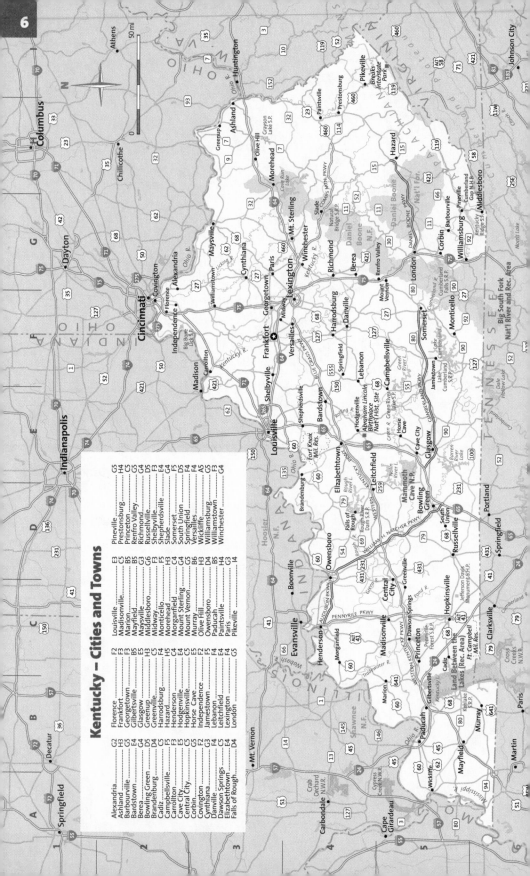

Kentucky – Cities and Towns

Louisville, KY

New Albany · **Clarksville** · **Jeffersonville**

311 · 131 · Spring St · Hamburg Pike · Middle Rd · Utica Pike · River Rd

62 · 64 · 150 · 111 · State St

Howard Steamboat Museum

Ohio R. · C.G. Cox Park · 71 · Klin Ln · 71 · 22

Brownsboro Rd · Westport Rd · E.P. "Tom" Sawyer State Park

Culbertson Mansion S.H.S. · Southwestern Pkwy · 1447 · Lyndon · A.B. Sawyer Park

Louisville Water Tower · Eva Bandman Park · Zorn Ave · 42 · 264 · Herr Ln · 146 · 1747

Shawnee Park · Market · St · Muhammad Ali Blvd · Brownsboro Rd · **St. Matthews** · 1699

Chickasaw Park · 264 · Hale St · Virginia Ave · Main St · Frankfort Ave · 60 · Shelbyville Rd

111 · Broadway · Lexington Rd · Breckenridge Ln · 64

Ohio R. · Dumesnil St · Oak St · Winter Ave · Cherokee Park · Beargrass · Cr. · Ln

Algonquin · Pkwy · Shelby St · **Louisville** · ALT 60 · 150 · 31E · 155 · Taylorsville Rd

Wilson Ave · 7th St Rd · 3rd St · Univ. of Louisville · 864

60 · Curchill Downs & Kentucky Derby Mus. · Poplar Level Rd · Louisville Zoological Gardens · 264 · Hikes Ln · **Jeffersontown** · N

Campground Rd · Cane Run Rd · 31W · **Shively** · 1020 · 61 · Bardstown Rd · 1932 · 1747

Crums Ln · Berry Blvd · Cardinal Stad. & Freedom Hall Col. · 65 · Col. H. Sanders Museum · 1703 · **Buechel**

Rockford Ln · HENRY WATTERSON EXPY · Preston Hwy · Produce Rd · Bardstown Rd · Fegenbush Ln

Manslick Rd · Taylor Blvd · Southern Pkwy · Louisville Int'l Airport · 1631 · Old Grade Ln · 864 · 2052

Dixie Hwy · Iroquois Park · 1931 · 1865 · Southside Dr · 1631

0 — 3 mi

Louisville, KY

Lansing, MI

27 · Clark Rd · Clark Rd · Webster Rd

Clark Rd · Forest Hill Rd · Francis Rd · Lowell Rd · 27 · 69 · Stoll Rd · Williams Rd · Rd · Chandler Rd · 69

96 · Stoll Rd · Airport Rd · Dewitt Rd · BUS 27 · 127

Wacousta Rd · BUS 96 · State Rd · Capital City Airport · N

Sheridan Rd · 69 · Delta River Dr · Grand River Ave · Turner Rd · East St · Wood St · 0 — 4 mi

Willow Hwy · 96 · Grand Woods Park · Tecumseh Park · Paulson Park · Lake · Lansing Rd · **East Lansing**

27 · Elmwood Ave · Willow St · Turner Dodge House · **Lansing** · Towar Park · BUS 69

Broadbent Rd · 43 · Saginaw St · BUS 69 · Oakland Ave · Saginaw St · 43 · M.S.U. Museum

Michigan Ave · St. Joe Hwy · State Capitol · Michigan Ave · 143 · Kresge Art Mus.

Canal Rd · Creyts Rd · 496 · Grand R. · Potter Park Zoological Gardens · Spartan Stadium

Mt. Hope Rd · Frances Park · Mt. Hope Rd · Fenner Nature Cen. & Arboretum · Crego Park · Mt. Hope Rd

Nixon Rd · Guinea Rd · Millett Hwy · Anderson Nature Park · Holmes Rd · Pleasant Grove Rd · Washington Ave · Cedar Ave · Pennsylvania Ave · Aurelius Ave · 496 · College Rd · Michigan State University · Hagadorn Rd

Davis Hwy · 69 · Woldumar Nature Cen. · Jolly Rd · Martin Luther King Jr. Blvd · Forest Rd · Jolly Rd

27 · Billwood Hwy · Hart Hwy · Waverly Rd · Miller Rd · Washington Ave · 127 · 496 · Sandhill Rd · 96

Pinch Hwy · Bishop Hwy · 99 · 96

Lansing, MI

10

Metro Detroit, MI

Birmingham	C2	Novi	A3
Bloomfield Hills	C2	Plymouth	A4
Farmington	B3	Rochester	D1
Farmington Hills	B3	Romulus	B6
Madison Heights	D3	Royal Oak	D3
Mt. Clemens	F2	Southfield	C4
Northville	A4	Troy	D2

Copyright ©2001 by Maps.com and Fodors LLC

11

Ann Arbor, MI

Barton Pond

Nixon Rd

Domino's Farms & Nat'l Cen. for the Study of Frank Lloyd Wright

Marshall Park

Plymouth-Ann Arbor Rd

153

Bird Hills Park

14

Black Pond Woods Park

Plymouth Rd

23

Dixboro Rd

Matthaei Botanical Gardens

Dexter Ave

Huron R.

Stearns Musical Collection

BUS 23

Miller Ave

Univ. of Mich. N. Campus

Fleming Cr.

94

Hands-On Museum

BUS 94

Gerald Ford Presidential Library

Fuller Rd

Geddes Rd

Dolph Park

Univ. of Michigan

Nichols Arboretum

Ann Arbor

Huron Pkwy

Superior Rd

Maple Rd

Stadium Blvd

Michigan Stadium

Huron

River Dr

Ypsilan

N

Scio-Church   Rd

Main St

State Rd

Packard Rd

Buhr Park

Washtenaw

17

Eastern Michigan University

Huron St

Waters   Rd

Cobblestone Farm & Mus.

Carpenter Rd

Ave

0   3 mi

94

Brown Park

BUS 94

Montibeller Park

Golfside Rd

Point Cr.

Wagner Rd

Ann Arbor-Saline Rd

Ellsworth   Rd

Ann Arbor Mun. Airport

12

94

N. B. Par

Sharon Woods Metro Park

Hoover Res.

Dublin

257

270

Westerville

33

Dublin-Granville Rd

Worthington

Ave

3

Dublin-Granville Rd

161

Antrim Park

161

Granville Rd

Ohio State Univ. Airport

23

71

Cleveland

Pike

Blendon Woods Metro Park

New Albany

Hayden Run   Rd

Bethel Rd

Henderson Rd

315

Cooke Rd

Morse Rd

Westerville

Alum Cr.

Rd

Hamilton Rd

Morse   Rd

62

270

33

High St

Oakland Park Ave

Innis   Rd

Rd

Hilliard Cemetery   Rd

Fishinger Rd

Kenny Rd

Agler Rd

Steltzer   Rd

Gahanna

Rocky Fk.

Havens Corners Rd

Upper Arlington

Lane Ave

Columbus

Scioto

Roberts Rd

Ohio State Univ.

Sunbury   Rd

Port Columbus Int'l Airport

317

Trabue   Rd

Hague Ave

McKinley Ave

5th Ave

Ohio Stadium

Ohio Hist. Cen.

670

E. Broad St

16

70

Wilson Rd

Grandview Heights

5th Ave

Bexley

Whitehall

270

Reynoldsbur

40

Lincoln Village

Sullivant Ave

Nationwide Arena (U.C.)

Mus. of Art

Franklin Park

James Rd

Main St

Big Walnut Cr.

40

State Capitol

Livingston Ave

Hamilton   Rd

Brice Rd

Clime Rd

Cooper Stadium

Lou Berliner Park

Parsons Ave

Lockbourne Rd

N

Norton Rd

Big Run Park

Frank Rd

Brown Rd

104

Alkire Rd

Gantz Rd

62

Refugee Rd

317

70

Bolton Field Airport

3

Grove City

104

Williams   Rd

Alum Creek Dr

33

Winchester Pike

Grove City Rd

Stringtown Rd

23

Three Rivers Park

Columbus, OH

71

270

Metro Cleveland, OH

Beachwood H3
Brecksville F6

Ohio – Cities and Towns

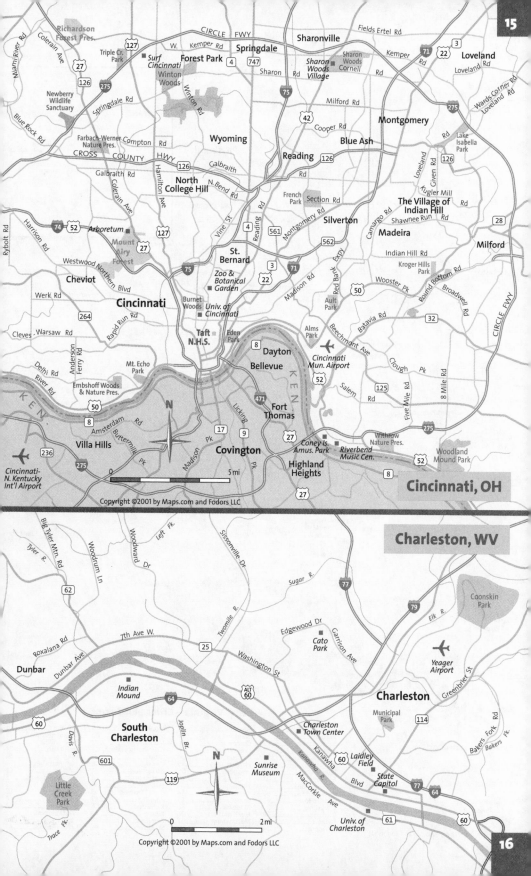

Cincinnati, OH

Charleston, WV

Copyright ©2001 by Maps.com and Fodors LLC

Copyright ©2001 by Maps.com and Fodors LLC

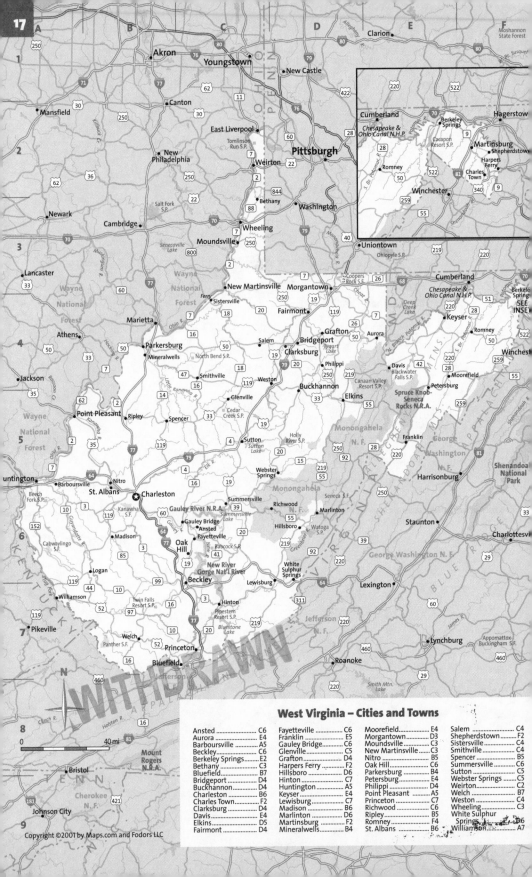

West Virginia – Cities and Towns

Ansted	C6	Fayetteville	C6	Moorefield	E4	Salem	C4
Aurora	E4	Franklin	E5	Morgantown	D3	Shepherdstown	F2
Barboursville	A5	Gauley Bridge	C6	Moundsville	C3	Sistersville	C3
Beckley	C6	Glenville	C5	New Martinsville	C3	Smithville	C4
Berkeley Springs	E2	Grafton	D4	Nitro	B5	Spencer	B5
Bethany	C3	Harpers Ferry	F2	Oak Hill	C6	Summersville	C5
Bluefield	B7	Hillsboro	D6	Parkersburg	B4	Sutton	C5
Bridgeport	D4	Hinton	C7	Petersburg	E4	Webster Springs	C5
Buckhannon	D4	Huntington	A5	Philippi	D4	Weirton	C2
Charleston	B6	Keyser	E4	Point Pleasant	A5	Welch	B7
Charles Town	F2	Lewisburg	C6	Princeton	C7	Weston	C4
Clarksburg	D4	Madison	B6	Richwood	C6	Wheeling	C3
Davis	E4	Marlinton	D6	Ripley	B5	White Sulphur Springs	D6
Elkins	D5	Mineralwells	B4	Romney	F4	Williamson	A7
Fairmont	D4			St. Albans	B6		

Copyright ©2001 by Maps.com and Fodors LLC

17 A B C D E F

1 2 3 4 5 6 7 8 9

0   40 mi